Brain Anatomy

Lateral view

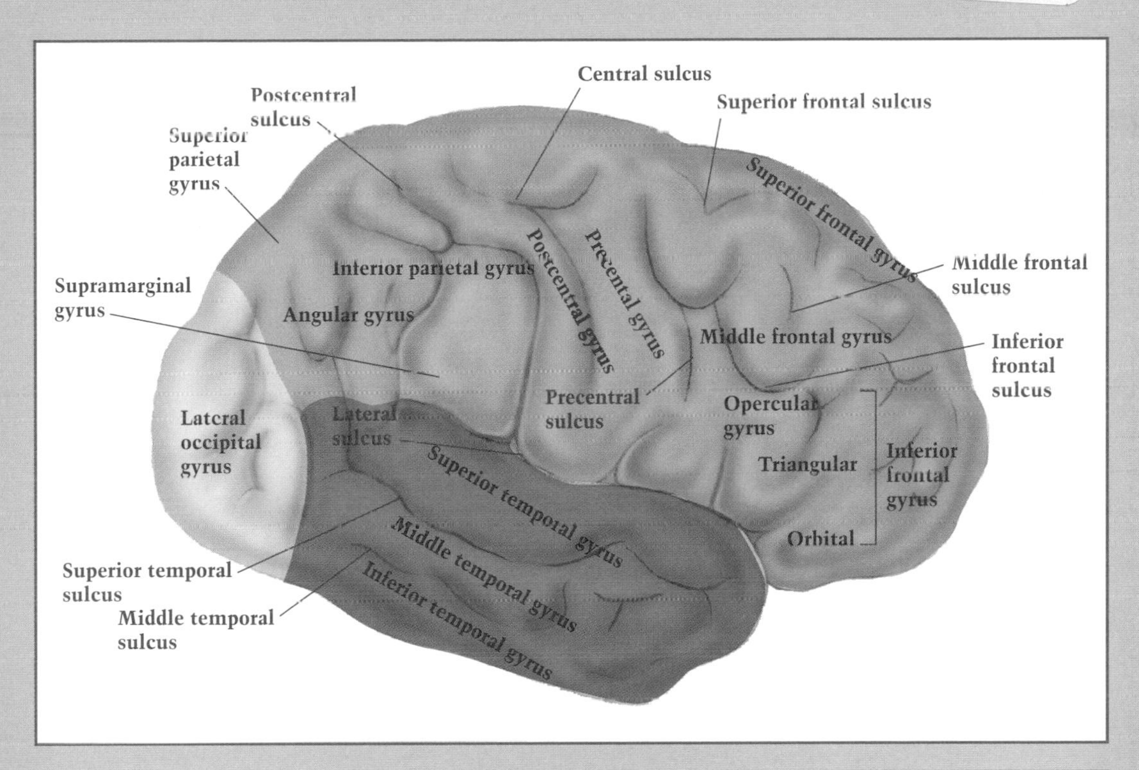

Medial view

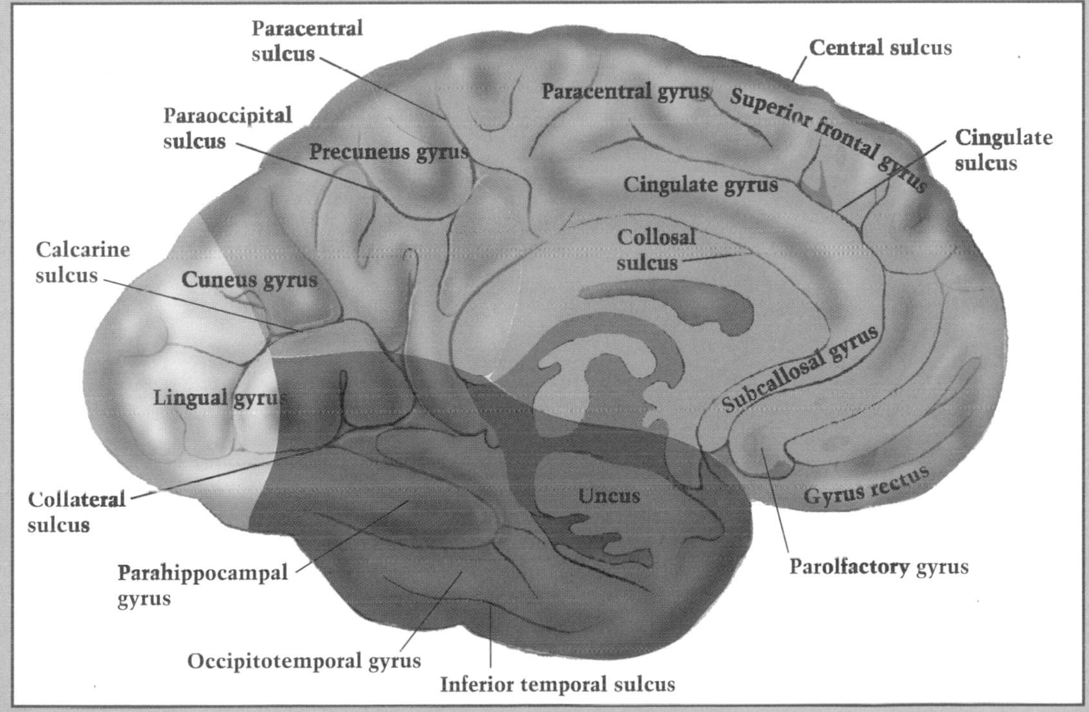

COGNITIVE NEUROSCIENCE AND NEUROPSYCHOLOGY

SECOND EDITION

MARIE T. BANICH
University of Colorado at Boulder

Houghton Mifflin Company
Boston • New York

To Dad, who taught me "You live, you learn"

To Mom, who taught me "You learn, you live"

& To Laura, who daily reminds me of the wonders to which words can lead.

Editor in Chief: Charles Hartford
Senior Sponsoring Editor: Kerry Baruth
Assistant Editor: Danielle Richardson
Senior Project Editor: Tracy Patruno
Senior Manufacturing Coordinator: Marie Barnes
Marketing Manager: Katherine Greig

Cover Photo/Art: *X-Ray of Skull with Electronic Brain* © Scott Tysick/Masterfile

Credits are listed on page 604, which is hereby considered an extension of the copyright page.

Printed in the U.S.A.

Library of Congress Control Number: 2002115725

ISBN: 0-618-12210-9

123456789-CW-07 06 05 04 03

BRIEF CONTENTS

CONTENTS

PART II NEURAL BASES OF MENTAL FUNCTIONS

PREFACE

THE SECOND EDITION of this book, although renamed and extensively revised, retains the spirit, organization, and many of the features of the first edition. Like the first edition, it provides a systematic introduction to the neural basis of mental function. Also like the first edition, it includes research from experimental work performed with humans and animals, as well as findings from clinical populations. New to this edition is the perspective on these issues that can be provided by computational models. The goal, as before, is to provide a balanced, synthesized, and integrated view of what we know both about the brain and about cognition.

The title of the book reflects not only a change in how the scientific community conceptualizes the area of study that investigates linkages between cognition and the brain, but also the fact that the book has been extensively updated to provide a state-of-the-art view of the field. Research findings from patients with neurological disorders are discussed side by side with findings from studies involving transcranial magnetic stimulation; computational perspectives are provided along with findings obtained from neuroimaging; and the results of research with animals are discussed in tandem with results from electrophysiological recordings in humans. In this regard, the material in the book clearly encompasses the field of cognitive neuroscience. Yet, at its core, the book also presents what we have learned and continue to learn from neuropsychological research, especially with clinical populations. Thus the title indicates the integration of these two perspectives on the neural bases of mental function.

TEXT ORGANIZATION AND FEATURES

Users of the first edition will find that, despite the title change, the book's soul remains very much the same as the following main features have been retained.

■ The book provides a systematic survey of the neural bases of a wide variety of mental functions.

The overall organization of the book is changed little from the first edition. The first section of the book, comprising the first four chapters, provides students with a basic foundation for the exploration of cognitive neuroscience and neuropsychology. The first chapter provides information about the basic parts and divisions of the central nervous system, while the second chapter, which is new, discusses the fundamentals of neural transmission. These two chapters are probably unnecessary for students who have already completed a course in physiological psychology, but will be of use to students who have not.

The third chapter acquaints students with the myriad of burgeoning techniques, both standard and novel, that are available to scientists and clinicians in their quest to understand the neural bases of mental function. The fourth chapter provides an overview of lateralization of function. The second part of the book, Chapters 5 through 12, provides a survey of the neural bases of mental function, with each chapter devoted to a distinct mental function. The chapter topics discussed are, in order, motor processes, object recognition, spatial processing, attention, language, memory, executive function, and emotion.

The last part of the book, comprising the last two chapters, looks at broad-based issues in cognitive neuroscience and neuropsychology. Chapter 13 examines neural plasticity from a life-span perspective, including not only developmental changes during childhood but also those that occur with aging. In addition, it discusses recovery of function in children and in adults, and the neural bases of developmental disabilities. Chapter 14 examines syndromes that are characterized by generalized cognitive disorders (rather than the specific disorders discussed in Chapters 5 through 12), including closed head injury, dementia, demyelinating diseases, disorders due to substance abuse or exposure to toxins, and epilepsy.

■ Both the sequence of the chapters and the information within them is designed for progressive learning.

The chapters have been carefully sequenced so that information in later chapters builds upon information in earlier chapters. Notably, the processes most linked to motoric and sensory functions are presented earlier, and those that depend on more integrative aspects of brain function, such as executive function and emotion, are presented later. For example, the chapter on object recognition directly precedes that on spatial processing, so that the student is introduced to the ventral and dorsal visual-processing streams in consecutive chapters. The chapter on memory is preceded by the language and object-recognition chapters so that the distinction between generalized memory disorders and the "memory" problems that are specific to certain domains (e.g., anomia in language or agnosia with regard to objects) is clear.

In each chapter that discusses a particular mental function, the student is first introduced to the basic neural circuitry that underlies that process. Then the student is introduced to how these parts function as a system to support the mental function. Finally, relevant clinical syndromes are discussed; a presentation of their phenomenology is followed by a discussion of the syndrome's implications for understanding brain-behavior relationships.

■ The book is designed to actively engage students in the process of learning.

Each chapter begins with an opening case history to pique the students' interest and preview issues that are discussed later in the chapter. For example, the opening case history in Chapter 5 discusses how Muhammad Ali's boxing career led him to have a Parkinsonian disorder, and the opening case history in Chapter 14 discusses the mental decline of my maternal grandmother due to dementia. The text is written in a conversational tone rather than in a technical style, to grab the students' interest and retain it. So that difficult conceptual issues can be presented in a tractable manner, analogies are used extensively. Each chapter includes information in a special-interest box focused on a particular issue in research in cognitive neuroscience or on the implications of neuropsychology for everyday life.

To keep students oriented to terminology, key terms are introduced in boldface and defined in a glossary at the back of the book. Chapter summaries allow students to review the material learned or preview what is to be discussed, and outlines at the beginning of each chapter provide a clear conceptual structure of the contents. All these features are designed to make this book as user-friendly as possible.

■ State-of-the-art knowledge in the field is presented without sacrificing accuracy or oversimplifying the material.

As a researcher who maintains a highly active and visible research program, the author is in a position to ensure that the book contains not only a discussion of the agreed upon and "classic" findings in the field, but also the cutting-edge portion of our knowledge. Never, however, are students overwhelmed with a laundry list of findings or with overly technical arcane issues. Rather, representative studies are used to highlight the nature of current debates, so that students can understand the conceptual issues under consideration. The author's extensive work in the field, as well as her experience teaching this course, allows her to present issues in a manner that is precise and sophisticated, yet also accessible and integrative.

WHAT'S NEW IN THIS EDITION

While the approach of the first edition has been retained, this second edition has nevertheless been extensively revamped. The main new additions are as follows.

■ The introduction of color.

In this edition, color has been introduced to enhance students' understanding of the material. Figures now highlight the regions of the brain that are being discussed so the reader can quickly see "where" and "what" in the brain are important. Data from patient populations under discussion are highlighted in graphs and figures by use of color. In addition, a full-color insert in the center of the book provide examples of the way in which data from new brain imaging techniques are providing insights into the bases of neural function. Color is also used to set off the glossary terms as well as the chapter summary, which is now provided in a concise bulleted format rather than paragraph format.

■ Ancilliary materials to aid in learning.

This new edition of the book is accompanied by a website that offers chapter quizzes written by Wouter Duyck of Ghent University. The quizzes cover the major topics discussed in the text and provide immediate feedback for students. For instructors, the site includes PowerPoint slides of the figures in the text to aid in lecture presentations.

■ A new chapter on the functioning of neurons and integration of new knowledge from genetics.

In response to many requests, the book now includes a chapter (Chapter 2) on how neurons function. This chapter provides a foundation for discussions later on in the book regarding the role of neurotransmitters in neuropsychological function. For example, in the emotion chapter, we discuss the importance of dopamine in reward systems and in schizophrenia, and in the chapter on memory and generalized cognitive disorders, we discuss the role of the cholinergic system. As an adjunct to this information, we also provide increased coverage of genetic mechanisms in neuropsychology, derived from the burgeoning knowledge supplied by the human genome project. For example, when discussing Alzheimer's disease, we discuss the genetic markers that have been linked to early versus late manifestations of the disorder, and we discuss the genetic findings that suggest a distinct etiology for nonverbal as opposed to verbal learning disabilities.

■ Extensive updating of the material to incorporate the acceleration of knowledge in the field.

Since the first edition, the fields of cognitive neuroscience and neuropsychology have exploded with new discoveries. As a result, most of the chapters of the book had to be extensively rewritten to incorporate this huge amount of additional knowledge, which is reflected in the over 700 new references in this edition. Much of this knowledge has been garnered from new techniques like functional magnetic resonance imaging (fMRI) and transcranial magnetic stimulation. The methods chapter has been extensively revised and enhanced to include a discussion of these techniques, as well as other promising ones on the horizon, such as optical imaging methods. The findings from studies using fMRI are discussed throughout the book and integrated with material from other methods. In addition, the insights that computational models can provide are presented.

Following is a summary of the main changes to each chapter:

CHAPTER 1

- Now focuses exclusively on the major section and subdivisions of the nervous system

CHAPTER 2—NEW

- Provides an introduction to the basics of neuronal transmission and the effect of neurotransmitters on cognitive and emotional function

CHAPTER 3

- Expanded coverage of functional MRI (fMRI) as a method

- New discussion of transcranial magnetic stimulation (TMS), optical imaging, and computational modeling

CHAPTER 4
- New coverage on the evolution of lateralization and handedness

CHAPTER 5
- Expanded coverage of the roles of distinct regions of premotor cortex in motor control
- New discussion of computational models of movement control

CHAPTER 6
- Expanded coverage of the distinct roles played by specific regions of the ventral visual-processing stream, emphasizing recent information gleaned from fMRI
- Updated discussion of computational models of object recognition
- Updated discussion of categorization of agnosias
- Expanded coverage of the degree to which faces are or are not processed differently than other objects

CHAPTER 7
- Updated with recent fMRI and ERP studies pertinent to spatial processing

CHAPTER 8
- Reorganized to emphasize both the component parts and the interrelationships in the network of brain structures that control attention
- Expanded coverage of the role of the anterior cingulate in attentional control
- Expanded coverage of neurobiological and computational models of the attentional network
- Expanded coverage of methods to ameliorate hemineglect and of the implications of hemineglect for our understanding of the neural bases of attentional control
- Expanded discussion of the neural bases of unconscious processing of information

CHAPTER 9
- Updated discussion of recent findings from fMRI and ERP studies pertinent to language processing, especially those related to the role of inferior frontal regions in language processing
- Added coverage of the neural basis of bilingualism and other language systems, such as American Sign Language

CHAPTER 10
- New section on mechanisms that support encoding, consolidation, and retrieval in memory
- New sections on working memory and skill learning
- New section on the interface between memory and emotion

CHAPTER 11

- New coverage of conflict and error-monitoring and their neural substrates
- Enhanced discussion of how frontal regions may act as an interface between working memory, goal-setting and executive processes

CHAPTER 12

- Reorganized to emphasize the myriad of brain regions involved in emotional processing, rather than highlighting the lateralization of emotional processes
- Expanded coverage of the role of the amygdala, prefrontal regions, and retrosplenial cortex in emotional processing
- New section on individual differences in affective processing

CHAPTER 13

- New coverage of genetic mechanisms that influence the neuropsychological profile of development disorders
- Expanded discussion of techniques that induce recovery of function after brain insult and of possible mechanisms for their effects
- New discussion of neurogenesis in adults and the factors that affect it
- Expanded coverage of changes in patterns of brain activity that accompany aging
- New section on how the changes in the brain that accompany aging may be reduced or slowed
- New discussion of neurochemical changes associated with development and of neurotransmitter mechanisms that are involved in developmental disorders

CHAPTER 14

- Expanded coverage of closed head injury related to sports
- New discussion of genetic influences in Alzheimer's disease
- Updated section on potential mechanisms involved in Alzheimer's disease and other neurodegenerative disorders
- Expanded coverage of Creutzfeldt-Jacob (i.e., "mad-cow") disease
- New coverage of the association of neurotransmitter systems with specific dementing disorders, substances of abuse, and toxins

ACKNOWLEDGMENTS

This book has benefited greatly from the generous help of a number of colleagues who reviewed it. I was genuinely touched by the amount of time and effort that these individuals took to improve the book. Their enthusiasm for the project bolstered me when the process seemed to be dragging on forever. They kept me on my toes, and although I may not have taken all of their advice, I thought about each and every one of their suggestions. I am most appreciative of their input.

Mark H. Ashcraft, Cleveland State University; Ruth Ann Atchley, University of Kansas; Mark Beeman, Northwestern University; Robert Bohlander, Wilkes University; Robert Bornstein, Ohio State University; Joan C. Borod, Queen's College of CUNY; Marie-Christine

Buhot, Centre National de la Recherche Scientifique, France; Brian Butterworth, University College London; Michael P. Caligiuri, University of California, San Diego; James V. Corwin, Northern Illinois University; Verne C. Cox, University of Texas, Arlington; Suzanne Craft, University of Washington; Tim Curran, University of Colorado; Martha J. Farah, University of Pennsylvania; Deborah Fein, University of Connecticut; Wim Fias, Ghent University; Susan M. Garnsey, University of Illinois; Siegfried Gauggel, University of Technology Chemnitz; Jordan Grafman, National Institute of Neurological Disorders and Stroke; Kenneth F. Green, California State University, Long Beach; Gary Greenberg, Wichita State University; Dai Jones, Cheltenham & Gloucester CHE; Daniel Kimble, University of Oregon; Karen E. Luh; James V. Lupo, Creighton University; Jennifer A. Mangels, Columbia University; Yuko Munakata, University of Colorado; Loraine K. Obler, CUNY Graduate School; Shelley Parlow, Carleton University; Michael Peters, University of Guelph; Graham Ratcliff, Healthsouth Harmarville Rehabilitation Center; Patricia Reuter-Lorenz, University of Michigan; John D. Salamone, University of Connecticut; Martin Sarter, Ohio State University; Carol A. Saslow, Oregon State University, Emeritus; Sid Segalowitz, Brock University; Matthew L. Shapiro, Mount Sinai School of Medicine; Myra O. Smith, Colgate University; Chantal Stern, Boston University; Christopher Sullivan, Butler University; James Tanaka, University of Victoria; Eli Vakil, Bar-Ilan University; Janet M. Vargo; X. T. Wang, University of South Dakota; David A. Westwood, Dalhousie University; and Daniel B. Willingham, University of Virginia.

I thank Doug Bernstein for his insights and wisdom regarding the textbook publishing process, which spared me many headaches with this and the prior edition, and to Jane Knetzger for helping me formulate a vision for this book during her work on the first edition. I also thank my editor on the second edition, Danielle Richardson, who always seemed to be available the instant I needed her, and who obviously took great care and thought regarding all decisions of the book, prodding me tactfully when I needed it. I have appreciated as well the support of Kerry Baruth, my sponsoring editor, who was an enthusiastic backer of the very extensive revisions that went into this edition. Furthermore, I am grateful to both Neal J. Cohen and Wendy Heller for their willingness to contribute yet again to the book, even though their schedules would have made it much more convenient for them to refuse.

I was most fortunate to have two very able assistants, Felicia Tomasko and Vanessa Currie, aid me in researching material for this book. I am even more pleased that I can now consider them among my friends. Felicia's dedication and doggedness in tracking down even the most arcane issues, in organizing the chaos of my papers and PDFs, in discussing the best ways to present a concept to make it accessible to students, and in catching those places where my fingers got ahead of my mind, were invaluable. Vanessa's ability and enthusiasm at filling in after Felicia left enabled me to keep the momentum going as I was coming down the home stretch.

In the end, however, the people most important to this revision are the three who made it possible, and to whom it is dedicated—my father, my mother, and my partner. One of my father's favorite sayings was, "You live, you learn." By that he meant that we all make mistakes. For him there was no shame in slipping up here and there as long as you harvested the seeds of your future success from today's mistakes. In doing a revision of this book, I took my father's words

from today's mistakes. In doing a revision of this book, I took my father's words to heart—vowing to let any shortcomings of the first edition teach me how to improve the second.

Although she never explicitly stated it this way, my mother's mantra is undoubtedly, "You learn, you live." To her, the essence of life is to continually learn. During my childhood she fashioned everything as an opportunity to learn, from trips to the grocery store, which became mini-lessons in nutrition, to family vacations, which were venues for improving map-reading skills. Those lessons taught me that learning makes the world come alive. As she goes off in her eighth decade of life to tackle the Internet, learn more about opera, or attend her first stockholders' meeting, she is showing me that learning keeps you young. And so it is with that spirit that I undertook this revision.

Finally, Laura Edwards, my soulmate and spouse, took fingers to keyboard and crafted words, sent with deliberate casualness via the Ethernet, that reinitiated a connection made during the days of my dissertation research and visited only intermittently over the intervening years. That small, single brave act has, to my exquisite good fortune, blossomed into the most enthralling experience of my life. She reminds me daily that words can open doors and vistas to worlds barely conceived of in the imagination. Even though my writing lacks the elegance and panache of hers, she inspired me to write yet again in the hope that I might be able to convey to some of my readers the wonders of the human brain and mind that have captivated me for over 20 years.

MARIE T. BANICH

PART I
FUNDAMENTALS

INTRODUCTION TO THE NERVOUS SYSTEM

What Are Cognitive Neuroscience and Neuropsychology?
Basic Building Blocks of the Nervous System
Neuroanatomical Terms and Brain "Geography"
Major Subdivisions of the Central Nervous System
- Spinal Cord
- Medulla
- Cerebellum
- Pons
- Midbrain
- Hypothalamus
- Thalamus
- Major Subcortical Systems
- Cerebral Cortex

A Closer Look at the Cerebral Cortex
- Cytoarchitectonic Divisions
- Primary Sensory and Motor Cortices
  - Motor Cortex
  - *[Discovery of the "Homunculus"]*
  - Somatosensory Cortex
  - Visual Cortex
  - Auditory Cortex
  - Olfactory Cortex
- Association Areas
  - Frontal Lobe
  - Parietal Lobe
  - Temporal Lobe

What Are Cognitive Neuroscience and Neuropsychology?

In this book, we explore how the neurological organization of the brain influences the way people think, feel, and act. Two areas of inquiry, **cognitive neuroscience** and **human neuropsychology,** are critical to our understanding of this linkage between brain and mind. Cognitive neuroscience comprises investigations of all mental functions that are linked to neural processes—ranging from investigations in animals to humans and from experiments performed in the laboratory to computer simulations. Human neuropsychology also focuses on understanding mental processes in humans, but with an emphasis on gaining such understanding from examining the results of brain trauma.

Since the mid-1970s, not only has our knowledge in the realm of cognitive neuroscience and neuropsychology grown rapidly, but so has the number of individuals who specialize in these areas of inquiry. *Cognitive neuroscientists* attempt to understand the relationship between the brain and mind from a variety of conceptual vantage points simultaneously. Borrowing from computer science, they view the brain as an information-processing system whose primary goal is to solve problems. Hence, these scientists attempt to understand how the brain is organized to perform specific computations, such as recognizing a face. To do so, they rely on integrating findings from different approaches. For example, they record the activity of cells to determine what stimulus makes them respond, use brain imaging to ascertain exactly which brain regions become active during a specific mental task, and build computer models to provide principles and gain insights into how different mental operations might be performed by the brain.

Experimental neuropsychologists work to understand the neural bases of cognition by doing scientific studies comparing individuals who have sustained brain damage with those who are neurologically intact. In their studies, these researchers use a variety of techniques to divide complicated mental functions into meaningful categories such as language and memory and to isolate the contribution of specific brain regions to each of these functions.

Clinical neuropsychologists work in health care settings, such as hospitals and clinics, with individuals who have sustained brain damage through either trauma or disease. They diagnose the cognitive deficits resulting from brain trauma, plan programs of rehabilitation, evaluate the degree to which an individual is regaining function, and determine how environmental factors (e.g., family structure, educational background, and so forth) may moderate or exacerbate the effects of brain dysfunction. In this book, we provide an overview of the current state of knowledge in cognitive neuroscience and neuropsychology as derived from findings in both the laboratory and the clinic.

The endeavor of understanding the relationship between the brain and the mind may be undertaken from two distinct vantage points, one that emphasizes the neurological organization of the brain and one that emphasizes the psychology of the mind. The neurologically oriented approach emphasizes the brain's anatomy; therefore, the major objective of this approach is to understand the function of specific circumscribed regions of brain tissue. For instance, a researcher might want to investigate a particular brain structure, such as the hippocampus, to determine its anatomical characteristics, its pattern of connectivity to other brain regions, and its role in mental functioning. Information derived from this approach can be extremely useful to medical personnel such as neurosurgeons who need to know what functions might be affected by different surgical approaches.

In contrast, the psychologically oriented approach emphasizes the brain's mental capabilities, so the major objective of this approach is to understand how different aspects of cognition, such as language, memory, and attention, are supported by the neurological organization of the brain. For example, cognitive neuroscientists and neuropsychologists may want to know whether the brain structures supporting the ability to read are the same as, or distinct from, those supporting our ability to write. One way of addressing this question is to determine whether the type of brain damage that compromises the process of reading always compromises the process of writing as well. In fact, both reading and writing are not always simultaneously lost after brain damage, a finding that tells us that although they are similar functions, they are controlled by separate brain regions.

In this book we lean more toward the psychologically oriented approach than the neurologically oriented one. This bias can be seen most clearly by taking a quick glance at the table of contents, which includes chapter titles such as "Language," "Memory," and "Attention," indicating that our discussion of the relationship between the brain and the mind emphasizes cognitive functions. If this book were written from a more neurologically oriented approach, the chapters would have been organized by brain regions and been titled "The Basal Ganglia," "The Cerebellum," and "The Frontal Lobes." Although we take a more psychologically oriented approach, a working knowledge and understanding of the neurological organization of the brain is indispensable, for only with that knowledge can we intelligently discuss the relationship between psychological functions and the specific regions of brain tissue that support those functions.

Cognitive neuroscience and neuropsychology, by the very questions they address, fall at the intersection of a variety of fields, including neurology, biological psychology, and cognitive psychology. To study such a cross-disciplinary subject, we must be willing not only to examine questions from different perspectives, but also to integrate the information provided from these alternative perspectives. You may find that you are already familiar with some of the concepts raised in the book through previous course work in either cognitive or biological psychology. However, the perspectives taken in this book are likely to be different because we integrate, interrelate, and synthesize material from both a biological and a cognitive vantage point. Although we cannot go into the detail that separate courses in each area would entail, we can provide a large-scale, integrative picture of the topic under study. For example, when discussing face recognition in Chapter 6, we learn not only which salient features enable people to recognize the face of someone they haven't seen for 30 years, but also which regions of the brain support such feats and why.

Now is a particularly exciting time to study cognitive neuroscience and neuropsychology. Vast advances in our knowledge in neuroscience, medical science, and cognitive psychology provide the opportunity to synthesize findings in ways that were impossible just a few years ago. Research in cognitive psychology has tremendously increased the sophistication of models of mental functioning. For example, we can take a complicated function such as language and divide it into specific subcomponents and subprocesses. At the same time, incredible advances in medical technology now allow us to examine the neuroanatomy and physiological functioning of the brain in ways unimagined even as recently as the 1980s. We discuss these advances in methods in more detail in Chapter 3.

Before we begin to attempt to link cognitive functions to the brain, however, we need some background knowledge, a common base of knowledge about the anatomy and physiology of the brain. The first two chapters are designed to provide this base of knowledge. The first chapter introduces the somewhat specific vocabulary scientists utilize when discussing the brain—the terms that describe the location of brain structures and their characteristics. Next there is a brief overview of the major regions of the brain that provides a glimpse of each region's major functions. After gaining a general familiarity with the nervous system the second chapter takes a closer look at how nerve cells communicate with one another, and how disruptions in this process can have important implications for mental functions.

Basic Building Blocks of the Nervous System

Our nervous system, which consists of the brain, spinal cord, nerves and ganglia, controls the body's response to internal and external stimuli. It is comprised of two main classes of cells: **neurons** and **glia.** Neurons are the cells in the nervous system that carry information from one place to another by means of a combination of electrical and chemical signals. Glia, which outnumber neurons by at least 10 to 1, are support cells.

Neurons have three main parts: a **dendritic tree,** a **cell body,** and an **axon.** The dendritic tree is the part of the neuron that receives input from other cells. The cell body is the part of the cell containing the nucleus and other cellular apparatus responsible for the manufacture of proteins and enzymes that sustain cell functioning. The axon is the appendage of the cell across which information is carried. It can vary in length; in some cases it is very short, extending a distance not much farther than the length of the dendrites and cell body. In other cases it is very long, spanning large distances between brain regions.

Some neurons, known as *sensory neurons,* bring information to the central nervous system. Others, known as *interneurons,* associate information within the central nervous system. Finally, *motor neurons* send information from the brain and spinal cord to the muscles. Although all neurons have these same basic component parts, they come in a variety of sizes and shapes (Figure 1.1).

Although glia are not the main carriers of information, they are critical to the functioning of the nervous system. Their tasks include influencing the communication between neurons by modifying the chemical milieu between them, aiding with reorganization after brain damage by removing dead neurons, and serving some of the nutritive needs of neurons. Glia are critical to maintaining the **blood-brain barrier,** which is the mechanism by which many harmful substances, such as toxins, are prevented from reaching the brain. The blood-brain barrier results from the tight packing of glial cells between blood vessels and neurons that keeps not only toxins but also nutrients, drugs, and cells of the immune system in the blood stream from directly reaching the nervous system.

Although we leave our discussion of neurons for now, in the next chapter we examine them in more detail. There we will present an overview of how neurons work, highlighting the aspects of neuronal function that are important to remember for discussions in later chapters.

Developmentally, glia guide neurons as they migrate from the site of creation to their final position within the brain. Compared with our knowledge about neurons, our knowledge about glia is scant, but it has increased tremendously in recent years (see Laming et al., 2000, for a recent review).

Now that we know the basic cells that form the nervous system, let's step back and view the system as a whole.

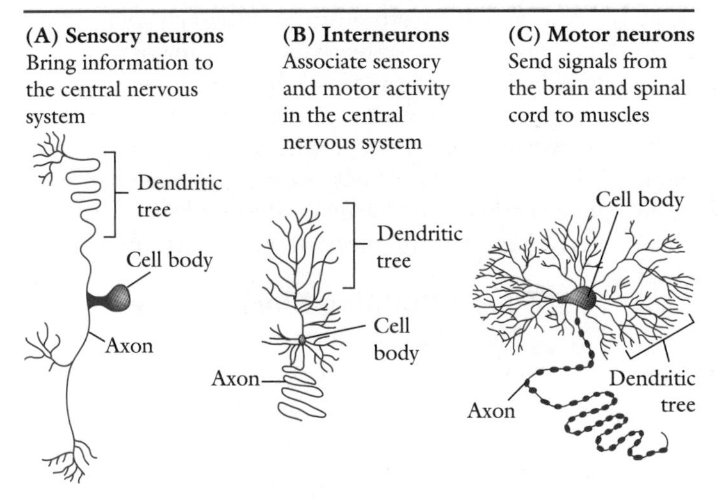

FIGURE 1.1 Examples of some nervous system cells (not to scale). (A) Sensory neurons, (B) interneurons, and (C) motor neurons. Note that the appearance of the different kinds of neurons is distinctive; the appearance of each kind of neuron is due to its function. A sensory neuron collects information from a source and passes it on to an interneuron. The many branches of interneurons suggest that they collect information from many sources. Motor neurons are distinctively large and collect information from many sources; they pass this information on to command muscles to move.

Neuroanatomical Terms and Brain "Geography"

Anytime you begin a long journey, you need a road map to guide your path, plus some understanding of common directional terms such as *north, south, east,* and *west.* So, to begin our trip around the "geography" of the central nervous system, we must identify the major neural regions and introduce terms that can help to orient us on our journey. Distinguishing between regions of the central nervous system, and in particular the brain, serves a function similar to that of drawing boundary lines on a map. Such lines on a map may tell us about differences not only in the geography of different regions, but also in the behavior, attitudes, and customs of the people on either side of a boundary. Likewise, boundaries between brain regions are often drawn to demarcate differences in structure and function of brain tissue. Sometimes we find that boundaries between brain regions are based on large and obvious anatomical landmarks, like major geographical features on a map such as rivers or mountains. In other cases, the physical distinction between regions is not as obvious from the neuroanatomical terrain.

We must first learn the anatomical equivalents of north, south, east, and west. Unlike most geographical maps, which have only two dimensions, the brain has three. Thus, we need terms not only for the brain's left, right, top, and bottom, but also for its back and front (see Figure 1.2). The front of the brain

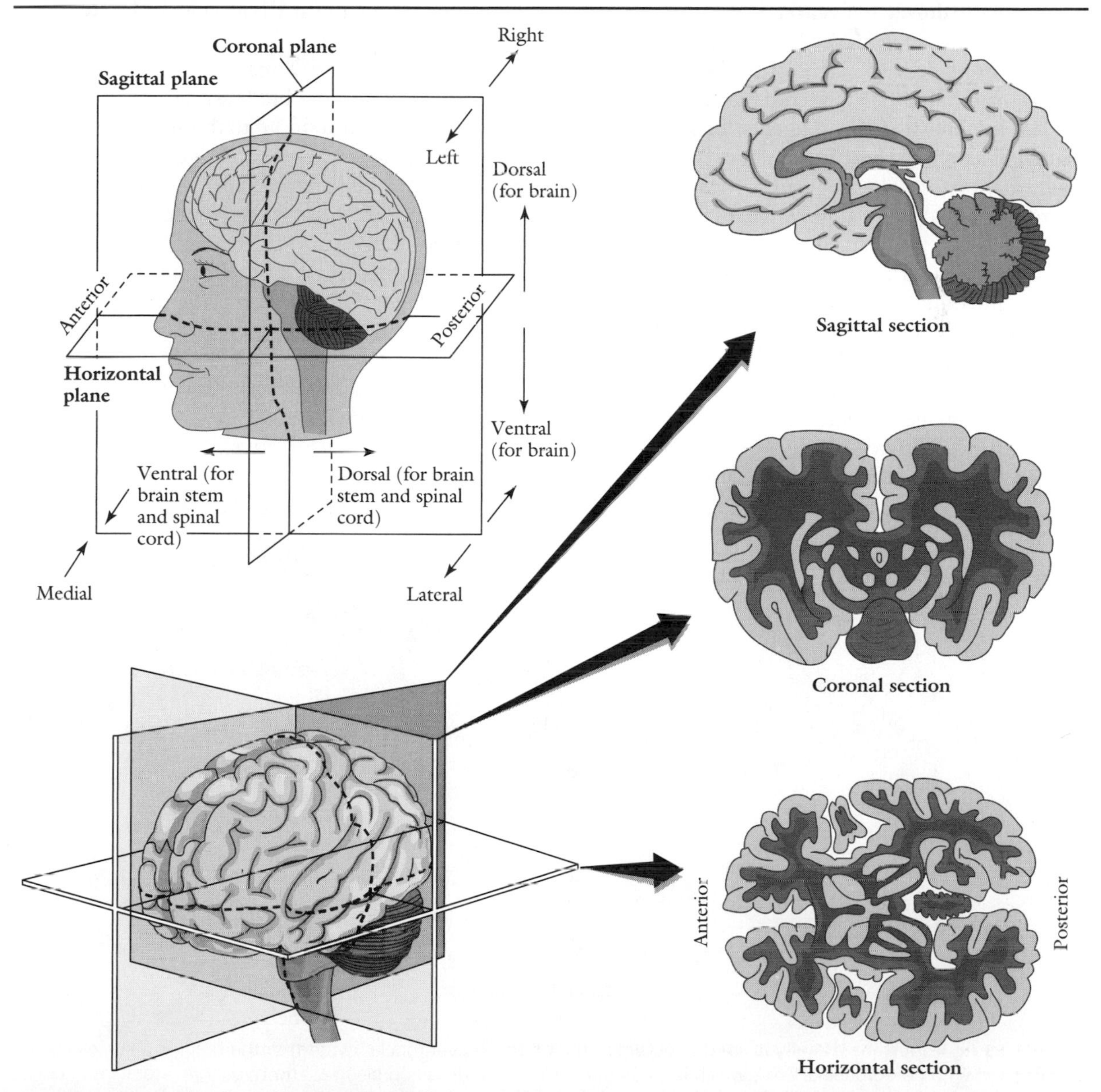

FIGURE 1.2 The main planes in which the brain is viewed. A sagittal section divides left from right, a coronal section divides front from back, and a horizontal section divides top from bottom.

is referred to as **anterior** and the back as **posterior.** Because the head of an animal is situated in front of its tail, regions toward the front can be referred to as **rostral** (toward the head), whereas regions toward the rear are referred to as **caudal** (toward the tail). The top of the brain is referred to as **superior,** and the bottom is referred to as **inferior.** With regard to the human brain, **dorsal** and **ventral** have meanings similar to superior and inferior, respectively. However, with regard to other portions of the central nervous system, such as the spinal cord, dorsal and ventral are better understood in reference to a four-legged animal or a fish. In these cases, dorsal means toward an animal's back, whereas ventral means toward an animal's stomach. If you have aquatic interests, you can remember that dorsal means top because the dorsal fin of a shark sticks out of the water. Finally, areas in the middle or center of the brain are referred to as **medial,** whereas areas that are toward the outside of the brain are called **lateral.**

Throughout this text, the brain is portrayed in one of three planes. When the brain is sliced ear-to-ear to separate the front from the back, the view, or slice, is **coronal**. If the brain is sliced front to back, so that the top of the brain is separated from the bottom, the view is **horizontal** (also sometimes referred to as *axial* or *transverse*). Finally, if the brain is cut top to bottom, so that the left side of the brain is separated from the right side, the view is **sagittal.** A sagittal slice down the middle of the brain is known as a **midsagittal,** or *medial,* section, whereas a section taken more toward one side is known as a *lateral* section.

Knowledge of these terms can help us understand the location of specific brain structures. For example, when we are introduced to the anatomical structure called the *lateral ventricle* (a ventricle is a space within the nervous system that is filled with fluid), we can deduce that it must be positioned away from the midline of the brain (i.e., laterally). Indeed, if you examine the picture of the ventricular system presented in Figure 1.3, you can see that the lateral ventricles are positioned toward the outside of the brain.

As another example, consider how we might go about locating **nuclei,** distinct groups of neurons whose cell bodies are all situated in the same region in a brain structure called the *thalamus*. As dis-

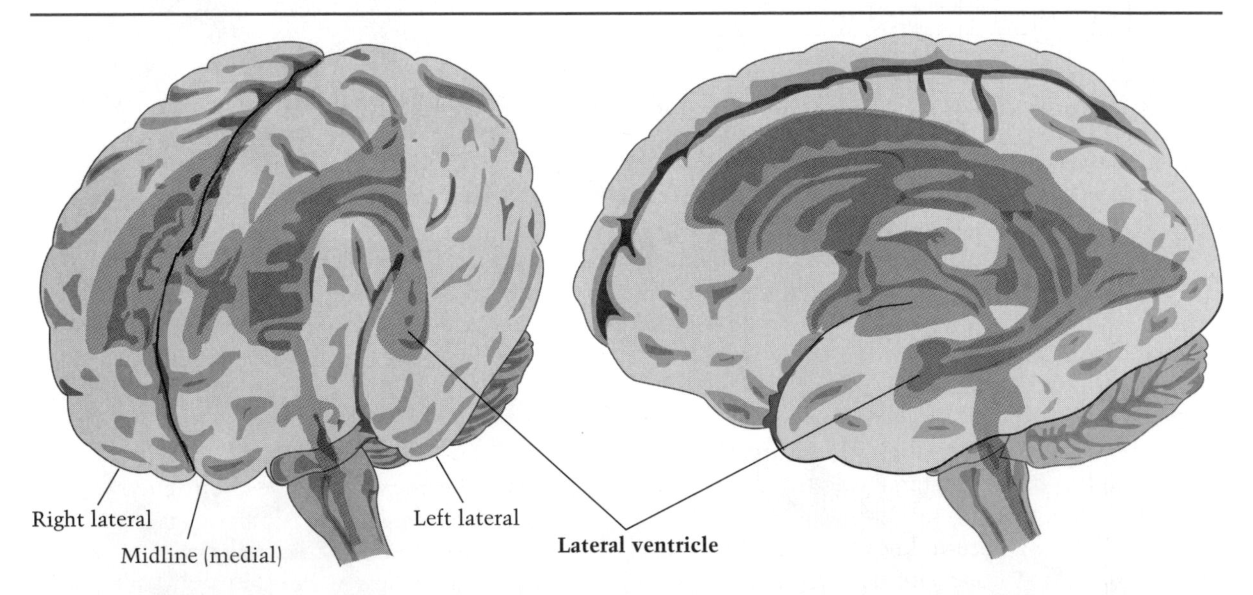

FIGURE 1.3 An important laterally located structure in the brain. The ventricular system of the brain is a system of canals filled with cerebrospinal fluid, which is similar in composition to blood plasma. The two large lateral ventricles are located toward the exterior surface of the brain and away from the midline.

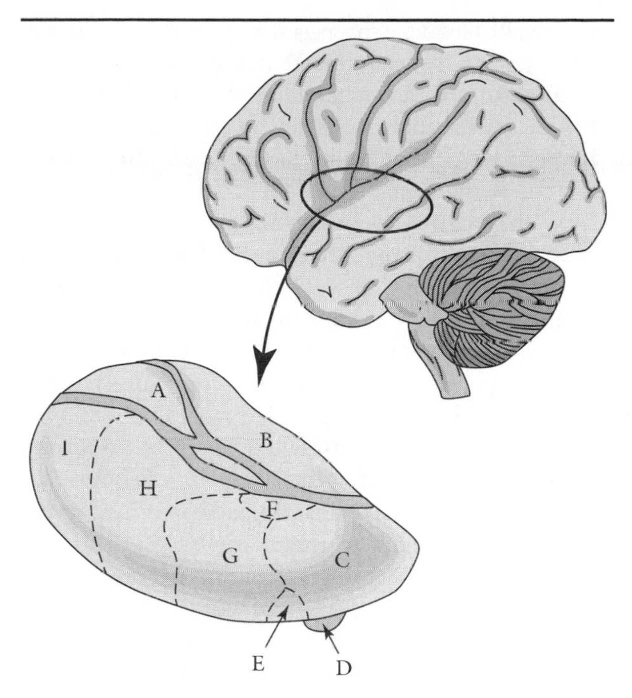

FIGURE 1.4 The different nuclei of the thalamus. (A) Anterior nucleus, (B) dorsal medial nucleus, (C) pulvinar, (D) medial geniculate nucleus, (E) lateral geniculate nucleus, (F) lateral posterior nucleus, (G) ventral lateral posterior nucleus, (H) ventral lateral nucleus, and (I) ventral anterior nucleus.

cussed later in this chapter, the thalamus helps to regulate and organize information coming from the outer reaches of the nervous system as it ascends toward the cortex and also modifies information descending from the cortex. If we need to find the anterior ventral nucleus of the thalamus, we now know from our discussion of anatomical terms that it should be located at the front and bottom part of the thalamus. You can give yourself a quick test of how well you learned these anatomical terms by trying to locate the dorsal medial nucleus, the ventral lateral nucleus, and the lateral posterior nucleus of the thalamus in Figure 1.4.

Other terms we need to know include **contralateral,** meaning on the opposite side from, and **ipsilateral,** meaning on the same side as. So, for example, the left half of your brain is contralateral to your right hand, whereas it is ipsilateral to your left hand. To make these definitions more concrete, remember the familiar adage that the right side of your brain controls the motor movements of the limbs on the left side of your body, and vice versa. Put in the terms we just learned, motor control occurs contralaterally.

When something, such as damage, is situated to only one side of the brain (or space) it is known as **unilateral,** whereas that which holds for both sides of space is known as **bilateral.** Other terms often used to describe brain regions and their relation to body parts are **proximal,** which means near, and **distal,** which means far. Thus, distal muscles are in your far extremities, such as your hands. Now that we know the spatial terms of directionality in the nervous system, we turn our attention to the major subdivisions of the nervous system.

Major Subdivisions of the Central Nervous System

We now start our journey across the different territories, or regions, of the **central nervous system.** The central nervous system encompasses the brain and the spinal cord, whereas the **peripheral nervous system** involves all neural tissue beyond the central nervous system, such as neurons that receive sensory information or that send information to muscles, and those that relay information to or from the spinal cord or the brain. Because of its fragility, the entire central nervous system is encased in bone. The spinal cord is enclosed within the spinal column and the brain within the skull. Although these bony structures protect the central nervous system, at times they can cause damage. For example, if the spinal column presses against the spinal cord, it can pinch a nerve and cause pain. Likewise, as discussed in Chapter 14, the brain can be damaged from compression against the skull.

Between the neurons and their bony encasements is **cerebrospinal fluid (CSF),** which is similar in composition to blood plasma. Essentially, the brain floats in CSF, which makes it buoyant and cushions it from being knocked around every time we move. CSF also serves metabolic needs, allowing nutrients to reach neurons. Typically, cells outside the nervous system receive nutrients from the blood. However, the blood-brain barrier precludes such transport to the brain. Rather, nutrients from the blood reach nerve cells through CSF.

The blood-brain barrier also acts to deflect bacteria and other infectious agents and to block the entry of toxins to the brain. However, molecules of the immune system, such as antibodies and phagocytes (cells, such as white blood cells, that engulf foreign bodies), also have difficulty crossing the blood-brain barrier. Thus, the immune system is prevented in large part from protecting the central nervous system against infection. When an infection does reach the brain it can be difficult to arrest because standard treatments used for infections in other regions of the body are unlikely to be effective. By drawing a sample of CSF from a region near the spinal cord (commonly known as a *spinal tap*), a neurologist can determine if the brain is being affected by an infectious or a toxic agent. An unusually high bacteria count in the fluid may indicate infection.

Having discussed the basic organization of the nervous system, we now turn to examine the seven main subdivisions of the central nervous system depicted in Figure 1.5: (1) the spinal cord, (2) the medulla, (3) the cerebellum, (4) the pons, (5) the midbrain, (6) the hypothalamus and thalamus (diencephalon), and (7) the cerebral cortex. In addition, we discuss two major subcortical systems, the basal ganglia and the limbic system.

Spinal Cord

The **spinal cord** is the portion of the nervous system whereby most (but not all) sensory neurons relay information on the way to the brain, and whereby motor commands from the brain are sent to the muscles. The *spinal column,* the bony structure housing the spinal cord, is composed of many sections, or vertebrae. At each vertebra, sensory information enters the cord and motor information leaves it. If the spinal cord were cut in cross section, two clumps of nerve cells, one located ventrally and another located dorsally, as shown in Figure 1.6b, would be prominent. Cells in the dorsal section of the spinal cord (remember, dorsal is located toward the back) receive sensory information. In contrast, cells in the ventral region (remember, ventral is located toward the stomach) are responsible for conveying motor commands to the muscles as well as for receiving input from the brain and from other regions of the spinal cord.

Damage to the spinal cord leaves an individual without sensation or motor control for all body areas that are connected to the brain by spinal cord segments distal to the point of injury. Impulses from the periphery cannot be carried up the spinal cord past the point of injury and therefore cannot reach the brain. Likewise, information from the brain cannot be relayed down past the point of injury to the muscles. How much of the body is paralyzed and how much sensation is lost depends on where in the spinal cord the damage occurs.

The vertebrae where information from each part of the body enters the spinal cord are shown in Figure 1.6a. Compression of the spinal column that causes a vertebra to be broken or crushed may result in a damaged or severed spinal cord. For example, when damage to the spinal cord occurs at the level of the fifth cervical vertebra (C-5; see Figure 1.6a), the person is often left quadriplegic, without control of muscles or sensation from either the arms or the legs (see Figure 1.6c). If, however, the damage is sustained at a lower level, perhaps waist level (e.g., at vertebra T-12, the twelfth thoracic vertebra), the person is often paraplegic, with loss of sensory information and motor control for just the bottom half of the body.

Medulla

The **medulla** is the section of the brain directly superior to the spinal cord. For our purposes, we should know a few main facts about the medulla. First, it is the region of the brain that contains many (though not all) of the cell bodies of the 12 **cranial nerves.** Whereas the spinal cord is the point of entry and exit for sensory and motor nerves of the body, some cranial nerves are responsible for receipt of sensory information and motor control of the head. Other cranial nerves are responsible for the neural control of internal organs. A list of the 12 cranial nerves and their functions, and a diagram of the region of the

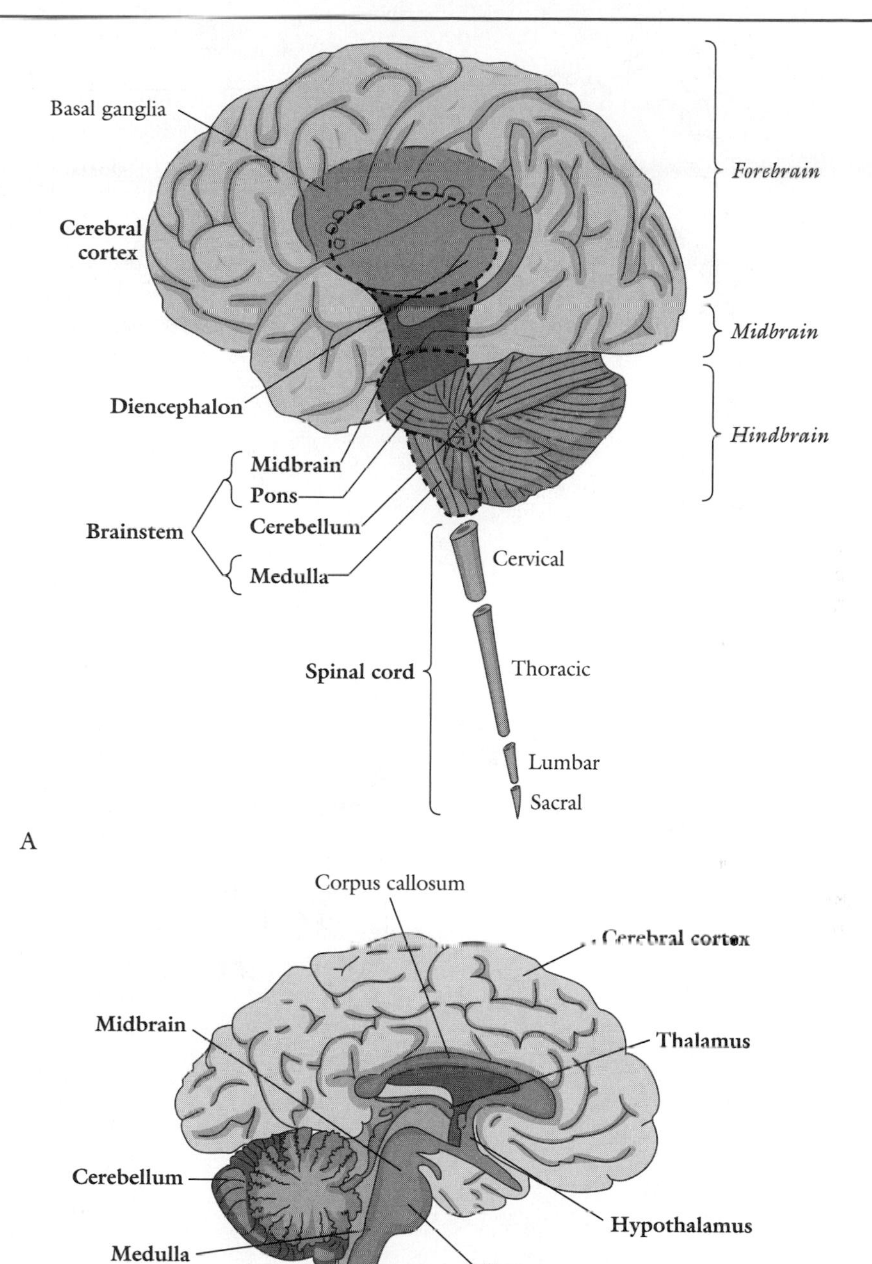

FIGURE 1.5 Major subdivisions of the nervous system. (A) Left hemisphere, lateral view of the major subdivisions: the spinal cord, medulla, cerebellum, pons, midbrain, diencephalon (thalamus and hypothalamus), and cerebral cortex. The medulla, pons, and midbrain are often referred to as the *brainstem.* Sometimes the brain is conceived of as having three broad sections: the hindbrain (medulla, pons, and cerebellum), the midbrain, and the forebrain (diencephalon and cerebral cortex). (B) Left hemisphere, midsagittal view.

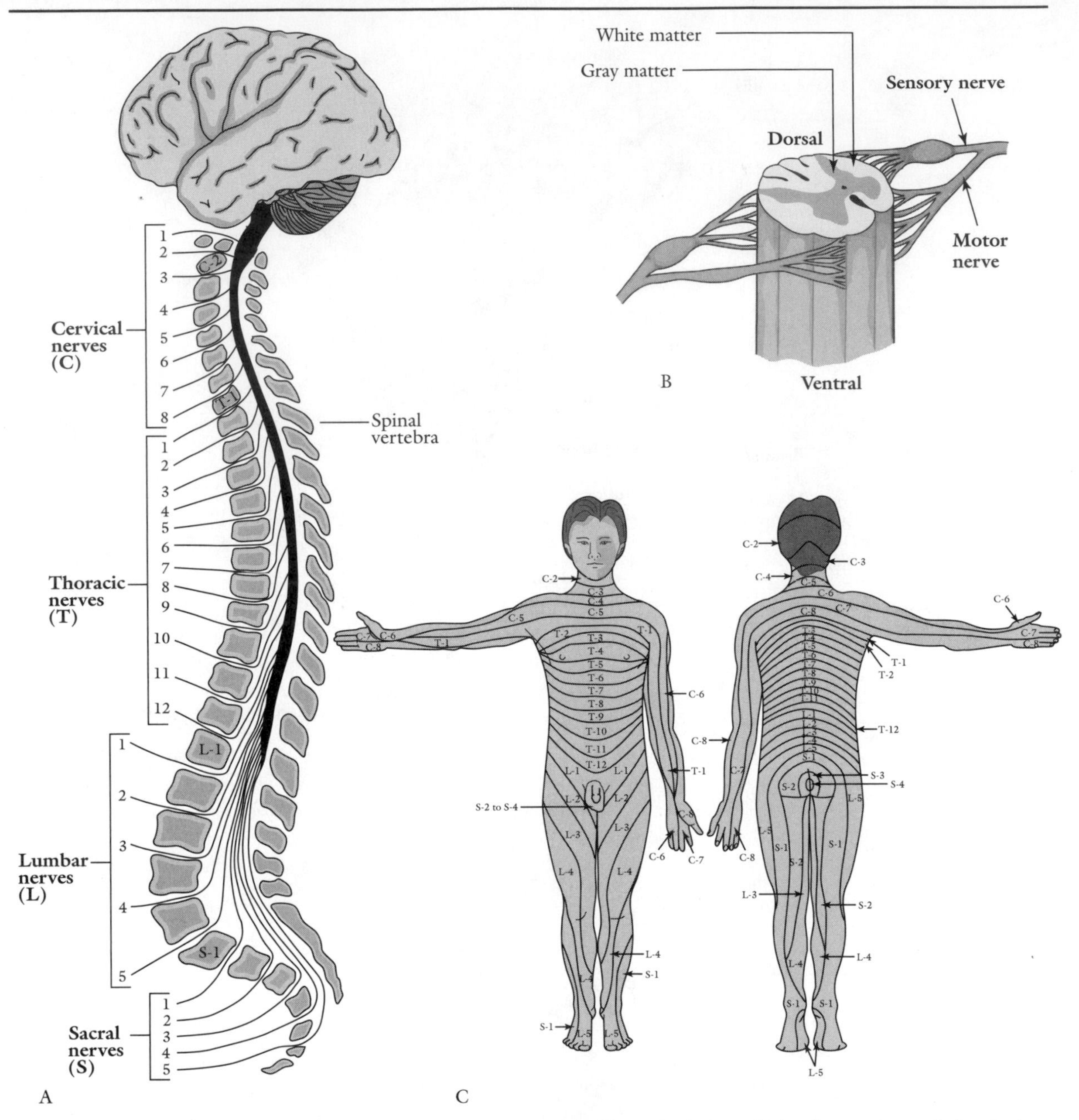

FIGURE 1.6 The spinal cord. (A) The four sections of the spinal cord: cervical, thoracic, lumbar, and sacral. A spinal nerve exists at each vertebra of the spinal column. (B) A cross section of the spinal cord. Sensory information enters the spinal cord through the dorsal region, and nerves exit through the ventral region to control muscle movements. The gray matter consists largely of cell bodies. The surrounding white matter is composed of myelinated axons that carry information to other levels of the spinal cord and the brain. (C) A map indicating which sensory nerve carries information from that portion of the body to the spinal cord. Determining the locations of sensory loss after trauma to the spinal cord by using such maps helps medical personnel determine the level of the spinal cord at which the damage occurred.

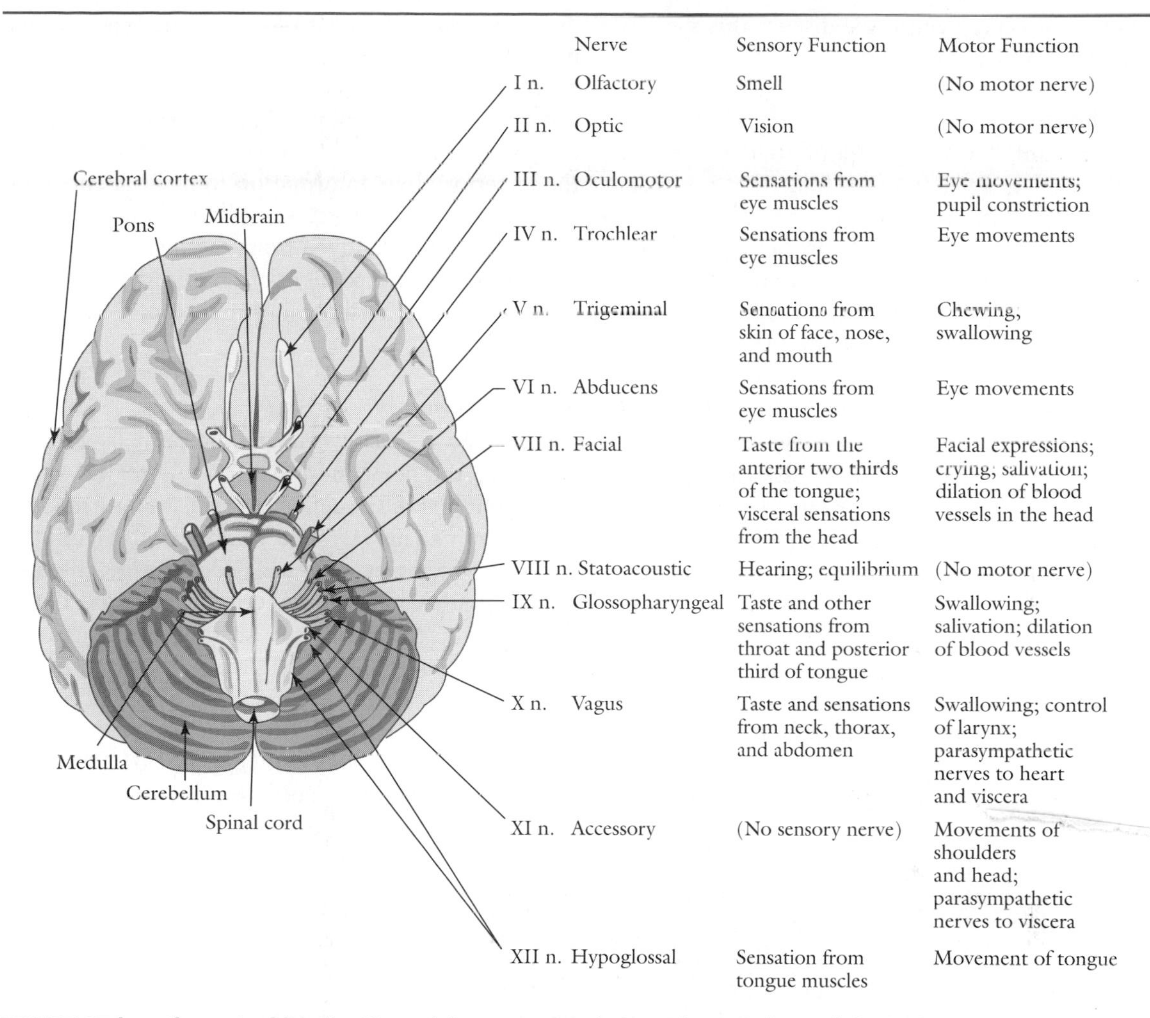

	Nerve	Sensory Function	Motor Function
I n.	Olfactory	Smell	(No motor nerve)
II n.	Optic	Vision	(No motor nerve)
III n.	Oculomotor	Sensations from eye muscles	Eye movements; pupil constriction
IV n.	Trochlear	Sensations from eye muscles	Eye movements
V n.	Trigeminal	Sensations from skin of face, nose, and mouth	Chewing, swallowing
VI n.	Abducens	Sensations from eye muscles	Eye movements
VII n.	Facial	Taste from the anterior two thirds of the tongue; visceral sensations from the head	Facial expressions; crying; salivation; dilation of blood vessels in the head
VIII n.	Statoacoustic	Hearing; equilibrium	(No motor nerve)
IX n.	Glossopharyngeal	Taste and other sensations from throat and posterior third of tongue	Swallowing; salivation; dilation of blood vessels
X n.	Vagus	Taste and sensations from neck, thorax, and abdomen	Swallowing; control of larynx; parasympathetic nerves to heart and viscera
XI n.	Accessory	(No sensory nerve)	Movements of shoulders and head; parasympathetic nerves to viscera
XII n.	Hypoglossal	Sensation from tongue muscles	Movement of tongue

FIGURE 1.7 Locations at which the 12 cranial nerves enter (sensory) or exit (motor) the brain, and each nerve's functions. A ventral (*bottom*) surface view of the brain is shown on the left. The majority of cranial nerves enter at the medulla and the pons. The cranial nerves and their sensory and motor functions are shown in the table on the right.

brain where their nuclei are located are presented in Figure 1.7.

Second, at the medulla, most of the motor fibers cross from one side of the body to the other, with the result that the left side of the brain controls the right side of the body, and the right side of the brain controls the left side of the body. Third, the medulla controls many vital functions and reflexes, such as respiration and heart rate. Because the medulla serves these functions, damage to it can be fatal. One common accompaniment of either diffuse or specific brain damage is swelling of the entire brain. When this swelling puts enough pressure on the medulla to interfere with its functions, death can result.

Fourth, the medulla is home to part of a set of the neurons known as the **reticular activating system.** These neurons receive input from the cranial nerves and project diffusely to many other regions of the brain. The reticular activating system is important for overall arousal and attention, as well as for regulation of sleep-wake cycles. We discuss this system in more detail in Chapter 8.

Cerebellum

The **cerebellum,** located posterior to the medulla (see Figure 1.5), is a region of the brain that is important for the regulation of muscle tone and guidance of motor activity. In large part, it is the region of the brain that allows a pianist to play a piece of music seamlessly or a pitcher to throw a ball fluidly. Damage to the cerebellum does not result in paralysis, but instead interferes with precision of movement and disrupts balance and equilibrium. The classic test that neurologists use to detect cerebellar damage is one in which the doctor asks a person to alternate between touching his or her own nose, and then the doctor's. Although a person with cerebellar damage can follow this command, the path taken by the hand from one nose to the other will be imprecise and jagged. Damage to the cerebellum also contributes to lack of balance and motor control. A common manifestation of temporary disruption to the cerebellum is seen in the *punch-drunk syndrome,* in which an individual temporarily loses balance and coordination after sustaining a hard blow to the head.

Traditionally, a specific region of the cerebellum, the *lateral cerebellum,* was thought of as a brain structure mainly involved in motor control and the learning of motor skills (e.g., the skill of precisely serving a tennis ball). More recent evidence suggests that this region also may be linked to certain aspects of cognitive processing, allowing for fluidity and precision in mental processes (Akshoomoff & Courchesne, 1992). It has also been suggested to be critical for timing information, acting as the brain's internal clock (Ivry, 1997).

Pons

The **pons,** which lies directly superior to the medulla and anterior to the cerebellum (see Figure 1.5), has a multiplicity of functions. Because of its anatomical location, it acts as the main connective bridge from the rest of the brain to the cerebellum. It is the point of synapse (or point of connection between neurons) of some of the cranial nerves, and it acts as an important center for the control of certain types of eye movements and for vestibular functions (e.g., balance). Finally, the pons is the site of the *superior olive,* one of the points through which auditory information is relayed from the ear to the brain. At the superior olive, information from both ears converges, and this convergence allows comparison of the information received from each ear. Such comparison is thought to be important for localization of sounds in the horizontal dimension (Masterton, 1992).

Midbrain

The **midbrain** lies superior to the pons (see Figure 1.5). Like the pons and medulla, this region of the brain contains the nuclei of the cells that form some of the cranial nerves. The midbrain also contains two important structures on its dorsal side, the **inferior colliculus** and the **superior colliculus,** which play a role in orienting us to stimuli in the auditory and visual modalities, respectively (Figure 1.8).

Like the superior olive, the inferior colliculus is a relay point for auditory information as it travels from the ear to the cortex and appears to be involved in sound localization. However, it also contributes to reflexive movements of the head and eyes in response to sound, which provides us with the rudimentary ability to orient toward salient auditory stimuli.

The superior colliculus is the visual system's equivalent of the inferior colliculus, allowing us to perceive and orient toward large moving objects in the periphery. So, if a car comes speeding toward you from the far left, the superior colliculus signals that something is approaching. The superior colliculus also aids, along with other brain regions to be discussed later, in guiding your eyes toward that large object so that it falls in the center of your vision, a process known as *foveation.* The midbrain visual system, however, cannot make fine discriminations of visual objects (e.g., recognize the object as a car); thus only after the object is in central vision can it be identified precisely by other brain regions that are specialized for object recognition. The role of the superior colliculus in orienting toward certain types of visual information and guiding the

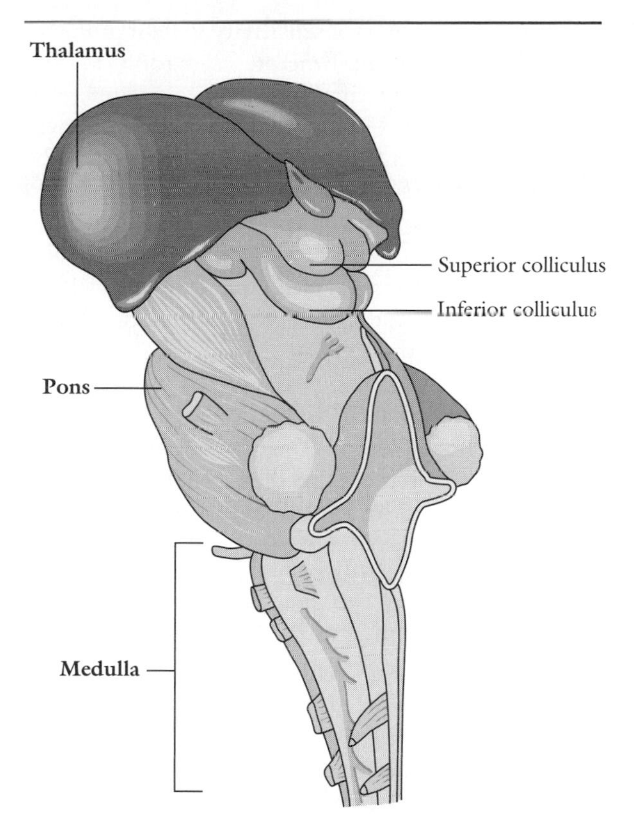

FIGURE 1.8 Brain stem, including medulla, pons, and midbrain. Note the position of the inferior and superior colliculi on the dorsal surface of the midbrain. Above the midbrain lies the thalamus, an important portion of the diencephalon.

eyes toward objects of interest is a subject revisited in Chapter 8.

Hypothalamus

The general role of the **hypothalamus** (see Figure 1.5b) is to control behaviors that help the body satisfy its needs so it can maintain equilibrium. When organisms have a particular need, they generally emit a behavior designed to bring the body back to a stable state (this stable state is known as *homeostasis*). For example, when hungry or thirsty, a person will engage in behaviors that lead to ingesting food or drink, or if cold, the person will search for a sweater or a blanket. The hypothalamus provides the signals telling the brain that these sorts of behaviors are called for.

Let's now examine the role of the hypothalamus in each of a variety of such functions in more detail. One of the main functions of the hypothalamus is to aid in feeding and drinking behavior. For example, research with animals has demonstrated that damage to the ventromedial region of the hypothalamus causes an animal to eat more than is required to maintain a normal body weight; such behavior eventually leads to obesity. Likewise, *lesions* (wounds, damage, or injuries) to dorsal and lateral regions of the hypothalamus can interfere with water intake. Another main function of the hypothalamus is to aid in regulation of body temperature. Some neurons in both anterior and posterior sections of the hypothalamus detect changes in the temperature of the skin or blood and are therefore similar to a thermostat in their function.

The hypothalamus also has an intimate relationship with the *hormonal system,* which is the system whereby chemical messengers are carried throughout the body by means of the bloodstream so as to exert their influence on target organs far from their point of production. The hypothalamus either secretes hormones itself or produces other factors that regulate activity of additional brain regions that secrete hormones. This linkage of the hypothalamus to the hormonal system helps explain its role in sexual behavior, daily (diurnal) rhythms, and fight-or-flight reactions.

Certain regions of the hypothalamus, such as the *sexually dimorphic nucleus,* vary in size between males and females, a difference seen in many mammalian species, including humans. Other regions of the hypothalamus, such as the *suprachiasmatic nucleus,* play a role in diurnal rhythms. The suprachiasmatic nucleus receives input from the retina and, in response, controls fluctuations in the release of hormones during the day. Finally, lateral areas of the hypothalamus are important for activating certain bodily responses such as the fight-or-flight reactions that animals have in threatening situations.

Thalamus

Along with the hypothalamus, the **thalamus** (see Figures 1.4, 1.5b and 1.8) is part of the **diencephalon.** It is a large relay center for almost all sensory information coming into the cortex and almost all motor information leaving it. A **relay center** is a brain region in which the neurons from one area of the brain synapse onto neurons that then go on to synapse somewhere else in the brain. Often, the pattern of connections between neurons at relay centers serves to reorganize information before it is sent elsewhere in the nervous system. For example, in the visual system, information from the retina comes, via the optic tract, to synapse onto the *lateral geniculate nucleus* of the thalamus. The pattern of connections is such that one layer of the lateral geniculate, the *magnocellular layer,* tends to receive input from cells that are extremely sensitive to low levels of light and quite insensitive to color, whereas the *parvocellular layer* receives information from cells that are color sensitive and need higher levels of light to function. Thus, at this relay point, information is reorganized on its way to the brain so that information about color and light intensity are segregated (Zeki & Shipp, 1988).

To give you a better sense of how certain brain regions, including the thalamus, act as relay centers, consider an analogy to the distribution of eggs laid by a group of chickens, each of which has a particular roost. In this case, eggs, rather than information, are being relayed from one point to another. Initially, each hen lays a set of eggs in her nest. These eggs are then sent down the conveyor belt toward the processing plant in a systematic order so that eggs laid by hens with roosts next to each other end up on the belt next to each other. However, as the eggs reach the plant, they are sorted into two piles on the basis of size; therefore, all the small eggs are packaged together and all the large ones are packaged together. Such a system preserves basic information about life in the henhouse (because eggs from hens with adjacent roosts get packaged next to each other), but nonetheless also sorts the information in a novel way (because the eggs are now segregated with regard to size).

Likewise, if we go back to the visual system, when information leaves the retina it does so with regard to where in the retina a cell is located but without regard to a cell's sensitivity to color or degree of illumination. However, the partitioning of information between the magnocellular and parvocellular layers ensures that the information leaving the thalamus is segregated on the basis of sensitivity to light intensity and color, at the same time preserving information about where in the retina those cells originated.

The connections of the thalamus are extremely complicated, and understanding all of them could be a course unto itself. For our purposes, we should know that the patterns of connections, both to and from the thalamus, are very specific. One particular region of the thalamus receives information from just one sensory system and projects to only one particular region of the cortex.

Major Subcortical Systems

Two important neural systems reside mainly within regions of the midbrain and diencephalon: the basal ganglia, important for motor control, and the limbic system, important for emotions. Because many or all the structures in these systems are located in regions below the cerebral cortex, they are referred to as *subcortical* systems.

The **basal ganglia** consist of the *caudate nucleus,* the *putamen,* and the *globus pallidus,* all of which are structures located near the thalamus (Figure 1.9). Degeneration or destruction of these areas leads to difficulty in motor control, generally characterized by involuntary movements. Damage to the globus pallidus leads to involuntary twisting and turning of the limbs, whereas damage to the caudate nucleus and putamen causes involuntary movements, such as tremors while the person is at rest, as well as the introduction of extra movements into a standard progression of voluntary movement such as walking. We discuss the role of these structures in motor behavior in much more detail in Chapter 5.

The **limbic system** is a series of subcortical structures that were initially believed to be a circuit for integrating emotional information between various parts of the nervous system. These structures were thought to allow mainly for the processing of emotional information by linking information from the sensory world and from an individual's internal state with information from the cortex. For example, if a small animal sees a larger one, it must integrate (1) information from its hypothalamus about fear, (2) information from its visual cortex identifying the large animal, and (3) information from the brain regions involved in memory that reminds the small

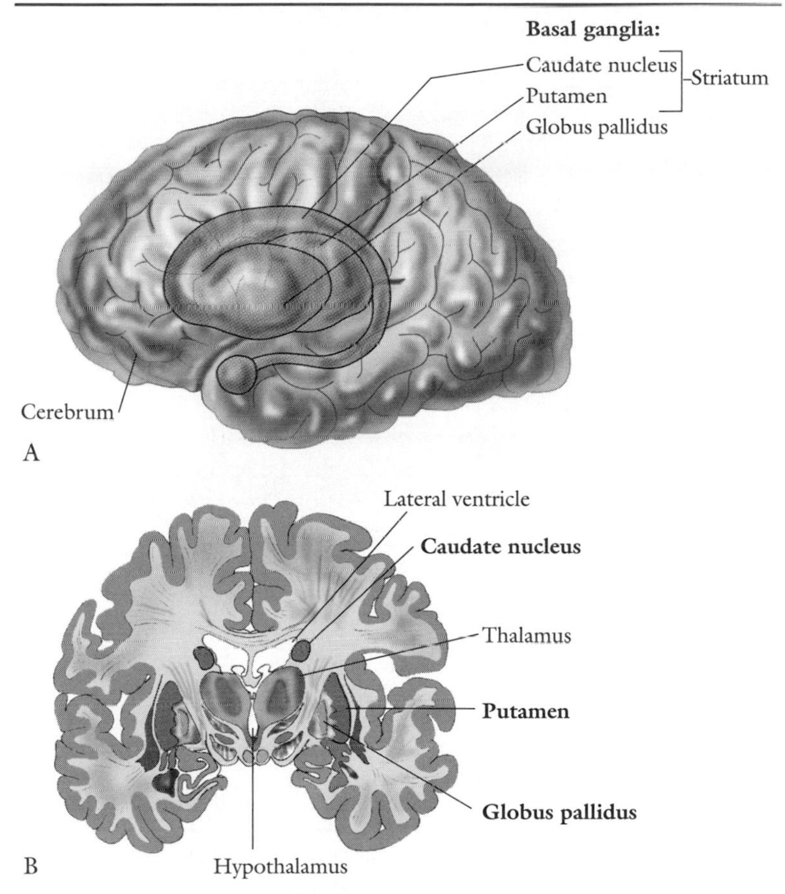

FIGURE 1.9 The location of basal ganglia in relation to other cortical and subcortical structures. (A) Left hemisphere, lateral perspective. (B) Coronal view.

animal whether previous encounters with this type of large animal were dangerous. Although the general concept of the limbic system has been retained, we know now that the structures comprising the limbic system play a much more complicated role in a variety of functions.

Limbic structures include the *amygdala,* the *hypothalamus,* the *cingulate cortex,* the *anterior thalamus,* the *mammillary body,* and the *hippocampus* (Figure 1.10). We discuss the roles of these structures in more detail in later chapters. For example, the amygdala has been implicated in the control of fear and is thought to play a prominent role in emotional functioning, as discussed in Chapter 12. The hippocampus plays an important role in memory, specifically the formation of new long-term memories, as described in Chapter 10, and the cingulate cortex has been implicated in motor control and in the selection of actions, as discussed in more detail in Chapters 5 and 8.

Cerebral Cortex

The cerebral cortex is the region that most often comes to mind when we think of the brain (see Figure 1.5). The cortex plays a primary role in the majority of functions that we discuss in the remainder of this text, such as object recognition, spatial processing, and attention. The cortex is divided into two physically separated halves, each called a **cerebral hemisphere.** Although at first glance these two hemispheres look similar, we learn in Chapter 4 that they differ both in function and in anatomy. Each convolution, or bump, of the brain is called a **gyrus** (plural: gyri) and is basically a giant sheath of neurons wrapped around the other brain structures just discussed. These convolutions serve to pack more brain tissue into a smaller space, much as rolling your clothes allows you to get more of them into your suitcase. Each valley between the bumps is called a **sulcus** (plural: sulci), and if it is deep it is known as a **fissure.** Every brain has the same basic gyral pattern, just as every face has the same basic pattern (i.e., eyes above the nose, mouth below the nose). However, subtle individual variations exist in the gyral pattern, just as facial configuration varies (e.g., some people have wide-set eyes, whereas in others the eyes are close together). The major gyri and sulci of the brain and their names are shown in the endpapers on the inside front cover of your book. They are located there so it will be easy for you to find the particular portions of the brain that we are discussing as you go through the book. Notice that the

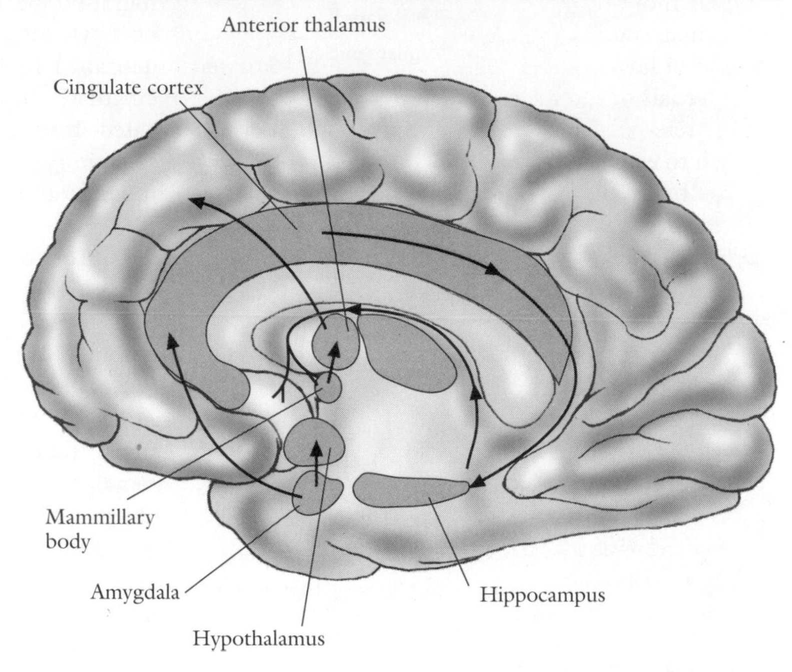

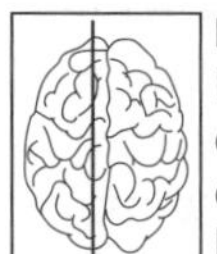

FIGURE 1.10 The structures that comprise the limbic system. Left hemisphere, medial view of the limbic system, which comprises the amygdala, the mammilary body, the cingulate cortex, the anterior thalamus, the hippocampus, and the hypothalamus.

labels for the gyri are in black ink whereas those for the sulci are in red ink.

Three major fissures serve as prominent landmarks in the brain because they provide a means for conceptualizing distinctions in function between major brain regions. The first of these is the **central fissure,** sometimes called the *Rolandic fissure,* which separates each hemisphere of the brain in an anterior-posterior dimension. In general, areas of the brain in front of the central fissure are more involved in motor processing, whereas those behind are more involved in sensory processing. The second major fissure is the **Sylvian (lateral) fissure,** which separates each hemisphere of the brain in the dorsal-ventral dimension. This division is important because the area of the brain below the Sylvian fissure is the temporal lobe, which plays an important role in memory, emotion, and auditory processing. The third major fissure is the **longitudinal fissure,** which separates the right cerebral hemisphere from the left. This division is important because each hemisphere has a unique specialization with regard to both cognitive and emotional functioning.

These three major fissures also divide each hemisphere into four major regions, or lobes. The area in front of the central fissure is known as the **frontal lobe.** The area below the Sylvian fissure is the **temporal lobe.** The region directly behind the central fissure but above the Sylvian fissure is the **parietal lobe.** The remaining region of the brain behind the parieto-occipital sulcus is the **occipital lobe** (see figures on the inside front cover of the book).

 A Closer Look at the Cerebral Cortex

Because the cortex plays a prominent role in many functions that we think of as uniquely human, we must examine it in more detail. We begin by briefly discussing the anatomical characteristics of the cortex and a system of how cortical regions can be distinguished on the basis of the pattern of cellular organization, often referred to as *cytoarchitectonics*. Then, we switch to examining regions of the cortex according to the functions that each serves. We discuss not only the areas of the brain that are important for receiving sensory information from the outside world, but also the areas that are important for controlling the motor output of the body. Finally, we examine an overview of the functions of the remaining areas of the cortex, most of which are devoted to cognitive and emotional function.

Cytoarchitectonic Divisions

Although all regions of cortex have five or six layers, or *laminae*, of cells, the relative thickness of each layer, as well as the size and the shape of cells within those layers, varies between brain regions. Neuroanatomists have identified the areas of the cortex in which the laminar organization and nature of cells within those layers are similar. From these findings has emerged what is known as a **Brodmann map** (named after its creator), divided into distinct areas, which is shown on the inside back cover of your book. It is useful to bear in mind that these boundaries on the Brodmann map are not always absolute. Sometimes, they reflect smoother transitions; therefore, the borders may be considered "fuzzy."

Although the distinctions between regions in the Brodmann map are made entirely on the basis of anatomy, with no regard to function, in some cases regions with distinct cytoarchitectonic characteristics also have distinct functions. In other cases, the correlation between neuroanatomy and function is less clear. One of the main reasons to be familiar with the Brodmann map is that use of this system has become very popular with cognitive neuroscientists as a way to refer to particular regions of brain tissue. In Chapter 3 we discuss the explosion of research utilizing brain imaging techniques that are designed to determine which regions of the brain are physiologically active during performance of a specific task. To convey the location of these regions to the reader, scientists often refer to the activated brain region by means of the number assigned to that region on the Brodmann map. For example, *Broca's area*, a region of the left hemisphere that is important to speech output, is often referred to in Brodmann's terminology as area 44 (abbreviated as BA 44, for Brodmann Area 44). Alternatively, this same region could be called the *frontal opercular region* (see endpaper on the inside front cover).

Primary Sensory and Motor Cortices

The first region in the cortex to receive information about a particular sensory modality (e.g., visual information) is known as **primary sensory cortex.** The **primary motor cortex** is the region of the cortex that is the final exit point for neurons controlling the fine motor control of the body's muscles. The locations of the primary sensory areas and primary motor cortex are presented in Figure 1.11.

The organization of primary sensory regions is dictated by the physical attributes of the world to which our sensory receptors are sensitive. Let's use *audition* (the sense or power of hearing) to illustrate this point. In some alternative universe, we might have evolved so that the sensory receptors in the cochlea of the ear, known as *hair cells,* were organized to allow certain receptors to respond only to loud sounds and others only to soft sounds. However, in our world this is not the case. Rather, the hair cells in the cochlea of the ear are differentially sensitive to sounds of different frequencies (i.e., low tones vs. high tones), which we perceive as tones of different pitch. Thus, frequency is the attribute of auditory information that is coded by the nervous system. Later in this chapter, we see that the sensitivity of the sensory receptors to frequency is reflected in the organization of primary auditory cortex in that some regions are active when high tones are heard and other regions are active when low tones are heard.

The primary sensory and motor areas share some general characteristics of organization that are worth noting now, before we discuss the specifics of each system. First, all these brain areas are organized so that specific attributes of the physical world are "mapped" onto brain tissue. For example, motor control of a specific region of the body is controlled by a specific region of primary motor cortex. Thus,

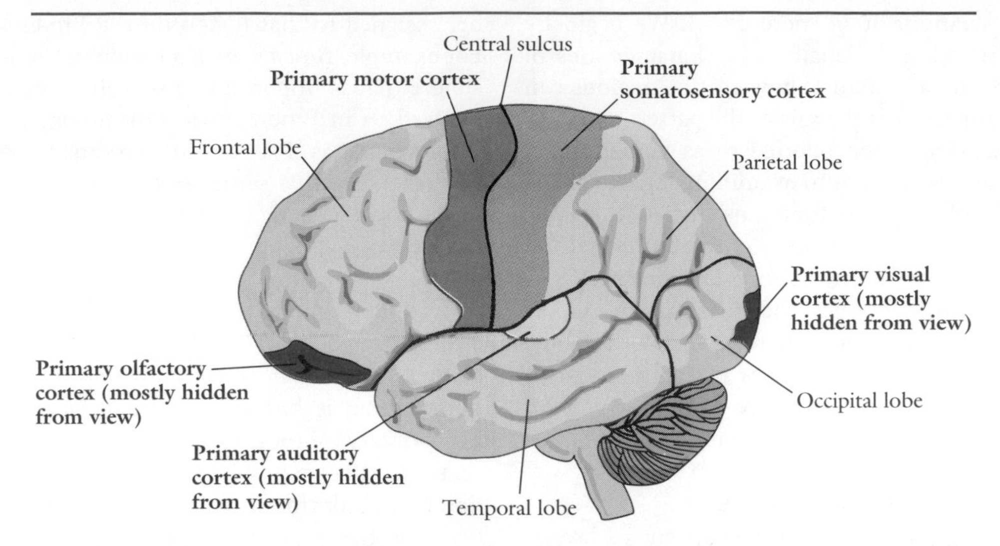

FIGURE 1.11 Primary sensory and motor cortices. All the primary sensory areas are posterior to the central sulcus, whereas primary motor cortex is anterior.

movement of the index finger is controlled by one specific region of the motor cortex rather than a multiplicity of areas. Second, these maps are distorted relative to the physical world. They appear to reflect the density of receptors (or effectors) within a system. For example, we have a much higher density of receptors at the fovea, the focal point of our vision, than for more lateral locations. Likewise, much more of the primary visual cortex is devoted to processing visual information from the central part of the visual world as compared with the periphery. Third, the mapping of the world onto brain tissue occurs in an upside-down and backward manner for vision, touch, and motor control. For example, information from the upper right-hand portion of the body or world is processed by primary sensory or motor cortex in the ventral portion of the left hemisphere.

• *MOTOR CORTEX* •

The *primary motor cortex* resides directly in front of the central fissure in a long, narrow band called the *motor strip.* It begins deep within the longitudinal fissure, rises up to the top of the brain, and then continues down to the Sylvian fissure. It falls mainly within Brodmann area 4. Look at Figure 1.12, which depicts the body regions that are controlled by each portion of the motor strip. This map is often referred to as the *homunculus,* meaning "little man." As you look at Figure 1.12, note that a couple of features bear out the generalizations we just discussed. First, notice that the mapping of the body onto the brain is inverted both with regard to top and bottom and with regard to left and right. The inversion left-right occurs because the left motor strip controls the right side of the body and the right motor strip controls the left side of the body. The inversion top-bottom occurs because the area of the motor strip controlling the toes and feet is at the top end of the motor strip, actually within the longitudinal fissure, and the control of the face is most ventral on the lateral surface of the brain.

Second, notice that the mapping is distorted in that the size of the area of brain tissue devoted to control of a particular body part is disproportionate to the size of that body part. Notice which regions of the body have large amounts of cortex devoted to their control despite their relatively small size: the face, the larynx, the vocal cords, and the hands. As you may surmise, the distortion of the map depends, in large part, on the degree to which we have fine motor control of a body part. The body parts for which we have a large degree of fine motor control, such as the face and the hand, have a

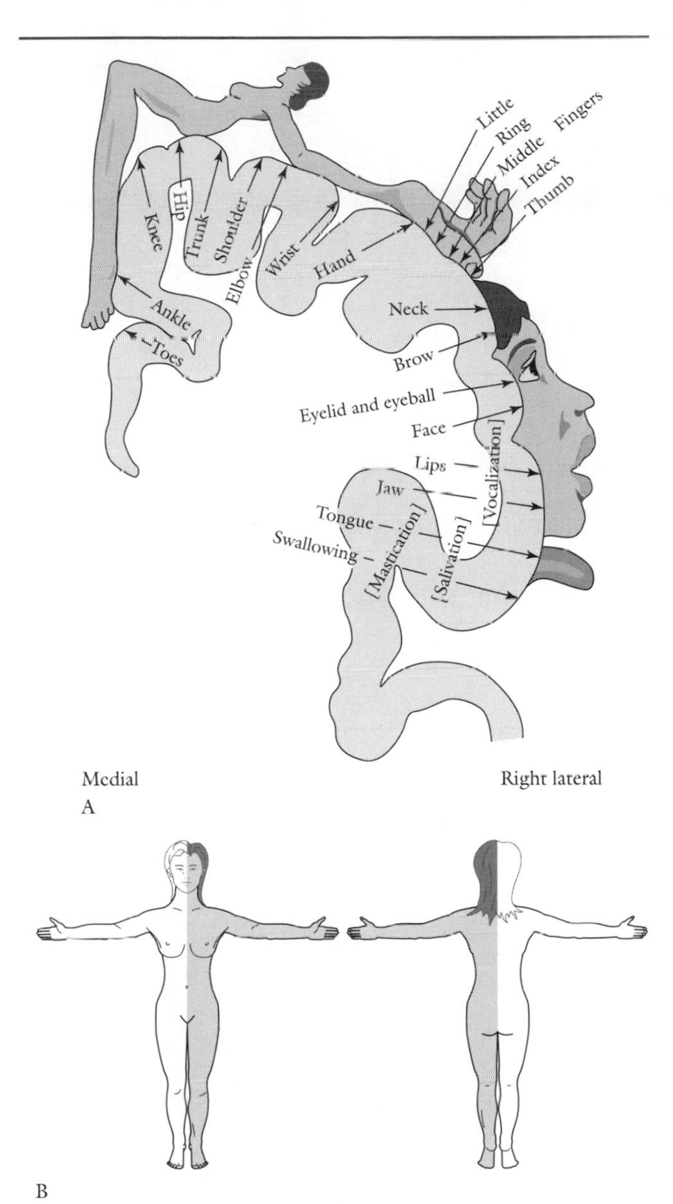

FIGURE 1.12 Motor homunculus in the right hemisphere. (A) The regions of the body for which we have precise motor control, such as the hand and vocal musculature, have a large region of motor cortex devoted to their control. In contrast, large body parts for which we have relatively poor fine motor control, such as the trunk, have a relatively small region of the cortex devoted to their control. (B) The motor cortex in the right hemisphere controls movement on the left side of the body as depicted by the shaded regions on the body.

disproportionately larger area of brain tissue devoted to their control than do areas of the body for which we have little fine motor control, such as the thigh.

The functional significance of this distortion can be understood when we consider the extremely precise fine motor control needed to express emotion, speak, and manipulate objects, actions that are performed by the face, the vocal apparatus, and the hands, respectively. Hence, large sections of the motor cortex are devoted to control of these body regions. In comparison, we have little fine motor control of the muscles of our backs, so only a small region of the motor strip is devoted to their control, even though the back is one of the larger regions of the body.

What are the effects of damage to the primary motor cortex? Because the neurons in the motor cortex control the amount of force to be applied by muscles, damage to primary motor cortex leads to muscle weakness on the contralateral side of the body. For example, damage to dorsal regions of the motor strip results in weakness of the bottom part of the body (recall the upside-down orientation of the homunculus), whereas damage to ventral regions of the motor strip often leads to weakness in face and arm muscles. As discussed in Chapter 5, the body has multiple systems for muscle control. Hence, damage to the motor cortex does not cause total paralysis because the other motor systems can compensate for the damage. However, the ability to move muscles independently of one another is lost, as are the abilities required for fine motor control, such as is needed to grasp something between the thumb and forefinger. When massive destruction to the motor strip occurs along with damage to the basal ganglia (as often occurs after stroke), paralysis on the contralateral side of the body is observed and results in a deficit known as **hemiplegia.**

• *SOMATOSENSORY CORTEX* •

The *primary somatosensory cortex* is the portion of the cortex that receives information about tactile stimulation, **proprioception** (the perception of the position of body parts and their movements), and pressure and pain sensations from internal organs and muscles. It is located directly posterior to the central fissure. It is located just behind the central fissue in Brodmann areas 1, 2, and 3.

The skin contains various nerve endings, or receptors, that are sensitive to different aspects of tactile information, such as pain, pressure, vibration, and temperature. This information travels to the cortex along two main routes. Crude tactile information, along with information about pain and temperature, is sent to the cortex by neurons that synapse at dorsal regions of the spinal cord. From there information is carried to the thalamus and then to the cortex. Information about fine touch and proprioception enters the spinal column but does not synapse until the medulla, from which point it crosses over and is carried to the thalamus and subsequently onto the cortex.

Like the motor homunculus, the map of the body onto the primary somatosensory cortex is inverted left-right and top-bottom. The distortion of body parts in the somatosensory map is proportional to the density of touch receptors. In general, areas that have a high density of tactile receptors have large areas of the somatosensory strip devoted to receiving information from them, and areas of the body that have relatively few tactile receptors have relatively small regions of brain tissue devoted to receiving information from them. The mapping of the body's sense of touch onto the somatosensory cortex is illustrated in Figure 1.13.

If you compare this map with that of the motor strip in Figure 1.12, you can see that the map of somatosensory cortex looks similar but is not identi-

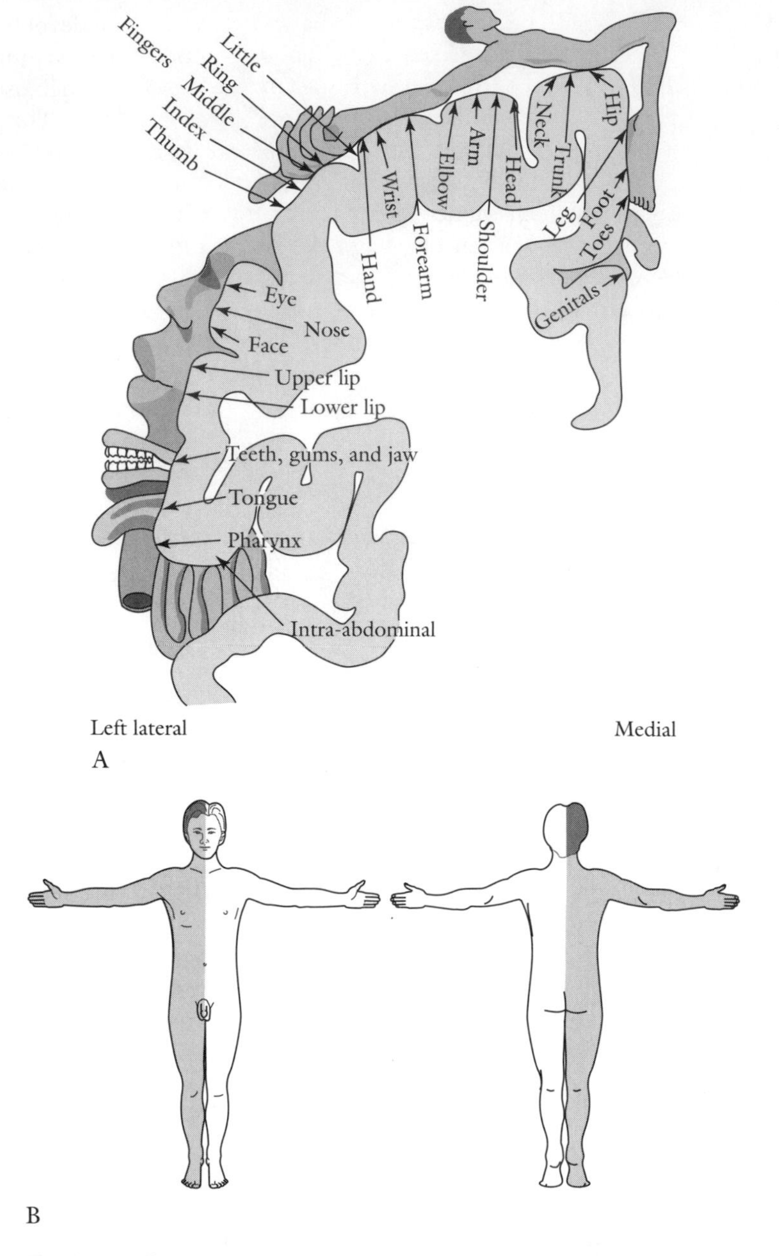

FIGURE 1.13 Somatosensory homunculus in the left hemisphere. (A) Like the motor homunculus, the somatosensory homunculus is distorted, with regions of high tactile sensitivity occupying large regions of cortex. Although the distortion is similar to that of the motor homunculus, it is not identical. (B) Sensory information from the right side of the body is sent to the primary somatosensory cortex of the left hemisphere.

cal to that of the motor homunculus. The differences clearly arise because what is being mapped in the somatosensory strip is sensitivity of touch, not precision of motor control. Yet, striking similarities are apparent. These similarities should not be surprising because the parts of our body for which we have fine motor control, such as our hands, are the same areas for which we need a fine sense of touch. Agile manipulation of an object requires not only that we be able to move our hands and fingers, but also that our sense of touch be equally fine so that we have tactile feedback on which to base our movements. If this relationship is not intuitively obvious, consider, for instance, how difficult it is to deftly manipulate something like your car keys in the winter when you are wearing a pair of gloves and your sense of touch is reduced.

What are the consequences of damage to the somatosensory strip? Rather than obliterating all sense of touch, such damage compromises fine discriminations of touch on the side of the body contralateral to the damaged primary somatosensory cortex. So, for example, if you put a piece of cloth in the hand of an individual who sustained damage to the somatosensory strip, that person would know something was placed there but would have difficulty determining whether the cloth was velvet or burlap. Furthermore, if touched multiple times in quick succession, that person likely would have trouble determining the number of times she or he had been touched. Finally, if that individual was touched in two places near each other (e.g., two places on the back of the palm about 5 mm apart), he or she would have difficulty knowing that the touch had occurred in two separate places. This type of discrimination is known as *two-point discrimination,* and our sensitivity to it varies depending on the body part. The distance required to perceive two points as distinct is smallest for the hands and fingers (with the largest number of receptors) and largest for the shoulders, thighs, and calves (with the smallest number of receptors).

One interesting aspect of the somatosensory map of the body is that it appears to provide a means for understanding some phenomena associated with *phantom limb pain,* a symptom common after the loss of a limb. With phantom limb pain, the limb is usually perceived to be in a particular position and may also be perceived to move. In addition to pain, other sensations, such as itchiness, may be perceived. However, reorganization of the primary somatosensory region after limb loss can lead to some atypical feelings. For example, in the case of an individual who lost a hand, touch on his face leads him to report that he feels the phantom hand. Although at first such a claim may seem odd, it isn't if you think about the organization of the somatosensory strip. By referring to Figure 1.13, you can see that the primary somatosensory region that receives tactile information from the hand is adjacent to the area that receives information from the face. In this individual, the reorganization of the somatosensory strip probably led neurons in regions previously devoted exclusively to receiving tactile information from the hand to interact with neurons that receive information from the face (Ramachandran, Rogers-Ramachandran, & Steward, 1992).

• *VISUAL CORTEX* •

The *primary visual cortex* is the first region of the cortex that processes visual information. It is located in Brodmann area 17. The information it receives first impinges on the nervous system in the retina via two types of visual sensory receptors: the *rods,* which are very sensitive to small degrees of light but are insensitive to color, and the *cones,* which are extremely sensitive to color but require a high degree of illumination to function. The light energy detected by these cells is transformed into a neural signal and relayed to the *ganglion cells,* which reside in the retina. The axons of the ganglion cells form the **optic nerve,** which, with the **optic tract,** is the conduit whereby information is carried from the eye to the brain. Ganglion cells synapse on the **lateral geniculate nucleus** of the thalamus, and cells in this brain structure project to primary visual cortex (Figure 1.14).

Although this is the basic outline of the major relay points from the eye to the brain, we must examine the visual system in a bit more detail for a number of reasons. First, doing so enables us to better understand the nature of the mapping of the visual world onto primary visual cortex. Second, a thorough understanding of the wiring of the visual

DISCOVERY OF THE "HOMUNCULUS"

Our knowledge about the organization of the motor cortex is derived in large part from the search for a therapeutic intervention for a particular disease—epilepsy. Although scientists knew from the late 1800s that the left motor strip controlled the right side of the body and vice versa, the precise nature of the homunculus was revealed only in the course of attempting to obtain a better understanding of epilepsy (Novelly, 1992). Observations by neurologists of a particular type of epileptic seizures known as *Jacksonian seizures* (named after the famous neurologist John Hughlings Jackson) revealed that the body was mapped onto the brain in an orderly fashion. In an **epileptic seizure,** neurons in the brain fire in an abnormal manner typified by great bursts, or volleys, of firing, often called *spikes*. In Jacksonian seizures, the tremors follow an orderly pattern, starting in one body part, such as the leg, and moving systematically to the trunk, then to the arms and face. Such a pattern indicates that the seizure begins in one part of the motor strip and proceeds along it in an orderly fashion.

The creation of therapeutic interventions to reduce and control epilepsy earlier in this century dramatically revealed the degree of distortion of the brain map of the motor area. Working at the Montreal Neurological Institute, Wilder Penfield pioneered the use of surgical interventions to excise regions of brain tissue that cause epileptic activity (Penfield & Rasmussen, 1950). Even today, when seizures originate from a specific brain region, often referred to as an *epileptic focus*, and cannot be controlled by drugs, physicians sometimes remove brain tissue at the focus. The rationale for this intervention is that continued seizure activity will recruit otherwise healthy neurons and cause them to become more prone to seizure activity. Although the neurosurgeon wants to remove the region of brain tissue that is misfiring, he or she must ensure that neither the incisions required to reach the focus nor the removal of the misfiring tissue will have devastating effects. Therefore, during surgery, the neurosurgeon needs the ability to map out precisely which regions of the brain control which functions. This is especially true for the motor strip because excision of portions of it can leave a person with severe muscle weakness on the contralateral side of the body.

Let's move into the operating room to see how the mapping is performed. The patient is lying on the operating table, covered with green surgical sheets that are used to form a tent of sorts, with one open side around the patient's head. The patient's face protrudes from under one side of the tent,

system is important to understanding how researchers can examine differences in processing between the two halves, or hemispheres, of the brain (which we learn more about in Chapter 4). Third, an understanding of visual processing is important because vision is one of the keenest senses that humans have. And fourth, our understanding of the neurology of the visual system probably surpasses that of any other sensory system.

To understand the organization of the visual system, take a look at Figure 1.15, and fix your eyes on the dot in the center of the arrow. When you look straight ahead, the information to the right of fixation, known as the **right visual field,** which in this case contains the arrowhead, projects to the left half of the retinas of both your eyes. Information to the left of fixation, known as the **left visual field,** in this case the arrow tail, projects to the right half of the retinas of both your eyes. Except for information in the far periphery of the visual world, all visual information reaches both eyes. The far peripheral portion of the left side of the visual world is detected only by the left eye (in part because the nose precludes the right eye's perception of that part of the visual world); likewise, the far right side is detected only by the right eye. Ultimately, information from the right visual field is directed solely to the primary visual cortex of the left hemisphere, and information from the left visual field projects only to the primary visual cortex of the right hemisphere.

The routing of information from each retina through the optic nerve and tract to the lateral geniculate is tricky. Information from the inside half of each retina, known as the *nasal hemiretina* (because this half of the retina is near your nose), crosses the midline of the body at the **optic chiasm** and projects to the contralateral lateral geniculate. In contrast, information from the outside, or *temporal, hemi-*

whereas the surgeon is situated on the other side at the opening of the tent. Procedure in this operating room is different from what you might expect: Instead of an unconscious patient on the operating table,this patient is alert and talking! Because the brain has no pain receptors, only local anesthetics are used as the surgeon removes a piece of skull to expose the brain underneath. After the brain is exposed, the surgeon places a small piece of metal known as an electrode on the brain. Then a sheet with a number is placed on the brain, adjacent to the electrode. Let's assume that the surgeon starts by placing the electrode directly in front of the central fissure at the most dorsal portion of the brain. Although the patient is lying perfectly still, as soon as the surgeon runs some current through the electrode, the patient's leg begins to twitch involuntarily! When the current is turned off, the twitching stops. The neurosurgeon then announces "Leg movement at position 4" and moves the electrode more ventrally, leaving the marker in place. She or he now places another marker number on the brain and stimulates at the next spot. The patient's thigh begins to twitch. The neurosurgeon continues in this fashion until the whole motor strip is identified.

The need for such mapping is important if you consider, as we already discussed, that each individual's brain is as distinct as each person's face. Although neurosurgeons know that the motor strip lies in front of the central fissure, they don't know exactly where. Consider by analogy the organization of the face. Just as we know that the eyes are always located above the nose, so the neurosurgeon knows that the motor strip is in front of the central fissure. However, this landmark alone is not enough, just as knowing where a person's nose is located does not tell you exactly where his or her eyes are situated. Likewise, precise mapping is needed to determine the extent and range of the motor strip.

In addition to mapping the motor area, a neurosurgeon will also map the primary somatosensory cortex during surgery. In this case, the active cooperation of the patient is even more critical. Only if the patient is conscious can he or she convey to the surgeon where the sensations, such as a tingle, a tickle, or an itch, are being felt as different regions of the somatosensory strip are stimulated. This mapping technique, originally designed to aid the neurosurgeon in therapeutic interventions for epilepsy, has provided extremely useful information about the organization of the primary motor and somatosensory areas as well as language areas. ■

retina projects to the ipsilateral lateral geniculate. This aspect of the visual system's wiring is important because at the lateral geniculate, for the first time, information from one side of space is confined to one half of the brain, and information from the other side of space is confined to the other side of the brain. From the lateral geniculate, information then projects back to the ipsilateral visual cortex.

In Figure 1.15, notice that information about the arrowhead that has landed on the nasal hemiretina of the right eye crosses the midline of the body at the optic chiasm on its way to the lateral geniculate nucleus of the thalamus in the left hemisphere. There it is joined by information about the arrowhead that has landed on the temporal hemiretina of the left eye. Likewise, information about the arrow tail that has landed on the nasal hemiretina of the left eye crosses midline to project to the right lateral geniculate, which is also receiving information from the temporal hemiretina of the right eye. From here information travels ipsilaterally to the visual cortex. Thus, if you trace the path of information separately for the arrow's head and the arrow's tail, you can see that information from the right visual field projects only to the left hemisphere and information from the left visual field projects only to the right hemisphere.

Because of the organization of the visual system, determining whether a difficulty in vision arises from a problem in the eye or a problem in the brain is relatively easy. If the source of the problem is in the eye, the world will look different depending on whether it is being viewed just by the right eye as compared to just by the left eye. For example, if part of the retina of the left eye is damaged, the visual problem will be noticeable when viewing the world with just the left eye open, but nonexistent when just the right eye is open. In contrast, if the problem resides in the brain, the problem is identical no

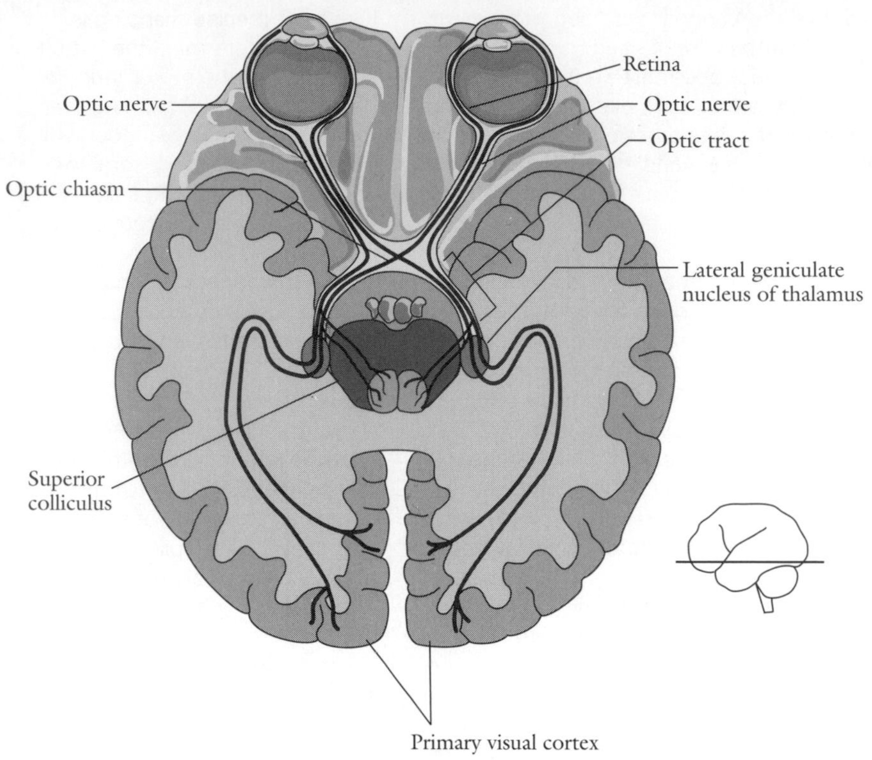

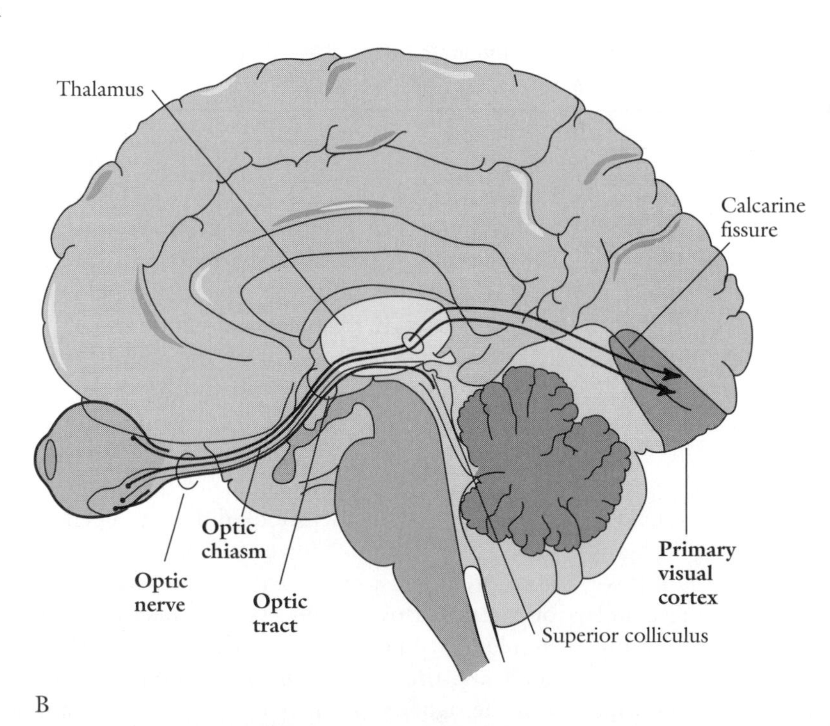

FIGURE 1.14 Pathway from the visual receptors in the retina to the brain.
(A) Horizontal view. The brain receives visual information through two routes. One goes from the retina by means of the lateral geniculate nucleus to visual cortex. The other goes from the retina to the superior colliculus in the midbrain. Information from the inside retina of each eye crosses over to the other side of the brain at the optic chiasm. (B) Right hemisphere, midsagittal view. The group of axons carrying information from the retina to the brain are called the *optic nerve* before they reach the optic chiasm, but the *optic tract* afterward.

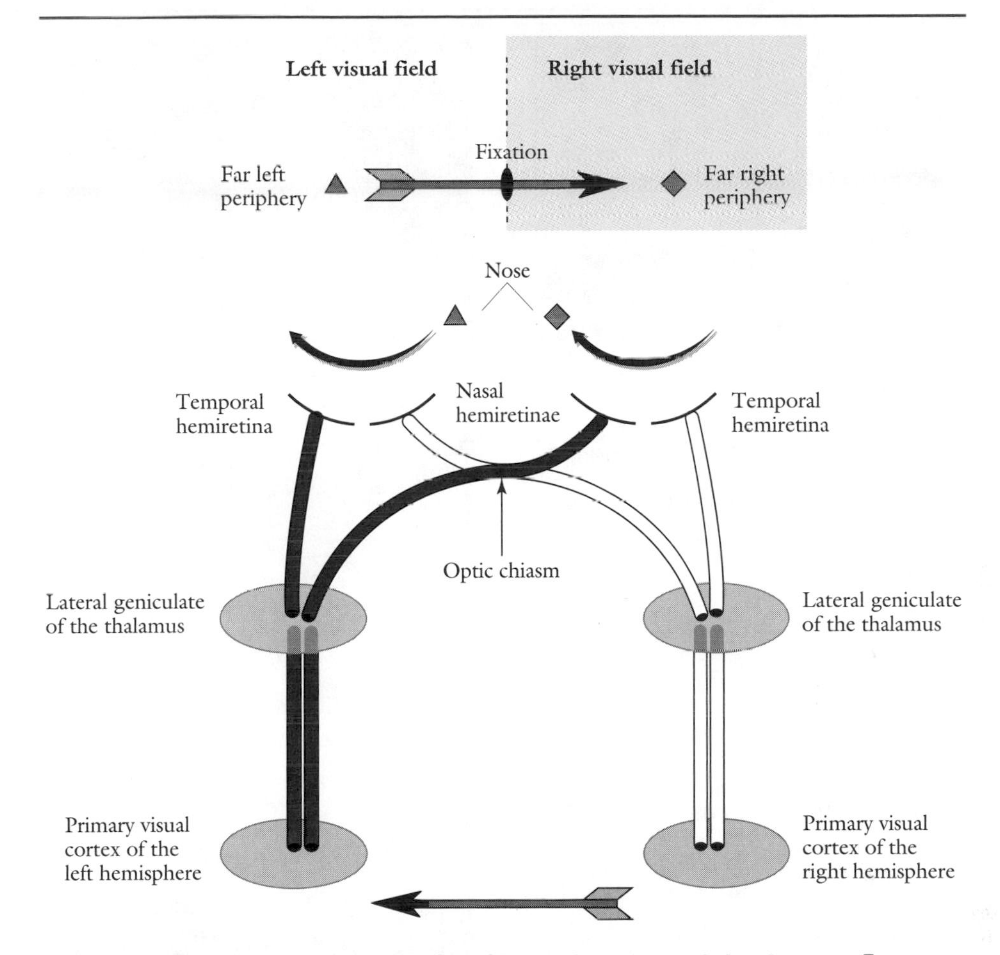

FIGURE 1.15 The mapping of the visual world onto the retina and visual cortex. Except for information in the far periphery, all visual information projects to both eyes. The image on the retina is inverted because light rays are bent as they pass through the eye's lens. Because information from the nasal hemiretinae crosses over at the optic chiasm, the arrowhead projects only to the left hemisphere, whereas the arrow tail projects only to the right hemisphere.

matter which eye is open because *all* information from a specific region of the visual world converges on the same region of the lateral geniculate or primary visual cortex, regardless of whether it was initially received by the right eye or the left. (This is why the crossover of information at the optic chiasm is so important—it allows information from a specific region of space detected by *each* eye to converge on the same region of brain tissue.)

Not only is the mapping of the visual world onto the brain reversed left-right, but as we have seen with other modalities, it is inverted top-bottom as well. Thus, information above the fixation point projects to ventral portions of the visual cortex, and information below the fixation point projects to dorsal portions of the visual cortex. Furthermore, as with the other senses already discussed, the map by which the physical world is transformed onto brain tissue is distorted. Once again, this distortion is related to the density of receptors. The greatest concentration of light receptors is in the *fovea,* or central region of vision. From there, the density of receptors decreases dramatically. Hence, a much larger area of the occipital cortex is devoted to processing information from the central part of vision than is devoted to processing information from more peripheral regions.

A Normal vision

B Quadranopsia

C Homonymous hemianopsia

D Far left peripheral visual field deficit

E Scotoma

F Quadranopsia

FIGURE 1.16 Visual field disorders. (A) The visual world as it appears to an individual with an intact visual system. Where would the damage be located to create the views in (B), (C), (D), (E), and (F)? *Answers:* (B) Ventral regions of the left occipital lobe, (C) all regions of right occipital lobe, (D) damage to the left eye, (E) damage to a small portion of the ventral region of the right occipital lobe, (F) damage to the dorsal region of the left occipital lobe.

Destruction of visual cortex results in an inability to perceive light-dark contrast. If the entire occipital cortex of only one hemisphere is damaged, no visual information can be detected in the contralateral visual field. This condition is known as a **homonymous hemianopsia.** Sometimes just the dorsal or ventral portion of occipital cortex is damaged, in which case just one quadrant of the visual world is lost, a disorder known as **quadranopsia.** In other cases, only small portions of the visual cortex are damaged, resulting in **scotomas,** particular regions of the visual field in which light-dark contrast cannot be detected.

To determine how well you understand the organization of the visual system, take a look at Figure 1.16. Each picture shows a view of the visual world as it appears to a person with damage in a

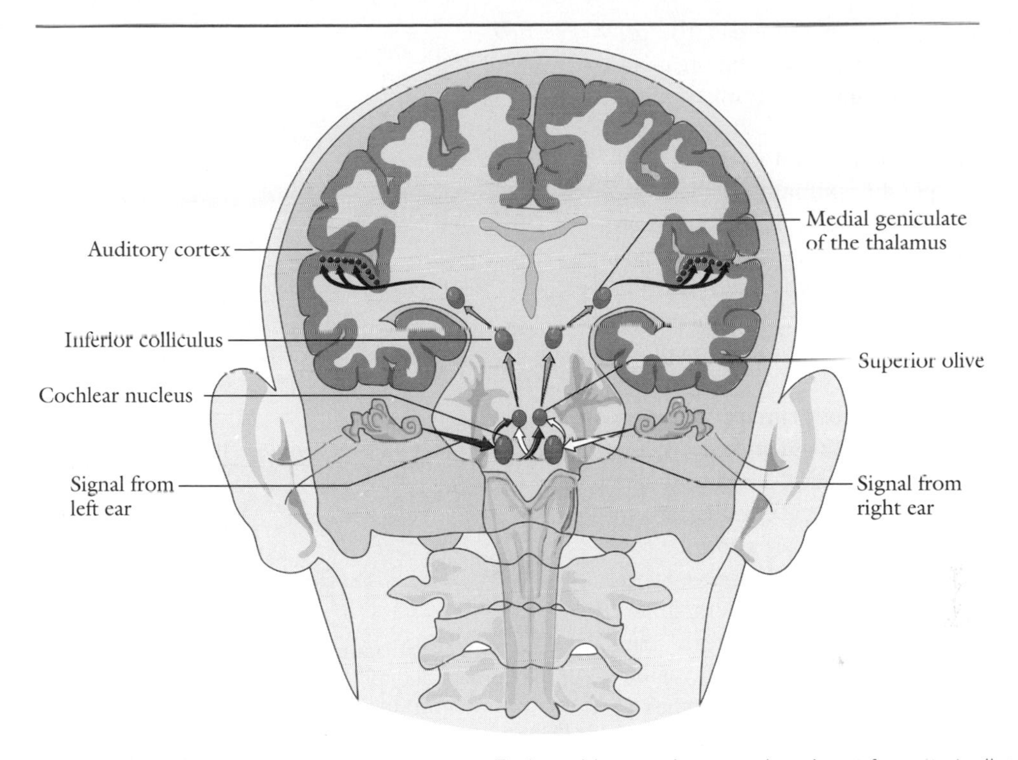

FIGURE 1.17 Auditory pathway from cochlea to cortex. Each cochlear nucleus receives input from its ipsilateral ear only. All subsequent connections, however, are both ipsilateral and contralateral.

particular portion of the visual system. Try to determine the location of the lesion in the visual system for each situation shown.

• *AUDITORY CORTEX* •

The human auditory system is sensitive to sound, which is essentially pressure waves in the air. The physical energy in sound waves causes vibration of the eardrum and the bones in the ear. These vibrations are transformed into pressure waves in a liquid in the cochlea, which contains hair cells that transduce pressure waves into a neural signal. Hair cells are aligned so that those nearest the bones in the ear are more sensitive to high-frequency sounds and those farther away are more sensitive to low-frequency sounds. These hair cells synapse on spiral ganglion cells, the axons of which form the **auditory nerve,** which is the main conduit of auditory information to the central nervous system, where it synapses on the *cochlear nucleus* in the medulla.

Unlike other sensory systems in which information from one side of the body projects solely to the contralateral hemisphere, the auditory system is organized such that there are both ipsilateral and contralateral projections from the ear to the brain. Hence auditory information received at the right ear projects to the left and right hemispheres. The point at which two copies of information are created is the cochlear nucleus in the medulla. There some nerve fibers cross the midline and synapse on the contralateral superior olive, whereas others remain ipsilateral and synapse on the ipsilateral superior olive. From the superior olive, information is sent to the *inferior colliculus,* then to the **medial geniculate of the thalamus** (the thalamic relay station of auditory information), and finally onto primary auditory cortex. In addition, some information projects directly from the cochlear nucleus to the inferior colliculus. The primary auditory cortex of the human brain is located in the superior portion of the posterior temporal lobe in an area called **Heschl's gyrus,** which is located in Brodmann area 41. The pathway whereby information is carried from the ear to the primary auditory area is depicted in Figure 1.17.

Like other primary sensory areas, the *primary auditory cortex* has a specific organization, described as **tonotopic,** meaning that it is organized with regard to the frequency of a tone. In the auditory cortex, information from cells that all respond maximally to the same frequency converge on the same region of cortex. The mapping of auditory cortex is such that the lowest tones are processed rostrally and laterally and tones of increasing frequency are processed more caudally and medially (Figure 1.18).

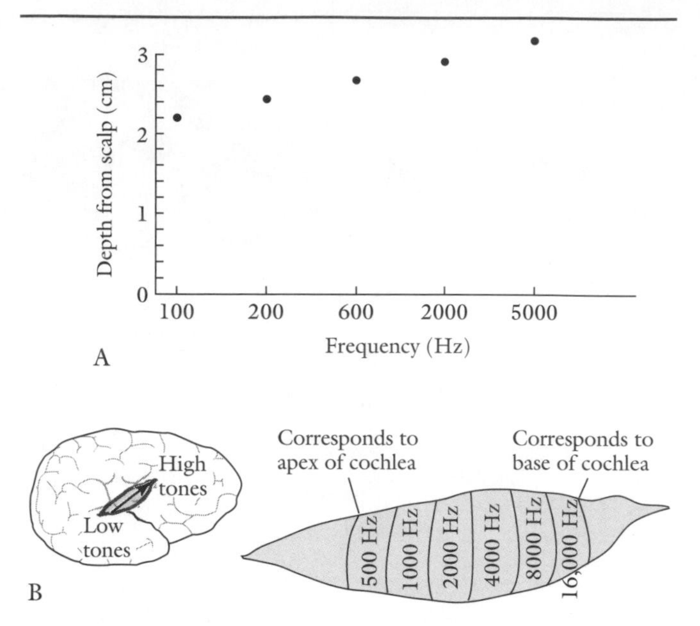

FIGURE 1.18 Organization of primary auditory cortex. (A) A map of the primary auditory cortex of the right hemisphere emphasizing depth from the scalp. Low-frequency tones are processed closer to the scalp, whereas high-frequency tones are processed more deeply within the cortex. (B) Right hemisphere, lateral view of the oblique angle at which the tonotopic map in primary auditory cortex is aligned.

Unilateral damage to primary auditory cortex does not impair the ability to perceive all sound because of the redundancy provided by both crossed and uncrossed connections in the auditory system. If primary auditory cortex in the right hemisphere is damaged, primary auditory cortex in the left hemisphere can still process sound from both ears because it receives information both ipsilaterally and contralaterally. So, what types of deficits are observed after damage is sustained by auditory cortex in one hemisphere? First, the softest intensity that can be perceived—that is, the *sound threshold*—becomes higher contralateral to the damaged hemisphere. In addition, the ability to perceive the location of a sound becomes poorer for the contralateral side of space.

If you have had a course in physiological psychology or perception, this finding should not be surprising. You may remember that the mechanisms used to determine the location of the sound involve a comparison of the difference in the intensity and time at which auditory information arrives at each ear. Quite simply, if a sound is located closer to your right ear than to your left, the sound will be louder at the right ear (and will arrive there sooner). Because unilateral damage to primary auditory cortex disrupts the ability to judge the loudness of sounds, you can see why individuals with such damage have difficulty localizing the source of a sound.

• *OLFACTORY CORTEX* •

Our sense of smell comes from receptors in the nasal mucosa that send information about odors to the **olfactory bulb.** Each of the two bulbs (one in each hemisphere) is a thin strand of neural tissue located directly below the frontal lobe (Figure 1.19). From the olfactory bulb, information is projected in one of two directions. One pathway, which probably mediates our emotional responses to smell, travels to various parts of the limbic system. Another projection is to the medial dorsal thalamus, which then projects to the cortex, specifically, the orbitofrontal lobe, which can hence be considered *primary olfactory cortex.* Olfaction is unique in humans because it is the only sensory system in which information is conveyed ipsilaterally. Hence, information received in the right nostril is sent to the right olfactory bulb, and information received in the left nostril is sent to the left olfactory bulb. Unlike the case of the visual and auditory systems, in which we know that light/dark contrast and sound frequency, respectively, are the critical dimensions of the sensory world that the nervous system processes, the basic dimension by

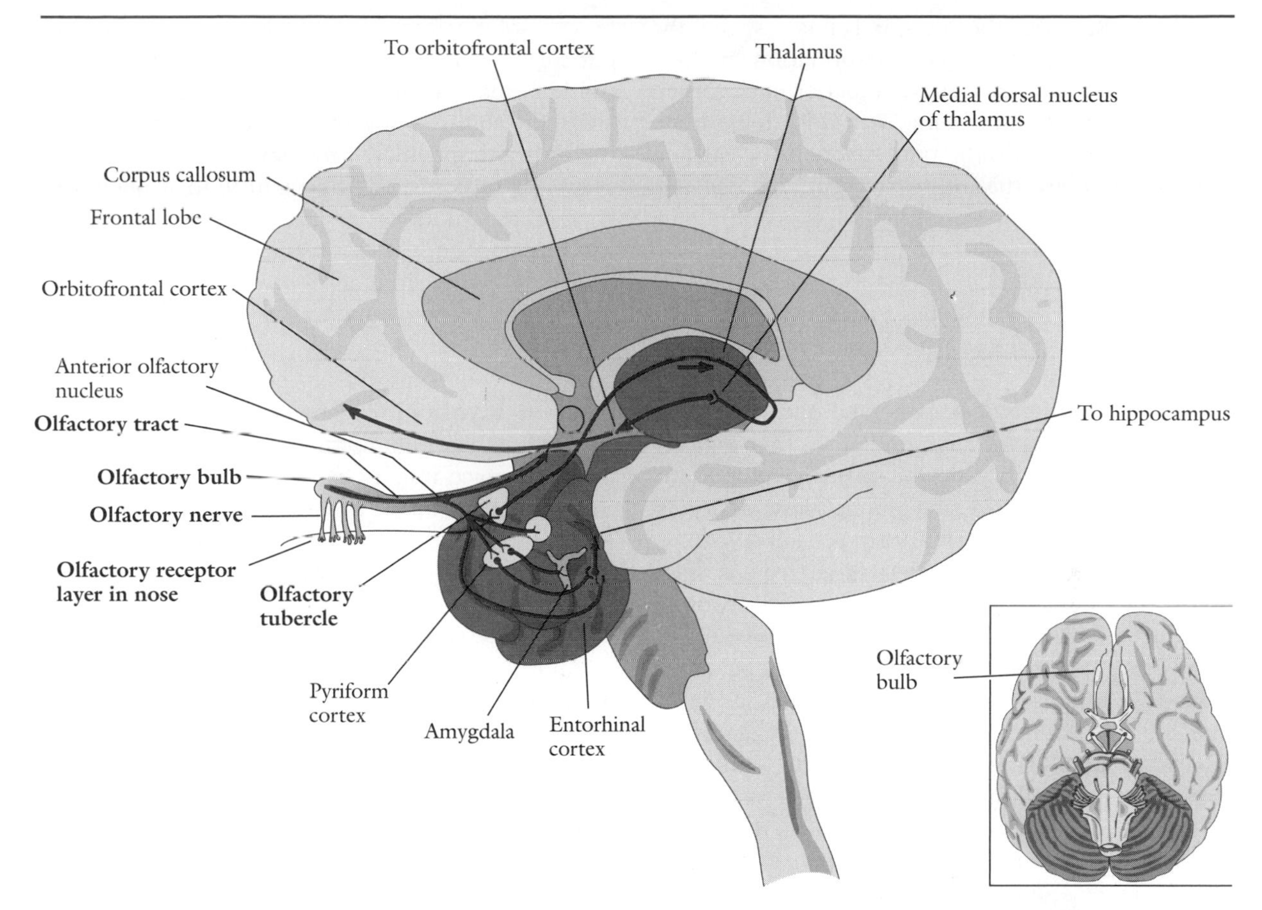

FIGURE 1.19 Path of olfactory information in the cortex. The connections from the olfactory bulb to the cortex from a right hemisphere, midsagittal view. Olfactory information can reach the cortex, specifically orbitofrontal cortex, via two main projections: one via the medial dorsal nucleus of the thalamus and the other via structures in the limbic system. (Inset) The position of the olfactory bulb from a ventral vantage point.

which smell is mapped onto the nervous system is unknown. What we do know, however, is that damage to primary olfactory cortex impairs odor discrimination in humans.

At this point, we have discussed how sensory information is initially handled by the cortex. After processing by primary sensory regions, the information is relayed to *secondary sensory cortex,* which, like primary sensory regions, processes information from only one sensory modality. However, secondary sensory cortex has a more specialized organization. For example, more than 30 regions of secondary visual cortex have been identified, each of which varies in its sensitivity to important visual attributes such as color, orientation, and motion. However, primary and secondary sensory cortices account for only a small proportion of the overall mass of the cortex. Next, we overview the type of processing performed by the remainder of the cortex.

Association Areas

An area of the brain where information from multiple modalities is processed is known as an **association area.** As we shall see, these regions of the brain support the abilities that we tend to think of as distinctly human, such as language, compassion, and foresight. Because the occipital lobe is mainly involved in processing visual information, it does not serve as large an associative function as the other three major lobes of the brain. We now turn to a brief overview of the multiplicity of functions by each of these three lobes: the frontal, the parietal, and the temporal.

• *FRONTAL LOBE* •

In discussing the frontal lobes, researchers and clinicians generally describe it as having three distinct regions: the *primary motor region* (previously discussed), the *premotor region,* and the *prefrontal region.* Prefrontal regions are often further divided into dorsolateral, orbital, and medial regions (see Figure 1.20). The distinction among these regions is based on major cytoarchitectonic subdivisions. Recent evidence suggests that these regions may play very different roles in mental functioning. Although we will talk about these subdivisions in more detail later on, it is important to note here that dorsolateral regions have been implicated in memory and attentional processing, orbital regions in emotional processing, and medial regions in judgment, decision making, and the detection of errors.

Frontal regions are often thought of as the source of some of the most uniquely human abilities. A good generalization about the role of frontal regions is that they are associated with the planning, guidance, and evaluation of behavior. Just as the head of a corporation oversees its day-to-day operations and plans long-term goals for it, the frontal lobes are considered the "executive" of the brain. Not only are the frontal regions important for organizing behavior coherently, but research also suggests that they may allow us to extrapolate forward in time, enabling us to realize the future consequences of our current behavior.

The abilities that are destroyed by frontal lobe damage are not easily categorized under a simple rubric, but the loss of these abilities can nonetheless be profound. For example, individuals with frontal lobe dysfunction may exhibit little decrement in performance when given standardized IQ tests that assess fact knowledge and academic skills, such as knowing the definitions of words, understanding how to solve arithmetic problems, knowing how to put together jigsaw puzzles, and so forth. Yet, disruptions may occur in any or all of the following areas: the ability to organize and sequence behavior; the ability to modulate behavior, especially its initiation or its cessation; the ability to generate an appropriate emotional response; and the ability to use strategies and tags for retrieving memories.

People with frontal lobe damage generally have difficulty knowing how to organize behavior to reach a goal. Although they may know the components or steps in a process, they are unable to put them together in a coherent manner to reach a goal. Thus, in making an omelet, a patient with frontal damage might beat the eggs, place them in the skillet, turn up the heat, and then add the butter. As this example illustrates, the individual knows that making an omelet requires eggs, grease, and heat, but the components cannot be organized in a systematic way to reach the desired endpoint.

Another problem observed in individuals with frontal lobe damage is an increase in what has been called *psychological inertia,* the force that must be overcome to either initiate a process or stop one. This handicap may take many forms. For example, persons with frontal lobe damage may not bathe and change clothes each day on their own volition but will do so if directed to by another individual. Or an individual may sit on a couch for hours without initiating any behavior. Initiating behavior seems to take a monumental effort that the person just cannot muster. Conversely, once involved in a behavior, an individual with frontal lobe damage may find it impossible to stop that behavior. Such patients are likely to **perseverate:** they perform a behavior repeatedly. There is now evidence that obsessive-compulsive disorders, which are characterized by engaging in the same stereotyped motor behavior to ward off some danger (e.g., constantly washing one's hands to prevent infection by germs), result from dysfunction of the frontal lobe, specifically the orbitomedial area, and the subcortical regions to which it connects (e.g., Malloy, 1987).

Developmentally, the frontal lobes are relatively immature in young children; thus, these youngsters often exhibit perseverative tendencies. You may

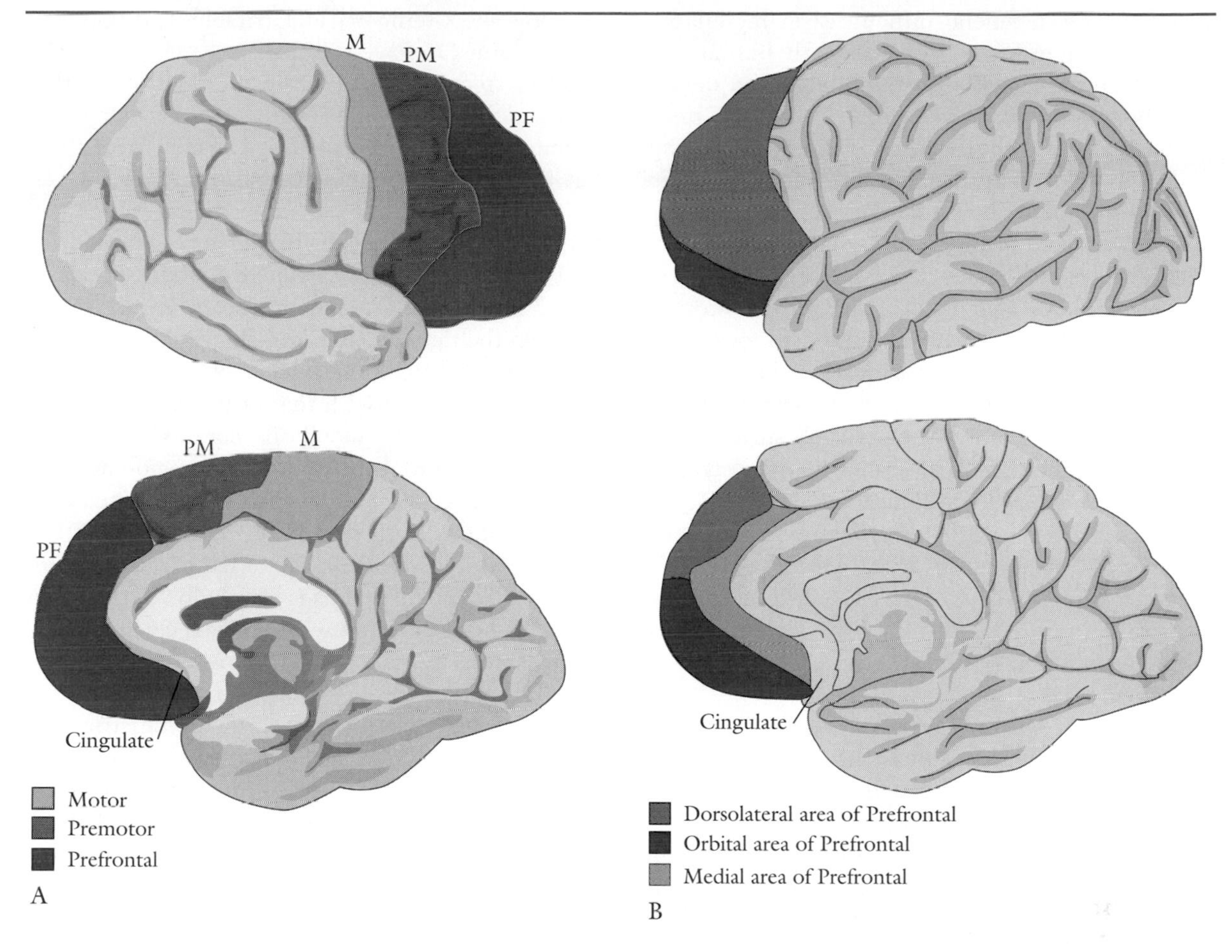

FIGURE 1.20 Divisions of the frontal lobe. (A) The three major divisions of the frontal lobe; primary motor (M), premotor (PM), and prefrontal (PF) regions. (Top) Right hemisphere, lateral view. (Bottom) Right hemisphere, midsagittal view. (B) The prefrontal regions are further divided into dorsolateral, orbital, and medial areas. (Top) Left hemisphere, lateral view. (Bottom) Right hemisphere, midsagittal view.

have had the experience of hiding a child's favorite toy behind one of many pillows. If the first pillow that the child removes does not reveal the toy, he or she will not try the other pillows but will instead go back to the first pillow, if it is replaced, and remove it again and again. Although the child appears to forget where the toy is hidden, research suggests that very young babies, only 2 to 2.5 months old, can remember the location of an object even when it is hidden behind another one (e.g., Baillargeon, 1994). The problem is not so much one of memory, but rather that the child seems to be locked into a perseverative behavioral loop in which the only way to look for the toy is to reach out and move that one particular pillow. This sort of behavioral loop is exactly the type of perseverative behavior that may be exhibited after frontal lobe damage. However, the young child engages in perseverative behavior not because frontal lobes are damaged but because they are relatively immature (A. Diamond, 1990).

Not only do individuals with frontal lobe damage have difficulty in starting and stopping behavior, but they have more general difficulties in modulating behavior. For example, patients with frontal lobe damage are often socially uninhibited and display socially inappropriate behavior. They may make unwanted sexual advances, may tell jokes at inappropriate times, may be insensitive to the social context in which they find themselves (such as a man dressed in a business suit, who after obtaining his boarding pass for an overbooked flight, skips past the remaining long line of haggard customers yelling, "It's Friday, be happy!"), and so forth. This inability to modulate behavior leads to a paradoxical effect: sometimes individuals with frontal lobe damage are insensitive to their social surroundings whereas at other times they are unduly swayed by them. For example, by talking about depressing topics, physicians and other medical personnel may cause an individual with frontal lobe damage to be moved to tears but can reverse the effect and put the individual in an ecstatic mood within minutes by talking about the person's favorite possessions or activities.

From what we just learned, you should not be surprised that frontal regions of the brain have been implicated in emotional functioning. Although we discuss the role of the frontal lobes in emotion in more detail in Chapter 12, let's briefly consider some important points. Commonly, the family and other loved ones of an individual who has sustained frontal lobe damage will comment that the individual doesn't really seem like him- or herself anymore. A formerly quiet and peaceful person may be described as argumentative and prone to outbursts, a previously conscientious and hardworking person may be characterized as irresponsible and lazy, and a previously kind and considerate person may now be found to be selfish and uncaring. In sum, people often say that the individual with frontal lobe damage has undergone a change in personality. One of the most famous early cases in which such changes were documented was that of Phineas Gage, a railroad worker. While he was helping to clear a way for the railroad in 1848, an explosion blew a steel rod through his skull, damaging sections of his frontal cortex. Family and friends complained that Phineas just "wasn't Phineas anymore." Whereas he had been agreeable and persevering before the injury, he was now short-tempered and irritable. The man they knew seemed to have vanished.

More recent research suggests not only that frontal lobe functioning influences personality, a characteristic considered to be constant over time, but that such functioning can also influence a person's internal emotional state, or mood, which can vary over time from happy to sad, from calm to frustrated, from peaceful to agitated. Certain aspects of mood are related to the difference in activation between the right and left frontal regions. In particular, relatively higher activation of the left frontal region as compared with that of the right is associated with positive mood. In contrast, relatively higher activation of the right frontal region as compared with that of the left is generally associated with negative or dysphoric mood (e.g., Davidson, 1992).

For example, after damage to left frontal regions, activation of such regions is clearly lower than that of right frontal regions—an imbalance associated with depressed mood. In fact, in one study approximately 60% of individuals with damage to left frontal regions due to stroke fit the psychiatric definitions of either major or minor depression (Starkstein & Robinson, 1988). You may be thinking, "Well, of course. Anyone who sustains brain damage would have a good reason to be depressed!" However, the probability of depression is much higher after left than after right frontal damage. Furthermore, the extent of the depression does not depend on the severity of the person's cognitive deficits, but is related to the location of the lesion within the left frontal lobe. We discuss these research findings in more detail in Chapter 12.

Frontal regions of the brain are also involved in what are known as **metamemory** functions, which can be thought of as the abilities that allow for the strategic use, deployment, and retrieval of memories. These functions clearly are related to memory, but they don't involve actually remembering a particular item, individual, or fact. In general, the difficulties in metamemory observed after frontal lobe damage are problems with the temporal sequencing or tagging of memories. For example, individuals with frontal damage are unable to determine which of two items in a sequence occurred more recently (B. Milner, Corsi, & Leonard, 1991), even though they can clearly distinguish between items that appeared in a sequence and those that did not (B. Milner & Petrides, 1984). Moreover, if you show individuals with frontal lobe damage a series of items in which some items randomly appear on multiple occasions (e.g., three times, five times, seven times), they have difficulty in estimating how often an item occurred, although they have no difficulty in discerning whether an item was previously viewed (Smith & Milner, 1988).

The frontal lobe, in particular the dorsolateral prefrontal region, is also considered important for keeping memory information online to be used in giving a response. Evidence for this function of frontal regions comes from various sources, including work with monkeys (e.g., Goldman-Rakic, 1990), young infants (A. Diamond, 1990), and adults. Young children, whose frontal lobes are underdeveloped, exhibit deficits in working memory that are similar to those observed in monkeys with damage to dorsolateral regions of the frontal lobe. Such findings are discussed in more detail in Chapter 11.

As this short review illustrates, the frontal regions of the brain are involved in a vast array of behaviors. Rather than being important for specific domains of cognitive activity such as language, spatial processing, or object recognition, frontal regions provide us with executive capabilities that are used across a vast number of domains and allow for flexible and novel behavior.

• *PARIETAL LOBE* •

The parietal lobe of the cortex plays a role in (1) integrating information from various sensory modalities, (2) integrating information from the sensory world with information stored in memory, and (3) integrating information about an individual's internal state with information from the external sensory world. Because this integrative function can occur in various ways, the deficits observed after parietal lobe damage are often diverse and difficult to conceptualize as all falling under the same rubric. However, if you keep in mind that the parietal lobe is critical for associating different forms of information, the array of functions performed by the parietal lobe will not seem all that disjointed.

One way to begin to conceptualize the role of parietal cortex is to consider the results of experiments done with macaque monkeys, because such results nicely illustrate some of the ideas discussed next. In these studies, an electrode is placed into the brain of an animal to record a single cell's activity. The investigator determines what type of stimulus will make the cell fire. This procedure is performed for a multiplicity of different cells all over the area of interest, until the researcher can deduce the critical characteristics required to make cells in that region fire. To understand the role of the parietal lobe, we need to consider what we would observe if we recorded from other brain regions as well. Let's suppose that a banana is in a monkey's field of view. If we recorded from a cell in *inferior temporal cortex* (discussed in the next section), we might find a cell that would fire consistently whenever the banana was within the monkey's field of view but would not fire when other visual forms, such as other monkeys, people, or objects, were within view. (This pattern would occur because regions of inferior temporal cortex are specifically involved in distinguishing between distinct visual forms.) If we recorded from a cell in the parietal lobe, however, we would find that it too would fire whenever the banana came into view, but if and only if the banana was within the monkey's reach. Alternatively, another cell in the parietal lobe might not fire at the sight of the banana alone, but would fire only if the animal was also hungry. Thus, in both cases, the cell would fire in response to some *conjunction* of attributes: the visual stimulus of the banana *and* its position in space, or the visual stimulus of the banana *and* the animal's internal state (e.g., Lynch, 1980). For this reason, we can say that processing by the parietal lobe is *multimodal* in nature.

In humans, the role of the parietal lobe in multimodal integration is seen in many syndromes that occur after damage to this region, including alexia, agraphia, and apraxia, all of which we now discuss in turn.

Alexia and **agraphia,** are, respectively, the inability to read and the inability to write as a result of brain damage. We discuss both these syndromes in more detail in Chapter 9. The fact that alexia and agraphia are caused by parietal lobe damage makes sense if you consider what is involved in reading and writing. What we must do is take a pattern of letters (e.g., d-o-g) and associate it with meaning (e.g., a favorite household pet). Hence, reading and writing, like other functions for which the parietal lobe is important, require different types of information to be linked.

Still another deficit observed after damage to parietal regions is **apraxia,** which is the inability to perform skilled motor movement in an abstract manner. Although we already discussed how almost all aspects of motor processing occur in frontal regions, the motor movements affected in apraxia are the exception. In the case of apraxia, basic motor control is intact; the individual is not paralyzed. Yet, these people have trouble linking motor movement to a representation. Individuals with apraxia can usually make skilled voluntary movements without difficulty but cannot pantomime them. Thus, an individual with apraxia might be able to put a spoonful of sugar into his or her coffee cup, but when asked to pantomime the same gesture, might use one finger to represent the spoon, rather than positioning the hand as appropriate for stirring sugar into coffee. Apparently, individuals with apraxia lack the capacity to program the motor sequences that allow for the representation of an act, but these persons have the capacity to perform the act itself. Apraxia is discussed more thoroughly in Chapter 5.

Other abilities affected by parietal lobe damage include disturbances in spatial processing. Damage to parietal regions disrupts the ability to localize points in space, to know the angle of lines, and to understand spatial relations between items. Parietal regions of the brain also enable us to link spatial maps across different sensory modalities, and to integrate spatial information with motor movements. Consider the situation in which you hear but do not see a bird with a particularly melodic song. You want to know whether this bird is as pretty as it sounds. On the basis of auditory information, your brain will be able to deduce the bird's probable location in space. But if you wish to see the bird, the spatial location in auditory space must be translated into coordinates in visual space. The parietal lobe is important for that translation. In addition, you will need to link such information with motor actions. To view the bird, you must move your eyes from their present location to the bird's probable location. Knowing how far to move your eyes to reach that spot—that is, the translation of visual space into motor coordinates—also relies on parietal regions.

The importance of parietal regions in maintaining a map of space is seen most prominently in the syndrome called **hemineglect,** or **hemi-inattention.** In this syndrome, individuals ignore information on one side of space, usually the left, and act as if that side of the world does not exist. It is not that such individuals have sensory deficits that preclude them from processing information from the neglected region; rather, they do not direct attention to one half of the world, acting as if that region has been erased from their spatial map of the world. Details about spatial processing and hemineglect are given in Chapters 4, 6, and 8.

As you can probably tell from this brief review, damage to the parietal regions can cause a heterogeneous array of syndromes. In general, however, they all are syndromes in which sensory information cannot be integrated either across modalities, with internal representations or memories, or with actions.

• *TEMPORAL LOBE* •

Temporal regions of the brain are associated with four main functions: memory, visual item recognition, auditory processing, and emotion. Classically, the temporal lobes have been associated with memory function, as documented most clearly in the famous case of H.M., who in early adulthood underwent bilateral removal of anterior portions of the temporal lobe for the relief of intractable epilepsy. Although the surgery was successful in reducing his seizures, he was left with the inability to learn almost all types of new information, even though most of his memories from the years before the operation were intact. This case was pivotal in demonstrating that specific regions within the temporal lobe, more notably the hippocampus, are critical for the formation of new long-term memories. Additional research by Milner and colleagues demonstrated that the memory deficit tends to be greater for verbal material after removal of only the left temporal lobe (e.g., Frisk & Milner, 1990) and greater for spatial information after removal of only the right temporal lobe (Smith & Milner, 1981). You will learn much more about the role of the temporal lobes in memory in Chapter 10.

In addition to being important for the formation of new long-term memories, temporal regions of the brain play important roles in visual processing, contributing to visual item recognition. Electrical recordings from single cells in the inferior temporal lobes of monkeys have revealed that these cells respond only to highly specific visual stimuli. Unlike cells in the primary visual cortex, which respond to bars of light oriented at particular angles and moving in particular directions, the cells of the inferior temporal lobe respond to very specific shapes, such as a hand, a brush, or a face (Gross, Rocha-Miranda, & Bender, 1972). In fact, some of the cells may respond only to faces of particular people or certain features on a face (e.g., eyes) (Perrett, Mistlin, & Chitty, 1987). This specificity of visual processing in temporal regions appears to be a characteristic of the mammalian nervous system. For example, certain cells in temporal cortex of sheep respond only to horned sheep, not unhorned sheep, whereas other cells respond only to sheepdogs, but not wolves or dogs with pointy ears that resemble wolves (Kendrick & Baldwin, 1987). In people, damage to temporal regions can lead to deficits in recognizing common objects such as cars and chairs (Farah & Feinberg, 2000) or, knowing that a given face belongs to a specific individual (DeRenzi, 2000). Thus, temporal regions appear to be important for identification of visual items. The role of the temporal lobe in visual item recognition is discussed in more detail in Chapter 6. This specialization of temporal regions for visual item processing seems to reflect a segregation of the processing of visual information in the mammalian brain into two streams or systems, one of which is important for processing the shape of items and the other of which is important for processing the location of items. On the basis of neuroanatomical, neurophysiological, and behavioral work with animals, researchers have suggested that visual information leaving primary occipital areas bifurcates into two pathways, one of which courses dorsally to the parietal lobe and the other ventrally to the temporal lobe (Ungerleider & Mishkin, 1982). The parietal visual processing system is considered the "where" system, responsible for localizing objects in space with little regard for the item's identity. In contrast, the temporal visual processing system is the "what" system, responsible for determining what an item is regardless of its location. One way to think about these two systems if you are a sports fan is to consider the contrast between a zone defense and a person-to-person defense. The parietal region of the brain treats items much the way a defender in a zone defense does. The job of these parietal regions is to process the location of items in space regardless of who they are. Thus, for parietal regions, localization of objects, not their identities, is important. In contrast, the temporal region of the brain treats items much the way a defender in a person-to-person defense does. These regions are sensitive to a specific person or object regardless of its location in space, just as a defender will stick to his or her person regardless of where on the court or field that person may wander.

Because auditory processing areas are located in the temporal lobe, damage to this region of the brain can have consequences for the processing of auditory material. For example, damage in the temporal lobe can lead to an inability to recognize common sounds, such a church bell, or to difficulties in the appreciation of certain aspects of music, such as melody. A modality-specific deficit in recognizing sounds or objects that occurs in the absence of major deficits in basic sensory processing is known as an **agnosia.** What we mean by *modality-specific* is that the person cannot recognize an object in one sensory modality but can recognize it in other modalities. Agnosias can occur in all modalities. Since visual and auditory agnosia are associated with temporal lobe damage, we will discuss them in a bit more detail here.

If an individual has a *visual agnosia,* he or she will be unable to identify an item as a rose merely by looking at it. However, if the person is pricked by a thorn or smells the flower, she or he will instantly recognize it. An important point about agnosia is that the deficit can be attributed neither to the inability to perform basic sensory processing nor to a memory deficit. Persons with visual agnosia are not blind. They can distinguish light from dark, and they can discriminate basic shapes (e.g., square from rectangle) (Warrington & James, 1988). So, for example, when looking at a rose, a person with visual agnosia can see that an object is there, describe its color, and maybe even crudely describe its shape, but cannot use this information to gather a visual impression of a rose. Furthermore, memory for an item is intact. Therefore, if a person with visual agnosia is asked what kinds of flowers compose the garland that is placed around the neck of the horse that wins the Kentucky Derby or which popular flower associated with romance has thorns, he or she could easily answer "rose."

In *auditory agnosia,* an individual knows that a sound has occurred but doesn't know its significance. For example, a person with auditory agnosia cannot identify a particular sound as a car horn even though she or he knows that some sound just occurred. Likewise, in *tactile agnosia,* objects cannot be recognized by touch. What is common to all these agnosias is that basic sensory processing in the affected modality is intact, as are memory processes. Agnosia is discussed in more detail in Chapter 6. For now, we should note that temporal lobe damage is most often associated with auditory and visual agnosia, whereas tactile agnosia is associated with parietal regions.

Finally, temporal regions of the brain have also been implicated in the processing of emotional information. Some structures in the temporal lobe are portions of the limbic system, which, as we learned earlier in the chapter, can act to integrate information from the sensory world with internal urges (e.g., urges for food, sex, and so forth). Moreover, disruptions of temporal lobe functioning can have emotional consequences. For example, some investigators have suggested that temporal regions may be dysfunctional in a certain proportion of persons with schizophrenia, most notably those suffering from delusions (Schroder et al., 1995).

In this chapter we have learned the terms used by scientists to talk about the nervous system and the brain, become familiar with the central nervous system's major subdivisions, and made brief acquaintance with the role that each of these subdivisions plays. In the next chapter, we will become more knowledgeable about how the main cells that comprise the nervous system communicate with one another.

SUMMARY

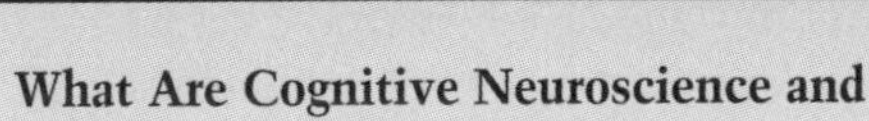

What Are Cognitive Neuroscience and Neuropsychology?

- Cognitive neuroscience comprises all investigations of mental functions that are linked to neural processes—ranging from investigations in animals to humans, and from experiments performed in the laboratory to computer simulations.
- Human neuropsychology is the specific study of linking brain function to mental processes in humans, usually inferred from examining the performance of individuals who have sustained brain damage.

Basic Building Blocks of the Nervous System

- Neurons are the cells that carry information by means of electrical and chemical signals.
- Glia are the support cells that serve as a conduit for transfer of nutrients to neurons and help repair damage to the nervous system.

Neuroanatomical Terms and Brain "Geography"

- Toward the front is known as anterior or rostral.
- Toward the back is known as posterior or caudal.
- Near the top of the head is known as superior or dorsal.
- Toward the bottom is known as inferior or ventral.
- Near the middle or midline of the body is known as medial.
- Toward the side of the head is known as lateral.

Major Subdivisions of the Central Nervous System

- The spinal cord is the main route for information coming into and leaving the nervous system.
- The medulla is important for controlling such life-sustaining functions as the beating of the heart and breathing, and for overall alertness and arousal.
- The cerebellum is important for skilled, fluid, motor movement.

- The pons is the brain region at which information from many of the cranial nerves enters the nervous system.
- The midbrain is home to two important structures involved in orienting toward sensory stimuli: the inferior colliculus, which processes auditory information, and the superior colliculus, which processes visual information.
- The hypothalamus is important for motivational behavior, such as seeking food, seeking a sexual partner, and fleeing.
- The thalamus is a major relay center in the brain whereby information from the sensory world is reorganized on its way to the cortex and information from the cortex is reorganized on its way to the periphery.
- Major subcortical systems are the basal ganglia, which is involved in the control of movement, and the limbic system, traditionally thought to be important for emotion but now known to be involved also in other functions, such as memory.
- The cerebral cortex is the main structure in the human brain; it is involved in processing sensory input, controlling motor output, and in higher-order mental functions such as object recognition, spatial processing, and memory.

A Closer Look at the Cerebral Cortex

- Primary sensory cortex is the first place in the central nervous system at which information about a particular sensory modality is received from the peripheral receptors.
- Motor cortex is the final exit point for neurons controlling the fine motor control of the body's muscles.
- Primary somatosensory cortex processes tactile information, including pain, pressure, texture, and the degree of pressure applied.
- Visual cortex processes the contrast between light and dark.
- Auditory cortex processes sound in regard to its frequency (pitch).
- The frontal lobe is the region of the brain that is involved in the planning, guidance, and evaluation of behavior.
- The parietal lobe is the region of the brain that is involved in multimodal processing—integrating information across sensory modalities, memory, and an individual's internal state.
- The temporal lobe is the region of the brain involved in memory, visual item recognition, emotion, and auditory processing, including the processing of music.

KEY TERMS

agnosia 37
agraphia 35
alexia 35
anterior 8
apraxia 36
association area 31
auditory nerve 29
axon 5
basal ganglia 16
bilateral 9
blood-brain barrier 6
Brodmann map 19
caudal 8
cell body 5
central fissure 18
central nervous system 9
cerebellum 14
cerebral hemisphere 17
cerebrospinal fluid (CSF) 9
cognitive neuroscience 4
contralateral 9
coronal 8
cranial nerves 10
dendritic tree 5
diencephalon 15
distal 9
dorsal 8
epileptic seizure 24
fissure 17
frontal lobe 18
glia 5
gyrus 17
hemi-inattention 36
hemineglect 36
hemiplegia 21
Heschl's gyrus 29
homonymous hemianopsia 28
horizontal 8
human neuropsychology 4
hypothalamus 15
inferior 8
inferior colliculus 14
ipsilateral 9
lateral 8
lateral geniculate nucleus 23
left visual field 24
limbic system 16
longitudinal fissure 18
medial 8
medial geniculate of the thalamus 29
medulla 10
metamemory 34
midbrain 14
midsagittal 8
neurons 5
nuclei 8
occipital lobe 18
olfactory bulb 30
optic chiasm 24
optic nerve 23
optic tract 23
parietal lobe 18
peripheral nervous system 9
perseverate 32
pons 14
posterior 8
primary motor cortex 19
primary sensory cortex 19
proprioception 21
proximal 9
quadranopsia 28
relay center 16
reticular activating system 13
right visual field 24
rostral 8
sagittal 8
scotomas 28
spinal cord 10
sulcus 17
superior 8
superior colliculus 14
Sylvian (lateral) fissure 18
temporal lobe 18
thalamus 15
tonotopic 30
unilateral 9
ventral 8

SUMMARY

CHAPTER 2

HOW NEURONS COMMUNICATE

Introduction

In this chapter we will discuss how neurons communicate with one another. You will learn about the electrochemical nature of this communication system, how it can be disrupted, and how it can be enhanced. Knowing how neurons work will provide a foundation that will allow for a more integrated perspective on a number of different issues discussed later in this book. For example, this knowledge will help you better understand why certain cognitive neuroscience methods can be so illuminating. Once you understand more about the electrical properties of neural conduction, you will see why *electroencephalography* (EEG) provides a good measure of brain function, and why the brain's activity can be disrupted by *transcranial magnetic stimulation.* Understanding more about the chemical nature of neural transmission will help you see how the depletion of certain chemicals in the brain can lead to mood disorders, such as depression, and why people may find taking certain drugs, such as amphetamines, enjoyable.

Electrochemical Signaling in the Nervous System

Neurons transfer information by means of a combination of electrical and chemical processes. There are two broad principles to this electrochemical signaling: information is relayed within a neuron by means of an electrical signal, whereas one neuron influences another via a chemical signal.

How Information Is Transferred within a Neuron

To better understand these principles, we need to examine the neuron in its typical resting state. Neurons have a difference in the electrical charge between the inside and outside of the cell. This difference in electrical charge is the neuron's **resting potential,** typically about −70 millivolts (mV). You may wonder how a cell in your body could have an electrical charge. The cell membrane of the neuron acts as a barrier separating *ions,* which are electrically charged particles, on the inside from those on the outside. These ions, such as sodium and potassium, can traverse the cell membrane only through special passageways known as *ion channels.* The channels are formed by protein molecules embedded in the cell membrane. When in specific configurations, these protein molecules create a passageway, allowing ions to flow in and out of the cell. In other configurations, the passageway is blocked, and ions cannot move from one side of the cell membrane to the other.

Neurons contain multiple ion channels, as channels are selective, allowing only certain ions to traverse them. When these channels are open, ions, which are found in different concentrations on either side of the membrane, begin to diffuse in the direction that will allow the concentration on both sides of the membrane to reach an equilibrium. Potassium, which has a higher concentration inside the cell than outside, travels out of the cell, whereas sodium, which has a higher concentration outside the cell than inside, flows inward. The net imbalance causes a potential, or electrical charge, across the membrane of approximately −70 millivolts.

Eventually diffusion would cause these ions to be equally distributed between the inside and outside, much the way a drop of ink eventually disperses equally throughout a glass of water. However, there exists a mechanism, known as the *sodium-potassium pump,* that pumps more positively charged sodium ions out of the cell than it pumps in positively charged potassium ions. The net result is that the inside of a neuron stays more negatively charged than the outside.

Input from other neurons causes the opening and closing of ion channels. The change in the ion concentrations on each side of the membrane drives the neuron's electrical charge away from its resting potential, making it either more negative or more positive. If the cell receives enough stimulation to reduce the voltage across the membrane to about −55 mV, a threshold is passed and the cell "fires." When a cell fires, the electrical charge of the neuron reverses quite rapidly from −55 mV to a peak of +40 mV. After reaching the peak—a state known as *depolarization*—the electrical charge then retreats toward the baseline resting potential, which is known as *repolarization.* The voltage then passes the resting potential, becoming even more negative, to about −90 mV, known as *hyperpolarization.* Following hyperpolarization, the neuron returns to the resting potential.

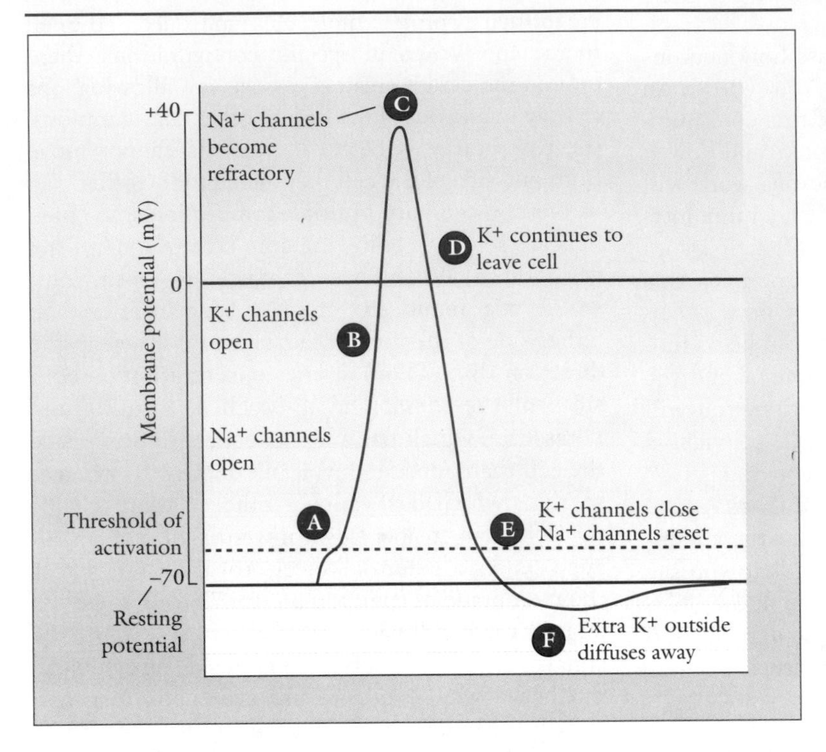

FIGURE 2.1 Phases of the action potential. (A) When the threshold of activation is reached, sodium (Na+) begins to enter the cell. (B) Potassium (K+) begins to leave the cell. (C) No more sodium enters the cell, and the voltage reaches its peak positive value. (D) The leakage of potassium drives the voltage in the negative direction. (E) The cell passes through its resting potential. (F) The cell hyperpolarizes and then stabilizes at its resting potential.

The whole sequence of events we have described, from resting potential and back again, is known as an **action potential.** The different phases of the action potential, along with the opening and closing of the different ion channels that drive each of these phases, are depicted in Figure 2.1.

This action potential has three very important properties. First, it is self-propagating, which means that once it is set in motion nothing else needs to be done—much as knocking down one domino causes all the others in a line to fall as well. Second, its strength does not dissipate with the distance that it travels. It remains +40 mV for its entire trip down the axon. In this characteristic it is quite unlike sound, for example, which loses energy the farther it travels. Third, the action potential is an all or nothing response—either the cell "fires" (i.e., has an action potential) or it doesn't. You can think of the action potential as working like a conventional camera. You either press the button down far enough to take a picture or you don't. Once you have depressed the button past a certain point, there is no turning back—the picture is taken. If you don't press hard enough to get to the trigger point, it makes no difference how far you partially depress the button—the picture is not taken.

Take a look at Figure 2.2, which shows the main parts of a neuron in detail. The action potential is produced at a specific part of the neuron near the cell body called the **axon hillock.** From there the action potential is carried along the entire length of the axon to the *terminal bouton,* which is the end of the road for the action potential. Here the electrical signal gets transformed into a chemical message. The terminal bouton contains little balloons filled with neurotransmitter, known as **synaptic vesicles.** Some of these synaptic vesicles reside in the bouton, whereas others are fused to the outside wall of the neuron. The action potential causes synaptic vesicles that are fused to the outside walls of the neuron to burst open, pouring their contents into the area between neurons known as the *synaptic cleft.* Once out of the vesicles, neurotransmitter diffuses across the cleft into the vicinity of the neighboring neuron. The side of the cleft from which the neurotransmitter is released is known as the *presynaptic side,* while the opposite side, containing the outside edge of the neighboring neuron, is known as the *postsynaptic side.* This region of contact between the neuron containing the terminal bouton, the synaptic cleft, and the postsynaptic region is called a **synapse.**

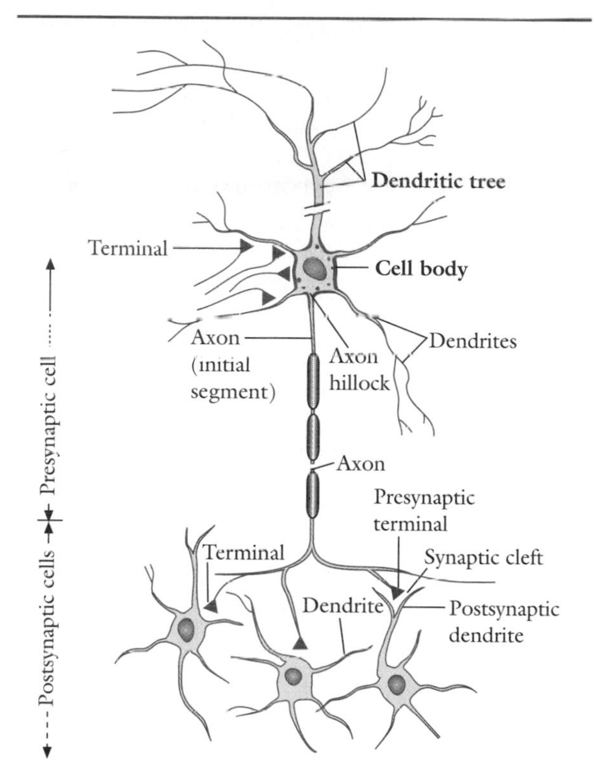

FIGURE 2.2 Basic parts of a neuron. The dendritic tree, made up of individual dendrites, is the main region that receives information from other cells. The cell body contains the nucleus and the machinery necessary to support basic cell functions. The axon hillock is the location at which a large electrical signal is generated. The axon is the long shaft of the cell across which this large electrical signal is propagated. The branches at the end of the axon contain bulbous-shaped terminals (or boutons), which have vesicles filled with neurotransmitters. These neurotransmitters, which can be either inhibitory or excitatory, are released into the space between adjacent neurons, which is known as the synaptic cleft. The neuron on the terminal side of the cleft is known as presynaptic and the neurons on the opposite side are referred to as postsynaptic. Some synaptic connections are made onto postsynaptic dendrites, whereas others are made directly onto the postsynaptic cell body. An axon can have many branches, synapsing with as many as 1,000 other neurons.

How Information Is Transferred between Neurons

The postsynaptic membrane of the dendritic trees of the adjacent neuron contains regions known as **receptors.** These receptors are specially configured proteins that are embedded within the postsynaptic membrane. As shown in Figure 2.3, when neurotransmitter reaches the postsynaptic membrane, it fits into a specific region of the receptor (called the *binding site*), much the way a key fits into a lock. The binding of the neurotransmitter changes the configuration of the receptor, which leads to a change in the electrical charge of the postsynaptic neuron in a small local area near the receptor site by altering the flow of ions across the membrane. Hence, at this point the chemical signal is transformed back into an electrical one.

There are two main classes of receptors, one that works directly to produce a local change in the voltage of the dendritic tree of the postsynaptic neuron, and one that works indirectly. **Ionotropic receptors** work directly to either open or close an ion channel. In contrast, **metabotropic receptors** indirectly control an ion channel. Metabotropic receptors are linked to a protein called *guanyl nucleotide-binding protein,* known as **G protein** for short. When the neurotransmitter binds to the receptor, it causes a subunit of the protein, known as the α (alpha) subunit, to break away. The α (alpha) subunit either binds directly to an ion channel, opening it so that ions can pass, or it activates the channel in a much more roundabout manner by attaching to and activating an enzyme situated in the postsynaptic membrane. An **enzyme** is any molecule that controls a chemical reaction, either by binding together two substances or by cleaving a substance into parts. The enzyme causes the production of another chemical, known as a *second messenger.* This second messenger causes a series of steps to occur that in turn open the ion channel. Although the postsynaptic potentials produced by metabotropic receptors are slower to start, they end up being more long-lasting than those produced by ionotropic receptors.

How Postsynaptic Potentials Can Cause an Action Potential

The local changes in the electrical potential that occur near the receptor sites can make the electrical charge of the cell either more positive than the resting potential, in which case they are known as **exci-**

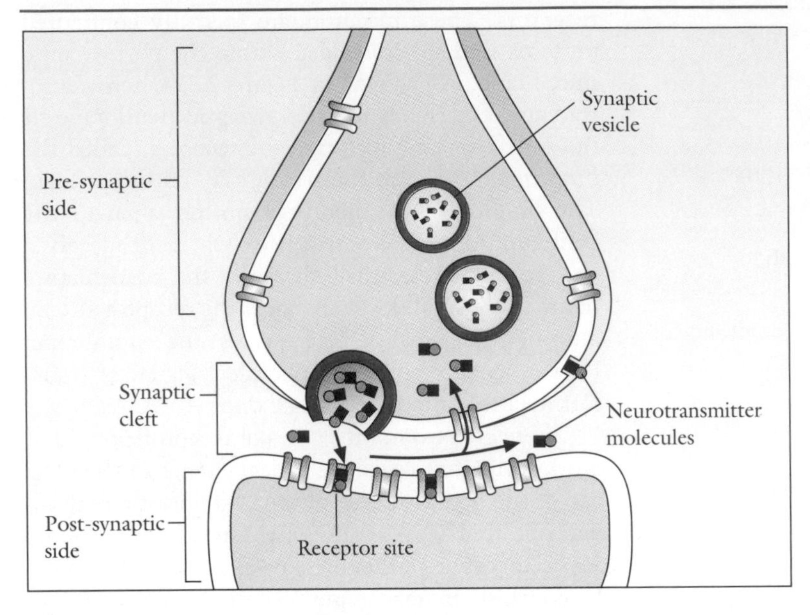

FIGURE 2.3 Important elements of the synapse. Within the presynaptic side are synaptic vesicles that contain molecules of neurotransmitter. When an action potential occurs, the neurotransmitter is released into the synaptic cleft. The neurotransmitter then binds with a receptor on the postsynaptic membrane, causing a local change in electrical voltage.

tatory postsynaptic potentials (EPSPs), or more negative than the resting potential, in which case they are known as **inhibitory postsynaptic potentials (IPSPs).** Whether a particular neurotransmitter has an excitatory or inhibitory effect depends not on the neurotransmitter but rather on the receptor type to which it binds. We will talk a bit more about the many different types of receptors later on in the chapter.

The postsynaptic potentials are much smaller in magnitude than the potential that occurs when an axon fires. If excitatory, the postsynaptic potential makes the cell's electrical charge a bit more positive—that is, it reduces the difference in electrical charge between the inside and the outside of the cell. This reduction brings the differential closer to the value of −55 mV at which the cell will fire. If inhibitory, the postsynaptic potential makes the inside of the cell a bit more negative than the outside and moves the cell farther away from the threshold at which it will fire.

Postsynaptic potentials differ from action potentials in three important ways. First, they are graded: The farther they travel from their source, the more they dissipate. Thus, unlike the action potential, which remains constant for the entire course of its journey, postsynaptic potentials weaken as they travel across time and space. Second, as already mentioned, postsynaptic potentials are much smaller in magnitude than an action potential, usually in the range of .5 to 5 mV. Third, whereas action potentials are always "excitatory" in that they make the cell fire, postsynaptic potentials can be either excitatory or inhibitory.

Because postsynaptic potentials are small and dissipate over space, one of them is highly unlikely to cause a cell to fire. Rather, it requires the combined effect of these potentials, both across time and across space, to make a neuron fire. Hence two EPSPs that occur close together in time have a greater influence than if a gap in time separated them. Likewise, if two EPSPs occur at the same part of the dendritic tree, they are likely to have a larger influence than if they occurred in spatially disparate regions of the dendrite. The complexity of this summation process can be appreciated if you consider that the average neuron has hundreds to thousands of other neurons synapsing upon it. Thus, whether a single cell fires depends not on a single voice from a neighboring neuron, but rather on the chorus of EPSPs and IPSPs produced by its neighbors and on whether those voices occur close together in time and space.

The cacophony of postsynaptic potentials is summated at the axon hillock. If the summed value of EPSPs and IPSPs manages to change the differential in charge across the membrane from its resting potential of −70 mV to around −55 mV, the cell will fire. If this value is not reached, the cell will not fire. Because the postsynaptic potentials are graded and lose their potency as they travel from their source to the axon hillock, potentials generated close to the axon hillock have a larger influence on whether or not the cell fires. Consequently, if we go back to our chorus analogy, the cells that synapse closer to the axon hillock have a louder voice in the chorus than those that synapse farther away. In general, excitatory synapses are located on a dendritic tree, whereas inhibitory synapses are located on the cell body. Hence, IPSPs are more likely to be generated closer to the axon hillock, where they can have a greater effect.

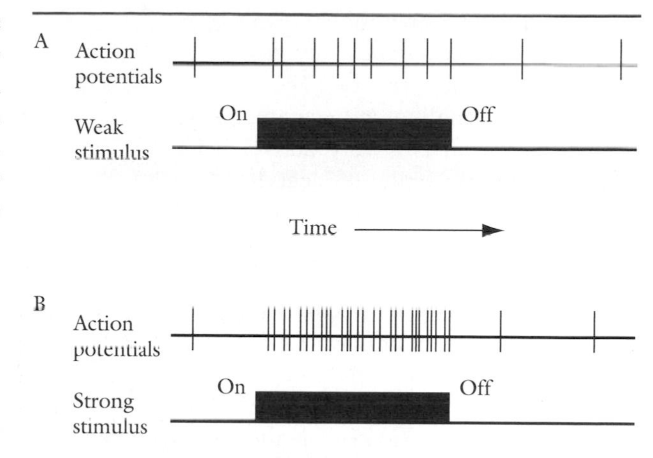

FIGURE 2.4 Neurons code the strength of a stimulus by the rate of firing. (A) When a relatively weak stimulus is encountered, the cell fires relatively infrequently. (B) When a strong stimulus is encountered, the cell fires many times.

Factors That Influence the Responsiveness of a Neuron

Let's consider the way the electrochemical processes of neuronal firing serve both to enable and limit the responsiveness of the neuron. Because the value of the action potential is always the same, neurons cannot code the intensity of a stimulus by the size of its electrical response. Rather, neurons code the intensity of a stimulus via the *rate,* or pace, of its firing. When there is a strong stimulus, the cell fires many times in succession; when there is a weak input, it fires only occasionally (see Figure 2.4).

To better understand this concept, let's go back to our analogy of neuronal firing being like taking a picture with a conventional camera. Consider a situation in which you find a person or vista interesting—you snap a picture or two. But what happens when you find someone overwhelmingly attractive or a vista breathtakingly beautiful? You snap lots and lots of pictures. Likewise, neurons code their "interest" in a stimulus by how many times they fire.

This firing rate, however, does have an upper limit, which is generally about 200 times per second. The ceiling exists because once an action potential has been initiated, it is impossible to generate another one during the depolarization and repolarization phases. After an ion channel opens and allows for the movements of ions, it then becomes blocked and cannot reopen until it is "reset." Much as you cannot take another picture with a conventional camera until it has been forwarded to the next frame, another action potential cannot occur until the channels are reset. During the hyperpolarization phase, another action potential can be produced, but stimulation must be substantially higher than for the prior action potential.

Even though there are temporal limits on the responsiveness of the cell, certain aspects of the electrochemical processes involved in neuronal firing enable it to respond repeatedly to multiple stimuli. One way of making a cell more responsive is to have a mechanism that can limit the postsynaptic potential. If such a mechanism did not exist, there would be little precision of firing. An event that occurred seconds ago could continue to have an effect. The postsynaptic potential can be terminated by clearing neurotransmitter from the synaptic cleft so that the postsynaptic receptors are freed for another influx of neurotransmitter, which can then produce IPSPs or EPSPs.

One method by which this is accomplished is **reuptake,** which is the rapid removal of neurotransmitter from the synaptic cleft back into the terminal bouton by special transporter molecules that are embedded in the presynaptic membrane. Another mechanism is **enzymatic deactivation,** in which an enzyme cleaves the transmitter molecules so they become incapable of binding to the receptor. This process occurs mainly for one neurotransmitter,

acetylcholine. An enzyme known as **acetylcholinesterase** divides acetylcholine into its two constituent parts, choline and acetate. This deactivation is a very active process—one molecule of acetylcholinesterase can destroy more than 5,000 molecules of acetylcholine per second!

A third mechanism occurs via glial cells in the vicinity of the synapse. A particular type of glial cell known as *astrocytes* (because they look like stars) takes up the neurotransmitter and destroys it by breaking it down. Another way of regulating the responsiveness of cells is through **autoreceptors.** These receptors are located on the presynaptic neuron and bind the same neurotransmitter as released by that neuron. When neurotransmitter released into the synaptic cleft binds to the autoreceptor, it decreases the activity of the presynaptic neuron. These autoreceptors work as a feedback mechanism, providing a way to keep the cell from becoming overactivated or overstimulated. Some tolerance effects to drugs are thought to be mediated by autoreceptors, as the cells downregulate their activity in response to repeated exposure to the drug. Finally, neurotransmitter may also be cleared from the synapse by diffusion: it simply floats away, putting it out of range of the receptors. The different mechanisms for modulating the degree of neurotransmitter in the synaptic cleft are shown in Figure 2.5.

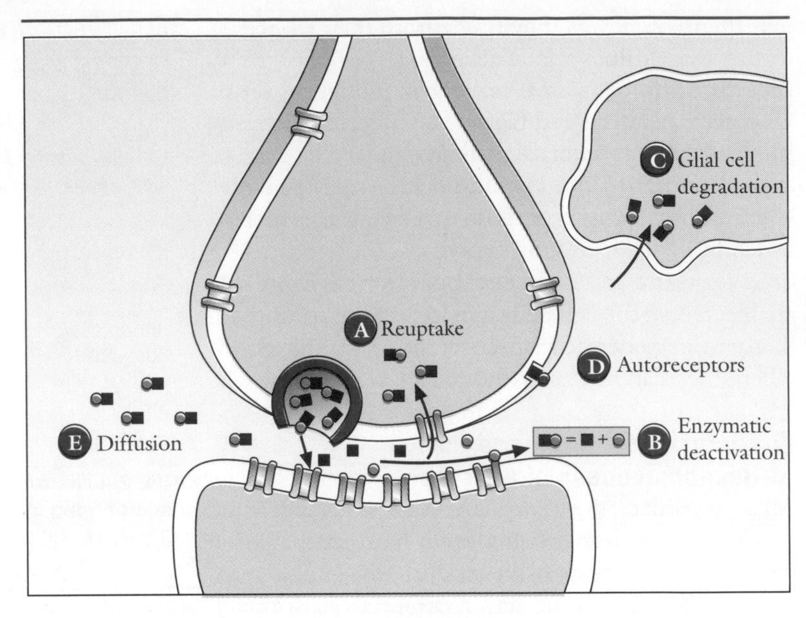

FIGURE 2.5 Mechanisms for modulating the amount of neurotransmitter in the synaptic cleft. (A) Neurotransmitter may be taken up by the presynaptic neurons via special transporter molecules. (B) The neurotransmitter may be broken apart by enzymatic deactivation. (C) Glial cells may take up neurotransmitter. (D) Neurotransmitter may bind to an autoreceptor. (E) Neurotransmitter may diffuse away from the synapse.

Neurotransmitters

Up until this point we have been discussing neurotransmitters in a generic manner, as if they came in only one flavor. In actuality, they come in a variety of flavors, and many aspects of neural transmission are influenced by the type of neurotransmitter released at the synaptic cleft. Although at one time it was thought that a neuron releases only one type of neurotransmitter, it is now clear that many types of neurons can release two or more neurotransmitters. In this section of the chapter we discuss those different types of neurotransmitters, their characteristics, the type of receptors to which they bind, and their influence on mental function. You should be aware that there are many more neurotransmitters and other chemicals that modulate neural activity (e.g., peptides) than we discuss here. In the discussion that follows, we focus primarily on those neurotransmitters that play a major role in the functioning of the central nervous system (CNS), while ignoring many issues regarding neurotransmitters that play a more prominent role in the peripheral nervous system.

As we have already mentioned, **neurotransmitters** are the chemicals that neurons utilize to communicate with one another. Traditionally, neurotransmitters are defined as having four major characteristics. First, they are chemicals synthesized within the neuron. Second, they are released when the cell is activated by an action potential and have an effect in a target cell, such as a neighboring neuron or muscle cell. Third, the same response is obtained in the target cell when the transmitter is placed upon it artificially, such as in an experimental situation. And fourth, when the release of the neurotransmitter is blocked, an action potential will not result in activity in the postsynaptic neuron.

Although a variety of chemicals can serve as neurotransmitters, our discussion focuses on two major classes of neurotransmitters that are found in the CNS. The first is that of the **amino acids,** the smallest and most basic building blocks of proteins. Amino acids act as the main excitatory and inhibitory neurotransmitters in the brain. The other main class of neurotransmitters are those organized into "systems" as they are produced by specific sets of neurons; their cell bodies are located subcortically and in the brain stem, and their axons project diffusely throughout the cortex.

Amino Acids

Amino acids are the most common type of neurotransmitter in the CNS. Because these substances are found in the nervous systems of very simple organisms, they are likely to have been the first neurotransmitters to evolve. The two main amino acids in the central nervous system that act as a neurotransmitter are **glutamate,** which has an excitatory effect, and **GABA** (gamma-aminobutyric acid), which has an inhibitory effect. There are two other amino acids that also serve as neurotransmitters: *aspartate,* which is excitatory, and *glycine,* which is inhibitory. Because their role is mainly confined to the brain stem and peripheral nervous system we will not discuss them in detail.

You might wonder why there are both inhibitory and excitatory neurotransmitters. If only excitatory inputs existed, the system might careen out of control. Inhibitory inputs serve to dampen down, or modulate, the system. Think about a car. Imagine that the only way that one could control a car was via the gas pedal—by modulating "excitatory" input. You could indeed take your foot off the gas to slow the car down, but you could not do so very precisely or quickly. There is a need for the "inhibitory" input provided by the brake. Likewise, there is the need within the nervous system both to be able to ramp up the activity of neurons and to tone them down.

• *GLUTAMATE* •

The main excitatory amino acid neurotransmitter in the CNS is glutamate. It has been estimated that this neurotransmitter is utilized at between 15 and 20% of synapses in the central nervous system. There are four major glutamatergic receptors. Three are ionotropic and named after the artificial chemicals that stimulate them: NMDA (N-methyl-D-aspartate), AMPA (alpha-amino-3-hydroxy-5-methylisoasole-4-proprionic acid), and kainate receptors. The fourth is the metabotropic glutamate receptor. Binding of glutamate to the AMPA and kainate receptors produces EPSPs. In contrast, the binding of glutamate to the NMDA receptor has special properties that allow it not only to regulate the entry of ions, but also allow those ions to act as second messengers to change the biochemical and structural properties of the cell. These changes are important for the production of new memories, as they initiate a cascade of events that leads to changes in the shape and number of spines at synaptic sites. We will learn more about these changes in Chapters 10 and 13.

Overactivity of glutamate (and also aspartate) in the brain is thought to play a role in the development of epilepsy, a disease in which an abnormal lowering of a cell's firing threshold causes it to misfire (Morselli & Lloyd, 1985). Drugs that treat epilepsy have been found to decrease the amount of glutamate and aspartate released from neurons. Too much glutamate can produce **excitotoxicity,** which is excessive activity of receptors that can literally excite neurons to death. These neurons get "fried" by too much stimulation. In fact, excitotoxicity appears to be an unfortunate consequence of a particular form of brain damage, known as **ischemia,** in which neurons die due to a lack of oxygen, most typically after blockage of a blood vessel in the brain. Glutamate and aspartate build up during ischemia because their reuptake mechanism is energy-dependent and hence relies critically on oxygen. Without oxygen, these neurotransmitters cannot be effectively cleared out of the synaptic cleft.

• ***GAMMA-AMINOBUTYRIC ACID (GABA)*** •

The main inhibitory amino acid neurotransmitter is gamma-aminobutyric acid (GABA). About 40% of receptors in the CNS are GABAergic. As you can see, the use of inhibitory input is rather common across the nervous system. GABAergic input is thought to occur mainly via interneurons. The inhibitory control provided by GABA is thought of as a mechanism that is important for "fine-tuning" the pattern of activation across the nervous system.

There are two main types of GABA receptors: $GABA_A$ and $GABA_B$. $GABA_A$ is an ionotropic receptor whereas $GABA_B$ is metabotropic. Both appear to be important in dampening oscillatory, reverbatory excitation between the thalamus and cortex that could lead to the seizure activity associated with epilepsy (e.g., Hosford, Clark, Cao, Wilson, Lin, Morriset, & Huin, 1992). Quite a number of substances that reduce the activity of the CNS bind to GABA receptors. One such group of substances is **barbiturates,** a class of CNS depressants derived from barbituric acid. Not surprisingly, these drugs reduce seizure activity and induce sedation and sleep. Other substances that bind to GABA receptors are tranquilizing drugs called **benzodiazepines,** such as diazepam (Valium) and chlordiazepoxide (Librium). These drugs are generally used to treat anxiety disorders but can also be used as antiseizure medication and to promote sleep and muscle relaxation. Alcohol also produces its *anxiolytic* (i.e., anxiety-reducing) and sedative effects by affecting GABA receptors.

Although GABAergic input tends to fine-tune the pattern of brain activation across the brain, in some systems it plays a more direct role. For example, as we will see in Chapter 5 on motor control, some of the changes in activation in the nervous system occur via modulation of the constant inhibitory input provided by GABAergic receptors. The system can be let to run free by "taking off the brakes" rather than by "pressing down on the gas," as would occur by excitation.

Neurotransmitter Systems

The other main group of neurotransmitters is distinct from amino acids in that they are organized into systems. They are produced by neurons whose cell bodies are located subcortically and in the brain stem, and whose axons project diffusely throughout the cortex. We have already been introduced to one neurotransmitter of this kind, *acetylcholine.* It is composed of acetate and choline. The three other such neurotransmitters are known as **monoamines,** as they derive from an amino acid that has undergone a chemical transformation via an enzymatic process. The monoamines are **dopamine, norepinephrine** and **serotonin.** Their molecular structure is very similar; hence there are drugs that affect the activity of all of them to some degree. For example, all three are affected by *MAO (monoamine oxidase) inhibitors,* which are used to treat depression. As you may be able to tell from the name, MAO inhibitors inhibit the activity of monoamine oxidase, which serves to break down monoamines. The end result is to provide the brain with more monoamines—dopamine, norepinephrine, and serotonin.

Two of these monoamines, dopamine and norepinephrine, derive from the same amino acid, *tyrosine,* and are known as **catecholamines.** Tyrosine is transformed by tyrosine hydroxylase, an enzyme, to L-dopa. (You can easily identify enzymes in our subsequent discussion as they all end in "–ase"). As we will learn in Chapters 5 and 14, L-dopa is used to treat Parkinson's disease, a disorder characterized by the death of dopaminergic cells, resulting in difficulties with the initiation of motor control and mental thought. L-dopa is then transformed by dopa decarboxylase to form dopamine. Finally, dopamine can be transformed into norepinephrine by dopamine beta-hydroxylase. The third monoamine, serotonin, derives from *tryptophan,* and is classified as an **indolamine** (as compared to a catecholamine).

Each of these neurotransmitters is released by a different set of neurons that form a neurotransmitter system: the cholinergic, dopaminergic, noradrenergic, and serotonergic systems. Because these systems project diffusely throughout the cortex, each one can affect a large variety of behaviors, some of which overlap. Nonetheless, each system has been found to have some degree of specificity not only with regard to behavior, but also how its breakdown manifests in specific neuropsychological impairment. Before we turn our attention to the particulars of each of these systems, however, we must introduce the idea of a neurotransmitter agonist and a neurotransmitter antagonist. **Agonists** are chemicals that mimic or facilitate the effect of a neurotransmitter on a target neuron, whereas **antagonists** oppose or diminish the effect on a target neuron. Much has been learned about the functions associated with these different neurotransmitter systems by examining the effects of agonists and antagonists on each system.

• *CHOLINERGIC SYSTEM* •

The *cholinergic* system utilizes acetylcholine as its neurotransmitter. The cell bodies of neurons of the cholinergic system are located in the basal forebrain nucleus and project to almost all portions of the cortex in a very diffuse and nonspecific manner. There are also cell bodies in the septal nuclei that project to the hippocampus. Both these nuclei are located between the hypothalamus and orbitofrontal cortex (see Figure 2.6). Because ACh is released in almost every cortical area, it tends to have a very general effect on neuronal and mental functioning.

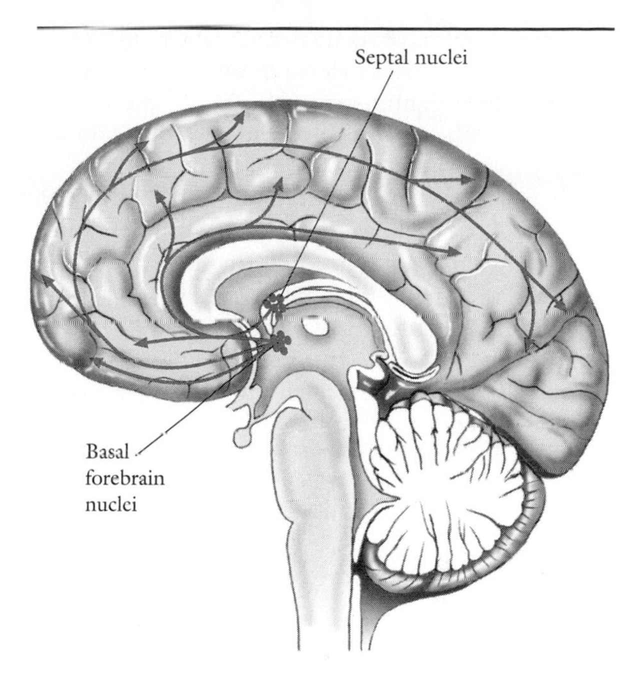

FIGURE 2.6 Pathways of cholinergic system.

There are two different types of ACh receptors, one ionotropic and one metabotropic, each of which is activated by a different drug. The ionotropic ACh receptor is known as the *nicotinic receptor* because it can be stimulated by nicotine, the drug found in tobacco leaves. In contrast, the metabotropic receptor is known as the *muscarinic receptor* because it can be stimulated by muscarine, a drug in the poisonous mushroom, *Amanita muscariam.*

The cholinergic system has been found to play a large role in maintaining overall cortical excitability. ACh levels are decreased during anesthesia when the brain is less active and are increased by convulsants, which are drugs that will produce seizure activity. ACh has also been linked to the production of REM (rapid eye movement), or paradoxical sleep, which is that portion of sleep during which we dream and our minds are a bit more active.

Given that ACh plays a role in overall cortical excitability, it may not surprise you that activity of the cholinergic system has been linked to paying attention (Sarter & Bruno, 1997). Cholinergic activity appears to be important for overall arousal or vigilance—the ability to stay alert, especially in boring or monotonous situations or over long periods of time (Wesnes & Warburton, 1984). For example, although depletion of ACh does not initially affect the ability of animals to differentiate between a target and non-target stimulus, it seriously erodes their ability to do so as the task drags on. In humans, nicotine, an acetylcholine agonist, can improve performance on tasks requiring sustained attention, ranging from those that are relatively simple, such as detecting three consecutive even digits in a row (Mancuso, Andres, Ansseau, & Tirelli, 1999), to those that are more complicated, such as landing a plane in a flight simulator late at night after having done the task a couple of times before (Mumenthaler, Taylor, O'Hara, & Yesavage, 1998). Moreover, the administration of tacrine, which inhibits the breakdown of acetylcholine, or nicotine, attenuates deficits in tasks of sustained attention in patients with Alzheimer's disease (Sahakian & Coull, 1994).

ACh has also been linked to *selective attention,* which is the ability to tune in certain information while tuning other information out. ACh appears to sharpen the responses of cells to the features of stimuli that are most likely to make them fire, while suppressing responses to less prominent features of a stimulus. In both humans and monkeys, cholinergic agonists aid the ability to orient toward important sensory information (Witte, Davidson, & Marrocco, 1997). It has been suggested that one of the reasons people like to smoke is that nicotine can help filter irrelevant and annoying information from the smoker's awareness, allowing him or her to focus on new and important information (Kassel, 1997).

Traditionally, neuroscientists have associated activity of the cholinergic system most closely with memory processing. Acetylcholine depletion is associated with Alzheimer's disease (Spillane, White, Goodhardt, Flack, Bowen, & Davison, 1977), which, although it affects a large number of cognitive functions (as we will learn in Chapter 14), has devastating effects on memory. Scopolamine, a drug that works as an antagonist by blocking muscarinic receptors, can induce deficits in learning new tasks in young healthy individuals comparable to those seen in older individuals (e.g., Drachman & Leavitt, 1974). These deficits can be reversed by drugs such as physostigmine that work to keep acteylcholine from being broken down in the synaptic cleft. Giving individuals a cholinergic agonist, such as arecoline, or a precursor of acetylcholine, significantly improves learning (Sitaram, Weingartner, & Gillin, 1978). We discuss this issue in more detail in Chapter 14 when we discuss Alzheimer's disease.

It is difficult to determine whether the effects of ACh on cognition are related more to attention or more to memory. Clearly, if you are not paying attention to information when you first learn it, it will be difficult to retrieve later on because it was never well stored in memory. Hence some researchers suggest that improvements in memory with cholinergic agents in both monkeys (Voytko, Olton, Richardson, Gorman, Tobin, & Price, 1994) and Alzheimer's patients using anticholinesterases (Lawrence & Sahakian, 1995) result from improvements in attention rather than memory (for a discussion of these issues see Bartus, 2000). Recently, studies have indicated that anticholinesterases increase activity in extrastriate regions during a working memory task, suggesting that these drugs augment the process of selecting specific information for storage in memory (Furey, Peitrini, & Haxby, 2000). Therefore ACh may affect both attentional and memory processes because it modulates an operation required in both—that of selecting, or highlighting, certain types of information while discarding, or ignoring, other types of information (Warburton & Rusted, 1993).

• *DOPAMINERGIC SYSTEM* •

The *dopaminergic system* uses dopamine as the main neurotransmitter. There are actually three major dopaminergic subsystems: the nigrostriatal, mesolimbic, and mesocortical. These subsystems, shown in Figure 2.7, are differentiated by the location of their cell bodies, the regions of the brain to which they project, and by the effect they have on behavior. In a moment, we will examine each of

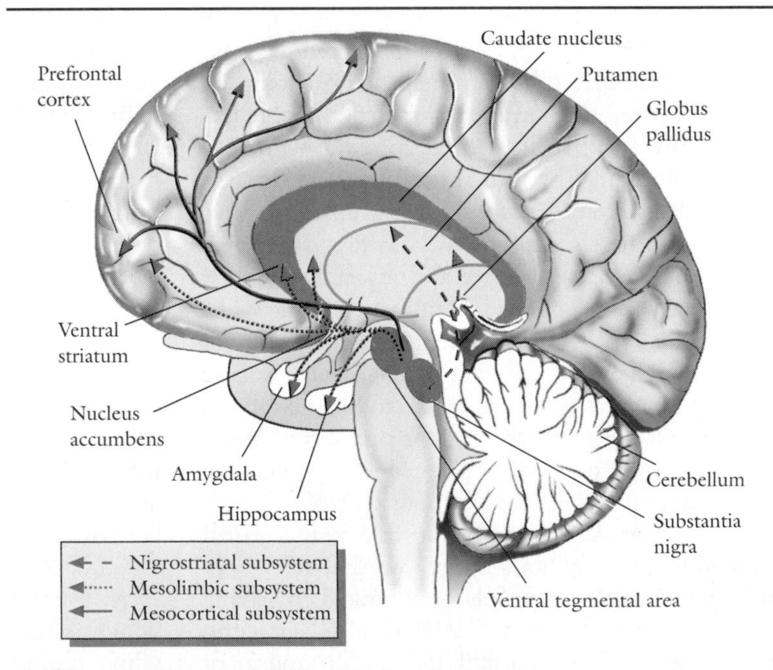

FIGURE 2.7 Pathways of dopaminergic systems.

them in more detail. Before we do, however, let's look at some characteristics common to all three subsystems.

• ***Overall Characteristics*** • There are a multiplicity of different dopaminergic receptors, all of which are metabotropic. The two main families of receptors are the D_1-like and D_2-like. D_1-like receptors, which are the D_1 and D_5 receptors, increase the production of a second-messenger, cyclic AMP. In contrast, the D_2-like receptors, which are the D_2, D_3, and D_4 receptors, all decrease the production of cyclic AMP.

D_1 receptors are located exclusively on postsynaptic sites, whereas D_2 receptors are located both postsynaptically, and presynaptically, where they serve as autoreceptors. Postsynaptically, dopamine can act to produce both excitatory and inhibitory potentials. Presynaptically, autoreceptors located on dendrites and cell bodies decrease neural firing by producing hyperpolarization. In contrast, those located in the terminal boutons suppress the activity of the enzyme tyrosine hydroxylase, decreasing the production of dopamine and ultimately its release.

We introduce the variety of dopamine receptors because they have been related to a wide variety of mental and emotional functions. In particular, the activity of D_1 and D_2 receptors has been linked to schizophrenia. Many antipsychotic drugs work as D_2 antagonists. For example, chlorpromazine, one common antipsychotic drug, blocks D_2 dopamine receptors. These drugs often reduce the "florid" symptoms of schizophrenia, which are the delusions, such as a belief that "The FBI is reading my thoughts," and the hallucinations, such as hearing voices that command a person to act in certain ways. However, they do not much alleviate the cognitive deficits and emotional withdrawal observed in schizophrenia.

Rather, the severity of these latter deficits in schizophrenic individuals has been linked to the level of binding of D_1 receptors (Okubo et al., 1997). It is known that either too little (Sawaguchi & Goldman-Rakic, 1991) or too much (Zahrt, Taylor, Mathew, & Arnsten, 1997) binding of D_1 receptors impairs working memory function (we discuss working memory more in Chapters 10 and 11). There is a narrow middle ground that allows for optimal function.

Designing effective drugs for schizophrenia is very difficult because the D_2 antagonists that are effective antipsychotic medications also have the effect of decreasing D_1 receptors. Remember that individuals with schizophrenia don't seem to be able to bind dopamine to D_1 receptors to an optimal degree to begin with, and that inadequate binding of D_1 receptors is associated with their emotional and cognitive deficits. Hence, if antipsychotic drugs reduce, or downregulate, D_1 receptors, that will serve only to exacerbate the cognitive and emotional problems. Consequently, a major challenge in designing new drug therapies for schizophrenia is to find drugs that optimize binding of both D_1 and D_2 receptors, reducing psychotic symptoms without having deleterious effects on cognitive and emotional functioning (e.g., Lidow, Williams, & Goldman-Rakic, 1998).

Other receptors in the D_2 family also have specific effects on aspects of cognitive and emotional processing. One of these, the D_4 receptor, acts postsynaptically and tends to be located in the limbic system and cortex. The expression of the D_4 receptor has been linked to a psychological trait known as "novelty seeking" (Benjamin, Li, Patterson, Greenberg, Murphy, & Hamer, 1996), which is characterized by exploratory behavior, excitability, and impulsiveness. All of these characteristics are hallmarks of individuals who have trouble regulating their attentional control, so it is not surprising that genetic variability in the nature of D_4 receptors may account for inherited aspects of attention deficit hyperactivity disorder (LaHoste, Swanson, Wigal, Glabe, Wigal, King, & Kennedy, 1996).

• ***Subsystems*** • The first subsystem that we discuss is the **nigrostriatal system.** The cell bodies of this system are located in the substantia nigra and project to the neostriatum (i.e., the caudate nucleus and putamen), especially the dorsal portion (refer back to Figure 2.7). You may remember from the last chapter that the caudate and putamen play a role in motor functioning, so it may not surprise you that this portion of the dopaminergic system is important in motor control. This subsystem doesn't control motor output as much as it regulates the selection, initiation, and cessation of motor behaviors. As we will learn in Chapter 5, it is the nigrostriatal dopaminergic subsystem that is affected in Parkinson's disease. In that disorder, the dopaminergic neurons in the substantia nigra die, depleting the caudate and putamen of dopaminergic input, leading to difficulties in motor control.

The second system, known as the **mesolimbic system,** has its cell bodies in the *ventral tegmental area,* which is medial to the substantia nigra. It projects to several parts of the limbic system, including the *nucleus accumbens* and ventral portions of the striatum, amygdala, and hippocampus, as well as prefrontal cortex. This dopaminergic subsystem has been linked to reward systems (refer back to Figure 2.7).

We will briefly discuss the behaviors related to each of the structures to which the mesolimbic system projects. Increased dopamine levels in the nucleus accumbens are found in response to both natural reinforcers, such as food, drink, and sex, as well as drugs of abuse, such as amphetamine and cocaine (Spanagel & Weiss, 1999). Activity within the ventral portion of the striatum has been linked to a wide variety of reinforcers. For example, the better one performs on a video game (Koepp et al., 1998), the greater is the release of dopamine and its subsequent binding to D_2 receptors in the ventral striatum. And this same region of the brain (along with other regions involved in the reward circuitry—see, for example, Kalivas & Nakamura, 1999) becomes active when people view a picture of a person they are madly in love with as compared to a close friend (Bartels & Zeki, 2000). Seeing or ruminating on the person you are crazy about is apparently very rewarding! The portion of the mesolimbic system that projects to the amygdala appears to be important for linking predictive cues to either a rewarding or aversive stimulus. Thus, inhibition of the portion of the mesolimbic system that projects to the amygdala impairs the ability of animals to respond to stimuli that they have learned to fear (Nader & LeDoux, 1999). Finally, inputs to prefrontal regions help to integrate what the organism is doing at that time with the appropriate behavioral response to the rewarding stimulus.

One prominent theory of how this dopaminergic subsystem affects mental activity posits that the dopaminergic signal is very specific. It does not code whether a reward has been received nor how an organism acts in response to the reward. Instead, dopamine appears to signal whether the reward *exceeds* or *falls short* of what was expected (Hollerman & Schultz, 1998). Dopamine production associated with an unexpected reward elicits a strong positive dopamine signal in the ventral tegmental area. With repeated presentation and learning this response declines, because with time the reward is no longer unexpected. Conversely, omission of a predicted reward leads to suppression of the dopamine signal. Now you know why a surprising success, like winning a raffle, feels so good!!!

The third dopaminergic subsystem, the **mesocortical system,** has its cell bodies located in the ventral tegmental area. The axons of these cells project to much of the cortex, especially motor and premotor cortex, as well as prefrontal cortex, where they influence a variety of mental functions. One of these functions is working memory, which allows us to keep information online for performance of tasks, planning, and strategy preparation for problem solving. Depletion of dopamine, but not of other neurotransmitters, produces a specific deficit in these cognitive functions of the dorsolateral prefrontal cortex (refer back to Figure 1.20) similar to those observed in animals who have had surgical removal of this area. This effect has been linked specifically to D_1 receptors (Sawaguchi & Goldman-Rakic, 1991). Moreover, this behavioral deficit can be reversed by giving the dopamine precursor L-dopa or the dopamine agonist apomorphine, but cannot be reversed by other neurotransmitter precursors (Brozoski, Brown, Rosvold, & Goldman, 1979).

• *NORADRENERGIC SYSTEM* •

Norepinephrine (or noradrenaline) is the neurotransmitter emitted by cells of the *noradrenergic system.* There are two main branches of the central noradrenergic system, those originating from the ventrolateral tegmental area and those originating from the locus coeruleus. The branch originating from the ventrolateral tegmental area projects to the hypothalamus and reticular formation and is associated mainly with sexual and feeding behavior. The branch that we will be more interested in is that originating from the locus coeruleus, as it is associated with cognitive function. From these regions, the neurons project to the thalamus, hypothalamus, and the cortex, most notably the prefrontal cortex (see Figure 2.8).

There are four main types of noradrenergic receptors: α_1, α_2, β_1, β_2. All are metabotropic, coupled to G proteins. Adrenergic receptors produce both excitatory and inhibitory effects.

The primary cognitive effect of increased activity in the noradrenergic system is to influence arousal and attention. Overall arousal is increased through actions at α_1 receptors in the thalamus and cortex, whereas decreased arousal is associated with decreased release of noradrenaline mediated through presynaptic α_2 autoreceptors. Noradrenaline also plays a role in sleep. The α_2 receptors in the thalamus put the brain in a sleep mode. Noradrenergic cells also shut off during REM sleep. Hence, the only difference between waking and dreaming is norepinephrine!

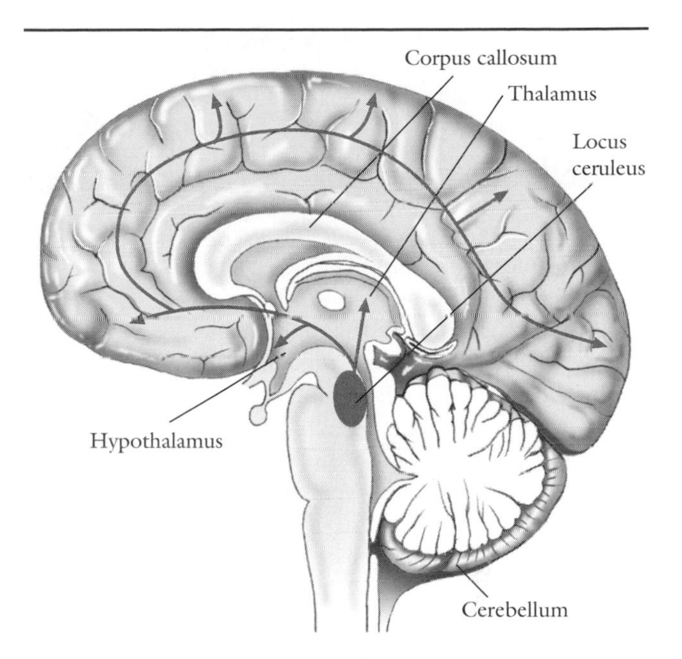

FIGURE 2.8 Pathways of noradrenergic systems.

Attention is influenced by α receptors as well. Giving humans low doses of clonidine, which down-regulates the release of noradrenaline via α_2 presynaptic autoreceptors, degrades performance when they have to be vigilant (Coull, Middleton, Robbins, & Sahakian, 1995), when they must keep their attention focused on a highly demanding task (Coull, et al., 1995), when attention must be maintained in the absence of sensory input (Smith and Nutt, 1996), and when they are "alerted" to the subsequent presentation of a stimulus by a warning cue (Coull, Nobre, & Frith, 2001).

Given the association of noradrenaline with attentional functions, it has been suggested that the functioning of noradrenaline may be disrupted in attention deficit hyperactivity disorder (for more details on this disorder, see Chapter 13). A class of antidepressants known as *tricyclics,* which affect catecholamine reuptake, particularly that of norepinephrine, as well as other drugs that affect the noradrenergic system have been utilized clinically to treat attention deficit hyperactivity disorder (Biederman & Spencer, 1999).

Functioning of the noradrenergic system in prefrontal cortex has also been linked to working memory. Research in monkeys suggests that noradrenergic functioning of α_2 receptors in prefrontal cortex aids working memory. This effect is relatively specific; α_2 receptor agonists improve performance on working memory tasks dependent on the prefrontal cortex but do not improve performance for perceptual and memory tasks that rely on different brain regions (Arnsten, 1998). In contrast, high levels of binding of α_1 receptors in prefrontal cortex, as is often associated with stressful events that an individual cannot control, impairs working memory (Birnbaum et al., 1999).

The activity of the beta-receptor system has been linked to long-term memory, especially that which has an emotional component. For example, administering propranolol, which is a beta-adrenergic antagonist, reduces the heightened memory for emotionally charged information in both rats (Cahill, Pham, & Setlow, 2000) and people (Reist, Duffy, Fujimoto, & Cahill, 2001).

If you are sitting here feeling that all you've just read seems eerily familiar, you are right. The cognitive effects of the noradrenergic system are suspiciously similar to those of the cholinergic system. At the end of this section we will discuss the reasons for those similarities, as well as interrelations between other neurotransmitter subsystems.

• *SEROTONERGIC SYSTEM* •

Serotonin, or 5-hydroxytryptamine (5-HT), is the neurotransmitter released by the *serotonergic system.* The cell bodies of the serotonergic system are found in nine clusters, located in the raphe nuclei of the midbrain, pons, and medulla. The most important clusters are found in the dorsal and medial raphe nuclei. For the most part, cells from both the dorsal and medial raphe nucleus project to similar sites in the brain. These include the hypothalamus, hippocampus, and amygdala, all of which are part of the limbic system. However, cells from the dorsal raphe project with greater density to the striatum, cortex, cerebellum and thalamus, while those from the medial raphe project more to the hippocampus and other limbic structures (see Figure 2.9). Due to its diverse sites of projection, this system influences a large variety of behaviors, including arousal, mood, anxiety and aggression, the control of eating, sleeping and dreaming, pain, sexual behavior, and memory.

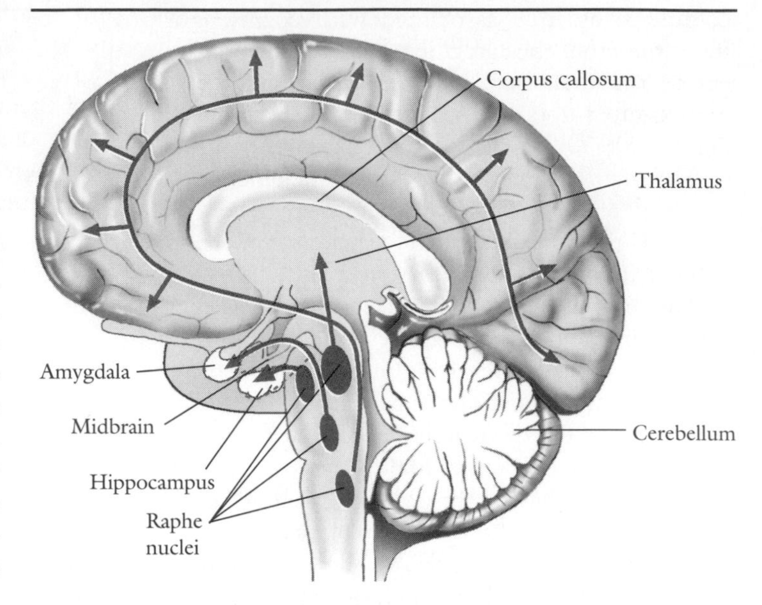

FIGURE 2.9 Pathways of serotonergic system.

There are over 10 different types of serotonergic receptors, all of which are metabotropic except for 5-HT_3. Some of these receptors are tightly linked to certain behaviors, whereas others affect a wide variety of behaviors. Here we will just touch upon some highlights.

One of the functions clearly associated with serotonergic function is sleep. 5-HT levels can influence the degree to which one falls asleep and the degree to which one goes into REM sleep, which is associated with dreaming. The dorsal, rather than the medial raphe nuclei are especially important for this function. The serotonergic receptors linked to sleep are the 5-HT_{1A} receptors, but these receptors are important in regulating a large variety of behaviors, including sexual behavior, appetite, aggression, and pain. Notice that many of these behaviors are those controlled by limbic structures and the hypothamalus. They are all regulatory behaviors that help to meet the basic needs of the organism.

Serotonin has been linked to mood states, most notably depression. Too little serotonin leads to depression, a state in which arousal levels are quite low (i.e., the person has no energy), and mood is continuously blue. Currently, some of the most popular drugs to treat depression are known as *serotonin-specific reuptake inhibitors (SSRIs),* because they do exactly that—they increase the amount of serotonin in the synaptic cleft by inhibiting its presynaptic uptake. You have probably heard of one of the best known SSRIs, fluoxetine, known commercially as Prozac.

Although serotonin can be very helpful in reducing depression, it has many other consequences as well. SSRIs can interfere with sleep, reduce appetite, and have deleterious effects on sexual performance, making an individual incapable of having an orgasm. Because of differences among individuals in their reactions to various SSRIs, a depressed individual may need to try a number of different SSRIs to find the one that has the best salutary effect on depression and the least adverse effect on eating, sleep, and sexual function.

With regard to mental function, serotonin has been linked most closely to memory, specifically the function of putting new memories into long-term storage (for a review, see Buhot, 1997). For example, individuals given a diet that does not provide tryptophan, a precursor to serotonin, show a specific deficit in forming new memories, whereas other cognitive functions, such as the ability to find a target item embedded in a bunch of distractors and the ability to make a speeded response to a sensory input, are unaffected (Riedel, Klassen, Deutz, van Someren, & van Praag, 1999). Individuals with a history of using the recreational drug "ecstasy" (3,4-methylenedioxymethamphetamine; MDMA), which is toxic to serotonergic neurons, tend to exhibit deficits in long-term memory (Morgan, 2000). Finally, deficits in learning and memory associated with aging and Alzheimer's disease appear to coincide with a decline in serotonergic function (Sirviö, 1999), specifically functions related to the 5-HT_4 receptor (Wong, Reynolds, Bonhaus, Hsu, & Eglen, 1996), although acetylcholine probably plays a larger role. Not surprisingly, there is a high density of 5-HT_4 receptors in the hippocampus, which, as we will learn in Chapter 10, is critical for the formation of new long-term memories. Because many serotonergic receptors are found in limbic regions, it is also thought that memories that have emotional connotations may be especially affected by compromise of the serotonergic system (Buhot, Martin, & Segu, 2000).

The serotonergic system has also been linked to the hallucinogenic effects of certain drugs. For example, LSD (lysergic acid diethylamide) acts as a direct agonist on 5-HT_{2A} and 5-HT_{2B} receptors.

As you can see, these neurotransmitter systems affect many different regions of the brain and have a variety of effects on cognitive and emotional processing. Table 2.1 summarizes the main attributes of each.

Interaction between Neurotransmitter Systems

Although we have treated these neurotransmitter systems as if they are independent, it should be

TABLE 2.1 The Four Main Neurotransmitter Systems

NEUROTRANSMITTER SYSTEM	TRANSMITTER	SITE OF ORIGIN	PROJECTION SITES	MAIN RECEPTOR TYPES	MAIN BEHAVIORAL EFFECTS
Cholinergic	Acetylcholine	Basal forebrain	Diffuse cortical regions	a. Muscarinic b. Nicotinic	Overall cortical excitability, attention, memory
Dopaminergic	Dopamine			a. D_1 family (D_1 & D_5) b. D_2 family (D_2, D_3, & D_4)	Working memory, novelty seeking, attention, psychotic symptomatology
Subsystems NIGROSTRIATAL		Substantia nigra	Dorsal striatum		Motor activity
MESOLIMBIC		Ventral tegmental area	a. Limbic regions b. Prefrontal cortex		Reward
MESOCORTICAL		Ventral tegmental area	Prefrontal cortex		Working memory, planning
Noradrenergic	Norepinephrine			α_1, α_2, β_1, β_2	
Subsystems		Ventrolateral tegmental area	Hypothalamus		Feeding, sexual behavior
		Locus ceruleus	a. Thalamus b. Hypothalamus c. Cortex		Attention, sleep, working memory
Serotonergic	Serotonin			At least nine different receptors	Sleep, mood, sexual behavior, eating, pain, memory, arousal
Subsystems		Dorsal raphe nucleus	a. Cortex b. Thalamus		
		Medial raphe nucleus	Limbic system		

SO CAN HERBS REALLY IMPROVE YOUR MEMORY, ATTENTION, AND MOOD?

Balm is sovereign for the brain, strengthening the memory and powerfully chasing away the melancholy (John Evelyn, 1699).

Although we may think that the use of herbal supplements and therapies as a new and trendy approach to treating a variety of disorders, in actuality it is a time-honored tradition, as attested to by this quotation. Long used in Eastern medicine, and now increasingly in Europe and to a lesser degree in the United States, herbal supplements are being favored in some cases over standard pharmaceutical products. For example, in the United Kingdom, rosemary, lemon balm (a member of the mint family), and sage are used by herbalists and aromatherapists for memory problems. Probably one of the most commonly touted substances for reducing memory problems is gingko, which is derived from the leaf of the *Ginkgo biloba* tree, a native plant of China. It is widely prescribed in Europe, especially in France and Germany, for dementia. St. John's wort, an aromatic perennial that is native to Europe, is frequently used in Germany and other European countries to treat mild to moderate depression. Its effects have been known for a long time, discussed by the ancient Greek and Roman physicians such as Hippocrates and Galen. Kava, derived from a shrub native to Polynesia and the Pacific island and traditionally taken as a beverage mixed with water and coconut milk, is taken to reduce anxiety and induce calm. Ginseng, derived from the root of a Chinese perennial, has been used to increase energy (see Beaubrun & Gray, 2000, for a brief review). Do these herbs have the claimed effect on thinking and mood, and if so, how do they work?

There is much controversy surrounding the answer to this question. One source of controversy is the fact that in the United States such substances are not regulated by the Food and Drug Administration, so dosages and purity are not monitored. It appears that in some cases, these herbs may have therapeutic effects. For example, there are some reports that ginkgo special extract EGb 761 slows the mental decline of individuals with Alzheimer's disease (LeBars, Katz, Berman, Itil, Freedman, & Schatzberg, 1997). Their effectiveness in slowing the disease in individuals with mild to moderate Alzheimer's has, in some cases, been found to approximate the level of standard pharmaceutical products, whose main action is inhibiting acetylcholinesterase (Wettstein, 2000). Benefits have also been found in normal middle-aged individuals—a combination of ginkgo and ginseng may actually improve memory performance (Wesnes, Ward, McGinty, & Petrini, 2000). In a recent large-scale study of patients in clinics in Germany, St. John's wort was found to be as effective as standard antidepressants and to have fewer side

clear from our discussion that they are highly interrelated. For example, we have seen that both dopamine and norepinephrine are implicated in attention deficit hyperactivity disorder, they both have receptors in prefrontal cortex, and they are both derived from tyrosine. Likewise, the serotonergic and cholinergic systems have been implicated in the formation of new long-term memories and sleep, and both project very diffusely to many regions of the brain. And both the cholinergic and noradrenergic systems influence attention and memory. Hence, much current research is centered on how these systems interact (e.g,. Steckler & Sahgal, 1995).

Because of these interactions, many new pharmacological interventions for a variety of disorders ranging from hyperactivity to schizophrenia to depression either attempt to capitalize on these similarities or try to disentangle them. One approach is to combine drugs to treat a disorder, such as attempting to modulate both the noradrenergic and cholinergic systems simultaneously to improve performance of individuals with Alzheimer's disease (e.g., Bierer, Aisen, Davidson, Ryan, Schmeidler, & Davis, 1994). Another approach is to more carefully pinpoint a pharmacological intervention to a very specific receptor type, such as designing antipsychotic drugs to affect only 5-HT_{2A} receptors (see

effects than conventional medications for treating mildly to moderately depressed individuals (Woelk, 2000), although it does not appear to be effective with more severely depressed individuals (Shelton et al., 2001).

So how do these herbs affect the brain? It appears that many of them work on some of the neurotransmitter systems that we have discussed in this chapter. Sage inhibits acetylcholinesterase (Perry, Court, Bidet, & Court, 1996) and binds with muscarinic cholinergic receptors (Wake et al., 2000), while balm inhibits acteylcholinesterase as well as binding with nicotinic receptors (Perry et al., 1996). Ginseng serves to facilitate the release of acetycholine (Benishin, Lee, Wang, & Liu, 1991) as well as the binding to muscarinic acetylcholine receptors (Kumar, Ghosal, & Bigl, 1997). Thus, many of the herbs that are thought to help memory work on the cholinergic system. St. John's wort works similarly to some more commonly prescribed antidepressants as it inhibits the uptake of serotonin and norepinephrine (Neary & Bu, 1999). Furthermore, some of these herbs have a very specific effect: for example, Indian ginseng affects only the cholinergic system, having no effect on GABAergic or glutaminergic receptors (Kumar, Ghosal, & Bigl, 1997), whereas gingko does not work as a monoamine oxidase inhibitor, affecting all the monoamine systems, but appears instead to be specific to the cholinergic system (Folwer et al., 2000).

It should be noted, however, that some of these herbs may affect the CNS through mechanisms other than neural transmission. For example, gingko has been found to cause dilation of the blood vessels, which may allow more oxygen to reach the brain. It also has been found to help in dealing with molecules known as "free radicals" that can interfere with oxygen metabolism. In Chapter 14, we will discuss the degree to which defects in oxygen metabolism may underlie a large number of neurodegenerative disorders.

So, should you suggest to your aging relatives that they start gobbling down scads of gingko, sage, St. John's wort, and ginseng to ward off the mental declines that can accompany aging? Probably not. As with any drug, paying attention to dosage and considering interactions with other drugs as well as effects on other bodily systems is important. For example, one 36-year-old woman who ate 70–80 gingko nuts in an attempt to improve her health unfortunately had a very different outcome than the one she expected—that of inducing seizures four hours later (Miwa, Iijima, Tanaka, & Mizuno, 2001). St. John's wort can affect blood pressure, intensify the effects of anesthetics, and increase the skin's sensitivity to sunlight. It can also interact with a multiplicity of drugs because it interferes with a metabolic pathway in the liver that is used by many drugs to enter the body. And ginseng can interfere with the functioning of cells in the blood that aid in clotting. ■

Dubovsky & Thomas, 1995, for a discussion of this general approach).

Chemical Modulation of Neural Transmission

Now that we have covered the basics of neural transmission and the different neurotransmitter systems, let us review in brief how communication between neurons can be modulated or disrupted. Many of the examples we provide are for the neurotransmitter acetylcholine. In addition to modulating cortical excitability in the CNS, this neurotransmitter is the one used outside the CNS at synapses of the neuromuscular junction, which is where neurons synapse onto muscles. When the neuron fires, it causes a contraction of the muscle tissue. Knowing this will help you appreciate some of the examples that follow.

There are three main ways of modulating neurotransmission: by affecting presynaptic mechanisms, by modulating the amount of neurotransmitter in the synaptic cleft, and by affecting postsynaptic mechanisms (refer back to Figure 2.5).

There are a number of ways to modulate presynaptic mechanisms. One way is to regulate the amount of neurotransmitter that is actually produced. For example, ingesting a diet high in choline helps to promote the production of acetylcholine.

Foods rich in choline include cauliflower and milk. Or one can influence the release of the neurotransmitter into the synaptic cleft. For example, the venom of the black widow spider promotes the release of ACh, allowing it to flood the synaptic cleft. Because the excess amount keeps a large amount of ACh bound to the postsynaptic receptor, the person cannot initiate any other motor actions, becomes paralyzed, can't breathe, and dies. Finally, one can modulate the action of autoreceptors. Remember from our discussion earlier in the chapter that when a neurotransmitter is bound to an autoreceptor it causes a *decrease* in the release of that neurotransmitter. Some drugs stimulate autoreceptors. The drug binds as if it were identical to the neurotransmitter, which then causes the cell to release less of that neurotransmitter. For example, at low doses clonidine binds the autoreceptors for norepinephrine, inhibiting its release, with a consequent degradation in attention. However, a drug that blocks an autoreceptor, displacing the neurotransmitter so that it cannot bind to the autoreceptor, will enhance the release of neurotransmitter and thus increase firing. The neuron will be stripped of the feedback mechanism that provides information about how much transmitter is in the cleft, and will not adjust release of the transmitter downward. As one example, some experimental antipsychotic drugs, such as amisulpride, at low doses block the D_3 autoreceptor, leading to increased release of dopamine.

A variety of mechanisms can modulate the amount of neurotransmitter in the synaptic cleft. One way is to affect reuptake mechanisms. For example, cocaine blocks reuptake of dopamine, leading to its stimulatory effects. Another way to modulate the amount of neurotransmitters is to inhibit the action of the enzymes that break them down. For example, insecticides, nerve gases, and herbicides all serve to inhibit acetylcholinesterase, allowing for the accumulation of ACh in the synaptic cleft. This eventually leads to neuromuscular paralysis. Notice that the end result here is similar to that observed with black widow spider venom. Both nerve gases and black widow spider venom have the same result: they lead to an excess of ACh. However, the mechanism by which this excess occurs is different.

The final major way to modulate neuronal activity is via postsynaptic mechanisms. A drug can increase activity by mimicking the effect of a neurotransmitter, thus serving as an agonist. For example, nicotine stimulates receptors to which acetylcholine binds. The physical structure of nicotine is similar enough to acetylcholine that it can fit into the binding sites of the postsynaptic receptor and be effective in opening the ion channels. Thought of this way, an agonist is like an alternative key that can open the lock. Because nicotine binds to cholinergic receptors, it stimulates this system, leading to effects such as increasing attention. On the other hand, a drug may block postsynaptic sites, precluding the neurotransmitter from doing so, and thereby act as an antagonist. For example, curare prevents acetylcholine from binding postsynaptically because it occupies the receptor site. Yet when in the receptor site, it does not open the ion channel. Its action is much like having a key that fits in a lock but can't turn it. It is jammed in there, preventing the correct key from being used. This jamming of the lock mechanism explains why curare acts to cause paralysis. Acetylcholine cannot bind with the receptor to produce muscle activity.

Myelination

So far we have discussed the mechanics of how information is propagated from one neuron to another. However, we have not considered how information can be carried over long distances in the nervous system. The speed at which neurons propagate electrical signals down their axons varies in large part according to the degree to which the axon is insulated by a fatty sheath called **myelin.** The larger the myelin sheath is, the greater the speed with which the electrical signal is propagated down the axon. The axons of some neurons have no myelin sheath. Unmyelinated neurons typically are small and do not carry information over long distances, generally synapsing on nearby neurons. In contrast, neurons whose axons project to distant places in the nervous system are typically myelinated because myelination decreases the time needed to transport information from one neuron to the next.

To demonstrate the increase in speed afforded by myelin, let's consider a specific type of neuron in the brain known as a **pyramidal cell,** which, among other things, is involved in controlling muscle movement. The axon of a pyramidal cell that controls movement of the right leg must extend from the brain to the bottom reaches of the spinal cord, a distance of more than 3 feet, or approximately 1 m. Unmyelinated fibers convey information at the rate of only about 0.5 mm/ms. If the pyramidal neuron were unmyelinated, it would take approximately 2,000 ms (i.e., 2 s) to convey information from the brain to the base of the spinal cord (2,000 ms × 0.5 mm/ms = 1 m). Such a time delay would not enable people to move or react very quickly. The myelination of pyramidal neurons allows information to be relayed at about 50 mm/ms, reducing the time between the generation of the signal in the brain to its arrival at the spinal cord more than a hundredfold, to about 200 ms.

The myelin sheath is not produced by the neuron but rather by a particular class of glia. In the brain, these are known as **oligodendrocytes.** A portion of the oligodendrocyte wraps itself around the axon much the same as a carpet wrapped around a cardboard tube; such wrapping creates a discrete section of myelin. The more turns there are around the neuron, the greater the insulation and hence the greater the conduction speed. Gaps between myelinated sections of an axon are known as **nodes of Ranvier.** Because the electrical signal must jump across these nodes, they serve to keep the electrical signal constant in size rather than degrading as it travels down the axon (Figure 2.10).

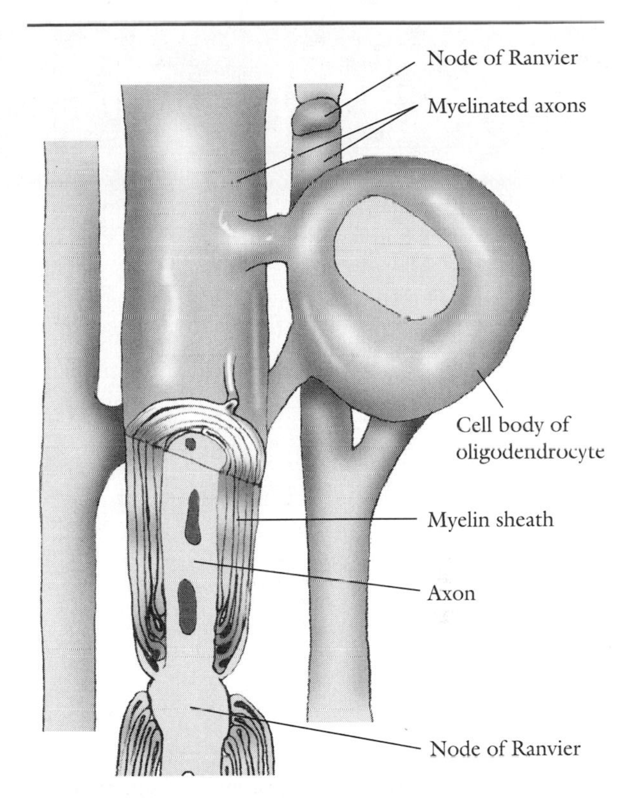

FIGURE 2.10 The structure of the myelin sheath around an axon. Oligodendrocytes in the brain form a short section of the myelin sheath on each of a number of adjacent neurons by wrapping a paddlelike process around each axon. Gaps between sections of myelin are known as nodes of Ranvier and help the electrical signal to be propagated at a constant strength along the axon.

Because myelin is fatty, it is white. Areas of the brain through which myelinated fibers run are known as the *white matter* of the brain. Concentrations of cell bodies, which are unmyelinated, constitute the *gray matter.* When a group of cells sends their axons to the same place, the group of axons is known as a **fiber tract,** and because these axons usually traverse long distances, they tend to be myelinated. For example, the *corpus callosum,* which is the main fiber tract connecting the two halves, or hemispheres, of the brain, is composed mainly of myelinated fibers, which allow a speedy transfer of information from a neuron in one hemisphere to a distant neuron in the other hemisphere.

Later in this book, we discuss the myelination of neurons in two contexts: with regard to development and with regard to certain diseases. As discussed in Chapter 13, myelination of the brain follows a developmental course in which sensory and motor regions myelinate early in life, but the connections between more distant regions involved in higher cortical processing do not become fully myelinated until as late as the teenage years or early twenties (Giedd et al., 1996). The result is that regions of the brain become functionally more connected with age. Some of the disease states we discuss later, such as multiple sclerosis (see Chapter 14), cause the myelin that is surrounding neurons to be thinned in a patchy, or haphazard, manner. This process leads to a significant disruption in neural processing, affecting both motor function and cognitive function (e.g., Peyser & Poser, 1986).

Electrochemical Signaling in the Nervous System

- Information is conveyed within a neuron via an electrical signal.
- An action potential, which is often referred to as the cell "firing," consists of a change in the differential electrical charge across the cell membrane from −70 millivolts to +55 millivolts and back again.
- An action potential causes neurotransmitter to be released, which diffuses across the synaptic cleft and binds with specific receptors on the postsynaptic side of neighboring neurons.
- This chemical binding causes the production of postsynaptic potentials, which when they summate in time and space, can cause an action potential.
- The responsiveness of a neuron is limited by the time needed to "reset" before it can fire again.
- The effect of postsynaptic potentials is temporally limited by reuptake of the neurotransmitter by the presynaptic neuron, enzymatic deactivation of the neurotransmitter, uptake of the neurotransmitter by nearby glial cells, and diffusion away from the synaptic cleft.

Neurotransmitters

- Neurotransmitters are chemicals that are synthesized within the neuron and when released produce an action potential.
- Amino acids are the most common type of neurotransmitter in the CNS. The main excitatory amino acid in the CNS is glutamate whereas the main inhibitory amino acid is gamma-aminobutyric acid (GABA).
- The other types of neurotransmitter are arranged into systems: acetylcholine is one type, and the monoamines—dopamine, norepinephrine, and serotonin—constitute the other type. The cell bodies for the neurons producing these neurotransmitters originate in subcortical and brainstem regions and project diffusely throughout the cortex.

Chemical Modulation of Neural Transmission

- Presynaptic modulation can occur by affecting the amount of neurotransmitter produced, the release of neurotransmitter into the cleft, or the feedback regulation that is controlled by autoreceptors.
- Modulation can occur in the synaptic cleft by affecting reuptake mechanisms or the breakdown of neurotransmitter.
- Postsynaptic modulation occurs by a substance binding with receptors or by blocking the receptor site.

Myelination

- Myelination is the process whereby oligodendrocytes wrap themselves around the neurons to provide an insulating fatty sheath around axons.
- Myelination reduces transmission time of information to and from disparate sites in the nervous system.
- Myelinated axons are referred to as white matter, in contrast to cell bodies, which are gray matter.

KEY TERMS

acetylcholine 46
acetylcholinesterase 46
action potential 42
agonists 49
amino acids 47
antagonists 49
autoreceptors 46
axon hillock 42
barbiturates 48
benzodiazepines 48
catecholamines 48
dopamine 48
enzymatic deactivation 45
enzyme 43
excitatory postsynaptic potentials (EPSPs) 44
excitotoxicity 47
fiber tract 59
G protein 43
GABA 47
glutamate 47
indolamine 48
inhibitory postsynaptic potentials (IPSPs) 44
ionotropic receptors 43
ischemia 47
mesocortical system 51
mesolimbic system 51
metabotropic receptors 43
monoamines 48
myelin 58
neurotransmitters 46
nigrostriatal system 51
nodes of Ranvier 59
norepinephrine 48
oligodendrocytes 59
pyramidal cell 58
receptors 43
resting potential 41
reuptake 45
serotonin 48
synapse 42
synaptic vesicles 42

CHAPTER 3

METHODS

Introduction

In this chapter we discuss the different methods that can be used to understand how the brain influences the way we think, feel, and act. Because cognitive neuroscience and neuropsychology are interdisciplinary fields of research, they require integration of information about the brain with information about behavior. The question under investigation has a major influence on which aspects of information about the brain and behavior will be examined. In terms of the brain, we may want to obtain information at the neuroanatomical, neurochemical, or neurophysiological level. At a neuroanatomical level, we may need information about the integrity of brain structures, their connections to other brain regions, and their relationship to particular behavioral patterns.

For example, knowing that people have specific difficulties in recognizing faces after sustaining trauma to the ventral regions of the right temporal lobe may allow us to infer a connection between that cognitive process and that brain region. We may also require information about the brain at the neurochemical level. For example, we may want to know how the disregulation of the neurotransmitter dopamine contributes to the symptoms observed in schizophrenia. Finally, at the neurophysiological level, we may want to observe which brain regions are electrically or metabolically active during performance of a specific task. For example, we may want to know the degree to which the right hemisphere is electrically responsive during a musical judgment task.

We can also observe behavior at different levels. On the one hand, we may want to observe the integrity of sensory processing in an individual, such as determining whether a person can distinguish high tones from low tones. On the other hand, we may need to examine more central aspects of mental processes, such as the integrity of the memory system. In still other cases, we may want to decompose specific mental abilities, such as determining whether a memory deficit is limited to learning new information or extends to retrieving previously learned information as well.

To investigate each of these issues requires particular tools: Research methods are cognitive neuroscientists' tools. The research methods and ideas introduced in this chapter are referred to throughout the book as we explore the neuropsychological underpinnings of mental activity. During all our discussions, understanding the strengths and limitations of different research methods is important because the adage "You need the right tool for the job" is as apt in cognitive neuroscience and neuropsychology as in carpentry. If you have ever tried to use a knife or a dime when you needed a screwdriver, you know that the correct tool can mean the difference between success and failure or between ease and hardship. In cognitive neuroscience, the proper tool may be a particular clinical population, a specific brain imaging technique, or a certain experimental method.

Cognitive neuroscientists and neuropsychologists must consider how the information they gather in any investigation is influenced by the choice of a particular population and a particular method. Each choice biases the researcher toward observing some aspects of functioning and not others. Consider, as an analogy, that the form of transportation you choose to take from one city to another influences what you see along the way. Taking a plane from one city to another will allow you to clearly see differences in the topography of land, between plains and forest, whereas taking a car will allow you to see differences in the regional architecture of buildings between farmhouses and row houses. Given the limitations imposed by any single method of neuropsychological inquiry, you may wonder how scientists can be certain of the conclusions that they draw about brain-behavior relationships. Are these scientists as foolhardy as the inhabitants of the Emerald City in *The Wizard of Oz,* who thought the city was emerald because they were wearing green eyeglasses?

As we discuss in more detail later in the chapter, the answer to the previous question is "no," because neuropsychologists and cognitive neuroscientists invoke a strategy akin to changing your eyeglasses often. In general, information is gathered on the same question by using a variety of methods with a variety of populations. This technique of examining whether all the answers obtained from a set of interrelated experiments lead to the same conclusion is known as the **method of converging operations.**

When researchers have examined a question from multiple perspectives and all answers point to the same verdict, the researchers can be relatively confident that they understand a basic aspect of the relationship between the brain and behavior. Let's consider an example of converging operations by examining three representative findings, from different methods, regarding the role played by the parietal lobe in directing attention to particular regions of space. Simultaneously, we'll also consider the potential pitfalls of each method.

First, research with monkeys indicates that the response of neurons in the posterior parietal cortex varies depending on the region of space to which the animal is directing its attention (e.g., Lynch, Mountcastle, Talbot, & Yin, 1977). Interpolating from animals, however, may sometimes be problematic because their repertoire of behavior and the organization of their brains are distinct from those of humans. Second, brain imaging in neurologically intact individuals reveals an increase in the metabolic activity of the parietal region when a person directs attention to a specific portion of visual space (Corbetta, Miezin, Shulman, & Petersen, 1993). However, brain imaging techniques usually provide an "average" of activity across a number of individuals, so conclusions about precise anatomical locations can sometimes be difficult to make. Third, after a person sustains a unilateral parietal lobe lesion, he or she often ignores the contralateral portion of visual space (e.g., Vallar & Perani, 1986). However, findings from patients with brain damage are always subject to variability among individuals both in the extent of the neurological damage and in the diversity of the individuals' experiences pre- and postdamage. Hence, although the evidence from any one of these studies alone is not convincing, evidence from all three methods of inquiry converges on the same conclusion, namely that the parietal region plays an important role in directing our attention to a given region of space. When such convergence occurs, researchers can have more confidence that the answer arrived at is accurate and that the inherent biases of each method are not so great as to obscure their usefulness. Notice that such a converging body of work usually cannot be performed by a single scientist but rather depends on a community of scientists with different areas of expertise.

We now turn our discussion to the specific subject populations and the specific methods used in examining the relationship between the brain and behavior. In this endeavor, we need three critical ingredients. First, we need a population of individuals on which to test our hypothesis about the relationship between the brain and behavior. The group of participants chosen will vary depending on the question asked. Second, we need a means of gathering information about the brain of each individual. Depending on the question, we may want information about brain structure, brain function, or both. Third, we need a way to measure behavior. In some cases, we may want to use specific measures of behavior, and in other cases, large batteries of tests. In the remainder of the chapter, we survey the options available for each of these three critical ingredients and outline the advantages and disadvantages conferred by each choice.

Populations of Research Participants

In this section of the chapter we examine the specific advantages and disadvantages of using three major populations—individuals with circumscribed brain damage, neurologically intact individuals, and nonhuman animals—to investigate questions in neuropsychology and cognitive neuroscience.

■ Patients with Circumscribed Brain Damage

Understanding mental functioning by examining patients who have sustained brain damage has a long and venerable history, stretching back some 2,000 years. In the time of the Romans, Galen, a physician who ministered to the wounds of the gladiators, noticed that contestants sustaining injury to the arm, leg, or torso retained their powers of thought, whereas those who sustained injury to the head or the brain did not. From these observations, he inferred that the brain was linked to thought, becoming one of the first scientists to use individuals with brain damage to understand brain-behavior relationships.

Galen's approach was a precursor of the logic we use today to determine which regions of the brain are important for a given mental function. If damage to a particular brain region results in an inability to perform a specific mental function, scientists usually assume that the function must have depended on that brain region, an approach known as the **lesion method.** During the history of neuropsychological investigation, this method has proved very powerful in expanding our knowledge about the neurological bases of thought and emotion. Importantly, it has led us to conceptualize the brain as being composed of different subsystems, or modules, each supporting a different mental function. Although scientists have different ideas about exactly what constitutes a module (e.g., Fodor, 1985), for our purposes it can be considered a portion of a processing system that is dedicated to a single function not performed elsewhere within that system (e.g., reading, verbal short-term memory, or face recognition). Furthermore, we now realize that these subsystems are located in specific regions of brain tissue, a concept called **localization of function.**

The brain was not always believed to work in the manner just described. In the early twentieth century, scientists debated whether functions were localized or whether the brain worked by **mass action,** meaning that all pieces of brain contributed to all functions. One of the most notable supporters of the mass action viewpoint was the psychologist Karl Lashley, who did much of his work in this area in the 1920s and 1930s (K. S. Lashley, 1929). He argued that the nature of cognitive deficits observed after brain damage hinged not on which region of the brain was destroyed but rather on the extent of the damage: The larger the amount of tissue destroyed, the greater were the decrements in performance. In contrast, researchers supporting the idea of localization of function argued that the site of brain damage, not just the overall amount of destruction, predicted the nature and degree of the deficit observed.

Today the debate has been resolved more firmly on the side of localization of function than on that of mass action. This resolution occurred in part because of improved techniques for measuring lesions (or in the case of animals, creating lesions), and because of more sophisticated methods for measuring behavior. With these improvements, researchers realized that not all lesions have the same effect on behavior and concluded that behavioral differences must occur because of differences in brain structure.

Even though localization of function biases us to conceive of the brain as being composed of distinct subsystems, we must not forget that the brain is comprised of about 50 billion *interconnected* neurons. Although any complex cognitive function will require activity in distinct modules, each of which is mainly responsible for some subcomponent of the task, it is the smooth and integrated functioning across these distinct areas that enables complex tasks to be performed. Consider by analogy a car. Although it is made of specific parts or systems such as an engine, a drive train, wheels, and a suspension, all these parts are useless for travel unless they are interconnected in a specific manner so that the power from the engine can be transferred to the drive train to move the wheels.

Throughout this book, we will see that the modular description of functioning is more useful for certain cognitive abilities than for others, which act in a more distributed manner. For example, the components of language—the comprehension of spoken language, the production of spoken language, reading, and writing—seem to be performed by quite distinct brain regions. In contrast, components of other cognitive functions, such as certain aspects of attention, are much more diffusely organized across many brain regions. Thus, we must remember that the brain relies both on localization of function and on distributed processing to carry out cognitive function in a seamless fashion. In fact, as we discuss later in this chapter, many computational models, which represent the brain's functioning in an abstract fashion using computer simulations, are precisely designed to capture the flavor of this diffuse processing.

• *USES OF THE LESION METHOD* •

The main strength of the lesion method is that it allows a specific region of brain tissue to be directly linked to a specific aspect of mental processing. Our ability to make such a linkage has been critically important to understanding many aspects of human cognition and emotion. Although research with nonhuman animals has historically provided much information on the relationship between the brain and behavior, limitations in the cognitive repertoire of nonhuman animals restrict our ability to address many important questions, such as the neural bases of language. Unlike animal models, in which scientists carefully create lesions in a certain region of the brain and then observe the effect on behavior, the lesion method in humans requires investigators to rely on cases of brain damage that result from unfortunate circumstances, such as war, accident, injury, or disease. Hence, the neuropsychologist has no control over the location, extent, and cause of the lesion in any given patient. A researcher interested in the role of a particular brain structure in cognition must work with medical personnel to identify patients who can be asked to participate in a research project. The success of this method depends critically on the cooperation, courage, and goodwill of these patients, who despite struggling with the ill effects of brain damage, agree to participate in studies. Although testing will starkly reveal the extent of their disabilities, these individuals nonetheless participate in the hope that the knowledge gained will help other individuals who find themselves in the same unfortunate circumstance in the future.

When using the lesion method, a researcher can take one of two conceptual approaches: one emphasizes knowledge about neural substrates, the other knowledge about cognitive function. The approach chosen has a large influence on the population recruited for a study. Throughout the book, we find many examples of these two different conceptual approaches, so we discuss them next in more detail.

If the researcher chooses to emphasize neural substrates by asking, "What functions are supported by a particular piece of brain tissue?" then she or he assembles a group of individuals in whom the site, cause, and extent of damage are as comparable as possible. An example of this approach is the work done by Brenda Milner and colleagues at the Montreal Neurological Institute examining the role of the temporal lobe in memory. Their population consisted of patients with epilepsy who underwent removal of areas of the temporal lobe because that brain region was the center of epileptic activity. For this procedure, the neurosurgeon excises a particular region of brain tissue and obtains documentation of the extent of tissue removal at the time of the operation; therefore, a relatively uniform population can be obtained. Using this approach, Milner and colleagues found that removal of a particular region within the temporal lobe, that associated with the hippocampus, leads to difficulties in forming new long-term memories (e.g., B. Milner, 1978).

Studies of this type usually include not only a group of patients who have had damage to or removal of the brain structure under investigation, but also one or more groups of patients with damage elsewhere in the brain. This practice allows researchers to determine whether the behavioral disruption is linked specifically to the brain structure under investigation and not others. Returning to the previous example, although damage to the hippocampal region disrupted the ability to form new long-term memories, it might be just one of many regions supporting this function. To rule out this possibility, Milner and colleagues typically included one or more groups of individuals with damage to a different brain region, such as the frontal lobe. Because individuals with damage to these other regions did not exhibit problems in forming new long-term memories, the researchers concluded that the hippocampal region specifically supports the formation of new long-term memories.

Because such an approach allows us to identify a particular brain region as critically important to a specific component of cognition, it can provide invaluable information to physicians, clinical neuropsychologists, and other medically related professionals. For example, neurosurgeons must know which cognitive functions are likely to be disrupted if a particular region of brain tissue is excised. Likewise, knowing the site of brain damage allows neuropsychologists to predict which intellectual abilities are likely to be compromised, to tailor their evaluation of cognitive deficits, and to plan for appropriate rehabilitation.

The other conceptual approach to the lesion method emphasizes cognitive function. When taking this approach, researchers are likely to select a group of individuals who exhibit the same behavioral symptoms; the selection is made with little regard for the location of the brain damage. For example, in the chapter on attention, we learn about a syndrome called *hemineglect,* which, as we discussed in the introductory chapter, causes individuals to ignore information on one side of space. Although most common after damage to parietal regions of the right hemisphere, hemineglect can occur after damage to many other regions of the brain, including the basal ganglia, the frontal lobes, and the thalamus. Hence, researchers may assemble a group of individuals who have hemineglect to be examined regardless of the location of the lesion that caused the hemineglect. For example, researchers might design a study to determine whether the neglect can be minimized if fewer rather than more objects are located in the environment. Obtaining answers to this question not only informs us about brain-behavior relationships but also can be useful in designing effective methods of rehabilitation.

Although this approach does not emphasize the neural organization of the brain, it may nonetheless be able to provide such information. By carefully examining the neurological records of the assembled group of patients (all of whom exhibit the same behavioral deficit), researchers can determine the locus of damage in each patient. Convergence or similarity of the location of damage across patients can help to identify the specific neural structure or set of neural structures likely to participate in that given function.

Comparing patterns of cognitive disability and cognitive sparing across individuals with lesions in different locations can provide important insights into the architecture of the mind. **Double dissociation** is a particularly powerful method that allows researchers to determine whether two cognitive functions are independent of one another (e.g., Shallice, 1988; Teuber, 1955). A double dissociation occurs when lesions have converse effects on two distinct cognitive functions: one brain lesion causes a disruption in Cognitive Function A but not Cognitive Function B, whereas a different lesion causes a disruption in Cognitive Function B but not Cognitive Function A. We infer that the functions are independent because the viability of one cognitive function does not depend on the viability of the other.

To make the concept of a double dissociation more concrete, let's consider a classic example, the dissociation between Broca's aphasia and Wernicke's aphasia, both of which are disruptions in language processing (we discuss both of these in more detail in the chapter on language). Without any background knowledge, we might think that all aspects of auditory language processing rely on the same region of the brain. If this were the case, we would predict that if a person lost the ability to understand auditory language, he or she would also lose the ability to speak. However, Broca's aphasia and Wernicke's aphasia illustrate that the ability to produce and the ability to comprehend spoken language are distinct. In Broca's aphasia, comprehension of auditory language is, for the most part, intact. However, individuals with this syndrome have great difficulty producing speech. In Wernicke's aphasia, the converse is observed. The individual cannot understand what is said to her or him but nonetheless fluently produces grammatically correct sentences (although, as we will learn later in the book, these sentences are usually nonsensical). Hence, disruptions in speech output are independent of whether a disruption in speech comprehension occurs, and vice versa.

The importance of the lesion method in expanding our knowledge in neuropsychology cannot be underestimated. It has led to classic conceptualizations about the neural underpinnings of language, memory, and perception, to mention just a few areas (see H. Damasio & Damasio, 1989, for further discussion). Throughout this book, we often discuss evidence provided by the lesion method, yet for all its power, this method, like any other, has its limitations. We now turn to a discussion of these limitations.

• *DIFFICULTIES WITH THE LESION METHOD* •

The lesion method imposes two major limitations on researchers. First, variability in characteristics of the participant population, as well as variability in the location and extent of the damage, can make straightforward inferences difficult. This variability is especially prominent when compared with that which occurs in animal experimentation. Second, although the lesion method has an obvious intuitive appeal and appears to allow straightforward inferences about the relationship between the brain and behavior, in some cases this logic can lead us to inaccurate conclusions. We discuss both sets of problems in turn.

Compared with lesion experiments done with nonhuman animals, research performed with people who have sustained brain damage is "messy" because the sample is much less homogeneous along a number of dimensions. In animal experiments, the population usually consists of littermates (which are genetically similar) raised in the same environment, given the same lesion at the same age, provided with the same experiences before and after the lesion, and assessed behaviorally at the same age. Thus, genetic and environmental characteristics of the sample are as comparable as possible.

In contrast, populations of individuals who have sustained brain damage are quite different. Individuals typically vary widely in age, socioeconomic status, and educational background. Prior to brain damage, these individuals had diverse life experiences. Afterward, their life experiences tended to vary too, depending on the type of rehabilitation they received, their attitudes toward therapy and recovery, and their social support network. Compared with research animals or the human subjects of standard psychology experiments (typically college sophomores), individuals with brain damage who participate in studies on the neural underpinnings of human cognition are quite a heterogeneous group. Even if we compare groups of individuals who have similar demographic characteristics, such as age, educational background, and gender, the participants still differ on a myriad of other individual characteristics. For example, extensive experience during childhood with playing a musical instrument that involves fine motor control of one hand (e.g., a violin) increases the size of brain tissue devoted to representation of the fingers of that hand (e.g., Elbert et al., 1995). Hence, two individuals who sustained lesions in the same location might nonetheless exhibit different degrees of deficit as a result of their varying experiences.

Furthermore, lesions sustained by humans are much less specific, both in extent and origin, than those created in animal experiments. Although a researcher can assemble a group of patients in whom the lesion is more or less in the same location (e.g., the dorsolateral region of the frontal lobe, the posterior parietal lobe), the size and severity of the lesions are likely to vary widely. While in animals we can induce lesions in a uniform manner (e.g., apply electrical current to destroy brain tissue), in humans the cause of damage can range from a bullet wound to a stroke to an infectious disease to surgical removal of a region necessitated by epilepsy or tumor. These different sources yield very different types of damage. For example, damage from stroke causes more diffuse effects and has a higher probability of involving subcortical regions than damage inflicted by a bullet or another missile does. Often researchers attempt to assemble groups of individuals with similar causes of brain damage, yet in some cases doing so may be impossible.

Thus, many factors—the diversity of characteristics among people who sustain brain damage, the heterogeneity of the cause of damage, variability in the size and location of lesions—can impede our ability to isolate the specific neural structures that influence a given behavior. When a relationship is uncovered, however, it is more likely to be robust because it was discerned despite variations in populations and differences in the nature of the damage.

The second major limitation of the lesion method is that we cannot directly observe the function performed by the damaged portion of the brain. Rather, all that can be observed is how the rest of the brain performs *without* that particular area. From these observations we then infer the previous role of the damaged region. Although such inferences are usually sound, they may have certain limitations and liabilities. First, only the regions of the brain *critical* to a given cognitive function can be identified, not the entire set of brain regions that may participate in that function. Second, behavioral impairment may result after damage to a region not because that region is critical to the task, but rather because that region *connects* other brain regions that must interact for the function to be performed correctly. Finally, a brain region's contribution to a particular cognitive function may be "silent," or masked, if the task can be performed in more than one manner. Individuals may remain competent at performing a given task by using an alternative strategy to that used before damage.

To appreciate the lesion method's limitations in identifying all the brain regions that are involved in performing a task, think about putting on a play. If the person playing the main character is ill (and there is no understudy), the show cannot go on; therefore, we can identify that person as critical for the performance of the play. But if one of the stagehands or prop masters becomes ill, the curtain still goes up, even though clearly the missing individual contributed to the production. The show can continue because the chores of the remaining crew are likely to be shuffled to compensate for the absence of this individual. Similarly, if brain damage destroys a region that participates in but is not critical for the performance of a function, behavior can appear to be more or less intact because other brain regions can act to support that function.

The lesion method is also limited in that it doesn't allow us to discern whether damage to a particular region of the brain alters performance because that region is critical to task performance or because it contains axons, known as *fibers of passage,* that connect two or more brain regions critical for the function. When damage occurs, information carried by these fibers, in effect, cannot be transmitted from one brain region to another. The result is a behavioral deficit called a **disconnection syndrome.** To understand this concept more clearly, consider a situation in which severe weather prevents food from the farms from reaching the city. Perhaps the farms were destroyed and are no longer producing food. This case would be similar to a brain lesion having damaged a portion of the brain critical for performance of a task. Alternatively, assume that the farms are intact but the highway between the farms and the city was ruined and thus the food cannot be transported. This situation would be similar to what occurs in a disconnection syndrome. Throughout the book, we find many examples of disconnection syndromes, including *split-brain syndrome* (discussed in the chapter on lateralization of function) and *conduction aphasia* (discussed in the chapter on language). We can sometimes identify disconnection syndromes by referring to brain anatomy. If the region of the brain that leads to cognitive deficits contains few cell bodies and many nerve fiber tracts, a disconnection syndrome is more likely to be an explanation for the deficit.

A final potential limitation of the lesion method is that it may cause us to underestimate the role of a specific brain region in a given cognitive function. After brain damage, a person may compensate by using a different strategy to perform the task, one that relies on intact areas. For example, suppose that after damage to Region A of the brain, a person navigates around her or his world without much difficulty, leading us to assume that the functioning of Region A is unrelated to the cognitive skill of navigation. Yet, in actuality, Region A *is* important for navigation, playing a role in constructing the geographical relationship between objects or places (e.g., that the post office is to the east of the main shopping center). However, Region B of the brain provides the ability to navigate point to point by means of landmarks (e.g., the post office is six blocks past the church). The ability to uncover the distinct roles of Regions A and B in navigation is possible only if we carefully break down general cognitive skills into their components and test each component individually, a task that sometimes can be difficult.

• *SINGLE-CASE VERSUS GROUP STUDIES* •

Our discussion of the lesion method would be incomplete without a review of the debate about single-case versus group studies of individuals with brain damage. In **single-case studies,** a single individual with brain damage is studied intensively with a variety of neuropsychological tests. In contrast, in **group studies,** individuals with brain damage who have similar characteristics (e.g., lesions in similar areas) are studied as a group. Some researchers argue that group studies may obscure patterns of behavior or cause misleading interpretations of data. They argue that a group of patients may be so heterogeneous in their patterns of performance that the group average does not typify the majority of individuals and may be a composite that is rarely, if ever, found in any individual (e.g., Caramazza & Badecker, 1989). Suppose, for example, as illustrated in Table 3.1, that researchers test a group of nine individuals with localized brain damage and a control group of nine neurologically intact people on three tasks. If you look at the average percentage correct for each group at the bottom of the table, you can see that on each of the three tasks, the group

TABLE 3.1 Hypothetical Example of Potential Distortion of Performance Patterns When Group Averages Are Used

INDIVIDUAL WITH BRAIN DAMAGE	PERFORMANCE AS MEASURED BY PERCENTAGE CORRECT		
	TASK 1	TASK 2	TASK 3
1	20	75	70
2	25	70	80
3	30	80	75
4	75	25	75
5	80	30	70
6	70	20	80
7	75	80	25
8	70	75	30
9	80	70	20
Average of nine individuals with brain damage	58.3	58.3	58.3
Average of nine neurologically intact individuals	78	80	83

The average score for the nine individuals with brain damage does not adequately reflect the performance of any given individual. Although the average for individuals with brain damage is lower than that of neurologically intact individuals for all three tasks, all individuals with brain damage score as well as neurologically intact individuals for two of the three tasks.

with brain damage gets a lower percentage correct than the control group. However, if you look at the pattern for each individual with brain damage, you should be able to identify three subgroups of patients: one group that does poorly on Task 1 (Individuals 1–3), one that does poorly on Task 2 (Individuals 4–6), and a third that does poorly on task 3 (Individuals 7–9). Although on average the individuals with brain damage do worse than the controls on all three tasks, no single individual with brain damage performs more poorly than the controls on all three tasks!

Because of the difficulties that arise when we generalize from group studies, some researchers endorse the single-case study. However, the single-case study approach also has its difficulties (for instances of problems with single-case studies, see Zurif, Gardner, & Brownell, 1989). One problem is that we may never know whether the pattern observed for a single individual is representative of people in general. For example, we know that left-handers, who compose about 10% of the population, have a neural organization for cognitive function that is distinct from that of right-handers. If handedness, genetics, or some special environmental influence causes an individual's brain organization to be atypical, the pattern of disability after damage may also be atypical. This issue is especially a problem when the behavioral syndrome and its causative lesion are so rare that they have been observed in only one or two individuals. In such cases, our power of interpretation is restricted.

If both group and single-case studies have limitations, what are researchers to do? One approach, known as the **multiple-case study approach,** is to validate research findings on a series of patients, each of whom is also treated as a single-case study. In this approach, data for each individual within each group are provided, so that researchers can determine the variability across individuals as well as the degree to which the overall group average typifies the behavior of individuals within the group (see Figure 3.1).

Multiple single-case studies have other advantages as well. A series of multiple single-case studies

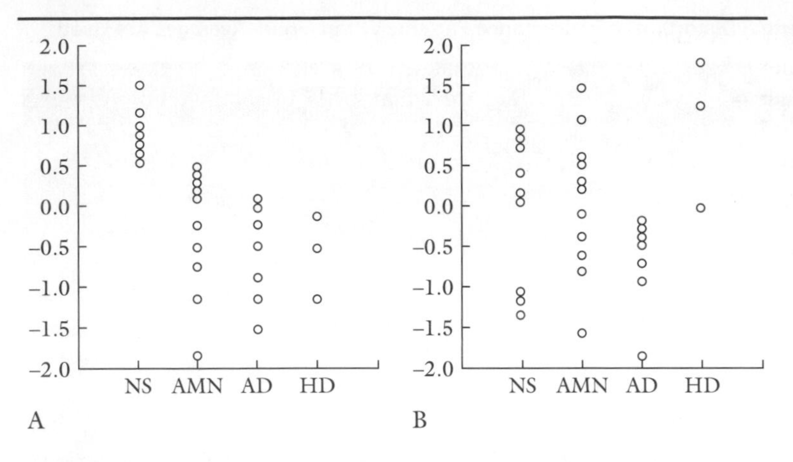

FIGURE 3.1 An example of the multiple-case study approach. To determine the extent of differences between patients with brain damage (AMN, patients with amnesia; AD, patients with Alzheimer's disease; HD, patients with Huntington's disease) and neurologically intact subjects (NS), the researcher treats each member of the group as a single-case study as well. (A) For a measure of recognition memory, every patient is performing at a level worse than that of the neurologically intact controls (0 indicates average performance, positive values represent above-average performance, and negative values below-average performance). (B) In contrast, for a measure of memory "priming" (i.e., facilitation of processing of material due to prior exposure), much more variability exists across the groups; the result is an overlap between the performance of the neurologically intact participants and that of the different patient populations. Whereas individuals with brain damage can clearly be characterized as having poorer recognition memory than controls, the same is not true for memory priming.

in which the individuals all have damage in the same general region may help clinicians to determine the cognitive profile of a "typical" patient with damage to that region. In addition, such studies can be used to examine whether a relationship exists between a cognitive deficit and some other factor of interest, such as the amount of tissue destroyed. For example, in a previous example in this chapter, Milner and colleagues found that the hippocampal region is involved in the formation of new long-term memories. They reasoned that additional confirmation for this relationship could be provided by demonstrating that the degree of hippocampal damage is proportional to the degree of memory loss. A single-case study cannot address this question, as it can reveal only whether the hippocampal region is related to memory, not whether the degree of damage predicts the severity of the memory problem. Thus, Milner and colleagues turned to a multiple-case approach, examining a group of patients with varying amounts of hippocampal damage and assessing the extent of memory impairment in each. As predicted, they found that the greater the damage to the hippocampal region, the greater was the memory loss (e.g., Pigott & Milner, 1993). This additional support for their claim could be obtained only by examining a group of individuals rather than a single patient.

Neurologically Intact Individuals

Studying neurologically intact individuals can also aid our understanding of the linkage between mental function and brain structure. First and foremost, these persons provide the important control group that allows us to determine the degree to which the performance of individuals with brain damage is compromised. Clearly, a problem is much more severe if, after brain damage, an individual performs worse than 98% of the individuals in a neurologically intact reference group than if he or she performs worse than 40% of those individuals. The larger the control group assembled for any given test, the more certainty researchers can have in such comparisons.

Well-designed neuropsychological studies must include careful consideration of the characteristics of the individuals composing the neurologically intact control group. These individuals must be matched, on a case-by-case basis, as thoroughly as possible with the individuals with brain damage for demographic variables such as age, gender, and educational history. In this manner, the study hones in on the degree to which the brain damage, and not other factors, affects performance on a particular task. Consider, for example, a hypothetical study in which the researchers do not match for educational history, with the end result that most patients have a college education, while most of the neurologically intact group have only completed high school. When tested, the two groups perform equivalently, leading the researchers to conclude that the brain damage was inconsequential. Yet, because the group with brain damage had more schooling, they would have *outperformed* the control group if they had been tested prior to injury. Thus, relative to their pre-injury state, the individuals with brain damage did experience a deficit, but it was masked by the poor choice of a control group.

When choosing a control group, we may also want to select individuals who are experiencing stresses similar to those of individuals recently brain damaged. For example, in some studies, individuals with brain damage are inpatients in a hospital. In such cases, the researcher will want to consider that hospitalization can be stressful. Patients lose control over the simplest aspects of their lives, such as their privacy and their eating schedule. They have anxiety about the outcome of their hospitalization and often worry about their finances as well. Because individuals under stress often perform poorly on cognitive tasks, a well-designed study should demonstrate that any cognitive deficit can be attributed to the brain damage and not to the stresses associated with hospitalization, illness, or misfortune. For this reason, neurologically intact individuals gathered from a different inpatient hospital population would be good controls because they are under similar stresses but do not have brain damage. One example of such a population is patients who, like those with brain damage, are in a rehabilitation unit, but who are there because of bodily injury rather than brain injury.

Neurologically intact individuals may aid our understanding of brain-behavior relations in other ways besides acting as a control group. They can shed light on how individual variations in the neuroanatomical structure of the brain are related to cognition. For example, as we learn in the next chapter, differences in neuroanatomical asymmetries in left-handers and right-handers, who differ in language lateralization, implicate particular brain regions as important for certain aspects of language processing (e.g., Ratcliff, Dila, Taylor, & Milner, 1980; Strauss et al., 1985). Finally, neurologically intact individuals are important as research participants because when brain imaging techniques (discussed later in this chapter) are used with them, scientists can obtain evidence on how brain structures work together under *normal* conditions. Such insights cannot be obtained from individuals with brain damage.

Nonhuman Animals

Until this point, we mainly have considered how studying people can aid our understanding of the neural underpinnings of cognition. However, our understanding of the neural organization for cognition also is derived from studies performed with nonhuman animals, most notably monkeys. Although the brains of monkeys and humans are distinct, they appear to share several basic organizational principles, some of which are exhibited in all mammalian brains. Because monkeys can be trained to perform sophisticated cognitive tasks, many mental functions can be investigated with these animals, such as object recognition (e.g., Gross, Rocha-Miranda, & Bender, 1972), attention (Moran & Desimone, 1985), and memory (Miskin, 1982). In numerous instances throughout the text, we discuss research of this nature.

For many of the reasons mentioned earlier in the chapter, such as better control over environmental conditions, the size and nature of lesions, and previous life experiences, research with animals can be more straightforward than that with people. In addition, certain techniques that we discuss later in the chapter, such as single-cell recordings, can be readily performed with animals, but only with very restricted groups of people. As with research involving humans, researchers must adhere to careful guidelines concerning the ethical treatment of their animal participants. Researchers are responsible for designing and following protocols that ensure the animals experience the minimal amount of pain possible and are not unduly traumatized by the procedures.

Now that we have discussed the different populations of individuals that are used to examine brain-behavior relationships, we turn our attention to the different methods available for both research and clinical work that inform us about brain anatomy, brain function, and behavior.

Techniques for Assessing Brain Anatomy

Linking specific regions of neural tissue to specific cognitive functions requires that researchers and clinicians be able to determine *where* damage was sustained in the brain. Our ability to make such linkages has been undergoing a revolution since the mid-1970s because of the advent of different brain imaging techniques. These techniques opened a new world to researchers, allowing the location of damage in living individuals to be pinpointed much more exactly than previously possible. Prior to this revolution, researchers had to wait for postmortem examination of the brain to localize damage that had occurred years or decades prior, or they had to guess the location of brain damage from scant medical records or exams. To appreciate the advances provided by these new brain imaging methods, look at Figure 3.2, which depicts the older methods. All they provide is information about what part of the skull is missing as a result of the entry of a bullet or another missile. Such records clearly give us no idea of how extensive or how deep the damage is, and they provide only a gross measure of the location of the damage.

The intricacies of some of the new brain imaging techniques can take a career to master. The goal of this section of the chapter is to present a practical overview of how these techniques work, the basic principles behind them, and, most important, the type of information they provide. We also consider the advantages and disadvantages for researchers and clinicians of each technique. We begin our discussion with the first of the modern brain imaging techniques, computerized axial tomography.

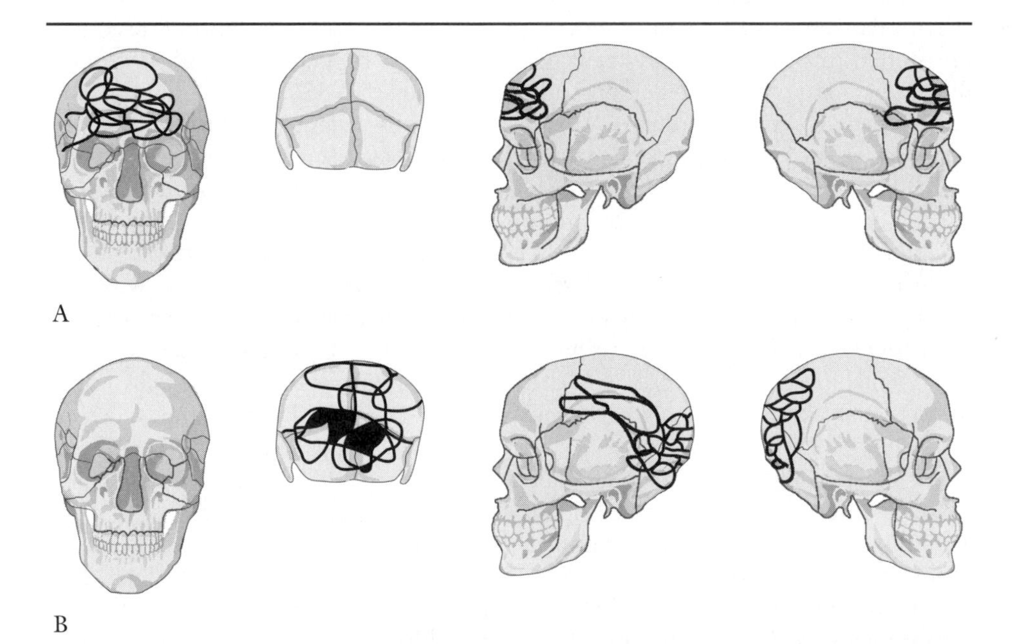

FIGURE 3.2 Composite diagrams of skull x-rays showing the entrance (and sometimes the exit) points of missiles that caused damage in two groups of 20 men. X-rays were used in the days before brain imaging techniques to infer the extent and location of brain damage. Localization was not precise and allowed only gross differentiation such as that shown between (A) individuals with anterior lesions and (B) those with posterior lesions.

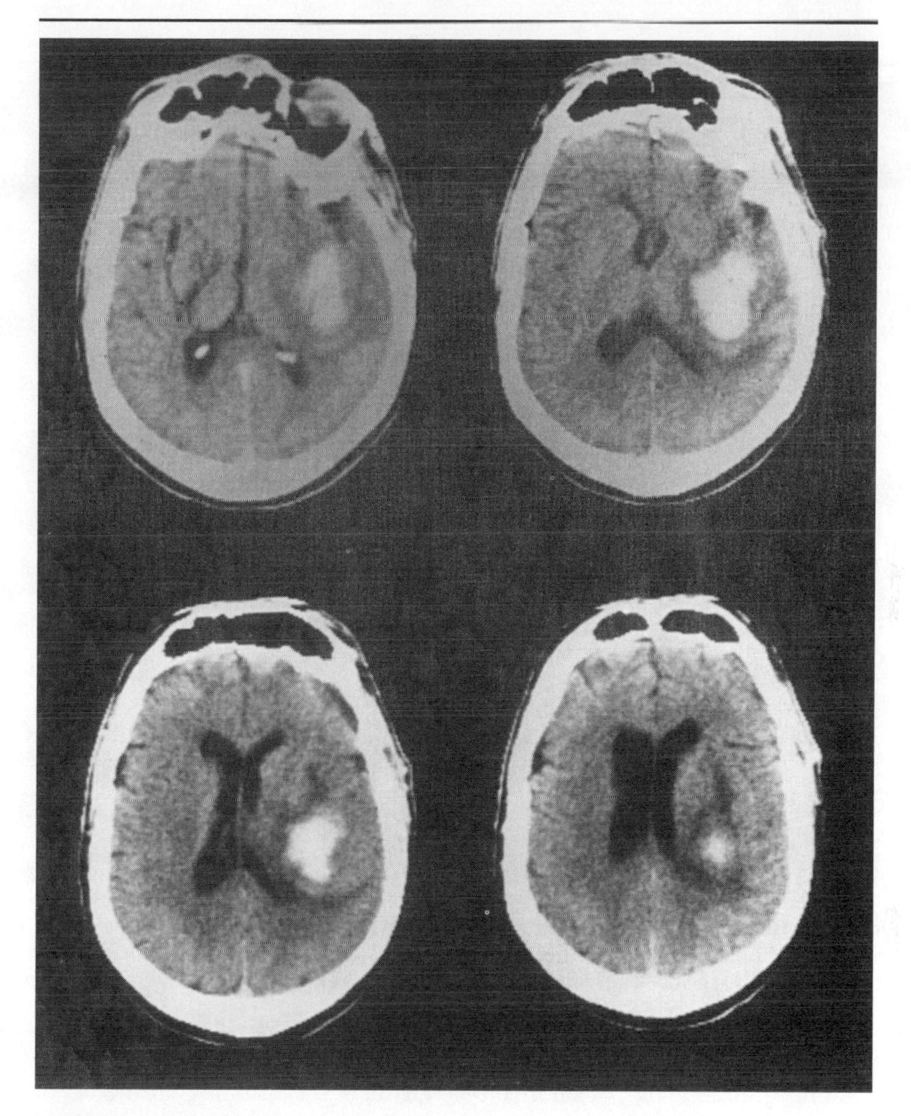

FIGURE 3.3 Slices of a computerized axial tomography (CAT) scan showing regions of high density. A collection of blood, (a *hematoma),* appears as an area of increased brightness in the right temporal lobe. The presence of the hematoma causes a displacement of the lateral ventricle on that side of the brain.

Computerized Axial Tomography

CAT, **computerized axial tomography** (sometimes called CT), uses x-rays to provide information on the density of brain structures. Cerebrospinal fluid (CSF) is less dense than brain tissue, which is less dense than blood, which is less dense than bone. In a CAT scan, dense tissue such as bone appears white, whereas material with the least density, such as CSF, appears black. Typically, CAT scans provide a series of slices of the brain (usually between 9 and 12), stacked one above the other. In CAT scans, regions of the brain that were damaged long ago appear darker than the surrounding tissue because they are filled with less dense CSF. In contrast, areas in which a hemorrhage has recently occurred are indicated by lighter areas because blood is denser than brain tissue.

When you look at a CAT scan (Figures 3.3 and 3.4), the slices appear to cut through the middle

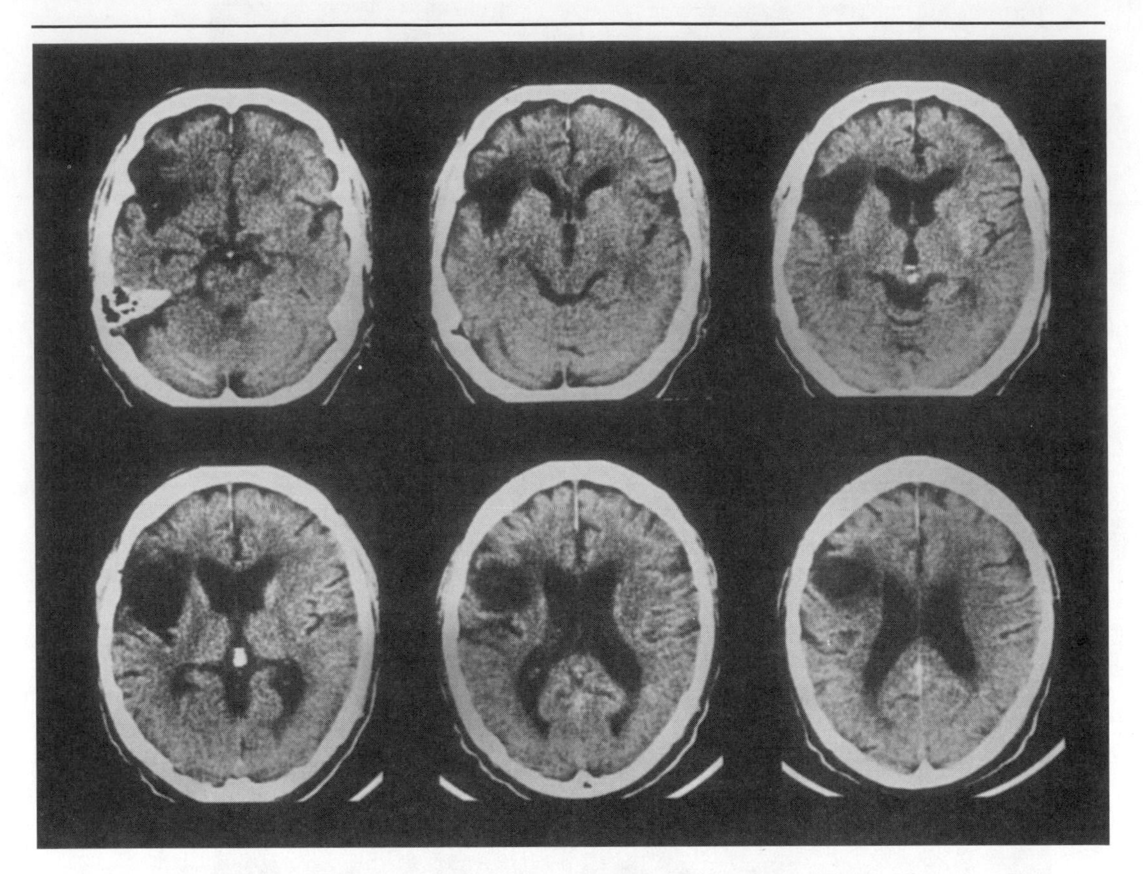

FIGURE 3.4 Slices of a computerized axial tomography (CAT) scan showing regions of low density. (A) The dark regions in the frontal lobe of the left hemisphere indicate the site of damage. As a result of a stroke, tissue in these regions was lost. They now appear dark because they are filled with cerebrospinal fluid.

of the brain in a manner similar to that of a horizontal slice. However, this is not the case; the slices provided by CAT are typically *oblique slices* through the brain. They are oblique because when an individual's head is positioned in the machine, a line is usually drawn from the eyes to the *meatus,* the point where your skull meets your neck in the middle of your head (if you place your hand about two-thirds of the way down the middle of the back of your head, you can feel an area of depression; this is the meatus). This line is known as the *orbitomeatal line,* which typically is at an oblique angle varying between 10 and 30 degrees.

To better understand what brain regions are depicted in each slice of a CAT scan, look at Figure 3.5. Depending on the depth of the slice, all lobes or just some of them will be imaged. For example, the top oblique slice provides information on just regions of the frontal and parietal lobes. Notice that the top four slices (numbered 8 to 11 in Figure 3.5) do not cut through the temporal lobes. As you go lower in the stack of slices, they course through regions of all four lobes: the frontal, temporal, parietal, and occipital lobes. The lowest slices provide information about only the frontal and temporal lobes.

The advantage of CAT scans is that they are relatively inexpensive and available in most hospitals. Furthermore, there are no restrictions on who can receive a CAT scan, as opposed to other methods we discuss later.

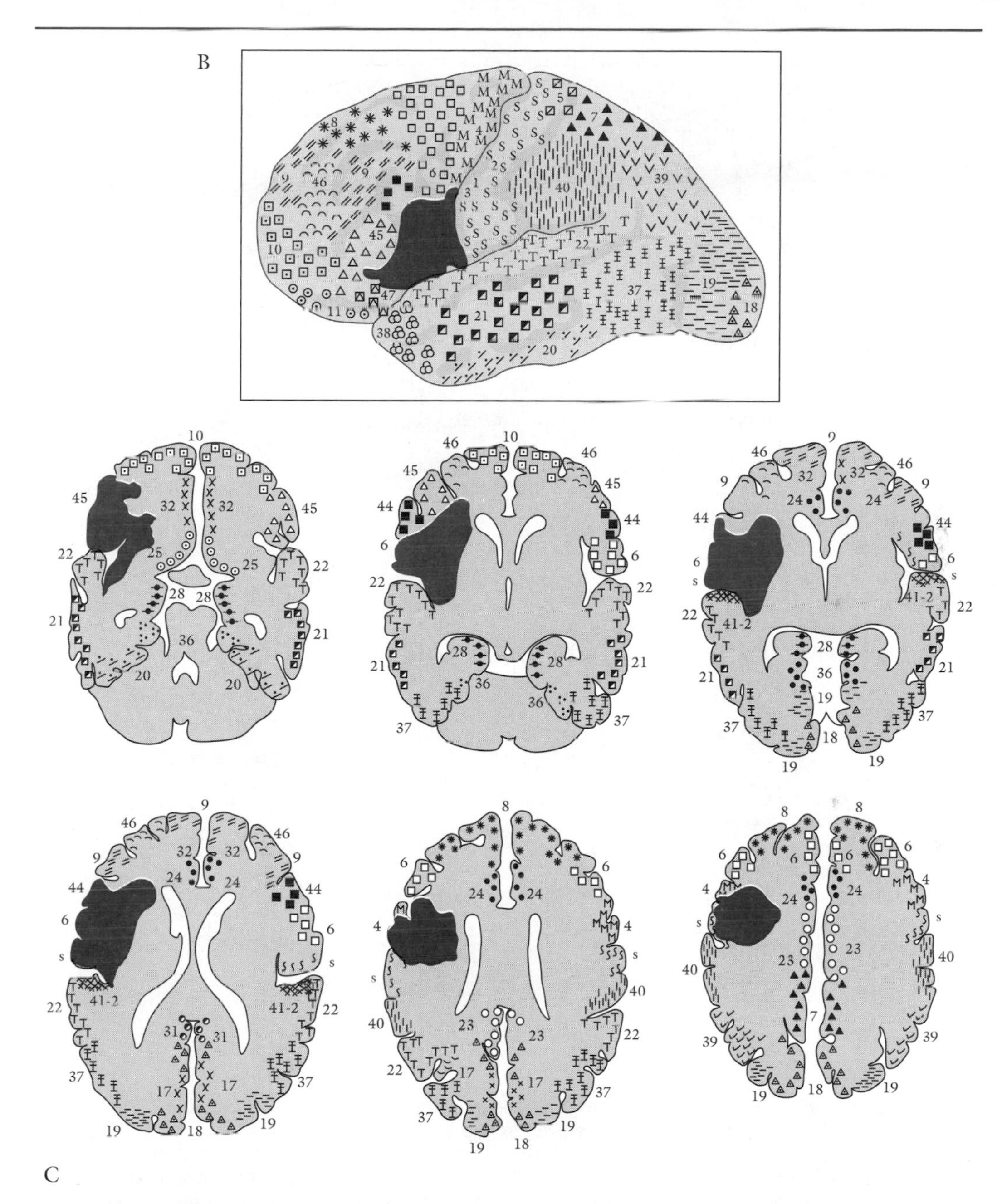

FIGURE 3.4 (Continued) (B) A lateral view of the brain showing the site of damage. (C) Maps of the affected brain regions with Brodmann's areas labeled. The slices depicted are at the same angles as Slices 3 to 8 in Figures 3.5A and 3.5B.

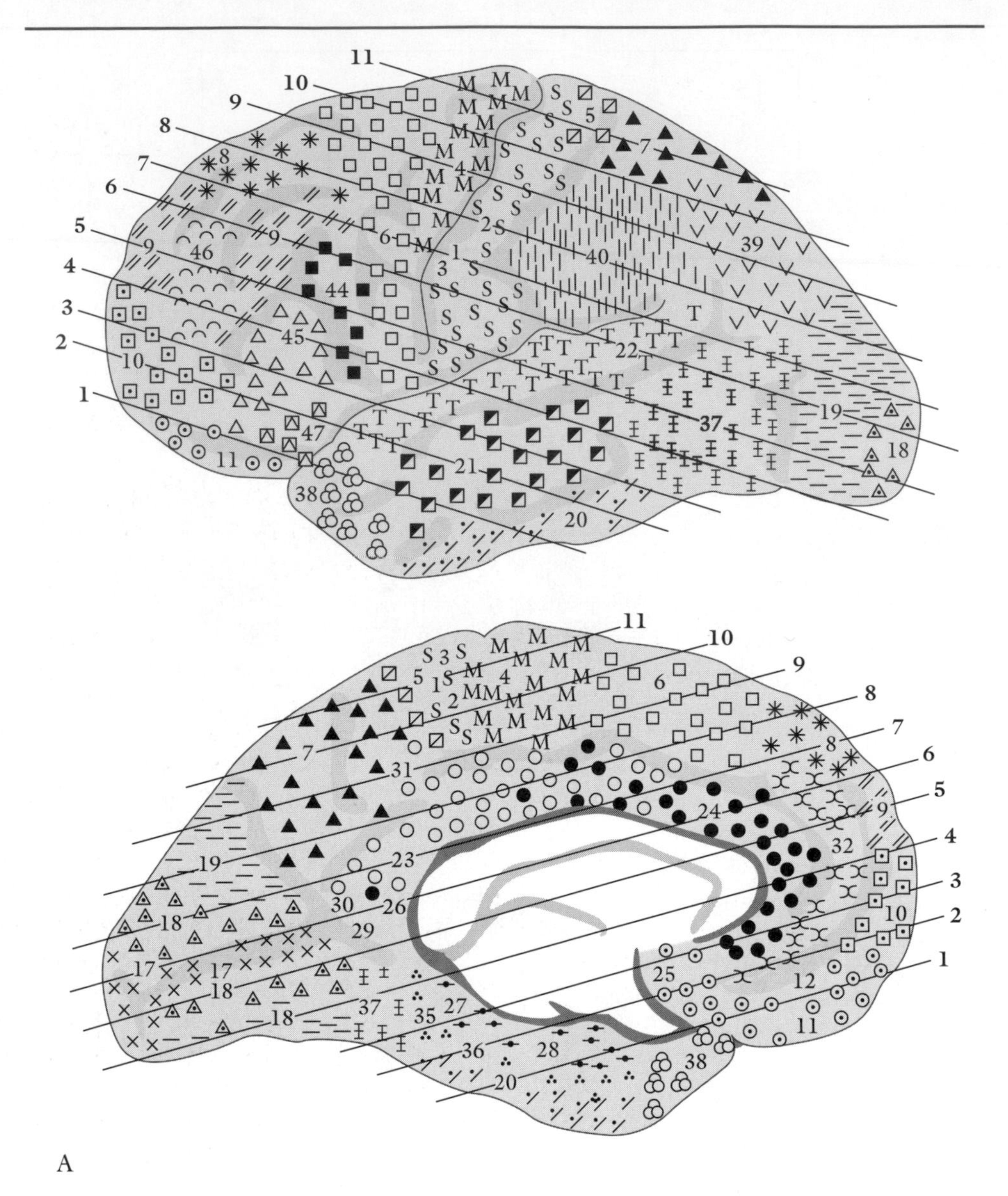

FIGURE 3.5 Typical oblique slices through the brain often provided by brain imaging techniques. (A) The location of the slices as seen from a left hemisphere, lateral view (top) and a left hemisphere, midsagittal view (bottom). The numbers on the brain represent the different Brodmann's areas (which are also differentiated in the diagrams by different symbols). (B) The slices corresponding to the locations depicted in (A). Note the correspondence between the figures. For example, look at Slice 7 in this figure and notice that the Brodmann's areas labeled around the lateral surface of the brain from front to back (i.e., 8, 6, M, S, 40, 22, 37, 19, and 18) are all transected by Slice 7 in the lateral view in A. Also note that the areas labeled medially at Slice 7 in this figure (i.e., 8, 24, 23, and 18) are all transected by Slice 7 in the midsagittal view in A.

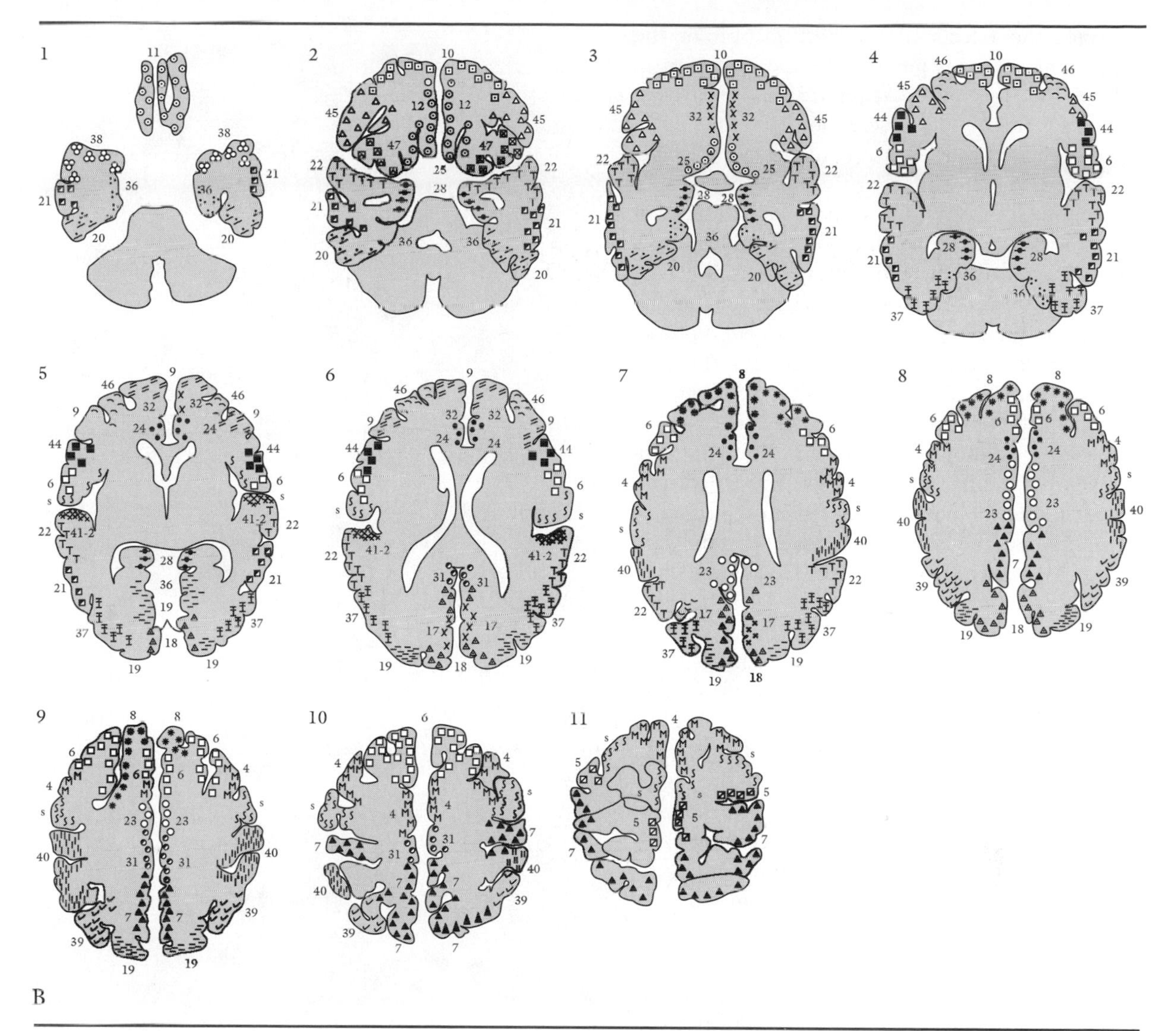

FIGURE 3.5 (Continued)

Magnetic Resonance Imaging

Although CAT scanning was a breakthrough, in many ways it has been superseded by **magnetic resonance imaging** (MRI), a technique that relies on the use of magnetic fields to distort the behavior of protons. The information gained on how long the protons take to recover from this distortion can then be used to create an image of the anatomy of the brain. The description of how this technique works is somewhat more complicated than that for CAT, so we examine it in a bit more detail.

MRI relies on three magnetic fields. The first is the **static field,** a constant magnetic field. MRI machines are classified by the strength of this field. Clinical machines generally vary in strength between 0.5 and 1.5 tesla (T), with "high-field" research machines generally being either 3 or 4 T (for a reference point, the magnetic field of the earth is 0.0001 T). This static magnetic field causes all the magnetically sensitive particles to align themselves in the same direction. Such uniformity is important because only if the particles are all acting in the same manner can we interpret the effects of the perturbation of the static field, which is provided by the second magnetic field, the **pulse sequence,** an oscillating magnetic field. The oscillation of the pulse sequence is "tuned" to a set frequency *(resonant frequency)* so that it affects only one particular substance, much the way that a particular frequency of sound makes only one but not all tuning forks vibrate. Typically, the pulse sequence is tuned to hydrogen atoms. The time it takes for the protons to revert to their original state, the *relaxation time,* is recorded through a radio-frequency coil that acts as a **receiver coil.** This coil is positioned around or near a portion of the individual's head.

Because hydrogen atoms in different substances have different relaxation times, we can adjust different parameters of the pulse sequence to maximize the ability to image certain substances. We may want to maximize our ability to visualize water if we are interested in obtaining information about the density of brain tissue, or we may want to maximize our ability to visualize fat if we are interested in imaging white matter. The intensity of the signal received by the receiver coil indicates the concentration of the particular substance in the brain, but by itself the signal intensity cannot provide information on the location in the brain from which it is coming. This information is provided by the third magnetic field, the **gradient field,** which varies in intensity over the area being imaged. It provides a way to identify particular locations, thus enabling identification of the location from which signals are emanating. The combination of spatial information from the gradient field and the signal intensity received after a series of radio-frequency pulses allows a three-dimensional image of the brain to be reconstructed (for a more advanced but readable discussion of this method and some of its applications, see Andreasen, 1989).

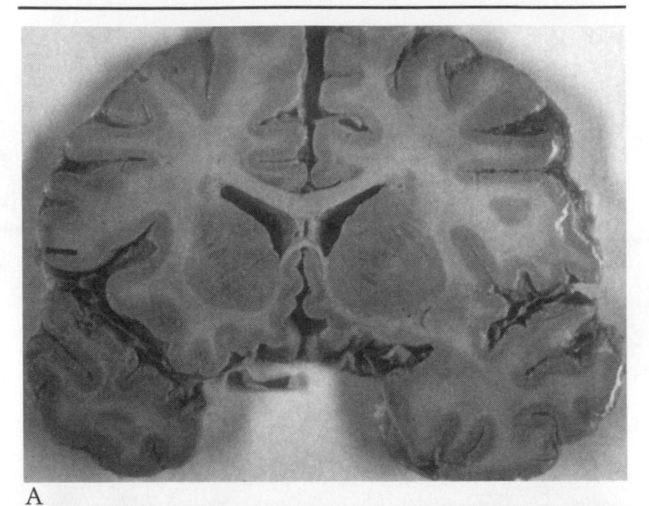

A

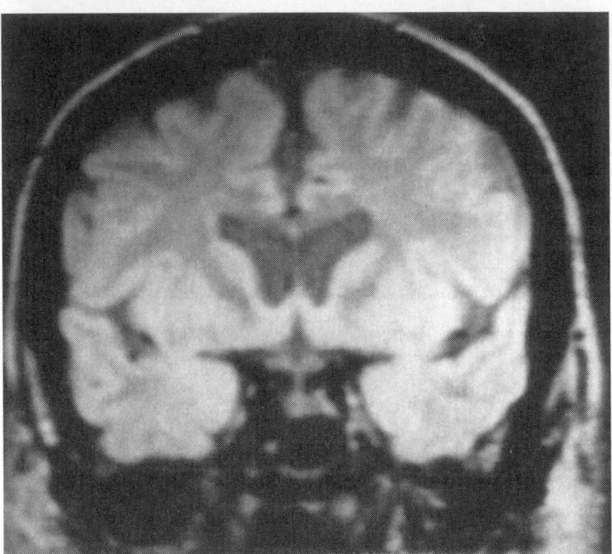

B

FIGURE 3.6 A comparison of the clarity obtained in anatomical dissection and magnetic resonance imaging (MRI). (A) A coronal section through the brain as seen on anatomical dissection. The temporal lobes, Sylvian fissure, putamen, globus pallidus, lateral ventricles, and frontal lobes can be seen. (B) The same coronal slice as imaged by MRI. Note how precisely the MRI reveals anatomical detail.

MRI has two main advantages over CAT. First, MRIs do not require x-rays and hence do not involve transmitting high-energy ionizing radiation through the body. Second, the clarity of the picture—that is, the *spatial resolution* of the image—is superior in MRIs. If you look at Figure 3.6A, which is a coronal section of the brain provided at autopsy, you can see how well a similar slice provided by MRI, in Figure 3.6B, compares with what is revealed on anatomical dissection.

Yet, not everyone can be subjected to an MRI scan. Because magnetic fields interfere with electrical fields, individuals with pacemakers (which generate electrical signals to the heart) cannot undergo

MRI. Also, any individual with metal in her or his body that is not connected to hard tissue (e.g., a clip on an artery or a metal shaving in the eye such as might be received from welding) cannot have an MRI taken because the attraction of the metal to the magnet could cause it to move or dislodge. (Metal embedded in hard tissue, such as the fillings in teeth, is not a problem). Other than these exceptions, MRI is becoming the anatomical imaging technique of choice because of its superior imaging capabilities and the lack of high-energy ionizing radiation.

A recently developed anatomical MRI method called *diffusion tensor imaging* has the potential to provide information not only about the structural integrity of brain regions, but also about the anatomical connectivity between different brain regions. This method detects differences in the degree to which water diffuses along each of the axes of nerve fibers. The axis along which water diffusion is greatest indicates the main directional orientation of white-matter tracts, while the degree of diffusion can provide information on the structural integrity of those tracts (Conturo et al., 1999). Since white-matter tracts connect distant brain regions, this method can be utilized to detect disorders that arise from a partial or complete disconnection between brain regions, or to investigate the effects of demyelinating disorders.

Techniques for Assessing Physiological Function

The brain imaging techniques we just discussed provide a picture of the anatomical structure of the brain. However, they cannot tell us about brain function. As an analogy, consider devices that measure the thickness of metal on a car's body as an index of how much a car has been affected by rust. Although these devices provide information about the structural integrity of the car, much the way anatomical brain imaging techniques provide information about the structural integrity of the brain, they cannot tell us how well the car runs. A similar limitation befalls anatomical brain imaging techniques.

For many reasons, neuropsychologists and cognitive neuroscientists often want to know how well the brain is functioning. But, just as is the case with cars, there exist many different ways to evaluate function—by the amount of "fuel" consumed, by the level of certain critical substances, and by the degree of electrical activity. Just as we might want to know how much fuel the car is using, we may want to know how much of the brain's fuel, such as oxygen or glucose, is being consumed by different regions. And as we might want to know the amount of antifreeze in the cooling system of our car, so we might want to measure the concentration of a specific neurotransmitter, such as dopamine, in the brain. Likewise, while we might want to see whether our car's battery is holding a charge, in the case of the brain, we might measure whether aberrant electrical signals are being generated, or we might want to record the sum of the brain's electrical activity.

Notice that we have been talking about the mechanics of how the car functions, not its overall behavior. We have not discussed ways to measure overall performance: how a car handles in sharp turns, how quickly it brakes, how it climbs steep, narrow roads. Similarly, in this section of the chapter we discuss methods for measuring the mechanics of brain function rather than its overall performance at such tasks as remembering or paying attention, the subject of a later section.

Functional Brain Imaging Methods

Not only has there been a revolution in the ability to image the brain anatomically, but there has also been a revolution in the ability to measure the functioning of the brain. In this section of the chapter, we discuss the methods that discern which areas of the brain are physiologically active by measuring changes related to blood flow and the metabolic changes in compounds used by different brain regions. The two main techniques are **positron emission tomography (PET)**, which uses a radioactive agent to determine the brain's metabolic activity, and **functional magnetic resonance imaging (fMRI)**, which uses a variation of the MRI techniques just discussed.

Although these functional brain imaging techniques are often used with individuals with known or suspected brain damage, these techniques can also be used with neurologically intact individuals to great advantage. They allow researchers to observe the degree to which a brain region in a neurologically intact individual is activated by a task, so that its contribution to task performance under normal circumstances can be directly observed. This technique contrasts with the lesion method, in which inferences about a brain region's contribution to a task are made as a result of dysfunction. These functional brain imaging methods also allow researchers to observe the entire network of brain structures that participate in performing a particular cognitive function by detecting all brain regions that are active.

• *POSITRON EMISSION TOMOGRAPHY* •

Positron emission tomography (PET) allows researchers to determine the amount of a particular compound being used by specific brain regions. Like CAT, PET relies on the use of high-energy ionizing radiation to obtain a picture of brain function, although in this case the radiation is emitted by a substance introduced into the body rather than by radiation passing through the body. Like MRI, this technique is somewhat complicated, so let's examine it in more detail.

In PET, molecules altered to have a radioactive atom are introduced into the blood supply and carried to the brain. Typically, this molecule is a radioactive form of sugar, such as 2-deoxy-2-fluoro-D-glucose, a physiologically inert sugar to which a radioactive fluorine atom (^{18}F) is introduced, or water containing a radioactive isotope of oxygen ($H_2{}^{15}O$). Radioactive molecules are unstable but reach a more stable, nonradioactive state by releasing a charged particle. PET uses a particular class of radioactive molecules, those that become stable by emitting a positively charged electron called a *positron.* When a positron is emitted, it collides with an electron, which has a negative charge of the same value, and they annihilate each other. As first realized by Einstein, the annihilation of matter produces energy. In this case, the energy is emitted in the form of two photons of light that travel from the site of annihilation exactly 180 degrees opposite each other.

A person having a PET scan lies with his or her head in a ring of photocells specifically designed to detect the coincident arrival of two photons of light from exactly opposite directions. (Because light travels at 186,000 mi/s, the arrival of the two photons is, for all intents and purposes, simultaneous.) Areas of the brain that are very metabolically active emit many photons of light, whereas those that are less active emit fewer. From the data received by the detectors, computers can extrapolate backwards to determine the point from which the photons emanated, allowing the activity of various brain regions to be determined. The time required to obtain a picture of the brain's functioning is linked to how quickly a given isotope goes from a radioactive state to a nonradioactive state (known as its *half-life*), because a significant number of photons must be detected to create an image. The process of acquiring a PET image is shown in Figure 3.7, and an image generated from this process is shown in Color insert 3.1.

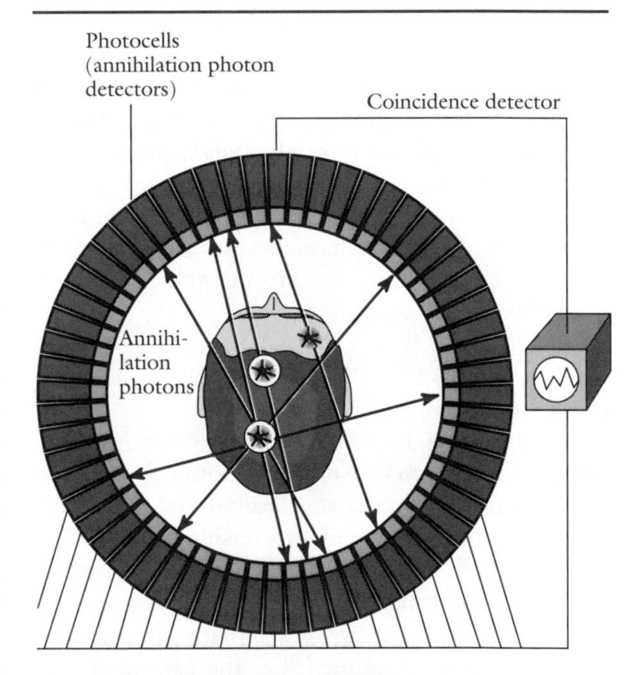

FIGURE 3.7 An explanation of positron emission tomography (PET). When a positron is annihilated by an electron, two photons of light traveling in opposite directions are emitted simultaneously. The coincidence of arrival of two photons 180 degrees apart is detected by photocells. Brain regions that are very active give off many photons, whereas those that are less active give off fewer. By extrapolating backward, the source of the photons can be determined.

A related technique, *SPECT (single photon emission computed tomography)*, uses a much scaled-down version of the same technique as PET. In this case, however, a small set of sensors rather than a ring of sensors is used. The smaller number of sensors reduces the spatial resolution, or clarity, of the obtained brain image. Moreover, the isotope used with these techniques usually takes longer to decay than the isotopes used with PET; therefore, the picture of the brain activity is less precise because it is averaged over a much longer time interval than with PET.

PET's main advantage is that it allows researchers to examine how the brain uses a variety of molecules, provided that a radioactive (positron-emitting) version of the molecule can be created. (If you are a cognitive neuroscientist performing such studies, it is helpful to have a clever biochemist as your collaborator.) Suppose we are interested in looking for regional increases in cerebral blood flow because we know that local changes in blood flow are associated with increases in neural activity (e.g., Sandman, O'Halloran, & Isenhart, 1984). To do so, we can inject research participants with radioactive water that contains the positron-emitting ^{15}O, which accumulates in the brain in direct proportion to the local blood flow (for a readable account of how this technique has been fruitfully applied to the study of a wide variety of cognitive functions, see Posner & Raichle, 1994). In contrast, if we are interested in the distribution of a neurotransmitter, such as dopamine, we can introduce a radioactively tagged substance that binds to receptor sites (e.g., Wong et al., 1986).

Another advantage of PET is that it can provide an absolute measure of regional cerebral blood flow (rCBF), which is directly related to oxygen and glucose consumption. Because the value obtained is not a relative measure, we can directly compare the rCBF from one person or population of persons to the next. For example, let's say a scientist wants to investigate whether cognitive declines with aging might be linked to a reduction in the brain's oxygen supply. PET would be a good method to investigate such an issue because one can directly compare the rCBF in elderly individuals who are exhibiting a cognitive decline with that of those who are not.

Despite these major advantages, PET has some drawbacks. First, like CAT, it involves ionizing radiation; therefore, the number of scans an individual can undergo a year is limited to somewhere between two and five scans. Second, the time periods required to obtain a picture of brain activity (which is determined by an isotope's half-life) are much longer than those typically used to measure mental activities in the brain. For example, 2-deoxy-2-fluoro-D-glucose will yield a picture of brain activity averaged over about 40 minutes, and ^{15}O provides an image of brain activity averaged over a minute and a half. Both these times are long considering that most people can make a cognitive decision, such as whether a letter string is a word or not, in seven-tenths of a second or less. This time lapse is a problem when you consider all the activity that may have occurred in the participant's mind in that amount of time—besides that related to the task she or he was instructed to do. All of the subject's thoughts (not just those related to the experiment) cause brain activity that ends up being conglomerated into one picture. An additional drawback of PET is that it requires an ongoing ability to create a radioactive isotope so it can be continually infused into the individual for the duration of the task. Such a procedure necessitates a machine called a *cyclotron* that is expensive and often available only at major medical centers.

A third disadvantage of PET is that it often cannot provide enough information from a single person to provide a reliable picture of brain activity. Rather, studies often portray the areas of the brain that are active during a specific task or activity averaged across numerous people. The process of averaging across individuals requires that each individual's PET scan be "normalized" by morphing it so it can be superimposed onto an "average" brain. Because brains are as unique as faces, this averaging will not allow for very precise localization of activity. Think about the variation in morphology of your friends' faces: some are wide whereas others are thin, some have eyes spaced far apart whereas others have eyes quite close, and some have prominent ridges at the eyebrows whereas others do not. If you imagine how your face would be modified to match that of the "average" person's face, you can get a sense of the potential distortion imposed by this averaging process. Hence, although PET can be used to determine, on average, whether different functions (e.g., speech output and speech comprehension) rely on different brain regions, it may not be as accurate at determining localization of function for a given individual (e.g., Hunter et al., 1999). Obviously, more precise localization is required if this technique (or any other) is to be used in a clinical setting to make decisions about the treatment of a given individual, such as determining which regions of the brain absolutely should not be excised during surgery.

Although many difficulties are associated with PET, it is still a good technique for identifying the multiplicity of brain structures involved in a cognitive function, and, at present, is uniquely suited to examining the brain's processing of certain substances such as neurotransmitters and acid-base balance (pH) (M. E. Raichle, 1994). If the researcher need not precisely locate active brain regions during short time periods, the advantages of PET can more than outweigh its disadvantages.

• *FUNCTIONAL MAGNETIC RESONANCE IMAGING* •

Although we previously discussed MRI as a means of obtaining images of brain anatomy, a variation of this method allows examination of certain aspects of brain function. This method is known as *functional magnetic resonance imaging (fMRI)* to distinguish it from MRI used to obtain neuroanatomical images of the brain. Because changes in neuronal activity are accompanied by local changes in other physiological functions, such as cerebral blood flow and blood oxygenation (e.g., Fox, Raichle, Mintun, & Dence, 1988), these local changes can be used to infer the activity levels of different brain regions.

In the last five years there has been a veritable explosion of research using a particular fMRI method known as BOLD (Blood Oxygen Level Dependent), which takes advantage of the fact that oxygenated and deoxygenated blood have different magnetic properties. It should not surprise you that blood has magnetic properties if you consider that a lack of iron in the blood causes anemia, which is the reason that many people, especially women, are encouraged to ensure that their diet contains enough iron. Oxygen-rich blood carried from the heart by the arteries is *diamagnetic,* meaning it has magnetic properties. As this blood passes through the capillary beds, oxygen is extracted and the blood loses its magnetic properties (a *paramagnetic* state). When a particular area of the brain is active, the local increase in oxygen-rich blood is greater than the amount of oxygen that can be extracted by the brain tissue. Thus, the relative proportion of oxygenated blood to deoxygenated blood increases in that local region, and it is from this increased signal that a picture of brain activation can be derived (e.g., Kwong et al., 1992). For example, when neurons in primary visual cortex fire in response to light, more oxygen is delivered to this region. Researchers can detect the *increase* in the signal as compared to the previous state when there was no light and the neurons were less active.

Because we are detecting a change in the signal from one state to another, the use of fMRI requires that we always compare two conditions—the condition of interest, such as "light on," to a baseline, such as "light off." In many of the studies we discuss later in the book, we will notice that researchers attempt to isolate the brain region involved in a particular function by carefully picking a baseline task against which to measure changes in brain activation associated with the task of interest. The selection of the baseline is critical for interpretation of the results. For example, if one wants to determine those regions *specifically* involved in processing faces above and beyond other objects, then brain activation while viewing faces needs to be compared to a baseline of brain activation while viewing non-face objects. On the other hand, if the researcher wants to determine all the brain regions involved in visually analyzing a face, then brain activation while viewing faces needs to be compared to a baseline of brain activation while viewing a very basic visual form such as a cross.

Notice that fMRI cannot measure a neuronal response directly but rather indexes a *hemodynamic response,* that of the vascular system to the increased need for oxygen of neurons in a local area. This response is slow, generally starting about 2 seconds after a stimulus is presented, peaking at about 8–10 seconds and falling off by 14–16 seconds. Although this response is drawn out over seconds, we can nonetheless obtain a measure of brain activity on about a second-by-second basis (see Figure 3.8). This temporal resolution is much faster than PET but it is slow compared to some other methods, such as EEG, that we discuss later on in the chapter.

For a number of reasons, fMRI is a particularly exciting method for making brain-behavior inferences. First, it is a widely available method as scans can be obtained with clinical MRI machines that have the appropriate upgrades to enable the procedure. Second, it is a noninvasive technique as no high-energy radiation is involved. Third, multiple scans can be run on a single individual, unlike the limitations imposed by PET. Multiple scans allow scientists to examine changes in the brain over time, such as those that occur with learning, and allow clinicians to observe changes occurring during the course of recovery or as a result of treatment regimens. A fourth advantage of fMRI is that it provides a measure of brain activity over seconds rather than minutes as is the case with PET. And finally, the precision of scans obtained from fMRI enables us to examine brain-behavior relationships for individuals rather than only for groups (as is often the case with PET), which makes fMRI particularly useful for clinical interventions such as neurosurgery (e.g., Schulder et al., 1998).

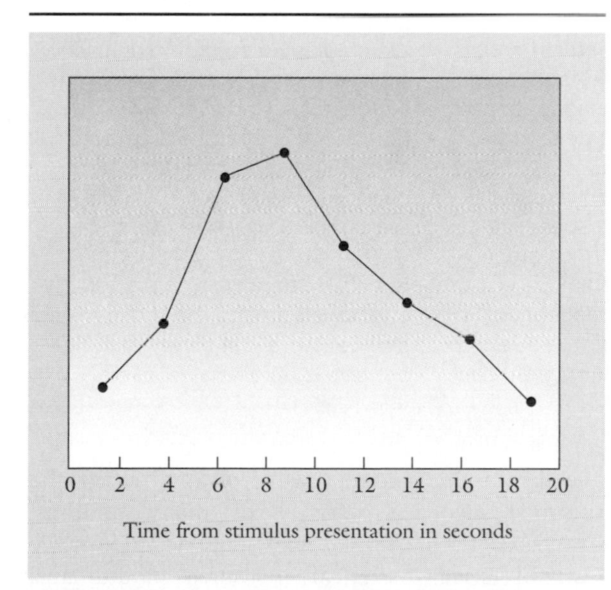

FIGURE 3.8 Time course of the fMRI signal from the onset of a stimulus. Notice that there is a lag such that the increase in oxygenation, which is picked up as an increase in MR signal intensity, starts only 2 seconds after the stimulus onset, peaks about 8 seconds later, and then returns to baseline after about 16 seconds.

fMRI techniques, although burgeoning, are still in the developmental stage. At present, the BOLD technique provides information only about the *relative* concentration of oxygenated and deoxygenated blood, so that absolute measurements of the amount of oxygen delivered to the brain across individuals, such as younger and older individuals, are not available. Currently, other fMRI methods, such as *arterial spin-labeling techniques,* are being developed and advanced in the hope that they will provide a method of recording cerebral blood flow such as that provided by PET (Thomas et al., 2001).

Because MRI can be tuned to specific atoms, it can be utilized to examine the concentration of other biologically active substances via a method known as *magnetic resonance spectroscopy.* These methods are limited, however, in two ways. First, they provide only very gross information on the location of these substances within the brain (e.g., within the frontal lobe). Second, the concentration of the substances that can be detected by this method must be quite high. For example, it remains to be seen whether these methods will be able to detect neurotransmitters. One substance that has been examined using this technique is *N*-acetylaspartate (NAA). This amino acid, which is found only within the nervous system, has the second highest concentration of any free amino acid (i.e., one that is not bound to another substance) in the nervous system. Although its exact role in neuronal processes is unknown, a reduction in NAA has been observed in conditions under which neuronal functioning is less than optimal, such as when pathological processes are acting upon neurons, as in demyelinating disorders, or when the energy metabolism of the brain is compromised. NAA levels have been linked to cognitive functions (Jung et al., 1999) such as working memory (Bertolino et al., 2000). The importance of magnetic resonance spectroscopy may increase in the future as high-field MR systems (i.e., 3T or higher) become more commonplace. These high-field systems will enhance the ability to detect sub-

PARTICIPATING IN A FUNCTIONAL MAGNETIC RESONANCE IMAGING STUDY

What is it like to participate in fMRI studies of brain function? I have been involved in these studies both as a researcher and as a participant, so I can provide a short description of some of this work from both perspectives. As an experimenter, it is often very helpful to be an initial participant before the actual data collection starts. It is not only a way of checking to make sure that everything is in working order, but allows you to determine what difficulties might arise during the course of the experiment. This was especially true for me and my colleagues back in 1993 when we first starting doing studies using fMRI. It was a relatively new technique then, so before asking anyone else to participate in a study using this new technique, we wanted to see for ourselves what it would be like. That way, we would know exactly what our participants would experience. Since the magnet is quite a different environment than the standard neuropsychology laboratory, we also wanted insights into the ways in which a "typical" neuropsychology experiment would be transformed by having to perform it in the magnet.

Our first study was very simple; it was designed to determine whether we could detect changes in blood oxygenation over the occipital lobe while a person stared at a checkerboard of red and green squares that reversed color seven times a second. I was one of the first participants. I could not just go and sit in the magnet to be tested. First, I had to carefully look over a checklist to make sure that I did not have characteristics that would preclude a scan. Such characteristics included having ever had a metal clip placed on any blood vessel during surgery, having a pacemaker, and even having "permanent" eyeliner! Next, I had to check that I had nothing on my person or in my pockets that would be attracted to the magnet or would be influenced by the strong magnetic field—this included belt buckles, jewelry, pens, credit cards, watches, coins, and paper clips, among other things. Such precautions are very important because the strength of the magnetic field in a 1.5 Tesla magnet (the strength of a standard clinical magnet) can draw a pen into the center of the magnet at more than 100 miles per hour! Denuded of any metallic objects, I actually entered the magnet room. There I was given a pair of earplugs, as MRI scans are very loud. At this point, I was positioned on my back on a table outside the magnet, which is a rather large cylinder, about 8 ft tall by 8 ft wide, with a small hole (known as the *bore*) in the middle, into which the person is placed (see accompanying figure, which, by the way, is not me).

When obtaining fMRI data, it is very important that a person's head remain motionless for a good image to be obtained. My colleagues placed pillows around my head to stabilize it before the receiver coil of the magnet, which is like an enlarged baseball catcher's mask, was put around my head. Finally, two angled mirrors positioned directly above my eyes were adjusted so that I could view a screen, positioned near my feet, on which the visual stimuli would be projected. Then I was moved into the machine headfirst. My head was placed in the middle of the magnet, which is where the best image can be obtained. Because I'm not tall, I was literally swallowed up into the magnet—my feet were just barely sticking out of the bore.

stances at lower concentrations than is currently available with standard magnets (e.g., 1.5 T).

Electromagnetic Recording Methods

The methods we discussed so far examine the metabolic activity of the brain. In other cases, however, we may want to record the electrical activity of the brain that results from neuronal firing or the magnetic fields induced by that electrical activity. In animals, we can place electrodes directly into or onto cells and determine what types of stimuli make a cell fire. In humans, we typically record the summed electrical activity of many neurons. Compared with the brain imaging techniques we just discussed, electrical measures in humans, including EEG, event-related potentials and magnetoencephalography, currently do a poor job of identifying where activity is occurring in the brain. Yet, the electrical methods provide an accurate measure of brain activity on a millisecond-by-millisecond basis, much more rapidly than even the fastest fMRI methods. Although the spatial resolution of these

I found the experience of being moved into the magnet somewhat disconcerting. The bore of the magnet is a small semicircular opening that leaves little room for even the smallest arm movements and places your nose just inches from the top of the magnet. If you are a spelunker (that is, a cave explorer), you'd probably feel comfortable, but for people who have any tendency to claustrophobia, the experience can be a bit nerve-racking. I must admit that the first time I was rolled into the magnet my heart started to race and I felt uncomfortable. But I chatted to my colleagues and forced myself to think about being safely and snugly tucked into bed rather than trapped in a magnet. By keeping my mind on that train of thought, I subsequently found the magnet a comfortable place to relax.

Once the screen at my feet was positioned for optimal viewing, the studies began. MRIs work by setting up a homogeneous static magnetic field around an object. Because a body and a head in the magnet disrupt that field, the machine has to be "shimmed," or adjusted, to take into account the peculiarities of the individual's head and body, and to optimize the signal that the machine will receive. While this was being done, the machine made low, deep "a-clump, a-clump, a-clump" noises, like the sound of a large steel horse slowly loping around a racetrack. After the shimming, an anatomical scan of my brain was taken. The first time I participated in this procedure, my colleagues thoughtfully let me know through an intercom system between the control room and the magnet that the structural scan revealed that I did indeed have a brain!

Because we were interested in visual processing, the machine was programmed to take a "slice" of my brain's activity that would pass through the calcarine fissure (see figures on the inside front cover of this book), which is where the primary visual areas of the brain are located. During each pair of scans, I first had to close my eyes, a task designed to provide a baseline of the activity level in my occipital cortex when it receives no visual input. Then a checkerboard was flashed to measure the response of my occipital cortex to visual stimulation. This comparison between a baseline condition and a control condition is a hallmark of the design of fMRI studies. The noise made by the machine became different, more tinny and staccato than previously. To round out the day, a high-resolution anatomical scan of my brain with 128 slices was obtained so that a computerized three-dimensional rendering of my entire brain could be constructed. About an hour after we started, my colleagues told me through the intercom that we were done, came into the magnet room, and wheeled me out of the magnet. Although being in the magnet was relaxing, I was glad to get out, stretch my legs, and hear more familiar noises. ■

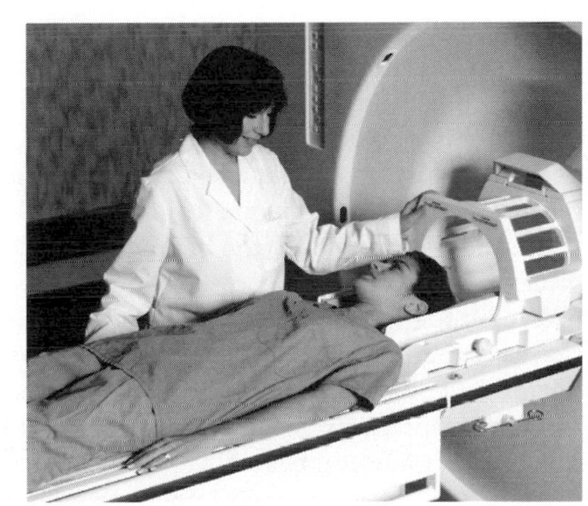

methods is poor, they offer neuroscientists the best available *temporal resolution.*

• *SINGLE-CELL RECORDINGS* •

Many of the studies performed with animals that we discuss in this book examine the electrical responses of cells in particular regions of the brain. In these studies, an electrode is placed into the brain region of interest and the experimenter records the electrical output of the cell or cells that are contacted by the exposed electrode tip. After establishing a baseline firing rate for a given cell, researchers attempt to discover the properties of a stimulus that will make a cell fire maximally above that baseline. Depending on the location of the cells being monitored, researchers may want to address various issues. They may want to determine whether the cells are sensitive to input in only one sensory modality or are multimodal in sensitivity, whether they respond to information from only specific places in the sensory world or from broad regions of space, and whether a cell's response is modified depending on whether or not the animal's attention is directed at the stimulus.

Studies involving single-cell recording techniques in animals have been enormously helpful in providing information about the organization of many brain regions. For example, such studies have demonstrated that cells in primary visual areas are responsive to basic orientation of bars of light whereas cells in higher-order visual regions are responsive to much more elaborate forms (e.g., Desimone, Albright, Gross, & Bruce, 1984), that frontal regions are important for keeping information available in memory during a short delay period (e.g., Funahashi, Bruce, & Goldman-Rakic, 1991), and that parietal areas are important for directing arm movements to particular regions of space (Georgopolous, Schwartz, & Kettner, 1986). Because studies such as these provide a basis for conceptualizing how particular regions of the human brain may be organized for certain cognitive functions, we discuss them throughout the text where appropriate.

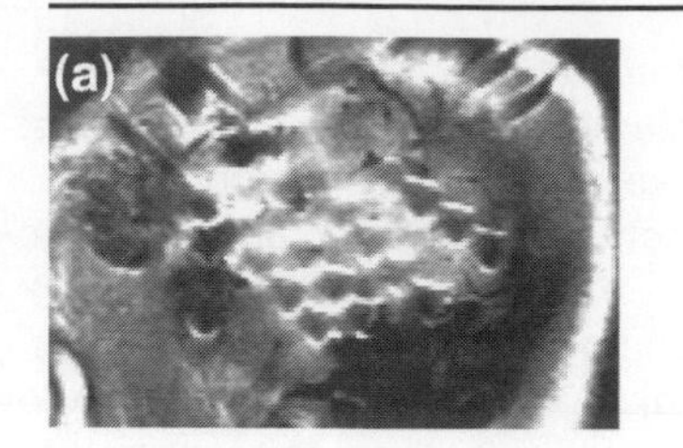

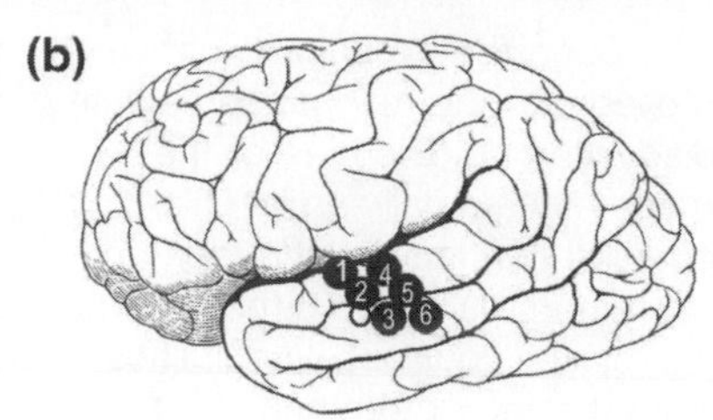

FIGURE 3.9 An example of an electrode array placed directly on the surface of the brain in an individual with epilepsy. (A) Shown here is the placement of electrodes as viewed in a sagittal section of an MRI scan. This image, as well as others, some of the brain more medially and some of the brain more laterally, were used to reconstruct the location of the 64-electrode array on the surface of the brain. (B) Shown here are locations of 6 electrodes in the array.

In humans, opportunities for such studies are limited. However, there are cases in which electrodes are implanted into the brain for about a week prior to surgery for the removal of epileptic tissue or placed on the surface of the brain during the operation to better isolate the source of seizure activity (Figure 3.9). Such procedures allow seizure activity to be more precisely located, making it less likely that useful tissue will be removed. These procedures that allow clinicians to gain important information for designing a patient's treatment, can also provide scientists the opportunity to determine what stimulus properties make cells in the region fire (e.g., Allison et al., 1994). In addition, small amounts of current can be passed through the electrodes and the effect on behavior can be observed. For example, researchers have isolated regions of the left hemisphere involved in language process-ing by identifying regions that when stimulated electrically, result in an arrest of speech (Ojemann, 1983). Because opportunities to study the firing of single cells in humans are so limited, researchers often rely instead upon measurements of electrical activity of the whole brain via methods we discuss next.

• *ELECTROENCEPHALOGRAPHY* •

Electroencephalography (EEG) is a method of recording the brain's electrical activity. Clinically, it is often used to detect aberrant activity such as that which accompanies epilepsy and sleep disorders. Experimentally, it is used to detect certain psychological states, such as drowsiness and alertness, because each of these states is associated with particular patterns of electrical activity.

In EEG, the electrical signals produced by the brain are typically recorded by metal electrodes positioned on the scalp (Figure 3.10) and then amplified. Each electrode (sometimes called a *lead*) acts as its own recording site or channel. Additionally, one electrode is attached to an electrically inactive site, such as the mastoid bone (located behind the ear), which acts as a reference that provides a baseline against which the activity at each of the other electrodes can be compared. An electrode simply placed on the skin is an inappropriate reference because it covers muscles, whose contractions are induced by electrical signals. To avoid mistaking eye movement for brain activity, researchers usually place an electrode near the eye muscles so that EEG signals from the time periods when eye movements occur can be discarded from further analysis.

The **electrical potential** recorded at an electrode on the scalp is the summed or superimposed signal

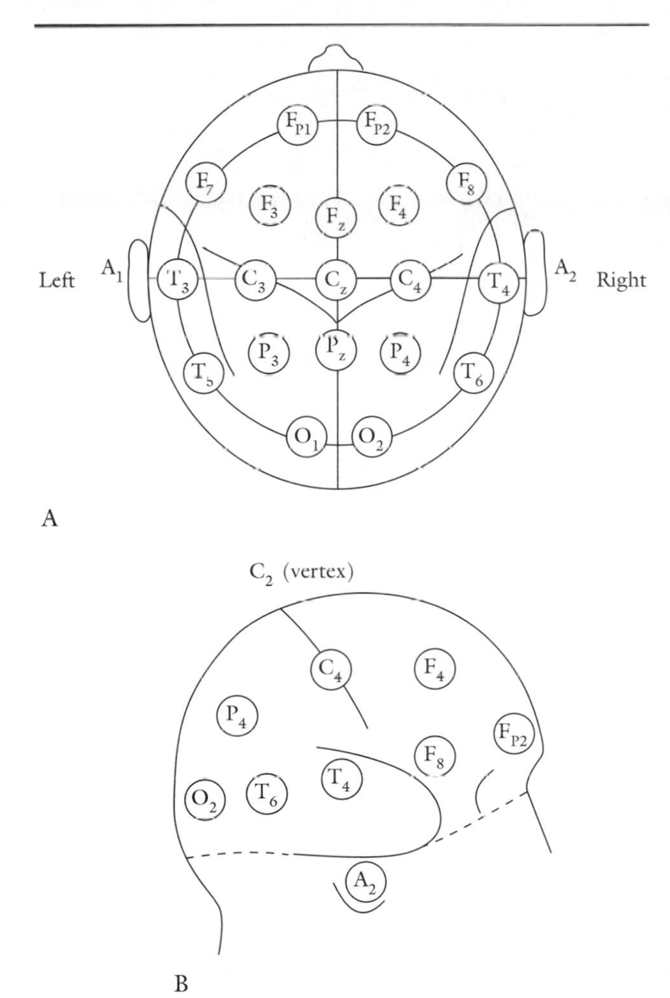

FIGURE 3.10 Standard placement of electrodes during electroencephalography (EEG) recording. Electrodes over the left hemisphere are labeled with odd numbers, those over the right hemisphere are labeled with even numbers, and those on the midline are labeled with a *z*. The uppercase letter is an abbreviation for the location of the electrode: A, auricle; C, central; F, frontal; Fp, frontal pole; O, occipital; P, parietal; and T, temporal.

The **electrical potential** recorded at an electrode on the scalp is the summed or superimposed signal of the postsynaptic electrical fields of similarly aligned neuronal dendrites. Recorded at the scalp as a waveform, the electrical potential has a particular voltage (which is a measure of its size) and a particular frequency, meaning that it oscillates at a specific rate (measured in Hertz; cycles per second). The frequency and form of the EEG signal vary according to a person's state. When a person is awake, the EEG shows a mixture of many frequencies, but those that are relatively fast (15 Hz), known as *beta activity,* tend to predominate. In contrast, when a person is relaxed, with his or her eyes closed, slower frequencies, or *alpha activity,* at 9 to 12 Hz, are much more common. During sleep, very slow frequencies of *delta activity,* at 1 to 4 Hz, predominate.

Clinically, EEG can detect epilepsy, which can be conceptualized as an electrical storm in the brain. Neurons normally fire in a synchronous manner, leading to the alpha, beta, and delta waveforms we just discussed. In epilepsy, however, rather than firing in a synchronous rhythm, neurons fire in large quantities at once (a burst, or "spike") at random times. The result is an increase in the amplitude of firing that can be observed on the EEG record. After an individual is treated with anticonvulsants, the EEG can be performed again to ensure that the spiking activity decreased.

EEG can also be used to examine experimental questions. Because alpha waves indicate that a person is relaxed and resting, the absence, or suppression, of alpha activity is often used as an indicator of the degree of activation of the brain. The degree of **alpha suppression,** as it is known, is examined to determine how active the brain is under different conditions. For example, in the chapter on emotion (Chapter 12), we discuss evidence that when individuals are depressed, they exhibit greater alpha suppression over right frontal areas than over left frontal areas. This finding indicates that depression is accompanied by greater activation of right frontal regions than of left frontal regions. Figure 3.11 provides some examples of different types of brain waves seen in neurologically intact individuals as well as those that occur in clinical conditions.

• *EVENT-RELATED POTENTIALS* •

Event-related potentials (ERPs) are recordings of the brain's activity that are linked to the occurrence of an event, such as the presentation of a stimulus. Therein lies their greatest strength—they can

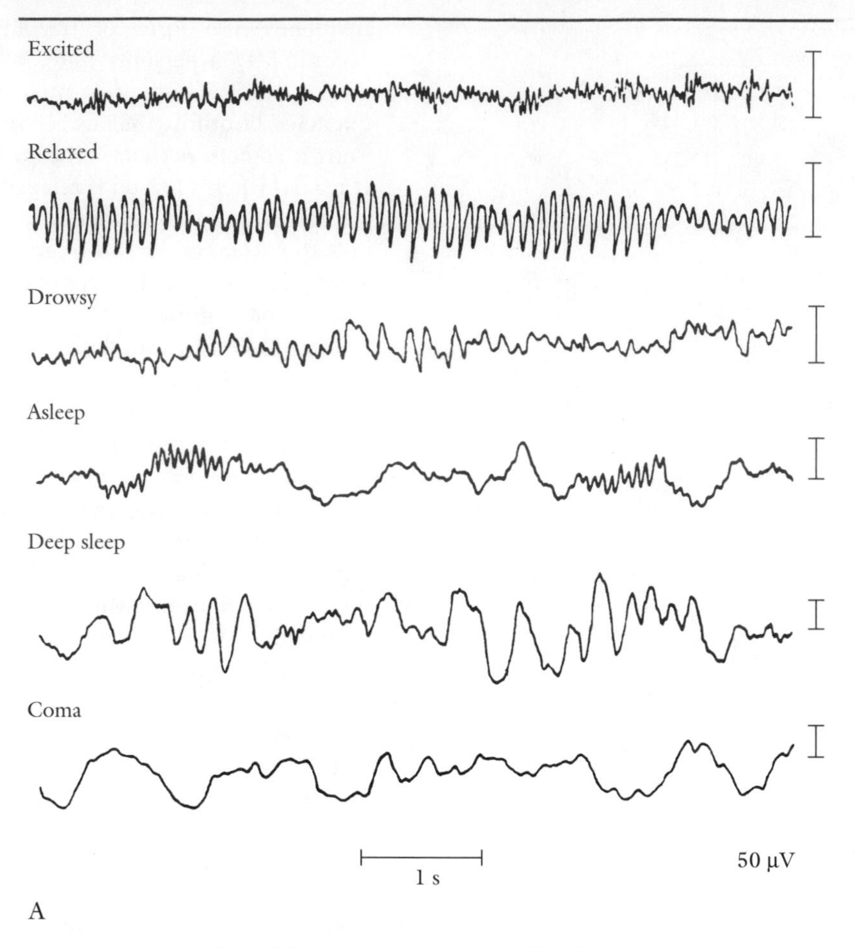

FIGURE 3.11 Examples of electroencephalography (EEG) recordings.
(A) Characteristic EEG activity during various mental states. Note the cyclicity of activity that can be observed, for example, when an individual is in a relaxed state.

provide some idea of "when" processes occur in the brain. Whereas EEG recordings provide a continuous measure of brain activity, ERPs are recorded in reference to a specific event. The common alignment and firing of dendritic fields in the brain after this event create a **dipole,** which is a small region of electrical current with a relatively positive end and a relatively negative end (hence *di*pole, or *two*-pole, system). Electrodes placed on the scalp can detect this dipole.

As time from the onset of the stimulus elapses, the active groups of neurons, and hence the locations of the dipoles, change. Thus, the waveform recorded on the scalp changes as well. The waveform can be divided into **components,** which are characteristic portions of the wave that have been linked to certain psychological processes, such as attention and memory. ERP components are usually given names that have two parts: a letter and then a subscript number (e.g., P_3). The letter is always a *P* or an *N* to denote whether the deflection of the electrical signal is positive or negative. The number represents, on average, how many hundreds of milliseconds (ms) after stimulus presentation the component appears.

Components are often divided into two categories: exogenous and endogenous. **Exogenous**

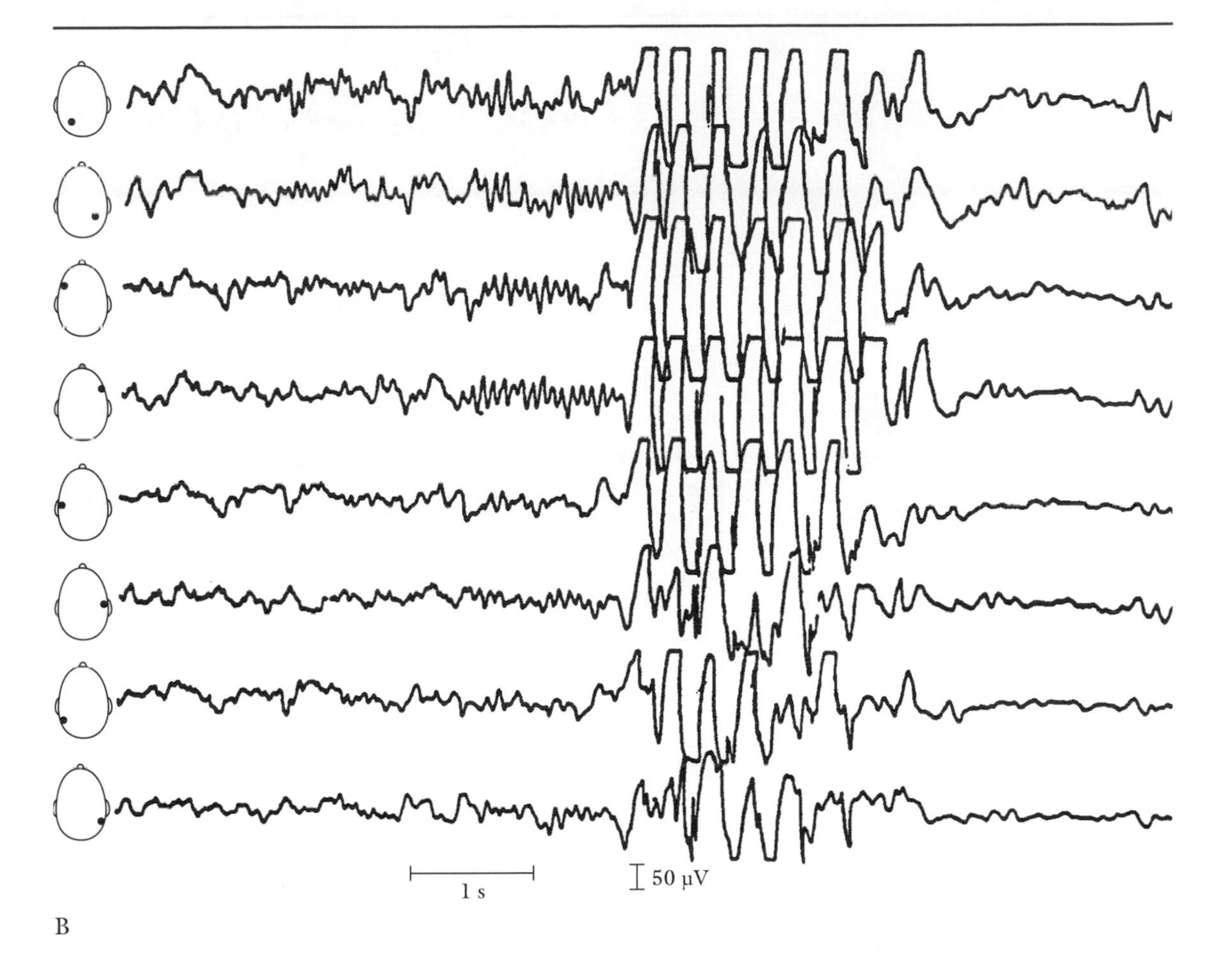

FIGURE 3.11 (Continued) (B) An example of "spiking" activity, which is a discrete increase in the voltage of the EEG, that accompanies epilepsy. In this case, the seizure occurred over many regions of the brain simultaneously, as can be seen by the occurrence of high-voltage activity over all electrodes. The position of the electrode for each line of recording is indicated by a dot on the diagram of the head on the left. The square shape of the wave during seizure activity is an artifact owing to limitations of the recording apparatus, which could not adequately record the intensity of the voltage associated with this seizure. More typical waveforms during seizure activity can be seen in the third recording from the bottom, in which square waves are less prominent.

components are linked to the physical characteristics of a stimulus and usually occur early in the waveform. (Because they are evoked by an external stimulus, they are sometimes referred to as *evoked potentials.*) In contrast, **endogenous components** appear to be independent of stimulus characteristics and driven by internal cognitive states. They typically occur later in the waveform. An example of a typical waveform with the different components is presented in Figure 3.12.

Next, let's discuss the major classes of important components, starting with those that occur earliest in time. The very early components, occurring within 100 ms of stimulus onset, are linked to sensory processing. This property makes them useful in assessing the integrity of nerve fiber pathways from the sensory receptors to the brain. For example, as information is relayed from the cochlea of the ear to the cortex, the points where neurons synapse are, in order, the cochlear nuclei (and superior olive) at the

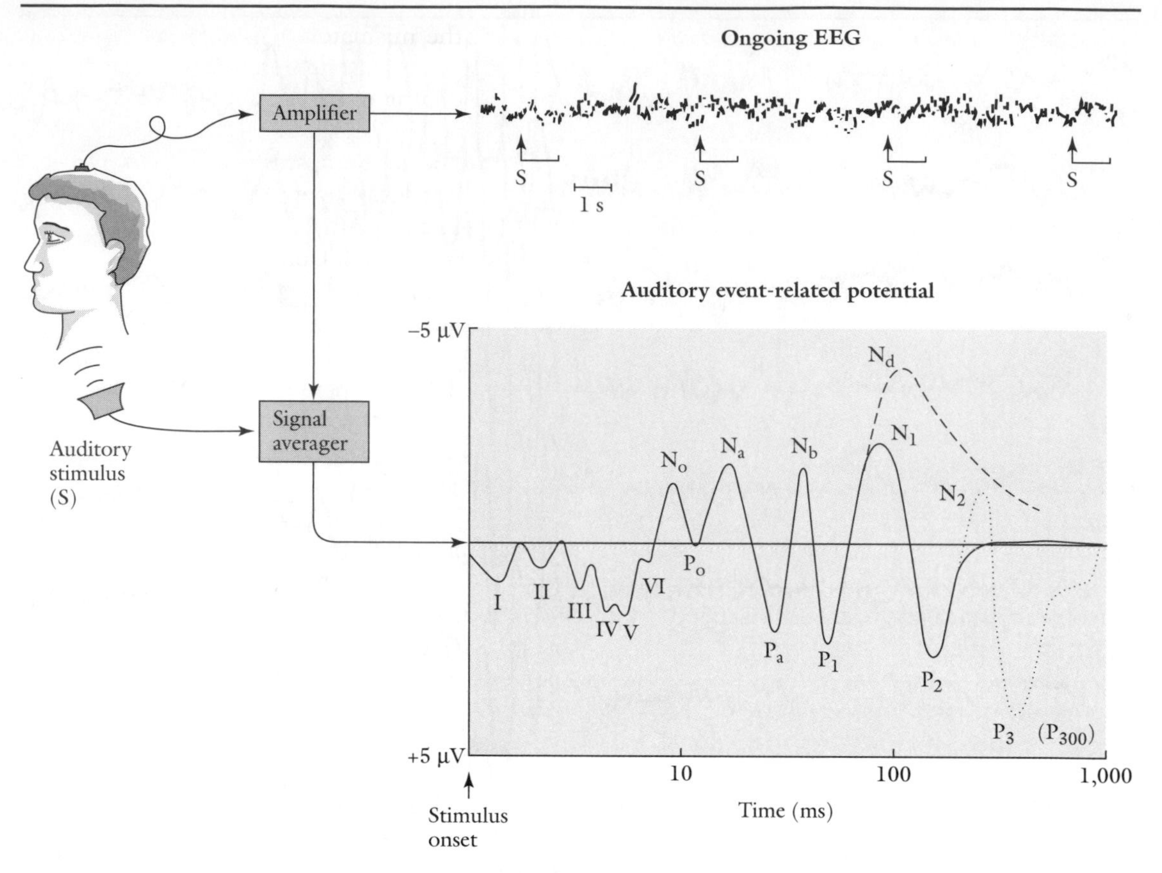

FIGURE 3.12 The method of recording event-related potentials (ERPs). The ongoing electroencephalography (EEG) (top) is recorded on the scalp through an amplifier. Every time a stimulus occurs (denoted by an *S* in the ongoing EEG), the electrical signal is recorded for a discrete period (e.g., 1 s). Signals from all such time periods are then averaged, because ERPs are too small to be detected in the ongoing EEG. The resulting ERP waveform to an auditory stimulus is shown below, with time plotted logarithmically to allow differentiation of early responses from the brain stem (Waves I–VI), early components (<100 ms) that indicate the response of the brain to sensory characteristics of the stimulus (N_o, P_o, N_a, P_a, N_b), and later (endogenous) components (>100 ms) that tend to be linked more to cognitive processes (N_d, N_2, P_2).

level of the medulla, the inferior colliculus, the medial geniculate nucleus of the thalamus, and then Heschl's gyrus, the primary auditory region of the brain (see Figure 1.18). Information takes time to reach each of these relay points, and when it does, a characteristic component of the waveform is produced. Hence, an abnormality in one of these early components implicates a disruption at a specific relay point in the flow of information from the sensory receptors to the cortex.

Components that appear approximately 100 ms after a stimulus is presented include the P_1 and N_1. At this point, ERPs are no longer driven solely by sensory information but can also be modulated by attention. The P_1 component is a positive deflection observed between 80 and 140 ms postpresentation, whereas the N_1 is a negative deflection observed about 100 ms postpresentation for auditory stimuli and between 160 and 200 ms postpresentation for visual stimuli. The effect of attention on these components can be demonstrated by asking individuals to pay attention to information presented in one place but not another, such as attending to information presented to the right ear but not the left. When an individual's attention is directed to the location at which the stimulus is presented, the size of the P_1 and N_1 are increased relative to when that same stimulus is presented but the individual's attention is directed elsewhere (Mangun & Hillyard, 1990). Notice that the stimulus in both cases is identical—all that varies is whether the individual is attending to the location at which it is presented.

The N_2, a negative deflection at about 200 ms postpresentation, is known as the *mismatch negativity*. It occurs when an individual is presented with an item that is physically deviant from that of the prevailing context. For example, if someone is listening to a series of tones, most of which are low in pitch, an N_2 is elicited by a high-pitched tone. Unlike the N_1, this effect occurs regardless of whether the individual is attending to the location in which the deviant stimulus appears (e.g., Näatanen, Gaillard, & Mantysalo, 1978).

One of the most studied components is the P_3, which is a positive deflection found approximately 300 ms poststimulus. Although researchers disagree on exactly what the P_3 measures, it appears to be related to attention and the updating of memory, as occurs when a person modifies his or her current model of the environment to include incoming information (Donchin & Coles, 1988). The P_3 occurs in numerous situations; however, the classic situation in which it is usually observed is in an experimental procedure called the *oddball paradigm*. In this paradigm, an individual hears a series of tones at consecutive intervals, most of which are at one pitch (e.g., a "beep") and a minority of which are at another pitch (e.g., a "boop"). A larger P_3 is generally elicited by the oddball, the boop, than by the regular items, the beeps. Typically a P_3 is observed when the individual must pay attention to an item, the oddball, and that oddball is distinct from the information currently held in memory (necessitating the updating of memory). The P_3 is distinct in two ways from the mismatch negativity that occurs when a physical deviance is detected. First, a P_3 can be elicited by the lack of sensory stimulation, such as silence. If, for example, a person hears a series of tones punctuated periodically by silence when a tone should occur, a P_3 is elicited to the silence because memory must now be updated. Furthermore, whereas the mismatch negativity appears to occur relatively automatically regardless of whether or not an individual is paying attention to the items, the person must be engaged in processing the stimulus for a P_3 to occur. Because of this feature, it has been used as an index of how much attention an individual is devoting to processing a stimulus (e.g., Kramer, Wickens, & Donchin, 1985).

Another late component that has been linked to psychological processing is the N_4. This negative-going component appears approximately 400 ms poststimulus presentation and occurs when individuals detect semantic anomalies. So, for example, if your ERP were being recorded at this moment, an N_4 would probably be observed as you read the last word of the following sentence: "Running out the door, Patty grabbed her jacket, her baseball glove, her cap, a softball, and a skyscraper." In contrast, the N_4 would be absent if the same sentence ended with the word "bat". The amplitude of the N_4 increases with the deviance of a word relative to the prior context of the sentence. For example, your N_4 to the following sentence, "Running out the door, Patty grabbed her jacket, her baseball glove, her cap, a softball, and a lamp," would be smaller than your N_4 to the first sentence because *lamp* is less deviant a word than *skyscraper* (i.e., Patty could actually grab a lamp, but not a skyscraper). However, an N_4 would still be elicited by the second sentence because you would expect Patty to grab another piece of softball equipment, not a piece of furniture (e.g., Kutas & Hillyard, 1980).

A review of the components and the psychological processes with which they are associated is presented in Table 3.2. (A more detailed review of ERPs and their relations to psychological processes is presented in Rugg & Coles, 1995.)

ERPs are extremely useful because they provide some information about the time course with which information is processed in the brain (e.g., attention acts to enhance processing of task-relevant materials by 150 milliseconds postpresentation). But they have some drawbacks. The pattern of brain activity on the scalp cannot tell us with certainty the location of the dipole or dipoles within the brain that are generating such a pattern. Any given pattern of activity on the scalp could mathematically be produced by a variety of generators or sets of generators within the brain, a

TABLE 3.2 Basic Components and Psychological Processes Associated with Event-Related Potential (ERP) Components

ERP COMPONENT	TIME PERIOD (MS)[a]	ELICITING CONDITIONS	ASSOCIATED MENTAL PROCESSES
Sensory components	0–100	After the receipt of sensory information	Transmission of sensory information from the periphery to the cortex
N_1–P_2 (N_d)	100–300	When subjects are paying attention to the portion of the stimulus stream in which the material was presented	Selective attention
Mismatch negativity (N_2)	200–300	When a stimulus is physically deviant from other recent stimuli; it is not much affected by whether the individual is paying attention to the portion of the stimulus stream in which the deviant item is presented	Detection of physical deviance
P_3	300–800	When individuals must pay attention to the rarer of two events, even if that rare event is the absence of sensory stimulation (e.g., silence)	Memory of context updating
N_4	400–600	When items deviate in meaning from what is expected	Detection of semantic deviance

[a]Indicates time postpresentation.

difficulty known as the *inverse problem.* For this reason, researchers have focused on utilizing computer models of the head that make certain simplifying assumptions to help them more precisely localize the neural generator or generators within the brain (e.g., Scherg, 1992). An example of dipole modeling of the source of a component is shown in Figure 3.13. Recently there has been a push toward developing recording systems with many more leads than in the standard placement system (refer back to Figure 3.10). The additional information provided by these high-density recording systems, which often have up to 128 leads, aids in the modeling process (e.g., Potts et al., 1996).

Another approach to expanding the utility of ERP recordings is to run identical experiments, one using ERP recordings and one using a complementary method such fMRI or PET. In this case, the data obtained from fMRI or PET about the location of brain activity during a mental process is utilized to constrain the set of possible locations for the possible dipoles. Then a researcher can examine whether the ERP data collected on the scalp is consistent with such a dipole. If there is a good fit, the researcher has information about both the probable location and the time course of a given mental process (see Mangun, Hopfinger, & Heinze, 1998).

• *MAGNETOENCEPHALOGRAPHY* •

A related method to EEG is **magnetoencephalography,** known as MEG. This method relies on the recording of magnetic potentials at the scalp, rather than electrical potentials, to index brain activity. Remember that in discussing ERPs, we mentioned that the synchronous activity in aligned fields of dendrites creates a dipole, which consists of a region that is relatively negatively charged at one end and relatively positively charged at the other end. If you have taken physics, you will have learned that a magnetic field exists around such a differential electrical potential, as shown in Figure 3.14A. This magnetic field can be used to locate the dipole because the dipole resides midway between the extreme high points of intensity of the magnetic field, as shown in Figure 3.14B.

MEG records these magnetic fields using devices called SQUIDs, which stands for *superconducting quantum interference device.* The critical portions of these devices will have superconducting properties only if they are kept at very low temperatures,

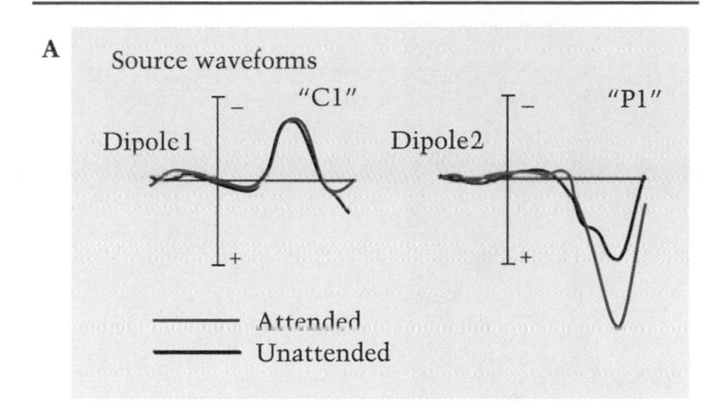

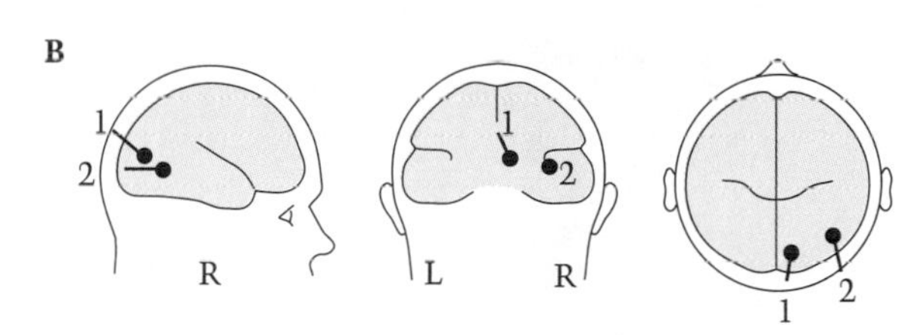

FIGURE 3.13 Results of a dipole modeling procedure. In this experiment, individuals were shown a simple visual stimulus, a circular checkerboard, and told to attend to information on the left side of space. (A) Shown here are the responses to attended items, depicted by the blue line, and unattended items, depicted by the black line. Dipole 1 models the source of the C1 waveform. Notice that its amplitude does not vary depending on whether an item is attended or not. Dipole 2 models the source of the P1 waveform, which reflects attentional modulation of sensory processing as indicated by the larger response to attended than unattended information. (B) The location of these two dipoles as seen from a lateral, coronal, and horizontal perspective. The location of Dipole 1 is near the midline of the brain and near the calcarine fissure, consistent with a position within primary visual cortex. Dipole 2, however, is positioned more laterally, consistent with a location in secondary visual processing areas.

close to those at which all molecular motion ceases (i.e., 0 degrees Kelvin). To obtain such temperatures, the SQUIDs are encased in devices called *dewars,* which contain liquid helium, a substance that is found at 4 degrees Kelvin or colder. Although originally systems contained only one or two sensors, modern systems now contain up to 122 sensor arrays. As you can see in Figure 3.15, the apparatus for collecting MEG data is quite involved, mainly because of the size of the helium dewars.

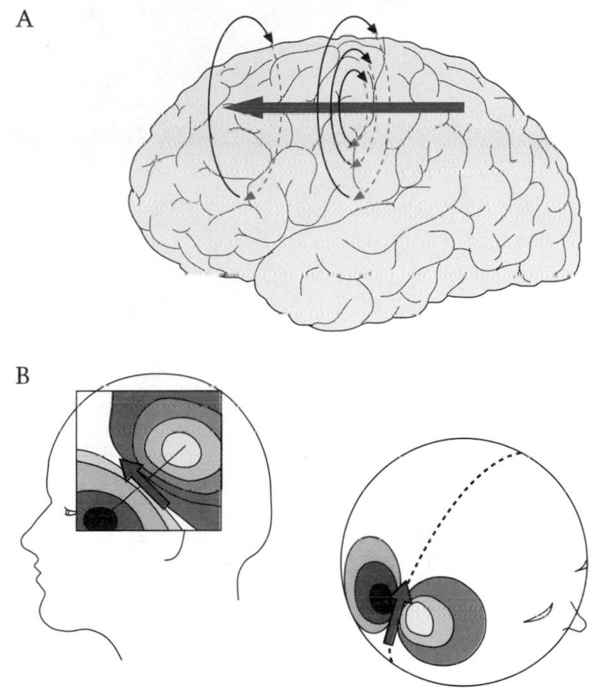

FIGURE 3.14 Relationship between electrical dipoles and magnetic fields. (A) The orientation of a magnetic field that occurs around a dipole. The magnetic field, shown here as solid and dashed lines, emanates in a clockwise manner around a dipole, shown here as an arrow, with the arrowhead representing the positive pole of the dipole. In physics this is known as the "right-hand rule," because if you stick the thumb of your right hand out to represent the dipole, with your thumb being the positive end, the curling of your remaining fingers represents the magnetic field around that dipole. (B) How the localization of an electrical dipole is derived from the distribution of the magnetic fields. The electrical dipole is located midway between the extremes of the magnetic signal. Just the way electrical signals are positive or negative, magnetic fields also have a sign: negative is shown here in black and positive in blue. In this figure, the intensity of the magnetic field is illustrated by the intensity of the color. Notice that the intensity of the magnetic fields drops off very close to the electrical dipole.

The two most common clinical uses of MEG are (1) to localize the source of epileptic activity and (2) to locate primary sensory cortices so they can be avoided during neurosurgical intervention (e.g., Forss, Mäkelä, Keränen, & Hari, 1995). MEG is especially helpful in cases where neither EEG nor a brain

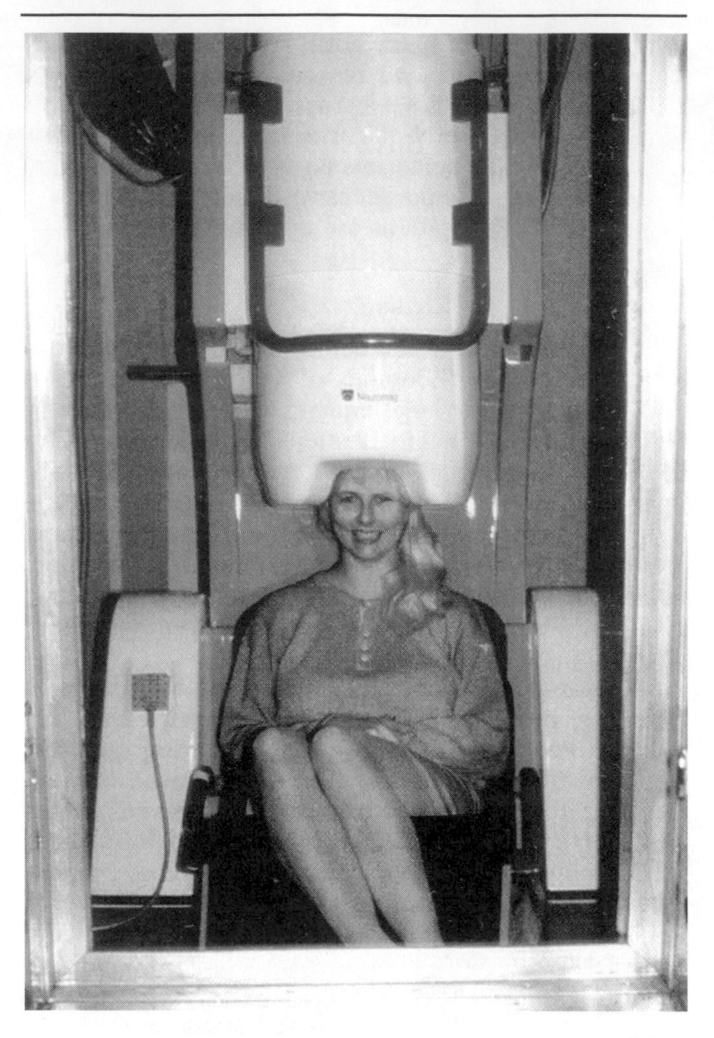

FIGURE 3.15 Apparatus necessary to record MEG. The sensors are located at the helmet-shaped bottom of the helium dewer, as close as possible to the participant's head.

imaging method such as fMRI or PET can definitely locate the source of epileptic activity or the location of primary sensory cortices (see Color insert 3.2).

MEG has also been used to understand more about the neurophysiology underlying psychiatric disorders such as schizophrenia. For example, one particular component of a MEG waveform, the M100, is thought to index the raw perceptual memory for auditory stimuli that lasts 150 ms or so after stimulus presentation (Lu et al., 1992). In people with paranoid schizophrenia, this component is generated at an atypical location in Heschl's gyrus (which, as you may remember from Chapter 1, is the location of primary auditory cortex) (e.g., Reite et al., 1994, 1997). Such findings lend support to the theory that people with paranoid schizophrenia have difficulties in filtering early sensory information appropriately (e.g., Boutros et al., 1999; Freedman, Waldo, Bickford-Wimer, & Nagamoto, 1991). MEG also has been used to examine a variety of cognitive processes, including language, object recognition, and spatial processing among others, in neurologically intact individuals. (See Lounasmaa, Hämäläinen, Hari, & Salmelin, 1996, for a readable introduction to MEG and its application to cognitive neuroscience.)

Why would one want to utilize magnetic currents when one can record brain activity with EEG or ERPs? Recording magnetic fields has some advantages over electrical potentials. First, electrical currents conduct through different media to different degrees. As you probably know, electrical currents are carried well in metal and water, but not so well in wood. Likewise, the electrical currents produced in the brain are carried in varying degrees through brain tissue, cerebral spinal fluid, the skull, and the scalp. The strength of magnetic fields, however, is not as influenced as electrical currents by these variations in tissue. Second, the strength of magnetic fields falls off from their source in a systematic manner (with the square of the distance). Thus, the strength of the magnetic field recorded on the outside of the head can help provide some information about how deep within the brain the source is located. One advantage of this characteristic is that it allows us to clearly differentiate the signals within the left hemisphere from those in the right. Such an ability is important, for, as we will learn in the next chapter, the hemispheres play very different roles in emotional and mental processes.

However, MEG is not without its drawbacks. The setup needed for such a technique is rather elaborate because the size of the magnetic fields produced by the electrical activity in the brain is very small—in the range of 50–500 femto Tesla (fT). This magnetic field is 100 millionth, or 1 billionth, the size of the earth's magnetic field. Not only do the recordings of such tiny fields require the superconducting technology used in SQUIDs, but they require a special shielded room. This room, usually made of aluminum (which is a nonmagnetic metal), shields not only against the earth's magnetic field but also other electromagnetic radiation, such as microwaves, radiation contained by electrical currents in everyday buildings, and the magnetic field generated by the sun.

Another drawback of MEG is that it cannot detect activity of cells with certain orientations within the brain. If you turn back to Figure 3.14, you will notice that the magnetic fields generated by electrical activity in cells aligned parallel to the plane of the surface of the brain will "emerge" from the brain and can be recorded by sensors. In contrast, magnetic fields created by cells with their long axes radial to the surface will be invisible. Fortunately, the activity of cells with radial orientations is best detected by EEG. Hence, these two methods complement each other in that each can detect activity that is "invisible" to the other.

Optical Recording Methods

A very new and exciting technique, **optical imaging,** provides cognitive neuroscientists with the ability to simultaneously obtain information about the source of neural activity as well as its time course. In this method, a laser source of near infrared light is positioned on the scalp. Detectors composed of optic fiber bundles are located a few centimeters away from the light source. These detectors sense how the path of light is altered, either through absorption or scattering, as it traverses brain tissue (see Figure 3.16).

This method can provide two types of information. First, it can be used to measure the absorption of light, which is related to concentration of chemicals in the brain. This measurement of the absorption of light is known as the *slow signal* and is so named because the time course is on the order of seconds: it starts about a second and a half after neuronal activity commences and subsides seconds after it stops. It is thought to reflect increased blood flow to areas engaged by task demands, similar to the information obtained with the BOLD signal in fMRI. However, unlike BOLD, which provides information only on the ratio of oxyhemoglobin to deoxyhemoglobin in the blood, optical imaging can actually tease them apart, because the degree to which light is absorbed by each of these substances can be determined separately. Second, it can measure the scattering of light, which is related to physiological characteristics such as the swelling of glia and neurons that are associated with neuronal firing. This information is known as the *fast signal* because it occurs contemporaneously with neuronal activity (Andrew & MacVicar, 1994).

A new method, *EROS* (event-related optical signal), takes advantage of this fast signal to record

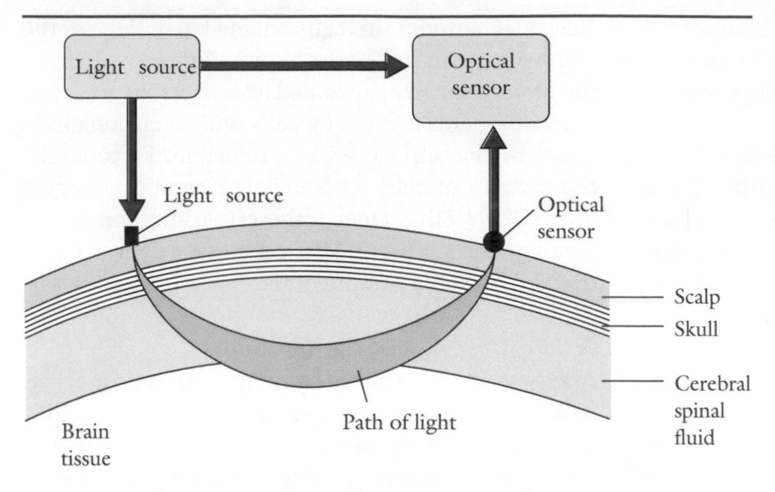

FIGURE 3.16 The principles of optical imaging. A light source at the surface of the head emits near infrared light that travels through the skull into the brain. The light then passes through the brain and emerges at the surface, where it can be detected. The path that the light takes through the brain can vary depending on a number of factors, including the geometry of the head. Hence, the set of possible paths are shown here as a crescent-shaped gray area. The optical signal is analyzed to determine how much light is absorbed, which results in a decrease in intensity, or how much the light is scattered from its ideal path, which causes a delay in its receipt at the sensor.

information locked to an event, much the way ERPs record the time-locked electrical response to a stimulus. The EROS method provides information about the source of activity within millimeters while providing temporal information on the order of milliseconds (typically recorded every 20 ms or so). Because this technique has not been utilized extensively, much work in recent years has centered on validation of its results both with regard to localization and time course. EROS provides information about localization of primary sensory and motor areas similar to that obtained with PET and fMRI, and also provides information about the timing of responses in different regions of visual cortex that is consistent with that obtained in ERP studies. More recent work has centered on expanding the capabilities of EROS to examine memory and attentional processes (for a review of how this method works, its validation and application to studying human cognition, see Gratton & Fabiani, 1998).

EROS has many advantages. First, as just discussed, it provides separate measures of the concentration of oxyhemoglobin and deoxyhemoglobin in the blood supplying the brain. Compared to PET and fMRI, it is much less costly and provides information about the timing of neural responses that cannot be obtained from either PET or fMRI. Finally, whereas patients must be transported to the PET or fMRI suite, EROS can be used at a patient's bedside. The major limitation of this method is that it cannot be used to obtain information about subcortical regions because too much light gets absorbed on the way to and from structures deep within the brain.

Techniques for Modulating Brain Activity

One of the most startling changes in the past five years regarding the methodology employed in cognitive neuroscience has been the advent of methods that actually modulate or change brain activity in neurologically intact individuals. The method that has been most utilized this way is **transcranial magnetic stimulation (TMS).** TMS can be conceptualized as akin to the reverse of MEG. Whereas MEG records the magnetic fields induced by the electrical activity of the brain, in TMS a coil or series of coils is placed on the scalp to produce a pulsed magnetic field that in turn induces an electrical field. Some examples of the types of coils used, along with the electrical fields that they produce, are shown in Figure 3.17.

This electrical field alters the membrane potential of neurons, causing them to depolarize synchronously, which in turn changes the probability that they will fire. Once the pulsed magnetic field is discontinued, the neurons can return to their previous state. Although TMS has been referred to as causing a "reversible" lesion, which would suggest that it blocks neuronal activity, it is better understood as scrambling neuronal activity—it causes neurons to fire in a random pattern rather than in a coherent manner.

There are two main types of TMS: *single-pulse TMS,* in which the stimulation is delivered at a pre-

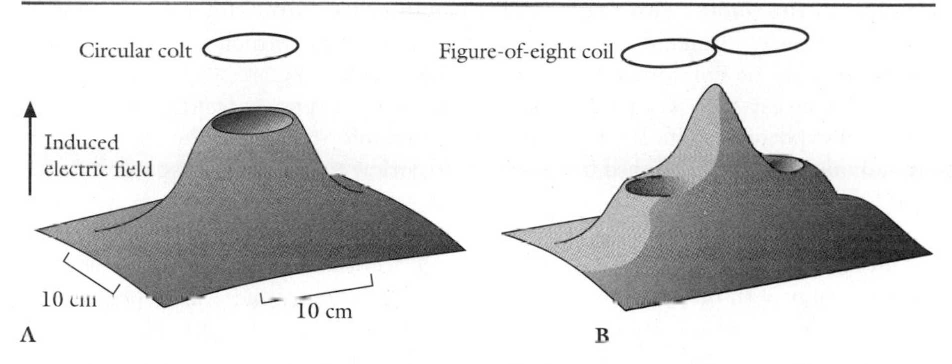

FIGURE 3.17 Shapes of magnetic coils and the distribution of the electrical field that they induce. On these graphs, the higher the peak, the greater the strength of the electrical field. (A) With a simple circular coil, the maximal electrical effect occurs directly below the coil, with much less of an effect occurring in the region in the middle of the coil. (B) With a figure-8 coil, the maximal intensity of the electrical field occurs at a much more restricted region, at the intersection of the two circles that comprise the figure 8.

cise time during performance of a task, and rTMS, which stands for *repetitive TMS* and involves multiple pulses with rates up to 50 Hz for tens, hundreds, or thousands of milliseconds. Although TMS can actually facilitate brain activity, such as inducing muscle movement, more typically it disrupts activity. For example, TMS applied over Broca's area leaves a person unable to produce speech (Pascual-Leone, Gates & Dhuna, 1991). Applying TMS over areas that process visual motion (area V5) leads to deficits in perceiving motion similar to those observed in patients with damage to this area (Walsh, Ellison, Battelii, & Cowey, 1998).

Therein lies one of the major advantages of TMS. It can be used to confirm findings from the lesion method that implicate a brain region as playing a critical role in a specific mental function. If a brain area is critical for a particular mental function, then applying TMS to the region should disrupt that function. For example, it has been suggested on the basis of a PET study that primary visual cortex is critically involved when an individual imagines an object, "picturing" it in his or her mind's eye (e.g., Kosslyn et al., 1995). Results from subsequent neuroimaging studies have been equivocal, with some studies yielding activity in primary visual cortex and others not. To resolve this ambiguity, researchers applied TMS over primary visual cortex and demonstrated that it produces deficits in visual imagery, indicating that these brain regions are critically involved in visual imagery (Kosslyn et al., 1999).

But this method has generated much excitement because it has many more potential applications. First, it can be used therapeutically. For example, as we mentioned earlier in this chapter, depression is associated with decreased activity of left frontal regions. Hence, if activity of this region can be increased by rTMS, depressive symptomatology might be reduced. In fact, successive trains of high-frequency rTMS applied over left frontal regions over a series of days alleviates the symptoms of depression (George et al., 1997). However, there remain at present many questions as to the optimal course of rTMS for treating depression. One problem is that trains of stimulation that are too infrequent or of low frequency may actually exacerbate symptoms of depression (Speer et al., 2000), apparently because they decrease rather than increase blood flow to the underlying region. Moreover, rTMS may be effective only for those individuals who exhibit low metabolic activity of prefrontal regions prior to treatment (e.g., Eschweiler et al., 2000).

Second, TMS can be utilized to show how the brain might reorganize, either with learning or as a result of sensory deprivation. For example, applying TMS to primary visual areas in normal individuals does not interfere with reading Braille, an alphabet felt with the fingers. We would anticipate such a result, as reading Braille would of course rely heavily on tactile regions of the brain. However, TMS applied to the visual cortex of blind individuals actually interrupts the reading of Braille (Cohen et al., 1997)! Such a finding suggests that as a result of sensory deprivation and exposure to Braille, the visual cortex of blind individuals has reorganized from processing visual information to processing nonvisual information.

Another potentially important use of TMS, when employed in conjunction with other methods, is to provide information on the connectivity between brain regions. The logic in these studies is to decrease or interrupt activity of one brain region using TMS, and then to examine the change in the pattern of activity across the whole brain with another imaging method, such as PET. Those brain regions intimately connected with and influenced by the region receiving TMS should also show decreases in activity. As an analogy, consider that just as cognitive neuroscientists can identify the subset of brain regions involved in a task, so does a teacher identify all the students taking her or his class. However, knowing who is taking the class doesn't provide the teacher with any information on which individuals in the class talk to each other.

Imagine that I temporarily disable the phone of one person in the class, much the way TMS can disrupt activity of a single brain region. I can now determine which individuals in the class talk to the person whose phone has been disabled by examining which individuals in the class are receiving fewer phone calls than normal. In the case of the brain, PET or some other method is used to determine which brain regions are showing a decrease in activation (rather than, in our analogy, a decrease in phone calls received). This logic has been utilized very effectively by researchers. For example, rTMS over the frontal eye fields, which are involved in voluntary eye movements, not only alters blood flow there but also in visual areas in superior parietal and medial parieto-occipital cortex, implicating these latter regions as being functionally connected to the frontal eye fields (Paus et al., 1997).

TMS can provide important information about whether behavior is critically dependent on a particular brain region or whether it results from the interaction between brain regions. For example, hemineglect (to which you were introduced in Chapter 1 and which you will learn more about in the chapter on attention) typically occurs after a right hemisphere lesion, leading individuals to ignore information on the left side of space. If paying attention to this side of space depends critically on an intact right hemisphere, then once the right hemisphere is damaged, patients should never be able to orient attention leftwards. However, applying TMS to the left hemisphere of these patients reduces the severity of neglect. Such a finding suggests that neglect results not so much from a right-hemisphere dysfunction, but rather from an imbalance of activation between the hemispheres. If the activity level of the left hemisphere is decreased via TMS, then the activation level of both hemispheres becomes more equivalent and neglect is reduced. Because the interconnectivity and functional interrelations between brain regions are sources of major unanswered questions in cognitive neuroscience today, TMS may become a very important tool in future research endeavors.

Despite its promise, TMS is a relatively new method that must be used cautiously because it can have adverse effects on brain function. Both single-pulse TMS in patients (Fauth et al., 1992) and too high a rate of stimulation of rTMS in neurologically intact individuals (Wasserman et al., 1996) can induce seizures. Furthermore, studies performed with animals suggest that longer term applications of TMS can have accumulating effects, actually causing significant structural changes in neurons. On a less severe level, in humans TMS can lead to mild headache (due to activation of scalp and neck muscles), muscle twitches, or nausea. Therefore, it must be utilized very carefully, and strict guidelines have been drawn up to minimize the potential for such adverse effects (Wasserman, 1998).

TMS also has some limitations as a tool for cognitive neuroscientists. As currently designed, the stimulating coils affect only the region of the brain closest to the surface. Hence at present it is not possible to stimulate deeper cortical neurons or subcortical structures without affecting the neurons that are on top of them. (For a short review of the many issues that can be addressed by TMS and the potential pitfalls of this method, see Fitzpatrick &

Rothman, 2000; for an in-depth discussion of many of the applications of TMS, see the February 1999 issue of *Neuropsychologia,* which was a special issue entitled *TMS in Neuropsychology*—Rushworth & Walsh, 1999).

In summary, in this section of the chapter, we discussed various techniques for assessing or modulating brain function. Because we need the proper tool for the job, the relative advantages and disadvantages of each method must be considered for each question to be investigated. A summary of the information provided by each method, as well as its spatial and temporal resolution, is presented on the inside back cover of this book. Table 3.3 lists the advantages and disadvantages of each method.

Techniques for Analyzing Behavior

Just as we need precise tools to measure brain anatomy and brain physiology, we also need precise tools to examine behavior. Careful and thoughtful behavioral testing is one of the most powerful tools we have for analyzing how the brain constrains and influences the way we think.

The Role of Cognitive Theories

Although we might assume that the deficits a person has sustained due to brain damage can be ascertained simply by observing behavior, this is not the case. Think for a moment about the many possible reasons a patient might not be able to provide a name when shown a picture of an animal, such as a zebra. Perhaps the visual attributes of the stimulus can't be processed because occipital regions were damaged and the person is blind. Or maybe basic visual processing is intact, but the patterns of light and dark cannot be interpreted as the black-and-white stripes of a zebra. Alternatively, maybe the physical form can be perceived (which we know because the patient can correctly choose a horse and not an elephant as looking similar to the zebra) and the patient's memory for zebras is intact (which we know because when asked which African animal is similar to a horse and has stripes, the patient correctly points to the word *zebra*), but the patient can't identify that particular form as a zebra. Or, perhaps the verbal label cannot be specifically accessed (that is, if you said "zebra," the patient could point to a picture of one, but if shown a picture of a zebra, he or she couldn't name it). Finally, the patient may have sustained some damage to the vocal musculature that does not allow production of the sound sequence of *zebra,* even though she or he knows that the picture is that of a zebra.

As this example demonstrates, what appears on the surface to be a simple problem may actually stem from numerous complex sources. Often the job of both clinical and experimental neuropsychologists is to carefully tease apart the possibilities and pinpoint the probable locus of the deficit. The degree to which we know how to parcel a cognitive ability into subcomponents relies not only on logic and common sense, but also to a large degree on having sound theories of cognitive functioning. For example, psycholinguists often describe language as being composed of three parts: phonology, syntax, and semantics. *Phonology* refers to the rules governing the sounds of language, *syntax* its grammar, and *semantics* its meaning. As we discuss in the chapter on language, individuals with brain damage may have deficits in only one of these domains. Why is it so important to be aware of cognitive theories? Let's suppose that a naive neuropsychologist doesn't know or consider psycholinguistic theories of language and encounters an individual who cannot correctly repeat a sentence spoken to her. The neuropsychologist might conclude, erroneously, that the patient doesn't "understand" the words in the sentence. However, if the neuropsychologist knew from theories of language that the ability to use grammar correctly can be separable from knowing what words mean, the neuropsychologist would not only test the patient's ability to repeat the sentence, but also would test her comprehension—for example, by asking her to point to a picture that depicted what she had just heard. The results might show that although the individual could not repeat the sentence, she could point to the picture depicting the sentence, indicating that she could indeed understand the meanings of words. The neuropsychologist would discover that the problem did not lie in comprehension and could go on to systematically test whether the individual had difficulties in producing the correct grammar or syntax.

TABLE 3.3 Advantages and Disadvantages of Different Methods Used in Cognitive Neuroscience

Methods of Assessing Brain Anatomy		
	ADVANTAGES	**DISADVANTAGES**
CAT (computerized axial tomography)	Can be used with almost all individuals	a. Involves the use of ionizing radiation b. Does not provide high spatial resolution
MRI (magnetic resonance imaging)	a. Can be used to detect different substances b. Does not involve radiation c. Good spatial resolution	a. Cannot be used with individuals who have metal in their bodies or pacemakers b. Can induce claustrophobia in some individuals

Methods of Assessing Brain Physiology		
Functional Brain Imaging	**ADVANTAGES**	**DISADVANTAGES**
PET (positron emission tomography)	Can be used to assess many aspects of physiological function	a. Involves the use of ionizing radiation (which limits an individual to 4–5 scans per year) b. Provides images that are averaged over times longer than thought processes require
fMRI	a. Provides good spatial resolution in relatively short periods b. Can be performed repeatedly on the same individual c. Does not require the averaging of data across individuals d. Widely available	a. Cannot be used with individuals who have metal in their bodies or pacemakers b. Limited ways of measuring physiological function *BOLD:* (1) Provides information only on relative oxygenation of the blood; (2) measures the brain's hemodynamic response that occurs on the order of seconds *Spectroscopy:* Doesn't provide information on location of activity
Electromagnetic Recordings	**ADVANTAGES**	**DISADVANTAGES**
Single Cell	Provides information on the type of stimulus to which a cell responds	Cannot be used in humans except under very specific circumstances
EEG (electroencephalography)	a. Provides information on the general state of the person (e.g., alert, drowsy) b. Provides excellent temporal resolution	a. Difficult to determine the source of activity from within the brain b. Difficult to detect activity of cells oriented parallel to the brain's surface
ERP (event-related potentials)	a. Provides information that has been linked to specific psychological processes such as memory and attention b. Provides excellent temporal resolution	a. Difficult to determine the source of activity from within the brain b. Difficult to detect activity of cells oriented parallel to the brain's surface
MEG (magnetoencephalography)	a. Provides better information about the source of the signal b. Not as susceptible to differences in conduction of tissue intervening between the brain and scalp	a. Set up is large and elaborate, requiring a shielded room b. Cannot detect cells with orientations radial to the brain's surface

TABLE 3.3 (Continued)

Optical Imaging	ADVANTAGES	DISADVANTAGES
Slow signal (metabolic)	a. Noninvasive b. Inexpensive c. Portable d. Allows the concentration of oxygenated and deoxygenated blood to be calculated separately	a. Relatively new and untested b. Cannot provide information on subcortical structures c. Can measure only the hemodynamic response of the brain
Fast signal EROS	a. Noninvasive b. Inexpensive c. Portable d. Detects a neuronal response rather than a hemodynamic response	a. Relatively new and untested b. Cannot provide information on subcortical structures
Methods of Modulating Brain Activity		
	ADVANTAGES	DISADVANTAGES
TMS (transcranial magnetic stimulation)	a. Can be used to confirm findings from lesion method b. Can be used therapeutically to treat clinical syndromes c. Can provide information on brain reorganization d. Provides information about the functional connectivity of brain regions e. Can be used to determine whether a deficit results from dysfunction of a region or disconnection of brain regions	a. Can have adverse effects on brain functions (e.g., induce seizures) b. Long-term effects are unknown c. Can only stimulate regions close to the surface

Throughout this book, we discuss different theories of mental function. They help to guide investigations into the relationship between the brain and behavior by providing a means of conceptualizing overarching cognitive functions such as "language" or "spatial ability" as actually consisting of a set of more specific cognitive capacities. These theoretical frameworks for understanding cognitive functions can help delineate the many possible causes of a behavior and allow behavior exhibited in either the clinic or the laboratory to be decomposed into its parts.

We must remember that not only do psychological theories inform neuropsychological investigations, but neuropsychological investigations can inform cognitive theories, especially differentiating those that are plausible from those that are not. For example, as discussed in the chapter on language, data from neuropsychological studies support the conceptualization of syntax and semantics as distinct aspects of language, because brain damage can disrupt one of these abilities while leaving the other intact.

Clinical Assessment of Behavior

In this section of this chapter, we discuss some of the methods commonly used in clinical settings for assessing the effects of brain damage. A **neuropsychological assessment,** which is performed by a clinical neuropsychologist, is used to determine the degree to which damage to the central nervous system may have compromised a person's cognitive, behavioral, and emotional functioning. The goals and uses of this assessment are numerous. First, the assessment provides a profile of the cognitive capacities exhibited by an individual. It can demonstrate both a person's strengths and weaknesses, identifying the domains likely to cause difficulty and highlighting the retained skills that can be used to offset potential problem areas. Second, the assessment provides a baseline from which to evaluate the person's progress during rehabilitation. As time passes from the insult, neuropsychologists often want to know whether the person is making additional gains in performance or whether a particular therapeutic regimen is helpful. Third, the assessment yields information that can be used to provide a prognosis. The individual, as well as his or her family and loved ones, must be given not only insight into the level of current functioning, but also reasonable expectations about the likely level of functioning in the future. If expectations are too high, the patient and family may become frustrated, and if expectations are too low, the person may not recover to her or his full potential (Lezak, 1995).

We begin by discussing the test-battery approach, in which a variety of cognitive abilities are assessed in order to obtain a profile of an individual's strengths and weaknesses. We next discuss several standard tests designed to measure overall intelligence. In some cases, more specific tests, such as those measuring memory, attention, spatial ability, and abstract reasoning, are used to elucidate a more fine-grained profile of an individual's strengths and weaknesses. Myriad tests can be used for assessing specific functions, far too many to be discussed here. If you are interested in knowing more about these specific tests as well as other aspects of clinical assessment of neuropsychological dysfunction, the definitive reference is Lezak (1995).

• *BATTERIES AND CUSTOMIZED APPROACHES* •

There is a tension in neuropsychological assessment between detecting the presence of brain damage regardless of its source and obtaining a fine-grained componential analysis of behavior that precisely delineates the specific cognitive or emotional functions that have been disrupted. To cast a wide net to detect brain dysfunction of either neurological or psychiatric origin, neuropsychologists often administer a **neuropsychological test battery.** These batteries typically assess a variety of mental functions, and have at least one test designed to measure overall intelligence.

Probably the most widely used neuropsychological test battery is the *Halstead-Reitan battery,* which consists of a number of tests that generally require about six to eight hours to administer. The abilities examined in this battery range from simple tests of sensory function to complex tests of reasoning, from tests of verbal function to tests of spatial function, and from tests of immediate recognition to tests of memory. In addition, the battery is used to assess functioning in different sensory modalities. A complete Halstead-Reitan battery for adults includes the tests described briefly in Table 3.4 (Boll, 1981).

Other test batteries, such as the Luria-Nebraska, can be administered in about half the time of the Halstead-Reitan. The tasks on the Luria-Nebraska are divided into 12 content scales: motor functions, rhythm and pitch, tactile and kinesthetic functions, visual functions, receptive language, expressive language, reading, arithmetic, writing, memory, intermediate memory, and intelligence. This battery is a formalized set of tests that reflects the philosophy of Alexander Luria, who believed the brain to be composed of three functional and interrelated systems: a brain-stem system that is important for overall tone and arousal, an anterior system that is important for the planning and output of behavior, and a posterior system that is important for the reception of information and its processing (Golden, 1981).

These batteries were designed to determine whether or not an individual suffered brain damage, and they are effective at discriminating patients with brain damage from neurologically intact individuals (e.g., Golden, Hammeke, & Purisch, 1978; Vega & Parsons, 1967). However, they may be less effective at discriminating between individuals with brain damage and persons with psychiatric disorders (e.g., Adams, 1980). In addition to providing data about the absolute level of performance, test batteries can provide data on the qualitative nature of performance—that is, the strategies an individual uses to perform a task. Such information can be important in gaining a more precise understanding of the cognitive deficit.

TABLE 3.4 Components of the Halstead-Reitan Neuropsychological Test Battery

TEST	WHAT IT MEASURES	HOW THE ABILITY IS MEASURED
MMPI-2 (Minnesota Multiphasic Personality Inventory—Second Edition)	Psychiatric symptomatology, such as depression and schizophrenia	The individual answers a large number of yes-no questions to provide a profile relative to individuals who have been diagnosed with specific psychiatric disorders.
Categories Test	Abstract reasoning	The individual views four items on the screen and pushes one of four buttons: different sets of items require different responses (e.g., push the button corresponding to the atypical item, push the button corresponding to the Roman numeral on the screen). The only feedback provided is a bell for correct answers and a buzzer for incorrect responses.
Rhythm Test	Auditory perception and timing	The individual decides whether two patterns of sounds are similar.
Speech Sounds Perception Test	Verbal abilities Attentional abilities	In each trial, the individual chooses a previously heard sound from among a number of choices. The sounds are nonsense syllables that begin and end with different consonants.
Finger Tapping Test	Motor function	The tapping rate of each index finger is determined.
Grip Strength Test	Motor function	The strength with which a dynamometer can be squeezed by each hand is assessed.
Trail Making Test	Visual search Attention	*Part A:* The individual's ability to draw a line connecting consecutively numbered circles is assessed. *Part B:* The individual's ability to connect, in an alternating manner, numbered and lettered circles (e.g., A1B2C3) is examined.
Aphasia Screening Test	Language	The individual's ability to use and perceive language, to pantomime simple actions, and to reproduce simple geometric forms is assessed.
Tactile Perception Test	Tactile ability	The individual is tested as to whether he or she can identify objects by touch (each hand separately), can identify letters traced on the fingertips (with the eyes closed), and can perceive being touched on different fingers of both hands.
Tactual Performance Test	Tactile memory Spatial localization	Without any visual input (blindfolded or eyes closed), the individual must place a set of felt shapes into a single board from which they were cut out. Afterward, with eyes open and the board obscured from view, the individual must draw each shape at its correct location on the board.
Sensory-Perceptual Exam	Sensory loss Hemineglect	The individual's perception of simple information in the visual, tactile, and auditory modalities is examined. To determine whether neglect is present, the investigator presents stimuli to just one side of the body or to both sides simultaneously.
WAIS-III (Wechsler Adult Intelligence Scale—Third Edition)	General intellectual abilities	Eleven subtests are used to assess various intellectual functions of the individual (see Table 3.5).

An alternative strategy to the test-battery approach is **customized neuropsychological assessment.** In such assessment, the examiner initially uses information from a small set of tests (e.g., WAIS-III [Wechsler Adult Intelligence Scale—Third Edition, 1997], Boston Diagnostic Aphasia Exam) to generate hypotheses about the set of particular abilities that were compromised by the brain damage. Each hypothesis is then evaluated with a specific neuropsychological test, and, depending on the individual's performance, the hypothesis is either pursued further by means of another test or abandoned (e.g., Lezak, 1995). If it is abandoned, a new hypothesis is generated, and the cycle is repeated until the behavioral deficit is well characterized. In such a situation, not only the level of performance, but also the manner in which an individual performs tasks can provide important clues as to the nature of the underlying deficit. Compared with a standardized battery, the individualized approach requires a more skillful examiner. Such expertise on the part of a neuropsychologist may be critical to elucidating the nature of the disorder, especially in atypical or unusual cases.

• *MEASURES OF OVERALL INTELLIGENCE* •

The Wechsler family of intelligence tests, probably the most widely used tests to assess intellectual abilities, include the WPPSI-R (Wechsler Preschool and Primary Scale of Intelligence—Revised [Wechsler, 1989]), for children aged 3 years 7 months to 7 years 3 months; the WISC-III (Wechsler Intelligence Scale for Children—Third Edition [Wechsler, 1991]), for children aged 6 years to 16 years 11 months; the WAIS-III (Wechsler Adult Intelligence Scale—Revised [Wechsler, 1997]); and the WAIS-NI (Wechsler Adult Intelligence Scale as a Neuropsychological Instrument [Kaplan, Fein, Morris, & Delis, 1991]). All these tests provide an overall, or full-scale, estimate of IQ (FSIQ) as well as two major subscale scores, a verbal IQ (VIQ) and a performance IQ (PIQ), which in general break down into verbal tests and nonverbal tests, respectively. Because our discussion centers mainly on adults, rather than on children, the subscales and tests that compose the WAIS-III are presented in Table 3.5. The WISC-III, WPPSI-R, and WAIS-NI contain many of the same subscales with some minor modifications and substitutions.

For many of the subscales in the Verbal portion of the test (e.g., Vocabulary and Similarities), responses are not timed but are scored according to the completeness and complexity of the answer. For example, if asked to define *commerce,* a person who answers "money" will receive 1 point, whereas a person who answers "a system of exchanging goods and currency" will receive 2 points. Likewise, if a carrot and celery are described as alike because they are both long and thin, 1 point will be given, whereas if the reply is that they are both vegetables, 2 points will be given. In contrast, on some of the Performance subtests, individuals must either respond within a set time to receive points, or receive fewer points the longer he or she takes to reach an answer. However, most recent versions of these tests have been revised to deemphasize the reliance on speeded performance.

The WAIS-III is useful because it provides a profile of abilities, not just a single score. In particular, the subtests are broken down into four separate index scores. The first index score, the Verbal Comprehension Index, provides a measure of knowledge acquired verbally and verbal reasoning. This index is assessed by examining performance on Vocabulary, Similarities, and Information. The Perceptual Organization Index is a measure of a person's nonverbal ability to utilize information in a flexible or fluid manner, attentiveness to detail, and visual-motor integration. It is computed as a function of scores on Picture Completion, Block Design, and Matrix Reasoning.

The Working Memory Index requires an individual to attend to information, to hold it briefly online in memory, and then to formulate a response. This index is assessed by performance on the Arithmetic, Digit Span, and Object Assembly subtests. The final index, the Processing Speed Index, is assessed by Digit Symbol-Coding and Letter-Number Sequencing. It is highly sensitive to many different neuropsychological conditions (WAIS-III, Technical Manual, 1997).

Another useful aspect of the WAIS-III is that the test is well-normed, based on a large sample of individuals who were chosen to match the demographics of the U.S. population with regard to gender, region of the country in which they reside, and type of environment (i.e., rural or urban). In addition, the WAIS-III provides different norms for different age ranges—an important feature. As a person ages, the ability to perform tasks quickly is compromised (e.g., Salthouse, 1985). Because superior scores on certain Performance subscales are obtained not only by performing the task correctly but also by performing it quickly, different norms are necessary for younger and older individuals to account for the slowing that accompanies aging.

Finally, the WAIS-NI (WAIS as a Neuropsychological Instrument) was designed specifically for use in neuropsychological assessment (Kaplan, Fein, Morris, & Delis, 1991). In this version of the test, certain items were changed in consideration of the way in which difficulties in motor output might unduly

TABLE 3.5 Wechsler Adult Intelligence Scale III (Third Edition)

SUBSCALE	WHAT IT MEASURES	HOW THE ABILITY IS MEASURED	INCLUDED IN INDEX SCORING
Verbal subtests			
Vocabulary	Vocabulary	The individual identifies a series of orally and visually presented words, such as *commerce.*	Verbal comprehension
Similarities	Abstract thinking	The individual answers questions such as "How are celery and a carrot alike?"	Verbal comprehension
Arithmetic	Arithmetic abilities; freedom from distractibility	The individual solves math problems, such as the following, in his or her head, without the aid of a pen and paper: "If it takes 18 days for 12 workers to manufacture one automobile, how many workers would it take to manufacture an automobile in 6 days?"	Working memory
Digit span	Verbal short-term memory; freedom from distractibility	The individual hears a string of digits ranging in length from three to eight and must repeat the string to the experimenter. In half the trials, the string must be repeated in the same order as presented (e.g., hear: "2-5-3" and respond: "2-5-3"), and in the other half in the opposite order (e.g., hear: "2-5-3" and respond: "3-5-2").	Working memory
Information	Factual knowledge	The individual answers questions such as "If you were to go from New York to Los Angeles, in which direction would you be traveling?"	Verbal comprehension
Comprehension	Social knowledge	The individual answers questions such as "If you were at a beach without a lifeguard and someone in the water was having trouble, what would you do?"	Verbal comprehension
Letter-number sequencing	Working memory; freedom from distractibility	The individual hears a series of letters and numbers presented in a random order. He or she has to repeat the numbers in sequential order and letters in alphabetical order, (e.g., hear: "8,5,G,B,W,3" and has to repeat back: "3,5,8,B,G,W").	Working memory
Performance subtests			
Picture completion	Visual processing	The individual views a series of pictures and within the allotted time must identify in each picture the critical portion that is missing (e.g., missing tail lights from a car viewed from the back).	Perceptual organization
Digit symbol-coding	Visuomotor ability; freedom from distractibility	The individual sees a series of symbols, each of which is associated with a number. The template is in front of the person. A series of numbers with blank boxes is given below and the corresponding symbol must be written in.	Processing speed
Block design	Visuomotor ability; spatial processing	The individual is given cubes that are red on two sides and white on two sides and two that are half red and half white (the color divide goes along the diagonal). The cubes must be arranged so that their tops match a picture.	Perceptual organization
Matrix reasoning	Visual processing; abstract reasoning skills	The individual views an incomplete gridded pattern with a section missing. He or she has to choose the correct missing piece to the picture out of five possible choices.	Perceptual organization
Picture arrangement	Visual processing; sequencing	The individual views a series of frames, much like those in a comic strip, and must put them in order so that they make a coherent story.	Perceptual organization
Symbol search	Visual processing	The individual views two groups of symbols, a target group and a search group. He or she must indicate whether either of the target symbols appears in the search group by marking yes or no.	Processing speed
Object assembly	Visuomotor ability; spatial processing	The individual must perform a task similar to completing a jigsaw puzzle, except the pieces are large and have few distinctive shapes or markings.	Perceptual organization

decrease an individual's test score. Let's consider an obvious but nontrivial example. On the Information subtest, the individual must answer specific "fact" questions, such as, "If you were to go from New York to Los Angeles, in which direction would you be traveling?" An individual with Broca's aphasia, a condition that makes speech output difficult but leaves language comprehension intact, might have difficulty saying "west" and thus would not receive credit for that question even if she or he knew the answer. To preclude such a situation, researchers designed the WAIS-NI so that Information questions can be given in a multiple-choice format. As a further aid, the written question and the four possible answers are shown to the patient while the examiner reads the question and the four answers aloud.

Another design feature of the WAIS-NI is that it provides the examiner with information on the strategies and approaches that a patient uses in solving problems. For example, the manner in which the individual attempts to arrange the blocks on the Block Design test can be informative. In the standard form of the test, the individual is scored only on the basis of whether he or she completes a particular design in the allotted time. However, there are numerous ways in which someone can fail to receive credit on items in this subtest. Some individuals receive no credit on this subtest because they perform the test too slowly or because they misorient just one of the blocks. Performance of this nature would indicate that, for the most part, visuospatial faculties are not compromised, except maybe with regard to how quickly they can be translated to motor output. Other individuals are unable to manipulate the blocks to form the correct overall shape (e.g., a square), performance suggestive of a larger problem in visuomotor or visuoperceptual processing.

The administration of the WAIS usually takes at least two hours, if not longer. If an individual is easily fatigued or if less time is available, another means of assessing general intellectual ability may be preferred. In some cases, this may involve obtaining an estimate of overall IQ by using just a subset of the WAIS-III tests, such as Similarities, Comprehension, Block Design, and Object Assembly. These subtests are used because the first two correlate well with the basic ability measured by the Verbal subscale, whereas the latter two correlate with that measured by the Performance subscale (Crawford, 1992).

• *MEASURES OF PREMORBID FUNCTIONING* • The test batteries and tests of general intellectual abilities discussed so far can tell us how well a person is functioning. When brain injury has profound consequences, these consequences are reflected in deviant scores on such tests. Yet in other situations the deficits may be more subtle or difficult to assess. Consider the case of a midlevel manager for a small business who, after a car accident, performs about average on the WAIS-III. How can a neuropsychologist differentiate between the possibility that this person initially had average intelligence and the possibility that brain damage compromised his functioning? To make such a distinction, neuropsychologists must obtain an **estimate of premorbid functioning**—that is, a reasonable guess of how well the person was performing before the injury. Sometimes a person's educational and occupational history can serve as such a standard, but in other cases it may be inadequate. The Vocabulary subtest of the WAIS-III has been used to estimate premorbid IQ because the abilities it measures seem relatively resistant to brain damage, even that which affects many different arenas of intellectual functioning, such as Alzheimer's disease. Another test used to estimate premorbid functioning is the National Adult Reading Test (Nelson, 1982), which is an oral reading test consisting of 50 words, most of which are short and irregular, meaning they don't follow normal rules of pronunciation (e.g., *ache*). Because the words cannot be sounded out, the ability to read them indicates some previous familiarity with them and hence provides an estimate of premorbid abilities (Crawford, 1992). When estimates of premorbid intelligence are much higher than present test scores, the results suggest that the brain damage adversely affected the individual's intellectual abilities.

Techniques for Modeling Brain-Behavior Relationships

In this final section of the chapter, we discuss another major method in cognitive neuroscience, the use of computer modeling techniques, generally known as **neural networks,** to simulate the action of the brain and its processes. Researchers create such models to help them create and test theories of neuropsychological functioning and to derive general principles regarding brain-behavior relationships.

The level at which brain processes are modeled can vary. Some neural networks actually model the electrical processes in dendrites (e.g., Anton, Granger, & Lynch, 1993), others the electrical properties of neurons (e.g., Gerstner, Kempter, van Hemmen, & Wagner, 1996) and some the interactions in a well-specified circuit of neurons that control some very fundamental behavior (e.g., the oculomotor circuit in the brain stem that is the final common pathway for movement of the eyes (Qian, 1995). These types of models will not be of large concern to us here, as they attempt to describe the behavior of the nervous system more than they are designed to model mental functioning in humans.

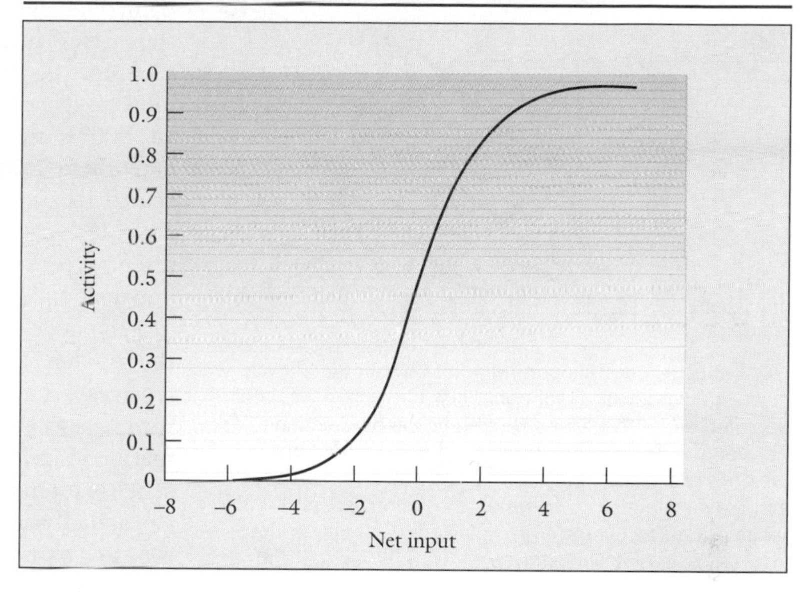

FIGURE 3.18 The sigmoid activation function that translates the sum of the input values to a unit of a neural network into an output value. Notice that the main changes in activation occur across a range of intermediate input values (e.g., between −2 and +2), rather than more extreme input values (e.g., less than −2 or greater than +2). This feature causes the activation of the unit to remain relatively stable when the inputs are either very high or very low, and very responsive to changes when inputs are in an intermediate range.

A variety of **computational models** can be used to simulate mental functions in humans (for an accessible overview, see Hinton, 1992). Here we will focus on **connectionist networks,** which are composed of interconnected layers of units that exhibit neuronlike behavior. Let's first talk about the basic components of such models. The following discussion will necessarily be a bit abstract since these models are not literal representations of mental and biological processes. The basic component of most computational models is a "unit," which one can think of as exhibiting neuronlike behavior. These units receive input from other units, which are summed to produce a net input. The summed input is then transformed via an *activation function* that produces an activation value, which is sent on to other units. Typically such models utilize a sigmoid function, shown in Figure 3.18, for transforming the net input to a unit into that unit's output. A sigmoid function is used because, as you can see in Figure 3.18, maximal changes in activation occur over the range of intermediate input values, whereas not much change in output occurs either when the input to a unit is very weak or very strong. As you will learn in a minute, this function aids in helping the system "settle" into a stable state.

These units are wired together in layers. Most models have an input layer that simulates the receipt of information from the outside world, an output layer that simulates the response of the system, and a "hidden" layer that is involved in the transformations that are necessary to perform the computation under investigation (see Figure 3.19). Units in one layer are connected to those in another via connection weights, which indicate the degree of influence that a unit in one level has on a unit on another level. The values of these weights usually

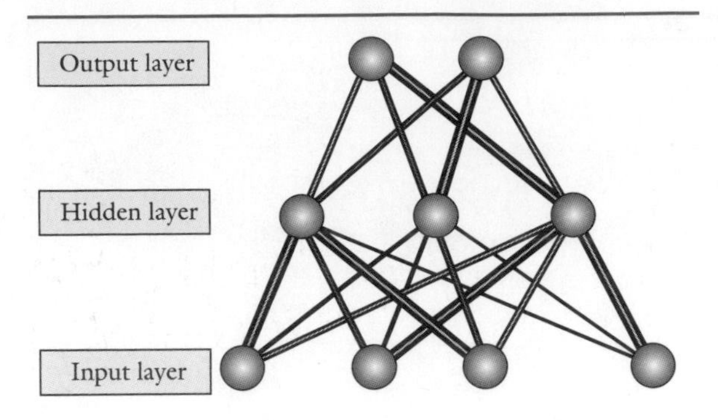

FIGURE 3.19 A simple connectionist network. Shown here is a hypothetical connectionist network. Units are depicted as circles. Lines represent the connections between units, and the strength of the connection weights is depicted by the thickness of the line. The input layer represents some type of information that is received by the system. The value for each unit in the input layer is typically either a "1" or "0." The output layer represents the response of the system. Here for example, one unit could represent a "yes" response and the other could represent a "no" response. The exact type of information that is coded by the middle layer, known as the hidden layer, is generally not easily determined.

vary between −1 and +1. Notice that the values can be either positive or negative. If positive, then activity in the first unit will increase activity of the next unit. If negative, then activity in the first unit will decrease activity of the next unit. If the absolute value of the weight is large (.9), then a large amount of the activity in the first unit will be passed onto the next one. In contrast, if the absolute value of the connection weight is small (.1), then not much of the activity of the first unit will be passed on to the other.

Let's look a little more closely at all of the layers in a model to understand their interrelation. The input layer typically encodes something about the external environment. In computer models it is impossible to code actual physical attributes of the physical world, so they are given an arbitrary code. The basic unit of currency for most computers is a 1 or 0, since current can either be on or off. Hence, each unit is assigned a value of either 1 or 0. For example, let's say that a stimulus might be in one of four positions, far left, left center, right center, or far right. The input layer would consist of four units (as shown in Figure 3.19). We might have the values for each unit be "1000" to indicate far left, "0100" to indicate left center, "0010" to indicate right center, and "0001" to indicate far right. In the example used here, there is an actual correspondence between the spatial location and the position of the "1" in the array. However, the four arrays could be used to represent green, red, blue, and yellow, or any other dimension of a stimulus.

Each node in this array then feeds information to the hidden layer. Notice that the hidden layer receives input from multiple input units. In this way it can act as a mechanism for integrating such information. Exactly what these hidden units "represent" is often obscure, although in some cases they can actually end up simulating the properties of neurons in a particular region of the brain (e.g., Zipser & Andersen, 1988). The hidden units then are connected to the output layer, which indicates the model's response. An output layer could have two units, one representing a "yes" response and the other a "no" response.

What is most notable about these models is their ability to "learn" without being provided specific rules, a property that simulates important aspects of human cognition. For example, once you were in school you learned the rules governing the grammar of your native language. In actuality, however, you had learned that grammar long before going to school, and no one taught you the "rules." Rather, your brain somehow extracted the regularities of language without formal training. These computational models learn in much the same manner as you learned your native language—by extracting the regularity of relationships with repeated exposure. In computational modeling this exposure occurs via "training" in which input patterns are provided over and over again. Learning within the system occurs via adjustment of the connection weights between units, typically those between layers. Notice that learning does not occur because of changes in the activation functions of the units themselves, but rather in the interrelationships between units. It is thought that similar changes occur in the nervous system with learning. The parameters that affect neuronal firing stay relatively constant (except in the cases of diseases such as epilepsy). It is the functional connectivity, the impact of one neuron's activity on another that changes with learning, a process known as *neuronal plasticity.* Such changes are thought to occur either because the influence of one neuron on another is increased (i.e., through increased efficacy of the synaptic connection) or because of a sprouting of new connections between neurons or a withdrawal of existing connections. We will talk more about this issue of plasticity in Chapter 13. In computational models, changes in synaptic efficiency are simulated by changes in the absolute value of the connection weight. A shift from a connection weight of 0 (i.e., no connection, no influence) to a nonzero weight is the equivalent of sprouting a new connection, whereas the reverse is akin to withdrawing a synaptic connection.

One of the most common methods for learning in computational models is *back propagation.* In this learning algorithm, the system is provided with an input and allowed to compute through a final output. The output obtained is then compared to the output that *should* have been given (e.g., the output yielded a "yes" response and the correct response would have been "no"). Starting at the output layer and going backward to the hidden layer, and then from the hidden layer to the input layer, small adjustments are made in the connection weights. If input from one unit helped push a connected unit toward the correct output, its connection weight is slightly increased; if it helped push a connected unit toward an incorrect output, its connection weight is slightly decreased. This process is performed over and over again until the system settles into a relatively stable state, in which increased training doesn't much change the performance of the system. Performance of the model can be evaluated in a number of ways. One way is to determine whether the pattern of results mimics that seen in people. Another is to pit models against each other and determine which one makes the fewest "errors" or reaches a stable state most quickly.

Simple systems such as these can model a remarkable amount of human behavior, ranging from learning the pronunciation rules and reading skills for the English language (Seidenberg & McClelland, 1989), to recognizing objects (e.g., Reisenhuber & Poggio, 2000) to accounting for our ability to store and retain new information in long-term memory (O'Reilly & Rudy, 2000). In addition, these models can mimic patterns of behavior seen after brain damage, such as dyslexias that impair reading ability (McLeod, Shallice, & Plaut, 2000) and attentional disruptions that lead to hemineglect (Mozer, Halligan, & Marshall, 1997). In these cases the models are "damaged" by reducing the number of connections or adding "noise" to the system, such as adding variability to the input/output function of units.

Computational modeling has a number of important strengths. First, when researchers create a model, they must be very explicit about the assumptions underlying their reasoning, and about the factors that they think contribute to a neural mechanism underlying mental processing. Basically, you can think of these models as keeping a researcher honest. Second, models can be manipulated systemically in ways that an experimenter may find impossible to do with animals or people. For example, lesions that do not occur or that occur rarely in real life can be simulated in a model. Finally, the outcome of modeling can provide researchers with novel predictions about the relationship between the brain and behavior that can be tested via many of the other techniques that we have discussed (e.g., by examining patients with lesions or using neuroimaging techniques). In later chapters we will discuss how computational models can provide better insight into the interrelationships between brain and behavior. The drawbacks of such models are that they obviously are only an abstraction of the brain or of a cognitive process. In addition, it is hard to determine how well the model "fits" or "explains" behavior, as no clear criterion for evaluating their validity is available.

Introduction

- The relationship between the functional architecture of the brain and behavior can be investigated by using a variety of populations and techniques. Depending on the question that researchers want to answer, the focus may be on the neuroanatomy or neurophysiology of the brain, or the way in which the brain controls behavior.
- Various techniques are often used in combination because converging evidence from different techniques is the most powerful tool for uncovering fundamental aspects of brain-behavior relationships.

Populations of Research Participants

- Patients with delineated brain damage allow researchers to determine which functions are lost as a result of damage to specific brain regions. This method cannot identify all brain regions that participate in a function, but rather identifies only the areas critical for task performance.
- Neurologically intact individuals provide (1) a baseline against which to compare performance of individuals who sustain brain trauma, (2) information on the basic neuroanatomical organization of the brain, and (3) when used in conjunction with brain imaging techniques, evidence on how brain structures work together.
- Nonhuman animals can provide useful information about the brain-behavior relationship because human brains share certain characteristics with other mammalian and primate nervous systems, especially those of monkeys.

Techniques for Assessing Brain Anatomy

- These methods provide information about the structural integrity of the brain.
- Computerized axial tomography (CAT) uses X-rays to provide information on the density of tissue, which can differentiate bone, blood, brain tissue, and cerebrospinal fluid.
- Magnetic resonance imaging (MRI) uses magnetic fields to provide a picture of the distribution of specific substances, such as water and fat, in the brain.

Techniques for Assessing Physiological Functioning

- Functional brain imaging methods provide information about the physiological activity in the brain that occurs as a by-product of neuronal firing, and as such provide very good information about *where* in the brain activity is occurring.
- Positron emission tomography (PET) uses a radioactively tagged molecule to provide a measure of physiological activity of different brain regions. It can be used to examine consumption of glucose and oxygen as well as binding of specific neurotransmitters.
- Functional magnetic resonance imaging (fMRI) typically works by detecting differences in the magnetic properties of oxygenated and deoxygenated blood, allowing the identification of those brain regions with active neurons.
- Electromagnetic recording methods record the electrical signals or the magnetic fields that accompany neuronal firing, providing very precise information on *when* neuronal activity is occurring.
- Single-cell recordings, which are used mainly in animals but in rare cases with people, involve inserting an electrode into single cells so researchers can determine what type of stimulus will make that cell fire.
- Electrocephalography (EEG) is used to examine the frequency of the summed electrical signal of synchronous firing in the dendrites of populations of neurons. It is useful for distinguishing states of alertness, drowsiness, and sleepiness and can be used for detecting the electrical spiking that occurs in epilepsy.
- Event-related potentials (ERPs) are electrical potentials that are recorded in response to an event and are time-locked. Different portions of

the ERP signal are linked to specific sensory or cognitive processes.

- Magnetoencephalography (MEG) provides information about the magnetic potentials that are associated with electrical activity in the brain. Different portions of the MEG signal are linked to specific sensory or cognitive processes.
- Optical recording methods supply information about the absorption and scattering of light through the brain. These can be used to infer regional changes in oxygenated and deoxygenated blood that occur on the order of seconds, and information about changes associated with neuronal firing that occur on the order of milliseconds.

Techniques for Modulating Brain Activity

- Transcranial magnetic stimulation (TMS), disrupts brain activity through magnetic fields on the scalp that interfere with the electrical firing of neurons.

Techniques for Analyzing Behavior

- Cognitive theories play a large role in helping to dissect the different component processes of mental functioning.
- Clinical assessment of behavior is done either via a test-battery that samples a large number of mental functions without going into a detailed examination of any one function or a customized approach that assesses very specific cognitive functions in addition to obtaining a measure of general intelligence.

Techniques for Modeling Brain-Behavior Relationships

- Computational models, composed of neuronlike units, can be used to make predictions about the way that the brain supports mental functions and to simulate what happens after brain damage.

KEY TERMS

alpha suppression 87
components 88
computational model 107
computerized axial tomography (CAT) 73
connectionist networks 107
customized neuropsychological assessment 102
dipole 88
disconnection syndrome 68
double dissociation 66
electrical potential 87
electroencephalography (EEG) 86
endogenous components 89
estimate of premorbid functioning 106
event-related potentials (ERPs) 87
exogenous components 88
functional magnetic resonance imaging (fMRI) 79
gradient field 70
group studies 68
lesion method 64
localization of function 64
magnetic resonance imaging (MRI) 77
magnetoencephalography (MEG) 92
mass action 64
method of converging operations 62
multiple-case study approach 69
neural networks 107
neuropsychological assessment 101
neuropsychological test battery 102
optical imaging 95
positron emission tomography (PET) 79
pulse sequence 78
receiver coil 78
single-case studies 68
static field 77
transcranial magnetic stimulation (TMS) 96

CHAPTER 4

HEMISPHERIC SPECIALIZATION

Close to the edge, a little off center,
More than a dreamer, a real believer,
Visual but I take heart,
I've been born right brained in a left brain world,
it's true!

—*Carrie Newcomer, folksinger, 1991*[1]

AS THE LYRICS to the song on the opening page of this chapter attest, it is common knowledge that the cerebral hemispheres are specialized for different aspects of cognitive and emotional functioning. We should not be surprised that the brain's functions differ left and right, because, as we learned in the introductory chapter, they also differ in the anterior-posterior and dorsal-ventral dimensions. The difference between the hemispheres in their processing is often referred to as **hemispheric specialization,** or **lateralization of function.**

Basics of Hemispheric Specialization

Although at first glance the hemispheres of the brain look like mirror images, this impression is deceiving in some important ways. In actuality, the hemispheres are distinct with regard to neuroanatomy, neurochemistry, and, most important, function. Many asymmetries in the neuroanatomy of the cerebral hemispheres have been noted. The right frontal lobe tends to extend farther forward toward the skull and is wider than the left frontal lobe, whereas the left occipital lobe extends farther back toward the skull and is wider than the right occipital lobe (e.g., Galaburda, LeMay, Kemper, & Geschwind, 1978) (Figure 4.1A). In most individuals, the Sylvian fissure extends farther in the horizontal dimension in the left hemisphere but takes more of an upward turn in the right hemisphere (Hochberg & LeMay, 1975; Rubens, Mahowald, & Hutton, 1976) (Figure 4.1B). This asymmetry has a long evolutionary history, having been observed in a Neanderthal fossil 60,000 years old (LeMay, 1976) and in australopithecine fossils dating back as far as 3.5 million years (Holloway, 1980). In addition, the region of the brain at the end of the Sylvian fissure in the temporal lobe, known as the **planum temporale** (i.e., temporal plane), usually is larger on the left than on the right, in fact, sometimes as much as 10 times larger (Geschwind & Levitsky, 1968) (Figure 4.1C).

These anatomical asymmetries are of interest because they may account for some hemispheric differences in functioning. For example, the planum temporale of the left hemisphere is an area that has been implicated since the late 1800s as being important in language comprehension, and asymmetry of this region, as measured by magnetic resonance imaging (MRI), is related to lateralization for language (Foundas et al., 1994). Another region of the brain that differs between the hemispheres is the frontal opercular area (see the inside front cover of your book). A portion of this region in the left hemisphere, Broca's area, is critically important for speech output (Falzi, Perrone, & Vignolo, 1982). Moreover, neurons in this region show greater branching of dendrites than those in the homologous region of the right hemisphere (Scheibel, 1984). Because animals raised in complex (rather than simpler) environments also exhibit greater dendritic branching (Greenough, 1975), this dendritic elaboration may indicate that neurons in this region have a larger or more specialized processing capacity. Another brain region, Brodmann's area 39 (see inside back cover), which is approximately akin to the angular gyrus (see figure inside front cover), is larger on the left than on the right side of the brain, a finding consistent with the specialization of this region in the left hemisphere for reading. In contrast, a more dorsal parietal area, which is hypothesized to be important for spatial processing, is larger on the right than on the left (Eidelberg & Galaburda, 1984).

Neurochemical differences between the hemispheres also abound, mainly expressed as asymmetries in neurotransmitter concentrations. For example, larger concentrations of norepinephrine can be found in certain regions of the right thalamus than in the left (Oke, Keller, Mefford, & Adams, 1978). A different brain region, the globus pallidus (which, as we learned in the introductory chapter, is a portion of the basal ganglia), has not only greater concentrations of dopamine in the left than in the right (Glick, Ross, & Hough, 1982), but also more terminals for the reception of dopamine in the left than in the right (Wagner et al., 1983). Because dopamine and

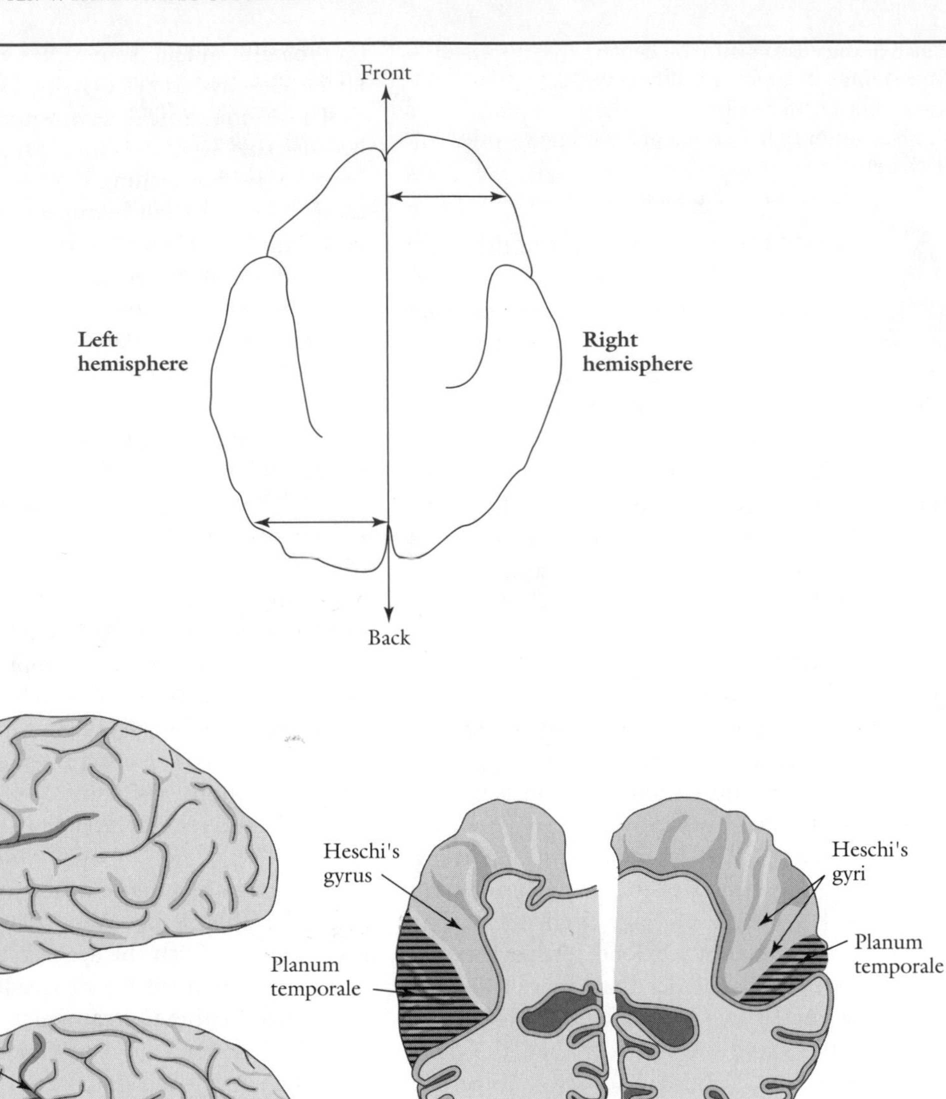

FIGURE 4.1 Some anatomical asymmetries of the human brain. (A) The right frontal region typically extends farther forward and is wider than the left frontal region, whereas for the occipital region the opposite is true: this region of the left hemisphere extends farther back and is wider. (B) The Sylvian fissure extends farther horizontally in the left hemisphere (top), whereas in the right hemisphere (bottom), it takes more of an upward turn. (C) The planum temporale, which can be clearly seen after the cortical tissue above the Sylvian fissure is removed, as is shown by the solid line in B, is typically larger on the left than on the right.

norepinephrine have different effects on behavior, these findings have led to the hypothesis that mental processes more dependent on dopamine, such as those that require a readiness for action, are lateralized to the left hemisphere. In contrast, processes more dependent on norepinephrine, such as those that aid a person in orienting toward new or novel stimuli, are lateralized to the right hemisphere (D. Tucker & Williamson, 1984). Most dramatic, however, are the differences in function between the hemispheres, a distinction that was first observed in the late 1800s. We now turn back the pages of time to explore how the distinct specialization of each hemisphere was uncovered.

Historical Perspective

The idea that the hemispheres have different functions first caught the attention of the scientific community in the 1860s, when Paul Broca, a French neurologist and anthropologist, provided evidence from numerous case studies that the left hemisphere, but not the right, was critical in language processing. The imagination of the scientific community may have been captured by Broca's findings in part because a hot topic of scientific inquiry in the late nineteenth century was the relationship between brain anatomy and mental function. Broca's discovery was sparked by a patient he met on his rounds who had an unusual syndrome. The man could utter only the syllable "tan," yet, because he could follow simple verbal commands, it was clear he could understand language. His problem was specific to speech output in that he did not exhibit paralysis of the vocal musculature or the vocal tract. When the man died relatively soon thereafter, Broca autopsied his brain and noticed that a specific region of the left hemisphere was damaged. Broca then proceeded to accumulate a small series of brains from individuals who had the same type of language problem. He noticed that in each case the damage was restricted to the same brain region, but more significant, it was always located in the left hemisphere. Furthermore, individuals with damage to the analogous area of the right hemisphere displayed no difficulties in language.

The importance of the left hemisphere for language processing was confirmed by other neurologists. Karl Wernicke noticed that damage to yet another region of the left hemisphere caused the converse syndrome of that discovered by Broca. In this syndrome, individuals lose almost all ability to comprehend language, although they retain their ability to speak fluently (even though what they say makes little or no sense). Like Broca, he found that this syndrome occurred only after left-hemisphere damage.

By the end of the 1860s, the English neurologist John Hughlings Jackson had introduced the idea of **cerebral dominance** (although he had not named it as such), which is the concept that one hemisphere dominates or leads mental function. At that time language was considered to be the quintessential mental act (following the logic that language equals thought). As a result, the left hemisphere came to be viewed as the dominant hemisphere, and even today you may find a research article in which the right hemisphere is referred to as the "nondominant hemisphere." Although Jackson documented the deficits that occur after right-hemisphere damage in the late 1800s, these findings were generally ignored. The prevailing thought was that the right hemisphere was important only for receiving sensory information from the left side of space and for controlling motor movement of the left half of the body. In this view, the right hemisphere was like a spare tire, available in case the left hemisphere sustained damage, but having few functions of its own (see Springer & Deutsch, 1993, for a discussion of the history of these ideas).

Building on a groundwork laid in the 1930s, research in the late 1950s and early 1960s performed around the globe dramatically changed scientists' conceptions of the functioning of the hemispheres, revealing each to have its own specialization. For example, studies performed by Brenda Milner and colleagues at the Montreal Neurological Institute demonstrated that the surgical removal of temporal regions of the right hemisphere for the relief of epilepsy did have consequences, such as disrupting memory for unfamiliar faces and other stimuli that could not be easily named (e.g., B. Milner, 1968). Other evidence for the role of the right hemisphere in specific tasks was provided by research performed by Henri Hécaen and colleagues in France (e.g., Hécaen, 1962) and by Arthur Benton and colleagues in the United States (e.g., A. L. Benton, 1969). Probably the most dramatic demonstration of differences in function between the hemispheres, however, came from the research of Roger Sperry and associates at the California Institute of Technology when they tested the competency of each hemisphere in a unique set of patients (e.g., Sperry, 1974). The findings from this research were so definitive and compelling that they were cited as part of the reason that Sperry was awarded the Nobel Prize for Physiology and Medicine in 1981. We turn next to this body of research.

Studies of Patients with Split-Brain Syndrome

Sperry came to demonstrate the distinct specializations of each cerebral hemisphere because he had been attempting to elucidate the function of the **corpus callosum,** the massive neural tract of more than 250 million nerve fibers that connects the hemispheres. While studying this structure in cats and monkeys, he found it to be critical in the transfer of information between the hemispheres of the brain. Around the same time, the neurosurgeons Joseph Bogen and Philip Vogel were severing the corpus callosum in a small group of people for a different reason—to control intractable epileptic seizures. These seizures did not diminish with anticonvulsant medication and were so frequent and severe as to make any semblance of a normal life impossible, and in some cases, had life-threatening consequences. The surgical procedure performed by Bogen and Vogel became known as the **split-brain procedure** because it severed the primary route by which the left and right cerebral hemispheres interact, thereby splitting the brain in half. This procedure is also sometimes referred to as *commissurotomy* because it severs the corpus callosum, one of the brain's *commissures* (brain structures that connect the hemispheres). Figure 4.2 illustrates the nature of the split-brain procedure.

When the callosum is intact, the hemispheres can coordinate their processing, shuttling information back and forth with great rapidity (in $\leq$ 20 ms) over millions of nerve fibers. However, with the callosum severed, information initially directed to one hemisphere cannot be sent to the other; essentially, the information is trapped within a hemisphere. Using specific techniques that take advantage of the neuroanatomy of the human nervous system, Sperry and colleagues were able to direct information to only one hemisphere. Since commissurotomy isolated that information to a single hemisphere, these researchers then could assess each hemisphere's individual competency to process such information.

• *BASIC FINDINGS* •

Because the observations of Broca and subsequent neurologists implicated the left hemisphere as dominant for speech output, one of Sperry and colleagues' first goals was to determine lateralization of speech output in the patients with the split-brain syndrome. To do so, these researchers asked the patients to feel objects with just one hand, either the left or the right. The objects were hidden from view so that the only source of information about them was tactile. Under this procedure, objects felt by a given hand are perceived exclusively by the contralateral hemisphere. Thus, objects felt by the right hand of a patient with split-brain syndrome would be perceived only by the left hemisphere and those felt by the left hand would be perceived only by the right hemisphere.

The patients were able to name the objects placed in the right hand but not those placed in the left. At this point, the researchers were faced with two possible explanations for their results. One was that the right hemisphere was indeed a stupid spare tire with little knowledge of the world, unable to identify even simple objects. The other was that, as Broca suggested 100 years earlier, only the left hemisphere can control speech output. When asked about the object in the left hand, the right hemisphere, which had felt the object, would be unable to reply because it is incapable of speaking. The speaking left hemisphere would respond appropriately by saying that it didn't know what the object was because it hadn't perceived it.

To distinguish between these possibilities, the researchers changed the task so that the patient had to demonstrate the correct use of familiar objects,

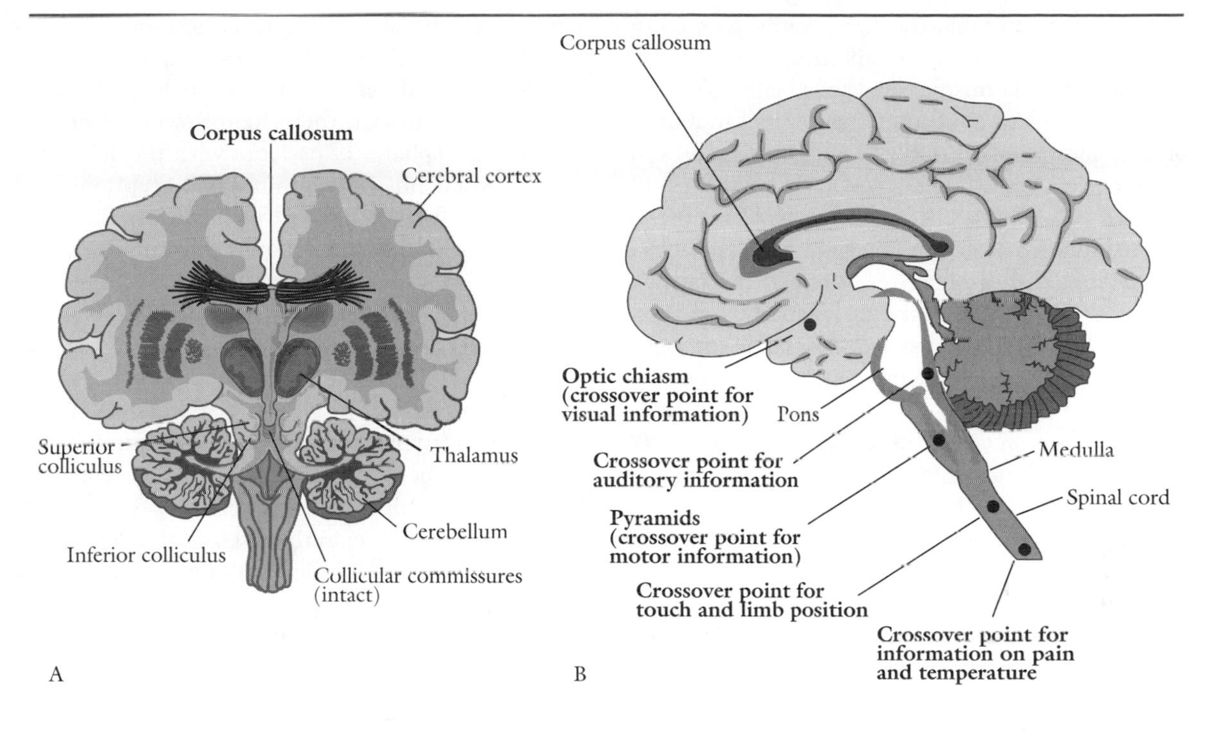

FIGURE 4.2 Split-brain procedure. (A) In this procedure, the hemispheres of the brain are separated, mainly by cutting the corpus callosum. With this pathway severed, information from one cerebral hemisphere cannot be transferred to the other. (B) The surgery does not affect the crossover of sensory and motor information from one side of the body to the opposite side of the brain because these crossovers occur before information reaches the cerebral cortex. Crossover points are noted by blue circles.

such as pencils, cigarettes, and drinking glasses. If the right hemisphere does know about the world but is merely mute, it should be able to demonstrate correctly the use of objects placed in the left hand, which it controls. In contrast, if the right hemisphere is only a spare tire, it should be dumbfounded when asked how to use the object. The researchers found that objects placed in the left hand could be used correctly, an indication that the right hemisphere does have knowledge about the world (Gazzaniga, Bogen, & Sperry, 1962).

Although the right hemisphere has been revealed to be much more than a spare tire, its linguistic capacity is somewhat limited, the exact degree of limitation remaining an issue of some debate (see, for example, the contrasting viewpoints of Gazzaniga, 1983a,b, vs. Levy, 1983, and E. Zaidel, 1983b). First, as we've already learned, the right hemisphere cannot control speech output. Second, it cannot understand complicated grammatical constructions, such as long, nonredundant sentences in which word order is important (e.g., "The dog that the cat chased ran under the table behind the garage that had been condemned by the sheriff last week") (E. Zaidel, 1978). Rather, its grammatical abilities are limited to simple distinctions (e.g., differentiating between "The boy went to the store" vs. "The boy did not go to the store"), and its vocabulary is limited to concrete words (that is, words that represent real objects or actions in the world) (e.g., E. Zaidel, 1990). Finally, it seems unable to break words down into their constituent sounds, a task known as *phonologic processing,* which is required to determine whether two words rhyme (e.g., Levy & Trevarthen, 1977).

Because the right hemisphere's language was revealed to be relatively poor in the patients with the split-brain syndrome, researchers began to focus their attention on what the right hemisphere *could* do. As they performed more experiments, they found that the right hemisphere excelled at tasks that could be described as spatial or nonverbal in nature. For example, when given the Block Design subtest of the Wechsler Adult Intelligence Scale—III (WAIS-III) (see page 105, Chapter 3), in which blocks must be arranged to form a pattern, the right hand performed in a hapless and disorganized manner. In contrast, the left hand performed the task rapidly and accurately. In addition, the left hand, but not the right, could depict three-dimensional structures in a two-dimensional plane, such as is required when a cube must be drawn on a piece of paper (Gazzaniga, 1970). On the basis of such findings, some researchers suggested that the right hemisphere was specialized for manipulative or motor aspects of spatial processing (Gazzaniga & LeDoux, 1978).

However, other studies revealed that the right hemisphere was superior on spatial tasks even when no manual manipulation was required. In a series of studies, patients with the split-brain syndrome were asked to view chimeric figures (i.e., figures composed of two different objects, such as those in Figure 4.3). Although these figures seem strange to us, the hemispheres of patients with the split-brain syndrome do not have a similar perception. Each hemisphere perceptually "fills in" the half-face. Because the hemispheres cannot communicate, they do not realize that they are viewing different faces.

Next, the researchers tested each hemisphere's competence by asking participants to use the contralateral hand to point to the object that was just viewed, precluding the need for manual manipulation. When a left-hand response was required, the right hemisphere, which controls the left hand, pointed with a high degree of accuracy to the face it had just seen, the one in the left visual field (LVF). In contrast, when the left hemisphere was required to respond (either through pointing with the right hand or a vocal response), performance was much poorer. This pattern was found not only for real-world

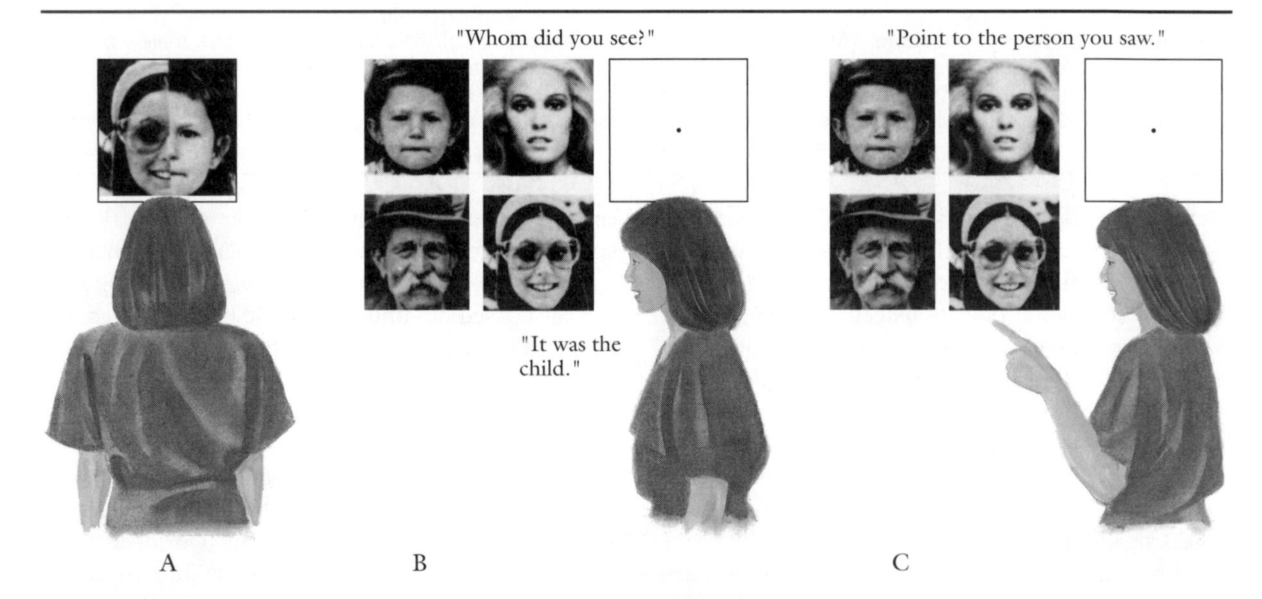

FIGURE 4.3 Examining the competency of each hemisphere in a patient with split-brain syndrome. (A) An example of a chimeric stimulus, composed of two half-faces, used with patients with split-brain syndrome. (B) When asked to indicate verbally which face was seen (a task under control of the left hemisphere), the patient names the child, whose picture was located in the right visual field. In such cases, accuracy is not high. (C) When asked to use the left hand to point to the face that was seen (a task under control of the right hemisphere), the patient points to the picture that was in the left visual field. Under these conditions, accuracy is higher, a finding that indicates a right-hemisphere superiority for face-recognition processing.

objects, such as faces, but also for abstract forms (Levy, Trevarthen, & Sperry, 1972). Therefore, the results of research on patients with the split-brain syndrome demonstrated the complementarity of the hemispheres for different aspects of mental functioning. The left is superior at processing verbal material, but the right has expertise in the spatial domain.

• *CAVEATS IN INTERPRETATION* •

Although studies of patients with the split-brain syndrome provide fascinating, compelling, and dramatic data, we must keep certain caveats in mind when interpreting these results. One potential problem is that the brains of these patients may not be typical. Their brain organization may be unusual as a result of their long-standing history of epileptic seizures. Furthermore, to sever the corpus callosum, which is located deep within the longitudinal fissure (see Figure 4.2), the surgeon must *retract* (pull back) the hemispheres, which provides the opportunity for damage to regions other than the callosum.

A second set of problems arises because the population of patients who have been extensively tested is small, only about five to seven (most individuals who undergo split-brain surgery have IQs so low as to preclude them from participating in research studies). Usually, no more than two or three individuals are included in a single study (see page 68 in the chapter on research methods for a discussion on the potential problems in studies with so few patients). Further compounding this problem, results from these patients can somctimes be difficult to interpret because different patients may exhibit distinct patterns of performance. For example, the patients vary not only in the degree to which their hemispheres truly act independently of each other (Sergent, 1990), but also in the competency of the right hemisphere for language (Sidtis et al., 1981). Hence, we need to be careful not to overgeneralize when drawing conclusions from the results of studies of patients with the split-brain syndrome.

Despite the issues just raised, some striking and consistent results observed with these patients have clearly demonstrated hemispheric specialization of function. Research with these patients was, and remains, very important, because it provides a means of examining hemispheric differences in a relatively intact, but isolated, hemisphere (see Reuter-Lorenz and Miller, 1998, for a recent appraisal of the role of split-brain research in cognitive neuroscience). In contrast, observing patients whose damage is restricted to a single hemisphere, a popular approach for determining hemispheric asymmetries, has the same difficulties as any other study involving the lesion method (see page 64 in the chapter on research methods): It cannot reveal how an intact hemisphere functions, but rather allows us to observe only how the rest of the brain functions when portions of one hemisphere are damaged. Because studies of patients with split-brain syndrome provide information on the functioning of a reasonably intact hemisphere, they continue to be a powerful tool in our attempts to understand asymmetry of function in the human brain.

Research with Individuals with Lateralized Lesions

While dramatic demonstrations of lateralization of function were being provided by split-brain research, studies with other neurological patients were also revealing the distinct capabilities of the hemispheres. Although scientists had known for some time that left-hemisphere lesions compromise language functioning, especially speech output, other methods provided converging evidence. One such method is the **Wada technique,** used to determine which hemisphere is responsible for speech output in patients about to undergo tissue removal to control epileptic seizures. Although the left hemisphere is almost always dominant (except in left-handers), the surgeon wants to know unequivocally which hemisphere is dominant for speech before beginning surgery. In this technique, a barbiturate (typically sodium amobarbital) is injected into one of the carotid arteries (which lead from the heart to the brain). Because the blood supply to the brain is unilateral, the barbiturate anesthetizes only one hemisphere. The onset of the barbiturate's effect can be readily detected because shortly after injection it causes paralysis on the contralateral side of the body. At this point, the neuropsychologist determines whether the individual can speak. If the person is mute, the anesthetized hemisphere is inferred to be responsible for speech output. This determination must be made quickly, in about five minutes, because after that point the barbiturate reaches the other side of the brain and the individual becomes groggy. Typically, the procedure is repeated some time later, ideally the next day, except then the opposite hemisphere is anesthetized to determine its contribution, if any, to speech output (Grote, Wierenga, & Smith, 1999). Research with this method has revealed that the left hemisphere is dominant for speech in 95% of right-handers, a finding consistent with those observed in patients who sustain unilateral brain damage (Rasmussen & Milner, 1977b). Because the Wada test is very invasive, much work is being performed to determine whether fMRI can be used to localize critical language areas prior to neurosurgery (e.g., Rutten et al., 2002).

In addition to confirming the role of the left hemisphere in language functions, studies of patients with lateralized brain damage have also demonstrated that right-hemisphere lesions have different consequences than left-hemisphere lesions. Whereas left-hemisphere lesions disrupt language-related processing, right-hemisphere lesions disrupt many spatial and visuospatial abilities. For example, individuals with right-hemisphere damage are poor at making judgments about line orientation (A. L. Benton, Hannay, & Varney, 1975), have difficulty recognizing objects that are not in a standard or canonical form (Warrington & Taylor, 1973), and are poor at distinguishing between faces that were previously viewed and those that were not (Yin, 1970). In addition, patients with right-hemisphere damage have difficulty distinguishing different pitches of sound or tones of voice (E. D. Ross, 1981) and cannot interpret the emotional expression of faces (Bowers, Bauer, Coslett, & Heilman, 1985). This body of research revealed the right hemisphere to have cognitive abilities equally sophisticated to those of the left hemisphere, albeit in nonverbal, nonlinguistic domains.

Research with Neurologically Intact Individuals

Examination of hemispheric differences in neurologically intact individuals is relatively easy because in most sensory modalities, information from one sensory half-world is directed initially to the primary sensory regions of the opposite hemisphere. The large body of evidence garnered in this manner provides a third converging approach that illustrates the specialization of the hemispheres for different cognitive and emotional processes. Before discussing this evidence further, though, we first turn to a discussion of the methods used to investigate lateralization of function.

• *METHODS* •

Lateralization of function is mainly investigated in the visual, auditory, and tactile modalities. Measuring hemispheric differences in the visual modality takes advantage of the arrangement of the neural pathways from the eye to the brain (see Figure 1.15). Most critical is the fact that information in the right visual field (RVF) projects exclusively to the primary visual cortex of the left hemisphere. Conversely, information presented in the LVF projects exclusively to the primary visual cortex of the right hemisphere. Studies that take advantage of this neural arrangement involve presenting information separately in each visual field, a technique often referred to as the **divided visual field technique.**

In divided visual field studies, two methods of presentation can be used: bilateral and unilateral. In **bilateral presentation,** two items are presented, one in each visual field. In **unilateral presentation,** a single item is presented entirely within one visual field. Regardless of the type of presentation, we infer how well each hemisphere can process information by comparing performance for items presented in the RVF versus the LVF. Performance is generally measured by either the speed or the accuracy of responding. For example, if the recall of information is, on average, superior when presented in the RVF than when presented in the LVF, the left hemisphere is assumed to be specialized for processing that type of information. In contrast, an advantage for information presented in the LVF is considered indicative of right-hemisphere specialization. Note that what we actually observe is an asymmetry in the perception of information depending on which part of the sensory system we stimulate. Hence, these differences in performance are often referred to as **perceptual asymmetries.** Because different parts of the sensory system project to different hemispheres, the perceptual asymmetries are then interpreted as reflecting hemispheric differences.

One constraint imposed by the divided visual field technique is that information must be presented for 200 ms (one-fifth of a second) or less because this is the amount of time required to move the eyes from one position to another. Only if the eyes are maintaining fixation on a single point will the region of space that constitutes the RVF and the LVF stay static. If an individual's eyes move to a new fixation point, different information will fall into each visual field and thus different information will be projected to each hemisphere than was intended by the researcher. By having a person fixate on a central point and by precluding eye movements, the investigator can ensure that information presented in the RVF will project initially to the left hemisphere and that information presented in the LVF will project initially to the right hemisphere. To ensure that the information presented is initially received by only one hemisphere, the researcher usually positions stimuli somewhat lateral (at least 1 or 2 degrees) from midline so that they fall exclusively within one visual field even if the individual is slightly off fixation. (The divided visual field technique is also sometimes referred to as *tachistoscopic presentation*, a term dating from the days before personal computers, when a machine called a *tachistoscope* and timers were used to control precisely the temporal duration of displays.)

Similar logic can be applied to investigate hemispheric differences in the somatosensory modality. In **dichaptic presentation,** a person is asked first to feel two items simultaneously, one in each hand, and then to identify these items in some manner (e.g., Witelson, 1974). Often, the items are behind a screen or the person is blindfolded so that information can be obtained only from the somatosensory modality and not other modalities (e.g., through vision). Because tactile information from the left side of the body projects to the primary somatosensory region of the right hemisphere, an advantage in processing information presented to the left hand is generally interpreted as a right-hemisphere superiority for the task. Likewise, an advantage in processing information presented to the right hand is generally interpreted as a left-hemisphere superiority for the task.

Examining hemispheric differences in the auditory modality is a bit more complicated. As you may remember from the introductory chapter, information from each ear connects both to the primary auditory cortex of the contralateral hemisphere and to the primary auditory cortex of the ipsilateral hemisphere. If each ear connects to both hemispheres, how are we to interpret differences in the ability to report information from each ear? Under special conditions known as **dichotic presentation** the situation becomes simplified. In dichotic presentation, *different* information is presented simultaneously to each ear so that each hemisphere receives two competing pieces of information, one from the ipsilateral ear and one from the contralateral ear. Because of this competition, information traveling to a hemisphere from the ipsilateral ear is suppressed relative to information from the contralateral ear (B. Milner, Taylor, & Sperry, 1968). Thus, information from the right ear is processed almost entirely by the left hemisphere and information from the left ear is processed almost entirely by the right hemisphere (Figure 4.4). In dichotic studies, individuals are typically asked to report what they heard in one ear or what they heard in both ears. In other situations, they are asked to monitor for a specific target item and to press a button as soon as they hear it.

• *RESEARCH FINDINGS* •

Empirical studies examining perceptual asymmetries have served as fertile ground for revealing differences in the processing capabilities of the hemispheres. Because these studies are relatively simple to undertake and can be performed on a variety of neurologically intact individuals, thousands of such studies have been performed. As a gross generalization, processing of verbal materials tends to be superior when directed initially to primary sensory regions of the left hemisphere. In contrast, nonverbal information tends to be processed better when directed initially to primary sensory regions of the right hemisphere. For example, in the visual modality, an RVF (or left-hemisphere) advantage is usually observed for words (e.g., S. C. Levine & Banich, 1982) and an LVF (or right-hemisphere) advantage for faces

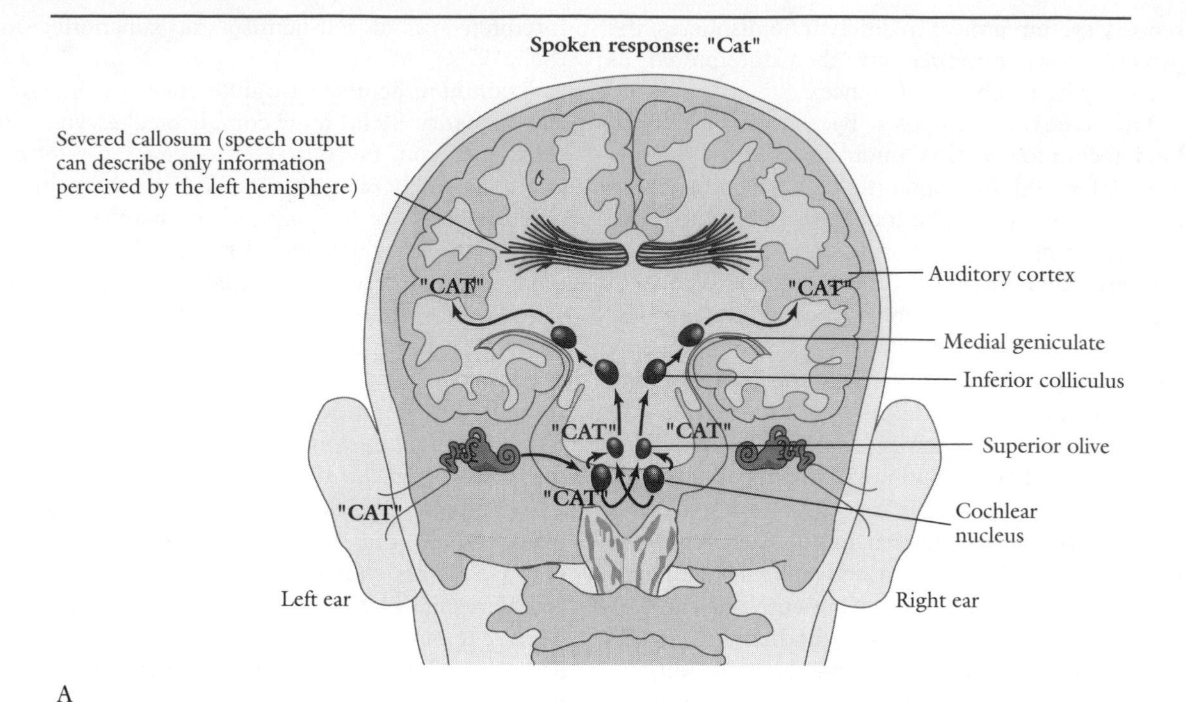

FIGURE 4.4 Ipsilateral suppression in the dichotic listening technique. (A) Under conditions of monaural stimulation (a stimulus presented to one ear), the left hemisphere of a patient with split-brain syndrome can name, with a high degree of accuracy, the word that was presented monaurally in the left ear. This ability must rely on the use of ipsilateral auditory fibers from the left ear to the left hemisphere because only the left hemisphere can produce speech output, and information received by the right hemisphere cannot be transferred to the left.

(S. C. Levine, Banich, & Koch-Weser, 1988). In the tactile modality, a right-hand advantage is found for identifying letters drawn on the palm (e.g., O'Boyle, Van Wyhe-Lawler, & Miller, 1987) and for identifying dichaptically presented letters made of sandpaper (Gibson & Bryden, 1983). In contrast, when individuals must feel two complex shapes simultaneously and match them to a visual array (e.g., Witelson, 1974) or otherwise identify them (e.g., Gibson & Bryden, 1983), a left-hand advantage is found. In the auditory modality, the report of or response to words (e.g., Kimura, 1967) and other speech sounds (e.g., Studdert-Kennedy & Shankweiler, 1970) is more accurate or faster when the words or sounds are presented to the right ear than when they are presented to the left ear. In contrast, the report of or reactions to nonverbal material, such as animal noises, sounds in the environment (e.g., doors opening, train whistles), and musical tones, are better processed when the material is presented to the left ear (e.g., H. W. Gordon, 1980).

The advantage in performance generally observed under divided visual field, dichaptic, or dichotic conditions is on the order of a 10% difference in accuracy and usually between 20 ms and 100 ms in speed of response. Although these differences may seem small, they are actually impressive if you consider that they occur even though the hemispheres are connected by the 250 million nerve fibers of the corpus callosum. How do such perceptual asymmetries arise in neurologically intact individuals given the vast network of interconnections between the hemispheres? No single account is agreed upon, but researchers have a number of ideas.

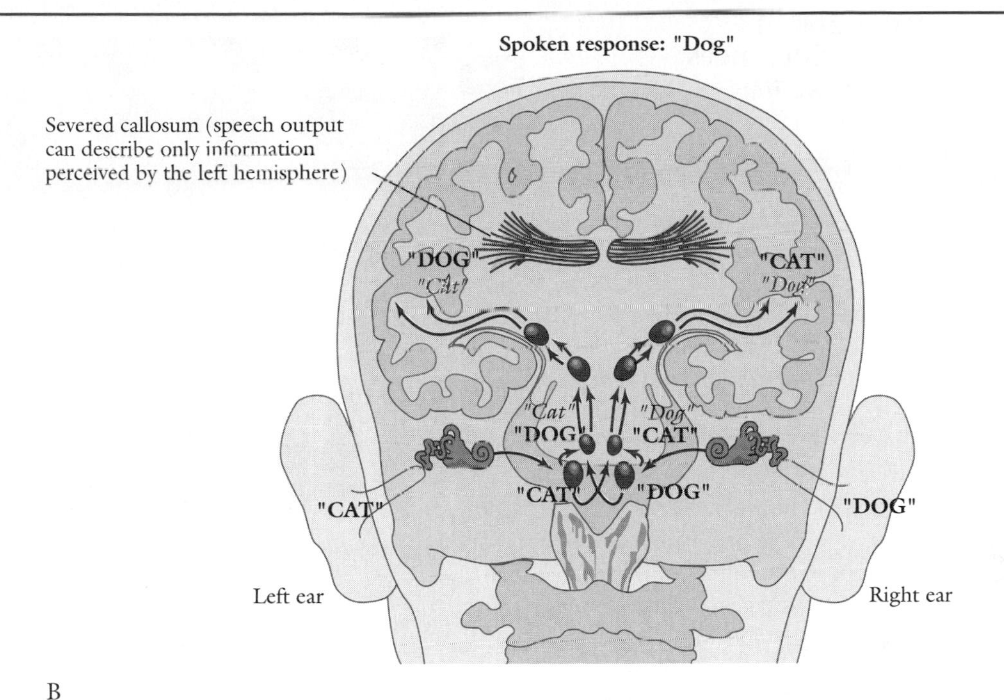

FIGURE 4.4 Continued (B) Under conditions of dichotic stimulation, the patient with split-brain syndrome cannot report both words. Only the word presented to the right ear, which projects contralaterally to the left hemisphere, can be reported with a high degree of accuracy. The word presented in the left ear is not reported because of the suppression of information carried through ipsilateral fibers. The fidelity of information at each brain region is noted by the font and case of the word. Words in capital letters indicate that the information is clear, whereas lowercase and italics indicate that the information is lost or compromised.

One idea, referred to as the **direct access theory,** assumes that the hemisphere receiving sensory information processes it. When information is received by the hemisphere less suited to a task, performance is poorer than if it is received by the hemisphere better suited to the task. Another idea, the **callosal relay model,** assumes that information received by the hemisphere less adept at a given task is transferred to the opposite hemisphere. This callosal transfer is believed to degrade the information and lead to poorer performance than if the information is received by the hemisphere more suited to the task (see E. Zaidel, 1983a, for a discussion of these issues).

A different type of model, known as the **activating-orienting model,** suggests that an attentional set or bias can contribute to perceptual asymmetries (Kinsbourne, 1975). According to this theory, engaging in a particular type of process (e.g., word recognition) causes greater activation in the hemisphere best suited to the task (e.g., the left hemisphere). This increased activity is thought to result in an attentional bias to the side of space contralateral to the more active hemisphere (i.e., the right side). As a result, perceptual information on that side of space is more salient, allowing it to be processed in a superior manner. Evidence for this model comes from studies in which larger visual field advantages are observed when tasks have just been preceded by a task that activates the same hemisphere rather than the opposite hemisphere (e.g., a larger LVF advantage is observed on a face task when preceded by a face task than when preceded by a word task) (Klein, Moscovitch, & Vigna, 1976).

Characterization of Hemisphere Differences

Until this point, we implied that the hemispheres are specialized for processing different types of material: verbal versus nonverbal. Yet the situation isn't quite so simple. In fact, a fair amount of debate has been generated regarding how to best characterize the differences in processing between the cerebral hemispheres. Some researchers posit that the hemispheres differ in their ability to process basic sensory features of information, and that these basic asymmetries in sensory processing underlie hemispheric differences for more complicated cognitive tasks. Another group of theorists suggests that the hemispheres differ not so much in *what* type of information they process, but rather in *how* they process information. These theorists suggest that the hemispheres have different modes of processing (e.g., holistic vs. piecemeal) and that certain materials or tasks are better handled by one mode than the other. We now examine these two classes of theories regarding hemispheric specialization.

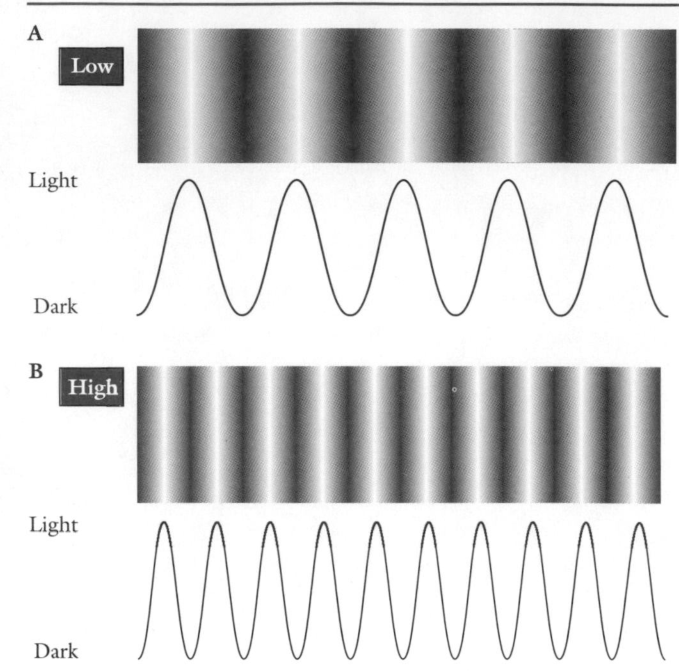

FIGURE 4.5 Information of varying spatial frequency. (A) Information of low spatial frequency. (B) Information of higher spatial frequency. As you can see, the change from light to dark occurs less often in A than in B.

Differences in Sensitivity to Particular Sensory Features

One group of theorists argues that the differences in hemispheric specialization arise early in processing, soon after receipt of sensory information, because the hemispheres differ in their ability to process basic sensory attributes of stimuli. One influential theory of this sort, the **spatial frequency hypothesis,** proposes that the hemispheres differ in their ability to process a particular attribute of visual information known as *spatial frequency* (e.g., Sergent, 1983). Visual information has a low spatial frequency if, over a given expanse of space, it oscillates slowly from black to white. In contrast, it has a high spatial frequency if information switches quickly from black to white. To obtain a better appreciation of visual information of high spatial frequency versus that of low spatial frequency, look at Figure 4.5. Visual information of low spatial frequency generally provides the broad outline of form without much detail. You can get a poor approximation of what low spatial frequency information is by squinting your eyes and looking at this page. Notice that you can perceive broad general forms but not details. Visual information of high spatial frequency provides the details.

Sergent's theory hypothesizes that the right hemisphere is more adept at processing low spatial frequency, whereas the left hemisphere is specialized for processing high spatial frequency. This distinction is somewhat akin to an earlier suggestion that in general the right hemisphere is specialized for coarse coding of information, whereas the left is specialized for fine coding of information (Semmes, 1968). To understand how differences in the processing of visual information of varying spatial frequencies might cause differences on more cognitively complicated tasks, let's consider the example of a face-processing task in which an individual decides whether two faces are identical. If the faces were to differ by only one feature, a left-hemisphere advantage would be observed, because detailed high spatial frequency information is required to differentiate between two similar faces. In contrast, if the faces were substantially different, a right-hemisphere advantage would emerge, because low spatial frequency information is best suited to determine whether the overall forms of the faces are identical (e.g., Sergent, 1985).

Results of investigations of the spatial frequency hypothesis have been equivocal; some, but certainly not all, studies have yielded results consistent with its predictions (see Christman, 1989, for a review). The discrepancies among some of these studies may have occurred because, as more recent research suggests, hemispheric differences are driven by the *relative,* rather than the *absolute,* spatial frequency of visual information. What is important, then, is not whether the spatial frequency of information is high or low on an absolute scale, but rather what the relative spatial frequency of information is within a given context (Kitterle, Hellige, & Christman, 1992).

These findings have been considered and expanded into a theory known as the *double filtering by frequency theory.* This theory posits that both hemispheres initially process all sensory information and do so symmetrically. However, after the task-relevant information has been identified, the hemispheres filter information differently. The filtering causes information of relatively higher spatial frequency to be preferentially processed by the left hemisphere and information of relatively lower spatial frequency to be processed by the right hemisphere (see Ivry & Robertson, 1998, for a book-length account and Robertson & Ivry, 2000, for a short, easily readable account of the highlights).

This theory is thought to apply to all sensory information regardless of modality, so here we will illustrate the idea using an experiment performed in the auditory modality (Ivry & Lebby, 1993). In this study, each participant decided whether a target tone was "higher" or "lower" than the average of all the tones within a set. In one set of trials, all the target items were of low frequency (e.g., 192–208 Hz) (Figure 4.6A). In another set of trials, all the target items were of high frequency (e.g., 1860–1940 Hz) (Figure 4.6B). If absolute frequency of information

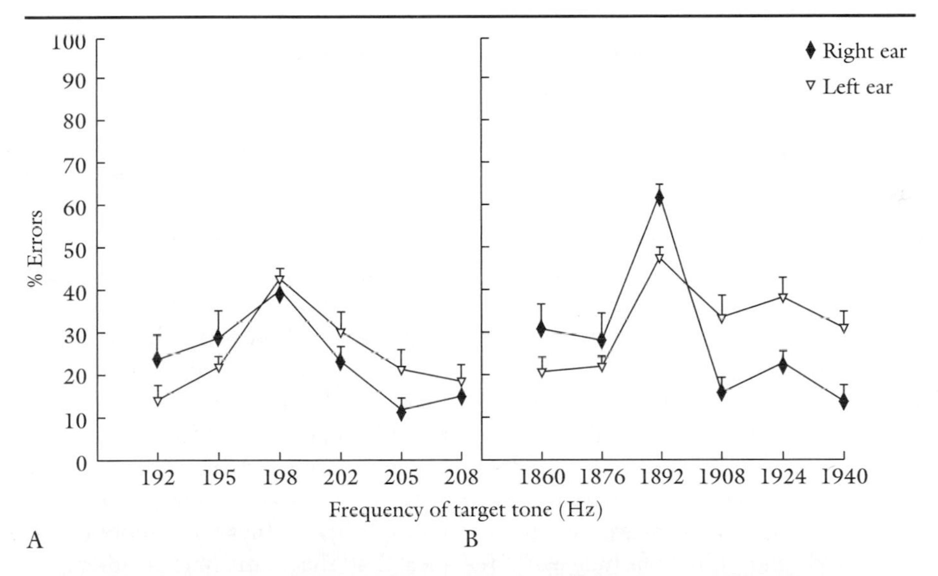

FIGURE 4.6 Hemispheric differences for the processing of different auditory frequencies. The percentage of errors in the tone-judgment task for the set of low-tone targets (left) and the set of high-tone targets (right). For relatively lower tones within both sets (192–198 Hz, and 1860–1892 Hz), fewer errors are made on left-ear trials (open inverted triangles) than on right-ear trials (solid diamonds). In contrast, for the relatively higher tones within each set (202–208 Hz, and 1908–1940 Hz), right-ear performance is superior. This pattern of performance indicates that the right hemisphere is specialized for processing information of relatively lower (rather than absolutely lower) frequency and the left for processing information of relatively higher frequency.

dictates hemispheric differences, a left-ear advantage (indicative of right-hemisphere superiority for the task) should be observed for detection of all target items (192–208 Hz) in the Low-Tone Set, and a right-ear advantage (indicative of left-hemisphere superiority) should be observed for all items (1860–1940 Hz) in the High-Tone Set. In contrast, if *relative* frequency is important, a different pattern should be observed: A left-ear advantage (indicative of right-hemisphere superiority) should be observed for low tones within *each* set (i.e., 192–198 Hz and 1860–1892 Hz), and a right-ear advantage should be found for the high tones within *each* set (i.e., 202–208 Hz and 1908–1940 Hz).

As we can see in Figure 4.6, the results are dictated by relative frequency rather than by absolute frequency. Within both the Low-Tone Set (Figure 4.6A) and the High-Tone Set (Figure 4.6B), a left-ear advantage is observed for lower frequencies and a right-ear advantage for the higher frequencies. Thus, the differences between the hemispheres appear not to be in what types of sensory information (e.g., high-frequency vs. low-frequency) are processed by each hemisphere but rather in what type of processing is performed on that sensory information (e.g., filtering of relatively high-frequency information vs. filtering of relatively low-frequency information).

Differences in Modes of Processing

Like the double filtering by frequency theory, other approaches to hemispheric differences also emphasize the differences in *how* the hemispheres process information rather than *what* kinds of information they each process (e.g., spatial vs. verbal). Although many dichotomies have been suggested to describe the differences between the hemispheres, they are well summed up by saying that the left hemisphere processes information in a piecemeal and analytic fashion with a special emphasis on temporal relationships, whereas the right hemisphere processes information in a gestalt and holistic fashion with a special emphasis on the spatial relationships.

The concept that the hemispheres are specialized for different modes of processing implies that both hemispheres can simultaneously contribute to performance. If only the left hemisphere processed verbal material and only the right processed nonverbal material, we would be left with a situation in which the right hemisphere would "take a nap" while we read and the left hemisphere would "snooze" while we tried to recognize a friend's face. Going around the world in such a half-brained manner doesn't seem, on the face of it, a good strategy. However, if each hemisphere can bring its own mode of processing to bear on any given task, having specialized hemispheres affords us two ways of examining the world at once. Even if one hemisphere is better than the other when tested head-to-head (no pun intended!), two modes of processing provide extra information than what could be obtained from one perspective alone.

One of the first studies to illustrate clearly that the hemispheres differ in processing styles was performed with patients with the split-brain syndrome (Levy & C. W. Trevarthen, 1976). In this study, researchers presented the patients with chimeric figures, such as those in Figure 4.7, under two conditions. In one condition, the patients were told to point to the item that "looks like" the one just seen. In the other, they were told to point to the item that "goes with" what was just seen. What was critically important in this study was that the stimuli were *identical* in the two conditions. All that varied was the nature of the decision, which, as it turns out, had profound effects on the patients' behavior. If they were told to point to the item that "looks like" what they just saw, they made a match on the basis of what had been presented in the LVF (viewed by the right hemisphere). However, given the same picture, but told to choose the item that "goes with" what they just saw, they made a match on the basis of what had been presented in the RVF (viewed by the left hemisphere). This experiment demonstrated that both hemispheres were capable of processing the information provided, so their differences were not adequately explained as a distinction between *what* types of information each could process. Rather, the findings were more consistent with the idea that the hemispheres differ in terms of *how* they process information, because the hemisphere that controlled the response varied depending on the task instructions.

Research with neurologically intact individuals has also demonstrated that the hemisphere most adept at processing can vary depending on the demands of the task, even when the stimulus remains the same. For example, remember that the

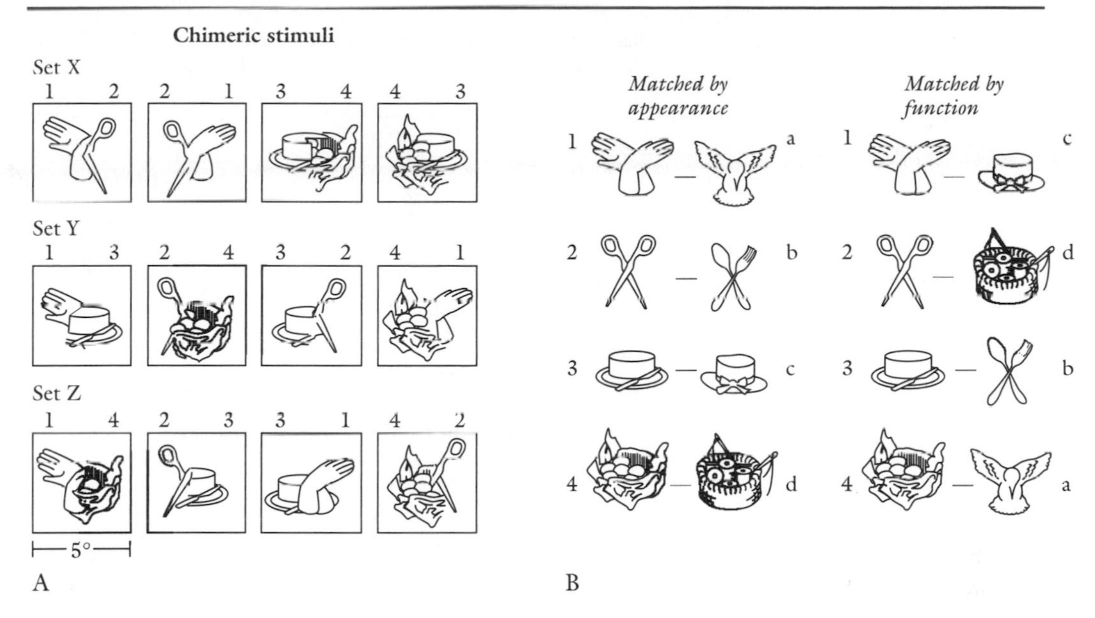

FIGURE 4.7 Demonstration of hemispheric specialization for different modes of processing. When patients with split-brain syndrome viewed these chimeric stimuli, they responded differently depending on whether they were instructed to match by appearance or by function. For example, look at the left-most stimulus in Set X. When instructed to match by appearance, the patient selected the dove (a) because it looks like the gloves (1) (which were viewed by the right hemisphere). However, when given the same stimulus but instructed to match by function, the patient chose the sewing basket (d) because it is similar in function to the scissors (2) (which were viewed by the left hemisphere).

right hemisphere is generally superior at deciding whether two faces represent the same person. However, if the faces differ by just one feature, such as the eyes, a left-hemisphere advantage is observed (Sergent, 1982a). We can interpret these results within theories of hemispheric specialization that emphasize differences in modes of processing by positing that a right-hemisphere advantage emerges for differentiating two distinct faces because this task can best be performed by a gestalt, or holistic, comparison between the faces. But when the faces differ by just one feature, the task can best be performed by paying attention to the details, a mode of processing at which the left hemisphere excels.

These differences in modes of processing between the hemispheres can also be observed by comparing the performance of patients with unilateral damage to the left hemisphere with that of patients with unilateral damage to the right hemisphere. For example, look at the figures in Figure 4.8, which are often referred to as *hierarchically organized figures.* After sustaining a right-hemisphere lesion, individuals have difficulty paying attention to the global form of the item (i.e., an *M* or a triangle) but have no difficulty paying attention to the local pieces or parts (i.e., the *Z*s or the rectangles). Conversely, after left-hemisphere damage, patients have difficulty paying attention to the parts (i.e., the *Z*s and the rectangles) but no difficulty with the global form (i.e., the *M* and the triangle) (for a review of this research, see Robertson & Lamb, 1991). Notice that a similar pattern is obtained regardless of the *type* of stimulus, either linguistic or nonlinguistic. As we can see, the hemispheres take complementary roles in processing. In this case, metaphorically, the right hemisphere pays attention to the forest while the left hemisphere pays attention to the trees.

In recent years it has become clear that both hemispheres contribute to performance on almost all tasks, albeit in different manners. Even those functions traditionally thought of as relying on one hemisphere, such as verbal abilities (which are typi-

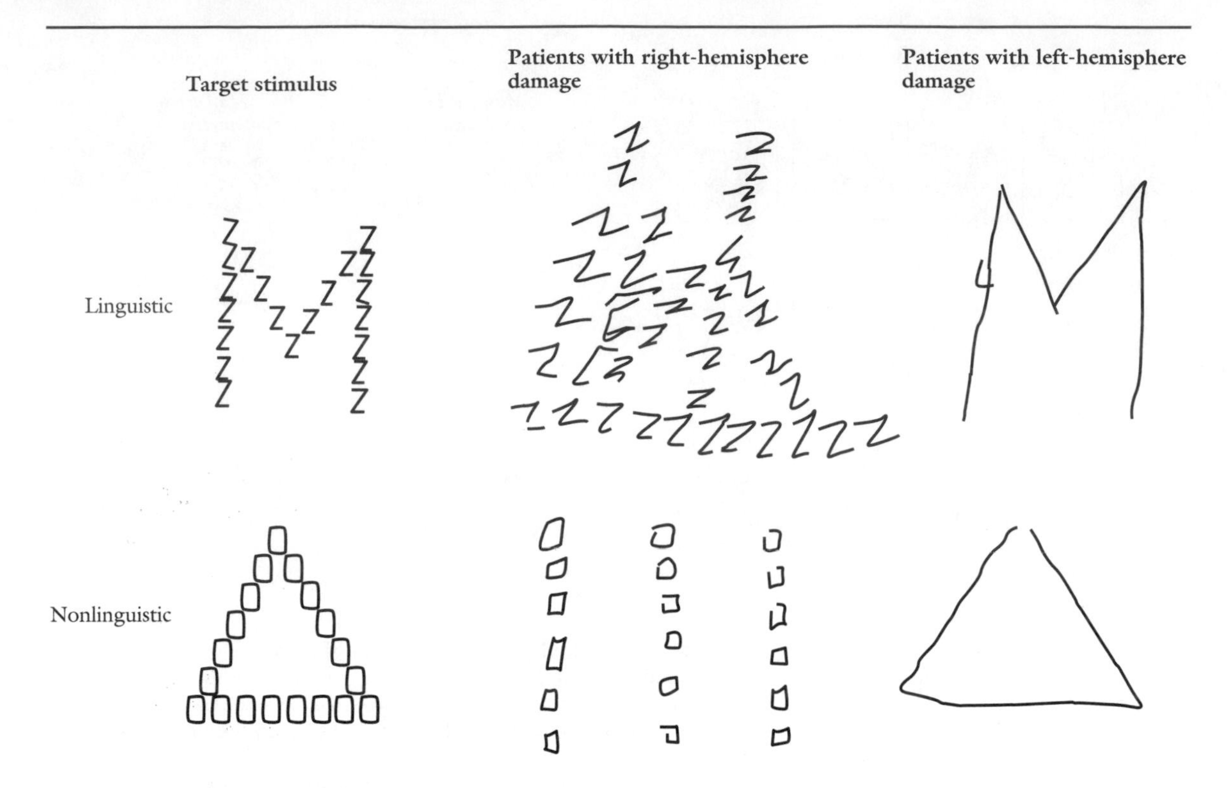

FIGURE 4.8 Hemispheric differences between global and local processing. Patients who sustain damage to the right hemisphere can correctly draw the local, or component, parts of the objects, as illustrated by the correct drawing of the Zs and the rectangles. However, the overall global form is incorrect; it is neither an M (in the case of the linguistic stimulus) nor a triangle (in the case of the nonlinguistic stimulus). In contrast, patients who sustain damage to the left hemisphere can correctly draw the global form of the items but not the local, or component, parts.

cally considered to rely on the left hemisphere) and spatial abilities (which are typically considered to rely on the right hemisphere) seem to rely on both hemispheres. For example, the processing of metaphor, the comprehension of a storyline, and the ability to make inferences across sentences, are all language-related processes that rely more on the right hemisphere (for an article-length discussion of the right hemisphere's contribution to language, see Beeman & Chiarello, 1998a; for a book-length discussion, see Beeman & Chiarello, 1998b). Similarly, the ability to discern top from bottom, right from left, and front from back are all spatial relations that rely more on the left hemisphere (Chabriss & Kosslyn, 1998). Now that we have a greater appreciation for how both hemispheres contribute to performing almost all cognitive tasks, we turn our attention to how the activities of each hemisphere are integrated.

 Integration of Information between the Hemispheres

Although our hemispheres are clearly specialized for different processes, our actions and everyday experiences reflect the unified processing of a single brain, not the output of two distinct minds. Thus, we must address the question of how the hemispheres manage to communicate with each other and coordinate processing to yield a seamless response. This issue has recently begun to receive more attention from researchers. In this section of the book, we focus on two aspects of this issue. First, we examine the properties of the main conduit through which the hemispheres communicate, the corpus callosum, and then we examine the functions served by interaction between the hemispheres.

Nature of Information Carried Over the Corpus Callosum

Although other subcortical commissures allow information to traverse from one side of the brain to the other, the corpus callosum is the main nerve-fiber tract whereby information is transferred between the cerebral hemispheres. Studies indicate that the callosum is a multifaceted structure with a specific anatomical and functional organization. Structurally, anterior sections of the callosum connect anterior sections of the brain, and posterior sections of the callosum connect posterior sections of the brain (Figure 4.9). Because of this organization, different types of information are transferred across different parts of the callosum depending on the brain regions connected by that section of the callosum. For example, information about motor signals is transferred in the middle of the callosum (known as the *body*), whereas visual information is transferred in the back of the callosum (a region known as the *splenium*).

Researchers can determine the nature of information transferred by the callosum by asking patients with the split-brain syndrome to compare items directed to different hemispheres. Because the callosum is severed in these patients, we can infer that if the patients are incapable of comparing two items, each of which is sent to a different hemisphere, such integration must rely on the callosum. If, however, the patients can make such a comparison, that comparison must rely on commissures other than the callosum, as those shown in Figure 4.10. Studies based on such logic have revealed that the detailed information required to uniquely identify an item can be transferred between the hemispheres only by the callosum. More general information can be transferred through subcortical commissures (see Gazzaniga, 2000, for a recent review of over 30 years of work on this issue). For example, researchers have reported that patients with the split-brain syndrome cannot determine whether two faces, each directed to a different hemisphere, are the same person (e.g.,

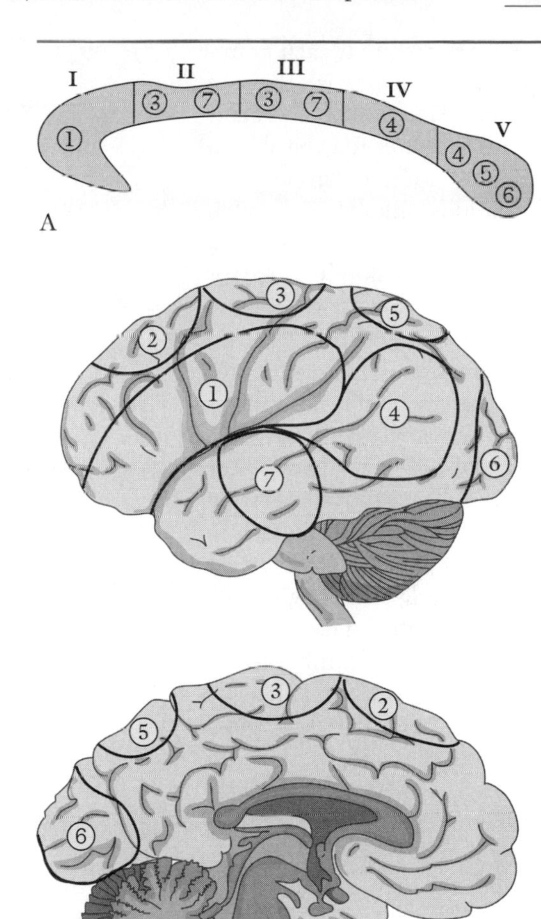

FIGURE 4.9 Different brain regions connected by different sections of the corpus callosum. (A) Diagram of the corpus callosum. The number shown in each section indicates the brain region depicted in B (top, left hemisphere, lateral view; bottom, left hemisphere, midsagittal view), which are connected through that section of the callosum. The connections occur in a topographic manner: Anterior sections (I) of the callosum connect anterior sections of the brain (Region 1, which is frontal), middle sections of the callosum (II and III) connect brain regions that are more central (Regions 3 and 7), and posterior sections of the callosum (IV and V) connect posterior sections of the brain (Regions 4, 5, and 6). Some brain regions, such as the frontal region labeled 2, have few, if any, callosal connections.

whether the face that each hemisphere is viewing is that of Madonna). However, the subcortical commissures may be able to transfer a limited amount of dichotomous information, such as whether the face is of a younger adult or an older one, or is a female and not a male (Sergent, 1990).

The subcortical commissures also appear to be able to transfer information about a person's own general emotional tone. For example, in one study, faces were shown only to the right hemisphere, and the left hemisphere had to attempt to signal its response to that face with a "thumbs-up" or "thumbs-down" sign made by the right hand. The left hemisphere could respond appropriately, giving the thumbs-down sign to pictures of people like Hitler and the thumbs-up sign to pictures of family members (Sperry, Zaidel, & Zaidel, 1979).

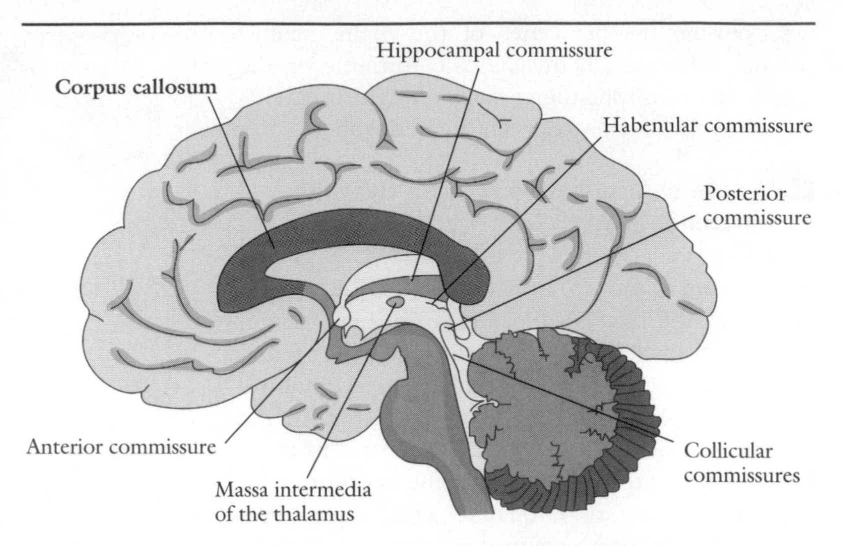

FIGURE 4.10 Position of the corpus callosum compared with the locations of other brain commissures. Information that allows an item to be uniquely identified can be transferred between the hemispheres only by the corpus callosum. Some evidence exists that other commissures can support the transfer of information coded in a dichotomous manner (e.g., old/young) or information about basic emotional tenor (e.g., positive/negative).

The conclusion from all these studies is that the corpus callosum is the major conduit for transfer of higher-order information between the hemispheres. Interhemispheric transfer of only basic and rudimentary information occurs through other brain commissures.

Functions of Interhemispheric Interaction

Part of the corpus callosum's function in interhemispheric interaction is to act much like an office messenger service, providing photocopies of each hemisphere's experience for the other and sending information that allows the hemispheres to coordinate processing. We first discuss this function of the callosum and then explore its additional roles, including that of helping the brain to deal with difficult or demanding tasks.

The callosum keeps the hemispheres aware of each other's doings by allowing for immediate transfer of information received by one hemisphere to the other. One way this fast transfer can be demonstrated is by examining event-related potentials (ERPs) to sensory stimuli. A response recorded over the hemisphere contralateral to presentation of a stimulus is followed only a few milliseconds later by a response over the other hemisphere (e.g., Saron & Davidson, 1989) (Figure 4.11). The difference in time between the peak of the ERP recorded over the hemisphere that received the information and the opposite hemisphere is often considered an estimate of callosal transfer time, which ranges from 5 ms to 20 ms in the average adult.

As we mentioned earlier when discussing the source of perceptual asymmetries, sometimes information acquired by means of callosal transfer may be somewhat "degraded" compared with the original, much as a photocopy is degraded compared with the original. Such degradation is most often observed in memory studies in which participants inspect a series of items, some of which appear in the RVF and some of which appear in the LVF. After a short delay (e.g., five minutes), the participant views a series of test items and decides, on each trial, whether the item was viewed in the inspection series. Some items in the test series are shown to the same hemisphere as in the inspection series (e.g., RVF/RVF), whereas others are shown to the hemisphere opposite that in the inspection series (e.g., RVF/LVF). In general, performance is superior when the item is initially and subsequently presented in the same visual field (not requiring interhemispheric interaction) than when the item is initially viewed by one hemisphere and subsequently seen by another (e.g., Banich & Shenker, 1994a). The inferior performance on these latter trials suggests that information received through callosal transfer can be poorer in quality than that received directly.

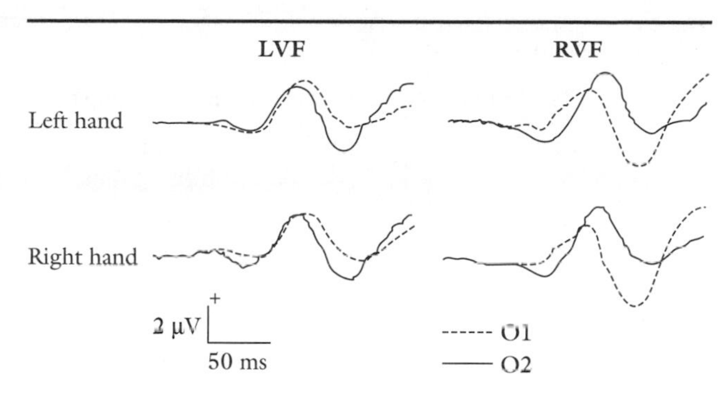

FIGURE 4.11 The rapid transfer of sensory information from one hemisphere to the other. Shown here are evoked responses to visual checkerboards presented either in the left visual field (LVF) or the right visual field (RVF). These responses were recorded at sites O_1 (occipital lobe, left hemisphere) and O_2 (occipital lobe, right hemisphere) (see Figure 3.10), when individuals were asked to respond to the presentation of the stimulus with either the left hand or the right hand. For LVF stimuli, the response occurred earlier over the right hemisphere (site O_2, solid line) and then later over the left hemisphere (site O_1, dotted-line) after the signal was transferred across the callosum. In contrast, for RVF stimuli, the response occurred earlier over the left hemisphere. The hand used to give the response did not influence the event-related potential (ERP) patterns because the electrodes were located over occipital regions and hence were detecting responses to visual information (as opposed to motor responses).

More recent evidence indicates that interaction between the hemispheres does not act merely as a message transfer service. It may, in fact, enhance the overall processing capacity of the brain under high-demand conditions. By high-demand conditions we mean (1) those in which processing is relatively complex and much information must be simultaneously processed within a short period or (2) those in which attentional demands are high—that is, when it is difficult to process the information that is critical for a task because of the necessity to ignore other information which is distracting or irrelevant (see Banich, 1998 for a review of the evidence). Figure 4.12 illustrates the types of experiment that demonstrate such a phenomenon.

To examine how interaction between the hemispheres influences the brain's capacity to process information, two types of trials are contrasted: those on which critical items, which have to be uniquely identified, are directed to opposite hemispheres and have to be compared (across-hemisphere trials), and those on which the critical items are directed initially to just one hemisphere (within-hemisphere trials). The only way the task can be accomplished on across-hemisphere trials is if the hemispheres interact, whereas on within-hemisphere trials no such interaction is necessary. When the task is relatively easy, such as making a simple decision about whether two items look physically identical (e.g., 2 and 2), processing is faster on within-hemisphere trials. Yet when the same type of stimuli are used but the task is more complicated, such as determining whether the sum of two numbers equals 10 or more (e.g., 2 and 8), an across-hemisphere advantage is observed. These more demanding tasks require not only that a physical form be recognized, but that additional processing be performed, such as adding one value to another (e.g., Banich & Belger, 1990; Belger & Banich, 1992, 1998).

Why is within-hemisphere processing faster and more efficient for easy tasks, but across-hemisphere processing superior for difficult ones? Researchers believe two different factors may be involved: the degree to which the processing capacity of a single hemisphere is taxed, and the communication "overhead costs" imposed by having to coordinate processing between the hemispheres. On easy tasks, the processing capability of a single hemisphere is not much taxed, so there is little advantage afforded by dividing processing across the hemispheres. Moreover, the time required to coordinate processing between the hemispheres entails a cost. Hence, a

Physical identity task

"Is the bottom item the same as either of the top two?"

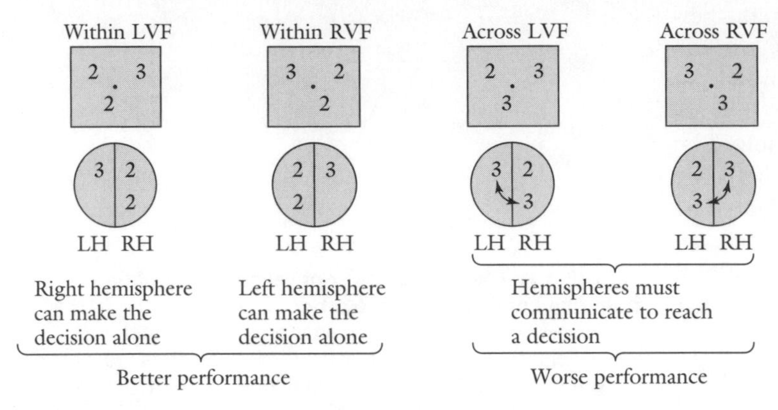

Ordinal task

"Does the bottom item plus one of the top two equal 10 or more?"

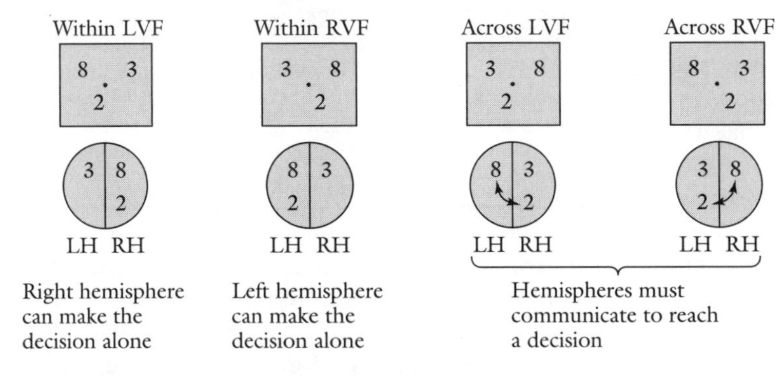

FIGURE 4.12 Example of interhemispheric interaction aiding in the performance of more demanding tasks. In the physical identity task, which is easier, individuals must simply decide whether the bottom item looks identical to either of the top two items, whereas in the more demanding ordinal task, individuals must not only identify the digits but also add them. Two types of trials are compared: those in which the critical items are directed initially to only one hemisphere and the correct decision can be reached without interhemispheric interaction (within-LVF and within-RVF trials) and those in which each hemisphere receives one of the critical digits and both hemispheres must communicate for the task to be performed correctly (across-RVF and across-LVF trials). Performance is better on within-hemisphere trials for the easier task, but requiring the hemispheres to interact, as is mandatory in across-hemisphere trials, leads to better performance on the more demanding task.

within-hemisphere advantage is observed. On hard tasks, however, the advantages afforded by a distribution of processing across the hemispheres is likely to outweigh the costs associated with recombining information. As a simple analogy, assume that you are taking a twentieth-century history class and your professor tells you to do your assignments in teams. If your task is easy, such as writing a one-paragraph summary of the major events of World War II, it will probably take you longer to communicate with a friend and work on the paragraph together than if you just sat down and wrote it yourself. But suppose you have the more difficult task of writing a 40-page term paper on the same topic. The time and effort required for coordinating with your friend and the subsequent time needed to meld your respective portions of the paper together will be small relative to the time you will save by having your friend research and write half the paper. Likewise, as tasks get harder, the brain seems to work better when both hemispheres contribute (see Banich & Brown, 1998, for a more detailed discussion of this model).

Recent evidence shows that the hemispheres actually couple and decouple their processing depending on the severity of task demands. To understand the logic behind the experiments demonstrating this phenomenon, refer back to Figure 4.12. You will notice that the typical conditions under which these types of experiments are performed are rather constrained. In the across-hemisphere condition the researcher designs the situation such that the hemispheres *must* communicate to perform the task, and the within-hemisphere condition is designed such that no communication is required. Although across-hemisphere processing is indeed advantageous under such conditions, it might be the case that the brain rarely if ever invokes across-hemisphere processing in everyday conditions to meet computational demands and does so in the laboratory only because those conditions have been artificially arranged by the researcher.

To see whether the hemispheres actually invoke across-hemisphere processing under difficult conditions, my colleagues and I designed "indeterminate" trial types, so called because in effect they provide the brain with the choice of using across-hemisphere or within-hemisphere processing to perform a task. We reasoned that if within-hemisphere processing is utilized under easy, or low-load, conditions, then the pattern of results on indeterminate trials under those conditions would be similar to results on within-hemisphere trials and distinct from those on across-hemisphere trials. Conversely, if under difficult, or high-load, conditions the brain uses across-hemisphere processing to respond to increased task demands, then the pattern of results on indeterminate trials would be similar to results on across-hemisphere trials and distinct from those on within-hemisphere trials. Such a pattern is exactly what we observed. Thus, we can conclude that the dynamic coupling and decoupling of the brain provides a flexible and adaptive system to meet the computational demands placed upon it.

A number of recent findings suggest that this hemispheric coupling is especially likely to occur in populations in which the capacity of a single hemisphere is less than that of a young, neurologically intact adult. For example, it has been shown that an across-hemisphere advantage emerges at a lower level of task difficulty in elderly adults as compared to young adults (Reuter-Lorenz et al., 1999). Young children are also more likely to show an across-hemisphere advantage for relatively easier "tasks" (Banich, Passarotti, & Janes, 2000). In both children and the elderly, a single hemisphere does not have as much processing capacity as it does in a young adult, so the hemispheres in these populations appear to couple sooner to meet computational demands.

Some diseases affect the integrity of the corpus callosum, such as multiple sclerosis or phenylketonuria, a genetic disorder we discuss in the chapter on development. We have speculated that the poor ability of the hemispheres to coordinate processing in these situations may account for some of the attentional difficulties observed in each of these disorders (see Banich, 2003).

What is clear from these and other studies is that one cannot think of the brain's activity as simply the sum of the processing of the two hemispheres. Rather, the sum of the parts is greater than the whole. The hemispheres act together as a unit in ways that one could not surmise from examining each hemisphere in isolation. For example, we have found that a manipulation of the font and case in which printed words are shown does not affect processing either on RVF trials, in which two items are directed to the left hemisphere, or on LVF trials, in which two items are directed to the right hemisphere. Changes in the font or case do, however, affect performance when both hemispheres are each given a word.

To summarize, the studies we have just discussed demonstrate that the brain's functioning does not depend exclusively on the specialization of the different regions of the brain, but also on the manner and degree in which they interact. The processing capacity of the brain is enhanced when the hemispheres interact, though only when task demands are high. This same interaction hinders performance when task demands are low.

Developmental Aspects of Hemispheric Specialization

Now that we have examined the manner in which the hemispheres are specialized and how they interact, we need to consider whether such patterns are observed from an early age or whether they change as a person develops. In his influential book, *Biological Foundations of Language,* Eric Lenneberg (1967) hypothesized that the hemispheres of the brain were equipotential at birth. That is, each hemisphere held the capacity to perform the same functions as the other. Lenneberg suggested that lateralization increased until puberty, after which it remained constant. He based this hypothesis, in part, on evidence that younger children who sustain left-hemisphere damage have less severe deficits than older children and adults with similar lesions. He posited that the recovery in younger children occurred because the right hemisphere, which he assumed was not yet fully specialized, took over language processing.

However, subsequent investigations suggest that the basic specializations of the hemispheres are in place at birth and that the degree of specialization is not modified much with development, except in cases of profound environmental influence such as occurs with traumatic injury to the brain. The evidence for the lack of an increase of lateralization of function comes from four major areas, each of which is briefly discussed next (one of the best early discussions of these issues is contained in Segalowitz & Gruber, 1977).

The first piece of evidence that a child's brain is lateralized at birth comes from neuroanatomy. As we discussed earlier in the chapter, neuroanatomical asymmetries exist in certain regions of the human brain; the most noteworthy is the asymmetry of the planum temporale. Because these neuroanatomical asymmetries have been related to asymmetries in function (e.g., Ratcliff, Dila, Taylor, & Milner, 1980), we would expect that if lateralization did develop with age, these neuroanatomical asymmetries would become more pronounced with age. However, this is not the case. The gyral patterns of the human brain are present before birth, sometime between the 10th and 31st gestational weeks, and the asymmetry in the planum temporale can be observed at this time (Wada, Clarke, & Hamm, 1975) and at birth (Witelson & Pallie, 1973). Thus, neuroanatomically, an infant's brain is already lateralized.

The second piece of evidence comes from studies examining the size of perceptual asymmetries in children. If asymmetry developed with age, the size of the left-hemisphere advantage for verbal material and the right-hemisphere advantage for spatial information would be smaller in younger children than in older children. Because many of the methods used to assess lateralization of function require a certain level of cognitive capacity (e.g., the ability to read), comparisons have focused on children of school age and older. A vast review of these studies revealed that the size of perceptual asymmetries does not increase with age, a finding suggesting that specialization of the brain does not increase between kindergarten and puberty (Witelsen, 1977).

The third piece of evidence that asymmetry does not increase with age comes from measurements of asymmetries in infants. Because standard techniques for assessing lateralization of function cannot be used owing to the limited cognitive repertoire of infants, clever techniques had to be utilized. Some researchers recorded the electrical brain activity of young infants while they were exposed to verbal materials, such as nonsense syllables (e.g., "pa" or "ba"), or to nonverbal materials, such as musical chords. In children as young as one week old, brain activation over the left hemisphere was greater for verbal material and over the right hemisphere was greater for nonverbal material (Best, Hoffman, & Glanville, 1982; D. L. Molfese, Freeman, & Palermo, 1975). In other cases, rather than recording brain waves, investigators determined whether the hemispheres are specialized at birth by relying on normal behaviors in the repertoire of babies, such as sucking on a pacifier. When young babies are interested in something, they suck at a fast rate, whereas when they get used to, or habituate to, a stimulus, their sucking rate decreases. Researchers found that when verbal material was played, the sucking rate was more affected by changes in sound in the right ear than in the left. In contrast, when nonverbal material was presented, the sucking rate was more affected by changes in the left ear (Bertoncini et al., 1989; Entus, 1977). Hence, the results of these studies suggest that the hemispheres of infants are as specialized as they are in older children.

The fourth piece of evidence comes from studies of young children who were born with one extremely small and malformed hemisphere. Because this malformed hemisphere often becomes a focus for epileptic activity, the prognosis for these children is better if the hemisphere is removed at birth, a procedure known as **hemispherectomy.** If the hemispheres are equipotent at birth, the performance of children with just a left hemisphere should be identical to those with just a right hemisphere, even years after the hemispherectomy. If the hemispheres are specialized at birth, however, performance should differ depending on which hemisphere was excised. On language tasks, most notably those in the domain of syntax, children who have only a left hemisphere outperform children with only a right hemisphere (Dennis & Kohn, 1975; Dennis & Whitaker, 1976). Likewise, children with only a left hemisphere do not acquire spatial skills to the degree of children with only a right hemisphere (Kohn & Dennis, 1974). Because the performance of children with only a left hemisphere differs from that of those with only a right hemisphere, the hemispheres are probably not equipotent at birth.

We should mention that these children do acquire some skills typically performed by the removed hemisphere, albeit not at a very high level. Children who have only a right hemisphere generally acquire the ability to speak and to comprehend language, but not to the degree of children with only a left hemisphere. Likewise, children with only a left hemisphere can acquire some spatial skills. Thus, we can conclude that each hemisphere is specialized for a particular type of processing and from birth provides the best neural substrate for its expression. However, under extreme circumstances, such as the removal of one hemisphere early in development, the opposite hemisphere is sufficiently *plastic* (capable of being shaped or formed) to take over those functions to at least a moderate degree. This extent of plasticity is lacking in adults (we discuss plasticity in more detail in the chapter called "Plasticity Across the Lifespan").

As the preceding sections of the chapter should have made clear, distinctions in processing that occur between the two hemispheres of the human brain are one of the fundamental aspects of the neurological organization of the brain. Throughout this book, we find that certain syndromes or cognitive dysfunctions are associated with damage to one hemisphere but not the other. We also observe hemispheric differences in processing for almost all the intellectual functions that we discuss in this book, including language, attention, emotion, and memory. We next turn our attention to the ways in which this basic pattern of brain organization may vary among individuals.

Individual Differences in Brain Organization

We have described the pattern of lateralization of function that is observed for most individuals, but this brain organization is not observed in *all* individuals. Some variability in brain organization appears to be linked to specific individual characteristics. In this section of the chapter, we discuss two of these factors: handedness and gender.

Handedness

Scientists have known for some time that the brain organization for left-handed individuals is distinct from that for right-handed individuals. Historically, left-handers have been believed to be different in a none-too-flattering way. For example, the Latin word for left is *sinister,* whereas the French word is *gauche.* In certain cultures such as in India, the left hand is never used to eat a meal (nor is it extended to someone for a handshake) because it is the hand reserved for bathroom functions. Even in the early to mid-twentieth century, individuals who wrote with their left hand were considered evil, stubborn, and defiant, and consequently they were often forced to write with the "correct" (right) hand. Left-handers often were subjected to such indignities because they compose a minority of the population, approximately 10%.

Although left-handers have been unfairly labeled with negative stereotypes, these people do appear to be different from right-handers, at least with regard to their brains. For right-handers, verbal processing is almost always lateralized to the left hemisphere and visuospatial processing to the right, but this is not the case for left-handers. Rather, their brain organization is heterogeneous, some being the same as that of right-handers (verbal, left hemisphere; visuospatial, right hemisphere), some the opposite (verbal, right hemisphere; visuospatial, left hemisphere), and some different (verbal and spatial processing performed by both hemispheres).

For example, whereas in 95% of right-handers, speech output is controlled by the left hemisphere and in 5% by the right, in 70% of left-handers speech is controlled by the left hemisphere, in 15% by the right, and in 15% by either hemisphere (Rasmussen & Milner, 1977b). Thus, when we average across all these types of left-handers, as a group they appear to be less lateralized than right-handers (e.g., Bryden, 1965). However, a given left-hander may not be less lateralized than a given right-hander.

Because on average left-handers are less lateralized than right-handers, the consequences of brain injury for a given function may not be as dire for left-handers. For example, after damage to the left hemisphere, left-handers may exhibit less severe language deficits than right-handers do, because language

IS BEING LEFT-HANDED A HEALTH HAZARD?

In 1991 two researchers made the provocative claim that left-handers are likely to have a shorter life span than right-handers (Coren & Halpern, 1991). By examining a 1979 yearbook providing information on professional baseball players, these investigators found that, on average, right-handers lived an extra eight months longer than left-handers. By examining death records in one community, the researchers found that the older the age of the deceased, the less likely the person was to be left-handed, so of the individuals who had died at an advanced age, few, if any, were left-handers.

The researchers proposed that left-handers might have an elevated death rate, in part because they are forced to live in a right-handed world, where everything from telephones to scissors are not made for them. Support for this conjecture came from findings that left-handers were 1.89 times more likely than right-handers to report injuries that required medical attention. However, the researchers also claimed that left-handedness may be a marker for a stressful birth and may be associated with a variety of maladies, including developmental disabilities, reduced immunological competence, and neural abnormalities, all of which could decrease life span.

As you can imagine, these findings sparked some interest not only among left-handers, who were concerned for personal reasons, but also among the research community in general. As with any new and intriguing finding, this result generated a large debate and a number of subsequent studies. Some researchers suggested that alternative explanations existed for the data (e.g., Harris, 1993a). For example, the individuals who went to school in the mid-1900s were likely to be under much less pressure to switch to being right-handed than those who attended school in the early 1900s. Thus, the decreased rate of left-handedness among the very elderly might not indicate that they had all died, but rather that they never existed because they had all been forced to become right-handers! Although the original researchers do not believe such an explanation, or other possible rationales (e.g., Halpern & Coren, 1993), there was debate over the interpretation of the original data (Harris, 1993b).

A number of researchers have examined the age of death in left-handers using a large number of very different samples. Although not all in agreement, most studies suggest that the death rates for left- and right-handers are similar. Such studies have included a reanalysis of the 1979 data on

output may be controlled by one hemisphere and language comprehension by the other (e.g., Naeser & Borod, 1986). Yet, such apparent sparing of function is misleading. Although right-handers often exhibit little to no visuospatial deficit after left-hemisphere damage, the deficit observed in left-handers usually is more severe (J. C. Borod, Carper, Naeser, & Goodglass, 1985).

These differences in lateralized functions between right- and left-handers may derive in part from differences in brain morphology between the groups. Anatomical asymmetries that are observed in the planum temporale, for example, are not as consistent or as large in groups of left-handers (e.g., Hochberg & LeMay, 1975). Furthermore, some researchers have suggested that physiological aspects of functioning may differ between left- and right-handers as well. One theory that has received much attention is that of Geschwind and Galaburda (1985a-c), which posits that the expression of patterns of lateralization (and left-handedness) are related to sex hormones, the immune system, and profiles of cognitive abilities. One of their specific suggestions is that left-handedness is associated with autoimmune disorders, in which the body incorrectly identifies its own tissue as foreign. However, evidence for this broad theory is sparse (see McManus & Bryden, 1991, for a thoughtful critique of the model; *Brain and Cognition, 26*(2), 1994, for a variety of commentaries on the theory; and Bryden, McManus, & Bulman-Fleming, 1995, for a response to those commentaries).

At this point, we know that the brains of left-handers differ from those of right-handers. However, the reasons for such variation and the ability to predict the pattern of brain organization for any given left-hander are beyond our grasp. Some have posited that handedness is a cultural phenomenon (see

baseball players (Fudin, Renninger, Lembessis, & Hirshon, 1993), an updated analysis of 5,441 players in a 1993 baseball yearbook (Hicks et al., 1994), data from death rates of Swedish soldiers (Persson & Allebeck, 1994), and death rates of individuals who play cricket (Aggleton, Bland, Kentridge, & Neave, 1994). These studies were all retrospective, meaning that the researcher looks at what has happened in the past. Obviously, in such a case, the researcher can't interview individuals about whether or not they were left-handed. In a prospective study, though, one can obtain that information and then determine the age of death as the population ages. This type of study gets around a number of issues that might obscure the true results, such as foggy memories by the relatives of the deceased regarding his or her handedness, a bias toward assuming that an individual was right-handed, and so forth. Prospective studies on the life span of left-handers paint a similar picture. Left-handers do not appear to die any earlier in studies that examined death rates for women in Iowa (Cerhan, Folsom, Potter, & Prineas, 1994), elderly adults in Boston (Salive, Guralnik, & Glynn, 1993) or Canada (Steenhuis, Østbye, & Walton, 2001).

So does that mean that left-handers can breathe a sigh of relief? Well, not exactly. There is some evidence of an elevated accident rate among left-handers (e.g., Merckelbach, Muris, & Kop, 1994), and among individuals who are neither strongly right-handed nor strongly left-handed (e.g., Hicks et al., 1993). College-age individuals who are not right-handed, either because they exhibit mixed-handedness or left-handedness, also have higher accident rates (Daniel & Yeo, 1994). Left-handed adolescents appear to be especially vulnerable. Reports from Scotland suggest that left-handed adolescent girls are more likely to sustain injuries, that the injuries are more severe, and more likely to require an overnight stay in a hospital (Wright, Williams, Currie, & Beattie, 1996). Among high-school athletes, left-handers are more likely to have sustained a injury, and to have required hospitalization or surgery for the injury (Graham & Cleveland, 1995). And driving a car may not be so safe either. Left-handed females are more likely to suffer traumatic brain injury, especially in automobile accidents (MacNiven, 1994), and left-handers are somewhat more likely to die in motor vehicle accidents (Persson & Allebeck, 1994). At present, it appears that although being left-handed may not doom one to a premature death, it may make life a little more hazardous. In any case, left-handers may still want to search out that pair of left-handed scissors: even if doing so doesn't reduce their chance of injury, it might make their lives a bit easier. ■

Provins, 1997) that arose from the fact that the right hand accrued symbolic significance in our human ancestors. This theory suggests that such symbolism predated tool usage and speech, and that lateralization for speech was driven asymmetrically so that the dominant hand would be controlled by the same hemisphere as that which controlled language output. This theory, however, does not explain how those cultural/symbolic biases arose in the first place, why this bias was retained over tens of thousands of years in disparate human populations, and why lateralization of function occurs in other species, such as apes, that do not have speech or symbolism.

Most researchers assume that there is at least some biological component to handedness. However, although various genetic models have been proposed, none seems to perfectly account for the distribution of right- and left-handed children, given different parent pairings (e.g., two right-handed parents, two left-handed parents, one right-handed and one left-handed parent). One prominent model (Annett, 1985, 1995) assumes that individuals either inherit from each parent what is called a right-shift (RS) gene, or they do not inherit such a gene. This right-shift gene shifts cerebral dominance for language to the left hemisphere, with the concomitant shift toward right-handedness. Individuals who inherit two RS genes will be likely to be strongly right-handed, those who inherit one RS gene will be less likely to be right-handed, and those who inherit no RS genes will exhibit a random distribution of handedness. A similar model assumes that handedness is controlled by two genetic codings, or alleles. One allele, D, specifies dextrality (right-handedness) and another, C, specifies chance (McManus, 1985). The D allele is similar to the RS gene, and the C allele is comparable to the *absence* of an RS gene, except that the C allelle must be specifically inherited. In general, these models assume that there is an intrinsic bias toward an asymmetry (in this case rightward), and the genes code for whether or not that bias is expressed. This idea is subtly different from the idea that genes code for the *direction* of handedness (left or right). Later, in the last section of the chapter, we consider why such an asymmetry may have evolved and how handedness might have derived from that.

Gender

One of the more heated debates about individual variations in brain organization revolves around differences between the genders. Not only is the question of whether gender is linked to neurological organization of interest, but also of interest is whether there are gender differences in cognitive function.

Much evidence in other species indicates that hormones influence brain organization and behavior for reproductive functioning (e.g., Breedlove, 1992). However, the degree to which these hormonal differences in other species influence nonreproductive aspects of behavior is less certain (e.g., van Haaren, van Hest, & Heinsbroek, 1990), although anatomical differences between the sexes have been noted in areas of the brain that are not associated with reproduction (for a review of these differences, see J. Juraska, 1991). Furthermore, in humans the degree to which hormones rather than patterns of learning and cultural influences contribute to mental function is difficult to determine. (For a critique of the overgeneralizations from animals to humans and an appraisal of some of the conclusions drawn about gender differences in lateralization of function, see Bleier, 1984, especially Chapter 4.)

For many years, researchers have debated whether lateralization of function is less pronounced in females than in males. If so, females would be more akin to left-handers and males more akin to right-handers. Although some researchers report such a pattern, others find no differences between men and women, and some even find women to be more lateralized (see McGlone, 1980, for the diverse spectrum of viewpoints on this issue). Two relatively recent reviews of hundreds of divided visual field studies (Hiscock et al., 1995) and dichotic listening studies (Hiscock et al., 1994) revealed that, depending on the criterion used as support for gender differences, between 5% and 15% of these studies yield results consistent with the idea that females are less lateralized than men. These authors concluded that although statistically the average degree of lateralization found for a group of men may differ from that found for a group of women, gender differences account for little of the variability (1–2%) in patterns of lateralization of function among individuals. Even if gender differences are observed, we must remember that they may result from other factors besides differences in neural organization. We will discuss the results of some sample studies in both the anatomical and behavioral domains to illustrate the factors that we must consider when interpreting gender differences.

One anatomical structure for which gender differences have been reported is the corpus callosum. A relatively consistent finding involves both sex and handedness: portions of the callosum are larger in non-right-handed men than in right-handed men, but the same is not true of women (e.g., Habib et al., 1991; Witelson & Goldsmith, 1991). This finding has been attributed to the effects of sex hormones (Witelson & Nowakowski, 1991). Furthermore, gender differences have been observed in the shape of the posterior section of the corpus callosum—the splenium—which is more bulbous in women than in men (e.g., L. S. Allen, Richey, Chai, & Gorski, 1991). However, the functional implications of this finding, if any, are unclear. (Originally, the callosum was reported to be larger in women than in men [deLacoste-Utamsing & Holloway, 1982], but this finding has not been replicated in numerous studies [e.g., Byne, Bleier, & Houston, 1988].)

One potential problem in interpreting any observed gender differences in anatomy is that they could be due to other factors that co-vary with gender, such as brain and body size. For example, because women are generally smaller than men, they generally have a smaller brain. Perhaps people with smaller brains have a more bulbously shaped splenium. Hence, a difference between men and women might be attributed to gender when it actually reflects differences between people with larger and smaller brains (regardless of gender). Consequently, investigating alternative explanations for gender differences and attempting to rule them out is extremely important. Accordingly, a researcher may want to compose a sample in which male and female individuals are matched for approximate overall brain size and then determine whether gender is related to the shape of the splenium.

Similar issues must be considered when we interpret the results of behavioral studies. For example, some functional brain imaging studies indicated differences between the genders in regional brain activation not only when the participants were at rest (R. C. Gur et al., 1995), but also during processing of linguistic information (Shaywitz et al., 1995; yet, also see a nonreplication of this effect in a larger sample—Frost et al., 1999). We must consider whether men and women may exhibit distinct patterns of brain activation on these tasks not because they have differentially organized brains, but because they use different strategies to perform a task (similar consideration should be given to gender differences in perceptual asymmetrics). If different cognitive or emotional strategies are employed, then a different pattern of brain activation will be observed. These differential strategies could arise from a large number of factors, including discrepant schooling, socialization, and other environmental factors. To definitively demonstrate that the genders have distinct brain organizations, researchers will have to show that dissimilar brain regions are activated in the genders even when both groups are using identical strategies to perform a task.

Because interpreting differences between the genders can be difficult, researchers have turned to other approaches to examine whether gender and hormonal influences on lateralized functioning exist. One approach is to examine differences in cognitive function during different phases of the menstrual cycle that vary in the levels of female hormones. For example, estrogen and progesterone are at high levels directly after ovulation and at low levels during menstruation. By testing women at different points in the menstrual cycle, researchers can determine whether fluctuations in the ability to perform lateralized tasks are related to hormonal levels. In this manner, researchers need not compare women with men, but can compare just the performance of a given woman at two points in time. The way a woman has been influenced by culture will be constant, so researchers can sidestep the cultural issue.

These types of studies have yielded some evidence that when female hormones are high, such as just after ovulation, women tend to perform better on certain fine motor tasks that are more likely to be lateralized to the left hemisphere and poorer on spatial tasks, such as the mental rotation of objects, that are more likely to be lateralized to the right hemisphere. Women exhibit the opposite pattern when female hormones are low, such as during menstruation (e.g., Kimura & Hampson, 1994). However, the differences in ability are small and are found for only a limited set of tasks. Put practically, the differences are not large enough that a woman would want to use the phase of her menstrual cycle to determine the best date to take a school entrance examination.

Variations in cognitive abilities have also been linked to variations in hormonal levels in men. Most evidence suggests that intermediate, rather than high, levels of testosterone are associated with superior spatial skills. Men tend to perform worse on spatial tasks in the morning and in the autumn, when their testosterone level is high, as compared to the afternoon and the spring, when their testosterone level is lower (Moffat & Hampson, 1996; Kimura & Hampson, 1994).

As we now know, the debate regarding gender differences in brain organization, and specifically lateralization, has not been satisfactorily resolved. In fact, public imagination on the issue is often fueled by sensational stories in the popular press. The bodies of men and women clearly differ in a number of anatomical features and physiological functions, and we would probably not be surprised to find that such differences apply to the brain as well. However, what is critically important is how differences in brain lateralization are interpreted, with regard to both their nature and their magnitude. When differences are observed, they tend to be relatively small, and the variations among individuals within a gender are much greater than any variation between men and women as a group.

Why Have a Lateralized Brain?

In this final section of the chapter we will consider the mystery of why and how the human brain became lateralized. There is evidence that anatomical and functional lateralization occurs in other animals, including parrots (e.g., Snyder & Harris, 1998), mice (Gasne et al., 2001) and rats (Crowne et al., 1992). Such asymmetries are also observed in other primates, including gorillas, chimpanzees, and monkeys. Like humans, the great apes show an asymmetry of the planum temporale (Hopkins et al., 1999). In fact, this asymmetry is observed in a larger proportion of the population in chimps than in humans (Gannon, Holloway, Broadfield, & Braun, 1998). Evidence of functional specialization ranges from left-hemisphere specialization for the recognition of vocal calls that have communicative significance in macaque monkeys (Petersen et al., 1984), to better discrimination of faces by the right hemisphere of split-brain monkeys (Hamilton & Vermeire, 1988) to a left-hemisphere advantage for processing local information in the chimpanzee (Hopkins, 1997). Yet in no other species is lateralization observed across so many domains—with regard to perceptual asymmetries, with regard to handedness, and with regard to anatomical asymmetries in the brain.

Although we cannot know for sure, there are various speculations about what lateralization of function provides the human brain, and how that might have been adaptive. As we discussed earlier in the chapter, a lateralized brain provides us with the ability to extract information from the environment in two different yet complementary manners simultaneously. But what evolutionary, or survival, benefits does lateralization provide? Although increased manual agility and the emergence of a vocal or gestural communication system are often suggested (see the December 1998 issue of *Cahiers de Psychologie* for a broad spectrum of viewpoints), there is no clear answer to that question. Rather there are a variety of opinions. One viewpoint suggests that lateralization of function may have been advantageous because it allowed for the best expression of these more complex manual or vocal skills (Corballis, 1997). Other theorists have placed more emphasis on motor functions, arguing that precise manual manipulation and throwing would be more efficient if feedback were received from somatosensory regions in the same hemisphere (Wilkins and Wakefield, 1995) and that motor functions would be best performed by a single hemisphere so as to avoid possible interhemispheric conflict (Corballis, 1991). For example, chimps that strongly prefer to forage for food sources such as termites with one hand do so more efficiently than chimps that don't have a strong hand preference (McGrew & Marchant, 1999). In contrast, other researchers put language lateralization in the forefront, suggesting that having language perception and language output in the same hemisphere would provide more reliable feedback than if language production and comprehension were lateralized to different hemispheres (Annett, 1985). Researchers in this group also suggest that the temporal precision required by language functions might have been impeded by delays in interhemispheric communication if language areas were not co-lateralized (Ringo, Doty, Demeter, & Simard, 1994). A final group of theorists have suggested that because both language and motor skills rely on efficient sequencing abilities, language and handedness became co-lateralized to the same hemisphere (Kimura, 1993).

The question then becomes, why isn't everyone in the population right-handed and strongly lateralized? One possibility is raised by evolutionary neuropsychologist Michael Corballis, whose two-allele theory of the genetic inheritance of handedness was discussed earlier in the chapter. He contends that neither extreme lateralization nor the lack thereof provides the optimal brain organization. Rather, left-hemisphere dominance, associated with the inherited D allele, is achieved at the expense of right-hemisphere functions, whereas the influence of the C allele, which reduces cerebral asymmetry, has a cost in verbal and manual manipulative abilities. Thus, there is an advantage to being heterozygous, meaning that the individual has one of each allele (i.e., one D allele and one C allele) (Corballis, 1997). Since these alleles are inherited independently from each parent, both need to be maintained in the gene pool. This fact leads to a distribution of individuals with different combinations of the D and C alleles. Some people are strongly right-handed (DD), some are less strongly right-handed (DC) and some range from right-handed to left-handed (CC). Some studies have supported this theory, showing that extreme right-handedness is associated with poor spatial and mathematical skills, whereas certain verbal difficulties are associated with a lack of right-handedness (for a dissenting interpretation of this data, however, see Provins, 1997).

In this chapter, we reviewed many, but not all, of the differences between the hemispheres in their anatomy and function. For a more extensive discussion of these topics and others related to cerebral asymmetry, you may want to investigate two very readable yet scholarly books on the topic, one by Springer and Deutsch (1993) and another by Hellige (1993a). A third good book on the topic is the edited volume by Davidson & Hugdahl (2nd edition, 2003). It dives into a bit more detail as the chapters are written by the individuals who are doing research on lateralization of function in a specific area (e.g., emotion, spatial processing).

Basics of Hemispheric Specialization

- Hemispheric differences were first demonstrated in the 1860s, when Paul Broca reported that damage to a posterior region of the left, but not the right, frontal lobe disrupted the ability to produce fluent speech.
- Karl Wernicke later observed that damage to a temporo-parietal region of the left hemisphere produced the opposite syndrome: disrupted language comprehension with intact production.
- These findings led to the idea of cerebral dominance, which is the notion that one hemisphere dominates or leads mental function.
- Studies of split-brain patients, in whom the massive nerve-fiber connection between the hemispheres, the corpus callosum, is severed for the relief of intractable epilepsy, revealed the left hemisphere to be superior for language processing, and the right hemisphere to be superior at visuospatial tasks.
- Research with individuals with lateralized lesions indicates that left-hemisphere lesions disrupt language processing, whereas right-hemisphere lesions disrupt a variety of abilities, including face recognition, judgment of line orientation, recognition of objects, and tonal processing of auditory material.
- Hemispheric specialization can be demonstrated in neurologically intact individuals by directing sensory information so that it is received initially by a single hemisphere.
- Generally, processing of verbal material is superior when presented to the right hand, right ear, or in the right visual field. In contrast, processing of spatial material tends to be superior when presented to the left hand, left ear, or in the left visual field.

Characterization of Hemisphere Differences

- One prominent theory suggests that the hemispheres initially process sensory information in an equivalent manner, but then filter it differently; therefore, the right hemisphere preferentially processes whatever portion is of lower frequency, and the left preferentially processes whatever portion is of higher frequency.
- Another class of theories suggests that each hemisphere applies a different strategy for analyzing information: the left hemisphere is most adept at analyzing information in a piecemeal, detailed, and time-locked manner, whereas the right hemisphere is most adept at analyzing information in a holistic, gestalt, and space-based manner.

SUMMARY

Integration of Information between the Hemispheres

- The callosum is critical for transferring information that can be uniquely characterized (e.g., a picture of Madonna's face), as compared with that categorized dichotomously (e.g., a female face rather than a male face).
- Interaction between the hemispheres increases the brain's processing capacity when tasks are demanding or difficult, but not when they are relatively easy.

Developmental Aspects of Hemispheric Specialization

- The basic pattern of hemispheric specialization appears not to change much during development.
- Anatomical asymmetries can be observed in utero and at birth, behavioral asymmetries can be observed in infants and remain constant during childhood, and children with only a single hemisphere develop skills associated with that hemisphere to a higher degree than those associated with the absent hemisphere.

Individual Differences in Brain Organization

- On average, left-handers have less of a division of labor between the two halves of the brain than right-handers do.
- Although it is often suggested that women are less lateralized than men, there is much debate about the validity of this claim.

Why Have a Lateralized Brain?

- Asymmetries in neuroanatomy are observed in other species besides humans, including other primates, but no species other than humans exhibit lateralization across so many domains—with regard to perceptual asymmetries, handedness, and anatomical asymmetries of the brain.
- Most theories of the evolution of lateralization in humans suggest that it may have been driven either by our acquisition of communicative skills via voice or greater manual dexterity.

KEY TERMS

PART II

NEURAL BASES OF MENTAL FUNCTIONS

CHAPTER 5

MOTOR CONTROL

The life story of Muhammad Ali, one of the twentieth century's most famous boxers, interweaves not only boxing and politics, but also the neural basis of motor control. Ali, who was known as Cassius Clay before his conversion to Islam, rose to prominence as an Olympic boxer. He eventually turned pro and became a world champion. Ali said that his boxing strategy was to "float like a butterfly, sting like a bee," meaning that his fancy footwork allowed him to flutter around the ring evading his opponents' punches until he could move in for a knockout. At the height of his career, Ali was drafted to serve in Vietnam, but refused induction because of his religious beliefs. He was convicted of draft evasion, stripped of his crown, and was not allowed to box in a sanctioned match for the next three years.

During his exile from the ring, Ali's ability to "float" deteriorated substantially. When he was allowed to resume his boxing career (shortly before the Supreme Court overturned his conviction), he adopted a different fighting style that capitalized on the strength he had gained during his hiatus from professional bouts. This new style, however, would have deleterious effects later in his life. Ali would let an opponent get him against the ropes in the early rounds, either blocking or absorbing an onslaught of punches that would have felled most men. This technique became known as the "rope-a-dope" style, because a boxer was traditionally considered a fool if he allowed himself to get caught against the ropes. However, Ali would patiently wait for the later rounds when his foe was exhausted, frustrated, and getting sloppy. Then he would throw the punch that would send his opponent reeling to the mat.

After his retirement from boxing, Ali became a popular speaker on the lecture circuit. As time passed, however, people began to notice that he was slurring his words and stumbling. When signing autographs, he was slow and his penmanship was more and more illegible. Naive observers assumed that Ali was drunk, but heavy drinking was never his style. Medical examinations revealed that Ali had sustained neurological damage and that he was most likely displaying signs of Parkinson's disease. In Parkinson's disease, motor control is disrupted so that previously simple motor acts become extremely difficult. The three basic attributes of Parkinson's are slowness of movement, rigidity of movement, and tremors—rhythmic, oscillating movements (which are usually observed when a person is at rest). Generally, Parkinson's is observed in older people as a progressive neurological disorder. But Ali, although well past the years when most boxers are in the ring, was only middle-aged. So what could explain these symptoms?

As best as his neurologists could surmise, years of boxing had taken their toll on Ali. Although he had never been knocked out, the barrage of punches Ali absorbed with his rope-a-dope style had the cumulative effect of damaging regions of his brain important for motor control. As we discuss later in this chapter, Parkinsonian symptoms begin to manifest themselves when a substantial proportion of the dopaminergic neurons in the substantia nigra are destroyed. As cells die, the remaining cells try to do all the work, but at some point the number of damaged cells is too great and motor control deteriorates. Thus, although Ali sustained the damage during his long and illustrious boxing career, only afterward did the effects of this damage become apparent (Hauser, 1991). ■

Introduction

Muhammad Ali's Parkinson's disease was caused by destruction to just one of the many brain regions that permit the great diversity of motor skills that humans display. Before we discuss these various brain regions, let us first consider several of the many types of movements that humans can exhibit. In some motor acts, such as when hitting a tennis serve, you must coordinate movement of the gross and postural muscles in a smooth and seamless fashion. When learning to serve, you break down the process into a series of steps: Start to toss the ball, dip your legs, bring the racquet behind your back, push up on your legs, extend the racquet skyward, rotate your torso, and hit the ball. Consider how different such a step-by-step process is from the smooth, well-learned tennis serve of professionals like Venus Williams and Andre Agassi. Rather than seeming like a concatenation of separate movements, the swing of a tennis pro or even a good amateur player appears to be one smooth, continuous motion. As we learn later in this chapter, such smooth, rapid movements are aided by the cerebellum.

Other actions require that fine motor movements be precisely timed. Touch-typing (that is, when you type with ten fingers instead of pecking with two), unlike a tennis serve, requires little gross muscle movement—because the position of your hands remains relatively static. Typing speed is increased by reducing the time between individual keystrokes. One way to accomplish this increased speed is to adjust the typing of a given key on the basis of the keystrokes that precede and follow it. Our ability to make such adjustments implies that we create an overall motor program of the series of movements that we want to produce, then invoke this program when a series of finger strokes is executed. As we learn later, these motor programs are probably produced by a specific brain region known as the *supplementary motor area.* This area transmits information about the motor program to other brain regions, eventually allowing for the activation of the specific muscles required to execute the program.

In other motor acts, performance is linked to specific external cues, such as when you press on the gas pedal upon seeing a green light and step on the brake upon seeing a red light. When movements require us to break well-learned associations (e.g., pressing the gas pedal for a *red* light and stepping on the brake for a *green* one), when they are novel, or when they are less well rehearsed, the anterior cingulate is called into action.

Motor acts often involve multiple brain regions because they require many types of motor control to occur simultaneously (e.g., control over both the fine and gross muscles). However, as this brief introduction should illustrate, specific brain regions may play a more prominent role in certain motor acts than in others. We begin this chapter by reviewing the major brain regions involved in motor control and by pointing out the important contribution each makes. Afterward, we examine clinical syndromes in which motor processing is disrupted. These syndromes fall into two major categories: those resulting from damage to subcortical regions of the brain and those resulting from damage to the cortex. The subcortical syndromes that we discuss—Parkinson's disease, Huntington's disease, Tourette's syndrome, and tardive dyskinesia—all involve a disruption in the form of movements. These syndromes may lead to slowness or imprecision in movement, or to movement that should not occur (e.g., tremors). In contrast, the cortical syndromes impair the conceptualizing, planning, and sequencing that underlie learned movements. In these cases, individuals have difficulty playing the piano or knowing how to program muscles to make the sign of the Christian cross.

Brain Structures Involved in Motor Control

As we mentioned, a multiplicity of brain regions are involved in motor control. In this section, we review the primary brain structures involved in such control starting with those located subcortically and then discussing those in the cortex.

Subcortical Regions

Before discussing the role of different brain regions in motor control, we must first discuss the basic underlying mechanism that makes muscles move. Muscles are composed of muscle fibers that can be either in a contracted state or in an uncontracted state. Muscle fiber contraction is caused by an impulse from a neuron. Typically, one motor neuron innervates a number of muscle fibers. The number of muscle fibers innervated can vary from two or three for muscles involved in very fine motor control to over a hundred for large antigravity muscles. A motor neuron and the muscle fibers it innervates are referred to as a **motor unit.** The synapse between a neuron and muscle fibers is larger and has a more specialized structure than a typical synapse. It is called the **neuromuscular junction** (see Figure 5.1). Hence, for muscles to move, information must be relayed from the nervous system to the muscles. Without such control, paralysis occurs.

• *MOTOR TRACTS* •

The brain has not one, but four basic routes through which information is transferred from the brain to the muscles: the corticospinal, corticobulbar, ven-

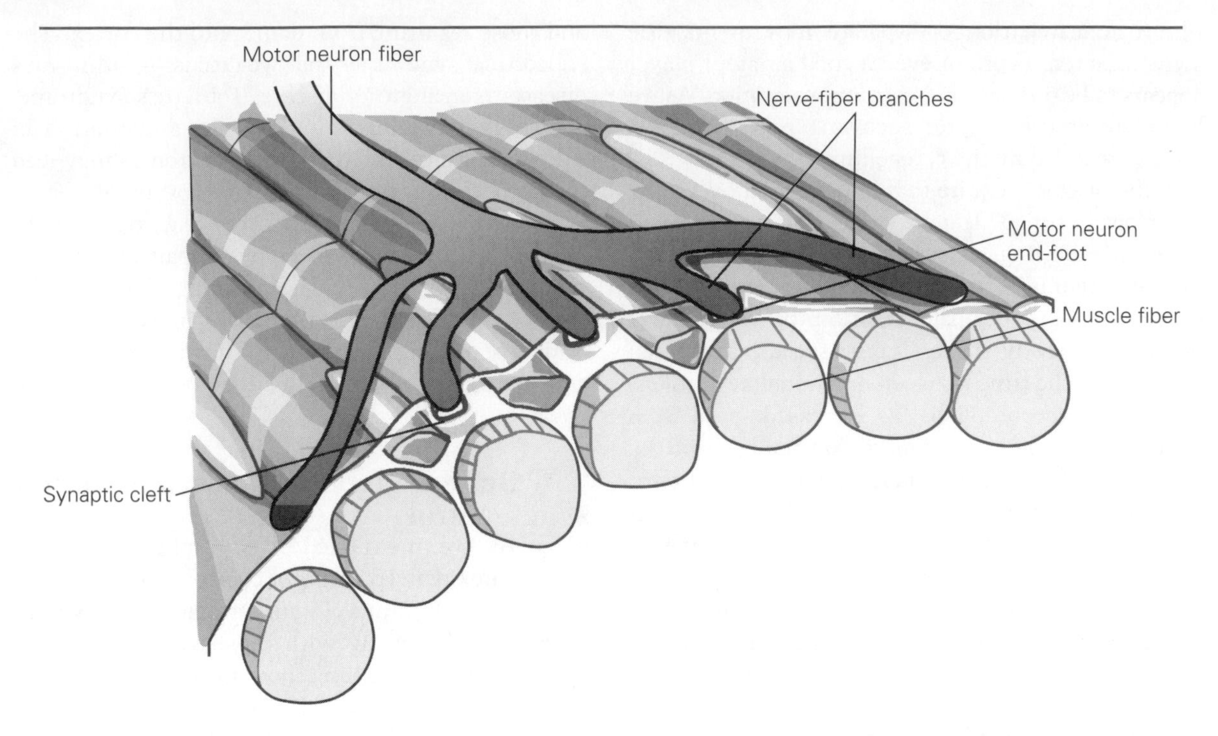

FIGURE 5.1 The neuromuscular junction. At this junction, a motor neuron fiber makes extensive contact with muscle fibers. When an action potential reaches the motor neuron end-foot, acetylcholine is released into the synaptic cleft. Then acetylcholine binds with nicotinic cholinergic receptors in special troughs in the membrane of the skeletal muscle, known as the motor endplate. This causes an action potential in the muscle membrane, resulting in muscle contraction.

tromedial, and rubrospinal pathways. Each of these routes innervates different types of target muscles (e.g., finger muscles vs. leg muscles) and hence is involved in different aspects of motor control (e.g., fine motor control vs. posture). These pathways are the mechanisms through which motor movements planned in the brain are sent to target muscles to be executed. To better conceptualize the role that these pathways play in motor control, we might consider them akin to the infantry in the army: they carry out the orders but do not make them. Instead, the subcortical and cortical regions that we discuss later are the key regions for determining the form, sequencing, and planning of these movements. The subcortical regions can be thought of as lieutenants who make sure that their platoons are moving along in proper form, whereas the cortical regions are more like generals who plan the actions of vast numbers of platoons. The lieutenants and generals do not cause the actual movement. Rather, the movement occurs because of the action of the infantry.

The basic characteristics of the major motor pathways, including their points of origination and termination, and their effects, are summarized in Table 5.1.

The first of the four pathways, the **corticospinal pathway,** links the cortex to the spinal cord, just as its name suggests. The cell bodies for these tracts are located mainly in the motor cortex. Two corticospinal tracts are of most importance. One, the **lateral corticospinal tract,** is responsible for the control of distal (i.e., far) limb muscles, such as those that innervate the arms, hands, fingers, lower leg, and foot. Damage to the lateral corticospinal tract has profound effects on the ability to reach and grasp objects and to manipulate them. For example, after damage to this tract, a person would have difficulty grabbing and manipulating a key or twirling a pencil

TABLE 5.1 The Four Major Motor Pathways and Their Characteristics

PATHWAY	ORIGIN	TERMINATION	TARGET MUSCLES	PURPOSE
Corticospinal	Motor cortex: 1. Finger, hand, arm, lower leg, and foot regions 2. Trunk and upper leg regions	Spinal cord	1. Fingers, hands, arms, lower legs, and feet 2. Trunk and upper legs	1. Grasping and manipulating objects 2. Locomotion and posture
Corticobulbar	Motor cortex: Face region	Pons: Nuclei of cranial nerves V, VII, X, and XII	Face and tongue	Face and tongue movements
Ventromedial	Superior colliculus, nuclei in the medulla and pons	Spinal cord	Trunk, neck, and legs	1. Posture 2. Coordination of eye movements with those of trunk and head 3. Autonomic functions (e.g., respiration) 4. Walking
Rubrospinal	Red nucleus of the midbrain	Spinal cord	Hands (not fingers), feet, forearms, and lower legs	Allows independent movements of forearms and hands from that of the trunk

with his or her toes (as some talented individuals can do). This motor tract crosses the midline entirely in the medulla. Thus, damage to cell bodies of this tract (which are in motor cortex) results in deficits in motor movement on the opposite side of the body. The other major tract within the corticospinal pathway, the **ventral corticospinal tract,** is important for controlling muscles of the trunk and upper legs, and it plays a more prominent role in the ability to walk and run (i.e., to locomote) and to maintain posture. This tract projects both ipsilaterally and contralaterally (Figure 5.2A).

The second major motor pathway is the **corticobulbar pathway,** which also has most of its cell bodies located in the motor cortex. However, instead of synapsing in the spinal cord, these cells synapse in the pons on the fifth, seventh, tenth, and twelfth cranial nerves (Figure 5.2B). As we learned in Chapter 1, these cranial nerves are important for innervation of the face and tongue, as well as the vocal apparatus and respiration. Some portions of the corticobulbar pathway have only contralateral projections, whereas other portions have both ipsilateral and contralateral connections. In particular, the regions of the motor cortex that control movements of the upper part of the face project both ipsilaterally and contralaterally. Therefore, the forehead area is usually unaffected by a unilateral cortical lesion to the motor cortex. As a result, people with unilateral lesions can still furrow their brows in frustration or raise their eyebrows in surprise, and they can wink each eye separately. In contrast, the regions controlling movement of the lower part of the face project only contralaterally. After damage to these regions, mouth movements are asymmetrical because one side of the mouth cannot move whereas the other can. Consequently, drooping of one side of the face is common after a stroke.

The two other major pathways, the ventromedial pathway and the rubrospinal pathway, do not originate in the cortex but mainly have their cell bodies in the brain stem. Both terminate in the spinal cord and have indirect linkages to primary motor cortex. The **ventromedial pathway** has a variety of functions. Primarily, it controls movements of the trunk and proximal (i.e., near) limb muscles. Along with the ventral corticospinal tract, it contributes to posture. A division of the ventromedial pathway is important for coordinating eye movements with movements of the head and trunk. The cell bodies of these tracts originate, not surprisingly, in the superior colliculus, which, as we learned in Chapter 1 (and discuss further

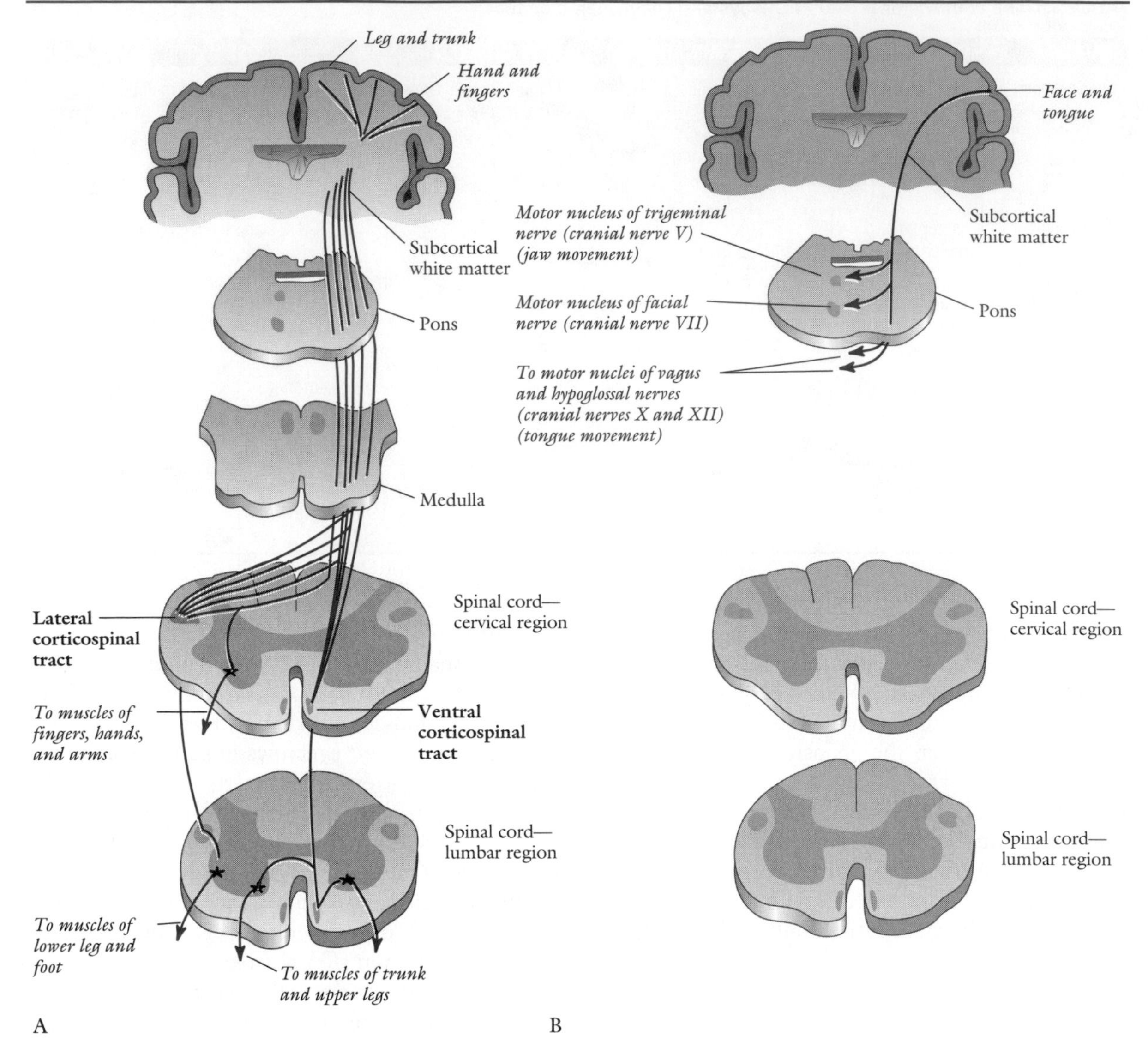

FIGURE 5.2 The four major motor pathways. (A) The lateral and ventral corticospinal tracts of the corticospinal pathway. The lateral corticospinal tract, which controls fine motor movement of the distal extremities, crosses the midline at the level of the medulla so that motor control by this fiber tract is exclusively contralateral. In contrast, fibers of the ventral corticospinal tract, which are important for posture and locomotion, synapse both ipsilaterally and contralaterally. (B) The corticobulbar pathway, which is important for motor control of the face and tongue. In contrast to the corticospinal pathway, this pathway crosses the midline at the level of the pons. (C) The ventromedial pathway. This pathway is important for controlling movement of the trunk and proximal limbs; contributes to posture; coordinates head, trunk, and eye movements; and controls muscles involved in autonomic functions. (D) The rubrospinal pathway, which is important for independent movement of the forearms and hands from that of the trunk. Although this tract originates mainly in the red nucleus of the midbrain, it projects to primary motor cortex as well as to the cerebellum.

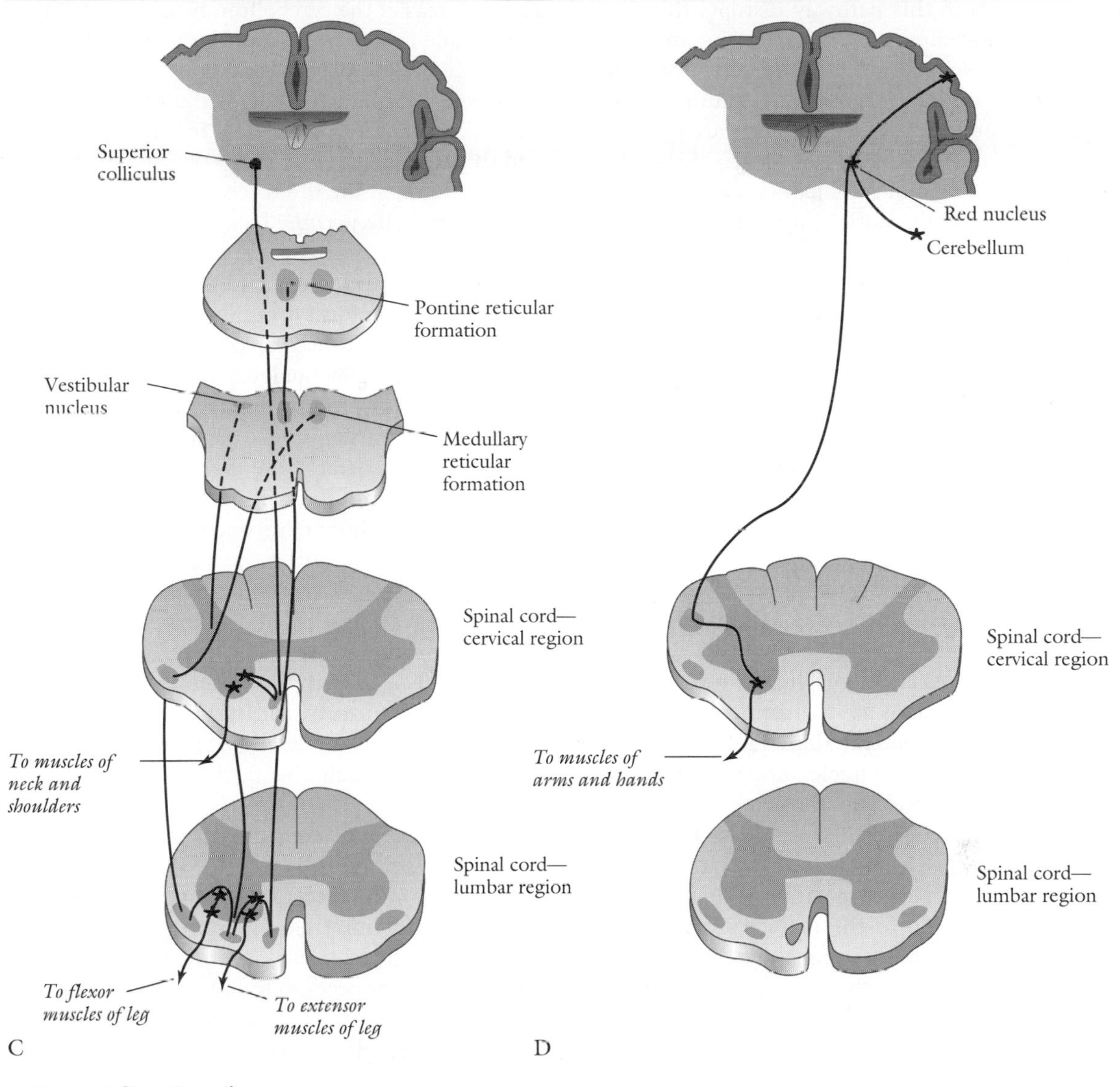

FIGURE 5.2 (Continued)

in the chapter on attention), is important in eye movements. Other tracts in the ventromedial pathway control muscles involved in autonomic (involuntary) functions, such as sneezing, breathing, and muscle tone, along with other motor functions, such as walking. The cell bodies for these tracts reside in the nuclei of the brain stem (such as the vestibular nucleus and the medullary reticular formation) and in the pontine reticular formation (Figure 5.2C).

The last major pathway, the **rubrospinal pathway,** originates mainly in the cell bodies of the red nucleus located in the midbrain. This nucleus receives input from both the motor cortex and the cerebellum, to which it also projects, forming a loop (Figure 5.2D). Loops in the nervous system usually provide an opportunity for modulation of control, and the role of the rubrospinal pathway can be well characterized as that of modulating motor movement. Damage to this pathway disrupts the ability to control movements of the forearms and hands that do not also involve movement of the trunk. When this system is damaged in animals, limb movements are clumsy and usually cannot be produced without associated movements of the trunk (e.g., an animal cannot raise just one limb and keep the rest of the body static) (Lawrence & Kuypers, 1968). In humans, this pathway appears to play a role in movement of the proximal muscles of the arm, and in relaying information from the cortex to the cerebellum.

• *CEREBELLUM* •

The **cerebellum,** looking much like a small cauliflower attached to the back of the brain, often does not receive much attention because it lies outside the cortex. Nonetheless, it plays an extremely important role in motor control, especially in the modulation of motor movements and in the learning of motor skills. The anatomy of the cerebellum is such that it contains two hemispheres and three divisions within each hemisphere. From the midline, the three divisions are the **vermis,** the **intermediate zone,** and the **lateral zone.** Embedded within the cerebellum are three nuclei, known as **deep cerebellar nuclei.** Each region of the cerebellum projects to a different deep cerebellar nucleus: The vermis projects to the **fastigial nucleus,** the intermediate zone projects to the **interpositus nucleus,** and the lateral zone projects to the **dentate nucleus.** The inputs and outputs to the cerebellum, as well as the location of the deep cerebellar nuclei are shown in Figure 5.3.

Before we examine how damage to each of these major zones of the cerebellum affects motor processing, a few general principles about the cerebellum are worth noting. First, the projection of information through the cerebellum often forms loops that connect with other brain regions important for motor functioning. In this way, the cerebellum is perfectly positioned to have a modulatory effect on motor processing, and it may act as a mechanism to determine whether the ongoing movement is matching the intended movement. Second, unlike the motor cortex, which acts on contralateral muscles, the cerebellum modulates *ipsilateral* muscles. Finally, areas of the cerebellum near the midline are responsible for functions associated with the body's center, including posture and control of speech. In contrast, more lateral areas of the cerebellum control the lateralized structures, including the limbs and the eyes.

We now examine the three main divisions of the cerebellum. The *vermis,* located on the midline of the cerebellum, receives input from the spinal cord regarding somatosensory and *kinesthetic* information, which is information about body movement derived from the muscles, skin, and joints. It projects to the fastigial nucleus, which in turn influences some of the ventromedial pathway tracts. As we discussed earlier in the chapter, these ventromedial pathway tracts are important for posture. Hence, damaging the vermis leads to difficulty with postural adjustments and movements such as walking. If you deactivate the fastigial nucleus unilaterally in a monkey, the animal tends to fall to the side of space ipsilateral to the deactivated cerebellar hemisphere (because of the ipsilateral cerebellar control). Other movements, such as those made with the arms and fingers, are unaffected because these are controlled by the corticospinal pathways, to which the fastigial nucleus has no connections.

The *intermediate zone of the cerebellum* receives information from the red nucleus (which receives projections in part from motor cortex) and somatosensory information from the spinal cord. This zone projects to the interpositus nucleus, which in turn projects to the red nucleus, creating a loop. Damage to the intermediate zone of the cerebellar cortex results in rigidity and difficulty in moving the limbs. In monkeys, deactivation of the interpositus nucleus causes tremors, which are observed most often when the animal reaches for something, such as a piece of food. Similar problems have been observed in humans with localized cerebellar atrophy and are most often characterized as an inability to make smooth movements to a target location. An affected person makes such movements in a staggered manner, especially as he or she zeroes in on the target. This behavior is sometimes referred to as an **action tremor** or **intention tremor** because it occurs during the performance of an act. This type of

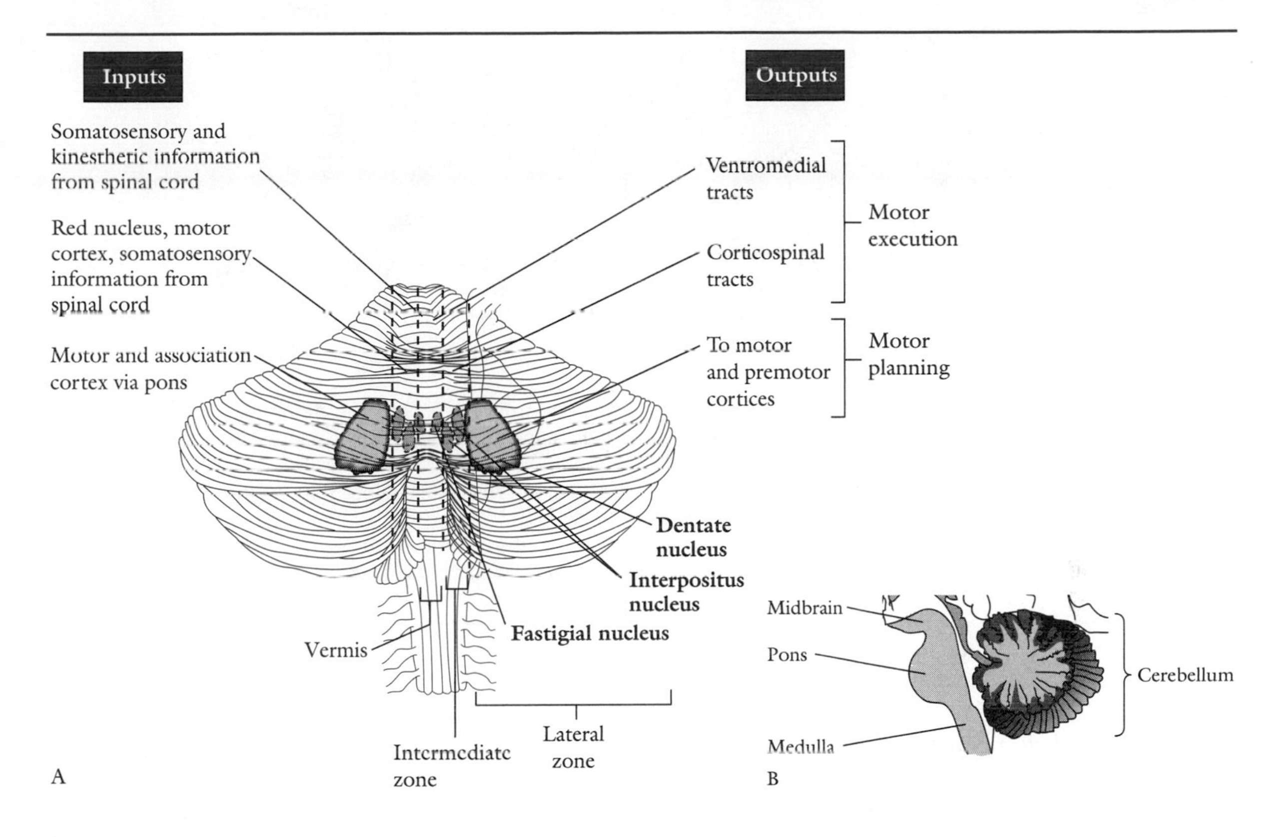

FIGURE 5.3 Structure of the cerebellum showing its inputs and outputs. (A) Main functional divisions of the cerebellum with their inputs, deep cerebellar nuclei, and outputs. (B) Midsagittal view of the cerebellum.

tremor is distinct from that seen with disorders of the basal ganglia, in which the tremor is much more likely to occur at rest. As mentioned in Chapter 1, neurologists often screen for cerebellar damage by having an individual touch his or her nose and then the neurologist's nose. An individual with damage to the intermediate zone of the cerebellum can perform this task, but the path the hand takes from one nose to the other is often staggered, jerky, and zigzag.

The *lateral zone of the cerebellum* receives input from both motor and association cortices through the pons. This zone projects to the dentate nucleus, which in turn projects back to the primary motor and premotor cortices through the red nucleus and the ventrolateral thalamus. Accordingly, whereas information from the vermis and intermediate zones projects down to the spinal cord (known as descending systems), that from the lateral zone ascends to the cortex. Damage to the lateral zone affects four types of movements. One type is rapid and smooth **ballistic movement,** meaning movement that occurs so quickly it leaves little or no time to be modified by feedback. In a ballistic movement, the precise time at which the movements of individual muscles start and stop is preprogrammed. The swing of a batter trying to hit a ball moving at 90 mph (144 km/h) is a good example of a ballistic movement. Although the adage says to "keep your eye on the ball," the ball moves so rapidly that the batter has no time to adjust the swing as the ball nears the plate, but rather must preprogram movements on the basis of the initial flight path of the ball soon after it leaves the pitcher's hand. (Often pitchers throw sliders or knuckleballs, in which the ball takes an irregular, curved path rather than a straight trajectory, to tax the batter's ability to produce the correct ballistic

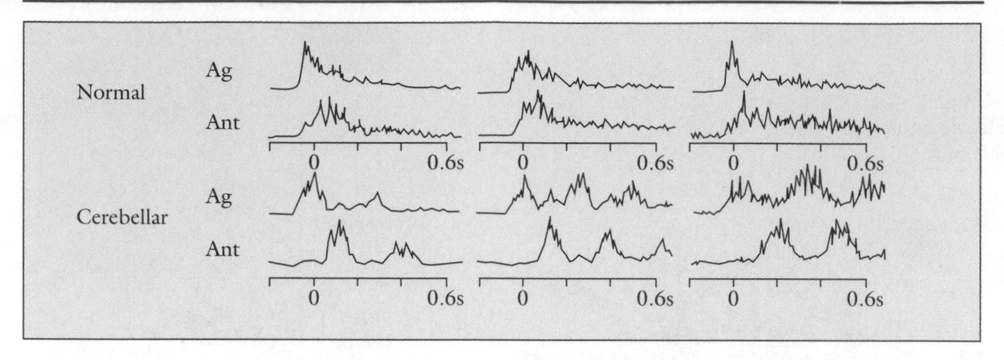

FIGURE 5.4 The mechanics that produce overshoot in patients with cerebellar damage. Shown here is the activity of agonist and antagonist muscles in a single-joint motion from a hand (A) unaffected by cerebellar damage and (B) affected by cerebellar damage. Time is depicted along the x axis and degree of muscle activity along the y axis. Note that for the normal hand, the activity of the antagonist muscle lags behind that of the agonist, acting as a brake on the movement. In contrast, for the affected hand, the antagonist muscle activity comes too late and too strongly. This induces more activity in the agonist, which then is poorly modulated by the antagonist, leading to both an overshoot of the target as well as tremor.

movement that will cause good contact with the ball.) The typical problem with ballistic movements after lateral cerebellar damage is an overshooting of the target (see Figure 5.4). This overshooting occurs because individuals cannot calculate when each muscle group must be turned on and then off to land at the target. Because these patients cannot program the correct movements in advance, they try to adjust only when they see that their arm or finger is almost at the target, which is too late (e.g., C. Marsden et al., 1977).

The second set of difficulties experienced by individuals with damage to the lateral cerebellar cortex involves the coordination of multijoint movements. Because multijoint coordination breaks down, movements are best accomplished by moving one joint at a time in a serial manner, a strategy known as **decomposition of movement.** For example, rather than lifting a glass by moving the entire arm, an individual with damage to the lateral cerebellar cortex is taught in rehabilitation to place an elbow on a table, lean forward, and bring the glass to his or her mouth. With the elbow stationary, the number of joints that must be moved is decreased, which increases the likelihood of a successful movement (Thach, 1992). In the monkey, inactivation of the dentate nucleus (which receives projections from the lateral cerebellar regions) results in both overshooting and lack of coordination of movements involving multiple fingers.

Third, damage to the lateral zone of the cerebellum can hamper the learning of new movements. Let's consider the case of throwing a dart at a target. The ability to coordinate eye fixation on a target with arm movement is an acquired skill. An individual with cerebellar damage who had decent eye-hand coordination prior to injury can throw a dart with relative accuracy. However, if this task is changed a bit so it requires new sensorimotor learning, deficits are exhibited. For example, if a person is wearing prism eyeglasses that displace the view of the world 15 degrees to one side, hitting the target will require a recalibration of the relationship between the position of the gaze and the arm movement. Neurologically intact individuals can gradually make this adjustment if given enough practice. When the prisms are removed, their throws are once again off target, but these individuals can learn to recalibrate the relationship between the gaze and the throw back to its original value (Figure 5.5A). In contrast, patients with cerebellar damage who are wearing prisms never learn to adapt their movement to hit the target, even after much practice. Because they never learn the new gaze-throw relationship, they, unlike the neurologically intact individuals, can hit the target as soon as the spectacles are removed (Figure 5.5B) (see Thach, Goodkin, & Keating, 1992, for a description of this research, as well as a general research review of the role of the cerebellum in the coordination of movement).

Finally, the lateral zone of the cerebellum seems to be important in the timing of not only motor movements, but cognitive functions as well. Lesions in this region compromise the ability to perform simple but precisely timed tapping movements. In addition, they impair the ability to make judgments about the temporal duration of events, such as whether the time gap between the presentation of two tones is longer or shorter than a reference interval (e.g., 400 ms) or which of two successive displays of dots is moving more quickly across the screen. These deficits do not result from a general inability to make comparative judgments, but are specifically linked to timing, as individuals with cerebellar damage are perfectly capable of determining which of two successively presented tones is louder (Ivry & Keele, 1989). Thus, this region of the brain seems to be critical in determining the temporal relationship between successive events (see Ivry, 1997, for a review). Rather than providing a single central clock that keeps a running track of time, as would a pacemaker, the cerebellum appears to contain a wide

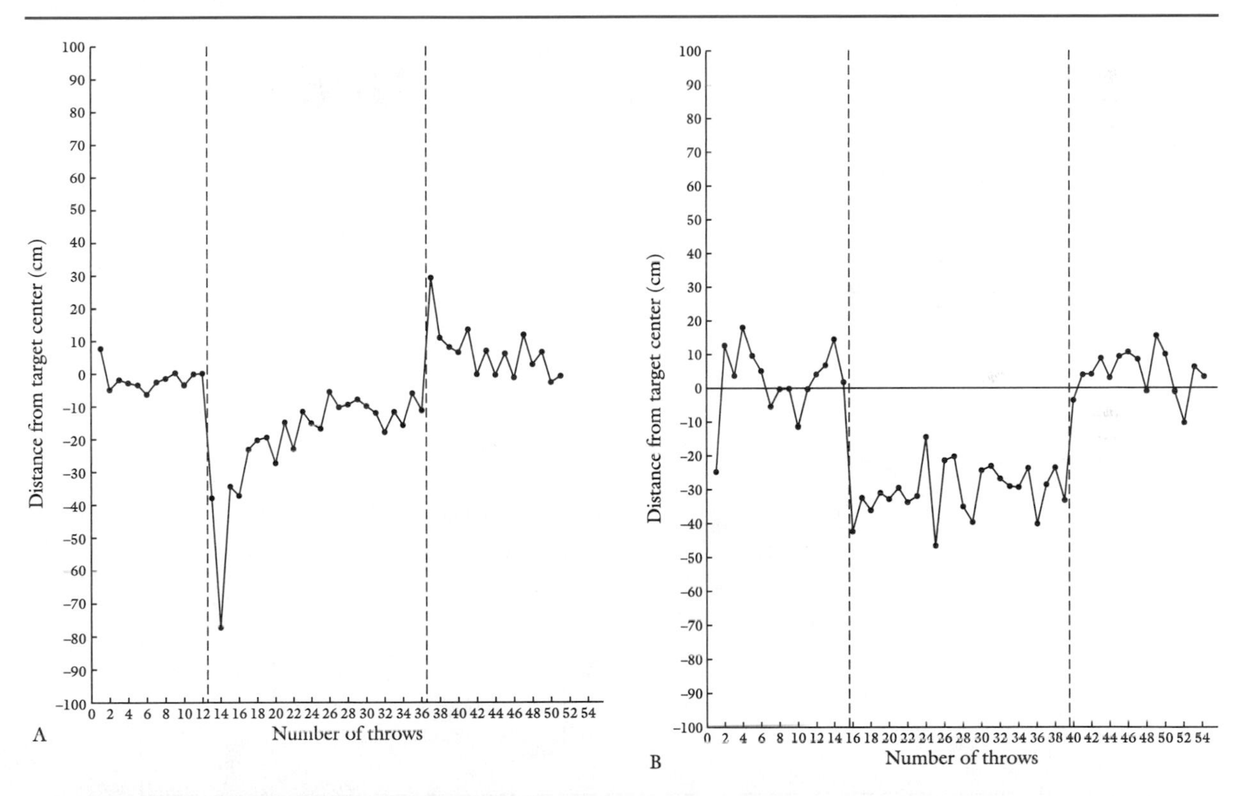

FIGURE 5.5 Role of the cerebellum in motor learning. Shown here are plots of dart-throwing accuracy for a series of throws by two individuals. The first dashed line indicates when the individual puts on the prism spectacles, and the second dashed line when they are taken off. (A) Plot for a neurologically intact individual. After putting on the prisms, the person's throw is far off target, but with practice, the individual's aim improves. After the eyeglasses are removed, the throw is off again but quickly becomes recalibrated. (B) Plot for an individual with cerebellar damage. The introduction of the eyeglasses leads to inaccurate throws, which are not adjusted with practice. Because no learning has taken place, the individual's accuracy returns to the preprism baseline almost immediately after the eyeglasses are removed.

range of interval-type timers (e.g., Ivry, 1996, Robertson et al., 1999). The difference between these two types of clocks is shown in Figure 5.6.

Such a timing function may explain the important role that the cerebellum plays in sensorimotor learning and other diverse aspects of cognitive functioning. A classic example of the role of the cerebellum in such learning is provided by eye-blink conditioning. In this paradigm, an animal (or person) hears a tone, which then predicts that a puff of air will be delivered to the eye. Blinking the eyes reduces the aversive effects of the air puff, but only if the timing of the blink relative to the tone is appropriate. It is well known that damage to the cerebellum interferes with the ability to learn to make an anticipatory response at the correct time interval and interferes with the response after it has been learned. Thus, it has been suggested that the cerebellum plays a critical role in sensorimotor learning because it allows the nature of the temporal relationship between events to be understood. Supporting such an idea, a recent fMRI study has demonstrated that as the temporal lag between hand and eye movements increases, making hand-eye

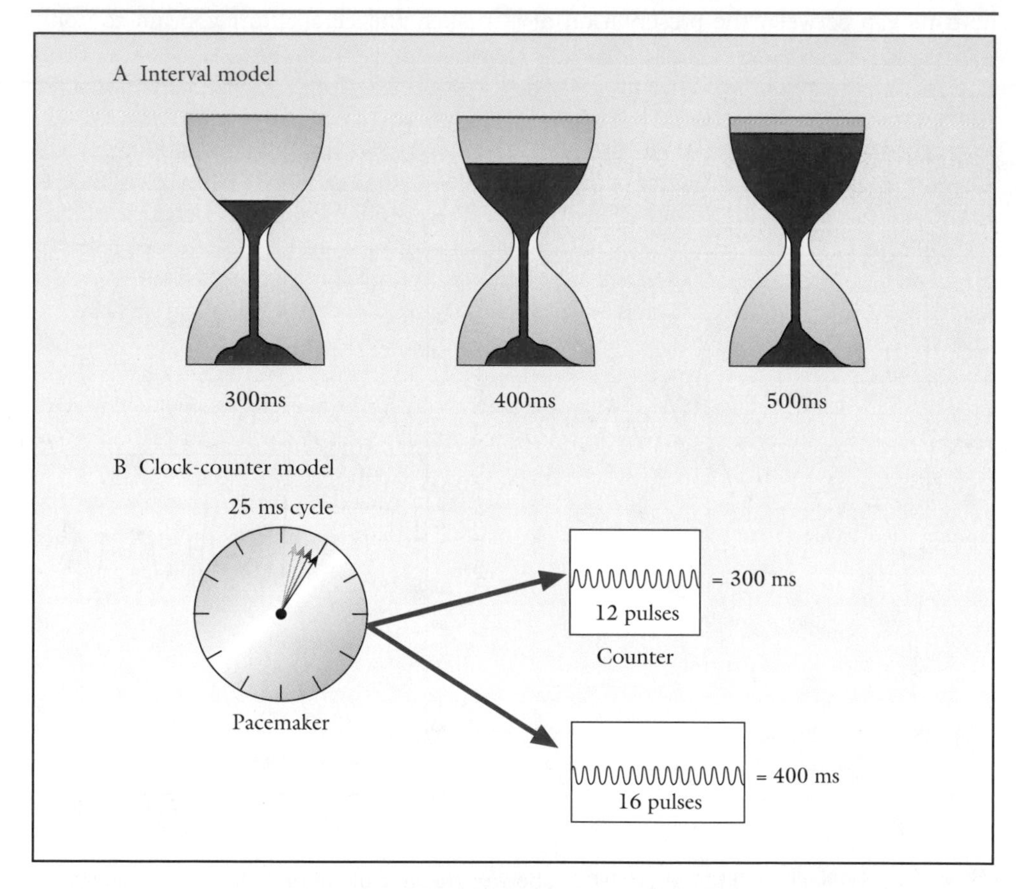

FIGURE 5.6 The nature of the time-keeping apparatus in the cerebellum. (A) The "clock" in the cerebellum is thought to consist of a set of timers, each of which is set to a specific time interval. Such timers do not tell how much time has elapsed on a continuous basis, but rather just note when a specific time period has elapsed, much as sand in a glass timer allows one to know when the time is up, but not how much time has passed. (B) This system stands in contrast to a pacemaker type of clock that oscillates, or completes a cycle (often to produce an output), at regular intervals (e.g, every 25 ms). The elapsed time can be calculated in such a clock by the multiplying the number of cycles by the time duration of the cycle.

coordination more difficult, the involvement of the cerebellum in task performance also increases (Miall, Reckess, & Imamizu, 2001).

Although traditionally thought to be involved in only motor control, the cerebellum has recently been suggested to play a role in higher-order cognitive function as well. Decreased cerebellar size has been noted in a number of developmental disorders that compromise either specific cognitive functions, such as attention deficit hyperactivity disorder (Berquin et al., 1998), or intellectual abilities in general, such as autism (Courchesne et al., 1988) and fragile-X syndrome (Mostofsky et al., 1998). (We discuss each of these disorders in greater detail in Chapter 13.) In addition, many neuroimaging studies have reported activation of the cerebellum during higher-level cognitive tasks. Findings such as these have been interpreted to suggest that the cerebellum plays an important role in mental processes, such as stimulus–response linkages (e.g., Thach, 1998) and emotion (Schmahmann, 1998). However, the observed relationships between cerebellar and cognitive function may not indicate that the cerebellum is directly involved in a specific cognitive function (see Desmond & Fiez, 1998, for a very good review). One notable possibility is that the cerebellum is a slave system required to provide the timing parameters that are important for higher-order cognitive tasks such as language and memory (Ivry, 1997).

As we just learned, the cerebellum has a multiplicity of roles with regard to motor control: it is important for posture, smooth movements, coordinated multilimb movements, and ballistic movements. It plays a prominent role in the coordination and learning of motor movements because of its role in the timing of motor movements (see Mauk et al., 2000, for a longer discussion of the interrelations between these functions). These different functions of the cerebellum are, in part, the province of different regions of the cerebellum. Damage to the cerebellum does not eradicate motor movements so much as it degrades motor capabilities.

• BASAL GANGLIA •

The **basal ganglia** are a complex collection of subcortical nuclei consisting of the **caudate nucleus, putamen,** and **nucleus accumbens** (known collectively as the *striatum*), the **globus pallidus** (or *pallidum*), the **substantia nigra,** and the **subthalamic nucleus.** These structures form a loop with cortical regions. The vast majority of all input to the basal ganglia goes to the caudate and putamen. Output from the basal ganglia is from the globus pallidus to the thalamus, which then projects back to the cortex. There are multiple versions of this loop, each from a different region of cortex through a distinct region of the striatum and global pallidus and back to cortex again. Each loop includes input from a frontal or limbic area to which information then returns.

In addition to input from the cortex, the striatum receives input from the substantia nigra via the **nigrostriatal bundle,** whereas the globus pallidus receives input not only from the striatum but also from the subthalamic nucleus (Alexander, DeLong, & Strick, 1986). In addition to affecting cortex, output from the basal ganglia can affect other motor regions of the brain. For example, its output can influence eye movements via the superior colliculus. The basal ganglia, thus, are at the crossroads of the neural circuits involved in motor control (for a description of the multiple anatomical connections of the basal ganglia, see Alexander & Crutcher, 1990, or Middleton & Strick, 2000), which positions them perfectly to modulate motor activity (see Figure 5.7).

Unlike the cerebellum, which plays a role in rapid ballistic movements, the basal ganglia are more important for the accomplishment of movements that may take some time to initiate or stop. The basal ganglia have been suggested to have multiple roles in motor control: "setting" the motor system with regard to posture, preparing the nervous system to accomplish a voluntary motor act, acting as an autopilot for well-learned sequential movements, controlling the timing and switching between motor acts, and, because both motor and nonmotor information feed into the basal ganglia, playing a role in motor planning and learning, especially when motor acts have motivational significance (i.e., lead to a reward) or have a large cognitive contribution (i.e., learning new input-output rules that override well-learned behavior). (See Graybiel, Aosaki, Flaherty, & Kimura, 1994, for a description of how the modular neural organization of the basal ganglia makes them particularly well-suited for learning.)

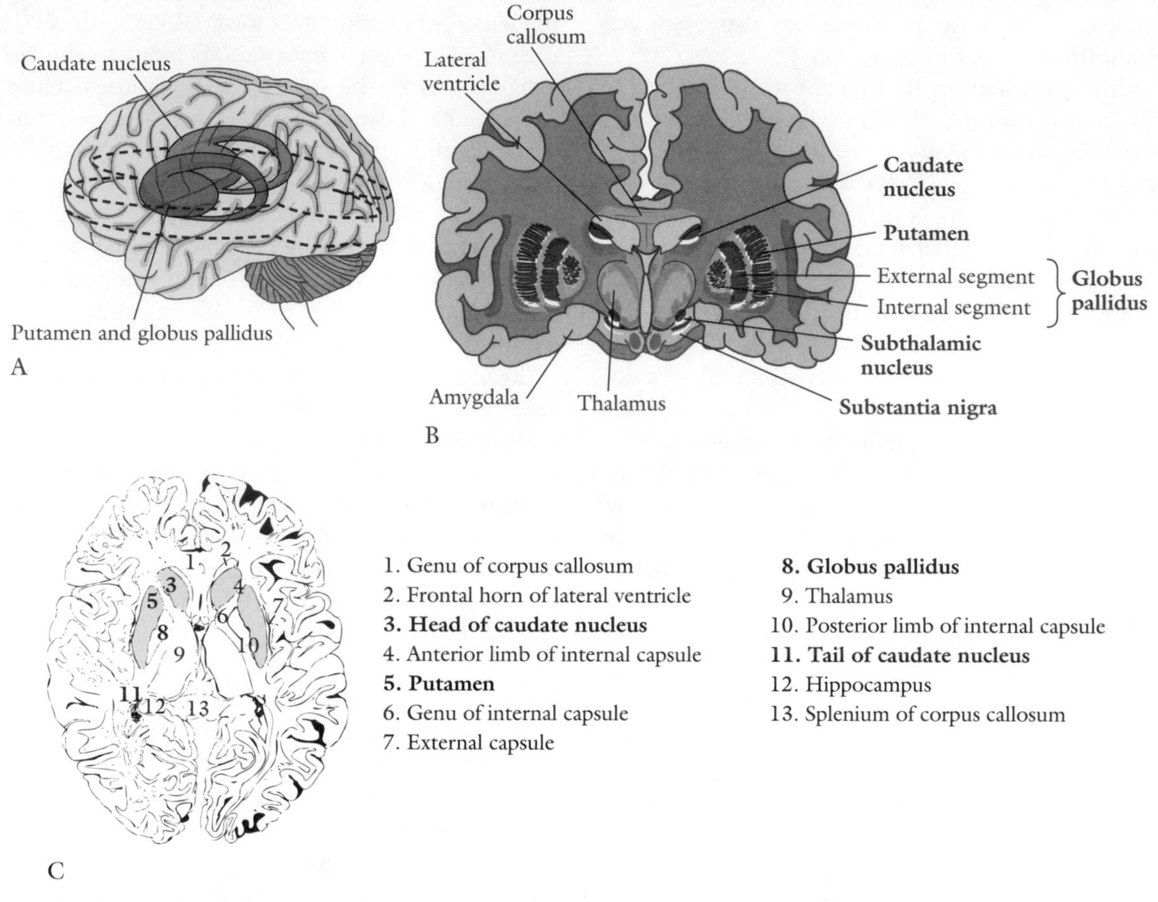

FIGURE 5.7 Basal ganglia in relation to other brain structures. (A) The basal ganglia in relation to the neocortex. (B) Coronal and (C) horizontal sections indicating the location of the basal ganglia.

To best understand the role of the basal ganglia in movement and movement disorders, look at Figure 5.8. The caudate and putamen, which receive most of the basal ganglia's input, connect to the main output region of the basal ganglia, the internal section of the globus pallidus, by two routes. One route, the *direct* route, directly connects these two regions in an inhibitory fashion. The internal section of the globus pallidus then has inhibitory connections to motor nuclei of the thalamus, which serve to excite the cortex. As a result, activity in the direct route normally causes inhibition of the internal sections of the globus pallidus so that it can no longer inhibit the thalamus from exciting the cortex. Therefore, activity in this route allows for sustaining or facilitating ongoing action (because inhibition of the thalamus is decreased). The other route, the *indirect* route, involves inhibitory connections of the caudate and putamen to the external (rather than the internal) section of the globus pallidus. This region has inhibitory connections to the subthalamic nucleus, which then has excitatory connections to the internal section of the globus pallidus. Thus, normal activity in the indirect pathway causes the subthalamic nuclei to activate the internal section of the globus pallidus, which suppresses thalamic activity. This pathway is thought to be important for suppressing unwanted movement.

Damage to the basal ganglia produces various motor disorders depending on which regions of the ganglia are affected. Parkinson's disease is characterized by **akinesia** (the inability to initiate spontaneous movement), **bradykinesia** (slowness of movement), and **tremors** (rhythmic, oscillating movements). In Parkinson's disease, the major problem is that the section of the putamen from which the direct pathway emerges is not receiving any dopaminergic input. This dopamine deficiency is caused by the death of cell bodies in the substantia nigra, which project to the basal ganglia through the nigrostriatal bundle. The death of cells in the substantia nigra (meaning "black substance") can be seen easily on autopsies of patients with Parkinson's disease because this region does not stain the usual dark color seen in neurologically intact individuals. Because there is no input to the direct pathway, the indirect pathway becomes overactive (see Figure 5.8), causing much activity in the internal portion of the globus pallidus, which in turn inhibits the thalamus and results in decreased motor activity (Albin, Young, & Penney, 1989).

If the striatum of the basal ganglia itself is damaged, as in Huntington's disease, a different set of motor problems is observed. **Hyperkinesias,** involuntary undesired movements, are common. One type of hyperkinesia is **chorea** (derived from the Greek *khoros,* meaning "dance"), which is uncontrollable, jerky movements such as twitching and abrupt jerking of the body. Another type is **athetosis,** defined by involuntary writhing contractions and twisting of the body into abnormal postures.

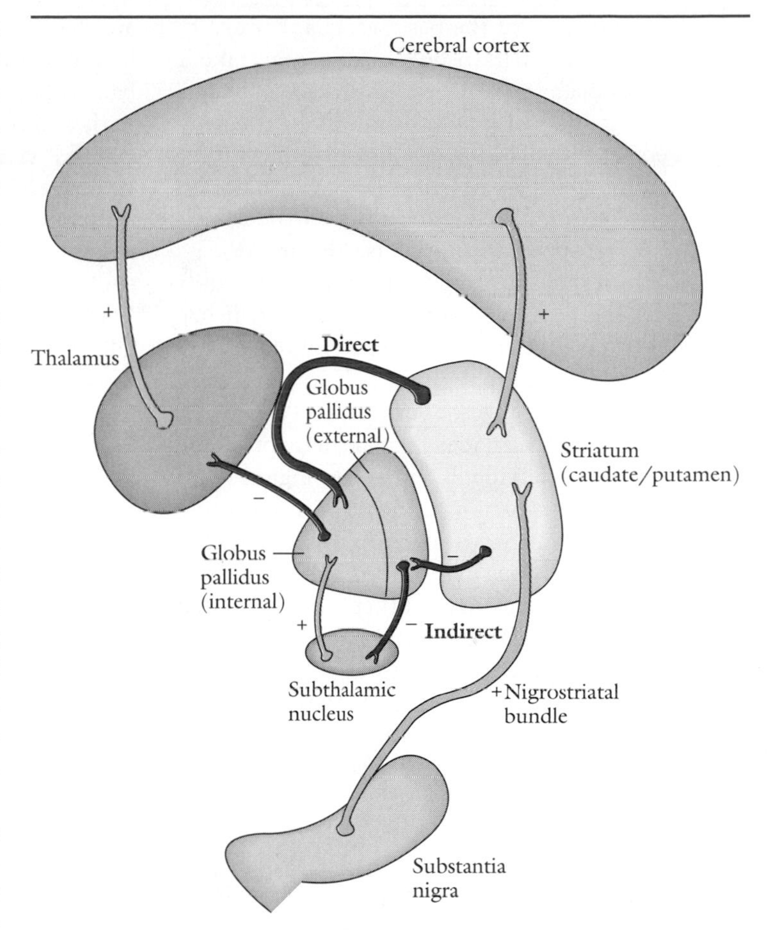

FIGURE 5.8 Connections between different sections of the basal ganglia. Inhibitory connections (indicated by a minus sign) and excitatory connections (indicated by a plus sign). Two routes exist between the caudate and putamen (which receive all the input to the basal ganglia) and the internal section of the globus pallidus (the main output region of the basal ganglia). One route is a direct route (inhibitory) between these two regions. The other is an indirect route from the caudate and putamen to the external section of the globus pallidus (inhibitory), to the subthalamic nucleus (inhibitory), then finally to the internal section of the globus pallidus (excitatory). The globus pallidus has inhibitory connections to motor nuclei of the thalamus. The motor nuclei of the thalamus serve to excite the cortex.

In Huntington's disease, there is a selective loss of striatal neurons that bind gamma-aminobutyric acid (GABA). These neurons give rise to the indirect pathway from the striatum to the globus pallidus, leading to underactivity in this pathway. More specifically, the loss of inhibitory input to the external globus pallidus causes excessive inhibition of the subthalamic nucleus. With this nucleus deactivated, the output from the globus pallidus is decreased. Decreased output in turn lessens inhibition of the thalamus and leads to more motor activity (see Figure 5.8) (Albin, Young, & Penney, 1989).

The role of the basal ganglia in the initiation and termination of movements, particularly those oriented toward a goal or in response to a stimulus, can be well illustrated by the symptoms observed when there is dysfunction of the basal ganglia. For example, a person with Parkinson's disease may take a long time to begin to walk across a floor, but once started, the individual may continue like a runaway train. People with Parkinson's also may have difficulty writing cursively because they can't maintain a steady velocity of production through the transitions from one stroke to another (see Figure 5.9).

Just as the basal ganglia may help to shift between different movements in a sequence, it has been suggested that they may help shift to a new rule or conceptual set that must guide behavior (e.g., Owen, Roberts, Hodges, Summers, Polkey, & Robbins, 1993). Such an idea is made more plausible by the fact that individuals with Huntington's and Parkinson's disease exhibit difficulties in cognitive as well as motor functions. Later in this chapter we discuss their difficulties in motor control, saving our discussion of the cognitive difficulties associated with these disorders for Chapter 14.

The basal ganglia are especially important for the control of movement that is guided internally rather than by external sensory stimuli. This is well illustrated in diseases that affect the basal ganglia. For example, patients with Parkinson's will be much better at initiating walking if there are markers on the floor to which they must move. Likewise, a person with Parkinson's disease may be unable to initiate the leg movement required to kick a stationary ball, but if the ball is rolled toward him or her, the ball will act as a trigger, and the person will respond with a kick (a nice illustration of this phenomenon can be seen in the movie *Awakenings* starring Robert DeNiro and Robin Williams). Conversely, the chorea observed in Huntington's disease may result from an inability to suppress a response to somatosensory and kinesthetic stimuli (see Albin, Young, & Penney, 1989, for a discussion of basal ganglia anatomy and how damage to them leads to motor disorders).

Cortical Regions

In contrast to the basal ganglia, which are important for internally guided movements, the major role of cortical regions in motor control is in externally guided movements, those that require the linkage of sensory inputs with motor outputs. Cortical regions support a range of motor abilities, including picking up an object, using a tool, producing a gesture in response to a verbal command, moving the eyes to explore the image of a face, and moving around our environment. As befits this long list of abilities, there is a large set of cortical regions involved in motor control. Before we describe each of their roles in more detail, we first need to become familiar with their locations in the brain.

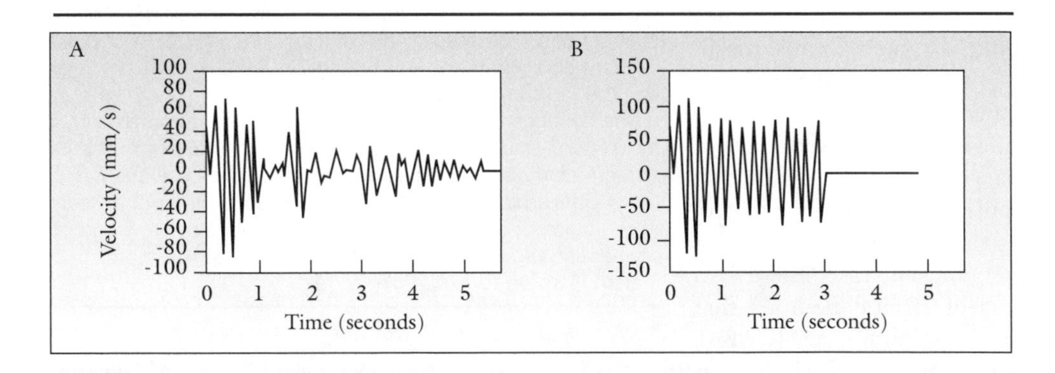

FIGURE 5.9 The disruption in writing as a result of Parkinson's disease. Shown here is the writing of the word "minimum" (A) by an individual with Parkinson's disease as compared to (B) a neurologically intact individual. In Parkinson's the ability to maintain the velocity of the movement as transitions occur across letters is disrupted, whereas in a neurologically intact individual the velocity can be kept constant across those transitions.

Take a look at Figure 5.10. The motor areas are distributed across the frontal lobe, located both on the lateral and medial surfaces. We'll start with a description of the regions on the lateral surface. First, notice the location of the primary motor cortex, directly in front of the central fissure, which encompasses most of Brodmann area 4. Although the majority of primary motor cortex is located on the lateral surface of the brain, it wraps from the dorsal section of the lateral surface down the horizontal fissure to the medial surface (where the representation of the leg and foot are located—refer back to Figure 1.12). Directly in front of primary motor cortex on the lateral surface is premotor cortex, located within Brodmann area 6. At the ventral end of this region but above Broca's areas are the frontal eye fields (also contained within Brodmann area 6, Paus, 1996).

Now let's look at the medial surface. Above the corpus callosum and below the cingulate sulcus, extending as far back as the central fissure is the anterior cingulate cortex. It resides mainly in Brodmann areas 24 and 32, but also in 25 and 33. Above the cingulate and in front of the primary motor region is the supplementary motor area (SMA), located in Brodmann area 6. There is one other portion of the brain involved in motor control, but it is not located within the frontal lobe. These are regions of the parietal lobe within Brodmann areas 7 and 40.

As a brief overview of the contributions of each of these regions to motor control, premotor, SMA, and frontal eye fields are involved in the planning, preparing, and initiating of movement, the anterior cingulate is important for selecting particular responses and monitoring whether the execution of those actions occurred appropriately, primary motor cortex controls the force and/or direction with which the motor plans are executed, and parietal regions are involved in linking motoric movements to extrapersonal space and sensory information as well as linking motor movements to meaning, as occurs in gesture.

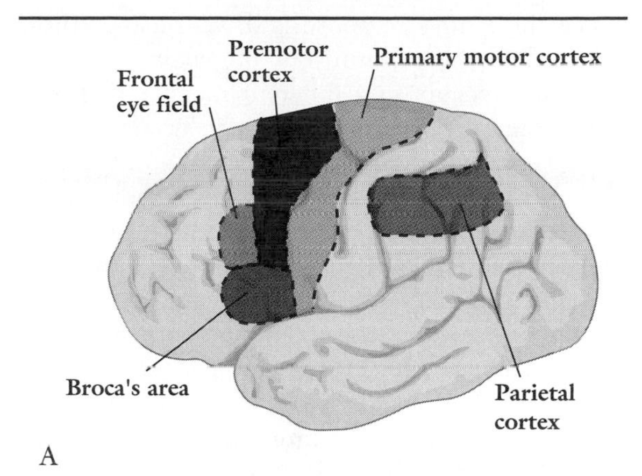

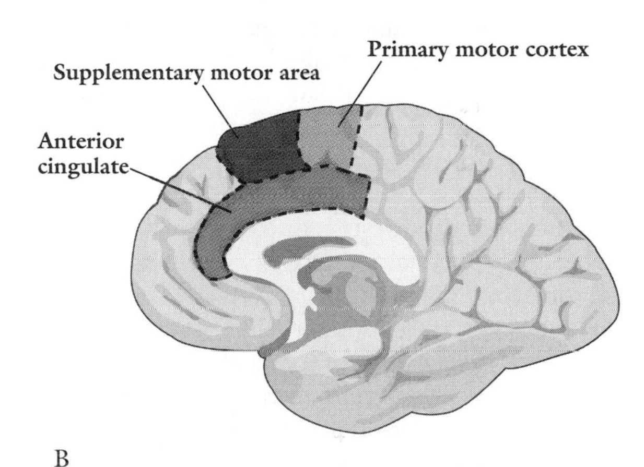

FIGURE 5.10 The major regions of the cortex involved in motor control. (A) Left hemisphere, lateral view. (B) Right hemisphere, midsagittal view.

• *PRIMARY MOTOR CORTEX* •

Primary motor cortex (sometimes referred to as M1) is the region of the brain that provides the command signal to drive motor neurons to make muscles move. Traditionally, it was thought that motor neurons coded for the force of movement and were organized similarly to other sensory systems that have a systematic, fine-grained organization to the sensory maps. For example, the region of occipital cortex sensitive to a particular region of visual space is further divided into columns, each of which responds strongly and preferentially to lines of a particular orientation (e.g., 90 degrees) but not lines of other orientations (e.g., 75 degrees, 20 degrees). A 90-degree line in the receptive field will just stimulate cells in one column with little or no increase in activity over baseline for cells in other columns.

Hence the brain's response is driven just by those cells within the column. But the coding of motor movement occurs in a different manner than this fine-grained micro-organization; it occurs in the form of a neuronal population vector.

Let's examine this concept in a bit more detail. Each neuron is tuned to fire maximally to movement in a certain direction. But for every movement it is the summed activity (the vector) across the entire set of neurons (the population) that influences the direction of the movement. For every movement, then, each and every neuron votes. If the movement is to be in a neuron's preferred direction, it fires a lot, and hence has a loud vote; if the movement is not in the direction preferred by the neuron, it fires less, having a smaller vote (Georgopoulos, Schwartz, & Kettner, 1986). If a monkey has to rotate the direction of movement in a systematic, continuous manner (e.g., slowly turn 90 degrees clockwise), the activity of the population vector can be shown to show a systematic change reflecting the rotation (Georgopoulos et al., 1989).

From a computational perspective, there has been much debate about exactly what the activity of neurons in M1 tells muscles to do—that is, what they are coding for. These cells seem to be sensitive not only to the direction of movement or the degree of muscle force and torque (rotational force) of joint acceleration, but overall trajectory and distance to target, among other things. Furthermore, activity of M1 can be sensitive to sensory information, suggesting that it may be involved in sensory-motor integration (Shen & Alexander, 1997). Recently, there has been an attempt to reconcile these varying viewpoints. It has been suggested that at the most basic level, neurons in M1 code for the force of movement, but the manner in which this control is implemented allows these other features, such as control of movement and posture to "emerge." (The model itself is explained in Todorov, 2000, but unless one has a background in engineering and physics, it will be incomprehensible. For a thumbnail sketch of the model, see S. Scott, 2000.)

Even though primary motor cortex programs the control of muscle movement, it can be influenced by cognitive aspects of performance (see Georgopoulos, 2000, for a review). For example, in adults, learning a new motor skill can change the size of the cortical regions in primary motor cortex that represent each finger (e.g., Karni et al., 1995, 1998). The regions of cortex devoted to fingers that are often used will expand, whereas those controlling fingers that are used less often will retract (we discuss this issue of changes in the neural substrates underlying mental function, known as plasticity, in more detail in Chapter 13).

• *SUPPLEMENTARY AND PREMOTOR AREAS* •

When the motor cortex is damaged, the force with which muscles are exerted cannot be controlled, and the result is weakness and imprecise fine motor movements. Yet, skilled movement requires more than being able to move the muscles: it also requires coordination and timing of muscle movements. For example, merely having the ability to move our muscles is clearly insufficient if we want to give a speech or play the piano. Such complicated motor tasks require a plan of action. Areas of the cortex distinct from primary motor cortex but connected to it are believed to be important for the creation of such plans. After first reviewing the concept of a motor plan, we examine the areas involved in creating such plans: the supplementary motor area (SMA) and premotor regions.

• *Concept of a Motor Plan* • A plan of action, or **motor program** as it is often called, is believed to be an abstract representation of an intended movement. It must contain not only general information about the goal that a series of movements is intended to achieve, but also specific information about the neuromuscular control that will allow the goal to be reached (see Keele, 1968). Suppose that the goal of the plan is to type the sentence, "The lazy white cat just languished in the sun as the bunny bolted across the yard." In this case, the motor program should contain information about which fingers will move, the order in which they will move, the direction in which they will move, the timing between movements, and so forth.

Evidence that the human brain creates an overall plan of a series of complicated motor movements

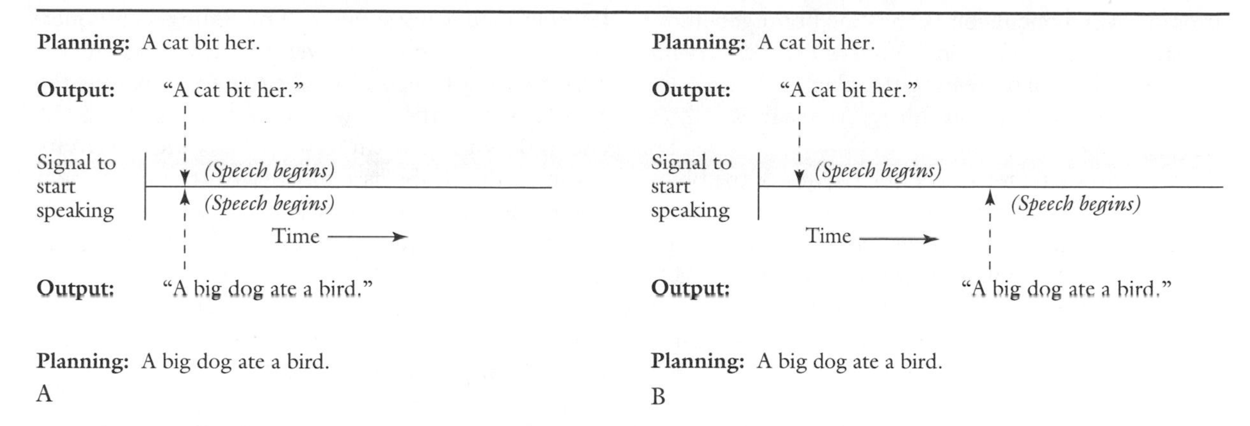

FIGURE 5.11 Testing for the existence of a motor program. (A) If the brain just plans a step or two ahead, the time required to initiate an utterance should not be affected by the length of the utterance—in this case, four versus six words. (B) In contrast, if the brain must plan the entire utterance before initiating speech, the longer the utterance, the longer the delay before its initiation.

comes primarily from studies examining motor control in the oral and manual domains. One phenomenon suggestive of motor planning is **coarticulation,** which refers to differences in how the vocal muscles produce sounds (most notably vowels) depending on what precedes or follows them. For example, the sound of the vowel "u" requires the lips to be rounded (unless you are a ventriloquist!). In contrast, consonants can be produced acceptably with or without lip rounding. Thus, if a series of consonants precedes a vowel requiring lip rounding, the consonants will be produced with rounded lips. Look at yourself in the mirror as you say "construe." Notice that your lips are rounded as you begin to say "str" of the second syllable. Now look in the mirror at the shape of your lips as you say "constrict." When you said the "str" of this word, your lips were not rounded, because the vowel "i" did not require it.

Examples such as these indicate that some preplanning of speech must have occurred. The question that arises is how far in advance this preplanning occurs. Are motor commands generated in a chainlike manner, allowing movements to be planned only a couple of steps ahead rather than requiring the entire sequence to be planned before an action begins? Or is the *entire* utterance planned in advance? (See Wright, 1990, for further discussion.) The answer appears to be that humans can indeed plan an entire motor sequence before initiating action. In their experiments, the researchers told their participants to produce a fluent stream of words, but only after a signal let them know to do so. The utterances were well practiced so that the subjects could produce them fluently. The critical variable in the study was the time an individual took to begin to say the utterance after the signal appeared. The researchers reasoned that if the motor plan were being continually created "online," the number of words in an utterance would not influence how long a person would take to start the utterance. The person would plan speech "on the fly," keeping a step or two ahead of what he or she was actually saying. Such a strategy would be invoked in the same way regardless of whether an utterance consisted of three words or seven. However, if a motor plan of the entire utterance is created before the person begins to speak, the time to initiate speech would be related to the length of the utterance. Because short utterances would require little time to plan, an individual would begin to speak these more quickly than a longer utterance, which would require more time to plan. The logic behind these experiments is shown in Figure 5.11. Results indicated that the time it took to begin speaking increased linearly with the number of words in the utterance, such that each word increased the latency to begin speaking by a set amount. The conclusion is that the brain generates an entire plan of action before movement commences rather than creating the plan as actions are being performed (e.g., Sternberg, Monsell, Knoll, & Wright, 1978).

As mentioned previously, the regions of the brain that are involved in creating these motor plans lie outside the primary motor cortex. As a brief overview, the supplementary motor area (SMA) comes up with the motor plan at the most abstract level—that of sequencing the critical pieces. Then the premotor areas code for the types of actions that must occur to meet that motor plan, and primary motor regions execute the commands to move the muscles. For example, if one wanted to uncork a bottle of wine, the SMA might code for the motor sequence needed: to steady the bottle with one hand and to use the other hand to position the corkscrew above the bottle, for twisting the corkscrew into the cork and then for pulling to retract it. Premotor areas might code for the fact that the bottle would need to be grasped a certain way, and that the corkscrew would need to be twisted in a particular direction and manner. Finally, primary motor areas would code exactly how the muscles would be controlled to implement the required grasp on the bottle and the force or torque with which the twisting of the corkscrew would need to occur. Evidence for such a hierarchical control of movement comes from studies that combine the anatomical precision of PET with the temporal precision of MEG (Pedersen et al., 1998). Activity in the SMA is observed 100–300 ms before an action commences. Activity in the premotor cortex is observed from 100 ms prior to the onset of movement, while activity in the primary motor cortex commences at movement onset and continues for another 100 ms. We now examine the function of each of these regions in more detail.

• ***Brain Regions That Create a Motor Plan*** • One of the main regions of the brain that plays a role in planning, preparing, and initiating movements is the **supplementary motor area (SMA)** (refer back to Figure 5.10). The SMA's role in motor planning has been demonstrated in studies with both animals and humans. In monkeys trained to plan a simple response to a stimulus, the firing of SMA neurons (as examined using single-cell recording techniques) was found to change systematically when the movement was being planned. By comparing the time at which the firing rate of a cell in the SMA changed with the time when electrical activity began in the limbs associated with the movement (remember, neuronal firing is necessary for a muscle to move), researchers determined that the firing rate in the SMA changed *before* electrical activity was recorded at the limb (Tanji, Taniguchi, & Saga, 1980). Thus, these data indicate that the SMA is involved in planning movement prior to initiation of an action.

Research with humans provides a similar picture of the role of the SMA in the planning of complex movement. First, functional brain imaging studies indicate that this area becomes active during tasks that require complicated motor sequencing. For example, an increase in SMA activity is observed when an individual must guide a finger by touch (not vision) to a specific place within a grid of rectangular rods, or when he or she must repetitively touch the limb of one hand to the fingertips in a 16-sequence set of movements (Roland, Larsen, Lassen, & Skinhøj, 1980). Thus, the SMA is specifically involved in *complex* movements. No increase in SMA activity occurs during a simple repetitive task, such as pressing a spring between the thumb and index fingers one time a second.

Second, the SMA is active even when participants are asked to imagine, but not actually perform, a complex finger-sequencing task. Although blood flow to the SMA increases about 20% under these conditions, blood flow does not increase over primary motor cortex; this finding indicates that the individuals were not performing the motor task but merely imagining it (Roland, Larsen, Lassen, & Skinhøj, 1980; see Goldberg, 1985, for a review of much research in animals and humans on the SMA and its role in motor planning).

Unlike motor cortex, whose output is mainly contralateral, each SMA projects to both the ipsilateral and the contralateral motor cortex, as well as to the contralateral SMA. This neuronal wiring allows one SMA to influence motor control on both sides of the body. Whereas unilateral damage to the primary motor areas produces difficulties only on the contralateral side of the body, unilateral damage to the SMA in nonhuman primates mainly produces difficulty in bimanual coordination. These animals are unable to execute different movements of the fingers on each hand because the hands no longer work independently but rather tend to make the same movement at the same time. The deficits are abolished when the corpus callosum is sectioned, a finding that suggests that connections between the SMAs in each hemisphere are also important for coordinating hand movements (Brinkman, 1984). In humans, activity in the SMA also is linked to the planning of movement of both hands. Even in tasks in which only one hand is moving, an increase in blood flow occurs *bilaterally* over the SMA in each hemisphere. In contrast, changes in blood flow over the primary motor cortex occur only contralateral to the hand that is moving.

The **premotor area** is aptly named, not only because that describes its position in front of the motor area but also because its role is to send commands to the primary motor area, making it just prior in the chain of command. Research with monkeys has provided important insights into the function of premotor areas. Single-cell recordings have revealed that a subregion, known as F5, contains neurons that fire in response to specific actions, mostly manual, such as "grasping with the hand," "holding," and "tearing." In some sense, these neurons can be thought of as a neural mechanism for representing basic actions.

Even more intriguing was the discovery of other neurons in this region known as *mirror neurons* that fire only when the monkey observes another organism mirroring a specific type of action that it can perform. In some cases, the correspondence between actions must be very tight. For example, a mirror neuron will fire only when the same precision grip involving the index finger and thumb is used both by the monkey and the experimenter. In other cases, the activation is broader: any type of hand grasping by the experimenter will cause neural firing. What purpose would such neurons serve? They appear to provide a neural substrate for understanding actions being performed by others and for imitating them. Such an ability is a basic prerequisite for any communication system—one must be able to understand the motor production of another individual in order to imitate it (see Rizzolatti & Arbib, 1998, for an excellent insider's review of this research as the first author was instrumental in elucidating the function of these neurons).

The idea that these neurons could form the substrate for a communication system is supported by the finding that their location in the monkey is homologous to Brodmann area 44 in humans, typically considered Broca's area. As we discussed previously, Broca's area is critical for the control of speech output. It may have been that these neurons first were involved in a manual communication system, and then evolved to support auditory language. Neuroimaging studies reveal a functional similarity between the activity in Broca's area in humans and that observed in F5 in monkeys. Broca's area exhibits a specific increase in activity when one has to make a motor movement in response to just having observed that same movement, as compared to viewing a more abstract representation of the motor movement (e.g., viewing one of five fingers being lifted as compared to seeing a photograph of fingers with an "x" on the finger that should be lifted) (Iacoboni, Woods, Brass, Bekkering, Mazziotta, & Rizzolatti, 1999).

• *ANTERIOR CINGULATE CORTEX* •

The role of the **anterior cingulate cortex** in cognitive functioning is one of the most hotly debated topics at present. Until recently, the function of the cingulate in humans was a relative mystery. Because of its location on the midline of the brain, it was rarely damaged in isolation, precluding the ability to determine the effect of a lesion to this region. But since the advent of brain imaging techniques, its important role in cognitive function has become much more obvious. Even a cursory look at the brain imaging literature reveals that the cingulate becomes activated across a huge range of tasks (e.g., Paus, Koski, Caramanos, & Westbury, 1998). The debate regarding the cingulate's function probably occurs in part because it covers a large expanse of brain tissue. Although referred to in general terms as the *anterior cingulate,* it has many distinct regions. Some of these regions are more likely to be involved in attentional control and emotional regulation, which we discuss in Chapters 8 and 12, respectively. Here we will focus on the role that the anterior cingulate plays in motor control.

The posterior portion of the anterior cingulate is specifically implicated in the control and planning of motor movements, especially when they are novel or require much cognitive control. Whereas lesions of the cingulate cortex interfere with motor function, extra activity in this region, such as that generated during epileptic seizures, causes increased motor activity. Moreover, stimulation of the anterior cingulate gyrus in monkeys leads to vocalization as well as to movements of the body, some of which can be complex (e.g., sucking). Evidence that the region is involved in the preparation for movement comes from single-cell recordings. Activity is observed in the anterior cingulate cortex before the beginning of hand movements, regardless of whether they are initiated internally by the animal (i.e., in self-paced tasks) or occur in response to a sensory signal from the environment (Vogt, Finch, & Olson, 1992).

A group of researchers at McGill University has suggested that the anterior cingulate cortex plays a role in modulating motor commands in humans, especially when the movements to be produced are novel or unrehearsed and therefore influenced by cognitive factors (Paus, Petrides, Evans, & Meyer, 1993). To test their hypothesis, these investigators recorded regional brain activity with positron emission tomography (PET) while individuals performed motor tasks that required manual, oral, or ocular movements. For each manner of movement (oral, manual, or ocular), the researchers administered two types of tasks: one that was well practiced and one that was not. For example, in the well-practiced oral task, after hearing "A," subjects responded "B," or after hearing "L," they responded "M." In the novel task, the stimuli were the same, but the task demands were different. In this task, when individuals heard "A," they responded "M," and when they heard "B," they responded "L."

The study revealed two important findings. First, these investigators found that the anterior cingulate cortex has a specific topography. Tasks requiring manual movements activated the most caudal region of the anterior cingulate cortex, those requiring oculomotor movements the most rostral, and those requiring speech, the area between. Hence, like the organization of primary and premotor motor areas, the organization of the anterior cingulate region is topographic. Second, the researchers found that this region was most active when a novel response was required (saying "M" in response to "A") but was not very active when the response had been ingrained over the course of a lifetime (such as saying "B" in response to "A") or over hundreds of trials preceding the PET scan. These findings suggest that the anterior cingulate cortex plays a role in linking motor and cognitive behavior, especially when that linkage is novel or newly learned.

We have also performed a study suggesting a very central role for the anterior cingulate in the selection of a motor response (Milham et al., 2001). In our study, individuals had to press one of three buttons to indicate the ink color (blue, green, yellow) in which a word was presented, a task called the Stroop task. In some cases, known as incongruent trials, the word actually names a different color than the ink color (e.g, the word "green" in blue ink). In other cases, the word is unrelated to color (e.g., the word "bond" in blue ink). The former trials are harder and responses take longer because the conflicting color information provided by the word must be ignored to make the correct response. This task is known to yield activation of the cingulate.

We wanted to specifically examine what aspect of processing was critical to produce cingulate activity. It might be that the cingulate was sensitive to conflict between the ink color and word because of factors that had nothing to do with motor processes, such as the fact that green brings to mind a different hue or has a different meaning from blue. However, we posited that the cingulate's activity was specifically linked to motor conflict, the idea that the motor planning involved in pressing the button to indicate green would slow down or interfere with pressing the button to indicate the correct answer of blue.

To examine this issue we compared regional brain activation for three types of trials: incongruent trials in which the distracting word named a possible response, known as response-eligible (e.g., the word "green" in blue ink when the possible choices are green, blue, and yellow); incongruent trials in which the distracting words did not name a possible response, known as response-ineligible (e.g., the word "red" in blue ink when the possible choices are green, blue and yellow); and neutral trials in which the distracting word had no relationship to color (e.g., the word "lot" in blue ink). We reasoned that if the anterior cingulate is *specifically* involved in response-related processes, it should show more activation on response-eligible than response-ineligible trials, since there is response conflict on response-eligible trials but not response-ineligible trials. Furthermore, activity should be no greater to response-ineligible trials than to neutral trials. Although response-ineligible trials contain conflicting information at the nonresponse level (e.g., the idea of red conflicts with the idea of blue), at the response level neither response-ineligible nor neutral word contains information that would lead to a conflicting response. We found that posterior portions of the anterior cingulate exhibited exactly such a pattern, reinforcing the idea that it plays a prominent role in response-related processes.

The motor system must not only be able to generate and select a response, but must also be able to detect when such selection is incorrect. A different region of the anterior cingulate plays such a role, determining when an *incorrect* response is being made. Recent neuroimaging studies have more precisely localized this function to a region of the cingulate sitting on top of the genu of the corpus callosum (Braver et al., 2001; Kiehl, Liddle, & Hopfinger, 2000). We discuss the role of this region in monitoring for errors in more detail in Chapter 11 on executive control. For now, it is important to know that the regions of the anterior cingulate involved in selecting responses are different from those involved in detecting errors (see Color insert 5.1).

• *FRONTAL EYE FIELD* •

Another region in the frontal lobes that plays a role in voluntary movement is the **frontal eye field,** which, as its name suggests, controls the voluntary execution of eye movements (Paus, 1996). Control of these movements can be lateralized, as in the case of *conjugate lateral eye movements,* which are rapid eye movements in a sideways direction. The frontal eye field of the right hemisphere controls movements in a leftward direction, and the frontal eye field of the left hemisphere controls movement in a rightward direction. The voluntary eye movements controlled by the frontal eye fields are distinct from the reflexive eye movements that occur when something such as a loud noise or a large, bright, moving object pulls a person's attention to a particular point in space. Such reflexive eye movements are under the control of the superior colliculus (which we discuss in Chapter 8). In contrast, the frontal eye field controls the voluntary eye movements that are involved in scanning the visual world, as when you look for a friend's face in a crowd, or visually pursuing a moving object, as when your gaze follows a bird in flight.

The neural system controlling voluntary eye movements (involving the frontal eye fields) and the system controlling reflexive eye movements (involving the superior colliculus) can work independently. For example, eye movements that occur when the frontal eye fields are stimulated in the monkey are not affected by removal of the superior colliculus (Schiller, True, & Conway, 1980). Yet both of these systems synapse on brainstem centers that direct the actual eye movements by means of the third, fourth, and sixth cranial nerves. Thus, the neural control of both voluntary and involuntary eye movements appears to occur through a final common output pathway, even though they can work separately.

If each of these two systems can control the eye-movement centers in the brain stem, why doesn't massive conflict occur? The conflict seems to be avoided because the frontal eye fields have precedence: they strongly influence the superior colliculus. In humans, damage to the frontal eye fields makes it difficult to suppress automatic eye movements that occur when an attention-grabbing stimulus appears in the periphery, because the frontal eye fields can't inhibit the response (Paus et al., 1991). In monkeys, cells in the frontal eye fields excite the cells in the superior colliculus that are important for moving the eyes in the same direction while inhibiting the cells important for movements in other directions (Schlag-Rey, Schlag, & Dassonville, 1992).

• *PARIETAL LOBE* •

The role of the parietal lobe in motor programming is twofold: First, it is involved as an interface

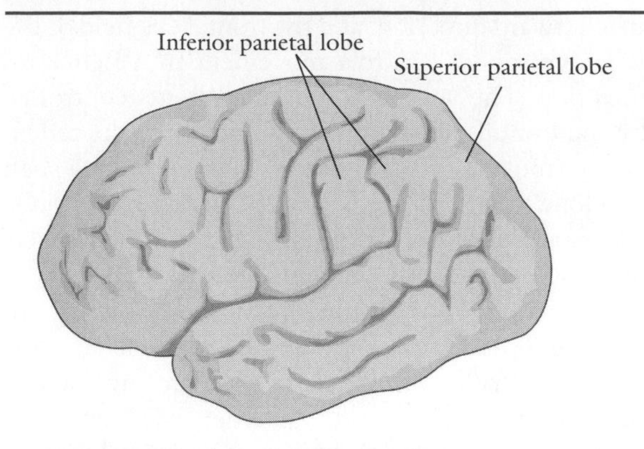

FIGURE 5.12 Superior and inferior regions of the parietal lobe involved in motor programming. The superior regions are important in controlling movements in space, whereas the inferior regions are important in the ability to produce complex, well-learned motor acts.

between movement and sensory information; second, it contributes to the ability to produce complex, well-learned motor acts. These two aspects of motor control appear to rely on different regions of the parietal lobe, the former on the superior regions and the latter on the inferior regions. These regions are depicted in Figure 5.12.

As demonstrated in both monkeys and humans, the superior parietal lobe acts to integrate sensory information with motor movements so that the limbs can be guided correctly during motor acts. Parietal regions are sensitive to *proprioceptive information,* a type of sensory information received from internal sensors in the body, such as that about the position of body parts relative to one another, as well as *kinesthetic* information about actual movement of body parts. This information can be sent forward to premotor and primary motor regions to enable the selection of appropriate motor programs, which in turn provide feedback to parietal regions. The motor feedback, as well as proprioceptive and kinesthetic information, can be used to ensure that movements are being executed according to plan and to allow for correction if they are not (e.g., Mountcastle et al., 1975). Damage to the superior parietal region in humans causes individuals to lose the ability to guide their limbs in a well-controlled manner and is often accompanied by a tendency to misreach (D. N. Levine, Kaufman, & Mohr, 1978).

The superior parietal lobe also plays a role in providing and integrating spatial maps drawn from different modalities to allow for the precise control of movement. For example, when a person reaches for an object, the object's location is taken from visual information and is in retinal coordinates. It must be translated into a spatial map in body-centered or head-centered coordinates so that the motor action can be directed to the correct location (for a review of much of what we know of these functions from single-cell recordings in monkeys, see Andersen, Snyder, Bradley, & Xing, 1997). We discuss more about the role of parietal regions in regard to spatial processing in Chapter 7.

Damage to more inferior regions of the parietal lobe can affect the ability to perform complex, well-learned motor acts. Damage to inferior parietal regions may cause apraxia. Apraxia is a syndrome in which an individual is unable to perform certain complex, learned motor tasks when asked to do so (Lezak, 1983) despite intact motor innervation of the muscles, an intact ability to coordinate sensorimotor actions spontaneously, and an ability to comprehend what is being asked. Apraxia is discussed in more detail later in this chapter.

The neural control of these aspects of motor function is lateralized because apraxia often results after damage to the *left* inferior parietal lobe. Researchers have hypothesized that the left parietal lobe links different types of information, such as visuokinesthetic information and internal conceptual representations, to motor programs. Considered this way, the performance of complex, learned acts falls well within the domain we characterized in Chapter 1 as the purview of the parietal lobe, namely, that of a multimodal association area. For example, the inferior parietal lobe might link the visual and kinesthetic information of a match and a matchbook cover with the motor act that involves lighting the match against the matchbook cover. Such linkages do not require a physical object, because the parietal lobe may also link motor acts to internal representations such as occur during pantomime or gesture (e.g., waving good-bye) (K. M. Heilman & Rothi, 1985).

Given the deficits in pantomime and gesture after parietal damage, it has been suggested that this region may be critical for generating a mental model of motor movements. For example, individuals with parietal lobe lesions were asked to imagine pressing each finger against the thumb sequentially in beat with a metronome. The speed of the metronome was increased every five seconds. The participants were asked to determine the point where their imagination of moving their fingers told them that they could no longer keep up with the metronome. Then they were asked to perform the task, and the actual breakpoint in their performance was compared to that which they had imagined. Their estimates were quite poor (Sirigu et al., 1996). Converging evidence is provided by neuroimaging studies indicating that the inferior parietal area (BA 40) becomes active when an individual has to imagine making complete sequential movements of the finger (Gerardin et al., 2000) or grasping an object (Decety et al., 1994).

The ability to create such models of sensorimotor states is important for a number of reasons. If one can predict what will happen with regard to motor movements, known as a **forward model** (since you are predicting what will happen forward in time), then one can predict the sensory consequences of motor plans. That prediction can be used to determine if the motion is being performed correctly (e.g., I am feeling what I think I should be feeling). Thus, if you decide to pick up a full carton of milk from a table, you have a model of how that should feel and how much force you will need to pick it up. If the carton turns out to be empty, you quickly realize that it doesn't fit with your model and can adjust your actions accordingly. The parietal lobe appears to play a large role in this adjustment process. The role of the parietal lobe was demonstrated in a study in which individuals were to move their arms to a visual target. Unbeknownst to them, after they started to move their arms, the target's location was moved. Online adjustment of the motor program based on the change in visual input was needed for them to correctly reach the target. If during this time period TMS was applied over the posterior parietal cortex, which should disrupt activity of this region, no adjustments were observed for the contralateral arm movement—it was incorrectly directed to the same position where the target originally was located (Desmurget et al., 1999).

At present there is some evidence that parietal regions may be aided in the building of an internal model by the cerebellum. For example, there is evidence that when a person is learning to use a new object, such as a new tool, the cerebellum may play a role in helping to create an internal model (e.g., Imamizu et al., 2000). The cerebellum also seems to be important for providing an internal model of the sensory information that is likely to accompany a movement. Having such a model can help the brain to "subtract out" the sensory feedback that is irrelevant to task performance. Have you ever noticed that it is near to impossible to tickle yourself? Well, that occurs in part because you create a motor model that has a sensory consequence. Since you already know what the sensory consequences of tickling yourself would be, you are relatively impervious to the results of your motor action. The cerebellum appears to play a role in this process as there is less cerebellar activity to a self-produced tactile stimulus than to one that is externally generated (Blakemore, Wolpert, & Frith, 1998).

Having a model of motor actions as is created by parietal regions is also important if one wishes to control motor actions to produce a desired sensory outcome. This control can be achieved via an **inverse model,** which conceptually is the opposite of a forward model. In an inverse model you construct the desired state at each point along a trajectory and translate those states into specific motor commands. Rather than predicting the sensory states that would be expected based on a motor program (a forward model), in this case you determine what motor actions are required to reach a particular state (an inverse model). For example, in visually controlled actions, one needs a model of how one's motor movements can be generated so that the arms will end up in the place to which they are being guided by sight (see Wolpert & Ghahramani, 2000, for a discussion of the range of computational problems that must be solved by the motor system, and the different possible ways of doing so).

At this point, we have reviewed the major regions of the brain that are involved in motor movement and have briefly outlined some of the motor disorders that occur after damage to these brain regions. It is important to keep in mind that despite the dif-

TABLE 5.2 Functions of major brain regions involved in movement

BRAIN REGION	COMPUTATION
Movement planning	
Inferior parietal regions	Generating an internal model of the movement
Supplementary motor area	Selection of the order of movements
Premotor area	Selection of the types of movements required (e.g., a grasp)
Frontal eye fields	Voluntary control of saccades
Posterior regions of the anterior cingulate cortex	Initiating novel responses and overriding prepotent responses
Movement specification and initiation	
Cerebellum	Temporal patterns of muscular activation
Basal ganglia	Switching between different patterns of movement initiation and cessation
Motor cortex	Motor execution of the force and/or direction of movement
Movement monitoring	
Anterior cingulate cortex	Detects when an action is erroneous
Parietal cortex	Uses sensory feedback to adjust movement online

ferent roles that each brain region plays, there remains a certain amount of overlap. For example, sequential movement requires the integrated functioning of many different brain regions. To gain an appreciation for how each of these individual brain regions might contribute to sequential motor processing, see Table 5.2.

Motor Disorders

We now turn our attention to the neurological basis of some of the more common motor disorders. In our discussion, we divide motor disorders into two categories: those that occur because of damage or disruption to subcortical areas and those that occur after cortical damage. As was discussed at the outset of this chapter, we can broadly characterize subcortical motor disorders as affecting the form and timing of movements, whereas cortical motor disorders affect the conceptual clarity of motor acts, either by disrupting the sequencing of complex motor acts or by disrupting the ability to have a motor act represent a concept.

Subcortical Motor Disorders

In this section of the chapter, we discuss the motor disorders that are characterized mainly by damage to subcortical regions: Parkinson's disease, Huntington's disease, Tourette's syndrome, and tardive dyskinesia.

• *PARKINSON'S DISEASE* •

As we learned earlier, **Parkinson's disease** results from damage to the cells of the substantia nigra, which stops producing the neurotransmitter dopamine. This damage may result from a variety of causes, including encephalitis, toxins, trauma, and neural degeneration. The behavioral effects of the disease are not evident, however, until 60% of nerve cells and 80% of dopamine are lost. The delay in symptom onset occurs because the brain tries valiantly to compensate for the loss of dopamine in a number of ways, such as by having the remaining dopaminergic neurons increase their synthesis of dopamine or by decreasing the inactivation or clearance of dopamine once it crosses the synaptic cleft (Zigmond et al., 1990). At some point, however, often later in life, when a person reaches age 60 or 70 years, these compensatory mechanisms fail. At this point, cell loss, which is a normal part of the aging process, reduces the population of cells in the substantia nigra below a critical point, and behavioral effects are observed.

The movement disorder of Parkinson's disease has four major symptoms: tremors, **cogwheel rigidity,** akinesia, and **disturbances of posture.** These symptoms are generally observed on both sides of the body (Bannister, 1992). However, in some cases, the dopamine depletion occurs in just one half of the brain, so symptoms are evident only on the contralateral side of the body; a condition known as *hemi-Parkinsonism.* Let us now examine each of the symptoms in more detail.

As we mentioned earlier, tremors are repetitive rhythmic motions. Parkinsonian tremors generally affect the arms and hands. These tremors are rarely seen during deliberate and purposeful movements but are most obvious when the person is at rest (e.g., just sitting in a chair listening to a conversation). Hand tremors are often described as looking like "pill-rolling" because they resemble movements of an individual who is rolling a pill between the thumb and forefinger.

The rigidity observed in Parkinson's disease occurs because increased muscle tone in the extensor and flexor muscles makes the person appear stiff. In fact, the mechanical nature of the movements is referred to as cogwheel rigidity. If you try to move a limb of someone with Parkinson's disease, the movement is resisted. If you push hard enough, however, the limb can be moved, but only so far until once again the movement is resisted. When sufficient force is applied, the limb can be moved again. Thus, rather than moving smoothly, the limb moves in specific, rigid steps, much as a cogwheel does.

Another symptom of Parkinson's disease is akinesia, a poverty of movement, or bradykinesia, a slowness of movement. Some Parkinson's patients sit motionless, like mannequins in a store window. Even facial movements can diminish to such a degree that these individuals are said to have a *Parkinsonian mask.* As we saw in the case of Muhammad Ali, this lack of movement can disrupt communication. Speech is affected because individuals have trouble producing sounds, and writing is affected because the production of letters is slow and labored.

Parkinsonian symptoms also include difficulty in posture and locomotion. Unlike tremors, which mainly affect the arms and hands, these other difficulties affect muscle groups throughout the body. The posture of a person with Parkinson's disease suffers because he or she has difficulty counteracting the force of gravity. For example, the person's head may droop or the person may bend so far forward as to end up on his or her knees. The posture required for sitting or standing may be impossible to maintain without support. The ability to make postural adjustments may also be impaired. For example, individuals with Parkinson's disease may fall when bumped because they cannot right themselves quickly after losing balance. Movements that require postural transitions are also difficult, such as standing up from a seated position. Walking is compromised not only because it requires continual postural adjustments, but also because it requires a series of movements, which akinesia renders difficult. When patients with Parkinson's disease walk, they tend to shuffle, much as normal individuals do when walking on ice or in other situations in which maintaining balance is difficult.

Although Parkinson's disease has been described as having four major symptoms, all these symptoms are not typically observed in any one person. Some patients have a rigid-bradykinetic-predominant form of the disease, in which their main symptom is slowness, whereas others have a more tremor-predominant form. These two varieties of Parkinson's differ not only with regard to behavior, but also in their biochemical bases, in the degree of intellectual impairment observed, and in the clinical course of the disease. The clinical course may decline more sharply and the intellectual impairment may be more severe in patients with the rigid-bradykinetic-predominant form than in those with the tremor-predominant form (Huber, Christy, & Paulson, 1991). Likewise, akinesia is associated with depletion of dopamine and **homovanillic acid (HVA),** a by-product of dopamine synthesis, in one part of the nigrostriatal system (the caudate nucleus), whereas tremor is associated with HVA depletion in another region (the globus pallidus) (Bernheimer et al., 1973).

As already noted, the causes of Parkinson's disease seem to vary. In some cases, the disease runs in families. In other cases, it may be related to carbon monoxide, toxins, syphilis, or tumors. Still other cases may be viral in origin. In the 1910s and 1920s, individuals with *encephalitis lethargica* (also known as *von Economo's encephalitis*) caught the flu and exhibited Parkinsonian symptoms either soon thereafter or as long as 20 years later. Parkinson's disease can also be caused by drugs that individuals voluntarily ingest. For example, in the mid-1980s, young adults in their twenties and thirties began appearing in hospital rooms exhibiting symptoms of the disease, especially those related to lack of movement. Because such symptoms are highly unusual in this age group, doctors looked for a commonality among the patients and discovered that all were drug users. As a result, the afflicted individuals were called "the frozen addicts." Some detective work revealed that these cases of Parkinson's disease could be linked to a synthetic heroin that was contaminated with the compound, MPTP (1-methyl-4-phenyl-1,2,3,6-tetrahydropyridine), which, when converted by the body into MPP^+ (methylphenylpyridinium), is toxic to dopaminergic cells.

Although Parkinson's disease cannot be cured, it can be treated, typically by drug therapy, either to increase the level of dopamine or to inhibit cholinergic receptors. Because the nigrostriatal pathways are damaged, dopaminergic pathways are underactive. To augment the level of dopamine, physicians give these patients a metabolic precursor of dopamine, **L-dopa,** because dopamine itself cannot cross the blood-brain barrier. This precursor, however, can reach the brain when taken orally. Damage to the nigrostriatal pathways also disrupts the usual balance between dopaminergic and cholinergic systems so that the cholinergic systems are relatively overactive. Thus, anticholinergic drugs are also given, which are particularly helpful in reducing tremors (Bannister, 1992).

Unfortunately, these drugs have numerous side effects. They may alter a person's mood, leading to euphoria or depression. Sometimes, they interfere with memory and the ability to pay attention. In other cases, people's thought patterns and their sexual behavior may be changed. In extreme cases, an individual may even experience hallucinations and delusions. These effects tend to go away when the person stops taking the drug or when the dosage is reduced (Cummings, 1991). Another unfortunate characteristic of these medicines is that they tend to lose effectiveness after a number of years.

Some experimental therapies for Parkinson's disease are being explored, but they are far from becoming standard treatment. One that has received much attention is the grafting of fetal tissue rich in dopamine-producing cells to the substantia nigra of an affected person. The strategy is for cells from the graft to produce dopamine and thus offset the loss of dopamine-producing cells in this region. The possibility of such a treatment was first demonstrated in monkeys whose substantia nigra was destroyed in a matter of days (as compared with years as is typical for Parkinson's) by the neurotoxin MPTP. Results with this procedure in humans have been inconsistent, probably due to variations in procedures (e.g., Olanow, Kordower, & Freeman, 1996), although at least some groups have reported significant improvements (e.g., Hauser et al., 1999).

Other approaches that have been explored involve the destruction of the internal segment of the globus pallidus (GP_i), known as *pallidotomy,* to reduce tremors, and chronically implanted electrodes to artificially produce stimulation in the subthalamic nuclei (which project in an inhibitory fashion to the GP_i), although both treatments are quite experimental and controversial.

• *HUNTINGTON'S DISEASE* •

Huntington's disease, an inherited neurologic disease caused by degeneration of the striatum, produces abnormal movements, cognitive deficits (eventually dementia), and psychiatric symptoms. As with our discussion of Parkinson's disease, we concentrate here on the motor aspects of Huntington's and leave a description of the intellectual and cognitive deficits for Chapter 14. Although Huntington's disease is rare (1.6 cases per million), when the Huntington's gene is inherited, it always expresses itself. This gene acts much like a time bomb that remains relatively dormant until some time between the ages of 30 and 45 years, when the symptoms begin to manifest themselves in earnest. Afterward, the disease involves a slow decline for 10 to 15 years and eventually leads to death.

The main motor symptom of Huntington's disease is chorea, a variety of rapid, jerky movements that appear to be well coordinated but are performed involuntarily and ceaselessly in an irregular manner. Although individuals with Huntington's disease initially seem to be fidgeting, the movements eventually increase until they are almost incessant. They never involve just one muscle but affect whole limbs or parts of a limb. Eventually, all movement becomes uncontrollable and the chorea affects most of the body, including the head, face, trunk, and limbs. In the later stages, not only is the person unable to communicate through speaking or writing, but other basic movements required for independent living, such as walking or swallowing, are also lost (Bannister, 1992).

Although chorea is considered the classic motor sign in Huntington's disease, individuals with this condition have additional motor difficulties. Some of these occur in the realm of initiation and execution of movement. For example, while neurologically intact individuals can use a cue to aid in performing a sequential button-pressing procedure, Huntington's patients are unable to use such advance information to initiate and execute movements. These difficulties may be a marker for the disease because they may even precede the onset of chorea, which is generally considered the definitive motor symptom of the disorder. Furthermore, difficulty in using cue information and initiating movement in the absence of other symptoms has been found in a subset of individuals who are at risk for Huntington's disease (because one of their parents had the disease). Researchers speculate that this group is likely to exhibit the disease later in life (Bradshaw et al., 1992).

Arm movements are not the only aspect of motor control affected in Huntington's disease; the speed and initiation of voluntary eye movements are also affected. As we discussed earlier in the chapter, voluntary eye movements are under the control of frontal brain regions. These regions are likely to be affected in Huntington's disease because the basal ganglia, which are damaged, project to the frontal eye field. For example, when required to visually track a target that moves predictably between positions, patients with the disease cannot direct their eyes to the correct location at the correct time. However, movements to an unexpected stimulus that appears in the periphery, which are under the control of the superior colliculus, a region unaffected in Huntington's diease, are normal (Tian, Zee, Lasker, & Folstein, 1991).

Destruction of the caudate in Huntington's disease has been directly linked to the severity of motor slowing (see Figure 5.8). Using magnetic resonance imaging (MRI) techniques, researchers measured the degree of caudate atrophy in a group of patients with Huntington's disease and found that it correlated not only with eye-movement abnormalities, disruptions on tests requiring writing speed, and tests of complex psychomotor processing, but also with the severity of cognitive impairment (Starkstein et al., 1988). However, no correlation was found between the caudate degeneration and the severity of chorea, a finding indicating that the atrophy was linked specifically to motor slowing and not to all the motor manifestations of Huntington's disease.

Researchers have also been attempting to discover what aspect of the motor control process for voluntary movement is compromised in Huntington's disease. Recently, it has been suggested that voluntary movements become jerky and variable because there is a loss of error feedback control. The initial phase of movements made by individuals with Huntington's disease or those who carry the Huntington's gene but who are as of yet asymptomatic (i.e., are not yet exhibiting chorea), appear to be like those of neurologically intact individuals. Hence, it appears that the feedforward control predicting how the movement should occur is intact. However, as they get to the second half of a reaching motion, in which they must slow down their movement to zero in a target, they exhibit error not shown by neurologically intact individuals. Furthermore, if their movements are disrupted by an external force, such as a push, they are much less able to correct for and counteract that disruption than are neurologically intact individuals. These findings suggest that control of motor movements via feedback is compromised.

• *TOURETTE'S SYNDROME* •

Tourette's syndrome is a relatively rare disorder that manifests itself as a variety of vocal and motor **tics**, which are repetitive involuntary movements of a compulsive nature that wax and wane in severity. This disorder can vary in severity from a few tics that occur only when the individual is tired or tense to between 30 and 100 tics per minute. Unlike the other motor disorders discussed so far, all of which affect individuals in their middle to late adult years, Tourette's syndrome is seen in childhood, usually before the age of 11 years. In the least severe form of the disorder, the tics typically involve the face and head, although the limbs, and even the entire body, may be affected. Complex movements, such as touching, hitting, and jumping, can also occur, movements akin to those seen in pogo dancing or the head banging of punk rockers (Lees, 1990).

The next level of severity includes cries and vocalizations. The onset of vocal tics usually follows the production of motor tics by several years. The most severe level is characterized by *echolalia,* the repeating of what has just been said, and *coprolalia,*

THE WEXLER FAMILY'S ROLE IN FINDING THE GENETIC BASIS OF HUNTINGTON'S DISEASE

Although a tragic and harrowing illness, Huntington's disease has an interesting history, and the discovery of its cause is a testimony to the efforts of personally involved and determined scientists. Even before the first medical description of Huntington's disease, investigators knew that choreas inherited in families were associated with a progressive dementia. For example, Vessie (cited in Kolb & Whishaw, 1990) claims that the disease was introduced to the United States by immigrants from England who were attempting to escape persecution as witches (a perception probably reinforced by their movement disorders).

Because the disease is most common among white persons of European descent and is rare in other racial groups, the introduction of the gene to a particular region of the world can usually be traced to one or two immigrants from Europe. For example, individuals with Huntington's disease in mainland China and Hong Kong generally have family origins from the coastal provinces of China, which suggests that the Huntington's gene was introduced into the Chinese gene pool by European travelers (Leung et al., 1992).

One family touched by Huntington's disease has played a prominent role in the discovery of its cause. Nancy Wexler, whose mother died of the disease, worked with molecular biologists to find the responsible gene. Research funds were provided in part by the Hereditary Disease Foundation, which her father helped to found. Tracking down the gene required a population not only with a high incidence of the disease, but also isolated enough so that the genetic status of most of the individuals within the population could be determined (a prerequisite for obtaining a highly complete genealogy). Accordingly, Nancy Wexler and other scientists packed their bags and headed for the small towns near Lake Maracaibo in Venezuela where the local population has one of the highest concentrations of people with Huntington's disease in the world. The scientists carefully charted the genealogies of these people and then painstakingly took blood and skin samples so that their chromosomes could be examined.

Then it was back to the laboratory. The scientists examined the chromosomes for a marker, a characteristic telltale portion of the chromosome that would be easily identifiable. This marker, although not the gene for Huntington's disease itself, would be positioned so close to the Huntington's gene that it would be inherited along with it. Although skeptics believed that finding such a marker would take 50 to 75 years, the twelfth marker tested, which was located on the short arm of

obscene speech. Because of the unusual behavior of these children, they are often misdiagnosed as having psychiatric disorders.

Tourette's syndrome appears to run in families and has been suggested to be caused by a single autosomal dominant gene (Kurlan et al., 1986). Yet the disease is much more common in males than in females. To account for this gender difference, some researchers have suggested that androgen acting at key developmental periods may potentiate the disorder (Petersen et al., 1992). Tourette's syndrome is also associated with obsessive-compulsive disorder. Half the children with the syndrome exhibit obsessive-compulsive behaviors, whereas approximately a quarter manifest a full-blown obsessive-compulsive syndrome. Like compulsive behaviors, in which an urge becomes stronger and stronger until relieved by the production of an act, people with Tourette's syndrome claim that the more they try to suppress a tic, the greater their compulsion to produce it; this compulsion is relieved only after the tic occurs (G. S. Golden, 1990). There is also evidence that Tourette's syndrome often co-occurs with attention deficit hyperactivity disorder (Matthews, 1988).

The association with obsessive-compulsive disorders, along with the effects of pharmacological agents on Tourette's syndrome, suggests that it involves dysfunction of the basal ganglia. A number of other motor syndromes that involve basal ganglia

chromosome 4, was the correct one (Gusella et al., 1983). Nancy Wexler said, "It was as though, without the map of the United States, we had looked for a killer by chance in Red Lodge, Montana, and found the neighborhood where he was living" (Murray, 1994, pp. 30-31).

The discovery of the gene, however, raised a number of gut-wrenching dilemmas. Once the gene was known, a genetic test for the disease was created. Imagine for a moment that one of your parents died of Huntington's disease, meaning that the chances that you have the disease are fifty-fifty and that you have a fifty-fifty chance of passing it on to your offspring. Would you *really* want to be tested to learn whether you have the gene? Would you make different decisions about your life, about marriage, children, and a career, if you definitely knew your fate, be it good or bad, than if all you knew was that you had a fifty-fifty chance of having the disease? What would you do if you found out that you had the Huntington's gene? Because the test would tell you only that you have the gene but not the age at which you would be affected nor the speed of your demise, how would you handle the uncertainty?

Because of the ethical and psychological dilemmas raised by the test, Nancy Wexler, trained as a clinical psychologist, has become a specialist in counseling individuals who are deciding whether to learn their status. She says that people often claim that if they knew their fate, they would live their lives differently, spending more time with their families or traveling. She points out to these people that they might not want to wait until they are diagnosed with a fatal disease to give themselves license to pursue their desires. Studies with individuals at risk for Huntington's disease suggest that they often want to be tested because of decisions about having children and planning for the future. The effect of counseling remains unclear. For example, a group study in Wales found that many applicants were ill prepared for what they learned and reacted negatively (A. Tyler et al., 1992), whereas other studies have suggested that the knowledge provided by the test increases the psychological well-being of individuals (e.g., Wiggins et al., 1992).

How has Nancy Wexler decided to deal with her own genetic legacy? When she was in her twenties and her mother was first diagnosed with Huntington's disease, Nancy decided not to have children. She will not say publicly whether she has been tested for the gene, believing that the issue is very personal and not wanting to influence others in their choice. She has stated, however, that she took many years to reach her decision. In October 1993 she received the Albert Lasker Public Service Award, one of the most distinguished awards in medicine, for "her groundbreaking work . . . toward finding a cure for Huntington's disease and for increasing awareness of all genetic disease" (Murray, 1994, p. 28). ■

dysfunction are also associated with obsessive-compulsive disorders (Rapoport, 1990), including von Economo's encephalitis and Sydenham's chorea (a motor disorder characterized by sudden, aimless, and irregular movements of the extremities that usually occur after rheumatic fever).

The dysfunction in Tourette's syndrome appears to be specifically related to the dopaminergic system, of which the basal ganglia are a major part. Drugs that block dopamine receptors ameliorate the disorder, whereas drugs that increase dopamine turnover aggravate the symptoms. Moreover, levels of HVA, a metabolite of dopamine, are lower than normal in children with Tourette's syndrome. In fact, the level of HVA predicts behavior: children with lower levels of HVA perform more poorly in school and have more motor restlessness. These findings are believed to indicate that dopamine receptors are hypersensitive and that negative feedback is sent to the presynaptic dopaminergic neurons so as to reduce their production of dopamine. Treatment for Tourette's syndrome usually involves agents that block the D_2 receptors, such as haloperidol, which have been found to reduce vocal tics in a majority (85%) of patients. Also implicating the D_2 receptor is a finding that the density of D_2 receptors may influence the severity of Tourette's syndrome (Wolf et al., 1996). However, haloperidol has side effects that include lethargy, increased appetite and weight gain, depressed mood, and in some cases, social phobias and avoidance of school. As a result, less than 12% of individuals continue to use this medication long-term. Other drugs may therefore be employed (see Leckman & Riddle, 2000, Table 1, for a nice summary of treatment options). In general, the advantages and disadvantages provided by drug therapy must be carefully considered case by case (G. S. Golden, 1990).

In general, Tourette's syndrome does not have major deleterious effects on cognitive functioning. Most children with the syndrome have normal IQs, although 35% also have difficulties in certain realms of learning, most often those related to visuomotor and visuographic skills. At present, scientists know neither the degree to which these difficulties are part of the core constellation of symptoms associated with the syndrome, nor how much these problems can be attributed to associated factors such as (1) the side effects of medication taken to relieve the disorder, (2) social stigmatization, or (3) difficulties in concentration because of frequent tics. Fortunately, the symptoms of this syndrome may ameliorate somewhat by adulthood, with the severity of childhood tics having little predictive value for later functioning (Goetz et al., 1992).

• *TARDIVE DYSKINESIA* •

Tardive dyskinesia is a movement disorder that has been estimated to occur in 20% to 40% of individuals who are long-term users of conventional antipsychotic drugs that act to block dopamine (e.g., Morgenstern, Glazer, Niedzwiecki, & Nourjah, 1987). As we learned earlier when discussing Parkinson's disease, decreased dopaminergic output causes slowness, lack of motor movements, and/or tremors. However, people with tardive dyskinesia do not tend to show Parkinsonian symptoms. Rather, they often exhibit increased motor movements that usually affect the face, especially the mouth and lips, and sometimes the trunk and limbs. Some of these motor movements include chorea, tics, **akathisia** (compulsive, hyperactive, and fidgety movements of the legs), and **dystonia** (painful, sustained muscle spasms of the same muscle groups frequently causing twisting and repetitive movements or abnormal postures).

How then are we to explain these abnormal motor movements? The answer at present is not clear. One possibility is that, just as in Tourette's syndrome, these motor movements result from a supersensitivity to dopamine of receptors in the striatum. This supersensitivity may result, in part, from the inactivation of dopaminergic neurons in the substantia nigra (Breggin, 1993). Supporting such an idea, the abnormal movements can be lessened in some patients by the blockage or depletion of dopamine, but unfortunately the symptoms are ameliorated in less than half of all individuals treated (Bannister, 1992). The answer to this riddle is bound to be complicated. Somewhat paradoxically, and by a mechanism that is not clearly understood, a significant number of individuals may have overlapping tardive dyskinesias and Parkinsonian symptoms. Findings such as these have led to some speculation that the relative balance of activation of different dopamine receptors, in particular, D_1 and D_2 receptors, may play a causative role. Other neurotransmitter systems have also been implicated, including a change in the GABAergic system, and the cholinergic system, as anticholinergic agents can also be clinically effective in the control of dystonias (Casey, 2000; Cardoso & Jankovic, 1997).

The motor-related problems induced by conventional antipsychotic medications are extremely troublesome for several reasons. First, determining which individuals will exhibit tardive dyskinesia is nearly impossible because the symptoms appear only after a person has been taking such drugs for at least three months. Research indicates that older individuals and females are more at risk for the disorder, and the risk may also be increased for patients with mood disorders and those who have sustained brain injury (Wirshing & Cummings, 1990). Second, once the symptoms appear, they are usually irreversible. Although lowering the dosage may help, complete eradication of the problem occurs in only about 30% of patients. Consequently, the patient and the person prescribing the medication often find themselves in a catch-22: starting the patient on a low dosage of antipsychotic drugs might help reduce the possibility of motor symptoms, but too low a dosage will not suppress the psychotic behavior.

Fortunately, recent advances in psychopharmacology have yielded new drugs, known as atypical antipsychotics, that tend to be associated with a much lower incidence of tardive dyskinesia but are still effective in diminishing psychotic symptoms. Unlike the typical antipsychotics, which block D_2 receptors, these newer drugs act in a different manner. Exactly how they work remains unclear: they may work via a different set of receptors—in particular, D_4 or serotinergic receptors—or they may bind D_2 receptors in different brain regions or in a different manner than typical antipsychotics (see Kapur & Seeman, 2001, for a longer discussion of this issue).

Cortical Motor Disorders

As we have learned, most of the subcortical motor disorders manifest as a slowness of movement or as an increase in movements. As we turn our attention to cortical motor disorders, we see that they have a different effect, tending to disrupt the ability to pursue specific plans of motor action or to relate motor action to meaning. We first examine one specific cortical disorder of motor control, alien limb syndrome, and then a family of such disorders, the apraxias.

• *ALIEN LIMB SYNDROME* •

One of the more unusual disorders of motor function is **alien limb syndrome.** Patients afflicted with this disorder feel as if one of their limbs is alien, either because it seems to move on its own, feels as though it doesn't belong to its owner, or seems to have its own personality. Patients with this disorder commonly complain that their limbs do not obey them or that they make involuntary and complex movements. The most typical types of movements displayed by the alien limb are groping and grasping. As described in one case study, "The left hand would tenaciously grope for and grasp any nearby object, pick and pull at her clothes, and even grasp her throat during sleep" (Banks, et al., 1989, p. 456). In almost all cases, only one limb is affected, and it is located contralateral to the site of the lesion, which is typically caused by a stroke.

Another common symptom among patients with this disorder is competition between the hands or difficulty in bimanual control. For example, one person noted that, while driving, one hand tried to turn the car to the left, while the other tried to turn it to the right. In other cases, each hand would try to hold a glass from a different side, or the hands would fight over which one would pick up the telephone. Not only do the difficulties in bimanual coordination result in power struggles, but they may also manifest as mirror movements, in which one hand mimics the motions of the other (Doody & Jankovic, 1992).

Any limb can be affected in this syndrome, although the distal parts of a limb (e.g., the hand and forearm) are usually involved. While the individual retains the ability to move the affected limb voluntarily, control of such movement is clumsy. The affected limb seems as if it can be controlled only from proximal regions (e.g., the shoulder), which allow only gross motor control, rather than from distal regions (e.g., the hand), which provide fine motor control. Under extreme conditions, the limb can take on a personality. In one case study, a patient thought her left arm was named Joseph and was a baby. When her limb acted in strange ways, she would make up a story to explain the alien limb's behavior in the context of her belief about the limb's personality. For example, when this arm acted on other parts of her body (like pinching her nipples), she interpreted this action as baby Joseph's biting her while nursing.

At present, no consensus exists about exactly which neural structures must be damaged for alien limb syndrome to occur. However, the syndrome is usually observed after an *infarction* (i.e., blockage of a blood vessel) in the territory of the anterior cerebral artery (the artery that supplies blood to the medial frontal cortex), the anterior two thirds of the corpus callosum, and the anterior cingulate cortex; thus, these structures are implicated as likely candidates (Gasquoine, 1993). The damaged areas of frontal cortex tend to include the SMA, which may help to explain some of the symptoms observed in alien limb syndrome. As you may remember from our discussion of the SMA earlier in the chapter (see page 164), in monkeys, damage to this region and the callosum affects bimanual control (Brinkman, 1984).

Although no cure exists for alien limb syndrome, several methods can be used to alleviate it. One approach is to keep the limb "busy" performing a repetitive motor activity or holding an object. Another approach is to use muscle relaxation or the application of warm water or a shower spray to calm the limb. Still another approach is to attempt to increase control over the limb by concentrating on it or by directing it with verbal commands.

• *APRAXIA* •

Apraxia is an inability to perform *skilled*, sequential, purposeful movement, an inability that cannot be accounted for by disruptions in more basic motor processes such as muscle weakness, abnormal posture or tone, or movement disorders (such as tremors or chorea). This disorder is more common after damage to the left hemisphere, although, as we discuss later, the exact region damaged varies depending on the type of apraxia exhibited.

Two main pieces of evidence suggest that apraxia is a higher-order motor deficit rather than a deficit associated with more low-level aspects of motor control. First, apraxia usually exhibits itself bilaterally. If the deficit were at a low level and concerned the control of specific muscles, it would be expected to be observed only for the limbs contralateral to the site of damage. Second, low-level motor processes are intact in some patients with apraxia because they can spontaneously perform skilled motor movements. They encounter difficulty only when the movement must be performed purposefully, as when imitating someone or responding to a verbal command (Poeck, 1986).

• *Dichotomous Classifications of Apraxia* • Apraxia can take many forms, and there is an ongoing debate as to how to classify them. A number of classification schemes dichotomously categorize the disorder. For example, some classification schemes focus on the part of the body affected (e.g., a limb vs. the face). Others categorize apraxias depending on whether simple or multisequence movements are affected, whereas still others distinguish between apraxias exhibited when objects are used and apraxias that are seen when objects are not used. We next briefly highlight and review these distinctions.

As mentioned, one method of classifying apraxia is to refer to the part of the body that is affected. If facial movements are disordered, the condition is known as oral (buccofacial) apraxia; if limb movements are affected, it is known as limb apraxia.

Oral (buccofacial) apraxia is associated with difficulties in performing voluntary movements with the muscles of the tongue, lips, cheek, and larynx. As is usually the case in apraxia, automatic movements are preserved. However, tasks such as sticking out your tongue, clearing your throat, blowing a kiss, and yawning are impaired. These difficulties may also extend to oral movements used to manipulate or act upon objects, such as blowing out a match or sucking on a straw.

Limb apraxia disrupts the ability to use the limbs to manipulate items such as screwdrivers, scissors, and hammers (e.g., DeRenzi & Lucchelli, 1988). It can also disrupt the ability to perform more complex series of movements, such as opening a can of soup or opening a door with a key (e.g., Poeck & Lehmkuhl, 1980). In addition, limb apraxia affects the ability to use motor movements in a symbolic way, as occurs in gestures like waving good-bye or saluting, and in pantomime (e.g., K. M. Heilman & Rothi, 1985). In pantomime, individuals with this type of apraxia commonly use a body part to represent the object that they would be manipulating. For example, if asked to imitate putting a spoonful of sugar into a cup of coffee and then stirring it, an individual with limb apraxia will extend the index finger below the others, as if to represent the spoon, and will move it around in a circular manner rather than rotating the wrist as would occur in a correct pantomime (see Figure 5.13). Their performance tends to be better when they actually perform the task, presumably because of the visual and tactile-kinesthetic cues they receive under those conditions.

The person with limb apraxia may also have difficulty copying and imitating meaningless motor movements or unfamiliar hand or arm positions (e.g., Kimura, 1977; Kolb & Milner, 1981). A frontotemporal lesion usually produces oral apraxia. More specifically, the lesion includes the frontal and central opercula, a small area of the superior temporal gyrus adjacent to these two frontal regions, and the anterior part of the insula, which is the region tucked into the Sylvian fissure (see Figure 5.14) (Tognola & Vignolo, 1980). In contrast, limb apraxia is generally associated with damage to left parietal or parietotemporal regions (see Figure 5.14) (e.g., DeRenzi, Motti, & Nichelli, 1980; Hecaen & Rondot, 1985).

Another, and classic, way of distinguishing between types of apraxia was introduced in 1905 by Liepmann, who differentiated between ideational and ideomotor apraxia. He suggested that **ideational apraxia** (sometimes also called conceptual apraxia)

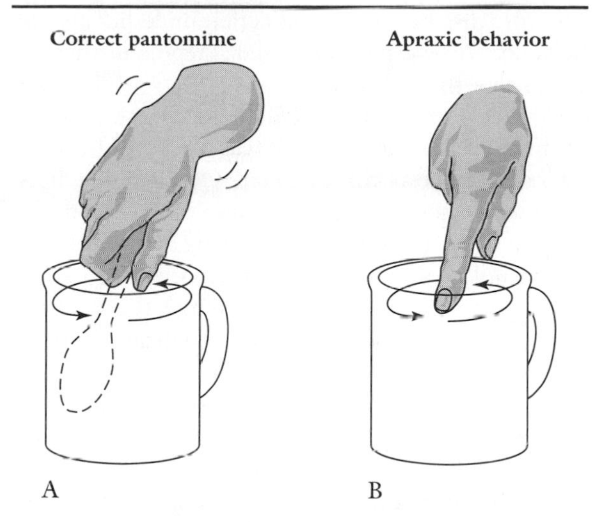

FIGURE 5.13 Example of apraxic behavior. When attempting to pantomime, an individual with apraxia often uses a limb to represent an object.

impairs the ability to form an "idea" of the movement, so that a person cannot determine which actions would be necessary and in what order they should occur. For example, a person would be unable to light a candle because he or she might not be able to sequence the necessary events (e.g., tear a match out of a matchbook, close the matchbook cover, strike the match against the cover, bring the match to the candle's wick). In contrast, each single, isolated act, such as striking a match against a matchbook or bringing the match to the candle's wick, would be undisturbed.

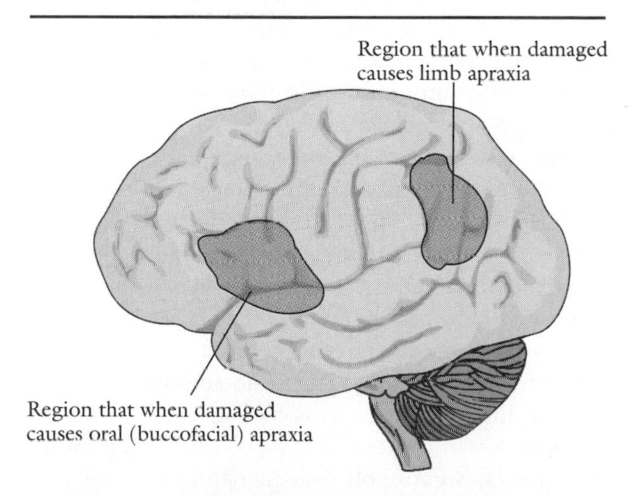

FIGURE 5.14 Locations of lesions associated with oral (buccofacial) and limb apraxia. A lesion in the frontotemporal region produces oral apraxia, whereas limb apraxia is often caused by a left parietal or parietotemporal lesion.

Conversely, Liepmann conceptualized **ideomotor apraxia** as a disconnection between the idea of movement and its execution. He believed that in this case, single simple actions, mainly gestures, would be impaired because the commands for action could not reach the motor center. These problems would be most pronounced for motor actions that were the least concrete (e.g., gestures, meaningless movements) or that had to be imitated, although the production of most everyday motor actions would be relatively undisturbed. Unlike individuals with ideational apraxia, these individuals would be able to sequence complex movements, although the constituent acts would be disrupted.

Regrettably, the degree to which Liepmann's types represent two separate syndromes is unclear. Some theorists have suggested that ideational apraxia might just be a more severe version of ideomotor apraxia (Zangwill, 1960). Still others differentiate between *ideational apraxia* and *ideomotor apraxia* quite differently than Liepmann did (see Mozaz, 1992, for an overview of how these different terms have been used and how one might distinguish between them). For example, one camp of researchers differentiates between ideomotor apraxia and ideational apraxia on whether the apraxia involves the use of objects (DeRenzi, Pieczuro, & Vignolo, 1968). For these researchers, the cardinal symptom of ideomotor apraxia is an inability to imitate gestures, such as making the sign of the cross or saluting, that are conceptual in nature and that do not act upon an object. (These are sometimes called *intransitive gestures,* because, like intransitive verbs, they do not have an object upon which they act.) In contrast, ideational apraxia is defined by an inability to use an actual object, such as a hammer, a toothbrush, or a pair of scissors. This syndrome is closely associated with aphasias caused by occipitoparietal lesions of the left hemisphere that disrupt language comprehension and hence these investigators argue that individuals with ideational apraxia may have disrupted "concept formation." Considered from this vantage point, ideational apraxia, as they define it, does not seem to be specific to the motor realm.

Still others view the distinction differently. Leiguarda and Marsden (2000) suggest that the cardinal symptom of ideational apraxia is an inability to associate objects with their corresponding actions (somewhat similar to the conclusions of DeRenzi and colleagues). Individuals with this disorder may pantomime shaving when asked to pantomime brushing teeth, may actually use a toothbrush as if it were a shaver or rip a piece of paper when asked to cut a piece of paper with a pair of scissors. They have problems in everyday life because they use tools or objects improperly, select the wrong tool or object for the task they wish to perform, or perform a complex sequential task in the wrong order (like making a cup of coffee). Unlike DeRenzi, however, Leiguarda and Marsden view ideomotor apraxia as mainly disrupting the speed and timing with which movements are made, either in real life or as a pantomime. According to them, patients with ideomotor apraxia are likely to make movements at irregular speeds (e.g., slow and hesitant buildup of hand velocity) in atypical orders, and with atypical configurations (e.g., loss of interjoint coordination, decoupling of hand speed and limb trajectory, use of body parts as objects).

Thus, researchers have not yet formed a clear consensus on how to divide the apraxias into meaningful subtypes. Because of the difficulties in distinguishing between types of apraxias on theoretical grounds, some researchers instead categorize them on descriptive grounds. Thus, rather than talking about ideational versus ideomotor apraxia (which may mean different things to different people), some researchers use descriptive terms such as "apraxias of symbolic actions" or "apraxias of object utilization" (e.g., Dee, Benton, & Van Allen, 1970). Another approach taken to understanding the apraxias is to determine what type of information (sensory, conceptual, memorial) cannot be linked with motor output (e.g., Westwood et al., 2001; Heath, Roy, Westwood, & Black, 2001).

• ***Nature of Underlying Deficit in Apraxia*** • Not only do researchers disagree on how to classify apraxia, but they also disagree over what deficit underlies apraxic behavior. As we just discussed, Liepmann thought that either the "idea" of a movement was disrupted (in what he called ideational apraxia) or the linkage of that idea to motor control was disrupted (in what he called ideomotor apraxia). Other researchers, however, consider what Liepmann called ideomotor apraxia to be a basic deficit in using action patterns or "visuokinesthetic motor" memories, which are stored in the angular and supramarginal gyri of the parietal lobe. Under this conceptualization, these memories of action patterns contain not only information about the selection and production of specific gestural actions, but also linkages to information about the visual and kinesthetic feedback that will occur during the performance of the motor act. Such action patterns are fed forward for execution by premotor and motor areas (K. M. Heilman & Rothi, 1985).

According to this viewpoint, apraxia can result either from the loss of the stored action pattern, in which case the person can neither perform gestures correctly nor discriminate between them (e.g., knowing the difference between the gesture for brushing your teeth and that for flipping a coin), or from a disruption between the stored program and motor control. In this latter case, the person can discriminate between correctly and incorrectly performed gestures made by others (because the stored program is intact) but cannot produce correct gestures (because the stored program cannot reach motor areas) (K. M. Heilman, Rothi, & Valenstein, 1982).

Other individuals argue that sequential aspects of motor processing are disrupted in apraxia. Some researchers suggest that apraxic individuals lack the ability to understand how motor actions are concatenated into a coherent sequence. These individuals cannot perform motor acts and have difficulty arranging a series of pictures about motor actions into a logical order. This deficit is not one of sequencing in general but specifically relates to motor acts, because other sequencing tasks, such as the picture arrangement task in the Wechsler Adult Intelligence Scale, and sequencing of everyday events, like shopping, can be performed without difficulty. Other researchers emphasize the transitions in postural adjustments that must be made in sequences of movements (e.g., Kimura, 1977). For example, in one test, individuals with apraxia have difficulty sequencing three relatively gross motor movements across three objects positioned on a box: pushing on a button (located at the top), pulling on a handle, and then pressing down on a bar (located on the bottom). In contrast, they have fewer problems repetitively turning a screw, even when it requires much greater fine motor control than the box task does (e.g., Kimura, 1980). Similar effects are found in the oral domain. For example, apraxic individuals have more difficulty saying "badaga" rather than "bababa," or, in sequence, opening the mouth, pursing the lips, and then clicking the teeth, rather than just blowing over and over again.

Unlike the distinction we made earlier between limb apraxia and buccofacial apraxia, Kimura (1982) conceptualizes the left hemisphere's control over manual and oral movements as falling under the rubric of a single system, called **praxis,** which is thought to control all aspects of movement, including those required for language output. This conceptualization is based in part on findings that difficulties in oral and manual movement often co-occur, as do aphasia and apraxia (e.g., Kertesz, Ferro, & Shewan, 1984). Moreover, Kimura and Watson (1989) found a high correlation in performance between tasks requiring speech production and nonspeech oral movements (e.g., blowing). This is not to say that motor control for language and nonlanguage systems can never be distinct, as in at least some cases a double dissociation occurs between apraxia and aphasia. Nonetheless, in many other cases, these two syndromes co-occur, a finding that indicates at least a fair degree of overlap between the systems (e.g., Papagno, della Sala, & Basso, 1993).

• ***Other Varieties of Apraxia*** • Some syndromes referred to as apraxia, in which a person has difficulty performing complex motor acts, arise from difficulty in the spatial domain rather than the motor domain. Two examples of such syndromes are constructional apraxia and dressing apraxia. In **constructional apraxia,** items cannot be correctly manipulated with regard to their spatial relations. For example, wooden blocks cannot be manipulated to copy an arrangement created by someone else. In **dressing apraxia,** the affected individual has difficulty manipulating and orienting both clothes and his or her limbs so that clothes can be put on correctly (e.g., opening a jacket so that the arm can be inserted, and properly putting an arm out and bending it at the elbow to put on the jacket). These syndromes are generally observed after right-hemisphere lesions and are often associated with spatial-processing difficulties and hemineglect. As such, many neuropsychologists do not consider these apraxias per se, but rather motor manifestations of visuoconstructive disorders.

Still other apraxias result from a disconnection syndrome rather than from difficulties in motor programming. We already discussed the idea that in certain cases of apraxia, visuokinesthetic programs may not reach motor areas because of a disconnection between parietal and frontal areas. Another type of apraxia that results from a disconnection syndrome is **callosal apraxia.** Unlike other apraxias that affect motor control bilaterally, this apraxia selectively disrupts the ability to perform movements or manipulate objects with the left hand in response to verbal commands. Callosal apraxia is associated with damage to the corpus callosum and has been suggested to occur because of a disconnection between the left hemisphere, which is specialized for skilled motor sequencing, and the right hemisphere, which controls motor functioning of the left hand (e.g., Rubens, Geschwind, Mahowald, & Mastri, 1977). According to this account, when a person is verbally instructed to perform a skilled motor act, the left hemisphere interprets the command and relays it to left parietal regions so that the appropriate motor program can be assembled. Once formed, the motor command is forwarded to the premotor and motor cortices of the left hemisphere. These areas receive an intact program, so there is no apraxia of the right hand. However, because of the callosal disconnection, the motor programs are trapped in the left hemisphere and have no way of reaching the right hemisphere, which controls the left hand. Because motoric information cannot reach the right hemisphere, the left hand is apraxic. Figure 5.15 diagrams the essential anatomical relations of this syndrome.

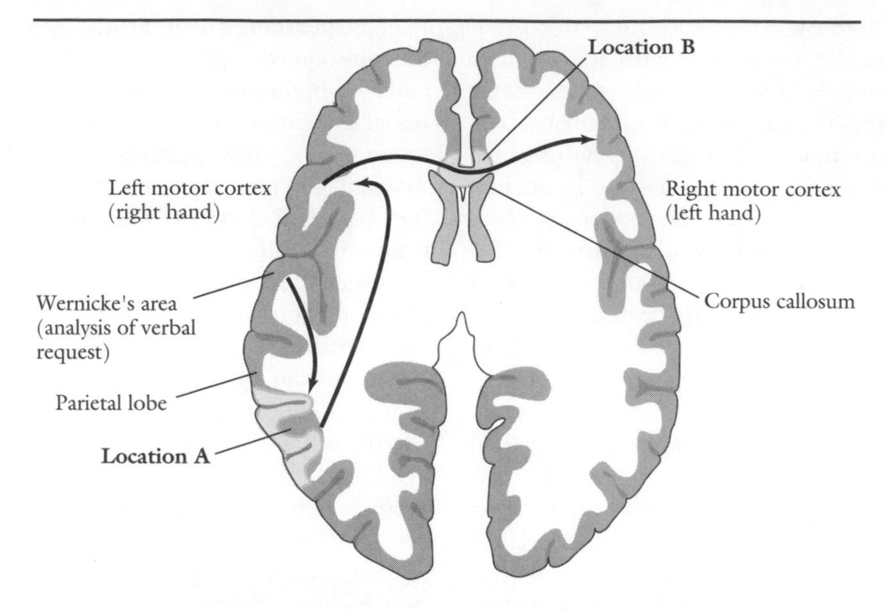

FIGURE 5.15 Anatomical mechanisms of unilateral and bilateral apraxia. Wernicke's area analyzes a verbal request and transmits this information to the left parietal region (Location A), where the correct movements are selected. If this region is damaged, bilateral apraxia results. In contrast, in unilateral apraxia of the left hand, the left parietal region is intact, so information about the correct movements is sent forward to the left motor cortex, where the motor commands are executed. Hence, the right hand is not apraxic. However, because of a lesion of the corpus callosum (Location B), the information cannot be relayed to the right hemisphere and apraxia of the left hand results.

SUMMARY

Brain Structures Involved in Motor Control

- Motor tracts transmit information from the brain to muscles.
- The cerebellum is important for gross posture, the smooth coordination of movements, ballistic movements (i.e., rapid movements that must be planned with little chance for feedback), the learning of skilled motor movements, and timing of movements.
- The basal ganglia are important for controlling the initiation and cessation of motor movements that are internally guided as well as playing a role in motor planning and learning.
- Primary motor cortex controls the force and/or direction of movement of specific muscles.
- The SMA is thought to provide a motor plan for an action, which is an abstract representation of an intended movement that is preprogrammed before the motor act is initiated.
- Premotor regions are thought to specify the type of motor action that is necessary, such as a grasp.
- The anterior cingulate cortex plays an important role in the selection of motor responses, especially when they are novel or atypical.
- The frontal eye field programs voluntary eye movements such as those involved in scanning visual space.

- The parietal lobe links movements with a representation of the space in which those movements occur, links information about motor programs with visuokinesthetic information about the motor acts as well as other sensory information, and links a motor act with its conceptual significance.

Motor Disorders

- Subcortical motor disorders affect the form and timing of movements, whereas cortical motor disorders affect the conceptual clarity of motor acts, either by disrupting the sequencing of complex motor acts or by disrupting the ability to have a motor act represent a concept.
- Parkinson's disease, which occurs because the putamen does not receive dopaminergic input due to the death of cells in the substantia nigra, results in an inability to initiate spontaneous movement (akinesia), a slowness of movement (bradykinesia), and rhythmic oscillating movements (tremors).
- Huntington's disease, which occurs because of damage to the striatum, results in involuntary undesired jerky and writhing movements.
- Tourette's syndrome, a rare disorder that manifests itself in childhood, is characterized in less severe cases by tics and twitching of the face, the limbs, and other regions of the body, and in more severe cases, by vocalizations, such as cries, grunts, and curses.
- Tardive dyskinesia is a disorder characterized by an excess of motor movements associated with the long-term use of typical antipsychotic medications that reduce the amount of dopamine in the brain.
- Alien limb syndrome, which results from damage to the SMA, causes an individual's appendage to seem to move of its own free will in ways that are destructive or unhelpful, often disrupting coordinated bimanual activity.
- Apraxia is a disorder that typically results from left inferior parietal lesions or left frontal lesions and prevents the individual from performing sequential skilled motor acts.
- Some classifications of apraxia emphasize the body part that is affected, others emphasize whether the idea of movement is lost or whether there is a disconnection between the idea of a movement and its execution, and still others emphasize the difference between movements required to use objects as compared with those that have symbolic significance.
- Other disorders that are not true apraxia are constructional apraxia, in which items cannot be correctly manipulated with regard to their spatial relations; and dressing apraxia, in which limbs and clothes cannot be manipulated to dress.
- In callosal apraxia the ability to perform movements or manipulate objects with the left hand in response to verbal commands is lost.

KEY TERMS

CHAPTER 6

OBJECT RECOGNITION

One crisp autumn night Betty yearns for a midnight snack when she remembers that some deliciously spiced tart apple pie is sitting in her refrigerator. She thinks, "That would be wonderful right now with a hot cup of tea!" Although for most people getting the pie out of the refrigerator and making a cup of tea would be simple, for Betty it will be a difficult task.

She walks into the kitchen and identifies the refrigerator by its large size and black color. But now she knows that she must find the pie, and that doing so will not be easy. As she peers inside the refrigerator, she sees a large, round object but deduces from its red color that it must be the leftover pizza pie, not the apple pie. Searching a bit more, she sees a tan, round-shaped object and reaches for it. But alas, as soon as she feels how flexible it is, she realizes it's the package of tortillas, not the desired pie. Searching some more, she spies another tan, round-shaped object. This one feels stiff, like a pie pan, and is covered with plastic wrap. She pulls it out, takes off the plastic wrap, and sniffs. Ah, it is the pie she has been searching for! She carefully places it on the breakfast table.

Now for the cup of tea. Because she knows that the stove is to the left of the refrigerator, her usual strategy is to leave the teakettle sitting on the stove so that she can easily find it. Unfortunately, it's not there. "Ah," she sighs, "why didn't I just put the teakettle back where it belongs?" Now she begins to feel all the objects on the counter next to the stove. Hmm, that one feels tall and thin and a little greasy—must be the bottle of olive oil. Another one feels cylindrical and as if it's made of paper—must be either the large container of salt or the carton of oatmeal. Soon after, she feels the distinctive curved arm of the teakettle and its wide, round body. Next to it, she feels the box of tea bags. That was fortunate, she thinks, or I would have spent the next five minutes searching for the tea bags. She carefully places the box of tea bags on the stove; the box is now easily identifiable because its bright green color stands out against the white stove.

She then turns around to the sink, which she knows is located directly across from the stove, and fills the teakettle with water. Waiting for the water to boil, she puts her hand in the silverware drawer, feels for the tines of a fork, and takes one out. Soon, the teakettle whistles. She makes her cup of tea, walks over to the breakfast table, and gets ready to eat her piece of pie. That was a bit of a trial and tribulation, she thinks, but after the first bite of pie and sip of tea, she knows that all her work was worthwhile. ■

AT THIS POINT, you are probably wondering what strange disorder this woman has. As you think about this story, a number of possibilities may come to mind. Maybe she has a visual problem and is blind. This seems unlikely. She recognized the pizza pie (if only by its distinctive round shape and red color) and incorrectly grabbed an item that looked similar to the apple pie, a package of tortillas, rather than something quite different in shape and size, like a milk carton. Another possibility is that she has a memory problem and can't remember where things are located or the specific attributes of an item. This possibility seems unlikely, too. She remembered the locations of the stove and the sink. Furthermore, her memory for specific items must be intact because she recognized the apple pie as soon as she smelled it and the kettle as soon as she felt it.

The neurological syndrome that this woman has emanates neither from a problem in basic aspects of visual perception nor from a memory problem. Rather, her disorder is visual agnosia, a syndrome that deprives an individual of the ability to link perceptual information in a particular sensory modality (in this case, vision) to meaning. The goal of this chapter is to examine the neural mechanisms that allow people to recognize objects in the visual modality as well as in other modalities. Our discussion, however, concentrates on visual object recognition because this process has undergone much study and because vision is a very salient human sense.

To set the stage for appreciating distinctions between types of deficits in visual object recognition, we begin the chapter by discussing the neural hardware, in both humans and other mammals, that allows us to recognize objects visually. This hardware is known as the *"what" visual system,* or **ventral visual system,** which we were introduced to in Chapter 1 (see page 37). We then consider what insights can be garnered about how the brain solves the problem of recognizing objects by examining computational models. Afterwards, we discuss clinical syndromes in which the ability to recognize visual objects is lost, and consider whether faces are a special class of visual objects that are analyzed by highly specific neural tissue. Following this, we examine disorders of object recognition that are limited to specific categories of objects, such as fruits and vegetables or human-made objects, and consider what these types of disorders imply about the neural mechanisms of object recognition as well as memory. To conclude the chapter, we briefly discuss object-recognition difficulties that occur in other modalities besides vision.

The "What" Ventral Visual System

A clear understanding of how the brain recognizes objects visually requires us to consider how the brain processes visual information after it leaves primary visual cortex. As we discussed in Chapter 1, information departing from primary visual cortex is funneled into two distinct processing streams, one that courses ventrally toward anterior temporal regions and one that courses dorsally toward parietal regions. As we learned in Chapter 1, the ventral visual system is important for item identification. We now examine this system in more detail.

The ventral visual-processing stream consists of the areas of the occipital, occipitotemporal, and temporal regions that are solely devoted to processing visual stimuli and are unresponsive to information from other modalities or to multimodal information. Much of our knowledge about the basic processing characteristics of the ventral visual system comes from research with other species such as monkeys in which techniques not typically used with humans, such as single-cell recordings, are employed.

The mammalian brain is confronted with a number of difficult problems to solve when attempting to recognize a visual object. One major problem is that information from the three-dimensional (3-D) world is projected onto the retina, a two-dimensional (2-D) plane. Hence, the brain must *reconstruct* the third dimension of a visual scene solely on the basis of 2-D information. Another major hurdle is that items must be recognized no matter where they fall on the retina and no matter how much of the retina they fall upon. For example, a cup in your hand projects onto a much larger area of your retina than a cup on a table across the room. Yet, in both cases, you must recognize the object as a cup. In addition, objects must be recognized regardless of the orientation in which we view them. Your brain needs to recognize that a cat walking directly toward you, facing forward, is the same object as when viewed sideways skittering across the floor in pursuit of a mouse. Recognition must occur even though the visual information you receive in each case is distinct. In sum, although the same object can project upon the retina in various ways, the brain must nonetheless interpret the object as being the same, regardless of variations in retinal size, retinal position, and orientation (see Plaut & Farah, 1990, for a discussion of these issues from both neuroscientific and computational viewpoints).

Evidence from Nonhuman Primates

By examining the response characteristics of cells in the ventral visual system with single-cell recording techniques, researchers can uncover many of the mechanisms that the brain uses to solve these problems. If information is recorded from various electrode sites in the ventral visual-processing stream, which is depicted in Figure 6.1, three important trends emerge regarding the types of stimuli that make the cells fire. The first trend is that relatively simple stimuli make the cells fire in posterior regions, but for anterior regions the stimuli must be more complex and specific. So, whereas the areas just beyond primary visual cortex, such as V2, are likely to respond to one or more simple stimulus qualities (e.g., color, texture, length, width, orientation, direction of motion, spatial frequency), the cells in inferotemporal (PIT and AIT) regions fire only in response to much more complex visual stimuli.

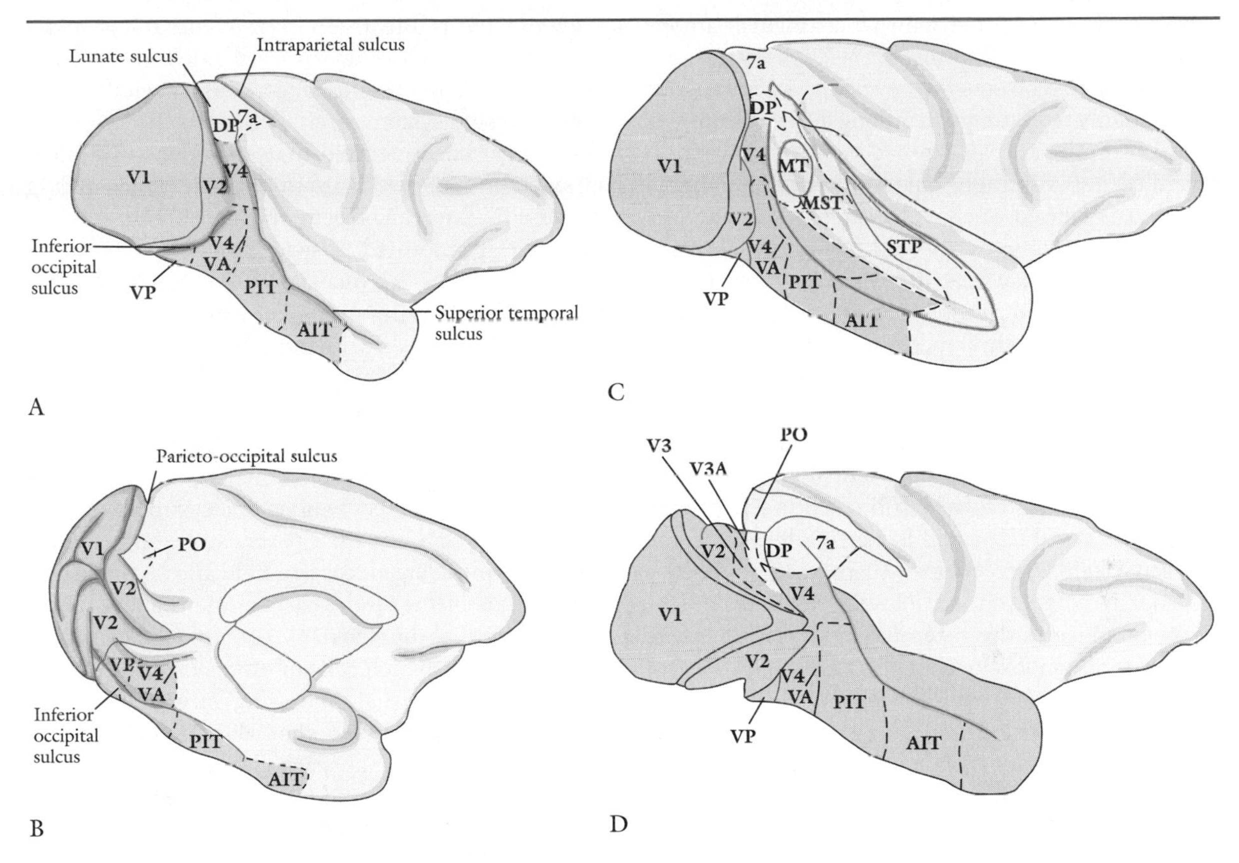

FIGURE 6.1 Ventral processing stream of the brain in the macaque. (A) Right hemisphere, lateral view. (B) Left hemisphere, midsagittal view. (C) View showing the areas buried within the superior temporal sulcus. (D) View showing the areas buried within the lunate, intraparietal, parieto-occipital, and inferior occipital sulci. The ventral processing stream (shown here shaded in gray) goes from V1, V2, V3, VP, and V4 to the posterior and anterior inferotemporal areas (PIT and AIT, respectively). DP, dorsal prelunate; VA, ventral anterior; VP, ventral posterior; PO, parieto-occipital; MT, middle temporal; MST, medial superior temporal; STP, superior temporal polysensory.

In fact, cells in the inferotemporal cortex of monkeys can be tuned to specific forms, such as hands (Gross, Bender, & Rocha-Miranda, 1969) or faces (Gross, Rocha-Miranda, & Bender, 1972). The discovery that these cells are so selective in their response occurred serendipitously. The researchers were having difficulty determining what type of stimulus would make cells in the inferotemporal region fire, and in frustration one of them moved a hand across the monkey's visual field. To their amazement, they found that the cell fired more strongly than it had to any other object! They then tested other complex visual stimuli and found that in all cases the cell fired only in response to highly specific forms (Figure 6.2),

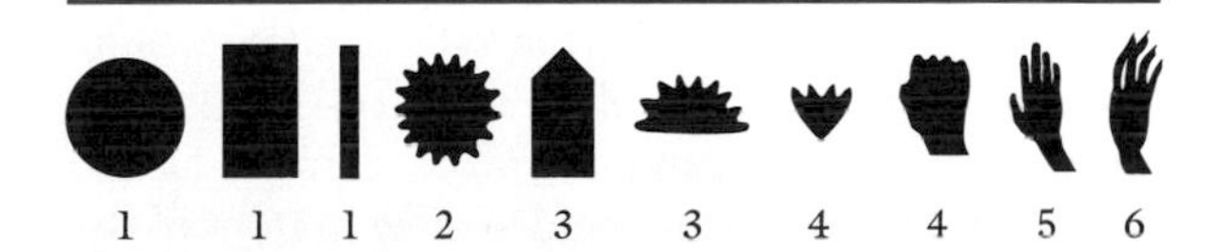

FIGURE 6.2 Examples of stimuli used to test the responsiveness of cells in the inferotemporal region of the macaque. These stimuli are arranged from left to right in order of the degree to which they elicited a response, from 1 (no response) to 2 and 3 (little response) to 6 (maximal response). Note that the forms that make the cell fire are complicated and specific.

a trait that enables the brain to distinguish among many complex visual forms.

To recognize objects, however, the brain must be able not only to distinguish among different complex visual stimuli, but also must recognize an object regardless of variations in the conditions under which it is viewed, such as lighting and orientation. In fact, the response of cells in inferotemporal cortex is unaffected by changes in retinal position, retinal size, and orientation (e.g., Desimone, Albright, Gross, & Bruce, 1984), a neural mechanism that allows us to recognize an object from various perspectives.

The second trend observed is that the receptive fields of cells are larger for anterior regions than for posterior regions. The **receptive field** of a cell is the area of visual space to which the cell is sensitive. If a stimulus to which a cell is tuned falls within the receptive field, the cell fires. If the same stimulus falls outside the receptive field, the cell does not fire. You can consider the receptive field of a cell to be similar to a window or a field of view. The view of the world through a window is limited, so if something is happening beyond the view provided by the window, you do not respond to it because you cannot see it. Cells in primary visual cortex receive information from only a limited region in space. Hence their receptive field is small and can be considered analogous to a peephole or a porthole on a ship. However, the farther the cell is positioned along the ventral visual-processing stream in an anterior direction, the larger the area of space to which it responds. For example, cells in area V4, a region beyond primary visual cortex and near anterior temporal areas, have receptive fields that are between 16 and 36 times larger than the receptive fields of cells found in primary visual cortex. The most anterior region of the ventral visual-processing stream, the inferotemporal area, has cells with large receptive fields that can encompass as much as 130 degrees of the 180-degree field of view in front of the head. In addition, the receptive fields of these cells *always* include the foveal, or central, region of processing (e.g., Desimone & Gross, 1979). In contrast to the peepholes of the primary visual cortex, which are distributed all over space, the receptive fields of the inferotemporal area can be considered analogous to a large picture window or glass wall that runs the length of one side of a house and always provides a view of what is directly in front. Figure 6.3 provides a comparison of the relative sizes of the receptive fields for cells in posterior and anterior regions of the ventral visual system.

A large receptive field that encompasses almost all of the visual field is useful for object recognition because it allows an object to be identified regardless of where it is located in space and regardless of its size (e.g., Gross & Mishkin, 1977). Consider that when you look out a peephole, you see just a small portion of an object, which often doesn't allow you to determine what you are viewing. Such is the problem with the small receptive field sizes of the more posterior regions of the ventral processing stream. However, as your field of view increases, so does your ability to detect whole objects, because the interrelations among their parts can be appreciated. Thus, having a large receptive field allows the cell to respond to objects on the basis of their global shape, rather than just the size or location of local contours (the features to which cells in more posterior regions of the ventral visual-processing stream respond). Having a receptive field that always includes the central region of visual space also aids object recognition. The region of the retina that receives information about the central area of visual space, the fovea, has the greatest density of sensory receptors and therefore the best acuity, providing for the highest possible resolution when attempting to recognize an object.

The final important attribute of cells in the ventral processing stream is that they are often sensitive to color (e.g., Zeki, 1980). Color is a visual attribute that aids in object recognition because it allows us to separate an object from the background in which it is embedded. This process is often referred to as **figure-ground separation.** Consider an average street scene including parked cars, trees, buildings, and parking meters. Color may aid in quick identification of a car if it is yellow or aqua, a color distinct from the red brick building, the gray parking meter, the tan sidewalk, and the green trees that surround the car.

At this point you have been introduced to the basic attributes of visual information that are important to cells in the ventral system and allow for object recognition as they have been discovered in nonhuman primates. We now examine the evi-

A

B

FIGURE 6.3 Receptive-field size for cells in primary visual cortex compared with that for cells in the inferotemporal region. The receptive field is the region of space to which the cell is sensitive. If the optimal stimulus for an object falls outside its receptive field, the cell does not respond. In these pictures, the receptive field of a cell is indicated by a dashed circle. Areas within the receptive field are *denoted in black, whereas those outside the receptive field are denoted in gray.* (A) In primary visual cortex, the size of a cell's receptive field is small. (B) In contrast, the receptive field of a cell in the inferotemporal region is much larger, usually encompassing a wide expanse of visual space that always includes the midline.

dence for a similar organization of the ventral visual-processing stream in humans.

Evidence from Humans

A spate of recent research using neuroimaging techniques has provided new insights into the organization of the ventral visual-processing stream in humans. These studies reveal that the organization of the human brain and that of the monkey appear to be quite homologous up to V4 (Sereno et al., 1995), after which the visual field is no longer mapped in a strictly retinotopic manner. Past that point, temporal regions that appear to play a role in object recognition in the human brain include the lateral occipital cortex (LOC), the fusiform face area, and the parahippocampal place area, which are shown in Figure 6.4.

What evidence would persuade scientists that a region of the brain is *specifically* involved in object recognition? First we would expect that the region should treat an object similarly regardless of whether an apple is depicted as the logo on a computer, is sitting on the table in front of you, or is depicted in a painting. This characteristic is known as *form-cue invariance,* meaning that the brain's response does not vary depending on the form of the visual cue that represents the object. Second, such a mechanism should recognize an object regardless of its position and size on the retina, the amount of illumination under which it is viewed, and the vantage point from which it is viewed, a phenomenon known as *perceptual constancy.*

The lateral occipital complex (LOC), located at the posterior portion of the fusiform gyrus directly anterior to Brodmann's area 19, meets these criteria (see Mazer & Gallant, 2000, for a review). How do researchers demonstrate such invariance and constancy? They typically utilize an approach known as an *adaptation,* or *attenuation paradigm.* We know that the brain's response to an item decreases if it has been seen before; that

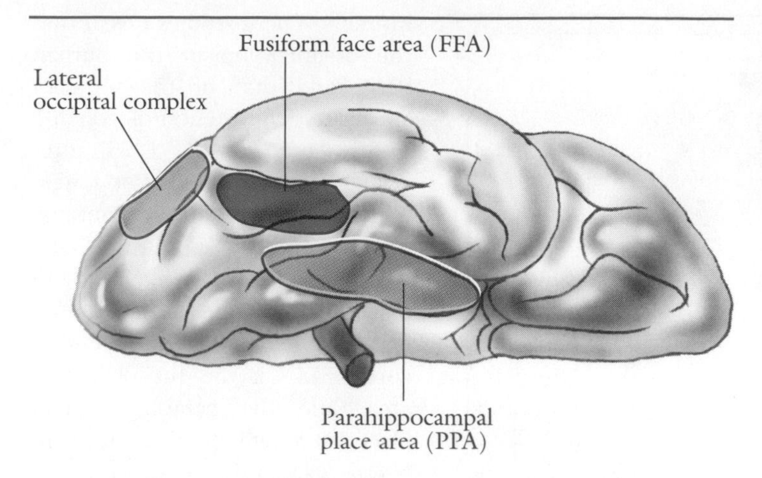

FIGURE 6.4 The relative locations of the fusiform face area, the parahippocampal place area, and the lateral occipital complex as shown in temporal regions of the right hemisphere.

is, the brain's response adapts, or attenuates, to the repetition. The logic here is that if a portion of the brain exhibits perceptual constancy, it will show as large a decrease in response when presented with two instances of the same object that vary in perceptual features as when presented with identical representations of the object. For example, the decrease in response should be the same size for two views of an object that differ in size as for two identical views of the object. In neuroimaging studies, the response of the LOC to an object is the same across variations in size, location, viewpoint, and illumination (Grill-Spector et al., 1998). In addition, activation in the LOC exhibits a similar response to both line drawings and photographs of the same object, indicating form-cue invariance (Kourtzi & Kanwisher, 2000). The question, however, remains as to whether the LOC is processing objects per se, or is involved in representing complex shapes. Suggesting the latter interpretation, this region exhibits equal responsiveness to line-drawings of 3-D objects, line drawings of partially occluded 2-D shapes that have depth but no 3-D structure, and simple 2-D line drawings with neither depth nor 3-D structure (Kourtzi and Kanwisher, 2000).

One group of researchers has suggested that the temporal lobe contains a multitude of object-processing regions, each of which is optimally sensitive to a different class of objects. One region, known as the *fusiform face area,* exhibits a greater response to faces than to other objects (Kanwisher, McDermott, & Chun, 1997). Another region, known as the *parahippocampal place area,* appears to process information related to places in the local environment (Epstein et al., 1999), while a third appears to respond preferentially to buildings (Aguirre, Zarahn, & D'Esposito, 1998). Finally, the *extrastriate body area* responds preferentially to human bodies and body parts over various inanimate objects and object parts (Downing et al., 2001). These findings would suggest that the temporal lobe has a variety of regions tuned to identifying very specific classes of objects.

However, other researchers have suggested that the organization of the ventral visual-processing stream in humans is quite different. They posit that these different types of objects are all processed across this entire set of brain regions, and what varies for each class of objects is the pattern of activation across the regions. The implication of this theory is that the organization is more distributed than localized. As evidence for their viewpoint, they demonstrate that the pattern of activation across the region is significantly higher for two objects of the same class, say two houses, than for objects from different classes, such as a house compared to a face, cat, bottle, scissors, shoe, or chair (Haxby et al., 2001).

These two viewpoints provide a very different take on the brain systems involved in object recognition, with one characterized by dedicated modules for specific classes of objects and the other characterized by a distributed network (for a discussion, see Cohen & Tong, 2001). Is there any way to reconcile them? It is possible that a hybrid model may be most accurate—that representations are distributed across a wide swath of the ventral visual-processing stream, but certain subpopulations of neurons may be more involved in helping to recognize certain types of objects (e.g., faces) than others. Later on in the chapter, we will revisit this issue and discuss whether the processing of faces is distinct from the processing of other classes of objects.

The ventral visual-processing stream also appears to be organized in a lateralized manner. As we discussed briefly in Chapter 4, the right hemisphere appears to filter visual information so that it preferentially processes global information, whereas the left hemisphere filters visual information so that it preferentially processes local information. As a result, there appear to be two distinct neural mechanisms involved in object recognition: one lateralized to the left hemisphere, important for analyzing the parts of objects, known as **local processing,** and another, lateralized to the right hemisphere, important for analyzing the wholes, known as **global processing.** Thus, it appears that the brain can treat the parts of an item separately from the whole.

Much research examining the separation of global and local processing has made use of a task invented by David Navon (1977) involving *hierarchical stimuli.* We were introduced to these stimuli briefly in Chapter 4 (see Figure 4.8, page 128). As a reminder, items (e.g., Zs) that are small (e.g., 0.25 in., or 0.64 cm) are arranged in a particular spatial array so that they form a large item (e.g., an M that is 2 in. or 3 cm square). On each trial, a hierarchical letter is shown. The individual is typically instructed to respond only to the information at one level (e.g., the global level) and to ignore the information at the other level (e.g., the local level). The participants in the study generally have to discriminate items; for example, they must press one button if a Z is present at the specified level and another button if an M is present.

Research both with patients with brain damage and with neurologically intact individuals suggests that the hemispheres play different roles in perceiving the global aspects of an object as compared to its parts. Whereas large lesions of the left hemisphere disrupt the ability to perceive local, but not global, aspects of an item, right-hemisphere lesions have the converse effect, disrupting the ability to perceive global, but not local, aspects of form (Delis, Robertson, & Efron, 1986). Such effects occur regardless of whether the hierarchical figures are composed of letters or geometric shapes (Doyon & Milner, 1991). The lesions most likely to cause such effects are those in the temporal region, consistent with the idea that these regions, which are part of the ventral visual-processing system, are specialized for object recognition (Robertson, Lamb, & Knight, 1988).

Confirmatory evidence for a distinction in the neural control of local and global processing comes from studies with neurologically intact individuals. For example, when shown hierarchical figures, these individuals exhibit a left visual field (LVF) advantage for detecting the letter at the global level and a right visual field (RVF) advantage for detecting it at the local level (e.g., M. Martin, 1979). Although not all researchers have found this exact pattern, the overall conclusion emerging from the half dozen or more studies on this issue is that the right hemisphere plays a greater role in global processing and the left in local processing (Van Kleeck, 1989).

Hemispheric differences in global and local processing suggest that these two processes can occur in parallel and somewhat independently. Evidence from other studies utilizing hierarchical stimuli is consistent with such a conclusion. On some trials, the small letter and the large letter are the same (e.g., a large *Z* composed of little *Z*s), which is known as the *consistent condition.* On other trials, the small letters lead to one response and the large letter to another (e.g., a large M composed of little *Z*s), which is called the *inconsistent condition.* Not surprisingly, there is interference in the inconsistent condition; that is, the person takes longer to respond than in the consistent condition. But this interference is much greater when the person must respond to the local information (e.g., respond to the little *Z*s) than when the response is to the global information (e.g., respond to the large M). This finding has been suggested to indicate **global precedence;** that is, the global information (i.e., the overall relationship among the parts) may be analyzed before the parts themselves. As such, global information interferes with the ability to extract local information, but the reverse is less likely to occur because global information has already been extracted before local information is analyzed.

These findings also imply that one may not need to build from the bottom up, recognizing the parts before the whole can be processed. For example, if a person were attempting to recognize a house, the right hemisphere would ascertain information about its global form (e.g., whether the house is an A-frame or a bungalow), and the left hemisphere would analyze the local features (e.g., whether the house is composed of bricks or shingles, or whether the windows have panes or not). Such findings have implications for the computational models of object recognition to which we now turn.

Computational Models of Object Recognition

As we mentioned earlier, visual object recognition requires elaborate computations and inferences not only because the brain must reconstruct a 3-D world from the 2-D information that falls on our retinas, but also because it must do so simply on the basis of light intensity and wavelength (color). Any automated computer system used to identify objects, such as those used in the military to define targets, must solve a similar problem. Accordingly, both neuroscientists and computer scientists have spent much time trying to understand the computations that the brain uses to solve this problem.

One classic computational model of object recognition was that provided by David Marr (1982), who was a computer scientist. He theorized that to recognize objects, the brain constructs a series of representations of the visual world by making inferences derived from basic retinal information. He proposed three main types of representations: the primal sketch, the $2\frac{1}{2}$-D representation, and the 3-D representation. The **primal sketch** is a "rough draft" of visual information in the visual world easily derived from information that reaches the retina. The initial raw primal sketch takes information about light intensity at different points in space and specifically computes the *changes* in light intensity across the visual array and their geometric relations. This information allows lines or edges to be specified, which are used to help define the edges of objects. The full primal sketch uses gestalt-like principles to group together lines that should be perceived as whole forms.

The **$2\frac{1}{2}$-D representation** is a more elaborate representation of the visual world that provides information about the relative depth of surfaces (e.g., whether something is in front or behind). Depth information is squeezed out of the primal sketch by various means. First, the difference in the retinal images received by each eye, known as **binocular disparity,** provides information about the relative depth of surfaces, as the disparity of information received by each eye is greater for items closer to the viewer rather than further away. Second, some depth information can be inferred from motion, because points moving in the same direction and at the same velocity tend to be associated with the same surface. Those moving more quickly are generally located closer rather than farther away from the viewer. Third, color, as already mentioned, allows for the separation of foreground from background, providing information on relative depth, and thus aids in the identification of objects. Texture helps in a similar way, because points of similar texture usually all reside on the same item, and objects nearer to the viewer generally have a finer grain than those farther away. Occlusion likewise provides relative depth information and helps to parse figure from background, because what is in front occludes the view of that which is in back. Although these many mechanisms provide information on relative depth, a full 3-D construct of the item is not yet available. Front and back or nearer and farther are identified, but the **volumetric representation** of an object—that is, the actual overall 3-D shape, including how far back one surface is from another, its center of mass, its principle axis of symmetry—is not yet specified.

According to Marr at the final level, a **3-D representation** of the object is constructed, which is a volumetric representation of the object that is **orientation invariant,** meaning that the relationships among different parts of an object can be specified regardless of the angle from which it is viewed. As such, the representation of the object is now considered an **object-centered representation** rather than a **viewer-centered representation.** In a viewer-centered representation, when the position of the viewer changes, so does the representation of the object, because the relative positions among the parts of an item change. For example, when a mug is viewed sideways, the distance in the retinal image between the handle and the main cylindrical body is far, but if the cup is turned so that the handle faces you, this same distance in the retinal image is substantially decreased. Thus, although a mug is being viewed in both cases, the representations are different because the viewer's position relative to the mug is different. In contrast, in an object-centered representation, the volumetric properties of the object have been ascertained, so the object and its parts are always referenced with regard to the same coordinate system. In the mug example, the distance between the handle and the main body of the mug in the 3-D representation remains invariant regardless of the angle from which the item is viewed, because parts of the object are specified with regard to volumetric properties.

Although Marr assumed that an object-centered representation was necessary for object recognition, currently there remains a large debate as to whether objects are recognized via viewer-centered or object-centered representations. Some researchers have followed in Marr's footsteps, suggesting that objects are represented as descriptions of spatial arrangements among parts in a 3-D coordinate system that is centered on the object itself (sometimes also referred to as *structural-description* models). One such model is the recognition by component (RBC) theory (Biederman, 1987). According to this model there are primitive and basic volumetric forms called geons. These geons specify basic volumetric forms, such as a cylinder, a curved "elbow," and so forth (see Figure 6.5). An object is specified as a particular set of geons arranged in a particular spatial configuration. In this way the geons can be considered basic units, or primitives, that are used to describe objects in the same way that phonemes (e.g,. /ba/ /t/) are put together to form words. To recognize familiar objects, a viewer-centered representation of the object is constructed from the volumetric primitives and then compared to descriptions of objects stored in the brain. Novel objects are recognized as such because they contain a new and unique set of geons and/or an existing set of geons in a new and different spatial arrangement.

Other researchers posit that objects can be recognized via the systematic integration or interpolation across a set of viewer-centered representations (see Tarr & Bülthoff, 1998, for a nice review of current thinking on these types of models from a computational, neural, and psychological perspective). These models vary in flavor. Some suggest that particular local areas of interest in the input are noted (e.g., areas of dark versus light) and the mutual constraints among how these local areas are arranged

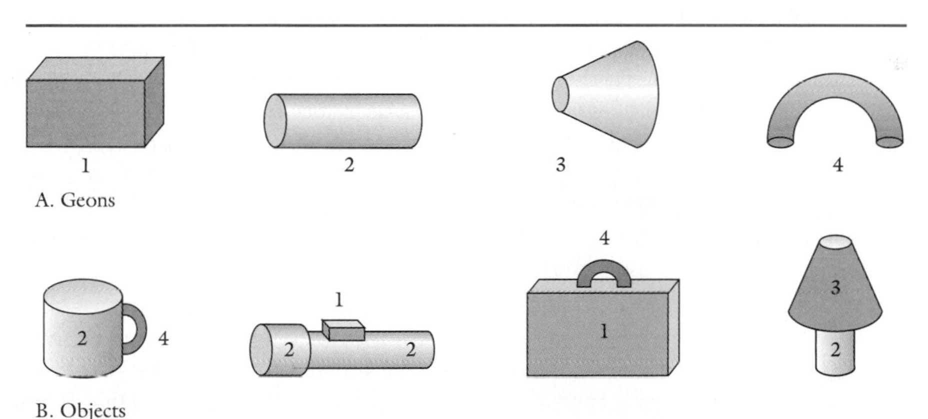

FIGURE 6.5 Geons, the basic volumetric primitives from which objects are suggested to be constructed. (A) Some basic geons. Geons vary with regard to whether their edges are curved or straight, their shape is symmetric or asymmetric, their size around the main axis is constant or expands, and their major axis is straight or curved. (B) Complex objects are composed of multiple geons. For example, the cup is composed of the geons labeled 2 and 4, the flashlight of 2 and 1, and so forth. The spatial arrangement of the same geons can create distinct objects. For example, if geon 4 were placed above geon 2 it would form a pail, not a cup.

are compared to stored descriptions of objects. For example, the area and angle of a horse's neck, its head, and its body create a very specific configuration that can be met only by mutual constraint satisfaction as being part of horse, not as being part of another object, such as a small truck or helicopter. Other models assume that the system makes a guess about what an object might be and compares that to stored representations of objects, measures the difference, and generates another hypothesis if the match is too poor. Notice that the former models emphasize more local processes, whereas the latter emphasize more global processes. In both cases, though, there is a heavy reliance on comparison with stored descriptions in the brain (see Riesenhuber & Poggio, 2000, for a good review of such models). Proponents of such viewer-centered models cite evidence of their biological plausibility by noting that most studies of single-cell recordings suggest that many more cells in temporal regions are view-specific than are view-invariant. Opponents note that such models rely heavily on a comparison with stored descriptions, which would make the identification of novel objects difficult.

How are we to reconcile these two different theoretical claims when empirical evidence exists for both? The solution may not be that the answer is either/or, but rather both, as these mechanisms may provide complementary information. Furthermore, their utility may vary across different stages of processing and across different objects. For example, some models suggest that geons are first coded in a viewer-dependent manner. These representations are then bound together to create a 3-D structural description (e.g., Hummel & Stankiewicz, 1996). As another example, other models suggest that structural descriptions based on component parts may be very helpful for accessing the basic-level category (e.g., bird) of an object if the object is composed of distinct parts. But such representations may not work well when attempting to distinguish within a class of objects, such as distinguishing robins from sparrows. Because they belong to the same basic-level category of bird, the basic components of robins and sparrows are the same—an elongated ovoid for a body, an ovoid head with a pyramidal beak, two thin cylinders for legs, and three smaller thin cylinders for feet. What distinguishes a robin from a sparrow is the relative proportions, distance, and relationship between each component. Consequently, distinguishing between a sparrow and a robin requires processing the configuration of the component parts. In this case, interpolating across a series of viewer-centered representations may provide the best way to differentiate between these objects (see Treisman & Kanwisher, 1998, for a good discussion of these issues).

Having discussed the brain regions that are important for object recognition and the types of computational strategies that may be employed, we now turn our attention to the way in which object recognition can break down after brain insult.

Visual Agnosia

As mentioned in Chapter 1, **visual agnosia** is an inability to recognize a visual object that is not attributable either to a basic deficit in processing of visual information or to a pervasive memory disorder. Furthermore, the deficit is modality specific, because the item can be recognized through other sensory channels. For example, a woman with visual agnosia might be able to describe an object as a fuzzy brown, white, and black ovoid balanced on four short, stocky cylinders with a triangular-shaped appendage at one end and a very thin, very pointy, appendage, constantly in motion, at the other end. This description would illustrate that her rudimentary visual abilities are intact. Furthermore, if this fuzzy ovoid nuzzled up to her so that she could feel its wet nose and whiplike tail, or if she heard its plaintive "boooaaaaahhhhhh, woooaaaaaahhh, woooooaaahhh" she would probably have little trouble identifying it as a dog, and possibly even as a beagle. Thus, although the woman cannot recognize the beagle in the visual modality, she can do so by the sense of touch or sound. Hence, her disorder is **modality specific,** meaning that it manifests in one modality or sense but not others.

The word *agnosia* is Greek, meaning "without knowledge." One of the most famous figures in psychology, a man who is not traditionally known for his contributions to neuropsychology—Sigmund Freud—first used this word to describe the neuropsychological disorder. He chose to call this syndrome agnosia because he argued that it was not the result of disruptions in sensory processes but rather reflected an inability to gain access to previous knowledge or information about a sensory experience.

Traditionally, visual agnosias have been divided into two types: apperceptive and associative. This distinction dates to the 1890s and has been attributed to Lissauer. He suggested that **apperceptive agnosia** is a fundamental difficulty in forming a *percept* (a mental impression of something perceived by the senses). Although visual information is processed in a rudimentary way (e.g., distinctions between light and dark can be made), it cannot be bound together so that a meaningful whole can be perceived. In contrast, in **associative agnosia** basic visual information can be integrated to form a meaningful perceptual whole, yet that particular perceptual whole cannot be linked to stored knowledge. If we consider this distinction differently, persons with apperceptive agnosia in some sense have trouble "seeing" objects, whereas persons with associative agnosia can "see" objects, but they don't know what they are looking at. We now discuss these two main types of agnosia in more detail (for the definitive, book-length review on agnosia, see Farah, 1990).

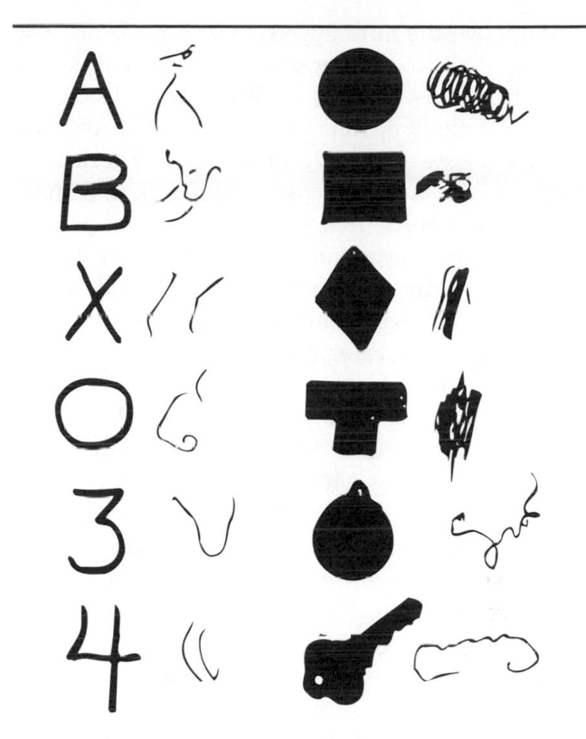

FIGURE 6.6 Example of the inability of a person with apperceptive agnosia to copy even the most basic of forms. The objects that the patient was asked to copy are on the left of each column, and the patient's attempts to do so are on the right.

Apperceptive Agnosia

In apperceptive agnosia, rudimentary visual processing is intact at least to the degree that basic perceptual discriminations involving brightness, color, line orientation, and motion can be made. However, the ability to coalesce this basic visual information into a percept, an entity, or a whole is lost. Persons with apperceptive agnosia have little or no ability to discriminate between shapes, regardless of whether they are objects, faces, or letters, and have no ability to copy or match simple shapes (Figure 6.6).

These individuals generally correctly perceive local features of an object, but suffer from an inability to group them together into the percept of a whole object (Farah, 1990). As an example of this deficit, look at Figure 6.7. An individual with apperceptive agnosia would not perceive the pattern as "this" because of the discontinuity between the parts of the "T" and the "H." He or she would read it as the number "7415" because that ability relies on perceiving the most simple of visual features, line orientation.

Generally individuals with such a severely compromised ability to recognize objects have diffuse damage to the occipital lobe and surrounding regions, a pattern of damage that most often occurs with carbon monoxide poisoning (Farah, 1990).

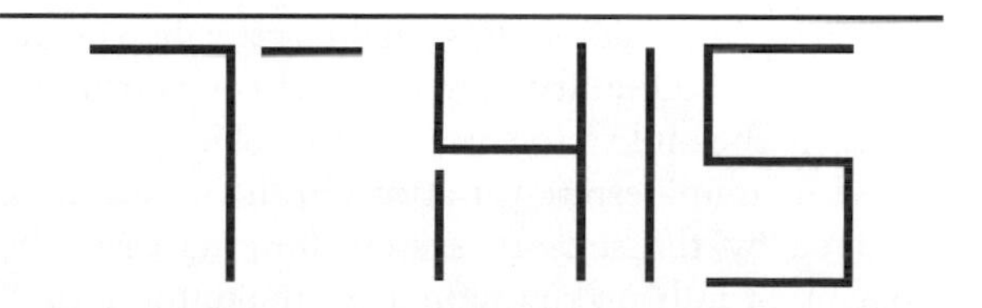

FIGURE 6.7 Limited local form perception in an apperceptive agnosic patient. The patient cannot read this visual pattern as the word "this" but rather reads it as "7415."

Although the term apperceptive agnosia has also been applied to a group of individuals with somewhat better visual abilities (Warrington, 1982), the nature of their deficits and the location of their lesions suggest that they may represent a distinct syndrome. These individuals typically have damage to the right hemisphere, in particular to the parietal region, which, as you know, is *not* part of the ventral visual-processing stream. The visual abilities of these individuals are much better than those of a classic apperceptive agnosic. They can distinguish two simple visual forms from each other, such as discriminating an oval from a circle and a square from a rectangle, and they can successfully find a fragmented letter, such as an X, in a mottled background. Hence, it appears that, unlike classic apperceptive agnosics, these individuals can at least coalesce *contour* information into a meaningful whole (Warrington, 1982). They sometimes exhibit difficulties, however, when the contour information is degraded and must be interpolated (Figure 6.8A) or when an object's contour must be disembedded from among other contours (Figure 6.8B).

They also have difficulty when an object is displayed in an atypical manner as a result of transformations of either position or lighting. In everyday life, we generally view most objects from a particular vantage point. For example, we usually view a pail from the side rather than from above (Figure 6.9A). Yet, when we encounter an "unusual view" of an object, such as that of the pail from above, we still recognize it as a pail (Figure 6.9B). Individuals with this particular disorder cannot recognize an item in an atypical position, even though they can do so when the same item is viewed in a prototypic, or usual, position (Warrington & Taylor, 1973).

Rather than being considered apperceptive agnosics, these individuals might better be considered to have difficulty in **perceptual categorization,** which is the ability to categorize an object as being the same item despite variations in the information received by the sensory system (in this case, the image that falls on the retina). To make the idea of perceptual categorization clear, consider an example from the auditory modality. Imagine that you heard two different cat meows. If asked what those sounds meant, you might not be able to link a gurgling sound to the meaning of "I'm happy," or a high-pitched mew to "I'm hungry," much the way persons with agnosia can't determine the meaning of visually presented objects. Nonetheless, you could perceptually classify the meows, determining that two high-pitched mews sounded similar and that both of these were different from a gurgle.

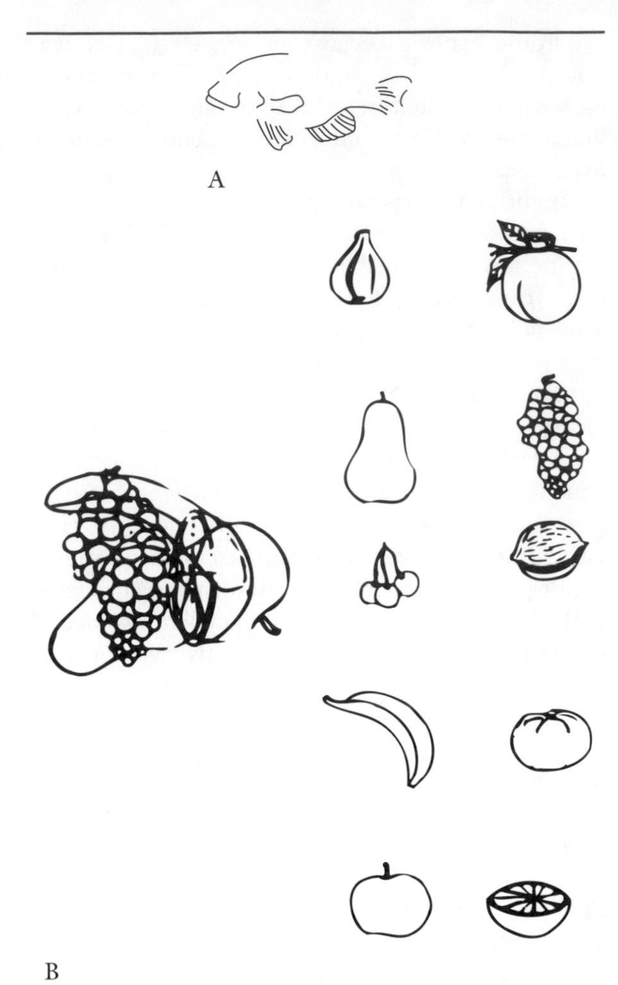

FIGURE 6.8 Examples of how the extraction of contour information is disrupted in individuals with perceptual categorization disorders as a result of right hemisphere damage. (A) These individuals have difficulty recognizing this object as a fish because they cannot interpolate the missing contours. (B) They also cannot disentangle the contours of the five items (grapes, apple, pear, banana, and orange) on the right that are superimposed in the overlapping figure on the left.

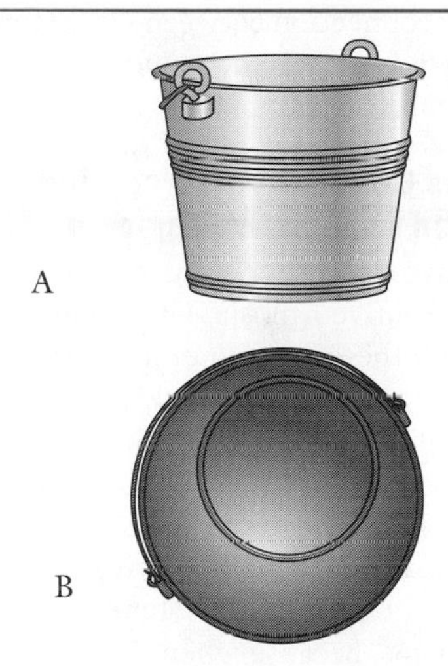

FIGURE 6.9 A common item viewed from a typical and nontypical perspective. (A) In this case, a pail is in the position from which we typically view it. (B) The same object but in an atypical, or nonprototypic, view. Persons with posterior right-hemisphere damage have difficulty recognizing the item in its atypical orientation.

Individuals with this posterior right-hemisphere damage cannot perform such categorization with visual stimuli, even when the linkage of meaning is not required. Asked to make a same/different judgment about two different models of the same object (e.g., an open umbrella and a closed umbrella; or a cat facing the camera and a cat turned away from the camera), they perform poorly (Warrington & Taylor, 1978). We can speculate that the right posterior damage in these individuals makes it difficult to extract some of the spatial invariants among objects that aids in their perceptual classification.

To summarize, although persons with apperceptive agnosia can process crude visual information, such as color and line orientation, the ability to derive more complex visual information, such as contour, is lost. The site of lesions in such cases is generally diffuse across the ventral visual-processing stream. There is also another set of patients, sometimes referred to as apperceptive agnosics, who are probably better thought to have difficulties in perceptual categorization of visual items. They have damage to right parietal regions and may have difficulty in perceptual classification as a result of difficulties in extracting spatial invariants across objects.

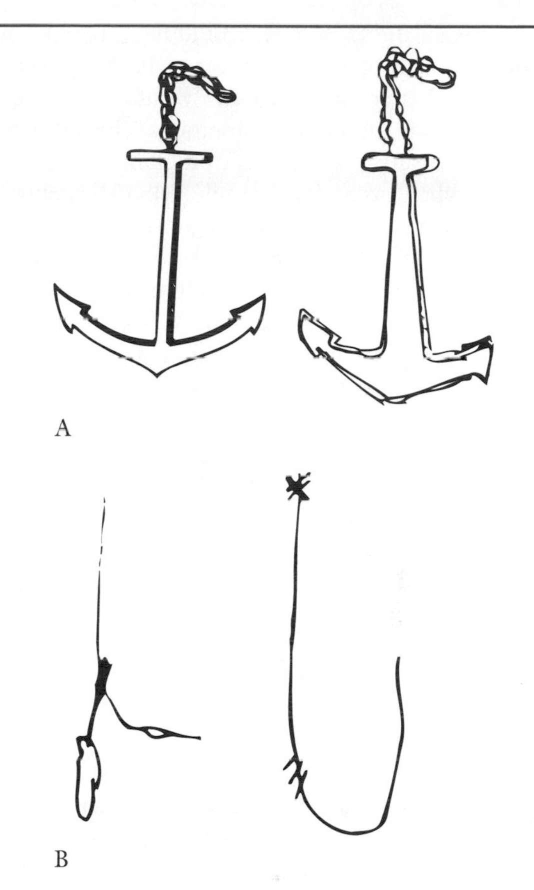

FIGURE 6.10 Drawing abilities of a person with associative agnosia. (A) The patient's copy (right) of the model (left). Compared with the copying ability of a person with apperceptive agnosia (see Figure 6.6), this patient's ability to copy is much better. Yet, despite the patient's ability to copy the figure and assert that an anchor is "a brake for ships," he could identify neither the model nor his copy as an anchor. (B) The patient's attempts to respond to the request to draw an anchor. He was unable to retrieve the correct visual form from memory.

Associative Agnosia

In associative agnosia, individuals retain the ability to perform the perceptual grouping that persons with apperceptive agnosia find difficult. Copying a picture, such as the anchor shown in Figure 6.10, is relatively easy for a patient with associative agnosia, even though the same task would be impossible for a person with apperceptive agnosia. However, a patient with associative agnosia would be unable to draw the same picture from memory. This difficulty does not arise from a general problem in memory, because when asked, for example, what an anchor is, an individual with associative agnosia can provide a reasonable definition, such as "a brake for ships" (Ratcliff & Newcombe, 1982). In some cases, persons with associative agnosia are able to extract enough information from a visually presented item to determine its superordinate category (e.g., mammal, insect, or bird) but cannot correctly determine other attributes (e.g., whether it is tame or dangerous) (Warrington, 1975).

Because individuals with this disorder can copy objects and can detect identical items from a set of similarly shaped objects, researchers originally presumed that their visual processing was intact—it was its linkage to semantic information in memory that was defective. More recent evidence suggests that the perceptual abilities of these people, although better than those of patients with apperceptive agnosia, are not truly normal. First, although individuals with associative agnosia can perform matching and copying tasks, they use a point-by-point or part-by-part comparison, which suggests that they are not obtaining a percept of the entire form. This strategy is different from that of neurologically intact individuals, who tend to draw the broad features first and then fill in the details. Furthermore, although they may be able to copy pictures in great detail, they are exceedingly slow.

Second, their deficits in object recognition become more severe as the input from a visual stimulus becomes more impoverished. They are best at recognizing real objects (which are least impoverished), next best with photographs, and worst with line drawings (which are most impoverished). Third, their errors are often ones of visual similarity, such as misidentifying a baseball bat as a paddle, knife, baster, or thermometer, rather than as a bat. Finally, they have difficulty in matching objects, such as unfamiliar faces and complex meaningful or novel shapes, which have no semantic association. If their visual processing were intact and the problem arose solely from a disconnection between visual form and semantics, they would have no trouble in matching these items (Farah, 2000).

Differences Between Apperceptive Agnosia and Associative Agnosia

Now that we have discussed the syndromes of apperceptive and associative agnosia, let's review the differences between these two syndromes. Individuals with associative agnosia can perceive much more detailed information than persons with apperceptive agnosia can, as evidenced by their ability to match items and to copy drawings with a fair degree of accuracy. In addition, patients with associative agnosia apparently can extract some information about general shape, because when they misidentify an item, they generally assume it to be an object that looks similar in shape (e.g., misidentifying a pig for a sheep). In contrast, individuals with apperceptive agnosia have a poor ability to extract shape information and must rely on other cues, such as color and texture, to segregate figure from ground. Common to both syndromes, however, is the loss of the ability to link visual information to meaning.

Given the differences in processing abilities between persons with apperceptive agnosia and associative agnosia, we would expect the site of brain damage to differ between these two populations, and indeed this is the case. A diagram summarizing the location of damage that is typically seen in each of these syndromes is provided in Figure 6.11. As you may remember from earlier in the chapter, persons with apperceptive agnosia who have only the most rudimentary visual functions usually have diffuse damage to the occipital lobe and surrounding areas. In individuals with associative agnosia, the lesion site varies but typically involves the occipitotemporal regions of both hemispheres. When damage is restricted to one hemisphere, the lesion tends to be in the region of the occipital lobe bordering on the posterior temporal lobe (Farah, 1990).

Now that we have some idea of the different ways in which visual object recognition can be disrupted, it is time to investigate face recognition, a process that appears to be distinct from other types of object recognition.

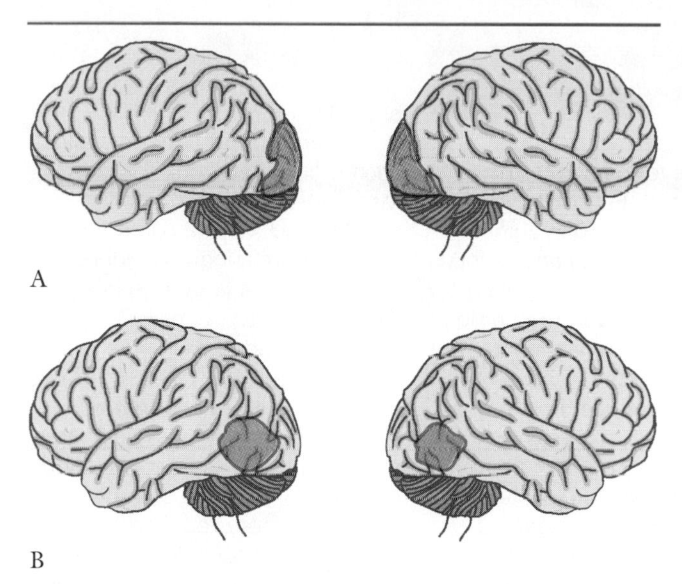

FIGURE 6.11 Regions of the brain typically damaged in apperceptive and associative agnosia. (A) In apperceptive agnosia, damage occurs diffusely across occipital regions. (B) In associative agnosia, the damage tends to be bilateral at the occipito-temporal border. The typical lesion in associative agnosia is more anterior than the lesion in apperceptive agnosia.

Face-Recognition Difficulties as a Special Type of Visual Agnosia

So far, we have discussed agnosia as a deficit in which the person loses the ability to recognize or identify all information within a specific modality. However, at least one type of visual agnosia is specific to a particular class of visual items, namely faces. This disorder is known as **prosopagnosia,** and it is a selective inability to recognize or differentiate among faces, although other objects in the visual modality can be correctly identified. Individuals with prosopagnosia can recognize a face as a face, which suggests that high-level visual processing is intact. In fact, they may even be able to determine the sex or relative age (old or young) of a person's face and the emotion that it is expressing (e.g., Tranel, Damasio, & Damasio, 1988). Yet, the ability to recognize a particular face as belonging to an individual person is lost. The impairment can be so severe that the patient with prosopagnosia may not be able to recognize her or his spouse, children, or even her or his own face! Like other individuals with agnosia, those with prosopagnosia do not have a general memory deficit. They can remember information about specific individuals and can recognize these people through other modalities, even when the individual's face cannot be recognized. Commonly, persons with prosopagnosia attempt to compensate for their deficit by relying on distinctive visual nonfacial information, such as a person's hairstyle or a distinctive piece of clothing, or by relying on information in a nonvisual modality, such as voice or gait (A. R. Damasio, Damasio, & Van Hoesen, 1982).

Researchers have been interested in face recognition not only because the syndrome of prosopagnosia suggests that faces may be a special type of visual object, but for a number of other reasons as well. As already mentioned, face recognition seems to be the task for which the right hemisphere is highly skilled, much as the left hemisphere is skilled for processing language. Thus, researchers are interested in understanding face recognition to gain better insight into the types of processes at which the right hemisphere is most adept. Another reason for the interest in faces is that findings from studies of patients with prosopagnosia seemingly indicate that the ability to identify an item as belonging to a specific category (e.g., determining that the visual pattern is a face) is distinct from the ability to remember the particulars about members within that category (e.g., determining that the face you are viewing is John's and not Tim's). As we discuss later, these findings have implications for how perceptual information is linked to memory. Still another reason for an interest in studying faces is that face recognition is an ecologically important task. The ability to distinguish among people's faces is critical for many aspects of social interaction and communication. Moreover, these abilities have probably been honed over evolutionary time. Whereas humans as a species have known how to read and write for only the last 5,000 years (which did not give the brain enough time evolve to specifically perform such tasks), the ability to distinguish family from

VISUAL IMAGERY: SEEING OBJECTS WITH THE MIND'S EYE

Have you ever imagined yourself on a tropical island in the Caribbean? Can you see the long, white, sandy beach? The blending of the water's colors from pale green to jade to aquamarine to royal blue? The palm trees with their fronds waving in the breeze? And, to complete the picture, your latest romantic interest looking perfectly enticing in an ever-so-alluring bathing suit? If so, then even though our discussion of objects has centered on recognizing objects in the real world, you realize that we also have the ability to examine and manipulate objects in our mind's eye by mental imagery.

The nature of mental imagery has been the subject of a long-running debate whose resolution was based, in part, on data from cognitive neuroscience. Stephen Kosslyn, a researcher at Harvard University, had proposed that mental imagery was much like visual processing, except in the mind's eye. Some support for this position came from studies in which he found that the time needed to "see" particular parts of an image was proportional to the distance that we would expect the mind's eye to have to move to get to that part. For example, participants were told to imagine an item (e.g., an airplane) and to focus on one end (e.g., the propeller). Then they were given the name of a particular feature to look for ("the tail") and instructed to press a button when they could see it. Kosslyn (1973) found that individuals took longer to press the button if the feature was located at the other end of the imagined item (e.g., the tail) than if it appeared in the middle (e.g., the wing).

In contrast, Zenon Pylyshyn (1973, 1981) argued that we don't actually draw mental images. Rather, he suggested, the results of Kosslyn's experiment could just as easily be explained by *propositional knowledge*. Propositional knowledge describes entities (e.g., a propeller, a wing), their relations (next to, behind), their properties (long, silver), and their logical relations (if). He argued that a person takes less time to decide about the wing than the tail because the individual must remember only that the wing is behind the propeller, which is fewer propositions than remembering that the tail is behind the wing, which in turn is behind the propeller.

The arguments for and against each theory oscillated for more than another 10 years, until Kosslyn and Martha Farah turned to neuropsychological evidence, which played a large role in settling the matter (for a more detailed but readable account of this debate, see Kosslyn, 1990). These researchers reasoned that if imagery does rely on producing a picture in the mind's eye, it should require some of the same neuronal machinery required by vision (e.g., Farah, 1988). Alternatively, if imagery tasks can be performed simply by resorting to propositional knowledge about objects in the world, then the memory and/or semantic-processing areas of the brain should be active, but visually related areas should not.

Studies of regional brain activation and of patients with brain damage as well as "reversible lesions" caused by transcranial magnetic stimulation (TMS) all suggest that visual areas play a major role in imagery. For example, Kosslyn and colleagues (1993) reasoned that if imagery relies on the visual cortex, some relationship should exist between the size of the imagined object and the area of visual cortex that is

friend and friend from foe on the basis of facial features has been of great importance for the survival of humans for a much longer period of time. In fact, the neural substrate for face-recognition abilities appears to have a rich evolutionary heritage, as the neural machinery for distinguishing among the faces has been found in other mammalian species. To provide a broader perspective, we now briefly review some of what has been learned about the neural substrates of face-recognition abilities in other species.

Face Recognition in Other Species

Many mammals appear to have a specific brain region that is important for recognizing faces, especially those of their own species. As we discussed in Chapter 1, single-cell recording in the temporal regions of sheep indicate that certain cells respond selectively to horned sheep, others to unhorned sheep, some to dogs that look like sheepdogs, and others to dogs that look like wolves (e.g., Kendrick & Baldwin, 1987). These findings provide evidence that

activated. This finding would be expected because, as we discussed in Chapter 1, visual space is mapped onto visual cortex in a retinotopic manner. Consistent with their hypothesis, these investigators found that when a person was imaging small letters in the center of the mind's eye, activation was greatest in posterior regions of the medial occipital lobes, which is the region that processes information from the fovea. In contrast, when a person was imaging larger letters, activation occurred over a larger area of visual cortex that included more anterior regions, which is where more peripheral regions of visual space are processed.

Additional evidence that imagery relies on visual cortex comes from an unusual case study in which an individual had elective surgery to remove the occipital lobe of one hemisphere because it was the source of intractable epileptic seizures (Farah, Soso, & Dasheiff, 1992). The researchers calculated the visual angle of the patient's mental image before and after the surgery (see the original article for details on how this was done). The researchers reasoned that if imagery relies on the visual cortex, after surgery the visual angle of images in the horizontal dimension should be half what it was previously, because the visual cortex of one hemisphere is responsible for processing information from one half of visual space. However, the visual angle of images should be unchanged in the vertical dimension, because the remaining intact occipital cortex would be able to process information from both the upper and lower halves of space. These investigators found, as expected, a reduction by approximately half for the visual angle of images in the horizontal dimension, but no change for the visual angle of images in the vertical dimension.

Finally, with the recent advent of TMS, it has been possible to disrupt processing of visual areas. If imagery relies on visual-processing regions of the brain, then disrupting them should also disrupt the ability to use imagery. To test this premise, Kosslyn and colleagues had participants memorize four sets of lines. Participants were given auditory information about which two sets of lines to compare and along what dimension (e.g., relative length, width, orientation or spacing between them). Compared to a control condition in which no imagery was required, the individuals exhibited activity in V1 (BA 17). They then applied TMS while the individuals were either performing the imagery task or a perceptual version of the task in which the stimuli were kept in front of the individual. TMS interfered with both perception and imagery, suggesting that primary visual areas are critical for this function (Kosslyn et al., 1999).

Does this mean that the regions of the brain involved in perception and imagery are identical? If so, then how would we ever be able to tell the difference between what we experience in a particularly vivid dream and our everyday perceptual experience? Although neuroimaging studies suggest a high degree of overlap, there are areas activated uniquely for each (Kosslyn, Thompson, & Alpert, 1997). Furthermore, there are case studies of individuals who have impaired object perception but intact imagery (Behrmann, Moscovitch, & Winocur, 1994), and also the converse—individuals with disrupted imagery but intact perception (Farah, Levine, & Calvanio, 1988). These findings suggest that at least some aspects of the neural control of imagery and perception must be separable, although in most situations they may rely on very similar brain structures (for a very readable and short review of this issue, see Behrmann, 2000). ■

the mammalian brain has the ability to divide a larger category of visual forms (e.g., sheep) into subcategories (e.g., horned sheep vs. unhorned sheep). Notice, however, that this evidence does not imply that, on the basis of visual cues, the sheep brain is capable of distinguishing different individual sheep from one another.

Single-cell recordings in monkeys provide additional evidence for a specific neural substrate underlying face recognition. As mentioned earlier in the chapter, cells in the inferotemporal cortex can be tuned to highly specific visual information. In some cases, the cells in this region are tuned to fire specifically in response to faces, regardless of whether the faces belong to monkeys or persons. Indicating their specificity to faces, these cells do not fire in response to other round objects, such as alarm clocks, or to other emotionally important stimuli, such as snakes. Even more specialized cells in the inferotemporal cortex fire in response to specific aspects of faces or only in response to faces that have particular characteristics. For example, just as global and local aspects of an item are processed by distinct neural systems in humans, there is also a specificity of cell responses, some firing only in response to a global facial configuration and others to certain facial features. Some cells in the inferotemporal cortex fire only when a specific facial feature, such as the eyes, is present, either when embedded within the whole face or when presented by itself. The critical feature varies from cell to cell. Some cells fire only when the mouth is present and others fire only when the eyes are present. In contrast, another class of cells is particularly sensitive to the configuration of features that form a face (e.g., two eyes positioned laterally above a nose on midline that in turn is positioned directly above a mouth). These cells fire in response to the components of monkeys' faces only if the components are correctly positioned but not if their positions are scrambled. Other cells have still different types of specificity. Some fire only in response to faces in particular orientations (e.g., those facing directly forward; those turned 45 degrees from front view). Others fire only in response to faces with a particular emotion. It appears, therefore, that cells within the inferotemporal cortex can be finely tuned for specific aspects of face processing.

As we discussed earlier in the chapter, recognizing an object requires that its equivalency be appreciated across variations in retinal size and orientation. Cells in the inferotemporal region of monkeys have this characteristic, being responsive to faces under a variety of illuminations and configurations (such as variations in facial orientation and viewing distance). A small number of cells are even more finely tuned, firing only in response to a specific person's face (usually that of an experimenter), regardless of orientation, size, color, or emotional expression on the face. Furthermore, these cells do not fire in response to other individuals (Perrett, Mistlin, & Chitty, 1987, provide a good review of these results). Taken together, these findings provide evidence that cells in inferotemporal cortex are highly sensitive to faces and to facial features, and, in some cases, are selectively responsive to individual faces.

Because these cells respond to specific aspects of faces and in some cases to specific people's faces, we might be tempted to think that these cells are *the* place in the brain where recognition of a particular face occurs. In fact, at one time a predominant theory posited the existence of the "grandmother cell" (see H. B. Barlow, 1985, for an account of this viewpoint). According to the **grandmother cell theory,** a small set of cells would fire only in response to a highly specific visual object, such as your grandmother, and no other objects. In other words, these cells alone would be the brain mechanism responsible for recognizing your grandmother. They would recognize a specific object because they received information from other cells that analyzed parts of that specific object and conjoined them (e.g., received information from cells that recognized your grandmother's nose, her hair, her eyes, her chin line, etc., to perceive her face). However, current understanding of brain organization reveals that a cell exhibiting a highly specific firing pattern isn't likely to be *the* place in the brain that recognizes your grandmother so much as it is part of a diffuse cortical network that *participates in recognizing* your grandmother. The reason that scientists think this scenario more likely is that although some cells show high specificity in their response for shape, most cells in inferotemporal cortex are simultaneously selective for a particular aspect of color, a particular aspect of shape, and a particular aspect of visual texture. Furthermore, these cells usually tend to give a small response to a variety of somewhat dissimilar stimuli. As a result, the brain probably codes a particular visual object as a highly specific pattern of activation across a population of neurons rather than having a small pool of neurons dedicated to responding to that object and no other (see Gross, 1992, for a good historical and theoretical description of this work and its relevance to face recognition).

Researchers have also moved away from the idea of a grandmother cell because they realize that although a cell can appear to be specific in its response (e.g., it responds only to a researcher's face), determining with certainty exactly which specific stimulus makes the cell fire is practically impossible. Consider the following rather contrived example, which nonetheless makes this point. Assume that an experimenter finds a cell that fires in response to the face of his grandmother but not that of his grandfather. He might conclude that this cell is highly specific for recognizing his grandmother. However, unbeknownst to the researcher, the same cell fires in response to potato chips (which the researcher doesn't know because he can't test all possible objects and potato chips didn't seem a likely candidate). The common denominator between the face of his grandmother and the potato chips that makes the cell fire is that they share a particular oval shape, a characteristic not shared by his grandfather's face, which is round.

As this theoretical example illustrates, ascertaining the specific visual configuration that makes a cell fire may be difficult in principle. Recent empirical evidence illustrating this difficulty comes from recordings of a subpopulation of cells that traditionally were considered "face" cells because they respond vigorously to faces. However, researchers found that a subpopulation of these cells also fire in response to views of the body, even when the face is occluded. These findings suggest that these cells might be more aptly described as "body" cells rather than "face" cells (e.g., Wachsmuth, Oram, & Perrett, 1994).

Overall, what implications do these findings in monkeys have for face-recognition abilities in people? They suggest that the brains of monkeys (and most likely people) have specific regions that are especially adept at performing the computations important for recognizing faces. Moreover, these same brain structures can in certain cases individuate among faces of different people. If these regions are damaged, disruptions of face recognition can occur. We now turn our attention to such disruptions seen after neurological insult in humans.

Face Recognition in Humans

As we mentioned in Chapter 4, much evidence exists from studies of patients with the split-brain syndrome, from divided visual field studies of neurologically intact individuals, and from individuals with right-hemisphere damage, that the right hemisphere of the human brain is particularly adept at recognizing faces. In fact, Yin (1970) suggested that posterior sections of the right hemisphere are specifically organized for recognizing faces above and beyond other types of complex visual stimuli. To investigate this hypothesis, he compared the ability of individuals with right-hemisphere damage to recognize faces with their ability to identify other visually complex stimuli that are also generally viewed in only one orientation, such as houses. In these studies, individuals viewed an inspection series of items (either faces or houses). Afterward, they were given a test series of items that contained, on each trial, a pair of items, one of which had appeared in the inspection series and one of which had not. The individuals were asked to pick the item viewed previously.

The participants were required to perform this task twice, once when the items in both the inspection and test series were in their regular upright orientation and once when they were presented in an inverted orientation. The rationale behind this manipulation is that, regardless of orientation, the items are identical in visual complexity, but when the items are inverted, configurational information is lost (e.g., the nose is no longer below the eyes, the chin is not at the bottom of the face). Yin theorized that this configurational information was especially important for recognizing faces.

To appreciate the role that configurational information plays in face recognition, let's consider the picture in Figure 6.12, which is a demonstration created by Thompson (1980). In the inverted orientation, the woman does not look very odd, although on closer inspection you may notice that in the right-hand picture her eyes and mouth seem a bit strange (because they are actually upside down). Now, turn your book upside down and view the woman in an upright position. In the picture on the left, her face should now look bizarre and somewhat ghoulish. Because we have a configuration for recognizing upright faces but not one for recognizing inverted faces, her face looks much more distorted when viewed upright than when viewed inverted.

Yin found that neurologically intact individuals exhibited an **inversion effect,** which is a greater difficulty in remembering inverted stimuli than upright stimuli. Of most importance was the fact that the inversion effect was significantly larger for faces than for houses, which suggests that configural properties play a more important role in recognizing

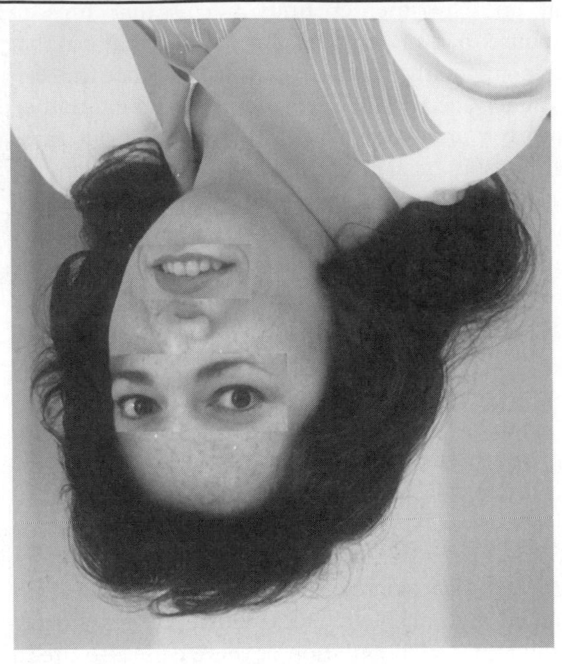

FIGURE 6.12 Example of the importance of configural information for recognizing faces. Examine the two faces and notice how from this vantage point they look similar. Now turn your book upside down so that the two faces are right-side up. You should immediately see a difference. This exercise, called the Thompson illusion, demonstrates the degree to which configural strategies are important for the processing of faces in the upright orientation and how they are minimized when the faces are inverted.

faces than in recognizing houses. In contrast, patients with right-hemisphere damage showed a reduced inversion effect for faces. Although these patients did as well as neurologically intact subjects at recognizing inverted faces, they were selectively poor at recognizing upright faces. These findings led Yin to suggest that the posterior section of the right hemisphere was specialized specifically for face recognition and for the configural processing that such recognition required. This suggestion is consistent with a vast literature on face-recognition studies of neurologically intact subjects. Typically, a LVF advantage is found for face recognition (e.g., Geffen, Bradshaw, & Wallace, 1971), but this effect diminishes when faces are presented in an inverted orientation (e.g., Leehey, Carey, Diamond, & Cahn, 1978).

Other researchers have attempted to build upon Yin's findings, with the idea of determining more specifically which regions of the brain are critical for face processing and also whether these regions are specialized for processing faces above and beyond other visually complex mono-oriented stimuli. At present, data from various converging methods, such as electrophysiological recordings, brain imaging studies, and analysis of lesion location in patients with prosopagnosia, confirm that faces are processed differently than other objects and that this ability relies on the posterior sector of the right hemisphere.

We now review some of this evidence. Recordings of electrical potentials are one source of information about the neural substrates of face processing. In neurologically intact individuals, there is a particular brain wave with a negative amplitude at about 170 ms poststimulus presentation (i.e., an N_{170}) that occurs when individuals are asked to view faces but not other categories of stimuli, such as cars, butterflies, scrambled faces. Moreover, it tends to be greater over the right hemisphere than the left (Bentin et al., 1996). Recordings from the surface of the brains of patients about to undergo surgery for the relief of epilepsy provide confirmatory evidence and a bit more information on the brain region likely to be generating this potential (Allison et al., 1994). The location of the source of this potential varies from patient to patient but generally is recorded bilaterally from fusiform and inferotemporal regions (Figure 6.13A). In any given patient, however, the size of the region providing such a response is small, perhaps only 1- to 2-cm wide, a finding suggesting a fair amount of anatomical variability with regard to the exact location of face-specific regions. Hemispheric differences have also been found in these recordings, with the right hemisphere, but not the left, exhibiting different responses to upright faces than to inverted faces (Figure 6.13B)

The findings from electrophysiological studies mesh well with those of functional imaging studies of face processing, with regard to the specificity of this region's response to faces but not other complex visual stimuli. Ten years ago, using PET, researchers identified ventral regions of extrastriate cortex in the right hemisphere as critical for discriminating among the physical features of faces, sometimes referred to as *physiognomy,* because these regions were more active in a gender-decision task for faces than for an object-recognition task (Sergent, Ohta, & MacDonald, 1992). These regions are highly similar in location to those identified more recently using fMRI—the fusiform face area described by Kanwisher and colleagues (Kanwisher, McDermott, & Chun, 1997) as well as the regions implicated in face processing by Haxby and colleagues (Haxby et al., 2001).

These findings are also consistent with data from brain-damaged individuals. As we discussed in Chapter 3, a double dissociation is a particularly powerful method for demonstrating that two mental processes can proceed independently of one another, and that they rely on different neural substrates. Such a double dissociation has been observed for face and object recognition. As mentioned earlier, prosopagnosia is a syndrome in which the identification of faces is impaired but the recognition of other objects is relatively normal. Recently there have been case reports of patients who exhibit the converse syndrome—they can recognize faces but exhibit agnosia for objects (e.g. Feinberg et al., 1994; Moscovitch, Winocur, & Behrmann, 1997).

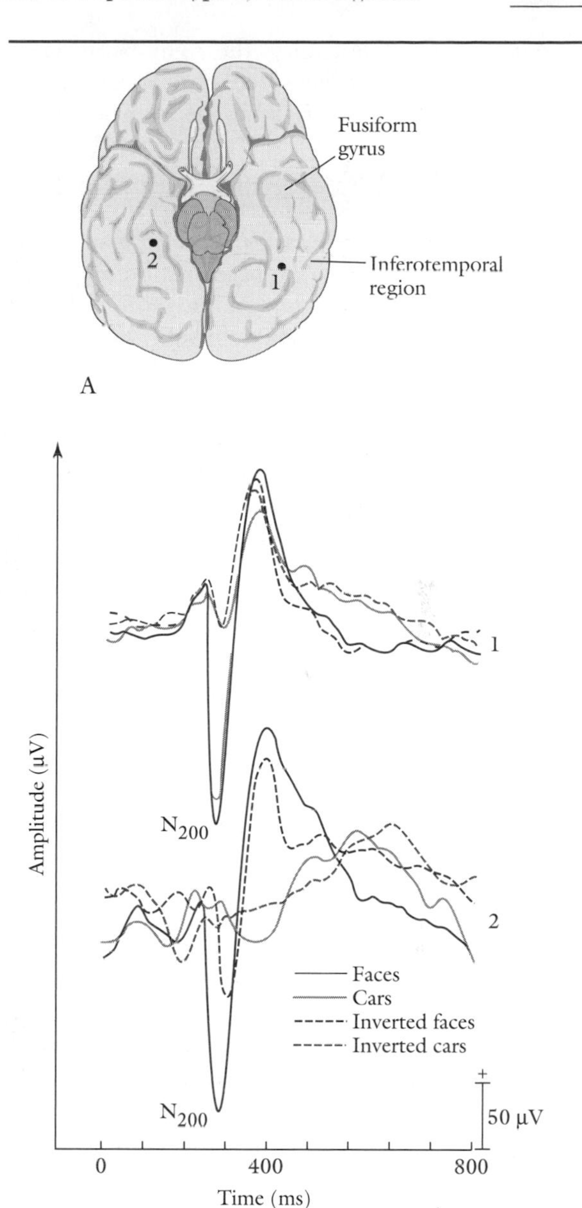

FIGURE 6.13 Examples of N_{200} responses to faces and cars recorded from the cortex of one individual about to undergo surgery for the control of epilepsy. (A) The sites (labeled 1 and 2) in the fusiform gyrus at which the potentials were recorded. (B) The potentials recorded over the left hemisphere (top) and over the right hemisphere (bottom). Note that the N_{200} response is larger to faces than to cars. Also notice that the larger response over the right hemisphere to upright faces than to inverted faces (bottom) does not occur for the left hemisphere (top).

With regard to laterality, the right hemisphere appears to play a critical or predominant role in face processing. Although initially it had been suggested that prosopagnosia occurred only after bilateral lesions (which was proposed to account for it being so rare; e.g., see A. R. Damasio, Damasio, & Van Hoesen, 1982), a more recent review of lesion locations in case studies of prosopagnosia indicates that this disorder can result from lesions restricted to the right hemisphere. In a small sample of patients whose MRI scans showed a lesion confined to the right hemisphere, reduced metabolism was found only for right hemisphere regions. This finding confirmed that the left hemisphere was functioning normally, implicating the right hemisphere as critical for face processing (see DeRenzi et al., 1994, for some of the empirical data and for a review of this literature). Further supporting the idea that face processing can rely solely on the right hemisphere are the results from patients who cannot recognize objects but can recognize faces. They have lesions in the left hemisphere that presumably leave the right-hemisphere face processing mechanisms intact, accounting for the dissociation between their object- and face-recognition abilities.

Both neuroimaging studies and studies of patients with prosopagnosia suggest that different regions of the brain are important for identifying the visual features of faces, which is what most of our discussion has centered on so far, as compared with the ability to specifically identify a face as belonging to a particular individual, such as the face of Sting as compared to Paul McCartney. As initially revealed by PET studies, anterior regions of the temporal lobe become active in both hemispheres when a face has to be identified as belonging to a specific person. But an important distinction in neural activity is observed for temporal regions of the right hemisphere: anterior areas of the fusiform gyrus and the parahippocampal gyrus are active only during a face-identification task but not during a gender-identification task; suggesting that these regions of the right hemisphere may be specifically specialized for the operations required to determine facial identity (Sergent, Ohta, & MacDonald, 1992). Subsequent fMRI studies also suggest activation of this region when people have to retrieve biographical information associated with faces (Leveroni et al., 2000), and damage to this region results in a selective impairment in semantic identification of famous faces (Tranel et al., 1997).

Additional evidence for the idea that anterior regions of the right hemisphere are involved in processing facial identity comes by a study in which single-cell recording was performed in patients who had implanted electrodes as part of the procedure involved in undergoing surgery for epilepsy. Consistent with recordings in monkeys, cells in the right anterior temporal regions were found to fire only in response to a specific category of items, such as animals or natural scenes. Of most importance for the current discussion, cells were found that responded to famous faces, but not to emotional faces of unknown actors. This finding indicates that they were not firing to faces per se, but rather to the fact that the identity of the face was known (Kreiman, Koch, & Fried, 2000) (see Figure 6.14).

Case studies of patients with prosopagnosia also suggest that different portions of the occipitotemporal area of the right hemisphere play distinct roles in different aspects of face processing. Case reports of two patients with prosopagnosia who had difficulty performing basic perceptual face tasks (such as determining whether two identical photographs of the same face represented the same individual) but who didn't have such difficulties with other objects, such as cars, were found to have damage in occipital regions and posterior parts of the medial temporal cortex. In contrast, two patients who were relatively unimpaired at matching pictures of faces but were unable to determine the identity of a given face had damage in more anterior regions of the right fusiform gyrus and/or the parahippocampal gyrus (Sergent & Signoret, 1992b).

There is yet one other area of the brain that appears to be involved in processing faces, the superior temporal sulcus. Single-cell recordings in monkeys have shown that cells in this region are sensitive to gaze and head direction, with most cells preferentially firing to full views of the face with eye contact and profile view of faces with averted gaze (D. I. Perrett et al., 1985). They are also sensitive to facial gestures, especially those involving the mouth, such as a grimace, teeth chatter, or threat display (D. I. Perrett & Mistlin, 1990). In humans,

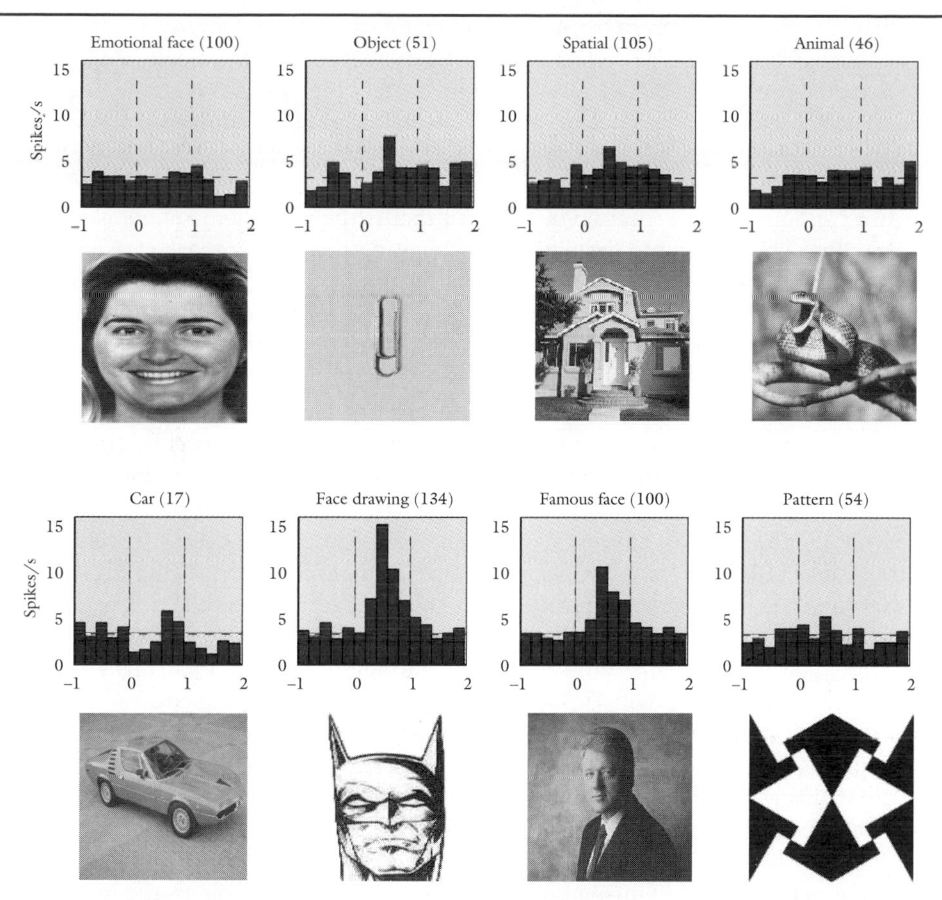

FIGURE 6.14 Responses of a cell in the right anterior temporal lobe that differentially responds to famous faces as compared with other objects. The histogram notes the number of spikes per second from one second prior to stimulus presentation to two seconds afterwards. The one-second presentation time is noted by the dashed lines. The picture below the histogram provides an example of the type of stimulus displayed. Notice that this cell does not respond to all faces, as indicated by the lack of a response over baseline levels to emotional faces, but only to famous faces, such as that of Batman (depicted as a face drawing) and Bill Clinton (depicted in a photograph).

attending to the eye-gaze direction causes greater activity in the superior temporal sulcus (STS) than the fusiform region, whereas paying attention to facial identity activates lateral fusiform areas more than superior temporal regions, suggesting a dissociation between these two areas (Hoffman & Haxby, 2000). Electrode recordings in individuals about to undergo surgery for epilepsy also indicate that certain cells within the STS show a specific response to mouth movement (Puce & Allison, 1999). This role of the STS in interpreting facial expression may be part of its larger role in interpreting movements in biological systems that have social significance (e.g,, eye gaze indicates whether someone is paying attention to you; for a good review of the role of the STS in interpreting visual cues of a social nature, see Allison, Puce, & McCarthy, 2000). It may also be that superior temporal regions are important for the changeable aspects of the face, such as perception of eye gaze, expression, and lip movement, while the lateral fusiform area is important for processing those aspects of the face that are invariant (and would lead one to be able to uniquely identify a face), (Haxby, Hoffman, & Gobbini, 2000).

The conclusion that can be drawn from these studies is that a broad range of areas within occipital and ventral temporal regions are involved in face processing, with the right hemisphere playing a predominant role. In general, posterior regions seem to be important for the perceptual processes that must be performed to create a configural representation of a face (as distinct from other objects) and to extract the invariants of the face that make it unique. In contrast, more anterior regions are involved in linking a particular facial representation to the pertinent biographical information about that person. Finally, regions of the STS are involved in processing those features of the face that change, such as eye gaze and expression, and thus provide critical information for social cues (see Haxby, Hoffman, & Gobbini, 2000, for a very good overview of the parts of the brain involved in face processing and how information derived from faces may aid in other cognitive functions, such as how processing of mouth movement aids in lip reading).

Role of Experience or Expertise in Face-Processing Capacities

Although the evidence we just reviewed clearly indicates that the right hemisphere is specialized for determining facial identity, we haven't directly addressed the degree to which the right hemisphere might be specialized for individuating among members of any general class of complex visual objects, of which faces is only one (for an example of this position, see DeRenzi & Spinnler, 1966). In the studies we just discussed, participants had to determine whether a given face belonged to a certain person, but similar demands were not required for other complex objects, such as requiring them to differentiate their own cat from the neighbor's cat.

To address this question, researchers considered the different pieces of evidence suggesting that the role of the right hemisphere in face processing was special; one such piece of evidence was the inversion effect (remember, Yin found that the inversion effect was greater for faces than for other mono-oriented stimuli). One group of researchers hypothesized that the inversion effect might be observed for any class of objects with which a person has had vast experience. According to these investigators, experience would allow a configural strategy to be developed for that particular class of objects, and this strategy would be disrupted by inversion. By their reasoning, the inversion effect is observed for faces because faces clearly are a class of objects with which we have much experience. The researchers further reasoned that if the right hemisphere is specialized for individuating members of any class of objects with which we are extremely familiar, as large an inversion effect should be found for that highly familiar class of objects as is observed for faces (R. Diamond & Carey, 1986).

The trouble these researchers faced in attempting to prove their hypothesis was finding such a set of objects. What other type of object besides faces requires extensive expertise in carefully individuating among members of a category over a long period? To solve this problem, these investigators devised a plan to compare how well college students and judges of show dogs could individuate among pictures of different dogs in a paradigm similar to that used by Yin. As expected, the researchers found that college students exhibited a much larger inversion effect for faces than for show dogs. The results for the show-dog judges, though, were different. They had as large an inversion effect for show dogs as for faces. Hence, the researchers concluded that expertise plays an important role in the inversion effect.

You should not be surprised to learn that experience influences the way we process not only faces, but also other stimuli. This point is well illustrated by the following study. The ability to remember a particular chest X ray that is abnormal and indicative of disease (e.g., congestive heart failure, pneumonia, collapsed lung) increases with expertise from someone with no medical training through medical residents, junior radiologists, and senior radiologists. On the other hand, if these same groups of individuals must remember X rays that don't indicate disease, greater expertise is associated with *poorer* performance, even though memory for other items, such as faces, is identical across the four groups (Figure 6.15) (Myles-Worsley, Johnston, & Simons, 1988).

Why are the highly trained radiologists significantly worse at remembering normal X rays? One likely explanation is that they have devised a system of encoding information about X rays that empha-

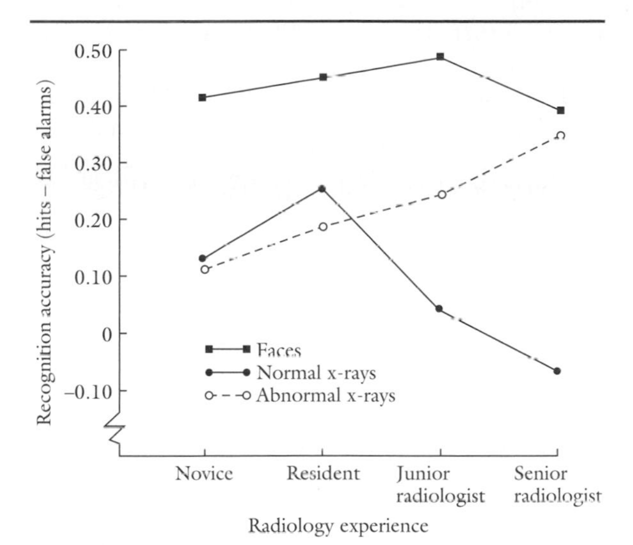

FIGURE 6.15 Example of how experience can influence the way in which visual information is processed. Shown here is the accuracy of identifying faces and x-rays for four groups of individuals who vary in their expertise in reading x-rays: novices, medical residents, junior radiologists, and senior radiologists. All four groups are equally skilled at remembering faces (scores depicted by black squares). Also, as might be expected, the greater the expertise with reading x-rays, the better the memory for abnormal x-rays (scores depicted by white circles). However, greater expertise with reading x-rays is associated with *poorer* memory for normal x-rays (scores depicted by black circles). These results suggest that expertise can hone the ability to observe certain visual characteristics, which has the effect of reducing the ability to observe other visual characteristics.

sizes certain markers associated with disease. When given X rays that are distinguished by other attributes unrelated to disease (e.g., thickness of the ribs), the radiologists do not pay attention to them, which makes remembering these X rays more difficult. Thus, this study illustrates how expertise can affect the way in which information is encoded and retrieved from memory.

Expertise also affects the ability to recognize faces. With experience, faces, like other classes of objects, can be well processed by using a configural strategy that likely relies more on right- than left-hemisphere processing. Evidence that experience aids in the configural processing of faces comes from both cross-cultural and developmental studies. For example, the inversion effect has been found to be greater for same-race faces, with which a person has had much experience, than for different-race faces. Thus, Chinese individuals exhibit a greater inversion effect for Chinese faces than for European faces, whereas European individuals exhibit the opposite pattern (Rhodes, Tan, Brake, & Taylor, 1989). These results probably occur because we have more experience with the configural nature of the faces of individuals of our own race than with that of other races. When asked to differentiate among faces, we can do so more easily if they fit into a configuration with which we are familiar.

A recent neuroimaging study suggests that the advantage for recognizing same-race faces relies on the specific right-hemisphere regions important for face recognition. In this study, the researchers located the area of each individual's brain that exhibited greater activation to faces than to other objects with configural properties, such as radios. This area was located in the right hemisphere for most of the individuals. They then observed that activation within this region was greater for same-race than different-race faces (Golby, Gabrieli, Chiao, & Eberhardt, 2001).

Developmental studies suggest that such a configural strategy for processing faces is not fully developed until about 12 years of age. Before that age, children tend to rely on salient features and can be fooled—by clothing, hairstyle, eyeglasses, or expression—into thinking that two individuals are the same person (Carey & Diamond, 1977). Also suggesting that the right hemisphere is important for this configural processing of faces is the finding that children do not show the typical right-hemisphere advantage for faces until 12 years of age, after which a LVF asymmetry emerges. We know that experience can speed up this process, because a LVF advantage can be found in younger children for faces with which they are highly familiar, such as their third-grade classmates. In contrast, no visual field asymmetry is observed for faces of other third-graders in either their own school or that of a neighboring town. The larger experience with their classmates probably allows these children to devise a configural strategy for this particular set of faces, a strategy that relies on the right hemisphere (S. C. Levine, 1984).

Given that expertise affects the recognition of faces and other objects, we now need to consider whether the right hemisphere is more involved in individuating among faces than among members of other well-known mono-oriented objects. To do so, we will consider data both from individuals who have sustained brain damage and from neuroimaging studies of neurologically intact individuals. In certain clinical case reports of patients with prosopagnosia, researchers have informally asserted that the ability to distinguish among members of other categories is also affected. In one case report, a farmer who became prosopagnosic could no longer distinguish among the cows in his herd (B. Bornstein, Sroka, & Munitz, 1969). In another case, a bird watcher could no longer individuate among birds of a given species (B. Bornstein, 1963). Yet in other case studies, these abilities dissociate: the ability to distinguish among faces was found to be disrupted while the ability to differentiate among cows (Bruyer et al., 1983) or to differentiate personal objects from other objects (e.g., DeRenzi, 1986) remained intact.

Two case studies are of particular interest because they directly address the issue of expertise. In one case, the individual with prosopagnosia was a car expert, possessing a set of miniature cars that numbered more than 5,000. To test his ability to distinguish among cars, researchers showed him 210 pictures of cars and asked him to identify each car's make, model, and year of production (within two years). He identified all three aspects correctly for 172 of the pictures, and of the remaining 38, he correctly identified the company in 31 cases and the model in 22 cases (Case R.M., Sergent & Signoret, 1992b). Thus, this individual retained his ability to individuate among cars even though he had lost the ability to do so for faces.

In another case, a patient who became a gentleman farmer after becoming prosopagnosic was able to learn the individual faces of his flock of sheep (as well as sheep he had never seen before), even though his inability to distinguish among human faces remained (McNeil & Warrington, 1993). Interestingly, this person's ability to identify sheep faces was superior to that of other new farmers. Such findings hint that he could use cues to recognize sheep faces unencumbered by the "human face schema" that the other farmers might have been imposing on sheep faces.

These data from patients with focal lesions suggest that the ability to individuate among faces can be distinct from the ability to distinguish among members of other well-known classes of objects.

Recent neuroimaging studies also have contributed to our understanding of how both expertise and individuating among classes of items are supported by right-hemisphere mechanisms. In these studies, the fusiform face area is identified individually for each participant by finding the brain region that exhibits a larger response to faces than other objects. In one study, 11 car experts and 8 bird experts, individuals who on average had 20 years of experience identifying such items, were asked to decide whether a previously seen item (car/bird) was the same as the present one. The car experts exhibited greater activity in the "face" region for cars than for other objects, a pattern not observed in the bird experts. Conversely, the bird experts exhibited greater activity in this region for birds than for other objects, but no such pattern was observed in car experts (Gauthier et al., 2000) (See Color insert 6.1).

Furthermore, activation in this "face" region increases as people become better trained to recognize novel objects. In one study, individuals were trained to become expert at recognizing novel objects, known as "greebles" (see Figure 6.16). Participants were trained with these objects until they were as fast at judging them at the individual level as they were at categorizing them at the "family" level, one index of expertise. Greeble experts but not greeble novices activated the right fusiform face area when viewing the greebles. Furthermore, the activation in the right fusiform area for upright as compared to inverted greebles increased with training (Gauthier et al., 1999). Remember that the inversion effect is taken as an index of configural processing. These findings have led some to suggest that the fusiform face area is really a "flexible fusiform area" specialized for subordinate level visual processing (i.e., differentiating individuals), which becomes automatized by expertise (Tarr & Gauthier, 2000; but see Kanwisher, 2000, in the same issue for a dissenting viewpoint).

What are we to make of the evidence that the fusiform face area is sensitive to greebles in greeble

A

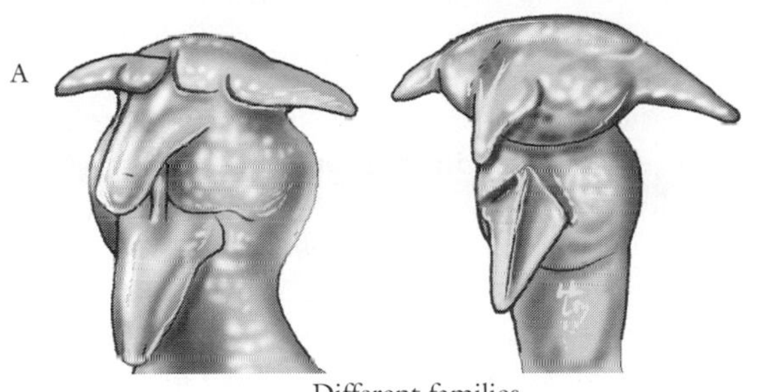

Different families

B

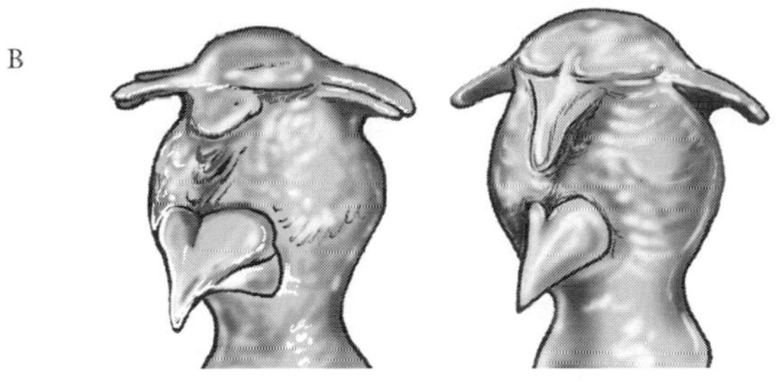

Different individuals

FIGURE 6.16 Other objects that can activate the fusiform face area. Shown here are "greebles," somewhat facelike objects that can activate the fusiform face area after individuals gain expertise in individuating them. (A) Two greebles from different "families," which are differentiated by their large central part. (B) Two greebles from the same family. Their central portions are similar, but the smaller parts are different. As an indication of expertise, greeble experts can distinguish between two members of the same family as quickly as they can distinguish between two greebles from different families.

experts, to birds in bird experts and to cars in car experts? Does it mean that the faces aren't special? As my colleagues and I noted over 10 years ago (S. C. Levine, Banich, & Koch-Weser, 1988), the right hemisphere is specialized for the types of visuospatial analyses, such as configural processing, that are required in face recognition. Evidence suggests that these abilities can be tuned by experience and honed with time. A basic right-hemisphere specialization for face recognition could be magnified with time because our vast experience with faces allows for the extraction of common configural aspects of faces. If other objects become processed in a more configural manner as expertise increases, it seems logical that they would rely on the same neural substrates as faces, since they are being processed in a similar manner. This leaves us in part with a chicken-and-egg question—which comes first? Is the basic specialization of the fusiform face area, so elegantly isolated by recent neuroimaging studies, really for configural processing but masquerading as a "face" area because we have more experience with faces than other objects? Or is this region specialized for processing faces, and as other objects become processed configurally as a result of experience, they then utilize that portion of the brain best suited for such processing, the fusiform face area?

For a number of reasons, the latter interpretation is likely to be correct. First, evidence from brain-damaged individuals suggests that the neural processing of faces is special to the degree that the neural mechanism allowing us to differentiate among individual faces has been found to be independent from the ability to distinguish among individuals of other classes of mono-oriented objects, such as cars or sheep. Second, a recent case study suggests that the right-hemisphere specialization of this region for processing of faces is at least partially innate. A 16-year-old boy who sustained brain damage in occipital and occipital-temporal regions at one day of age, has always been and remains prosopagnosic—profoundly impaired at recognizing faces but not other objects (Farah, Rabinowitz, Quinn, & Liu, 2000). These findings suggest that this region of the brain is initially the fusiform *face* area, but that does not preclude it from being used *flexibly* with expertise.

Implicit Recognition of Faces

One intriguing aspect of face processing that has been revealed by studying individuals with prosopagnosia is that in some cases they can recognize faces even though they do not have conscious access to that information! Such evidence stands in contrast to the classic conception of agnosia as a disruption in the ability to link perceptual patterns to information in memory. Covert processing of faces has been demonstrated in two major ways: through measurements of electrodermal skin conductance and through behavioral priming studies.

Although individuals with prosopagnosia cannot verbally distinguish between familiar and unfamiliar faces at more than a chance level, electrodermal skin conductance is greater to previously known faces than to unknown faces (Tranel & Damasio, 1988).

The electrodermal skin conductance response (which is basically a lowering in the impedance to electrical current as a result of sweat and is the same method used in a lie-detection test) is related to activity of the autonomic nervous system, although its exact source is unknown. As a reminder, the autonomic nervous system is the part of the nervous system responsible for control of smooth muscles (such as those that cause goose bumps and the hair on your arms to stand up), the heart, and glands (including sweat glands).

Other evidence for covert recognition of faces in patients with prosopagnosia is the existence of interference effects that would not occur if the individual truly lacked access to information about facial identity. In one study, a patient was taught (to the limited degree possible) face-name pairs for a set of faces. Some of the faces in the set were faces he had previously known but now could not identify and claimed not to know. However, he had more difficulty learning to associate these faces with incorrect names than with correct names. Thus, at some level, information about the face had to be accessed; otherwise, no interference would have occurred when he was learning a new name for an already-known face (Bruyer et al., 1983).

In another study, a patient had to read a person's name or after reading the name had to classify the person by occupation (e.g., a musician or a politician). A prior study with neurologically intact individuals had demonstrated that such tasks take longer if the name is situated next to the face of someone in a different occupation than if it is situated next to the face of the correct person or someone in the same occupation. If the patient is not retrieving any information about faces, the face should have no effect on how quickly the name is read or how quickly the person's occupation is classified. The patient demonstrated covert recognition of the faces because, like neurologically intact adults, he took longer to read an individual's name when it was situated next to the face of someone in a different occupation (De Haan, Young, & Newcombe, 1987). This interference effect occurred even though the individual with prosopagnosia did not recognize the faces, being able neither to name them nor to sort them according to occupation. Examples similar to the type of stimuli used in this study are shown in Figure 6.17.

The results of all these studies suggest that a subset of patients with prosopagnosia retain some information about faces in memory, although it is not available in a way that allows explicit naming or categorizing of faces. These cases of prosopagnosia do not fit well with a model that presumes a total disconnection in the linkage between a face's perceptual features and its associated biographical information in memory. Rather, the amount of visual information that can be encoded from a face by these individuals may be scant, or the threshold for recognizing a face may be so increased that gaining access to information is impossible under ordinary conditions but can nonetheless influence performance under other very particular conditions. Computational modeling provides support for such an idea. A connectionist network trained to identify faces was then "lesioned" by the reduction in the number of hidden units available. This model could not overtly recognize faces but could do so covertly (Farah, O'Reilly, & Vecera, 1993). We revisit the issue of implicit memory in more detail in the chapter on memory.

Category-Specific Deficits in Object Recognition

So far we have discussed agnosia as a deficit in which the person loses the ability to recognize or identify information within a specific modality. However, in other cases a person has trouble identifying a certain category of objects even though the ability to recognize other categories of items in that same modality is undisturbed. This disorder is known as a **category-specific deficit.** An example would be difficulty identifying fruits and vegetables but not in identifying human-made objects (Warrington & Shallice, 1984). These deficits are perplexing because they are difficult to understand within the framework in which we previously considered agnosias.

When discussing agnosias, we emphasized that they do not arise from a fundamental disruption in basic sensory processing. Rather, apperceptive agnosia has been conceptualized as an inability to use basic sensory attributes to form a percept.

FIGURE 6.17 Examples of stimuli used to demonstrate covert recognition in a patient with prosopagnosia. In studies such as these the patient was asked to read the name inside the bubble. Then three types of trials were given: in some the name of the individual (such as Dianne Feinstein, an American politician) was paired with (top) her own face, (middle) in others with the face of another American politician (in this case, Patricia Schroeder), and (bottom) in still others with the face of a nonpolitician (in this case, Barbara Walters). Although the individual with prosopagnosia could not recognize any of the faces, she was still slower to read the name when it was paired with an individual from a different profession, than when it was paired with either the individual or someone in her profession.

Associative agnosia has been conceptualized as a difficulty in linking meaning to a particular visual pattern (e.g., the visual form of a chair), which itself can be categorized perceptually (e.g., matched to an identical chair). How then are we to understand these category-specific deficits? Clearly, neither of these problems arises here. First, the ability to form percepts must be intact, because objects outside specific categories can be recognized. For example, although apples and oranges cannot be recognized, cars and trains can, which indicates that an overall ability to form a visual percept is intact. Second, in limited cases, the percept can be linked to meaning, as evidenced by the fact that items in the nonaffected category can be recognized.

Most data suggest that such deficits are not agnosic deficits. Rather, they arise either from difficulties within the semantic memory system (i.e., the system for meaning) or from difficulty in being able to name certain items, which is known as *selective anomia.* For example, Warrington and Shallice (1984) found patients who could neither recognize a particular class of objects when they were presented visually, nor provide an adequate definition of those items when told the names of the objects (remember that individuals with agnosia *can* provide definitions for items they can't identify). Such findings suggest that these individuals have lost access to memory for the affected class of items. In other cases, individuals cannot name certain categories of items, such as fruits and vegetables, but their deficit is limited to naming and therefore appears to be a problem in word retrieval rather than in semantic memory (e.g., J. Hart, Berndt, & Caramazza, 1985).

How could such category-specific deficits in memory arise? One possible explanation is that gaining access to information in memory about certain items, such as fruits and vegetables, is more difficult than doing so for other items, such as human-made objects. However, this possibility is unlikely since other patients exhibit the converse syndrome—they have more difficulty recognizing human-made objects than fruits and vegetables (Warrington & McCarthy, 1987). If the problem were merely one of difficulty in gaining access to certain portions of memory, we would not expect to find the categories that are the most difficult for some individuals to be the easiest for others.

Another argument against the idea that gaining access to certain categories of items is more difficult is the finding that access may be hampered only for specific attributes of the affected category. In one case report, researchers described a patient who could retrieve nonvisual aspects of information about living things (e.g., "Are roses given on Valentine's day?") and nonliving things (e.g., "Was the wheelbarrow invented before 1920?") equally well but had difficulty gaining access to information about the visual form of living things (e.g., "Are the hind legs of a kangaroo larger than the front legs?") compared to nonliving things (e.g., "Is a canoe widest in the center?"). If gaining access to information from memory about living things were truly harder than for nonliving things, the same pattern would be expected to hold regardless of the type of information that was being retrieved from memory (i.e., the type of question asked) (Farah, Hammond, Mehta, & Ratcliff, 1989).

An alternative explanation is that memory is organized so that the "living things" section is distinct from the "nonliving things" section (Caramazza & Shelton, 1998). In this case, the argument would be that in category-specific deficits, one section of memory can be accessed and retrieved whereas another cannot. The problem with this account is that some individuals can *generally* distinguish one semantic category from another (e.g., living vs. nonliving items) but exhibit important exceptions to the rule. For example, one patient can't recognize fish, flowers, or fruit, all of which are living. Yet he recognizes body parts perfectly well, which are also living. Likewise, although nonliving items such as clothing, kitchen utensils, and vehicles can be identified, musical instruments cannot. Such findings cast doubt on the idea that the deficit in these patients is restricted to a specific topical area (e.g., living items, nonliving items) (Warrington & Shallice, 1984).

A more likely explanation for the deficits is that when a person is accessing memory, information from different modalities may have a differential weight or influence (see Farah & McClelland, 1991, for a computational model that mimics the patterns seen in brain-damaged individuals). For example, when recognizing human-made objects, we generally differentiate them according to function. Chalk, crayons, and pencils are all used for drawing and writing, but they are distinguished from one another by the surfaces on which they are used (blackboard, construction paper, and writing paper, respectively). Nothing inherent in the sensory attributes of the items might point to this distinction in function. However, this is not the case for living things. The best way to distinguish a leopard from a lioness and a tiger is by sensory attributes in the visual modality (the leopard has spots, the lioness is all one tawny color, and the tiger has stripes). According to this explanation, a more severe deficit might arise in recognizing animals than in identifying writing utensils because the information in memory relies more heavily on the visual attributes of the item (see Warrington & Shallice, 1984, for the original articulation of this idea).

Yet even this explanation is lacking. We still need to be able to explain why some patients have trouble recognizing fruits and vegetables but can recognize other items such as flowers, all of which are probably differentiated on the basis of visual attributes, and why other patients can recognize certain objects such as keys and pens but not airplanes and helicopters, even though they all are probably differentiated on the basis of function. One possible explanation is that particular channels of information within a sensory modality may be more affected by a brain lesion than other channels are. In our discussion of visual processing, we noted that different visual attributes, such as color, shape, motion and location, are processed in different regions of the brain (see page 186). Thus, the nature of brain damage may be such as to affect the processing of certain visual attributes more than others. Depending on the area damaged, identification of certain items is more likely to be affected than that of others.

Consider the case of round fruits such as oranges, peaches, and apples. For these items, color is the visual attribute that most helps us to differentiate among them. In contrast, differentiating among flowers is much less likely to rely on color. For example, the various colors of violets can overlap with those of irises and hyacinths. The distinguishing feature among these flowers is their shape. Thus, depending on where the damage is, one patient may have a greater disruption in gaining access to information about one channel (e.g., color) than another (e.g., shape), which is a possible explanation for the seemingly strange dissociations observed in patients with category-specific deficits (Warrington & McCarthy, 1987).

Recent neuroimaging studies of object recognition are consistent with the idea that the channel of information (e.g., visual, motoric) by which objects are linked to semantic memory varies across different classes of objects. In one such study (Perani et al., 1995), individuals viewed two objects and had to decide if they depicted two examples of the same object (e.g., "yes" to two dogs, "no" to a dog and a cat). Compared to the baseline of a shape-discrimination task, the sight of living objects activated areas of the occipital and inferior temporal regions of both hemispheres, whereas the sight of nonliving things activated more anterior areas, including the lateral inferior frontal cortex. Similar results were found when individuals had to name living items or nonliving items compared to viewing meaningless objects (Martin et al., 1996). This pattern suggests that whereas information concerned with perceptual properties was important for recognizing living things (as indicated by activation of occipital and inferior temporal regions), information on the uses of nonliving things was most important for recognizing them (as indicated by activation in motor control regions) (see Humphreys, 1996, for a longer discussion).

One other possibility is that memory could be organized into modality-specific meaning systems (e.g., Warrington & McCarthy, 1994). This suggestion has been based in part on a case report of a patient who had a category-specific disorder that appeared to be limited to a single modality, the visual one. The deficit was shown to be category specific because he could name line drawings depicting animals and flowers but was poor at doing so for other objects. The difficulty was shown to be modality specific because, when asked, he could easily and quickly define items whose pictures he could not recognize. Furthermore, when given the name of an object, he could pantomime its use flawlessly (an indication that he did not have difficulties in word retrieval and that he had intact memory for objects), but he was poor at pantomime when shown the object visually. Thus, he appeared to have a specific difficulty in retrieving information about objects through the visual modality. This individual's brain damage was located in the right parietal lobe and the inferior left occipitotemporal region; therefore, at least some disruption in the ventral processing stream was likely.

At present, no one knows exactly which of these theories provides the best explanation of the available data. These category-specific deficits do, however, suggest that sensory information from different modalities may allow for differential access to a memory system and/or that memory itself is organized in some way with regard to sensory/functional attributes.

Agnosias in Other Modalities

Much of our attention in this chapter has been directed to agnosias in the visual modality. However, we must remember that agnosias can occur in other modalities as well. In this section we discuss the characteristics of auditory and somatosensory (tactile) agnosias.

Auditory Agnosia

Auditory agnosia, like other agnosias, is characterized by unimpaired processing of basic sensory information but an inability to link that sensory information to meaning, despite the fact that memory, as assessed through other modalities, appears to be normal. The integrity of basic auditory processing is generally assessed through **pure-tone audiometry.** In this method, an individual is tested on the ability to perceive a tone that consists of only one frequency (e.g., 1000 Hz). In the test, a large number of trials are given so that the ability to process these pure tones is assessed over the range of frequencies that can be detected by humans (e.g., ~125–8000 Hz). Individuals with auditory agnosia do well on tests of pure-tone audiometry. They can perceive when a sound occurs and at thresholds generally equivalent to that of the average person without agnosia.

In real life, though, sounds are typically made up of a complex pattern of tones that are overlaid much the way that chords in music are the result of combining different single notes. When persons with auditory agnosia hear a complex sound, they cannot classify it. Auditory agnosia usually manifests in one of three ways. In **verbal auditory agnosia** (also known as **pure-word deafness**), words cannot be understood, but the ability to attach meaning to nonverbal sounds is intact. In **nonverbal auditory agnosia,** the ability to attach meaning to words is intact, but the ability to do so for nonverbal sounds is disrupted. In **mixed auditory agnosia,** the ability to attach meaning to both verbal and nonverbal sounds is affected.

In verbal auditory agnosia, or pure-word deafness, the individual can read, write, and speak normally, an indication that this condition is not a disorder of linguistic processing. However, patients with this type of auditory agnosia complain that although they know that a noise has occurred, speech sounds like "an undifferentiated continuous humming noise without any rhythm" or "like foreigners speaking in the distance." Likewise, in nonverbal auditory agnosia, which is rarer than verbal auditory agnosia, the individual knows that a sound has occurred but cannot categorize it, either as for example, a car horn, a dog bark, or a lawn mower. This difficulty can be quite a problem in real life. For example, if a car's driver is honking a horn as a warning for people to move out of the way, an individual with auditory agnosia would hear a noise but might not hurry across the street because the sound was "unintelligible, sort of like how I remember crickets chirping or static on a telephone line." In contrast, persons with mixed auditory agnosia can recognize neither verbal nor nonverbal sounds, although they can determine whether two sounds are identical or different and whether one sound is louder than the other. That is, their ability to *hear* the sounds is intact, and they are not deaf.

Just as we discussed for visual agnosias, the degree to which higher-order perceptual problems can account for such disturbances is an issue debated by researchers and clinicians. Some authorities claim that one form of pure-word deafness involves the compromise of some important basic aspects of auditory perception (e.g., Auerbach et al., 1982). This type of verbal auditory agnosia is associated with bilateral damage to the temporal lobe, and because such damage interferes with the ability to process basic acoustic parameters, it has been suggested that higher-order auditory processing cannot occur in these cases (e.g., M. L. Albert & Bear, 1974). For example, compared with neurologically intact individuals, patients with pure-word deafness require a much longer separation in time between two tones to perceive them as distinct.

As we learn in more detail in the chapter on language, fine temporal discrimination is an important aspect of language processing. Similar difficulties have been reported for patients with mixed auditory agnosia. For example, one particular patient required 250 ms to perceive sounds as separate, whereas neurologically intact subjects could do so with only a 15-ms interval. Indicating that the problem was limited to the auditory modality, the length of time required to perceive two flashes of light as separate was normal (H. A. Buchtel & Stewart, 1989).

In addition to difficulties in sequencing sounds, individuals with auditory agnosia may have difficulty determining the duration of tones. In contrast, the ability to judge the pitch (frequency) of a sound and its intensity is much less affected (Mendez & Geehan, 1988). Thus, at least some persons with auditory agnosia appear to have what might be considered an apperceptive disorder because they cannot integrate component sounds into a whole, much the way patients with visual agnosia can't integrate local features of light and dark into a meaningful gestalt.

Why processing of the same types of acoustic parameters should be affected in individuals with pure-word deafness and nonverbal auditory agnosia is unclear. In part, the distinction between verbal auditory agnosia and nonverbal auditory agnosia may arise according to the degree to which the perception of specific acoustic parameters is impaired. For example, speech and nonverbal sounds tend to occur at different frequencies, and speech is also noteworthy for the transient nature of some of its acoustic cues. Our understanding of the conditions that produce pure-word deafness as compared with those that produce nonverbal auditory agnosia is likely to improve when the specific acoustic parameters compromised in each of these disorders become better characterized.

A disruption in the processing of different acoustic parameters may also account for two proposed varieties of pure word deafness (e.g., Auerbach et al., 1982), one that involves a disruption in relatively basic auditory processing and another that involves a more specific disruption of processing of the constituent sounds of language (this type of pure-word deafness is associated with left temporal lobe lesions). The first type of word deafness (as well as mixed auditory agnosia) results from difficulty in processing cues that are related to the location in the vocal tract where a sound is produced (for example, the "p" in "pot" is produced at the lips, whereas the "g" in "got" is produced toward the back of the mouth) (e.g., Miceli, 1982). These sounds may be difficult to differentiate because they rely on quick temporal transitions in the frequency of the acoustic signal (S. E. Blumstein, Tarter, Nigro, & Statlender, 1984). In contrast, in the other form of word deafness, cues that relate to the temporal offset between particular sounds are more likely to be compromised (e.g., voicing contrasts such as the difference between "b" and "p," which relate to when the vocal tract begins to vibrate relative to the burst of air produced at the lips). (We discuss some of these contrasts in more detail in the chapter on language; see page 295.)

In sum, the evidence suggests that auditory agnosia disrupts the ability to coalesce sounds into a percept that allows meaning to be obtained. The particular acoustic parameters that cannot be integrated may vary among verbal, nonverbal, and mixed auditory agnosias, but in all cases, the processing of temporal parameters seems to be more affected than the processing of the parameters involved in pitch or intensity.

Somatosensory Agnosia

Somatosensory agnosia, or **tactile agnosia** (sometimes referred to as *astereognosia*), is a condition in which a person is unable to recognize an item by touch but can recognize the object in other modalities. As with other agnosias, two types have been proposed, one in which the affected person has an inability to use tactile information to create a percept, and another in which the percept is more or less intact but cannot be linked to meaning. This latter agnosia is sometimes called **tactile asymbolia** because the tactile information cannot be linked to its symbolic meaning (e.g., a small metal object that is big at the top and thin at the bottom with a jagged edge and is about 1 in., or 2.5 cm, long cannot be linked to the concept of a key). Although these two distinct types of tactile agnosia have been proposed, researchers disagree as to whether tactile asymbolia actually exists.

As with the other agnosias we discussed, the degree to which sensory impairments preclude object recognition is also a debated issue for the tactile modality. Some researchers have argued that deficits in recognizing objects in the tactile modality occur only in the presence of sensory deficits, such as difficulty in two-point discrimination and pressure sensitivity. For example, in one study, most individuals (83%) who exhibited unilateral difficulties in recognizing objects through the tactile modality had severe sensory loss for the affected hand as well as damage to the hand area of the contralateral postcentral gyrus (Corkin, Milner, & Rasmussen, 1970). Although these sensory deficits often lead to poor object recognition, they do not always do so because many different cues can be used to recognize an object tactilely, such as its shape, texture, weight, temperature, and so forth. If the ability to process some of these cues remains intact, some object recognition may still be possible.

At least some authors (e.g., Semmes, 1965) have argued the opposite, namely that tactile recognition of objects can be disrupted even when no sensory deficit exists. These researchers found that individuals were impaired in the ability to identify an item's shape, although they could tell whether the item was smooth or scratchy, hard or soft, large or small. Although their intact perceptual-processing abilities would suggest an agnosia, the deficit did not appear to be modality specific because these individuals also had trouble identifying the same items visually. Hence, these individuals appeared to have difficulties in visuospatial processing that exhibited itself in multiple modalities.

A detailed case study (Reed & Caselli, 1994; Reed, Caselli, & Farah, 1996) of a woman with unilateral tactile agnosia provides evidence that tactile agnosia can occur when basic and intermediate sensory functions are intact; her difficulties could clearly be attributed to forming a percept of the item or to linking that percept to information in memory. Basic sensory functions for the affected hand were intact. She exhibited normal thresholds for detecting touch, vibration, and proprioception, and she had normal two-point discrimination (i.e., the distance required so that two touches are perceived as occurring in separate locations rather than the same location was normal). She also performed well with the affected hand on tests of more elaborate somatosensory functions, such as distinguishing objects of different weights and different textures, and identifying simple shapes. Moreover, her difficulties did not appear to be caused by an impaired ability to acquire sensory data, because the types of motor behaviors she exhibited when exploring objects was similar for both the affected hand and the unaffected hand. Nonetheless, she was deficient with the affected hand in identifying complex objects that she could identify visually and tactilely with the unaffected hand. For example, she misidentified a pine cone as a brush, a ribbon as a rubber band, and a snail shell as a bottle cap. It was shown that such problems were not due to a higher-order spatial deficit (as spatial processing in other modalities was fine), and that her deficits were limited to identifying "what" an item was, not where it was. Furthermore, the more complex the shape, the greater was her difficulty in identifying the item. This individual had a lesion in the left inferior parietal area (Brodmann's area 40 and, to a lesser degree, Brodmann's area 39—the ventromedial area of the somatosensory association cortices), as has been observed in other case reports of tactile agnosia (e.g., Caselli, 1993) (see Figure 6.18).

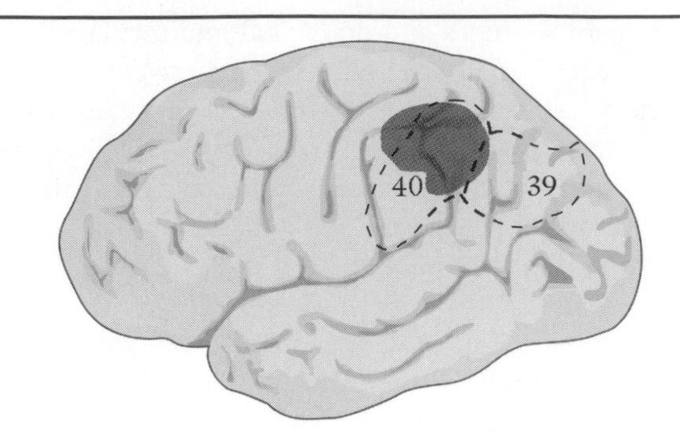

FIGURE 6.18 Location of the lesion that typically causes tactile agnosia. Damage to the left inferior parietal area (Brodmann's area 40 and, to a lesser degree, Brodmann's area 39 typically causes tactile agnosia.

The evidence reviewed in this section illustrates that agnosia can occur in modalities besides the visual one. The distinctions between apperceptive and associative disorders do not seem to be as clear-cut in the auditory and tactile modalities as observed in the visual modality.

SUMMARY

The "What" Ventral Visual System

- This brain system, which plays a major role in the ability to recognize objects, courses ventrally from the occipital regions toward the anterior pole of the temporal lobe.
- Lesions of the anterior temporal region create difficulties in recognizing objects.
- Single-cell recordings in monkeys indicate cells located more anterior in the ventral visual processing stream fire to specific forms, have a

larger receptive field, and are sensitive to color, attributes that are all helpful to recognizing specific objects.
- In humans, different portions of the ventral visual processing stream are specialized for processing different types or classes of objects.
- The lateral occipital cortex (LOC) is involved in processing complex shapes; the fusiform face area exhibits a greater sensitivity to faces than to other objects; the parahippocampal place area processes information related to places in the local environment; and the extrastriate body area responds preferentially to human bodies and body parts.
- Hemispheric differences in object processing also occur as the left hemisphere is more adept at processing the local elements or parts of an object, while the right hemisphere is more adept at processing the global form or overall shape of an object.

Computational Models of Object Recognition
- One class of computational models assumes that items are recognized from basic component parts to yield an object-centered representation, which provides a model of an object regardless of the orientation and conditions under which it is viewed.
- Other computational models assume that an object is recognized by interpolating across viewer-centered representations (which change depending on the vantage point of the viewer relative to the object) to yield a match to a stored template of the object in memory.

Visual Agnosia
- Apperceptive agnosia is an inability to process basic features of visual information that precludes perception of even the simplest forms (e.g., an "X").
- In associative agnosia the basic perceptual properties of visual information can be processed but not to a high enough degree to allow for object recognition.
- Whereas apperceptive agnosia is associated with diffuse bilateral damage near and extending into occipital regions, associative agnosia is associated with bilateral damage near the occipitotemporal border.

Face-Recognition Difficulties as a Special Type of Visual Agnosia
- The ability to recognize faces seems to have a long evolutionary history because specialized cells for recognizing faces are found in the temporal lobes of other species, such as sheep and monkeys.
- Evidence from brain-damaged individuals, neuroimaging and electrophysiology indicate that faces are processed differently than other classes of objects.
- Determining the physical characteristics of a face, linking that physical description to information about the person's identity, and recognizing facial features that can help convey social or emotional information each occur in distinct regions of the temporal lobe, mainly in the right hemisphere.
- Regions of the right hemisphere that are specialized for recognizing faces can be recruited to help recognize other classes of objects as one gains expertise with that class of objects.
- In some cases of prosopagnosia, which is the inability to recognize faces but not other objects, some aspects of the faces can be recognized implicitly, even though the person can't identify or otherwise classify the face.

Category-Specific Deficits in Object Recognition
- Some disorders, which are neither modality specific nor limited to the naming of items, affect the ability to recognize items within certain categories (e.g., fruits and vegetables), but not other categories (e.g., items manufactured by humans).
- The most plausible explanation for these disorders is that we gain access to memory for different classes of items through different means. For example, damage to visual areas will impair recognizing items differentiated on the basis of visual forms, such as flowers and plants, whereas damage to motor areas will affect objects that we differentiate on the basis of how they are manipulated and used, such as tools.

Agnosias in Other Modalities

- Auditory agnosia precludes the ability to recognize verbal sounds, nonverbal sounds or both.
- Somatosensory, or tactile, agnosia, impairs the ability to recognize items by touch.

KEY TERMS

$2\frac{1}{2}$-D representation 192
3-D representation 192
apperceptive agnosia 195
associative agnosia 195
auditory agnosia 215
binocular disparity 192
category-specific deficit 212
figure-ground separation 188
global precedence 191
global processing 191
grandmother cell theory 202
inversion effect 203
local processing 191
mixed auditory agnosia 216
modality specific 194
nonverbal auditory agnosia 216
object-centered representation 192
orientation invariant 192
perceptual categorization 196
primal sketch 192
prosopagnosia 199
pure-tone audiometry 216
pure-word deafness 216
receptive field 188
somatosensory agnosia 217
tactile agnosia 217
tactile asymbolia 217
ventral visual system 186
verbal auditory agnosia 216
viewer-centered representation 192
visual agnosia 194
volumetric representation 192

Data from Brain Imaging Techniques

COLOR INSERT 3.1 **(See page 80)**

Example of a PET image. This PET scan comes from a study in which radioactive carbon was attached to a drug that can provide a measure of the activity of dopaminergic cells. Low levels of activity are depicted by blue and green whereas higher levels of activity are shown by yellow and red. Notice that even after 80 days of detoxification, there is less activity of dopaminergic neurons in the brain of a methamphetamine abuser than in someone who does not use drugs. One of the strengths of PET is that it allows insights into neurotransmitter function in the brain.

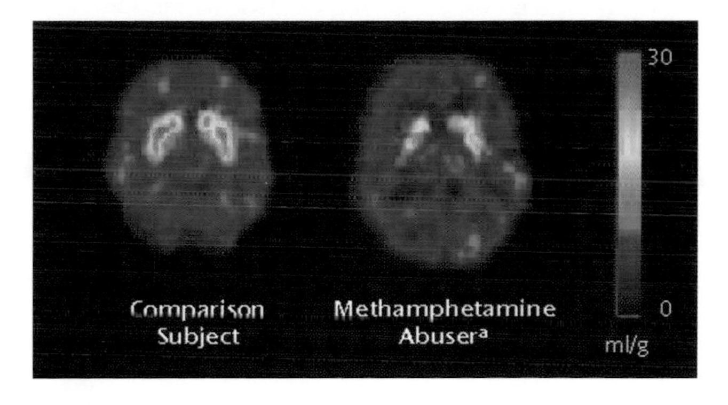

COLOR INSERT 3.2 **(See page 93)**

Example of localization of neuronal activity using MEG. Shown here are the localization of primary somatomotor regions that activate in response to movement of different body parts. Notice that whereas activity of the mouth (shown in lilac) occurs over both hemispheres, activation of regions receiving touch information from the right finger (shown in yellow) occurs only in the left hemisphere, and activation of the regions receiving touch information from the left finger (shown in red) occurs only in the right hemisphere. Notice also that the brain regions responding to stimulation of the nerves that supply somatosensory information (shown here as dots labeled "SEF") correspond well with the responses to somatosensory information derived from movement of the same body part. The tibial nerve conveys information from the legs whereas the median nerve conveys information from the hand.

COLOR INSERT 5.1 **(See page 167)**

Two distinct regions of the anterior cingulate cortex that play different roles in motor control.

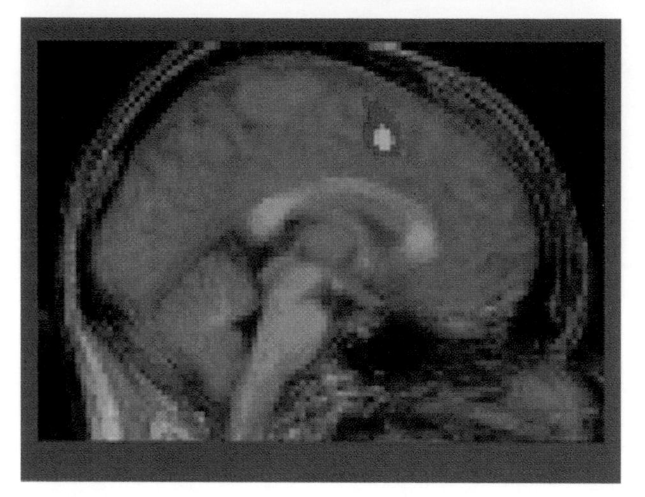

(A) The caudal and dorsal portion of the anterior cingulate is involved in selecting a response.

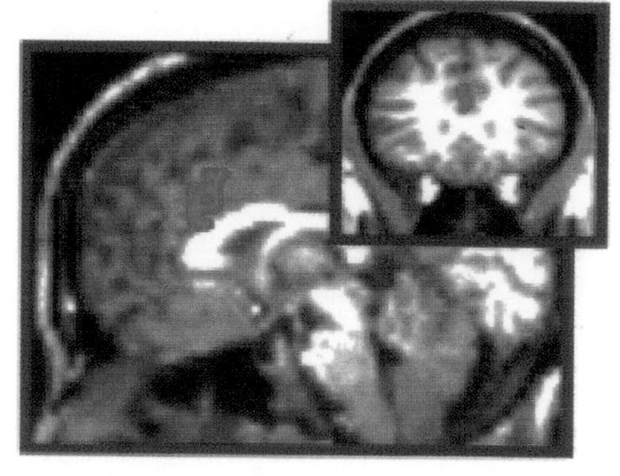

(B) In contrast, the more rostral and ventral area is involved in situations in which errors are likely, such as when there is a high degree of conflict with regard to the appropriate response.

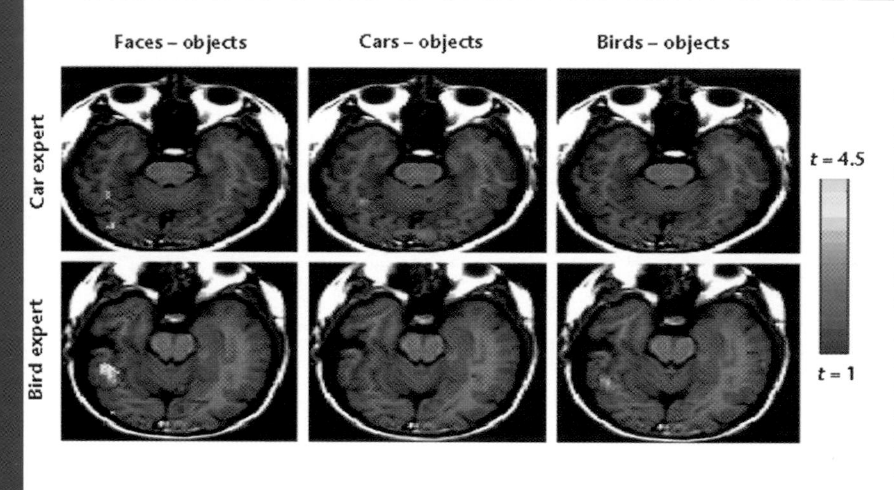

COLOR INSERT 6.1 **(See page 210)**

The sensitivity of the right fusiform face area to expertise in individuating members among a class of objects. Shown here are patterns of activation for faces, cars and birds versus other objects (in columns 1, 2, and 3 respectively), in a car expert (top row) and a bird expert (bottom row). The brain slices here are shown in radiological convention so that the right side of the brain is shown on the left. Notice that in the car expert a similar region is activated for faces and cars, but not birds. In contrast, this region is activated in the bird expert for faces and birds, but not cars. The redder the color, the greater the activation.

COLOR INSERT 7.1 **(See page 231)**

The brain regions involved in perceiving motion. This figure depicts those brain regions that are more activated when dots are moving in a random manner rather than being static. Notice the large amount of activity in area V5, which is considered analogous to area MT in the monkey. SOG = Superior Occiptial Gyrus.

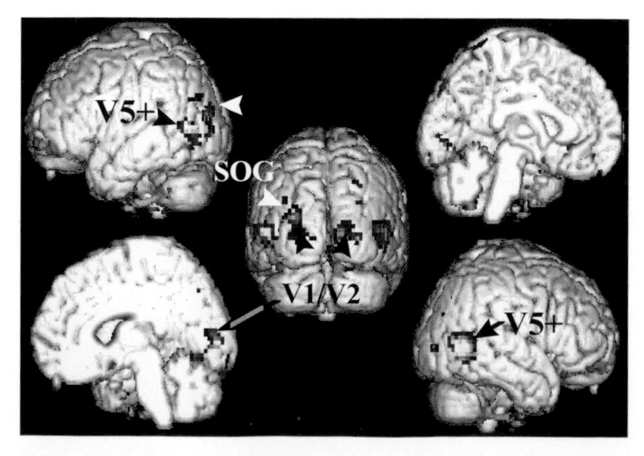

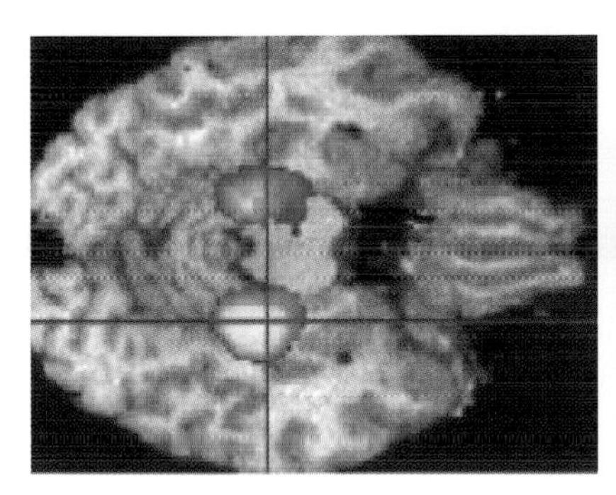

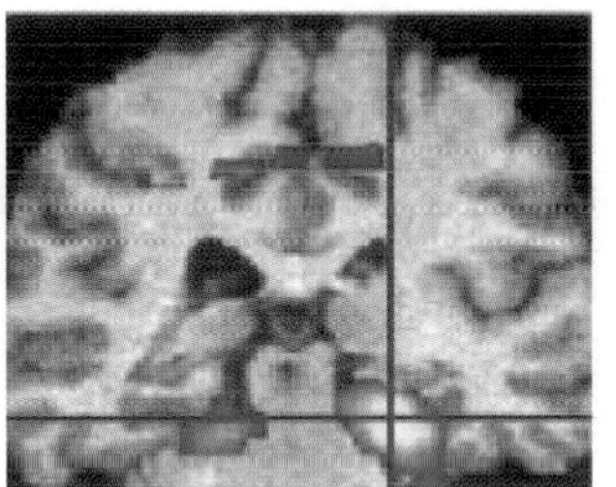

COLOR INSERT 7.2 (See page 243)
Brain regions involved in topographical memory. Shown here are regions that exhibit more activation when someone is viewing film footage of an individual navigating through a town as compared to viewing a scene from a stationary position with objects moving in and out. Notice that there is activation of the hippocampus and parahippocampal regions in the right hemisphere, along with activation of parahippocampal and parietal activation in the left hemisphere. Yellow indicates the most intense activation.

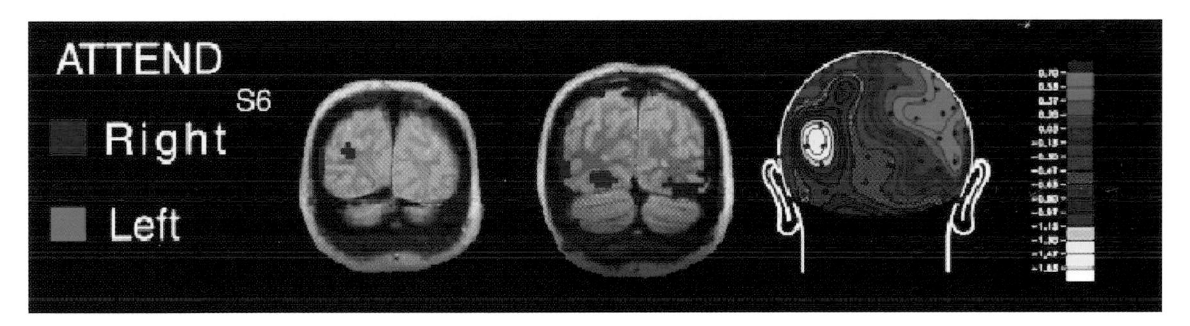

COLOR INSERT 8.1 (See page 264)
Contralateral control of spatial attention as shown by fMRI and ERPs. The two figures on the left show activation in extrastriate cortex as measured by fMRI. Areas shown in red (or yellow) are those activated when the individual attended to the right side of space. Notice that they are restricted to the left hemisphere. In contrast, the areas shown in blue are those activated when the individual attended to the left side of space. Notice that these regions are restricted to the right hemisphere.The drawing to the right shows the P_1 ERP component that occurs 100–140 ms after stimulus onset. Red and yellow indicate increased activity when attention is directed to the right side of space.

COLOR INSERT 8.2 (See page 283)
Overlap between brain regions activated when there is conscious versus unconscious perception of an item. In this study the individual did not consciously perceive items in the left visual field (LVF) under conditions of bilateral stimulation. Shown on the right side of the figure are those brain regions in striate (top row) and extrastriate (bottom row) cortex that exhibited more activity on unilateral LVF trials than RVF trials. On the left side of the figure are those brain regions in striate and extrastriate cortex that exhibited more activity to extinguished stimuli in the LVF as compared with the RVF. Notice that although they were not consciously perceived, the extinguished stimuli evoked activity in similar regions as when they were consciously perceived, although to a smaller degree.

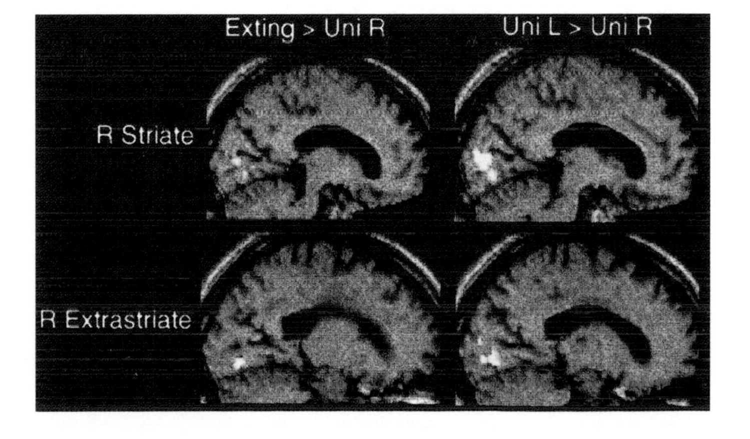

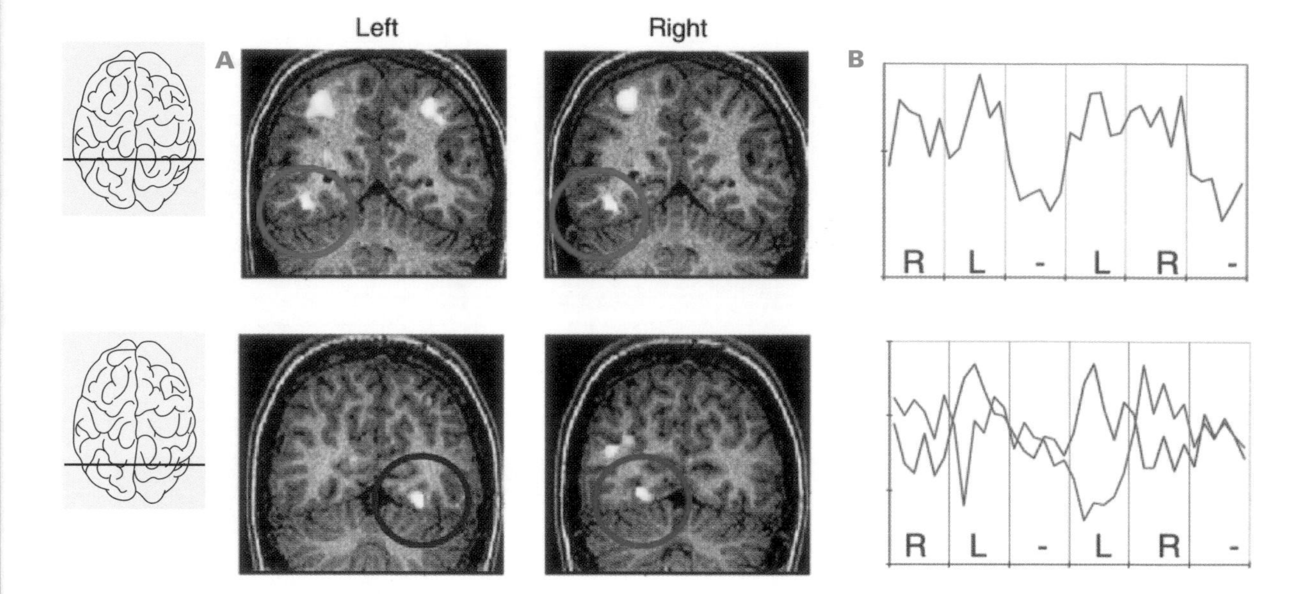

COLOR INSERT 9.1 (See page 308)
One putative location of the visual word-form area. In this study, individuals viewed three different types of blocks of trials: words presented in the RVF (R), in the LVF (L), or no words presented at all (–). (A) Shown here are the fMRI images of the location of activation. In the upper panel, notice that the same region of the left hemisphere is activated regardless of the visual field in which words are presented, which led these researchers to conclude that this region was the visual word-form area. In the lower panel, notice that words presented in the LVF lead to activation of extrastriate regions of the right hemisphere (red circle), whereas words presented in the RVF lead to activation of extrastriate regions of the left hemisphere (blue circle). (B) Shown here is the time course of activation for each of these areas across the blocks. Notice how activity of the left hemisphere region (depicted by the red line) is highest for those blocks in which trials were presented in the RVF, whereas activity of the right hemisphere region (depicted by the blue line) is highest for those blocks in which trials were presented to the LVF.

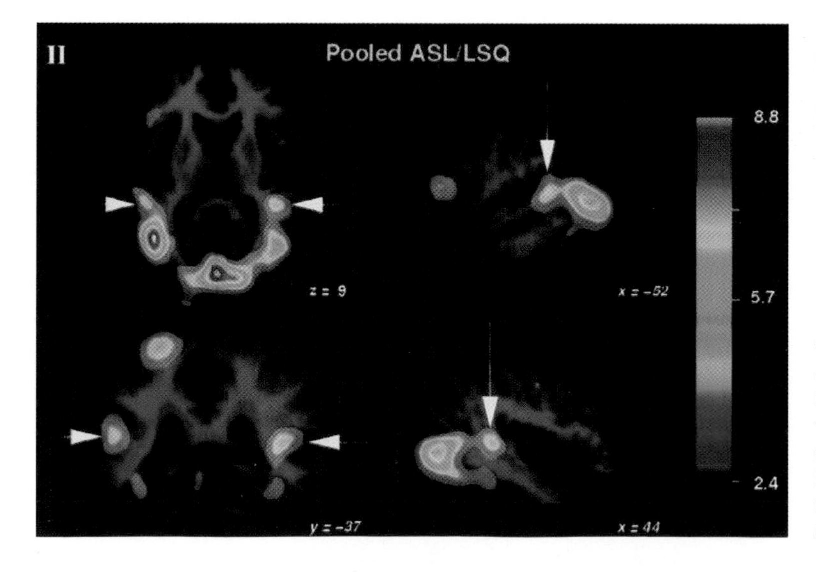

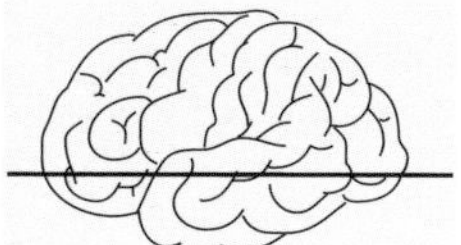

COLOR INSERT 9.2 (See page 313)
Activation of "auditory" areas in deaf individuals. Shown by the arrows is activation in the superior temporal gyrus of speakers of American Sign Language (ASL) or the Sign Language of Quebec (SLQ) while they are reading words or legal nonwords in sign. Red shows the highest area of activity.

COLOR INSERT 9.3 (See page 314)
Early right anterior negativity (mERAN) as recorded using MEG.

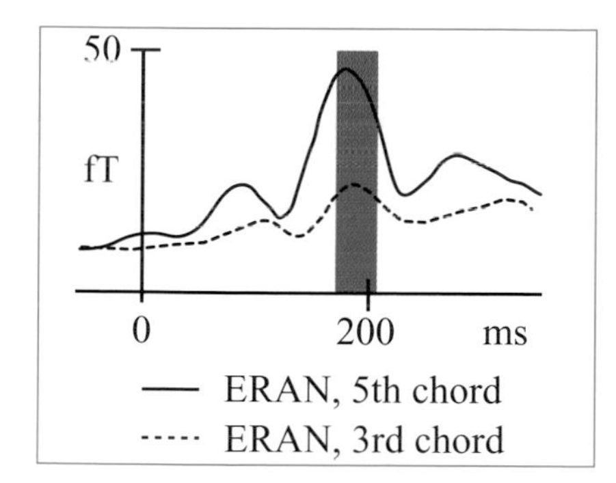

(A) Notice that the negativity is greater to an anomalous chord, the Neapolitan 5th, as compared to a standard chord, the third.

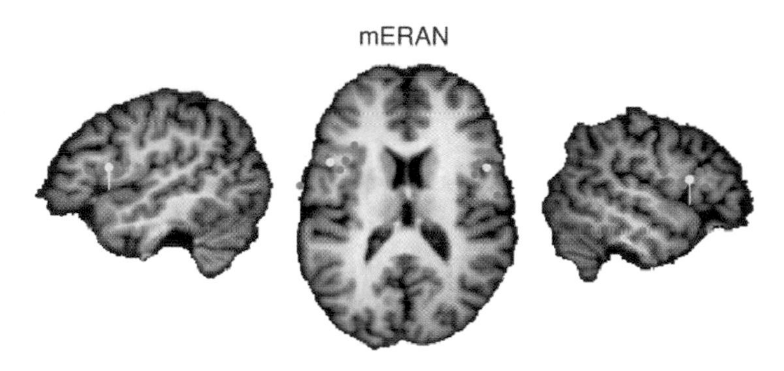

(B) The average source of the ERAN, shown in yellow. Note that it is located in Broca's area. The individual locations for each participant in the study are shown in blue.

COLOR INSERT 9.4 (See page 317)
Brain organization in Broca's and Wernicke's area for native and second language in six bilingual individuals who learned second language later in life. For anterior language regions, each language activates a separate subregion. In contrast, the posterior brain regions activated by each region overlap.

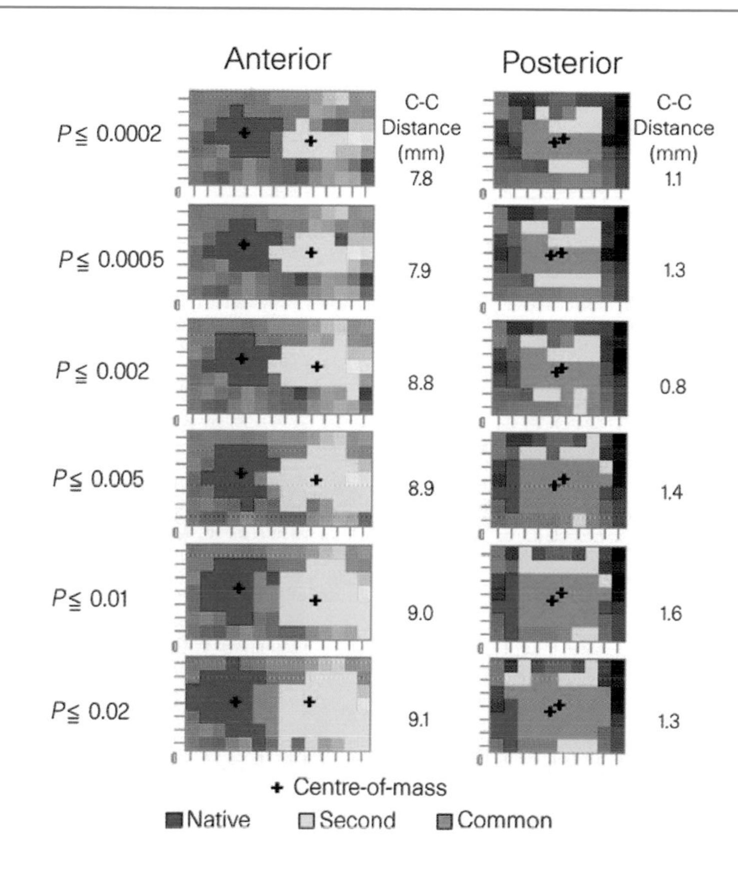

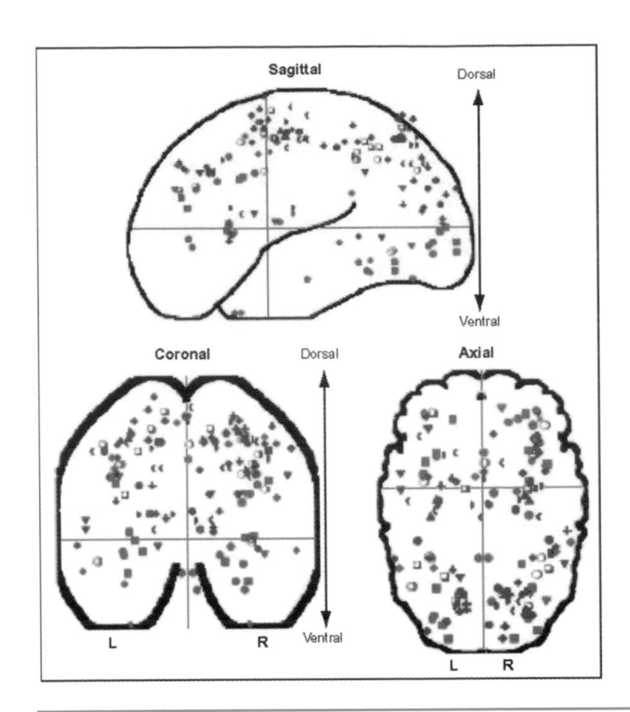

COLOR INSERT 10.1 (See page 346)
Distinctions between regions of cortex involved in working memory for space versus objects. Shown here are the centers of activations from a variety of brain-imaging studies examining working-memory. Areas activated during object working-memory tasks are shown in red, whereas those activated during spatial working-memory tasks are shown in blue. Notice that in prefrontal regions, as in posterior regions, more activation is seen in dorsal regions of cortex for spatial working memory whereas for object working memory more activation is seen in ventral regions. This distinction for prefrontal cortex is best shown in the coronal view.

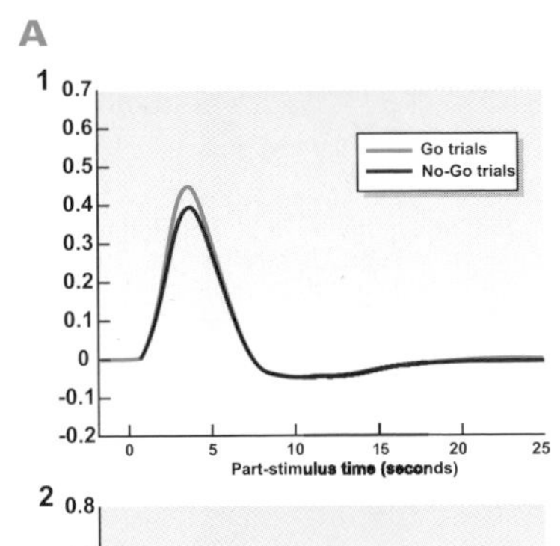

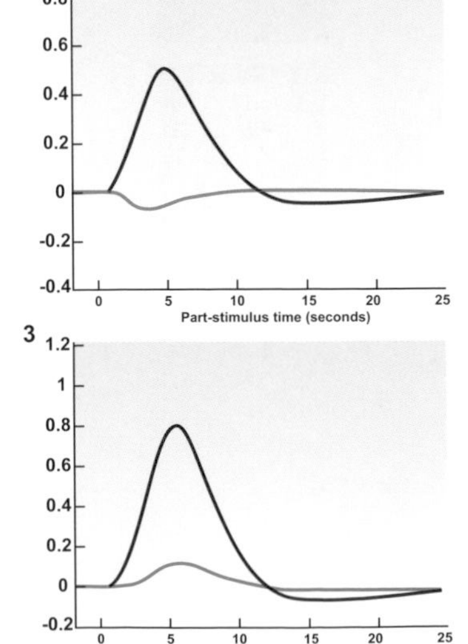

COLOR INSERT 11.1 (See page 371)
The role of different brain regions in response inhibition. (A) Shown here are the hemodynamic responses as assessed by fMRI to Go trials in green and No-Go trials in red for three different brain regions when Go and No-Go trials occur equally often. From top to bottom they are (1) anterior cingulate, (2) left inferior frontal, and (3) right inferior frontal. Notice that the activity in the cingulate is equivalent for Go and No-Go trials, whereas the inferior frontal regions show activity only when a response must be inhibited (i.e., on No-Go trials). (B) Inferior frontal regions involved in response inhibition on No-Go trials as viewed in coronal slices. (C) Right inferior regions active on "No-Go" trials as viewed in a horizontal slice. The activity peaks five seconds after the presentation of the stimulus to which the individual must refrain from responding. Greater activity is indicated by the color red.

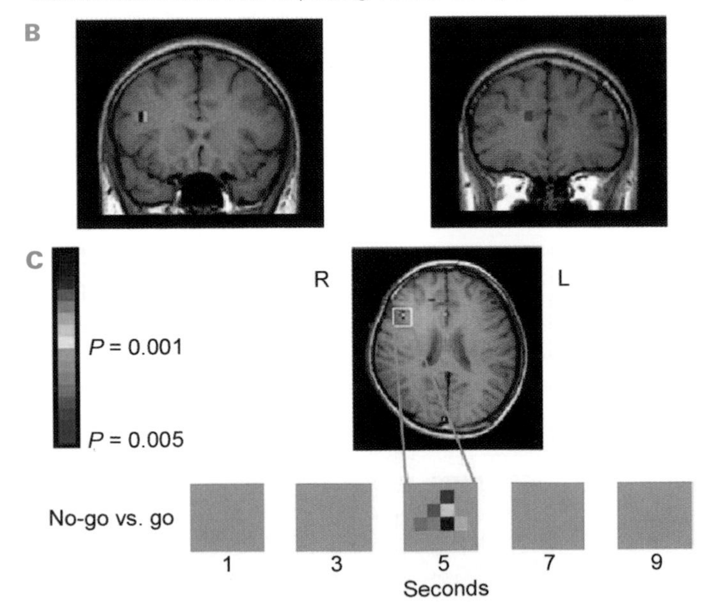

COLOR INSERT 11.2 (See page 376)
Activation of dorsolateral prefrontal cortex when an individual must impose and maintain an attentional set. Shown here are areas that become activated for maintaining an attentional set in the face of distracting information. Regions in blue denote results for a color-word Stroop task in which an individual must identify ink color. These regions are more active when the word conflicts with the ink color (e.g., "blue" in red ink), and hence is more distracting, than when it does not (e.g., "lost" in red ink). Regions in orange are for a spatial-word Stroop task in which an individual must identify the location of a word relative to a box (above, within, below). These regions are more active when the word's meaning conflicts with its location (e.g., the word "above" positioned below the box) than when it does not (e.g, the word "bond"). Purple denotes areas activated in both tasks.

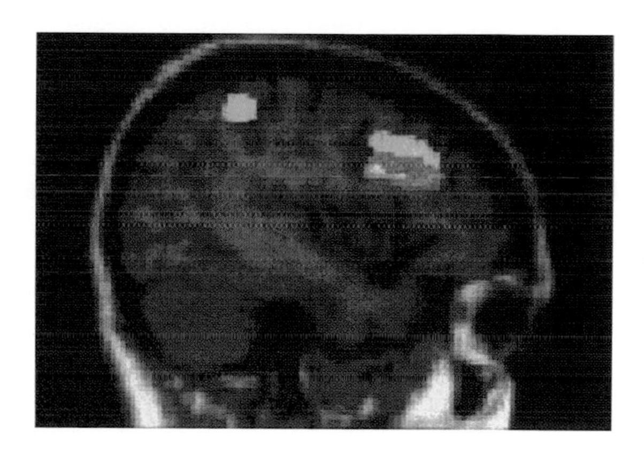

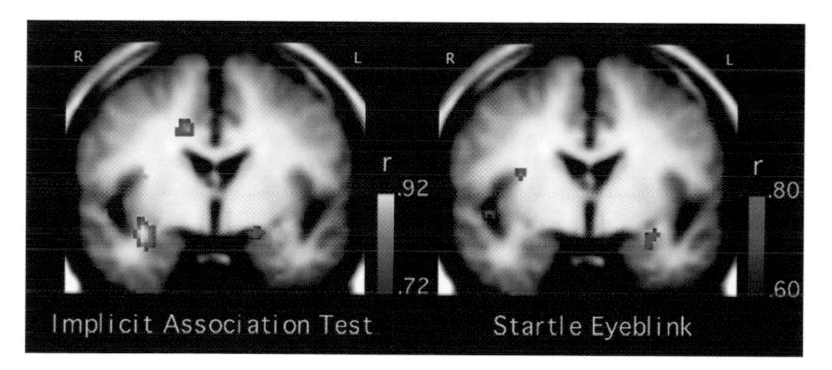

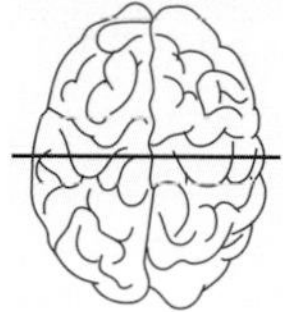

COLOR INSERT 12.1 (See page 401)
Amygdala activation associated with measures of unconscious racial bias on the part of Caucasian American participants. Notice that the more an individual reacted differently to African American and Caucasian American faces, the greater the degree of amygdala activity.

COLOR INSERT 12.2 (See page 403)
The distinct regions of the anterior cingulate involved in emotional as compared with cognitive processing as shown across a large number of studies. (A) Sites of activation (red circles for cognitive tasks and blue squares for emotional tasks). (B) Sites of deactivation (red circles for cognitive tasks and blue squares for emotional tasks). Notice the reciprocal pattern such that areas activated by cognitive tasks are deactivated by emotional tasks, and vice versa.

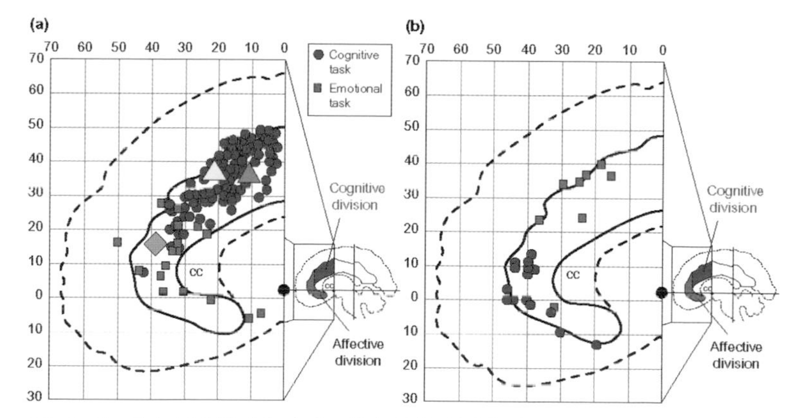

COLOR INSERT 12.3 (See page 411)
Pattern of activation across brain regions for expressionless faces versus emotional ones. The regions in green depict brain regions that exhibit more activity in response to neutral faces than to scrambled faces. The other regions depict more activity in response to faces showing a given emotion than to neutral faces: red represents angry; purple, frightened; yellow, happy; and blue, sad. Notice that whereas some areas of activation in response to emotional faces overlap with those that are activated by the sight of neutral versus scrambled faces (e.g, portions of fusiform cortex), other regions are activated only by the sight of emotional faces (e.g., orbitofrontal regions in response to happy faces).

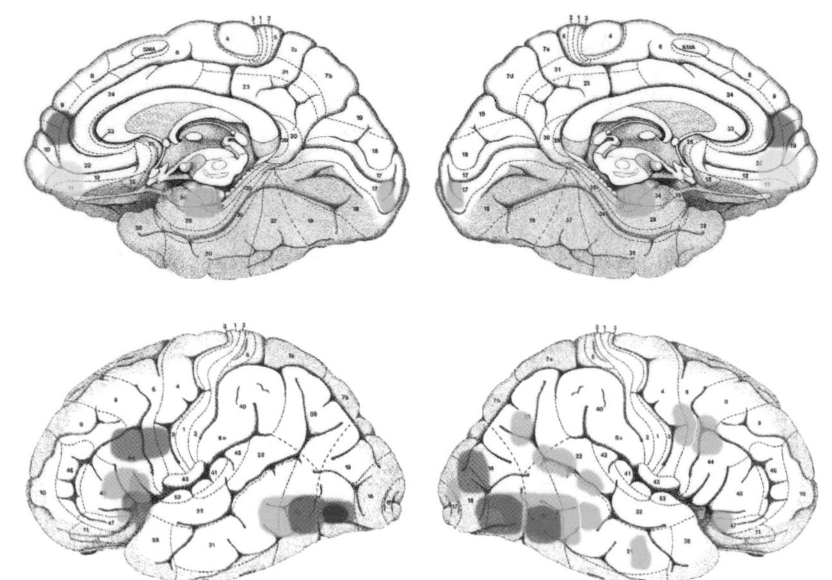

COLOR INSERT 13.1 (See page 473)
Changes in brain activation associated with aging. Notice that across a large variety of tasks brain activation is more bilateral in older adults than in younger adults.

Young Adults **Old Adults** **Young Adults** **Old Adults**

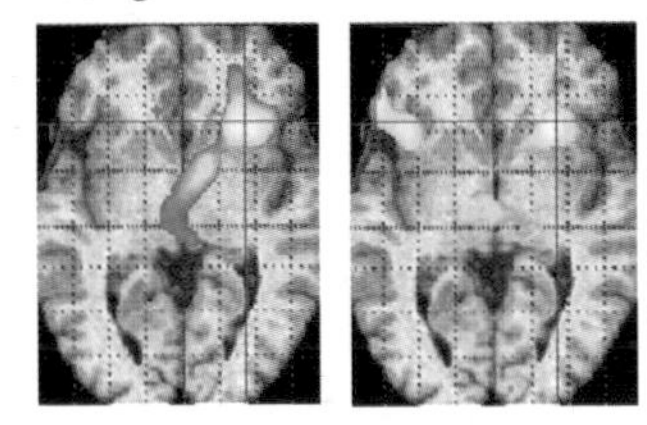

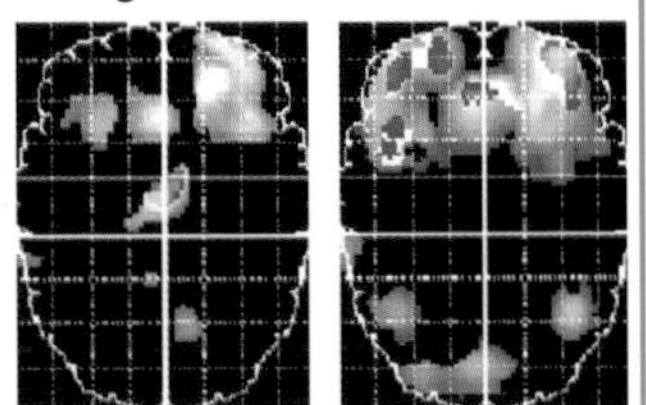

A. Word-Pair Cued-Recall **C. Word Recognition**

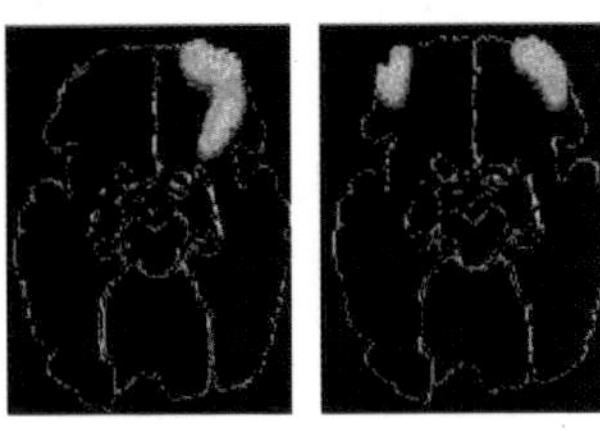

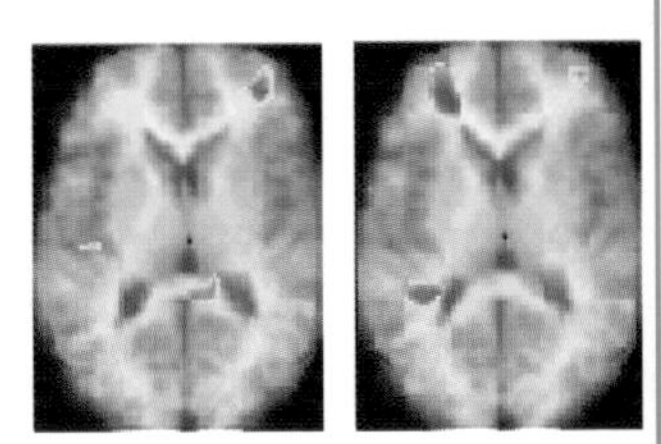

B. Word-Stem Cued-Recall **D. Face Recognition**

COLOR INSERT 14.1 (See page 500)
Dysfunction of basal ganglia in Parkinson's disease. Regions shown here are those that are significantly more activated in neurologically intact individuals than in individuals with Parkinson's disease when such individuals are performing a complex planning task. Red indicates the highest degree of activation.

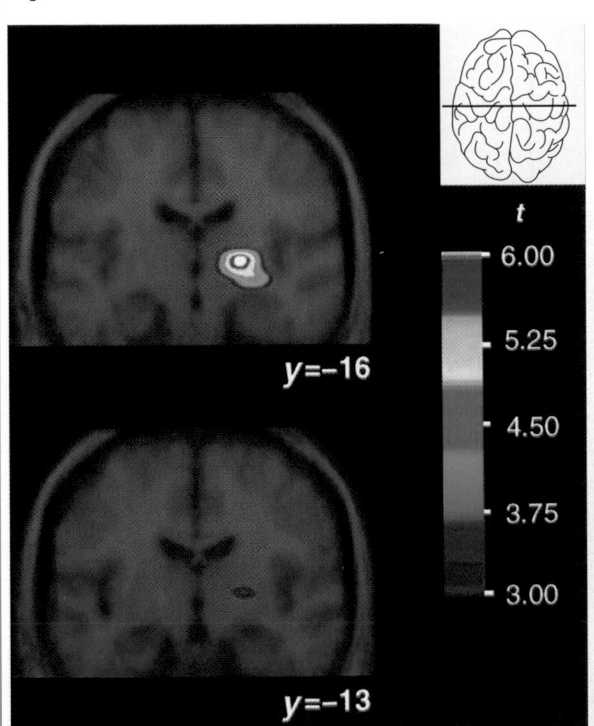

CHAPTER 7

SPATIAL PROCESSING

A fun-loving middle-aged woman, C.J. had spent her entire adult life as an outdoor enthusiast. Then she suffered a mild stroke that damaged a small portion of the posterior section of her right hemisphere. She hated the confinement of the hospital and eagerly awaited her chance to spend some time outdoors again. Because her basic visual-processing abilities were intact (an indication that the lesion had spared primary and secondary visual areas), she didn't anticipate having any problems doing the things she loved—hiking, skiing, and backpacking.

A few weekends after being released from the rehabilitation unit, C.J., along with her friend Sarah, decided to take a day hike up to a mountain pass. They started up the trail on a beautiful, crisp autumn day, with great views of the valleys below unfolding before them. They hiked for about an hour, passing a number of turnoffs until they entered a more forested area, where the trail became less well defined and had many switchbacks. The hiking was difficult, but C.J. was feeling like her old self again. Soon afterward, they came to a fork in the trail. They knew from the map that their cutoff should be nearby, but they weren't sure exactly where, so C.J. decided to pull out the map and compass. Once she had them out, though, she had difficulty determining how to align the map with reference to the compass. Having had a strong sense of direction previously, C.J. was surprised to find herself confused as to which way was north, east, south, or west. At that point, Sarah called out, saying that she had found a trail marker indicating that they wanted the rightward fork. C.J. was relieved to realize that despite her trouble with the map and compass, she had no trouble correctly distinguishing the rightward fork of the trail from the leftward one.

They reached the top of the pass after a couple of hours and were rewarded with a spectacular view of mountains all around them. As was their usual routine, they pulled out their map and tried to identify the surrounding peaks. Even though both the compass and the position of the sun could be used for orienting their direction, C.J. once again found herself confused. She was unable to translate the fantastic vista in front of her to the representations on the map. Although she and Sarah would usually disagree about the position of at least one mountain (after which a lively discussion would ensue), this time C.J. just listened carefully, startled at her own confusion.

C.J. was subdued on the hike down. Usually fit, she was a bit out of shape from her hospital stay, and as with any trauma, her body had not yet fully recovered. Sarah asked C.J. whether she was feeling OK, and although C.J. said that she was just tired, her mind was elsewhere. She was wondering whether her stroke might have had some unexpected consequences that would interfere with one of her favorite pastimes. ■

The story about C.J. helps to illustrate that spatial processing is not a simple cognitive function but consists of many different abilities. Some of C.J.'s spatial abilities, such as understanding the relationship between the map and the surrounding terrain, and knowing geographical points of reference (north, south, east, and west), were compromised. Other abilities, however, such as determining left and right, were unaffected. In this chapter, we examine the many ways in which spatial relations among items can be computed and the brain systems that underlie these computations.

To understand spatial relations, we start by examining basic spatial processes, including localizing points in space, perceiving depth, determining the orientation of lines, understanding the geometric relations among parts of objects and whole objects, perceiving motion, and rotating items mentally. These basic spatial skills underlie more complex spatial operations, which we examine afterwards, such as being able to construct items in either two or three dimensions and understanding how to read a map and follow a route. We then examine the ability to understand how your body relates to the external spatial world and the spatial relationships among parts of your body. As you will learn, most of these abilities rely on the regions of the parietal lobe.

After discussing these spatial skills, we examine their interplay with two other mental processes, memory and attention. We learn that the neural structures supporting the retention of long-term spatial representations rely on right temporal and hippocampal regions and are independent of the spatial operations performed by the right parietal region. We also examine how particular disturbances in attentional processing can have profound effects on the ability to process spatial information.

In many places throughout this chapter, we learn about the importance of the right hemisphere for spatial processing. In fact, the right hemisphere plays such a large role in spatial processing that is often referred to as the *spatial hemisphere.* However, as is the case with almost all mental processes, both hemispheres contribute to spatial processing, albeit in different ways. Therefore, we close the chapter not only by discussing the ways in which the left hemisphere contributes to spatial operations, but also by considering a theoretical framework that outlines the complementary roles of the hemispheres in spatial processing.

The "Where" Dorsal Visual System for Spatial Processing

As we learned in Chapter 6, research with nonhuman primates has provided many clues as to how the brain is organized for processing visual information. In that chapter, we examined this research to gain insights into the functioning of the ventral visual-processing stream. In this chapter, we examine similar research to learn about the contributions of the dorsal visual-processing stream. This processing stream, which supports spatial processing, projects from primary visual areas to parietal regions. Its location in the monkey is shown in Figure 7.1.

Just as the properties of cells in the ventral visual system make them well suited for the task of object recognition, so properties of cells in the inferior parietal area (area 7) of the monkey make them well suited to process spatial information. These cells are sensitive to different attributes than those that stimulate cells in temporal regions. Unlike cells in the ventral processing stream, cells in parietal areas are not particularly sensitive to form or color, making them ill-suited to detecting the visual properties from which shape can be derived. Furthermore, they are not particularly sensitive to items positioned in central vision, where acuity is the highest, a fact that serves as additional evidence that these cells do not play a large role in object recognition.

Cells in area 7 are most responsive to attributes of visual information that are useful for processing spatial relations. First, their receptive field generally encompasses almost all of the contralateral visual space as well as a substantial portion of ipsilateral space. Thus, information can be obtained about the locations of items across a large expanse of space. Second, the cells seem to fire in response to a specific direction of motion, either inward toward the center of the visual field or outward toward the periphery. Such sensitivity provides a means for objects to be tracked as they move across space. Third, the velocity of movement optimal for making these cells fire is about that at which objects would appear to be moving if the animal were not stationary but rather walking or running (Motter & Mountcastle, 1981). Sensitivity to this range of speeds provides a way to analyze space and update the positions of items as the animal is locomoting. Fourth, cells in this area appear to be responsive to a combination of the retinal location of the visual stimulus and the position of the animal's eyes and/or head (e.g., Andersen & Mountcastle, 1983), which allows for the creation of a stable spatial map of the world. Because a particular region of space falls on a specific region of the retina, the mapping of a spatial location to a retinal location changes as soon as the animal turns its head or moves. If the animal needs to respond to a particular portion of space (e.g., needs to reach for an object located in a certain location), it must be able to reference that position in a spatial map of the world that is constant regardless of head or retinal position. This constant framework can be considered the spatial equivalent of the constancy provided by inferior temporal neurons, which respond to a particular object regardless of variations in lighting, size, and orientation.

Lesion studies with monkeys provide converging evidence for the role of the parietal region in spatial

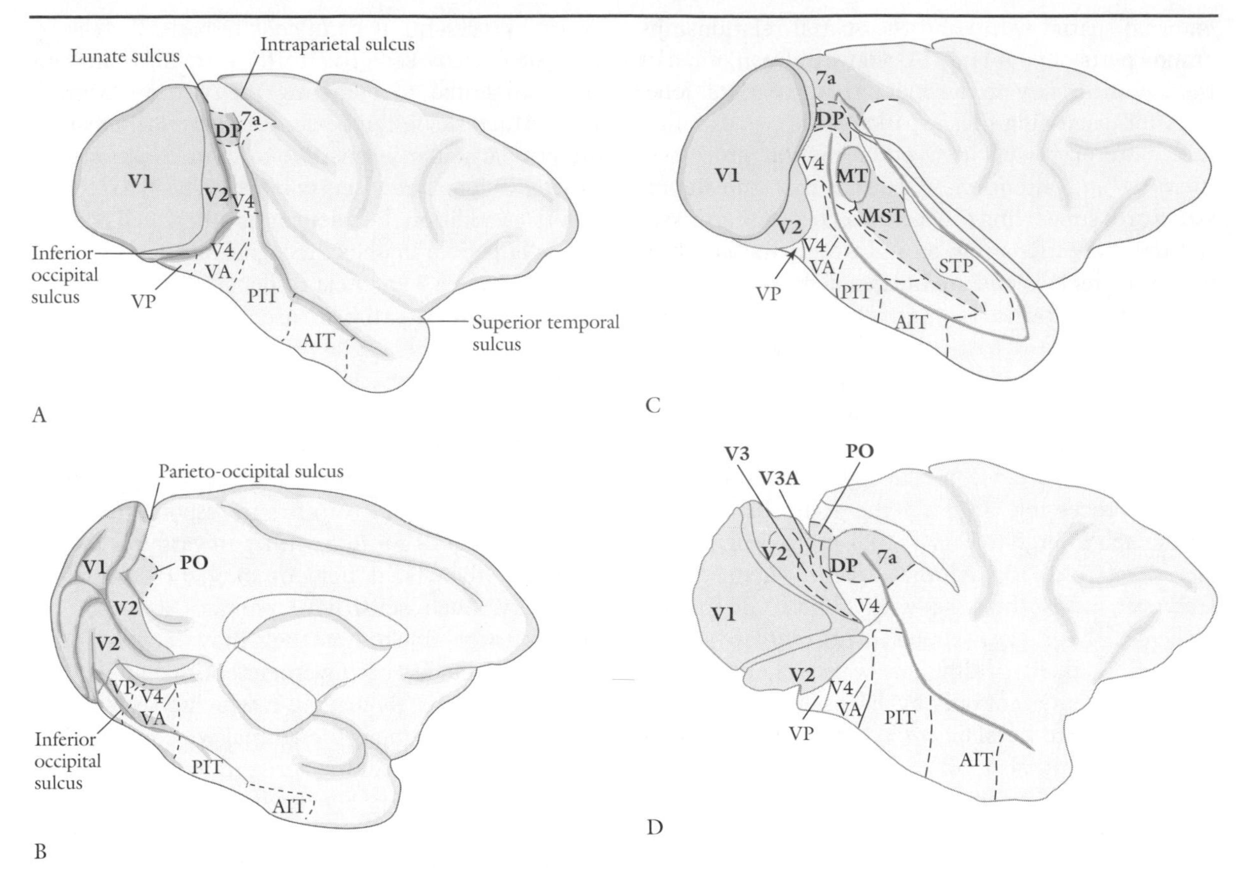

FIGURE 7.1 Dorsal visual stream of the brain in the macaque. (A) Right hemisphere, lateral view. (B) Left hemisphere, midsagittal view. (C) View showing the areas buried within the superior temporal sulcus. (D) View showing the areas buried within the lunate, intraparietal, parieto-occipital, and inferior occipital sulci. The dorsal processing stream, shown in gray, includes areas V1, V2, V3, and V3A; the middle temporal (MT) area; the medial superior temporal (MST) area; the dorsal prelunate and parietal-occipital areas; and area 7a of the parietal lobe. DP, dorsal prelunate; VA, ventral anterior; VP, ventral posterior; PIT, posterior inferotemporal; AIT, anterior inferotemporal; PO, parieto-occipital; STP, superior temporal polysensory.

processing. Monkeys with parietal lobe lesions are impaired on tasks that require the animal to compute spatial relations among items. In one such task, monkeys are shown two food wells that have identical covers. A small tower, which acts as a landmark, is situated closer to one of the covers than the other. The position of the landmark changes from trial to trial; sometimes it is closer to the right food well and sometimes it is closer to the left food well. However, it is always positioned nearer the well containing the food. Thus, the animal must be able to encode relative position to know that the reward is hidden under the well nearer the landmark (Figure 7.2A) (e.g., Pohl, 1973).

Furthermore, an object-based variation of the same task demonstrates that damage to parietal regions does not interfere with object discrimination. In this version of the task, the monkey is familiarized with an object placed in a central location (e.g., an elongated, striped pyramid). This object is then placed over one food well, whereas another object (e.g., a checkered, three-dimensional rectangle) is placed over the other food well. In each trial, the reward is hidden under the object with which the animal was *not* familiarized (i.e., the novel object), in this case the checkered, three-dimensional rectangle. This procedure is known as a *nonmatch-to-sample paradigm*.

As you might expect on the basis of what we learned in Chapter 6, animals with temporal lobe lesions find this task difficult even though they can perform the spatial-location task with ease (Figure 7.2B) (Mishkin, Ungerleider, & Macko, 1983). This dissociation between the performance of animals with temporal lesions and the performance of those with parietal lesions provides additional evidence for a functional distinction between the dorsal and ventral visual-processing streams (see Andersen, 1988, for a review of the anatomical, physiological, and behavioral research implicating parietal regions in spatial processing).

Before we end our discussion of the distinction between the dorsal and ventral processing systems, one additional point should be mentioned: At least some researchers suggest that the distinction between these two systems is not so much a distinction between "what" and "where" as between "what" and "how" (e.g., Goodale & Milner, 1992; see Goodale and Humphrey, 1998, for a more recent and lengthy review). From this perspective, the role of the dorsal system is to know *how* motor acts must be performed to manipulate an object—for example, how the hands and fingers must be positioned to grasp an object. Support for this idea comes from both monkeys and humans.

A double dissociation observed in human patients suggests the independence of a "what" system from a "how" system. In one case study, a patient with bilateral parietal damage could recognize line drawings of common objects but couldn't adjust the gap between her index finger and thumb to grasp items, such as a block, even though she could correctly move her hand to the region in space where the item was located (Jakobson, Archibald, Carey, & Goodale, 1991). In contrast, patients with damage to ventral extrastriate regions cannot recognize the size, shape, and orientation of visual objects, yet they can accurately guide both the hand and fingers to these same objects (e.g., A. D. Milner et al., 1991).

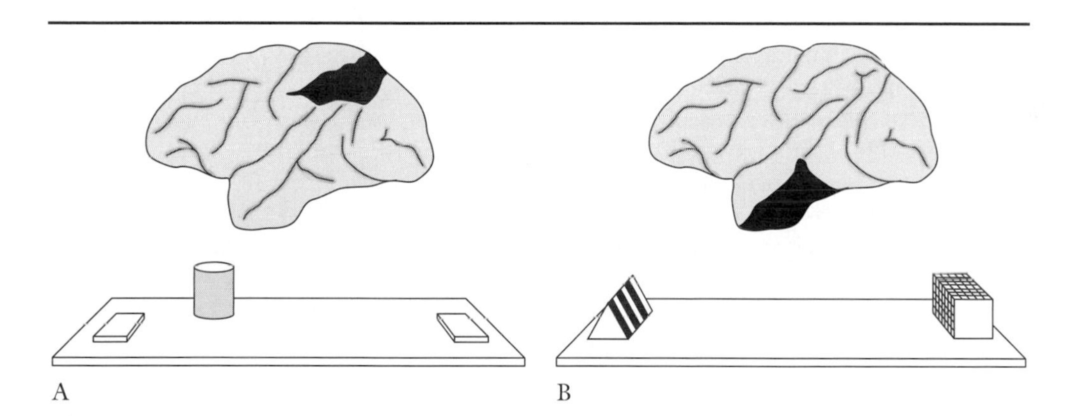

FIGURE 7.2 Tasks sensitive to dorsal vs. ventral stream damage in monkeys. (A) In the landmark-discrimination task, the monkey sees two identical food-well covers and a landmark. A reward is hidden under the food-well cover closer to the landmark. The position of the landmark varies randomly from trial to trial, sometimes closer to the left food well and sometimes closer to the right well. When bilateral damage to the posterior parietal region, shown in blue, is sustained, monkeys cannot perform this task. (B) In the object-discrimination task, the monkey sees two distinct food-well covers, one with which it has been familiarized prior to the trial. A reward is hidden under the food-well cover that was not previously viewed. This task is known as a *nonmatch-to-sample paradigm* because the animal must choose the well covered by the object that was not viewed previously. When bilateral damage to inferotemporal areas, shown in blue, is sustained, the monkey cannot perform this task.

Single-cell recordings in monkeys and neuroimaging results in humans are in agreement that parietal regions are involved in spatial aspects of motor control. Neurons in the inferior parietal lobe of monkeys are active when the animal directs motor acts to particular locations, such as reaching, fixating on an object, or tracking an item with the eyes. Because these cells exhibit both sensory- and movement-related activity, some researchers have suggested that these areas of the brain are important for integrating external information about space with the commands for motor actions in extrapersonal space (e.g., Lynch, Mountcastle, Talbot, & Yin, 1977; Mountcastle et al., 1975). Moreover, some cells in parietal regions are sensitive to the visual qualities of an object that influence how the hand and fingers should be positioned if the object is to be grasped (Taira et al., 1990). Studies using neuroimaging in humans also provide evidence for a role of posterior parietal cortex in guiding movements in space. This region is activated when individuals are engaged in visually guided movements, whether they be of the eyes, as in saccades, or of the hands, such as in reaching or grasping movements (Matsumura et al., 1996). Just as the regions within the ventral visual-processing stream seem to differentiate in their activation on the basis of the type of objects (e.g., faces vs. places), regions of the dorsal processing stream differentiate on the basis of the type of movement [e.g., eye movements vs. manual pointing movements (Kawashima et al., 1996)].

Recently it has been suggested that these two views of the parietal processing stream, that of a "where" system as opposed to a "how" system, may be able to be reconciled, as the former may rely more on inferior regions of posterior parietal cortex whereas the latter may rely more on superior posterior parietal regions (Creem & Proffitt, 2001). Regardless of the exact perspective taken, much evidence from research with monkeys and humans supports the idea that the parietal lobes play an important role in spatial processing in primates. Let us now turn to evidence on the neurological basis of spatial processing in humans.

Basic Spatial Processes in Humans

As suggested by the results of studies with monkeys, posterior parietal areas in humans are important for computing the location of an object in space and for integrating information about location with bodily movements so that a person can direct his or her movements, either limbs or eyes, to a particular location. Traditionally, much of our knowledge of the role of parietal regions in spatial processing comes from examining difficulties after damage to these regions, which can take numerous forms. Individuals may have difficulty because (1) they switch, elongate, or truncate the main axes on an item to be copied; (2) they cannot correctly represent the relationships among parts of an item; (3) they give an item an incorrect form; (4) they make lines intersect that should not; or (5) they rotate lines or object parts. Spatial difficulties may also affect other mental skills. For instance, an individual may be unable to perform arithmetic because he or she cannot keep columns straight, or a person may have an inability to use maps for navigation (e.g., McFie, Piercy, & Zangwill, 1950).

Because many of these spatial abilities appear to rely on a confluence of spatial skills, researchers have attempted to extract the basic component abilities that contribute to these more complicated spatial skills and identify the neural hardware required for each. Hence, we now examine the neural substrates of six fundamental spatial skills: localizing points in space, perceiving depth, judging line orientation, understanding geometric relations, perceiving motion, and rotating items mentally.

Localization of Points in Space

Probably the most basic aspect of spatial processing is the ability to find a point in space. Back in 1918, Holmes noted that such an ability could be compromised by brain damage. He reported on patients who could recognize objects, like a fork, placed directly in front of them. But if the objects were placed somewhere else, such as on a table set for dinner, they would act as if blind, groping and misreaching for the item. Localization in all three dimensions of space was affected because patients would reach too near or too far, too much to the left or too much to the right, or too high or too low. And these individuals were at just as much of a loss at determining relative position (e.g., determining which of two objects was farther left) as they were at determining absolute position (i.e., determining the precise point in space

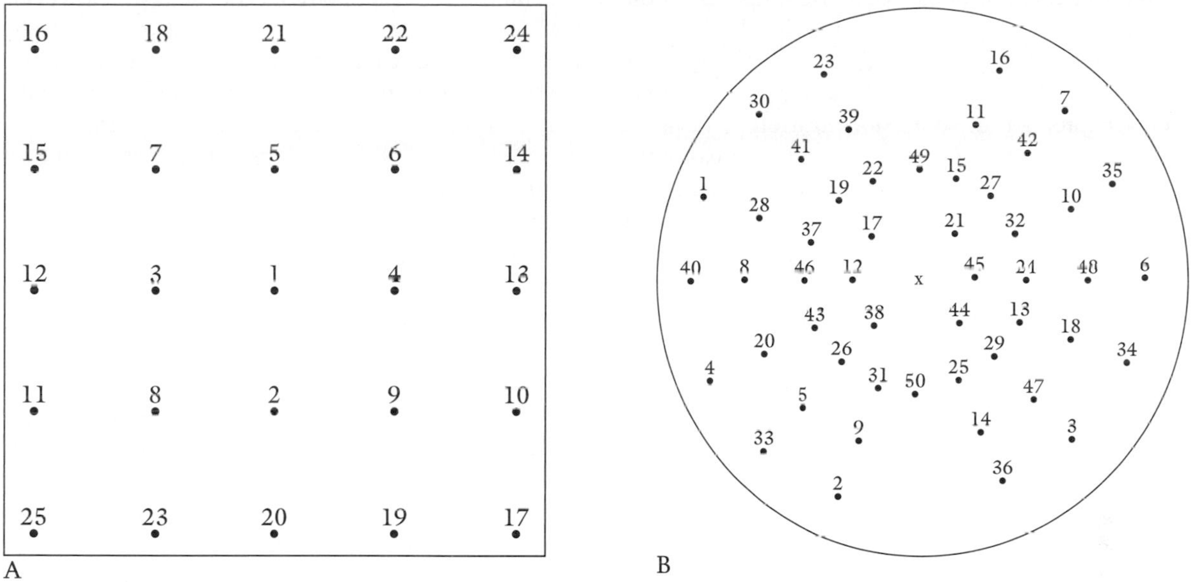

A B

FIGURE 7.3 Two choice arrays used in divided visual field studies to assess the ability of each hemisphere to localize points in space. A single dot is shown on a trial and the individual must point to the corresponding location on the choice array. (A) A choice array arranged in Euclidean coordinates (rows and columns). (B) A choice array arranged in polar coordinates.

at which an object was located). As you might imagine, such deficits greatly disrupted these patients' lives.

The syndrome that Holmes observed could not be called a specific deficit in spatial localization, because his patients exhibited various other disruptions in spatial processing as well. Nonetheless, the location of damage in these patients, which typically involved the parietal lobes of both hemispheres, hinted at the involvement of this region in spatial localization. Since the time of Holmes, the evidence has become clearer. Unilateral damage to superior regions of the parietal lobe can cause an inability to accurately reach for items on the contralateral side of space, regardless of the arm used, while leaving accuracy of localization for ipsilateral targets intact (e.g., Cole, Schutta, & Warrington, 1962; Ratcliff & Davies-Jones, 1972).

In the cases we have discussed so far, difficulty in spatial localization was demonstrated by an inability to direct movement toward a particular position in space. We might therefore want to investigate whether similar regions are important for *perceiving* the location of a point in space. Such investigation can be done in the laboratory in diverse ways—for example, by asking individuals to decide whether two dots, presented successively, appear in the same location, or by displaying a dot on the screen briefly and then asking the individual to locate its position among an array of dots.

Although some variation occurs across studies (e.g., Hannay, Varney, & Benton, 1976; Warrington & James, 1988; Warrington & Rabin, 1970), deficits are most likely to be observed on such tasks when individuals have damage to posterior regions of the right hemisphere. Converging evidence for the role of the right hemisphere in this function comes from divided visual field studies with neurologically intact individuals. Although the results are not always consistent (Bryden, 1976), a left visual field (LVF) advantage is often found regardless of whether the point must be localized with a Euclidean coordinate system (Figure 7.3A) or a polar one (Figure 7.3B) (Kimura, 1969).

Not only does the parietal region play a role in localizing information in visual space but it plays a similar role for auditory space as well. Lesions of the parietal lobe disrupt the ability to localize sounds (e.g., Pinek, Duhamel, Cave, & Brouchon, 1989; Ruff, Hersh, & Pribram, 1981). You may remember from Chapter 1 that sound localization can also be disrupted by damage to primary auditory areas of the temporal lobe, but this disruption occurs for a different reason. Whereas parietal lobe damage interferes with sound localization because it disrupts a spatial map of the world, damage to primary auditory cortex disrupts sensitivity to interaural differences in intensity and timing that are used for localizing sounds in space.

Although the results of studies of patients with brain damage disagree as to whether left or right parietal lobe damage is more likely to disrupt auditory spatial localization, research with neurologically intact individuals suggests that, at least for nonverbal noise, the right hemisphere is better at localizing sound. Monaural localization of a sound is better with the left ear than with the right (R. A. Butler, 1994) and for positions on the left side of space than for those on the right (K. A. Burke, Letsos, & Butler, 1994). Information received by the left ear or from the left side of space is assumed to be processed preferentially by the contralateral hemisphere because patients who undergo hemispherectomy have deficits in sound localization on the contralateral side of space (e.g., Poirier et al., 1994).

Before we leave this discussion, it is important to mention that there are a variety of different spatial frames of reference by which points might be localized. Work with monkeys has suggested that the brain contains a variety of spatial maps, some of which are centered with regard to the viewer's head, eyes, or trunk for space within the organism's reach, *egocentric space,* and others that are for regions beyond the organism's reach, *extracentric space.* These maps are then combined to produce an *allocentric map* that is independent of the viewer and is a representation of the absolute location of points in the environment, as well as the distances and direction between them.

Although we can make an educated guess, it is not exactly clear what coordinate system is being used to perform each of the tasks we have discussed thus far. The reference frame or frames used may depend on the exact demands of the task. However, we can speculate on the types of tasks that might rely more on one frame than another. For example, tasks such as pointing to locations in space within reach would likely be accomplished within an egocentric framework, noting the relative position of a chair and table located across the room might be accomplished within an extracentric framework, and determining the fastest route from your residence to the university library would probably require an allocentric framework.

Depth Perception

Most of the research that we just discussed involves localization in a two-dimensional plane. However, space has three dimensions. Thus, another basic spatial ability is the ability to perceive the third dimension—depth. Depth perception, also known as **stereopsis,** is the specific ability that helps us to localize items in the near-far plane. Because each eye is in a slightly different position with regard to our focus point, a different portion of the visual image falls on corresponding points of each retina. This offset is known as **binocular disparity** and is one of the important visual cues for relative depth (i.e., knowing which locations are closer to and which are farther from the viewer).

In general, there are two types of depth perception: local and global. Local stereopsis, or *stereoacuity,* is the ability to use comparison of local detailed features of objects in a point-by-point manner to determine relative position. For example, differences between information reaching each eye about particular local cues, such as the front leg of a chair and the right-hand corner of a table, can be compared to determine whether the chair or the table is nearer the viewer. This type of depth perception can be disrupted by either right- or left-hemisphere lesions (e.g., Danta, Hilton, & O'Boyle, 1978).

In contrast, global depth perception requires that the disparity between information reaching each eye be computed over the whole visual scene. This ability cannot be tested with ordinary stimuli but must be examined with specially constructed stimuli known as *random-dot stereograms* (Julesz, 1964). These stereograms are two large squares that consist of a patchwork of many smaller squares, each of which is randomly determined to be either dark or light. The patchwork pattern in the two large squares is identical except that the pattern in one is shifted a couple of small squares relative to the other. When viewed binocularly, one of the two large squares appears to be in front of the other. Because no discrete object can be seen in these stereograms, depth cannot be computed on the basis of local cues. Rather, perceiving depth requires an individual to calculate disparity across the entire display. This type of stereopsis, *global stereopsis,* appears to depend on portions of the ventral visual processing stream in the right hemiphere, including extrastriate regions in the right hemisphere and inferotemporal cortex (Ptito et al., 1993; Ptito & Zatorre, 1988).

Orientation of Lines

So far in our discussion we have assumed our interest is in finding a particular point in space. Yet, often in our visual world we must be able to calculate the location and orientation of a string of points, which together constitute a line. The ability to judge the orientation or angles of lines is another basic visuospatial ability that appears to rely on the right hemisphere. Disruption of this basic ability can have troublesome effects in everyday life. As a simplistic example, think of how difficult reading a clock face would be if you couldn't determine the angle at which the arms were pointing.

One task commonly used both in the laboratory and in the clinic to assess this ability requires individuals to differentiate among a set of 11 lines, all of which radiate at different angles from the same point. The individual views a display with 2 lines and must identify them from the set of 11 (see Figure 7.4). Right-hemisphere damage compromises the ability to perform either a visual or a tactile version of this task (e.g., A. L. Benton, Hannay, & Varney, 1975). Because deficits in the two modalities are correlated (Meerwaldt & Van Harskamp, 1982), the deficit is truly spatial and not modality specific. Neuroimaging studies suggest that the brain region most responsible for judgment of line orientation resides in the ventral extrastriate cortex (BA areas 18, 19). Converging evidence for the role of the right hemisphere in line orientation comes from studies of neurologically intact individuals who exhibit a LVF advantage on this task (e.g., Atkinson & Egeth, 1973; Umilta et al., 1974). However, this effect is limited to orientations whose positions cannot be easily verbalized, unlike "vertical" and "horizontal."

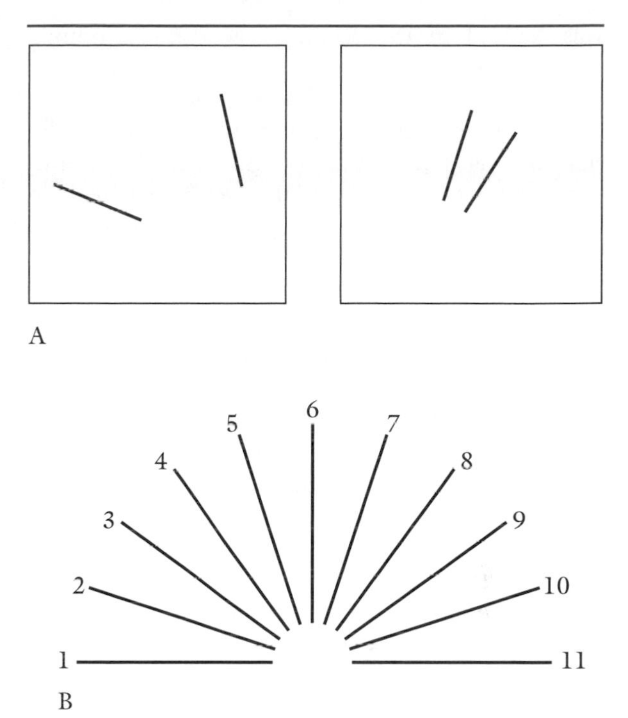

FIGURE 7.4 One test commonly used in assessing the ability to judge the orientation of lines. (A) Two sample trials from the test. In each trial, the two lines must be matched to the lines in the choice card shown in (B).

A LVF advantage for judging certain orientations but not others raises the important point, which we revisit frequently in this chapter, that alternative modes of processing can be used to perform the same spatial task. For example, as we just discussed, a RVF advantage may occur for line orientation if certain angles can be described verbally (e.g., horizontal, vertical); otherwise, a LVF advantage occurs. As another example, consider the Euclidean dot-localization tasks described earlier. Although on each trial only a single dot is seen, the array of dot positions from which an individual must choose follows a regular pattern (e.g., the dots are placed in rows and columns). After some experience with the task, an individual could estimate a dot's location with a verbally mediated strategy ("That dot seemed like it was located in the second row, third column"), which would minimize the role of the right hemisphere. We discuss this issue in more detail at the end of this chapter, but for now we should consider that inconsistent findings with regard to hemispheric differences in spatial tasks may reflect, in part, differences in strategies that individuals use to perform a task.

Geometric Relations

As we think about processing the components of our spatial world, we can progress from the ability to perceive points and lines to the ability to perceive the spatial relationships among parts of basic forms, which we refer to under the umbrella term of *geometric relations.* As with the abilities discussed so far, these tend to depend more on the right hemisphere than the left.

One ability that falls under the rubric of geometric relations is that of determining whether different forms have similar spatial properties. For example, a LVF advantage is observed for judgments of curvature (Longden, Ellis, & Iversen, 1976) and for deciding whether an arc has the same curvature as a circle (Hatta, 1977). Similarly, the left-hand (right-hemisphere) performance of patients with the split-brain syndrome is superior to that of the right when they are asked to tactilely feel arcs and match them to circles. Left-hand performance is also superior to that of the right when the pattern inherent in an array of raised dots must be detected and when a solid object must be felt and matched to an "exploded" visual depiction of that object in which its pieces retain the same spatial relationship but are no longer connected (Nebes, 1978).

The neural substrates of geometric spatial processing can also be investigated by examining the capacity of each hemisphere of split-brain patients to process four major classes of geometric relationships: Euclidean, affine, projective, and topological. Euclidean geometry is the type we learned in school; it provides mathematical equations for the properties of simple forms that can be easily verbalized (e.g., the area of a triangle = width $\times \frac{1}{2}$ height). Topology is the branch of geometry that relates to curved spaces and forms. As we move from Euclidean to affine to projective and then to topological geometry, the characteristics or constraints that define similarity among forms become fewer and fewer. Whereas the right hemisphere was equally good at all four types of geometry, the performance of the left, although equal to the right for Euclidean geometry, declines systematically from there (Franco & Sperry, 1977).

Another way to examine the ability to process geometric relations among item parts is to investigate the ability to remember complex figures that do not represent anything in real life. Because the complex figure has never been seen in the individual's lifetime, the person must process the spatial relations of the item's parts to encode the item into memory. This process is somewhat different than that required to recognize common objects, because in those cases the individual can refer to a template stored in memory (e.g., a template for the shape of birds). Studies with neurologically intact individuals generally reveal a LVF advantage when the person must determine whether a given complex figure was previously viewed (e.g., Fontenot, 1973; Umilta, Bagnara, & Simion, 1978), although some studies do not yield this result (Hannay, Rogers, & Durant, 1976). Some variations in findings may be accounted for by the degree to which a verbal label can be assigned to a particular nonsense shape. For example, the degree of the LVF advantage for remembering nonsense designs is smaller for items that are judged easy to label verbally than for items judged hard to label (Figure 7.5) (J. I. Shenker, M. T. Banich, & S. Klipstein, unpublished observations, 1993).

Motion

So far we have considered a spatial world in which the relations among points in space or geometric relations are static. But these relations can change with time; that is, they may involve motion. Thus, motion is another basic process underlying competence in spatial processing that we need to consider.

Research with monkeys has shown that a particular region of the brain—the superior temporal gyrus, known as MT (or V5), which is an area at the border of parietal, temporal, and occipital regions—contains cells that are especially sensitive to motion (e.g., Dubner & Zeki, 1971; Komatsu & Wurtz, 1988) and are active when an animal is visually tracking a moving object (e.g., Sakata, Shibutani, & Kawano, 1983). Evidence both from brain mapping and lesion

FIGURE 7.5 Some examples of complex nonsense shapes. These stimuli vary in how easily people can provide a verbal description of them. Although individuals had difficulty providing a verbal label for the stimuli shown in A, these persons were more likely to provide a label for those shown in B, which, from left to right, might be described as a pile of rocks, a nose with eyeglasses, a leaf, and interlocking horseshoes. A left visual field advantage in recognition is more likely to be observed when verbal labels cannot be easily applied to the figures, as for the items shown in A.

studies suggests a similar location for a motion-sensitive area in humans—the posterior lateral temporal cortex. Neuroimaging studies using positron emission tomography (PET) find activity in this region when stimuli similar to those presented to monkeys are used (e.g., Zeki et al., 1991), and when a target must be tracked with the eyes across space (Colby & Zeffiro, 1990), findings that are confirmed with fMRI (Tootell et al., 1995). Furthermore, when an individual must selectively attend to the speed of a moving object, similar regions become active (Corbetta et al., 1991). As this brain region is situated in the visual-processing stream past primary and secondary visual areas, it takes a bit of time after stimulus presentation for motion to be detected. The results of combined fMRI and ERP studies suggest that the analysis of motion starts to occur in these regions approximately 130 ms and peaks around 150–180 ms post-presentation (Ahlfors et al., 1999).

One case study is particularly informative by suggesting that the analysis of motion in humans has a separate neural substrate than that which supports other spatial skills. Although the woman in this study lost her ability to perceive motion in all three dimensions, her other basic visual and spatial functions, including visual acuity, binocular vision, color discrimination, discrimination of visual objects and words, and localization of items in space, were all intact (Zihl, Von Cramon, & Mai, 1983). Moreover, her difficulty in perceiving motion could not be accounted for by difficulties in integrating visual information across time (which in turn might selectively impair the ability to detect movement). As you might imagine, her disorder created much difficulty in her life. When she was pouring liquids, such as tea or coffee, the flowing stream would appear to her as a glacier or a snapshot, much the way such a stream does in magazine ads. Because she could not see the rising level of fluid in a container, it was impossible to determine when to stop pouring. Even more troublesome was her difficulty in judging the speed of cars (which she had no trouble recognizing). This impairment made crossing streets extremely dangerous. In describing her dilemma, she said, "When I'm looking at the car, first it seems far away. But then, when I want to cross the road, suddenly the car is very near" (Zihl, Von Cramon, & Mai, 1983, p. 315). Eventually, she learned to rely on auditory cues, such as the loudness of a car, to estimate how close or far away it was.

In this woman, damage occurred in a broad range of parietal regions in the right hemisphere and a more restricted range in the left hemisphere, as well as the middle and superior temporal gyri bilaterally (Hess, Baker, & Zihl, 1989). A subsequent case report of an individual who had difficulty perceiving motion (but in this case in only two, not all three, dimensions) had also sustained damage in a similar location, namely bilaterally in posterior temporoparietal areas (Vaina et al., 1990).

To summarize, results from these case studies and from neuroimaging studies suggest that the analysis of motion occurs in an area at the temporoparietal junction, as shown in Color insert 7.1,

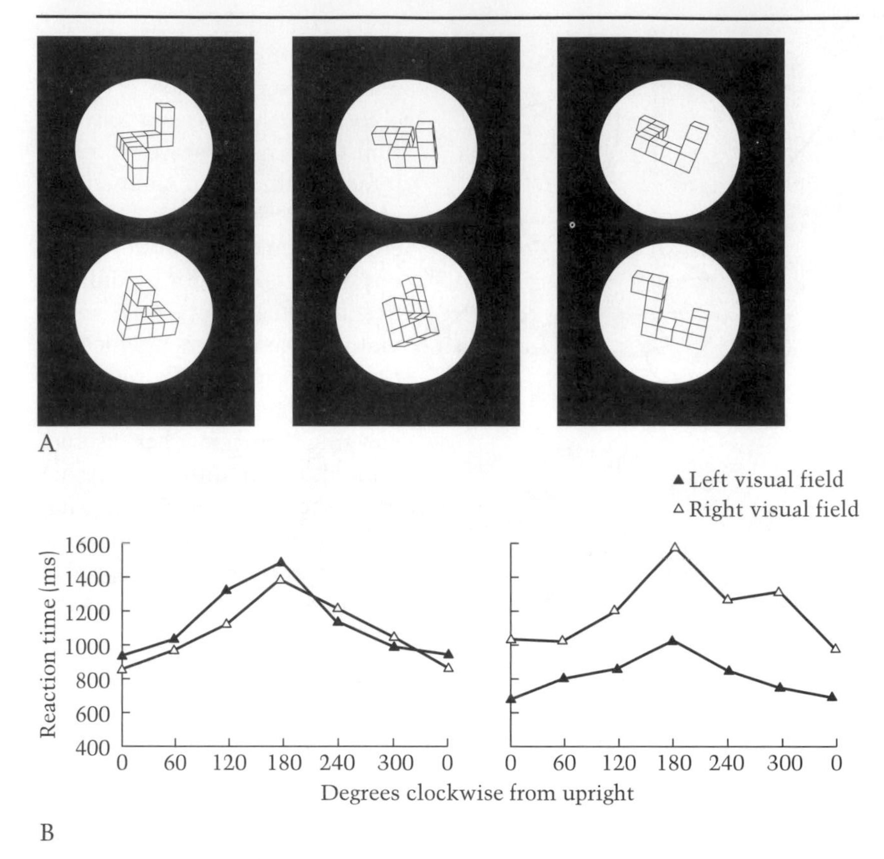

FIGURE 7.6 Classic paradigm for examining mental rotation. (A) The type of three-dimensional stimulus often used to assess the ability to rotate objects in three dimensions. Whereas the left two pairs can be rotated to match each other—the first by an 80-degree rotation in depth and the second by an 80-degree rotation in the sideways plane—the final pair cannot because the forms are mirror images. (B) Typical performance on such rotational tasks for a group of neurologically intact individuals (left) and for a patient with split-brain syndrome, L.B. (right). For both L.B. and the neurologically intact individuals, the more rotation required, the longer the reaction times. However, whereas L.B. showed a strong left visual field (right hemisphere) superiority for the task, the neurologically intact control subjects did not.

and that this basic spatial ability can be distinct from other aspects of spatial processing.

Rotation

To finish our review of basic spatial skills, we examine the ability to detect rotation, which might be considered a special class of movement detection. Rather than movement from one location in space to another, rotation is movement around an axis. Just as single-cell recordings in monkeys reveal that some cells are sensitive to the detection of motion, cells in the superior temporal regions (e.g., Saito et al., 1986) and the inferior parietal region (e.g., Sakata, Shibutani, Kawano, & Harrington, 1985) are sensitive to rotation, especially in a rotary manner (e.g., clockwise or counterclockwise). Other cells respond to rotations in depth (e.g., front to back).

In humans, the ability to rotate objects mentally has been studied extensively by Shepard and colleagues (for a review, see R. Shepard, 1988), who found that the greater thc degree of mental rotation required to align two 3-D objects (Figure 7.6A), the greater is the time required to decide whether they are identical. For example, if two items are positioned 180 degrees apart in rotation, a person will take longer to decide whether they are identical than if they are only 60 degrees apart (Figure 7.6B).

The vast majority of studies suggest that the parietal regions are responsible for rotational abilities. For example, increased blood flow to the right hemisphere is found during a rotation task similar to that depicted in Figure 7.6A (G. Deutsch, Bourbon, Papanicolaou, & Eisenberg, 1988), and when simplified versions of the same stimuli are used, rotational abilities are more disrupted by right parietal lobe damage than by left parietal lobe damage (e.g., Ditunno & Mann, 1990). Further compelling evidence for right parietal involvement in this task has been provided by more recent brain imaging studies that exploit the fact that increased reaction time is associated with an increased

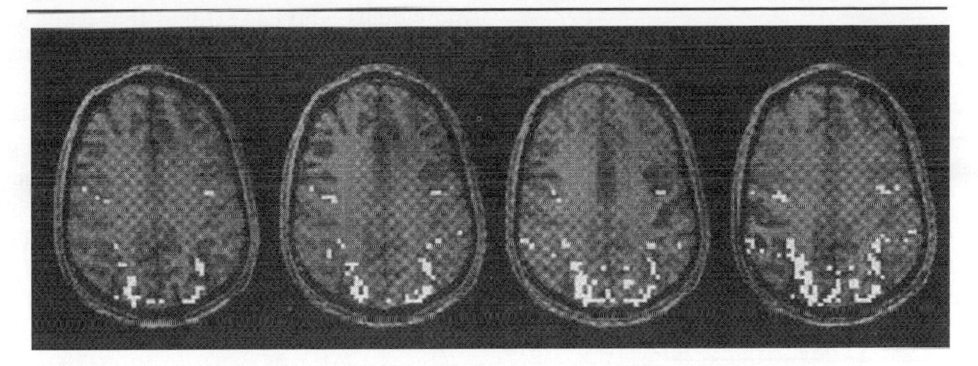

FIGURE 7.7 Increasing brain activation with increasing degree of mental rotation. Shown here is a slice through the ventral portion of the superior parietal lobe, near the intraparietal sulcus. From left to right the pictures depict the degree of activation associated with 0, 40, 80, and 120 degrees rotation. Notice that the degree of activity increases as more rotation needs to be performed.

degree of rotation. Researchers designing these studies reasoned that the brain region specifically involved in rotation should similarly show a specific relationship between the degree of activity and the degree of rotation (e.g., Carpenter et al., 1999). Methods that utilize such an approach converge very nicely in their findings to suggest that activation associated with the mental rotation task is specifically localized to the superior parietal lobule (BA 7), mainly in the right hemisphere but involving both hemispheres (e.g., Carpenter et al., 1999; Richter et al., 2000; Ng et al., 2001), as shown in Figure 7.7.

The results from divided visual field studies of rotational abilities provide hints that the lateralization of parietal involvement may be influenced by two other factors, the nature of the stimuli and the direction of the rotation. Verbal stimuli appear to be more likely to yield a RVF advantage, whereas spatial stimuli may be more likely to yield a LVF advantage (e.g., Corballis & McLaren, 1984). Consistent with this finding, a PET study of letters found greater activation in the left than in the right posterior-superior parietal cortex (Alivisatos & Petrides, 1997). Furthermore, differential hemispheric involvement in rotation may depend on the direction of rotation required. In particular, the right hemisphere seems to be superior for clockwise rotation and the left hemisphere for counterclockwise rotation; therefore, each hemisphere appears to be specialized for rotation inward toward the center (Burton, Wagner, Lim, & Levy, 1992; Corballis & Sergent, 1989). Although no clear explanation exists for this effect, perhaps it provides a conceptualization of space that allows mirror-image motor movements to be performed.

Now that we reviewed the neural bases of basic spatial processes, we turn our attention to more complex spatial skills.

Constructional Abilities

We have examined the ability to *perceive* spatial relations but have not yet discussed the ability to motorically produce or manipulate items so that they have a particular spatial relationship. These latter abilities are often referred to as **constructional praxis.** In everyday life such abilities can be critical for the performance of tasks ranging from putting groceries into the refrigerator to manipulating a key so that it fits correctly into a lock.

In the laboratory and the clinic, constructional skills are examined by means of tasks that are relatively simpler than the real-life instances just discussed. Such tasks can include copying a complicated nonsense drawing, building a block world, and manipulating and arranging colored cubes to match a particular pattern. The Rey-Osterrieth Complex Figure shown in Figure 7.8A is often used to assess spatial-constructional skills and perceptual skills. For the most part, such abilities

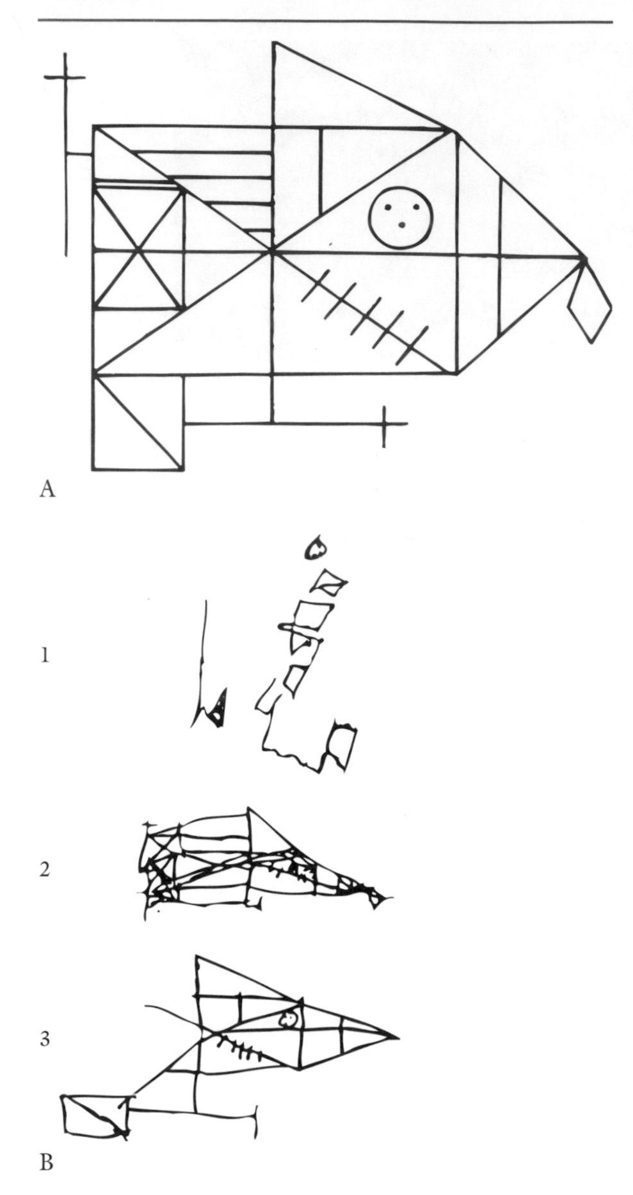

FIGURE 7.8 The testing of visuospatial drawing abilities. (A) The Rey-Osterrieth Complex Figure. (B) Examples of attempts to copy this figure by three individuals with damage to posterior sections of the right hemisphere.

are disrupted by damage to the right hemisphere (e.g., A. L. Benton, 1967). The role of the right hemisphere in such tasks can be seen by looking at the copies of the Rey-Osterrieth figure drawn by three individuals who had strokes that damaged the temporoparietal region of the right hemisphere (see Figure 7.8B).

Although deficits in spatial-constructional skills are typically associated with right-hemisphere damage, such is not always the case (e.g., Black & Strub, 1976). Inconsistency across studies probably occurs for one of two reasons. First, although all these tasks measure constructional abilities, they are likely to involve other subskills as well (e.g., fine motor control plays a larger role in copying than in manipulating large blocks). Thus any given task may be disrupted as a result of damage to additional regions besides the one critical for the constructional component of the task. Second, it is likely that many of these tasks can be performed with a variety of strategies and varying degrees of verbal mediation. For example, Figure 7.9 shows a Block Design subtest that requires an individual to arrange blocks with colored sides (either solid white, or with the black hill on a white background, or a white hill on a black background) so that the top of the blocks matches a template pattern (Figure 7.9A). One way to perform such a task is to analyze the spatial relationships in a given template (e.g., notice that, clockwise from the upper left, each corner item in Figure A is rotated 90 degrees clockwise from the prior one). Another approach is to use a verbal strategy to perform the task, such as saying, "I need a solid white block and must place that to the left of a block that has the black design at the bottom with the white part on top." Sometimes such differences in strategy can be detected by qualitative differences in how individuals perform the test. For example, after right-hemisphere damage, a distinctly different type of error is seen, one involving the overall arrangement of the blocks (Figure 7.9B), than that observed after left-hemisphere damage, which is much more likely to involve a specific piece of the pattern (Figure 7.9C).

 Route-Finding and Topographical Skills

In our lives we are often called upon not just to perceive spatial relationships but to understand their ramifications so that we can skillfully negotiate or navigate a route from one point to another.

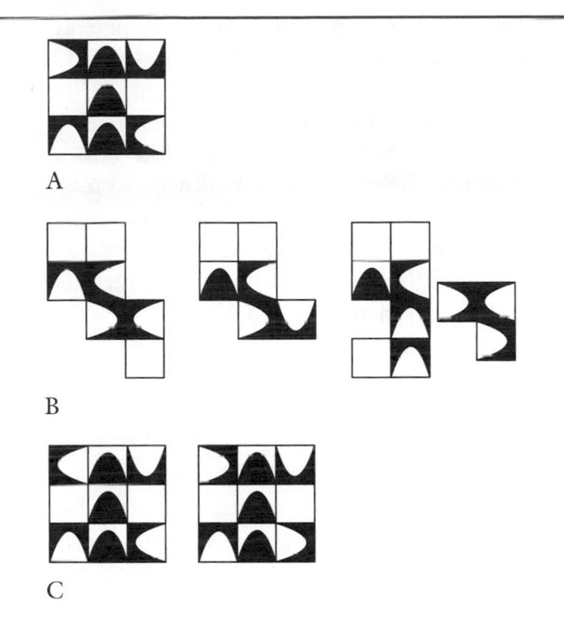

FIGURE 7.9 Constructional skills as measured by a Block Design subtest. (A) An example design that individuals must copy. (B) Three steps in an attempt to copy the design by an individual with right hemisphere damage. The patient does not even recognize the basic square pattern of the design. (C) The first and second attempts to copy the same figure by an individual with left hemisphere damage. The overall configuration is correct, but the details are incorrect. In the first attempt, the block in the upper left-hand corner is rotated 180 degrees from the correct position, whereas in the second attempt, the block in the lower right-hand corner is rotated 180 degrees.

Although we may know the direction of travel between the beginning and endpoints of our journey, navigation is often not simple as we can rarely travel a straight line between the two. Whether traveling from one building on campus to another or driving from home to the grocery store, our route probably takes us around other buildings, trees, people, and cars. What is common in each scenario, though, is that we must follow a route to reach our destination.

The ability to follow a route appears to require different neural substrates depending on the framework in which the locations are embedded. In this section we discuss how the ability to perceive spatial relations in extrapersonal space dissociates from the ability to do so in a personal framework. In the former case, you must perceive the relationship between two points in space, whereas in the latter you must perceive the relationship between your body and a point in space (e.g., you perceive that your body is to the left of a table).

In this section we also learn that the ability to comprehend spatial relations on a large scale, such as that required for reading a national map, may dissociate from route-finding abilities as applied to either a town or a neighborhood. Moreover, these abilities may be separable from finding the way around your house or hospital corridors, which in turn may be separable from knowing whether you turn left or right at the next landmark, which in turn may be separable from knowing your left hand from your right. All of this is said not to confuse you, but to indicate that we have a multiplicity of spatial frameworks with which to understand relationships between points. We compute some relationships between points in space that are within our range of view, we compute others between points that are outside our range of view (and can be symbolized on maps), and in some cases we compute relationships between points in space and our bodies.

Often damage to right posterior areas disrupts these route-finding abilities because, as we learned earlier, this region of the brain is important for the construction of a spatial map of the world. Yet, certain types of route finding may place additional burdens on an individual, and as a consequence, other brain regions may come to play a prominent role. For example, the route-finding abilities that have memory demands can also be affected by damage to temporal regions, whereas those that have a strong planning component may be more affected by frontal damage.

One task often used in the laboratory to assess route finding is the stylus maze task, in which the individual must maneuver a stylus through an orderly array of bolt heads to reach a goal (Figure 7.10). All the bolt heads are identical, and the person learns the maze because whenever she or he moves in the wrong direction, a counter clicks loudly to indicate the mistake. The ability to perform this task is compromised by damage to

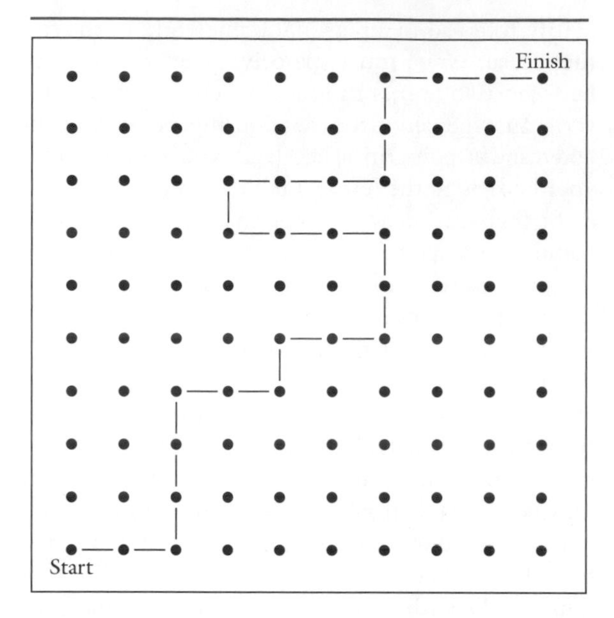

FIGURE 7.10 Example of a path that might have to be learned through the stylus maze. The maze is an array of identical metal bolt heads, depicted here by black circles. Although the path is shown in this diagram, it is not presented to the individual. Rather, each time the person touches an incorrect bolt head, a loud click occurs. Thus, the individual must discover the correct direction of movement at each choice point and remember information about previously discovered portions of the maze.

posterior and parietal regions of the right hemisphere (Newcombe, 1969). Because this task involves learning a spatial sequence of movements, individuals with damage to the right hippocampal region and those with right frontal damage show deficits. The former group seems to have difficulty remembering the series of turns that must be taken, whereas the latter group may have more difficulty with the sequential nature of the task (first right, then left, then left again, etc.) (B. Milner, 1965).

Another type of route-finding ability requires an individual to maneuver him- or herself through a maze (rather than moving an object through a maze as in the stylus maze task) (Ratcliff & Newcombe, 1973). In one such task, the locomotor maze, a series of nine dots are placed on the floor of a large room, in a grid (Semmes, Weinstein, Ghent, & Teuber, 1955). The individual is given a map on which is designated a route, from start to finish, that the person is to walk as quickly and accurately as possible. For orientation, one wall of the room is designated "north," and the person must always hold the map so that north is at the top and south is at the bottom. (In other words, the person is not allowed to rotate the map when changing directions as some people do when driving!) Poor performance on this task is associated with damage to the parietal region; some researchers claim that task performance is compromised by right-hemisphere damage (Semmes, Weinstein, Ghent, & Teuber, 1963) while others suggest that bilateral damage is required for such a result (Ratcliff & Newcombe, 1973). As we discussed with regard to other spatial tasks, this discrepancy may arise because alternative strategies are available for performing the task: one that relies more on mental rotation and the right hemisphere and another that is verbally mediated (turn left, turn right) and depends more on the left hemisphere. Perhaps deficits are most easily observed after bilateral damage because the ability to invoke either strategy is compromised.

Although the ability to perform this maze and the stylus maze can be impaired simultaneously, some patients show a dissociation between the two: either they are impaired at performing the stylus maze but not the locomotor maze, or vice versa (Ratcliff & Newcombe, 1973). Various reasons have been postulated to explain this dissociation. First, the stylus maze task is much smaller in scale. The individual can view the entire map in a bird's-eye fashion while maneuvering through it. This is not the case with the locomotor maze. Second, in the stylus maze task, a person's orientation with regard to the maze remains constant, whereas in the locomotor maze task, even though the map direction stays static, the individual's orientation relative to the map constantly changes. Another difference is that in the stylus maze task the individual must remember the route, whereas in the locomotor maze task the route is given.

Yet another way to test route-finding abilities is with the Money (1976) Standardized Road-Map Task, in which a person is shown a path through a fictional town and at each choice point must determine whether the direction turned to follow the route is right or left. Rather than being affected by parietal lobe damage, performance on this task is compromised by frontal lesions (e.g., Butters, Soeldner, & Fedio, 1972), possibly because movements must be planned in a sequential, orderly manner. This task seems to assess a different aspect of route finding than the locomotor maze does. In the road-map test, a person must determine her or his personal spatial orientation (e.g., turning right, turning left) at different points in the route; whereas in the locomotor maze, the person's orientation is irrelevant and the important factor is the relationship between two points in space relative to each other.

In the case of geographical knowledge and orientation, we are required to understand topographic spatial relations over much larger expanses than those just discussed. These types of spatial relations can be assessed by such diverse means as asking the direction of travel from one major city to another within a person's homeland or requiring major cities of a familiar country to be located on a map. Such abilities do not appear to depend on one specific brain region and can be disrupted by both right- and left-hemisphere brain damage (e.g., A. L. Benton, Levin, & Van Allen, 1974). As with route-finding abilities, different strategies may be available to perform such tasks. A right-hemisphere strategy would be based on topographical relations, whereas a left-hemisphere strategy would rely on verbal and analytic mediation. For example, verbal reasoning would allow one to locate Nova Scotia reasonably well on a map of Canada. One could do so by knowing that Nova Scotia is located on the southern portion of Canada's Atlantic Coast, knowing that the Atlantic Ocean is off Canada's east coast, knowing that east is on the right-hand portion of maps, and knowing that north is on the upper part of maps. As another example, an individual might deduce that the direction of travel from New York to Los Angeles is west by knowing that New York is three time zones ahead of L.A.

Brain damage may affect the ability to construct a mental representation of geographical space even when basic map-reading skills are intact. For example, in one study, neurologically intact individuals and individuals with right-hemisphere lesions, were asked, with no map in front of them, to estimate the distance between each of 36 pairs of cities (this represented all possible pairings of nine major cities in the United States). From their responses, a map could be produced showing where the nine cities would have to be located given their estimates. As you can see in Figure 7.11, the estimates of patients with brain damage were farther from the actual locations of the cities than the estimates of neurologically intact individuals. These difficulties could not be attributed to a lack of knowledge about the nine cities' locations or from general difficulty in estimating distance. When given an outline map of the U.S. cities, the patients with brain damage accurately located the cities, and when asked to estimate the distance between geometric forms arranged in a similar configuration to that of the nine major cities, they did no worse than neurologically intact individuals.

Thus, the deficit appears to be specifically in their ability to use an internal representation about the geographical relations between cities to guide their

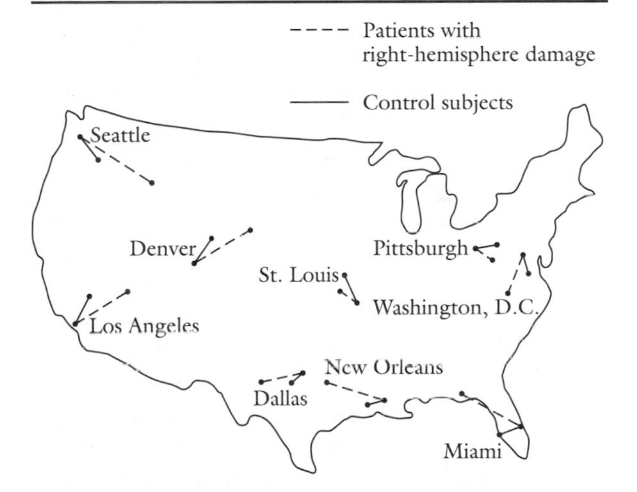

FIGURE 7.11 Difficulties in the mental representation of geographic space after brain damage. The locations of nine major U.S. cities and the locations of the same cities based on mileage estimates between each possible pair of cities (e.g., Denver and Seattle, Denver and Los Angeles, Denver and Dallas, etc.) provided by individuals with right hemisphere damage and by neurologically intact control subjects. The displacement of the cities from their actual locations is greater for individuals with right hemisphere damage (dotted lines) than for the control subjects (solid lines).

estimate of distance. Whether such deficits are limited to patients with right-hemisphere lesions is unclear from this study because a left-hemisphere control group was not tested (L. Morrow, Ratcliff, & Johnston, 1985).

In this section we reviewed the varieties of disruptions in route-finding and topographic skills that can occur as a result of brain damage. We also illustrated why these disruptions should not be considered to represent the same underlying function, as many functional dissociations can occur between the abilities to perform these different topographical tasks. These findings suggest that we use multiple frames of reference to understand our spatial world.

Body Schema

In this section we explore the inability to comprehend spatial relations among parts of one's own body, deficits that are generally conceptualized as disturbances of **body schema.** Apparently, the ability to understand the topography of the body dissociates from the ability to recognize the other topographies that we just discussed.

Probably the most well-documented disturbance of body schema that arises after brain damage is the inability to tell right from left. Traditionally, right-left confusion has been most often associated with damage to the left parietal region (e.g., McFie & Zangwill, 1960). Yet, when a spatial transformation is required to make such a discrimination, such as determining right from left on a person facing you, the ability can be disrupted by right-hemisphere damage (A. L. Benton, 1985).

Right-left disturbances have been linked to other types of disturbances in body schema, especially **finger agnosia,** which is a bilateral inability to recognize or localize one's own fingers. In the 1920s and 1930s, Gerstmann proposed that the association of finger agnosia and right-left disturbances along with *dysgraphia* (an inability to write) and *dyscalculia* (the inability to perform arithmetic) represented a specific syndrome—**Gerstmann syndrome**—that was indicative of damage to the left parietal cortex (Gerstmann, 1957). Although case reports of a pure Gerstmann syndrome (without any accompanying deficits such as aphasia) have been reported after damage to the left angular gyrus (e.g., Mazzoni et al., 1990), these four symptoms co-occur no more frequently than other signs of parietal damage (A. L. Benton, 1961). Hence, they do not appear to form a unique syndrome that is diagnostic of left parietal damage. In fact, finger agnosia seems to be associated with many types of damage, including diffuse damage and lesions in the posterior parietal, frontal, and temporal areas (A. L. Benton, 1985). When caused by a more circumscribed lesion, finger agnosia is usually associated with a left-hemisphere lesion that leads to an aphasic disorder in which a lack of language comprehension is the most prominent sign (e.g., Gainotti, Cianchetti, & Tiacci, 1972; Kinsbourne & Warrington, 1962). Thus, it is fair to say that most of the disturbances of body schema induced by left parietal lesions tend to be those associated with linguistic representations of the body.

There is another set of disturbances of body image that are associated with damage to the posterior parietal lobe of the right hemisphere (see Melzack, 1990, for a review), in this case characterized as loss of representation or as distortion of body parts. For example, individuals with hemiplegia may exhibit **anosognosia,** in which a unilateral disturbance of body schema exists because they deny, with both verbal and nonverbal behaviors, that the affected limb is paralyzed. They might claim that the hemiplegic limb is not paralyzed, and when asked to move it, make facial expressions and orient their gaze in a manner consistent with watching the limb being raised. Because this syndrome is usually observed after a stroke associated with the right middle cerebral artery, it often co-occurs with hemineglect, a syndrome in which an individual does not pay attention to the side of space contralateral to a lesion.

One might wonder whether such disorders truly represent a distortion of body schema or whether the person doesn't use or pay attention to the limb because it falls on the unattended side of space. Since case studies indicate that the syndrome can be observed in the absence of hemineglect, it appears that the right parietal region is important for representing the body's schema (Guariglia & Antonucci, 1992).

In other cases, individuals exhibit **somatoparaphrenia,** which is the loathing, non-belonging, or denial of body parts (Moss & Turnbull, 1996). Interestingly, at times this syndrome can extend to items that are commonly associated with body parts, such as rings typically worn on one hand (e.g., a wedding band). When taken off the hand, the object is recognized instantly (Aglioti, Smania, Manfredi, & Berlucchi, 1996). And in still other cases, individuals experience a sensation of having supernumerary (extra) limbs, usually of the hands or feet (Halligan, Marshall, & Wade, 1993). Also suggesting a role for right parietal regions in body schema, the feelings of a phantom limb in amputees can be suppressed by a lesion to this region (Berlucchi & Aglioti, 1997).

In some neurological disorders, most notably epilepsy, individuals have the sensation that parts of their body are either too big, known as **macrosomatagnosia,** or too small, known as **microsomatagnosia.** For example, in one case described by Williams (cited in Trimble, 1988), an 11-year-old boy had an epileptic disturbance centered in the left temporal lobe. During seizure activity, his hands would "seem too big, they were unnatural, he could not understand why they were there." Seizure activity may also make the relation of the person's body to the outside world feel distorted. Microsomatagnosia and macrosomatagnosia can occur with migraines, drug-induced psychoses, and schizophrenia. Because both epilepsy and schizophrenia have been associated with temporal lobe dysfunction (e.g., Trimble & Rogers, 1987), the temporal lobe appears to aid in creating a mental map of our bodies, especially in regard to the emotional aspects of body schema. The region of the temporal lobe most likely to be involved is the insula, as seizures in this region cause individuals to experience somatic hallucinations (Roper, Levesque, Sutherling, & Engel, 1993) (see Berlucchi and Agliotti, 1997, for a longer discussion of the neurological bases of body schema as well as changes in the brain that accompany amputation).

Spatial Memory

So far in this chapter we have centered our attention mainly on the ability to *perceive* spatial relations, which appears to depend on right parietal regions, rather than on the ability to *store* these relations in memory. Like the perception of spatial relations, memory for spatial relations relies on the right hemisphere. However, different regions are important. For short-term storage of spatial relations, the frontal lobes play a central role, whereas the right temporal lobe and especially the hippocampus play a prominent role for spatial abilities that require long-term storage of information.

Short-Term Spatial Memory

Short-term memory, or **working memory,** is the memory that allows us to hold information "online" for a brief amount of time as we perform a task. Storage in this type of memory is generally considered to be limited to about seven items, and the information dissipates quickly if not rehearsed. We were introduced to the idea of verbal short-term memory in Chapter 3 when we discussed the Digit Span subtest, in which a person hears a series of digits and then must recite them in order (similar to when you are trying to remember someone's telephone number). There exists a similar short-term memory for spatial information. One way to assess this ability is through the Corsi Block Tapping Test (B. Milner, 1971), which was designed to be a nonverbal equivalent of the Digit Span subtest. In this task, the individual sees a series of identical blocks that are spatially dispersed across a board. The sides of the blocks facing the subject have no identifying marks, whereas those facing the experimenter are numbered to aid in test administration. The experimenter taps the blocks in a specific order and the individual is required to immediately tap the blocks in the same sequence (Figure 7.12). In another version, similar to backwards verbal Digit Span, the experimenter taps the blocks in a specific order and the individual must touch the blocks in the reverse order. Patients with damage to the posterior sections of either the right or left hemisphere have difficulty with this task (e.g., DeRenzi & Nichelli, 1975), having spans of only about three items rather than the five or six exhibited by neurologically intact individuals.

The lack of clear-cut lateralization for this task may occur because individuals can use either a spatial strategy or a verbal sequential one (e.g., first block upper left, second block in the middle, etc.). Hence other researchers have devised other tasks to

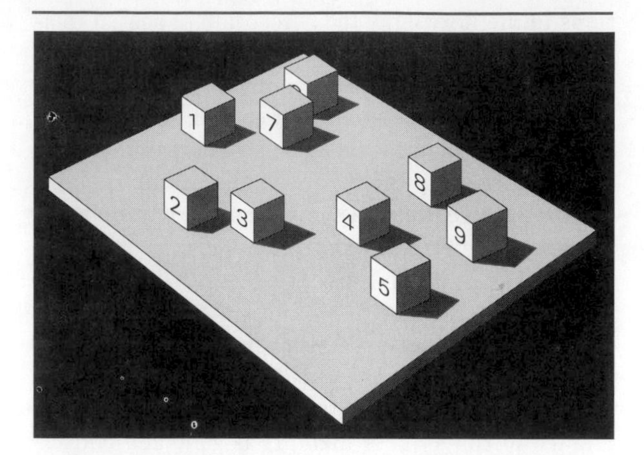

FIGURE 7.12 Corsi Block Tapping Test as seen by the experimenter. The individual being tested sees only an array of nine identical blocks. The experimenter taps a series of blocks (e.g., 4-1-3-9-2). Depending on the condition (forward or backward), the individual taps the blocks either in the identical order or in the reverse order.

determine whether verbal and spatial working memory can be clearly differentiated. Results with these tests, which place more demands on an individual to keep spatial information online simultaneously, without the sequential component inherent in the block tapping test, reveal that the right frontal region plays a prominent role in short-term visual memory. For example, in one study, individuals were given a series of patterns to remember briefly (for either 2 or 10 seconds) (Pigott & Milner, 1994). Each pattern was composed of small squares, which were randomly arranged so that half were white and half were black. After initially viewing the pattern, participants were shown it again, except this time one white box was missing, and the individual had to indicate where in the pattern the white box should be. The patterns increased in difficulty from the first pattern, which consisted of only two boxes, a single white one and a single black one, to a pattern containing 30 squares (see Figure 7.13). Whereas individuals with right frontal damage on average remembered only patterns composed of about 16 squares (Span Level 8 in Figure 7.13), neurologically intact individuals and those with right temporal lobe damage could remember patterns composed of about 22 squares (Span Level 11 in Figure 7.13).

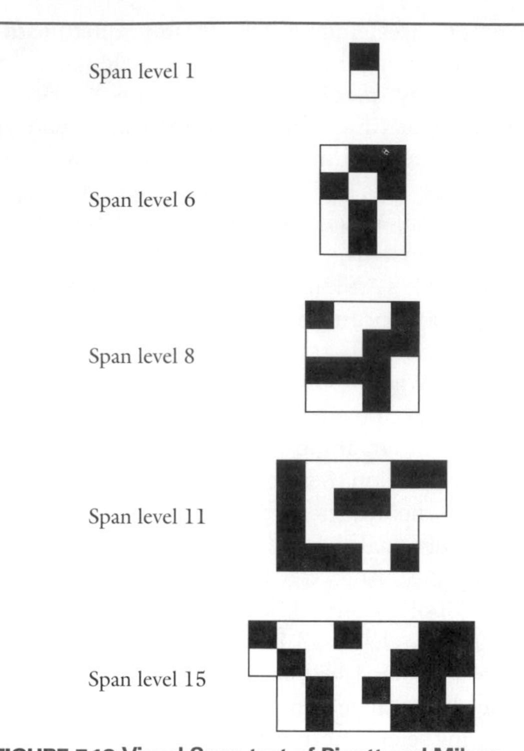

FIGURE 7.13 Visual Span test of Pigott and Milner (1994). Each individual was shown a simple pattern such as the one at Span Level 1 and was instructed to remember it. Then, after a short delay, the person was shown the same pattern except one of the small white boxes was missing. The individual was told to indicate the location where the white box should appear. After each correct response, the person was shown a more complicated pattern with two additional boxes and the process was repeated until he or she made two errors. Whereas neurologically intact individuals could remember patterns at Span Level 11 (consisting of 22 small squares), individuals with right frontal damage could remember patterns only up to Span Level 8 (consisting of 16 small squares).

Converging evidence from brain imaging studies also implicates right frontal regions as important for spatial working memory. For example, in one PET study, activation during a working-memory condition in which a spatial location had to be held online was compared with activation during a perception condition in which no memory load was imposed (see Figure 7.14). The difference in activation between the working-memory condition and the perception condition occurred most prominently

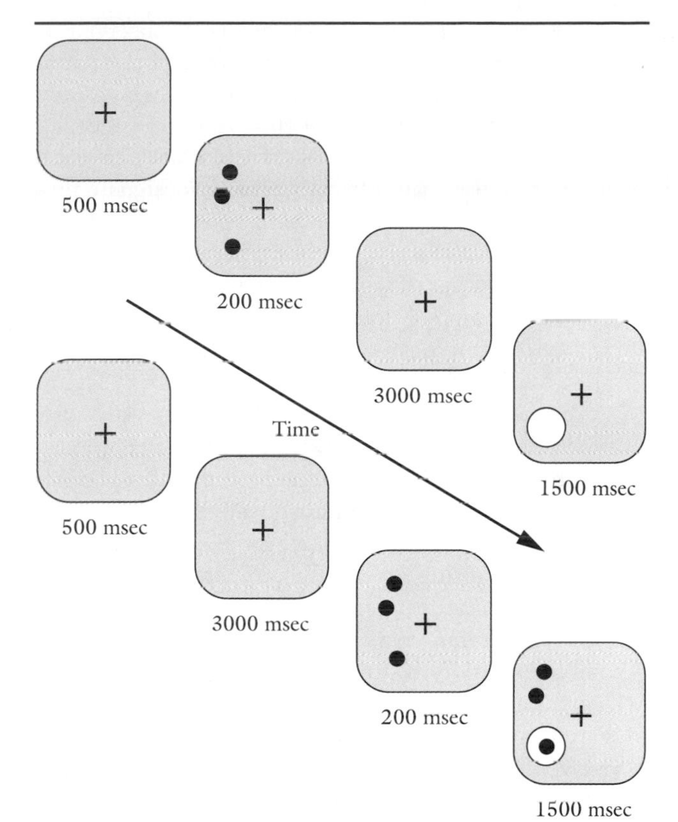

FIGURE 7.14 Task comparison used to isolate brain areas involved in working memory. In the working-memory condition (shown at top), individuals saw three dots briefly. The screen then went blank for three seconds, at which point a circle appeared. The participants had to decide if any of the previously presented dots had appeared within the circle. Hence, they had to keep in mind the position of the dots during the blank delay period. The perception condition was identical except that the circle appeared immediately after the initial presentation of the dots, and the circle and dots were presented simultaneously. As in the memory condition, individuals had to decide whether the circle surrounded the position of one of the dots. Unlike the working-memory condition, no information needed to be held in memory to accomplish the task under these conditions.

over the right frontal region, an indication that this area is important for spatial working memory (Jonides et al., 1993). In fact, using neuroimaging, a direct comparison of the brain regions activated by verbal and spatial working memory showed them to rely on different hemispheres. Right prefrontal regions tended to be active during spatial working-memory tasks but not during verbal working-memory tasks, whereas left frontal regions tended to be active during verbal working-memory tasks but not during spatial working-memory tasks (Smith, Jonides, & Koeppe, 1996; for an analysis across a variety of studies, see Smith & Jonides, 1999).

In addition to being distinct from verbal working memory, spatial working memory is distinct from working memory for objects. You should not find such a dissociation surprising, given the distinctions between the "what" and "where" systems that we discussed earlier in this chapter. Single-cell recordings in monkeys suggest that more ventral regions of dorsolateral prefrontal cortex are involved in object working memory than in spatial working memory (Wilson, O Scalaidhe, & Goldman-Rakic, 1993). Similarly, neuroimaging studies in humans suggest that tasks activating spatial working memory activate a more dorsal region of dorsolateral prefrontal cortex than those assessing object working memory (Smith & Jonides, 1999).

Long-Term Spatial Memory

Right-hemisphere damage affects a variety of long-term spatial-memory abilities, including the ability to remember spatial locations, spatial patterns of movement from one location to another, the locations of objects in space, and nonverbal spatial patterns such as nonsense designs. For the most part, these long-term spatial memory deficits are observed after damage to temporal regions rather than frontal regions, which, as we just learned, are more important for spatial working memory.

Patients with damage to right temporal regions, especially the hippocampus, have difficulty remembering the locations of positions in space. In such cases, the basic ability to perform the task remains intact, but the ability to retain such information over time is lost (Kessels, de Haan, Kappelle, & Postma, 2001). Likewise, temporal lobe damage does not interfere with the ability to retain a spatial span on the Corsi Block Tapping Test if the individual mimics the pattern immediately. However, when the delay before recall is extended to 8 or 16 seconds, or the number of items to be learned exceeds the individual's short-term span by more than two items, individuals with right-hemisphere damage exhibit a deficit (DeRenzi, Faglioni, & Previdi, 1977).

The right hippocampus is also important for remembering where in space objects are located (e.g., Smith & Milner, 1981, 1984). This effect was demonstrated in a group of individuals who underwent removal of large sections of the right hippocampus and adjacent regions. Their memory for object location was tested by viewing 16 small objects positioned on a board in an essentially random manner. Immediately after viewing the board and then 24 hours later, the patients were given a piece of paper and asked to place the objects in the same locations in which they had appeared. Compared with neurologically intact individuals, patients with right temporal lobe resection that included the hippocampus had more difficulty remembering item locations both immediately after viewing the board and 24 hours later. Such a deficit extends to more naturalistic visual scenes (as compared with the essentially random nature of the displays we just discussed). Individuals with right temporal lobe damage have difficulty remembering, after a 15-minute delay, a variety of aspects of a complex scene (e.g., a beach scene) that contains multiple objects (e.g., a person, a sandcastle, a pail and shovel, a beach towel, a motorboat, a sailboat, a sea gull). The patients could not detect when an object's position within the scene had been moved laterally or when an object had been removed from the scene. Furthermore, if the damage impinged on the hippocampus, they were unable to detect changes in a scene when the locations of two objects were switched (Pigott & Milner, 1993).

It should be noted that the ability to remember the objects themselves is unimpaired by such damage. This finding is consistent with the idea of a dissociation being the "what" and "where" portions of the visual system. Furthermore, the ability to remember the location of a point in space is independent from the ability to link specific objects to those locations. Although both are disrupted by damage to posterior sections of the right hemisphere, a double dissociation has been observed in patients: Some patients cannot remember spatial locations when given an empty frame on which they must mark locations, but if the locations are designated, they can place the correct object in each location. Other patients can correctly designate previously viewed locations within an empty grid, but cannot associate a given object with a given location (Kessels, Postma, Kappelle, & de Haan, 2000).

Right temporal lobe damage also disrupts the ability to remember complex spatial patterns, such as nonverbal nonsense designs (refer back to Figure 7.5). As we discussed earlier in this chapter, this task places special demands on spatial processing because the nonsense designs cannot be remembered with reference to spatial schemata already stored in memory, such as can be invoked for common objects. Deficits resulting from right temporal lobe damage result in difficulty remembering nonsense figures when there is a delay between initial presentation and the memory test. Damage to right hippocampal regions causes difficulty in recognizing the entire pattern of a large nonsense figure that was initially viewed piece by piece and then built into a whole (Jones-Gotman, 1986a) and compromises the ability to learn a list of abstract designs (Jones-Gotman, 1986b). Thus, all these findings implicate right temporal/hippocampal regions in long-term spatial memory.

Topographical Memory

Topographical memory is the spatial memory that enables an individual to store information about his or her way around a new environment and to remember routes through familiar places. Research with brain-damaged individuals and neuroimaging with neurologically intact individuals has provided insights into the brain mechanisms underlying such abilities. First, we discuss the findings from brain-damaged patients and then those from neuroimaging.

Topographical disorientation is a disorder resulting from brain damage that compromises the ability to remember routes around the environment, while sparing short-term and long-term spatial memory as well as the ability to recognize buildings and landmarks. These topographical abilities are distinct from geographical knowledge, as some individuals with topographical disorientation can nonetheless identify countries from outline maps, and name cities within a country when their location on a map is identified by a dot (Incisa della Rocchetta, Cipolotti, & Warrington, 1996). We know that this topographical disorientation does not result from a general problem in route-finding abilities, because these patients can learn the stylus maze within normal limits (e.g., Habib & Sirigu, 1987).

In some cases of topographical disorientation, the difficulty arises only in environments encountered since the brain trauma. Such individuals may have great difficulty negotiating the corridors of the ward in the hospital but few difficulties negotiating around their own house. Likewise, they may be able to traverse familiar paths through their hometown but have difficulty navigating new routes through the same town. In other cases, the ability to find their way in both old and new environments is lost (e.g., Habib & Sirigu, 1987). The underlying problem that these individuals have is unclear. One suggestion is that their damage prevents them from linking the sensory information about the relations of points in the environment with information in memory (much the way a person with agnosia cannot link sensory information about objects with information in memory) (e.g., Landis, Cummings, Benson, & Palmer, 1986). Another suggestion is that these individuals have a highly specific amnesia in which a personal route through space cannot be remembered (e.g., Habib & Sirigu, 1987). The location of the lesion that typically causes such a syndrome—the medial temporal region of the right hemisphere, including almost all of the lingual and parahippocampal gyri that border the occipital lobe—is consistent with either an impairment to memory itself or the linkage of information to memory.

Findings from neuroimaging studies converge to suggest an important role for right medial temporal and hippocampal regions in such skills. In studies such as these, a comparison is made between a condition that is thought to involve topographical memory and one that provides similar sensory input but has no memory demands. In one study, the condition designed to tax topographical memory required participants to view a film of what a person would see as he or she were navigating a path through an urban area. This condition enabled the participant to construct a mental spatial map of the environment. The baseline condition to which this was compared was one in which participants viewed a similar urban scene, but from a stationary perspective, with cars, people, and other objects moving in and out of the field of view. Overall sensory demands in this baseline condition were similar to those of the topographical-memory condition, but the baseline condition did not allow participants to build a mental map of the area. The regions that exhibited more activation in the topographical memory condition than the baseline were medial parietal regions, the parahippocampal cortex, and hippocampus in the right hemisphere (Maguire et al., 1996) (see Color insert 7.2). Similar activation of parahippocampal regions has been obtained with fMRI that examined activation as a person learned to maneuver around a "virtual," or simulated, environment (Aquirre et al., 1996).

The right hippocampus is involved not only when individuals are learning routes but also when they are recalling them. Showing the degree to which a carefully selected participant population can be very helpful in answering scientific questions, Maguire and colleagues (1997a) recruited taxi drivers in London to study topographical memory. These individuals made ideal participants because official London taxi drivers are experts at knowing the topography of the city: they must train for approximately three years and pass a stringent test to obtain their license. Compared to when they just had to remember landmarks, the taxi drivers exhibited significantly more activation of the right hippocampus when asked to remember specific routes (see Maguire, 1997b, for a nice overview of this issue).

 Attentional Disturbances in Spatial Processing

Our discussion heretofore has centered on the inability to process spatial material because of difficulties either in constructing a spatial map of the world or in comprehending the spatial relationships among parts of items or locations in space. But in a variety of syndromes, spatial processing is disrupted not so much because the relationships among items cannot be comprehended, but because of difficulties in directing attention to a particular spatial location. In everyday life, we often direct our attention to a particular sector of space, such as when we go to the airport to pick up a friend and direct our attention to the area around a specific gate while ignoring the activity and people at other locations. When attention cannot be allocated to certain regions of space, the ability to process spatial relations in that region suffers. The two main syndromes in which attentional problems interfere with spatial processing are Balint's syndrome and hemineglect.

Balint's Syndrome

Balint's syndrome has three major characteristics: **optic ataxia,** which is the inability to point to a target under visual guidance; **ocular apraxia,** which is the inability to voluntarily shift gaze toward a new visual stimulus; and **simultanagnosia,** which is the inability to perceive different pieces of information in the visual field simultaneously because the person cannot direct attention to more than one small location in the visual world at a time (A. R. Damasio, 1985). The last component defines this syndrome as a disruption of spatial attention rather than a disruption of spatial processing.

Individuals with Balint's syndrome often appear as if they are blind for all but the most limited area in the visual world. For example, if a doctor holds a pencil at arm's length in front of the face of a person with Balint's syndrome, the pencil is recognized but not the doctor's face or any other object in the room. These individuals do not have cortical blindness because they can view objects anywhere in their visual field, but only one at a time. A case of Balint's syndrome observed by Godwin-Austen (1965) and discussed in Farah (1990) illustrates this phenomenon well. The individual was asked to describe a drawing similar to that shown in Figure 7.15. She described the pieces one after the other, first mentioning the helmet, then the handlebars, and finally the car. Only after quite a bit of time did she infer that the girl was waving to flag down the car, but she never really understood why, because she never noticed that the front tire was disconnected from the bicycle. She could never "see" the whole picture but could comprehend only parts at a time. Subjectively, individuals with this syndrome report that one object in the world comes into focus while all the others fade. Additionally, such patients have little control over what is in focus and when that focus switches.

FIGURE 7.15 A picture used to reveal simultanagnosia, an inability to direct attention to more than one part of the visual world at a time. When asked to describe this picture, an individual with this syndrome could describe the handlebars, the car, and the helmet but could not perceive why the girl was trying to flag down the car.

The incidence of Balint's syndrome is relatively low because the causative lesion is rare. The syndrome is typically observed after a **watershed lesion,** which is caused by lack of oxygen to brain regions especially susceptible to oxygen deprivation since they fall between the main "watershed" areas of the arterial blood supply. The lesion that causes Balint's syndrome falls in a watershed region between the supply of the posterior and middle cerebral arteries and often occurs after a sudden and severe drop in systemic blood pressure. In almost all cases of Balint's syndrome, a bilateral lesion can be found in the dorsal occipitoparietal region (A. R. Damasio, 1985). Because of the dorsal location of the lesion and the individual's inability to pay attention to more than one location in space simultaneously, Balint's syndrome is sometimes known as **dorsal simultanagnosia** (Farah, 1990).

Hemineglect

As we discuss in more detail in the next chapter, damage to parietal regions is associated with hemineglect. Studies of patients with hemineglect are important for the purposes of the present discussion because they have revealed that what constitutes a "side" of space can be influenced by different spatial frameworks. For example, we can map the world not only by a spatial framework with regard to the body, but also by a spatial framework with regard to the head. When you are standing and looking straight ahead, these spatial frameworks coincide, but tilt your head or lie on one side and these spatial frameworks dissociate. The distinction between these spatial frameworks is revealed by patients with hemineglect, as what they ignore is influenced not only by what is to the left of body midline, but also by what is to the left of the midline of the head (e.g., Ladavas, 1987).

In summary, both Balint's syndrome and hemineglect reveal that when attention cannot be directed to particular regions of space, the ability to comprehend spatial relations in that region is disrupted as well.

Role of the Left Hemisphere in Spatial Processing

For most of this chapter, we have emphasized the predominant role of the right hemisphere in visuospatial processing. However, there were various occasions on which we noted deficits in spatial processing appearing after left-hemisphere damage as well. We argued these deficits arose because those spatial tasks were being performed by strategies that rely on the left hemisphere. One way to uncover the nature of such strategies is to examine the compensatory mechanisms invoked by individuals with right-hemisphere damage when they must perform visuospatial tasks. An illustrative example is provided by a young woman who wanted to become an architect even though she had sustained right-hemisphere damage and in whom researchers assessed many of the visuospatial functions that we discuss in this chapter (Clarke, Assal, & DeTribolet, 1993).

For several of the tasks given her, this woman used a piecemeal strategy in which spatial relations were computed on a point-by-point basis rather than in a holistic manner. For example, when copying the Rey-Osterrieth figure (see Figure 7.8A), she did not perceive its overall rectangular form (which probably jumps out at you), but rather copied the figure, small piece by small piece. Although she did manage to include all the basic elements of the figure, she misplaced half of them relative to one another and added extraneous details. Her piecemeal strategy was also evident in the house plans that she drew for her architecture classes. If she had to change the scale of the plan, she would misplace the subparts in relation to one another, although she could meticulously reproportion all the subparts to the correct size. Moreover, she used a feature-by-feature approach when trying to recognize pictures of European towns or villages in her native Switzerland. She managed to recognize many towns by some distinctive feature, such as a castle or a riverside. However, such a strategy led her to mistake towns with similar features for one another because she could not take into account the spatial composition of those features (e.g., a castle with a central tower that sits high above a lake vs. a castle with a side tower situated at a lakeside). Because her sense of the direction from point to point was impaired, sometimes off by more than 45 degrees, her method of remembering a route through an unknown town was to use a verbal point-by-point strategy. In all cases, her compensatory strategies seemed to be verbally mediated, detailed, and linear, in which the relations among different locations in space were processed in a point-to-point manner.

Exactly how does the left hemisphere contribute to spatial processing? Some researchers have suggested that the left hemisphere plays a larger role when distracting or extraneous information is included in the spatial array, when complex spatial processing is required to perform a task (as opposed to just a single basic process such as detecting the orientation of a line), and when Euclidean geometric

HOW THE NEUROPSYCHOLOGY OF SPATIAL ABILITIES INFLUENCES AVIATION

Although successful piloting requires a multiplicity of skills, including the ability to divide attention and the ability to prioritize tasks, spatial abilities are undoubtedly critical. Unlike earthbound mortals in cars, pilots must navigate in three, not two, dimensions and under conditions in which their major landmarks, the earth and the horizon, may sometimes be obscured from view. Neuropsychological evidence suggests that certain types of spatial processes are distinct from one another and may rely on distinct neural subsystems. The dissociations among spatial processes provided by neuropsychological research may have implications for the design of aircraft and for the type of spatial skills required for competent piloting. We now look in more detail at how two specific issues—the dissociation between different frames of reference and the distinction between categorical and coordinate processes—may be relevant to aviation.

As we discussed, neuropsychological evidence suggests that processing information with regard to a personal frame of reference is distinct from processing it with regard to positions in extrapersonal space. To the degree that these systems are separate, they may involve fundamentally distinct cognitive operations that are not very compatible. In fact, displays used by pilots tend to provide either a personal frame of reference or an extrapersonal frame of reference, but not both. One system, known as track-up alignment, provides a view of the world that is aligned perfectly with the world outside the cockpit window: What is straight ahead of the window is straight ahead on the map. As the plane turns, the alignment of the display turns with it so that the pilot has an egocentric, or personal, frame of reference (Box Figure 7.1A). The other system, known as north-up alignment, provides a map of the world that remains static; north is always straight ahead regardless of the direction in which the plane is moving. This map provides an earth-based, or extrapersonal, frame of reference (Box Figure 7.1B).

The advantage of the track-up map is the direct mapping between locations on the display and locations outside the cockpit window. Its disadvantage is that it hinders a pilot's ability to build a static mental map of the world because the display constantly changes. In contrast, the north-up map, which provides an earth-centered frame of reference, aids in composing a cognitive map, but it requires the pilot to mentally rotate either the display or the view outside the cockpit so that both are aligned, an operation that takes time (Aretz, 1991; Aretz & Wickens, 1992).

Psychologists interested in cockpit design have attempted to invent new displays that will maximize the benefits of each system while reducing their costs (e.g., Aretz, 1991) or to determine which type of map is most advantageous under specific conditions. For example, aircraft such as helicopters that are flown close to the ground may be best guided by track-up maps so that the map is continuously aligned with terrain, whereas aircraft flown at higher altitudes may be best guided by north-up maps (e.g., Harwood & Wickens, 1991).

As we also learned, neuropsychological evidence suggests that processing spatial relations in a categorical manner is distinct from processing them in a metric manner. It is specifically metric spatial relations, such as judgments about the distance between spatial locations, at which pilots excel compared to non-pilots. In contrast, they are no better than non-pilots at processing coordinate spatial relations, such as knowing whether one location is above or below another. Pilots have also been found to be superior at mental rotation, a skill required to use a north-up display effectively. As we discussed earlier in the chapter, these two types of spatial abilities, metric spatial processing and mental rotation, appear to place particular demands on right-hemisphere processing (see Dror, Kosslyn, & Waag, 1993, for a discussion of the spatial skills at which pilots excel and their neural bases). Thus, some test batteries designed to screen aviators for neuropsychological dysfunction due to disease or substance abuse are heavily weighted toward testing the spatial processes that rely on the right hemisphere (e.g., Banich, Stokes, & Elledge, 1989; Stokes, Banich, & Elledge, 1991). ■

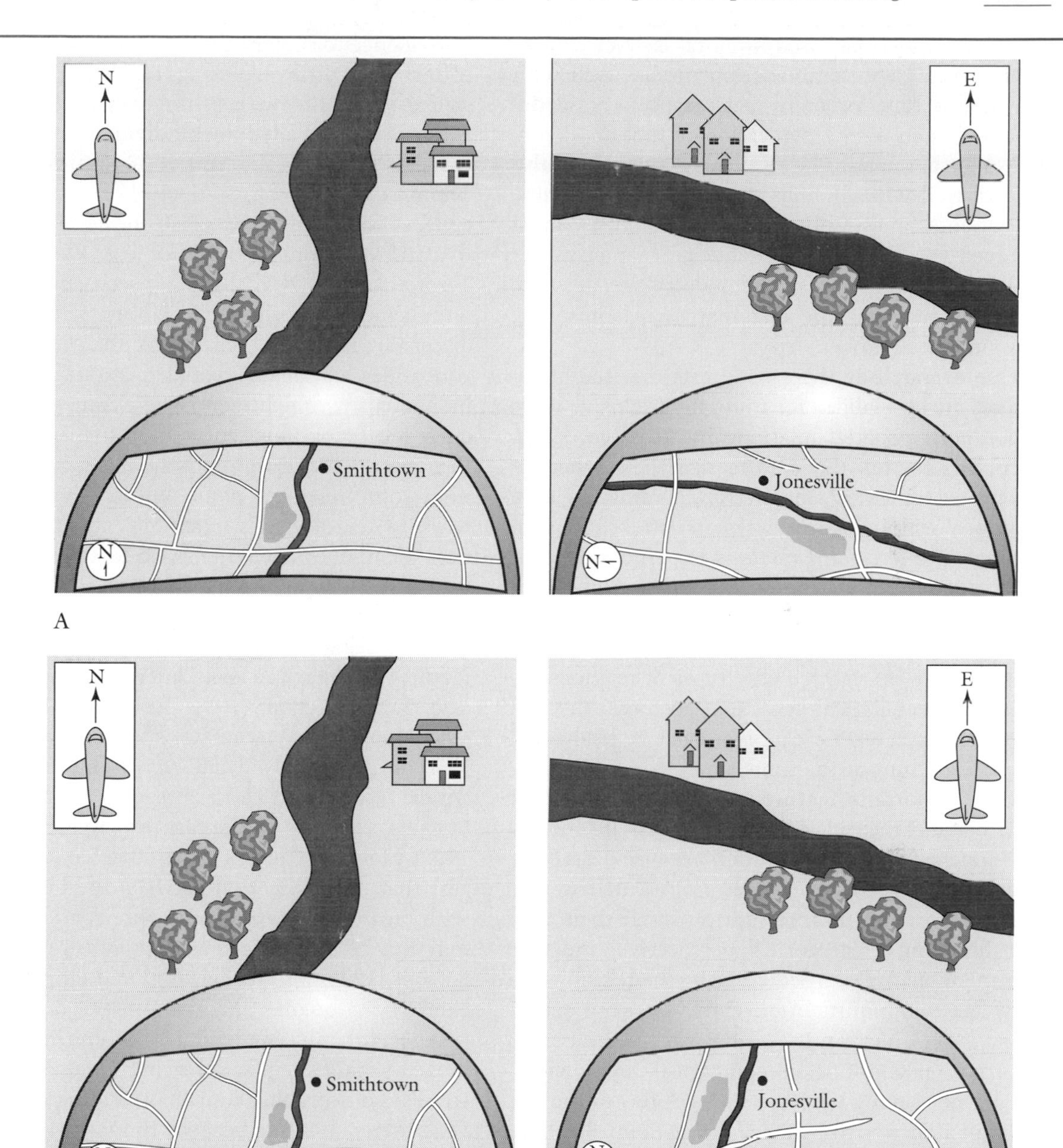

BOX FIGURE 7.1 Two navigational systems that rely on different frames of reference. (A) An example of track-up alignment: what is outside the cockpit window corresponds directly with the map. (B) An example of north-up alignment: the map always provides a constant view of the space; therefore, the pilot must mentally rotate it to align it with the view outside the cockpit window. In both A and B the letter above the plane icon indicates the direction in which the plane is heading. The letter in the circle indicates the direction of north on the pilot's display.

principles must be used (Mehta & Newcombe, 1991). Such a conceptualization meshes well with the finding that for many basic aspects of spatial function, such as the perception of motion, depth, and so forth, the right hemisphere is superior. It also meshes well with findings that the left hemisphere of patients with split-brain syndrome is most involved in performing Euclidean geometry. Yet such a description does not provide an overall rubric for conceptualizing the role that each hemisphere plays in spatial processing.

One overarching theory suggests that the hemispheres are specialized for mutually exclusive ways of computing spatial relationships (Kosslyn, 1987). According to this theory, the right hemisphere is specialized for computing **metric (coordinate) spatial relations,** or the distance between two locations. In contrast, the left hemisphere is hypothesized to be especially skillful at determining **categorical spatial relations,** or the position of one location relative to another (e.g., above vs. below, top vs. bottom, front vs. back, left vs. right). These types of relations are considered categorical because a position must fall into a single category (e.g., you can't be below and above something at the same time).

One important feature of this model is that metric and categorical spatial relations are considered independent of each other, because describing relations between two points from a metric perspective provides no information about their relationship from a categorical perspective, and vice versa. For example, if we describe the relationship between two points metrically, by saying that Point A is 3 feet from Point B, we are giving no information about their categorical relationship. We are not saying whether Point A lies to the left of Point B or whether it lies above Point B. These two processes appear to be somewhat mutually exclusive as computational models indicate that these processes can be carried out better by two distinct subsystems than one (see Kosslyn, Chabris, Marsolek, & Koenig, 1992, for an initial computer simulation of the computational advantages of two distinct subsystems and Baker, Chabris, & Kosslyn, 1999, for a follow-up). As such, it would make sense that they are performed by distinct hemispheres.

Evidence to support the distinction between categorical and metric processing comes from a variety of sources: patients with brain damage (e.g., Laeng, 1994), neurologically intact individuals (e.g., Kosslyn et al., 1989), brain imaging studies (Kosslyn, Thompson, Gitelman, & Alpert, 1998), and studies of epilepsy patients who have had one hemisphere deactivated by sodium amobarbitol (e.g., Slotnick, Moo, Tesoro, & Hart, 2001). As we discussed, individuals with left-hemisphere damage often have difficulty discerning right from left, a task that involves categorical descriptions of spatial relations. In contrast, individuals with right-hemisphere damage have difficulty localizing items in space, which implies that they are unable to compute the distance of an item from some reference point within a spatial framework. In neurologically intact subjects, divided visual field techniques have been used to assess responses to the same type of spatial stimuli, but under two separate conditions, one that requires a judgment about categorical spatial relations and one that requires a judgment about metric spatial relations (e.g., Kosslyn et al., 1989; Hellige & Michimata, 1989) (see Figure 7.16 for two such examples).

Typically, a RVF advantage is found for the categorical task, and a LVF advantage for the metric task. But this is not always the case (e.g., Rybash & Hoyer, 1992). Nonconfirming studies have led some to suggest that the distinction between the hemispheres, with regard to how they compute spatial relations, may not be as clear-cut as originally proposed (see Sergent, 1991, for a conceptual and empirical criticism of the original theory). Yet, the discrepancies may result because individuals become highly familiarized with a small set of stimuli and change their strategy during the course of testing (Banich & Federmeier, 1999) or because the tasks are not adequately demanding (Slotnick, Moo, Tesoro, & Hart, 2001). The results from brain-imaging studies and research on patients with lesions suggest that parietal regions form the neural substrate for the distinction between metric and categorical spatial relations (e.g., Kosslyn, Thompson, Gitelman, & Alpert, 1998; Laeng, 1994).

Before we leave our discussion of categorical and metric spatial relations, one fact worth mentioning is that knowledge about categorical spatial relations

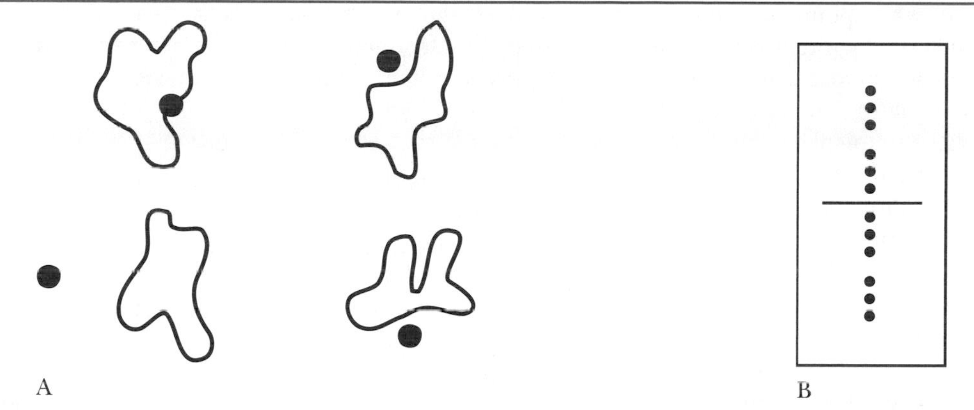

FIGURE 7.16 Examples of stimuli used in divided visual field studies to investigate the difference between categorical and metric spatial relations. (A) Each of these four stimuli was shown individually. In the categorical task, an individual was asked to decide whether the dot was on or off the blob. In the metric task, the person was asked to decide whether the dot was near or far from the blob. (B) In this task, the bar and one dot were shown in each trial. The figure depicts the 12 possible locations of dots. In the categorical task, subjects decided whether the dot was above or below the bar. In the metric task, they decided whether the line was near (within 0.79 in., or 2 cm) or far away (farther than 0.79 in., or 2 cm) from the dot. Generally for both tasks, an RVF advantage is observed in the categorical task and an LVF advantage for the metric task.

may be particularly important for object recognition. As we discussed in Chapter 6, objects must be recognized across various orientations and positions. Generally, the categorical relations among the parts of an item are invariant regardless of how and where the object is positioned in space. For example, we need to recognize a cat as the same object regardless of whether it is sitting curled up on the windowsill or scampering across the floor after a mouse. In both cases, the cat's ears are *above* its whiskers. These invariants in categorical relations may aid in the ability to recognize an object across a variety of transformations (Kosslyn, 1987).

The "Where" Dorsal Visual System for Spatial Processing

- The perception of spatial relations depends heavily on the parietal lobe, which is part of the dorsal, or "where," visual system.
- Single-cell recordings indicate that cells in the parietal region are sensitive to information over a wide expanse of the visual field (especially those outside the fovea), are sensitive to a combination of eye and head position, and are sensitive to motion in the range of speeds at which animals locomote—all of which make them well suited for processing spatial relations and constructing a map of external space.
- Monkeys with lesions to the parietal area cannot make decisions about the relative positions of items in space but can recognize objects.

Basic Spatial Processes in Humans

- The ability to localize a point in space relies on superior regions of the right parietal lobe.

SUMMARY

- Depth perception, when point-by-point cues are used, can be disrupted by either right or left hemisphere lesions, whereas depth computed across an entire visual image, is disrupted by damage to the right hemisphere.
- Judgment of line orientation relies on right hemisphere extrastriate areas, at least for those orientations that cannot be easily verbally labeled.
- Studies with split-brain patients and divided visual field studies with neurologically intact individuals indicate that the right hemisphere is better at perceiving geometric relations.
- Studies of brain-damaged patients and neuroimaging studies indicate that a very specific region of the brain, area MT (V5) at the juncture of the parietal and temporal lobes, is critically important for perceiving motion.
- Neuroimaging studies suggest that perceiving rotation is dependent on the superior parietal lobule.

Constructional Abilities
- Constructional abilities, which are those required to make the correct motor movements to manipulate items into a particular spatial relation, are generally disrupted by right-hemisphere damage.

Route-Finding and Topographical Skills
- Disruptions in route-finding abilities can take many forms: individuals may not be able to perform simple maze tasks, may be unable to use a map to follow a route around a room, may lose the ability to follow a route through a city, or may lose the ability to comprehend the relation between two landmarks.
- Although compromised by right-hemisphere damage, route-finding and topographical skills are sometimes affected by left-hemisphere damage, especially in cases when verbal strategies can be used to perform the function.

Body Schema
- Disturbances in understanding the relationship between body parts are typically caused by left-hemisphere lesions. In contrast, distortions in body schema that make body parts seem especially large or small or non-existent usually involve right-hemisphere damage.

Spatial Memory
- Right frontal regions play a prominent role in short-term, or working, spatial memory, which is the ability to store spatial information for relatively brief periods of time.
- Right temporal regions are important for retaining spatial information during the course of minutes, hours, or days.
- Topographical memory, which involves remembering spatial information that allows one to negotiate or navigate a route from one point to another, relies on the right temporal lobe and hippocampus, except when sequencing turns and "talking" through the route is important, at which point left-hemisphere mechanisms become more important.

Attentional Disturbances in Spatial Processing
- In Balint's syndrome, the individual has difficulty processing spatial relations because attention can be directed to only a single position in space.
- In hemineglect, the individual has difficulty processing spatial relations because information on one side of space is ignored.
- Studies of patients with hemineglect provide converging evidence that we map our spatial world according to multiple spatial frameworks (e.g., a head-centered framework, a body-centered framework).

Role of the Left Hemisphere in Spatial Processing
- When the left hemisphere processes spatial relations, it tends to use a verbal point-to-point strategy.
- The left hemisphere is specialized for determining categorical spatial relations, in which the relationship of two points is described according to categories of locations (above vs. below, to the left vs. to the right), whereas the right hemisphere is specialized for computing metric (coordinate) spatial relations, which specifies the distance between two points.

KEY TERMS

anosognosia 238
Balint's syndrome 244
binocular disparity 228
body schema 238
categorical spatial relations 248
constructional praxis 233
dorsal simultanagnosia 245
finger agnosia 238
Gerstmann syndrome 238
macrosomatagnosia 239
metric (coordinate) spatial relations 248
microsomatagnosia 239
ocular apraxia 244
optic ataxia 244
simultanagnosia 244
somatoparaphrenia 239
stereopsis 228
topographical disorientation 242
topographical memory 242
watershed lesion 244
working memory 239

CHAPTER 8

ATTENTION

What Is "Attention"?
Brain Structures Involved in Attention
- Reticular Activating System
- Superior Colliculus
- Thalamus
- Parietal Lobe
- Anterior Cingulate Cortex
- Frontal Lobe

The Time Course of Attentional Selection
Selection by Spatial Location, Objects, and Features
Models of Attentional Control by a Cortical Network
- Component Processes by Discrete Brain Areas
- Distributed Network Models
- Computationally Influenced Models

Hemineglect: Clinical Aspects
- Clinical Features
- Theories Regarding the Underlying Deficit
- Treatment

Hemineglect: Implications for Understanding Brain-Behavior Relationships
- Multiple Spatial Frames of Reference
- Space-Based vs. Object-Based Attention
- *[Neuropsychological Bases of Consciousness]*
- Hemispheric Differences in Attentional Control
- Processing of Unattended Stimuli

As he did every morning after waking, Bill went into the bathroom to begin his morning ritual. After squeezing toothpaste onto his toothbrush, he looked into the mirror and began to brush his teeth. Although he brushed the teeth on the right side of his mouth quite vigorously, for the most part he ignored those on the left side. Then he stepped into the shower and began rubbing a bar of soap to produce a frothy lather. After generously distributing the suds over the right side of his body, he began to rinse off without lathering the left side of his body.

After getting dressed, Bill went to his favorite local diner for breakfast. He ordered the daily special of two eggs, toast, bacon, and hash browns; the last two items were his favorites. When his order arrived, the waitress placed the plate in front of him with the fried eggs and the toast toward the right, and the bacon and hash browns to the left. He took one bite each of bacon and of hash browns, and then turned to the eggs and toast. Strangely, once he started eating the eggs and toast, he never took another bite of hash browns or bacon. While Bill was sipping his coffee, a busboy, walking to the kitchen off to Bill's left, dropped a stack of dirty dishes, creating a commotion. Bill, like everyone else in the diner, watched the rattled busboy clean up the mess. Afterward, Bill resumed eating his breakfast and now heartily consumed the hash browns and bacon he had previously ignored.

When Bill asked for the check, the waitress placed it on the left side of the table. After a few minutes, he waved the waitress over and complained, saying, "I asked for my tab five minutes ago. What is taking so long?"

She looked at him quizzically, pointed to the bill on the table, and replied, "But sir, it's right here. I put it there a while ago."

"It's not such a great idea to hide the bill from the customer," he replied. With that, Bill rose to leave, and the waitress, still bemused by the whole encounter, watched him bump into the left-hand part of the door frame as he walked out into the street. As she turned to clean the table, she saw that Bill had left a generous tip. Shrugging, she said softly to herself, "I guess the customer is always right." ■

THE SEEMINGLY BIZARRE behavior that the gentleman in this story displayed can be attributed to a syndrome known as **hemineglect,** or **hemi-inattention.** Despite having intact sensory and motor functioning, individuals with hemineglect ignore, or do not pay attention to, one side of space. Hemineglect is mainly considered a space-based phenomenon because the neglect of information occurs with reference to a spatial frame (i.e., information contralateral to the lesion is ignored) and because all types of information, regardless of modality, are ignored on the neglected side of space. Given what you learned in the last chapter about the important role that the parietal lobe plays in spatial processes, it should not surprise you that hemineglect is typically observed after a parietal lobe lesion.

Because attention is a multifaceted process that has been conceptualized in different ways, we begin the chapter by briefly discussing what attention is and how it influences behavior. Next, we identify and discuss the multiplicity of brain structures that play a role in attention. Unlike the other mental abilities we have discussed so far in this book, attention is controlled by a large and distributed network of brain structures. Then we discuss both the time frame and the manner in which attentional control is exerted. The latter half of the chapter is a detailed discussion of hemineglect. This syndrome has received much attention (no pun intended) not only because the pattern of deficits is so bizarre and intriguing, but also because it can provide much insight into how the brain is wired to help us to pay attention.

What Is "Attention"?

Attention is a concept often invoked by psychologists, but one that does not have a standard, universally accepted definition. Nonetheless, most psychologists agree that the brain has inherent limitations to the amount of information it can process at any one time. Therefore, it can function effectively only if there is a means to select specific information for further processing. This selective process is known as **attention.** In discussing attention, cognitive psychologists often divide it into four general categories: alertness and arousal, vigilance, (sustained attention), selective attention, and resources (capacity) (see D. L. LaBerge, 1990, for a short review of the different varieties of attention and some of the major theoretical debates). We will now briefly discuss each of these four categories.

Alertness and arousal represent the most basic levels of attention; without them a person is unable to extract information from the environment or to select a particular response. Our alertness and arousal are low when we are tired or sleepy, which is why at these times you may miss important information or have trouble choosing the correct action. In some extreme cases, such as a coma, alertness and arousal are so disrupted that the person is almost totally unresponsive to the outside world and has no control over his or her responses.

Another general category of attention is **vigilance,** which is also known as *sustained attention.* Vigilance is the ability to maintain alertness continuously over time. In common parlance, we often say that someone has a "short attention span" when he or she cannot maintain attention for long periods. Vigilance is important when a task must be performed in a nonstop manner—when "tuning in" and "tuning out" would be deleterious. Your ability to sustain attention is especially challenged whenever you try to listen to every word of a lecture for an entire class period. (And if the lecturer is particularly boring, your ability to remain alert and aroused may be taxed as well!).

A third general category of attention is **selective attention,** which involves the selection of information essential to a task. This selection process can be performed on incoming sensory information, on information that we are keeping "in mind," or on the set of possible responses. For example, as you read this page and try to understand what is written on it, you cannot simultaneously listen to a song on the radio and monitor the movements of people around you. Selective attention is the cognitive mechanism that allows you to select—from all the possibilities before you—the words on the page and the task of comprehension as the most salient aspects of processing that need to be accomplished at this time.

A fourth way in which attention has been conceptualized is as the **resource,** or effort, that is required to process information. Originally, these resources were conceptualized to be undifferentiated; that is, they were assumed to be the same. When either multiple tasks or a multifaceted task had to be performed, these resources would be doled out for different component processes until none were left (e.g., Kahneman, 1973). Picture a stack of U.S. dollar bills. You can use some of them to buy breakfast, another to buy a newspaper, some more to buy a bus ticket. It doesn't matter which particular bills you use for any of these purchases. However, **multiple-resource theory** suggests that a limited set of distinct resource pools may exist, each of which can be applied to only certain types of processes, much as only U.S. dollars can be spent in the United States, only Euros can be spent in Europe, and only yen can be spent in Japan. For example, spatial and verbal processes appear to rely on different resources, as do auditory and visual processes.

The brain's processing capacity is larger when tasks draw from different resource pools than from the same one (e.g., C. D. Wickens, 1980). Thus, it is easier to perform an auditory and a visual task simultaneously than it is to perform two visual tasks at the same time. We now turn our attention to what cognitive neuroscience can tell us about these different aspects of attention.

Brain Structures Involved in Attention

Attention relies on complex interaction among many neural areas (e.g., D. L. LaBerge, 1990; Mesulam, 1981; Posner & Petersen, 1990). The six main brain areas that are conceptualized as forming the neural network controlling attention are depicted in Figure 8.1. These areas, distributed throughout the central nervous system, are (1) the reticular activating system, whose cell bodies are located in the brain stem; (2) the superior colliculus, located in the midbrain; (3) the thalamus, which is a subcortical structure; and, in the cortex, the (4) parietal lobe, (5) anterior cingulate cortex, and (6) frontal lobe. The nature of attentional control

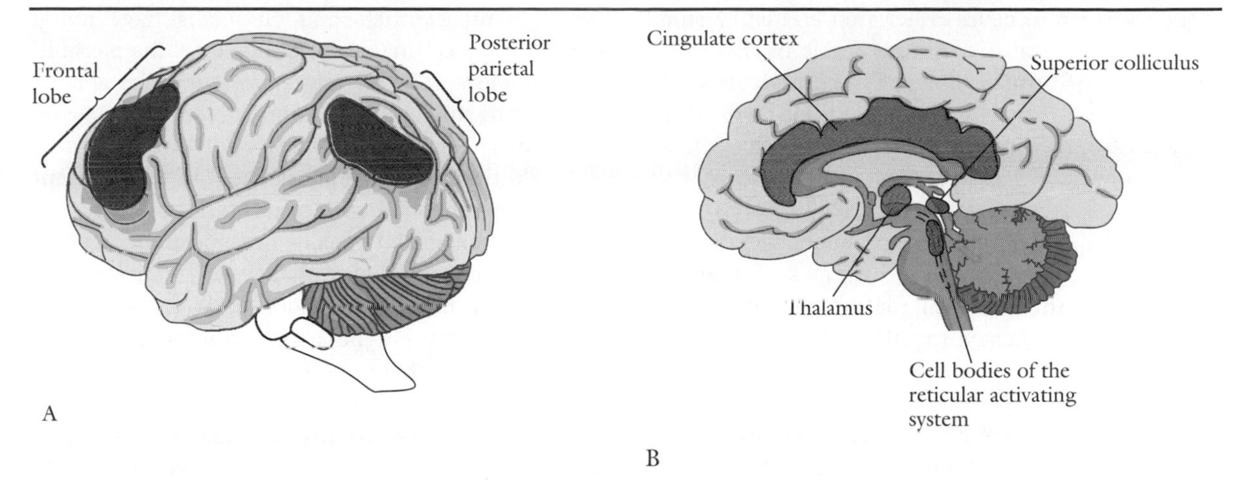

FIGURE 8.1 The six major components of the neural system responsible for controlling attention. These six components are the reticular activating system, the superior colliculus, the pulvinar of the thalamus, the cingulate cortex, the posterior parietal lobe, and the frontal lobe. (A) Left hemisphere lateral view. (B) Midsagittal view of the right hemisphere.

exerted by these areas varies from the basic, as in the case of the reticular activating system, to the much more sophisticated, as in the case of parietal and frontal regions.

Although attention is controlled by a network of interacting brain structures with overlapping functions, each brain region plays a somewhat more prominent role in certain attentional functions than in others. We outline each of these prominent roles next.

Reticular Activating System

At the most basic level, the ability to pay attention requires the nervous system to be receptive to stimulation. The brain system responsible for the alerting and arousal aspects of attention is the **reticular activating system (RAS).** Not surprisingly, this system is also responsible for controlling sleep-wake cycles. The cell bodies of the RAS are located in the brain stem and have diffuse connections to most regions of the cortex (Figure 8.2), which allows it to modulate the arousal and alertness of the entire brain. To the degree that this system keeps the brain in a constant attentive state (also known as tonic arousal), it contributes to sustained attention.

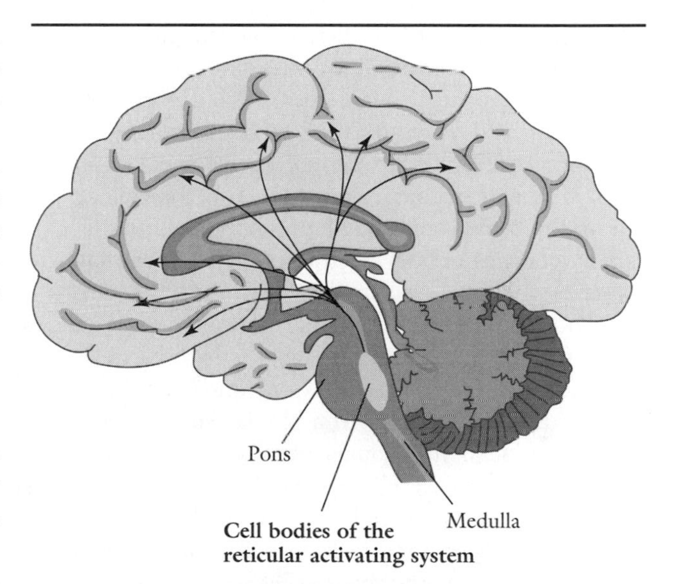

FIGURE 8.2 Reticular activating system. This system is the portion of the attentional network responsible for overall attention and arousal. The cell bodies of the reticular activating system are located in the medulla and the pons, but they project diffusely to many areas of the cortex (arrows). Coma results from bilateral damage to this system.

The RAS is so critical to alertness that coma results when it is damaged or disrupted. Individuals in a state of **coma** are seemingly unresponsive to most external stimuli. In severe cases, they may not even exhibit defensive movements to noxious or painful stimuli; although in less severe cases they will do so. Coma occurs either after bilateral lesions to the RAS or because of diffuse problems that interfere with RAS functioning. In some instances, the causative factor affects the brain but not the body, as in the case of meningitis, a tumor, hemorrhage, head trauma, or seizures. In other instances, the causative factor affects other regions of the body as well, as in the case of a metabolic disorder, an abnormal gas in the blood (e.g., carbon monoxide), lack of a certain vitamin (e.g., thiamine), or the presence of a toxin (e.g., alcohol or heavy metals) (Weiner & Goetz, 1989).

In some cases of coma, the person never regains consciousness and enters a **chronic vegetative state,** in which some RAS elements are intact, allowing basic bodily functions to be maintained (Plum & Posner, 1980). Individuals in a chronic vegetative state often regain some sort of sleep-wake cycle, have control of autonomic and respiratory functions, respond with primitive reflexes, and may even follow people with their eyes. However, they have no additional awareness of the outside world or their internal needs, are unable to voluntarily control movement, and have no ability to communicate. If their physical condition can be maintained at an optimal level (e.g., nutrition by a feeding tube, elimination by bladder management, peripheral circulation by changes in body positioning, etc.), they may survive for years (Gunderson, 1990).

In other cases, an individual may come out of coma, for example, after a metabolic disturbance is corrected or as time passes from an acute brain trauma. Before returning to a regular state of consciousness, such individuals usually progress to a state of **stupor,** in which they can be aroused when shaken vigorously or called by name but cannot speak rationally and fall back into unconsciousness quickly. Generally, the longer that someone is in a coma, the worse the long-term prognosis for regaining consciousness. Recently, brain imaging has been used as a window to examine how much information the brain is processing during a comatose state. In one case study, a comatose woman was found to show greater activation in the mid-fusiform gyrus of the right hemisphere to familiar faces as compared to scrambled versions of those same faces. Four months later she began to recognize faces (Menon et al., 1998). Neuroscientists and clinicians have found such results exciting because they offer the possibility that measures of brain activity may be able to provide prognostic information regarding the severity, duration, and possible dissipation of coma.

In addition to tonic arousal, the RAS is important for alerting the brain that it should get ready to receive information or make a response. In fact, the brain's electrical activity changes as it moves into such an expectant state. Soon after an individual receives a warning signal about an imperative stimulus, one to which a response must be made, a long, slow-going negative shift in the brain's electrical activity called the **contingent negative variation (CNV)** starts to appear. The CNV is thought to reflect some general aspect of the brain's arousal and alerting capacity as it can be decreased by depressant drugs (e.g., Tecce, Cole, Mayer, & Lewis, 1977) and enhanced by stimulants (e.g., Tecce & Cole, 1974).

Superior Colliculus

Paying attention requires more than simply being alert and awake; we must also have a means of directing our attention. To flexibly allocate attention, we must be able to move it from one position or object to another. The midbrain structure that has been implicated in this process, at least for visual stimuli, is the **superior colliculus** (Figure 8.3).

Although our focus of attention need not be the same place as our eyes, the position on which our eyes are fixed and our focus of attention most often are the same. The superior colliculus aids in shifting attention to new locations or objects by controlling eye movements responsible for bringing peripheral stimuli quickly into foveal vision. This process is accomplished by a **saccade,** an eye movement in which the eyes, rather than moving smoothly across space, jump from one position to the next with no processing of the intervening visual information. Saccades come in two varieties: express saccades and regular saccades. *Express saccades,* which are fast and take about 120 ms, tend to be reflexive and are triggered by the appearance of a novel visual stimulus in the periphery. Research with monkeys indicates that they are programmed by the superior colliculus, because when this structure is damaged, such saccades are extinguished.

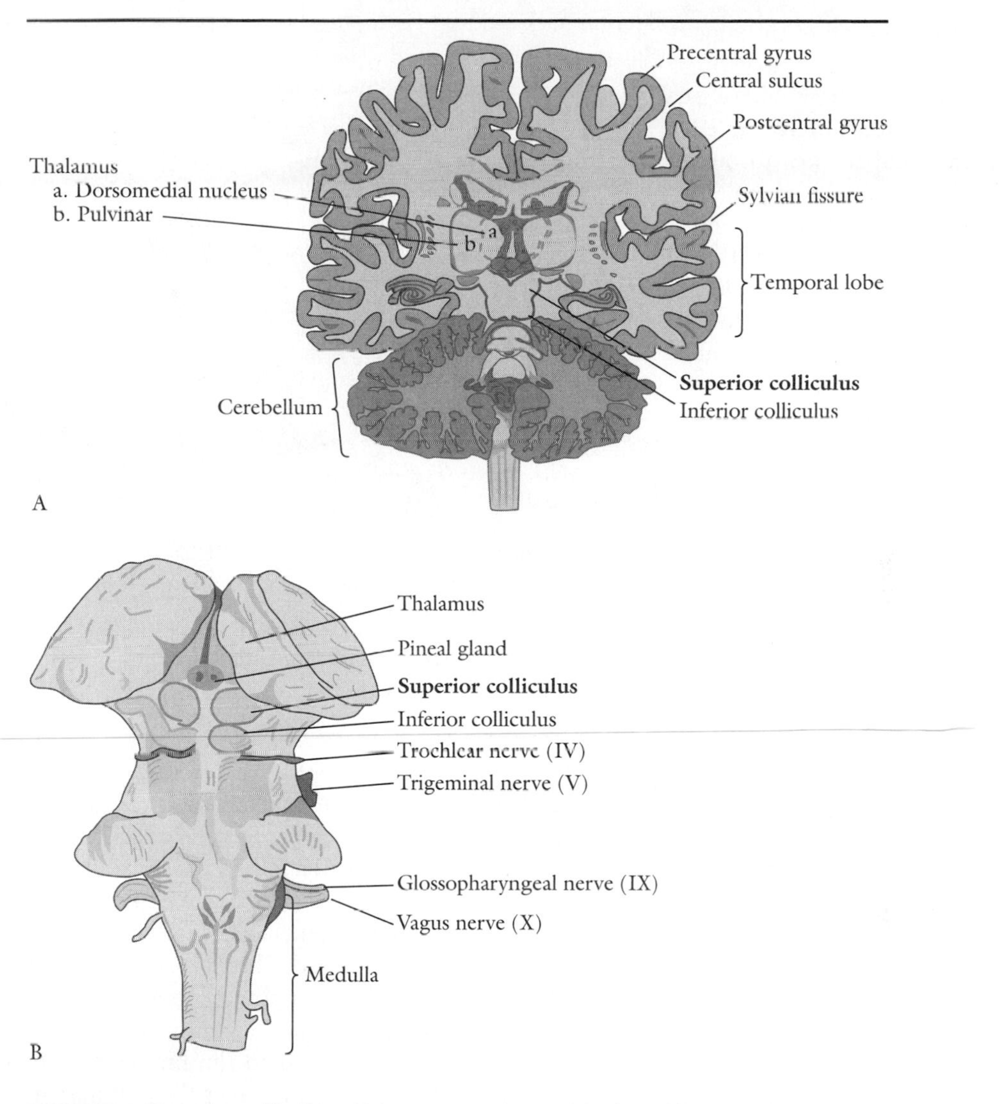

FIGURE 8.3 Superior colliculus. This structure, located in the midbrain, is responsible for moving attention to particular points in space. (A) Coronal view. (B) View from above with the overlying cortex removed.

In contrast, *regular saccades* are under voluntary control and take longer, about 200 to 300 ms (Schiller, Sandell, & Maunsell, 1987). They are not affected by damage to the superior colliculus, but are instead disrupted by damage to the frontal eye field, which we discussed in Chapter 5 (see page 167) (Guitton, Buchtel, & Douglas, 1985). From an anatomical perspective, the superior colliculus is well situated for controlling reflexive eye movements. Portions of it that receive sensory and motor information are tightly coupled to the oculomotor regions of the brain stem that serve as the final common pathway for control of eye movements (R. H. Wurtz & Goldberg, 1972).

The role of the superior colliculus in attention in humans has been aided by the study of individuals with *supranuclear palsy,* which is characterized by degeneration of parts of the basal ganglia as well as specific degeneration of the superior colliculus. In everyday life, these individuals often behave as if blind. Researchers have noted, "They often fail to turn towards those who approach them, to maintain eye contact during conversation, or to look at their plates when eating, even though they may still be able to do so on command" (R. D. Rafal et al., 1988, p. 268). In the laboratory, researchers have demonstrated that the main problem these patients have is in being able to move their attention from one point in space to another. We revisit these difficulties later in the chapter when we discuss a specific neural model of the control of visual attention (i.e., Posner, Inhoff, Friedrich, & Cohen, 1987). Before we leave our discussion of the superior colliculus, it is important to note that the inferior colliculus is believed to play a similar role in attention for information in the auditory modality.

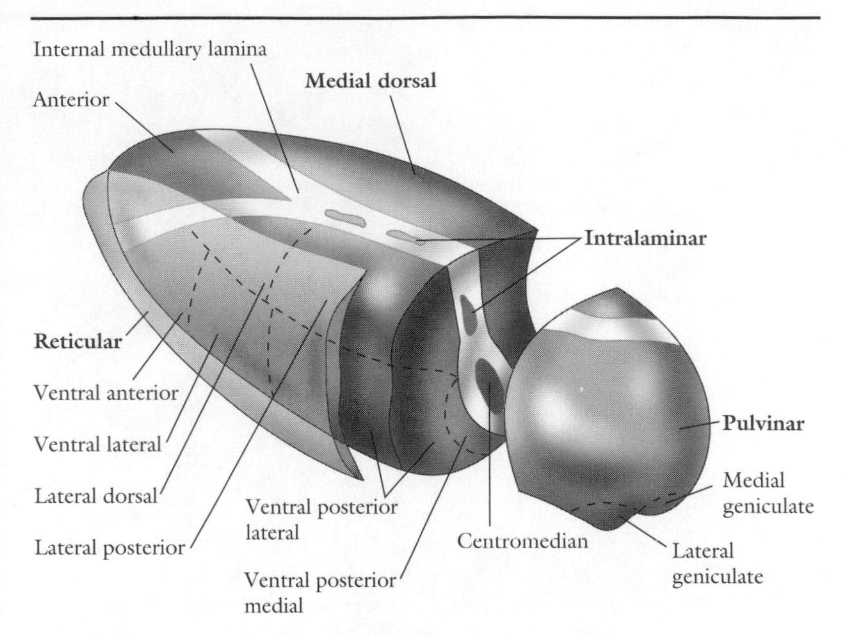

FIGURE 8.4 The nuclei of the thalamus that are thought to be involved in modulating attention. These nuclei include the reticular, intralaminar, and dorsomedial nuclei as well as the pulvinar.

Thalamus

The thalamus plays two important roles in attention. Some of the nuclei of the thalamus, in particular the **medial dorsal, intralaminar,** and **reticular nuclei,** help to keep us alert and awake by modulating the level of arousal of the cortex. Another nucleus, the **pulvinar,** plays an important role in selective attention. These nuclei are shown in Figure 8.4.

Portions of the thalamus receive information from the RAS. These areas are thought to be important for arousal, feeding forward to the cortex in a positive manner via the reticular nucleus. Neuroimaging studies have revealed activation of the intralaminar nucleus when a person must be alert and a quick response must be given to a visual or somatosensory stimulus (Kinomura et al., 1996). Furthermore, during a 60-minute auditory vigilance task, the activity in midline thalamic regions, probably reflecting activity of the intralaminar nucleus and the dorsal medial nucleus, decreased systematically with the degradation in performance over time (Paus et al., 1997).

Experts have suggested that other regions of the thalamus, such as the pulvinar, play a role in gating, or filtering, the barrage of sensory information that constantly impinges upon our brain. As we mentioned in Chapter 1, information from sensory receptors is relayed to the brain through the thalamus. Hence the position of the pulvinar at this crossroads makes it a logical structure to act as a gatekeeper for incoming information being sent to the cortex.

Studies of patients with brain damage and neuroimaging studies of neurologically intact adults provide evidence that the pulvinar plays such a role in attentional control, while event-related potentials (ERP) and magnetoencephalography (MEG) recordings provide complementary information on the time course of such activity. When individuals have damage to the thalamus, it deters their ability to engage attention to a particular location and filter out information at other locations (R. Rafal & Posner, 1987). Thus, they cannot use spatial location as a means for early gating. Positron emission tomography (PET) studies indicate that the thalamus is more engaged when filtering of information is required. For example, it exhibits greater activation when an item must be detected in the midst of eight other items as compared to when it is seen alone (D. LaBerge & Buchsbaum, 1990)—such as when one letter of the alphabet must be distinguised from eight other letters versus being recognized when it is alone. ERP and MEG studies indicate that such filtering occurs very early on after the receipt of a stimulus. An ERP component known as the P_{50} occurs 35 to 85 ms after receipt of auditory information. To measure sensory gating, an auditory stimulus is presented, followed 500 ms later by the same auditory stimulus. The measure of gating is the degree to which the amplitude of the P_{50} is diminished on the second presentation as compared to the first (Smith et al., 1994). This diminution of the P_{50} indicates that your brain says, "Oh, I just heard that—I don't need to pay that much attention to it again." There are certain populations of individuals who have difficulty in such early sensory gating, schizophrenics being the most notable (Freedman et al., 1991). Not surprisingly, they do not show a diminished P_{50} on the second presentation of an auditory stimulus.

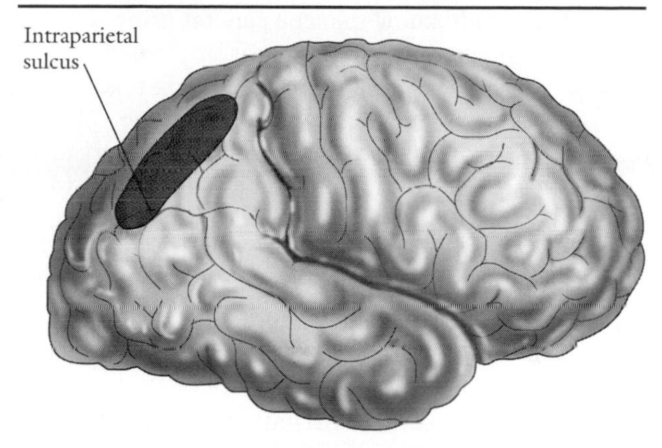

FIGURE 8.5 Regions bordering the intraparietal sulcus that are important for many different tasks involving visual selective attention.

Parietal Lobe

After the early gating of sensory information, more fine-grained selection is required. This task falls to the parietal lobe, which is important for visual and spatial aspects of attention. In addition, the parietal lobe has another attentional function: that of the overall allocation of attentional resources to a particular stimulus or task. We discuss each of these in turn.

Single-cell recordings in monkeys indicate a role of this region in visual attention—the firing rate of cells in this region is enhanced any time attention is directed to a visual object. Furthermore, this increase cannot be attributed to motor actions toward a stimulus, because it is independent of eye or arm movements to the stimulus (e.g., R. H. Wurtz & Goldberg, 1988). Single-cell recordings have also indicated that a portion of the parietal lobe, the lateral intraparietal region, is important for the representation of attended or salient spatial locations (Colby, Duhamel, & Goldberg, 1996). Suggesting that cells in this region are responding specifically to an attended location, they respond regardless of whether the information about location is auditory or visual and whether or not the monkey makes a motor response to the location.

Similar evidence is provided by research with humans. Neuroimaging studies indicate increased activation in parietal regions, more specifically the intraparietal sulcus shown in Figure 8.5, across a variety of tasks that involve increased visual attention, including those directed to spatial locations, those directed toward objects, and those involving the co-occurrence of visual attributes. However, this region is not activated by highly demanding tasks in general, as no increased activation is seen for a more difficult language task (semantic categorization) compared to a simpler one (characterizing the height of letters) (e.g., Wojciulik & Kanwisher, 1999).

In addition, neuroimaging studies indicate increased activation in superior parietal regions when an individual must make shifts in spatial attention (e.g., Nobre et al., 1997), and when a response must be selected on the basis of spatial attributes (e.g., Iacoboni, Woods, & Mazziota, 1996). Lesions to inferior parietal regions are likely to cause hemineglect (Vallar & Perani, 1986), which, as explained earlier, results in inattention to one side of space.

As you already know that the parietal is involved in sensory integration, it should not surprise you to find out that it also plays a role in binding together visual attributes with their position in space. This function is important because a prominent theory of attention suggests that such binding allows us to select information for further processing. According to this viewpoint, "attention" is the glue that lets you know that a particular item is at a particular location. Before we review the evidence for the parietal lobe in such a function, we need to discuss this theory in a bit more detail.

According to *feature integration theory,* basic visual features, such as color (e.g., green) and form (e.g., X), are detected relatively automatically. But we cannot know which of these features go together unless we direct our attention to a particular location. Thus, attention acts as the glue to bind those features together to form the percept of an item, such as a green X. A classic illustration of this point is provided by experiments in which an individual must find a target item in a visual display that contains many non-targets. When a target can be differentiated from all the non-target stimuli on the basis of a simple visual attribute, the time required to find the target tends *not* to vary with the number of non-target items. For instance, a target such as a red X will "pop out" of a field of non-targets, such as green Xs , no matter how many green Xs there are in a display. Similarly, a red X will pop out of a field of red Os. In such situations, processing is said to be "preattentive," which means that attention needn't be implemented to find the target. On the other hand, when a target item, such as a red X, must be identified on the basis of a conjunction of basic visual attributes (e.g., both shape and color) from among a mixture of non-targets, such as red Os (which share the same color as the target) and green Xs (which share the same shape as the target), the time required to find the target increases with the number of non-targets.

This increase in the time necessary to detect the target occurs because attention can be directed to only one point at a time. The more items in the display, the more locations that must be sampled before the target is located. The important concept for the purposes of the present discussion is that directing attention to a point in space *precedes* the identification of information, which means that directing attention to a particular spatial location allows the features at that location to be bound together so that an item can be identified. (A. Treisman & Gelade, 1980). If items are located at unattended locations, their features become "free-floating" and can be combined in illusory manners. For example, if a red X and a green O are at unattended locations, an individual may report having seen a red O, incorrectly combining one item's color with another item's shape (A. M. Treisman & Schmidt, 1982).

The parietal region plays a critical role in this binding process. Bilateral damage to parietal regions disrupts the ability to bind together features. Individuals with such deficits cannot detect conjunction of features, whereas their ability to detect a single attribute remains intact (e.g., Friedman-Hill, Robertson, & Treisman, 1995). In addition, transcranial magnetic stimulation (TMS) applied to the right parietal cortex of neurologically intact adults increases the time for conjunction searches but not simple feature searches (Ashbridge, Walsh, & Cowey, 1997).

The other major role that the parietal lobe plays in attention is that of the overall allocation of attentional resources. Evidence for this proposition comes from a variety of sources. We discuss just a few here. First, this region is activated during tasks that require sustained attention to either visual or somatosensory information (Pardo, Fox, & Raichle, 1991). Obviously, attentional resources must be allocated if one is to sustain attention. Second, although different types of attention activate different regions of parietal cortex, common overlapping regions of activation are found regardless of whether attention is directed to particular regions of space or particular periods of time (Coull & Nobre, 1998) or to spatial locations or objects (e.g., Fink et al., 1997). For example, spatial orienting of attention relies more on regions within the right inferior parietal lobe, whereas the temporal orienting of attention relies more on regions of the left intraparietal sulcus. Yet, both these regions are distinct from other areas of the inferior parietal lobe and intraparietal sulcus that show activation for both tasks. Third, damage to the parieto-temporal junction, but not other regions, such as the frontal lobe, eliminates the P_{300} (R. T. Knight, Scabini, Woods, & Clayworth, 1989). This finding is significant because the amplitude of the P_{300} has been found to index the degree of attentional resources that an individual voluntarily allocates to a particular stimulus or task. For example, when trying to perform two tasks simultaneously, attention can be divided equally between the tasks (50% to Task A, 50% to Task B) or unequally (e.g., 80% to Task A, 20% to Task B, or 20% to Task A, 80% to Task B). The more attention an individual allocates to a given task, the greater the P_{300} to that task. So, for example, if 80% of attention is directed to Task A and only 20% to Task B, a larger P_{300} is elicited from Task A than from Task B (A. F. Kramer, Wickens, & Donchin, 1985).

Anterior Cingulate Cortex

Thus far, we have discussed how the brain becomes alert and aroused, how it orients toward previously nonattended information, how it performs early gating of sensory information, and then how it performs more fine-grained selection of sensory information. Once the brain has accomplished all these processes, it needs to also select a response. The region of the brain that is responsible for doing so is the **cingulate cortex,** which can be thought of as an interface between subcortical and cortical regions (refer back to Figure 8.1).

The role of the anterior part of the cingulate cortex may be particularly important in the selection of appropriate responses, especially when it is difficult to emit such responses. You may remember that in Chapter 5 (see page 166) we discussed a PET study in which the anterior cingulate cortex was found to be particularly active when a new or novel response had to be emitted (e.g., responding "L" to "A" and "M" to "B" rather than responding "B" to "A" and "M" to "L") (Paus, Petrides, Evans, & Meyer, 1993). This task requires attentional control over response selection because the person must use effort to inhibit a typical and automatic response to produce an appropriate action. Also as we discussed in Chapter 5, the incongruent conditions of the Stroop task is another in which a fair amount of control must be exerted to inhibit an automatic, but incorrect, response. As a reminder, in this condition, a person must identify the color of ink in which a word is printed (e.g., blue) when the word itself spells a conflicting color name (e.g., red). Because reading is so automatic, the individual usually wants to identify the color as red and must use attention to suppress this response and produce the correct one (e.g., "blue"). This author has found that a specific portion of the cingulate, shown in Color insert 5.1A, exhibits activity when the word names a conflicting response (e.g., the word "blue" in green ink, when the possible responses are blue, green, and yellow), but not when the word is incongruent without naming a conflicting response (e.g., the word "purple" in green ink, when the possible responses are blue, green, and yellow) (Milham et al., 2001). These findings implicate the cingulate as critically involved in response selection.

Cingulate activity is observed in neuroimaging studies not only when there is a need to select between directly conflicting responses, but when selecting the correct response is demanding or complicated. For example, cingulate activity is observed when there are multiple possible responses, such as when a person is given a noun (e.g., *wood*) and must choose one verb from a larger set of verbs with which that noun is associated (e.g., *chop*) (Petersen et al., 1988). Greater cingulate activity is also found when the determination of a response is complicated because it relies on multiple attributes of a stimulus (e.g., color, form, speed) rather than a single one (e.g., color) (Corbetta et al., 1991).

It should also be mentioned that in addition to being involved in response selection, some theorists have suggested that portions of the activity of the anterior cingulate may reflect general task demands. Activity of the anterior cingulate is commonly found in neuroimaging studies. The more difficult or demanding the task, the more likely it is to evoke cingulate activity (Paus et al., 1998). Given the connections of the RAS to the cingulate, this activity may reflect the need for greater arousal and attention as task demands increase. Moreover, this activity can be specific to increased cognitive demand rather than any stimulus that is likely to grab attention. Recordings of the activity of single cells in particular portions of the anterior cingulate of humans (who undergo this procedure as a precursor to surgery in this region) exhibit modulation of activity while a person is performing an attentionally demanding cognitive task, but no modulation of activity when they are given a noxious stimulus, such as a pinprick, which would also be likely to grab attention, albeit in a more general manner (Davis et al., 2000).

Frontal Lobe

So far we have discussed how selection occurs for input to the brain and how selection occurs for output. But we have remained mum about selection for more abstract characteristics, such as selecting words that have particular meanings or selecting information that must be held "online" in memory. These attentional functions are performed by the frontal lobe, but because they are considered executive processes, we save our discussion of them for Chapter 12.

In addition to performing these executive aspects of attentional control, frontal regions aid in selecting, initiating, and inhibiting motor responses. In monkeys, unilateral damage to the dorsolateral frontal area causes a hemispatial hypokinesia in which the animals fail to move the limbs contralateral to the lesion (Watson, Miller, & Heilman, 1978). Similar effects are observed in humans after frontal damage. Frontal damage can cause a directional hypokinesia in which extra time is required to initiate movements in the direction contralateral to the lesion (e.g., leftward movements in individuals with right-hemisphere lesions) (K. M. Heilman et al., 1985). In addition, frontal lesions cause a motor neglect that exhibits itself as an inability to make motor movements toward the neglected side of space (e.g., A. R. Damasio, Damasio, & Chui, 1980). This deficit is distinct from the neglect of sensory information, which is typically associated with parietal lobe damage (e.g., Bisiach et al., 1990).

Frontal regions are involved in the control of eye movements as they are linked to attentional control. As we discussed earlier in the chapter, directing attention to a particular region and moving our eyes there usually go hand in hand. The frontal eye field is important for volitionally directing the eyes to a particular point in space, whereas orbital and medial regions are important for inhibiting or overriding the reflexive eye movements that are controlled by the superior colliculus (Paus et al., 1991). The need for such an inhibitory control mechanism becomes obvious if you consider how difficult maintaining your attention on a location would be without it. Every time a novel object occurred in the periphery, your gaze would be directed toward it. For example, your attention would be drawn away from the road in front of you every time a car on the other side of the median passed you!

The Time Course of Attentional Selection

One of the major questions that psychologists studying attention have tried to answer is *when* selection occurs. Does it occur relatively soon after the receipt of sensory information or later? There have been two schools of thought. The **early-selection viewpoint** suggests that attentional selection occurs at an early stage of processing, before items are identified (e.g., Broadbent, 1958). The **late-selection viewpoint** argues that selection occurs only after sensory processing is complete and items have been identified and categorized (e.g., J.A. Deutsch & Deutsch, 1963). The debate has raged on, in part, because the measures of standard cognitive psychology experiments, recording accuracy and reaction time, could not provide the critical information to distinguish between these two possibilities.

ERP studies, though, are perfectly suited to answer this question, and they have demonstrated that it is not an either/or question, because attention can occur both early and late. In ERP studies, the effects of attention are assessed by comparing two conditions: one in which a stimulus receives attention, and another in which the identical stimulus does not receive attention. Because the stimuli are identical, any difference in the ERP response to the two conditions must be attributable to the attentional manipulation.

In a classic example of this type of experiment, individuals are instructed to listen and count the number of target tones, such as long tones, interspersed within more frequent non-targets, such as short tones. They are told, however, to attend only to information in one ear (e.g., the left). Responses are compared for targets when they are attended (e.g., left-ear targets when attention is directed to the

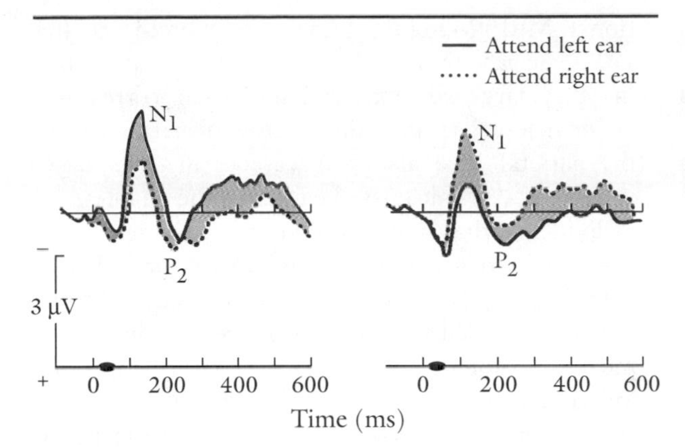

FIGURE 8.6 Modulation of early event-related potential (ERP) components by attention. The response to the stimulus is enhanced when it is presented in the attended location as compared with when it is not. (Left) For example, the amplitude of the N_1 is greater to a left-ear tone when the individual is attending to the left ear (solid line) than when the same tone is heard but the individual is attending to the right ear (dotted line). (Right) Likewise, the response to a right-ear tone is greater when the right ear is attended (dotted line) than when the left is (solid line). The difference between these two waveforms (shaded area) is the N_d component. This effect begins relatively soon after stimulus presentation, within the first 100 ms.

left ear) as compared to when they are unattended (e.g., left-ear targets when attention is directed to the right ear). Researchers can obtain an estimate of when attention begins to exert its influence by noticing the point in time when the amplitude of the ERP to the attended stimulus begins to diverge from that of the unattended stimulus. In this case, the ERP in the attended condition begins to become more negative in amplitude than that in the nonattended condition approximately 80 ms after stimulus presentation, a difference that may continue for some time (Hillyard, Hink, Schwent, & Picton, 1973). This increased negative shift for the attended stimulus is often called the *N_d (negative difference) component* and is shown in Figure 8.6.

Although we used auditory stimuli in this example, a similar negative electrical shift can be observed for visual (Van Voorhis & Hillyard, 1977) and somatosensory (Desmedt & Robertson, 1977) information. These findings suggest that the early negativity in the ERP reflects a general attentional process that is not modality specific. Because the onset of the N_d occurs as soon as 80 ms after stimulus presentation, attention can exert itself relatively early in the stream of processing, though not immediately after receipt of information by the cortex.

Preceding the N_d (usually referred to as P1/N1 component in the visual modality) is an even earlier component known as the C_1, which occurs 50–90 ms post stimulus presentation. Unlike the P1/N1, this component, which appears to index activity of primary visual cortex, does not vary in amplitude depending on attention (e.g., Clark & Hillyard, 1996). Although fMRI studies have found changes in activation in primary visual cortex as a result of attentional manipulations, the joint recording of ERPs has indicated that this activity in primary visual cortex does not occur in the "first pass" but rather reflects feedback from higher-order sensory areas whose activity is modulated by attention (e.g., Martinez et al., 1999; Olson, Chun, & Allison, 2001).

Attention can act at later stages as well, as demonstrated by the effect of attentional manipulations on later ERP components. In addition to the early negativity for attended information, there is the N_{2pc} that occurs approximately 180–280 ms post presentation that is thought to reflect the focusing of attention to potential target items in a display (e.g., Luck & Hillyard, 1994). (It is labeled as "pc" because it is recorded maximally over *parietal* areas *contralateral* to the position of the target.) The P_{300} (which occurs at least 300 ms post presentation) is found only when an individual is paying attention and monitoring the sensory world for a target (e.g., Donchin, 1981). This component is thought to index the degree to which an item given attention is task-relevant (and hence requires an update of working memory), or the amount of attention paid to a task (e.g., C. Wickens, Kramer, Vanasse, & Donchin, 1983).

Selection by Spatial Location, Objects, and Features

Psychologists studying attention have also spent much time attempting to determine exactly what aspect of the sensory world is used when selecting information. The debate has revolved around whether attention is directed on the basis of locations in space, the **space-based viewpoint of attention,** or whether it is directed on the basis of particular objects, the **object-based viewpoint of attention.** To make the distinction between space-based and object-based attention more concrete, let's assume that you have arranged to pick up your friend on a specific corner outside a train station. When you arrive and begin to look for your friend, you can direct your attention in a space-based manner to that particular corner and not other locations at the train station. In contrast, you may direct your attention in an object-based manner if you know that your friend will be wearing her long oversized wool coat. As you look for your friend, you can selectively pay attention only to particular objects, long oversized wool coats, while ignoring other objects such as ski jackets, short coats, and parkas.

Studies using a cognitive neuroscience approach have provided evidence that both types of selection can occur, as well as evidence that selection can occur on the basis of the attributes of specific items. We start by discussing the evidence for selection on the basis of spatial location, then on the basis of item attributes, and finally on the basis of whole objects.

Neuroimaging studies have provided evidence that regions of both visual and parietal cortex mediate space-based attentional effects. As you may remember from our discussion of the visual system, the mapping of the visual world in early visual-processing areas (V1–V4) is retinotopic so that a specific region of space is processed by a specific region of visual cortex. Of most importance for the current discussion, this mapping of visual space is inverted so that information in one visual field is processed by the contralateral visual cortex. Indicating that attention has space-based properties, attending to information in one visual field increases activation over extrastriate (V2–V4) regions of the opposite hemisphere (Heinze et al., 1994). ERP studies indicate that this space-based attentional modulation occurs relatively early on in processing, approximately 100 ms after stimulus presentation. The amplitude of the P_1 component to a visual target is enhanced when the item appears in the attended location as compared to the unattended one (Heinze, Luck, Mangun, & Hillyard, 1990). Both PET and dipole modeling (Heinze et al., 1994), as well as functional MRI (Mangun, Buonocore, Girelli, & Jha, 1998), suggest that the source of this component is in secondary (i.e., extrastriate) visual cortex (see Color insert 8.1). In addition to extrastriate cortex, the parietal lobe also plays a role in space-based selection, as we discussed earlier in the chapter.

Evidence that information can be selected on the basis of item attributes or features is provided by neuroimaging studies. In one such classic study, participants decided whether two successive displays of moving colored shapes were identical or not. Individuals were told to base their decision on one of the attributes (e.g., color) and to ignore the others (e.g., speed and shape) (Corbetta et al., 1991). Thus the perceptual information was equivalent across conditions, with variations only in what attribute should be attended. When the person was attending to color, ventral visual regions sensitive to color, such as V4, were most active. When the person was attending to shape, greater activation was found in portions of the ventral visual-processing stream. When the person was attending to speed, activation was greatest in area MT, the portion of the dorsal processing stream that is sensitive to motion. ERP data suggest that selection on the basis of stimulus attributes, such as color and shape, occurs about 250–300 ms after stimulus presentation (Anilo-Vento, Luck, & Hillyard, 1998).

Attentional selection can also be object-based. To demonstrate object-based attention, one needs a paradigm in which the spatial location of objects is held constant, so that spatially based selection can be ruled out. Typically, paradigms used to assess object-based attention involve overlapping figures, one of which must be attended to and the other of which must be ignored. In one such study, displays included both faces and houses. When attention was directed to an attribute that associated with faces, increased activation was observed in the fusiform face area. In contrast, when attention was directed to an attribute associated with houses, increased activation was observed in the parahippocampal place area (O'Craven, Downing, & Kanwisher, 1999). This modulation of attention appeared to occur relatively early on in processing when visual features are first recognized as forming a particular object. As you may remember from Chapter 6, there is a specific

ERP component, the N_{170}, that is elicited specifically by faces as compared to other objects. The amplitude of the equivalent magnetoencephalographic component, the M_{170}, can reflect the effects of object-based attention. When a display contains overlapping faces and houses, the amplitude of the M_{170} is greater when individuals attend to faces as compared to houses (Downing, Liu, & Kanwisher, 2001).

The evidence we have just discussed suggests that attention can act to select information in a variety of manners: on the basis of spatial location, on the basis of item attributes, or on the basis of objects. The neural bases of these effects exhibit an interesting and important pattern. When selection is based on a particular characteristic, activation is increased in the brain region specialized for processing that characteristic. For example, if selection occurs on the basis of space, increased activation is observed in sensory areas that are organized with regard to space, such as early visual-processing areas, and regions that provide a spatial map of the world, such as parietal regions. When attention is directed to an object, increased activation is observed in areas that process objects, such as the ventral visual-processing stream. And if attention is directed to a certain characteristic, such as motion, increased activation is observed in the region of the brain most sensitive to motion, MT.

Thus, you can see that attention does not reside in one particular region of the brain. Rather, it acts to influence the processing of distinct brain modules, ramping up their activity if they are processing information that is attentionally relevant. Recent evidence suggests that attention may also decrease the activation of brain regions processing information that is task-irrelevant (Rees, Frith, & Lavie, 1997). Hence, we know that attention is a modulatory process.

Models of Attentional Control by a Cortical Network

As we have just discussed, attention is a function that relies on multiple brain regions. Therefore, we need a way to conceptualize how these regions might interact and coordinate their processing to allow for attentional control. To provide a flavor for how this might occur, we briefly introduce you to a series of models of attentional control. In some there is a degree of modularity: specific attentional processes are performed by specific brain regions. In others the control of attention is more diffuse. We end this section by discussing how computational models can help illuminate our understanding of attentional control.

Component Processes by Discrete Brain Areas

In this section, we discuss one model for how the brain allows us to move our attention from one spatial location to the next, a process known as *visual selective attention.* To understand the evidence, we need to first discuss a classic experimental paradigm for demonstrating space-based selection (Posner, 1980). In this paradigm an individual sees a display consisting of a central cross and two peripheral boxes. While the person is fixating on the central cross, a cue occurs. Typically, it is either the brightening of one of the two peripheral boxes, or the appearance of a central arrow pointing to one of the boxes. Shortly afterward, a target to which the person must respond, such as an asterisk, appears inside one of the boxes. In approximately 80% of the trials, known as *valid trials,* the cue correctly identifies the location of the target. For the remaining 20% of the trials, known as *invalid trials,* the target's location is not correctly identified by the cue. Thus, the cue, on average, is helpful in performing the task. The essentials of this paradigm are shown in Figure 8.7.

Suggesting that attention can be directed in a spatial manner, responses to trials with valid cues are faster than to those with invalid cues. Since the cue is helpful, once it appears, you move your attention (but not your eyes, which remain fixed on the cross) to the cued location. When a target appears in the same location (valid trials), you respond quickly because your attention is already directed to that position in space. In contrast, if the target appears in the other location (invalid trials), your responses will be slower because your attention must be moved from the cued location to the target's position. Changing attention from one spatial location to another, as needs to occur on invalid trials, has been theorized to rely on three component operations. First, attention must be *disengaged* from the spot at which it is currently located. Then it must be *moved*

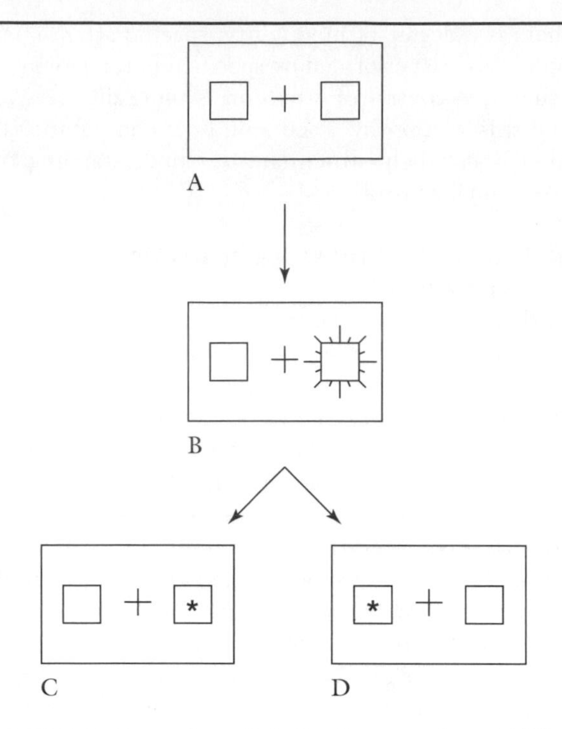

FIGURE 8.7 Posner's spatial attention paradigm. (A) The individual is told to fixate on a central location (the cross) for the duration of the trial. (B) At some point a cue occurs, which is the brightening of a peripheral box. This cue predicts with a high degree of accuracy the location of the subsequent target. The target, to which the individual must respond, an asterisk, appears after a variable interval. Two types of trials are given; those in which the cue correctly predicts the location of the subsequent target, *valid trials* (C), and those in which the cue incorrectly predicts the location of the subsequent target, *invalid trials* (D). Responses to invalid trials take longer because the individual must move attention from the cued location to the location of the target.

to a new location, and finally it must be *engaged* at the new location.

It has been proposed that a different neural structure is responsible for each of these three functions: the *disengage* operation is performed by parietal areas, the *move* operation is performed by the superior colliculus, and the *engage* operation is performed by the thalamus (e.g., Posner, Inhoff, Friedrich, & Cohen, 1987). Support for this idea comes from the pattern of performance of patients performing the visual-attention task just described who have lesions in each of these areas. Individuals with unilateral parietal lobe damage can engage attention as shown by normal responses when both the cue and the target appear contralateral to the damage. However, when the cue is ipsilateral to their lesion and attention must be *disengaged* to respond to a contralateral target, they are exceedingly slow to respond (Posner, Walker, Friedrich, & Rafal, 1984).

Individuals with supranuclear palsy exhibit delayed facilitation from a valid cue, indicating that they are slow to *move* their attention. Remember that when a cue is presented, individuals must move their attention from the fixation cross to the cued location. If attention has been successfully moved to the cued location by the time the target appears, responses should be facilitated. But if the movement of attention is slow, it will not get to the target location in time to facilitate a response. Whereas a 50-ms interval between the cue and the target is typically enough time to allow for facilitation of responses, these patients require an interval of approximately 350 ms (R. D. Rafal et al., 1988). Patients with thalamic damage exhibit yet a different pattern. Anytime a target appears contralateral to the lesioned hemisphere, regardless of whether the cue is valid or invalid, their response to the target is delayed. Such findings suggest that these patients have difficulty *engaging* attention contralateral to the lesion (R. Rafal & Posner, 1987).

Distributed Network Models

Other models of attentional control perceive the role of brain regions as less circumscribed than that just described. One classic model proposed by Mesulam (1981) views directed attention as being controlled by a diffuse cortical network that is simultaneously specialized and redundant. In this model, each region in the network has some specialization because the role it plays is not exactly like that of any other, yet this specialization is not absolute in that lesions to different areas of the network can have similar effects. Thus, this model takes neither a strict localizationist approach nor one of mass action (see page 64 in Chapter 3 regarding debates about these two positions).

According to this model, each of four major brain regions plays a prominent, but not necessarily exclusive, role in controlling a certain aspect of attention. The main role of the RAS is to maintain vigilance and arousal; the main role of the cingulate cortex is to impart motivational significance to information; the main role of the posterior parietal region is to provide a sensory map of the world; and the main role of frontal regions is to provide the motor programs for moving the attentional focus around the world by exploring, scanning, reaching, and fixating. Because this model views attention as being supported by an interconnected neural network, it has three important implications regarding the relationship between the brain and behavior. First, it implies that even though a lesion is confined to a single brain region, the lesion will affect not only attentional behaviors, but other behaviors as well. For example, although frontal regions are part of the attentional network, they also are involved in executive functions. Second, the same complex function can be impaired as a result of a variety of lesions in different locations. For example, as we discuss in more detail shortly, hemineglect has been reported after lesions to many different regions of the brain. Third, the most severe disruption of a complex function will be observed after damage to more than one region that is involved in the network. Thus, neglect would be expected to be more severe if damage occurred to both frontal and parietal regions rather than just parietal regions.

Still other models take a more broad-based approach, distinguishing between anterior and posterior portions of the brain. The *posterior attentional network* is thought to play a prominent role in the selection of information based on sensory attributes, whereas the *anterior attentional network* is important for selecting items in terms of more abstract representations, such as the degree to which an item is task-relevant or in regard to an item's meaning (e.g., Posner, 1992). These systems are conceptualized to be mainly independent but somewhat overlapping systems (e.g., Posner, Sandson, Dhawan, & Shulman, 1989).

Another distinction that has been made is between brain regions that are the sources of attentional control as compared to the sites of attentional control. *Sources of attentional control* send a signal to bias processing toward particular information, such as that which is most relevant to a task. In contrast, a *site of attentional control* is where modulation of processing is exerted. Evidence for such a model is provided by a neuroimaging study in which individuals had to detect a target under two conditions, one more attentionally demanding than the other. On some trials, a cue indicated where individuals should direct their attention. In the time period after the cue but before the target, a large increase in activity was observed in frontal regions and in the superior parietal lobule. With the onset of the visual stimuli, no additional increase in activity was observed in frontal and superior parietal regions, regardless of whether detecting the target was demanding or not. This pattern suggests that these regions serve as sources of attentional control, setting the bias for subsequent processing, but are not involved when selection must actually occur (i.e., after onset of the visual display), as their activity is not affected by how hard the actual selection process is (i.e., whether detecting the target is easy or hard). In contrast, activity of posterior visual regions (e.g., V4) also increased after the cue, but to a much smaller degree than frontal and superior parietal regions. It was as if these posterior regions were put "on alert" by biasing signals from frontal and parietal regions. After the target appeared, however, their activity increased substantially, suggesting that they were actively involved in the selection process and acted as sites of attentional control (Kastner, Pinsk, De Weerd, Desimone, & Ungerleider, 1999).

Computationally Influenced Models

Certain models take a more computational approach to explaining the processes involved in attention. Most such theories suggest that there is some form of competition between item attributes, item locations, or items themselves. Single-cell recordings in monkeys provide evidence for such an idea. In these studies, the scientist records the cell's response to a set of visual items, each individually when that item is the only one located within the cell's receptive field. For the sake of this example, let's say that item A makes the cell fire at a moderate rate, and item B makes it fire at a slow rate. If the cell is responding to the additive effect of all items within the receptive field (i.e., response to A plus response to B), then when both items are shown together, the firing rate of the cell should be greater than observed for either item alone. In actuality, however, when both items are within the receptive field, the cell's response is an average of the responses to each item. Thus, item B, which doesn't drive the cell's response very well, actually suppresses, or lowers, the response of the cell to item A (e.g., Reynolds, Chelazzi, & Desimone, 1999). Thus, there is competitive interaction between all task-relevant items within the receptive field.

Given this state of affairs, then how does any information stand out? A prominent model, *the biased-competition model,* assumes that attention puts a bias into this competition (Desimone & Duncan, 1995). This bias can be induced in a bottom-up manner from sensory regions or in a top-down manner from frontal regions. An example of a bottom-up influence would be stimulus intensity—a brighter stimulus is more likely to capture attention than a dimmer one. An example of a top-down bias would be the relevance of the stimulus to the task—a spoon is more likely to capture your attention than a fork if your goal is to eat soup. The results of such biasing can be observed neurophysiologically. For example, in humans, directing spatial attention to a particular location eliminates the suppressive effects of other items in the visual field, biasing the competition in favor of the item at that location (Kastner, DeWeerd, Desimone, & Ungerleider, 1998).

Computational models of attention instantiate this competition through winner-take-all networks, in which one unit's activation wins out above the rest (e.g., Mozer & Sitton, 1998). Thus, competition influences what is ultimately selected and what is ultimately discarded. So, for example, computational models of the Stroop effect have a module representing a word's ink color, and another representing the color described by the word. Within each module, activation is winner-take-all. Activity in the unit representing the ink color of green inhibits activation of other units in that module, such as those representing the ink color of red or blue.

In the brain, within-module competition would presumably occur in V4 for selecting ink color and within posterior language areas for selecting word meaning. Corresponding information between modules is thought to be linked by mutually excitatory connections—activation of the green unit in the word module activates the green unit in the ink-color module. Another module provides for top-down control, serving to bias the relative activation levels of the ink-color and word-reading modules. For example, the demands of the Stroop task in which the ink color of a printed word must be identified can be mimicked in computational models by having the top-down module provide greater activation to the ink-color module than to the word-reading module, which in turn influences the outcome of the system (O'Reilly & Munakata, 2000; Cohen, Braver, & O'Reilly, 1996). In the brain, frontal regions are likely to provide such top-down biasing.

Hemineglect: Clinical Aspects

Now that we have discussed the different brain regions that contribute to attentional control and the ways in which they may interact, we spend the rest of the chapter concentrating on one of the most prominent syndromes in which attentional dysfunction occurs: hemineglect. First we describe the clinical aspects of neglect and then discuss how this syndrome has increased our understanding of the cognitive neuroscience of attention (for a good short review on both these aspects of the syndrome, see Vallar, 1998).

Clinical Features

In this section of the chapter we discuss the clinical features of neglect. We first describe the typical way in which this disorder is manifested. Then we examine the features in a bit more detail to illustrate how the disorder cannot be explained merely as a consequence of sensory deficits, and is indeed one of attention.

• *TYPICAL MANIFESTATION* •

As mentioned previously, hemineglect, sometimes referred to as hemi-inattention, is a syndrome in which an individual ignores, or does not pay attention to, the side of space contralateral to the lesion. The side of space ignored is usually defined with reference to body midline but, as we discuss later, may occur with regard to other spatial reference frames as well (e.g., information to the left of the head's midline when the head is not at body midline). This inattention is seen regardless of the modality in which information is presented. Depending on the severity of hemineglect, individuals might fail to eat food on the left side of the plate, draw the left side of objects, read the left side of words, or use the left side of the body.

In severe cases individuals may even deny that the left side of the body belongs to them. Two case studies illustrate the sometimes bizarre consequences of this denial. In one case, a patient with hemineglect protested to a nurse with great agitation that one of the staff had played an extremely cruel and inappropriate joke on him by placing a severed leg in his bed. At that point, he attempted to throw the offensive leg out of bed, which happened to be his own, and thus managed only to hurl himself onto the floor (Sacks, 1985)! In another case, a woman repeatedly affirmed that her left upper limb was not hers but the examiner's. When the examiner brought the patient's left arm into view and asked whose it was she answered, "It's not mine. I found it in the bathroom, when I fell [during her stroke she fell in the bathroom]. It's not mine because it's too heavy; it should be yours. It can move and do everything; when I feel it too heavy, I put it on my stomach. It doesn't hurt me, it's kind." When asked where her own arm was, she answered: "Behind the door" (Rode et al., 1992, p. 204). This syndrome, although rare, has been recognized since the late 1800s and is called **somatoparaphrenia.** Other than denying ownership of a limb, and claiming that it belongs to someone else, the rest of the patient's reasoning is normal.

Neglect is usually observed after vascular damage to the supramarginal gyrus of the parietal region, which extends into subcortical regions (e.g., Vallar & Perani, 1986; K. M. Heilman, Watson, & Valenstein, 1985) (see Figure 8.8). Neglect is observed more commonly and is more severe after right- than left-hemisphere lesions (e.g., M. L. Albert, 1973; Ogden, 1985). Hence neglect is observed more often for the left than for the right side of space. Although occurring most commonly after damage to the right parietal lobe, neglect can also occur after damage to frontal regions (e.g., K. M. Heilman & Valenstein, 1972), the basal ganglia (e.g., A. R. Damasio, Damasio, & Chui, 1980), and the thalamus (e.g., Watson, Valenstein, & Heilman, 1981).

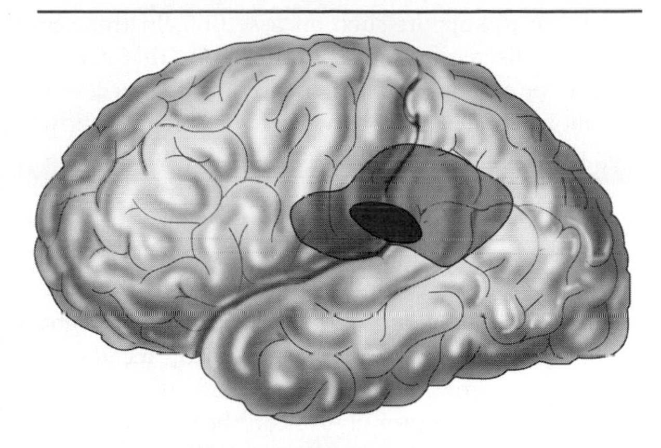

FIGURE 8.8 The region of the brain most commonly associated with hemispatial neglect. Most individuals with hemineglect have sustained damage to the portion of the supramarginal gyrus sitting at the junction with temporal regions as a result of a vascular insult. The region most highly associated with neglect is shown in blue, while that in grey is also associated, but to a lesser degree.

The degree of neglect is usually severe at first: all items on the neglected side of space are ignored. Within weeks to months, this profound neglect usually dissipates so that some information on the neglected side is processed. For example, patients become able to detect a single item on the neglected side of space. However, neglect rarely, if ever, disappears completely (K. M. Heilman, Watson, & Valenstein, 1985). This residual deficit is most noticeable when there is competing information on both sides of space. To test for residual deficits, neurologists and neuropsychologists often use the **double simultaneous stimulation technique,** in which the patient is confronted with two similar items simultaneously, one on each side of space. The simple question asked is, "How many items have been presented, one or two?" Typically, under double simultaneous stimulation, the patient will say that he or she sees, hears, or feels only a single item, ignoring the item on the neglected side.

• *NOT DUE TO SENSORY DEFICITS* •

So far we presented the neglect syndrome as a deficit in attentional processing but have not discussed the evidence to support such an assertion. In this section, we discuss findings demonstrating that neglect cannot be attributed to deficits in sensory processing. Then, in the next section we discuss evidence showing that neglect is modulated by attentional factors.

To evaluate the possibility that neglect could result solely from deficits in sensory processing, let us reconsider the chapter's opening vignette. Initially you may have thought that the gentleman's odd behavior might be explained by right-hemisphere damage that precluded receipt of sensory information from the left side of space and interfered with motor control on the left side of his body. On closer investigation, though, you can see that this explanation is not plausible. He could perform motor acts competently, as evidenced by his ability to shave, shower, dress, and eat. Despite such competence, however, motor acts were mainly confined to the right side of his body. Furthermore, when his attention was drawn to the neglected side (by a loud noise), his performance improved. Thus, the motor acts themselves were probably not disrupted. Rather, the ability to direct these acts to the left side of body was impaired.

Is it possible that a sensory deficit in the visual modality could explain his behavior? You might hypothesize that he had a dense hemianopsia of the left visual field (LVF) because, as we learned in Chapter 1, that would make him functionally blind for all information to the left of fixation. Yet this explanation cannot account for a general inattention to visual information to the left of body midline, because patients with hemianopsia can process visual information on the left side of space. They do so simply by moving the center of their gaze to the far left.

For a fuller appreciation of this point, look at Figure 8.9A. Assume that you have left hemianopsia and are sitting at the center of the table. Previously, you lit a candle and placed it on the left side of the table. Now you want to make sure that it is not dripping wax. If your gaze is fixed straight ahead, you will be blind to all information to the left of body midline including the candle. However, simply turning your head and fixating your gaze on the left edge of the table, as shown in Figure 8.9B, will enable you to see the candle because it now falls entirely within your right visual field (RVF). Thus, even though the candle remains to the left of body midline, it can be perceived merely by changing the point of visual fixation. Hence, visual deficits cannot account for the fact that patients with hemineglect ignore what is on the left side of space. It is important to demonstrate that visual deficits cannot account for hemineglect, because the lesion that causes it often

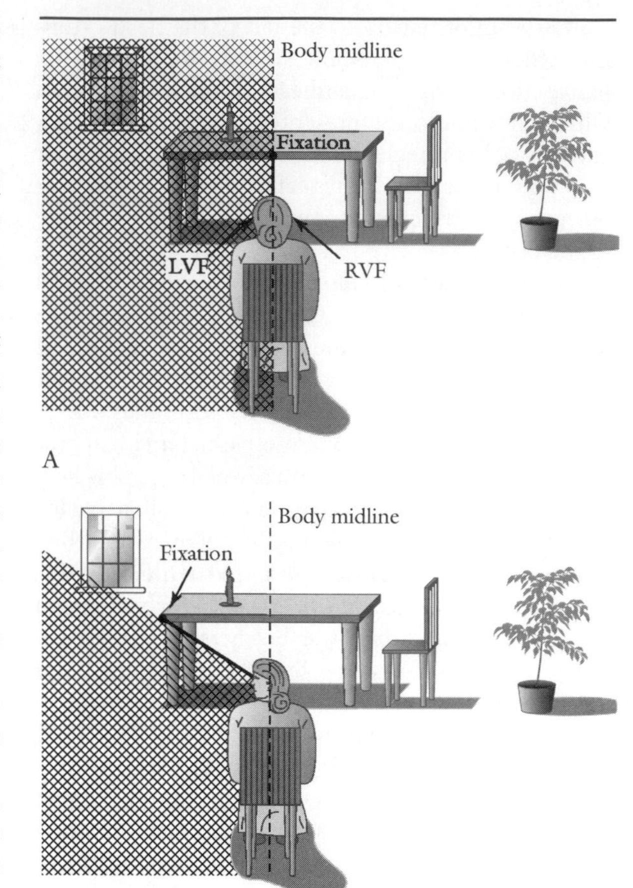

FIGURE 8.9 The influence of head position on the information that falls in each visual field. (A) When someone is looking straight ahead, information to the left of body midline falls in the left visual field (LVF) and information to the right of body midline falls in the right visual field (RVF). If the individual has hemianopsia for the LVF (gray crosshatching), the candle in this picture will not be visible. (B) However, the individual can view the candle by simply turning her head so that the candle now falls within the good visual field, the RVF. Although patients with hemineglect who simultaneously have visual field defects could use such a strategy, they do not, because they ignore the left side of space.

extends into the occipital lobe, leading to cuts or scotomas (i.e., blind spots) in the visual field. Consequently, there may indeed be regions of space for which the patient with hemineglect is functionally blind. Nonetheless, the presence of such visual deficits cannot fully explain the hemineglect.

Our analysis of the gentleman's deficits so far should make you skeptical of the idea that hemineglect can be explained by sensory loss in the visual modality. Is it, however, possible that individuals with hemineglect are relatively insensitive to *all* sensory material received by the damaged hemisphere? This hypothesis would rest on the fact that the posterior regions of the brain damaged in hemineglect are important for sensory processing. However, we now entertain this hypothesis just long enough to disprove it!

If this hypothesis were true, then the severity of neglect would be predicted by the degree to which information in a given modality is processed by the contralateral hemisphere. For the purposes of this discussion, let us assume that the person is ignoring information on the left as the result of a right-hemisphere lesion. Because only the right-hemisphere receives visual and somatosensory information from the left, this hypothesis would predict neglect of visual and somatosensory information from the left, but intact processing of this same type of material from the right. In the auditory modality, inattention to material on the left would be less severe because some information from the left ear projects ipsilaterally to the intact left hemisphere. Concomitantly, some neglect of auditory information on the right would be expected because the right hemisphere would be unable to proficiently process information from the right ear that is received through ipsilateral pathways. Finally, because the left nostril projects to the left hemisphere and the right nostril to the right hemisphere, no neglect would be observed for smells on the left, but neglect would be evident for smells on the right. In sum, if the neglect resulted from an inability of the right hemisphere to process sensory information, it would be exhibited by an extreme insensitivity to visual information in the LVF and tactile information from the left side of the body, less extreme neglect for auditory information on the left side of space, and no neglect for olfactory information on the left side of space. But such variations in the degree of neglect across modalities are not observed in cases of hemineglect. Instead, information from the contralateral side of space is generally ignored regardless of whether it is presented in the visual, tactile, auditory, or olfactory modality. Thus, the evidence we reviewed illustrates that neglect does not appear to have a sensory basis.

• *MODULATED BY ATTENTIONAL FACTORS* •

Now that we know that hemineglect is not the result of sensory malfunction or damage, we examine the evidence demonstrating that it arises specifically from a disruption in attentional processing. Let's return to the scenario at the beginning of this chapter. One odd aspect of the gentleman's behavior was that information on the left side of space seemingly ignored on one occasion was not ignored on others. So although he initially ignored his hash browns and bacon, he eventually ate them, but only after his *attention* had been drawn leftward by the ruckus produced by the crashing dishes. Furthermore, even though his attention was drawn leftward by an auditory event, all information on that side of space, regardless of the modality through which it was perceived (e.g., visual, auditory), was processed.

As this scenario suggests, neglect can be moderated by attentional factors. According to anecdotal reports, particularly salient or emotional information in the neglected half of space will not be ignored, such as a long needle in the hands of a nurse. Even in experimental situations, neglect can be diminished by the manipulation of attention. For example, a classic sign of hemineglect is the inability to bisect a line correctly (see Figure 8.10). Patients with hemineglect most often place the halfway point about one quarter of the way from the

FIGURE 8.10 Typical example of line bisection by an individual with hemineglect. Because the person with hemineglect ignores the left half of space, the line is bisected far to the right, as if it extended only from its midpoint to its right endpoint.

line's right end and three quarters of the way from the left end (e.g., Reuter-Lorenz & Posner, 1990). They act as if the line extends only from the middle to the right and has no left side. However, line bisection can be improved (although it is still not totally accurate) if attention is first drawn to the left side of space by a preceding task. Typically, this directing of attention is accomplished by placing a salient marker at the left edge of the line that must be identified, such as a digit or letter that must be named (e.g., Riddoch & Humphreys, 1983).

Furthermore, if information on the neglected side of space is critical for the understanding or comprehension of material, it tends to receive attention. For example, if a patient with hemineglect for the left side of space sees the word *antiballistic* centered on the page, he or she is much more likely to read the word as *ballistic,* even though the letters to the right of midline are only *llistic.* Thus, patients with hemineglect attend to information from the left side of space to the degree that it is needed to devise a reasonable interpretation of sensory information.

Finally, motivational factors can also mitigate the degree to which attention is allocated to the left. In one case study, a patient with hemineglect was asked to perform a letter-cancellation task that requiring crossing out all the As on a page full of letters. Whereas on the first occasion, he was just simply told to perform the task, on the second occasion, he was promised a certain amount of money for every A correctly detected. When he was provided with a motivation to direct attention to the left side of space, his neglect was reduced, as indicated by his ability to detect more As on the second occasion than on the first (Mesulam, 1985).

We have just seen that neglect can be decreased by manipulations that draw attention to the left. These manipulations include external factors, such as the presence of particularly salient items or emotionally charged information. Attention to the left can also be increased by internal factors, such as a pressing motivation to process the left side of space or the need to do so in order to make sense of the world.

Theories Regarding the Underlying Deficit

One of the most striking aspects of hemineglect is that individuals who have it seem to have no awareness that they are ignoring one side of space. Often when first learning about hemineglect, students comment, "I just don't understand. If a person is ignoring the left side of space, why can't you just point out that it is important to pay attention to the left?" Because individuals with hemineglect do not realize that they are ignoring one side of space, telling them to orient in that direction is of little use. For them, that region of space does not exist at a conscious level.

As an analogy, consider how you usually conceptualize the area of space behind your head. Generally your attention is focused on the world in front of you and you give little thought to the region behind you. Even if you were instructed to pay attention to what is behind you, you might start out by looking over your shoulder every few seconds, but would soon stop doing so. However, you'd probably do it for a longer period if you were paid a certain amount of money every time you reported on an event that occurred behind you. Or you might pay attention to the world behind you if some extremely significant information were coming from that region, such as the sound of quickly approaching footsteps when you were walking down a dark street alone at night. The patient with hemineglect treats one side of space the way you normally treat the space behind your back.

Researchers have tried to uncover why this profound neglect occurs. One suggestion is that these patients lack an internal mental representation of the neglected side of space. For them, that side of space doesn't even exist! Supporting such an idea, neglect can occur whether or not the individual is receiving sensory information. When placed in a totally darkened room, patients with neglect move their eyes only to positions in the non-neglected half of space, as if they didn't perceive that the other half exists. In contrast, neurologically intact individuals move their eyes to positions all over both sides of space (Hornak, 1992). Although this study demonstrated that sensory stimuli are not required to produce neglect, it didn't directly address whether these patients lack the conception of one side of space.

This issue was directly addressed, however, in a particularly ingenious (and classic) study by Bisiach and Luzzatti (1978) involving two patients from Milan, Italy, who had hemineglect for the left

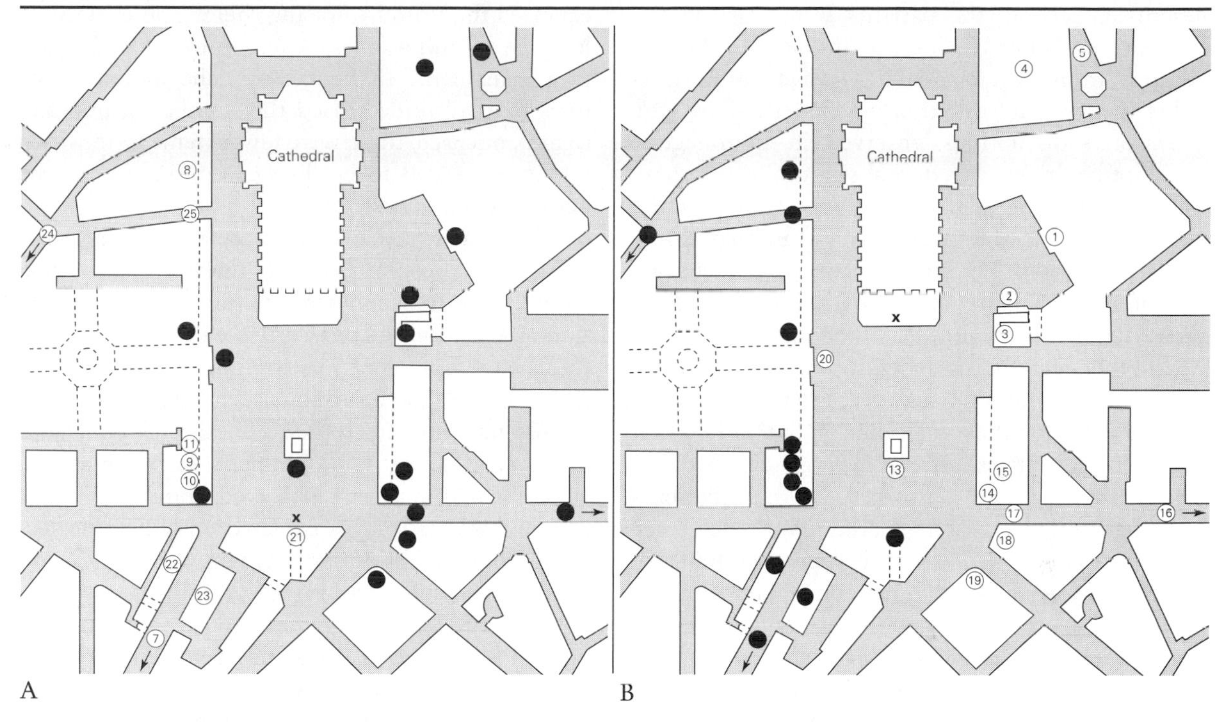

FIGURE 8.11 Maps indicating which structures were reported by patients with hemineglect when they imagined standing in the Piazza del Duomo in Milan, Italy. The position in the plaza where the individual imagined him- or herself to be standing is marked with an *X*. The landmarks that the patients described are designated by filled circles. (A) The landmarks mentioned by patients when they imagined themselves facing the cathedral. These landmarks are situated mainly on the right. (B) The landmarks mentioned when the patients imagined themselves standing on the steps of the cathedral and facing away from it. Once again, mainly the landmarks on the right are mentioned. These individuals' memory for the square is intact because they mention most of the square's major landmarks across the two imagined positions.

side of space. While the patients were in their hospital room, the researchers asked them to imagine an extremely famous plaza in Milan that contains a variety of buildings, including the city's renowned and ornate cathedral. Because this plaza is a major Milanese landmark, the two individuals had visited it many times and could be expected to have an excellent mental representation of the area. First, the patients were asked to imagine standing at the end of the plaza opposite the imposing cathedral and then to describe what they saw. The landmarks that the patients mentioned are designated by black circles on the map of the square shown in Figure 8.11A.

Notice that the patients could aptly describe the major landmarks on the right but not those on the left. Why not? Perhaps in their mind's eye, they were exhibiting neglect of information on the left. But there was an alternative explanation—maybe their memory for the buildings situated in that part of the plaza was poor. To distinguish between these two possibilities, the researchers next asked the patients to imagine being at the opposite end of the plaza—standing on the steps of the cathedral with their backs toward it—and then to describe the plaza. As shown in Figure 8.11B, they described a whole new set of landmarks—those that were previously to the left but were now to the right.

We can draw a number of conclusions from this study. First, clearly the patients' memory for the entire plaza was fine, as across their first and second imaginings of the plaza, all aspects of it were described. Second, the patients were missing the conception of one side of space, in this case the left, because from either mental vantage point, they failed to report information on the left. Third, the attentional disruptions observed in hemineglect need not be driven by external stimuli. In this case, the patients were in their hospital rooms, not the plaza, imagining the square. These findings imply that patients with hemineglect fail to represent one side of space or fail to pay attention to one side of their mental representations of the world.

Another explanation of hemineglect suggests that the problem is not so much that the left side of space doesn't exist for these individuals, but rather that the pull of sensory stimuli on the non-neglected side of space is so salient as to prevent these patients from attending to the information on the neglected side. Consistent with this idea are a number of pieces of evidence. As you may remember from earlier in the chapter, we noted that patients with parietal lesions often have difficulty disengaging attention from the non-neglected field (refer back to page 266). However, they can normally engage attention when a cue draws their attention to the neglected field. In this latter condition, there is no competing information in the non-neglected field from which attention must be disengaged. Likewise, we discussed how the long-lasting deficits in hemineglect are likely to occur under conditions of double simultaneous stimulation, once again a condition in which there is competing information in the non-neglected field. In contrast, individuals with hemineglect can attend to information in the neglected field when it is presented alone.

An interesting demonstration of the degree to which information in the non-neglected field influences performance was provided by a study in which patients with unilateral neglect performed two versions of a cancellation task often used to assess hemineglect (Mark, Kooistra, & Heilman, 1988). In this task, a series of lines are randomly distributed across the page, and the person must "cancel" as many as possible. In one version, individuals canceled the targets on a dry-erase board by writing over them in darker color ink. In this way, the lines remained even after they were canceled. In the second version, individuals were given an eraser and canceled the lines by erasing them. The neglect for left-side stimuli was less severe in the second condition than in the first. Because cancellation of the lines by erasure decreased the number of items in right hemispace, there were fewer items from which attention needed to be disengaged, and hence the neglect was less severe.

These data can also be interpreted to suggest that hemineglect results from an uneven competition between the hemispheres for controlling the direction of attention. As we learned earlier in the chapter, the notion of competition is fundamental to many models of attentional control. When both hemispheres are intact, the competition is equal, but after brain damage, the competition becomes lopsided and hemineglect is observed. Some of the most compelling data for this explanation of hemineglect come from studies of patients with unilateral brain damage who suffer from neglect and were administered TMS. The researchers reasoned that if neglect occurs because of an imbalance between the hemispheres, then giving TMS to disrupt processing of the intact hemisphere should restore such a balance, and reduce neglect. In fact, that was exactly what they found (Oliveri et al., 1999)!

Treatment

As we mentioned earlier, although hemineglect may dissipate with time, it rarely if ever disappears. Hemineglect can be vexing because of the degree to which it can interfere with everyday life. Think about how having hemineglect would make it dangerous or even impossible to drive a car or cross the street! Finding an effective means of reducing neglect, therefore, is of great clinical interest.

Some intriguing recent findings suggest that different types of sensory stimulation can modulate the degree of neglect observed. One simple method for reducing neglect is to either actively or passively move the limb on the neglected side of space within the neglected hemispace (e.g., Frassinetti, Rossi, & Ladavas, 2001). This method appears to work by making the left side of space more salient. Other techniques use different types of sensory stimulation. One technique known as **caloric stimulation** can lead to temporary remission of a variety of the symptoms in patients with hemineglect, including somatoparaphrenia, whether given soon after damage (Bisiach, Rusconi, & Vallar, 1991) or as long as six months later (Rode et al., 1992). Water at least 7° C colder than body temperature is poured into the ear canal, which induces motion in the semicircular canals of the vestibular system. Various studies have found that vibration of the left neck muscles (often referred to as *neck-proprioceptive stimulation*) can also reduce neglect (e.g., Karnarth, Christ, & Hartje, 1993).

At present, the mechanism by which these types of stimulation reduce neglect remains an issue of debate. One possible link is that unilateral vestibular stimulation increases brain activation (as measured by regional blood flow) in the temporoparietal region of the brain (Freiberg et al., 1985); thus, caloric stimulation may modify parietal functioning, which in turn reduces neglect. Because both caloric and neck-proprioceptive stimulation result in an illusion that straight ahead is shifted to the left (Karnath, Sievering, & Fetter, 1994), they may cause a shift in the individual's spatial frame of reference, moving midline of the body toward the left (e.g., Vallar, Guariglia, & Rusconi, 1997). Consistent with this idea, these types of stimulation reduce neglect not only in the sensory and motor realms, but also with regard to mental representations (Cappa, Sterzi, Vallar, & Bisiach, 1987; Rubens, 1985; Vallar et al., 1990).

Unfortunately, these methods cannot be used regularly, not only because they would be impractical but because they have side effects—for example, caloric stimulation induces vertigo and nausea (Gunderson, 1990). Nonetheless, they may provide important insights into the mechanisms of neglect that could lead to an effective method of reducing it.

Hemineglect: Implications for Understanding Brain-Behavior Relationships

Now that we have discussed the clinical aspects of hemineglect, we turn our attention to a number of issues regarding brain-behavior relationships that can be illuminated by this syndrome. We explore the degree to which hemineglect reveals the multiple frameworks that we use to understand our spatial world, how it provides additional evidence for object-based attention, how it expands our understanding of hemispheric asymmetries in attention, and how it provides insights into the degree to which the nervous system processes unattended stimuli. Where relevant we present converging evidence from other techniques used in cognitive neuroscience.

Multiple Spatial Frames of Reference

In Chapter 7, we discussed evidence that the maps we build of our spatial world can be constructed with reference to multiple spatial frameworks. For example, the ability to negotiate through space with regard to an egocentric framework can be distinct from the ability to do so with regard to an extrapersonal framework. In this section, we discuss how hemineglect also provides evidence for distinct spatial frameworks, especially with regard to left and right.

• *FRAMES OF REFERENCE WITH REGARD TO LEFT AND RIGHT* •

So far in our discussion of hemineglect, we have used body midline as the frame of reference from which to determine left and right. However, left and right can be determined with regard to a number of other reference points, including the retina, the head, and gravity. Often we experience a world in which these different spatial frames are all aligned. For example, what is to the left of our head is also to the left of our body, which in turn is to the left side of space as determined by gravitational coordinates. But these frames of reference can be dissociated, for example by turning the head to one side so that head and body coordinates dissociate or by leaning to one side so that egocentric (head and body) coordinates are disentangled from gravitational (environment-centered) coordinates.

Research with monkeys suggests that these spatial frames of reference may be dissociable. Different regions of the parietal cortex are involved in representing spatial locations with reference to an allocentric framework, such as a testing room, as compared to parts of the body, such as the head and trunk (Snyder, Grieve, Brotchie, & Andersen, 1998). Neglect provides a powerful way to determine whether these frames of reference can be perceived independently in humans. If they can, the degree of neglect should depend not only on the location of a region of space with regard to one frame of reference (e.g., the head), but also on the location with regard to another frame of reference (e.g., the body).

To make this idea more concrete, let's consider a specific example in which researchers investigated whether neglect for information to the left side of the body can dissociate from neglect for information to the left side of the environment (Calvanio, Petrone, & Levine, 1987). Normally, as shown in Figure 8.12A, body-centered and environment-centered coordinates are the same. Quadrants 1 and 3 are to the left of body midline, and also to the left of the environment as defined by gravity. Likewise, Quadrants 2 and 4 are to the right, both with regards to body midline and gravity. However, when an individual reclines, these frames of reference dissociate. Although left and right in regard to environment-centered coordinates remain the same, body-centered coordinates change. As shown in Figure 8.12B, when a person reclines with the head to the right, Quadrants 3 and 4 (not 1 and 3) are to the right and Quadrants 1 and 3 (not 2 and 4) are to the left of body midline. Also as shown in Figure 8.12C, when a person reclines with the head to the left, Quadrants 3 and 4 are now to the left of body midline, and Quadrants 1 and 2 are to the right.

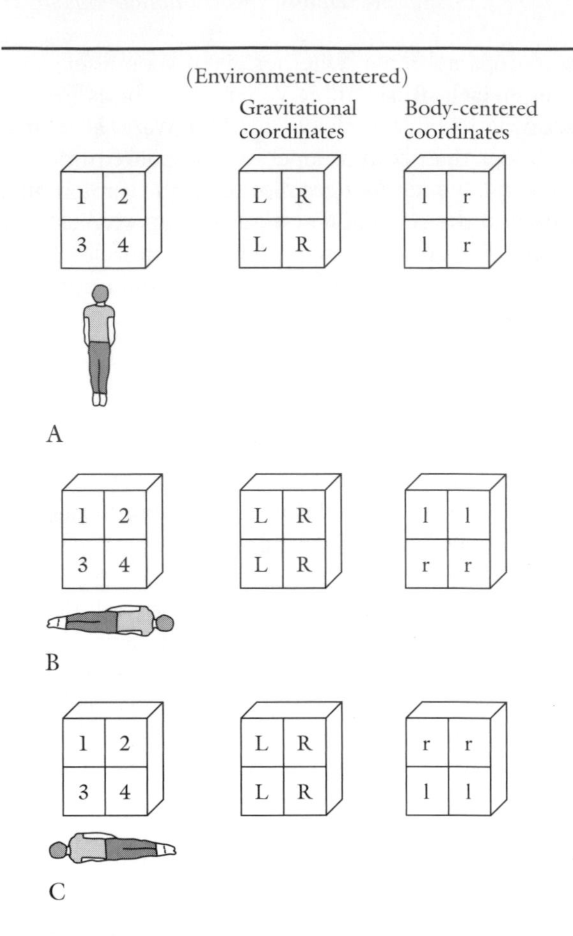

FIGURE 8.12 Examples of how body-centered and gravitational (environment-centered) frames of reference can dissociate. (A) When a person is looking straight ahead, information that is to the left of the body is also to the left as defined by gravity. (B) When the person reclines with the head to the right, the frames dissociate so that information to the left of gravitational midline, Quadrants 1 and 3, is distinct from that to the left of the body, Quadrants 1 and 2. (C) When the person reclines with the head to the left, information to the left of gravitational midline, Quadrants 1 and 3, is distinct from that to the left of the body, Quadrants 3 and 4. Both gravitational and body-centered frames of reference influence what patients with hemineglect ignore.

The degree of neglect was influenced by *both* environment-centered and body-centered coordinates, which suggests that these frames of reference are separable. The neglect is most severe for the quadrant that is left with regard to the body *and* left with regard to gravity (e.g., Quadrant 1 when the head is turned right and Quadrant 3 when the head is turned left), whereas it is least severe for the quadrant to the right of both body midline and the gravitational midline. Across other studies of patients with neglect, dissociations among retinotopic, head-centered, body-centered, and gravity-centered coordinates have also been demonstrated (e.g., Bisiach, Capitani, & Porta, 1985; Ladavas, 1987).

• *FRAMES OF REFERENCE IN OTHER DIMENSIONS* •

To this point, we have discussed neglect only with regard to the horizontal plane (i.e., left and right). However, our three-dimensional world has two other planes—the top-bottom (vertical) plane and the near-far plane. If these three dimensions are dissociable in our mapping of space, we might expect to find specific cases of neglect for each of these dimensions in space as well.

In fact, evidence from case studies indicates that neglect can occur with regard to the vertical plane, which has been dubbed **altitudinal neglect** (for top vs. bottom) (Rapcsak, Cimino, & Heilman, 1988). In one case, the individual could detect a single stimulus in all four quadrants of her visual field. However, when shown two objects, one above the horizontal meridian and one below (which makes this situation similar to the double simultaneous stimulation example discussed earlier in the chapter), she always ignored the one below. When required to find the midpoint of vertically oriented sticks of wood, she estimated the midpoint significantly above the true midpoint of the rod whether she inspected the rod just visually, just tactilely (with the eyes closed), or both visually and tactilely. These findings suggest that her difficulties arose in paying attention to the bottom portion of space rather than from a problem in a specific sensory domain (e.g., visual, tactile).

A case of an individual with the opposite problem, neglect of the upper part of space, has also been reported. Behaviorally, he bisected vertical lines below their midpoint and ignored the upper portions of visual stimuli (Shelton, Bowers, & Heilman, 1990). This patient exhibited another interesting neglect phenomenon. He seemed to have neglect for far portions of space because he consistently bisected radial lines too close to his body. Because this patient ignored both the upper part of space and the far part of space, the researchers wondered whether the patient we just discussed, who had neglected the lower part of space, might also show a neglect of near space. Upon retesting, she was found to have a significant tendency to bisect radial lines too far away from her body, an indication of neglect of near space (Mennemeier, Wertman, & Heilman, 1992).

Hence, in both these patients, representation of space in the vertical dimension was linked to representation of space in the near-far dimension. One patient neglected both the upper half and far region of space, while the other patient neglected both the lower and near part of space. Although it remains conjecture, these two reference frames may be coupled inasmuch as information at the top of our visual world is usually far away (e.g., the horizon), whereas information near to us is usually lower in our visual world. More exploration of this issue is warranted, since the available evidence is based on just a few case studies.

Finally, studies of patients with hemineglect also provide evidence that the spatial framework for extrapersonal space can dissociate from the framework for personal space. In one case, an individual exhibited no neglect for the extrapersonal world; he was attentive to all aspects of his surroundings and used objects to perform activities on both sides of space (e.g., serving tea or dealing cards). Yet, he exhibited neglect for personal space because when objects such as razors and combs had to be used on his own body, he ignored the left side of his body. So severe was this neglect that in one instance he woke up his wife in the middle of the night and asked her for help in finding his left arm (Guariglia & Antonucci, 1992).

Space-Based vs. Object-Based Attention

Most of our discussion of neglect so far has been with regard to a spatial framework. However, earlier in the chapter we discussed how attention can be directed either to certain regions of space or to certain objects. Additional evidence for object-based attention could be garnered if neglect were found for certain portions of objects (rather than certain regions of space). To make this distinction clearer, consider, for example, that whereas spatially based neglect for the left half of space would cause a failure to read all words on the left half of the page, object-based neglect would cause a failure to read the left *half* of words, regardless of where they occur on the page.

A number of case studies of object-based neglect have been reported both for nonverbal and verbal material (e.g., Behrmann & Moscovitch, 1994; Driver, Baylis, Goodrich, & Rafal, 1994). In the nonverbal realm, one case study described a patient who exhibited a specific neglect for the left half of faces but not for the left half of other objects, such as cars (Young, DeHaan, Newcombe, & Hay, 1990). Although this individual could recognize people from a full view of the face or just the right half of the face, he made many errors in identification when shown just the left half. When shown chimeric faces, which consist of two different

NEUROPSYCHOLOGICAL BASES OF CONSCIOUSNESS

How are we aware of who we are and the world around us? What makes us conscious, willful beings? The question of consciousness has intrigued philosophers for centuries, and now increasingly is intriguing neuroscientists as well. In Descartes's view, the answer boiled down to "I think, therefore I am." Holding to a basic premise of neuropsychology and cognitive neuroscience that the brain is critical for mental function, we might update Descartes by saying, "I have a brain, therefore I am."

Does consciousness emanate from a special place in the brain? In Descartes's view, the pineal gland (a structure that hangs from the base of the brain) was the likely source because it was the only brain structure that did not have two halves. Some neuroscientists say there is a central control region in the brain that guides our actions and thoughts, whereas others believe that consciousness emerges from the complex interactions of neurons (see Dehaene & Naccache, 2001, and other articles in that volume for recent perspectives).

What is clear, however, is that changes in brain function can alter what we often conceive of as consciousness. As we discussed earlier in the chapter, damage to the reticular activating system (RAS) can alter responsiveness to sensory information and impair the ability to perform willful acts on a basic level. In epilepsy, an alteration of consciousness, known as an *aura,* often precedes a seizure. These auras usually are distortions of sensory experience, such as experiencing an intense characteristic smell or a feeling of an alteration in the size of certain body parts. In some cases, individuals even experience visual hallucinations (for a particularly interesting self-report of such visual hallucinations as a result of viral encephalitis, see Mize, 1980). At least some investigators have speculated that certain "visions" seen by particular religious figures of the Middle Ages may have been the result of a neurological disorder (Sacks, 1985). These distortions of experience can extend to a sense of time and place as well.

Brain injury can often cause a seeming lack of awareness or knowledge about certain aspects of the world (see Prigatano & Schacter, 1991, for a multifaceted discussion of this issue). In fact, one of the most vexing aspects of neuropsychological rehabilitation after brain trauma is that patients often lack an awareness of their dysfunction. Self-awareness of the problems to be overcome is critical for effective adjustment to deficits. Without it, a patient is unlikely to engage in behaviors—whether they be restructuring the physical environment or devising compensatory strategies—that will mitigate

half-faces merged at midline, the patient's behavior was dictated solely by the right half of the face and not at all by the left. Moreover, the researchers demonstrated that the neglect was not spatially based. The patient exhibited no neglect for the left half of space on a standard item-cancellation test. In addition, the neglect for the left half of the face occurred regardless of the face's position in space. For example, the neglect of the left side of the face was observed even for the rightward of two faces presented side by side. Cases of left-sided neglect for other objects have also been reported (e.g., Young, Hellawell, & Welch, 1992).

Evidence for object-based neglect in the verbal domain comes from two case studies of patients, who, regardless of a word's length and position in space, ignored one side of the word. The neglect did not exhibit itself with relation to body or head midline, but rather with regard to where letters were located in the overall frame of the word. For example, one patient who had sustained left-hemisphere damage made errors when reading the right half of words, regardless of the length of the word. She tended to read the first half of the word correctly, but not the second half, reading *fabric* as "fable" *banister* as "banish," and *familiar* as "family" (Caramazza & Hillis, 1990). Another patient, who sustained a right parieto-occipital lesion, made reading errors on the left half of words regardless of word length. The farther a letter was from the right end of the word, the more likely it was to be misread (Hillis & Caramazza, 1991).

These case studies are important because they demonstrate that attention can be object-based

the effects of brain damage (see Chapter 13 for a more detailed discussion of compensatory strategies). For example, a brain-damaged patient with left hemiplegia was about to be discharged from a rehabilitation hospital where she had spent an hour a day learning to use a set of handrails to enable her to get in and out of the bathtub. Yet when asked what renovations she was planning for her bathroom at home to accommodate her disability, she replied, "Oh, I won't need to do any."

In certain syndromes, such as hemineglect and amnesia, the lack of consciousness occurs within particular domains of space and time. As we just discussed, hemineglect causes a lack of awareness for one side of space while at the same time consciousness for the non-neglected side of space seems perfectly normal. In cases of amnesia (which we discuss in more detail in Chapter 10), consciousness is intact for memories of the immediate moment and for the period of time prior to the brain injury, but not for time after the insult. As stated by H.M., one of the most famous patients with amnesia, "You see, at this moment everything looks clear to me, but what happened just before? That's what worries me. It's like waking from a dream; I just don't remember" (B. Milner, 1966, p. 115). (See Newcombe, 1985, for a review of alterations in consciousness as a result of brain damage and the way that they may be similar to experiences that we may have in our everyday lives, such as waking from sleep or sensory deprivation.)

At the same time that these syndromes demonstrate how consciousness of time and space can fractionate, they also demonstrate that information that seemingly appears to evade consciousness can nonetheless influence an individual's actions. For example, as we discussed previously, in hemineglect, information that is in the neglected field will, under certain conditions, prime behavior. Furthermore, as we discuss in more detail in Chapter 10, information that is not recognized by amnesic patients may influence a behavioral or physiological response. And as we have just discussed, brain imaging studies with neurologically intact individuals have provided evidence of brain activation to information that primes or influences behavior yet is not recognized or categorized by the individual (e.g., Dehaene et al., 1998). Typically these studies indicate that the pattern of brain activation is a subset of that observed during conscious recognition (e.g., Beck, Rees, Frith, & Lavie, 2001). These laboratory findings, which indicate that the nervous system is processing information even though it doesn't appear to be doing so, have caused a heightened awareness among clinicians about different levels of consciousness. For example, such findings have been used, in part, to justify coma stimulation therapy, in which patients in a coma are given specific types of stimulation even though they appear unresponsive (for a sample description of such therapy, see Freeman, 1991). ■

rather than spatially based. In all cases, neglect was exhibited for a particular portion of the object regardless of the object's position in space.

■ Hemispheric Differences in Attentional Control

One of the most striking aspects of the hemineglect syndrome is that it is much more prominent and severe after right-hemisphere damage than after left-hemisphere damage. Theorists have wondered why this might be the case. Here we will discuss some possible explanations.

Some theorists have proposed that the hemineglect exhibited after right-hemisphere damage reflects the effects of two distinct factors: an attentional bias of each hemisphere for information on the opposite side of space and a larger role of the right hemisphere in overall attention and arousal. We next discuss the evidence for each of these two factors and then examine how they might combine to cause the effects observed in hemineglect.

Various pieces of evidence suggest that each hemisphere exhibits an attentional bias for information located in the contralateral space. As discussed earlier in the chapter, when individuals direct attention to one visual field, such as the LVF, the ERP recorded over the occipital lead on the contralateral hemisphere is larger than that over the ipsilateral hemisphere (e.g., Mangun & Hillyard, 1988). When task demands activate one hemisphere, it induces an attentional bias to the contralateral side of space, enhancing the processing of material in that location (Kinsbourne, 1974). For example, performing a verbal task will enhance the size of the

RVF advantage on a subsequent divided visual field task as compared to performing a nonverbal task. The verbal task activates the left hemisphere, which induces an attentional bias to the opposite side of space, increasing the RVF advantage (e.g., Klein, Moscovitch, & Vigna, 1976).

Such attentional biases for one side of space can be observed even when items are presented in free vision. Take a look at Figure 8.13. Which of the two faces looks happier to you? If you are right-handed, you are likely to have said A. Because the right hemisphere of right-handers is better at processing of faces and in interpreting emotional expression, it becomes more activated. This leads to a bias for the contralateral side of space, in this case, the left. The half-face located there will be more salient and hence judged as happier. Notice that this bias is completely induced by the brain, as the two pictures are mirror images, which means that on the basis of perceptual factors, there is no reason to perceive one as happier than the other (Levy, Heller, Banich, & Burton, 1983b).

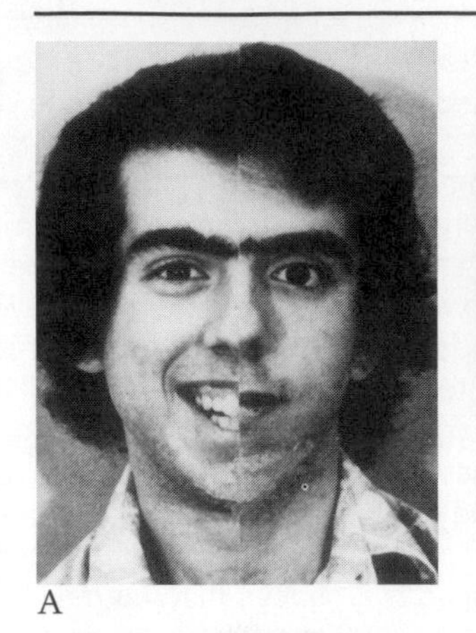

A

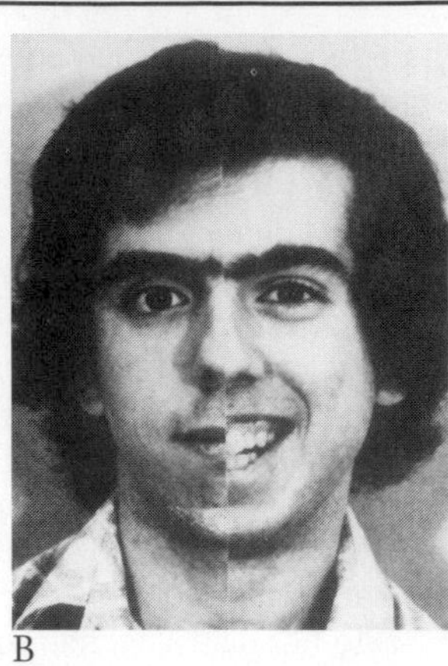

B

FIGURE 8.13 Examples of chimeric faces that demonstrate attentional biases to one side of space. Although these faces are identical except that they are mirror images, most right-handed individuals perceive the face in (A), which has the smile on the left, as happier than the face in (B), which has the smile on the right. Experts think that the left half-face is perceived as more expressive because the right hemisphere is more adept at processing emotional and facial information, which causes an attentional bias toward the left side of space. Hence, information located on the left is perceived as more salient.

Finally, PET studies indicate that when attention has to be shifted among various locations, all of which were restricted to one visual field, activation is greatest over left superior parietal and left superior frontal cortex for RVF locations, and over right superior parietal and right superior frontal cortex for LVF locations (Corbetta, Miezin, Shulman, & Petersen, 1993). On the basis of evidence of this nature and others (e.g., Reuter-Lorenz, Kinsbourne, & Moscovitch, 1990), each hemisphere appears to have an attentional bias for the contralateral side of space.

The evidence for a large right-hemisphere role in alerting and arousal also comes from various sources. After right-hemisphere damage, patients exhibit slow responses to simple stimuli. Although brain damage slows the responses of almost all individuals, damage to the right hemisphere, and more specifically the right posterior regions, causes the greatest decrement in performance (Coslett, Bowers, & Heilman, 1987). Heart-rate responses to warning signals are also disrupted by right-hemisphere damage (Yokoyama et al., 1987), and passive-vigilance tasks are performed more poorly by the isolated right hemisphere than the isolated left hemisphere of patients with the split-brain syndrome (e.g., Dimond & Beaumont, 1973). Moreover, PET studies indicate that the right hemisphere is important in sustaining overall attention, for example in vigilance tasks (e.g., R. M. Cohen et al., 1988).

These two factors, a hemispheric attentional bias for the contralateral hemispace and greater right-hemisphere involvement in attention and arousal, may combine to explain why neglect is more severe after right-hemisphere damage. The manner in which they combine was demonstrated in a study in which an item-detection task was given to three groups of individuals: patients with right-hemisphere damage, patients with left-hemisphere damage, and neurologically intact individuals (Weintraub & Mesulam, 1987). These individuals were asked to circle as many target items as they could find within a visual display; the results are presented in Table 8.1. As expected, the neurologically intact individuals missed practically no targets on either side of space. The results for patients with

TABLE 8.1 Number of Items Missed in the Visual Search Task Used by Weintraub and Mesulam (1987)

GROUP	AVERAGE NO. OF ITEMS MISSED LEFT SIDE	RIGHT SIDE
Patients with left hemisphere lesions	1.25	2.38
Patients with right hemisphere lesions	17.13	8.00
Neurologically intact control subjects	0.56	0.30

Patients with unilateral lesions miss more items on the side of space contralateral to the lesion than on the ipsilateral side. Overall, the patients with right hemisphere damage miss many more targets than those with left hemisphere damage do.

two important findings. First, regardless of whether individuals had right- or left-hemisphere damage, they missed more targets on the side of space contralateral, rather than ipsilateral, to the lesion. These results provide additional evidence that each hemisphere is primarily responsible for attention to information in the contralateral hemispace. Second, as you can see in Table 8.1, the overall performance of patients with right-hemisphere damage was worse than the performance of patients with left-hemisphere damage; that is, they missed more items overall on both the left *and* right sides of space. In fact, patients with right-hemisphere damage missed more items in their *non-neglected* hemispace (i.e., right hemispace) than patients with left-hemisphere damage missed in their *neglected* hemispace (i.e., right hemispace)! This piece of evidence, along with the others cited previously, suggests that the right hemisphere may exert more influence over overall attention and arousal than the left.

Another explanation for the greater severity of hemineglect after right hemisphere lesions is that the hemispheres differ in the way they direct attention across space. Unlike the model we have just discussed, which assumes that each hemisphere is specialized for processing information in the contralateral hemispace, this model suggests that both hemispheres can attend to both sides of space. But they do not attend to all locations equally. Rather they do so via an *attentional gradient.* For the left hemisphere, attention is directed maximally to the farthest right point of space and falls off systematically to a minimum for the far left side of space. The pattern for the right hemisphere is the opposite: attention is directed most strongly to the far left and least to the far right. Importantly, however, the decrement of this gradient across space is thought to be less drastic for the right hemisphere than the left (Kinsbourne, 1993), as illustrated in Figure 8.14.

Support for this idea comes from findings that even within the non-neglected hemispace, patients will show more neglect for the portion of that hemispace closer to midline than that further to the periphery (Ladavas, Petronio, & Umilta, 1990). Other support is provided by the TMS study on patients with unilateral damage and neglect that we discussed earlier in the chapter. If each hemisphere is responsible for directing attention only to the contralateral side of space, then once that hemisphere is damaged, it should be difficult or impossible to direct attention contralaterally. According to this idea, TMS to the intact hemisphere should have no effect on the degree of neglect. But as we learned, TMS to the intact hemisphere restores the ability to attend to the neglected side (Oliveri et al., 1999). Such a finding is much more consistent with competing gradients of attentional control in the hemispheres than the idea that each hemisphere attends only to the contralateral side of space.

Processing of Unattended Stimuli

Thus far we presented attention as a mechanism whereby the brain can choose what it wants to process from the vast array of information available. But what is the fate of unattended stimuli? Do they fall into a black hole of mental consciousness, leaving not even a trace of their existence, or are they processed but to a much lesser degree than attended stimuli? In Chapter 6, we discussed the fact that patients with prosopagnosia appear to be able to extract some information about faces that they cannot recognize. Such findings provide evidence that information may be processed to some degree even if it doesn't reach consciousness. Next, we examine evidence that although patients with hemineglect appear to ignore all information on the unattended side of space, under certain conditions this information can nonetheless influence their behavior.

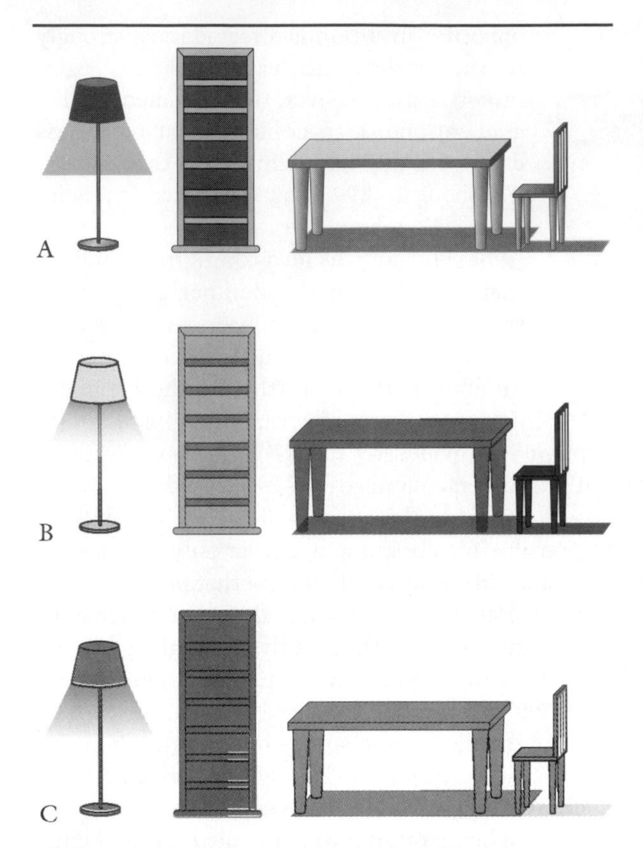

FIGURE 8.14 Hemispheric differences in the attentional gradient. (A) A visual scene. (B) The attentional gradient for the left hemisphere, with darker color indicating a greater allocation of attention. Notice that there is quite a difference between the left and right sides of space. (C) The attentional gradient for the right hemisphere. Once again the intensity of color indicates the intensity of attention allocated to that object. Here the difference between attentional allocation to the right and left sides of space is not as salient.

One of the first hints that patients with hemineglect might process information in their unattended half of space came from the case of a patient with left-sided hemineglect who was shown drawings of two houses that were identical except for flames coming out of the left side of one (J. C. Marshall & Halligan, 1988). Although the patient claimed to detect no difference between the houses, when asked which house she would prefer to live in, she picked the one without flames. Subsequent studies failed to replicate this particular finding (e.g., Bisiach & Rusconi, 1990), but other researchers have found evidence that information in the neglected field can be processed. Some of this evidence comes from priming studies in which information on the left that cannot be explicitly recognized nonetheless influences performance. In one study researchers determined the speed with which patients with right-hemisphere damage, who exhibited a neglect of the contralateral space, could categorize a picture in the RVF (their non-neglected field) as an animal or fruit. The important factor in this study was that 400 ms earlier a picture from either the same category or a different category was presented in the neglected field (i.e., the LVF). Responses to information in the RVF were faster when a related rather than an unrelated item was presented in the neglected field. This finding suggests that information in the neglected field was being processed to some degree, since it could influence processing of material in the non-neglected field (Berti & Rizzolatti, 1992). In contrast to individuals with neglect, individuals with hemianopsia for the LVF do not show such priming effects as they are truly blind for information in that portion of space (McGlinchey-Berroth et al., 1993).

Recently fMRI studies have provided some insight into how brain regions might support such priming effects. These studies suggest that residual or low-level activation of brain regions allows for priming but precludes conscious recognition. One case study demonstrating such a phenomenon was of a man who exhibited hemi-inattention after a right inferior parietal lobe infarction (Rees et al., 2000). Shown items singly he could identify them in each hemi-field with over 95% accuracy, yet under conditions of bilateral simultaneous stimulation he identified only 2 trials as bilateral and said the remaining 58 contained just a single item in the RVF. The researchers compared brain activation for the bilateral condition in which he reported seeing only the RVF item to those trials in which he truly saw only a single item in the RVF. Thus, the patient's response was the same in these two conditions even though the stimuli were distinct (bilateral as compared to unilateral).

In particular, the researchers wanted to examine the degree of activation in the visual cortex of the hemisphere contralateral to the neglected field, in this case the LVF. Even though the patient reported not seeing anything, there was activation in this region, albeit somewhat reduced as compared to that observed when an item was presented solely in the LVF (and could be correctly detected by the patient) (see Color insert 8.2)

ERP evidence also suggests that in the early stages of processing, neglected and non-neglected stimuli are treated similarly by the brain. For example, a normal N_{170} is recorded to faces that are neglected under conditions of bilateral simultaneous stimulation (Vuilleumier et al., 2001). Yet activation in higher-order visual areas was absent. It appears, therefore, that neglected stimuli are not processed as deeply or as thoroughly as non-neglected stimuli. Nevertheless, the degree of processing that they do receive allows them to influence performance—just not at a conscious level.

What is "Attention"?

- Attention is the cognitive ability that allows us to deal with the inherent processing limitations of the human brain by selecting information for further processing.
- In discussing attention, cognitive psychologists often divide it into four general categories: alertness and arousal, sustained attention (vigilance), selective attention, and resources (capacity).

Brain Structures Involved in Attention

- The reticular activating system (RAS), which resides in the brain stem, plays a role in the regulation of alertness and arousal.
- The superior colliculus, located in the midbrain, plays an important role in automatically orienting attention to particular locations in space.
- Portions of the thalamus act as a gating mechanism for selecting or filtering incoming information, whereas other portions of the thalamus help activate the cortex.
- The posterior parietal lobe provides a spatial frame of reference for attentional processing, binds together features, such as color and form, so items can be uniquely identified, and is likely involved in allocating overall resources needed to meet attentional demands.
- The cingulate cortex aids in selecting motor responses and may also aid in processing when tasks are attentionally demanding.
- Frontal regions are important for top-down attentional control, and motor aspects of attentional control, such as the voluntary control of eye movements to information that is to receive attention.

The Time Course of Attentional Selection

- Cognitive neuroscience has indicated that selection can occur at multiple points in time—soon after sensory attributes are initially processed and also after items have been identified.

Selection by Spatial Location, Objects and Features

- Attention can be directed to a particular position in space, to a particular item attribute, such as color, or to a particular object.
- In general, attention acts to increase processing in brain regions that are responsible for processing the type of information to which attention is directed.

Models of Attentional Control by a Cortical Network

- Some models propose that each component of attentional control relies on a specific brain region.
- Other models assume that different brain regions play distinct but overlapping roles with one another in controlling attention.
- Still other models suggest that attention is controlled by two subsystems: the posterior

subsystem plays a prominent role in selection of information based on sensory attributes, while the anterior subsystem plays a role in selecting items on the basis of abstract representations, such as an item's meaning or how relevant it is to a task.
- Computational models emphasize the degree to which attention acts via competitive interaction among items, in a winner-take-all fashion, with attention acting to bias this competition.

Hemineglect: Clinical Aspects
- In hemineglect, which is most often observed after vascular damage to the posterior parietal region, an individual ignores information on the side of space contralateral to a brain lesion.
- The neglect is not due to sensory deficits, as the severity of neglect for the contralateral side of space does *not* vary with sensory modality, and individuals with a severe sensory deficit for the contralateral side of space do not exhibit neglect for that side of space.
- Neglect can be modulated by factors that draw attention to information on the neglected side of space, such as high emotional saliency, motivational factors, and a need to process such information to allow for understanding or comprehension of material.
- Theories regarding the main underlying deficit in neglect include one suggesting that patients lose the mental conception of the neglected side of space, and another suggesting competition between the attentional biases of each hemisphere to the opposite side of space.
- Treatments for neglect include sensory stimulation of body parts located on the neglected side of space, and, to yield a temporary reduction, caloric stimulation therapy, in which cold water is introduced into the ear canal.

Hemineglect: Implications for Understanding Brain-Behavior Relationships
- Neglect demonstrates the existence of multiple spatial frames of reference with regards to left and right: with regard to either body-centered coordinates, head-centered coordinates or gravitational coordinates.
- Neglect can demonstrate the existence of other frames of reference: with regard to the vertical plane (top-bottom) and the depth plane (near, far).
- Neglect also illustrates that attention can be either space-based or object-based.
- The fact that neglect is more common and more severe after right-hemisphere damage, suggests that the right hemisphere is more important for overall arousal and attention and/or that the attentional gradient for the contralateral versus the ipsilateral side of space is steeper for the left hemisphere than the right.
- Material in the neglected field that cannot be identified by patients with hemineglect can nonetheless influence performance by priming certain responses, and appears to undergo early stages of processing that allow for unconscious but not conscious access.

KEY TERMS

alertness and arousal 254
altitudinal neglect 277
attention 254
caloric stimulation 274
chronic vegetative state 256
cingulate cortex 261
coma 255
contingent negative variation (CNV) 256
double simultaneous stimulation technique 269
early-selection viewpoint 262
hemi-inattention 253
hemineglect 253
intralaminar nucleus of the thalamus 258
late-selection viewpoint 262
medial dorsal nucleus of the thalamus 258
multiple-resource theory 254
object-based viewpoint of attention 264
pulvinar 258
resource 254
reticular activating system (RAS) 255
reticular nuclei 258
saccade 256
selective attention 254
somatoparaphrenia 269
space-based viewpoint of attention 264
stupor 256
superior colliculus 256
vigilance 254

CHAPTER 9

LANGUAGE

Dr. Sheila Chorpenning, a neurologist, had just joined the staff of a hospital for U.S. Army veterans. In the large patient recreation room, she noticed two men sitting on a sofa, one middle-aged and one younger. The middle-aged man, Bill Rieger, had been a rising star in high school—academically talented and a top athlete. But then his mother died unexpectedly. Confused by her death, he turned down a scholarship to college and joined the army. During a combat mission in Vietnam, he was hit by shrapnel that damaged his left frontal lobe as well as parts of his parietal lobe. Dr. Chorpenning introduced herself and asked Bill to tell her about his history. He replied:

> "My un mother died . . . uh . . . me . . . uh fi'tenn. Uh, oh, I guess six month . . . my mother pass away. An'uh . . . an'en . . . un . . . ah . . . seventeen . . . seventeen . . . go . . . uh High School. An uh . . . Christmas . . . well, uh, I uh . . . Pitt'burgh" (Goodglass, 1976, p. 239).

He told the story with much effort, and the words seemed to explode as they came out of his mouth. His intonation was uneven, which made his speech difficult to follow initially, but with time Dr. Chorpenning found him easier to understand.

The younger man, who was in his late twenties, was named Jim Hurdle. He had had a carotid artery aneurysm (the ballooning, then breaking of the carotid artery), which had caused brain damage. As Dr. Chorpenning began to converse with him, he attempted to explain that he didn't live at the hospital but had just been brought there by his father to have some dental work performed:

> "Ah . . . Monday . . . ah, Dad and Jim Hurdle [referring to himself by his full name] and Dad . . . hospital. Two . . . ah, doctors . . . , and ah . . . thirty minutes . . . and yes . . . ah . . . hospital. And, er Wednesday . . . nine o'clock. And er Thursday, ten o'clock . . . doctors. Two doctors . . . and ah . . . teeth. Yeah, . . . fine" (Goodglass, 1976, p. 238).

Like the first man, Jim spoke in a slow, halting cadence, and his words were produced in a harsh and guttural manner.

Despite their difficulties in speaking, both men seemed to understand most of what Dr. Chorpenning said to them. When she mentioned that the weather was springlike, Bill pointed to the open window through which a warm breeze was blowing. When she discussed what a relief the present weather was compared with the cold, hard winter that they had been experiencing, Jim pulled his sweater tightly around himself and imitated a shiver. Before she left, she thanked both men for chatting with her, realizing how frustrated they were with their inability to communicate. ■

LANGUAGE IS THE mental faculty that many people consider most uniquely human and that most distinctly separates us from the other species that inhabit the earth. It is such a wonderful communicative tool that for more than a century scientists have tried to understand how the brain's organization endows us with such a superb faculty. In fact, language difficulties such as those experienced by Bill Rieger and Jim Hurdle first led Paul Broca in the late 1800s to realize that the hemispheres have different functions, an event that heralded the advent of modern-day neuropsychology. Broca noticed that a lesion to a specific region of the left hemisphere causes a loss of fluent speech even though the person's speech comprehension is relatively spared. This syndrome, known as **Broca's aphasia** (*aphasia* is the loss of a language-processing ability after brain damage), has revealed more than just hemispheric specialization: it has also provided a window to understanding the neurological organization for language.

In this chapter, we discuss a variety of aphasias, gleaning from each some lessons about the neurological organization for language. We consider the neural underpinnings for spoken and written language and examine the degree to which their neural substrates are similar and the degree to which they are distinct. Although most of our discussion is on the neural organization for Indo-European languages, such as English, we also consider the neural underpinnings for other languages, including those from Asia and languages created by persons who are deaf. We take this broader view because if some aspects of the neurological organization for language are universal, they should reveal themselves despite the different grammatical structures found across languages (e.g., Indo-European vs. Asian languages) and despite differences in the modality in which the information is conveyed (e.g., sound in English vs. hand movement in American Sign Language). We end the chapter by examining how the right hemisphere, which was initially thought to be relatively uninvolved in language, contributes to language comprehension.

Neurological Bases for Auditory Language Processing

Our discussion of the neural bases for language begins by taking the classic approach used since the mid-1800s, namely, characterizing patterns of language impairment that accompany specific brain lesions. Afterward, we consider the degree to which evidence from other more modern methods converges with the conclusions drawn from the study of individuals with brain damage. In this section, we focus mainly on auditory language, saving our discussion of written language for later in the chapter.

Evidence from Studies of Patients with Brain Damage

At the beginning of this book, we discussed how the relationship between the brain and mental function can be examined from either of two vantage points—one emphasizing the neurological organization of the brain and one emphasizing the psychological processes performed by the brain. These two vantage points are extremely well illustrated by the differing perspectives on language breakdown after brain trauma. The early advances in this field, made in the late 1800s, came squarely from a neurological, or medical, perspective. Because damage to particular regions of the cortex can each produce distinct language problems, the early *aphasiologists* (i.e., people who study aphasia) proposed that each region of the cortex had a specific role in language processing: one area was deemed critical for recognizing sound images of words, and another critical for producing speech. As we learn shortly, according to these models, the brain processes language much as a factory manufactures products along a conveyor belt. Input is received at one region, then is packaged and sent to another region for output. From this perspective, these models have a "knee bone is connected to the thigh bone" flavor about them.

Since the 1960s, psycholinguists have examined the neurological bases for language from a different perspective. In attempting to understand the results of brain damage on language processing, these researchers have emphasized the organization of language rather than the organization of the brain. This approach has led them to ask very different questions about aphasia. For example, they have used aphasia to help test theories about the fundamental components of language.

In this chapter, we examine language processing from both perspectives: the neurological and the psychological. Because each can provide useful information, these views should be considered complementary rather than mutually exclusive ways to conceptualize the brain organization for language. After discussing each perspective (according to historical precedent—the neurological viewpoint first and the psychological second), we determine the generalizations about language that can be made regardless of the viewpoint taken.

• *NEUROLOGICAL PERSPECTIVE* •

As we mentioned, the two men discussed in the opening vignette of the chapter, Bill and Jim, had an aphasia similar to that experienced by Broca's patients. If you reread what the two men said, you may be struck by certain characteristics. You may have noticed the paucity of speech output: people with Broca's aphasia have great difficulty producing words. Broca deduced that the deficit he observed in his patients was specifically linguistic in nature because their difficulty with speech output was not accompanied by motoric problems of the vocal musculature, such as paralysis. The patients could utter sounds, albeit not linguistic ones, and were sometimes able to use the mouth and lips to perform orofacial movements, such as blowing out candles.

Because the deficit appeared to be limited to the language domain, Broca conceptualized the region of the brain that now bears his name as the area that is critical for programming speech output.

Although difficulty in speech output is a glaring symptom of Broca's aphasia, you may have noticed other characteristics from Bill and Jim's dialogue as well. For instance, the sentences do not fit a standard structure but seem more like a telegram (e.g., "Need help, send money"). This characteristic is often referred to as **telegraphic speech** because the words produced tend to be only content words, such as nouns and verbs. Function words and word endings are missing. Function words, although they convey little information, are nonetheless important for speech comprehension because they provide information about the relations among words. Conjunctions (e.g., *but, and*) and prepositions (e.g., *around, behind, about*) are function words. Word endings also convey meaning that is important for language comprehension. For example, *-ing* and *-s* appended to the end of a word designate, respectively, an action that is happening at the present time, and more than one item. We return to a discussion of these characteristics in the next section, when we discuss the psychological perspective on this type of aphasia.

Until this point, we have not discussed the specific location of the lesion that causes Broca's aphasia other than to say that it is in the left hemisphere. However, the knowledge we have gained in the previous chapters should enable us to make a well-educated guess as to its general location. First, guess whether the lesion is located anterior or posterior to the central fissure. Here's a hint: remember that the most prominent behavioral deficit in Broca's aphasia is a disruption of speech output with relatively spared comprehension. Given that hint, you can reason that the lesion causing Broca's aphasia is anterior to the central fissure, because anterior regions are specialized for motor output. Now, decide whether the lesion must include the motor strip. You should conclude that it does not, because Broca's aphasia is not a result of facial or vocal muscle paralysis. Finally, consider whether the lesion causing Broca's aphasia is located ventrally or dorsally in the frontal lobe. This decision is more difficult, but if you remember the organization of the motor strip, you might be inclined to choose ventral, because the head and the face are represented at the inferior portion of the motor strip. In fact, the lesion that typically causes Broca's aphasia is in the frontal region, just anterior to, but not in, the section of the motor strip that is responsible for control of the face (see Figure 9.1) (e.g., H. Damasio, 1991a).

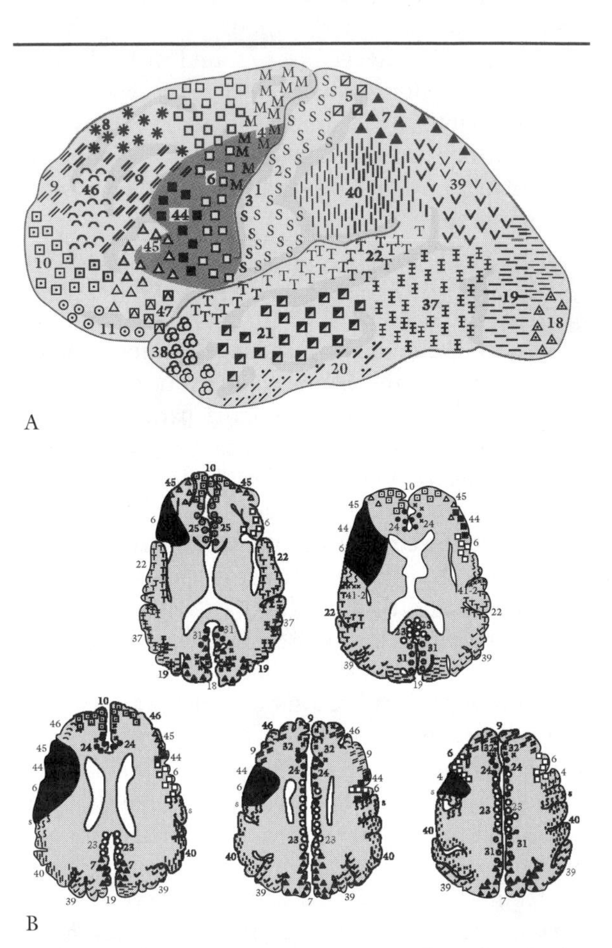

FIGURE 9.1 Site of damage that causes Broca's aphasia. Shown here is the location of the lesion in one patient with Broca's aphasia, as viewed (A) laterally and (B) in oblique brain slices that go from the lowest region of the brain that is affected (top row, left-hand slice) to the highest region (bottom row, right-hand slice). The damage in this patient involves not only Broca's area proper (Brodmann's areas 44 and 45), but also other areas that are often damaged, such as the motor and premotor areas (areas 4 and 6).

As we discussed in Chapter 4, about 20 years after Broca characterized his aphasia, Karl Wernicke described the converse syndrome—disrupted speech comprehension along with fluent (but nonsensical) speech output—which became known as **Wernicke's aphasia.** *Fluent* is the operative word in describing this syndrome because the output occurs without hesitation, the sounds are well formed, and all parts of speech are present. Yet, what these individuals say makes little sense; their output is a jumble of words, often referred to as a *word salad.* In fact, the speech of a person with Wernicke's aphasia can be so disjointed that someone without proper training in a medically relevant field might be tempted to refer the individual to a psychiatrist rather than a neurologist. Following is an example of speech from a 70-year-old man who acquired Wernicke's aphasia after blockage of part of his middle cerebral artery. Unlike the speech of individuals with Broca's aphasia, his speech was produced at a normal rate and rhythm and with an intonational pattern that was, if anything, exaggerated: "I feel very well. My hearing, writing been doing well, things that I couldn't hear from. In other words, I used to be able to work cigarettes I don't know how. . . . This year the last three years, or perhaps a little more, I didn't know how to do me any able to" (Goodglass, 1976, p. 239).

The speech of persons with Wernicke's aphasia is hard to comprehend not only because the words are combined in a way that makes little sense, but also because of errors in producing specific words, known as **paraphasias.** Paraphasias manifest in numerous forms. In a **semantic paraphasia,** the substituted word has a similar meaning to the intended one (e.g., substitution of "barn" for "house"). In a **phonemic paraphasia,** the substituted word has a similar sound to the intended one (e.g., "table" becomes "trable" or "fable"). On other occasions, persons with Wernicke's aphasia produce sounds known as **neologisms** that follow the rules by which a language combines its sounds yet are not words (e.g., "galump," "trebbin").

Despite the fluency of their output, individuals with Wernicke's aphasia generally have much trouble understanding language. They may not even be able to understand enough to follow simple commands such as "Point to the blue square" or "Pick up the spoon." Wernicke originally postulated that these individuals cannot link the "sound images" of language to meaning.

From what we just learned about the behavioral manifestations of Wernicke's aphasia, you should be able to make an educated guess as to the location of the lesion that typically results in this disorder. Is the lesion anterior to or posterior to the central fissure? You should have guessed posterior, because those regions of the brain are involved in interpreting sensory information. But where in posterior cortex? Consider that Wernicke described this aphasia as an inability to link a sound image to meaning or stored information. What posterior brain regions might that bring to mind? Because we are discussing a sound image, you might consider regions in the superior temporal lobe near Heschl's gyrus, which is the primary auditory area. Because the retrieval of meaning is important, other regions of the temporal lobe might be considered plausible candidates. Finally, because a sensory input must be linked to meaning, the parietal lobe might also be a viable candidate. As you can see in Figure 9.2, the lesion that typically causes Wernicke's aphasia is close to all these areas; it is situated typically at the junction of the temporal lobe with parietal and occipital regions, near Heschl's gyrus.

Not only did Wernicke discover the aphasia that bears his name, but he also postulated the existence of other aphasic syndromes, some of which were later documented. Wernicke assumed a basic blueprint for the neurological organization for language in which Broca's area is responsible for speech output and Wernicke's area is responsible for speech comprehension. He went on to suggest that damage severing the connection between these two areas should also result in yet another aphasic syndrome, one characterized by difficulty repeating what was just heard. If the damage that severed the connection nevertheless spared both Broca's and Wernicke's areas, both language comprehension and speech production would be intact, yet the person would not be able to repeat what was just heard, because sound images received by Wernicke's area could not be conducted forward to Broca's area to be produced. Wernicke's speculations were correct, and this syndrome has come to be known as **conduction aphasia.** When individuals with conduction aphasia are asked

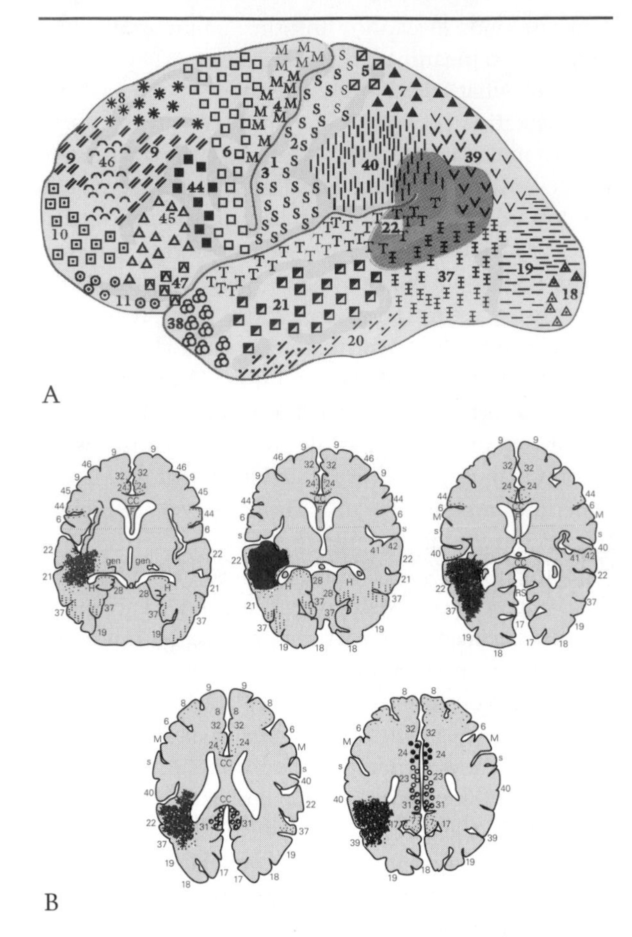

FIGURE 9.2 Site of damage that causes Wernicke's aphasia. This diagram shows a composite of the lesions observed in patients with Wernicke's aphasia, as viewed (A) laterally and (B) in oblique brain slices that go from the lowest region of the brain that is affected (top row, left-hand slice) to the highest region (bottom row, right-hand slice). In general, not only is Wernicke's area (Brodmann's area 22) affected, but so is primary auditory cortex (areas 41 and 42). The lesion sometimes extends into regions of the middle temporal gyrus (portions of areas 37 and 21) and the angular gyrus (area 39).

to repeat words, they often make phonemic paraphasias, may substitute or omit words, or may be unable to say anything.

You may remember from Chapter 3 that syndromes caused by severed connections between intact brain regions are called *disconnection syndromes.* Conduction aphasia is one such syndrome in that the behavioral dysfunction does not arise from damage to either the brain region that processes the sound image (Wernicke's area) or the region of the brain that produces the output (Broca's area) but instead from an inability to relay information from one intact area to another intact area. It is as if a communication cable between the two regions were broken. In fact, a large nerve-fiber tract, known as the *arcuate fasciculus,* connects these two regions, and part of this tract is almost invariably damaged in conduction aphasia, along with surrounding tissue (see Figure 9.3).

Lichtheim and other aphasiologists of the late 1800s elaborated Wernicke's model to include not only a brain region that was responsible for speech output and a brain region that processed sound images, but another region as well, the *concept center,* which was thought to be the place in the brain where meanings were stored and from where they originated. This three-part model is shown in Figure 9.4. Although the model itself is flawed—in actuality there is not a single "concept center" in the brain—it was used to predict the existence of certain aphasic syndromes that do occur regularly. We next discuss the characteristics of these syndromes.

Aphasiologists were interested in what difficulties would arise as the result of a disconnection between the proposed concept center and the other components of the language-processing system. These researchers reasoned that if the concept center were disconnected from the output center (Broca's area), most of speech output would be disrupted inasmuch as ideas could not be translated into speech. However, if Broca's area itself was spared, at least some degree of output would be possible if access to this area could be gained by another route.

As the model in Figure 9.4 shows, the sound image system, housed in Wernicke's area, is connected to the output center, Broca's area, not only via the meaning system, but also directly. Hence, the aphasiologists predicted that this intact direct route should enable the person to automatically feed-forward what was just heard for speech output, resulting in intact repetition. A syndrome with this behavioral profile has been observed, **transcortical motor aphasia.** Symptomatically, these patients show the same deficits as those shown by patients

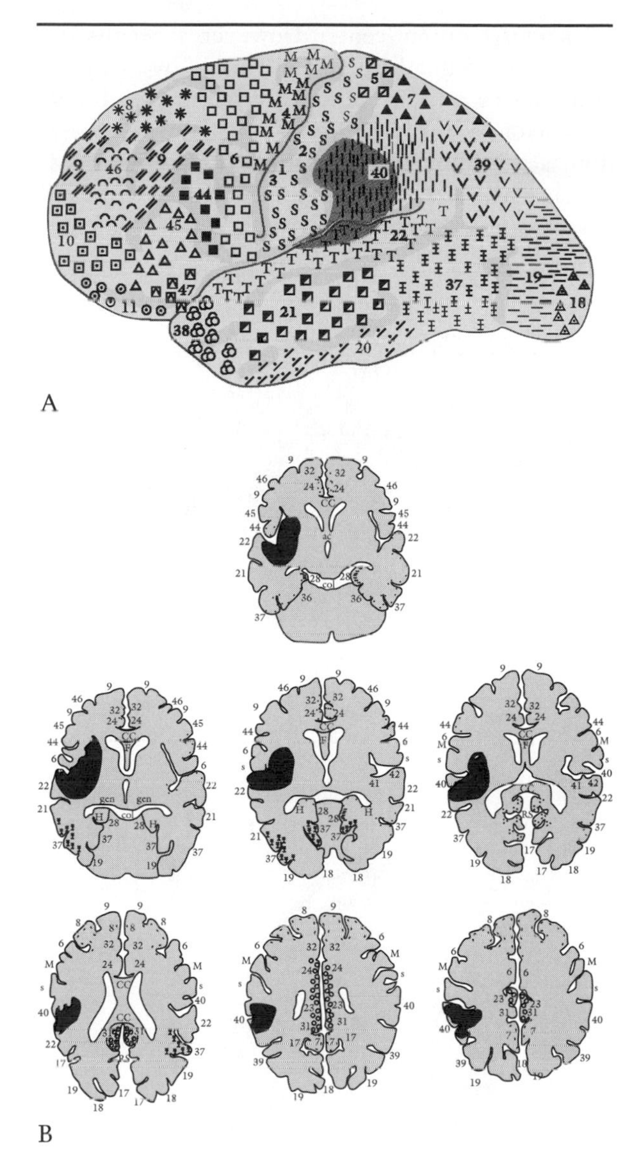

FIGURE 9.3 Site of damage that causes conduction aphasia. This diagram shows a composite of the lesions observed in six patients with conduction aphasia, as viewed (A) laterally and (B) in oblique brain slices that go from the lowest regions of the brain that are affected (top row) to the highest region (bottom row, right). The lesion generally affects an area in the insula (the region tucked into the Sylvian fissure) that includes Brodmann's areas 22, 41, and 42. More superior regions of the supramarginal gyrus (area 40) are often affected as well. Notice that the damaged area depicted here is located between those shown in Figures 9.1 and 9.2.

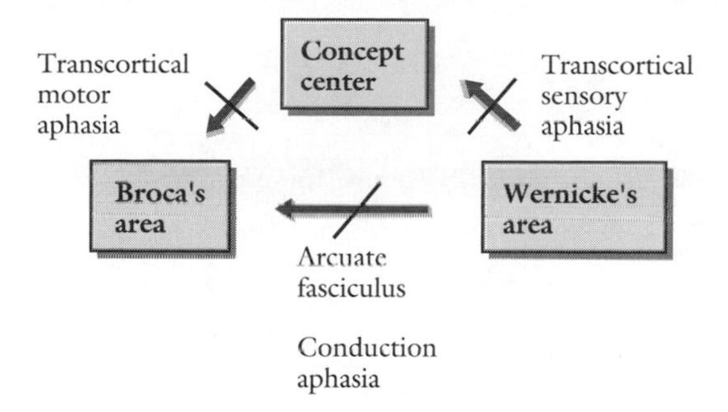

FIGURE 9.4 Lichtheim's model of language processing. In Lichtheim's conception, Wernicke's area processes the sound images of words, and this information is then fed forward through a nerve-fiber tract, the arcuate fasciculus, to Broca's area, which is responsible for speech output. Damage to the region between Broca's area and Wernicke's area leads to conduction aphasia. Language disruption can also occur if either the input from Wernicke's area is disconnected from the concept center (which causes transcortical sensory aphasia), or the output from the concept center cannot reach Broca's area (which causes transcortical motor aphasia).

with Broca's aphasia, except they retain the ability to repeat. They often do so compulsively, a characteristic known as **echolalia.** The area of brain tissue typically damaged in this syndrome is shown in Figure 9.5.

The aphasiologists also considered the behavioral consequences of a disconnection between the region processing sound images of words and the concept center. Such a disconnection, they reasoned, should prevent an individual from interpreting the meaning of words. Nevertheless, the remaining connection between the intact sound image and the output area would enable words to be repeated (refer back to Figure 9.4). A syndrome with this behavioral profile has also been observed, **transcortical sensory aphasia.** Patients with this syndrome have symptoms similar to those of patients with Wernicke's aphasia, except they can repeat words and they exhibit echolalia. The damage typically associated with this syndrome is shown in Figure 9.6.

Finally, the aphasiologists speculated that individuals who had extensive damage to multiple parts of the system (e.g., the output center and the sound image center) would be left with neither the ability to comprehend language nor the ability to produce

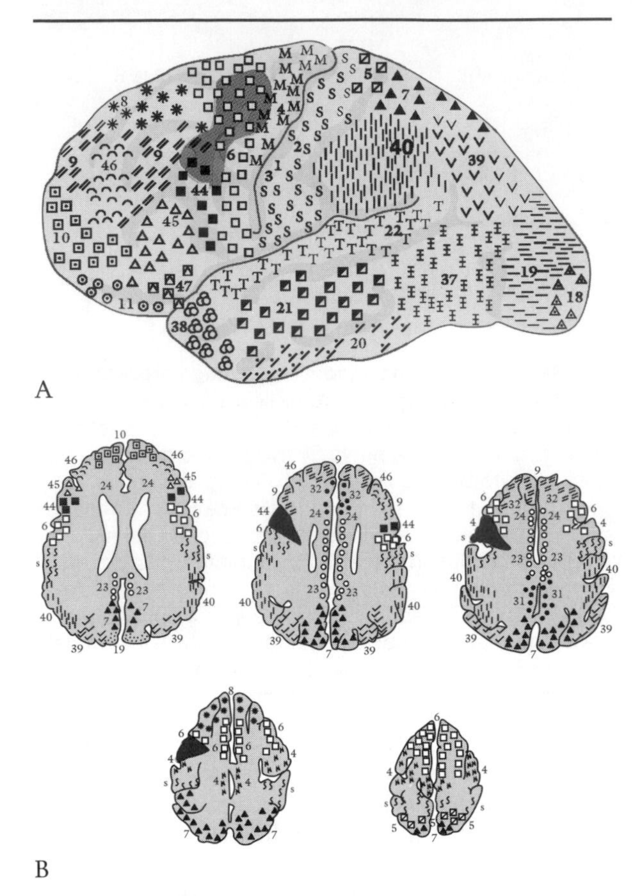

FIGURE 9.5 Site of damage in a typical case of transcortical motor aphasia. Shown here is the damage as viewed (A) laterally and (B) in oblique slices that go from the lowest region of the brain affected (top row, left) to the highest region (bottom row, right). In general, the lesion is located outside Broca's area and is either more anterior or more superior. In this particular case, left premotor and motor cortices, just above Broca's area, are affected.

it. Behaviorally, such a syndrome has been observed, **global aphasia.** This syndrome is associated with extensive left-hemisphere damage that typically includes not only Wernicke's and Broca's areas, but the area between them as well (Figure 9.7).

Although useful, the three-part model of Lichtheim and other nineteenth-century aphasiologists does not provide an adequate explanation of the symptomatology in aphasia. For example, the model posits that Broca's aphasia is caused by damage to the language-output center. However, as we discuss next, the difficulties experienced by patients with Broca's aphasia are not limited to speech output. Before we analyze the symptoms of aphasia from a psycholinguistic perspective, see Table 9.1, which lists the major aphasic syndromes observed clinically and their characteristics. Because different

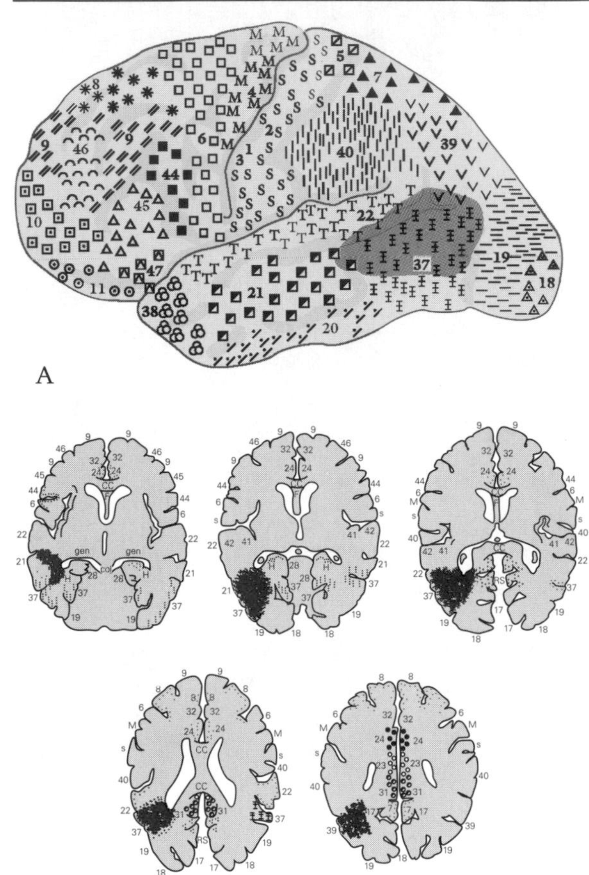

FIGURE 9.6 Site of damage in transcortical sensory aphasia. This diagram shows a composite of the lesions observed in six cases of transcortical sensory aphasia, as viewed (A) laterally and (B) in oblique brain slices that go from the lowest region of the brain that is affected (top row, left) to the highest region (bottom row, right). In this type of aphasia, Wernicke's area (area 22) is never completely damaged, but more posterior regions of the temporal lobe (area 37) are always damaged. Sometimes the angular gyrus (area 39) and extrastriate regions (area 19) are also affected.

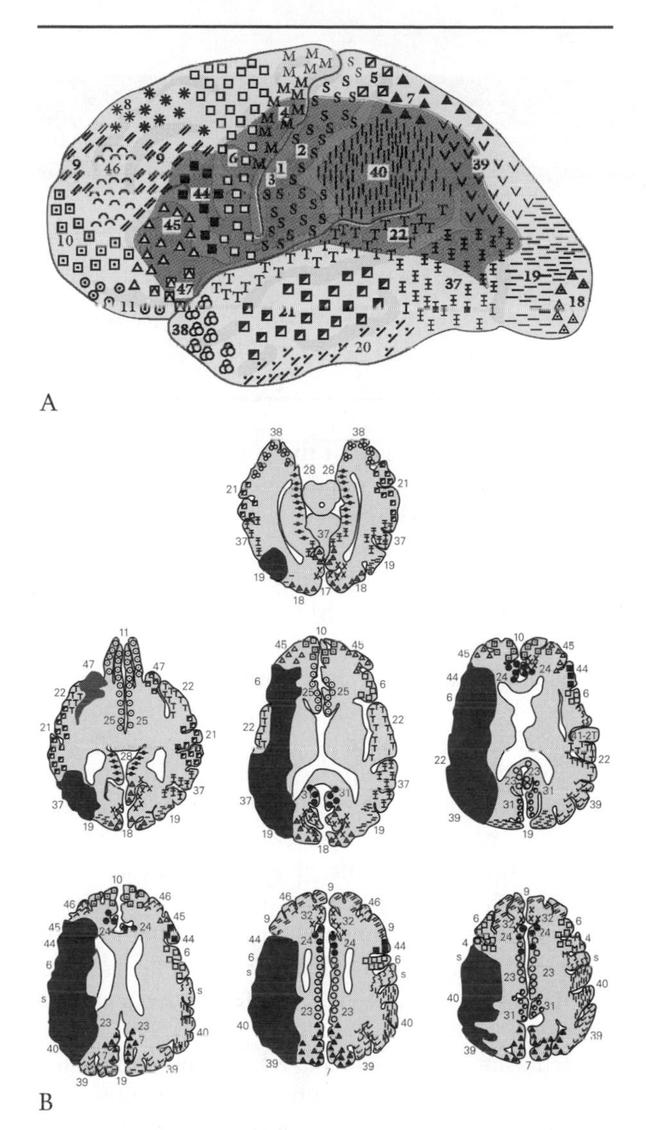

FIGURE 9.7 Site of damage in one case of global aphasia. Shown here is the damaged area as viewed (A) laterally and (B) in oblique brain slices that go from the lowest region of the brain that is affected (top row) to the highest region (bottom row, right). The massive left hemisphere damage affects almost all regions implicated in causing the other types of aphasias.

nomenclatures are used for these various syndromes, you may also find Broca's aphasia referred to as *nonfluent, agrammatic,* or *anterior aphasia,* whereas Wernicke's aphasia is also sometimes referred to as *fluent,* or *posterior, aphasia.* Figure 9.8

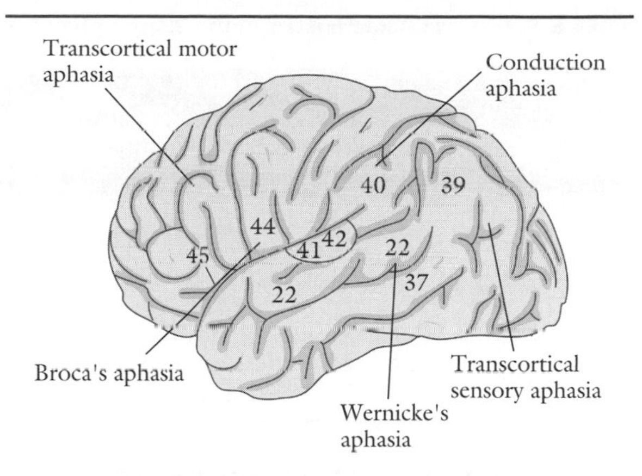

FIGURE 9.8 Composite diagram indicating the regions associated with the various major types of aphasias. The numbers in this diagram refer to Brodmann's areas.

provides a summary schematic of the typical lesion locations for each type of aphasia discussed in Table 9.1.

• *PSYCHOLOGICAL PERSPECTIVE* •

Since the 1960s, interest in aphasia has been renewed by psychologists and psycholinguists using aphasic disorders as a window into uncovering the mental structure for language (for a detailed and scholarly discussion of this approach, see Caplan, 1987). The way in which language breaks down in aphasia provides evidence either for or against theories about the organization of language. To appreciate what aphasia tells us about language processing in the human brain, we must first have some knowledge about the basic components of language as conceptualized by psycholinguists. They consider language to have three main components: phonology, syntax, and semantics. Roughly speaking, **phonology** examines the sounds that compose a language and the rules that govern their combination, **syntax** is the rules of grammar, and **semantics** is the meaning of language. We now discuss each in more detail.

• *Phonology* • As we just mentioned, phonology refers to the rules governing the sounds of language. Linguists have conceptualized two ways of representing the sounds of speech: phonemically and phonetically. A *phoneme* is considered the smallest unit

TABLE 9.1 Basic Characteristics of the Major Aphasic Syndromes

TYPE OF APHASIA	SPONTANEOUS SPEECH	PARAPHASIA	COMPREHENSION	REPETITION	NAMING
Broca's	Nonfluent	Uncommon	Good	Poor	Poor
Wernicke's	Fluent	Common (verbal)	Poor	Poor	Poor
Conduction	Fluent	Common (literal)	Good	Poor	Poor
Transcortical motor	Nonfluent	Uncommon	Good	Good (echolalia)	Poor
Transcortical sensory	Fluent	Common	Poor	Good (echolalia)	Poor
Global	Nonfluent	Variable	Poor	Poor	Poor

of sound that can signal meaning. For example, /b/ and /p/ mean nothing by themselves (/ / is used to symbolize a linguistic sound, allowing, for example, the sound /b/ to be differentiated from the letter *b*), but they nonetheless cause /bat/ and /pat/ to have different meanings. In contrast, the *phonetic* representation of a speech sound describes how it is produced on particular occasions or in particular contexts. For example, /p/ can be articulated in a number of ways. The /p/ in *pill* is created differently than the /p/ in *spill.* In *pill,* the /p/ is aspirated (produced with a burst of air), whereas the /p/ in *spill* is not aspirated. Different phonetic representations of the same phoneme are known as *allophones.*

Persons with Broca's aphasia, and other groups with aphasia whose speech is nonfluent, have difficulty producing the correct allophone of a phoneme (S. Blumstein, 1991), meaning that they cannot produce the correct *phonetic* representation of a speech sound. The production of different allophones of the same phoneme requires precise control over the articulatory muscles, with each version varying in subtle but important ways, a precision lacking in individuals with Broca's aphasia. In contrast, patients with Wernicke's aphasia (and other fluent aphasias) have little difficulty producing the correct allophone of a given phoneme. Thus, although the phonetic representation of a speech sound is disrupted in Broca's aphasia, it is not disrupted in Wernicke's aphasia.

Even though individuals with Wernicke's aphasia have no difficulty producing the correct phonetic representation of a speech sound, they often have difficulty producing the correct phoneme. This dissociation indicates that the phonemic representation of a speech sound is distinct from its phonetic representation. Thus, whereas a person with Wernicke's aphasia would be highly unlikely to produce an aspirated /p/ for a nonaspirated one, he or she might substitute a /b/ for a /p/. Patients with Broca's aphasia, however, appear to have difficulty producing both the correct phonetic and the correct phonemic representations of a speech sound (see Nespoulous et al., 1984, for a somewhat different perspective but a similar conclusion that persons with anterior aphasia have difficulty with the execution of word sounds).

The disruption of the phonemic representation of a speech sound in aphasia occurs systematically and can be well explained by a psycholinguistic perspective that considers speech sounds as being composed of a set of distinctive features. To explain this idea, we need a short digression on how certain speech sounds are produced. According to linguistic theory, consonants vary in distinctive features, two of which are place of articulation and voicing. Both of these bear on the voyage of air from the lungs out of the vocal tract. **Place of articulation** describes *the location* in the vocal tract where airflow is obstructed. This distinction is very obvious with *stop consonants,* which are the consonants in which airflow is initially stopped completely. For example, /b/ and /p/ are known as *labial stops* because obstruction occurs at the lips, /d/ and /t/ are *alveolar stops* because the obstruction occurs from tongue placement at the alveolar ridge behind the front teeth, and /g/ and /k/ are *velar stops* because the air is obstructed at the velar, or soft, palate in the back of the mouth. Say these sounds to yourself right now and it will become obvious how the airflow is obstructed in different places. **Voicing** describes the timing between the release of the air for the stop consonant and the vibration of the vocal cords. When a consonant is voiced, the release of air and the vibration of the vocal cords coincide (/b/, /d/, /g/), whereas in an unvoiced consonant (/p/, /t/, /k/), the vocal cords don't begin to vibrate until after the release. Hence, the only difference between a /b/ and a /p/, which are both labial stops, is that vocal cord vibration and air release are coincident in time for a /b/, whereas for a /p/ the air release precedes vocal cord vibration by a mere 40 to 80 ms! As such, incredibly precise timing in the movements of the vocal apparatus is necessary to correctly produce a /b/ that is distinct from a /p/, and equally precise temporal resolution of the auditory apparatus is required to perceive the difference between a /b/ and a /p/. (Perhaps you'll appreciate the precision of your brain a bit more the next time you utter or hear a sentence like "Pat, it's your turn to bat.")

A phoneme's distinctive features have been found to influence both the production errors of patients with aphasia as well as some of their receptive difficulties. Studies have demonstrated that when making phonemic errors, persons with aphasia are much more likely to substitute a sound that differs on the basis of only one distinctive feature (e.g., /b/ for /p/ since they differ only in voicing) rather than two (e.g., /b/ for /t/, which differ in both voicing and place of articulation). Phonemic errors of this nature are observed in both fluent and nonfluent aphasias (S. Blumstein, 1991).

With regard to perception, researchers have found that most persons with aphasia exhibit some problems in discerning these features (e.g., Miceli, Gainotti, Caltagirone, & Masullo, 1980). Not all distinctive features have equal saliency, though, because some may be less resistant to confusion than others. For example, errors based on place of articulation (e.g., /pa/ vs. /ta/) are more common than errors based on voicing (e.g., /pa/ vs. /ba/) (e.g., E. Baker, Blumstein, & Goodglass, 1981). In some cases, individuals are able to distinguish the acoustic differences between the sounds (i.e., distinguish the time offset between vocal cord vibration and airflow release) but have difficulty ascertaining the linguistic value of the sounds that they can discriminate. Thus, they may know that /ba/ and /da/ sound different but can't identify the latter as /d/ either by pointing to a card with the letter D or by saying "d" (S. E. Blumstein, Cooper, Zurif, & Caramazza, 1977).

Interestingly, an aphasic individual's degree of difficulty in linguistically categorizing the acoustic patterns of speech sounds does not predict the level of auditory comprehension (S. E. Blumstein, Baker, & Goodglass, 1977). Some individuals with aphasia who have great difficulty linguistically labeling certain speech sounds may have adequate comprehension. You can probably appreciate this effect if you've ever experienced hearing a word and knowing what it means but are unable to break it down into its constituent sounds well enough to spell it correctly. Persons with aphasia may also use information about sentence structure, the legal combination of sounds in words, and the context in which words are presented to make educated guesses that compensate for their difficulties in linguistic categorization. Conversely, some patients can linguistically label acoustic patterns yet have poor comprehension. Knowing each phoneme in a word does not ensure that you can extract meaning from words and sentences (S. Blumstein, 1991). You can probably appreciate this dissociation if you've known all the sounds in a word well enough to spell it but had no idea of its meaning.

Phonological theory describes not only the sounds of language, as we have just been discussing, but also the rules by which sounds can be combined. So, for example, in English a valid combination of sounds would be "casmeck," whereas an invalid combination would be "*cnamzik." (Linguists denote a word or a sentence that is not legal in a language by preceding it with an asterisk.) As you may remember from our earlier discussion, patients with aphasia, most notably Wernicke's aphasics, often construct novel series of sounds called *neologisms.* These neologisms *could* be words because they follow the rules for combining sounds, but the particular combination used does not constitute a valid word. In this sense, persons with aphasia appear to respect the rules of phonology for the language that they speak.

In summary, phonologic processing can be disrupted in aphasia in two major ways. First, phonetic representations of phonemes are often disrupted in patients with nonfluent aphasias (but remain intact in patients with fluent aphasias). Second, phoneme substitution in production and difficulty in phoneme discrimination are common occurrences in both fluent and nonfluent aphasias and appear to be governed by the similarity of phonemes to each other along the dimensions of distinctive contrasts. Analysis of language breakdown in aphasia suggests that the phonetic and phonemic representations of sounds are distinct in that the phonemic representation may be compromised even when the phonetic representation is intact. Despite these difficulties, the rules that govern the combination of specific phonemes are preserved in aphasic speech.

• ***Syntax*** • The second fundamental component of language, syntax, describes the rules governing how words are put together in sentences. For example, in English we generally use a subject-verb-object (SVO) word order, as in the sentence "The cat sat on her lap." This is not true of all languages. In Turkish, for example, the standard word order is subject, object, verb (SOV). Within a language, various syntactic forms or frames are often allowed. SVO word order in English is considered the active voice, and OVS is considered the passive voice, as in the sentence "The robber [object] was chased [verb] by the police officer [subject]."

Persons with certain types of aphasia, most notably those with anterior lesions, often have specific difficulties with the syntactic aspects of language processing. If you reread the opening vignette, you should notice that function words and word endings are missing in the gentlemen's speech, and that the words are not structured in a standard syntactic frame. Historically, researchers assumed that persons with anterior aphasia failed to produce function words and prepositions not because they had difficulty with syntax, but because they found it so hard to produce speech that they carefully chose those words that would convey the most meaning for the least effort—nouns and verbs. If this explanation were correct, then syntactic difficulties would be limited to production and not affect comprehension. More careful examination has revealed this not to be the case.

Individuals with anterior aphasia have a deficit in both the production *and* the comprehension of grammatical aspects of language and are therefore sometimes said to have **agrammatic aphasia.** For example, persons with anterior aphasia often have difficulty discerning the difference between active and passive sentences such as "The cat chased the kitten" versus "The cat was chased by the kitten." In the former case, the word structure is in the standard SVO (subject-verb-object) form, whereas in the latter it is in the nonstandard OVS (object-verb-subject) form, as signaled by the grammatical markers of the auxiliary verb *was* and the preposition *by.* Because of their insensitivity to syntactic markers, these patients assume an SVO word order for both sentences. When asked to select a picture representing the meaning of each sentence, these individuals select the same picture for both sentences, one of an adult feline chasing an immature feline.

Because languages vary widely in their syntactic structure, many opportunities exist to obtain converging evidence for the role of anterior brain regions in the processing of syntax (see Bates, Wulfeck, & MacWhinney, 1991, and related articles in the same issue of *Brain and Language* for a discussion of the commonalities and peculiarities of aphasia across different languages). For example, in English, we have only one definite article, *the,* and our nouns are not gendered (male, female, neuter). However, in many other languages, one *the* is used for male nouns, another *the* for female nouns, and yet another *the* for neutral nouns. Furthermore, *the* for a noun that is the subject of the sentence may differ from *the* for a noun that is the object. For example, in German, *the* for male nouns that are the subject of the sentence is *der,* whereas when a male noun is the object of a sentence, *the* becomes *den* and an *-n* is added to the end of the noun. Hence, the sentence "Der Junge küsste das Mädchen" means "The boy kissed the girl," whereas "Den Jungen küsste das Mädchen" means "The girl kissed the boy." The *den* and the *-n* at the end of *Junge* indicate that the boy is playing the role of the object. Given these two sentences, persons with anterior aphasia who are fluent in German have difficulty realizing that the boy is being kissed in the second sentence because they assume SVO word order (von Stockert & Bader, 1976).

Despite having problems differentiating between different syntactic constructions, patients with anterior aphasia have little trouble understanding sentences such as "The ice-cream cone was eaten by the boy" because their ability to understand the meaning of words (i.e., semantics) limits the interpretation of such sentences. When faced with the sentence just mentioned, an individual with anterior aphasia knows that ice-cream cones cannot eat boys (unless one is watching some very bizarre horror movie) and hence is not confused by the OVS word order. In contrast, because cats can chase kittens and kittens can chase cats, who is chasing whom is not constrained. Anterior aphasics have difficulty only when syntax must be relied upon to determine meaning.

In contrast, persons with posterior aphasia appear to have little difficulty processing syntactic aspects of language. As mentioned at the beginning of the chapter, their speech is fluent and contains all the grammatical markers (e.g., verb endings, prepositions, auxiliary verbs) that would normally be found in intact speech production (although what they say is largely devoid of meaning). Thus, their knowledge of syntax appears to be spared.

• ***Semantics*** • The third fundamental component of language, semantics, is concerned with the meaning of words and word combinations. Sentences may have different syntactic structures yet have approximately the same meaning. For example, "The beaver appeared among the reeds on the far side of the lake from where I was standing" has the same basic meaning as "On the side of the lake opposite from where I was positioned, the beaver appeared among the reeds."

The ability to extract meaning from language or to use words to produce meaning is seriously compromised in patients with posterior aphasia. In severe cases, even simple commands such as "Point to the blue circle" and "Point to the big red square," which are included in a quick screening device for aphasia known as the *Token Test* (DeRenzi, 1980), may not be understood. In less severe cases, simple nouns are understood but comprehension of more complicated linguistic material is difficult. Furthermore, this difficulty in comprehending the meaning of language is pervasive across modalities, extending to both auditory and written language. This finding indicates that the meaning system itself, as compared with some modality-specific (e.g., auditory) access to that system, is disrupted. Posterior aphasics read and write no better than they can understand speech, and their speech output conveys no more meaning than they appear to extract from spoken language. In contrast, patients with anterior aphasia appear to have intact semantic processing. They can usually follow simple commands with ease, although, as mentioned previously, they might exhibit minor problems in comprehension when syntax plays a large role in interpreting sentences. For example, if told, "Place the blue circle *on top of* the big red square," patients with anterior aphasia might react by putting the blue circle *next to* the big red square. Their problems with syntax would hinder their ability to comprehend the prepositional phrase that describes the desired relationship between the two items.

• *COMPARISON OF NEUROLOGICAL AND PSYCHOLOGICAL VIEWPOINTS* •

We have conceptualized the difference between anterior and posterior aphasias in two distinct manners. On the one hand, we have viewed anterior areas as important for speech output and posterior areas as important for speech comprehension. On the other hand, we suggested that anterior areas are important for syntactic processing and that posterior areas are involved in semantic processing. Each of these models has some validity, but a melding of the two probably best characterizes the manner in which these brain areas process language.

Regardless of how the processing difficulties experienced in the two types of aphasias are distinguished (input-output or syntactic-semantic), these syndromes represent a double dissociation in language processing. On a theoretical level, this dissociation tells us that no *unitary* language center or language system exists in the brain. Rather, the system has specific components that can act more or less independently of one another. This knowledge

TABLE 9.2 Control of Speech Output in a Sample of Left- and Right-Handed Patients as Determined by the Wada Technique

		SPEECH REPRESENTATION (%)		
HANDEDNESS	NO. OF CASES	LEFT	BILATERAL	RIGHT
Right	140	96	0	4
Left	122	70	15	15

is important both for understanding the neural control of language more completely and for practical reasons. Since the input and output of auditory language are governed by different systems, we know that therapies geared toward speech production are likely to have little effect on comprehension. Likewise, since a language's grammar and its meaning are under separate neural control, we know that being tutored in the rules of grammar is unlikely to aid a person with aphasia who is having difficulty producing sentences that make sense.

In sum, the human brain appears to have two distinct and separable subsystems that play different roles in language functioning. Although the anterior and posterior systems are intimately linked and interact seamlessly in the normally functioning brain, their separability can be revealed by brain damage.

Until this point, our discussion of the neurological bases for language has centered on evidence from individuals with brain lesions. However, as mentioned in Chapter 3, converging evidence from different neuropsychological techniques is what gives validity to our conclusions. We turn next to such evidence.

Converging Evidence from Other Research Methods

In this section of the chapter, we examine the converging evidence that exists for two important generalizations we have made about language. First, we present additional evidence that the left hemisphere plays a special role in speech output. Then we analyze further evidence for a distinction between anterior and posterior language systems.

Evidence for the left hemisphere's special role in speech production comes not only from patients with anterior aphasia and those with the split-brain syndrome (as discussed in Chapter 4), but also from two methods used during surgery for epilepsy to isolate brain regions involved in language processing. One of these, the Wada technique, was discussed in Chapter 4 (see page 119). As a reminder, this procedure involves the injection of sodium amobarbital, a barbiturate, into one of the two carotid arteries. The injection anesthetizes only one of the hemispheres. After the drug takes effect, the test administrator asks the patient to name a series of items depicted on cards that the patient was able to name prior to injection. If the anesthetized hemisphere is responsible for speech output, the person will be unable to name the items.

To ensure that only one hemisphere is capable of speech output, the usual practice is to repeat the procedure, preferably the next day (Grote et al., 1999), except the barbiturate is now injected into the other carotid artery to anesthetize the opposite hemisphere. The second procedure is necessary because in a relatively small percentage of cases, speech output is controlled by both hemispheres. Table 9.2 presents the percentages of left- and right-handed individuals who have left-hemisphere, right-hemisphere, and bihemispheric control of speech output as determined by the Wada test (Rasmussen & Milner, 1977a). These percentages accord well with more recent data on lateralization for language obtained from fMRI in neurologically intact individuals (Springer et al., 1999). As you can see from the table, speech output is rarely controlled by the right hemisphere in right-handed individuals, and in no case is speech output controlled by both hemispheres. This information is consistent with the clinical observation that **crossed aphasia**—that is, aphasia resulting from a right-hemisphere lesion in a right-hander—occurs with a frequency of 1% or less (Benson & Geschwind, 1972).

Knowing which hemisphere is responsible for speech output in left-handers is a more difficult proposition. Although left-handers, like right-handers, are most likely to have speech output controlled by the left hemisphere, in a significant proportion of left-handers the *right* hemisphere is specialized for speech output. Furthermore, in still other left-handed individuals, each hemisphere is capable of producing speech, a pattern rarely if ever observed in right-handers.

Another means of investigating the localization of auditory language processing in the brain is to stimulate the brain electrically before or during surgery for the removal of epileptic tissue. This stimulation is performed in much the same manner as discussed in Chapter 3 (see page 86) to determine the location and extent of the motor and somatosensory regions. This method reveals language to be lateralized to the left hemisphere in nearly all right-handers, a finding consistent with the results of lesion studies. Such stimulation also reveals, however, that the exact locations within the left hemisphere that are responsible for specific aspects of language processing vary considerably among individuals (Figure 9.9).

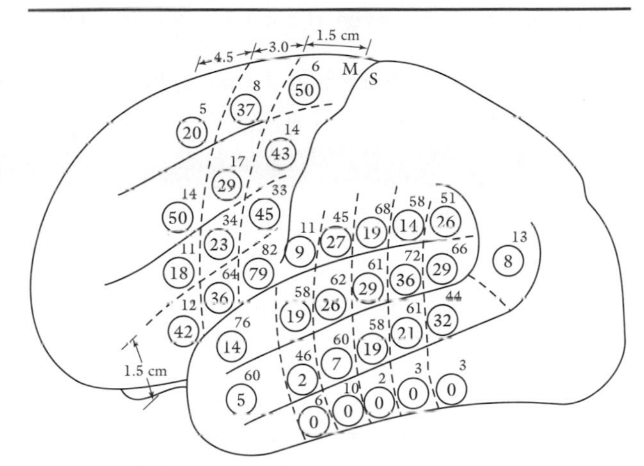

FIGURE 9.9 Language localization in the left hemisphere as determined from electrical stimulation studies. Variability among 117 patients for the regions of the left hemisphere that when electrically stimulated disrupt the ability to name objects. The number within each circle denotes the percentage of individuals whose language was disrupted by stimulation at that point, whereas the number above indicates the absolute number of individuals who produced naming errors when stimulated at that point. *M* and *S* mark the locations of the motor and somatosensory cortices, respectively. Variability can be seen among individuals both for anterior regions (which control the production of the object's name) and for posterior regions (which are involved in gaining access to the object's name).

Brain imaging studies have contributed substantially to our knowledge about language organization in the brain. First, they have provided converging evidence that anterior and posterior regions of the left hemisphere play different roles in language. For example, increased activity in the superior temporal regions of the brain, especially those of the left hemisphere, which Wernicke described as processing sound images of words, is observed when individuals must distinguish aurally presented words from aurally presented nonwords (e.g., Frith, Friston, Liddle, & Frackowiak, 1991). In contrast, Broca's area, which is implicated in speech production, becomes active when words must be repeated rather than just heard (Petersen et al., 1988). Brain imaging studies also support the idea that anterior regions of the left hemisphere are more involved in processing syntax while posterior regions are important for semantics. For example, there is more activation in Broca's area (BA 44) when individuals must process syntactically more complex sentences such as "The limerick that the boy recited appalled the priest" as compared to those that are less complex, such as "The biographer omitted the story that insulted the queen" (Stromswold, Caplan, Alpert, and Rauch, 1996). And activation is observed in the left posterior temporoparietal cortex (BA 39), near Wernicke's area, when individuals make semantic decisions, such as deciding whether a word names a living or nonliving object (Price et al., 1997). Greater activation is also observed in neighboring regions (BA 22) for sentences or stories as opposed to unrelated words or sentences (Price, 1998).

Second, neuroimaging studies have illustrated that the patterns of activation across these language-processing regions can vary depending on experience or practice. For example, in one study, researchers examined the brain regions that are involved in generating a verb in response to a noun (M. Raichle et al., 1994). When participants were naive to either the task or the particular set of stimuli used, activation occurred over the regions of the left hemisphere that when damaged typically cause Wernicke's aphasia. But when the individuals were given a familiar and well-practiced set of stimuli, activation was more anterior, in an area typically associated with conduction aphasia (which, as you should remember, disrupts the ability to repeat sequences).

Third, neuroimaging studies have expanded our knowledge of the cortical anatomy underlying language processing. They indicate that much larger regions of the left hemisphere besides those traditionally considered "language" areas (e.g., Broca's, Wernicke's) are activated during language tasks. Many of these regions are in the temporal lobe outside Wernicke's area (Binder et al., 1997). Probably one of the most surprising findings is the degree to which the left inferior prefrontal cortex plays a role in receptive language tasks, such as word reading (e.g., Kelley et al., 1998; Fiez and Petersen, 1998). The particular region of left inferior prefrontal cortex activated appears to depend on whether phonological or semantic processing is paramount. When an emphasis is placed on phonological processing, such as how a word sounds compared to how it looks (Fiez et al., 1995), when a specific phoneme must be detected (e.g., /pa/), or when a decision about the final consonant in a word is required, activation is observed in Broca's area (Zatorre, Meyer, Gjedde, & Evans, 1996). In contrast, activation is observed in more anterior and inferior prefrontal regions when semantic processing is emphasized (BA 45/47) (Wagner, 1999).

Haven't we mentioned many times in this chapter that the left frontal region is involved in speech production and syntax? So now what are we to make of talk of these regions being involved in phonological and semantic aspects of receptive language tasks? Is the classical model all wrong? Probably not. It just needs some refinement. The consensus is that whereas long-term storage of phonological and semantic knowledge is dependent on posterior regions, frontal regions are involved in the effortful retrieval, short-term maintenance, and/or strategic control of phonological and semantic information.

These left inferior prefrontal regions may aid in accessing a particular word, such as when you are searching for just the right word to describe something, and/or serve as working memory buffers to hold language-related information online. For example, nonaphasic individuals with bilateral prefrontal damage do as poorly as Alzheimer's individuals when asked to name as many animals as possible in 15 seconds. Is their semantic knowledge gone? No, because when given a cue every 15 seconds (e.g., animals found on a farm, animals that live in water), they outperform the Alzheimer's patients and do as well as normal individuals (Randolph et al., 1993). Thus, they have specific difficulty accessing the relevant information without a cue to help them search their memory (see Fiez & Petersen, 1998, for a nice discussion of this issue).

Fourth, brain imaging has refined our understanding of the correspondence between specific language functions and the brain tissue that supports them. In addition to providing a greater understanding of the role of frontal regions, it has illuminated the function of posterior brain areas involved in language as well. For example, although the classical viewpoint was that regions in the planum temporale processed only language-related sounds, these areas appear to be equally activated by linguistic (words) and nonlinguistic stimuli (tones), suggesting that they are important for extracting parameters of acoustic information in general (Binder et al., 1996) rather than acoustic parameters specifically related to language as suggested by Wernicke. The region that is involved specifically in phonological analysis, regardless of whether the item is presented auditorily (Zatorre et al., 1996) or visually (Pugh et al., 1996), appears to be a slightly different region in the left middle posterior temporal area (within BA 22). This region is also more active when hearing words than pseudowords, suggesting that it is crucial for activating a word's phonological form (Price et al., 1994). Furthermore, this region is specifically responsive to phonological information, as it is not activated by tasks that involve the extraction of semantic information (e.g., deciding if a word represents a living or nonliving item).

In sum, results from brain imaging studies are more parsimonious with the idea that brain regions for language are organized into discrete systems for phonology, syntax, and semantics versus tasks, such as speaking, repeating, and listening, as emphasized by classical models (e.g., Friederici, Opitz, & von Cramon, 2000). A summary of the critical regions involved in each of these language processes is shown in Figure 9.10.

Research from electrophysiological techniques also supports the conclusion that the brain segregates syntactic from semantic processing. As you may remember from Chapter 4, a specific component, the N_{400}, is elicited when an auditory word in a sentence violates semantic expectation, such as "He spread the warm bread with socks" or "The girl dropped the sky on the table." As shown in Figure 9.11A, this component tends to be large over parietal (and also central) recording sites and tends to be larger over the left hemisphere than the right (Hagoort & Brown, 2000a). In contrast, a different component is elicited when words occur that render a sentence ungrammatical, such as "The spoiled child *throw* the toys on the floor." This component, the P_{600} (also sometimes referred to as the SPS, for syntactic positive shift), is observed both over posterior and anterior recording sites as shown in Figure 9.11B. This component is known to be specifically sensitive to syntax regardless of the particulars of a given syntactic system since it has been observed across a variety of languages, such as German, English, and Dutch (Friederici, Hahne, & Mecklinger, 1996; Osterhout & Holcomb, 1992; Hagoort & Brown, 2000b). Suggesting a dissociation between syntax and semantics, a P_{600} can also be found when the sentence makes no sense semantically but nonetheless has a grammatical violation, such as "The boiled watering-can *smoke* the telephone in the cat" (Hagoort & Brown, 1994). Thus, ERP studies provide converging evidence that the brain processes syntax and semantics in distinct manners (for a short review, see Osterhout, McLaughlin, & Bersick, 1997).

Thus far we have learned that besides lesion studies, various methods—such as electrical stimulation, Wada procedures, brain imaging, and electrophysiological studies—all provide evidence of left-hemisphere specialization for speech output, for different roles for posterior and anterior regions in processing auditory language, and for distinct neural systems for processing syntax and semantics. Now we turn our attention to how the brain processes visual language.

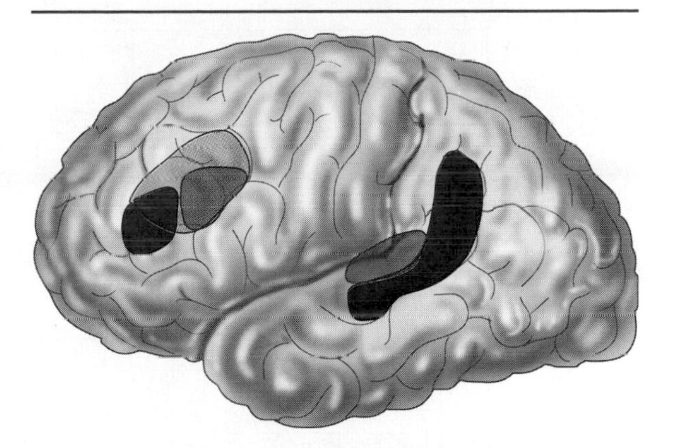

FIGURE 9.10 Main brain regions involved in semantic, syntactic, and phonological aspects of language processing. In this diagram, regions involved in semantics are shown in dark blue, regions involved in syntax are shown in light blue, and regions involved in phonology are shown in grey. Anterior language areas, such as Broca's area, are involved in syntactic processing. They also are involved in effortful retrieval of phonological and semantic aspects of words. Posterior language areas are involved in semantic processing as well as phonological processing.

Neurological Bases for Visual Language Processing

Portions of the neurological system that support processing of written language functions are distinct from those that support auditory language functions, although in right-handers both reside within the left hemisphere. We should not be surprised that the neural machinery for auditory and written language is somewhat distinct. First, these two types of language processing occur in different modalities. To the degree that they interact with different sensory regions of the brain, they might be presumed to differ in their neural organization. Second, although auditory language has existed for some time, written language is a relatively new invention. Whereas the organization of the brain is likely to have undergone evolutionary pressure for the development of auditory language, not enough time has passed for that to be the case for written language. Third, as we see in the following section, interpretation of written language does not always rely on

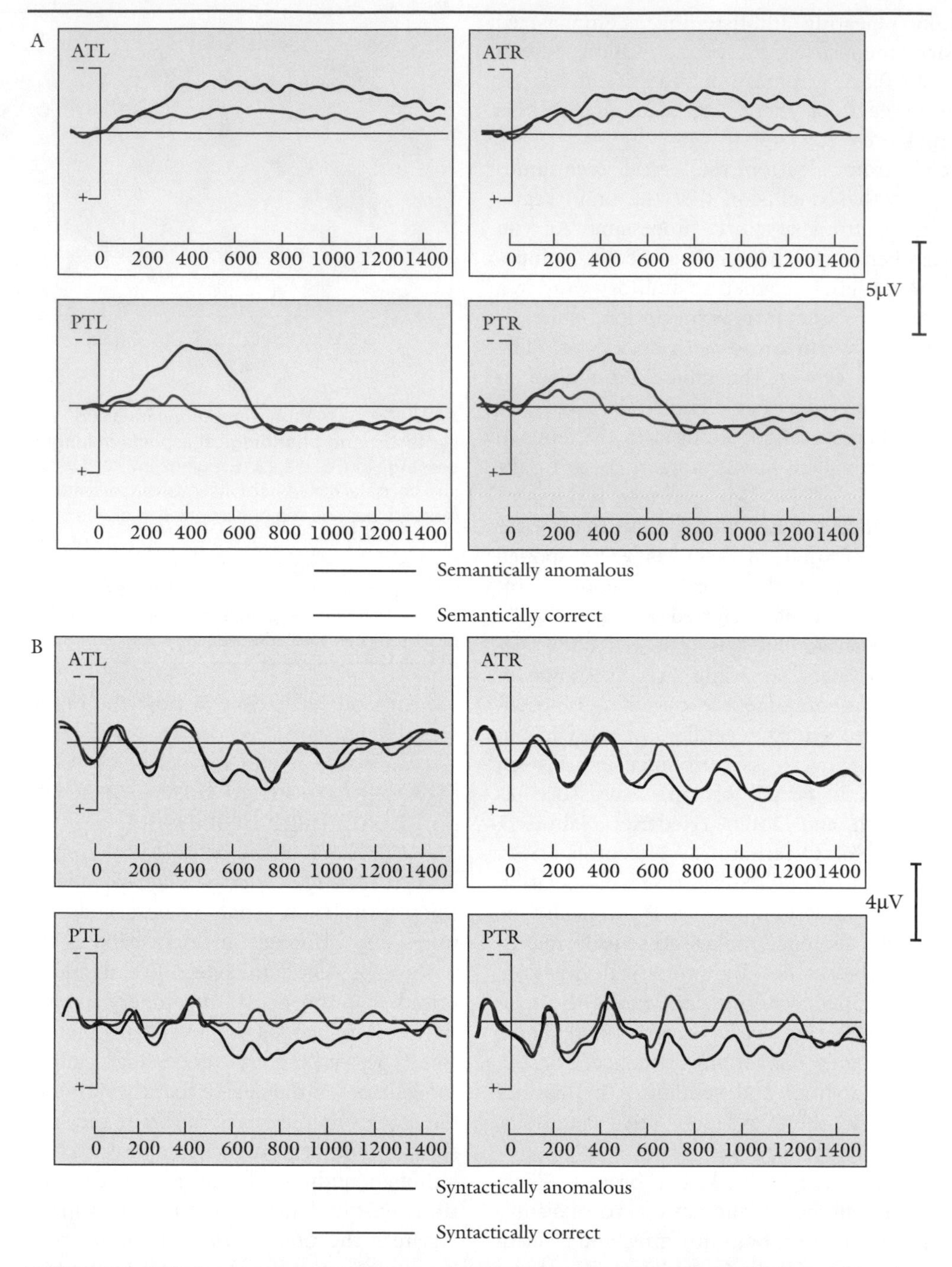

FIGURE 9.11 ERP components sensitive to aspects of language processing. (A) Shown here is the N_{400} that occurs in response to semantically anomalous material in the auditory modality. Notice that it is larger over posterior regions of the brain (panels labeled PT) than anterior regions (panels labeled AT) and larger over the left hemisphere (panels labeled L) than the right (panels labeled R). (B) Shown here is the P_{600} that occurs in response to syntactically anomalous sentences. Notice that unlike the N_{450} it is observed over both anterior and posterior regions.

using spoken language as an intermediary. To the degree that processing visual words is independent of spoken language, these two types of language processing might be expected to have different neurological bases. We now turn to a more detailed discussion of the neurological bases for visual language.

Evidence from Studies of Patients with Brain Damage

As we did when discussing the neurological bases for auditory language processing, we begin this section by examining the information about written language that can be gleaned from studies of patients with brain damage. Then we discuss converging evidence from other methods.

• *ALEXIA VERSUS AGRAPHIA* •

Just as the production of auditory language is distinct from the perception of auditory language, so too is the production of written language (writing) distinct from the perception of written words (reading). When, as a consequence of brain damage, the ability to read is lost, the ensuing syndrome is known as **alexia.** When instead the ability to write is lost, the deficit is known as **agraphia.** Although alexia and agraphia typically co-occur after damage to the angular gyrus (which is located in the ventral region of the parietal lobe above the Sylvian fissue), the two can dissociate. In some cases individuals have alexia without agraphia (e.g., Greenblatt, 1973) and in other cases agraphia without alexia (e.g., Hécaen & Kremin, 1976). These dissociations can lead to some strange situations. Although an individual who has alexia without agraphia can write a sentence with little difficulty, that person is unable to read sentences, including those that she or he previously wrote! Likewise, individuals who have agraphia without alexia are unable to write sentences but can read without much difficulty.

As you should recognize by now, the syndromes of alexia without agraphia and agraphia without alexia are examples of a double dissociation. In this case, the double dissociation indicates that the neural control systems for reading and writing are separable to some extent and do not critically rely on each other. Hence, we do not have a single module in the brain that is important for written language; instead, we have distinct systems, one for interpreting written language and one for producing it.

• *READING* •

To better understand how the brain processes written language, we first examine the cognitive processes underlying written language. In the discussion that follows, we use reading as an example, then later describe how these findings generalize to writing.

• *Phonological versus Direct Route to Meaning* •

Researchers have proposed two distinct routes whereby information in a visual linguistic format can be linked to meaning (e.g., Meyer, Schvaneveldt, & Ruddy, 1974). The first route is known as the **phonological route to reading** because sound is a mediator in the process of associating print with meaning. It is likely you used this route when you learned to read, being taught that each letter has a different sound. When confronted with a written word for the first time, such as *cat*, you were told to identify each letter (*c, a, t*), sound out each letter (/k/, /a/, /t/), and then blended the three sounds to produce a word ("cat"). Once you pronounced the word, you could recognize its meaning because you already associated this sound pattern with the concept that it represents ("a small, furry household pet with claws that is known for its taste for tuna and mice and for an aloof and independent demeanor"). Thus, the auditory sounds were the intermediary allowing you to link print to meaning.

The rules whereby print is associated with sound are known as **grapheme-to-phoneme correspondence rules.** *Graphemes* are the smallest units of written language that are combined to make words. For example, the visual pattern "c" is a grapheme, and this grapheme can take many forms, such as "c," "*c*," "C," and "**C.**" Grapheme-to-phoneme correspondence rules let us know how each grapheme should sound (e.g., "c" is usually pronounced /ka/) and how graphemes should be combined. For example, these rules dictate that for most words ending in *vowel-consonant-"e"* (e.g., *lake, mike*), the first vowel is long and the final "e" is silent.

The second route is known as the **direct route to reading** because print is directly associated with meaning, without the use of a phonological intermediary. For a certain proportion of words in the English language, the direct route *must* be used because these words, known as **irregular words,** do not follow grapheme-to-phoneme correspondence rules and so are impossible to sound out correctly. If grapheme-to-phoneme correspondence rules are used to pronounce *colonel,* for instance, the result will be the incorrect "koe-loe-nell," rather than "kur-nel." When the direct route is used, an association is made between a particular visual form of a word (e.g., *colonel*) and its meaning (e.g., "a high-ranking military officer whose rank is just below that of a general").

Whether neurologically intact readers use the phonological route or the direct route was, at one time, a source of much debate among cognitive psychologists. According to one viewpoint, the phonological route was mainly used when a person was acquiring the ability to read and whenever a skilled reader encountered a new word (as we usually attempt to sound out unfamiliar words). For known words, skilled readers were assumed to use the direct route because sounding these words out was no longer necessary. Consequently, the intermediate step of linking print to sound was mostly abandoned because it was time-consuming and unnecessary (e.g., Taft, 1982). According to a second viewpoint, even skilled readers were assumed to rely heavily on a phonological route (e.g., Chastain, 1987).

• *Neuropsychological Evidence for These Two Routes* • Using information from patients with brain damage provided a way to resolve this issue. To index the integrity of the phonological route in individuals with brain damage, researchers determined whether patients with brain damage could read words that they had never seen before and whether they could read nonwords. Reading new words would rely on the phonological route because no prior linkages from the visual form to meaning would exist, making direct access impossible. Similarly, the phonological route must be used in reading nonwords because they have no meaning. (For instance, until now, you probably never saw the nonword *glimay,* but you can read it using your knowledge of grapheme-to-phoneme correspondence rules.) Likewise, these investigators assessed the integrity of the direct route by determining how well the patients could read words that do not follow the grapheme-to-phoneme correspondence rules (i.e., common irregular words), such as *colonel* and *yacht.*

Such neuropsychological investigations demonstrated that both routes are available and that each can be used independently of the other. One set of individuals, who have a syndrome known as **surface alexia,** was found to have a disruption in the direct route but not in the phonological route. Their syndrome is so named because the individuals cannot link the surface information—that is, the visual form of a word—directly to meaning. Persons with surface alexia cannot read irregular words correctly. They sound out the words (using the phonological route) and hence misread them. They often confuse *homophones,* words that sound the same but have different meanings, such as *beat* and *beet.* Thus, when asked to define the word *pane,* these patients may say "to feel distress," or when asked to define *mown,* they may say "to complain." Their spelling errors also indicate their reliance on the phonological route because their spellings are often phonologically correct but graphemically incorrect (e.g., writing *whisk* as *wisque,* or *mayonnaise* as *mayenaze*) (e.g., Coltheart, 1982; Shallice, Warrington, & McCarthy, 1983). In contrast, when given nonwords or regular words to read, these individuals do well because they can use the intact phonological route. Even though before damage they probably read regular words by means of the direct route (e.g., read *cat* by recognizing the visual pattern), they retain the ability to read such words after damage because regular words can just as easily be read by using grapheme-to-phoneme correspondence rules. The lesion that causes surface alexia usually involves inferior temporal structures in the left hemisphere, although the exact location varies (Vanier & Caplan, 1985).

Individuals with the contrasting syndrome, **phonological alexia,** have a disrupted phonological route but an intact direct route. They have relatively little trouble reading previously learned words because regardless of whether the words are regular or irregular, these individuals can extract meaning directly from the visual form. Their disability becomes apparent only when they are asked to read nonwords or words with which they are unfamiliar. In these cases, the direct route does not suffice because either they do not have an association between the visual form and meaning (as is the case with unfamiliar words) or no such association exists (as in the case of nonwords) (e.g., K. Patterson, 1982). The lesion that causes such a deficit has not been well localized but, as might be expected, usually involves posterior regions of the left hemisphere.

Let's see how well you understand the distinction between phonological and surface alexia. Consider the following three tasks in which an individual is shown two pairs of items and must decide which pair contains two items that sound identical. The first task involves regular words (e.g., *sail/sale* vs. *sail/salt*), the second task irregular words (e.g., *berry/bury* vs. *ferry/fury*), and the third task nonwords (e.g., *fex/phects* vs. *fex/phox*). If you were a person with phonological alexia, which pairs would cause you difficulty? Remember that in phonological alexia the grapheme-to-phoneme route is disrupted, but the direct route is intact. Therefore, the direct route can be used to read real words with little difficulty, regardless of whether they are regular (e.g., *sail/sale*) or irregular (e.g., *berry/bury*). Once the visual form has been linked to meaning, the form can be used to generate the correct sound. For example, seeing *sail* allows a person with phonological alexia to gain access to the idea of a piece of cloth on a ship that is used to capture the wind's energy and propel the ship forward. Once meaning is obtained, the individual with phonological alexia can conjure the name of the word, just as seeing a picture of a sail or thinking about a sail allows you to say "sail." In contrast, nonwords (e.g., *fex/phects*) cannot be distinguished since gaining access to the sounds of nonwords relies on grapheme-to-phoneme correspondence rules, which are lost.

What type of performance would you expect from a person with surface alexia? Because the phonologic system is intact, little difficulty with the nonwords (e.g., *fex/phects*) and regular words (e.g. *sail/sale*) would be expected as these pairs can be translated into sound according to grapheme-to-phoneme correspondence rules. In contrast, because the direct route is damaged, correct pronunciation of irregular words (e.g., *berry/bury*) would be difficult—using grapheme-to-phoneme correspondence rules would lead to the wrong pronunciation. A word like *bury* would probably be mispronounced because it does not follow the same grapheme-to-phoneme correspondence rules as words like *fury* and *jury* do.

It should be mentioned that there is a syndrome related to phonological alexia known as **deep alexia.** Individuals with this disorder show many of the deficits exhibited by persons with phonological alexia (such as the inability to read nonwords), so much so that some researchers have suggested that phonological alexia is just a milder form of deep alexia (e.g., Glosser & Friedman, 1990). But the patients with deep alexia exhibit additional difficulties. First, when reading, they often make **semantic paralexias,** which are reading errors in which a word is misread as a word with a related meaning. For example, *forest* may be read as "woods" and *tulip* as "crocus." Second, these individuals have more difficulty reading abstract words (e.g., *sympathy, faith*) than words that represent concrete entities in the physical world (e.g., *refrigerator, basket*). Third, these patients have difficulty reading small function words that serve as grammatical markers. Because of this constellation of symptoms, Coltheart (1980) suggested that the syndrome may represent reliance on the right hemisphere for reading. As demonstrated by the reading performance of the isolated right hemisphere in patients with the split-brain syndrome, this hemisphere is better able to read concrete words than abstract words, has no ability to use grapheme-to-phoneme conversion rules, and cannot distinguish among the meanings of words that are closely associated (E. Zaidel, 1990).

• *WRITING* •

Just as two routes to reading can be used, studies of patients with unilateral brain damage suggest that two routes can be used to transform thoughts into writing. One route goes from thought directly to writing, whereas the other uses phoneme-to-grapheme correspondence rules as an intermediary. In **phonological agraphia,** individuals can manually or orally spell regular and irregular words to dictation but perform poorly with nonwords (e.g., Shallice, 1981). In **lexical agraphia,** the opposite occurs: a reasonable spelling, both manually and orally, can be produced for virtually any regular word or nonword, but spelling of irregular words is poor (e.g., Beauvois & Derouesne, 1981). Just as is the case for reading, writing seems to entail two routes, a direct one and a phonological one. Although you may have anticipated such a distinction on the basis of what we learned about reading, this needn't have been the case, because even though reading and writing are similar, the process of writing is not just reading in reverse order. For example, phoneme-to-grapheme rules are not the opposite of grapheme-to-phoneme rules. Consider the following case in point. Although /k/ is the most common sound for the grapheme "k," the most common grapheme for the sound /k/ is "c."

The dissociation between these two routes to writing is supported by findings that the location of the typical lesion that causes each syndrome differs. Damage that causes phonological agraphia, in which the sound-based route is disrupted, tends to involve the left supramarginal gyrus, an area of the parietal lobe directly above the posterior section of the Sylvian fissure (Roeltgen & Heilman, 1984). This location makes sense if you consider that it is situated near parietal regions implicated in reading and is close to regions that are known to process sound-based aspects of language. In contrast, the location of the lesion that causes lexical agraphia is more posterior, at the conjunction of the posterior parietal lobe and the parieto-occipital junction (Roeltgen & Heilman, 1984). In this case, the lesion is closer to areas involved in processing visual representations, which is consistent with the loss of an ability to go directly from a word's meaning to its graphemic (i.e., visually based) representation.

• *OTHER COMPONENTS OF VISUAL LANGUAGE PROCESSING* •

The syndromes we discussed so far are sometimes called *central* alexias or *central* agraphias because the problem arises in the linkage to or from meaning. In contrast, the peripheral processes required for reading and writing, such as the ability to analyze letters visually or to produce the motor patterns for writing graphemes, are intact. An individual unable to recognize many types of visual forms would not be considered to have a specific problem in reading. Yet if these difficulties were limited to processing visual forms of linguistic relevance, such as letters, we would be more inclined to categorize the problem as one that involved reading. When a specific disruption in the reading process occurs outside the linkage of form to meaning, it is sometimes referred to as a *precentral* alexia (when the difficulty arises prior to gaining access to meaning) or as a *peripheral* alexia. These disruptions include the inability to process more than one letter at a time, to read all the letters in a word, or to appreciate the overall form of a group of letters.

Some precentral dyslexias result from a disruption in attentional processes that affect only reading. In a syndrome known as **attentional dyslexia,** the individual can recognize a single letter or a single word in isolation but cannot recognize the same letter or word if it is presented along with items of the same kind (i.e., other letters or other words) (e.g., Shallice & Warrington, 1977). This attentional problem is similar to that observed in Balint's syndrome (also known as *dorsal simultanagnosia*), which we discussed in Chapter 7. At present, the lesion critical for causing this syndrome is unknown, but typically individuals have posterior left-hemisphere damage that includes subcortical structures. In **neglect dyslexia,** the individual consistently misreads the beginning or the end of a word, such as misreading *this* as "his" or misreading *discount* as "mount" (e.g., Ellis, Flude, & Young, 1987). This syndrome is similar to hemineglect, and, not surprisingly, neglect dyslexia involves damage to the parietal lobe. As we mentioned in Chapter 8, neglect may occur not only with regard to an external frame of reference, but also with regard to a frame of reference inherent to an object. In this case, the neglect is exhibited for a particular portion of a word regardless of its length or orientation (Caramazza & Hillis, 1990). In one case study of a patient with this syndrome (who had sustained a lesion to the parietal lobe of the left hemisphere), the last half of the word was neglected despite variations in orientation.

In another syndrome, known as **letter-by-letter reading** (sometimes referred to as *spelling dyslexia* or *pure alexia*), individual letters can be identified, but they cannot be integrated to form a word (e.g., K. E. Patterson & Kay, 1982; Warrington & Shallice, 1980). Individuals with this syndrome use oral spelling as a means to reading; they say each letter aloud and then use that information to deduce the word. Thus, a letter-by-letter reader sees the word *cat* and identifies it by saying "*C, a, t,* oh, that must be *cat*!" The lesion that typically causes such a syndrome is located in inferior portions of the occipital lobe bordering on the temporal lobe of the left hemisphere.

In review, studies of patients with neurological disorders demonstrate that difficulties in visual language can occur either in the linkage to meaning or in other processes specific to visual language skills. We now examine converging evidence about the neurological bases for visual language.

Converging Evidence from Other Research Methods

In this section we will discuss what converging methods can tell us about how the brain performs both the precentral (i.e., prior to meaning) and central (i.e., linking form to meaning) aspects of reading.

• *PRECENTRAL ASPECTS OF READING* •

We start by discussing how brain imaging studies, electrophysiologic studies, and behavioral studies of neurologically intact individuals provide insights into how the brain processes visual word form. These studies suggest that this process is supported by two separate systems, which are located in opposite hemispheres. The right-hemisphere system encodes words in their specific visual form, whereas the left-hemisphere system appears to extract an abstract representation of word form that is common across different instances of a word, such as variations in font or case. Let's explore, in more detail, evidence that the right hemisphere extracts the specifics of the visual form of a word. Positron emission tomography (PET) studies reveal that activation over the right hemisphere is greater when people are presented with strings of letter-like forms that look similar to distorted letters from the Cyrillic alphabet or with consonant letter strings (e.g., JVJFC) (Petersen, Fox, Snyder, & Raichle, 1990). Eighty to 120 ms after the presentation of words or nonsense strings, ERP studies reveal a larger positive amplitude (P_{100}) over the right posterior cortex than that over the left (Posner & McCandliss, 1993). Moreover, divided visual field studies indicate that the right hemisphere can better distinguish among different fonts of the same letter than the left (Bryden & Allard, 1976). Finally, priming studies of neurologically intact subjects reveal that if a particular physical shape of a word (e.g, uppercase) is presented to the right hemisphere, subsequent processing of that word is facilitated to a greater degree when it appears in the same case (i.e., uppercase) than when it appears in a different case (i.e., lowercase) (e.g., Marsolek, Kosslyn, & Squire, 1992). As ascertained in PET studies, this priming effect for words of identical visual form appears to activate the lingual gyrus of the right hemisphere but not the left (Squire et al., 1992).

In contrast, the left hemisphere appears to be less influenced by the specific visual form of a word. Rather, it has a more abstract or general representation of words. In neurologically intact individuals, the left hemisphere is facilitated by previous exposure to a word to an equal degree regardless of whether the word appears in identical physical form or altered form (e.g., another font) to the original presentation (e.g., Marsolek, Kosslyn, & Squire, 1992). Furthermore, left-hemisphere damage is associated with syndromes that appear to indicate a disruption of a word's abstract form. For example, as we discussed earlier, individuals with damage to the left ventral occipital area can read only one letter at a time, which suggests that they cannot integrate the letters into a general word form (e.g., Reuter-Lorenz & Brunn, 1990). We also mentioned a case in which a left parietal lesion resulted in neglect of the end of all words regardless of how they were oriented in space (e.g., horizontally, backward, vertically). Hence, the neglect exhibited by this individual was with regard to a framework of a word's general abstract form (rather than a framework linked to a specific form, spatial position, or orientation of the word).

• *CENTRAL ASPECTS OF READING* •

Additional studies have provided more refined information on brain systems that support the central aspects of the reading process. The left hemisphere appears to have specific mechanisms that are sensitive to the rules that govern how letters are combined, known as *orthography*, and/or the phonological status of a letter string. These processes occur after early visual analysis of words, as the ERP waveforms in response to real words and pronounceable nonsense words begin to diverge from the waveforms observed for consonant strings 200 ms after exposure (Posner & McCandliss, 1993). Around this point in time, ERPs in response to words also converge regardless of whether a word is presented in the RVF or the LVF, suggesting a common processing mechanism in the left hemisphere (Cohen et al., 2000).

Other evidence has provided additional information on the possible separation of systems within the left hemisphere that are responsible for processing words in an orthographic (i.e., direct) versus a phonological manner. The exact localization of the left hemisphere system that allows print to be directly linked to meaning is, at present, the source of much debate. A number of brain imaging studies indicate that ventral regions of extrastriate cortex (i.e., fusiform gyrus) BA 37 are more active during tasks that require orthography as compared to those that don't (e.g., the reading of real words as compared to consonant strings (Petersen, Fox, Snyder, & Raichle, 1990; Pugh et al., 1996; Cohen et al., 2000) (see Color insert 9.1)). This region has also been identified by intracranial recordings designed to isolate specific regions sensitive to word stimuli (Nobre, Allison, & McCarthy, 1994).

Consistent with such an interpretation, there exists a case study of a girl with damage to this region who cannot read irregular words (i.e., has lost the direct route from orthography to semantics), but who can read and spell regular words, suggesting that the route from orthography to phonology (to semantics) has remained intact (Samuelsson, 2000). However, given that her lesion was congenital, it is not clear whether this pattern represents the typical brain organization or one that has evolved in response to reorganization of the brain after an early trauma.

On the other hand, some studies obtain activation in this region bilaterally, not just in the left hemisphere (Hagoort et al., 1999), or find that the degree of activation in this region is related to the visual complexity of written word–like stimuli (e.g., how hard a font is to read) (Indefry et al., 1997). These studies suggest that this region is not specifically suited for gaining access to word meaning, but rather is related to the difficulty of extracting visual information from letter-like stimuli. Other neuroimaging studies (e.g., Beauregard et al., 1997; Howard et al., 1992; Menard et al., 1996) have suggested that the region more likely to be involved in linking visual form to linguistic information is a region of the middle temporal gyrus. In either case, the brain region involved seems to be associated with the ventral visual-processing stream.

Brain imaging studies also provide more information about the areas involved in the translation of orthography to phonology than can be gleaned from the relatively rare case studies of phonological alexia. Whereas the direct route relies on a more ventral processing stream within the temporal lobe, brain imaging suggests that the phonological route relies on more dorsal temporal and ventral parietal regions. The left supramarginal gyrus (BA 40), which is the anterior part of inferior parietal cortex, and the angular gyrus tend to be more active when one has to read pseudowords, which critically rely on a translation of orthography to phonology, as compared to regular words (Price, Wise, & Frackowiak, 1996) or irregular words (Herbster et al., 1997). Converging evidence comes from studies that compare word naming to picture naming. This comparison is used because naming either a picture or a word requires a linkage of phonology and semantics, but only in word naming will there also be a translation of orthography to phonology. This contrast reveals activation in the supramarginal gyrus (Price, 1998).

Yet, many studies have not shown greater activity in the angular gyrus during the comparison of nonwords as compared to words (e.g., Hagoort et al., 1999), nor greater activation for words than pictures (e.g., Bookheimer et al., 1995). Rather, these studies suggest that activation of this region may be linked to the amount of attentional demand placed on an individual, not language-related processing (e.g., Hagoort et al., 1999). These findings indicate that classical models of language processing are probably incomplete.

One alternative suggested by computational models of word reading is that there are not two discrete and separate routes from orthography to meaning, but just one system (e.g., Seidenberg & McClelland, 1989). In these models pseudowords can be considered to be read "by analogy" to real words, and hence do not activate a separate phoneme-to-grapheme route. Portions of words are linked to pronunciation units, and their degree of association is coded by the connection weights, which are modified with learning (e.g,. Plaut, 2003). Damage to these computational models can, in fact, mimic some aspects of reading impairments resulting from brain damage (K. E. Patterson, Seidenberg, & McClelland, 1989).

Although one might think that neuroimaging data could ascertain whether one or two routes exists, it cannot, because it is not clear exactly what pattern of brain activation would differentiate between the two possibilities (see Fiez and Petersen, 1998, for a discussion). The neuroimaging data, however, do make clear that there is a high degree of overlap between patterns of activation observed when a phonological translation is required or when there is a more direct route to meaning (e.g., Rumsey et al., 1997). This finding should not be surprising, as it is reasonable to suppose that fluent readers probably mix the degree to which they use each route depending on task demands.

One way of investigating the one- vs. two-route issue further is to examine the correlation between the degree of activity in the angular gyrus, which classically has been assumed to be critical for reading, and other brain regions during the reading of pseudowords (which would activate a phonological route) and real words (which would tend to preferentially engage the direct route). In fact, neuroimaging studies have revealed that during the reading of pseudowords, activity is most highly correlated with other areas that are regions involved in phonological processing, such as superior temporal regions (BA 22) and Broca's area. In contrast, during the reading of real words, activity is more highly correlated with regions in occipital and ventral temporal cortex, which are more often associated with the direct route (Rumsey et al., 1997). These findings suggest that one might not want to think of the brain regions involved in word reading as being tightly localized, but rather as consisting of a diffuse set of regions whose components become more or less activated depending on task demands (e.g., Rumsey et al., 1997; Tagamets et al., 2000).

All the evidence we discussed so far has come from studies involving speakers and readers of Indo-European languages. We now turn our attention to other linguistic systems to provide more insight into the cognitive neuroscience of language.

Processing of Non-Indo-European Languages and Other Symbolic Systems

Many languages are used around the world, some of which do not rely on the kind of phonological system that is used in English. By investigating the organization of the brain for other types of languages, we can determine the degree to which certain aspects of brain organization for language are universal.

Kana and Kanji

Because not all writing systems in the world use a phonetic alphabet based on phoneme-to-grapheme correspondences as in English, cognitive neuroscientists can look to other language systems to investigate the distinction between phonological and direct routes to meaning. Japanese provides one such opportunity. It consists of two writing systems: one known as kana, which is syllabic and sound-based, the other, known as kanji, which is logographic and derived from Chinese (Paradis, Hagiwara, & Hildebrandt, 1985). We discuss the characteristics of each of these types of systems in turn.

In a syllabic writing system such as kana, each symbol is linked to a whole syllable rather than to an individual phoneme. For example, a syllabically based language might have a symbol for the sound "tor," which would appear as the first of three symbols in a three-syllable word such as *torrential,* and the second of two symbols in the two-syllable word *motor.* Because syllabic systems are sound based, these words can be read using a phonological route. In contrast, in a logographic writing system, such as kanji, each symbol stands for a concept, and the visual form of the word has no systematic relationship to how it is pronounced. Typically, thousands of basic logographs are used in such languages; the reader must be able to associate each different symbol with a different word. Logographic systems require a direct route because little or no information in the symbol provides hints to its pronunciation. Some examples of kana and kanji characters are presented in Figure 9.12.

After brain damage, the ability to read words in kana can dissociate from the ability to read words in kanji, implying a distinction between direct and phonological routes to meaning. Sometimes individuals who lose the ability to read kanji retain the ability to read kana, whereas other times individuals who retain the ability to read kanji lose the ability to read kana (Sasanuma, 1980). Furthermore, case studies (e.g., Kawamura et al., 1987; Kawahata, Nagata, & Shishido, 1988) and neuroimaging studies using both fMRI (e.g., Sakurai et al., 2000) and PET (Tokunaga et al., 1999) suggest that these two systems may rely on different regions of the brain. The reading of kana appears to be primarily dependent on more dorsal regions of the left hemisphere, including the angular gyrus and temporoparietal junction, while the reading of kanji appears to rely more on inferior posterior temporal regions bordering on the occipital lobe. As with English, however, there is also substantial overlap (e.g., Koyama, Kakigi, Hoshiyama, & Kitamura, 1998). These findings provide converging evidence from a language other than English that access to meaning through a sound-based reading system can be independent of access to meaning through a visually based system.

FIGURE 9.12 Examples of kana and kanji. (A) Almost all of the 77 symbols in kana represent a consonant-vowel combination. (B) In kanji, the symbol has little relation to how the word is pronounced. Pictured here are various symbols, all of which are pronounced "kan" but each of which has a different meaning.

American Sign Language

Other evidence about the neurological organization for language can be derived from examining "spoken" language systems that are not aurally based but are instead completely visual. American Sign Language (ASL), the language used by most deaf individuals in the United States, is one such language.

• *BASIC STRUCTURE OF ASL* •

To evaluate the evidence that ASL provides about the neural organization of language, we first need a brief introduction to the structure of this language. Each noun in ASL is represented by a particular hand shape that is made in a particular way at a particular location in space with regard to the body. Just as distinctive contrasts exist among phonemes (e.g., voicing), distinctive contrasts can be seen among signs in ASL. One distinctive feature that can be used to distinguish among different words is hand shape itself. Place of articulation is another important feature. The same hand shape placed on the side of the face has a different meaning than if it is placed on the chin. An example of three words in ASL that differ only in place of articulation is presented in

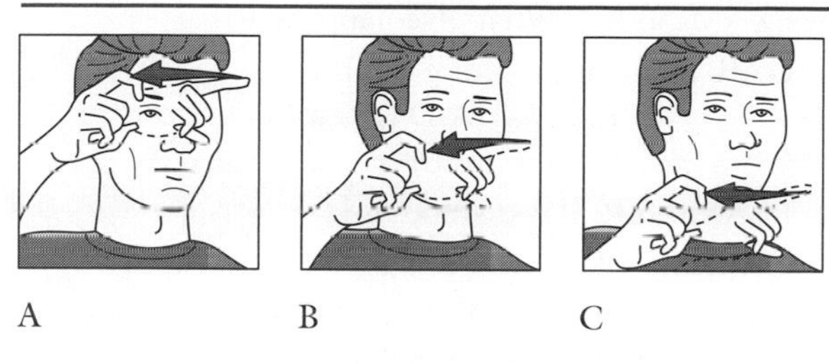

FIGURE 9.13 The distinctive contrast of place of articulation in American Sign Language. The same hand shape has a different meaning depending on where the shape is produced. (A) If produced at eye level, this sign means "summer"; (B) if produced at nose level, it means "ugly"; and (C) if produced at the chin, it means "dry."

Figure 9.13. The nature of the hand movement can also distinguish between two words.

Syntactic structure in ASL differs from that of spoken language. In ASL certain aspects of syntax are communicated through the position of the hands in space rather than through word order (e.g., SVO vs. OVS) or by the type of hand movement rather than by word endings (e.g., *-ly*). When a sentence is produced in ASL, a noun is placed within a frame, or theater of space, that is directly in front of the speaker's body. A speaker of ASL will make a hand shape for a noun and point to a particular location within this theater. Each noun in the sentence is given a different location in this theater. A sign designating a verb (e.g., "bit") is made from the location of noun acting as the subject (e.g., "dog") to the location of the noun acting as the object (e.g., cat). Thus, the syntactic distinction between subject and object is made spatially, by the direction of hand movement, as shown in Figure 9.14.

The type of hand movement also provides syntactic information, such as inflections of a verb, which in English are indicated by different word endings (e.g., *-ed*, *-ing*). For example, if a person wants to say that something occurred repeatedly, the hand movement is different than if the event happened only once, just as in English an ongoing action is indicated by an *-ing* ending. Examples of some of these distinctions are provided in Figure 9.15.

• *NEUROPSYCHOLOGICAL INVESTIGATIONS OF ASL* •

Now that we know the basics about the structure of ASL, we can discuss how it provides insights into the neural organization for language. If anterior portions of the left hemisphere are specialized for syntax, and posterior areas are specialized for semantics, this distinction should be observed in signers of ASL. Case studies of native speakers of ASL who have become aphasic reveal that such is the case: the distinction between anterior and posterior language systems holds for ASL signers (Poizner, Klima, & Bellugi, 1987). Those with anterior damage exhibit a paucity of signs and a lack of fluency. Their production of ASL is agrammatic with disruptions of hand movements that serve as syntactic markers and loss of the elaboration of hand movements that act as inflections. In contrast to these difficulties, the signs produced are semantically correct, although some errors in "phonological" processing might occur (such as mis-signing a word by producing it at the wrong place of articulation). Following is an example of the language capabilities of one native speaker of

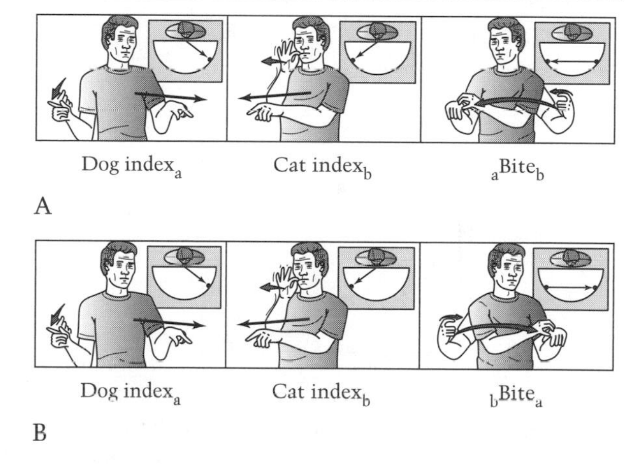

FIGURE 9.14 Spatial frame of reference in American Sign Language to make a syntactic distinction between subject and object. (A) In this case, the individual is signing the sentence "The dog bit the cat." First, the speaker makes the sign for the word "dog" and notes a particular spatial location for this noun (left frame). Then he makes the sign for "cat" and notes a different spatial location to denote this noun (middle frame). He next makes the sign for "bit," moving his hand from the "dog" position to the "cat" position (right frame). (B) In this case, the individual is signing the sentence "The cat bit the dog." The procedure of signing this sentence is identical to that for the other sentence, except the motion is made from the spatial position denoting "cat" to the one denoting "dog."

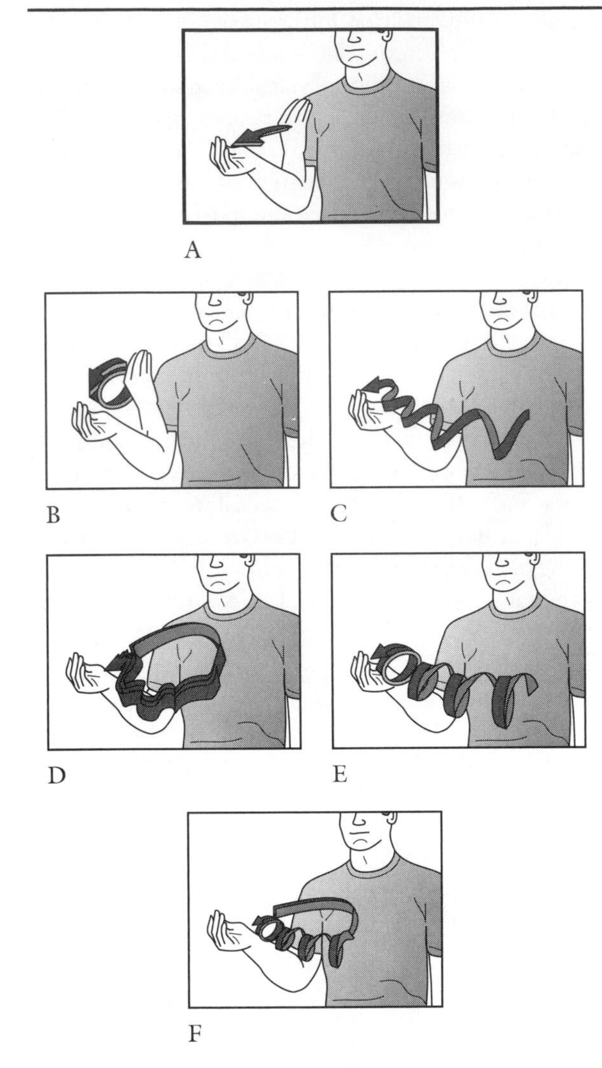

FIGURE 9.15 Examples of how variations in hand movement denote verb inflection in American Sign Language. (A) The basic sign and hand movement for "give." (B-F) Variations indicating the duration of the action and to whom it is directed. The various signs mean (B) "give continuously"; (C) "give to each"; (D) "give to each, that action recurring with time"; (E) "give continuously to each in turn"; and (F) "give continuously to each in turn, that action recurring with time."

ASL who sustained a large lesion to her left frontal lobe. Here she was attempting to relate a story from her childhood. Notice that she had little difficulty comprehending the examiner's questions.

EXAMINER: What else happened?
GAIL D.: car . . . drive . . . brother . . . drive . . . I . . . S-T-A-D [attempts to gesture "stand up"]
EXAMINER: You stood up?
GAIL D.: Yes . . . I . . . drive . . . [attempts to gesture "wave good-bye"]
EXAMINER: Wave goodbye?
GAIL D.: Yes. . . brother . . . drive . . . dunno . . . [attempts to gesture "wave good-bye"]
EXAMINER: Your brother was driving?
GAIL D.: yes . . . back . . . drive . . . brother . . . man . . . mama . . . stay . . . brother . . . drive

(Poizner, Klima, & Bellugi, 1987, p. 120)

Another signer whose damage included anterior regions but in this case also extended posteriorly exhibited a linguistic profile that was more like that of a person with Wernicke's aphasia. Although his comprehension was adequate, it was impaired compared with that before his stroke. His signing in ASL was fluent but did not have much meaning. As with Wernicke's aphasia, these difficulties transcended "spoken" language and affected his writing as well. Following is a translation of a sample of his signing in which he described the layout of his apartment, which had a glass-enclosed patio off the living room:

> And there's one (way down at the end) [unintelligible]. The man walked over to see the (disconnected), an extension of the (earth) room. It's there for the man (can live) a roof and light with shades to (keep pulling down). And there's a glass wall with four different. . . . He hammered. The man (makes hands), makes mobiles, many on the wall. A wonderful (always brillianting) man. (Poizner, Klima, & Bellugi, 1987, p. 98)

These case studies illustrate that the same neurological systems underlie the processing of many different language systems, including those that are visual and mark syntax spatially rather than with word order or word endings. These studies also suggest that anterior regions of the left hemisphere are specialized for syntactic aspects of language and language output, whereas posterior areas are specialized for semantic aspects of language processing.

Brain imaging studies have the ability to provide other insights into the neural bases of processing sign languages because specific populations can be selected to make important conceptual contrasts. For example, if one wishes to disentangle the degree to which deafness influences brain organization as compared to experience with sign language, one can compare patterns of brain activation for deaf individuals who are native signers of ASL with hearing individuals who are bilingual from birth in spoken English and ASL (these individuals are typically born to deaf parents). Such an investigation indicates that both groups activate classic language areas of the left hemisphere when processing language materials. But, in addition, language tasks also tend to activate homologous regions of the right hemisphere for native signers, both hearing and deaf (Neville et al., 1998). One might think that activation merely reflects the fact that this language is visual and spatial. However, at least some areas in the right hemisphere, such as the angular gyrus, are activated only in native speakers, not in those who learn sign language after puberty (Newman et al., 2002). Accordingly, the activation in native speakers appears to indicate a recruitment of right-hemisphere regions for language processing.

In addition, one can examine the pattern of activation across different sign languages. Just as English and Chinese are distinct languages, so are different sign languages. Knowing ASL will not help a person understand Chinese Sign Language. To look at the commonalities across sign languages, researchers have compared patterns of brain activation in speakers of ASL to patterns in speakers of Langue des Signes Québécoise (LSQ), which is a sign language used in Quebec and other parts of French Canada. They found that the pattern of activation does not vary significantly depending on the type of sign language used. Moreover, they found interesting parallels between speakers of sign languages and speakers of spoken languages. Left posteror inferior prefrontal regions that are usually involved in "phonological" processing were activated not only in hearing individuals but also in deaf individuals. More surprisingly, regions within the superior temporal gyrus that were considered dedicated to processing information in the auditory modality produced activation when deaf individuals processed sign nonwords! These results suggest the possibility that these regions are not auditory per se, but are dedicated to processing basic units of a complex pattern in rapid temporal sequence, an ability that could underlie either an auditory or visual language (Petito, Zatorre, Gauna, Nikelski, Dostie, & Evans, 2000) (see Color insert 9.2).

Music

Like language, music is an abstract symbolic system. Consequently, investigating how the brain processes music can provide insights into the basis of the left hemisphere's specialization for language. If a region of the brain is active during language because it is specialized for processing an abstract representational system based on auditory information, such activation should be observed not only for language, but for music as well. In contrast, if a brain region is truly specialized for language, then it should not be utilized when processing music. At present, the data suggest that there may be some truth in both viewpoints.

PET studies of brain activation during the performance of musical tasks suggest that with regard to reading, at least, different brain regions are used for language as compared to music. When a person reads a musical score, activity is centered in the left occipitoparietal junction, in a region dorsal to that activated during the reading of language. This more dorsal region's location probably reflects the larger demands on spatial abilities imposed by reading musical notation than imposed by reading words. In musical notation, specific notes have particular spatial positions on the musical staff. The position of the note on the staff indicates how high or low its pitch is, and the distance between two notes indicates their difference in pitch (see Figure 9.16).

Researchers also examined the areas of the brain that are activated while a person is listening to music and following its musical score. Like reading, this task requires a translation between a visual notation system and sound. Under such conditions, activation is observed in superior and posterior parts of the supramarginal gyrus, adjacent to but not identical with the area that when damaged typically causes alexia with agraphia.

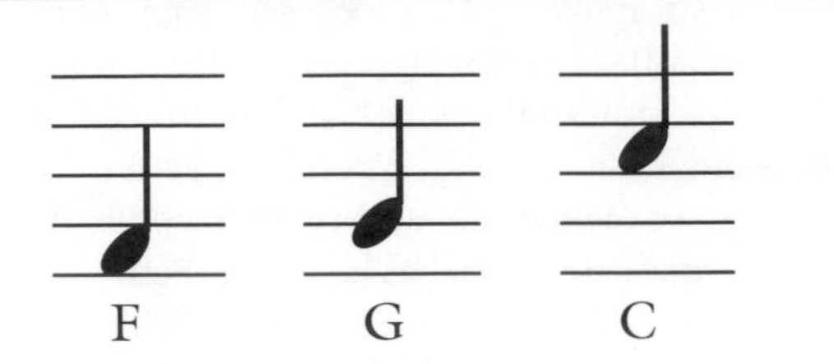

FIGURE 9.16 Spatial aspects of musical notation. In musical notation, each note has a particular location on the musical staff (which comprises five lines); either between two lines (as in the case of the notes F and C) or intersecting a line (as in the case of the note G). The higher the location is the higher the pitch (e.g., F at 343 Hz is lower in pitch than G at 384 Hz, which in turn is lower than C at 512 Hz). The relationship between the pitch of two notes is depicted in musical notation by the spatial distance between the notes. Because G is only slightly higher in pitch than F, it is located just a little above F, whereas because C is significantly higher in pitch than G, it is located substantially above G.

In contrast to the separateness of brain regions required for reading language as compared to reading music, there is some evidence that processing "syntax" in both language and music may rely on a similar neural substrate. As we discussed earlier, Broca's area is important for detecting a violation of syntactic structure, such as when a word in a sentence makes it ungrammatical. Similarly, one can determine what brain region reacts when a chord is played out of sequence, since the expectation of typical sequences in music can be considered akin to the syntactic structure of language. As with language, magnetoencephalography reveals a component that responds to a chord in an anomalous position. It occurs approximately 200 ms after presentation of the chord, with dipole modeling indicating a source located in Broca's area (Maess, Koelsch, Gunter & Friederici, 2001) (see Color insert 9.3).

Language and the Right Hemisphere

Since Broca, the left hemisphere's role in language has been considered so central that this hemisphere is often referred to as the *verbal* hemisphere. However, more recently researchers have come to appreciate that the right hemisphere is not a silent partner in language processing. Thus, we next turn our attention to the ways in which the right hemisphere contributes to language processing (for a recent short review of research in this area, see Beeman & Chiarello, 1998a, and for a book-length treatment, see Beeman & Chiarello, 1998b).

Right-Hemisphere Contributions to Language Processing

As we discussed in this chapter and in Chapter 4 (see page 117), although the right hemisphere of split-brain patients can comprehend written and auditory language, its abilities are limited. It has a poor understanding of complicated syntax, cannot produce speech or use phoneme-to-grapheme correspondence rules, and has a vocabulary restricted mainly to concrete words as opposed to abstract words. Despite these limitations, the right hemisphere contributes to the extraction of meaning from linguistic material in two main ways. First, the right hemisphere is involved in processing certain aspects of **prosody,** which is the intonation pattern, or sound envelope, of an utterance. Second, the right hemisphere plays an important role in narrative and inference. **Narrative** refers to the ability to construct or understand a story line, whereas **inference** refers to the ability to "fill in the blanks" and make assumptions about material that is not explicitly stated (i.e., material that is implied). We now examine these two contributions of the right hemisphere in more detail. Afterwards, we examine the role that the right hemisphere may play in the development of language abilities. We end our discussion by considering why the right hemisphere is not specialized for language processing.

• *PROSODY* •

Prosody, the sound envelope around words, can be useful in providing information about interpretation of a statement. For example, in English, a declarative statement is usually accompanied by a decrease in the pitch of one's voice, whereas a question is usually accompanied by a rising intonation pattern. In some cases, intonation pattern may be the only cue that can differentiate between two interpretations of an ambiguous sentence. Consider how prosody could differentiate the meaning of the four words "She did it again." as a response in the following dialogue:

LYNN: Alice is way into this mountain-biking thing. After breaking her arm, you'd think she'd be a little more cautious. But then yesterday, she went out and rode Captain Jack's. That trail is gnarly—narrow with lots of tree roots and rocks. And last night, I heard that she took a bad tumble on her way down.

SARA: *She did it again.*

If said with a rising intonation, Sara is asking whether Alice hurt herself again. On the other hand, if Sara said these same words emphatically with a falling pitch (e.g., "She did it again!"), the intonation would indicate that she is asserting what she already knows: Alice has managed to injure herself once more.

For the most part, the right hemisphere is superior to the left in its ability to interpret prosodic cues (e.g., whether a tone of voice is warm and friendly, sarcastic, condescending, or excited). Even though patients with severe aphasia (and hence left-hemisphere damage) can distinguish between questions and statements on the basis of prosodic cues (e.g., K. Heilman, Bowers, Speedie, & Coslett, 1984), evidence from patients with the split-brain syndrome, individuals with epilepsy, individuals undergoing the Wada test, and dichotic listening studies suggests that the right hemisphere is extremely important in the perception of prosody (e.g., Benowitz et al., 1983). A role for the right hemisphere in understanding prosody is not limited to situations in which prosody implies an emotional state (e.g., a brief high-frequency monotone might imply surprise), but can also be found when prosodic information is emotionally neutral (i.e., rising and falling intonation contours) (e.g., Weintraub, Mesulam, & Kramer, 1981; Zatorre, Evans, Meyer, & Gjedde, 1992). The right hemisphere's perception of prosodic cues appears to depend on the tonal aspects of the stimuli because poor tonal memory has been found to correlate with an inability to interpret prosody (e.g., C. Tompkins & Flowers, 1985).

In contrast to the right hemisphere's predominance in interpreting prosodic cues, both hemispheres seem to play a role in the production of prosody, but each makes a different contribution. Prosody consists of two classes of cues: those related to pitch or tone and those related to timing. Consistent with a left hemisphere superiority for temporal aspects of processing and a right hemisphere superiority for tonal processing, different types of prosodic deficits are observed after right-hemisphere damage than after left-hemisphere damage. For example, **aprosodic** speech observed after damage to anterior regions of the right hemisphere can be attributed to the individual's speaking all at one pitch (Behrens, 1988), which is not surprising considering that pitch perception depends more on the right hemisphere than on the left (e.g., B. Milner, 1962a). After damage to the left hemisphere, speech is not so much aprosodic as **dysprosodic,** meaning that it has disordered intonation. The dysprosodia seems to result from the ill-timed prosodic cues. For example, neurologically intact individuals tend to elongate the final word rather than the initial word of an utterance. In contrast, persons with Broca's aphasia do the opposite, elongating the first word rather than the last (e.g., Danly & Shapiro, 1982) (for a thorough and recent review of the literature on prosody, see Baum & Pell, 1999). Before we end our discussion of prosody, one point is worth mentioning: The production of prosody can be disrupted by damage to other regions of the brain besides the cerebral hemispheres. Prosody can be compromised by damage to the basal ganglia and cerebellum (e.g., Cancelliere & Kertesz, 1990; Kent & Rosenbek, 1982), but such damage simultaneously disrupts various other processes that depend on precise timing of motor control.

• *INFERENCE AND NARRATIVE* •

Because the meaning of language is not always clear, readers and listeners use certain strategies to aid comprehension. For example, determining the theme of a story can help in interpreting ambiguous information, in making inferences about what has not been explicitly stated, and in anticipating what information will be presented next. To demonstrate this effect, read the following sentence: "With mosquitoes, gnats, and grasshoppers flying all about, she came across a small black bug that was being used to eavesdrop on her conversation." Because of the way the initial part of the sentence biased you, you probably did a double take to reinterpret the meaning of *bug.* This sentence is an example of how we build upon previous information to make

BRAIN ORGANIZATION IN BILINGUALS

One issue that has intrigued neurolinguists for some time is whether the neural organization for language in bilingual individuals differs from that observed in monolinguals. In part, this discussion is motivated by recent findings that the language processing of bilinguals cannot be considered the equivalent to having the language-processing systems of two monolinguals residing within one person. For example, if one examined how French-English bilingual persons pronounce a particular vowel, such as /a/, one would find that their English version of an /a/ is shifted toward a French pronunciation as compared with an individual who speaks only English. Likewise, their French version of an /a/ is shifted toward an English pronunciation compared to a monolingual French speaker (Mack, 2003).

Traditionally, neuropsychologists have tried to understand the bilingual person's brain by examining the pattern of language disability in both languages as the result of a brain lesion. If the organization for both languages is controlled by the same neural apparatus, we would expect that language loss in one language would parallel language loss in the other. In contrast, if organization for each language is controlled by a different neural apparatus, any linguistic problems exhibited in one language would be independent of (that is, not correlated with) language loss in the other language. Unfortunately, the results in this area are not so clear-cut as to provide a definitive answer—an extremely wide variation in the pattern has been observed. Further complicating the picture, the pattern observed soon after injury may differ from that observed later (e.g., Paradis, Goldblum, & Abidi, 1982).

Scientists' attempts to understand the relation between brain structures and language processing in bilinguals are complicated by a number of factors, including the age at which the second language is acquired, the individual's relative facility in each language, and the amount of time in each linguistic environment (Paradis, 1977).

Whereas almost all individuals start to learn their initial language, often called the *mother tongue,* at birth, bilinguals acquire the second language either simultaneously with or at some point later in time after they acquire their first language. Some bilinguals have equal facility in both languages; others do not. Facility in a language needn't be correlated with its age of acquisition. For example, an individual who spoke the mother tongue until the age of three years might have a poorer grasp of its grammar and a more restricted vocabulary in that language than in a second language that was spoken exclusively for the next 20 years. The type of linguistic environment (e.g., a French-speaking environment) in which a person has spent the most time and how recently the person has been in that environment can also have an influence. As you might imagine, disentangling the contributions that each of these factors may play in the brain organization for language in bilinguals is a daunting task. The task can be especially hard if one is examining bilingual individuals who have suffered brain damage, because systematically varying these factors is not feasible.

Two particular issues remain the source of some debate. First, there has been a debate as to whether

inferences about upcoming words. Individuals with right-hemisphere damage have difficulty with the types of tasks just discussed: following the thread of a story (e.g., J. A. Kaplan, Brownell, Jacobs, & Gardner, 1990), making inferences about what is being said (e.g., Beeman, 1993), and understanding non-literal aspects of language such as metaphors (e.g., H. Brownell, 1988). These difficulties manifest themselves across spoken and written sentences, and in stories, dialogues, and paragraphs. We now examine these specific difficulties in more detail.

To comprehend language, we superimpose structure upon discourse. This structure allows us to organize information so that clauses within sentences, or episodes or events within stories, can be linked to one another, and so that material is presented in an orderly fashion, building upon that presented previously. Individuals with right-hemisphere damage have difficulty building such structures. They have difficulty ordering sentences so that they form a story (e.g., Delis, Wapner, Gardner, & Moses, 1983), ordering words so that they form a sen-

the right hemisphere plays a larger role in language processing in bilinguals than in monolinguals (e.g., Berquier & Ashton, 1992; Paradis, 1992). Recent brain imaging (e.g., Dehaene et al., 1997) and ERP studies (Weber-Fox & Neville, 1996) suggest that whereas there is strong activation of the left hemisphere for the native language, a later acquired second language tends to cause a more bilateral pattern of activation that is idiosyncratic across individuals.

The second aspect of neural organization in bilinguals that has been the source of much debate is whether the brain regions *within* the left hemisphere that are activated during processing of one language are somewhat distinct from those activated during processing of the other language. For example, naming an object in one language can be disrupted by electrical stimulation of a different region of the brain than that which disrupts naming in another language (e.g., G. A. Ojemann, 1983). A similar separation of regions involved in processing different languages has been observed during oral language processing (e.g., object naming) as well as during written language processing both at temporoparietal and frontal sites. More recently, brain imaging studies have suggested that the degree of separation may depend both on the brain area and the age of language acquisition. In one study, it was found that Wernicke's area was similarly activated by both languages regardless of age of acquisition of the second language. In contrast, activation in Broca's area overlapped only in those bilinguals who had acquired both languages at the same time, whereas distinct regions were activated for each language in bilinguals who had acquired their second language later in life (Kim, Relkin, Lee, & Hirsch, 1997) (see Color insert 9.4).

As a way to explain this pattern, researchers have proposed that the neural apparatus required to learn to move the vocal articulators when a first language is learned may prevent this brain region from programming these same articulators to be used in a different way later on. Hence, a distinct, and possibly suboptimal, region of brain tissue becomes involved in programming speech output for the second language. This may explain in part why it is so very difficult to speak a second language as a nonnative speaker without an accent. In contrast, since posterior brain regions are specialized for extracting meaning, there may be a common semantic reference regardless of how accessed ("dog" and "chien" both refer to the panting household pet). In fact, when access of semantic information is directly compared in two languages, one acquired earlier in life and the other acquired later, no difference is found in the brain regions activated regardless of whether the two languages are Spanish and English (Iles et al., 1999) or English and Mandarin (Chee, Tan, & Thiel, 1999), as long as individuals have high proficiency in both languages. Only when there is a difference in proficiency between the two languages is less extensive activation of posterior left hemisphere regions observed for the language acquired second (Perani et al., 1996). This effect is observed regardless of age of acquisition (Perani et al., 1998). Thus, proficiency in a language, rather than age of acquisition, appears to play a more important role in determining the degree to which posterior regions of the left hemisphere are involved in language processing. ■

tence (Cavalli, DeRenzi, Faglioni, & Vitale, 1981), and determining whether an utterance is relevant to a conversation (that is, determining whether it builds upon previously presented material) (e.g., Rehak, Kaplan, & Gardner, 1992). Individuals with right-hemisphere brain damage also have difficulty extracting the theme of a story (e.g., Moya, Benowitz, Levine, & Finklestein, 1986) or using information about a story's theme to help them in other tasks, such as arranging sentences into coherent paragraphs (e.g., Schneiderman, Murasugi, & Saddy, 1992).

Converging evidence for the role of the right hemisphere in these operations is provided by neuroimaging studies. Activation of the middle temporal gyrus of the right hemisphere is observed when individuals are told to pay attention to the general theme or moral of an Aesop's fable as compared to being asked specific information about an attribute of a fable character (Nichelli et al., 1995). More activation is also observed in this region when individuals read an untitled paragraph and have to deduce its main theme as compared to reading a paragraph when the title provides such information (St. George, Kutas, Martinez, & Sereno, 1999). Thus, this brain area appears to be involved in extracting the overall meaning of sentences or paragraphs.

One interesting ramification of this inability to comprehend a coherent theme in stories is that patients with right-hemisphere brain damage have difficulty comprehending jokes. Certain researchers have suggested that jokes are funny because most of a joke forms a coherent story, but then the punch line contains a surprise or twist that nevertheless coheres with the overall story. Given that individuals with right-hemisphere damage have difficulty following the thread of a story, we can easily see why they have difficulty selecting the correct punch line for a joke. They are likely to pick a surprising ending but not one that is compatible with the previously presented material (e.g., H. H. Brownell, Michel, Powelson, & Gardner, 1983).

Some authorities have suggested that individuals with right-hemisphere damage may have difficulty comprehending discourse, in part, because the right hemisphere gains access to the meaning of words in a different manner than the left hemisphere does. Experts have known for some time that when we hear or read a specific word, such as *nurse,* it primes our ability to process a network of words related in meaning, such as *doctor, hospital, needle,* and so forth. Divided visual field studies have demonstrated that the network of associated words that gets primed by a given word is more restricted in the left hemisphere than in the right. For example, whereas the right hemisphere retains activation of both meanings of an ambiguous word (e.g., *bank*) for about 1 second, the left hemisphere retains only the dominant meaning (e.g., "repository for money"), not the subordinate one (e.g., "side of a river") (e.g., Burgess & Simpson, 1988; Chiarello, 1991). Furthermore, weakly related words facilitate the processing of a word presented in the left visual field (LVF) but not a word presented in the right visual field (RVF) (e.g., Rodel, Cook, Regard, & Landis, 1992). These results have been interpreted to suggest that the semantic aspects of words are coded relatively more coarsely in the right hemisphere than in the left hemisphere (e.g., Beeman, 1998). Whereas fine semantic coding by the left hemisphere allows information occurring close together in a sentence to be integrated, the coarser and more diffuse semantic processing of the right hemisphere has been suggested to play an important role in integrating information over larger linguistic expanses (Beeman et al., 1994). Supporting such an idea, when an individual must generate a word to finish off a sentence that has many possible endings (e.g., "He went into the *house, garden, bank, office, store,* etc.), there is activation of the right temporal lobe relative to merely reading a sentence with one of those possible endings (Kircher et al., 2001).

Because individuals with right-hemisphere damage often have trouble understanding or maintaining the overall coherence of a story, they also have difficulties making inferences or using discourse to distinguish the meaning of an ambiguous phrase. For example, after hearing "John walked in the water near some glass" and "John grabbed his foot and called the lifeguard for help," most people infer that John cut himself. In contrast, individuals with right-hemisphere brain damage have difficulty doing so (Beeman, 1993).

Individuals with right-hemisphere brain damage also have difficulty with the non-literal aspects of language such as metaphors and indirect requests. For example, individuals with such damage may be horrified to hear that someone was "Crying her eyes out" because they interpret the sentence literally, so as to visualize a gruesome scene. When asked to point to a picture of someone who has a "heavy heart," an individual with right-hemisphere brain damage is likely to point to a picture of a large heart rather than to a picture of someone who looks sad (Winner & Gardner, 1977). When given a sentence such as "Can you open the door?" an individual with this type of brain damage might respond defensively, saying, "Of course I can open the door. Why do you ask? Do you think I'm such a weakling that I can't even open a door!?" when what was really meant was "Please open the door for me" (e.g., Foldi, 1987). Consistent with these findings, fMRI studies indicate that processing the metaphorical aspects of language leads to changes in activation in the right hemisphere, most notably the middle temporal gyrus and the frontal pole (e.g., Bottini et al., 1994).

The deficits in language processing exhibited by individuals with right-hemisphere damage are not so severe as to disrupt their ability to comprehend language and convey meaning. Yet, these deficits do dilute the linguistic experience. The aspects of language that we may find most appealing, such as a wonderful metaphor or an unexpected twist or turn of phrase, go unappreciated or are left unsaid.

• *THE DEVELOPMENT OF LANGUAGE ABILITIES* •

Recent research suggests that the right hemisphere may play a substantial role at various stages of language development, although the left hemisphere plays a predominant role by adulthood. For example, damage at birth to the right hemisphere results in deficits in the size of a child's vocabulary between the ages of 10 and 17 months, but not thereafter, suggesting that the right hemisphere may play a large role specifically during this time period (Nass, 1997). Similar shifts in the relative balance of power between the hemispheres in language processing are also observed during this time period in neurologically-intact children. For example, at 13 months, the ERP response to known words distinguishes itself from unknown words across broad regions of both hemispheres. By 20 months, however, the effects are consistently found only over temporal and parietal regions of the left hemisphere (Mills, Coffey-Corina, & Neville, 1997). Divided visual field techniques suggest that later on in childhood when children are learning to read, the right hemisphere once again plays a larger role. This lasts up until about 10 years of age, the time at which most children have 5 years of reading experience. After this point, the left hemisphere becomes more dominant (Waldie & Mosley, 2000). A similar effect has also been observed in Israeli teenagers learning to read English. Although they all exhibited a RVF advantage for reading Hebrew, those with only 2 years of experience learning English exhibited a LVF for English words, whereas those with 6 years of experience exhibited a RVF advantage (Silverberg et al., 1979). Thus, these findings suggest that the role of the right hemisphere in language may be linked both to the age of the individual and the level of language capabilities in a given language.

Why Isn't the Right Hemisphere Specialized for Language?

The differences in the right and left hemispheres' abilities to process language are one of the most basic and fundamental aspects of human brain organization. Because the distinction is so striking, you might wonder, "Why does the left hemisphere have special language capacities?" Three main answers have been proposed to this question: The first suggests that the left hemisphere is specialized for all symbolic and abstract processing (e.g., J. Brown, 1977), the second says that the left hemisphere is specialized for precise temporal control of oral and manual articulators (e.g., Kimura, 1982), and the third says that the left hemisphere is specifically specialized for linguistic processing (e.g., D. Corina, Vaid, & Bellugi, 1992).

According to the first perspective, all expression and comprehension of symbols occurs in the left hemisphere. Language is considered just one other symbolic system (e.g., the word *dog* becomes a symbol for a common household pet) and hence is lateralized to the left hemisphere. Such a perspective does not take a flattering view of right-hemisphere capabilities, ignoring many of the ways in which the right hemisphere can perform symbolic associations (e.g., interpreting the symbolic aspects of a map).

According to the second perspective, language is lateralized to the left hemisphere because it relies on precise timing in the motor control of oral articulators. From this vantage point, apraxia and problems in speech output arise from the same system, and that system is lateralized to the left hemisphere. In fact, oral and manual movements are often linked. For example, during the oral recounting of a story, gestures related to the story line are much more often made with the right hand than with the left in right-handers. The interpretation of this finding is that a single left-hemisphere system controls both the oral articulators for speech and the manual articulators for gesture (which must be precisely coordinated with speech). In contrast, self-touching movements that have nothing to do with the story line, such as moving your hair, occur equally often with either hand (e.g., Lavergne & Kimura, 1987).

According to the third perspective, the left hemisphere is specifically lateralized for linguistic processing, regardless of whether linguistic information is conveyed in speech, as in conventional English, or in hand symbols, such as in ASL. The argument is that the left hemisphere's contribution to language is above and beyond that which occurs for gesture.

Support for this viewpoint is provided by a single case study of a deaf signer who, after sustaining a left-hemisphere lesion, could neither produce nor comprehend ASL but retained the ability to communicate by using gestures in nonlinguistic domains (D. P. Corina et al., 1992). These findings suggest that we do not have one unitary linguistic-gestural system; rather, the control of language and the control of nonlinguistic gesture are distinct.

At present, the debate between the last two positions continues. One camp argues, on the basis of deficit patterns in ASL signers, that the left hemisphere is specialized for language. They say that all symbolic processing is not lost because these individuals can use symbolic gestures to pantomime. Furthermore, these researchers assert that their signers with aphasia do not necessarily have apraxia. Thus, apraxia and aphasia are not linked. The other camp retorts that the tests of apraxia in this special population have not been sensitive enough. Given that speakers of ASL are more sophisticated than most individuals in the use of manual movements, they argue, more stringent tests are required to reveal deficits, and if such tests were given, a correlation between aphasia and apraxia would be found.

Although this debate remains unresolved, the hemispheres clearly differ in their contributions to language functioning. The left hemisphere has a much more elaborate language system, but the right hemisphere plays an important role as well. Like many other cognitive skills discussed in this book, the complete functioning of language skills relies on an entire brain, not just one hemisphere.

SUMMARY

Neurological Bases for Auditory Language Processing

- A breakdown in language functioning after brain insult is known as aphasia.
- Anterior regions of the left hemisphere, more specifically Broca's area, are specialized for speech output.
- Posterior regions of the left hemisphere, most notably Wernicke's area, are specialized for speech comprehension.
- Phonology, which refers to the rules by which sounds in a language are formed and the rules by which they can be combined, is disrupted in both anterior and posterior aphasias, although the ability to produce the correct sound for a given phoneme (i.e., phonetics) is more disrupted by anterior damage.
- Syntax, which refers to the rules of grammar dictating the ways in which words are conjoined to form sentences, is disrupted in anterior aphasias.
- Semantics, which is the aspect of language that specifies meaning of words and sentences, is disrupted after damage to posterior regions of the left hemisphere.
- The Wada test, in which one hemisphere is anesthetized, provides evidence of left-hemisphere specialization for speech output in all but a fraction of right-handers.
- Brain imaging and electrophysiological studies also support the idea that anterior and posterior regions of the brain are specialized for syntax and semantics, respectively.

Neurological Bases for Visual Language Processing

- Alexia is the loss of reading ability as a result of a brain insult.
- Agraphia is the loss of the ability to write as a result of brain damage.
- The phonological route to meaning links the orthography (graphic form) of a word to its phonology (sound), which is then linked to meaning. This route is required for words one has never encountered and non-words (e.g., glimp) that could be a real word but are not, and is lost in phonological alexia.
- The direct route links the orthography directly to the meaning. It is used to read irregular words,

such as "colonel" that do not follow the typical grapheme-to-phoneme correspondence rules, and is lost in surface alexia.
- In phonological agraphia, individuals cannot spell using phoneme-to-grapheme correspondence rules.
- In lexical agraphia, individuals cannot spell using the direct route.
- The exact location of the left hemisphere system that links word form directly to meaning is of some debate, with some investigators suggesting that it is located in the ventral regions of extrastriate cortex and others arguing that it is located in the middle temporal gyrus.
- The location of the system that links phonology to meaning is thought to reside in regions of the supramarginal and angular gyri that border on the temporal lobe.

Processing of Non-Indo-European Languages and Other Symbolic Systems
- Kana is a syllable-based system in which each symbol is related to sound, much like the alphabetic system in English, and hence can rely on the phonological route.
- Kanji is a logographic system, in which the symbol for each word is unique, and relies on the direct route.
- Evidence from both brain-damaged patients and brain imaging suggests that these two systems are dissociable.
- In American Sign Language, information is conveyed visually by hand symbols rather than auditorally by sounds, and syntax is marked not only by word order, as in English, but also by the spatial location where a symbol is made and by the type of hand movement.
- Anterior damage causes speakers of ASL to become agrammatic and posterior damage results in impaired comprehension of ASL, suggesting that anterior and posterior regions of the left hemisphere are specialized for different aspects of language processing regardless of the mode of language production, manual or oral.
- The reading of music and the reading of words rely on similar, but distinct, regions of the left hemisphere, suggesting they are separable.

Language and the Right Hemisphere
- The perception of prosodic cues, which are the intonation contour and timing parameters of speech that can help disambiguate the meaning of utterances, is performed mainly by the right hemisphere.
- The right hemisphere plays a major role in discourse by aiding a person in comprehending a story line, making inferences based on previously presented material, and extracting the main theme or moral of a story.
- By activating a more diffuse and remote set of semantic associations than the left hemisphere, the right hemisphere aids in the metaphorical and non-literal use of language.
- The right hemisphere may also play a role in language processing when a language is just being acquired.
- The left hemisphere may play a large role in language either because it is specialized for fine motor control of the vocal and manual muscles, or because it is specialized specifically for language.

KEY TERMS

agrammatic aphasia 296
agraphia 303
alexia 303
aprosodic 315
attentional dyslexia 306
Broca's aphasia 286
conduction aphasia 289
crossed aphasia 298
deep alexia 305
direct route to reading 303
dysprosodic 315
echolalia 291
global aphasia 292
grapheme-to-phoneme correspondence rules 303
inference 314
irregular words 303
letter-by-letter reading 306
lexical agraphia 305
narrative 314
neglect dyslexia 306
neologisms 289
paraphasias 289
phonemic paraphasia 289
phonological agraphia 305
phonological alexia 304
phonological route to reading 303
phonology 293
place of articulation 294
prosody 314
semantic paralexias 305
semantic paraphasia 289
semantics 293
surface alexia 304
syntax 293
telegraphic speech 288
transcortical motor aphasia 290
transcortical sensory aphasia 291
voicing 295
Wernicke's aphasia 289

SUMMARY

CHAPTER 10

Contributed by Neal J. Cohen and Marie T. Banich

MEMORY

In response to a seizure disorder that could not be controlled effectively by anticonvulsant medications, a young man underwent an experimental surgical procedure involving the removal of medial temporal lobe structures that we only now know are critical to memory. Although the surgery in 1953 was successful in bringing the seizure disorder under control, it resulted in a profound deficit in memory. This young man was unable to remember the events of his life or the people with whom he has come into contact since the surgery, such as his physicians and other caregivers, or to learn new facts about the changing world around him. This deficit has persisted to the present day. Thus, at this time, he does not know his age, the current date, or either his recent history (such as where he lives and how long he has lived there) or "our" recent history (such as the people in the public eye and the public events in which they have figured). Strikingly, he has on occasion misidentified a current picture of himself as a picture of his father.

Yet, this man still manages to express a wide range of memory abilities. He can reason and solve problems, recognize objects, perform voluntary and reflexive motor acts appropriate to all manner of objects and situations, and demonstrate a full range of linguistic skills, thereby exhibiting a considerable store of knowledge that he acquired early in life before the surgery. His ability to remember the remote past seems largely intact. Also spared is his ability to hold on to information in memory temporarily while he is working with it, but only if he is not interrupted.

He enjoys solving crossword puzzles and watches many television programs. But he is likely to do the same crossword puzzles or watch the same television shows repeatedly without noting the repetition. Understanding television shows is difficult for him because the commercials interspersed throughout a show cause him to forget the story line. Especially difficult are those shows that feature an ensemble cast in which many or all of the actors have continuing, interwoven story lines (e.g., as in soap operas); following the plot lines of such shows is beyond his capabilities.

This man can hold a perfectly reasonable conversation with you, except that his conversation is devoid of current content; he cannot tell you about recent weather conditions, the latest books that he read, the movies that he saw recently, or the people or events currently in the news. If you were to avoid such topics in your conversation with him, you would be hard pressed to notice any memory deficit at all, unless your conversation was interrupted and you left for a short while. Even if the interruption lasted only a few minutes, upon returning you would find not only that he could not remember what you were conversing about minutes earlier, but, most likely, he could not remember having ever met you.

This latter deficit— a near-total inability to recollect his experiences—is striking. Just as striking, however, is an intact ability to be shaped by his experiences. Thus, remarkably, he is able to acquire and express a variety of new skills, such as improving his performance in visuomotor tracking tasks, despite being unable to remember the specific training events or the materials to which he was exposed. In addition, like neurologically intact individuals, his improve-ment in performance with practice is larger for the specific items on which he trained, making him faster and more accurate for the particular words, faces, or objects that he recently experienced than for items being presented for the first time, which is exactly how we all perform. But in this case the improved performance with repeated items occurs despite the fact that he is unable to judge which items were the repeated ones, and he has no sense of familiarity for those items. ■

THE PATIENT IN the opening vignette of this chapter, who is known by the initials H.M., has been studied extensively ever since his surgery, initially by Brenda Milner and her colleagues, and then over the last several decades by Suzanne Corkin and her colleagues at the Clinical Research Center at MIT (where the first author had the good fortune to spend several years). H.M.'s memory loss is known as **amnesia,** which in his case is remarkably profound and pervasive. Since his surgery, H.M.'s impairments have been documented exhaustively (e.g., see Scoville & Milner, 1957; Corkin, 1984, 1991; Milner, Corkin, & Teuber, 1968; Corkin, 2002) and have been shown to include memory for such materials as words, text, names, faces, spatial layout, routes, geometric shapes, nonsense patterns, tunes, tones, public events, and personal episodes. H.M.'s amnesia apparently affects all aspects of his life and has been said to cause him to forget the events of his daily life "as quickly as they occur" (Scoville & Milner, 1957, p. 15). It is an irony that while H.M. is undoubtedly the most famous and intensively studied patient in the annals of neurology or neuropsychology, his memory impairment is so severe that he has no idea of his fame.

The disorder of memory seen in H.M. and in numerous other cases of amnesia, studied by various investigators in the field, tells us much about what memory is and about how it is accomplished by the brain. Because memory can be compromised in apparent isolation from other cognitive abilities, amnesia demonstrates a basic functional independence of memory from other cognitive capacities. Because amnesia can be so selective, affecting only certain memory capacities while leaving other aspects of memory fully intact, it indicates that there are different kinds of memory. Like other functions we have discussed in this book, memory must be thought of as a collection of abilities supported by a set of brain and cognitive systems that operate cooperatively, each system making different functional contributions. Normal memory performance involves various systems, which ordinarily operate together so seamlessly that it is difficult to gain any intuitive appreciation of the separateness of the contributions made by the various systems. Only through careful and converging neuropsychological, neuroimaging, psychophysiological, and neurophysiological studies can we infer the distinct roles and contributions of the various brain and cognitive systems that collectively mediate memory. This chapter lays out our current understanding of the different systems and their functional roles.

What Is Memory?

We begin our examination of memory by posing the most basic question right from the start: What *is* memory? Perhaps the best answer to this question is that memory is the group of mechanisms or processes by which experience shapes us, changing our brains and our behavior. Tennessee Williams said, "Life is all memory except for the present moment that flies by so quickly we can hardly catch it going by." For our purposes, memory is the ability to capture each successive "present moment" within the nervous system so that we are forever changed by it. How and where memory is captured within the nervous system is what needs to be understood.

We can also ask what is memory *for*? To this question, there are many answers: Memory is for holding onto the details of everyday life; remembering to take our keys, coat, or lunch; recalling where we parked the car, left our backpack, or placed the groceries; remembering scheduled appointments, class assignments, or plans for the evening; and knowing the names, appearance, and defining characteristics of people we have met. But memory is also for holding information in mind for just a short time while we work on it, such as doing mental arithmetic or keeping the phone number of the pizza delivery place in mind while we place the call. Memory is also for remembering the events of our lives, and the people who inhabit them and for identifying, appreciating, and responding appropriately to various objects and situations and the interactions between them. Finally, memory is for capturing the regularities in the world—the correlations and patterns of co-occurrence (of the letter combinations we type, of sights and sounds of related objects, or of smells and tastes of common foods)—and adapting our brains and behavior in accordance. And all of this, as we shall see later, occurs whether or not we are aware of those regularities and how we adapt to them.

However we look at it, memory encompasses a large collection of capabilities that share a common label. The brain, in accomplishing memory, must support all these different capabilities or functionalities. To do so requires a set of mechanisms supported by a set of brain systems. We turn now to identifying and characterizing those systems and the roles they play.

Amnesia—A Disorder of Long-Term Memory

Work on the neuropsychology and cognitive neuroscience of memory has focused disproportionately on one particular form of memory disorder, namely amnesia. From the study of amnesia, scientists have learned about many of the fundamental aspects of how the brain supports memory processing. Because this work has been so influential, we begin our examination of memory in the brain by discussing it.

This section starts by outlining the various etiologies of amnesia. We then talk a bit about the temporal extent of amnesia—how far into the future and how far into the past from the point of injury the memory disorder extends. Following that we examine the fundamental aspects of the amnesic syndrome. First, we note that amnesia is a global phenomenon, affecting memory in all sensory modalities, and across all types of material. Then we discuss two types of memory that are not affected—working memory and skill learning. Next we examine various theories that have been proposed to explain the constellation of impaired and spared abilities observed in amnesia. To conclude the section we discuss converging evidence and additional insights into amnesia provided by studies with nonhuman animals.

Although our discussion will include evidence from cases of amnesia resulting from varying etiologies, we will focus on the most famous case of amnesia, that of H.M. This particular case has been critical to our understanding of amnesia because it resulted from a surgical resection. Prior to the development of technology for CT or MRI scans of the brain there was no way to clearly identify the structural damage to the brain in a given neuropsychological patient, so the fact that H.M.'s amnesia resulted from a surgical resection was crucial. It meant that we knew specifically which structures were lesioned. In addition, we knew exactly which aspects of memory were impaired by the lesion because H.M. had been evaluated prior to the surgery that left him amnesic.

Etiologies

The case of H.M. was the first to indicate that amnesia results from extensive damage to the hippocampal region (including the hippocampus, dentate gyrus, subiculum, amygdala, and neighboring parahippocampal area: the parahippocampal, entorhinal, and perirhinal cortices) (see Figure 10.1).

Subsequent work has confirmed that amnesia results from extensive damage to the hippocampal region, regardless of how that damage is sustained, whether by surgical resection, as with H.M., or any of a number of other etiologies involving loss of blood supply to the region, as in stroke or as a result of anoxia, or in certain disease processes that target this region, as in herpes simplex encephalitis. In addition, amnesia can also result from damage to the closely related **midline diencephalic region,** involving particularly the dorsomedial nucleus of the thalamus and the **mammillary bodies** of the hypothalamus. Damage to this region can originate in a number of ways—for example, as occurs in Korsakoff's disease, following chronic alcohol abuse. The most frequently observed etiologies of amnesia are listed in Table 10.1. Regardless of etiology, the fundamental nature of the deficit is an inability to form most new long-term memories.

Across the various instances of amnesia, there are some differences, specifically with respect to the onset and duration of the memory disorder, its severity, and the extent to which it is associated with additional cognitive deficits. Most of the etiologies of amnesia listed in Table 10.1 produce chronic, stable impairments; these people never regain the ability to create new long-term memories. However, some instances of amnesia are associated with a more temporary impairment, as in the case of **posttraumatic amnesia** following closed head injury (see Chapter 14). Memory in these patients typically recovers over time, sometimes nearly completely. A temporary amnesia is also associated with some forms of bilateral **electroconvulsive therapy (ECT)** for depression, which involves inducing seizures (we discuss the rationale for this treatment more in Chapter 12, page 421). The resulting amnesia accumulates across treatments, but memory recovers during the weeks and months following the end of the treatment series.

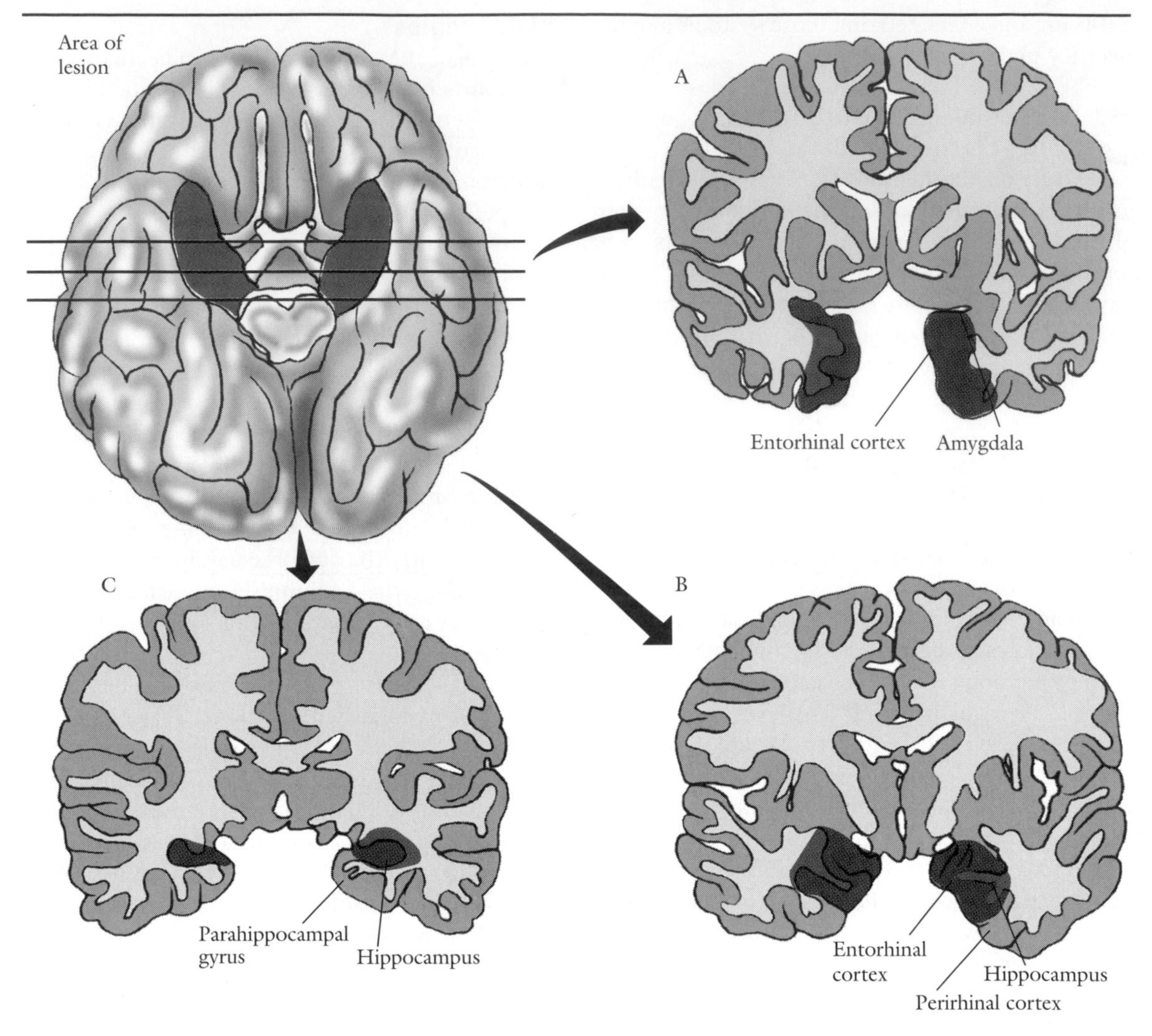

FIGURE 10.1 Brain structures removed during H.M.'s surgery. H.M.'s surgery involved bilateral removal of the anterior section of the medial temporal lobes (A–C). Three coronal sections, from rostral to caudal show the regions removed. The regions excised included not only most of the amygdala, as shown in A, but also the hippocampus, entorhinal and dorsal perirhinal cortex, as shown in B, while sparing most of the parahippocampal gyrus, as shown in C.

The onset and progression of memory impairment also differs across etiologies of amnesia. Whereas the amnesias caused by closed head injury or stroke have a sudden onset, others are more gradual and insidious. This is the case with amnesias associated with certain slow-growing tumors that impinge upon diencephalic memory structures, and with the **dementias,** such as that seen in **Alzheimer's disease,** a syndrome discussed in more detail in Chapter 14.

The severity of memory impairment varies considerably among different instances of amnesia. For example, the recall of H.M. and patients with amnesia from herpes simplex encephalitis is near zero. Their ability to recognize information that they should have acquired since the onset of their disorder is near chance or at chance on almost every test of memory reported. Other patients, while still being markedly impaired compared with the norm, show less severe symptoms. As an example, whereas

TABLE 10.1 Causes of Amnesia

CAUSE	DESCRIPTION
Medial temporal lobe damage causing amnesia	
Herpes simplex encephalitis	A virus that tends to affect medial temporal and orbital frontal areas; it can also compromise lateral temporal neocortical areas.
Vascular accident	For example, a blockage of the posterior cerebral artery preventing a normal blood supply.
Hypoxic ischemia	Oxygen deprivation leading to brain damage, especially hippocampal damage.
Closed head injury	For example, head injury from a motor vehicle accident; it tends to cause damage to medial temporal and frontal areas.
Bilateral electroconvulsive therapy (ECT)	A series of ECT treatments for the relief of depressive illness; when administered bilaterally, ECT produces a memory deficit that disappears with time.
Alzheimer's disease	A disease producing damage to medial temporal lobe structures as well as to various cortical areas, apparently as a result of primary damage to nuclei in the basal forebrain that project to those areas. Memory impairment is frequently the earliest sign and the most telling deficit in the early stages, although it is complicated by additional cognitive (and memory) deficits that are part of a progressive dementia.
Midline diencephalic damage causing amnesia	
Korsakoff's disease	The most frequently studied instance of amnesia, resulting from many years of chronic alcohol abuse and a thiamin (vitamin B_1) deficiency that causes hemorrhaging of midline diencephalic structures.
Vascular accident	For example, a stroke affecting the paramedial artery and preventing a normal blood supply to midline thalamic structures.
Third-ventricle tumors	For example, a pituitary tumor; the tumor may press on critical thalamic and hypothalamic structures.

the typical amnesic patient can recover very little information contained in paragraphs or visual figures studied 30 minutes earlier, H.M. cannot recollect even the fact that paragraphs or visual figures were presented 30 minutes earlier.

Temporal Extent

There are two different categories of memory impairment: anterograde and retrograde amnesia. So far we have emphasized **anterograde amnesia,** which is the deficit in new learning that results in impairment in memory for information acquired after the onset of amnesia. Yet, anterograde amnesia virtually always occurs in association with at least some retrograde amnesia. **Retrograde amnesia** is the impairment in memory for information that was acquired *prior* to the event that caused the amnesia, a deficit stretching back in time to some point before the onset of amnesia (see Figure 10.2). The degree and temporal extent of retrograde amnesia varies greatly across patients, from a week to decades. Nonetheless, some generalizations can be made. As long as the damage is limited

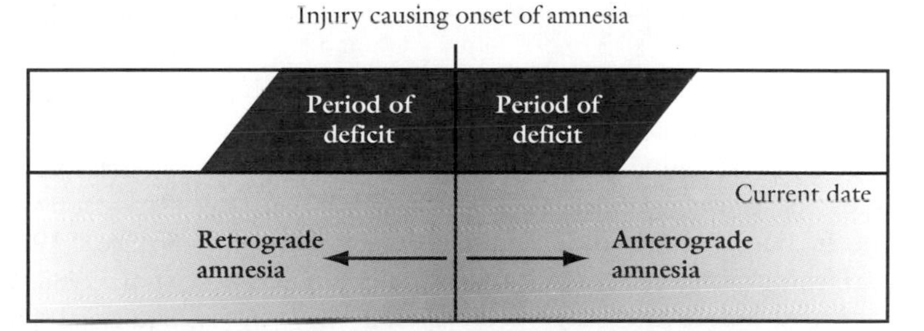

FIGURE 10.2 Timeline illustrating anterograde and retrograde components of amnesia. Any memory deficit that extends forward in time from the onset of amnesia and prevents the formation of new, enduring memories is known as *anterograde amnesia.* Any memory deficit that stretches backward in time from the onset of amnesia and prevents retrieval of information acquired prior to the onset of the amnesia is known as *retrograde amnesia.*

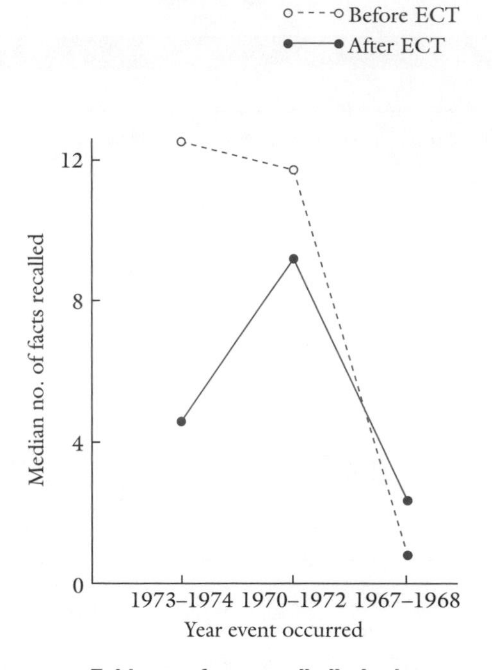

FIGURE 10.3 Evidence of temporally limited retrograde amnesia in patients who have undergone electroconvulsive therapy (ECT). Before and after a series of ECT treatments, 20 individuals were asked to recall information about former television programs that aired for just one season. Shown here is a graph of the median number of facts recalled. Before ECT (dashed line), patients showed a normal forgetting curve; their best recall was for shows from the most recent time period, and their poorest recall was for shows from the most remote time period. After ECT (blue line), a selective impairment occurred in the recall of shows from the most recent time period.

to the hippocampal system and does not involve extensive additional damage to neocortical brain regions, these individuals will have intact memory from the remote past, such as their childhood or youth. Furthermore, they retain the basic perceptual, motor, linguistic, and intellectual competence they had before the onset of amnesia. They also retain information learned early in life about language, objects, and the world in general. We now discuss the temporal aspects of amnesia in more detail.

Most instances of amnesia are associated with a **temporally limited retrograde amnesia.** For example, in *closed head injury* (associated with car accidents and falls), the retrograde amnesia extends back less than a week before the injury in more than 80% of patients (Russell and Nathan, 1946). Temporally limited retrograde amnesias are not always brief, however: they can extend to years, as in the case of the amnesia associated with bilateral electroconvulsive treatment (ECT). For example, when asked to remember information about television programs that had aired for just one season, patients who had received ECT were disproportionately impaired in recalling information about shows aired one to two years earlier. They couldn't even remember the single most salient fact about the shows, such as that it was a sitcom or a "cop show." But they could remember much more, including even specific episodes, about shows that aired farther back in time (Squire & Cohen, 1979) (see Figure 10.3).

The amnesia associated with H.M.'s surgery is more extensive, extending back 11 years (Corkin, 1984; Sagar, Cohen, Corkin, & Growdon, 1985). However, it is difficult to know how much of this retrograde amnesia results from his surgery and how much of it is related to his seizure disorder, which started about 11 years prior to his surgery. Studies of retrograde amnesia in patients with damage restricted to the temporal lobe following encephalitis or anoxia show the extent of retrograde amnesia to be quite variable, ranging from years to decades (e.g., see Reed & Squire, 1998; Kapur & Brooks, 1999). As a generalization, more extensive retrograde amnesia seems to occur in those patients who have sustained damage beyond the hippocampus proper—that is, including the parahippocampal region and (lateral) temporal neocortex.

Temporally extensive retrograde amnesia that can span back decades is often seen in patients with progressive disorders like Korsakoff's, Alzheimer's, Parkinson's, or Huntington's disease (e.g., Cohen & Squire, 1981; Brandt & Butters, 1986; Sagar et al., 1988; Wilson, Kaszniak, & Fox, 1981; Reed & Squire, 1998; Kopelman, Stanhope, & Kingsley, 1999). In dementias, this kind of amnesia is seen only later in the progression of the disease (e.g., Weingartner, Grafman, Boutelle, & Martin, 1983), when there is loss of tissue not only in the hippocampus but other cortical regions as well. For example, when asked to name the current U.S. pres-

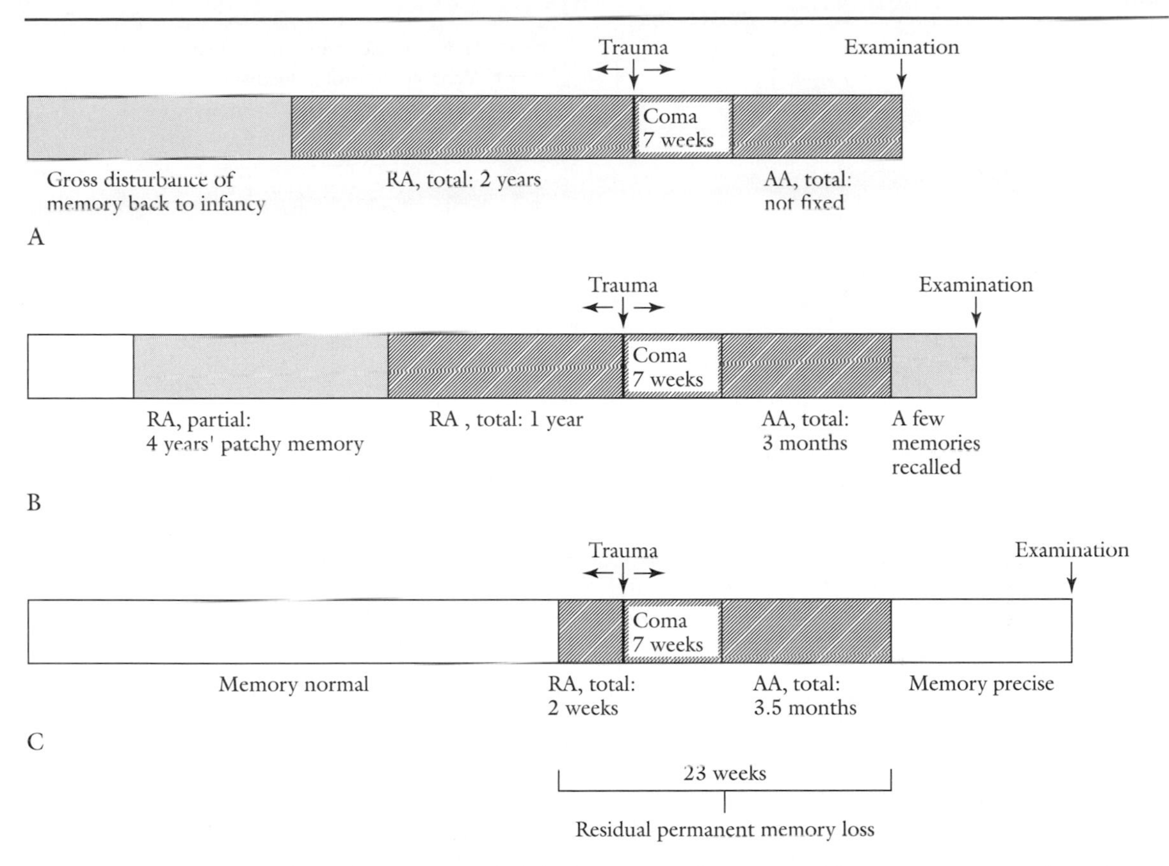

FIGURE 10.4 Illustration of the phenomenon of shrinking retrograde amnesia. The memory status of a patient was assessed at three examination times: (A) 5 months, (B) 8 months, and (C) 16 months after closed head injury. The time of the head injury is indicated by the heavy vertical line in each time line. The portion of time for which memory was impaired is depicted by diagonal lines, and times of patchy impairment are represented by lightly shaded areas. The portions of time affected to the right of the heavy vertical line indicate the extent of the anterograde amnesia (AA). The portions of time affected to the left of the heavy vertical line indicate the extent of the retrograde amnesia (RA). Across the three time lines, the retrograde amnesia shrinks from an initially extensive impairment encompassing years to a more limited amnesia affecting only weeks.

ident, these patients are likely to name someone whose presidency occurred during his/her youth, such as Harry Truman or Dwight Eisenhower (whose terms ran from the mid-1940s through the late 1950s).

Having discussed the amount of time over which retrograde amnesias extend, we can ask whether the deficits are equal across that time period. Typically, in temporally limited retrograde amnesia there is greater compromise of more recent memories than more remote memories. This effect is often referred to as the **temporal gradient** of retrograde amnesia and is now known as **Ribot's Law,** after the nineteenth-century scientist, Theodule Ribot, who first noted it (Ribot, 1881/1882). A good illustration of this effect can be seen in the shrinking retrograde amnesia after closed head injury (see Figure 10.4). The amnesia is much more extensive immediately after the injury, and then resolves over time. Its shrinks from an amnesia that includes the remote past to one that covers only the recent period (Benson & Geschwind, 1967).

The temporal gradient can also be seen in patients, such as those with Korsakoff's disease, in

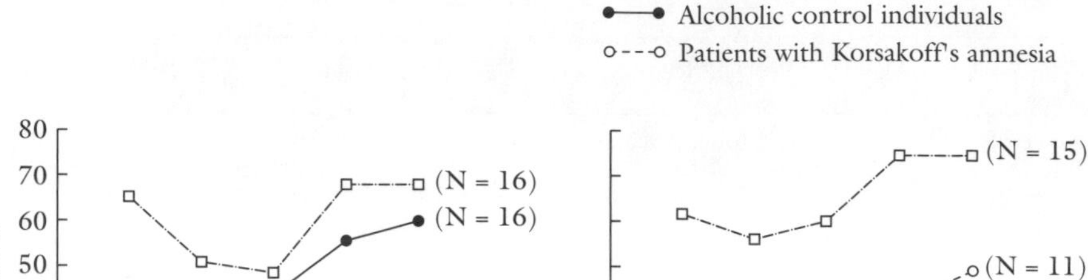

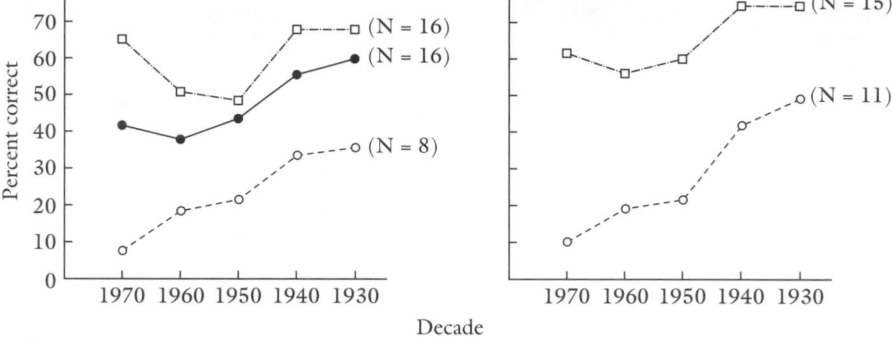

FIGURE 10.5 Evidence of the extensive retrograde amnesia in patients with Korsakoff's disease. Alcoholic and nonalcoholic control individuals and patients with Korsakoff's disease were asked to identify photographs of public figures who became prominent during different decades from the 1930s through the 1970s. Across all decades, the performance of patients with Korsakoff's disease was impaired compared with that of the control individuals. (Left) Results of research by N. J. Cohen and Squire (1981). (Right) Results of research by M. S. Albert, Butters, and Levin (1979).

whom the retrograde amnesia extends back decades (e.g., Cohen & Squire, 1981; Kopelman et al., 1999). In studies, such patients were asked to identify the faces of public figures who were famous across many decades (Albert, Butters, & Levin, 1979): Patients were more likely to correctly identify them in older photographs (such as Ronald Reagan as the 1930s- to 1950s-era actor) than in more contemporary photographs (Ronald Reagan as the 1970s- to 1980s-era politician). The gradient of retrograde amnesia points to the dynamic nature of memory, indicating that memory undergoes change during the time after learning, an issue we will revisit later in the chapter (see Figure 10.5).

Not all forms of amnesia exhibit a temporal gradient, however. Instead, some are relatively uniform across time periods. Such "flat" gradients have been observed in Alzheimer's disease (Wilson, Kaszniak, & Fox, 1981) and in Huntington's disease (see Chapter 14), as well as in some etiologies of amnesia with hippocampal system damage (e.g., Sanders & Warrington, 1971; Cermak & O'Connor, 1983; Mayes et al., 1994). It may be that these flat retrograde amnesias occur most often in degenerative disorders in which there is much additional damage to neocortical areas.

In very rare cases, retrograde amnesia is very extensive and completely out of proportion to whatever anterograde deficits might be exhibited (e.g., see Parkin, 1996; Kopelman, 2000; Kapur, 2000). The cause of this phenomenon is somewhat controversial, and may require a different explanation than the other memory disorders considered thus far. In other cases in which there is no evidence of brain damage and *no* anterograde amnesia, the individual may be exhibiting *functional amnesia* (or *psychogenic amnesia*) from a psychological rather than a neurological trauma (see Kihlstrom & Schacter, 1995; Treadway, McCloskey, Gordon, & Cohen, 1992).

Global Nature of the Deficit

One of the most fundamental aspects of amnesia is that it is global with regard to modality and material. For example, H.M.'s impairment has been shown to be modality general, affecting memory of material presented in the visual, auditory, somesthetic, and even olfactory modalities (see Corkin, 1984; Milner, Corkin, & Teuber, 1968). The deficit in amnesia is equally material general, affecting memory of both verbal and nonverbal material, spatial and nonspatial information, meaningful and nonsense stimuli, and so forth.

The modality- and material-generality of amnesia has been crucial in identifying the disorder as specifically one of *memory* functions rather than any perceptual, linguistic, or other cognitive processing functions. Damage to the cortical brain systems critical for processing language, visual objects, or motor sequences can cause memory problems, but these are invariably modality- and/or material-specific. For example, in a visual agnosia the patient fails to identify objects presented visually, but has no problem identifying the same objects by touch or sound (see Chapter 6). *Unilateral* damage to the hippocampal system can produce **material-specific memory disorders.** After left hemisphere damage, memory is selectively impaired for verbal material, whereas after right hemisphere damage, memory is impaired for nonverbal materials (e.g., B. Milner, 1971; see page 115, Chapter 4). When there is bilateral damage, as in the case of H.M., a material general impairment is observed.

This modality- and material-general aspect of memory can be observed regardless of how memory is assessed. Consider a paradigm in which the patient is read a list of 15 words to remember (e.g., *motel, cathedral, broker, bowl, cyclone . . .* etc.), and then is tested 30 minutes later. Profound impairment following extensive hippocampal system damage can be seen regardless of how memory is tested, whether using **free recall** (the subject is told, "Report all of the words on the study list"), **cued recall** (the subject is told, "Report all the words from the study list that were examples of buildings or that began with the letter 'b' "), or **recognition** (the subject is given 15 word pairs, each containing one item from the list and one novel item, and for each pair is asked, "Which of these two words ['cabin' or 'cathedral'] was on the study list?").

Deficits can also be found under training paradigms. For example, the individual could be trained on the list—that is, tested repeatedly on the same list until it is learned to some criterion level of performance—then after 30 minutes one can determine how many fewer trials are required to reach the criterion as a result of the prior experience, a measure known as *savings in relearning.* Amnesic patients are impaired in this measure as well.

Spared Working Memory

The deficit in amnesic patients is one of long-term memory, which is the ability to retain information for as long as a lifetime. In contrast, working memory, which is the ability to hold a limited amount of information online over the short term while it is being actively processed, is unaffected. An experiment by Drachman & Arbit (1966) illustrates this dissociation. H.M.'s performance on a **digit span task** in which he had to report back in order digits read one at a time by the experimenter was within the normal range (7 +/− 2 items). However, once his working-memory span was exceeded, his performance suffered. This deficit was demonstrated by an **extended digit span** task, in which the same digit string is presented on each trial but with an additional digit added to extend the span. For example, persons whose digit span is 7 items are repeatedly given a string of digits that surpasses their digit span by one digit (e.g., 2-7-9-1-3-4-8-6) until it can be correctly recalled. Then they are given multiple trials with the same initial string but with an additional digit at the end (e.g., 2-7-9-1-3-4-8-6-5) until it can be recalled, and so forth. Although neurologically intact subjects can recall strings of at least 20 digits using this procedure, H.M. could not recall even a single string that was one digit larger than his span, despite 25 repetitions of the same string.

Because patients with amnesia have intact working memory, they perform normally when the delay between the exposure to information and the memory test is short, or when the amount of material to be remembered is small. Thus, they can comprehend episodes and events normally if they unfold over a relatively short time, and they can engage in reasonable discourse if it remains on topic. However, because their memory impairment "emerges" over significant delays, they are unable to retain this information for the long term. Consequently, these individuals exhibit little cumulative learning across events or episodes. For

A UNIQUE OPPORTUNITY TO EXAMINE THE NATURE OF TEMPORALLY GRADED RETROGRADE AMNESIA

After decades of alcoholism, patients with **Korsakoff's amnesia** have a temporally graded retrograde amnesia. Such individuals show poorer memory for information from recent years than for information from more remote decades, a fact that poses a difficult question for scientists: does this temporal gradient result from the cumulative effects of alcohol abuse, or is it a graded amnesia from the onset of the amnesia, caused by hemorrhaging of midline diencephalic structures during a severe drinking binge?

To answer this question a neuropsychologist would need insight into a person's life well prior to the onset of the amnesia. Ideally, one should have a record of the events and facts that the individual considered of consequence at the time. This material could then be used to assess the degree of the patient's amnesia for the recent and remote past. How would such information be obtained? In a stroke of good fortune, two researchers, Butters and Cermak, found an individual who provided just such an ideal situation. They were able to study a man who, after a long history of drinking, developed Korsakoff's amnesia shortly after completing his autobiography. In his book, this man, who was a scientist, discussed many events from his long and rich career. In addition, his autobiography included references to many other scientists and to many conceptual issues that were prominent during different periods of his career. The timing of these two events—the completion of his book followed by the onset of his amnesia—was fortuitous. The investigators were able to test his memory for information from different periods of time with the certainty that he had recently been able to remember the information well, since the events were included in his book. They found that, like other individuals with amnesia, he exhibited a temporally graded retrograde amnesia. Thus, such a gradient exists even full-blown at the acute onset of Korsakoff's amnesia. ■

example, you can comprehend this paragraph and then integrate it not only with the knowledge acquired from the previous paragraphs in this chapter but information from the preceding chapters as well. Patients with amnesia, such as H.M., cannot do this, and, indeed, patients with the most severe amnesias often comment on the difficulty that reading presents to them. As a result of their amnesia, they cannot learn new facts and data about themselves or about the world.

The dissociation between a deficit in long-term memory with fully functional working memory is also seen in nonhuman primates with hippocampal damage. This effect is demonstrated in a variant of the **delayed nonmatch-to-sample task** (e.g., Gaffan, 1974; Mishkin & Delacour, 1975). On each trial in this task, an animal is exposed to one of a large set of objects. Following a delay, the object just viewed is presented again, this time together with another from the set of available objects. To receive a reward, the animal must select the object that was not previously presented (i.e., the nonmatch object). Following extensive hippocampal system damage, performance is markedly impaired for delays longer than about 10 seconds, but normal for shorter delays (e.g., Gaffan, 1977; Mishkin, 1978, 1982; Zola-Morgan & Squire, 1985).

It is important to reemphasize that work with amnesic patients indicates that the hippocampal system is particularly critical for the *formation* of new long-term memories. Patients such as H.M. can remember events prior to their hippocampal damage, indicating that the hippocampus is not critical for those memories. Thus, damage to the hippocampal system affects only new learning and memory for the recent past, not memory for the remote past.

■ Spared Skill Learning

Because H.M. is such a unique case, he has been studied extensively and intensively over decades. As we have just discussed, the aspect of his disorder that so impressed researchers was just how profound and global is his long-term memory impairment. But in the course of all this testing, a funny thing happened. The researchers began to discover that in spite of this pervasive impairment there were some tasks on which H.M. exhibited evidence of learning. Furthermore, even though H.M. exhibited such learning, he seemed to be totally unaware that he was learning anything!

Let's discuss some of the tasks on which H.M. and other amnesics show evidence of spared learning. In general, these tasks involve appreciating regularities in the environment that allow for increasingly improved performance. One main category of preserved learning is **skill learning,** which refers to the acquisition—usually gradually and incrementally through repetition—of motor, perceptual, or cognitive operations or procedures that aid performance.

One of the first examples of skill learning observed in H.M. was on a **mirror tracing task,** which involved tracing the outline of a figure (such as a star) by looking in a mirror (Corkin, 1968; B. Milner, 1962b). Across sessions, the number of times H.M.'s drawing fell outside the outline of the figure and the time it took him to complete the task decreased. Similar learning is demonstrated by amnesics on another perceptual-motor skill, that of **rotary pursuit.** In this task an individual has to track a circularly moving target. With practice, amnesics show an increase in the time spent on target (e.g., Brooks & Baddeley, 1976; Cermak, Lewis, Butters, & Goodglass, 1973).

Notice that in these tasks, the individual is doing exactly the same task over and over again. Researchers wondered whether amnesics were learning the specific instances of these tasks (e.g., mirror drawing of a star) or a skill in general. To examine this question, they used a **mirror-reading task** (Cohen & Squire, 1980) to determine whether the skill would generalize to new exemplars, not just items seen before. For this task word triplets are presented in mirror-image orientation, and the viewer reads them aloud as quickly and accurately as possible (see Figure 10.6A). Of critical importance, half of the word triplets are presented multiple times, appearing once in each block of trials (left-hand panel of Figure 10.6B), and half are presented only once during the experiment (right-hand panel of Figure 10.6B). With practice, neurologically intact participants learn to read with increasing speed and accuracy not only the mirror-imaged words they have seen before but also the new mirror-imaged words. In this way they acquire the basic skill of reading any word presented in mirror-imaged text (Figure 10.6B). Notice that amnesics, regardless of the etiology of the disorder, exhibit the same pattern—they also show increased speed in reading new, as well as old, mirror-imaged words.

This generalization of skill learning can also be found for complicated cognitive tasks, in which amnesic patients learn to perform in accordance with the statistical structure of complex sets of materials. For example, having been exposed to a series of letter strings generated by *artificial grammars* (made-up rules specifying which letters can follow which other letters), amnesics learned to classify as "grammatical" or "ungrammatical" new letter strings that do or do not follow the rules, even though they cannot identify which items had been previously studied (Knowlton et al., 1992) (see Figure 10.7). Showing that the effects are not restricted to verbal material, a similar effect is seen with the learning of categorization of dot patterns (Knowlton & Squire, 1993).

What is even more remarkable is that this spared learning occurs even when the patients cannot recollect the training events during which the new skills are acquired, cannot recall or recognize the material on which the increasing skill is demonstrated, and have no insight into their improved performance. That is, the amnesic patient is likely unable to remember having been in the laboratory, having been asked to draw in a mirror or to read mirror-reversed text words, and has no idea why his or her performance seems to have improved.

Another major category of preserved learning and memory in amnesia, and one that has been most extensively studied, is **repetition priming,** in which performance is enhanced, or biased, as a result of previous exposure to an item, even though individuals are not directly or explicitly asked about the item. One of the earliest demonstrations of repetition priming in patients with amnesia used figures from the *Gollin Incomplete Pictures* task (Milner, Corkin, & Teuber, 1968; Warrington & Weiskrantz,

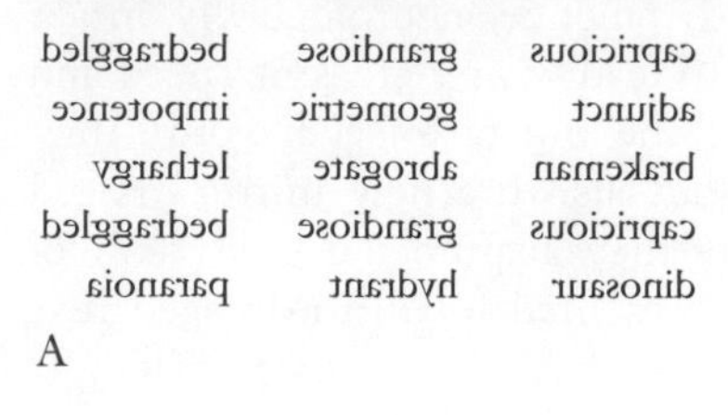

A

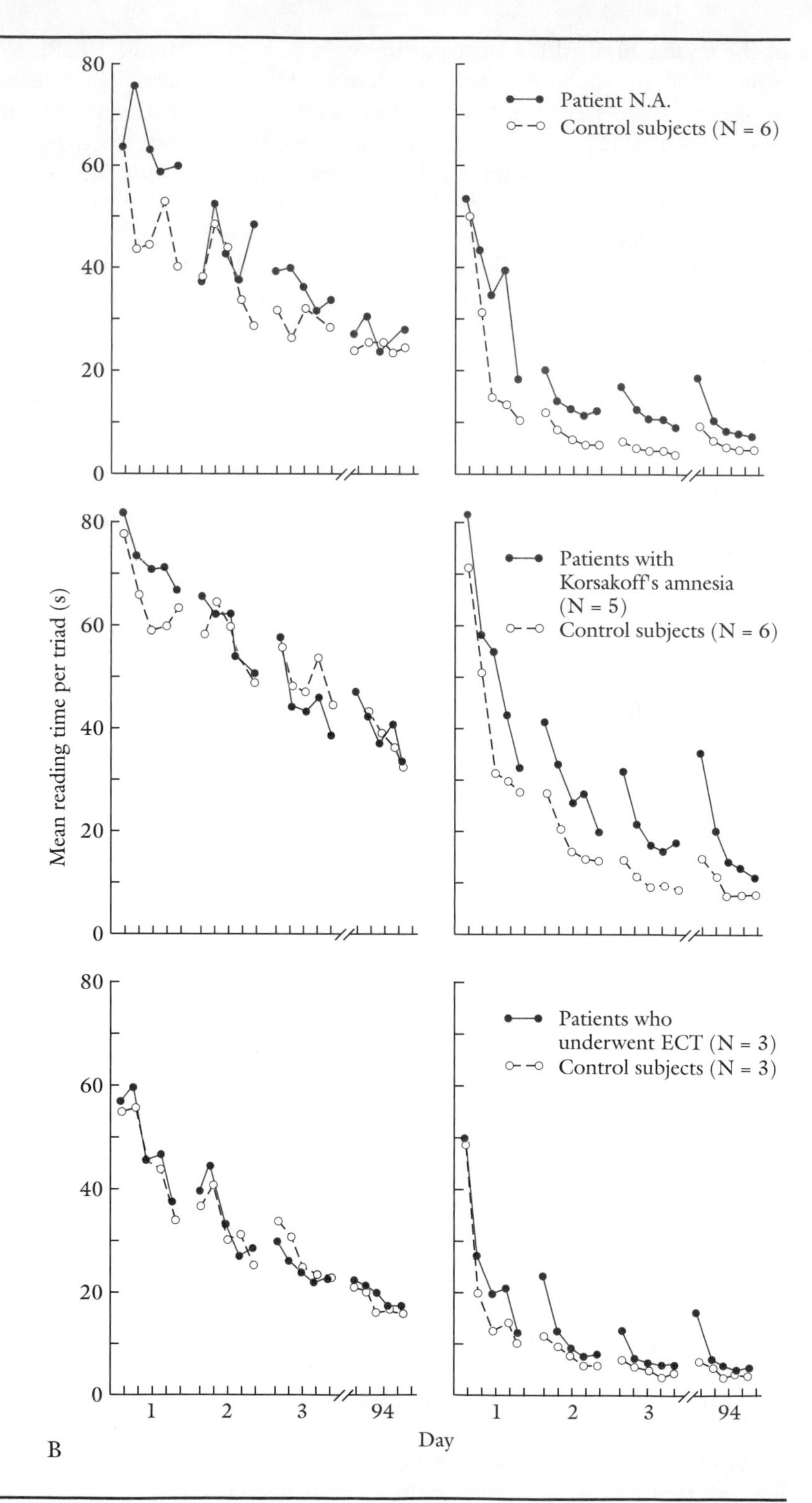

FIGURE 10.6 Example of spared perceptual skill in patients with amnesia. (A) Examples of the mirror-image word triads used in a mirror-image reading task (N. J. Cohen & Squire, 1980). (B) Just like control individuals, patients who have amnesia from different causes increased the speed with which they could read the triads. Patient N.A., who has midline diencephalic damage (top) is compared with patients with Korsakoff's amnesia (middle) and patients who underwent electroconvulsive therapy (ECT) (bottom). This increase in all these patients occurred not only for repeated triplets (triplets that they saw before; graphs on the right), but also for new (nonrepeated) triads (graphs on the left). The increase in the reading times for novel triplets indicates that the patients with amnesia were learning the perceptual skill of mirror-image reading.

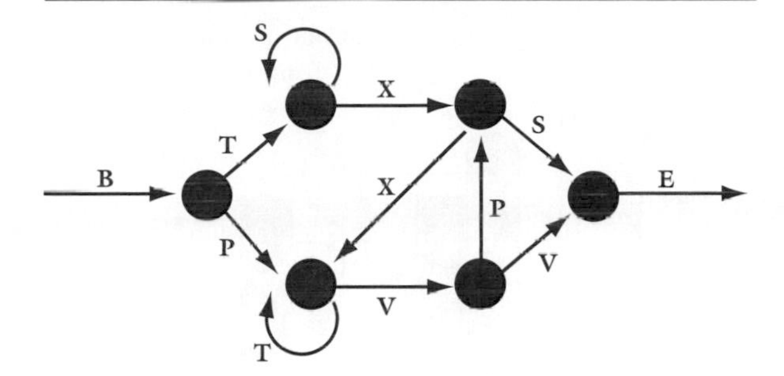

FIGURE 10.7 Example of rules for an artificial grammar. This is a flowchart showing rules for legal letter strings in an artificial grammar. Straight arrows indicate letters that can follow one another whereas circular arrows indicate the ability for a letter to repeat. Hence, in this grammar "BTSSX" would be a legal string but "BPTTX" would not.

1968, 1970). In this task, patients are shown very degraded and incomplete line drawings of objects (see bottom row of Figure 10.8), which they are to name. For those that cannot be named, somewhat less degraded drawings of the same objects are presented (see the row of figures above the bottom row of Figure 10.8). This procedure is repeated with sets of increasingly complete drawings of the objects until the patient can correctly name all the objects, and the number of trials required to correctly name each object is recorded. After a delay, the procedure is repeated once more.

All participants, including patients with amnesia, benefited from the previous exposure. They were able to identify the objects from more degraded, less complete versions than they could the first time. Similar effects were observed with a perceptual identification paradigm with words (Gabrieli et al., 1995). When words are shown very briefly, amnesic patients can identify the ones previously viewed in a study list at a shorter duration of presentation than novel items that were not on the list.

The dissociation in amnesia between the ability to exhibit repetition priming and the inability to remember the items to which one has been exposed is probably best illustrated by the **word-stem completion task** (Graf, Squire, & Mandler, 1984). In this task individuals are given a list of words to study. After a delay, memory for the words is then tested in two ways, both of which involved the presentation

FIGURE 10.8 Example of visually degraded line drawings for which patients with amnesia show repetition priming. Individuals are shown line drawings of three objects in different stages of completeness, ranging from very degraded (bottom row) to fully complete (top row), and the level of completeness at which an individual can first recognize the figures is determined. When shown the figures again after some delay, neurologically intact individuals recognize the objects at a less complete stage than initially, which indicates that prior exposure to the items influenced their performance. Individuals with amnesia show the same effect, which is indicative of repetition priming.

of three-letter stems (e.g., *mot, cyc*). In one condition, the cued-recall condition, participants are asked to recall the word from the study list that started with those same three letters. Not surprisingly, patients with amnesia perform poorly in this condition compared with neurologically intact control participants. In the other condition, the word-stem completion condition, individuals are to report "the first word that comes to mind" that completes each stem. The measure of performance was how much more often than chance an individual completes the stem with a word from the study list, like ***mot***el and **cy**clone, as compared to a word not on the list with the same initial three letters, such as ***mot***her and **cy**cle. Patients with amnesia performed normally on this task, being biased to complete the stems with items from the study list, just as were neurologically intact adults (see Figure 10.9).

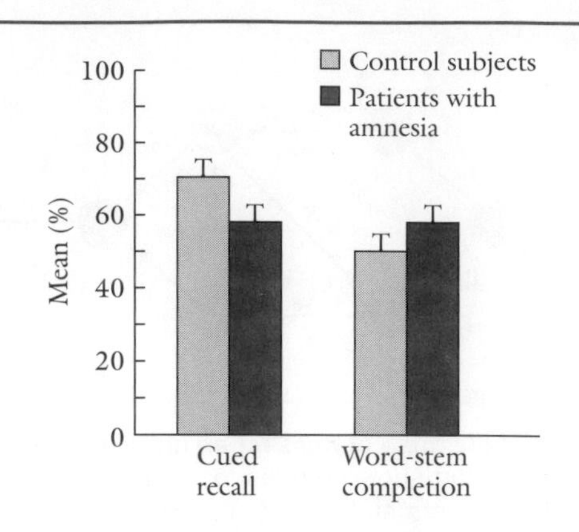

FIGURE 10.9 Evidence of a dissociation between disrupted cued recall and intact word-stem completion in patients with amnesia. Patients with amnesia are impaired relative to control individuals on cued recall of words from a previously studied list (left). However, when asked to complete the word stems with the "first word that comes to mind," these individuals are just as biased as neurologically intact control individuals to report the word that they saw previously on the list (right). Hence, the prior exposure primes their behavior even though they cannot explicitly recall their experience.

In all of the preceding examples, we have been able to infer an aspect of preserved memory in amnesia on the basis of increases in response accuracy or decreases in reaction times as a result of prior exposure to materials. A different line of evidence demonstrating preserved memory in amnesia comes from **eye-movement monitoring,** in which the eye movements of individuals are recorded. For both faces and scenes, eye movements elicited by stimuli to which the individual has been repeatedly exposed are different than eye movements elicited by novel stimuli. This repetition effect occurs for amnesic patients and neurologically intact control participants alike, indicating that their performance is influenced by prior exposure to the materials (Althoff et al., 1993; Althoff & Cohen, 1999; Ryan et al., 2000).

Explanations of the Deficit

As we have seen, amnesics show a very specific pattern of memory loss. They are unable to remember most of the information to which they are exposed but retain intact working memory. Although their ability to remember their encounters with information is lost, under certain conditions (e.g., those of skill learning) they exhibit performance that indicates they have learned and remembered. What can explain such a pattern? There has been a large discussion among scientists as to what explanation best captures the essence of what is retained and what is lost in amnesia. Here we outline some of the proposals that have been widely discussed in the scientific literature.

Remembering our past often has an experiential component; that is, it involves the conscious recollection of particular events or experiences. But not all instances of remembering involve conscious awareness, and not all memory performances require it. Indeed, as we have just seen, much modern work on human memory and amnesia has examined differences between performance on memory tasks that require conscious recollection of prior learning experiences as compared to those that do not. **Direct (explicit) tests of memory** (see Graf & Schacter, 1985; Richardson-Klaven & Bjork, 1988; Schacter, 1987) depend on conscious recollection of a particular study episode or a particular learning event. Being asked to provide information about what one did on a particular date or in a particular class are examples of memory being tested directly, or explicitly. Much of the regular social interaction we have with friends and family is of this nature, where, in sharing the details of our lives, we consciously hark back to specific events and recount the things that happened. Direct (explicit) tests of memory are also the norm for most formal assessments of memory. Standard memory tests instruct participants to recall the items from a specified study list or test recognition memory by asking, "Which of the following items did you see on the previous list?" To respond appropriately, the person must refer back to the specific event or context in question (e.g., the study list) and then inspect the contents of memory for it. This is often called *explicit remembering.*

By contrast, **indirect (implicit) tests of memory** are those that do not require conscious recollection of any given prior learning experience. One example is the word-stem completion task we discussed earlier. If individuals are biased toward completing the stems with words from the study list, it provides evidence that their recent experience with those words has influenced their performance. These types of task instructions do not require participants to refer explicitly or consciously to any specific prior experiences and hence do not test memory directly. Instead, they tap memory indirectly, gaining an implicit assessment of memory for prior experience.

Memory performance as assessed by indirect (implicit) measures can be independent of memory performance as assessed by direct (explicit) measures. More specifically, the facilitation, or bias, of performance by previous exposure, revealed by implicit measures, does not depend upon subjects' explicit remembering the previous exposure (see Roediger, 1990; Richardson-Klaven & Bjork, 1988), although they can co-occur. Amnesia provides, perhaps, the most compelling example of this dissociation. The preserved learning and memory capacities we discussed previously all occurred when the amnesic's memory was assessed by indirect (implicit) tests of memory. In contrast, patients with amnesia were impaired on direct (explicit) tests of memory. This contrast seems to capture a key aspect of amnesia: a normal ability to acquire and express skilled performance but an absence of the ability to consciously recollect learning experiences (see Cohen & Squire, 1980; Cohen, 1984). Because these patients cannot consciously engage in introspection about the contents of their knowledge, they are said to have "memory without awareness" (Jacoby, 1984; Moscovitch, 1994). Rarely, if ever, are neurologically intact individuals so devoid of familiarity while nonetheless exhibiting memory for their previous exposure. Therefore, some researchers see memory without awareness as a key aspect of amnesia.

Another major conceptualization of the nature of amnesics is that of a deficit in **relational learning**—learning that occurs in tasks or situations where performance depends on acquiring memory for the relations among items, especially items associated only arbitrarily or accidentally. Amnesic patients have exceptional difficulty in learning the arbitrary relations among items with which we are challenged in our everyday lives, such as learning the names connected with particular people's faces or the addresses and telephone numbers that we learn to associate with them. These relations are arbitrary in that people's real names are rarely, if ever, derived from people's appearance (e.g., my parents did *not* give me my name because they decided that I looked like a "Neal"); nor are telephone numbers and addresses in any way meaningfully related to people's names or appearance (e.g., the telephone company did *not* assign me my particular number because it seemed an especially good match to my particular name or my particular face). Retrieving the name of the person whom you met yesterday and remembering his or her phone number cannot be accomplished by deriving such information from other knowledge about the person; rather, you must access a memorized relationship among the name, face, and number. This real-world relational memory task is a challenge for anyone, but it is particularly challenging for patients with amnesia. For example, after all this time, H.M. still does not know the face-name pairings of any of the people who see and test him each year, is unable to report *any* personal events since the time of his surgery (or for the preceding 11 years), and shows marked impairment on various formal tests that assess memory for public events that occurred after the onset of amnesia (Corkin, 1984; Sagar et al., 1985).

This deficit in memory for relations can also be observed in the laboratory. One test often used to investigate this aspect of memory is **paired-associate learning.** In this task the individual is presented with arbitrarily paired words or other items that have no preexisting association, such as *obey-inch, crush-dark,* and so forth. Immediately afterward, participants are presented with one member of each pair (e.g., *obey, crush,* etc.) and must report its partner. Patients with hippocampal damage are profoundly impaired at performing this task. Some patients fail to learn *any* arbitrarily related pairs, even with multiple exposures to the identical item. For this reason, paired-associate learning is one of the subtests of the Wechsler Memory Scale.

As it turns out, memory for relations is also tested on most list-based recall or recognition memory tasks. In such memory tests, individuals study a list of common words, faces, or visual objects. They are then asked to report (in recall tests) or to judge (in recognition tests) which items appeared on that particular study list. Because all of the stimuli are familiar from previous experience, remembering specific items requires their identity to be linked to this particular occasion, the study context, or particular study list. Patients with hippocampal damage are markedly impaired on these tasks.

Of note, this deficit in relational learning can also be observed even without asking individuals to explicitly recall their experiences, as is required by the tasks we just discussed. A study was done in which eye movements were recorded after individuals viewed images of real-world scenes two times each. On the third presentation, individuals viewed one of three types of scene: a scene identical to the initial presentation (repeated scenes) (see Figure 10.10A), a scene in which a subtle but important manipulation of the relations among some of the elements of the scene were changed (manipulated scenes) (see Figure 10.10B), or an entirely new scene (novel scenes). Eye movements elicited to the different types of scenes revealed two distinct effects in neurologically intact individuals. One was a repetition effect, exhibited as a reduction in the sampling of locations in previously viewed scenes versus novel scenes. Amnesic patients show this repetition effect, indicating that they are affected by their prior experience with the material, much as is observed with repetition priming.

A second effect observed in neurologically intact individuals was a *relational manipulation effect,* exhibited as increased viewing directed to the regions of change in the manipulated scenes relative to the original scene. Such an effect indicates a sensitivity to the relations among the constituent elements of the originally studied scenes. Amnesics failed to show the relational manipulation effect, thereby revealing a selective deficit in memory for relations among items, even though it was tested implicitly (Ryan, Althoff, Whitlow, & Cohen, 2000) (see Figure 10.10C).

Functional neuroimaging studies of humans using PET and fMRI provide converging evidence that the brain region damaged in amnesia, the **hippocampal system,** is associated with memory for relations. When tasks place a high demand on memory for the relations among items, disproportionate activation of the hippocampal system is observed (see the review by Cohen et al., 1999). One such demonstration comes from a PET study by Henke et al. (1997), in which neurologically intact individuals were shown a series of pictures, each showing a person and a house. In one condition, participants had to make separate decisions about the person (*is it male or female?*) and the house (*is it an exterior or interior view?*). In the other condition, participants made subjective decisions about the relation between the person and the house (*is this person an inhabitant or just a visitor to this house?*). There was no right or wrong answer—individuals were simply asked to make a decision based on the person's age and stereotypes they had about people and the types of houses they might live in. Although the stimuli were identical in the two conditions, greater hippocampal activation was found when the materials were encoded relationally than when they were encoded separately.

Amnesia in Nonhuman Animals

One of the strengths of conceptualizing the deficit in amnesia as an inability to form memory for relations is that it allows us to better understand deficits seen in animals after damage to the hippocampal system. Obviously, it is difficult (if not impossible) to ascertain whether an animal's learning is dependent on implicit as compared to explicit memory, since it is not possible to ask it to recall its experience. But the contribution of the hippocampal system to learning the relations among objects or events has been

FIGURE 10.10 Eye-movement monitoring to assess implicit memory. (A) example of an original scene in a relational manipulation experiment. Participants viewed the scene twice, then saw either the original scene again or (B) a manipulated version in which relations among the objects in the scene were changed. Superimposed on the scenes in A and B are eye movements made by one of the neurologically intact participants in the study (the circles represent the eye fixations). When the participant viewed the original version, most eye movements were directed to the three objects in the center foreground: the person, the wooden trash receptacle, and the sign. When viewing the manipulated scene, the participant looked to the position where the person had been standing, even though it was empty and the person was positioned elsewhere. Hence, eye movements provide an implicit measure of the person's knowledge about the scene. *(continued)*

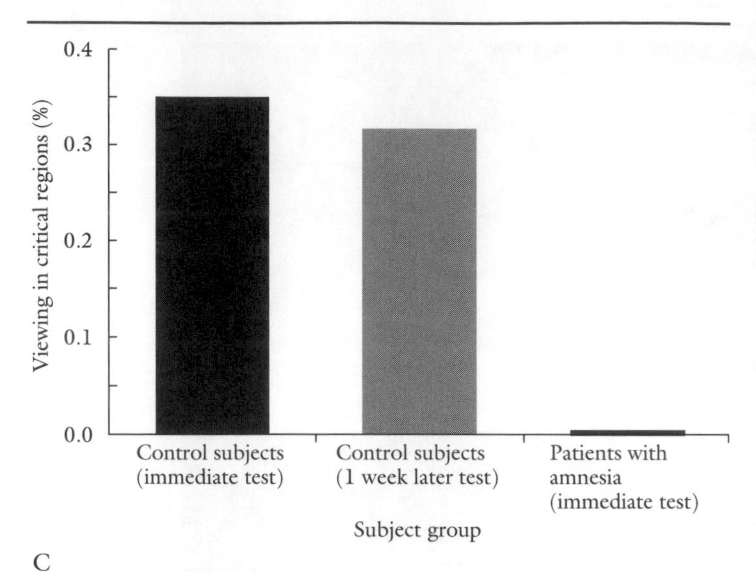

FIGURE 10.10 (Continued)
(C) A graph of data from this experiment. Control individuals tested either immediately after viewing the scenes or one week later (at which point they were at chance in explicitly distinguishing between the manipulated and unmanipulated scenes) exhibited implicit memory for the relations among objects because they spent much time viewing the region of the scene in which the relations had been manipulated. In contrast, patients with amnesia did not spend time looking at that region, an indication that they lacked the ability to remember relational information even when it was assessed implicitly.

clearly seen in work with both rodents and nonhuman primates.

Rats with damage to the hippocampal system exhibit marked deficits in learning and remembering spatial relations, such as required in the **Morris water maze** (Morris, 1981) (see Figure 10.11A). In this task, the rat is placed in a circular tank filled with an opaque liquid that obscures a slightly submerged platform. The platform is positioned at a constant location relative to various visual cues outside the maze (i.e., objects placed around the room, such as light fixtures, doors, and windows). From trial to trial, the animals are placed into the tank at different locations around the circumference of the pool. Across trials, normal animals learn the position of the platform in relation to the extra-maze cues, and thus the time it takes them to swim to the platform decreases rapidly (see Figure 10.11B). In contrast, a rat with hippocampal system damage does not learn the relations among the cues (see Figure 10.11C) and must search exhaustively each time for the platform's location, not reaching it any quicker from trial to trial (e.g., Schenk & Morris, 1985; Sutherland, Whishaw, & Kolb, 1983). Yet, if relational information is not necessary to perform the task, such as when the platform is visible and can guide swimming, animals with hippocampal damage show no impairment (Eichenbaum et al., 1990; Whishaw et al., 1995).

Research with animals on the neuroanatomy and physiology of the hippocampal system indicates that it possesses the anatomical connections and the neural mechanisms required to support relational memory. From an anatomical perspective, the hippocampal system receives inputs from the diverse cortical brain regions that perform different mental operations, such as object recognition and spatial processes, and from regions that process information of different modalities, such as vision and audition. The hippocampus thereby receives highly pre-processed input about the "items" encountered in the environment. In turn, the hippocampus projects back to these cortical processors. Accordingly, it is in a position to receive, and bind, information about the other organisms and objects present in the environment, the spatial relations among them, the events in which they play roles, the temporal relations among those events, and the affective and behavioral responses they elicit.

Furthermore, electrical recordings in animal tissue indicate that the hippocampal system also has a neuronal mechanism that allows for processing the conjunctions or co-occurrences of inputs. It exhibits a phenomenon called **long-term potentiation** (LTP), in which brief, patterned activation of particular pathways produces a stable increase in synaptic efficacy lasting for hours to weeks. LTP is mediated by a class of neurotransmitter receptors (*N*-methyl-D-aspartate [NMDA] receptors) that constitute superb conjunction detectors, being activated specifically by converging inputs arriving in close temporal con-

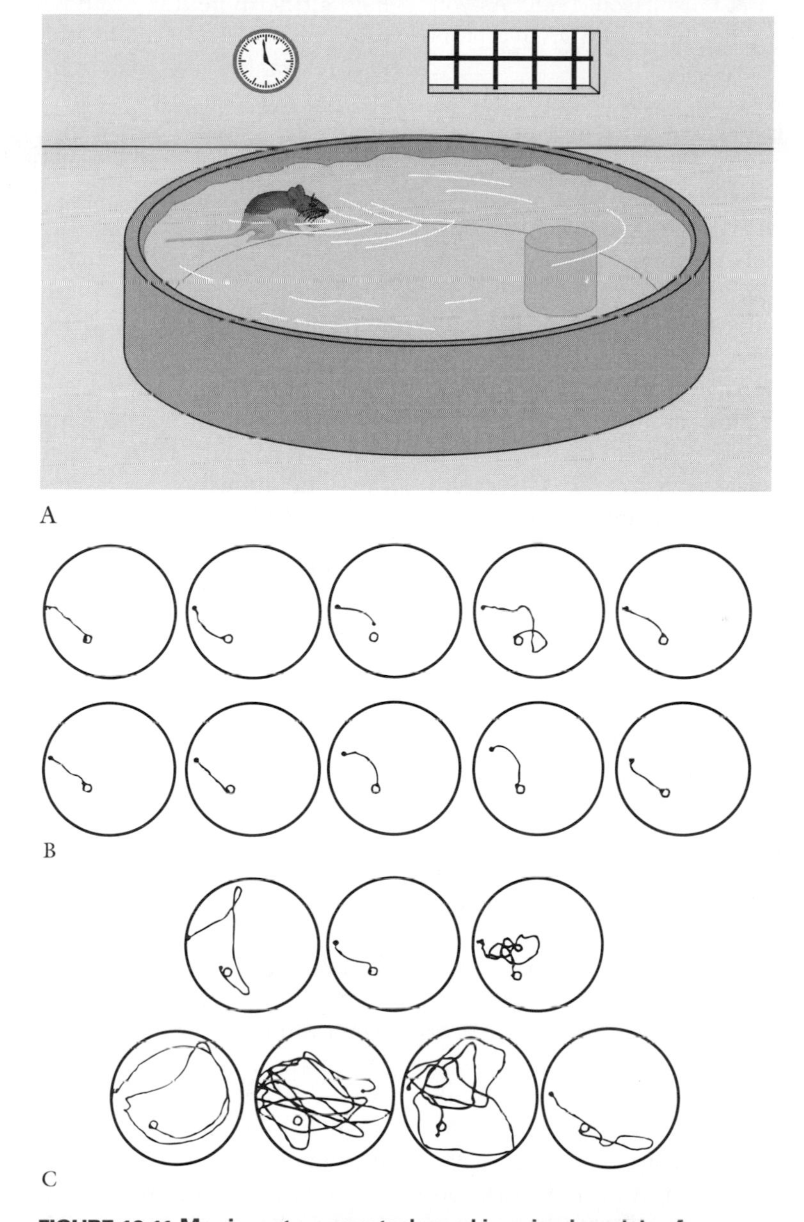

FIGURE 10.11 Morris water maze task used in animal models of amnesia. (A) The rats are placed in a circular pool near the perimeter. Submerged in the pool is a platform on which the animal can rest, but which is hidden from view because the liquid in the pool is opaque. The position of this platform is constant relative to various objects around the room. (B) The path (black line) from a specific starting point to the escape platform for each of 10 normal rats who had only sham lesions. Normal animals can learn the location of the escape platform, which permits them to swim short, direct paths to the platforms. (C) The paths for 7 animals with hippocampal system damage. Because these animals fail to learn the location of the escape platform, they spend much time swimming around the pool.

tiguity (e.g., Wigstrom & Gustafsson, 1985). As you may remember from Chapter 2, NMDA receptors are a type of glutamate receptor.

Furthermore, the electrophysiological response of hippocampal neurons indicates that they are sensitive to various relationships among significant cues or objects in the environment. For example, when rats actively explore their environment, hippocampal neurons have **place fields,** meaning that they fire preferentially when the animal is in a particular "place" in the environment (O'Keefe & Dostrovsky, 1971). Of most importance, firing of these cells does not depend on any specific environmental stimulus, but rather on the relationships among them. If the relative positions of some of the relevant cues are shifted in some systematic way (e.g., rotated 90 degrees clockwise), the place fields often are correspondingly shifted (e.g., Shapiro et al., 1997). When the environment being explored (e.g., a cylindrical enclosure) is scaled up in size, the place fields may correspondingly scale up (Muller et al., 1987). And when the boundaries of the environment that is being explored are moved outward, the place fields may be stretched out in size (O'Keefe & Burgess, 1996). Thus in all cases, the cells are responding not to an exact spatial location, but rather to the relative position between items (Figure 10.12).

Activity of hippocampal cells is not driven exclusively by relations of a spatial nature. In one study, hippocampal activity was recorded in rats during a task in which the relationship between the odors found at a particular location on the current and prior trial (match/non-match) indicated whether or not digging at the location would yield a food reward (Wood, Dudchenko, & Eichenbaum, 1999). While some hippocampal neurons fired preferentially for one attribute (e.g., a particular spatial location, a particular odor), the activity of most neurons was associated with one or another of the conjunctions of odor, location, match versus nonmatch, and movement (digging or no digging) (Wood et al., 1999).

Activity of hippocampal neurons also can be driven by a variety of higher-order relationships between spatial location and the animal's behavioral activity (see Eichenbaum et al., 1999). Neuronal activity while the animal is in the place field depends heavily on the speed with which the animal is moving and the direction in which it is heading and turning. Furthermore, the same neurons have different firing properties depending on which behaviors are task relevant at any given time. For example, these neurons can have a preference for one place in the behavioral apparatus when the animal is engaged in spatial navigation but a preference for a different place in the same apparatus when the animal is engaged in an olfactory discrimination task.

Taken altogether, the study of memory, amnesia, and the hippocampal system in humans and animals implicates this brain system as being critical for the formation of new long-term memories that depend on relational information. In contrast, the hippocampal system does not play a critical role in either working memory or skill learning. We now turn our discussion to these types of memory to explore the brain regions that support them.

Working Memory

In this section of the chapter we discuss the neural substrates of working memory, which is the ability that allows us to retain limited amounts of information for a short amount of time while we are actively working on it. As with long-term memory, much of our knowledge about the neural substrates of working memory was obtained from patients who have a selective deficit in this type of memory. We first discuss these findings and then findings gleaned from other methodologies.

Evidence from Patients

As we have already discussed, while hippocampal damage impairs long-term memory, it leaves working memory intact. In contrast, there are patients who exhibit a selective impairment in working memory, demonstrating a deficit in temporarily maintaining in an active state the information they are currently processing (see Shallice & Warrington, 1979; Vallar & Baddeley, 1984a,b). Their working memory is so compromised as to preclude immediate verbatim recall of as few as two items (e.g., two digits). The first well-recognized patient with such a disorder was a man known as K.F., who had a lesion in the left temporo-parietal area, and showed a profoundly reduced capacity to hold in working memory even short strings of words or digits (Shallice & Warrington, 1970). Nonetheless, he had intact long-term memory for word lists, paired associates, and

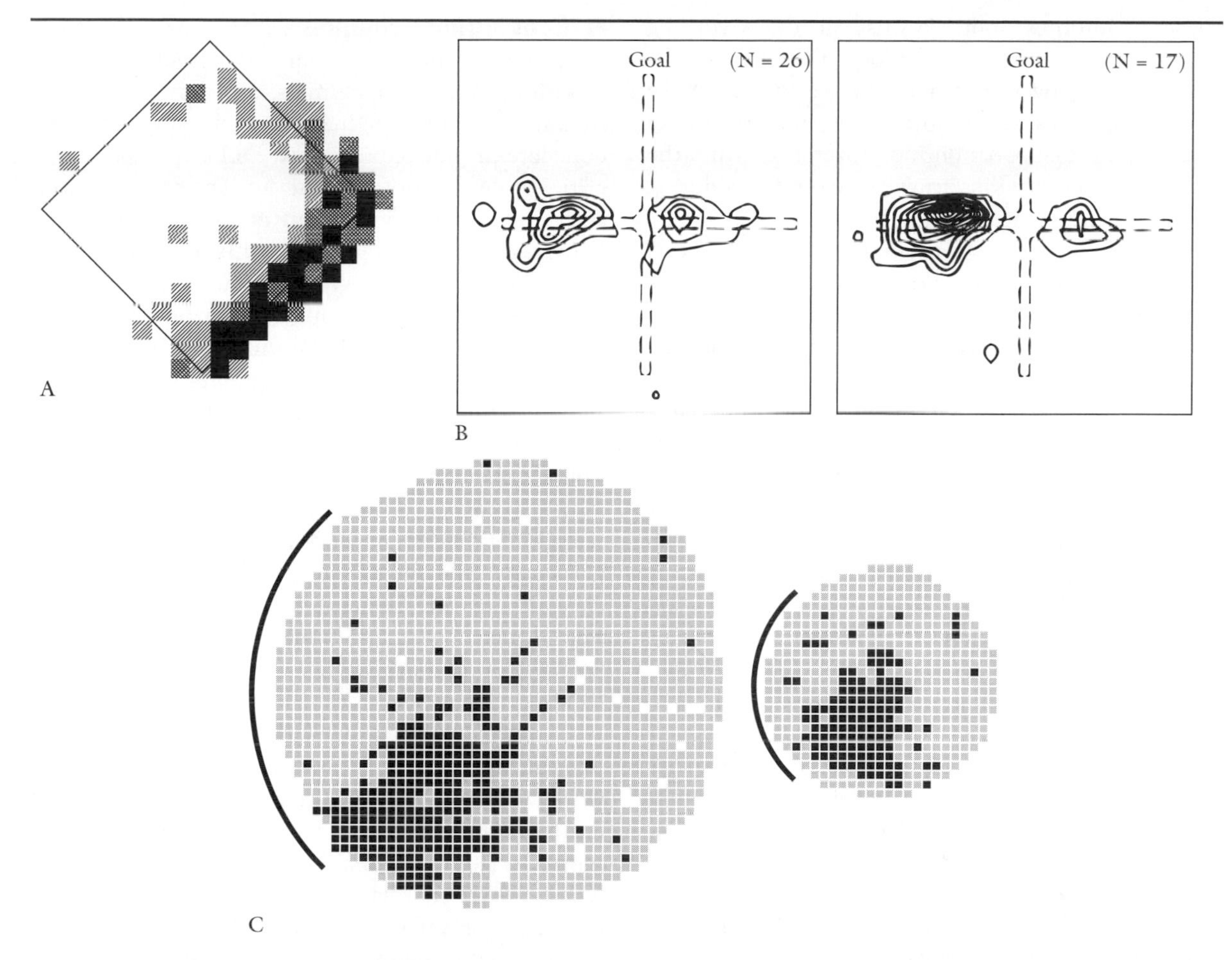

FIGURE 10.12 Examples of firing rates and patterns of hippocampal neurons with place fields in rats as they explore their environment. (A) This display indicates the rate of neuronal firing as a function of the animal's location in the environment. The darker the box, the higher the firing rate. Note that the neuron fired preferentially and at the highest rate when the animal was in one specific place in the environment, namely along the lower right edge of the diamond-shaped environment. (B) Shown here is the firing pattern of a neuron whose place field (within the contour lines) caused it to fire preferentially when the rat was in two arms of the maze (dashed lines); the neuron fired more so in response to one arm than in response to the other. A similar pattern occurred both when the animal could see the surroundings (perceptual condition, left) and when those cues were taken away after the animal had been oriented within the environment (memory condition, right). (C) These figures show the firing rate of a neuron (dark, high; light, low) when an animal was in a given location within an environment. When the animal was placed within a small circular environment (right), the cell fired preferentially to a location within that environment. When the animal explored the larger circular environment (left), the neuron's place field was "scaled up": The neuron still fired preferentially to the same quadrant of space even though that quadrant now encompassed more total area.

the content of stories and discourse across significant delays.

The fact that a deficit in working memory does not also cause a deficit in long-term memory is in some ways surprising and helps to clarify the nature of the relationship between these memory systems. Earlier theories of memory had suggested that working memory and long-term memory handled information in a strictly serial manner. Information was first held in a short-term store, which served as the gateway to the long-term store. The neuropsychological findings of a double dissociation between these syndromes indicate instead that working memory and long-term memory must be seen as systems working in parallel. The working-memory system operates to maintain information in an active state to support online processing, while the long-term memory system works to create enduring records of experience for later use.

Deficits of working memory tend to be tied closely to individual information-processing systems, occurring for a narrow domain of processing. Thus, the best-known example of a working-memory deficit, as in the case K.F., involves impairment of **auditory-verbal working memory,** or what is currently known as the *phonological store.* This deficit consists of difficulty in repeating aloud and verbatim the contents of the immediately preceding verbal utterance, such as is required in the digit span test. Nevertheless, patients with working-memory deficits can retain and recover basic content of a verbal utterance and can even learn word lists. Importantly, their working memory for other processing domains, such as spatial processing or arithmetic, is perfectly intact.

Some researchers have reported further specificity among verbal working-memory deficits with buffers linked to different aspects of language processing—that of comprehension versus production (Caramazza, Miceli, Silveri, & Laudanna, 1985). They suggest that the **input phonological buffer** holds auditory-verbal information received by the listener online while an utterance is being parsed, whereas the **output phonological buffer** holds the phonological code online as a speaker is preparing his or her own utterance. Other patients have deficits in **visual-verbal working memory,** which involve difficulty in the ability to hold visual-verbal information online during reading. Still other deficits occur in what Baddeley (1986) refers to as the **visuospatial scratch pad,** which involves deficits in the ability to hold nonverbal visual information while performing perceptual analyses of the stimulus array. Thus, each of these deficits is tied to a very specific processing domain, leaving working memory for other processing domains intact. This pattern suggests the existence of multiple working-memory capacities, each intimately tied to the operation of specific information-processing systems in the brain.

Converging Evidence

Evidence from lesion and electrophysiological recording studies in animals, and functional neuroimaging studies in humans, both implicate the dorsolateral prefrontal cortex (DLPFC) as playing a critical role in working memory. The role of frontal cortex in a short-term form of memory has been known since 1935, when Fulton first used the spatial delayed-response task with dogs. In each trial of this task, the experimenter put food in one of several food wells in view of the animal and then covered them. After a delay interval, the animal was given the opportunity to choose one of the food wells to obtain the food reward (see Figure 10.13). Following frontal lobe damage, the animal was unable to perform this task, even with delay intervals as short as 1 second. Subsequent work by various investigators has shown that the deficit in performing such tasks does not require damage to large portions of the frontal lobes but can instead be limited to dorsolateral prefrontal cortex (DLPFC) (see Goldman-Rakic, 1988).

The way in which the DLPFC plays a critical role in working memory is powerfully illustrated by the work of Goldman-Rakic and colleagues with an oculomotor version of the delayed-response task in monkeys (e.g., see Funahashi et al., 1993; Goldman-Rakic, 1995). In this paradigm, the monkey maintains fixation on a central spot on a display. As the monkey is doing so, one of eight possible target locations is briefly lit. Afterward, there is a short delay period during which the monkey must continue to maintain fixation. When the light at the fixation point is turned off, the monkey must move its eyes to the location where the target was presented in order to obtain its reward. During this choice period, no information in the display provides a clue as to the correct location. Rather, the monkey's response must be guided by information held in working memory during the delay period (see Figure 10.14A).

Lesions to the DLPFC produce an impairment in the performance of this task. The monkeys are unable to correctly guide their eye movements by memory. And the longer the delay, the greater the deficit. In contrast, eye movements guided by visual information are unaffected, indicating that

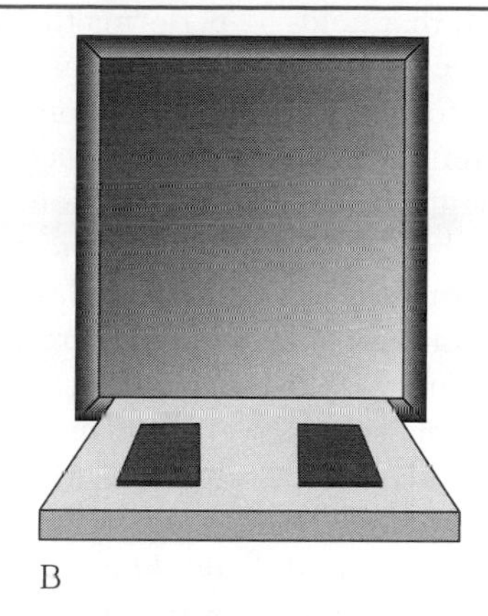

FIGURE 10.13 The delayed-response paradigm, used with monkeys, that illustrates the importance of dorsolateral prefrontal areas for working memory. (A) In the cue period, the animal watches as the experimenter places a piece of food in one of two recessed food bowls, which are then concealed by identical cardboard covers. (B) Then a screen drops, preventing the monkey from viewing the bowls. (C) After a delay of 1 to 10 seconds, the screen is raised and the animal gets to choose one of the two covers, obtaining the food morsel if the correct choice is made (response phase). Monkeys with dorsolateral prefrontal damage cannot perform the task when the delay is longer than 1 second.

the deficit is selective to memory-guided eye movements, not the control of eye movements in general.

The activity of neurons in the DLPFC provides converging evidence for the role of this region in holding information online. Neurons in this region maintain firing during the delay period, when the animal must maintain the position of the target in memory. These cells fire for as long as the delay period lasts, whether it be just a few or many seconds long (see Figure 10.14B). Moreover, the pattern of firing of these neurons is related to the animal's behavior. This firing is maintained only during the delay period for trials on which the monkey correctly remembers the target location; it is absent on trials on which errors are made.

Single-cell recording studies in monkeys have shown that the

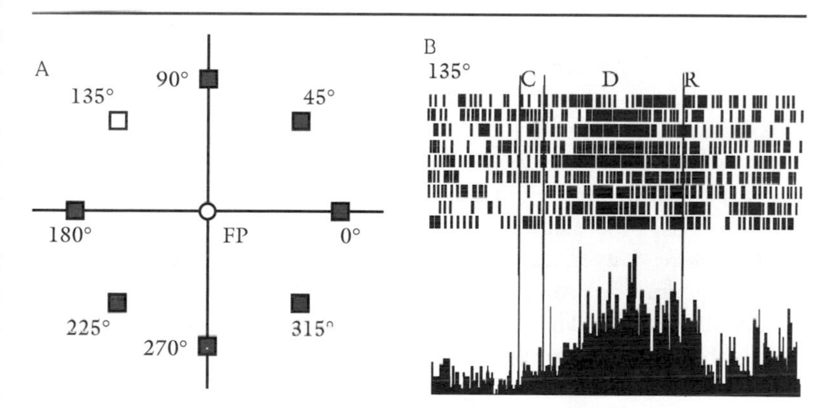

FIGURE 10.14 Activity in cells of dorsolateral prefrontal cortex in the monkey across a short time delay on the order of seconds. (A) The task involves a display with a fixation point (FP) and eight possible cue locations. Whenever the light is on at fixation, the monkey's eyes must remain there. Three-quarters of a second after the onset of the light at fixation, one of the cue locations lights up for half a second. Then there is a three-second delay, after which the fixation light goes off and the monkey must respond by moving its eyes to the location at which the cue was presented. (B) A recording of activity in a neuron in DLPFC. Notice that activity increases during the delay period (D) relative to the time period of the cue (C) and the response (R). Because of this increased activity during the delay period, it has been suggested that these neurons play an important role in working memory.

exact region of the prefrontal cortex (PFC) that holds information online varies depending on the nature of that information. Cells in DLPFC appear to fire preferentially when locations must be remembered across the delay, in the lateral PFC when objects must be remembered, and in yet another region when motor responses must be remembered. Moreover, damage to the various prefrontal subdivisions in monkeys causes deficits in different types of delayed-response performance, either for spatial locations, objects, or motor movements. As shown in Color insert 10.1, imaging studies of humans reveal a similar distinction between the more dorsal region of the DLPFC, which is involved in holding information online about spatial location, and the more ventral regions, which are involved in holding information online about objects (Smith & Jonides, 1999).

Each of these subdivisions of PFC that are involved in working memory receive distinct and non-overlapping inputs from other brain regions. The region of the DLPFC that maintains information about location receives information from the inferior parietal gyrus, which is part of the dorsal visual-processing stream and is involved in spatial processing (see Chapter 7). The region of the PFC that maintains information about object identity receives information from the inferotemporal cortex, which, as we learned in Chapter 6, is part of the ventral visual-processing stream important for item identity (see Ungerleider, 1995; Goldman-Rakic, 1996). And motor projections go to yet a different subdivision of PFC. Thus, there is an organization in which those regions of the brain that process a particular type of information (e.g., spatial information) are intimately connected with frontal regions that can hold that information online.

The data we have discussed so far emphasize the role that working memory plays in the maintenance of information. Yet various investigators, beginning principally with Baddeley (Baddeley & Hitch, 1974; Baddeley, 1986, 1992, 1996), have strongly advocated distinguishing storage, or maintenance, properties of working memory from control, or executive, processes of working memory. In Baddeley's model of working memory, specialized subsystems mediate the storage process, and a distinct **central executive** performs the mental work of controlling these slave subsystems and forming strategies for using the information they contain. This model includes two distinct slave subsystems, the visuospatial scratch pad mentioned previously, which maintains nonverbal images, and a **phonological loop,** which maintains auditory verbal information in support of speech perception and subvocal rehearsal of verbal materials.

The distinction between the maintenance and manipulation portions of working memory helps to make clear at least one of the reasons that the term *working memory* is preferred to the term *short-term memory.* Working memory involves the important addition of mental "work" that is performed by the central executive above and beyond the more passive retention capability of a short-term store. Sometimes all that is demanded of working memory is the maintenance portion, such as when we have to recall verbatim a phone number we have read in the phone book or heard from the operator just long enough to dial it. But more often working memory is required to do more, such as when we are preparing an ambitious meal or doing mental arithmetic. Clinically, these two aspects of working memory, the maintenance and executive portions, are tested in a task that requires individuals to count backward from 100 by 7s. One has to maintain the initial numerals (7 and 100), and then manipulate that material via subtraction to store the new value (93). After that, the next two relevant numerals must be selected (7 and 93), and the subtraction must be performed on them to store the new value (86). Thus, this task iteratively requires both the manipulation and maintenance portions of working memory.

Studies of monkeys with lesions, along with functional neuroimaging studies, have made considerable progress recently in delineating those regions of the brain involved in the maintenance of information in working memory as compared to the active manipulation of such information (for a good review of the empirical work on this issue, see Petrides, 2000). Across various studies using PET or fMRI to characterize prefrontal contributions to working memory, activation of ventrolateral regions is observed when the task emphasizes a passive retention of items—that is, maintenance of information. In contrast, activation extends to dorsolateral regions when the task requires involvement of continuous monitoring and manipulation of information (Owen et al., 1997).

The working-memory challenge used in many neuroimaging studies, the *N-back task*, typically involves both executive, or control, functions and maintenance functions. In this task, a series of items is presented one at a time and the task is to respond affirmatively when an item matches one that is *N* (either one, two, or three) items back. For example, in a two-back task, if the sequence is 4-2-9-2-7-5-7, the person would begin answering after the third item, with the correct responses being "no, yes, no, no, yes." Thus, on each trial of a two-back condition, a person must maintain in working memory the current item as well the last two items. Then he or she must compare the current item to the earlier ones, responding affirmatively only if it matches the item that was shown two places back, not one or three back. After each trial, the contents of working memory need to be updated to include the newest item while the item that is more than two back needs to be discarded. Thus, the task requires maintaining, comparing, updating, and inhibiting, among other operations.

Understanding that there is an executive, or information-manipulation, component of working memory helps to make sense of why working memory ends up being so dependent upon PFC. The PFC plays an important role in various aspects of executive functions, involving the planning, organizing, and monitoring of behavior, which we discuss in more detail in Chapter 11.

Skill Learning

As we discussed earlier, skill learning is preserved in individuals with amnesia, despite their inability to retain memories that are involved in forming a conjunction between items or events. Thus, we know that such learning can occur independently of the hippocampal system. In this section of the chapter, we turn our attention to the brain systems that support motor skill learning, as well as sequence learning and other aspects of habit learning involving the acquisition of stereotyped and unconscious behavioral repertoires.

Our knowledge of the neural substrates of skill learning comes in part from neuropsychological studies of patients with either Parkinson's disease or Huntington's disease. The assessment of skill learning in these patients is complicated because they have profound motor deficits that are quite separate from deficits in learning and memory. In addition, drug treatments administered to these patients have cognitive consequences. To demonstrate that skill learning in general is affected in these patients, we will not only discuss their difficulties in skill learning in the motor domain, but also in other domains. As we learned in Chapter 5, Parkinson's and Huntington's disease occur from dysfunction and damage of the striatum, so deficits in these patients implicate these regions as critical for skill learning. As we will see, acquiring and expressing skill results in changes in behavioral performance as a result of experience. Hence, these changes clearly qualify as memory.

Patients with Huntington's and Parkinson's disease show deficits on many of the skill-learning tasks on which amnesics exhibit intact performance. One category of skill learning in which they are impaired is **habit learning,** which, while gradual and incremental, may *not* necessarily generalize to new exemplars. We have already been introduced to one task of this type earlier in the chapter, the rotary pursuit task, which involves tracking a target on a circularly moving platter with a handheld stylus. The striatal damage in patients with Parkinson's disease or Huntington's disease keeps them from having as large an increase in time on target as do neurologically intact individuals (Gabrieli, 1995). In contrast, in neurologically-intact individuals, changes in activation of the striatum correlate with learning on this task (Grafton et al., 1992).

Another example of the deficit in habit learning in these patients can be observed on the *serial reaction time (SRT) task*. In this task, one of a number of different locations on a computer screen is flashed on each trial, and the individual presses a button corresponding to that location. Unbeknownst to the individual, the locations are flashed in a particular repeating order. Learning in this task is shown in two ways: by a gradual decrease in reaction time across blocks in response to the repeating sequence, and by an increase in the degree to which performance is disrupted when individuals are switched to a block of trials in which stimuli are presented in random order. Such learning can be considered implicit because individuals get better on the task even though they are not aware of the repeating sequence. Several reports have indicated deficits in learning on this task in patients with Parkinson's disease or Huntington's disease (Willingham & Koroshetz, 1993; Ferraro et al., 1993; Pascual-Leone et al., 1993). Converging evidence comes from functional neuroimaging work, in which activity associated with learning on this task has been observed in the striatum (Grafton, Hazelton, & Ivry, 1995), as well as on similar tasks such as finger sequencing (Seitz et al., 1990; Seitz & Roland, 1992).

Other skill learning generalizes across a range of exemplars in the trained domain (for reviews, see Gabrieli, 1995; Salmon & Butters, 1995; Knowlton et al., 1996). Patients with striatal damage have been found to be impaired on such tasks as well. One example is a deficit in the mirror-reading task exhibited by patients with Huntington's disease (Martone et al., 1984). Moreover, functional neuroimaging data indicate that learning to read mirror-reversed text is associated with activation of striatal and left prefrontal regions as well as temporal lobe and cerebellar regions (Poldrack, Desmond, Glover, & Gabrieli, 1998; Poldrack & Gabrieli, 2001).

In addition to the evidence provided by mirror reading, there is other evidence that the role of the striatum in skill learning is not restricted to the motor domain. Patients with Parkinson's disease are impaired at probabilistic learning in the *weather prediction task* (Knowlton et al., 1996). The task involves predicting which of two outcomes (*rain* or *shine*) follows from cues presented on cards. On each trial, one to three cards from a deck of four is presented. Each card is associated with the sunshine outcome only probabilistically: either 75%, 57%, 43%, or 25% of the time. The outcome with multiple cards is associated with the conjoint probabilities of the cards presented in any of 14 configurations. On each trial, the cards are presented, then the individual chooses between rain and shine, after which he or she is given feedback. The probabilistic nature of the task makes it somewhat counterproductive for individuals to attempt to recall specific previous trials, because repetition of any particular configuration of the cues could lead to different outcomes. Instead, the most useful information to be learned concerns the probability associated with the mapping of outcomes with particular cues and combinations of cues—information acquired gradually across trials.

Over a block of 50 trials, neurologically intact individuals showed significant and gradual improvement in their weather prediction performance, but patients with Parkinson's disease failed to show significant learning. Converging evidence for the role of the striatum in learning on such probabilistic tasks is provided by neuroimaging studies (e.g., Poldrack, Prabharkarn, Seger, & Gabrieli, 1999). Thus, a variety of evidence suggests the striatum is fundamentally important for skill learning, both in the motor and cognitive domains.

Multiple Memory Systems

The striking dissociation between memory abilities that are impaired and memory performances that are spared in amnesia has led to the view that there are multiple long-term memory systems. In particular, one of these memory systems is thought to rely on the hippocampal system, whereas the other does not. Although researchers agree on this point, they do not agree on exactly what dichotomy distinguishes between these two systems. Some of the most influential distinctions that have been proposed (e.g., Cohen & Squire, 1980; Cohen, 1984; Cohen & Eichenbaum, 1993; Gabrieli, 1998; Schacter & Tulving, 1994; Eichenbaum, 1997, 1999; Eichenbaum & Cohen, 2001; Squire, 1987, 1992) are listed in Table 10.2. In the following discussion we focus in particular on one way this distinction has been drawn.

The Declarative/Procedural Distinction

As offered by Cohen and Eichenbaum (see Cohen & Eichenbaum, 1993; Eichenbaum & Cohen, 2001), the system selectively affected in amnesia, and critically dependent on the hippocampal system, is that of long-term **declarative memory.** The declarative system is critical for memory of relations between

TABLE 10.2 Some Proposals of Multiple Memory Systems

Proposals
Declarative memory versus procedural memory
Explicit memory versus implicit memory
Episodic memory versus semantic memory
Knowing "that" versus knowing "how"
Memory with record versus memory without record
Memory with awareness versus memory without awareness
Memory versus habit
Locale (place) versus taxon
Representational memory versus dispositional memory
Working memory versus reference memory

the different pieces of an experience. It supports representations of relationships among the constituent elements of a given scene or event. Thus, for each successive event it represents the information about the co-occurrences of people, places, and things, along with the spatial, temporal, and interactional relations among them, that constitute the event. It also supports representations of relationships among various events, providing the larger record of one's experience over time. In contrast, the system unaffected in amnesia, and hence independent of the hippocampal system, is that of **procedural learning.** This system supports the acquisition and expression of skill. Learning in this system is probabilistic, integrating information across events rather than storing each of them separately. This system depends on the striatum and other structures (see Table 10.3).

It is important to note that the relations that are the domain of declarative memory are not limited to events. Declarative memory equally includes relations among the facts that constitute our knowledge of the world. This point is relevant to the distinction offered by Tulving (1972) between **episodic memory,** containing autobiographical records of personally experienced events occurring in specific temporal and spatial contexts, and **semantic memory,** consisting of world knowledge stored in a context-free fashion. For example, your ability to remember the circumstances of purchasing this textbook involves episodic memory, whereas the knowledge you have managed to glean about cognitive neuroscience from this book, from class lectures, and from all other possible sources, involves semantic memory. Some investigators have suggested that amnesia constitutes a selective impairment of episodic memory. However, amnesic patients show impairment in learning and memory for all kinds of relations, both episodic and semantic. Patient H.M. is profoundly impaired in memory for both personal (autobiographical) and

TABLE 10.3 Features and Characteristics of Declarative and Procedural Memory

Declarative	Accumulates facts and events
	Represents the outcomes of processing operations
	Binds the inputs converging onto the hippocampal system, creating relational memories
	Supports representations of experience that are fundamentally relational
	Is accessible to various processing systems
	Can be retrieved flexibly and used in novel contexts
Procedural	Supports the acquisition and expression of skilled performance
	Involves tuning and modifying specific processing systems
	Supports representations that are dedicated to the modified processors (and thus unavailable to other processors)
	Supports representations of experience that are fundamentally individual (nonrelational)
	Can be expressed only inflexibly, only in a repetition of the original processing situation

public (non-autobiographical) events since the onset of his amnesia, just as he is severely impaired in semantic memory for current technology (e.g., computers, fax machines, cell phones, and the Internet) and current politics (various wars, political alliances, etc.).

One good example of the compromise of semantic memory in H.M. is his inability to learn new vocabulary (Gabrieli, Cohen, & Corkin, 1988). He cannot recall, recognize, or even correctly decide whether words added to *Webster's Dictionary* after the onset of his amnesia in 1953, such as *jacuzzi* and *granola,* are real English words. Furthermore, he is unable to learn new low-frequency words of the type that appear on graduate record exams (GRE), such as *tyro, cupidity,* and *manumit.* His failure to learn these words is exhibited regardless of whether knowledge is assessed by the study and testing of definitions (e.g., *cupidity,* "an inordinate desire for wealth"), the study and testing of synonyms (e.g., *cupidity = greed*), or use of words to complete sentence frames (e.g., "The king demanded excessive taxes from the people in order to satisfy his "_____") (see Figure 10.15). Taken together, neuropsychological studies of the impairment in amnesia reveal a marked deficit in memory for all manner of relations, whether episodic or semantic, spatial or nonspatial, and so forth, thereby tying memory for relations (declarative memory) to the hippocampal system.

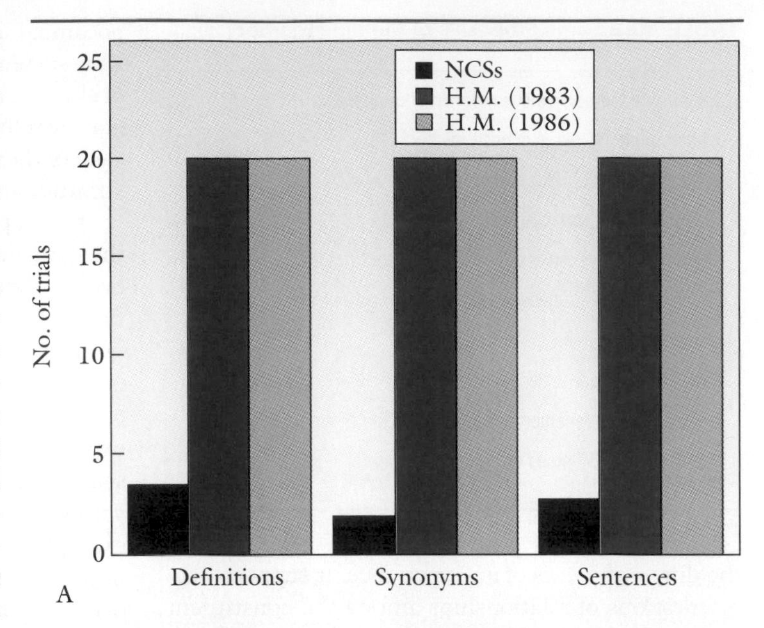

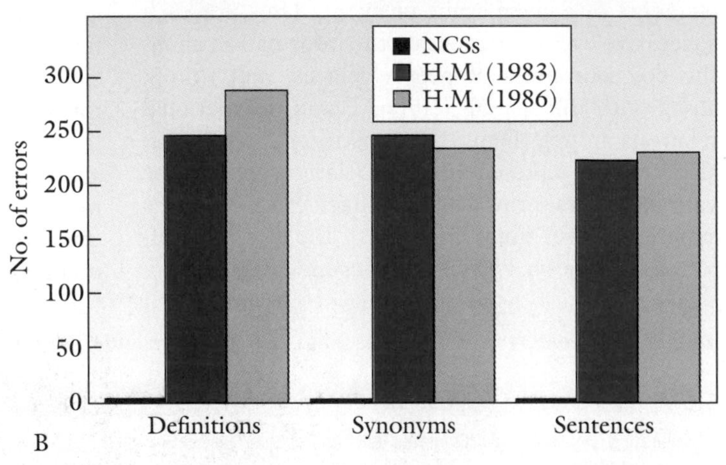

FIGURE 10.15 Illustration of profound inability of H.M., a patient who underwent bilateral removal of the temporal lobe, to acquire new information. In this study (J. D. Gabrieli, Cohen, & Corkin, 1988), H.M. and neurologically intact control subjects (NCSs) were taught the definitions of vocabulary words that they did not previously know. (A) This graph depicts the number of trials required to meet the learning criterion. Note that when tested in both 1983 and 1986, H.M. received the maximum number of trials, 20, whereas the NCSs could learn the definitions, synonyms, and appropriate sentence frames for words in fewer than 5 trials. (B) In learning to select either the appropriate definition, the appropriate synonym, or the correct sentence frame for these vocabulary words, the NCSs showed almost no errors, whereas H.M. made more than 200 errors in each case never learning any of the words.

Implications for Memory Storage

The theoretical distinction between declarative and procedural memory also provides a way of understanding where in the brain memory is stored. This issue has intrigued researchers and motivated empirical work for the last century. Although we will discuss this issue in more detail in a moment, as a preview let us note that declarative memory appears to be stored in a distributed fashion among various cortical processors (e.g., language-processing regions, visual-processing regions), with the hippocampus as critical for mediating the interaction between information in each of these cortical processors. In contrast, procedural memory is stored within individual cortical processing systems. Experience tunes and modifies the action of the processors.

• *DECLARATIVE MEMORY* •

As we experience the world, the various elements or attributes of the parts that make up that experience are handled by different cortical processors, each with its own specialization: vision, audition, language, and spatial processing, to name a few. These same cortical processors also provide the substrate for storing the outcomes of their processing. Memory for visual elements of the experience is stored in visual-processing areas, memory for linguistic elements is stored in language-processing areas, and so forth. In this way, memory for the entire experience is stored in a distributed fashion across multiple cortical areas.

This concept that memory storage occurs within the brain region that initially processes that information is well illustrated by considering activity within the ventral visual-processing stream that supports visual object recognition, which involves *inferotemporal cortex (area TE)* in the monkey and includes the *fusiform gyrus* in humans. Anatomical, neurophysiological, neuropsychological, and neuroimaging data all indicate that this region of the brain both processes information about visual objects and acts as the site of long-term storage of memory for those objects. As discussed in Chapter 6, this region is at the end of the "what" visual pathway, which in turn, projects to the hippocampal system (see Mishkin, 1982). Damage to this region results in visual agnosia, which both prevents individuals from identifying previously known visual objects and from learning the visual form of new objects. This association suggests that damage to this region affects both perception and memory of visual objects.

One good example of how this region is involved in both perception and memory is illustrated by a single study conducted by Sakai and Miyashita (1991). As we learned in Chapter 6, neurons in area TE in the monkey are responsive to specific visual objects. The visual object that is preferred by a neuron—that is, the one that elicits maximal firing—differs from neuron to neuron. In this study, the researchers assessed the responsiveness of neurons to various visual forms, permitting them to determine the objects for which the cells had a preexisting preference and those for which they did not. Then monkeys were trained to associate one preferred item with one for which the cell had no preexisting preference. After this training, when the monkeys were tested with the items individually, the neurons now fired robustly to the newly trained objects, the ones for which they had no previous preference. Presumably this occurred because the newly trained items were able to elicit cued recall of the preferred objects based on the associations formed during training (see Figure 10.16). A follow-up study by Naya, Yoshida, and Miyashita (2001) found that responses to the newly trained items emerged more slowly after stimulus onset than did responses to the preferred stimuli, possibly reflecting the time taken for reactivation of the preferred stimuli by the presentation of the associated nonpreferred item.

Other evidence for a tight coupling of visual processing and visual memories comes from functional neuroimaging studies of neurologically intact humans. The same regions of the visual ventral stream, particularly the fusiform gyrus (e.g., Grady et al., 1992; Haxby et al., 1994; Sergent, 1994) become active when an individual reactivates visual form information in the absence of the visual stimulus itself. In one study, participants studied words that were paired with either a picture or sound. At test, they were presented with words individually and had to recall whether they had previously been associated with a visual form or with a sound. When individuals were able to recall the pictures associated with the word, fusiform activation was similar to that observed during the initial presentation of the picture (Wheeler, Petersen, & Buckner, 2000).

Two studies of mental imagery strengthen and extend these findings (Ishai, Ungerleider, & Haxby, 2000; O'Craven & Kanwisher, 2000). In these stud-

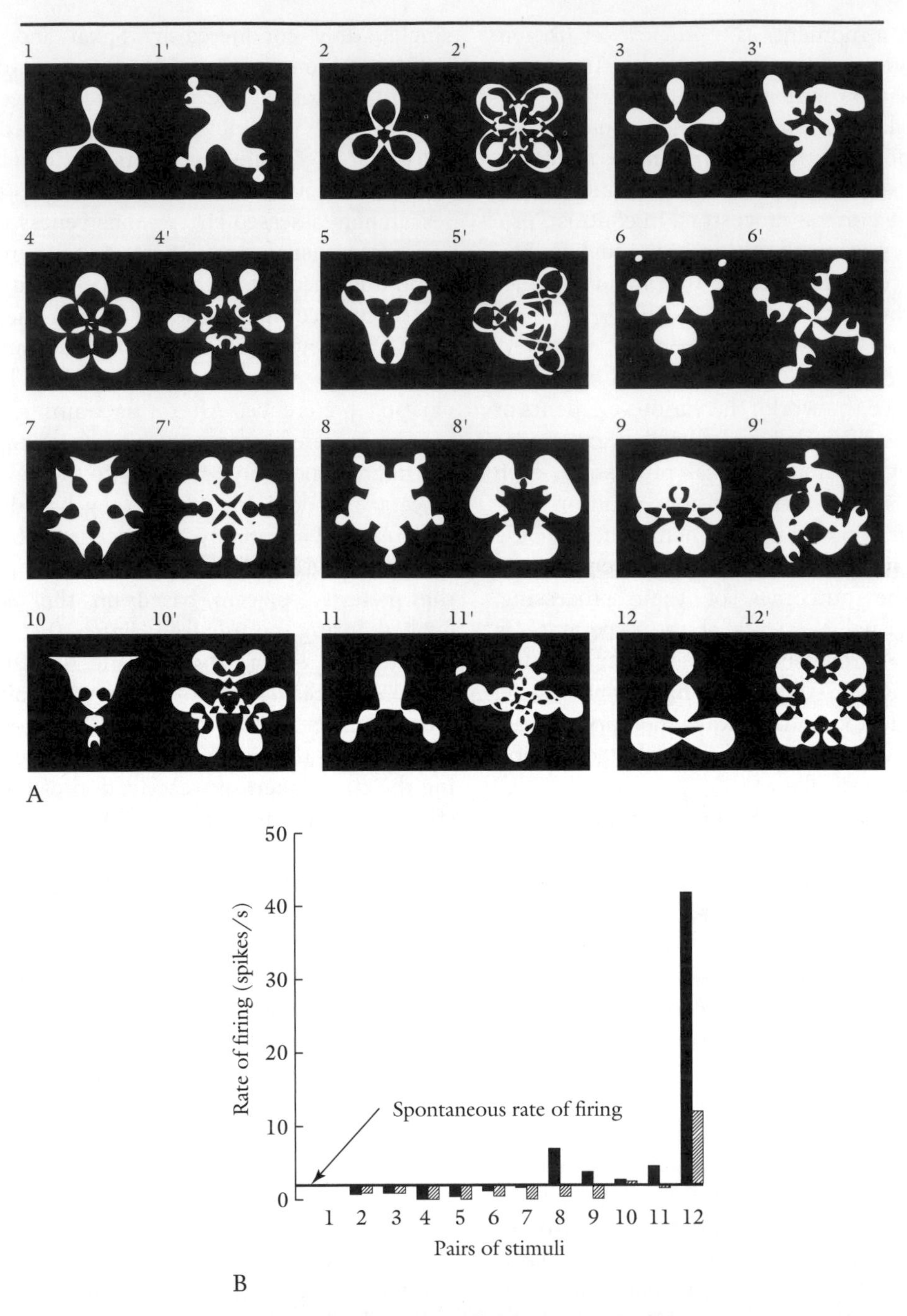

FIGURE 10.16 Evidence that inferotemporal cortex is involved in the memory for visual objects. (A) In the experiment of Sakai and Miyashita (1991), the monkey had to learn to associate specific pairs of these 24 visual shapes. (B) Neurons in temporal cortex that were responsive to a specific visual shape developed sensitivity to the visual shape that was arbitrarily paired with it during training. In this case, the cell was differentially sensitive to item 12 and during the course of learning also became sensitive to item 12′.

ies, researchers first isolated the specific region of the ventral visual-processing stream that was activated when viewing a particular category of visual objects (faces, houses, and chairs in Ishai et al., 2000; faces and buildings in O'Craven & Kanwisher, 2000). This same specificity of activation was also found when participants were to imagine the appearance of such stimuli. This is not to say that the neural machinery for perception and imagery completely overlap. Rather, visual object processing and visual object memory heavily rely on the same networks. Taken together with the earlier results, we can see that the same regions are activated for the initial processing as well as for the recall of perceptual information, indicating that these cortical sites are engaged in both processing and memory functions.

This relationship between initial processing and subsequent recall that we have discussed for the visual object system also holds for multimodal cortical areas, such as those involved in language, spatial processing, and the planning of behavioral acts. For example, in the Wheeler et al. (2000) study, mentioned previously, recalling the sounds associated with words caused similar activation in the auditory regions of the superior temporal gyrus as observed when the sound was initially presented. Extending beyond sensory systems, remembering recently performed actions can produce activation of motor system regions.

Finally, neuropsychological disorders that affect particular, circumscribed domains of world knowledge such as impairment in face recognition or spoken-language comprehension, manifest both as the loss of previously acquired knowledge in that domain as well as the inability to acquire new information in that domain. Each semantic-knowledge deficit thus seems to reflect damage to the cortical substrate for both the initial processing and memory of that domain of semantic knowledge.

But each of these domains represents only specific elements of our semantic knowledge. Just as memory for an entire experience is represented in a distributed fashion across multiple processors tied together by virtue of their interconnections with the hippocampal system, so too is world knowledge distributed across processors. For example, knowledge of objects includes information about their visual form, their function, how they feel or taste (e.g., for a food item), sound (e.g., for a musical instrument) or move through space (e.g., for a tool), and the words we use to name them. It is the nature of declarative memory that the constituent elements are represented in a distributed fashion across different cortical processors and the relations among them mediated via the hippocampal system.

As you can see, the representations in multiple neocortical sites must interact with hippocampus. Yet the evidence from the temporal gradient of retrograde amnesias tells us that the role of hippocampus diminishes with time, as more remote memories are spared in amnesia. Thus, it is a considerable challenge to model this form of memory. The most ambitious model of this system is a computational model offered by McClelland, McNaughton, and O'Reilly (1995). It incorporates a number of critical properties of earlier theoretical accounts of Marr (1971), Squire, Cohen, and Nadel (1984), Halgren (1984), and Teyler and DiScenna (1986), among others. One critical property is that the hippocampus provides a mechanism for rapid acquisition but temporary storage of information. A second is that the hippocampal system then mediates the creation of permanent memory representations in specific neocortical sites, maintaining a hippocampal-neocortical interaction for a considerable time after learning. A third is that the hippocampal-neocortical interaction over time produces richer and more interconnected representations within neocortex.

In the McClelland et al. (1995) model, memory involves the systematic organization of relational information that is stored in parallel, multidimensional hierarchies. Such elaborate, parallel distributed networks can readily be trained to store a large set of items. One problem, however, is that once a set of hierarchical organizations is established and stabilized, it is difficult to incrementally add new items without causing significant changes in the already established networks. These changes, unfortunately, result in what McCloskey and Cohen (1989) termed **catastrophic interference** for the already existing items, destroying the representations for the preexisting items. Such interference is a problem for all sequential learning conditions, that is, conditions in which training cannot be provided for all the to-be-learned information at the same time.

McClelland and coworkers' (1995) solution to the problem of catastrophic interference in sequential learning was to add a new small network—a *hippocampus*—that could very rapidly acquire a representation of a new item through rapid changes in the synaptic weights of the network. This small network could then gradually "train" the large (*cortical*) network, with very slow and incremental changes in synaptic weight. The hippocampal network also would mediate reactivation of already stored information, a process that is cued by information in the current input stream. This ensures that the cortical model is also repeatedly exposed to the old information whenever it is exposed to new information, thereby resulting in an "interleaved learning" regimen. Interleaving reactivations of old representations with presentation of new representations prevents catastrophic interference, permitting new knowledge to be integrated into the cortical networks.

Eventually, this process of interleaving produces an asymptotic state—the overall state of the cortical representation does not change. At this point, cortical representations no longer benefit from hippocampal reactivations, and thus no longer depend upon the hippocampal system. In this fashion, the model exhibits gradual **consolidation** which can be thought of as strengthening of the memory. The duration of consolidation required would depend critically on the nature and extent of new information to be obtained, which is likely to differ among various domains of knowledge. For domains for which the acquisition of new information is expected to continue throughout one's lifetime, consolidation should be conceived of as a lifelong evolution of cortical networks, whereas for other knowledge, the asymptotic state would be reached more quickly. This concept of consolidation can help us understand at least some of the mixed results regarding the duration and nature of temporal gradients in retrograde amnesia.

A number of other computational models have appeared that implement various aspects of the ideas we have just discussed, implementing and extending them in interesting ways (e.g., see McNaughton & Morris, 1987; Treves & Rolls, 1994; McClelland et al., 1995; Alvarez & Squire, 1994; Gluck, 1996).

• *PROCEDURAL MEMORY* •

Unlike the case with declarative memory, the storage of **procedural memory,** which supports the acquisition and expression of skilled performances such as typing or speedier reading of mirror-reversed text, is accomplished through the tuning and modification of the specific processing systems engaged in performing the given task. As performance is gradually and incrementally shaped by experience, activation of the processing networks involved in accomplishing the task at hand are modified and tuned. Thus, rather than being distributed among processors of various domains, procedural memory is tied to domain-specific processors (e.g., motor regions for motor skills). Furthermore, procedural memory neither relies on hippocampal involvement nor requires the mediation of the hippocampal system over an extended period of time.

In an earlier section, we identified the striatum as a brain region that is critically important for procedural learning manifested in skill learning. Thus, the striatum is one brain region in which procedural memory is stored. But there are other regions as well. For example, in neuroimaging studies, the learning of specific finger-movement sequences resulted in changes in activation of various portions of the motor system critical for the performance of the skill, including changes in the distribution of activation in motor cortex (Seitz et al., 1990; Grafton et al., 1995; Karni et al., 1995) and the cerebellum (Friston et al., 1992; Jenkins et al., 1994; Kim et al., 1994). Changes in motor cortex during the course of learning have also been documented in the rotary pursuit task (Grafton et al., 1992, 1994), and changes in cerebellum during learning in the SRT task (Hazeltine et al., 1997) as well as in drawing or tracking tasks (Seitz et al., 1994; Flament et al., 1996), all of which are normal in amnesia and do not rely upon hippocampal involvement. Procedural learning in these tasks will therefore rely on motor regions.

Similarly, procedural learning as represented by repetition priming effects for visual materials results in activation across visual-processing regions. Remember that repetition priming is the form of learning in which items are responded to more quickly or accurately upon subsequent presentations than at initial presentation. Behavioral evidence of such learning is accompanied by changes in activation of the same extrastriate areas that are engaged in processing these visual materials (e.g., see Buckner et al., 1995, 1998). This conclusion is also supported by neuropsychological findings in two single-case studies of individuals who had damage to extrastriate regions. Lesions of these regions in patient L.H. (Keane et al., 1992) and patient M.S. (Gabrieli et al., 1995) resulted in impaired perceptual priming for visual materials. This deficit was selective, as neither individual showed difficulty in explicit remembering of the same visual materials, nor did they exhibit deficits in priming in other sensory modalities, such as audition.

Electrophysiological and anatomical studies in animals clearly show that experience changes the functional and structural aspects of the networks involved in the basic perceptual and motor processing areas. For example, the sensitivity of neurons in the primary auditory cortex of guinea pigs can be altered to be more sensitive to tones associated with shock (Weinberger, 1995). Similarly, Recanzone and colleagues (1993) found that training monkeys to discriminate among tones of certain frequencies resulted in a larger representational area for those frequencies in auditory cortex. Furthermore, this change correlated with increments in behavioral performance.

Similar changes in the basic processing machinery of the brain as a function of experience are seen also in somatosensory and motor cortices. As a result of tactile discrimination training in monkeys, neurons representing the "trained" areas of the skin's surface developed larger receptive fields (Merzenich, Recanzone, Jenkins, & Grajski, 1990; Recanzone et al., 1992). Moreover, training on a task that emphasized skilled movements of the digits of the hand to pick up small objects increased the representation of the hand in primary motor cortex, while training on a task that emphasized movement of the forearm to turn a key likewise increased the representation of the forearm (Nudo et al., 1996). Clearly, the networks that support basic perceptual processing in this domain are changed by experience, supporting procedural memory.

Finally, there is evidence that experience can cause structural change, a rewiring of the brain, if you will. These changes include the creation of new synapses (synaptogenesis) in areas such as motor cortex. For example, rats who learned acrobatic motor skills necessary to traverse an obstacle-filled course showed an increased number of synapses per neuron in motor cortex, an increase that correlated with the increase in performance (Black et al., 1990; Kleim et al., 1996). In this case, as in the others just mentioned, the very brain systems necessary for the performance of a given task showed changes as a function of experience in that task, providing the substrate for procedural memory.

The Relationship between Memory Systems

We can now ask the question of how these two brain systems, declarative and procedural memory, interact. Do they act in tandem, or in opposition, or do they interact in some other manner? At present, little definitive information exists on this issue. Some of the best evidence probably comes from recent fMRI studies using the weather prediction task (Poldrack et al., 2001). As a reminder, the task involves predicting which of two outcomes (*rain* or *shine*) follows from cues presented on cards. The outcome is associated with the conjoint probabilities of the cards presented in any of 14 configurations. This fMRI study suggests that the striatal- and hippocampal-dependent memory systems can compete with each other during this form of learning. In one experiment, fMRI was used to examine the trial-by-trial changes in the striatal and hippocampal systems during learning of the basic weather prediction task. Activation was seen in the hippocampal system very early in training, then declined across trials, with the hippocampal system eventually becoming deactivated. In contrast, striatal activation increased across time, suggesting that the gradual learning of probabilistic stimulus-response contingencies here is aided by inhibiting the use of a more declarative-memory-based performance strategy.

In another experiment, fMRI data were collected from individuals performing a standard version of the task and individuals performing a variant that emphasized declarative memory in a paired-associate learning format. Whereas striatal regions were engaged by the standard version, hippocampal regions were engaged by the latter version. Furthermore, activity in one region was negatively correlated with that in the other: high activity in the striatum was associated with low activity in the hippocampus, and vice versa. The apparent competition between the learning of stimulus-response contingencies, dependent upon striatal circuits, and memory for relations, dependent on the hippocampal system, is also strongly supported by a variety of studies in rodents (Packard & McGaugh, 1996; White & McDonald, 1993).

Brain Systems That Support Encoding, Consolidation, and Retrieval

In the prior section of this chapter, we spent some time discussing where memories are stored and maintained. But we do much more than just store memories. Memories have to be created—that is, information must be *encoded* so memories can be stored. While they are stored, they may undergo *consolidation,* or strengthening, as we touched on briefly in the last section. Finally, for a memory to be useful, we need to be able to access it; that is, we need to be able to *retrieve* it. In this section of the chapter, we examine which regions of the brain make these processes possible.

Hippocampus

The question of what role the hippocampus plays in these various memory processes arose in much of the early neuropsychological work on memory, which attempted to determine which of these different stages of memory processing is damaged in amnesia. Deficits in memory seen at some lengthy delay after learning could reflect impairment in any of these stages of memory. Impairment in the initial encoding of memories would prevent information from being fully processed or from being stored in a robust enough form for later retrieval. Alternatively, impairment in the storage, maintenance, or consolidation of memories would cause information to decay abnormally rapidly over time. Finally, impairment could occur in the retrieval of memories despite the information having been stored and maintained in memory normally. Unfortunately, no definitive answer about which of these stages is the locus of the impairment in amnesia was provided by these early studies.

However, the results of these studies taken together with newer methods in cognitive neuroscience, have provided a more complete answer. It turns out that through its interactions with other brain systems, the hippocampal system exerts its effects at multiple times in the lifetime of a memory: at encoding time, during the time after learning, and at retrieval time. These will be discussed in turn.

Evidence for the participation of the hippocampal system at encoding time comes from functional neuroimaging studies. Numerous studies have indicated that the hippocampal system is activated during encoding of faces, words, scenes, or objects (e.g., Kelley et al., 1998; Martin et al., 1997; Brewer et al., 1998; Wagner et al., 1998; Kirchhoff et al., 2000). There is more hippocampal activity when individuals are trying to memorize or just passively viewing a series of items than when only a fixation point or a single item is presented repeatedly. Hippocampal activation is lateralized to the left and right hemispheres during encoding of verbal and nonverbal materials, respectively, showing the same material specificity seen in the memory deficits following unilateral damage to the hippocampal system. Additionally, fMRI studies show that the amount of hippocampal activity at the time an item is first seen and encoded predicts how well that item is remembered later on (Brewer et al., 1998; Wagner et al., 1998; Kirchhoff et al., 2000). This is the **subsequent memory effect**: subsequently remembered items are associated with greater brain activation at encoding than items that are not subsequently remembered.

This finding meshes well with earlier ERP research demonstrating that activity recorded at the scalp at the time of encoding is associated with subsequent memory performance (e.g., Paller et al., 1987; Fabiani & Donchin, 1995). At the time of that research, it was not possible to identify the particular brain systems that produced the effect. More recent work using depth recordings in the hippocampus, however, has yielded the same ERP effects (Fernandez et al., 1999), providing good correspondence with the fMRI results. Taken together, this work illustrates that the hippocampal system is active at the time of information acquisition and memory formation, and that this activity is predictive of subsequent memory performance. The way in which such processes or operations contribute to memory formation is not yet particularly well illuminated by current methods.

In addition to the temporal gradients observed in amnesia, studies with animals provide most of the evidence that the hippocampus plays a role in consolidating information during the time after learning. The specific details of the processes underlying **memory consolidation** are not well understood. It has been suggested that reactivation of already stored memories during the time after learning plays a critical role in consolidation, and there is some interesting evidence tying such reactivation to activity in the hippocampus during sleep subsequent to the learning event. For example, some researchers noted that hippocampal neurons active during an animal's exploration of the spatial parameters of an environment went on to fire at an elevated rate during subsequent slow-wave sleep (Pavlides & Winson, 1989). Other researchers (Wilson & McNaughton, 1994; Skaggs & McNaughton, 1996) showed that sets of hippocampal cells with a high degree of coactivity when an animal was exploring particular locations in an environment went on to show a high co-activity during subsequent sleep. Moreover, the sequential ordering of firing in co-active cell pairs during sleep tended to replicate the preferential firing order observed during the previous exploration. Such activity is taken as evidence of reactivation in memory of the earlier event and of a role of the hippocampal system in interacting with other cortical areas to consolidate memories (e.g., McClelland, McNaughton, & O'Reilly, 1995; Squire, Cohen, & Nadel, 1984).

Finally, still other evidence indicates that hippocampal system activation occurs during retrieval (see Lepage et al., 1998; Schacter & Wagner, 1999), particularly, on some accounts, in posterior regions of hippocampus. The degree of hippocampal activation during retrieval may be related to how well information is remembered (Nyberg et al., 1996) and may be disproportionate for retrieving the specifics of a previous episode rather than the general sense that something is familiar (Eldridge et al., 2000). The neuroimaging evidence for hippocampal involvement in retrieval does not specify the nature of the processes or operations performed at that time, just as was the case for encoding. One possibility is that the hippocampus may be participating in the reactivation of long-term memories. When some aspect or component of an event is experienced at test time, the interaction of the hippocampal system with neocortical storage sites may allow the rest of the information that was originally bound with that component to be retrieved. In this manner, the hippocampus can be seen as allowing for **pattern completion**—one piece can be used to reconstitute the whole (see Halgren, 1984; Eichenbaum, 2000).

Frontal Regions

In addition to supporting working memory, frontal regions are involved in both the encoding and retrieval of long-term memories. Ventrolateral regions of the PFC are robustly and reliably active at the time of the acquisition of information and encoding in various long-term memory tasks (see Buckner, 1996; Buckner & Koutstaal, 1998). Like the hippocampal system, lateralization of activity is observed depending on the nature of the material being encoded (Kelley et al., 1998; Poldrack & Gabrieli, 1998; Wagner et al., 1998). For example, when individuals are told to remember items, disproportionate activity is observed over the left PFC for words, which are coded verbally, while disproportionate activity is observed over right PFC for unfamiliar faces, which are coded spatially. Activity is distributed over both left and right PFC for namable objects, which can be coded both verbally and spatially (Kelley et al., 1998).

Ventrolateral PFC activity is seen whether individuals are purposefully trying to encode information, known as *intentional encoding,* or are just doing so passively, *incidental encoding* (Buckner, Wheeler, & Sheridan, 2001). As with the hippocampal system, this activity is predictive of subsequent memory performance. Items that are subsequently remembered elicit greater activation at the time of encoding than do items that are not subsequently remembered (Brewer et al., 1998; Kirchhoff et al., 2000; Wagner et al., 1998).

These findings point to a critical collaboration between the hippocampal system and ventrolateral prefrontal circuits in performing operations at encoding that enable the successful formation of memories. Given our discussion in the immediately preceding section about the role of PFC in strategically mediated aspects of memory, we surmise what these operations might be. The PFC might enable the focusing and organizing of such processes, perhaps by inhibiting irrelevant information and encoding information in such a way that it can later be easily retrieved. Interestingly, there is a reduction in PFC activation for recently processed items (Buckner ct al., 1998, 2001), as if the operations required for encoding are already known and hence less involvement of the PFC is necessary. It should be noted that the contribution of the ventrolateral PFC to encoding is distinct from that of the hippocampal system, as normal activation of the ventrolateral PFC is seen even in patients with hippocampal system damage, who exhibit severely impaired memory.

Other regions of PFC are reliably and robustly active at the time of memory retrieval. A number of investigators have pointed to deficits in patients with prefrontal damage when there are minimal cues at test time to aid memory performance, as is the case for tests involving recall (e.g., Gershberg & Shimamura, 1995; Wheeler, Stuss, & Tulving, 1995). The PFC is probably involved in organizing and monitoring memory retrieval as patients with damage to this area tend to *confabulate*, generating narratives that include false memories (e.g., Moscovitch, 1995). In addition, they tend to show an increased proportion of false positives in recognition-memory tasks (Schacter et al., 1996), saying that they viewed items that in actuality were not seen.

At least two regions of PFC are reliably activated during retrieval. One is a posterior area, near Brodmann area 44/6 and extending into DLPFC. The other is an anterior frontopolar region, near Brodmann area 10 (e.g., see Buckner, 1996; Buckner & Wheeler, 2001; Nyberg, Cabeza, & Tulving, 1996) (see Figure 10.17). Activity in posterior PFC at retrieval time is lateralized depending on whether the material being retrieved is verbal or nonverbal (McDermott et al., 1999; Wagner et al., 1998). These laterality effects are similar to those we discussed with regard to encoding. For example, left posterior PFC is activated by verbal tasks including word generation, word classification, and word memorization. Thus, the role of this region should not be viewed as restricted to memory retrieval, as has been suggested (Nyberg, Cabeza, & Tulving, 1996).

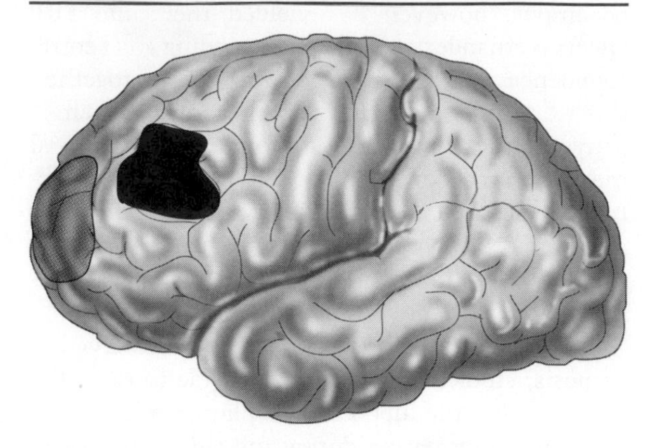

FIGURE 10.17 Frontal regions involved in memory retrieval. Two main areas are involved in retrieval, one in posterior regions by BA 44 and 6 (shown in darker blue) and one more anterior, near the frontal pole in BA 10 (shown in lighter blue).

Interestingly, activity in posterior PFC is more related to retrieval attempt than to retrieval success (Buckner & Koutstaal, 1998; Konishi et al., 2000; Buckner & Wheeler, 2001). That is, the amount of activation is related to the effort required when retrieval is being attempted. When retrieval is more difficult because encoding of the items was relatively poor, there is greater posterior PFC activation than when retrieval is less difficult because the items were well-encoded. Moreover, the amount of activation is independent of whether or not the item is successfully remembered.

Activation of the anterior frontopolar PFC region at the time of retrieval tends to be right lateralized, regardless of the type of information (Buckner, 1996; McDermott et al., 1999). Furthermore, this activation does not vary with how hard or easy it is to retrieve the information. It is more often elicited in free recall or cued recall tests, when one must generate the correct information, than it is for forced-choice recognition tests, in which information is already provided and the only decision to be made is about the available choices (Christoff & Gabrieli, 2000). These findings map nicely onto the neuropsychological data, which emphasize that deficits in recall but not recognition are observed in patients with prefrontal damage. We will discuss this pattern in more detail in Chapter 14, when we examine the cognitive deficits associated with dementias that affect subcortical-frontal systems.

Taken together, these PFC subdivisions appear to make contributions to strategic and executive aspects of memory. Rather than being involved in the storage and/or retrieval of the actual contents of memory of experience, they appear to aid in the organization, selection, monitoring, and evaluation of processing that occur at both encoding and retrieval.

Left Parietal Cortex

Recent evidence suggests that the left parietal cortex plays a general role in memory retrieval, regardless of the nature of the content (e.g., verbal, nonverbal) or the modality (e.g. auditory, visual) of the memory. In fMRI studies of recognition memory, left parietal cortex exhibits more activation for studied items correctly identified as "old"—that is, correctly remembered—than novel items correctly identified as "new," regardless of the nature of the materials (Henson et al., 1999; Konishi et al., 2000; Sanders et al., 2000). This result conforms with those of other neuroimaging studies in which more left parietal lobe activity is found for old items than for new items (see Habib & Lepage, 2000) even when no recognition-memory decision is required (Donaldson, Petersen, & Buckner, 2001).

The comparison of correctly remembered old items versus new items also produces a distinct ERP effect over left parietal electrode sites at about 400 ms after stimulus presentation (Curran, 2000). The fact that correct remembering is associated with parietal cortex activity, independent of the nature of the remembered material, suggests that this activity reflects retrieval success. The brain activity may indicate that the current item has made contact with a previously stored memory (see Buckner & Wheeler, 2001).

The Amygdala: An Interface Between Memory and Emotion

As we will discuss in more detail in Chapter 12, the amygdala plays a large role in the analysis of affective information and the expression of emotional output. Here we emphasize its role as an interface between memory and emotion. The initial evidence for this role of the amygdala came from the amnesic patient H.M. His surgery, which included bilateral removal of his amygdala, left him with a decreased ability to access information about his internal states. In a systematic study of his responsiveness to pain and hunger (Hebben et al., 1985), H.M. differed from other amnesic patients, in whom the amygdala is intact, and from neurologically intact individuals, as he failed to identify pain stimuli as "painful" no matter how intense they were. He also failed to show changes in his ratings of hunger before and after meals. Indeed, on one occasion, he rated his hunger as 50 on a scale of 0–100 both before and after a full dinner. Afterward, he was engaged in conversation with the experimenters and then given another full dinner. He did not remember the earlier dinner, ate the second dinner at his usual pace, and when done, still rated his hunger as 50.

Since those initial studies, we have learned that the amygdala plays two distinct and critical roles in the interaction of emotion and memory (see Eichenbaum & Cohen, 2001). First, it mediates the learning and expression of emotional responses to stimuli whose emotional significance is not automatic but has been learned via association. Second, it allows emotional experience to modulate certain aspects of long-term memory. Each of these roles will be discussed in turn.

The amygdala is critically involved in emotional memory and the learning of emotional responses. Perhaps the best studied example of emotional memory involves the brain system that mediates Pavlovian **fear conditioning** (e.g., LeDoux, 1992, 1994; Davis, 1992, 1994), in which a stimulus comes to invoke fear because it is paired with an aversive event. For example, rats are placed in a chamber in which they are presented multiple times with a 10-second pure tone that is terminated with a brief electric shock through the floor of the cage. They come to exhibit conditioned fear to the subsequent presentation of just the tone, since it was paired with the shock. This fear is expressed by changes in autonomic responses, such as arterial blood pressure, and in motor responses, such as stereotypic crouching or freezing behavior, and suppression of the urge to drink sweetened water, which they usually like. Animals with selective lesions in the lateral amygdala show dramatically reduced conditioned autonomic and motor responses to the tone.

Intact animals also exhibit **contextual fear conditioning,** meaning that their fear response is selective to the context, or environment, in which conditioning occurs. When intact rats are again placed in the conditioning chamber after initial exposure, they begin to freeze even *before* the tone is presented. Their reactions have been conditioned both to the tone and to the environmental context in which tones and shock have been paired. If placed in a different environment, they do not freeze unless a tone is presented. Amygdala lesions block this contextual fear conditioning, just as they block Pavlovian fear conditioning. In contrast, damage to the hippocampus selectively blocks contextual fear conditioning because it requires memory for the relation between the conditioning and the specific context or environment.

Analogous effects can be observed in humans. One such study examined autonomic conditioning in three patients who had sustained selective damage to either the hippocampus or amygdala, or both (Bechara et al., 1995). In this study, the researchers examined skin-conductance responses to a previous neutral stimulus (e.g., a monochrome color or a pure tone) that had been paired with a loud sound (e.g., a boat horn). As you might expect, neurologically intact individuals showed skin-conductance responses to the boat horn. After multiple pairings, they also showed a similar response to the pure tone alone, which indicates a robust effect of conditioning. Because the neutral stimulus could, as a result of conditioning, evoke the same response as the stimulus to which it was paired, it is referred to as a conditioned stimulus (CS+). The patient with selective hippocampal damage showed robust skin-conductance responses to the boat horn and normal conditioning to the CS+ stimulus. Both the patient with selective amygdala damage, and the patient with combined amygdala and hippocampal damage, showed normal skin-conductance responses to the boat horn but failed to develop conditioned responses to the CS+ stimuli. Yet, when asked about their experiences in the experiment, the neurologically intact individuals and the patient with selective amygdala damage showed good memory for the session, whereas both the patient with selective hippocampal damage and the patient with combined hippocampal and amygdala damage were severely impaired in recollecting what had transpired. These findings clearly demonstrate a double dissociation, with a form of emotional conditioning disrupted by amygdala damage and long-term declarative memory for the learning situation impaired by hippocampal damage.

A variety of other paradigms show that the amygdala is critical for learning stimulus-reward associations. One particularly nice example of this comes from a study by White and McDonald (1993) on radial arm maze performance of rats. Animals with amygdala damage failed to develop a preference for the maze arm consistently associated with a food reward compared to an arm in which they spent an equivalent amount of time but without a food reward. Yet, the same animals were fine in the standard "win-shift" variant of the radial maze task, in which they learned to sample each of the eight arms once before revisiting any of them; and they were fine in a "win-stay" variant of the task in which they learned to visit only arms that were illuminated by light and to avoid dark arms. Animals with hippocampal damage or damage to the striatum had no difficulty learning the place-preference task, but were each impaired on the "win-stay" or the "win-shift" tasks, respectively. Thus, amygdala damage produced a selective impairment in learning the reward significance, or the stimulus-reward association, necessary to develop a preference for a single rewarded arm.

The second contribution of the amygdala to memory involves the modulation of memory by emotional experiences. Perhaps the best evidence for this comes from a paradigm developed by Cahill and colleagues for studying human memory (1995, 1996, 1999). Their test involves presentation of a single series of slides and two alternative narratives, one of which is emotionally charged (e.g., a story about a mother and son involved in a traumatic accident), and one of which is not (e.g., a story about a safety drill). In subsequent delayed-memory testing, neurologically intact individuals showed a selective enhancement of recall for the emotional component of the tragic story but not the analogous portion of the neutral story. Bilateral damage to the amygdala in a patient with Urbach-Wiethe syndrome selectively wipes out the enhancement of memory for the emotional part of the tragic story without affecting memory for the neutral components of the story. This damage also did not prevent such individuals from appreciating the emotional content of the tragic story. In a complementary brain imaging study with neurologically intact individuals, one using a similar design, the amygdala was activated during the viewing of emotional material, and this activation was related to subsequent memory for emotional material. Amygdala activation was not, however, at all related to subsequent memory for neutral material. Finally, interfering with the normal interaction of the amygdala system with other brain systems by giving subjects a beta-adrenergic antagonist was found to selectively wipe out the facilitation of memory for the emotional component of the emotional story without affecting memory performance for the other parts of the story or for the neutral story. The beta-adrenergic agonists did not interfere with the ability to appreciate the emotional nature of the story—ratings of the story's emotionality remained the same. The effect was selective to the modulation of memory by emotional experience.

At this point we have considered all the major brain regions that are involved in memory processing; these include the hippocampal system (including the hippocampus and parahippocampal area), frontal lobes, left parietal cortex, amygdala, and the striatum, which are depicted in Figure 10.18.

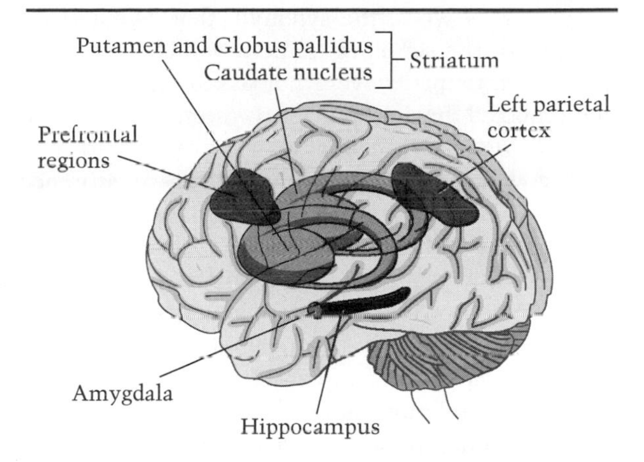

FIGURE 10.18 Network of structures underlying the ability to remember and learn. Shown here are the major structures involved in memory: the hippocampal system, including the hippocampus and surrounding entorhinal cortex, the amygdala, the striatum, the left parietal cortex, and the prefrontal regions.

Memory and Consciousness

To end this chapter we discuss whether recollective experience and consciousness are related to the nature of the deficit in amnesia and hence to hippocampal function (e.g., Gray, 1998; Moscovitch, 1994). It is important to note that the hippocampal system does not itself produce conscious awareness, nor is it critical for conscious awareness to be produced. Large lesions of the hippocampal region, resulting in profound memory impairments, have no demonstrable effect on consciousness in humans. Furthermore, conscious recollection of remote memories is still possible after amnesia, although that for recent memories is not. Finally, and most critically, the degree to which tests require conscious recollection does not seem to be the critical determinant of whether memory performance is impaired or spared. There have been several demonstrations of patients with amnesia failing to perform normally on indirect, implicit tests of memory when they had to learn relations among arbitrarily associated items.

Consider first the vocabulary-learning experiment mentioned earlier, in which H.M. failed to learn the definitions for uncommon words, such as *tyro* and *cupidity* (Gabrieli, Cohen, & Corkin, 1988). In each of the three test phases of this experiment, an indirect, implicit test of memory was used. It was not necessary to make reference to or consciously recollect any specific learning experience in order to select from a list of choices the definition that "went best" with a word, the synonym that "went best" with it, or the sentence frame it would "best complete." Participants were not asked whether they remembered having previously seen or had conscious awareness of previous experience with any of the words, definitions, synonyms, or sentence frames. Although H.M. shows normal performance on any number of indirect, implicit tests of memory, in this task requiring memory for the relations between new words and their meanings H.M.'s performance was profoundly impaired.

The independence of conscious recollection and memory for relations is made in an even more compelling manner in the eye-movement study by Ryan, Althoff, Whitlow, and Cohen (2000) discussed earlier. In that study, eye movements elicited during viewing of images of real-world scenes provided an indirect, implicit measure of memory. There was no requirement to make reference to any prior learning experience, or to consciously recollect the previous presentation of any of the scenes. In neurologically intact viewers, the pattern of eye movements indicated that they had both memory for a whole scene and, simultaneously, memory for the relations among the constituent elements of scenes. Eye movements were different when the relation between items had been changed, and this effect was observed whether or not the viewer showed explicit knowledge of the changes. Whereas the pattern of eye movements of the amnesic patients indicated they had a memory for the whole scene, their eye movements did not show any sensitivity to changes among the relations of the items within that scene. These results demonstrate a selective deficit in memory for relations among items, even when tested indirectly and implicitly without any requirement for conscious recollection. Accordingly, we can conclude that the deficit in amnesia, and the nature of the role of the hippocampal system, is not about conscious recollection but rather about memory for relations.

Rather than viewing the hippocampal system as mediating conscious recollection, it seems more reasonable that the hippocampal system provides the information about relations among people, places, objects, and actions on which conscious recollection and introspective reports can be based. This view, in addition to accounting for the human amnesia data, permits us to make contact with the animal work on hippocampal-dependent memory without having to address the thorny issue of the degree to which the "conscious recollection" of animals is or is not similar to that of humans. Damage to the hippocampal system in rodents and nonhuman primates produces a dissociation among memory capacities that is every bit as compelling as that seen in human amnesia. Such animals show impairments in learning and remembering spatial relations among environmental cues, configurations of multiple perceptually independent cues, contextual or conditional relations, and comparisons among temporally discontinuous events—all requiring a relational form of memory. Yet the same animals can show normal learning and remembering of a large variety of conditioning, discrimination, and skill tasks, none of which requires a relational form of memory but only gradual, incremental changes in bias or reactivity to individual items with repeated exposure. This dissociation parallels closely the dissociation observed in human amnesia.

In sum, conscious recollection and conscious awareness probably depend on a multiplicity of brain regions, including frontal cortex. These regions interact with the hippocampal system to mediate conscious recollection because the hippocampus provides information on the relational aspects of experience.

SUMMARY

What Is Memory?

- Memory is the group of mechanisms or processes by which experience shapes us, changing our brains and our behavior.

Amnesia—A Disorder of Long-Term Memory

- Amnesia occurs after damage to the hippocampal region, or to midline diencephalic structures, such as the dorsomedial nucleus of the thalamus and the mammillary bodies of the hypothalamus.
- Anterograde amnesia is the deficit in new learning, resulting in impairment in memory of information acquired after the onset of amnesia.
- Retrograde amnesia is the impairment in memory of information that was acquired normally *prior* to the onset of amnesia, a deficit stretching back in time from amnesia onset.
- Retrograde amnesias often have a temporal gradient affecting more recent memories to a greater degree than more remote memories.
- Amnesia occurs for information regardless of the sensory modality and the nature of the material (e.g., verbal, non-verbal), and regardless of the mode of testing, such as free as compared to cued recall.
- Amnesia selectively disrupts the process of developing new long-term memories, particularly of the relations among the elements of a scene or event, while leaving intact the ability to form short-term memories.
- Amnesics retain the ability to learn new skills and habits, and can exhibit priming, in that their performance is speeded or aided by the prior exposure to materials.
- Although amnesics exhibit a deficit in explicit tests of memory, as they are unable to recollect a particular study episode or learning event, they typically exhibit intact performance on implicit tests of memory, as their performance can be influenced by past experience when the learning event need not be recalled.

Amnesia in Nonhuman Animals

- Animals also exhibit memory deficits following damage to the hippocampal system, being unable to remember the relations between different aspects of an experience.
- Two characteristics of cells in the hippocampus of animals—their ability to exhibit long-term potentiation and their ability to act as place fields—provides evidence that this brain region has attributes that enable it to play an important role in the formation of new long-term memories.

Working Memory

- Some patients exhibit a specific deficit in working memory while retaining their long-term memory.
- The double dissociation between these patients and amnesic patients indicates that working memory and long-term memory are supported by distinct neural systems.
- Impairments of working memory are closely tied to domain-specific processing systems such as auditory verbal working memory or visuo-spatial working memory.
- Single-cell studies in animals indicate that cells in the dorsolateral prefrontal cortex fire during a delay when information must be held "online," suggesting that they play a role in sustaining information in working memory.
- Working memory has two distinct portions: one of which is a buffer that maintains information online and is associated with ventral regions of prefrontal cortex, while the other is important for manipulating the contents of those buffers, and is associated with the dorsolateral prefrontal cortex.

Skill Learning

- Skill learning is the acquisition, usually gradually and incrementally through repetition, of

SUMMARY

motor, perceptual, or cognitive operations or procedures that aid performance.
- Patients with damage to the striatum exhibit deficits in skill learning, even though their long-term memory for the learning experiences remains intact.
- The double dissociation between the pattern of memory deficits in patients with striatal damage and patients with amnesia indicates that skill learning is separate from the long-term memory affected by amnesia.

Multiple Memory Systems
- The dissociations between the affected and spared abilities in amnesia suggest that the brain contains multiple memory systems.
- One viewpoint suggests that the declarative memory system, which depends critically on hippocampal regions, allows the relations between the different pieces of an experience or event to be remembered, while the procedural memory system, independent of the hippocampus, allows for the acquisition and expression of skill through gradual incremental learning.
- Declarative memories are stored in a distributed network throughout the brain in those regions that initially process the material, and these regions are reactivated during recall.
- Procedural memory relies on changes to the domain-specific neural processors involved in a skill, such as motor regions involved in learning of a finger sequencing task.

Involvement of Brain Regions in Encoding, Consolidation and Retrieval
- The hippocampus is involved at the time that memories are being encoded, during consolidation, and at recall.
- Ventrolateral regions of prefrontal cortex are involved in the encoding of new long-term memories.
- Two regions of prefrontal cortex, a posterior region near Broca's area and one at the frontal pole, are involved at the time of retrieval.
- Activation in left parietal regions is associated with the successful retrieval of information from memory.

The Amygdala: An Interface Between Memory and Emotion
- The amygdala plays an important role in fear conditioning, linking events and stimuli to a fearful experience.
- It also plays a role in learning stimulus-reward associations, and in the modulation of memory by emotional experiences.

Memory and Consciousness
- Although the hippocampal system is required for conscious recollection of a learning situation, consciousness does not rely on the hippocampus.

KEY TERMS

Alzheimer's disease 326
amnesia 324
anterograde amnesia 327
auditory-verbal working memory 344
catastrophic interference 353
central executive 346
consolidation 354
contextual fear conditioning 360
cued recall 331
declarative memory 348
delayed nonmatch-to-sample task 332
dementia 326
digit span task 331
direct (explicit) tests of memory 336
electroconvulsive therapy (ECT) 325
episodic memory 349
extended digit span 331
eye-movement monitoring 336
fear conditioning 359
free recall 331
habit learning 347
hippocampal system 338
indirect (implicit) tests of memory 336
input phonological buffer 344
Korsakoff's amnesia 332
long-term potentiation (LTP) 340
mammillary bodies 325
material-specific memory disorders 331
memory consolidation 357
midline diencephalic region 325
mirror-reading task 333
mirror tracing task 333
Morris water maze 340
output phonological buffer 344
paired-associate learning 338
pattern completion 357
phonological loop 346
place fields 342
post-traumatic amnesia 325
procedural learning 353
procedural memory 354
recognition 331
relational learning 337
repetition priming 333
retrograde amnesia 327
Ribot's Law 329
rotary pursuit 333
semantic memory 349
skill learning 333
subsequent memory effect 356
temporal gradient 329
temporally limited retrograde amnesia 328
visual–verbal working memory 344
visuospatial scratch pad 344
word-stem completion task 335

CHAPTER 11

EXECUTIVE FUNCTION

Dr. P. was a successful middle-aged surgeon who used the financial rewards of his practice to pursue his passion for traveling and playing sports. Tragically, while he was undergoing minor facial surgery, complications caused his brain to be deprived of oxygen for a short period. The ensuing brain damage had profound negative consequences on his mental functioning, compromising his ability to plan, to adapt to change, and to act independently.

After the surgery, standard IQ tests revealed Dr. P.'s intelligence to be, for the most part, in the superior range. Yet, he could not handle many simple day-to-day activities and was unable to appreciate the nature of his deficits. His dysfunction was so severe that not only was returning to work as a surgeon impossible for him, but in addition his brother had to be appointed his legal guardian. As a surgeon, Dr. P. had skillfully juggled many competing demands and had flexibly adjusted to changing situations. Now, however, he was unable to carry out all but the most basic routines and then only in a rigid, routinized manner. Furthermore, he had lost his ability to initiate actions and to plan for the future. For example, his sister-in-law had to tell him to change his clothes, and only after years of explicit rule-setting did he learn to do so on his own. He managed to work as a delivery truck driver for his brother's business, but only because his brother could structure the deliveries so that they involved minimal planning. Dr. P. could not be provided with an itinerary for the deliveries of the day because he was incapable of advance planning. Rather, his brother would give him information about one delivery at a time. After each delivery, Dr. P. would call in for directions to the next stop.

Dr. P. also was totally unaware of his situation. He seemed unconcerned and uninterested in how he was provided with the basic necessities of life, such as clothes, food, and lodging, and was totally complacent about being a ward of his brother and sister-in-law. Formerly an outgoing man, he now spoke in a monotone and expressed little emotion. He did not initiate any activities or ask questions about his existence, being content to spend his free time watching television. ■

THE CASE OF DR. P. illustrates how brain damage can cause deficits in **executive functions**—which include the ability to plan actions toward a goal, to use information flexibly, to realize the ramifications of behavior, and to make reasonable inferences based on limited information. As illustrated by the case, difficulties in executive function can arise despite normal functioning in other domains of intellectual processing, such as those generally measured by IQ tests (e.g., retention of knowledge, vocabulary, spatial-processing abilities, and so forth).

As we learn in this chapter, *executive function* is a term that covers many abilities, and thus it is a difficult concept to define precisely. To better understand the types of abilities that we discuss throughout this chapter, let's consider, by analogy, the skills and attributes required of a company executive. First, an executive must have a master plan, or a general conception of how the company should work. For example, the executive's goal may be to increase customer satisfaction, diversify markets, or raise production. He or she must be able to translate that general goal into specific actions, whether by increasing quality control, expanding the sales force, or automating factories. Second, the executive must be able to assimilate new information and use it to modify plans as the need arises; that is, the executive must be flexible and responsive to change. For example, fluctuations in the stock market or political changes in foreign governments may necessitate a modification of plans or a new course of action. Such planning ability and flexibility are not usually required of assembly-line workers, who in many cases are told what task to perform, how to do it, and when to do it. Third, an executive must keep track of multiple tasks simultaneously and understand the relationships among them, knowing which should come first and which should come second. As a result, the executive must often prioritize both decisions and actions. For example, if limited cash flow does not allow for a simultaneous increase in the sales force *and* the automation of factories, priorities must be set. In a related vein, the executive must be able to assess the effect of each decision and to estimate its relative worth. Finally, an executive must be a person who projects the company image and serves as its spokesperson. As such, this job requirement calls for a certain amount of social skill and political savvy and the ability to get along with other people.

These abilities—to create a plan and follow through with it, to adapt flexibly, to sequence and prioritize, to make reasonable projections, and to interact in a socially astute manner—are multifaceted and share many characteristics. For example, the ability to prioritize often requires creating a plan and being flexible. When prioritizing, you must have an overall plan so that you can determine which actions will best help you reach your goal. Furthermore, you must be flexible because you need to consider a variety of paths toward your goal (rather than invoking a rigid rule). Because of the multifaceted nature of these executive functions, more than one function usually contributes to performance of many of the complex tasks we discuss in this chapter. Consequently, linking one particular type of function to a specific brain region, as we did in previous chapters (e.g., linking reading to the angular gyrus of the left hemisphere), is difficult to do for executive functions.

Even though executive function describes a family of related abilities, the concept has been useful to neuropsychologists and cognitive neuroscientists because it provides a way to understand a constellation of deficits. Although these deficits can occur after posterior damage (e.g., Anderson, Damasio, Jones, & Tranel, 1991; Grafman, Jones, & Salazar, 1990), they are most commonly observed after damage to prefrontal regions (refer back to Figure 1.20B). Such damage is often sustained, along with diffuse axonal damage, after closed head injury associated with vehicular accidents or falls (Stuss, 1987). In this chapter we will discuss how executive abilities are compromised by brain damage and then provide converging evidence from brain imaging and electrophysiological methods for the role of prefrontal regions in such abilities.

Executive Function and Goal-Directed Behavior

We now turn our attention to how each set of abilities referred to as an executive function is related to prefrontal function. Here we will not discuss how frontal areas are related to emotional processing but will reserve that discussion for the next chapter. However, as you read this chapter you should remember that emotional and social abilities can influence other executive functions. For example, Dr. P.'s flat affect, apathy, and lack of concern about his condition surely interfere with his ability to plan, initiate, and sustain activity.

Initiation, Cessation, and Control of Action

One difficulty often observed in individuals with executive dysfunction is what Luria (1966) and Lezak (1983) have referred to as **psychological inertia.** Inertia is the tendency of a body at rest to stay at rest or a body in motion to stay in motion unless acted upon by an outside force; it is resistance or disinclination to motion, action, or change. Thus, individuals with executive dysfunction are poor at starting an action or a behavior, but once engaged in it, they have great difficulty stopping it.

As illustrated by the vignette at the beginning of the chapter, difficulties in overcoming psychological inertia can permeate much of the existence of individuals with prefrontal damage. Dr. P. took no initiative in terms of his personal hygiene or his day-to-day activities, did not inquire about either the state of events in his life or those in the world, and tended not to speak unless spoken to. In fact, patients with left frontal lobe damage often exhibit a marked reduction in spontaneous speech (B. Milner, 1971). Yet the difficulties go beyond that. A waitress explaining why she had lost her job after frontal lobe surgery said, "You have to have a 'push' to wait on several tables at once, and I just didn't have it any more" (Malmo, 1948, p. 542, cited in Dunkin, 1986). Once engaged in a course of action, individuals with executive dysfunction have difficulty deviating from that path. They appear to get caught in a behavioral loop, engaging in repetitive behavior that is often referred to as **perseveration.**

Difficulties in overcoming psychological inertia can be detected on various neuropsychological tests that are commonly used to assess executive function. One such class of tests evaluates fluency, either verbal (Thurstone & Thurstone, 1943) or nonverbal (Jones-Gotman & Milner, 1977). These tests do not assess how coherently the individual can output information, as might be assessed in a patient with aphasia, but rather how easily, fluidly, and imaginatively a person can draw upon knowledge.

In these tests of fluency, an individual must, within a limited amount of time (e.g., four minutes) generate as many items as possible that meet certain constraints. For example, in the case of verbal fluency an individual might be asked to think of words beginning with the letter *s*. In the case of nonverbal fluency, the person might be asked to create as many figures as possible that can be constructed solely from four straight lines. Damage to the left frontal lobe is associated with poor verbal fluency (B. Milner, 1964) whereas right frontal lobe damage is associated with poor nonverbal fluency (Jones-Gotman & Milner, 1977). When told to begin, neurologically intact individuals launch into the task immediately and continue to produce items during the entire time period. In contrast, individuals with executive dysfunction typically appear to mull over the possibilities, seeming to deliberate as they slowly begin to start the task. For example, whereas a neurologically intact person might reel off, "snail . . . snake . . . soil . . . shark . . . stem . . . stuck . . . stencil . . . storage . . . sullen," a person with executive dysfunction might generate just a few items such as "snake.......................stand.................stall," and then continue with "............snake.....................snow ....snaked." Few words are produced, and many are likely to be identical to or similar to those already mentioned.

Another test used to assess difficulties in overcoming psychological inertia is the **Wisconsin Card Sorting Test (WCST).** In this test, four cards are lying on the table in front of the individual. Each card is distinct from all the others on the basis of three attributes: the number of items on the card (one, two, three, or four), the shape of the items on the card (circle, triangle, cross, or star), and the color of the items on the card (red, green, yellow, or blue). For example, one card might have three yellow crosses and another two green stars (see Figure 11.1). The person is then given a stack of cards and is told to sort them into four piles below the four cards already on the table. However, no explicit criteria for sorting are given. Rather, as the individual places each card onto one of the four piles, the experimenter indicates only whether the response is correct or incorrect. From the experimenter's feedback, the person must deduce the dimension on which the card should be sorted (e.g., color). An example of this procedure is shown in Figure 11.1.

After the individual correctly sorts 10 cards on the basis of one particular attribute, such as color, the experimenter, without explicitly telling the individual, changes the criterion for sorting the cards (e.g., to shape). Neurologically intact individuals quickly realize that although their behavior previously led to a correct response, it no longer does so. Hence, they adjust their responses accordingly. In contrast, individuals with executive dysfunction perseverate, continuing to sort the cards by the same attribute despite the negative feedback.

You may be wondering what traps such individuals into their perseverative behavior. Often their behavior is triggered by some object in the environment, which has been referred to as an **environmental dependency syndrome** (e.g., Lhermitte, 1983; Lhermitte, Pillon, & Serdaru, 1986). It is as if their actions are impelled or obligated by their physical and social environment (see some examples of such behaviors in Figure 11.2). For example, when individuals with this syndrome see a computer keyboard, they will begin to type on it, even though the computer does not belong to them. As you can imagine, this sort of behavior makes the person appear as if he or she is acting impulsively. Social influences can be compelling as well. For example, a patient came for a session with a doctor. Interspersed throughout their ensuing conversation, the doctor suggested that if the patient was thirsty, he should have a glass of water.

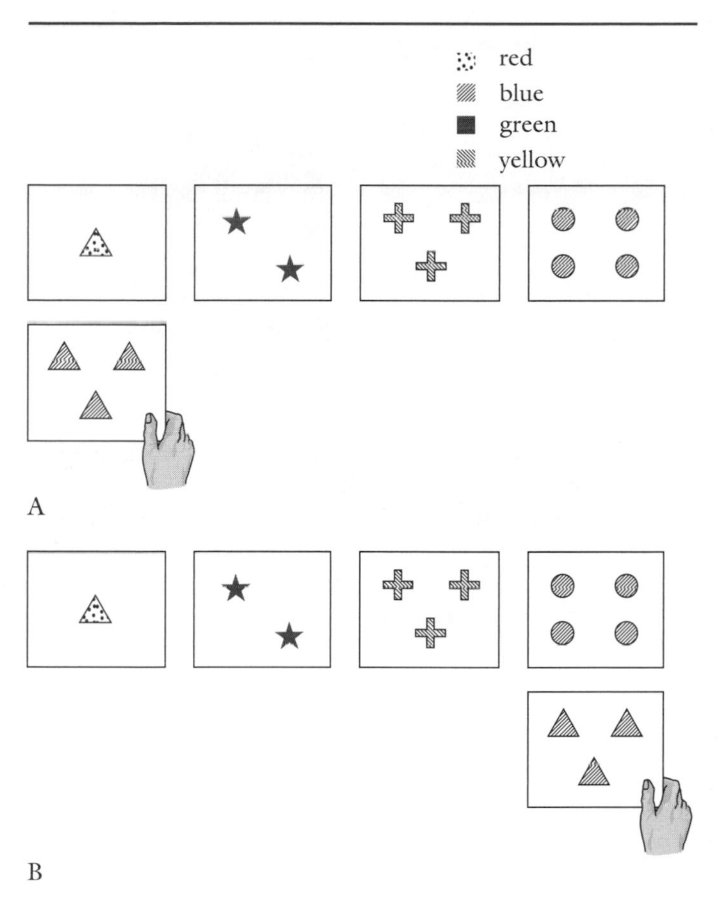

FIGURE 11.1 Two examples of sorting behavior on the Wisconsin Card Sorting Test (WCST). In this particular series of trials, the subject must sort on the basis of color. (A) An example of an incorrect sort because the individual matched the card on the basis of shape instead of color. (B) An example of a correct sort because the individual matched the card on the basis of color rather than shape or number.

Each time he heard this suggestion, the patient poured himself a full glass of water and drank it. However, when simply asked if he was thirsty, he claimed not to be. Because of difficulties such as these, some researchers have wondered, philosophically, whether individuals with this type of executive dysfunction have lost their "free will."

This environmental dependency syndrome can often be expressed in different forms depending on an individual's personal history prior to injury. Consider the following cases of two patients with executive dysfunction, each of whom was attending the same buffet dinner (Lhermitte, 1986). One patient, a man from an upper-class background, behaved like a guest expecting to be served. In contrast, the other patient, a woman who had been a modest housekeeper for most of her life, immediately began serving the other guests.

A noteworthy aspect of the lack of control of action exhibited by these patients is that it can occur even when the person appears to "know" how to act. This suggests that the deficit may in part be characterized as a disconnection between thought and action. A classic example of such behavior is observed in patients performing the WCST. Many anecdotal reports exist of individuals who persist in sorting on the basis of a previously correct but now incorrect category even as they state that they *know* their action is wrong (e.g., B. Milner, 1964). Another example of this disconnection between thought and action can be observed when such individuals are given a problem in which partial information toward a solution is given one step at a time. Although individuals with frontal lobe damage can provide a reasonable estimate of how many clues they will need to solve a sample problem successfully, they nonetheless attempt to solve the problem with fewer clues than they estimated they would need (L. A. Miller, 1992).

Brain imaging studies also provide converging evidence for the role of prefrontal cortex in such abilities. Clearly, it is difficult to adopt many of the tasks or situations we have just discussed into paradigms that can be used in a neuroimaging environment. However, certain basic components of such abilities can be investigated with neuroimaging. For example, one can look at the inhibition of responses. One paradigm used to investigate this function is the Go/No-Go task. On some trials, the appropriate response is to push a button (Go trials) and on others the appropriate response is to withhold a response (No-Go). One can make response inhibition difficult if the No-Go trials are relatively rare. Under such conditions, one finds a large amount of activity in dorsolateral (BA 46/9) and ventrolateral (BA 44) prefrontal regions of the right hemisphere as well as the anterior cingulate (e.g., Braver et al., 2001). Similar

A

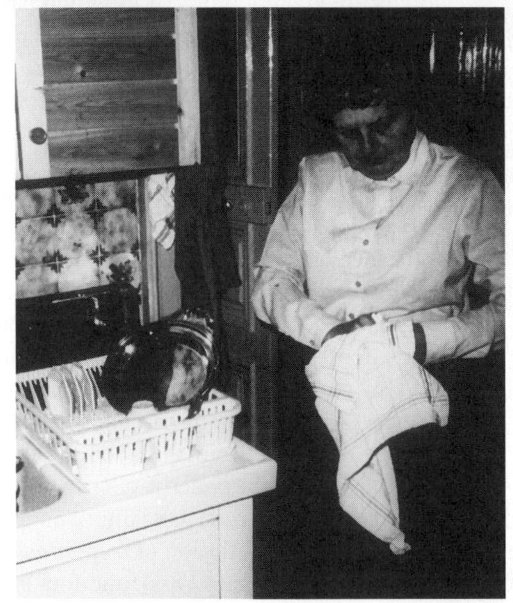

B

FIGURE 11.2 Two examples of the environmental dependency syndrome exhibited by patients with frontal lobe damage when they visited their physician's home. (A) The man, upon seeing two pictures lying on the floor, picked up a hammer and nails and hung the pictures on the wall. (B) The woman, upon seeing dishes in the kitchen, began to wash them.

regions are activated when individuals perform another task that involves inhibiting responses, the Stop-Signal task. In this task, a minority of trials contain a signal to stop responding shortly after (e.g., one-quarter of a second) the individual is shown the stimulus to which he or she usually responds (Rubia et al., 2001).

The exact role of inferior prefrontal regions as compared to that of the anterior cingulate in response inhibition has not been clearly delineated. However, at least some researchers suggest that the cingulate is engaged in the initiation and monitoring of decisions, because this region shows equivalent activity on Go and No-Go trials when they are equally probable (50/50). In contrast, inferior prefrontal regions, especially those in the right hemisphere, are thought to play a more specific role in inhibiting responses, because they exhibit greater activity on No-Go trials than on Go trials (Liddle, Kiehl, & Smith, 2001; Garavan, Ross, & Stein, 1999; Konishi et al., 1999) (see Color insert 11.1).

Abstract and Conceptual Thinking

Another deficit exhibited by individuals with executive dysfunction is an inability to process material in an abstract rather than a concrete manner. Although some individuals with frontal lobe damage exhibit only perserverative tendencies on the WCST, others cannot even figure out the criterion by which the cards should be sorted. Because they were not given concrete instructions (e.g., sort the cards into piles based on the color of the items), they cannot figure out how to perform the task.

These difficulties in conceptualization (rather than perseverative tendencies) are well revealed by use of a modification of the standard WCST (Delis, Squire, Bihrle, & Massman, 1992). In this test, an individual is given a set of six cards that must be sorted into two equal piles. Each card contains an animal's name and a triangle placed against a background of lines. The cards are constructed so that eight possible dimensions can be used to divide them into piles. For example, cards can be divided on the basis of whether the animal lives on land or in the water, whether the triangle is black or white, or whether the position of the animal's name is above or below the triangle (see Figure 11.3).

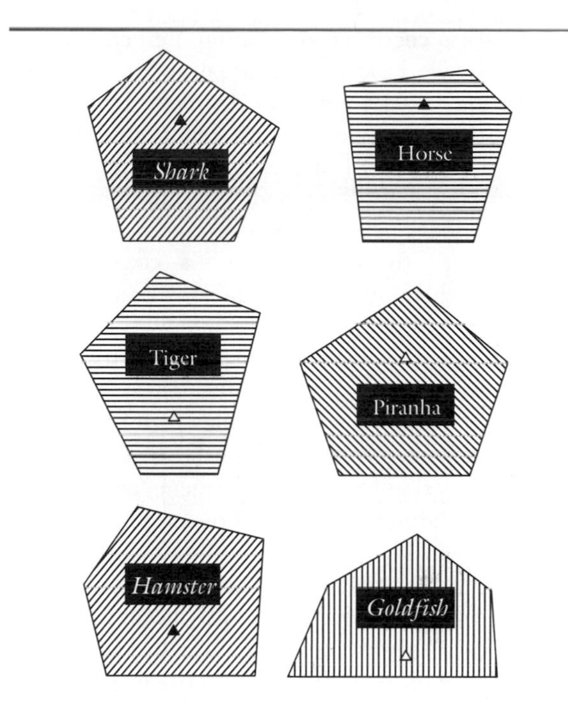

FIGURE 11.3 Examples of stimuli similar to those used to demonstrate abstraction difficulties in patients with frontal lobe damage. These cards can be sorted into two equal groups on eight dimensions: (1) whether the animal lives on land or in the water, (2) whether the animal is domestic or dangerous, (3) whether the animal is large or small, (4) whether the triangle is above or below the word, (5) whether the triangle is black or white, (6) whether the lines are oblique or nonoblique, (7) whether the animal's name is five letters or longer, and (8) whether the animal's name is written in block letters or cursive letters. Patients with frontal lobe damage have difficulty sorting the cards into meaningful piles and sometimes cannot even do so when given concrete cues ("The animals are either man-eating or domestic").

The difficulty that individuals with frontal lobe damage have on this task highlights the underlying problem in abstract conceptualization. The patients are often deficient at describing the rule by which they sort. For example, they are unable to state something to the effect of "The animals on the cards I am putting in this pile live in water, whereas the animals on the cards in this pile live on land." Even when the examiner sorts the cards into piles, the individuals cannot identify the rule used to sort the items. They also have difficulty sorting the cards into meaningful groups when given either abstract cues, such as "It has to do with how these animals behave around people," or even more concrete ones such as "These animals are ferocious or tame." This latter problem may reflect difficulty either in abstraction or in translating thought into action, a problem we discussed previously. These difficulties in abstraction may contribute, in part, to difficulties in strategy formation, which we discuss in more detail later.

Cognitive Estimation and Prediction

A third type of deficit often observed in individuals with executive dysfunction is an inability to use known information to make reasonable judgments or deductions about the world, a process often referred to as **cognitive estimation.** Remember that the knowledge base of individuals with executive dysfunction usually remains relatively unaffected; that is, these individuals can retain information such as the year of Canada's independence or the name of Henry VIII's second wife. In some cases, such knowledge can be used effectively. As we discussed earlier, these patients are as competent as patients with temporal lobe damage or neurologically intact individuals at judging how many clues they will need to solve a puzzle (although they don't let such information guide their response). And their estimates for judging how well they perform on concrete tasks, such as preparing meals, dressing themselves, and caring for personal hygiene, concur well with their relatives' estimates (Prigatano, Altman, & O'Brien, 1990).

However, if the estimate requires more inference or becomes a bit more abstract, they begin to exhibit difficulties. For example, patients with frontal lobe damage have difficulty estimating the length of the spine of an average woman. This type of information is not usually stored in memory nor easily obtained from reference materials, such as an encyclopedia. Instead, making a realistic estimate requires inference based on other knowledge, such as knowing that the average woman is about 5 feet 6 inches tall (168 cm), and the spine runs about one-third to one-half the length of the body, yielding an estimate of 22 to 33 inches (56–84 cm). Patients with frontal lobe damage have difficulty making such estimates, often stating absurd or outrageous values (Shallice & Evans, 1978). Likewise, patients with frontal lobe damage are poor at estimating the price of items, such as cars and washing machines, when shown a miniature replica (which is a somewhat abstract representation of the item). In fact, they provide bizarre estimates on 25 percent of all responses (e.g., 10 cents for a washing machine) (Smith & Milner, 1984). Their ability to estimate more abstract aspects of their own daily performance also is compromised. For example, in comparison with the ratings provided by relatives, patients with anterior lesions coupled with diffuse axonal injury grossly overestimate how capable they are of performing tasks such as scheduling their daily activities, fending off depression, or preventing their emotions from affecting daily activities (Prigatano, Altman, & O'Brien, 1990).

Estimation of information in the temporal domain can also be affected, in particular estimating how frequently an event or item has occurred. In one paradigm (Smith & Milner, 1988), individuals are shown a series of nonsense items, some of which appear only once, whereas others appear nonconsecutively three, five, seven, or nine times. After the individual has viewed the initial series of items, a series of test items is given, some of which were viewed previously and some of which were not. The person decides whether each test item appeared in the initial sequence, and if so, how often it occurred. Although individuals with frontal lobe damage have no difficulty determining whether an item was in the inspection series (an ability that is compromised by temporal lobe damage, as discussed in Chapter 10), they have difficulty estimating how frequently an item occurred, especially if it occurred often.

This difficulty in determining relative frequency of occurrence might not reflect just difficulties in cognitive estimation. It might also reflect a more general difficulty in memory for temporal information, such as *how often* and *when* something occurred, which is distinct from remembering *whether* it occurred. As we learn later in the chapter, individuals with executive dysfunction and frontal lobe damage are impaired on a variety of sequencing tasks. Thus, an inability to estimate frequency of occurrence may arise from both difficulty in cognitive estimation and difficulty in temporal sequencing. A significant repercussion of losing this ability is that planning, or prioritizing behavior, becomes much more difficult.

Individuals with frontal lobe damage also have trouble making attributions about other people's mental states that would allow them to predict the behavior of others. This capacity, known as **theory of mind,** is the ability to represent other people's mental states, such as beliefs and intentions. One way to assess this ability is to ask someone to predict the behavior of an individual who can be assumed to hold a mistaken belief. For example, take the scenario in which each occupant of a house always locks the door by pushing in the button on the door knob when leaving. If one housemate isn't sure whether another one heard him leave, theory of mind lets him infer that when the other housemate leaves, she will attempt to lock the door, even though, in fact, the door does not need locking. An inability to have a theory of mind is independent of other aspects of executive control (Rowe, Bullock, Polkey, & Morris, 2001).

Cognitive Flexibility and Response to Novelty

Individuals with executive dysfunction have trouble being cognitively flexible—that is, looking at situations from a multiplicity of vantage points and/or producing a variety of behaviors (Fuster, 1985). Such flexibility is paramount when dealing with novel or new situations. Novelty, of course, is a relative concept, but we define it as an event, a situation, or an action that has a low probability of occurring given a particular context. Flexibility is required not only in novel situations but also when a new reaction must be made to an old situation. Cognitive inflexibility can be considered distinct from, but related to, the perseverative tendencies and environmental dependencies we discussed earlier. It is difficult to respond or act in an atypical or novel manner if your history of prior actions biases you to act in a particular manner or if your responses are strongly triggered by objects in the environment.

Electrophysiological studies implicate frontal regions as playing an important role when a novel stimulus captures attention. As we have mentioned in Chapters 3 and 8, an oddball stimulus that must be attended causes a P_{300} that is maximal over parietal regions (this P_{300} is sometimes referred to as the P_{3b}). A similar component, known as the P_{3a}, occurs when a novel or unexpected stimulus captures attention. This component is maximal at frontocentral leads, with an occurrence 20 to 50 ms earlier than the P_{3b}. For example, the P_{3b} is elicited if an individual must count or attend to the rare boops interspersed within a series of frequent beeps. If a totally unexpected or novel item, such as a dog bark, is inserted into the series of beeps and boops, a P_{3a} is elicited (R. T. Knight, 1991). We can be relatively certain that frontal regions of the brain contribute to the generation of this potential because (1) the P_{3a} decreases in amplitude after lesions to prefrontal cortex (Yamaguchi & Knight, 1991), (2) the amplitude of the P_{3a} is correlated with the volume of gray matter in the frontal lobes in neurologically intact men (Ford et al., 1994), and (3) high-density electrode arrays suggest a frontal source (Spencer, Dien, & Donchin, 1999). Furthermore, neuroimaging studies indicate that the middle and inferior prefrontal regions become more active when processing novel stimuli (e.g., Kiehl et al., 2001) (see Figure 11.4).

The ability to be cognitively flexible in response to novelty may help contribute to performance on some other tasks of executive function that we already discussed. For example, fluency tests may, in part, measure response to novelty because individuals must apply knowledge in a fluid, novel, and flexible manner. Yet, as we discussed, these tasks also require a person to successfully initiate behavior. Therefore, we might be interested in disentangling the relative contribution of each function—cognitive flexibility and initiation of behavior—to fluency tasks. To do so, researchers compared the word-fluency task we discussed earlier (think of all the words you can beginning with the letter *s*) with a task involving fluency in knowledge of animals, requiring individuals to name all the animals that they can think of. Both tasks obviously involve the initiation and cessation of behavior. However, the animal-naming task is not as novel as the word-naming task because we are often required to search our memory for items that are categorically related. In contrast, we rarely ever have to search our memory for words beginning with the same letter (unless you spend hours watching educational television programs for children such as *Sesame Street*!). Patients with frontal lobe damage exhibit more severe deficits on the word-naming task (B. Milner, 1964) than the animal-naming task (Newcombe, 1969), suggesting that the frontal lobes help not only in initiating behavior, but also in enabling novel actions.

Researchers have attempted to clarify exactly what aspects of flexible behavior are most difficult for patients with frontal lobe damage. Two factors seem to stand out: (1) the degree to which learned behaviors or associations must be overridden or superseded, and (2) the degree to which information in the environment is available to guide behavior

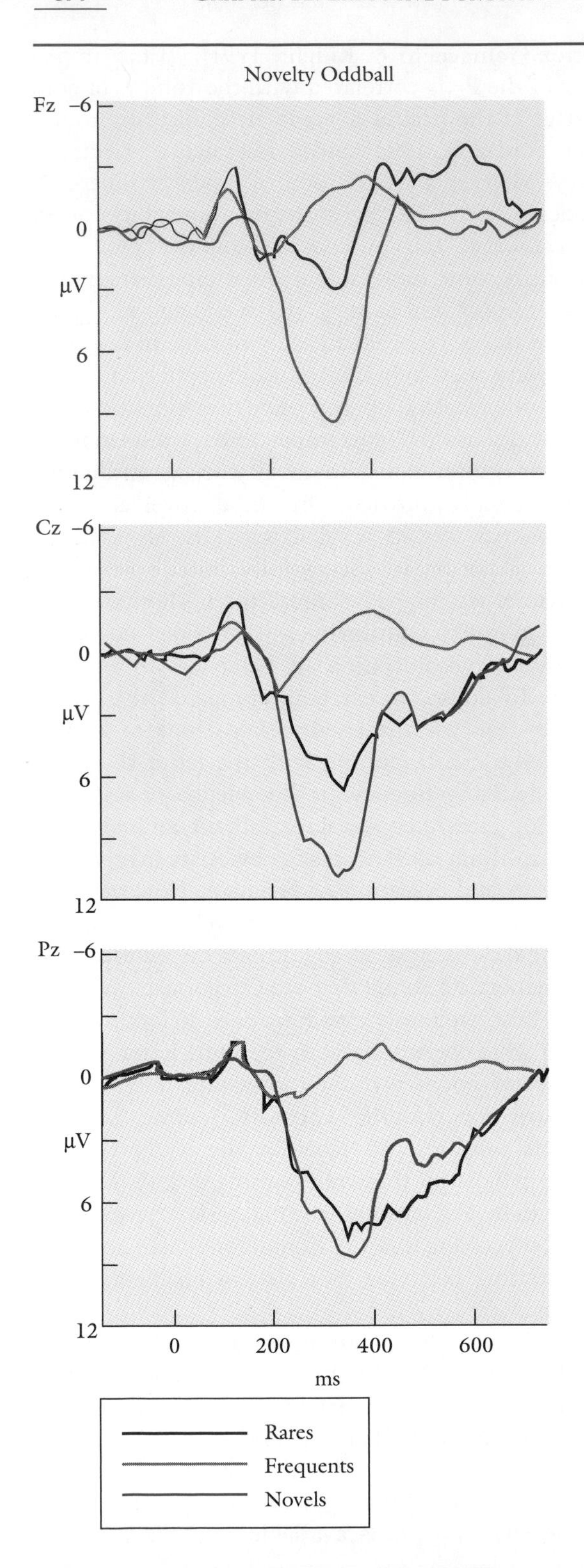

(R. W. Butler, Rorsman, Hill, & Tuma, 1993). Patients with frontal lobe damage perform poorly when well-linked associations must be overridden. For example, when the stimulus-response pairing is somewhat arbitrary, patients with frontal lobe damage can exhibit normal **reversal learning,** in which an individual reverses a previous response. Thus, after learning to press the right-hand key when a blue light appears and the left-hand key when a yellow light appears, patients with frontal lobe damage can learn to press the right-hand key when the *yellow* light appears and the left-hand key when the *blue* light appears. This task is unimpaired because the pairing of the color and the position of the key is arbitrary. However, they have difficulties when they must move a joystick to the left in response to a rightward-moving target and to the right in response to a leftward-moving target (Gauggel, 1996). In this case, they must overcome the tendency to move the joystick rightward in response to a rightward target. They also have difficulty when the environment provides little information to guide their behavior. For example, even a small degree of frontal lobe damage disrupts performance on the Alternative Uses Test, in which the individual must devise novel uses of an object (e.g., using a shoe as a bookend).

In contrast, larger amounts of frontal damage are needed to impair performance on design and verbal fluency. In verbal fluency, the manner in which an individual must search through memory is specified (i.e., by a designated letter), and in design fluency the components to be used to create a novel figure are specified (i.e., four straight lines). In contrast, nothing in the Alternative Uses Test suggests how to generate novel uses for a shoe. Not only is the Alternatives Uses Test much more open-ended than the fluency task, but it also taxes the ability to break old associations (e.g., between shoes and footwear). Generating words to a letter or creating

FIGURE 11.4 Evidence for the role of prefrontal regions in novelty. Shown here are the ERP responses to frequent, rare, and truly novel (i.e., unique) stimuli. Notice that the difference in the response to novel as compared to rare events is greatest over frontal leads (Fz) and practically indistinguishable over posterior leads (Pz), with an intermediate pattern over central leads (Cz).

novel figures does not require old associations to be overridden.

As we learned in this section, executive dysfunction is characterized by a lack of flexibility in performance. This inflexibility can manifest as a person's inability to vary his or her response or as inflexibility in the manner in which information is conceptualized or retrieved. Regardless of whether the problem occurs in terms of conceptualization or responding, executive dysfunction is usually characterized by an especially keen difficulty in being able to override well-learned associations. We revisit this issue later in the chapter when we discuss a theory of frontal lobe function that suggests the frontal lobes control behavior in nonroutine situations (Stuss & Benson, 1986).

Goal-Directed Behaviors

The final executive ability that we discuss is the ability to organize behavior toward a goal. Such an ability is multifaceted, and, as we will learn shortly, the loss of any facet of goal-oriented behavior can cause the entire plan to be derailed.

Consider the multiple aspects of the simple task of making yourself a peanut butter and jelly sandwich. First, the ultimate goal must be kept in mind throughout the procedure. For example, even though you are in the kitchen, which contains many other foods, you need to keep focused on the peanut butter and jelly. You must also keep this goal in mind even though subgoals must be met along the way. For example, although locating the bread may be the first step in making the sandwich, after attaining that subgoal, you must remember the ultimate goal and switch to finding the peanut butter or the jelly. Second, attaining the goal requires flexibility and adaptability. If you remember that the jelly is on the top shelf of the refrigerator but do not find it there, you must devise an alternative strategy, such as searching the other shelves or looking among the racks on the door. Third, for you to reach the ultimate goal, the completed portions of the task must be distinguished from those yet to be attained. Thus, after locating the jelly, you must remember not to turn your attention to finding some pieces of bread (because you already completed that part of the task). Fourth, you must evaluate the actions that will best help you to reach the goal. For example, you must realize that although a fork is in front of you, it is not the utensil best suited for making your sandwich. Instead, you must decide that the best course of action is to search through the silverware drawer for a knife. Finally, actions must be sequenced toward the goal. Only after you find the ingredients—the bread, the peanut butter, and the jelly—as well as the necessary utensil, the knife, do you proceed to make the sandwich.

In describing the construction of a peanut butter and jelly sandwich, we listed a number of skills: staying on task; sequencing, or planning, information; modifying strategies; using knowledge in your plans; and monitoring your actions. We now examine each of these components of goal-oriented behavior and determine how it is affected by brain dysfunction.

• *STAYING ON TASK* •

Probably one of the most basic prerequisites for meeting a goal is the ability to stay on task. Individuals with frontal lobe damage are notorious for not monitoring themselves or their performance, a tendency that manifests most noticeably as "wandering off task." For example, if asked to draw a square, persons with frontal lobe damage may start drawing a square but then begin to incorporate words from a nearby conversation into the drawing without seeming to realize or care that such actions are incompatible with what they set out to do (Luria, 1966). This behavior contrasts with that of individuals with nonfrontal lesions in similar situations. For example, a person whose visuospatial abilities have been compromised by a right posterior lesion will have difficulty drawing the square but will nonetheless continue in the attempt rather than engaging in some irrelevant activity.

Neuroimaging data suggests that dorsolateral prefrontal regions aid in maintaining an **attentional set,** which can be thought of as the process that designates which information is task-relevant. Consider the Stroop task in which one is told to identify the ink color in which a word is printed while ignoring what the word means. In this case, there is an attentional set for determining ink color rather than getting distracted by reading the word. This attentional set is hard to maintain because we read words automatically and it is hard to ignore them. Conversely, if attention should be paid to the word rather than the color, no increased dorsolateral activation is noted. Thus, it appears that prefrontal areas help us stay on task, especially when irrelevant information is particularly distracting (Banich et al., 2000) (see Color insert 11.2).

Additional evidence for the role of the dorsolateral prefrontal cortex in creating an attentional set comes from another Stroop task, similar to the one just described except that on each trial, a precue 1.5 seconds before the actual stimulus indicates whether to report the color information contained in the word or the ink color. The greater the degree of activation in left dorsolateral prefrontal cortex after receiving the color-naming instruction, the smaller is the degree to which a competing color name slows responses (MacDonald, Cohen, Stenger, & Carter, 2000).

• *SEQUENCING* •

One of the basic processes involved in reaching a goal is determining what steps to take to attain the goal, and the order or sequence in which they must occur. Little in life can be accomplished in just one step, and even the most basic functions, such as feeding yourself, require multiple steps. In this section, we review evidence that such sequencing and planning abilities rely mainly on frontal regions. As we discussed in Chapter 5, anterior regions of the brain are important for sequencing movements. Here we learn that they are important for the sequencing of mental thoughts as well.

A basic ability required for sequencing behavior is to know what comes before and what comes after. Compared with individuals who have brain damage in other cortical regions, individuals with frontal lobe damage have difficulty in this arena (B. Milner, 1982). One task that reveals these deficits requires an individual to inspect a series of items, such as line drawings. After the inspection series, test trials, containing two items per card, are shown. On *recognition trials,* the participant must identify which one of the two items was presented in the inspection series. On *recency trials,* the participant must decide which of the two appeared more recently, as both appeared in the inspection series. In this manner, the task can be used to assess both recognition memory ("Which one have you seen before?") and memory for item order ("Which one was seen more recently?") (see Figure 11.5).

These two types of memory are dissociable and rely on different neural substrates. The ability to remember whether an item was presented in the inspection series is disrupted by damage to temporal regions (as you might have expected from Chapter 10). In contrast, the ability to remember the sequence in which information was presented is disrupted by damage to frontal regions, but such damage leaves recognition memory unaffected.

The severity of deficits in remembering item order is affected by which hemisphere is damaged and the nature of the material whose order must be remembered. Left frontal damage results in deficits of remembering the order of presentation of words but relatively little impairment of order for abstract designs or line drawings of common objects. In contrast, right frontal lobe damage creates difficulty in remembering the order of presentation of words and even greater problems with order of abstract designs and line drawings. These results suggest that frontal regions of the right hemisphere play a larger role in recency judgments than left frontal regions, which seem to be involved only when the material is verbal.

In the study just described, the individuals passively watched a sequence of events whose order was controlled by the experimenter. We might want to consider the possibility that these patients' performance might be better if *they* could control the order of events. However, this is not the case. Because the procedure used to assess such abilities, known as the **self-ordered pointing task,** is complicated, we discuss it now in some detail.

In the self-ordered pointing task, individuals are shown an array of items, anywhere from six to twelve, all of which are from the same category (e.g., abstract designs or high-imagery words). Assume for the moment that we are using a six-item array. On each trial, the participant is given six sheets of paper presented sequentially. Although each sheet contains all six items (arranged in a two-by-three matrix), the position of each item in the array varies from sheet to sheet. On each sheet, the participant must point to an item that was not previously chosen. Because a given item appears in a different location on each

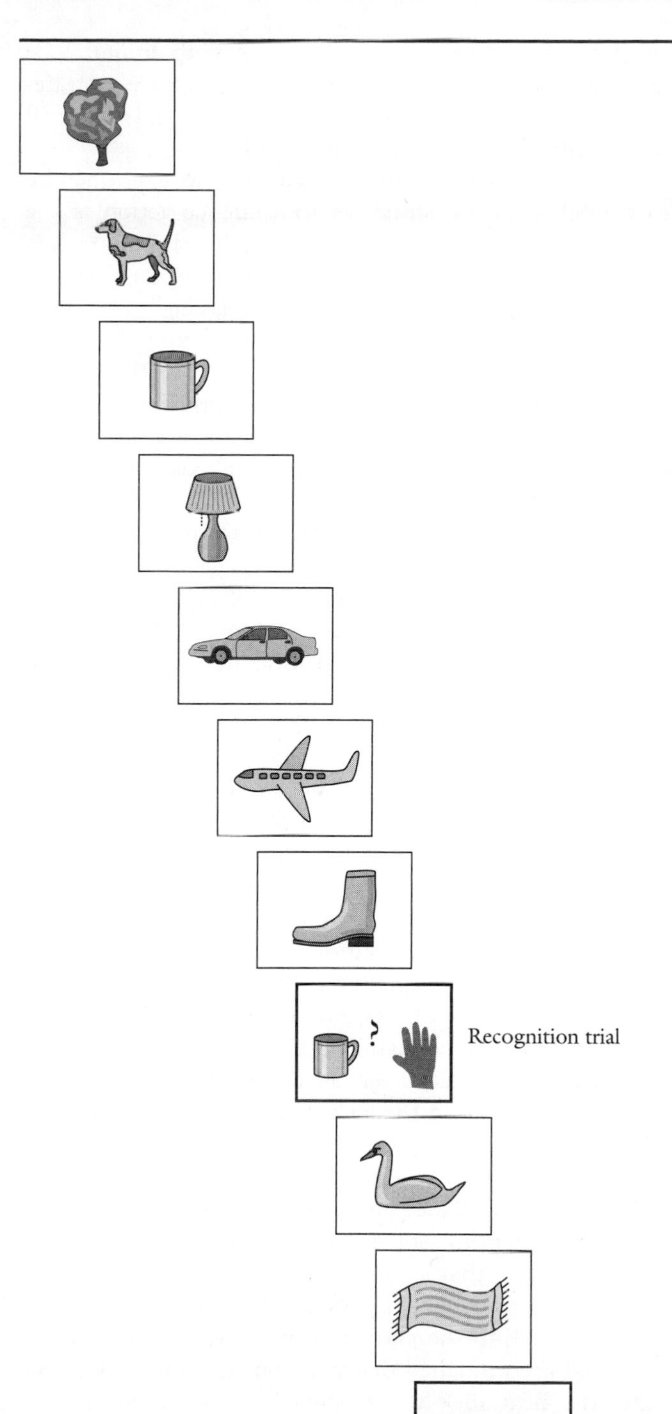

FIGURE 11.5 Example of format of recency judgment task. First, the participant views an inspection series of line drawings. Then, in each trial, the individual must point either to the item that was previously viewed (recognition trial) or to the item viewed more recently (recency trial). Individuals with frontal lobe damage exhibit no difficulties on recognition trials but poor performance on recency trials.

page, the individual must keep track of which items were previously selected (see Figure 11.6). To prevent the person from using strategies that would make the task too easy, examiners do not allow participants to point to the same position on each page (e.g., point to the bottom left-hand item on each page) or in the case of words or items with names, to point to them in alphabetical order (Petrides & Milner, 1982).

Damage to frontal but not temporal regions disrupts performance on this task. However, the regions of the frontal lobe that are important for self-ordered sequencing are different than those needed for recency judgments. For the self-ordered pointing task, deficits are most profound after left frontal lobe damage, whereas for recency judgments, where order is determined by outside forces, deficits are most noticeable after right frontal lobe damage. Damage to left frontal regions may cause the most profound disruptions in the self-ordered version of the task because, as we discussed in the motor control chapter and the chapter on language, the left hemisphere plays a large role in the sequencing of motor behavior.

The frontal lobes may contribute to the self-ordered pointing task and the recency-judgment task not only because these tasks involve sequencing, but also because they require working memory. As we have learned previously, working memory is used to keep information online to control behavior and as a sort of mental scratch pad during everyday actions. Working memory is important in the self-ordered pointing task because the person must keep track of which items have been pointed to and which remain to be selected. Likewise, the recency- judgment task requires an individual to keep information online in working memory so as to maintain information about the order in which events occurred. In fact, damage to lateral regions of the frontal lobe, which has been implicated in working memory, disrupts recency judgments more than damage to other regions of the frontal cortex (B. Milner, Corsi, & Leonard, 1991).

Thus far, we have discussed sequencing abilities from two perspectives: being able to appreciate the sequence in which events occur and being able to generate sequential behavior. Another important aspect of sequencing behavior is the ability to choose which sequence or strategy best allows a goal to be attained. Compared with individuals with damage to other brain regions, patients with frontal lobe damage are less likely to report that they use strategies, and when a strategy is used, it tends to be ill defined or invoked inconsistently.

One task designed specifically to examine the ability to use strategies to sequence action is the Tower of London task (Shallice, 1982). This task is shown in Figure 11.7. The apparatus for the task consists of three prongs of varying height and three colored balls with holes that allow them to be placed on the prongs. The first prong can hold three balls, the second can hold two, and the last can hold only one. The task requires the individual to move the balls, one at a time, from an initial position to a target configuration in as few moves as possible while keeping in mind the constraints imposed by the height of each prong.

Individuals with frontal lobe damage, most notably in the left hemisphere, are both inefficient and ineffective at performing this task (Shallice, 1982). They are inefficient because they take many moves to reach the end position and are ineffective because they engage in behaviors that are aimless rather than directed toward the goal.

Corroborative evidence for the role of frontal regions in the Tower of London task comes from experiments measuring regional blood flow by means of single photon emission computed tomography (SPECT) in neurologically intact individuals performing a computerized touch-screen version of the task (R. G. Morris, Ahmed, Syed, & Toone, 1993). To explicitly examine the planning-sequencing aspect, the researchers asked individuals to perform two versions of the task that were identical in their sensorimotor requirements but differed in the degree to which they required planning. In the first, or control, version, the person was passively guided by the computer to solve the puzzle. An X marked each disk that should be moved, and after the individual touched the disk, the computer moved the disk to the correct position. When the individual then touched that position, an X appeared over the next disk to be moved. In the experimental condition, the individual saw the same displays and made the same movements, except he or she had to plan the sequence of the moves (rather than being guided by the computer). Greater activation was observed in left prefrontal regions when participants

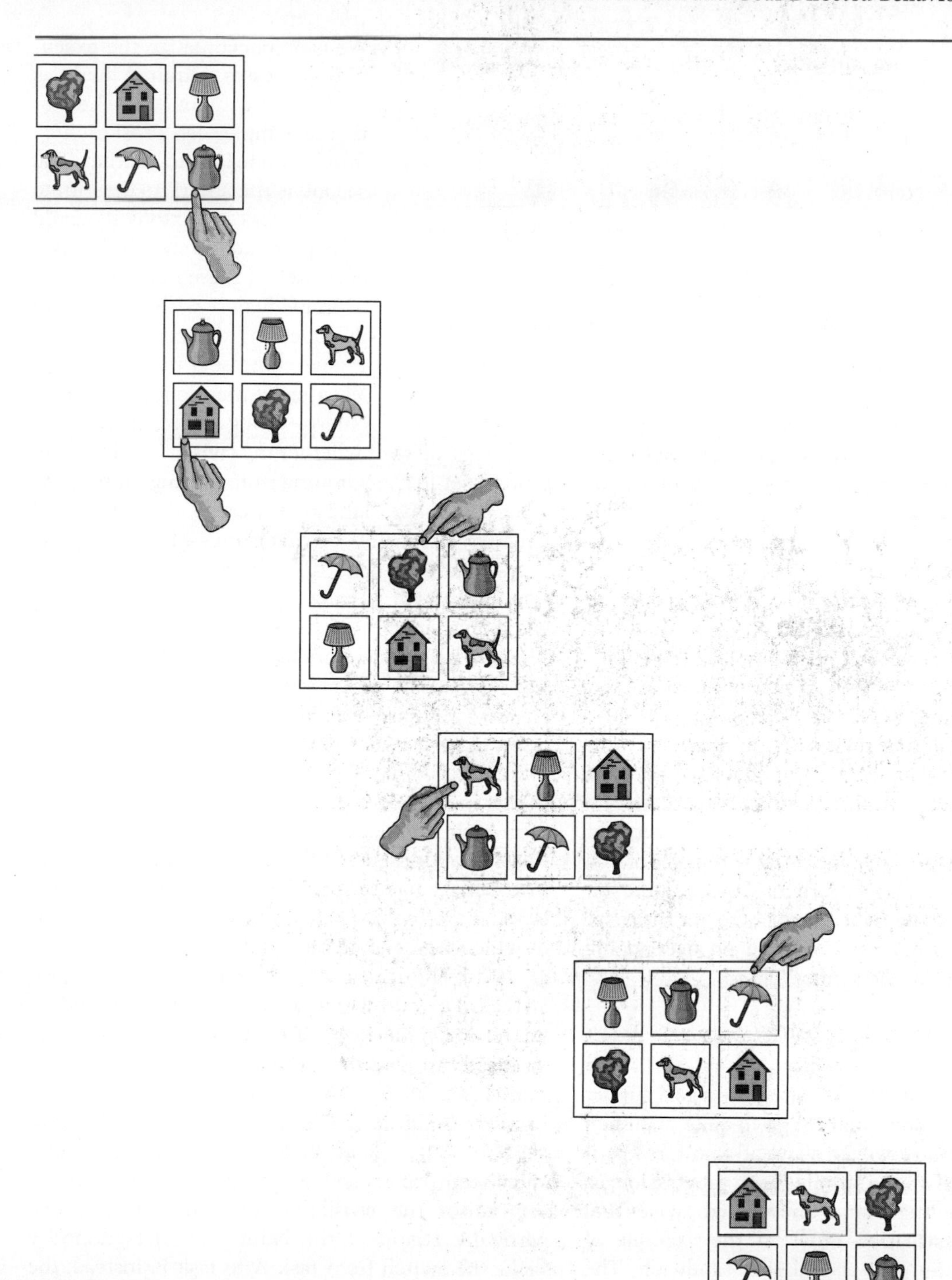

FIGURE 11.6 Example of correct performance on six-item self-ordered pointing task. The person must point to a different item on each page, and the position of each picture varies from page to page.

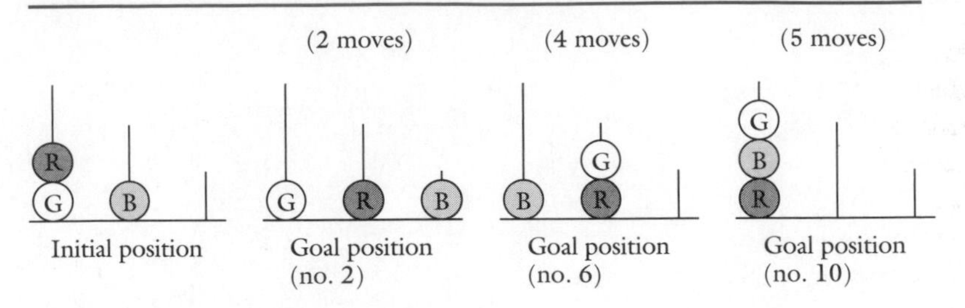

FIGURE 11.7 Example of three problems in Tower of London task. The same initial position is used in each problem. The balls must be moved to the goal position one at a time in as few moves as possible. The number of moves required to reach each goal is noted. R, red; G, green; B, blue.

had to actively plan the moves than when they were passively guided. Furthermore, the *degree* of activation of these regions in the experimental condition relative to the control condition predicted how well an individual performed the task. The individuals who solved the puzzle in fewer moves exhibited greater activation of left prefrontal areas than the participants who took longer. Thus, this study provides converging evidence for the role of frontal regions in planning sequential behavior.

In this section, we reviewed the many ways in which the conceptualization, understanding, and production of sequential behavior are disrupted by frontal lobe damage. Even though some aspects of sequencing depend more on frontal regions of the left hemisphere, whereas others depend more on frontal regions of the right hemisphere, for the most part, these skills appear to depend on overlapping neural structures in the frontal lobes.

• *SHIFTING SET AND MODIFYING STRATEGIES* •

So far we have presumed that attaining a goal simply requires determining what steps to take and then performing them. However, as we all know, the path to a goal is not always a simple linear progression, as we often encounter some unexpected twists and turns. Such a situation arose in the example of preparing a peanut butter and jelly sandwich. The plan called for retrieving the jelly from the top shelf of the refrigerator, but, alas, the jelly was not there. At this point, a modification of strategy, or a deviation from a previously invoked plan, was necessary. We can conceptualize the executive processes required here as having two components. The first is the simple *act of switching* from any one task to another. The second is the ability to determine to what task or actions it would be appropriate to switch. We discuss each of these in turn.

Individuals with executive dysfunction exhibit difficulties in switching sets in many ways. We already mentioned some that emerge during sorting tasks. These occur regardless of whether the switch involves conceptual set (e.g., switching from sorting animals by where they live, land or water, to their degree of ferocity, domestic or dangerous—Delis, Squire, Bihrle, & Massman, 1992) or perceptual set (e.g., switching from sorting based on color to sorting based on shape).

Evidence from neurologically intact individuals suggests that switching between two tasks is not easy for anyone. It is easier to keep doing what you are doing than to switch from one task to another. Task switching is directed by an executive control system that is independent of the systems that actually perform each task (e.g., Allport, Styles, & Hsieh, 1992; Rogers & Monsell, 1995). Patients with left frontal lobe damage have a specific deficit in task switching, especially when there are no strong or obvious cues as to which task should be performed when (Rogers et al., 1998). The critical role of prefrontal regions in task switching is corroborated by brain imaging studies. Interestingly, however, these studies do not converge in suggesting that one particular portion of the prefrontal region is critical (e.g., Dove et al., 2000; Kimberg, Aguirre, & D'Esposito, 2000; Nagahama et al., 2001; Rogers et al., 2000). Rather, the region activated seems to depend on task demands. Such a pattern raises the possibility that there is not one particular region of the brain that metaphorically flicks the switch from task A to task B. Instead, the brain region critical for the shift may vary with task demands. But set switching usually involves inhibiting a prior response. Thus, it is not surprising that during set shifting, activation is seen in the same ventral and inferior prefrontal regions as in inhibiting a response (Konishi et al., 1999).

The degree of difficulty that individuals with frontal lobe damage have in making a shift depends, in part, on the nature of the shift. Look at the task illustrated in Figure 11.8, which was originally designed for use with animals. Individuals are first taught to discriminate between two items (e.g., two black shapes) and to respond to only one of them (Figure 11.8A). Then another dimension is added to the items (e.g., a simple white line pattern), which is to be ignored (Figure 11.8B). At this point, new stimuli consisting of novel shapes and novel white line patterns are introduced. In one condition, the intradimensional shift condition, the discrimination is to be made solely on the basis of the same dimension used previously (e.g., on the basis of the black shapes while ignoring the white line pattern) (Figure 11.8C). In the other, the extradimensional shift condition, the participants must respond to the dimension that was previously ignored (e.g., the white line patterns) (Figure 11.8D).

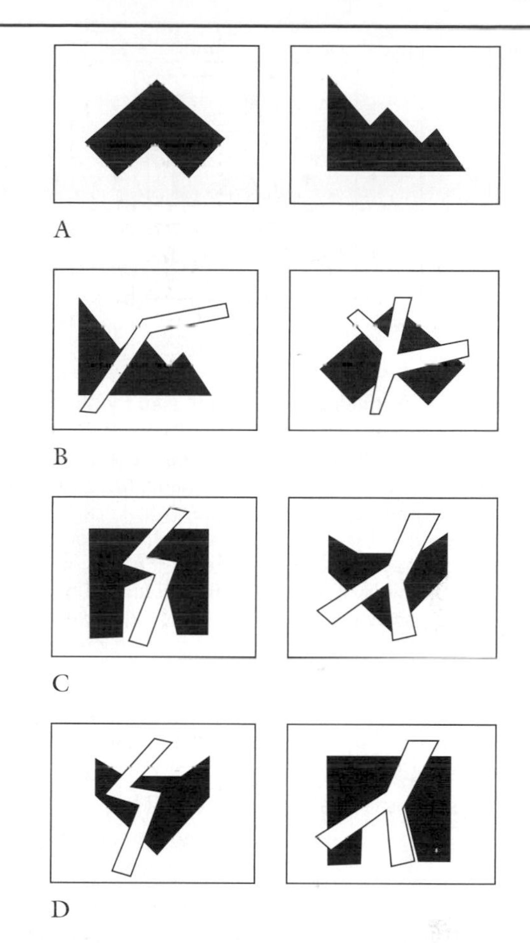

FIGURE 11.8 Examples of different types of conceptual shifts. (A) In simple discrimination, an individual must simply learn to discriminate between two black shapes. (B) Compound discrimination requires ignoring the white shapes and responding just on the basis of the black shapes. (C) In the intradimensional shift condition, the person must learn to discriminate between the two new black shapes while continuing to ignore the white shapes. (D) In the extradimensional shift condition, the person must discriminate between the two white shapes, which is a feature that was previously ignored. Individuals with frontal lobe damage have difficulty with this extradimensional shift.

Compared with patients who have temporal lobe lesions and with neurologically intact individuals, patients with frontal lobe damage are deficient at the extradimensional shift but not at the intradimensional shift (Owen et al., 1991). If a new strategy is similar enough to the old one, performance is unimpaired. However, patients with executive dysfunction are deficient in their ability to generalize rules to situations that are dissimilar from those in which the rules were originally learned. This difficulty may, in part, explain why individuals with executive dysfunction have difficulty on the WCST. They are unable to make the extradimensional shifts between color, form, and number.

Reminiscent of the perseverative problems we discussed earlier, patients with executive dysfunction may have difficulty switching sets because they cannot generate alternative plans of action, or because they become "locked" into one way of dealing with information, which precludes discovery of alternative responses. This phenomenon can be illustrated with the task shown in Figure 11.9, in which the individual is to choose one of the two items shown on every trial in order to deduce the correct dimension on which the items should be selected (e.g., always select the black item). Each item can be characterized on four dimensions (whether the item is black or white, large or small, an X or a T, and to the left or to the right). A pretest is given to ensure that the individual has the conceptual skills to discover the rule for the problem's

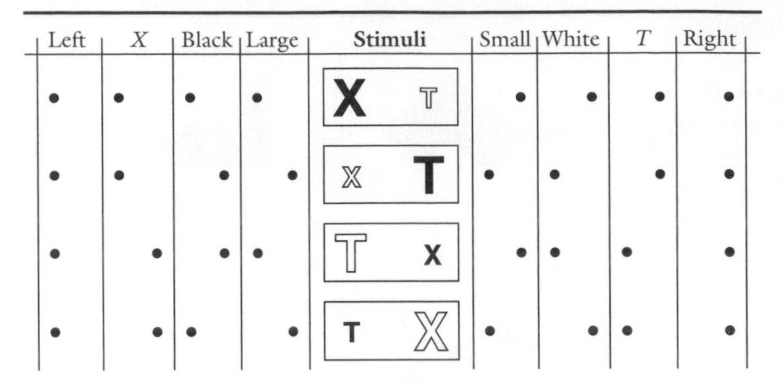

FIGURE 11.9 Examples of the stimuli used by Cicerone, Lazar, and Shapiro (1983). Each item on a card (under the Stimuli column) can be classified according to four variables: its position (left, right), its identity (*X*, *T*), its color (black, white), and its size (large, small). Individuals must deduce, or hypothesize, which one of the variables is important (e.g., letter name but not color, size, or position) and then the item that they should choose (e.g., the *X*s but not the *T*s). The position of the circle (left, right) within each column indicates which of the two items would be chosen to be consistent with the hypothesized critical feature listed at the top of the column.

solution on the basis of the examiner's feedback as to whether each choice is correct or incorrect. Only afterwards do the test trials begin. These are used to examine the generation of strategies and the switching of hypotheses (Cicerone, Lazar, & Shapiro, 1983). Patients with frontal lobe damage have difficulty forming a strategy for performing the task because they use fewer appropriate hypotheses than patients with damage to posterior brain regions do.

Moreover, they may focus on an incorrect hypothesis even though enough information has accrued to eliminate it as a possibility. They may be unable to switch to a new hypothesis because once they decide that a particular attribute is salient, their "tunnel vision" keeps them from switching their focus to another attribute that might lead to the correct solution (Cicerone, Lazar, & Shapiro, 1983).

The tendency of individuals with frontal lobe damage to start down a particular path and not consider alternative solutions is demonstrated by another task in which a series of items, such as words or pictures, must be ordered (Della Malva, Stuss, D'Alton, & Willmer, 1993). In this task, two types of trials are used. In one type of trial, two items that form a common association are presented in succession and needn't be separated to form a valid sequence. An example is "sky/the/lit/*full*/*moon*/a," which should be ordered to read "A *full moon* lit the sky." In the other type of trial, the associated items must be separated, as in the set "of/full/the/was/*coffee*/*cup*," in which *coffee* and *cup* must be moved to correctly order the sentence to read "The *cup* was full of *coffee*." Although patients with frontal lobe damage have no trouble ordering the sentence when the associated words do not need to be separated, the association of two related words appears to prevent them from successfully generating a valid reordering of the words when they must be separated.

In other situations, patients with frontal lobe damage appear to follow through on an appropriate hypothesis only to abandon it later. For example, in a case described by Grafman, Sirigu, Spector, and Hendler (1993), a patient was asked to play the game Twenty Questions, in which the player attempts to determine the object about which another individual is thinking by asking 20 or fewer yes/no questions. In this case, the object was the motor vehicle "tank." The patient had already determined that the object was inanimate and a vehicle. Yet after guessing a series of vehicle names, he suddenly stopped and asked if the object was an animal.

• *USING INFORMATION ABOUT CONTINGENCIES TO GUIDE BEHAVIOR* •

The effective and efficient attainment of a goal often requires available information to be evaluated so that the appropriate strategy for a given situation can be selected. One set of conditions may favor one strategy, whereas a different set of conditions may favor an alternative strategy. In at least some cases, individuals with frontal lobe damage do not use information that would enable them to effectively guide subsequent action. One such example comes from a study in which participants decided whether a letter that could be in various degrees of rotation

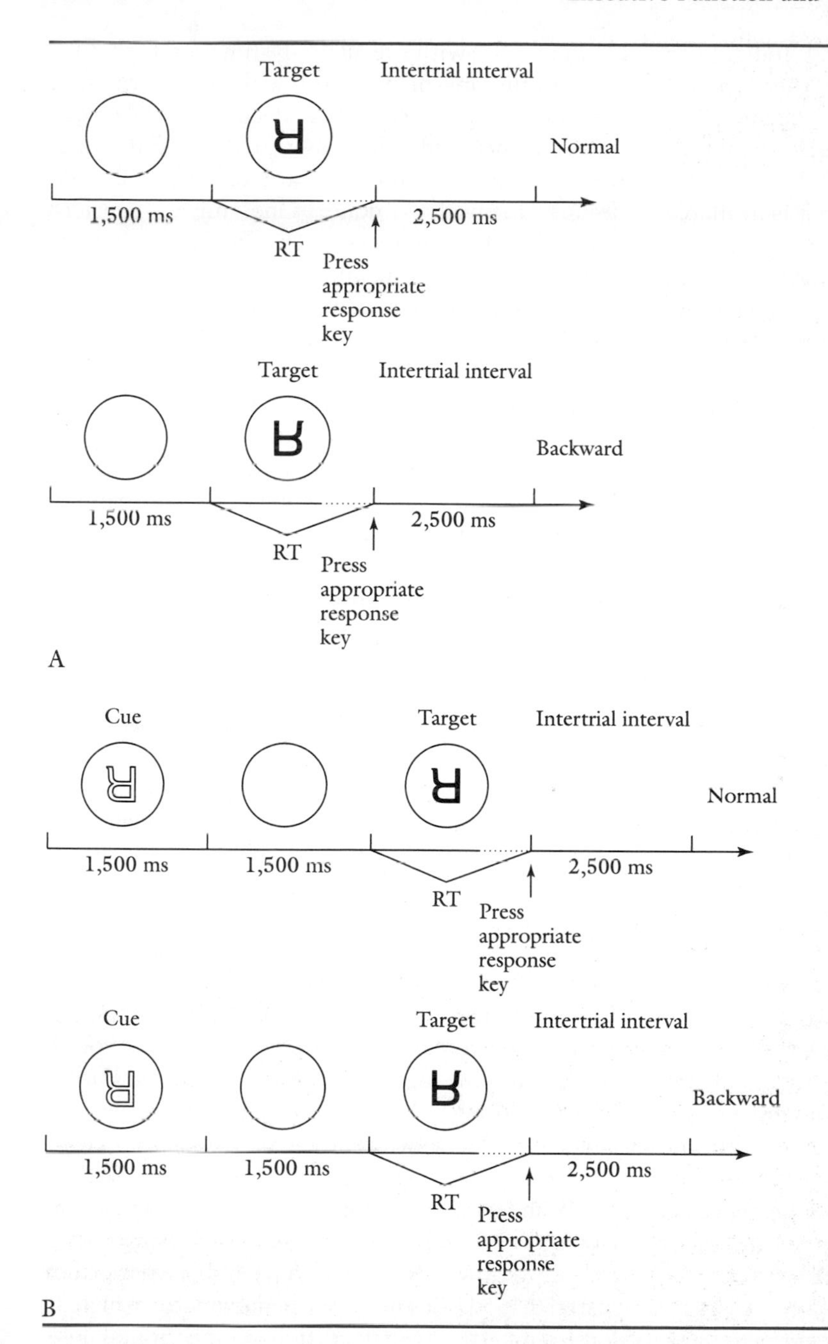

FIGURE 11.10 Example of an advance information paradigm. (A) In the standard (no-information) condition, the individual must decide whether the target item is in its normal orientation (top row) or is backward (bottom row). In general, the more the item is rotated from upright, the longer an individual takes to respond because he or she must rotate the letter mentally before answering. (B) In the advance-information condition, a cue that is always in the normal orientation is given, followed after by a brief delay by a target. This cue makes mental rotation unnecessary. If the cue and the target have identical orientations (top row), the individual should know immediately that the target is in the normal orientation, whereas if they have different orientations (bottom row), the individual should know that the target is in its mirror-image (backward) orientation. Individuals with frontal lobe damage do not use such information but instead continue to rotate the target letter mentally to reach their decision. RT, reaction time.

from upright was in the normal or mirror-image orientation. In one condition no precue was given and the individual had to mentally rotate the item to upright to make the decision. The other condition contained a precue that if paid attention to, precluded the need to mentally rotate the item (see Figure 11.10). Thus, if the participant was using the precue effectively, the degree of rotation of the item would no longer predict the speed of a response.

Although patients with temporal lobe lesions and neurologically intact subjects used the cue to avoid mental rotation of the letter, individuals with frontal lobe damage did not (Alivisatos, 1992). Individuals with frontal lobe damage do not use other types of cues either, such as those that indicate the position in space at which a target will subsequently appear (Alivisatos & Milner, 1989). Hence, they frequently appear not to use extra information that is available in their environment that would allow them to effectively plan and guide their behavior.

Another situation in which contingencies must be taken into account occurs when subgoals are embedded within a hierarchy. For example, one might be fixing dinner and the phone might ring. You need to answer the phone to deal with that subgoal while at the same time maintaining the goal of fixing dinner. Thus, as you are engaged in the phone conversation, you are likely to have to maintain the process of making dinner. Notice that this is somewhat different from task switching. It is not that you are engaged in making dinner, finish that process, and then switch to a phone conversation. Rather, here the processes are interleaved. You may be chopping vegetables, then greet the person on the other end of the line, switch to heating butter in a skillet to sauté the vegetables, and then commence talking about your latest romantic adventure. Notice that this interleaving of subgoals requires two tasks to be performed in succession, similar to task switching, as well as holding information over a delay (remembering what was last said before starting to the sauté the vegetables). Neuroimaging has been used to isolate those regions that are specific to this ability to handle hierarchical subgoals. To do so, activation requiring hierarchical subgoals was compared against two baseline conditions, one in which a task switch occurred but without retention of information during a delay, and another in which information had to be retained, but without a task switch. This comparison revealed activation in the most anterior regions of the prefrontal cortex, the orbitofrontal region (Koechlin et al., 1999).

• *SELF-MONITORING* •

The last skill we discuss that is important for attaining a goal is the ability to evaluate whether your performance is actually bringing you closer to your goal. Stated more simply, it is the ability to accurately answer the question, "How am I doing?"

Individuals with executive dysfunction have difficulty evaluating or monitoring their performance. For example, given cards that need to be rearranged in a sequence, individuals with executive dysfunction may simply move a card or two and then declare themselves done. One might consider whether lack of motivation or concern about their performance level accounts for some of these difficulties, especially considering the changes in emotional processing that accompany frontal lobe damage (which we discuss in Chapter 12). Lack of motivation, however, is unlikely to be the sole explanation for these difficulties because, as discussed earlier, in some situations patients verbally declare that they should do something but then fail to follow through. The verbal declarations provide some evidence that the individual is actually engaged by the task and has a degree of interest in reaching the goal. However, the ability to monitor performance or to specifically translate that idea into action is disrupted.

Another critical aspect of monitoring one's performance is detecting when one has erred. We appear to have a particular brain mechanism that helps monitor for errors. Evidence for such a mechanism comes from an ERP signal known as the **error-related negativity (ERN).** This component occurs approximately 100 ms after an error has been made (Gehring et al., 1993) (see Figure 11.11). It has been specifically linked to error monitoring because its amplitude increases under conditions in which accuracy of response is emphasized versus speed, and because the larger the error (pushing the button with the wrong hand as well as the wrong finger), the larger the amplitude of the ERN.

Dipole modeling (Dehaene, Posne, & Tucker, 1994) and neuroimaging studies (Kiehl, Liddle, & Hopfinger, 2000), suggest that this component, causally known as the "blunder blip," arises from rostral regions of the anterior cingulate, which is located on the medial portion of the frontal lobe (refer back to Color insert 5.1B). The region of the cingulate that is involved in error detection is distinct from that involved in inhibiting responses or selecting among responses.

The exact role of the cingulate with regard to error processing is currently a matter of debate. One

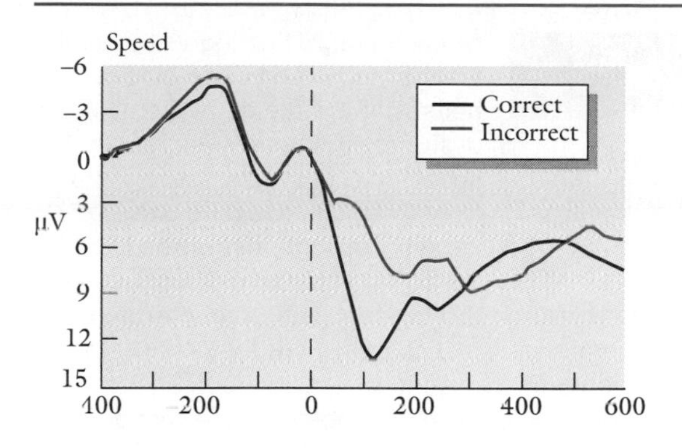

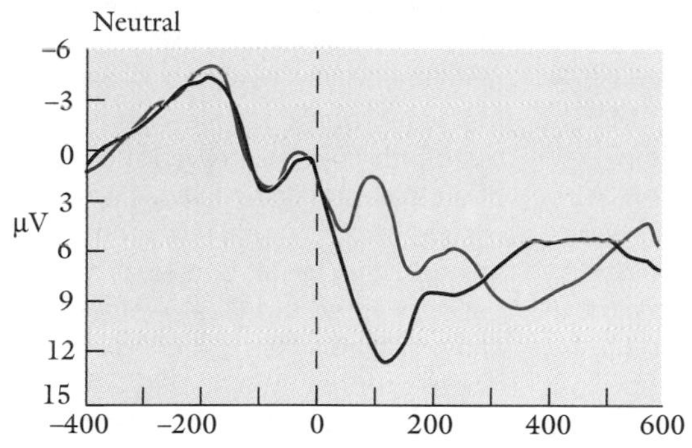

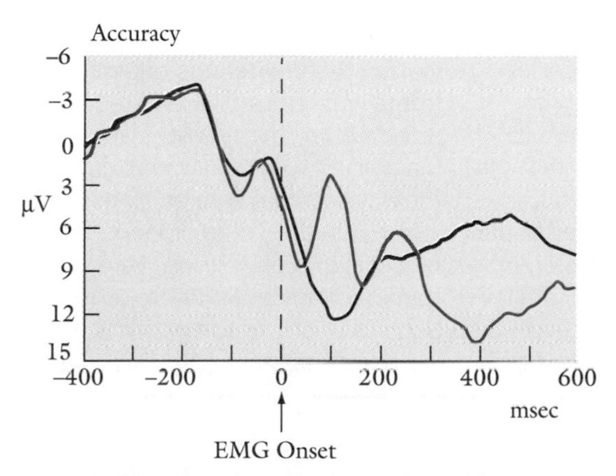

FIGURE 11.11 The error-related negativity (ERN). In these graphs negative electrical potentials are plotted on the upper portions of the graphs and positive potentials are on the lower portions. Notice that the response to errors (shown in blue) peaks about 100 milliseconds after the beginning of the muscles' movement (as denoted by EMG onset). Also notice that the size of the ERN is much greater when accuracy is stressed (bottom panel) as compared to speed (top panel).

viewpoint is that the cingulate actually detects errors (e.g., Scheffers et al., 1996). Another is that the cingulate monitors for conflict, and thus it is active during error detection because error detection usually occurs when there is conflicting information (e.g., Carter et al., 1998). Still another viewpoint argues that lateral prefrontal regions determine the need for control, while the cingulate implements that control (Posner & DiGirolamo, 1998). Obviously, the implementation of control would go awry when an error is made.

Evidence from patients with lesions in prefrontal cortex suggests that the anterior cingulate does not act alone in detecting errors. Patients with such damage show as large an ERN to correct trials as they do to incorrect trials. Furthermore, their behavior suggests poor monitoring of errors. Often, in reaction-time tasks, people know when they've made an error and go on to press another button, a self-corrective action. Furthermore, the force with which a response is made is usually less on error trials, as if the system is detecting conflict and "holding back" a bit. Patients with damage to lateral PFC exhibited neither of these traits when making errors (Gehring & Knight, 2000). Thus, these findings suggest that interactions between prefrontal regions and the anterior cingulate are important in the monitoring of action and detection of errors.

Before we leave our discussion of this topic, it is worth noting that some people have argued that the ERN really reflects the subjective evaluation of performance ("Oh damn, I think I just messed up") rather than whether you did indeed make an error. Support of such a viewpoint comes from findings that an ERN-like component, albeit of smaller amplitude, can be detected on correct trials (Vidal, Hasbroucq, Grapperon, & Bonnet, 2000), that the amplitude of the ERN is influenced by mood, such as high levels of subjective distress (Luu, Collins, & Tucker, 2000), and that the size of the ERN increases the longer a person delays in responding after a deadline (Luu, Flaisch, & Tucker, 2000).

 Theories of Frontal Lobe Function in Executive Control

So far in this chapter we have reviewed the many types of difficulties in executive functions that can occur after frontal lobe damage. We now turn our attention to the issue of whether any general conceptual framework exists that can help us to understand this diversity. Although we do not

FRONTAL LOBOTOMY AS A "CURE" FOR SCHIZOPHRENIA

In the 1930s, 1940s, and 1950s, frontal lobotomy was touted as a procedure to cure schizophrenia and other mental disorders. The history of the extensive use of this procedure is shameful but worth discussing because it provides useful lessons about the ethics of research with human participants and the methods used for evaluating the efficacy of new types of therapies.

Scientists often find that knowledge gained in animal studies is invaluable in their understanding of the human brain and in the design of new therapies. However, in the case of frontal lobotomy, this transfer of information from animals to humans ran amuck as a result of the ambitions of Egas Moniz, a Portuguese neurologist. Attending a conference in 1935, Moniz heard about a case study in which frontal lobectomy had made one of two chimpanzees tamer and less belligerent. Because psychiatrists were having minimal success in treating schizophrenia, Moniz was intrigued by this finding. Just three months later, Moniz, with little or no sound theoretical basis but this single case report, began performing bilateral frontal lobectomies on humans as a cure for schizophrenia. Compounding the problem was Moniz's seriously flawed method for evaluating the success of his operations. He examined his patients between 11 days and 2 months postoperatively—a time frame in which the generalized effects of brain trauma such as edema (swelling) are often still present. Thus, although Moniz observed reduced agitation in his patients, it probably reflected a groggy and stuporous state resulting from the brain surgery, not a cure induced by the specific removal of frontal tissue. Moniz's grand claims about his informal and poorly controlled studies led him to win the Nobel Prize in 1949 for "his discovery of the therapeutic value of prefrontal leukotomy in certain psychoses." Awarding this prize to Moniz has to rank up there as one of the worst decisions that the Swedish Academy ever made.

The rationale provided for frontal lobectomies was that delusions (e.g., thinking that Martians are broadcasting messages to earthlings through your brain) and hallucinations (e.g., hearing voices that are commanding you to burn down houses) were fueled by frontal lobe dysfunction. It was reasoned that such behavior would cease if the frontal regions could be disconnected from the rest of the brain. Today we know that disconnecting the frontal lobes is counterproductive. Not only are they critical for executive function, but, as we will learn in Chapter 12, they are actually *underactive,* not overactive, in patients with schizophrenia. Not only was this reasoning flawed, but medical professionals earlier in the twentieth century viewed the lack of an initiation of behavior that resulted from frontal lobectomy as a positive result because the patients acted out less. We now know that this lack of behavior doesn't represent a solution but is instead indicative of a problem in executive control.

Naturally, the question arises as to why the deleterious effects of frontal lobectomy weren't recognized earlier. The answers are many. First, psychiatry was groping for ways to deal with an illness for which it had no cure. Patients, their families, and physicians were all frantic for any possible treatment. Second, many of the patients were wards of the state, which meant

resolve this issue with a simple solution, we discuss some major approaches to conceptualizing the role of frontal regions in executive function. The premise of the first approach is that the dorsolateral prefrontal cortex is critical for working memory. Deficits in working memory preclude sequential analysis and the organization of behavior toward a goal. The underlying assumption of the second approach is that there are two ways to control behavior, one that is relatively automatic and one that is more controlled. Frontal lobe damage is believed to specifically disrupt the controlled processes. According to a third approach, the frontal lobes allow for complex behavior because they store memories for scripts that indicate the conditions under which actions should occur, the organization of those actions, and the end state that indicates those actions should cease. Damage to frontal areas leads to loss of these scripts and thus to executive dysfunction. A fourth approach, influenced by work in artificial intelligence, machine learning and computational modeling, suggests that frontal regions

that family members didn't need to be consulted prior to the procedure and often weren't around to provide impressions of their relative's postoperative state. Third, a neurologist in the United States, Walter Freeman—who was thought to be knowledgeable because he was associated with the most famous U.S. military psychiatric hospital, St. Elizabeth's—took it upon himself to proselytize the use of frontal lobotomy as he practiced it. The technique was barbaric, so you might want to brace yourself for the description that follows. To avoid the use of anesthetics, Freeman administered electroshock to the patient, which would rack the person's body with convulsions until consciousness was lost. At this point, Freeman gained access to the brain through the eye socket, using a specifically designed tool that he slipped between the eyeball and the skull. Then, by moving a blunt scalpel back and forth, he destroyed frontal tissue. The entire procedure could be performed in 15 minutes. Because of these factors, many years passed before the uselessness of frontal lobotomy became apparent (a longer and very readable account of this and other misuses of psychosurgery is provided by Valenstein, 1986).

What did result, however, from this unfortunate period in the annals of psychiatry was a much greater sensitivity to the notion of the rights of individuals who participate in experiments and better methods of experimental design to evaluate if an experimental treatment is an effective therapy. Today, in the United States and elsewhere, government-mandated and regulated procedures must be used to obtain consent for participation in an experimental procedure of any sort, whether it is a simple study of behavior or clinical trials for a new medical therapy. These rules state explicitly that a person cannot be coerced into participation and that individuals must be informed not only of a study's potential benefits, but of all its possible risks as well. In addition, researchers must follow special guidelines for including individuals who may have difficulty understanding the notion of voluntary consent, such as individuals with a psychiatric illness, brain damage, or mental retardation. In terms of evaluating a new therapy, the status of individuals who receive treatment generally is compared with that of those who receive no treatment. To prevent any experimenter bias, a researcher who is "blind," not knowing whether a given participant is in the treatment group or not, evaluates that person's performance or responses. Furthermore, a therapy's efficacy must be proved on a small sample of individuals before trials with a larger population can begin.

These government rules are enforced at the local level of the university or hospital where the experiment occurs by a Human Subjects Rights committee. The members of this committee are not only scientists and medical professionals, but also ethicists, members of the community and clergy. This committee may also enlist the help of other members of the community to aid them, such as having students in high-school English classes review consent forms to ensure that they are written in plain language and are not filled with jargon. The panel reviews experiments and consent procedures to make certain that they meet the government guidelines, which were created with the goal of ensuring that situations such as those surrounding frontal lobectomy never occur again. ■

modulate behavior in service of attaining goals based on the situation at hand. Proponents of this approach posit that frontal lobe damage prevents such modulation from occurring.

All these approaches need not be mutually exclusive, and each may shed light on how to conceptualize the role of the frontal lobes in executive functioning. As you read each theory, you may find it instructive to pause for a moment and evaluate it. You might, for example, want to consider how well each theory can explain Dr. P.'s problems.

■ Role of Working Memory

As we discussed in the last chapter, much converging evidence from monkeys and humans has demonstrated that dorsolateral prefrontal cortex is critical for working memory. The disruption of this underlying fundamental function of the prefrontal cortex may explain some of the deficits seen in executive function. To better understand the linkage between working memory and executive function, let's briefly review some of the characteristics of working memory. As discussed in Chapters 7 and

10, working memory is a limited-capacity system that keeps information online for use in performing a task. It allows us to retain about seven items for short time periods (e.g., 10 seconds). Working memory is to be distinguished from long-term memory, which is believed to be important for storing material for later retrieval. An extensive series of research performed on monkeys has documented the critical role of dorsolateral prefrontal cortex in different types of working memory, including that for spatial locations and objects (Goldman-Rakic, 1998). Neuroimaging with humans confirms the important role of these regions not only for these forms of object and spatial working memory, but for verbal short-term memory as well (Smith & Jonides, 1999).

How might difficulties in working memory account for some of the deficits in executive functioning? First, such difficulties may interfere with the ability to keep a goal in mind and thus with a person's ability to direct behavior toward a goal or to formulate a strategy that allows the goal to be attained. Second, difficulty in keeping information online may disrupt a person's understanding of temporal relations between items and events. If what has just happened cannot be kept online, its relation to subsequent happenings will be lost. In such cases, advance information that can aid in solving problems will be of little use, and deficits in self-ordering and recency judgments will also occur. Third, because of a lack of working memory, behavior may be driven by the immediate stimuli in the environment or by recently rewarded behavior, which may explain some aspects of environmental dependency and perseveration observed in patients with frontal lobe damage. Accordingly, difficulties in working memory may account for a number of the difficulties that are observed in cases of executive dysfunction (for a computational model demonstrating that a disruption in working memory can lead to deficits on four tasks on which patients with frontal lobe damage have difficulty, such as the WCST, see Kimberg & Farah, 1993).

Role of Controlled versus Automatic Processes

Two classic theories (Shallice, 1982; Stuss & Benson, 1986) emphasize the role of the frontal lobes as critical for more controlled processing as compared to automatic processing. We first discuss the model of Shallice (1982). He suggests that a two-pronged system influences the choice of behavior. One part, **contention scheduling,** is a cognitive system that allows for relatively automatic processing. This automaticity is engendered over time with learning. Stimuli or situations become linked to actions, routines, or processing schemes, and then groups of these routines become linked to one another. In this manner, a single stimulus may result in a relatively automatic string of actions, just as seeing a red light when you are driving automatically causes a series of actions. Once any action is initiated by this system, it continues to be active until inhibited by a mutually incompatible process. The other part, the **supervisory attentional system,** is the cognitive system required to effortfully direct attention and guide action through decision processes. It is active only in certain situations: when no processing schemes are available as in novel situations, when the task is technically difficult, when problem solving is required, and when certain response tendencies must be overcome. Although initially thought of as a unitary system, it has been more recently thought to have different parts that provide top-down control of different processes, such as monitoring the levels of activity in different processing schemas, energizing certain schemas, and inhibiting particular schemas (for a recent discussion of this class of model, see Stuss, Shallice, Alexander, & Picton, 1995).

According to this theory, frontal lobe damage disables the supervisory attentional system and thereby leaves actions to be governed totally by contention scheduling, a situation that has a number of implications. First, it means that individuals with frontal lobe damage will show few deficits, if any, in fairly routine situations in which the appropriate response is evoked by a stimulus in a simple and obvious way. So, for example, their performance is the same as that of neurologically intact people on many tests assessed in a standard IQ battery, because these tasks, such as providing a definition for a word, are often familiar and well practiced. However, when a situation is novel or requires flexibility, people with frontal lobe damage fail to respond appropriately because no schema is available in contention scheduling.

Second, these individuals will appear to act impulsively because their behavior is triggered by stimuli in the environment. For example, upon seeing a pen on a desk, they may pick it up and begin to write. This action occurs because over time one learns that a desk with writing implements on them are linked to certain actions—picking up the implements and using them to write—and when the supervisory attentional system is lost, the typical schemes of contention scheduling are invoked automatically.

Third, this theory explains why individuals with frontal lobe damage often perseverate. Once a strong trigger activates a scheme or an action, this process will continue to be invoked until some mutually incompatible process is activated. Without the supervisory attentional system, iterative actions triggered by contention scheduling are difficult to interrupt, resulting in perseveration.

Like Shallice's theory, the theory of Stuss and Benson (1986) suggests that the frontal lobes are especially important in regulating behavior in nonroutine situations or in situations when behavior must be carefully constrained. Their model links the degree of control to particular neural substrates in a hierarchical manner. At the lowest level, sensory information and simple tasks are processed by posterior regions of the brain in a relatively automatic manner that varies little from day to day. Processing of such information is difficult to control consciously. The next level of control is associated with the executive, or supervisory, functions of the frontal lobe. At this level, lower-level sensory information is adjusted so that behavior can be guided toward a goal. Control of behavior is effortful and slow and requires conscious control. The highest level of control involves self-reflection and metacognition. Self-reflection allows an individual to have self-awareness and to understand the relationship of the self to the environment, while metacognition is the ability to reflect upon a process. Such a level allows for an abstract mental representation of the world and the way one chooses to act in the world. This process is considered to be under control of the prefrontal cortex.

Clearly, such a model can explain deficits in goal-oriented behavior, because it posits that organizing such behaviors is one of the main functions of frontal regions. It can also explain deficits in dealing with novelty and lack of cognitive flexibility because the frontal lobes are assumed to be important for nonautomatic behavior. This account can also explain why damage to frontal regions produces the *environmental dependency syndrome*. The syndrome would occur because responses to sensory stimuli would be automatic. The model could also explain the inability to consciously control action because these functions would be compromised by frontal lobe damage. Finally, the inability to self criticize or self monitor could be explained by this model as resulting from prefrontal region damage, which would leave patients devoid of any ability to reflect upon themselves or the processes in which they become engaged.

Use of Scripts

Another approach to understanding the role of the frontal lobes in executive function borrows from work examining how individuals represent stories or events in their lives. According to this viewpoint, knowledge is organized into a set of events, actions, or ideas that are linked to form a unit of knowledge often referred to as a script (schema) (e.g., Schank, 1982). In this theory, managerial knowledge units (MKUs) are memories that are stored in prefrontal cortex and contain information on how to perform, use, or manage simple actions that have a single unifying theme (e.g., paying a bill). In general, an MKU specifics information about the setting in which such an event occurs, the set of events that must occur to achieve the goal, and the end event that terminates the action. Furthermore, these MKUs are organized hierarchically (Grafman, 1989). At the top of the hierarchy may be an abstract MKU that represents any series of events that has a beginning, a goal, an action, and an ending. Next is a MKU that represents a general behavior such as eating a meal. At a still lower level is a representation of how a person eats a meal in a restaurant. Even farther below are more specific rules, such as "Wait for the host or hostess to seat you." The linkage among these MKUs is believed to occur through learning and experience, and the more commonly a particular MKU is invoked, the more likely is that behavior.

This theory also can account for some of the deficits observed in patients with frontal lobe damage. First, because scripts provide a means for conceptualizing actions needed for a goal, the loss of them will severely compromise goal-directed behavior. Second, because novel events occur less frequently, frontal lobe damage will compromise the ability to retrieve an MKU for a relatively novel event, such as eating in a Nepali restaurant, as compared with something more common, such as eating in an Italian restaurant. Third, because the MKU specifies the starting and stopping conditions for many behaviors, deficits in the initiation and cessation of action will also occur.

Guidance of Behavior Toward a Goal

Another approach to understanding the role of frontal regions in executive control emphasizes the role that they play in guiding behavior toward a goal. This perspective has been influenced by artificial intelligence and machine learning. One version of such a class of theories suggests that a person has a list of task requirements or goals that she or he wants to achieve—a *goal list.* Typically a variety of behaviors or strategies can be used to reach a goal, and each must be evaluated as to how well it will enable the goal to be met. According to this theory, frontal lobe damage disrupts the ability to form a goal list. Because this list is so fundamental to guiding behavior, the loss of this list should lead to difficulties across a large variety of domains. Indeed, individuals with frontal lobe damage have difficulty in many arenas, including abstract thinking, perceptual analysis, verbal output, and so forth. The loss of a goal list would also imply that an individual would have difficulty staying on task (because the goal that would guide behavior is missing), would be unduly influenced by environmental stimuli (because no internal goal would be guiding behavior), and would have difficulty organizing actions toward a goal, all symptoms exhibited by individuals with frontal lobe damage (Duncan, 1986).

Another similar model argues that prefrontal cortex represents goals and the means to achieve them (Miller & Cohen, 2001). Prefrontal cortex provides bias signals to the rest of the cortex, involving systems ranging from sensory processing to memory, emotion, and response output. The effect of the signals is to bias the flow of information to appropriate pathways from input to internal states to outputs required to perform a task. As an analogy, you can consider the role of frontal cortex as setting switches on a series of railroad tracks to ensure that a train arrives at the correct destination. The correct destination, however, will vary depending on the context in which the individual finds him or herself.

Another aspect of this model is the need for sustained maintenance of the goal while the task is being performed. For example, individuals with frontal lobe damage may prepare their coffee by pouring coffee into their cup, stirring it, and then adding cream. Here the tasks have not been executed in a manner consistent with the goal of mixing the cream with coffee, even though the individual steps are being executed correctly. In this case, the train has not been derailed so much as it has arrived at the wrong station. Without sensitivity to context and the ability to modulate behavior based on goals, individuals will perseverate and engage in routine acts that may not be suited for the particular task at hand. Furthermore, their behavior will appear disorganized and off the mark.

An Integration

In this closing section of the chapter, we examine some final issues regarding the neural substrates of executive function. At present, there remains a debate as to how the prefrontal cortex is organized to support executive function. Some theorists suggest that executive function and the associated higher-order mental processes arise from the dynamic and distributed activity across prefrontal cortex (e.g., Carpenter, Just, & Reichle, 2000; Duncan & Owen, 2000). These theorists cite the fact that executive tasks appear to cause activation in a broad expanse of prefrontal cortex, with seemingly little similarity for a group of tasks that all tap the same category of executive function. As an example from earlier in the chapter, there does not appear to be a specific region of the brain that is engaged across all tasks requiring a switch from one task set to another.

Other theorists suggest that there is a more modular organization to the neural control of executive function. According to these models, different portions of prefrontal cortex each play a distinct role. Ventrolateral and inferior regions of frontal cortex maintain goal-relevant representations. Dorsolateral regions monitor and select among the relevant representations (Wagner, Maril, Bjork, & Schacter, 2001). Finally, orbitofrontal regions are thought to be involved in the selection of higher-order processes or subgoals (Fletcher & Henson, 2001). Thus, in these models, the coordinated activity of these modules, or regions, functions to select and maintain information that is needed to achieve a particular goal. As such, the line between two processes we have treated as distinct—working memory and attention—is blurred.

If you think about it, you can see that these functions clearly are related. Working memory allows you to keep in mind your ultimate goal as well as the type of information to which you should be attending (e.g., de Fockert, Rees, Frith, & Lavie, 2001). For example, working memory allows you to keep in mind that the goal of your foray to the shopping mall is to buy a present for your friend, and that she needs a scarf and that purple is her favorite color. Likewise, attention is required to determine what information is selected to be maintained in working memory, and which of the contents of working memory are most relevant for current task demands (Milham et al., 2002). Suppose you are at an airport listening to the announcements. Working memory allows you to keep what you've just heard in mind. But you need attention to select only that information associated with your flight number or your destination. Furthermore, when the announcement comes indicating the gate at which your flight number is embarking, you need to select the gate number but not your destination to be maintained in working memory. Thus, we can synthesize many of the perspectives presented in this chapter by suggesting that it is the interrelationship between regions of prefrontal cortex, and the interrelationship between working memory and attentional control, that is at the heart of executive functioning.

Executive Function and Goal-Directed Behavior

- Executive functions cover a variety of skills that allow one to organize behavior in a purposeful, coordinated manner, and to reflect on or analyze the success of the strategies employed.
- Although these abilities can be disrupted after damage to a variety of brain regions, executive functions are most typically impaired after frontal lobe damage.
- Executive dysfunction is often characterized by psychological inertia, which is the disinclination to initiate, change, or end an action.
- Individuals with executive dysfunction often have difficulty organizing information according to abstract categories or rules.
- Executive dysfunction causes difficulty in making reasonable inferences about the world and estimating the frequency of events.
- Individuals with executive dysfunction cannot predict the behavior of others when they must infer their beliefs or intentions.
- The ability to deal with novelty or reacting flexibly is compromised by executive dysfunction.
- Executive dysfunction is characterized by difficulty in staying on task or maintaining an attentional set for information that is most task-relevant.
- Individuals with executive dysfunction have difficulty remembering the sequence of events or successfully sequencing their own behavior to reach a goal.
- Individuals with executive dysfunction are poor at switching strategies, becoming locked onto one particular method of solving a problem even though that method cannot bring them any closer to the solution.

SUMMARY

- The ability to utilize the relationships or contingencies among events to help govern behavior is lost in individuals with executive dysfunction.
- Individuals with executive dysfunction are poor at evaluating their performance in both cognitive and social realms.

Theories of Frontal Lobe Function in Executive Control

- According to one theory, executive dysfunction occurs from disruptions in working memory that prevent information from being held online to meet task demands.
- Another set of theories argues that executive dysfunction is due to the loss of the ability to control behavior in nonroutine situations and to override typical stimulus-response associations.
- A third theory posits that scripts about actions and the context in which they occur are lost in executive dysfunction.
- A fourth approach, influenced by computational perspectives, suggests that executive dysfunction represents the inability to keep a goal list in mind or an inability to utilize the current context to select which stimuli and actions are most relevant for reaching a goal.
- Some theories argue that executive functioning arises from distributed functioning of activity across prefrontal regions.
- Other theories suggest that distinct regions of prefrontal cortex are involved in each of the following functions: maintaining items in working memory, selecting and manipulating the contents of working memory, and choosing among different subgoals or different processes needed to reach those goals.

KEY TERMS

attentional set 375
cognitive estimation 372
contention scheduling 388
environmental dependency syndrome 368
error-related negativity (ERN) 384
executive functions 366
perseveration 368
psychological inertia 367
reversal learning 374
self-ordered pointing task 376
supervisory attentional system 388
theory of mind 372
Wisconsin Card Sorting Test (WCST) 368

CHAPTER 12

Contributed by Wendy Heller

EMOTION

Joe Gray joined our family when I was 15 and he was 60. He and my mother had grown up on neighboring ranches in southern New Mexico. After my father's death, he came to Philadelphia to support her. Although my brothers and I had never met him before, he became a friend, mentor, and guide. Joe lived with us until he ended his life at 72.

Although some of Joe's past is shrouded in mystery, there were certain facts of his life about which we were sure. As a young man, we see him in photos astride a horse, handsome and confident. He knew how to ride and shoot and handle animals. He was a scholar, and a man of intense curiosity who read widely in many disciplines. Educated at Princeton University, he studied the Spanish language. We knew that he had spent time as an undercover agent for the United States during the cold war in South America, allowing him to combine his sense of adventure and his intellectual pursuit of Spanish among other things, but he never told us any of the details. We also knew that he became an alcoholic and was a member of Alcoholics Anonymous for many years. When Joe came to live with us, he had retired and had been living in Albuquerque, New Mexico. But his zest for life continued—whether going to listen to bluegrass and folk music, training a puppy, repairing a faucet, or teaching us to drive.

Joe had his first stroke when I was in graduate school. I was home for the holidays. One day we noticed that although Joe, ever talkative, was speaking, what he was saying was incoherent. Even so, he did seem to follow, more or less, what we were saying. I had enough training by then to realize that it was a symptom of a brain injury, most likely Broca's aphasia. Indeed a neurological exam confirmed that Joe was suffering the consequences of a left hemisphere stroke. Joe worked hard in therapy to regain his spoken-language abilities, and took comfort that reading, one of the pursuits he enjoyed most in life, was not lost. His progress was quite good, until he had a second stroke. After that, he couldn't read, or drive, or find the right words to converse. It was then that his demeanor also changed.

Although often cantankerous, Joe had always been upbeat about life, retaining his sense that life was an adventure. But now his moods could be positively dark and the energy he once had for life had noticeably ebbed. He began to threaten suicide. He tried several times. He took an overdose of pills one night but woke up eventually, in mid-afternoon, and was groggy for a day or two. He drank a fifth of scotch, after not having touched alcohol for 20 years, but passed out on the kitchen floor before any major damage was done. I convinced him to see a psychiatrist who got him so angry he forgot to be depressed for a while. We tried to cheer him up, telling him how important he was to our family, taking him to his favorite places, and buying him a brand-new pair of western cowboy boots.

Finally, he decided to hang himself, and this time he succeeded in his suicidal intent. My mother came home from work on a Friday afternoon to find cardboard taped to the front door window so that no one could see inside, and Joe, somehow having fallen from the noose, lying dead on the floor in the hallway. He was wearing his new boots.

Perhaps it will come as no surprise to the reader that much of my research since graduate school has focused on the role of brain mechanisms in depression. ■

AS IN OTHER AREAS of neuropsychology and cognitive neuroscience, much of what we know about the brain and emotion has an important history based on observations of individuals with damage to the brain. The depression that led Joe Gray to suicide was most likely due to much more than his inability to accept his impairments, although no doubt the loss of independence and reduced intellectual capacity contributed to his despair. Research has shown that damage to parts of the left hemisphere, especially frontal regions, often leads to clinical depression.

Findings such as these underscore the importance of particular brain regions for specific aspects of emotional functioning as well as psychiatric disorders.

We begin the chapter by discussing exactly what emotion is, and then survey the different brain regions that are important in emotion. As you will see, emotion involves a multiplicity of brain regions, some of which provide more automatic emotional responses, such as a flash of anger, and others of which provide a more controlled and evaluative emotional response, such as the feeling of sadness that comes over you as you read a tragic story. Next we consider neural models of basic aspects of emotional experience, such as the desire to approach something pleasant and retreat from something annoying or offensive. Afterwards we consider differences among individuals in their affective or emotional style, those aspects of brain functioning that make one person excitable and another calm. Then we conclude the chapter with a discussion of the recent work in cognitive neuroscience that has led to a greater understanding of how the brain's processing of emotional information can lead to psychiatric afflictions such as depression, anxiety disorder, and schizophrenia.

What Is Emotion?

It has been said that everyone knows what an emotion is until they are asked to define it (LeDoux, 1996). The *American Heritage Dictionary of the American Language* defines *emotion* as "1. Agitation of the passions or sensibilities often involving physiological changes. 2. Any strong feeling, as of joy, sorrow, reverence, hate, or love, arising subjectively rather than through conscious mental effort." At first glance, this description seems to capture our everyday sense of the concept of emotion. However, when we examine this definition more closely, we begin to appreciate the complexity of trying to understand emotion. Embedded in this passage are some topics that have aroused heated debate in the literature. For instance, what does it mean for a feeling to arise "subjectively rather than through conscious mental effort"? The question of whether cognition is a prerequisite for feelings to occur continues to engender controversy. Most of us would recognize the role that conscious mental effort can play in generating or maintaining emotions. Imagine the jealous lover who dwells on thoughts of the beloved in someone else's arms, making him- or herself more and more miserable in the process. However, much of the processing that is associated with emotion occurs outside conscious awareness. We may know how to describe a feeling we are experiencing, but we are often unaware of how that feeling was generated. For example, many studies have shown that we like things better when they are familiar, even when the stimuli have been exposed to us *subliminally* and we have no conscious awareness of ever having seen them before (i.e., the so-called mere exposure effect, e.g., Compton, Williamson, Murphy, & Heller, 2002).

Another debate highlighted by this definition is the role of physiological change in emotion. Historically, changes in heart rate, electrodermal response (the degree to which the skin conducts electricity depending on the amount of perspiration), blood pressure, and skin temperature have been viewed as generalized indicators of emotionality. As S. S. Tompkins (1984) described, "It had been known for centuries that the face became red and engorged with blood in anger. . . that in terror the hair stood on end and the skin became white and cold with sweat . . . that the blood vessels dilated and the skin felt warm and relaxed in enjoyment" (p. 190). An oft-cited quote from 1890 by William James stated that "bodily changes follow directly the perception of the exciting fact, and our feeling of the same changes as they occur is the emotion" (p. 449). If this is true, different emotions should be associated with very distinct physiological signatures (see Figure 12.1).

James's ideas led to a great deal of work in which researchers tried to identify specific physiological states that would uniquely characterize each emotion. Such studies were relatively unsuccessful. An alternative view was eventually introduced by physiologists Walter Cannon (1927, 1931) and Philip Bard, who argued that people could experience emotions even without the perception of bodily changes. For example, people who are completely paralyzed from the neck down and who have little awareness of sensory stimulation can still experience emotion. Furthermore, research has revealed that the same physiological states occur in many different emotions.

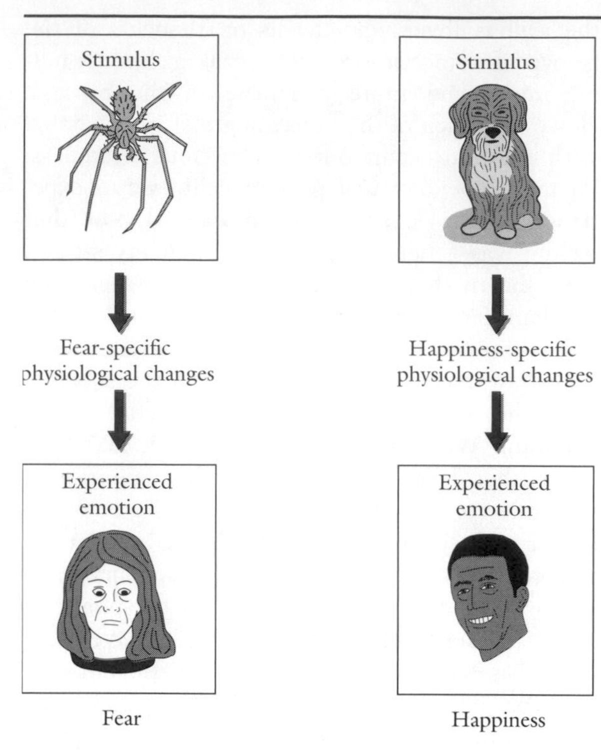

FIGURE 12.1 James-Lange theory of emotion. The underlying assumption of this theory is that the perception of an event or an object causes a specific pattern of physiological changes that evoke a specific emotional experience. For example, seeing a hairy spider causes physiological reactions that are distinct from those that occur when you see a puppy. The pattern of physiological change associated with seeing the spider induces an experience of fear, whereas the change associated with seeing the puppy induces the experience of happiness.

An extreme case of the latter view was put forth by Stanley Schachter in the **two-factor theory** of emotion, which suggests that emotional experience is the outcome of physiological arousal and the cognitive attribution of a cause for that arousal (see Figure 12.2). In a well-known study, Schachter and Singer (1962) used a chemical substance to induce a state of physiological arousal in their subjects. They then manipulated the situation, giving it a different emotional tone by changing the actions of the experimenters (e.g., in some cases the experimenter was rude and annoying; in other cases he was jovial and happy). As a result of their research, they claimed that "given a state of [physiological]

FIGURE 12.2 Two-factor theory of emotion. According to this theory, no unique physiological reaction is associated with each emotion. Instead, the physiological state can be interpreted in various ways. Thus, two factors, the physiological state and the causal attribution, dictate the emotional experience. Although the person in these pictures is having a similar physiological reaction, that of sweating and shaking, the context determines how the physiological reaction is interpreted.

activation . . . human subjects can be readily manipulated into states of euphoria, anger, and amusement" (p. 396).

More recent research, however, has shown that different emotions do have certain physiological signatures (e.g., Levenson, Eckman, & Friesen, 1990), although not to the dramatic extent that was once envisioned. Subtler, but nonetheless distinct, patterns of heart rate, electrodermal response, and physiological changes in the brain have been associated with specific emotions. Figure 12.3 shows different patterns of physiological responses as a function of different emotions.

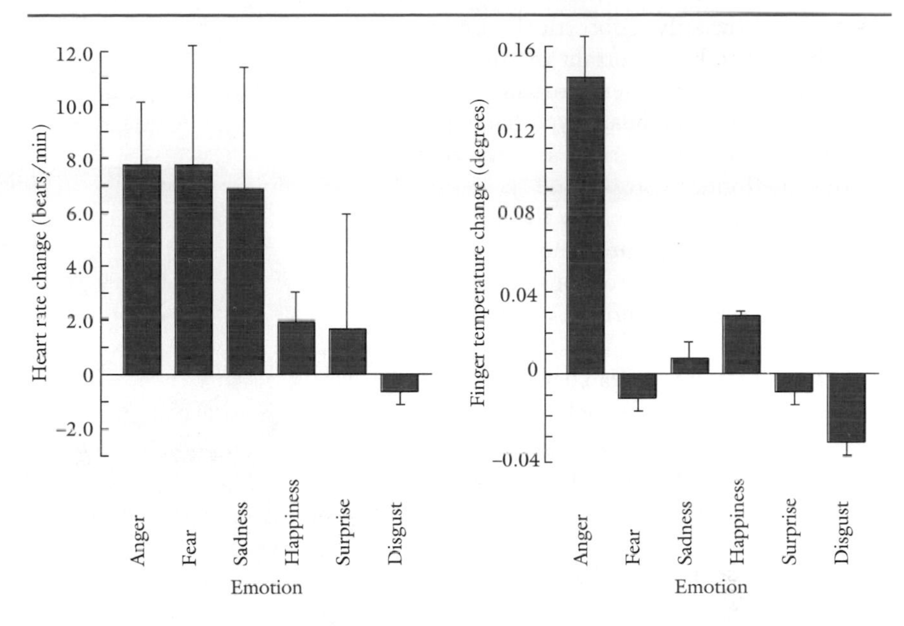

FIGURE 12.3 Examples of the unique physiological signatures of different emotions. These graphs show that heart rate and finger temperature can vary with particular emotions. For example, anger is associated with marked increases in both heart rate and finger temperature, whereas fear is associated with a marked increase in heart rate but a slight decrease in finger temperature.

Why are these issues important to our understanding of the neuropsychology and cognitive neuroscience of emotion? As we learned in previous chapters, distinct regions of the brain handle different kinds of processes. If conscious cognition plays only a minor role in emotion, perhaps the most important regions of the brain for emotion are subcortical structures, known to be associated with "emotional" behavior in animals. In contrast, if conscious cognition plays a major role in the experience of emotion, perhaps the cerebral cortex plays a larger role, possibly modulating subcortex by facilitating or inhibiting emotional behavior.

You will not be surprised to learn that research in neuroscience has shown that both subcortical and cortical areas of the brain play an important role in emotional behavior and experience. These results are compatible with the evidence that although many emotional processes unfold outside conscious awareness, effortful thought can influence them. Emotions can arise spontaneously, bypassing our conscious control (e.g., when we fall in love). But, they can also be modulated by our appraisals of the situation (e.g., whether or not this person's characteristics make him or her a good potential mate).

Rather than thinking of emotion as a unitary construct, it can be conceptualized as a set of processes that include perception, attention, appraisal, and feeling, as well as visceral and motor responses. Situations are perceived and subsequently interpreted in the context of a personal history of experiences. Once a situation has been appraised, actions must be taken, such as orienting the attention toward the stimulus, communicating or suppressing responses (an aspect of emotional regulation), and preparing the body for action (e.g., fight or flight). Some of these processes may be accessible to consciousness and some may not. If emotion is construed as a set of processes, it follows that there is no "emotion" center in the brain. Instead, multiple brain regions will be required to implement all these functions. Under normal circumstances their activities are coordinated and their outputs integrated in a seamless manner.

The evidence suggests that the brain regions involved in emotion include the so-called limbic system (a primarily subcortical circuit, long thought to be important in emotion, containing, among other structures, the amygdala, hippocampus, hypothalamus, and cingulate cortex), various subdivisions of the prefrontal cortex, and posterior regions of the brain such as the parietal lobes, posterior cingulate, and retrosplenial cortex. These major regions important for the processing of emotion are depicted in Figure 12.4.

Although various researchers place differential emphasis on which part of the brain is most important, or most involved, in affective computations, most agree that human emotion is a product of the interaction of these interconnected regions. Thus, we typically experience an emotion as having a "feeling" component (often linked with a physiological experience—"rigid with fury" or "flushed with shame") accompanied by both sensory and cognitive processes (e.g., evaluation, attention) that allow us to interpret and act upon the signals we perceive in the environment. We now examine in more detail the roles that these various brain regions play in emotion.

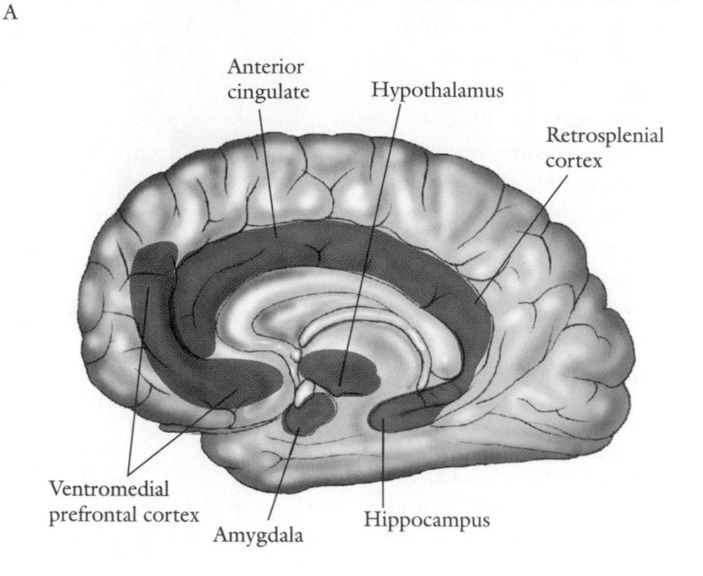

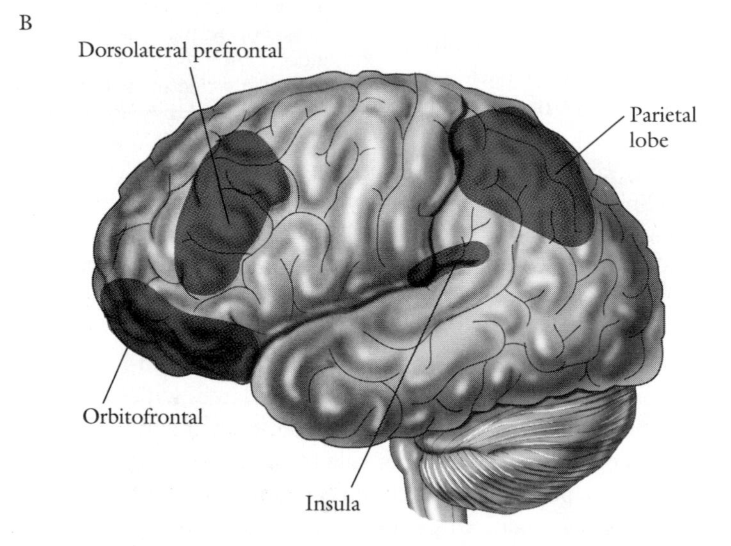

FIGURE 12.4 Major brain regions involved in emotional processing. (A) Medial view. Regions include the hypothalamus, hippocampus, amygdala, ventromedial prefrontal cortex, anterior cingulate, and retrosplenial cortex. (B) Lateral view. Regions include the parietal lobe, insula, and dorsolateral and orbitofrontal regions of frontal cortex.

 Subcortical Brain Regions Involved in Emotion

In our survey of the brain regions involved with emotion, we begin by discussing those non-cortical regions that are likely to be involved with more automatic or subconscious aspects of emotion.

Many emotions are uncomfortable to experience. However, their survival value is obvious. When a person is threatened, the body needs to mobilize its resources and take some kind of protective action: withdrawal (flight), perhaps, or aggression (fight). Furthermore, these responses often must be made quickly. As a result they are often made before the person has time to perform elaborate conscious cognitive computations and assessments of the situation (e.g., LeDoux, 1996).

Research with animals suggests that at least some brain regions strongly involved in emotion are presumed to be older in evolutionary terms. When animals have lesions or are stimulated in certain subcortical areas, emotional responding is often affected. On the basis of these observations, in 1937 James W. Papez (rhymes with "grapes") described a particular brain circuit involved in emotion that included the hypothalamus, hippocampus, anterior thalamus, and cingulate cortex (see Figure 12.4). Paul MacLean (1949, 1952) carried the idea further and proposed that these structures were part of what was termed the *limbic system*, the innermost of three brain layers (what he called the *triune brain*) that developed during the course of evolution. His conception of the structure of the brain is depicted in Figure 12.5.

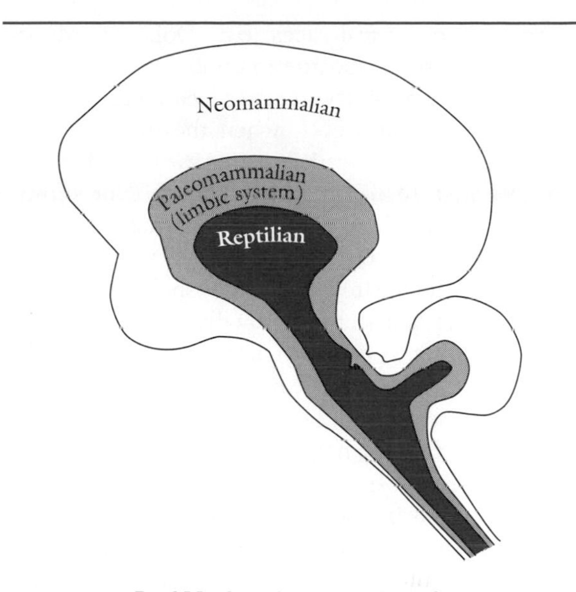

FIGURE 12.5 Paul MacLean's conception of the evolution of neural structures. MacLean proposed that three main neural levels—the reptilian brain, the paleomammalian brain, and the neomammalian brain—reflected anatomical and biochemical commonalities with reptiles, early-evolving mammals, and late-evolving mammals, respectively. The paleomammalian brain includes the structures that compose the limbic system.

Although investigators agree that emotions depend on the limbic system, scientists' ideas about exactly which structures constitute this system have changed over time (Brodal, 1998). For example, the hippocampus, once thought to be the hub of the limbic system, is actually relatively more important in memory functions than in processing emotion per se. In contrast, the amygdala, which in the past was not identified as a key component of the limbic system, has been receiving a great deal of attention from neuroscientists who study emotion (LeDoux, 2000). Brodal (1998) prefers to refer to limbic "structures," since the term "system" implies functional unity. In reality, the cell groups of neural structures involved in emo-tion, although they are highly interconnected, show differences with regard to connections, neurotransmitters, properties of single cells, and effects of selective lesions.

Amygdala: Fear and Emotional Learning

Scientists first became aware of the role of the amygdala in emotion when it was discovered to be important for the set of behavioral changes known as the *Kluver-Bucy syndrome* that resulted from large temporal lobe lesions in monkeys. These monkeys showed extremely abnormal reactions to the environment. They stopped being afraid of things they had feared in the past, attempted to engage in sexual behaviors with other species, and tried to ingest objects indiscriminately, including feces and rocks. Kluver and Bucy (1937) called the disconnection between the animals' ability to process the sensory properties of objects and their understanding of the affective properties of these same objects a *psychic blindness*.

Although the effects of amygdala damage in humans appear to be more modest, subsequent research has demonstrated that lesions of the amygdala interfere with the processing of emotional information. Case studies of people with amygdala damage indicate that they lose the ability to detect aversive emotional cues embedded in visual and auditory stimuli. They have difficulty identifying fearful facial expressions as well as fearful or angry sounds (Aggleton & Young, 2000). We mentioned earlier that people prefer stimuli that are familiar to them. When patients with damage to the amygdala, however, are asked to judge faces for trustworthiness and approachability, they rate unfamiliar photographs as more trustworthy and approachable than neurologically intact individuals do (Adolphs, Tranel, & Damasio, 1998). In addition, a number of neuroimaging studies have shown increased activity in the human amygdala in response to fearful as compared to neutral faces (e.g., Dolan & Morris, 2000) and during exposure to unpleasant as opposed to pleasant stimuli (Irwin et al., 1996). Furthermore, this effect is found even when the information is exposed subliminally (Whalen, 1998) and hence is not available to conscious awareness. Not surprisingly, activation of the amygdala has also been demonstrated in people with phobias when they are exposed to their feared object (e.g., spiders or snakes).

The amygdala seems especially involved in emotional learning, as has been demonstrated repeatedly in studies that examine fear conditioning. As we discussed in Chapter 10, in these paradigms, a neutral stimulus develops a negative emotional connotation by virtue of its association with an aversive stimulus. After pairing a neutral image with a very unpleasant noise, for example, people will eventually respond to the previously neutral image as if it were inherently aversive. This emotional response is reflected in physiological responses such as heart rate, skin conductance (which measures sweating), and the *startle response,* which is a blink that occurs when a puff of air is blown into a person's eye. If the individual happens to be gazing at a pleasant stimulus, the startle response is attenuated. In contrast, if he or she is gazing at an unpleasant stimulus, the startle response is larger, an effect referred to as *potentiation.* Increases in heart rate, skin conductance, and startle are all indications that the body is preparing itself for the actions that would be helpful in responding to a threat.

In one study, a patient with bilateral amygdala damage was trained to associate a colored slide with an unpleasant noise. After conditioning, neurologically-intact control subjects reacted to the slide by increased skin conductance. Although the patient was able to remember the pairing explicitly, or consciously, she did not show the expected autonomic conditioned response. The emotional impact of the noise appeared to be brand new every time she heard it (Bechara et al., 1995). In another study, a patient with a focal lesion of the right amygdala failed to show the normal increase in startle in response to an aversive as compared to neutral stimuli (Angrilli et al., 1996). Controls, however, did show potentiation to the same stimuli. Other work with patients who have amygdala lesions suggests that despite their lack of startle potentiation, their conscious evaluation of the aversive stimuli is similar to controls, rating them just as negatively.

Normally, the greater the emotional intensity associated with an event or experience, the better it is remembered, a phenomenon known as the *memory enhancement effect.* Consistent with the findings just described, amygdala damage also seems to interfere with this memory enhancement effect (Cahill, Babinsky, Markowitsch, & McGaugh, 1995; Adolphs, Cahill, Schul, & Babinsky, 1997). Using PET to investigate this pattern further, researchers found that better memory for emotional versus neutral film clips was correlated with glucose metabolic rate in the right amygdala of people without brain damage (Cahill et al., 1996).

LeDoux (1996) argues that two important pathways involving the amygdala exist for communicating sensory information to a network of brain regions that process emotion. One pathway seems to be important for quick, instinctive, emotional responses. For example, this pathway allows a jogger to leap away from a shape on the road that looks like a snake before the conscious mind has even had the thought "That might be a snake." This pathway projects straight from the anterior thalamus to the amygdala. Another pathway connects the sensory areas of the neocortex to the amygdala—a corticoamygdala projection. This pathway seems to provide a more comprehensive context for processing emotional information. For example, after leaping to safety, the jogger might study the shape more carefully and realize that it is only a stick and therefore not something to be feared. Thus, the amygdala appears to receive a progressively more complete image of the same information, like the photograph produced by a Polaroid camera in which the image emerges in more and more detail while you watch. Consequently, the thalamoamygdala pathway would carry a crude, preliminary sketch of some basic properties of the stimulus—not enough to clearly identify the object, but enough, perhaps, to ready a response. In contrast, the corticoamygdala pathway, which is slower because it involves more synapses, would deliver enough information to give rise to an affective reaction that takes into account the complexity and details of the situation.

You may have noted that the amygdala seems to be especially involved in representing unconscious aspects of the emotional response to stimuli. This phenomenon has been exploited as a means of studying an important aspect of social cognition, *race evaluation*, or attitudes regarding members of a different racial or social group. Even if people consciously rate or judge individuals in another group as positively as individuals in their own group, unconscious judgments might belie those beliefs. For example, when researchers use measures that indirectly assess emotional judgments, Caucasian Americans who espouse pro-African-American beliefs may still demonstrate an unconscious bias to associate African-American faces with negative words. In a recent neuroimaging study, researchers showed that two measures of unconscious racial bias were correlated with activity in the amygdala (Phelps et al., 2000). The two measures of bias were a task of startle potentiation and the Implicit Association Test (IAT) (Greenwald, McGhee, & Schwartz, 1998; for a demonstration of selected IAT procedures, visit www.yale.edu/implicit). The greater the unconscious bias according to these measures, the more activity there was in the amygdala, particularly on the left (see Color insert 12.1).

Quite a few studies report laterality effects with regard to activation of the amygdala. To date, however, the functional significance of these asymmetries is not clear. There has been some speculation that they may reflect the nature of the stimuli, with visual material more often associated with right amygdala activity and verbal material more often associated with left amygdala activity (Phelps et al., 2001). The degree of verbal and/or conscious representation regarding the fearful stimulus or event may also influence the asymmetry. For example, left amygdala activity occurred in an experiment where people were told to expect an uncomfortable shock but never actually received it (Phelps et al., 2001). These researchers attributed the activity in the left amygdala to input from a cortical pathway that provided a verbal or cognitive representation of the feared situation. They speculate that in contrast, in classic fear conditioning, there is a more immediate and direct impact by a threatening or aversive stimulus. Thus, under these conditions an increase in right amygdala activity is more likely. Supporting such an idea, activity was observed in the right, but not the left amygdala when angry faces are shown briefly and then followed by a visual display, known as a mask, that prevents them from being consciously perceived. When the same faces were not masked, and hence could be perceived, activity was found in both the right and left amygdala (Morris, Ohman, & Dolan, 1998). Providing indirect support of this idea, explicit processing of facial expressions was associated with activity in the temporal lobe of the cortex, whereas implicit or automatic nonconscious processing was associated with activity in the amygdala, especially on the right (Critchley et al., 2000).

Hippocampus: Putting Emotion in Context

The hippocampus, which (as we discussed in Chapter 10) is critical in allowing for declarative long-term memory storage, is important in providing the contextual and relational information that frames a particular event. This clearly is an adaptive response, as context often provides important information on whether real-world situations are dangerous or not. For example, someone wrapping their arms around you tightly and squeezing you is not threatening if the action is performed by a loved one, whereas the same action signals danger if it is performed by a stranger in a dark alley late at night. Hippocampal lesions made before training interfere with the acquisition of conditioned responses to the experimental context, but not with learning the specific cue-punishment contingency. In other words, imagine that every time a jogger is on a particular path, she hears a rattling sound and a snake appears. The jogger will learn that when the rattle sounds, a snake will appear, and will develop a fear response to the sound of the rattle. Over time, the jogger will also develop a fear of the path. If the jogger had a hippocampal lesion, however, she would learn to fear the rattle, but not the path.

The ability to process contextual information may also be very important in emotional regulation. For example, Davidson (2000) has suggested that a fundamental problem in many mental disorders is not the experience of extreme emotion, but rather its expression in inappropriate contexts. Thus, it is not necessarily that anxious people feel anxiety that is more intense than the rest of us, but rather that they feel anxiety in situations in which most of us don't. For example, a combat veteran suffering from posttraumatic stress disorder (PTSD) might hear a bang or pop while walking through a mall or another safe setting and suddenly reexperience the intense fear of a battle. Some research has indicated that PTSD is accompanied by hippocampal atrophy, thought to be caused by the release of large doses of glucocorticoids (for example, cortisol, which is a chemical produced by the adrenals in response to stress). Hence, impaired functioning of the hippocampus may contribute to the emotional dysfunction seen in PTSD.

The role of the hippocampus in emotional learning and memory may be temporally limited. In a study where rats were conditioned to be afraid of a particular environmental context, hippocampal damage interfered with contextual fear memory for recent events but not for events in the more distant past. These results suggest that after a certain amount of time, the hippocampus no longer plays a significant role in memory storage, at least for some types of information (see Chapter 10, page 355, where this issue is also discussed).

Hypothalamus: Get Ready to Run

The hypothalamus, part of the subcortical system that allows for the quick processing of emotional information, is important for many regulatory physiological functions. It mediates some of the autonomic phenomena (such as heart rate) and endocrine reactions (such as the release of hormones associated with stress) that we discussed earlier as typical manifestations of emotional states. For example, this region of the brain helps to coordinate the physical events that prepare the organism for approach or withdrawal ("fight or flight") such as an increase in blood pressure when confronted with a threatening stimulus. The hypothalamus is intimately connected with amygdala, serving both as an important relay station for information going into the amygdala as well as receiving information from the amygdala.

Cingulate Cortex: Interfacing Emotion and Cognition

The cingulate has been viewed as a component of the limbic system since Broca first described *le grande lobe limbique* in 1878 (for review, see Allman et al., 2001). It wraps around the corpus callosum like a collar, or *cingulum*, and has been considered part of the paleomammalian brain, or the middle layer of MacLean's *triune brain*. However, more recent neuroimaging studies have demonstrated that the anterior cingulate is an important brain structure in a variety of cognitive functions as well, and there is some debate as to whether it should be considered a neocortical, as opposed to a subcortical, structure. Allman and colleagues (2001) argue that although it has five layers of cells and is therefore distinct from much of neocortex, which contains six, the anterior cingulate is similar to adjacent motor areas in its laminar organization. Thus, rather than being more primitive than neocortex, the anterior cingulate may be a specialization of the neocortex involved in higher-order functions such as emotional self-control, error monitoring, and a variety of other executive functions, as we discussed in the last chapter. One especially well-developed layer of cells in the cingulate has lots of connections to the subcortical regions involved in emotion, suggesting that the neuroanatomical substates are present for the anterior cingulate to integrate a variety of inputs regarding emotion. As we will discuss shortly, both views may have some merit, as some regions of the cingulate may be more involved in emotional functions and others in more cognitive functions.

• *ANTERIOR CINGULATE GYRUS* •

Lesions of the anterior cingulate cortex have been noted to result in a variety of emotional sequelae, including apathy, inattention, emotional lability, and changes in personality (for review, see Bush, Luu, & Posner, 2000). It is also involved in pain, receiving input from subcortical structures that have neurons specialized to respond to noxious stimuli. PET studies have shown activation in anterior cingulate when painful heat is applied (Davis et al., 1997) as shown in Figure 12.6. Indeed, surgical removal of the cingulate has been used to treat intractable pain. In a recent study, Cohen and colleagues (1999) investigated the psychological functioning of a set of patients who had received small lesions in the anterior cingulate as a treatment for pain. The patients said that they still had pain but it

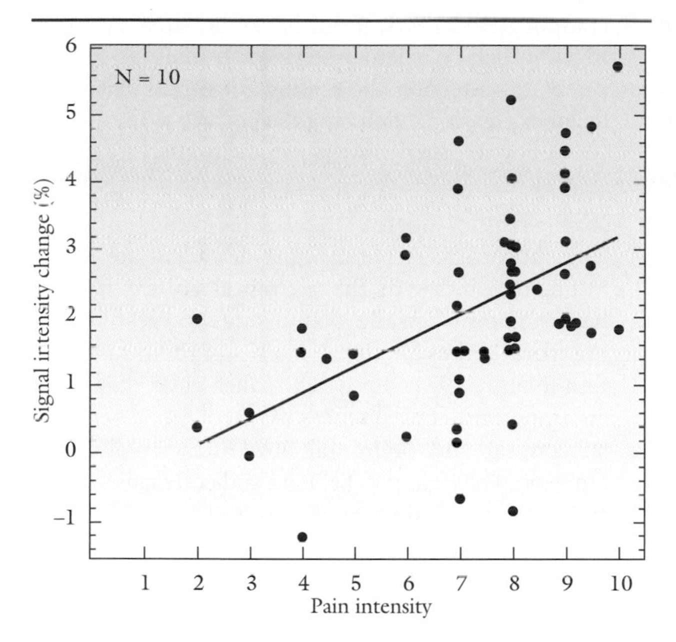

FIGURE 12.6 Relationship between the perceived intensity of pain and activation in the anterior cingulate. The more intensely individuals felt pain, the more activation was observed in the anterior cingulate.

no longer bothered them as much. They also showed lower levels of spontaneous behavior. These findings are consistent with earlier reports of apathy and inattention in patients with cingulate lesions.

Neuroimaging studies have allowed us to be much more specific about the functional specialization of the anterior cingulate. In a meta-analysis of 64 functional neuroimaging studies, Bush and coworkers (2000) were able to show that emotional tasks were associated with activations primarily in a rostral or ventral portion of the anterior cingulate, while cognitive tasks were associated with activations primarily in a caudal or dorsal portion (see Color insert 12.2). The cognitive subdivision, as we learned in Chapter 8, is part of a distributed attentional network and has connections with lateral prefrontal cortex, parietal cortex, and motor areas. The emotional subdivision is connected to many of the areas we have already described as important in an emotional network, including the amygdala, the hippocampus, the hypothalamus, the insula, and the orbitofrontal cortex.

Neuroimaging studies have also revealed an interesting relationship between these two subdivisions of the anterior cingulate. Deactivations are commonly found in the emotional division of the anterior cingulate during cognitive task performance, and vice versa. The cognitive division of the anterior cingulate has also been shown to be deactivated in people who have severe depression, are anticipating pain, and/or are watching emotional films. These results suggest that there may, under some circumstances, be an important reciprocal dynamic between emotion and cognition, with strong emotion functioning to shut down certain cognitive systems. Conversely, focused attention and concentration may function to suppress strong emotion. This notion seems intuitively appealing, as many of us have experienced for ourselves the degree to which an emotional state can interfere with paying attention to a nonemotional task. It is likely that many of us have also had occasion to "lose ourselves in our work" for the purpose of coping with some emotional stress or trauma.

These findings should not be taken, however, to suggest a strict and rigid dichotomy between the functions of the two regions, as at times they may work together. For example, the personality traits of approach versus withdrawal as well as induced positive versus negative emotion were found to predict the degree of activation in the so-called cognitive division of the anterior cingulate during a working-memory task (Gray & Braver, 2002). These results indicate that at the very least the neural networks involved in attention are modulated by emotional processes, and not always reciprocally.

Another indication of the cingulate's role in the interface of emotion and cognition is provided by results obtained using the error-related negativity (ERN). As we discussed in the last chapter, the ERN is an electrical response that occurs when people are aware of making an error, which dipole modeling suggests emanates from the anterior cingulate. The amplitude of the ERN has been shown to be larger in obsessive-compulsive patients and in people who are highly motivated to do well. It also gets larger when people become more concerned about making late responses on a speeded task (Luu, Flaisch, & Tucker, 2000). These findings led Luu and fellow researchers to the hypothesis that the anterior cingulate is best conceptualized as involved in evaluative self-monitoring along an affective dimension. These findings are consistent with research indicating that people who are more socially aware show more activation of the anterior cingulate cortex during an emotionally arousing task (Lane et al., 1997).

• *RETROSPLENIAL CORTEX* •

The retrosplenial cortex, so named because it sits right behind the splenium or most caudal part of the corpus callosum (refer back to Figure 12.4), is part of the posterior cingulate cortex. While the anterior portion of the cingulate is considered to be involved in executive functions, the posterior portion is thought to be involved in evaluative functions (Vogt, Finch, & Olson, 1992). Traditionally the retrosplenial cortex has been thought to be important in memory processing, but more recent functional neuroimaging studies have suggested that it interfaces such memory processes with emotion (see Maddock, 1999 for a nice, succinct review). The retrosplenial cortex is well positioned anatomically to mediate an interaction between emotional and cognitive processes. It receives major inputs from the orbital and dorsolateral prefrontal cortex, the anterior cingulate, parahippocampal cortex, superior temporal sulcus, the precuneus of the parietal lobe, and thalamic nuclei. These inputs can provide sources of information about the emotional and motivational significance of ongoing stimuli and events. The retrosplenial cortex has been suggested to be involved in the evaluation rather than the experience of emotional information, and in integrating those processes with episodic memory, although the exact nature of that interaction remains to be defined.

Cortical Regions Involved in Emotion

Having just examined the roles that noncortical regions play in emotion, we now turn our attention to the functions of cortical regions focusing on the prefrontal cortex, the insula, and parietal regions. Although an oversimplification, subcortical regions enable us to have an emotional response to stimuli quickly, whereas cortical regions are important for using those reactions to influence more complicated aspects of our behavior, such as deciding whether a particular behavior is likely to lead to a reward, inferring the feelings of others based on facial expression, and using the correct tone of voice to convey to others how we are feeling.

Prefrontal Cortex

The subcortical structures just described are richly interconnected with the prefrontal cortex. In fact, neuroanatomist Walle Nauta once suggested that the frontal lobes are the neocortex of the limbic system (Nauta, 1971). Research makes clear that there are important consequences of interactions between subcortical and prefrontal structures involved in emotion. For example, LeDoux and colleagues found that following lesions to the orbitofrontal regions of prefrontal cortex in rats, it was extremely difficult to extinguish conditioned fear. These findings suggest that this region plays an important role in keeping the amydgala apprised of current events and contingencies (see the following discussion). In the absence of input from this part of the brain, the amygdala seems to respond as if past conditions were still in effect.

Several regions of the prefrontal cortex have been identified as important in emotion. These include the orbitofrontal prefrontal cortex (OFC), the ventromedial prefrontal cortex (vmPFC), and the dorsolateral prefrontal cortex (DLPFC) (refer back to Figure 12.4). These regions have been differentiated by their cellular architecture as well as their involvement in different aspects of emotional functioning.

• *ORBITOFRONTAL REGION: REWARD AND PUNISHMENT* •

Case studies have shown that people with damage to the OFC exhibit disinhibited behaviors (e.g., blurting things out that other people find too personal), socially inappropriate behaviors, and irresponsibility. They seem to have difficulty anticipating the consequences of their actions and make poor decisions that result in negative outcomes; they also do not seem to learn from their mistakes (Rolls, Hornak, Wade, & McGrath, 1994; Bechara, Damasio, Damasio, & Anderson, 1994). Bechara and colleagues (1994) have termed their behavior a "myopia" for the future. These behaviors are especially remarkable because such patients show no deficits at all in intellectual ability. Such clinical findings have long suggested an important role for the OFC in emotional functions.

Recent research has allowed us to define more specifically the ways in which the OFC is involved in emotion and social behavior. This region of the brain seems to be strongly involved in evaluating reward and punishment contingencies, and in responding adaptively to changes in these relationships. For instance, under some circumstances, you might choose to "gamble" on a particular outcome, given your understanding of the cost-benefit contingencies in a particular situation. Suppose you are in business and are bidding for a job. You know that the client is more interested in whether you understand the company's vision than in whether you have a detailed plan for how you will complete the job. If you are short for time, you will most likely try to emphasize your understanding of their vision, and you will hope that they won't press you for details. In contrast, if you know a different client is more interested in the details, you will tell that client exactly how many workers you will employ on the project and who will be performing which functions, but skimp on the particulars of how you will organize the overall project. You will be gambling that in this manner you will maximize the payoff—getting the job—and minimize the loss—losing sleep trying to do everything perfectly.

Single-cell recording studies in nonhuman primates show that neurons in the OFC respond to the rewarding value of taste, smell, and visual stimuli, and that some neurons respond only when the reinforcement contingencies change (Rolls, 1999). People with damage to the OFC also show impairments in the ability to change their behavior when the contingencies change and when what previously was right is now wrong, a function referred to as *reversal learning.* For example, let's say you were taught to press the left button when the red light comes on and the right button when the green light comes on. In reversal learning, you now press the left button when the green light comes on and the right button when the red light comes on. These findings are consistent with PET data showing activation in the OFC when a monetary reward is received (Thut, 1997) and when getting positive and negative feedback during a guessing task (Elliott, Frith, & Dolan, 1997).

People with damage to the OFC do poorly on "gambling" tasks in which they choose a particular stimulus that results in them either winning or losing money (O'Doherty et al., 2001). These tasks are designed probabilistically so that people cannot simply associate one stimulus with one outcome. Over an initial period of time one stimulus is most profitable, but then the contingencies change and another stimulus becomes more profitable. People with damage to the OFC tend to go for the larger immediate reward even though over time it leads to losses. The behavior of these individuals is similar to that of a child who cannot resist the impulse to eat a piece of candy despite knowing that they will be punished for it, or that by eating too many pieces of candy they will get an upset stomach (Bechara, Damasio, & Damasio, 2000). In fact, such impairments in decision making may be related to substance abuse, where people also make decisions on the basis of immediate gratification while ignoring the long-term consequences. Some researchers have gone even further with this reasoning, suggesting that the OFC may provide the substrate for the development of moral behavior, comparing people with damage to this region to those with the psychiatric disorder of psychopathy, a failure of empathy often seen in violent criminals (Anderson et al., 1999).

A recent functional magnetic resonance imaging (fMRI) study suggests that different regions of the OFC are involved in different aspects of the reward and punishment contingencies. The lateral area of the OFC is activated following a punishing outcome in a gambling task, whereas the medial area is activated following a rewarding outcome (O'Doherty et al., 2001). These two regions appear to act in a reciprocal manner; the medial region showed increased activation to reward and decreased activation to punishment, whereas the lateral orbitofrontal region exhibited the opposite pattern. Furthermore, the magnitude of the activations reflected the magnitude of the reward or punishment delivered. The authors suggest that these findings help to explain some of the deficits seen in with OFC damage on gambling tasks. If they are unable to represent the magnitude of rewards and punishments, they will be insensitive to the degree to which a particular stimulus choice is advantageous on the basis of cumulative monetary gain.

Based on these findings, Davidson (2000) has suggested that the OFC is likely to play an important role in emotional regulation, since the capacity to relearn, or restructure previous stimulus-incentive associations, is important for responding adaptively to changes in emotional and social situations.

• *VENTROMEDIAL REGION: QUICK, HOW DOES IT FEEL?* •

Researchers are less clear about the exact role of the ventromedial prefrontal region (vmPFC) in emotion processing. Some theorists have speculated that the vmPFC is most likely involved in the representation of basic positive and negative affective states without more detailed consideration of incentives or contingencies (Davidson, 2000). For example, single-cell recordings of neurons in the right vmPFC were responsive during encoding of the emotional value of aversive visual stimuli (Kawasaki et al., 2001). Of interest, these cells responded within 120–170 msec of stimulus presentation, suggesting that neurons in this region can provide a rapid and coarse categorization of the emotional valence of a stimulus.

• *DORSOLATERAL REGION: ACTING ON FEELINGS* •

The dorsolateral prefrontal cortex (DLPFC), known to be important in working memory and attentional control, appears to be involved in the representation of goal-directed behaviors (see the discussion in Chapter 11, pages 375 and 388). To respond in an adaptive way to the environment, we would expect goal-directed behaviors to be influenced by positive and negative emotional states (Davidson, 2000). For example, an unpleasant emotional state should be associated with the goal of withdrawing from the situation that produced the feeling, and a pleasant state should be associated with the goal of approaching the situation that produced the feeling. These motivational states (withdrawal, approach) have been linked to hemispheric asymmetries in prefrontal cortex, with right hemisphere activation associated with withdrawal, and left with approach (see the section on "Models of Emotion" for further discussion of these findings).

Regions in the DLPFC have recently been found to be sensitive to an integration of cognition and emotion (Gray, Braver, & Raichle, 2002). Participants in this study watched emotional videos intended to induce either pleasant, approach-related states, or unpleasant, withdrawal-related states. After each video, they were scanned using fMRI while performing a difficult working-memory task using both words and faces. Consistent with the findings we discussed in Chapter 10, word stimuli preferentially activated the left DLPFC and face stimuli preferentially activated the right DLPFC. However, emotional state also affected cognitive processing. Performance on the word task was enhanced by a pleasant state and impaired by an unpleasant state whereas the opposite was true for the face task. This result should not be surprising as approach or positive states are associated with greater left than right DLPFC activity, and performance of verbal working memory tasks relies preferentially on the left DLPFC. In contrast, an unpleasant video would induce higher right than left DLPFC activity, and performance of nonverbal working-memory tasks would rely more on the right than the left DLPFC.

• *FUNCTIONAL ASYMMETRIES IN PREFRONTAL ACTIVITY AND EMOTION* •

A wealth of evidence suggests that the contributions of the prefrontal cortex vary by hemisphere. People with right hemisphere damage display different emotional behaviors than those with left hemisphere damage (Gainotti, 1972). Left frontal damage tends to cause what has been dubbed a **catastrophic reaction,** in which patients seem emotionally volatile and are prone to sad moods and tearfulness. In contrast, right frontal damage causes a **euphoric-indifference reaction,** in which patients seem inappropriately cheerful, are prone to laughter, and display a remarkable lack of awareness with regard to their disabilities and other consequences of changes wrought by brain damage.

The location of the lesion within the prefrontal region is strongly associated with these differential emotional responses. In a series of studies of patients with unilateral brain damage, 60 percent of the patients with left frontal lobe lesions had the symptom cluster of a major affective disorder as described by *Diagnostic and Statistical Manual of Mental Disorders* (*DSM*) criteria, the standard diagnostic criteria used by psychiatrists and psychologists in the United States to identify depression. Importantly, the more anterior the lesion in the left hemisphere, the more severe were the depressive symptoms (e.g., Robinson & Szetela, 1981; Morris, Robinson, Raphael, & Hopwood, 1996) as shown in Figure 12.7A. In contrast, lesions of the right frontal lobe were associated with indifferent or euphoric behavior. Here lesion location and depression correlated in the opposite direction to that observed in the patients with left hemisphere damage. In this case, the more anterior the lesion, the less likely the person was to be depressed (see Figure 12.7B).

Similar emotional responses have been described in patients undergoing the sodium amobarbital test (which was discussed first in Chapter 4 and then in Chapter 9, see pages 119 and 298, respectively). When an injection of this barbiturate deactivates the left hemisphere, a catastrophic reaction is usually observed, whereas when an injection deactivates the right hemisphere, a euphoric-indifference reaction is usually observed (e.g., Lee, Loring, Meader, & Brooks, 1990).

Converging evidence for differential involvement of the hemispheres in positive versus negative mood

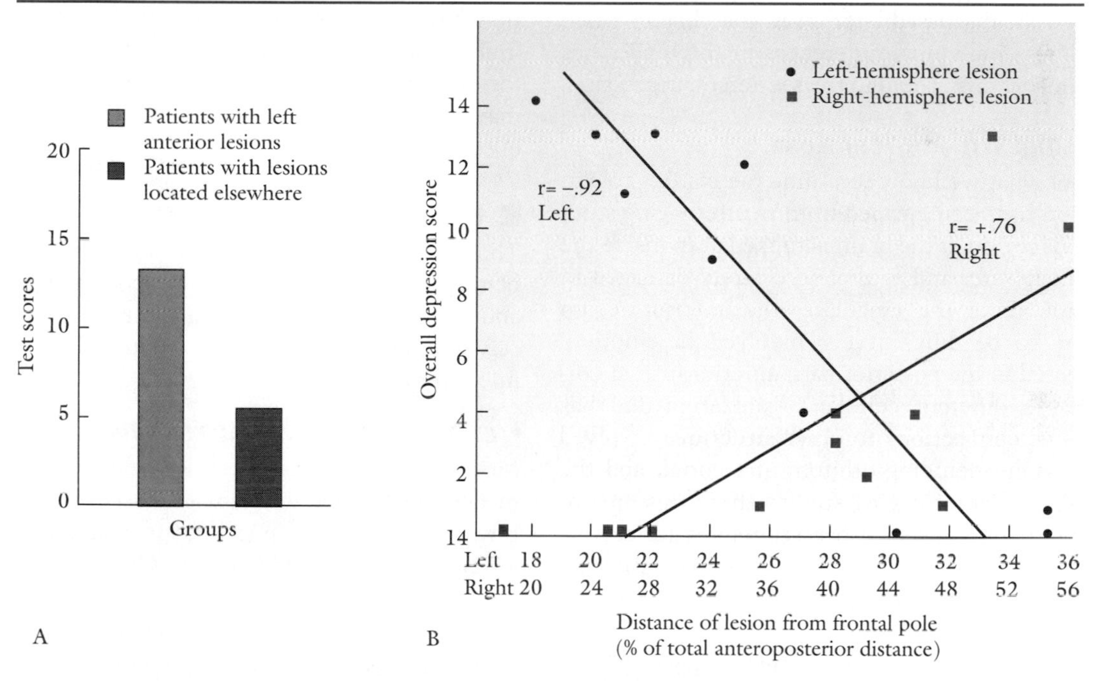

FIGURE 12.7 Relationship between degree of depression exhibited after cerebral insult and location of lesion. (A) Patients with damage to anterior regions of the left hemisphere often exhibit depressive symptomatology. Depicted here are scores on the Hamilton Depression Scale, a commonly used measure in clinical settings. A higher score indicates more severe depression. The average score for patients with left anterior lesions (blue bar) is higher than that for patients with lesions in other brain regions (grey bar). (B) The relationship between lesion location and degree of depression differs between the hemispheres. The closer the lesion is to the most anterior portion of the left frontal lobe, the higher the overall depression score, as indicated by a significant negative correlation ($r = -.92$) between depression score and distance of the lesion from the frontal pole. The opposite is true of the right hemisphere: the closer to the most anterior region, the lower the depression score, as indicated by a significant positive correlation ($r = +.76$) between depression score and distance of the lesion from the frontal pole.

states is provided by studies measuring EEG (e.g., Davidson, 2000). When positive affect is induced by procedures such as showing people funny movies or pictures of warm, cuddly animals, more activity is seen over the left relative to the right prefrontal cortex. When negative affect is induced by showing people upsetting movies or pictures of horrific events, the reverse pattern is observed.

A similar relationship between hemisphere of activation and mood state has been observed in clinical populations with affective disorders. For example, during a resting, eyes-closed condition, individuals with depression showed more activity in the right prefrontal region than in the left (Schaffer, Davidson, & Saron, 1983). Individuals who were not depressed showed the opposite pattern. These findings will be discussed later on in the chapter when we address individual differences in the tendencies to be upbeat or sad, and in the section on depression.

Insula: Wrinkle Your Nose

Most of what we know regarding the insula's role in emotion has been gleaned from neuroimaging studies. This region of the brain is tucked deep inside the Sylvian fissure, and is therefore rarely damaged in isolation. Like the cingulate, the anterior region appears to be differentially involved in emotion. Compared to the posterior part, anterior insular cortex has a different cellular organization and has extensive connections to other structures involved in emotion, including orbitofrontal cortex and the amygdala. Neuroimaging studies show this area to be sensitive to various processes related to feeding, such as odor, taste, tongue somatosensory stimulation, swallowing, thirst, and hunger (for review, see Small et al., 2001).

In an interesting study linking this region to the affective aspects of feeding, PET scans were performed on people eating chocolate, which has been identified as the single most craved food in studies of food cravings. The insula was one of the brain regions that became activated, especially when people first started eating it and were finding it a rewarding experience. Activity in this region decreased as individuals had more than enough chocolate and began to find it unpleasant (Small et al., 2001). These findings are consistent with a neuromodulatory role of the insula for various aspects of feeding.

The insula also seems to be involved in emotional functions that are not related directly to feeding. Activation of this region has been observed during symptom provocation in patients with phobias, the recollection of negative events in neurologically intact individuals, the induction of fear, the perception of facial expressions of disgust, and imagery of aversive stimuli (for review, see Shin et al., 2000). While many of these functions appear to be rather primitive and basic, activation has also been found in this region, along with activation in the anterior temporal poles and anterior cingulate, for a task in which healthy individuals recalled and imagined a personal event involving the most guilt they had ever experienced (Shin et al., 2000). These findings suggest that the insula may play a modulatory role in a variety of affective experiences, and may be particularly sensitive to the rewarding value of sensory stimuli.

Parietal Lobes

The parietotemporal region, particularly in the right hemisphere, appears to play an important role in the ability to interpret emotional information—to perceive, comprehend, and recall emotionally meaningful material.

• *COMPREHENDING EMOTION* •

Most of us take for granted knowing that a frown means something different from a smile. Sometimes, a frown means puzzlement, suggesting a need for clarification or explanation. Often, a frown signals displeasure or disapproval. It might cue us that something we said or did annoyed or disturbed another person. That facial expression then becomes an important piece of information that we can take into account as we engage further in the interaction. We can decide to ignore the frown and continue on our path, knowing that we are in danger of a confrontation, or we can decide to avoid the confrontation and steer clear of the disturbing conversation or behavior. Since human beings usually coexist with one another in highly complex social structures, they depend on such nonverbal signals to communicate effectively.

Several channels are used to express nonverbal signals, including tone of voice, often referred to as *prosody*, facial expression, and gestures. As we discuss next, the parietotemporal region of the right hemisphere has often been identified as important in perceiving these types of information.

• ***Prosody*** • Suggesting that the right hemisphere is more involved in processing auditory emotional information, left-ear advantages have been found for judging emotional tone of voice (e.g., Ley & Bryden, 1982) and for discriminating vocal nonspeech sounds such as shrieking, laughing, and crying (e.g., King & Kimura, 1972). Another source of auditory emotional information is tone of voice.

One of the first individuals to argue that language consists of more than finding the right word and putting it in the appropriate position with reference to other words was Monrad-Krohn (e.g., 1947). He coined the term *prosody* to refer to aspects of communication that are related to tone of voice, including pitch or frequency, stress and intensity, and timing. Two types of prosody have been described. **Affective prosody** communicates the emotional context or tone of an utterance; for example, "My mother is coming to dinner" could be stated in a way that expresses elation or in a way that expresses dismay. **Propositional prosody** communicates lexical or semantic information—for example, "What's that in the road ahead?" versus "What's that in the road, a head?"

Clinical studies have suggested that compared with patients with left hemisphere lesions, patients with right hemisphere lesions in parietal and parietotemporal regions are significantly impaired in comprehending prosody (e.g., K. M. Heilman, Scholes, & Watson, 1975; D. M. Tucker, Watson, & Heilman, 1977; Ross, 1981). Using a comprehensive battery for assessing emotional function, Borod and colleagues (1998) found that right-brain-damaged patients were more impaired than left-brain-damaged patients and controls in identifying prosodic emotions. Nonetheless, there is some debate in the literature as to how lateralized comprehension of prosody really is (see Pell & Baum, 1997; Van Lancker & Sidtis, 1992). Findings that left hemisphere damage can also be accompanied by prosodic dysfunction led some researchers to suggest that the right hemisphere is important for comprehending affective prosody (e.g., understanding emotional tone of voice) and the left hemisphere for comprehending propositional prosody. During the past decade, however, a variety of studies have failed to demonstrate a clear lateralization for comprehension of affective prosody to the right, and comprehension of propositional prosody to the left hemisphere. Researchers in this area have attributed some of the inconsistencies to methodological differences between studies.

Neuroimaging studies have not helped to clear up the confusion. Two PET studies found regions in right prefrontal cortex to be activated during detection of affective prosody (George et al., 1996; Imaizumi et al., 1997). Areas of right prefrontal cortex were also activated in an fMRI study using exactly the same task for both emotional and nonemotional conditions (Buchanan et al., 2000). In one condition, participants were asked to identify the emotional intonation of spoken words, whereas in the other they were asked to detect a target word. However, consistent with at least some findings from studies on patients with brain damage, this study found significant activity in the right inferior parietal lobe for the emotional condition. Since, as we have seen, the prefrontal cortex is intimately involved in most emotional processes, it seems likely that it would be active during any emotional task. Taken together, the lesion and imaging data suggest that the right hemisphere may be more involved in the perception of prosody, but it remains to be seen exactly which regions are most important.

• ***Facial Expression and Emotional Scenes*** • Patients with right hemisphere brain damage also perform more poorly than patients with left hemisphere damage when (1) asked to discriminate between emotional faces or to name emotional scenes (e.g., DeKosky, Heilman, Bowers, & Valenstein, 1980), (2) matching emotional expressions (e.g., Cicone, Wapner, & Gardner, 1980), and (3) grouping both pictorially presented and written emotional scenes and faces (e.g., N. L. Etcoff, 1984; Kolb & Taylor, 1981). Patients with right hemisphere damage are also impaired in the comprehension and appreciation of humorous or affective aspects of cartoons, films, and stories (H. Gardner, King, Flamm, & Silverman, 1975; Wapner, Hamby, & Gardner, 1981). More recently, Borod and coworkers (1998) found patients with right hemisphere damage to be more impaired in tasks of emotion identification (name or point to the correct label for an emotional expression depicted on a slide) than patients with left hemisphere damage or controls. Some of the facial expressions that individuals with right hemisphere damage have difficulty distinguishing among are depicted in Figure 12.8. The most severe impairments in emotion recognition have been attributed to damage of the right parietal cortex. However, right anterior temporal lobectomy, a common treatment for medically intractable epilepsy, has also been shown to cause impairments in processing emotional information, especially negative emotion in faces (see Adolphs, Tranel, & Damasio, 2001).

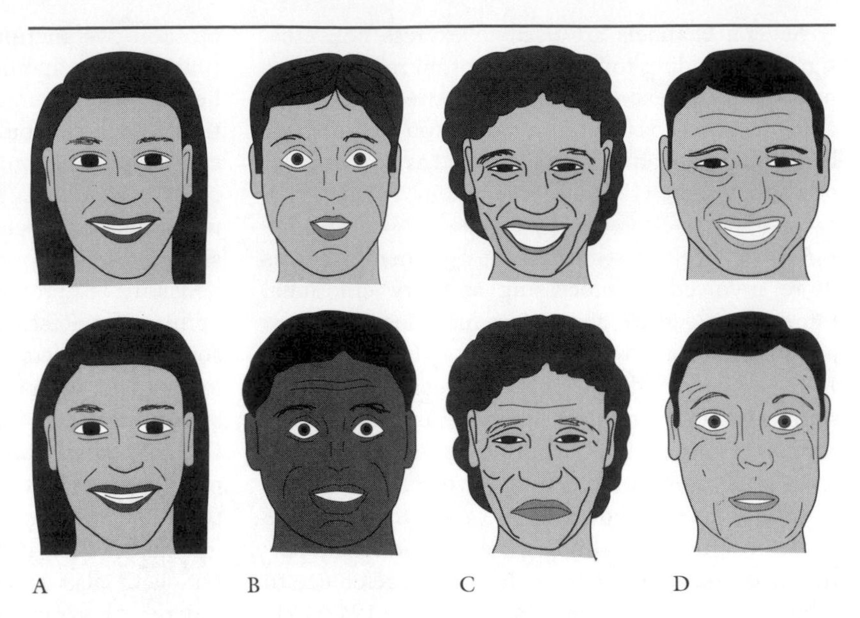

FIGURE 12.8 Examples of facial expressions of emotion that individuals with right-hemisphere damage have difficulty distinguishing between. Individuals with right-hemisphere damage are likely to have difficulty on a test such as the one shown here, in which they must decide whether the two faces in each column are expressing the same emotion. To ensure that the subject is not using other facial cues to perform the task, such as the poser's facial features, researchers use the following technique: in half of the trials the poser's identity remains constant, and in half it is changed. (A) Same face, same expression. (B) Different face, same expression. (C) Same face, different expression. (D) Different face, different expression.

The conclusion that the right hemisphere plays a special role in understanding emotional information has also been supported by behavioral studies with neurologically intact participants. Using divided visual field techniques, various researchers have found a left visual field (LVF), or right hemisphere, advantage on tasks that require participants to (1) discriminate among emotional expressions on faces (H. Buchtel, Campari, de Risio, & Rota, 1978; Ladavas, Umilta, & Ricci-Bitti, 1980; Pizzamiglio, Zoccolotti, Mammucari, & Cesaroni, 1983; Strauss & Moscovitch, 1981), (2) remember emotionally expressive faces (Suberi & McKeever, 1977), and (3) match an emotional face to a spoken word (Hansch & Pirozzolo, 1980) or to a cartoon drawing of a face (Landis, Assal, & Perret, 1979). Thus, the evidence converges to implicate the right hemisphere as playing an important role in appreciating the emotional significance of visual information.

• ***Is Facial Emotion Special?*** • One question that has engaged the interest of researchers is whether the right hemisphere is involved in processing the sight of emotional faces above and beyond that of faces in general. As you may remember from Chapter 6 (see page 210), a large amount of evidence from PET, fMRI, EEG, and MEG studies indicates that the fusiform region of the right hemisphere is differentially involved in processing such visual information (for review, see Halgren et al., 2000). Not surprisingly, the fusiform "face" area also becomes active in response to the sight of emotional faces (Dolan et al., 1996, Kesler/West et al., 2001). Furthermore, the greater the intensity of the sad expression, the greater was the activation in the right inferior and middle temporal gyri (Blair et al., 1999). On the basis of these findings one could argue that activation in the fusiform "face" area occurs in response to emotional faces because they are particularly expressive faces, not because they are specifically *emotional.*

Yet, data from studies of patients with unilateral lesions suggest that emotional-face processing may be dissociable from processing face identity. Cases have been reported of patients with prosopagnosia (i.e., people who can't recognize the faces of specific individuals) who can identify facial emotions (Tranel, Damasio, & Damasio, 1988). Conversely, other patients can recognize faces but can't identify facial emotion. Still other studies suggest a dissociation between spatial tasks other than face processing and emotion processing. For example, researchers have found subgroups of patients with right hemisphere damage who are not impaired on a nonemotional visuospatial task, but are impaired on an emotional one (DeKosky, Heilman, Bowers, & Valenstein, 1980). Likewise, other investigators have identified a group of patients with right hemisphere damage who were impaired relative to neurologically intact individuals and patients with left hemisphere damage on several emotional tasks, even when the patient groups performed equivalently on a measure of general visuospatial ability (Bowers, Bauer, Coslett, & Heilman, 1985).

The imaging data, though, are less supportive of such a clear-cut distinction. Some evidence suggests that the same regions, mainly those in right fusiform areas, are involved in processing both emotional and nonemotional faces. Emotional faces just seem to activate these regions to a greater degree (Dolan et al., 1996; Kesler/West et al., 2001, for angry faces only). Other evidence, however, suggests that there are brain regions uniquely involved in processing the emotional aspects of faces above and beyond faces in general (e.g., anterior cingulate: Kesler/West et al., 2001) (see Color insert 12. 3).

• *Clinical Implications* • How much is a person's quality of life disrupted by the inability to identify emotional signals? The answer is severely. Patients with right hemisphere damage can be extremely difficult to deal with on a daily basis. They often seem to have lost the most basic social skills, such as knowing when to take turns in a conversation (typically cued by facial expression and voice intonation) or knowing how close to stand to someone while engaged in a conversation. They tend to be talkative, but listeners often describe the content of their conversation as shallow and inconsequential. These patients laugh at inappropriate moments, or they display other emotions that don't seem to fit the context. To the dismay of those around them, they seem to have difficulty putting themselves in someone else's shoes and often alienate their family members and friends. These problems sound similar, in some ways, to those that occur after damage to orbitofrontal cortex (OFC). However, in this case there is typically a clear pattern of intellectual deficits that are specific to processing nonverbal and visuospatial information. Thus, the ability to comprehend nonverbal signals is probably at the root of many of their problems. In trying to help these patients and their families adjust, one focus of rehabilitation is to help the patient become more sensitive to emotional and social cues.

Even more of a problem, these patients often seem to be unaware of their disabilities, a syndrome called *anosognosia,* in which persons with brain damage fail to appreciate the fact that they are disabled or that their behavior has changed (Such difficulties are also observed in hemi-neglect, see Chapter 8). Patients with anosognosia do not realize that they are not thinking clearly or that they cannot do all the things they used to do. For example, an airplane pilot who had sustained a right hemisphere stroke with resulting left hemiparesis talked about going back to work the next day, ignoring even the fact that he was in the hospital. Clearly, such deficits in self-evaluation constitute a fundamental roadblock on the path to independent living and optimal rehabilitation. Thus, one of the main challenges facing rehabilitation professionals is to devise ways that enable such patients to become more aware of their disabilities.

The difficulty that patients with right hemisphere brain damage have in understanding social situations seems to extend to a difficulty in contextualizing all sorts of information. In an interesting study, Gardner and colleagues asked patients with right hemisphere damage and patients with left hemisphere damage to listen to a series of narratives (H. Gardner, Brownell, Wapner, & Michelow, 1983). The narratives were designed so that each included something that didn't make sense in the context of the story. When asked to recall the story, the patients with left hemisphere brain damage and the neurologically intact individuals either changed the nonsensical detail to fit the story or simply left it out. In contrast, the patients with right hemisphere brain damage not only remembered the detail but tried to make the rest of the story fit around it. This process caused them to sacrifice the essence of the narrative and end up with a highly implausible construction. On the basis of these results, the investigators suggested that the right hemisphere houses a system that assesses the plausibility of events. This system, they suggest, is important for the ability to judge the likelihood or probability that an event could actually take place. This notion fits well with some other data showing that patients with right hemisphere damage violate the contextual reality of objects (drawing things like a "potato bush," for example, even though potatoes grow underground). These results might also remind you of the situation we discussed previously in which the airplane pilot with right hemisphere damage seemed to be unaware of the magnitude of his deficits—an example of another way in which these patients seem out of touch with reality.

The idea that the right hemisphere is in a special position to judge the reality of something seems to be compatible with its other specializations, such as the ability to judge spatial relationships (as we discussed in Chapter 7) and the ability to distribute attention across both sides of space (as we discussed in Chapter 8). The fact that patients with right hemisphere damage have difficulty understanding the gist of a narrative suggests that skills associated with the right hemisphere are also important for judging relationships among many kinds of concepts, and for understanding how to put things in an appropriate context.

• *Sometimes the Left Hemisphere Is Right* • The left hemisphere, however, is not without any role in interpreting emotion. According to Bowers and colleagues, who have studied many patients with right hemisphere damage, the ability to understand emotional information depends upon a knowledge base that stores nonverbal information about the meaning of emotion—that is, a **nonverbal affect lexicon** (Bowers, Bauer, & Heilman, 1993). These investigators contrast this ability, which depends on the right hemisphere, with a type of emotional information processing that is not hemisphere specific, **emotional semantics,** the ability to label emotions and to understand the links between certain situations and specific emotions.

This idea is well illustrated in a behavioral study by Safer and Leventhal (1977), who asked participants to rate the emotionality of passages that variedin both emotional tone of voice and emotional content. Sometimes the emotional content was consistent with the emotional tone of voice (e.g., a story about something happy described in a happy tone of voice), and sometimes the emotional content was inconsistent with the emotional tone of voice (e.g., a story about something happy described in a sad tone of voice). The passages were presented to either the left ear or the right ear. These researchers found that participants who attended to the left ear based their ratings of emotionality on tone of voice, whereas participants who attended to the right ear based their ratings on the verbal content of the passages. In this study, therefore, the hemispheres relied on different sources of information to make judgments about the emotion presented in the passage: The right hemisphere used the nonverbal emotional content, and the left hemisphere used the verbal emotional content. These data are consistent with Bowers and colleagues' notion that the right hemisphere is important for nonverbal understanding of emotion but that the left hemisphere is able to process certain ideas about emotion. These findings are extended by neuroimaging studies, which have identified a variety of specific regions in both the right and left posterior hemispheres that appear to be involved in processing emotion (e.g. Iidaka et al., 2001).

• *EXPRESSING EMOTION* •

The expression of emotion is an extremely important component of social communication. For example, in Western culture it is considered rude not to look at a person's face when he or she is speaking to you. Many of our opinions about people are based on aspects of facial expression, and we often hear statements such as "He has a shifty look on his face" or "She has kind eyes." On the basis of facial expressions, we make judgments about all sorts of personal traits and qualities, such as whether a person is honest or dishonest; whether the person is attracted to us or dislikes us; whether she or he is kind, compassionate, cold, or cruel; and whether a person is sensible or "spacey." Both the phenomena of "love at first sight" and "I took an instant dislike to him" are frequently a function of the response to a person's face. Tone of voice carries a similar weight in affecting our emotional reactions to other people; a person who is soft-spoken is often believed to be gentle and nonjudgmental, whereas a person who is loud is perceived as arrogant and pushy.

• ***Prosody*** • We have discussed some brain mechanisms involved in the perception of emotion as expressed in a person's tone of voice, referred to as affective prosody. Various studies of patients with lateralized brain damage have supported the proposition that the right hemisphere is involved in *producing* affective prosody (for a review, see Borod, 1993). A common approach in such studies has been to present patients with neutral sentences and to ask them to repeat the sentence in different tones of voice (e.g., happy, sad, angry, or indifferent). Typically, individuals with right hemisphere damage speak in more of a monotone (e.g., D. M. Tucker, Watson, & Heilman, 1977). Furthermore, difficulty in producing prosody (i.e., **aprosodia**) appears to be a specific deficit, not just the result of an overall impairment in emotional functioning associated with right hemisphere damage (E. D. Ross & Mesulam, 1979). In one case, for example, a 39-year-old schoolteacher who had lost the capacity to convey emotion vocally and spoke in a monotone was still able to decode the emotions of other people and seemed to have a normal experience of emotion and an awareness of her own emotional state. These observations are also consistent with the evidence that different aspects of emotional function are implemented by different brain regions.

Some current work with clinical populations has focused on examining whether more specific components of the production of prosody, such as the basic frequency at which an utterance is made (known as the *fundamental frequency*), intensity, and timing parameters, may be differentially lateralized. Evidence suggests that deficits in producing fundamental frequency may be associated with right hemisphere damage, and deficits in producing timing parameters may be associated with left hemisphere damage (Pell, 1999).

• ***Facial Expression*** • Researchers have taken a variety of approaches to studying the neuropsychology of facial expression, but two are the most common. In one approach, the faces of patients with left or right hemisphere brain damage are photographed or videotaped while they are talking, watching emotional films, or doing other tasks. The photographs or videotapes are then rated, either subjectively by judges or by using coding schemes to identify the muscle movements in the face (such as the Facial Action Coding System developed by Paul Ekman; see Ekman, Hager, & Friesen, 1981). For example, if the corrugator muscles that control creasing of the eyebrows are judged to be active, the person can be inferred to be frowning, and if the zygomatic muscles that lift the edges of the mouth are judged to be active, the person can be scored as smiling (Figure 12.9). The emotion is then inferred from the facial expression.

In another approach, typically used with neurologically intact individuals, the emotional expression appearing on the left side of the face is compared with that appearing on the right. Often, we can observe facial asymmetries merely by looking at a face, as shown in Figure 12.10. However, one way to quantitatively evaluate facial asymmetry is to cut a picture of a person's face in half and to splice each half-face together with its mirror image to create a composite. The result is two chimeras, each consisting of two left half-faces or two right half-faces. When this is done, we can instantly see large differences in the appearance of the two sides of the face (see Figure 12.11).

Some of the earliest comments about these differences between the two sides of the face are

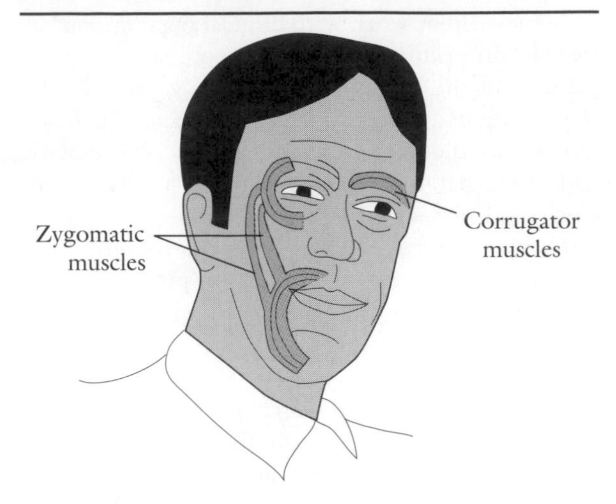

FIGURE 12.9 One method of studying facial expression. This method involves using a coding scheme that catalogs movements of specific facial muscles. For example, contraction of the zygomatic muscles is important for smiling, whereas contraction of the corrugator muscles is important for frowning.

interesting. Hallervorden (1902, 1929; cited in Borod, 1993), using the composite photograph technique, described the right side of the face as "apperceptive, thinking capably, lucid, and active" (p. 310). In contrast, the left side of the face was "perceptive, affective, having dark unformed content, and directionless" (p. 310). Somewhat later, Wolff (1933; cited in Borod, 1993) suggested that the right side of the face projects the social facade, whereas the left side reveals the passive unconscious self. Current descriptions based on these kinds of studies are less fanciful and poetic, although they sometimes parallel the previous descriptions. Generally, the left side of the face is found to be more expressive than the right side for both posed and spontaneous expressions, particularly for negative emotions (see Borod for an overview, 1993). These results are most consistently found in studies that examine neurologically intact adults. In contrast, the two sides of the face are more often judged to be symmetrical for positive emotions, such as smiles. This reduction in asymmetry for positive faces may occur because positive emotional expressions are more related to the conventions of social communication (e.g., in a public setting a person is perceived as more polite if he or she looks pleasant and smiles). Hence, they may be less likely to reflect sincere emotional experience.

It should be noted that findings across studies, especially among those examining facial asymmetry in individuals with brain damage, vary widely. Multiple factors besides which hemisphere is damaged may affect facial expression (for a good review, see Borod, 1993). These include the location of the lesion (anterior or posterior), the gender and age of an individual, and the cause of damage. If these factors all influence or moderate the degree to which the right hemisphere is involved in facial emotional expression, inconsistencies across studies would not be surprising.

A

B

C

D

FIGURE 12.10 Striking asymmetries in facial expression of emotion. Although we think of people's faces as symmetrical, asymmetries can be seen. Note the asymmetrical expressions on some well-known faces: (A) the Mona Lisa, (B) Marilyn Monroe, (C) Elvis Presley, and (D) John Wayne.

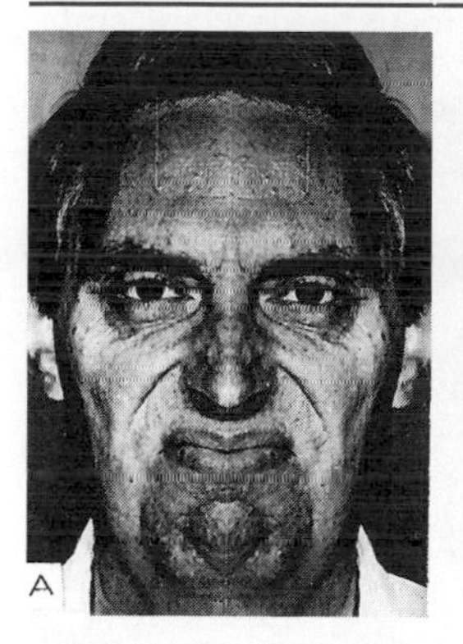

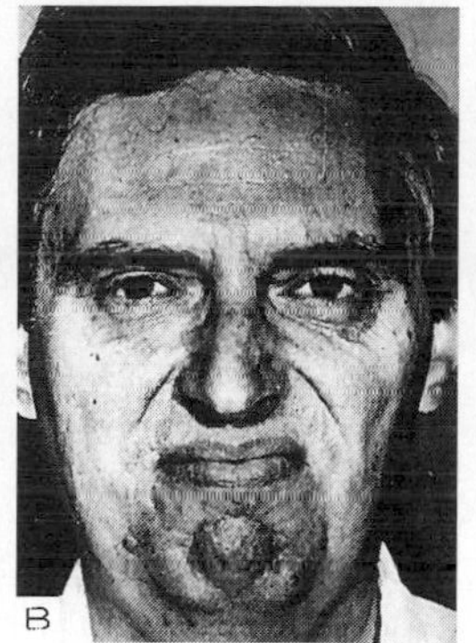

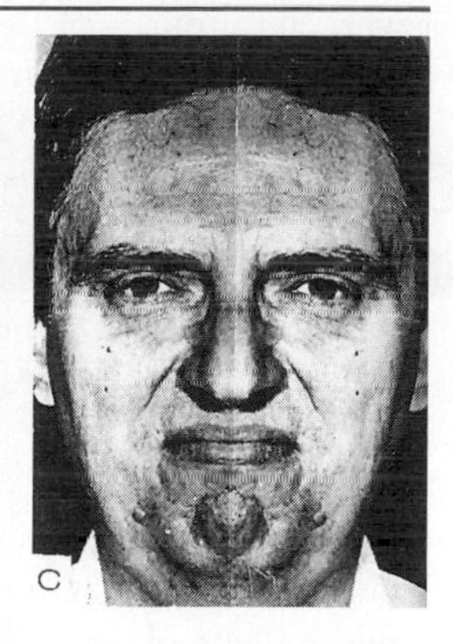

FIGURE 12.11 One method for demonstrating asymmetry of emotional facial expression. An original photograph of the face, shown here in B, is bisected. Then, each half-face is spliced together with its mirror image to create a composite. Note the difference between the two composites depicted in A and C. Which one looks more emotionally intense to you? Usually, individuals choose the composite composed of two left half-faces, depicted in A, as more intense than the composite composed of two right half-faces, depicted in C. This result suggests that the right hemisphere, which controls the lower left half of the face, has a larger role in producing facial emotional expression.

The inconsistencies may also arise because of the use of different methods. In studies in which judges rate the faces, the right hemisphere is typically found to play a more important role, whereas in studies in which coding systems are used, usually no special role is reported. Although debate continues about the reasons for these differences, one possibility is that something about the configuration, or combinations, of movements (as opposed to the exact muscle movements) that signal emotion may be affected by right hemisphere damage in a way that human perceivers can discern but that are not detected by coding schemes.

Models of Neural Organization of Emotion

In this section of the chapter we examine the ways in which many theorists have tried to provide a broader conceptualization that integrates the multiplicity of findings regarding brain functioning and emotion processing. We start with an historical perspective on some of the thinking on this topic, and then discuss the range of models that have been proposed. Afterwards, we focus on two specific models (approach/withdrawal and valence/arousal) that link basic dimensions of emotion to neural substrates.

Overview of Models of Emotion Processing

Early models of emotion and the brain speculated that the hemispheres had different emotional biases (for reviews, see Heller, 1990; Borod et al., 1998). The left hemisphere was suggested to be specialized for positive, or cheerful, affect, and the right hemisphere was suggested to be specialized for negative, or depressed, affect. This type of theory has been called a **valence theory** because its main premise is that the emotional state of one hemisphere has a particular valence (e.g., positive), whereas the emotional state of the other hemisphere has the opposite valence (e.g., negative). This theory seemed to be supported initially by findings from EEG recordings taken during different emotional states, and from the catastrophic response observed after left hemisphere damage and the euphoria/indifference reaction observed after right hemisphere damage. According to these valence models, damage immobilizes or diminishes the functioning of the damaged hemisphere, revealing the basic emotional tenor of the intact hemisphere. Another prominent early theory held that the right hemisphere was specialized for processing all types of emotion. This theory was based on evidence from studies of patients with brain damage indicating that right hemisphere damage interfered with the ability to understand emotional information (as was discussed earlier).

How can these findings be integrated? As long as *emotional experience* was considered indistinguishable from the ability to interpret *emotional information,* the findings remained contradictory. However, eventually investigators realized that just because a hemisphere is associated with a particular emotional state, that hemisphere is not necessarily "specialized" to process information corresponding to that emotion. Evidence from patients with brain damage and other clinical populations suggests that "feeling" an emotion can be distinguished from "knowing" about an emotion. Just as speech output seems to be localized to one region of the left hemisphere (Broca's area) and speech comprehension to another (Wernicke's area), a neuropsychological system involved in feeling can be independent of another system involved in the interpretation of that feeling. Therefore, the right hemisphere could be specialized for the interpretation of emotion without necessarily being specialized for the regulation of emotional experience.

Most researchers would currently agree that although the evaluation of emotion and the experience of mood may not be entirely independent of each other, they do need to be distinguished (Davidson, 1993; Heller, 1990). Furthermore, they appear to depend primarily upon different regions of the brain. In particular, the evaluation of emotion appears to be differentially processed by the posterior regions of the right hemisphere, whereas experiential aspects of emotion seem to be associated with asymmetric activity of the prefrontal regions.

Yet even such a distinction does not capture all the complexity of the situation. For example, neuroimaging studies have indicated that different subsections of the prefrontal cortex are involved in different aspects of emotional experience. Furthermore, the distinction between evaluation and experience is not always clear-cut. Thus, it has become extremely important to be as specific as possible about *what aspect* of emotion processing is under investigation when looking for its neural substrates (Borod et al., 1998).

Current theories of the neural bases of emotion range from general representations of the brain-behavior relationships to a description of the specific circuits involved in particular emotional processes. As an example of a model at a more general level, Lane (2000) argues that different types of emotion are represented by distinct circuits that involve different brain structures. The interactions between these circuits are hierarchically organized according to the complexity of the emotional process and the degree to which it is accessible to conscious awareness. In this model, unconscious emotional responses are implemented by more primitive brain structures, mirroring MacLean's conception of the evolution of brain structures.

Some of the circuit models focus on a specific emotion as a prototype (e.g., fear, as proposed by LeDoux, 2000) whereas others emphasize other higher-order constructs that represent different ways of conceptually organizing emotional behaviors. For instance, Dolan and Morris (2000) propose a model based on the notion that there are brain systems that have evolved to regulate responses to the environment by signaling the "value" of a stimulus or event. All of these models describe a set of proposed brain regions and the connections between them that would constitute a circuit that implements the behaviors.

Still other models examine underlying dichotomies in emotional processing and link them to specific neural systems, rather than describing a circuit that is linked to a particular emotional response. We now examine in a bit more detail two such models.

Approach/Withdrawal Model

The first model we examine, proposed by Davidson and his colleagues (see Sutton, 2002, for a review), posits that there are distinct brain systems for approach and withdrawal. Approach and withdrawal are considered by many to be the most basic and rudimentary actions that organisms take in responding adaptively to the environment. As emotions evolved, they became associated with already established approach-and-withdrawal action systems. Hence, the left frontal region is posited to house a system involved in approach behaviors, and increased activity of the left frontal area is associated with emotions that tend to be accompanied by approach behaviors, including most positive emotions. Some negative emotions, such as anger, that tend to be associated with approach behaviors are also suggested to be associated with increased activity of the left frontal region. In contrast, the right frontal region is posited to house a system involved in withdrawal behaviors, and increased activity of the right frontal area is associated with emotions that are accompanied by withdrawal behaviors, such as fear, disgust, and depression.

Davidson views the frontal region as a convergence zone where information from the posterior perceptual processing regions, such as the parietal cortex, is combined with information from subcortical areas involved in attributing emotional significance to sensory input, such as the amygdala. This notion is compatible with the view of LeDoux (1993) that emotional function is regulated by a system involving multiple regions of the brain. Both researchers would likely agree that the frontal region of the cortex is important for the most complex and coordinated decision making and action planning. As such, it would be crucial for it to have access to the various sources of emotional information processed or stored in other areas of the brain.

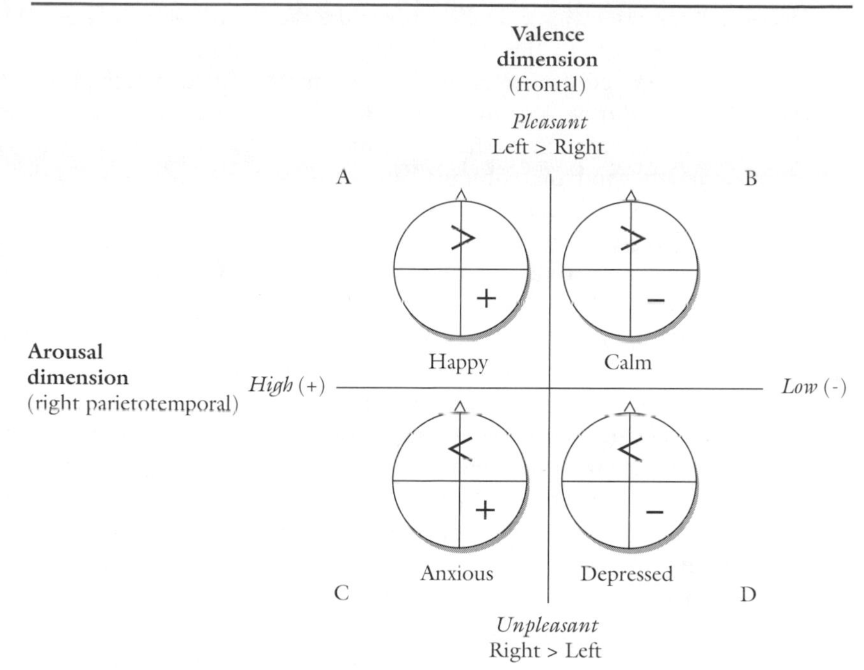

FIGURE 12.12 Model of regional brain activity and mood proposed by Heller (1993a). This model posits that the valence dimension of mood (positive, or pleasant, vs. negative, or unpleasant; *y* axis) is mainly affected by activation of frontal regions of the brain, whereas the arousal dimension (high vs. low; *x* axis) is mainly affected by activation of the right posterior region. Depicted here are the patterns of brain activation for four mood states. (Top left) When activation of left frontal regions is greater than that of right frontal regions (which leads to pleasant emotion) and the right posterior region is highly activated (which leads to arousal), the individual is happy. (Top right) The pattern of activation is identical over frontal regions for a calm state, but the activity over the right posterior region is reduced, which leads to a lower level of arousal for a calm state than for happiness. (Bottom left) In anxiety, higher right than left frontal activation leads to a negative valence, and high activity in the right posterior region leads to increased arousal. (Bottom right) Finally, the brain activation in depression is similar to that of anxiety in that higher right than left frontal activation leads to a negative valence. However, the low activity in the right posterior region causes the decreased arousal that differentiates depression from anxiety.

Valence/Arousal Model

Another model of emotion advanced by this author and her colleagues conceives specific patterns of brain activity to be associated with different emotional states, or moods (Heller, 1993a,b; Heller & Nitschke, 1998). Previously we discussed how research indicates that the evaluation of emotion needs to be distinguished from the experience of emotion. Our model focuses on this latter aspect of emotion. The model is founded on theories suggesting that emotions can be described by two fundamental dimensions: valence (pleasant vs.unpleasant, or positive vs. negative) and arousal (high vs. low) (e.g., Feldman, Barrett, & Russell, 1999). According to the model, frontal regions are involved in the valence aspect of emotion while the posterior right hemisphere is involved in the arousal aspect (see Figure 12.12). Earlier in the chapter we discussed the association of emotional valence with activity in frontal regions, such as the catastrophic reaction after left frontal damage and the euphoric reaction after right frontal damage. Although we have discussed the arousal aspect of emotion in terms of the physiological and autonomic functions described at the beginning of this chapter as critical components of emotion, we have not discussed evidence linking it to functioning of the posterior section of the right hemisphere. Now we do so.

The right hemisphere appears to play a special role in the regulation of autonomic and physiological responses (for review, see Heller, Nitschke, & Lindsay, 1997). Damage to the right hemisphere is associated with marked decreases in electrodermal responses (e.g., L. Morrow, Vrtunski, Kim, & Boller, 1981) and with slowing on certain reaction-time tasks above and beyond that observed in patients with other types of brain damage (e.g., A. Benton, 1986). In neurologically intact individuals, emotional stimuli presented to the right hemisphere but not the left, have been found to affect heart rate and blood pressure (Walker & Sandman, 1979; Wittling, 1990). Similarly, the right hemisphere seems to play a special role in the secretion of cortisol, which is a physiological response to certain stressful emotional events. For example, significant changes in salivary cortisol secretion occur when an emotionally aversive film is projected to the right hemisphere but not when it was projected to the left hemisphere (Wittling & Pflüger, 1990). Self-reported arousal (ratings of fatigue and energy) also shows a relationship to right hemisphere processing; the higher the energy level, the larger the left hemispatial bias on the Chimeric Faces Test (Heller et al., 1997: see Chapter 8, page 280)

This model has been particularly helpful in differentiating the patterns of brain activity that characterize depression and anxiety. Note that anxiety and depression are expected to be similar with regard to activity of the prefrontal cortex (i.e., greater right frontal than left frontal activation), but are expected to show activity in opposite directions for the posterior regions of the brain (high right posterior activity for anxiety, low right posterior activity for depression). Because anxiety and depression often co-occur, opposing patterns of activity could make it difficult to distinguish the two.

In a series of EEG and behavioral asymmetry (dichotic listening) studies, Bruder and colleagues (1997, 1999) have in fact shown that depressed people with an anxiety disorder differ from those without an anxiety disorder. When there is no anxiety disorder, depression is associated with evidence for decreased activity in posterior regions of the right hemisphere, both in terms of EEG recordings and in reduced behavioral asymmetries in favor of the right hemisphere. When an anxiety disorder is present, there is a propensity to show greater activation of the right hemisphere, as Heller's model would predict. Notice that in this model, certain emotional states or processes do not reside in particular regions of brain tissue. Rather it is the pattern of *relative* activation across a series of brain areas that is related to emotion processing, more specifically mood.

Individual Differences in Affective Style

In previous sections of this chapter we have seen that different patterns of regional brain activity are associated with different kinds of emotions; for example, sad moods are typically accompanied by more right than left prefrontal cortex activity, and anxiety is often accompanied by more right than left posterior cortex activity. These findings imply that people might differ in their characteristic tendencies to show different patterns of regional brain activity, and therefore may differ in a variety of personal and psychological dimensions, including their "affective styles" (Davidson, 2001), their risk for psychopathology (Heller et al., 2002), or their sensitivity to incentives or threats (Sutton, 2002).

Affective styles refer to individual differences in emotional reactivity, which could include things like how quickly a person calms down after a scare or emotional challenge, and dispositional mood, or a tendency to respond to things with an optimistic or a pessimistic outlook (Davidson, 2001). Asymmetries in both frontal and posterior regions have been linked to these individual differences in affective styles.

EEG measures reveal that people differ in the degree to which they show more right than left or left than right prefrontal activity during a resting baseline condition. These asymmetries predict dispositional mood, with more left frontal activity associated with a more optimistic or positive outlook and more right frontal activity associated with a greater reactivity to negative stimuli. They are even related to the functioning of the immune system, with greater left frontal activity predicting a more robust immune response. These patterns were replicated in 10-month-old infants, who were more likely to cry when separated from their mothers if they had more right than left prefrontal activation.

Moreover, children were more likely to be socially wary if they had more right than left prefrontal activation. In fact, these researchers have now described similar patterns in rhesus monkeys, who show higher levels of the stress hormone cortisol if they have more right than left prefrontal activation (Davidson, 2001).

Individual differences in asymmetries of posterior brain regions also have been found to predict risk for psychopathology (Heller et al., 2002). Across a number of studies with college students, behavioral measures and EEG results indicate that depression is associated with reduced right hemisphere acti-vity, and anxiety with increased right hemisphere activity.

Neural Bases of Mood and Emotional Disorders in Psychopathology

For the most part, we have discussed emotion processing in the brains of individuals who do not have psychiatric disorders or who had normal emotional functioning prior to the brain insult. In this section, we consider whether the same brain mechanisms that we have already discussed also play a role in psychopathology.

Depression

Depression is considered to be a mood disorder characterized by chronic feelings of sadness and hopelessness, and loss of interest or pleasure. Depression can also be seasonal, defined by the existence of a regular temporal relationship between the onset of an episode of depression and a particular 60-day period of the year (i.e., as the days become shorter). A milder state of chronic depression has been termed *dysthymia* (or depressive neurosis). It is diagnosed if a person has experienced symptoms of depression for at least two years (one year for children or adolescents). Typical symptoms of depression, in addition to sadness, hopelessness, and loss of interest or pleasure, include poor appetite or overeating, insomnia (difficulty falling asleep or early morning awakening) or hypersomnia (too much sleeping), low energy or fatigue, low self-esteem, and poor concentration or difficulty making decisions.

A number of brain regions have been implicated in depression. Not surprisingly, some of these will be familiar to you, since you have already seen that they are involved in normal mood states. Many studies have identified a deficit in activity of the prefrontal cortex (see Mohanty & Heller, 2002). Evidence from a variety of paradigms, ranging from those that examine individuals in resting states to those in which people must perform a task, show that depression generally is associated with reduced regional cerebral blood flow and metabolism in prefrontal cortex, anterior cingulate gyrus, and basal ganglia (for review, see Videbach, 2000). In addition, there is evidence that an asymmetric pattern of less left than right prefrontal activity is superimposed on this overall suppression (Heller & Nitschke, 1998). Some studies suggest that this asymmetry might be due to a hypoarousal of the left frontal region in particular (e.g., Henriques & Davidson, 1991).

Consistent with EEG findings, positron emission tomography (PET) studies have reported a decrease in regional cerebral blood flow (rCBF) in the left dorsolateral prefrontal cortex in depression (Baxter et al., 1989; Bench et al., 1993; Bench et al., 1992; George et al., 1993, 1994; Martinot et al., 1990). The hypoarousal of the left frontal region may reflect a vulnerability to dysfunction in the approach system housed in this brain region (Henriques & Davidson, 1991). Although not everyone with reduced activation of the left frontal region will become depressed, people who display such a pattern are more vulnerable to depression if other disturbing life events occur. This concept might explain why, although many studies have revealed that a higher proportion of patients with left frontal lobe lesions are depressed (e.g., Robinson et al., 1984), some have not (e.g., Gainotti, 1989). If hypoarousal of the left frontal region (relative to the right) increases vulnerability, other factors (such as distressing life events, degree of social support, financial worries, or personality traits) would play an important role in whether a person becomes depressed after experiencing brain damage. This kind of conceptualization is called a **diathesis-stress model,** in which environmental factors (the stressors) interact with or exacerbate a biological predisposition (the diathesis).

As one might expect from our discussion in the last chapter, abnormal activation of the prefrontal cortex has an impact on a variety of important cognitive functions (Heller & Nitschke, 1997; Mohanty & Heller, 2002). Findings from neuropsychological studies indicate that depression is associated with deficits in important executive functions, including set shifting, inhibition, and updating. For example, a number of studies have shown that depression is associated with impairments in working memory (e.g., Elliott et al., 1996). Individuals with depression exhibit deficits on a working-memory task that are accompanied by event-related potential (ERP) abnormalities consistent with dysfunction of a central executive system (Pelosi et al., 2000). Furthermore, individuals with depression do poorly on tasks that depend on aspects of executive functioning such as the Tower of London planning test (Elliott et al., 1997; Elliott et al., 1996). Similar results have been reported for the Stroop color word test (Trichard et al., 1995; Degl'Innocenti et al., 1998) (see Figure 12.13).

Researchers have also investigated whether executive functioning deficits persist in individuals with depression even when they are no longer in a depressed mood. There is some evidence that residual deficits remain. For example, after recovery from a depressed episode, some individuals still have difficulty in set shifting (Paradiso et al., 1997), simple and choice reaction times, verbal fluency (Beats et al., 1996), and the Stroop task (Trichard et al., 1995). Currently, it appears that residual deficits in mnemonic and executive functions persist in some patients with a history of depression. However, the relationship of these deficits to epidemiological variables such as age, treatment, duration, and chronicity of illness and number of episodes remains to be more clearly determined (Austin et al., 2001).

As we have discussed, depression is accompanied by a relative decrease in activation of posterior regions of the right hemisphere (Heller, 1993b, e.g., Deldin, Keller, Gergen, & Miller, 2000; Kayser et al., 2001). Thus, it is not surprising that depressed individuals also exhibit relatively poor performance on various neuropsychological tasks that depend on the right hemisphere, such as judgment of line orientation, three-dimensional constructional skills, face recognition, spatial association learning, and performance with the nondominant hand on the

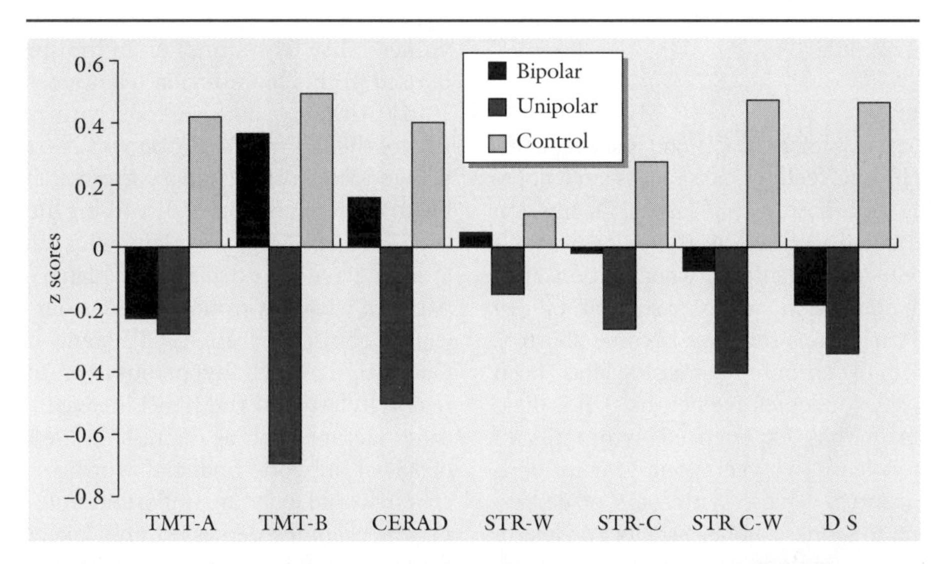

FIGURE 12.13 Deficits in patients with unipolar depression on a number of tasks dependent on prefrontal regions. Shown here are scores for patients with unipolar depression (blue bars), bipolar disorder (i.e., mania or mania with depression) (black bars), and neurologically intact controls (grey bars). TMT = Trail-making test; CERAD = a dementia rating scale, STR = Stroop test, DS = digit span. A Z-score of 0 is average. Positive scores indicate good performance, and negative scores indicate poor performance.

Tactual Performance Test (Mohanty & Heller, 2002; Heller & Nitschke, 1997). Consistent with these findings, depressed patients diagnosed according to *DSM* criteria with either bipolar illness or *melancholia* (i.e., sad mood along with possible disrupted sleep cycle, psychomotor slowing, excessive guilt, and weight loss) criteria have also been found to show abnormal perceptual asymmetries on lateralized tasks as a result of impairments in right hemisphere performance (Bruder et al., 2002).

Therapy for depression typically involves medication as well as psychotherapy. There are a variety of medications. Most of them alter the balance of neurotransmitters, in particular serotonin and dopamine. The most commonly used are called selective serotonin reuptake inhibitors (see Chapter 2, page 54). They make more serotonin available to the brain by interfering with the rate at which it is broken down. Serotonin seems to increase the overall arousal of the brain and body and leads to improved mood. A common psychotherapy technique, cognitive-behavioral therapy, works by helping people to change their self-defeating beliefs and attitudes.

An interesting new approach to the treatment of depression uses repetitive transcranial magnetic stimulation (TMS) to interrupt or augment cortical activity. Daily left prefrontal TMS to enhance activation in this region was found to improve mood in patients with depression (George et al., 1997). This therapeutic approach is currently undergoing intensive research in clinical trials as a possible treatment for depression. Recent findings (Mosimann et al., 2000) caution that not all studies have been able to demonstrate changes in mood, and call for larger sample sizes in future research.

Anxiety Disorders

The most common cognitive characteristic of anxiety, documented in all the anxiety disorders as well as in individuals who are put in an anxiety-producing situation, is an attentional bias to potential threat (for review, see McNally, 1998). These biases have been elicited very reliably across a variety of paradigms in which potentially threatening information is better at capturing attention in individuals with anxiety disorders than in controls. One task often used to assess this bias is the *emotional Stroop task*, a variant of the classic color-word Stroop task. Like that task, the person must name the color of words while ignoring their meaning. However, in this task the words are emotionally disturbing words rather than color words. Typically, when people are anxious, it takes them longer to identify the color of the emotionally disturbing words than of emotionally neutral words. Thus, we can conclude that their attention has been captured by the *meaning* of the disturbing word, interfering with their attention to the task at hand, which is to identify the word's color. For people who have had traumatic experiences, and who are suffering from posttraumatic stress disorder (PTSD) in response to combat or assault, such biases can be strongly elicited by using trauma-related stimuli, such as combat-related words (for review, see McNally, 1998). However, attentional biases can be elicited even in people without clinical disorders, especially in individuals who score higher on self-report measures that are designed to gauge anxiety (Compton et al., 2000).

Cognitive biases have also been observed in anxious individuals in how they interpret information and what they remember. Across a number of different paradigms involving ambiguous stimuli that can be interpreted as threatening or neutral, anxious people choose the threatening meaning. Accruing evidence suggests that anxiety disorders are also accompanied by enhanced memory for negative or threatening information under certain conditions (see McNally, 1998, for more details).

Such biases in attention and memory may be linked to a right hemisphere system involved in "emotional surveillance" (Compton et al., 2000; Nitschke, Heller, & Miller, 2000), a term coined by Bear (1986). This system is hypothesized to be part of a broader network that not only governs withdrawal and avoidance behaviors (Davidson, 1998) but also attends to the external environment on an ongoing basis with regard to threat. It is hypothesized to monitor for threat, to orient toward potential threat, to appraise the context for information regarding the possibility of threat, and to exert hierarchical control over the autonomic and somatic functions for responding to threat (Nitschke et al., 2000). Evidence for such a system is provided by a variety of behav-

CAUSES OF GENDER DIFFERENCES IN DEPRESSION: BIOLOGY, ENVIRONMENT, OR BOTH?

The rates of depression in our society constitute a significant mental health problem, one that is receiving growing attention from government agencies such as the National Institutes of Health in the United States. The problem is particularly acute for women: Many studies have revealed a female-to-male ratio of approximately 2 to 1 (Weissman et al., 1984).

Much literature has been generated on the causes of depression; researchers have examined factors inherent to the individual (e.g., genetic, neurochemical, and neuropsychological traits), as well as factors related to the environment, such as extreme loss (e.g., death of a parent), socialization processes that foster helplessness, and severe trauma (e.g., physical or sexual abuse). In general, it seems most likely that a complex interaction between biological vulnerability and environmental stress predisposes some people to depression.

In the attempt to explain gender differences in depression, many researchers have focused on the differing neurobiological functions that occur in the brain of a woman as compared to that of a man. Some researchers have argued that neurochemical messenger systems in a woman's brain are more finely tuned and therefore are more likely to become chronically disrupted or disregulated if normal developmental processes are interrupted or modified. For example, various regions of the brain that regulate reproductive hormones (e.g., hypothalamus, pituitary gland) are linked to the part of the body that produces adrenaline, a chemical that mediates a physical response to stress and threat. Early experiences of threat or stress may cause a greater dysregulation of this linkage in females than males, making the system overly responsive to stress. That could then in turn lead to a greater vulnerability toward depression in later years.

Another neurobiological phenomenon that has been identified in depression has to do with the relative level of activation of the cerebral hemispheres. As we have already described, two laterality effects are prominent in depression. First, people who are depressed exhibit lower activity of left than right frontal region compared with nondepressed individuals. Second, functions of the right posterior hemisphere are impaired in persons who are depressed, but not in individuals without depression.

Do these findings with regard to laterality tell us anything about gender differences in depression? Unfortunately, few researchers have examined this issue. Although little

ioral studies showing a right hemisphere bias in response to threat, lesion studies showing a pathological lack of anxiety after right brain damage, and EEG and PET studies showing increased right hemisphere activity in populations characterized by anxiety or experimental paradigms eliciting anxiety (e.g., Compton et al., 2000; Heller, Etienne, & Miller, 1995; Van Strien & Heijt, 1995).

Although anxiety is often referred to as a homogenous construct, neuropsychological data clearly indicate that unique patterns and heterogeneity exist both among and within the various anxiety disorders. Inconsistencies across studies may be explained by the fact that anxiety is not a unitary phenomenon and that different types and symptoms of anxiety are associated with particular cognitive patterns. It has been argued that distinctions should be drawn between panic, or **anxious arousal,** typically defined as an acute state associated with many physiological symptoms (including changes in heart rate, muscle activity, and temperature; see D. H. Barlow, 1991), and worry, or **anxious apprehension,** defined, for example, by Carter, Johnson, and Borkovec (1986) as an "uncontrollable verbally mediated cognitive activity, or thoughts, about self-relevant issues, such as interpersonal relations, finances, and work . . . concerned primarily with future events" (p. 193) (Heller & Nitschke, 1998; Nitschke et al., 2000).

Empirical data on brain activity and anxiety support such a distinction. Those studies focusing on individuals diagnosed with panic disorder or on states of anxious arousal yield indications of higher right hemisphere activity (e.g., Reiman et al., 1984). These findings are consistent with overactivation of the emotion-surveillance system of the right hemisphere. In contrast, studies focusing on anxious apprehension or worry yielded either no asymmetry

direct research has occurred in this area, we can consider some alternatives. It is possible that a greater proportion of females than males are born with relatively higher right frontal activity than left frontal activity. This would result in a greater proportion of females being vulnerable to depression. Another possibility is there are just as many males as females with a neurological vulnerability to depression (i.e., relatively reduced left frontal activity), but more of the females with this vulnerability develop depression as a result of a disparity in the number and intensity of environmental elicitors. For example, convincing evidence suggests that childhood sexual abuse is associated with depression later in life, and females are much more likely than males to be sexually abused. Similarly, women are socialized to be passive and feel helpless more often than men. To resolve these issues, future research will need to include groups of both males and females, and patterns of gender differences will need to be examined across the life span, from infancy through adulthood. Only then will researchers be able to untangle the alternative explanations for the observed gender differences in depression.

Furthermore, differences between the genders in the strategy used to cope with depression may influence the degree to which abnormal patterns of brain activity can be normalized. More specifically, Nolen-Hoeksema (1987) found that women are more likely to ruminate when depressed, whereas men are more likely to involve themselves in a distracting activity, such as a sport. Engaging in athletic activity may be particularly helpful when depressed, because recent research indicates that exercise produces a shift in cerebral activation such that the left frontal region becomes more active relative to the right (Petruzzello & Landers, 1992). Interestingly, physical activity has been found to enhance the self-concept of women who are depressed. Thus, perhaps the rate of depression in women versus men is also affected by the choice of behavioral coping strategies (e.g., engaging in athletic activities), which in turn influence the neurophysiological mechanisms underlying different emotional states.

To date, no definitive conclusions can be drawn about the reasons why more women than men are depressed. However, a number of promising pathways are open for investigation. Regardless of the methodology or aspect of brain function or psychology under investigation, researchers must consider the interplay of environmental and biological factors when attempting to construct hypotheses about brain-behavior relationships. This consideration is particularly important in light of the evidence for potentially large differences in the social and educational forces that are at play in the lives of women and men. ■

or higher left hemisphere activity (e.g., Carter, Johnson, & Borkovec, 1986; Reiman, Fusselman, Fox, & Raichle, 1989; D. M. Tucker, Antes, Stenslie, & Barnhardt, 1978; S. K. Tyler & Tucker, 1982). These findings are consistent with the notion that worry relies on verbal ruminations about the possibility of future catastrophic events. It is important to note that these two forms of anxiety are not mutually exclusive and likely exist in all individuals with anxiety disorders to varying degrees. Pronounced differences across individuals in the expression of both forms of anxiety are also likely, as are intraindividual differences across time.

In addition to hemispheric differences, there is evidence that specific aspects of anxiety disorders can be linked to a wide variety of brain regions. Anxiety disorders engage brain regions involved in threat perception (e.g., right hemisphere regions), anxious arousal (right posterior regions), fear (e.g., amygdala), vigilance for motivationally salient events (e.g., amygdala), decoding of motivationally relevant emotional information such as the reward and punishment value of a stimulus (e.g., orbital frontal cortex), worry (e.g., left hemisphere regions), response conflict (e.g., anterior cingulate cortex), and memory (e.g., hippocampus) (see Nitschke & Heller, 2002, for a review).

This is not to say that any particular anxiety disorder affects all these brain regions. Rather, the difference variants of anxiety disorders affect some of these regions more than others. For example, PTSD is the only disorder to be accompanied by memory deficits and by reduced hippocampal volume, whereas visual spatial deficits have been observed for obsessive compulsive disorder and social phobia but not the others.

Treatment for anxiety disorders typically involves the use of medications, known as *anxiolytics,* which are designed to reduce anxiety. Most of these drugs include benzodiazepines, such as Valium, that tend to act as agonists on GABA receptors. As you may remember from Chapter 2, GABA receptors tend to be inhibitory. It is thought that there is global decrease in binding of GABA receptors in the amygdala, orbitofrontal cortex, and insula of individuals with anxiety disorders, leading to overactivation of regions of the nervous system sensitive to fear and negative states. These drugs mainly act to circumvent a state of anxious arousal, but cannot be used long-term because of their potential for addiction. For more long-term treatment, cognitive-behavioral psychotherapy is usually employed. An example of this type of therapy is *systematic desensitization,* which teaches a person to link a calm state with the situation or item that provokes anxiety. Psychotherapy that provides insight as to what makes the individual anxious and how to avoid such situations or cope with them is also helpful (see Julien, 2001, Chapter 6).

Schizophrenia

Schizophrenia is a serious mental disorder that is the primary diagnosis for approximately 50 percent of all people in mental institutions in the United States. Currently, schizophrenia is viewed as a brain disease, although a diathesis-stress model has been strongly supported in its etiology.

Schizophrenia is currently classified into five types: disorganized, catatonic, paranoid, undifferentiated, and residual. Each type presents a somewhat different clinical picture, and the symptoms vary considerably among the types. Typically, however, patients show a combination of symptoms from a set of eight categories (Table 12.1). Given the background you now have in neuropsychology, you can see, by looking at these eight categories, that many regions of the brain might be involved in schizophrenia. Content and form of thought might be related mainly to frontal regions; perception and affect, mainly to the right hemisphere and subcortical areas; and sense of self, volition, and psychomotor behavior, to the frontal areas and to subcortical regions. Indeed, current perspectives on schizophrenia view it as fundamentally characterized by neurological dysfunction (Harrison, 1999).

A variety of techniques have been used to gain insight into the structure and function of the brain in schizophrenia. These have included measurement of anatomical features using magnetic resonance imaging (MRI) and data examining cellular architecture, as well as measures of more dynamic patterns of activity as indexed by fMRI, by electrical poten-

TABLE 12.1 Symptom Categories in Schizophrenia

CATEGORY	SYMPTOM(S)
Content of thought	A delusion or false belief.
Form of thought	A formal thought disorder involving abnormalities in the way a person's thought processes are organized. "Loose association," in which ideas shift from one unrelated topic to another, is a common example of this type of symptom.
Perception	Hallucinations or the reporting of experiences for which no observable eliciting stimuli appear to exist.
Affect	Disturbed emotions. Most common are emotions that are blunted, flat, or inappropriate to the situation.
Sense of self	Confusion about self-identity. The person may feel unreal or controlled by outside forces.
Volition	Reduced motivation and interest in pursuing almost any sort of goal. These symptoms interfere severely with a person's ability to work.
Relationship to the external world	Withdrawal from the external world and preoccupation with internal fantasies and odd ideas. These symptoms are sometimes called *autistic*.
Psychomotor behavior	Abnormalities of movement, including rocking, pacing, stereotyped actions, and bizarre behavioral rituals. Some patients diagnosed with schizophrenia become almost totally immobile; others take on a disheveled look or dress oddly, against social norms.

tials on the scalp (EEG, MEG, and ERP recordings) and blood flow (measured by PET). However, the findings across studies are varied, and although brain abnormalities are persistently found, an integrated model of neural pathology in schizophrenia remains elusive.

Neuropathologies in a number of brain regions have been identified in terms of both structural and functional anomalies. Structurally, the most robust findings relate to enlargement of the lateral and third ventricles (Sponheim, Clementz, Iacono, & Beiser, 2000), and loss of cortical thickness, particularly in the temporal lobes (Lawrie & Abukmeil, 1998). The frontal lobes and the basal ganglia have also been implicated, and Buchsbaum (1990) argued that these three areas might be part of a single neural system that is dysfunctional in schizophrenia.

Early studies using divided visual field techniques argued for pathology of the left hemisphere accompanied by its overactivation (R. E. Gur, 1978). Subsequent examinations using brain imaging techniques and electrophysiological recording have upheld the notion that some type of problem exists in the left temporal lobe. An overall reduction in the normal amplitude of the P_{300} component of the ERP has been replicated a number of times in patients diagnosed with schizophrenia (see McCarley et al., 1993). Furthermore, these abnormalities correlate with reductions in the amount of brain tissue present in the left temporal regions as measured by magnetic resonance imaging (MRI) (McCarley et al., 1993). These findings are intuitively appealing given the often dramatic symptoms of thought disorder, including bizarre verbalizations and nonlinear thinking, that such patients demonstrate.

Other studies have pointed to possible pathology in the right hemisphere as well. The flat affect often shown by these patients has been compared to the deficits in prosody that clinical studies have described in patients with right brain damage (Ross et al., 2001). In one study, 38 of 45 schizophrenic patients showed an aprosodia (84.4 percent); furthermore, their deficit profile on a set of four affective-prosodic tasks was very similar to that of patients with right, but not left, brain damage (Ross et al., 2000). Other studies have shown marked deficits in facial emotion discrimination in schizophrenics (see Gooding, Luh, & Tallent, 2001). Suggesting that the deficit is specific to emotion, and reflects right hemisphere dysfunction, schizophrenics showed reduced left hemispatial biases on an emotional chimeric faces test (CFT), but not on a nonemotional CFT where the faces were split male/female and participants had to identify which of the two was more "feminine" (Gooding et al., 2001). These findings are also intuitively appealing, in that social and emotional deficits are a notable feature of schizophrenic pathology; indeed, social withdrawal is one of the earliest signs of schizophrenia.

In other studies, researchers have found evidence for frontal lobe pathology on behavioral tests like the Wisconsin Card Sorting Test (WCST) (Weinberger, Berman, & Illowsky, 1988); a number of functional imaging studies have also found hypofrontality during the performance of such tasks (for review, see Fletcher, 1998). Some evidence has also been found for tissue loss in these areas (Raz, 1993) and in related subcortical areas. Again, these findings make sense, given the difficulty with volitional behavior often seen in patients with schizophrenia. Similarly, frontal lobe and basal ganglia pathology seem likely to be implicated in the abnormalities of motor behavior, such as rocking, pacing, and stereotyped motor movements, often exhibited by such patients.

In addition to evidence for regionally specific structural and functional abnormalities, there has been some suggestion that a hypothesis of functional disconnection between brain regions can more directly capture the predominant symptoms and impairments that characterize schizophrenia. A review of the empirical work suggests that the putative disconnection is most likely between the temporal and frontal regions. For example, the typical inverse relationship between activation in frontal and temporal regions in a verbal-fluency task relative to word repetition was absent in patients (Friston et al., 1996). This finding was replicated in an acutely ill, unmedicated sample of individuals (Grasby et al., 1994), and in an fMRI study of verbal fluency in people with schizophrenia (Yurgelun-Todd, Renshaw, & Cohen, 1995). Using PET, Heckers and colleagues (1998) found that schizophrenics showed abnormal patterns of activation in both prefrontal and medial temporal regions during

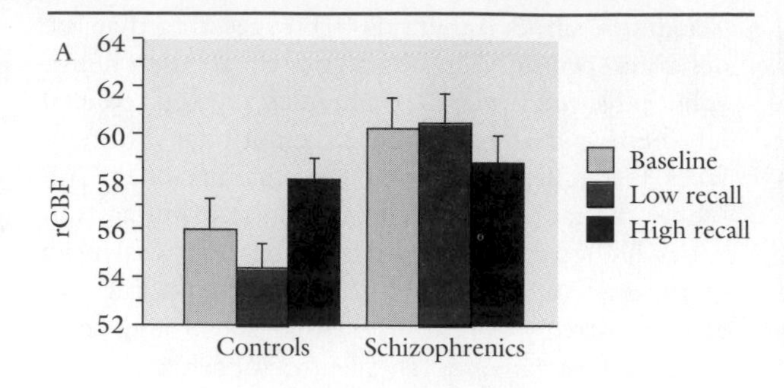

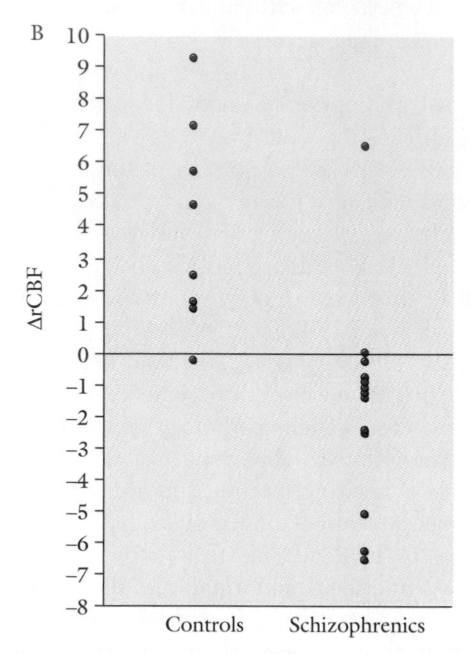

FIGURE 12.14 Impaired recruitment of the hippocampus in schizophrenics during recall. (A) The degree of activation as measured by regional cerebral blood flow (rCBF) during baseline (grey bars), low-recall (blue bars) and high-recall (black bars) conditions for controls and schizophrenics. Notice that whereas control showed the least activation during the low-recall condition and the most during the high-recall condition, the pattern of activation across all conditions was equivalent for the schizophrenics. (B) The difference in hippocampal activation in the high- and low-recall conditions. Notice that only one out of the thirteen individuals with schizophrenia exhibited an increase in activation in the hippocampus during high recall.

a verbal-memory task. In this case, the hippocampus was overactivated during rest, and its activity level did not increase with a challenging memory task, as did activity levels in controls' hippocampus (see Figure 12.14). More activity was also seen in prefrontal and parietal regions in schizophrenics compared with controls, a pattern interpreted as representing an "effort to compensate for the failed recruitment of the hippocampus."

A hypothesis of aberrant functional connectivity is also consistent with some microscopic findings in the literature that suggest abnormalities of neural connections (for review, see Harrison, 1999).

Because schizophrenia has a strong neurological component, treatment typically involves antipsychotic medication. These drugs tend to act on the dopaminergic system and their effects are thought to be linked to their action on the prefrontal cortex (see Chapter 2, page 50).

What Is Emotion?

- Emotion can be conceptualized as a set of processes that include perception, attention, appraisal, and feeling, as well as visceral and motor responses.
- Some of these processes may be accessible to consciousness and some may not.

Subcortical Brain Regions Involved in Emotion

- The amygdala is involved in learning the emotional significance of information and in providing for a quick, instinctive, emotional response.
- The hippocampus is likely to be important in providing the contextual information that frames how a particular stimulus configuration is interpreted with regard to emotion.
- The hypothalamus mediates some of the physiological phenomena associated with emotional states, such as changes in nervous system and endocrine function that are associated with fleeing or fighting.
- The anterior cingulate acts as an interface between cognition and emotion, being important for executing emotional regions and integrating the evaluation of emotional experience with episodic memory.

Cortical Regions Involved in Emotion

- Orbitofrontal cortex is strongly involved in evaluating reward and punishment contingencies and in responding adaptively to changes in these relationships.
- Ventromedial prefrontal cortex is involved in the representation of elementary positive and negative affective states in the absence of immediately present incentives.
- Dorsolateral prefrontal cortex appears to be most directly involved in the representation of goal states toward which more elementary positive and negative emotional states are directed.
- Positive affect is associated with more activity over the left than the right prefrontal cortex, whereas negative affect is associated with the reverse pattern: greater right prefrontal than left prefrontal activity.
- The insula is involved in the olfactory, gustatory, and autonomic functions associated with emotion.
- Right parietal and parietotemporal regions are important for comprehending emotional information whether it be understanding tone of voice or facial expression, or categorizing scenes based on emotional content.
- The ability to process emotion in a face may be independent from the ability to determine a person's identity from a face.
- Deficits in emotional processing can have profound repercussions, as patients with right-hemisphere damage often seem to have lost the most basic social skills.
- The left hemisphere plays a role in comprehending emotion by linking it to verbal meaning.
- The right hemisphere plays a predominant role in producing prosody that is related to emotional affect and the regions of the face controlled by the right hemisphere are judged as more expressive.

Models of the Neural Organization of Emotion

- Neural models of emotion vary as to whether they link general patterns of emotion processing to brain systems, or whether they discuss a particular circuit that processes a particular emotion, such as fear.
- Other models link basic underlying dimensions to particular brain systems, such as a model that posits different brain systems for approach and avoidance, and another model that posits brain activation being determined by valence (positive, negative) and arousal (high, low).

Individual Differences in Affective Style

- Patterns of brain activation have been linked to differences among people in affective style, such

SUMMARY

as how quickly a person calms down after a scare or emotional challenge, or a tendency to respond to things with an optimistic or a pessimistic outlook.

Neural Bases of Mood and Emotional Disorders in Psychopathology

- Depression has been linked to an overall reduction in activity of prefrontal cortex, less left than right prefrontal activity, and decreased activation of posterior regions of the right hemisphere, which leads to poorer performance on visuo-spatial tasks and executive functions including set shifting, inhibition and updating.
- Aspects of anxiety that are characterized by worry are linked to left hemisphere processes, while those characterized by immediate fear and panic symptoms are linked to right hemisphere processes.
- Schizophrenia is characterized by a pathology of the left temporal lobe, right hemisphere, and prefrontal cortex, as well as a disconnection between the temporal and frontal regions.

KEY TERMS

affective prosody 409
anxious apprehension 422
anxious arousal 422
aprosodia 413
catastrophic reaction 406
diathesis-stress model 419
emotional semantics 412
euphoric-indifference reaction 406
nonverbal affect lexicon 412
propositional prosody 409
two-factor theory 400
valence theory 415

PART III

BROAD-BASED PHENOMENA

PLASTICITY ACROSS THE LIFE SPAN

To all who knew him, Dan appeared to be a relatively intelligent 12-year-old with a friendly and cooperative manner. Yet, he was struggling in his schoolwork, especially in spelling and reading. These troubles were nothing new. Despite considerable remedial training, these subjects had always been difficult for him. When a school counselor suggested neuropsychological assessment, his parents agreed willingly, hoping that it might shed some light on his problems.

Neuropsychological testing revealed no evidence of gross brain damage. His sensory, perceptual, and motor abilities all appeared normal and his overall IQ was in the average range. A more detailed analysis of his abilities revealed that his visuospatial skills were quite good. His score on the Performance subscale of the Wechsler Intelligence Scale for Children (WISC), which emphasizes visuospatial abilities, was above average, and he performed well on a number of tests assessing nonverbal problem solving. In contrast, his performance on the Verbal subscale of the WISC was below average. A number of additional verbal tests revealed that he had little appreciation for the phonemic structure of words. He read words by guessing what they were on the basis of their salient visual features or configuration, rather than by trying to sound them out. For example, he read form as "farm," theory as "those," grieve as "great," and tranquility as "train track." He exhibited similar problems in the spelling of orally presented words, spelling square as "s-c-a-r," cross as "c-o-r-s," and triangle as "t-r-e-r-e."

Given that his difficulties were long-standing and that remediation so far had not been effective, the neuropsychologist diagnosed Dan as having a specific verbal learning disability that is commonly known as dyslexia. She suggested that further intervention for reading be geared to capitalize on Dan's good visuospatial abilities, such as teaching him to carefully distinguish words on the basis of their visual features and using flash cards to drill him on the form of words. An incremental approach could be taken; he could first acquire knowledge about simple words and then apply it toward reading more complicated material. For example, once Dan could learn to recognize fly, he could then use that knowledge to help read other words, such as butterfly. The neuropsychologist also explained to Dan's parents that even with such remediation, he would probably never become a fluent reader, which meant that some aspects of formal schooling would remain difficult. However, she also emphasized that such difficulties did not preclude future occupational success for Dan, especially if his parents encouraged him to pursue areas of study and interests that would capitalize on his above average visuospatial abilities. ■

THE CASE STUDY in the opening vignette of this chapter illustrates some of the important ways in which neuropsychological disorders observed developmentally can differ from those observed later in life. In adults, the inability to read is often associated with insult to particular regions of the left hemisphere (see Chapter 9, page 303). However, in Dan's case, no evidence of localized brain damage was apparent. Whereas adults with alexia have acquired the ability to read and then lost it, Dan never acquired the ability to read with a reasonable degree of proficiency.

The case of Dan and children with other developmental disorders should help us to realize something that we may have inadvertently been lulled into forgetting, namely that the brain exhibits **plasticity,** meaning that it has the ability to change. Although this plasticity is most apparent during development, it occurs throughout an individual's life, providing the brain with a way of being continually responsive to environmental input. In this chapter, we examine plasticity from a life-span perspective, centering on changes early in development as well as changes that occur with old age. The developing brain and the aging brain are substantially different from the brain of a young adult, so we examine the consequences of these differences for cognitive and emotional processes. We also consider how the brain can adapt in response to damage or insult.

Developmental Cognitive Neuroscience and Neuropsychology

In this section of the chapter, we examine developmental aspects of neuropsychological function. To provide some perspective on the differences between the immature brain and the mature brain, we begin by discussing brain changes during development and how these changes are influenced by the environment.

Changes in the Brain during Development

Early in fetal development, after the simple primordial fertilized egg differentiates into specific types of tissue (e.g., muscle, skeletal, cardiovascular, nerve), the spinal cord and brain are nothing more than a hollow tube. With time, the tube folds, twists, turns, and expands to become the fetal brain, while the hole becomes the ventricular system (see Figure 13.1). Around the sixth week of gestation, the

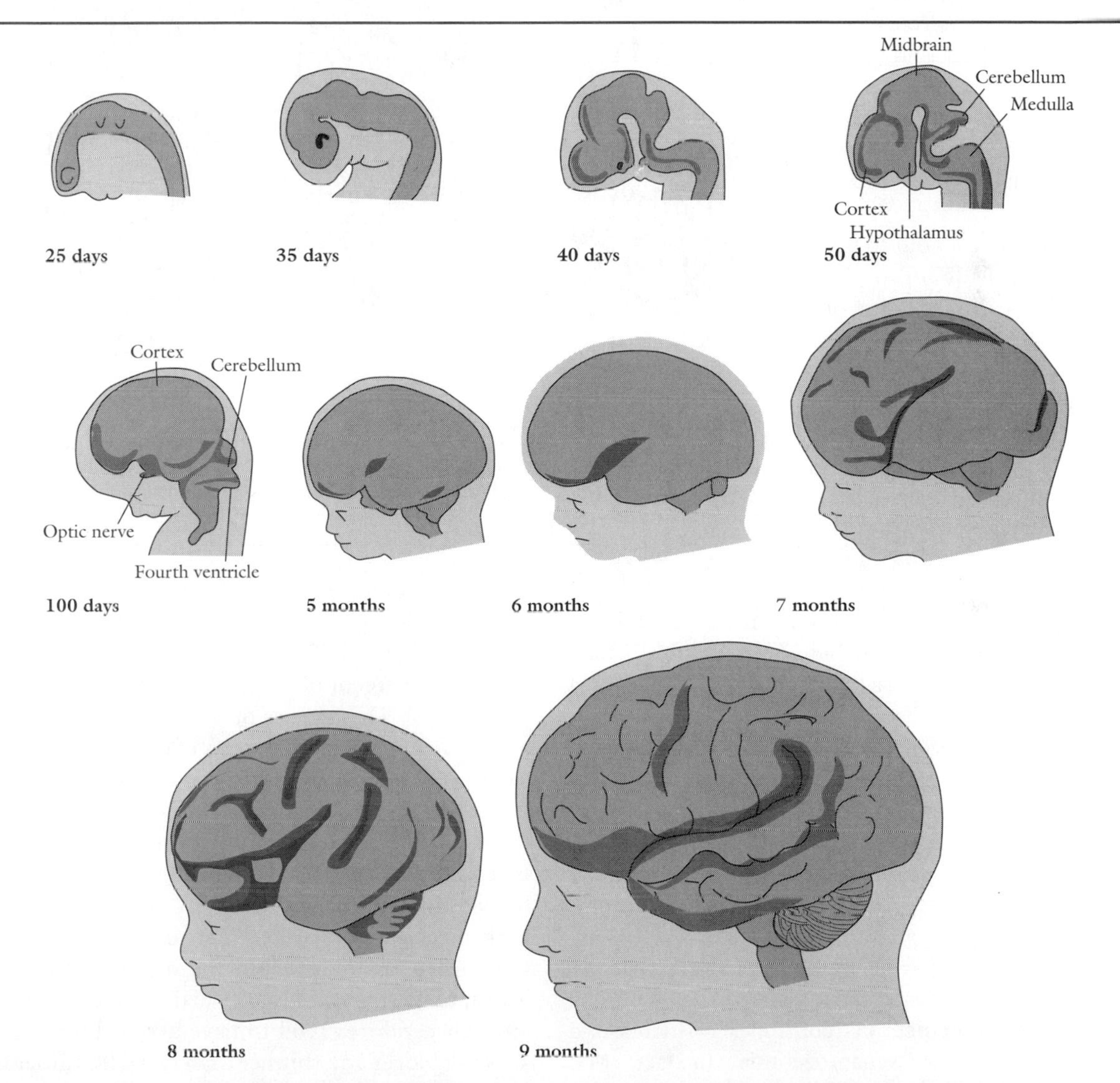

FIGURE 13.1 Development of the human brain from embryonic stages to birth. During the first 2 months of development the nervous system evolves from a hollow, curved tube to a structure that is folding and starting to differentiate into discrete sections. By 100 days, the major divisions of the cortex have been formed. From then until birth, the brain continues to expand and to develop gyral patterns, all of which are present at birth.

nerve cells (and glia) near the inside of the tube divide, proliferate, and then begin to migrate outward. In this process, the tube acts much like a port around which the initial neural settlers will reside. As more neurons are generated, a process known as **neurogenesis,** the initial core, or central areas, become settled, and then the new neurons, like new immigrants to a city, must traverse farther out to find a place to live. As the brain grows, new neurons travel farther and farther out to the metaphorical suburbs of the brain. Thus, the six layers of cortex are built from the inside out; the first set of cells migrates to the deepest layer of the cortex (the sixth), the second to the fifth, and so forth (e.g., Marin-Padilla, 1970). By six months after gestation, most neurons have been produced.

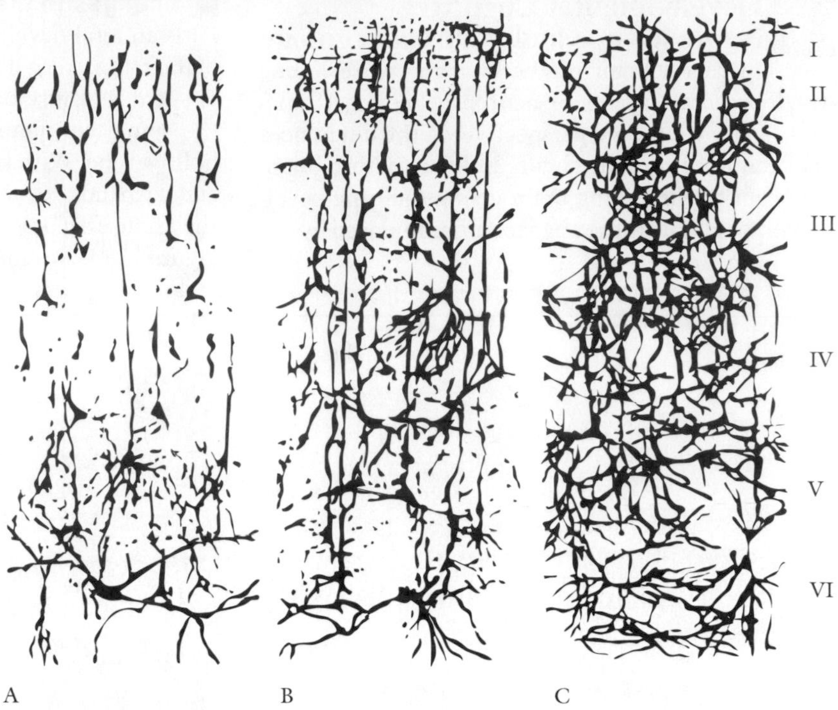

FIGURE 13.2 Increases in the dendrites of neurons and their interconnections during early development. Shown here are representative sections of the brain of (A) a 3-month-old child, (B) a 15-month-old child, and (C) a 24-month-old child. The Roman numerals to the right of C indicate the six layers of cortex.

Although it was initially thought that an individual could not acquire more brain cells after birth, new evidence that we discuss later in the chapter indicates that this is not the case. Nonetheless, neurons do not have nearly the regenerative capacity of other cells in our body, so the basic blueprint of the nervous system is indeed set in place by birth. Yet the newborn's brain is different from that of an adult because it continues to undergo changes during development. We will now discuss those changes, beginning with the cells themselves: neurons and glia.

One of the largest changes after birth is that the number of connections (synapses) that these neurons make with other neurons continues to increase, a process known as **synaptogenesis.** In fact, this process occurs so rapidly within the first year of life that the total number of synapses increases more than tenfold. The increase in the complexity of the neurons themselves and their connections with other neurons within the first two years of life can be seen in Figure 13.2; by this time the brain has reached 80 percent of its adult weight (Kretschmann et al., 1986). The process of synaptogenesis does not occur equally across all regions of the human brain at the same point in development—there are regional differences (Huttenlocher & Dabholkar, 1997).

The importance of this neuronal elaboration is made clear by neuroanatomical findings in the brains of individuals who have disorders associated with mental retardation. Their brains show reductions in the complexity of the dendritic trees, the length of dendrites, or both. Furthermore, the spines on their dendrites tend to have atypical form, such as being longer and thinner than usual (Kaufmann & Moser, 2000).

The two main changes that occur in regard to glia are that their functions become more complicated with age and that they proliferate during the course of development. Early in life, extra glia are not produced in response to injury; later in life they are. Furthermore, a baby's brain is relatively unmyelinated, which means that it lacks oligodendrocytes that insulate neurons. Hence, brain regions cannot interact quickly.

The process of myelination is a long drawn out one, with a developmental course that varies widely by brain region. Myelination first begins to appear between the fourth gestational month and the first year after birth. Not surprisingly, the brain regions that are most myelinated early in life, such as the spinal cord and the medulla, are those that support basic functions. During the first year after birth, basic sensory and motor systems become myelinated (see Figure 13.3). Later on in childhood, myelination occurs for connections between integrative systems, such as those connecting cortical and subcortical areas and those linking different cortical regions. For example, myelination of the corpus callosum continues through the late teens (e.g., Giedd et al., 1996; Yakovlev & Lecours, 1967). The net result of all this myelination is that the relative amount of white matter increases during childhood and the teenage years (Reiss et al., 1996) while the amount of gray matter decreases after age 12 (Giedd et al., 1999). The functional consequence of this process of myelination is that communication between brain regions increases. It is as if the baby's brain were connected by a series of old country roads meandering from town to town. This system doesn't make for fast travel. Myelin transforms this infantile system into a faster one—to continue with our analogy, the old country roads become regional highways, and even more myelin transforms them into national superhighways, over which large volumes of traffic can travel quickly. For example, the nerve-conduction velocity between the hemispheres reaches the adult value of approximately 5 ms during the late teen years, which is four to five times as quick as that observed in children aged four years (Salamy, 1978). Some developmental disorders, which we discuss later in the chapter, such as variants of autism, have been suggested to result from neurodevelopmental anomalies in white-matter development (e.g., Ellis & Gunter, 1999).

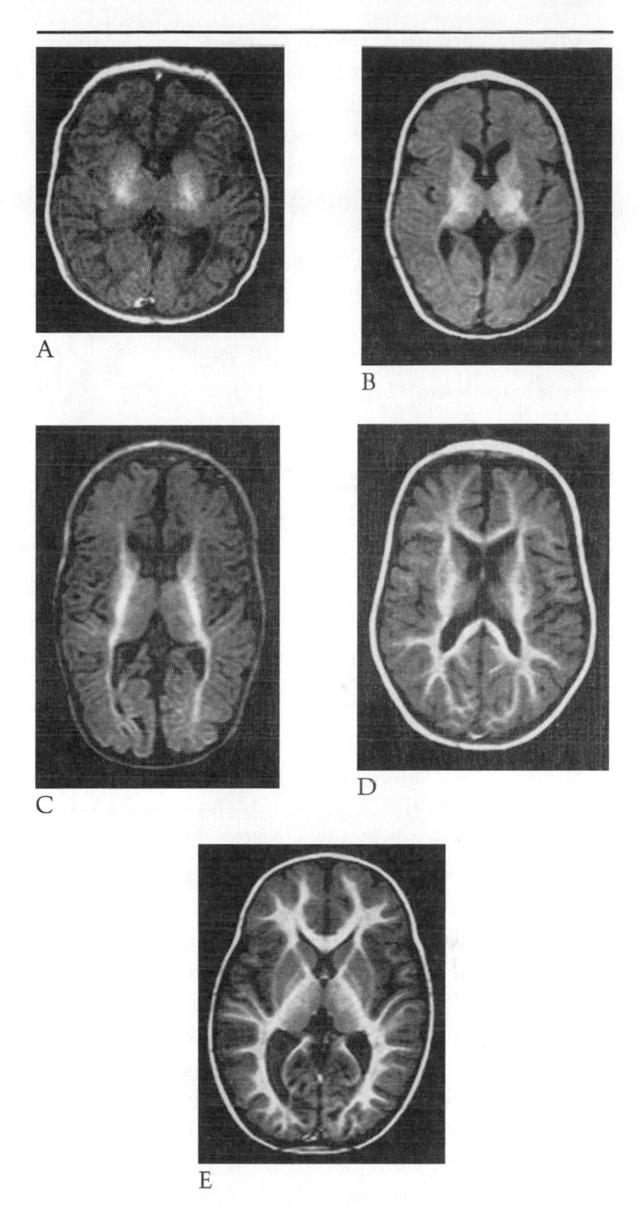

FIGURE 13.3 Increased myelination of the brain during infancy. In these figures, myelin is shown as white. (A) age 1 month, (B) 2 months, (C) 3–6 months, (D) 7–9 months, and (E) older than 9 months.

Other generalized changes also occur in the brain, such as those relating to electrical and biochemical activity. Two main trends emerge with regard to electrophysiological activity: the dominant frequency of activity increases and the pattern of electrical activity becomes more cyclic. During the first two years of life, electrophysiological activity tends to be of low frequency (delta rhythm, <3.5 Hz). Such low-frequency activity is not typically observed in awake adults. Between the ages of one year and five years, the dominant frequency band is theta (4–7 Hz), which in awake adults is associated with relaxation with the eyes closed. After the age of five years, the alpha rhythm (8–13 Hz) becomes discernible, a frequency band associated with relaxation but alertness in adults. In adults, the specific suppression of this band of electrical activity as compared with other frequencies is thought to index higher brain activity. By age 10 to 13 years, the alpha rhythm becomes similar to that of adults, and beta activity (>14 Hz) becomes discernible. As for the cyclicity of electrophysiological activity, no pattern is obvious in the infant, but as the child grows older, a clear sleep-wake cycle develops (Harmony, 1989).

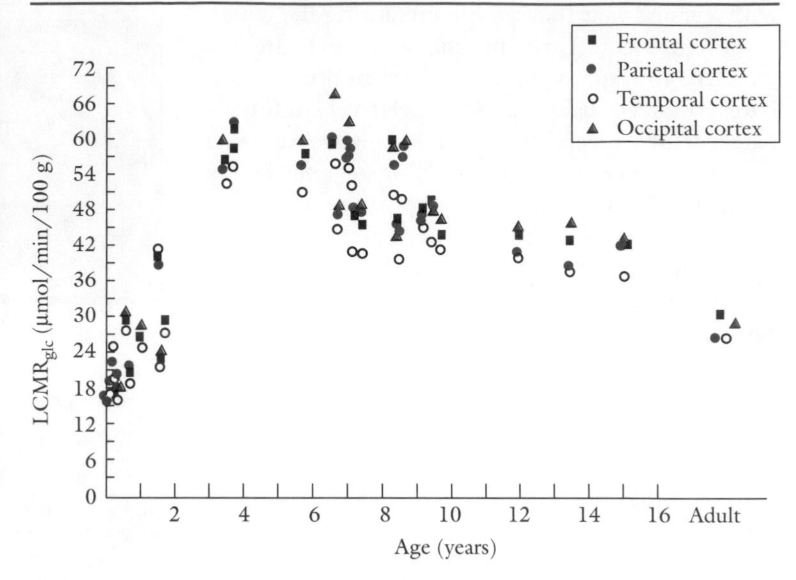

FIGURE 13.4 Changes in metabolic rate of the brain's four major lobes during development. During the first few years of life, metabolic rates are less than those of an adult (far left-hand side of the graph). However, in preschool years the rate of brain metabolism begins to accelerate, reaching a peak value around the age of 8 years, after which the metabolic rate slowly declines through the teenage years to adult values. $LCMR_{glc}$, local cerebral metabolic rate for glucose.

Biochemical changes also occur in the brain during development. Aspects of brain metabolism, such as the rate of glucose consumption, change during childhood. As shown in Figure 13.4, during the first year after birth the metabolic rate of the entire cerebral cortex, as indexed by positron emission tomography (PET), is less than that for adults. After this point, the metabolic rate climbs steadily until it is double the adult value between the ages of three and eight years. After this peak, it begins to decrease, but remains above adult levels during the early teen years. The changes in brain metabolism do not occur equally across the brain, but, like myelination and synaptogenesis, vary across brain regions with age. For example, during the first year of life, the highest metabolic rate occurs in subcortical structures. High metabolic rates for the cortex are observed only after that time (Chugani, Phelps, & Mazziotta, 1987).

The pattern of glucose consumption during childhood suggests that the brain needs fuel to support structural changes occurring during this time. The oligodendroglia may need extra energy to generate myelin, and neurons may need energy to undergo both elaboration and pruning, a topic to which we turn next. Before we do, however, let us note that changes in the concentration of neurotransmitters also accompany these processes. Acetylcholine and glutamate appear to be important in the plasticity of the developing nervous system, as they are involved in the creation, maintenance, and stabilization of synapses (Court et al., 1993), whereas GABA levels appear to support overproduction of synapses and then drop when pruning begins to occur (Davies et al., 1998).

One important characteristic of the development of the mammalian nervous system is an initial proliferation of neurons and their connections, which is then followed by a process of pruning. Pruning during development in the human cortex occurs by the **elimination of synapses,** in which the number of connections between neurons is reduced. The rate at

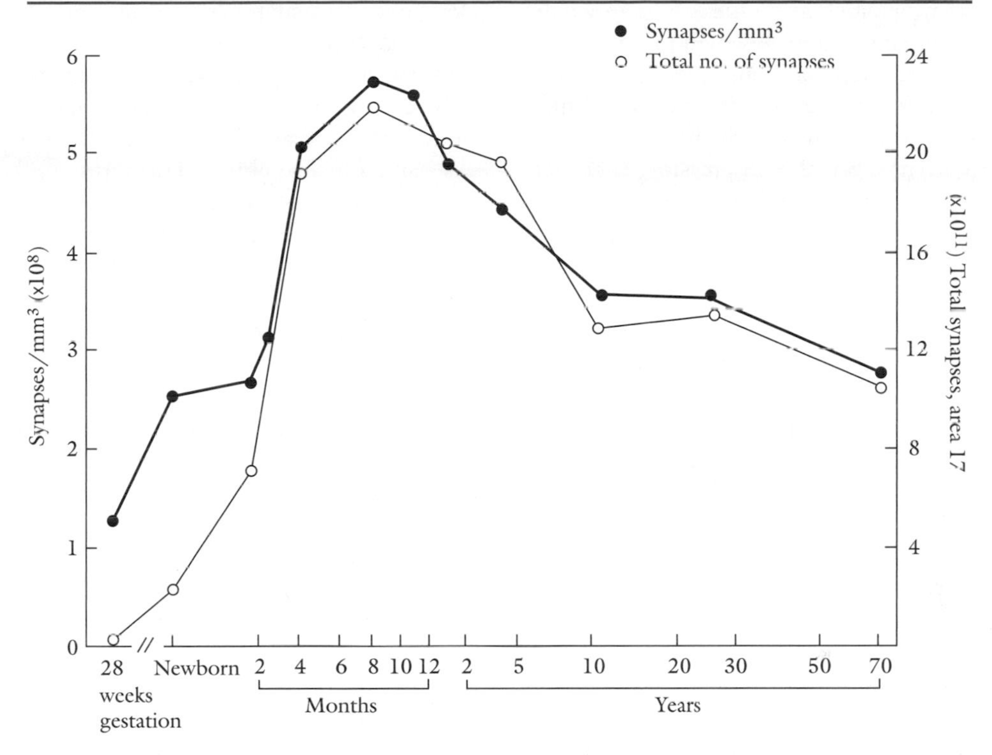

FIGURE 13.5 Proliferation and pruning of synaptic connections in the human visual cortex. Within the first year of life, the total number of synapses (white) and the density of synapses (black) increase substantially. Pruning begins toward the end of the first year and continues until age 10 years. Thereafter, the number of synaptic connections remains static until the effects of aging begin to cause loss.

which the pruning of neuronal connections can occur is staggering. For example, researchers estimate that as many as 60 axons per *second* in the corpus callosum are lost during the first few weeks of a monkey's life (LaMantia & Rakic, 1990), and they speculate that in humans the loss may be even greater—as many as 200 axons per second (Rakic, 1991). The time course of synaptic elimination can vary among cortical regions in humans; for example, it is complete in the visual cortex by age 10 years but continues until adolescence in the frontal cortex (see Figure 13.5) (Huttenlocher, 1979). What is constant across regions, however, is that the number of synapses in the adult is about 40 percent less than that observed during the peak value during childhood (Huttenlocher & de Courten, 1987). This neuronal or synaptic overproduction is thought to be the mechanism that allows the brain to initially have maximal capacity to respond to the environment, providing for a multiplicity of possible connections. Then, during development, the neurons or connections that don't receive much stimulation or are little used wither away (Huttenlocher, 1990), providing the brain with the capacity to fine-tune and specialize itself for its environment (Huttenlocher, 1990; 1994). For example, although the structure of the human brain has evolved in a way that allows almost all members of the species to process language, the actual linguistic environment into which an individual is born will vary. A large set of synaptic connections may aid in the capacity to learn any of the languages spoken around the world, but the pruning may allow for fine-tuning for acquisition of a specific language system. The importance of synaptic pruning for normal cognitive development is illustrated by certain disorders associated with mental retardation, such as fragile X (which we discuss later on in this chapter), which are associated with a higher than normal density of spines along dendrites, suggesting a failure of synapse elimination (Irwin, Galvez, & Greenough, 2000).

You should not get the impression that once synaptic pruning occurs, the connections in the cortex remain totally static. Some degree of plasticity must be retained across the lifetime so that new knowledge can be integrated and incorporated while prior knowledge is reorganized. One proposed mechanism for such plasticity is a change in the strength of a given synaptic connection. According to this viewpoint, often used synaptic connections become stronger and more effective; whereas those that are little used become weaker (this idea is sometimes referred to as a *Hebbian synapse,* after Donald Hebb, who suggested this type of mechanism). Another possible mechanism for plasticity is synaptogenesis, as the nervous system retains its ability to form new synapses throughout the lifetime. Early in development these connections are generated at random, but later in life, it has been proposed, the creation of new synapses becomes more specific and selective, guided strongly by the animal's experience (see Greenough, 1987, for a discussion of such a viewpoint).

The way in which experience influences the connections between neurons has been conceptualized as occurring in two major ways. Some systems, known as **experience-expectant systems,** are common among all individuals. They are designed to be plastic, requiring information to be gleaned from the environment at a particular point in development. This period is thought to coincide with the overproduction and subsequent pruning of synapses. Learning a language is one such example. All humans' brains have evolved so that they expect to be exposed to a linguistic environment that will provide the input necessary to acquire a language. The final brain organization for language, however, is critically influenced by linguistic environment of the *developing* brain. This environment engenders the selection of a certain set of synaptic connections that "cements" that system into place. In contrast, **experience-dependent systems** are those that vary across individuals and are based on their unique experiences. In such systems, synaptic connections are made throughout the lifetime. The acquisition of musical skills is one such example. Some people will acquire no musical ability, others will acquire modest musical ability, and still others will acquire extensive musical ability. Furthermore, the acquisition of these abilities can be acquired at all phases of the lifetime. The extent to which such skills are acquired will be closely tied to the degree of experience and training one has in music. This contrasts with language acquisition, which all humans acquire to approximately the same degree, and which is not highly dependent on the amount of exposure (Greenough, Black, & Wallace, 1987).

All these changes in brain physiology, such as changes in metabolic rate, myelination, and synaptic density, are mirrored by changes in the behavioral repertoire of the child. In the motor domain, newborns exhibit a characteristic set of basic reflexes. Some of them are the rooting, grasping, and Babinski reflexes (see Figure 13.6). These reflexes, which are relatively primitive responses controlled by the brainstem, aid in the infant's survival. For example, the rooting reflex, in which the infant turns toward the side of the face that is touched, helps the infant orient to the mother's breast. With age, these reflexes disappear because cortical areas inhibit their expression. When observed in an adult, they indicate that cortical damage has been so severe as to release these primitive reflexes from inhibition. (For this reason, checking for the Babinski reflex is a standard part of the neurological examination, because this test provides a gross but quick method of ascertaining the extent of cortical damage after brain trauma). As the child ages, motor control moves out of the realm of reflexes into more controlled actions. At first the child's motor control is so poor that he or she cannot even turn over. With time, the child masters this skill, begins to crawl, and by age 18 months or so begins to walk.

Not only do the physical capacities of a child change with age, but so do higher-order cognitive functions, such as language. The child progresses from cooing to babbling to speaking.

Children in all cultures tend to acquire both cognitive and motoric skills in an orderly fashion: Babbling precedes speaking, and crawling precedes walking. Furthermore, specific abilities are acquired

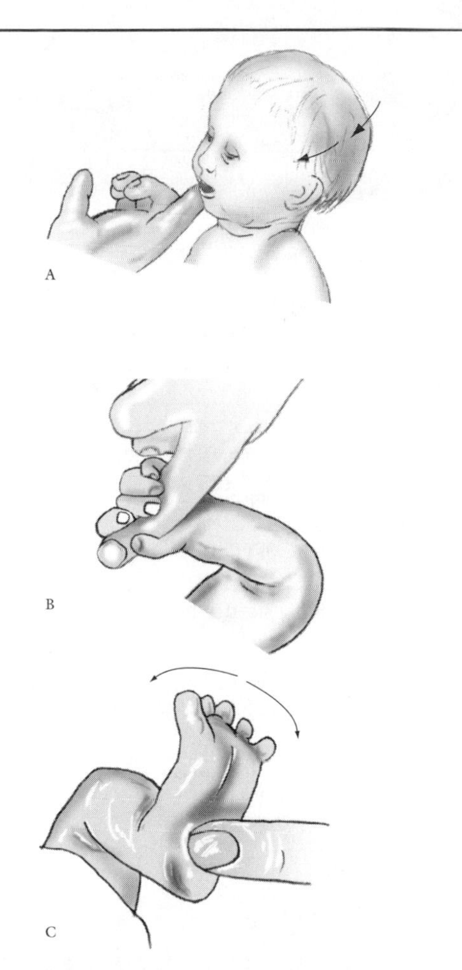

FIGURE 13.6 Three of the basic reflexes observed in infancy. Shown here are the (A) rooting, (B) grasping, and (C) Babinski reflexes. As the child matures, these reflexes become inhibited by higher cortical control and disappear. After head trauma, neurologists often test for a Babinski reflex as a gross means of quickly determining the severity of brain damage. If the reflex is observed, cortical damage has occurred.

within specific age ranges. Because these changes occur in an orderly fashion and at a particular age, they are known as **developmental milestones** (Spreen et al., 1984). The major physiological and behavioral changes during development are listed in Table 13.1. (For an excellent review of the multiplicity of changes in the brain during childhood see Webb, Monk, & Nelson, 2001.) Although development undoubtedly entails changes in brain functioning as well as changes in behavior, finding a direct one-to-one link between a change in a specific aspect of neural functioning and the emergence of a certain cognitive function has proved surprisingly difficult. Currently, there are relatively few cases in which we can point to a biological marker that predicts development of a specific cognitive process. Furthermore, even when we do find such a marker, the connection between the physiological process and the cognitive function is unclear. To illustrate this difficulty, we examine some research conducted by Molfese and colleagues. They found that an infant's electrical response to speech sounds (i.e., an AER—auditory evoked response) recorded a week or so after birth can predict how competent a child will be at processing language three years later (Molfese & Molfese, 1994). Follow-up studies indicated that the AER can still predict language abilities at age five (Molfese & Molfese, 1997) and language and reading abilities at age eight (Molfese, Molfese, & Espy, 1999). Although the AER appears to act as a biological marker for future language competence, we do not know exactly what aspect of nervous system function that is indexed by the AER is related to language. Moreover, we do not know how variations in that function lead to varying competence in language. In response to this dilemma, D. Molfese has speculated that a larger AER may reflect a heightened capacity to discriminate among different speech sounds. Thus, children who can make fine discriminations sooner may have a head start in learning words early in life, which in turn helps them to have more developed language capacities at later ages.

Another case in which speculative linkages can be made between brain development and behavior involves changes in visual cortex that appear to parallel changes in visual processing. At birth, few synaptic connections are present in visual cortex—only about 20 percent of those at adulthood. This neural state is accompanied by low visual alertness and difficulties in tracking moving objects efficiently. At four months, a rapid burst in synaptogenesis is associated with a sudden increase in visual alertness. At this age, binocular perception, which depends on cortical regions, begins to emerge. Synaptic density remains high until four years of age, at which point it decreases. After this age, the ability

TABLE 13.1 Development Changes During Early Childhood

AGE	VISUAL AND MOTOR FUNCTION	SOCIAL AND INTELLECTUAL FUNCTION	EEG*	AVERAGE BRAIN WEIGHT (g)
Birth	Exhibits sucking, rooting, swallowing, and Moro reflexes; engages in infantile grasping; blinks to light	—	Asynchronous; low voltage, 3-5 Hz; period of flattening; no clear distinction awake or asleep	350
6 weeks	Extends and turns neck when prone; regards mother's face; follows objects with eyes	Smiles when played with	Similar to birth records, with slightly higher voltages; rare 14-Hz parietal spindles in sleep	410
3 months	Exhibits infantile grasping and sucking modified by volition; keeps head above horizontal for long periods; turns to objects presented in visual field; may respond to sound	Watches own hands	When awake, asynchronous 3-4 Hz, some 5-6 Hz; low voltages continue; sleep better organized and more synchronous; more spindles but still often asynchronous	515
6 months	Grasps objects with both hands; will place weight on forearms or hands when prone; rolls supine to prone; supports almost all weight on legs for brief periods; sits briefly	Laughs aloud and shows pleasure; emits primitive articulated sounds, "gagoo"; smiles at self in mirror	More synchronous; 5- to 7-Hz activity frequent; many lower voltages, slower frequencies; drowsy bursts can be seen; humps may first be seen in sleep	660
9 months	Sits well and pulls self to sitting position; uses thumb-forefinger grasp; crawls	Waves bye-bye; plays pat-a-cake; uses "dada," "baba"; imitates sounds	Mild asynchrony; predominant frequencies, 5-7 Hz and 2-6 Hz, especially anteriorly; drowsy bursts frequent; humps and spindles seen frequently in sleep	750
12 months	Is able to release objects; cruises and walks with one hand held; exhibits plantar reflex (50% of children)	Says two to four words with meaning; understands several proper nouns; may kiss on request	5-7 Hz in all areas; usually synchronous; some anterior 20-25 Hz; some 3-6 Hz; humps often seen in sleep and usually synchronous	925
24 months	Walks up and down stairs (using two feet a step); bends over and picks up objects without falling; turns knob; can partially dress self; exhibits plantar reflex (100% of children)	Uses two- to three-word sentences; uses "I," "me," and "you" correctly; plays simple games; points to four to five body parts; obeys simple commands	6- to 8-Hz activity predominates posteriorly, with some 4-6 Hz seen, especially anteriorly; humps in sleep always synchronous	1,065
36 months	Goes up stairs (using one foot a step); pedals tricycle; dresses and undresses fully except for shoelaces, belt, and buttons; visual acuity 20/20	Asks numerous questions; knows nursery rhymes; copies circle; plays with others	When awake, synchronous 6-9 Hz predominates posteriorly; less 4- to 6-Hz activity seen; in sleep, spindles usually synchronous	1,140

*EEG, electroencephalogram.

to modify certain aspects of visual processing is lost. For example, strabismic amblyopia (i.e., crossing of the eyes), which is a relatively common condition of childhood, can be reversed if it is treated prior to this age (Huttenlocher, 1990). After that point, the condition is irreversible. Researchers have suggested that the decrease in synaptic density after four years of age may be related to a decrease in plasticity.

Even if more specific linkages can be found between biological markers and developmental changes in mental ability, researchers will have difficulty determining whether the biological marker is indexing a neural process that is critical for a developmental change in behavior or whether the marker is just indexing a general level of brain maturity, which in turn predicts the onset of behavior. To make this distinction more concrete, think about the case of visual processing that we just discussed. Perhaps the biological process indexed by synaptic density specifically determines a child's competence in visual processing. Alternatively, synaptic density may not *directly* affect visual processing but may be only one measure of overall brain maturity, which is also reflected by increased myelination, changes in metabolic level, increased electroencephalographic (EEG) coherence, and so forth. Although a deeper understanding of such linkages has evaded researchers, the general assumption is that a particular neurobiological substrate must be in place before specific motoric, cognitive, and emotional abilities can manifest themselves during development.

Influence of Environment on the Developing Brain

In discussing the biological timetable for development, we mentioned but did not elaborate upon the idea that environmental input has profound influences on the developing brain. We now review in more detail some of the evidence from research on animals that illustrates the substantial effects that environmental input can have on the structure and organization of the brain during development.

One well-known effect observed in animals is that an enriched or stimulating environment can affect the structure of neurons (e.g., Rosenzweig, Bennett, & Diamond, 1972) by causing the dendrites of the neurons to become bushier and the number of synapses per neuron to increase (e.g., Turner & Greenough, 1985). In the laboratory, an enriched environment for the rat consists of a complex spatial and social environment (see Figure 13.7A). In contrast, the control environment consists of a small standard-issue clear plastic cage that the animal lives in alone (see Figure 13.7B). Dendritic elaboration and increasing synaptic connectivity as a result

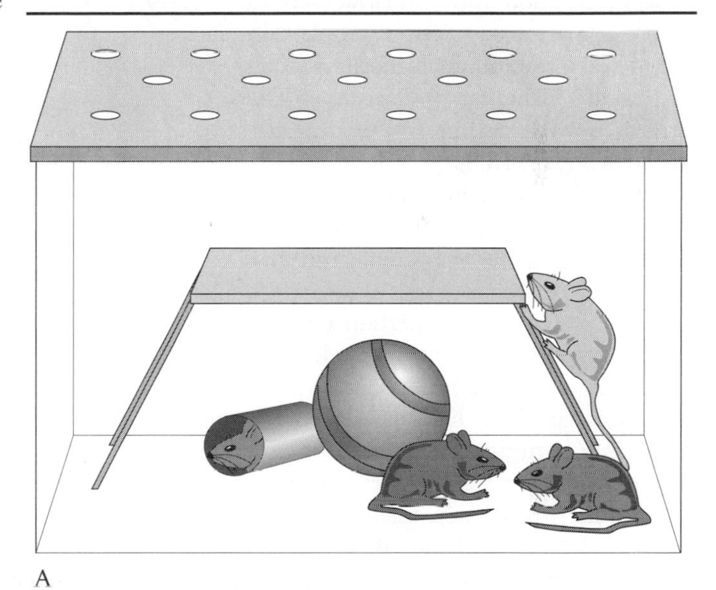

A

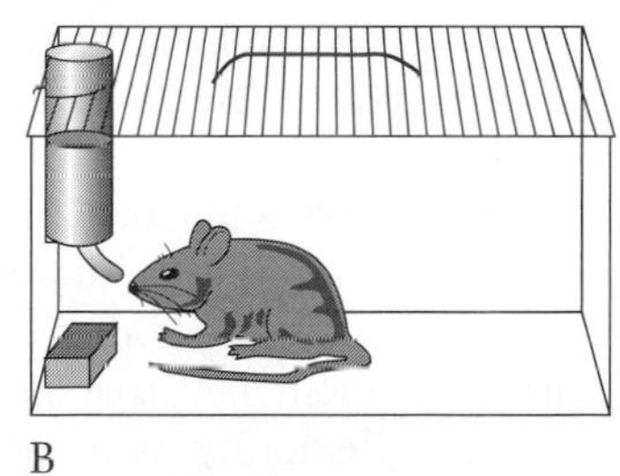

B

FIGURE 13.7 Conditions used with rats to investigate effects of different environments on brain structure and behavior. (A) In the complex environment condition, the animals are allowed to spend hours each day in an environment characterized by a large area in which the spatial arrangement of items and toys is changed daily (for variety) and in which the rats have the opportunity to interact with other rats. (B) In contrast, in the control condition the rat remains alone in a small plastic cage all day.

of an enriched environment occurs not only early during development but also in adulthood (e.g., Greenough & Chang, 1988). These neural changes may provide for more and varied connections, increasing the brain's computational power so that it can effectively deal with a more cognitively demanding and complicated environment. In fact, animals raised in complex environments are superior to control animals in solving various maze-learning tasks (e.g., Juraska, Henderson, & Muller, 1984). Likewise, sparse dendritic elaboration may preclude certain mental processes. For example, in humans, the mental deterioration associated with Alzheimer's disease is also associated with a thinning of dendritic branches (Figure 13.8).

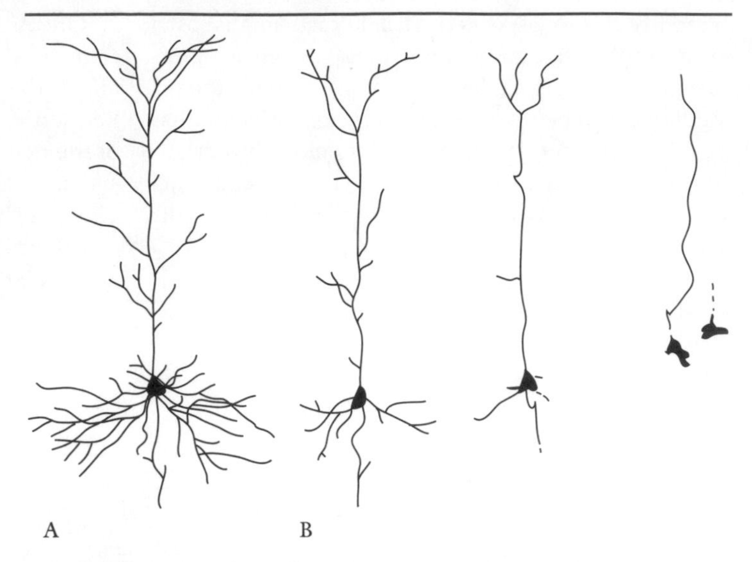

FIGURE 13.8 Loss of dendritic elaboration accompanying mental deterioration. (A) Shown here is a neuron from the brain of a normal adult human. Note the dark cell body in the lower part of the figure and the many dendrites feeding into it. Also note the axon emanating upward away from the cell body. (B) Neurons in individuals with increasing degrees of deterioration (left to right) as a result of Alzheimer's disease. Note the reduction in dendritic elaboration and other neuronal processes.

Although certain environmental effects can influence the organism across a lifetime, as in the case of dendritic elaboration, in other cases the organism is particularly sensitive to certain external stimuli only during a specific developmental period. This time is known as a **sensitive period** and generally has a specific onset and offset. Such time periods allow the brain to incorporate information from the environment and then to "lock" that information in. An example of a sensitive period that we already discussed is the limited time period during which intervention can correct walleye or crossed eyes. If the problem is not corrected during that time, irreversible difficulties in depth perception result.

A more cognitive example of a function that has a sensitive period is language. When children are born, they are able to perceive almost all phonetic contrasts that occur in different language systems around the world. Such flexibility is important because the linguistic culture into which a child will be born is unpredictable. Within the first year of life, however, the child's ability to perceive particular contrasts is honed, becoming more sensitive to the contrasts relevant for the baby's linguistic environment and less sensitive to contrasts important in other languages (Kuhl et al., 1992).

The examples just provided illustrate a salient feature of sensitive periods: the neural organization that develops during the sensitive period is relatively irreversible. For example, the ability to acquire sophisticated grammatical competence in a second language appears to be limited by the age at which the second language is acquired. If acquisition occurs before the ages of five to seven years, the person's competence will be equivalent to that of a native speaker (see Figure 13.9A). For each year that passes after the age of seven years without exposure to the second language, an incremental decline is seen in the ability to understand the particular grammatical constructions of that language. After this time period, age of acquisition becomes unimportant (Figure 13.9B) and other factors, such as how long the person has been in the environment in which the second language is spoken and the degree to which the second language is spoken at home and in the workplace, exert more influence. Such a pattern of results suggests that the ability to acquire a high degree of grammatical competence in a second

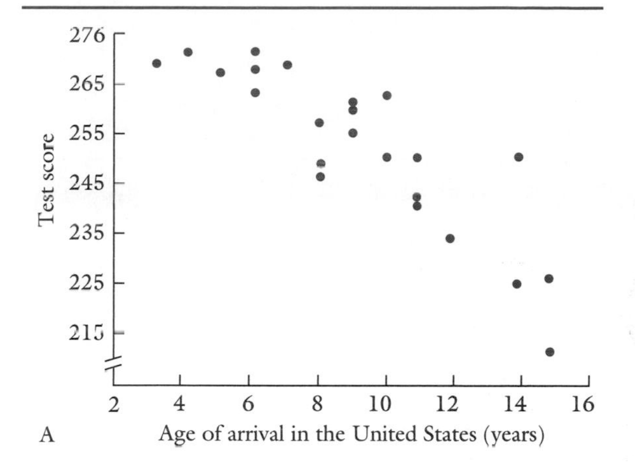

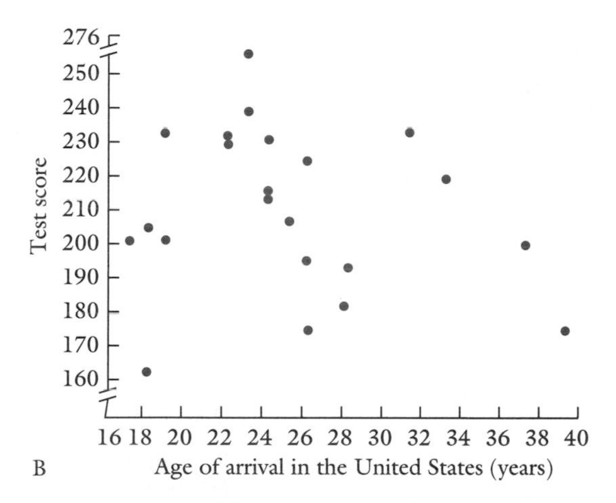

FIGURE 13.9 A sensitive period for the acquisition of grammatical competence in a second language. (A) The relationship between age of arrival in the United States and grammatical competence for individuals arriving between ages 3 and 15 years ($r = -.87$). With each year that passes after the age of 5 years, the ability to acquire grammatical competence decreases. (B) In contrast, after the age of 15 years, the age at which an individual arrives in the United States does not predict the person's grammatical competence ($r = -.16$). The relationships between competence and age of arrival shown in A and B suggest that the sensitive period for acquisition of sophisticated grammatical competence in a second language ends around the age of 15 years.

language is limited by biological factors that signal the end of the sensitive period around the age of 15 years (Johnson & Newport, 1989). Although these biological factors remain to be identified, they may be associated with the onset of puberty as the sensitive period ends around that time.

Developmental Disorders

Because the brain is developing in children, the nature of neuropsychological disorders observed in children is distinct from the nature of those occurring in adults. In this section we review some of the more common developmental disorders that appear to have neurological involvement. Some of these have identifiable causes and others do not.

Learning Disabilities

Learning disabilities are syndromes in which a child has difficulty acquiring cognitive skills in only one particular domain or area. The two major subtypes of learning disabilities that we discuss here are those that affect skills in the verbal domain and those that affect skills in the nonverbal/spatial domain.

DYSLEXIA AND OTHER VERBAL LEARNING DISABILITIES

Dyslexia is a specific inability to learn to read at an age-appropriate level, despite adequate opportunity, training, and intelligence (it is sometimes referred to as a *specific reading disability*). Usually, an individual is considered to have dyslexia when his or her general intelligence is adequate to support the cognitive demands imposed by reading, other cognitive functions seem to be age and grade appropriate, and exposure to written language and instruction in reading have been provided. For example, an eight-year-old child with a specific reading disability would be unable to read but could perform age-appropriate math problems such as simple multiplication. As the child gets older, acquisition of knowledge in other subjects besides written language is likely to be compromised because of the heavy reliance in schools on reading materials for conveying such information.

Dyslexia is one of the more common developmental disorders, affecting approx-imately 5 percent of all children. In the United States alone, for example, more than 11 million persons have a severe reading disability (Hynd & Cohen, 1983). The number of individuals affected by dyslexia surpasses the combined total of those affected by cerebral palsy, epilepsy, and severe mental retardation.

Although most people assume that the cardinal sign of dyslexia is writing letters backward, children without reading disabilities commonly write letters backward, so this is not a specific sign of dyslexia. Instead, most persons with dyslexia (85 percent) have difficulties in phonological processing: linking a particular letter, which is a linguistic symbol, to a particular sound, and in parsing words into their constituent phonemes. This disorder is sometimes referred to as *dysphonetic dyslexia.* The remaining 15 percent of persons with dyslexia have specific difficulty with visuospatial aspects of language (Boder, 1973). These individuals are said to have *dyseidetic dyslexia.*

Although the brain of a person with dyslexia appears normal on gross examination, researchers have postulated since the late 1920s, when Orton first introduced the idea, that dyslexia might result from some type of neural miswiring (e.g., Orton, 1937). At present, three major classes of theories exist that might explain the neural basis for dyslexia. One prominent theory is that a developmental anomaly disrupts left hemisphere function, specifically of parietal regions, which in adults are associated with processing written language (see page 307–309, Chapter 9). Some support for this viewpoint has been provided by various studies. First, postmortem anatomical examination of the brains of patients with dyslexia reveal anatomical anomalies not only in the angular gyrus, but in other regions of the left hemisphere as well (Galaburda et al., 1985; Humphreys, Kaufmann, & Galaburda, 1990) (see Figure 13.10). Second, brain regions activated during reading in neurologically intact individuals are either engaged ineffectively or not at all in dyslexics (e.g., Rumsey et al., 1992; Shaywitz et al., 1998). Even more importantly, the more the left angular gyrus is activated in normal readers, the better their reading scores on a variety of single-word reading tests. In contrast, the more this area is activated in dyslexics, the poorer their reading scores (Rumsey et al., 1999). In contrast, in dyslexics, better reading scores were associated with activation of regions of the *right* hemisphere. This finding raises the possibility that whatever reading skills are acquired by dyslexic individuals rely on a different neural mechanism from that utilized by normal readers.

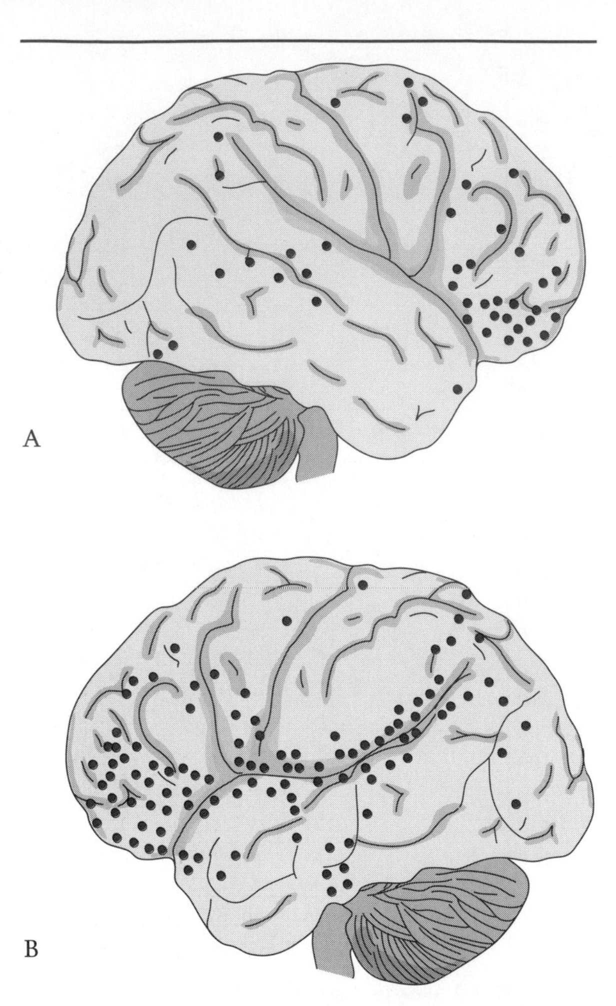

FIGURE 13.10 Locations of developmental anomalies in the brains of males diagnosed with dyslexia. Shown here as blue circles are sites that on postmortem examination were found to exhibit abnormalities in brain structure in (A) the right hemisphere and (B) the left hemisphere. Many more abnormalities can be seen in the left hemisphere than in the right. These abnormalities tend to occur in the peri-Sylvian area (in the vicinity of the Sylvian fissure) and in frontal regions.

A second viewpoint argues that a critical process required for the acquisition of reading is lacking, namely, **phonological awareness.** This is the ability to identify, think about, and manipulate the individual sounds in words (Pennington et al., 1987). If you think back to the discussion on language in Chapter 9, you may remember that we described two routes from print to meaning, the phonologic route and the direct route. Learning to read is critically dependent upon the phonological route because it allows new words encountered in print to be sounded out and linked to words already known in spoken language. You may be thinking at this point, "Well why can't they learn to read using the direct route?" Doing so is quite difficult because each new word must be memorized. Furthermore, the reliance on visual form causes readers with dyslexia to make errors not typically made by normal readers—such as misreading *house* as "hose," a word that looks similar but sounds dissimilar.

There is, however, disagreement on exactly why such phonological awareness is compromised. Some researchers suggest the lack of phonological awareness results from a specific difficulty within the domain of language processing, because similar deficits are not observed in nonlinguistic domains such as the processing of nonlinguistic sounds (e.g., Bishop, Carlyon, Deeks, & Bishop, 1999). Others, however, argue that the requisite perceptual mechanisms for acquiring phonological awareness are disrupted. These researchers suggest that difficulty with the fine temporal analysis of auditory information can interfere with language processing (e.g., Tallal et al., 1996). Such a difficulty would prevent dyslexics from processing the critical acoustic parameters, such as voicing, that distinguish between phonemes on the basis of a mere 40 ms (refer back to Chapter 9, page 295). Indeed, evidence suggests that individuals with reading impairment do indeed have difficulty with certain aspects of auditory processing (Wright, Bowen, & Zecker, 2000).

More controversial work suggests that individuals with dyslexia have particular difficulty in processing visual information that is associated with the magnocellular system, which leads from the rods in the retina to the dorsal visual-processing stream. In contrast, processing of information associated with the parvocellular system, which leads from the cones in the retina to the ventral visual-processing stream, is intact (see Stein & Walsh, 1997, for a review, and Stein, Talcott, & Walsh, 2000, and Skottun, 2000, for current evidence pro and con). Dysfunction of the magnocellular system could disrupt reading by interfering with the ability to determine the order in which visual stimuli are perceived (e.g., Slaghuis & Ryan, 1999) or by disrupting eye movements (e.g., Stein, 1994), confusing the process of visual perception.

A final viewpoint argues that dyslexia results from a disconnection syndrome between brain regions required to acquire the skill of reading. One version of this position argues that dyslexia is caused by dysfunctional interaction between the cerebral hemispheres (e.g., Bakker, 1973). Such a suggestion seems reasonable, considering that learning to read necessitates visual discrimination and recognition of letters, a purported right hemisphere function (e.g., Hellige & Webster, 1979), which must be linked via the corpus callosum with their phonetic representations, a purported left hemisphere function (e.g., Levy & Trevarthen, 1977). Thus, children with dyslexia might have difficulty reading because information processed by the right hemisphere cannot be translated to the left. Evidence for this viewpoint comes from both the anatomy and functioning of the corpus callosum. Some studies have reported correlations between reading ability and the size of the corpus callosum (e.g., Hynd et al., 1995; Robichon & Habib, 1998). Other studies find disrupted transfer of information between the hemispheres of dyslexics, both with regard to how well information is transferred (e.g., Gladstone, Best, & Davidson, 1989) and how quickly (e.g., Markee, Brown, Moore, & Theberge, 1996).

Another version of this position argues that there is a disconnection between regions of the left hemisphere itself (rather than a disconnection between the hemispheres) in dyslexia. Consistent with this viewpoint, dyslexics fail to coactivate temporoparietal and frontal regions during a rhyming task and exhibit less myelination of connections between left frontal and temporoparietal regions (Klingberg et al., 2000) relative to neurologically intact individuals (for a longer review of the potential problems in neurocognitive functioning in dyslexia, see Banich & Scalf, 2003).

Although a clear picture of the neurological contributions to dyslexia remains elusive, the disorder does appear to have a genetic component. Dyslexia tends to run in families (Olson, 1999), and monozygotic twins, who share all the same genes, have a higher concordance rate for dyslexia (i.e., both twins are dyslexic) than do dizygotic twins, who share only half their genes (Vellutino, 1987). The numerous attempts to isolate the specific portion of the genome linked to reading disability have met with only moderate success. Some findings suggest that regions on chromosomes 1, 6, and 15 are associated with dyslexia, but none of these findings is definitive as of yet (see Grigorenko, 2001, for a review).

Before we leave the topic of dyslexia, we should note that although it is one of the most common developmental disorders, it is not the only developmental disorder involving language. Whereas dyslexia is a specific problem in reading, **developmental dysphasia** is a disorder of expressive language in which children have difficulty understanding and producing speech. As reviewed by Rapin, Allen, and Dunn (1992), many aspects of developmental dysphasia remain a mystery. Information on its prevalence varies widely; lower estimates are 2 percent and upper estimates are 14 percent. Because most children who receive a brain insult usually retain the ability to acquire language, the cause of developmental dysphasia is unlikely to be a specific lesion but may involve dysfunction of various regions of both hemispheres. To date, however, a clear causative neurological factor has not been isolated. Neither has a direct link been found to environmental toxins, intrauterine exposure to alcohol, drugs, or an impoverished linguistic environment. Like dyslexia, though, developmental dysphasia appears to have a genetic component. Children with developmental language delays were more likely than matched control individuals to have a relative (parent, sibling, or more distant relative) who also had a developmental language disorder or learning disability.

Because language is the medium by which we most often communicate and the medium by which we are schooled, developmental disorders in language processing, regardless of the domain, visual or oral, can have profound implications for the subsequent level of achievement in school and work. Hence, individuals with developmental language disabilities must find alternative ways to acquire information, and persons with dyslexia often choose careers that do not emphasize the written word. Although acquiring information through reading is not impossible for persons with dyslexia, it is indeed difficult.

• *NONVERBAL LEARNING DISABILITIES* •

Although developmental disabilities in the language domain have received much attention and study, learning disabilities are not limited to this arena. Another class of learning disabilities, **nonverbal learning disabilities,** is characterized by difficulty in acquiring spatial and nonverbal skills while verbal abilities remain relatively unaffected. Whereas developmental language disabilities tend to affect processes performed by the left hemisphere, nonverbal learning disabilities tend to affect those performed by the right hemisphere.

Children with nonverbal learning disabilities are doubly at risk because their difficulties in the nonverbal domain affect not only cognitive functions but also emotional functions. Although any child with a learning disability must deal with its social implications (e.g., being called "stupid," being excluded from play by other children), the compromise of emotional processing in children with nonverbal learning disabilities compounds the problem. We first examine the cognitive aspects of nonverbal learning disabilities, then the emotional ones.

Children with nonverbal learning disabilities exhibit a broad range of cognitive difficulties. Overall, they have difficulty appreciating the significance of nonverbal information despite having normal verbal intelligence. The identifying features are thought to include tactile-perceptual deficits and poor psychomotor coordination, more often on the left side of the body; deficits in visual-spatial abilities, non-verbal problem solving, a reliance on rote learning, difficulty with the spatial aspects of arithmetic, such as aligning numbers correctly; verbosity of speech; and deficits in social perceptual, social judgment, and interactions (Harnadek & Rourke, 1994). Anecdotally, their parents report that these children rarely play with toys that require visuoconstructive skills, such as puzzles and blocks. Despite these difficulties, nonverbal learning disabilities are considered to be underdiagnosed, in part because the intact verbal skills of these children do not alert teachers and parents to their problems.

In addition to the cognitive deficits, these children exhibit a concomitant constellation of social and emotional difficulties. As we learned in Chapter 12, the right hemisphere is especially important for the interpretation and expression of emotion. In general, these children lack the ability to understand the social environment. Their difficulties may be exhibited in many domains. Perceptually, they may lack an ability to understand facial expression or gesture, to understand tone of voice, and to link those signals with verbal messages. In terms of production, their speech tends to be either flat and monotonous or hyperemotional and effusive. Such difficulties are accompanied by troubles in comprehending the social world. These children avoid new situations, lack friends, and don't learn from past social encounters. Their poor social competence manifests itself in social encounters by their lack of empathy and their attempts to keep a listener's attention with a lot of verbal jargon that does little to foster communication or dialogue. Because of these difficulties, such children tend to show elevated levels of anxiety, withdrawal, and depression on personality tests (Strang & Rourke, 1985). Learning can be difficult for these children, not only because they have difficulty acquiring information in certain content areas, but also because they cannot process the social signals that are critical to the interactive nature of learning environments.

Recently researchers have found that a morphological syndrome (velo-cardio-facial syndrome) is associated with both the cognitive and emotional profile of children with nonverbal learning disability: good verbal skills in the face of poor visuospatial and visuoperceptual abilities, poor motor skills, and poor visual attention (Swillen et al., 1999). Interestingly, they have intact object memory, indicating a specific impairment in spatial processing as compared with visual processing in general. The finding that individuals with this syndrome have a deletion on chromosome 22 at location q11.2, suggests that this region of chromosome 22 may harbor a gene or genes involved in the etiology of nonverbal learning disabilities (Bearden et al., 2001).

Autism and Pervasive Developmental Disorders

Pervasive developmental disorders, the most well known of which is probably **autism,** have four basic characteristics: qualitative impairment in social interaction; delays and abnormalities in language as well as other aspects of communication; restricted, repetitive, and stereotyped patterns of behaviors, interests, or activities; and an onset of the problems in at least one of these three areas before the age of three years [American Psychiatric Association, *Diagnostic and Statistical Manual of Mental Disorders,* 4th ed. (*DSM-IV*), 1994]. This disorder affects about 1 child in every 2,000 (Tanguay, 2000).

Most children with pervasive developmental disorders (75 percent) are also mentally retarded, meaning that their IQs are significantly below average. Unlike children who are mentally retarded but not autistic, autistic children have profound social deficits. Children with mental retardation seek interaction with adults, smile, and appreciate being held when hurt. Autistic children, on the other hand, are more likely to want to engage in routinized robotic behavior such as hand flapping, scream if approached as if being seriously intruded upon or violated, and avoid the gaze of other people. They appear not to care whether people are present, and when others are around seem to act as if they were pieces of furniture or "look through" them as if they didn't exist. When these children do become attached to something, it is usually an inanimate object, such as a piece of string or a rubber band (Fein et al., 1986).

Children with autism tend to do best on cognitive tasks that do not require human interaction or are not learned through human interaction. For example, their performance on certain mathematical or constructional puzzles (which require little human interaction) is much better than their performance on language tasks would predict. On recognition tests, they often can identify inanimate objects, such as a screwdriver, more readily than objects representing something human, such as a face. Their cognitive interests are usually narrow and unemotional, such as an obsession with baseball statistics or an absorption with mechanical movement, such as the spinning of an electric fan. They lack flexibility, becoming upset if any aspect of a routine is broken, and exhibit stereotypical and repetitious motor behaviors (e.g., hand flapping, head banging) (*DSM-IV,* 1994).

Throughout the history of thought on autism, a disorder that Kanner first described in 1943, people have debated whether it is primarily cognitive or emotional, and the debate continues today (e.g., Sigman, 1994). Early theories attributed autism to factors in the child's social environment, such as "cold mothering," which would leave the child socially isolated from the world and emotionally disturbed (Bettleheim, 1967). Such an emotional disconnection was hypothesized to preclude the types of interaction that would allow autistic children to acquire adequate cognitive skills. Although environmental models of autism have fallen by the wayside, many neurologically based models of autism view disturbances in emotional functioning as a primary component of the syndrome. This position is based on evidence that other developmental syndromes characterized by severe cognitive deficits are not accompanied by such profound defects in emotional functioning and that even when autistic individuals have adequate cognitive skills, they still manifest difficulty in the social realm (see Fein et al., 1986, for the details of this position).

Other theorists suggest that the basic problem in autism is not one of emotion but rather of cognition. They base their position on findings that wide and severe cognitive problems, especially in language, can linger even if the child's social withdrawal improves with age. According to this viewpoint, the autistic child has a basic cognitive problem in understanding and modifying rules, using information symbolically, or using information in a sequential manner (e.g., Rutter, 1983). The central cognitive deficits would make the world, to an autistic child, a weird and incomprehensible place, a place to be avoided. Viewed from this perspective, the social and emotional deficits result from the lack of an adequate cognitive system to handle the demands of social interaction.

Although the debate over the basic underlying problem in autism remains, most individuals will agree that autistic children seem to avoid interacting with the environment and people and act as if the world around them is intrusive, behavior that leads to both social isolation and cognitive deprivation. The cognitive and emotional deficits may be intertwined. For example, it has been suggested that individuals with autism do not develop *joint attention,* in which attention is coordinated between the individual, another person, and an object or event (McArthur & Adamson, 1996). Although this problem can be viewed as an attentional one, such coordination is obviously necessary for social and emotional interaction as well. It also has been suggested that they lack a theory of mind (Baron-Cohen, 1995), which, as we discussed in the previous chapter, is necessary to understand that other people may have different mental states from one's own and that these mental states can be deduced through social signals. For example, a look of surprise on someone's face can be a clue as to the particular mental model under which that person has been operating. Once again, such an ability involves an interface between cognitive and emotional functioning.

At present, autism is assumed to be a heterogeneous disorder with many potential causes, including genetic disorders, infectious disease, birth injury, metabolic diseases, and structural disorders of brain development (e.g., Coleman, 1987). The constellation of brain structures involved in autism remains unclear, although a number of regions have been implicated. The potential contribution of each is beyond the scope of this chapter, so they are mentioned only briefly here. Some researchers have suggested that autism is caused by abnormalities in the cerebellum, particular brainstem nuclei, the amygdala, and other limbic structures (Courchesne et al., 1988). According to this viewpoint, the cerebellar and brainstem abnormalities would explain the difficulties in learning novel mental and motor skills and in acquiring a smooth coordination of mental skills. The damage to the amygdala and other limbic regions would explain the abnormal emotional aspects of autism. Because these regions undergo neurogenesis during the fifth week of gestation, it is suggested that autism may result from insult during that time period (Courchesne, 1997).

Other investigators have emphasized the role of medial temporal areas (Bachevalier, 1994), and a dysfunctional frontal-limbic system (A. R. Damasio & Maurer, 1978), which would explain some of the communication and emotional disturbances. It has been suggested that damage to these areas might arise later in development, during the late prenatal or early postnatal period. Thus, autism may arise from different types of neural insult, which might explain some of the heterogeneity in the expression of the disorder (see Gillberg, 1999, for a review).

Notice that all the regions purported to be involved in autism share two main characteristics. First, a number of them, such as regions of the limbic system and temporal lobe, are typically associated with emotional functioning. Second, they tend to be part of a system that involves many different brain regions. The diffuse nature of brain structures affected in autism likely explains why this disorder affects so many aspects of intellectual and emotional functioning, in contrast to the specific verbal and nonverbal developmental disorders considered earlier, which affect a more circumscribed set of abilities.

No clear treatment for autistic disorders exists at present. Such children typically need a combination of treatments designed to deal with the problems in emotional and social interaction as well as the intellectual and language deficits. Plus, the additional problematic behaviors, such as ritualistic stereotyped actions, must also be addressed. Generally, prognosis is better if treatment is started early, by two to three years of age, rather than later than age four. Recently a variety of pharmacological agents have been used to try to alleviate some of the symptoms of autism, but there is no clear consensus on their effectiveness (see Tanguay, 2000, for an overview).

Attention-Deficit Hyperactivity Disorder

Attention-deficit hyperactivity disorder (ADHD) is a developmental disorder in which the affected child is much more inattentive and distractible than is typical for the average child of the same age. Furthermore, individuals with ADHD tend to be hyperactive and impulsive (*DSM-IV,* 1994) and are often guided by environmental dependencies similar to those discussed in Chapter 11. These children *are* capable of paying attention and sitting still, because they may spend hours playing a video game, but overall their ability to do so is much less than is typical for their age. ADHD often impedes a child's progress in learning, especially in a structured environment, because the child's impulsivity and distractibility do not allow him or her to sit still long enough to absorb material or to listen to instructions. Because of these tendencies, such children may find themselves cherished by neither teachers nor parents. If their behavior leads to difficulty with peers and authority figures, they can be at risk for engaging in antisocial behavior. Moreover, although ADHD is a distinct disorder, it can occur simultaneously with other learning disabilities such as dyslexia.

The nature of the underlying problem in attentional control in ADHD is not clear. Some individuals argue that the core attentional problem is in executive control (Barkley, 1998), whereas others suggest that alerting and orienting functions are also impaired (Swanson et al., 1998). Still others more precisely pinpoint inhibition of processing as being the main aspect of executive function that is disrupted (Nigg, 2001). Not surprisingly, various regions of the attentional network appear to be dysfunctional in ADHD. Studies have indicated hypometabolism of frontal regions (e.g., Zametkin et al., 1993), which would be associated with lack of executive control, and dysfunction of parietal regions (Sieg, Gaffney, Preston, & Hellings, 1995), which would be associated with difficulties in orienting. In addition, there is dysfunction of inferior prefrontal regions and the striatum (Rubia et al., 1999) during motor inhibition, and dysfunction of the anterior cingulate when salient information must be ignored (Bush et al., 1999).

A variety of evidence links ADHD specifically to a problem in the dopaminergic system. Anatomically, this system originates in brain stem regions and projects diffusely to many target areas, including frontal cortex. The symptoms exhibited by children with ADHD are sometimes reminiscent of those exhibited by individuals with damage to the frontal lobe (e.g., Barkley, Grodzinsky, & DuPaul, 1992), a region that receives many dopaminergic projections. The primary means of treating children with ADHD is with drugs that modulate dopaminergic transmission, such as those derived from amphetamine (trade names Dexedrine, Adderall) (Gadow, 1981), methylphenidate (trade name: Ritalin) and pemoline (trade name: Cylert). Methylphenidate affects the dopaminergic neurotransmitter system by slowing the rate of dopamine reuptake on postsynaptic sites. For children with ADHD, these medications have been found to improve cognitive performance (e.g., Barkley,

1977), classroom behavior (e.g., Whalen, Henker, & Dotemoto, 1981), and interaction with parents (e.g., Barkley, Karlsson, Pollard, & Murphy, 1985).

Brain imaging studies comparing brain activation in children with ADHD in medicated versus non-medicated states also implicate the dopaminergic system, as these drugs affect activation of the frontal-striatal system. For example, off methylphenidate, the children had hypoperfusion (less activity) in the caudate, putamen, and globus pallidus (i.e., the striatum), as well as in frontal regions, whereas primary sensorimotor areas were overactivated. With methylphenidate, activation of striatal regions increased, whereas that of primary sensory regions decreased (Lou et al., 1989). Also, the way in which methylphenidate affects striatal function differs between children with ADHD and those without, also suggesting a dysfunction of the frontal-striatal system (Vaidya et al., 1998). Finally, genetic studies link ADHD to the dopaminergic system. The expression of particular genes is linked to the severity of ADHD symptoms, and such genes run in families (for a review, see Swanson et al., 2000). One such gene is the DAT-1 (dopamine transporter gene), which may be linked to the hyperactive reuptake of dopamine (Cook et al., 1995) and another is the DRD4 gene, which may be linked to subsensitivity of the postsynaptic receptor (LaHoste et al., 1996). In both cases, it is assumed that disruption of dopaminergic transmission is linked to ADHD.

As we reviewed in the last three sections, developmental disorders can seriously hamper a child's ability to proceed along the normal developmental course with regard to the acquisition of cognitive and emotional skills. These disorders either affect specific areas of cognition, as in the case of dyslexia and nonverbal learning disabilities, or impair a broad array of cognitive functions, as in pervasive developmental disorders and ADHD. Developmental disorders may affect social functioning directly, as in pervasive developmental disorders, or indirectly, as in the case of dyslexia, because of their present and future effects on a child's social status. Because the problems rarely disappear with age (although they may dissipate), interventions that can mitigate the child's disabilities (e.g., tutoring, counseling) should be started as early as possible.

Mental Retardation

Many of the developmental disabilities that we have discussed so far manifest in relatively specific ways, such as the inability to read or the inability to pay attention. When children fail to acquire intellectual abilities across most cognitive domains at a normal rate and manner, and when they have difficulties in adaptive functioning, such as self-care, the disorder is termed **mental retardation.** Mental retardation is generally divided into four categories based on severity. This classification system and the characteristics of individuals in each category are presented in Table 13.2. Mental retardation can be caused by numerous factors, including infections, genetic disorders, toxins, anoxia, and malnutrition. In the discussion that follows, we describe these as **risk factors,** which means that although they increase the likelihood of an event occurring, they do not ensure that one will occur. These risk factors act much the way that a drunken driver, a slippery road, and bald tires act to increase the probability that the driver will be involved in a vehicular accident, although they don't ensure that an accident will ensue. The major predisposing factors for mental retardation are provided in Table 13.3. As we learned earlier in the chapter, the developing brain is plastic and can be affected by the environment to a greater degree than can the adult brain. Although the virtues of this plasticity are that the brain can fine-tune itself to the environment, it is also more vulnerable to influences that can affect it negatively, such as the risk factors for mental retardation. Risk factors can exert themselves either prenatally or postnatally. A growing public appreciation for the prenatal risk factors for mental retardation is reflected in public service announcements and packaging labels directed at pregnant women, cautioning them to limit their ingestion of certain substances (e.g., alcohol), to ensure adequate nutrition, and to avoid contact with people who have certain infectious diseases, such as German measles (rubella). We will now consider each of these risk factors for mental retardation in some detail.

• *INFECTIONS* •

A variety of infections may damage the developing fetus by crossing the *placenta,* which is the membra-

TABLE 13.2 The Four Classes of Mental Retardation Based on Severity

DEGREE OF RETARDATION	IQ LEVEL	PERCENTAGE*	TYPICAL PRESENTATION
Mild	50-55 to 70	85	Previously known as "academically educable." Develop normally during preschool but don't acquire academic abilities above the 6th-grade level. As adults can usually be self-supportive although at times may need supervision and guidance.
Moderate	35-40 to 50-55	10	Previously known as "academically trainable." Can acquire communication skills during early childhood. As adults, need supervision for living and work.
Severe	20-25 to 35-40	3-4	Can learn some elementary self-care and language skills. As adults, can perform simple tasks in closely supervised settings.
Profound	< 20-25	1-2	Usually have an identifiable neurologic disorder that accounts for the retardation. Have impairments during childhood in sensorimotor functioning. Need highly structured environment with constant supervision by an individual caregiver.

*Percentage of all mentally retarded children who fall into that category.

nous organ by which nutrients and blood are passed from the mother to the fetus. These infections, which are thought to occur in as many as 2 percent of all newborns, include toxoplasmosis, rubella, cytomegalovirus, and herpes simplex. One of the best known of these is rubella. If acquired by the mother before the 13th gestational week (even if during the last menstrual period before conception), rubella affects 50 percent of all infants and is associated with mental retardation and behavioral disorders (e.g.,

TABLE 13.3 The Various Causes of Mental Retardation

CAUSE	CASES (%)	EXAMPLE MECHANISMS	EXAMPLE SYNDROMES
Heredity	5	Error of metabolism Chromosomal aberrations	Phenylketonuria (PKU) Fragile X syndrome
Early alteration of embryonic development	30	Prenatal exposure to a toxin	Fetal alcohol syndrome (FAS)
Problems in pregnancy and perinatally	10	Infection Maternal malnutrition	Rubella Low birth weight
Medical conditions in childhood and infancy	5	Poisoning Malnutrition	Ingestion of lead Kwashiorkor
Environmental influences	15-20	Deprivation	No parental nurturance
No clear cause	30-40	?	?

Chess, Fernandez, & Korn, 1979). The herpes virus is also a problem because it may exist undetected in many adults yet have devastating consequences for a developing organism. In addition to causing mental retardation, many viruses may cause anomalous development of the auditory tract, which leads to deafness and hampers the acquisition of speech and other aspects of language (e.g., Eichhorn, 1982).

• *GENETIC DISORDERS* •

Many genetic disorders cause mental retardation. In this section, we briefly review only the major syndromes. Like the infections just described, genetic disorders affect not only the brain, but other aspects of physical development as well.

One of the major genetic disorders leading to mental retardation is **Down syndrome,** which occurs in 1 in 100 cases. Then retardation is usually severe, and IQs are typically lower than those exhibited by less than 2 percent of the unimpaired population. This syndrome is caused by a defective egg or sperm, defects in early cell division, or more rarely because chromosomes translocate (move to other positions) during mitosis (the replication and subsequent division of DNA). It can also be caused by trisomy 21, a condition in which the 21st pair of chromosomes contains three chromosomes (hence *tri*somy) rather than the usual two. One well-known risk factor for Down syndrome is the mother's age. The probability of having a Down syndrome child increases significantly if the mother is older than 35 years (e.g., Lilienfeld, 1969). As they enter the fourth or fifth decade of life, many individuals with Down syndrome begin to exhibit symptoms similar to those of Alzheimer's disease (which we discuss in Chapter 14), and postmortem examination of the brain reveals the tangles and plaques typical of Alzheimer's disease (e.g., Karlinsky, 1986; Oliver & Holland, 1986).

Another commonly inherited form of mental retardation is **fragile X syndrome** (sometimes referred to as *Martin-Bell syndrome*), which affects 1 in 1,500 boys and 1 in 2,500 girls (e.g., Webb, Bundey, Thake, & Todd, 1986). Because of this high incidence rate, some localities, such as Alberta, Canada, routinely screen newborns for this genetic disorder. In this syndrome, an individual inherits an X chromosome (from the mother in the case of boys or from either parent in the case of girls) with a fragile section. At this section of the chromosome, a normally repeating sequence of genetic material occurs an unusually large number of times, much like a genetic stutter (see C. A. Ross, McInnis, Margolis, & Li, 1993, for a discussion of unusually large repeating sequences causing not only fragile X syndrome but other neuropsychiatric disorders). If a male receives this gene, he has an 80 percent chance of being mentally retarded, whereas for girls the chance is 30 percent. The degree of retardation varies, ranging from profound to borderline in boys and from mild to borderline in girls (see Table 13.2) (S. T. Warren & Nelson, 1994). Like Down syndrome, which is associated with a specific morphology of the body and face (Figure 13.11A), individuals with fragile X syndrome often have a characteristic look, although it is much more subtle than that of Down syndrome. Fragile X syndrome produces a tendency toward a long, narrow face; a long, prominent chin; and large ears (Figure 13.11B) (Cianchetti et al., 1991). Because the physical characteristics of this syndrome are not striking, screening for the disorder is not routine in many places, and because the manifestations of the disorder can vary, children with fragile X syndrome are often not diagnosed until later in childhood. They come to the attention of parents and teachers when they begin to fall behind their peers in development.

Another genetic disorder that leads to severe mental retardation if left untreated, is **phenylketonuria (PKU),** which occurs in 1 of every 18,000 births. In this disorder, individuals lack phenylalanine hydroxylase, an enzyme that allows phenylalanine, a specific amino acid, to be converted to tyrosine. As a result, phenylalanine builds up in the blood, and there is a deficit in tyrosine and tryptophan, a metabolic precursor to the neurotransmitter dopamine. Hence, the brain is deprived of a critical neurotransmitter, and mental retardation results. Currently, newborns are screened for PKU. Such screening allows dietary measures that restrict the intake of phenylalanine to be instituted immediately after birth. (You may already be aware of PKU if you noticed labels on diet soda cans warning people with PKU, phenylketonurics, that the soda contains phenylalanine.)

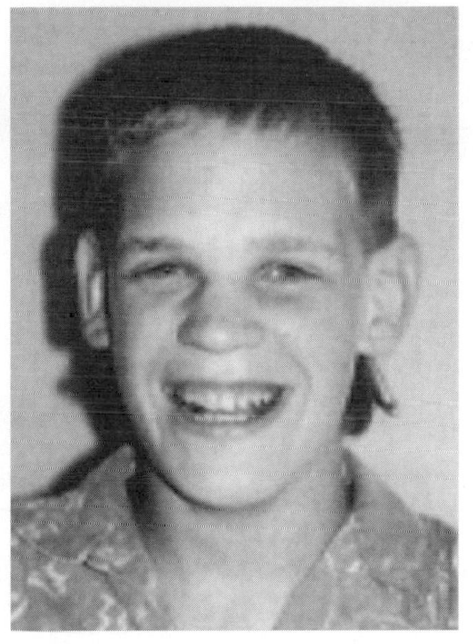

FIGURE 13.11 Physical features associated with genetic causes of mental retardation. (A) Individuals who have Down syndrome typically have certain physical features that make this type of retardation relatively easy to detect in infancy. These features include an upper eyelid that, at the corner of the eye, folds over the bottom eyelid, and a face with a relatively flat profile. (B) In fragile X syndrome, the associated physical features are much less pronounced. As shown here in this adolescent male who has the syndrome, they include a long face, a prominent forehead, and large ears. However, as can be seen, these features are not so out of the ordinary as to make the diagnosis obvious.

Although control of what these children eat can ameliorate some of the negative mental consequences of this condition, problems can still arise because the children typically dislike this very restrictive and bland diet and want to "cheat." Even with early and continuous treatment, children with PKU can still exhibit intellectual deficits, underscoring the importance of keeping phenylalanine levels low (Huijbregts et al., 2002). Deficits occur mainly in executive control (e.g., Diamond, Prevor, Callender, & Druin, 1997) and attention (e.g., Craft et al., 1992). These deficits are considered to be related to the effect that PKU has on the brain. In this disorder, prefrontal cortex does not get the requisite dopaminergic input, compromising executive control. PKU also affects myelination, which doesn't allow the integration of information across brain regions, such as the cerebral hemisphere, compromising attentional control (Banich et al., 2000).

Other genetic disorders can affect specific aspects of intellectual functioning. One such disorder is **Turner's syndrome,** which affects 1 in every 3,000 to 5,000 females. In this disorder, a female inherits just one X chromosome (XO) rather than two (XX). (Typically, fetuses that inherit just a Y chromosome are not viable.) Although these individuals' overall intelligence is normal and their verbal abilities tend to be above average, their spatial and perceptual skills are below average. Recently it has been suggested that the manifestation of Turner's syndrome varies depending on whether the sole X is that inherited paternally from the father (X^P) as compared to maternally, from the mother (X^M). Women who inherit an X^P tend to have better social skills than those who inherit an X^M (Skuse et al., 1997). In contrast, the inheritance of an additional X chromosome in both males (XXY) and females (XXX) is associated with poor verbal skills (e.g., Netley & Rovet, 1982; Pennington, Puck, & Robinson, 1980). Another recent suggestion is that the core cognitive deficit in females with Turner's syndrome is in visuo-spatial working memory (Buchanan, Pavlovic, & Rovet, 1998). Although a number of neuroanatomical abnormalities as well as atypical patterns of brain activation have been observed in these individuals, none of them appear to be a defining characteristic of the disorder.

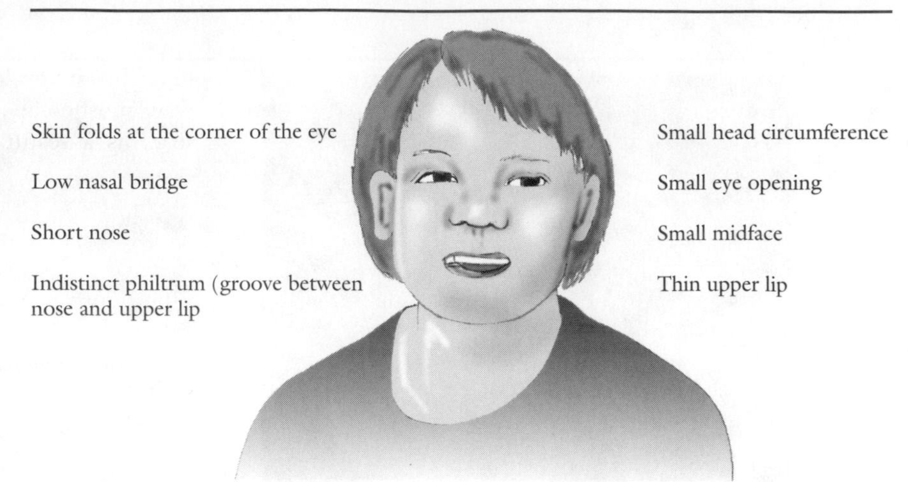

FIGURE 13.12 Physical facial features associated with fetal alcohol syndrome.

The exact mechanism whereby these genetic anomalies cause disruption in mental functioning is not yet clear. Because no cure exists, the emphasis is on prevention or early intervention. Genetic counseling can help individuals decide whether they want to have a child, and amniocentesis can help women decide whether they want to carry an affected fetus, such as one with Down syndrome, to term. Screening for disorders at birth allows for intervention early in life (as in the case of PKU).

• *TOXINS* •

Toxins are another cause of mental retardation. Recently, the public has been made more aware of this association because of discussion in the media and admonishments on cigarette packages and liquor bottles regarding the negative effects of tobacco and alcohol, respectively, on the developing fetus. The long-term effects of alcohol abuse by the mother during pregnancy are clear-cut and result in **fetal alcohol syndrome (FAS),** which is a leading cause of mental retardation (and is entirely preventable if the mother refrains from excessive drinking). The prevalence rate is about 1 in 1,000.

FAS causes hyperactivity, poor attention span, social and emotional difficulties, difficulties in learning and memory, executive dysfunction, retarded physical growth, and abnormalities of the face and cranium as shown in Figure 13.12 (see Mattson, Schoenfeld, & Riley, 2001, for a short, readable discussion of the effects of FAS on brain and behavior, and Warren & Foudin, 2001, for other characteristics of FAS). It is associated with changes in brain structure in the regions of the basal ganglia, corpus callosum, cerebellum, and hippocampus.

To provide some perspective, the amount of alcohol that these mothers typically consume is between 24 and 32 shots of hard liquor a week (or about 3.5 to 4.5 a day). Recent evidence suggests that risk is not so much associated with the total amount of alcohol consumed, but rather with the number of drinks consumed on a given occasion (Maier & West, 2001). Therefore, binge drinking, which leads to a higher blood alcohol level, is more likely to have deleterious effects on the developing nervous system than the same total number of drinks spread out over more than one occasion. Lower, but excessive, alcohol consumption during pregnancy, especially the early stages, can cause less severe effects, which are known as **fetal alcohol effects.**

Another drug whose negative effect on the developing fetus has received much attention is cocaine. However, some studies suggest that certain effects in crack babies (i.e., babies whose mothers are addicted to cocaine that is smoked) may be transient (e.g., L. F. Allen et al., 1991) and that with adequate support, children of crack-addicted mothers can make adequate academic progress. Nonetheless, difficulties in social interaction have been noted in children of substance abusers. For example, as infants they may not be responsive to a mother's touch or attention (e.g., Beckwith et al., 1994). Whether these early difficulties have future negative implications for their ability to sustain relationships in academic, occupational, and personal arenas is a question that will be answered only by longitudinal research on these children as they grow older.

Ascertaining the specific effects of the mother's drug abuse on the subsequent mental status of the developing fetus is often difficult because other factors typically associated with the mother's cocaine use, such as poor nutrition, can also lead to mental retardation (a point often overlooked in the media's discussion of this issue) (e.g., N. L. Day & Richardson, 1993). At this point, the oldest children followed longitudinally are about 10 years of age, with the majority just reaching school age. The pattern emerging from research is that these children may have difficulties in regulating arousal and attention, especially in the face of novel or stressful situations. These difficulties appear to be related to altered functioning of the norephinephrine system (Mayes, Grillon, Granger, & Schottenfeld, 1998), which, as we learned in Chapter 2, is important for control of overall activation of the central nervous system. But, on the whole, when other demographic factors are accounted for, their performance appears not to differ significantly from that of other school-age children (Richardson, Conroy, & Day, 1996).

• *ANOXIA* •

The brain is the most metabolically demanding of all organs, and because oxygen is critical for the conversion of glucose into energy, deprivation of oxygen, known as *anoxia,* for as few as three minutes is sufficient to cause brain death. Oxygen is even more critical for the developing nervous system because, as we learned previously, the metabolic needs of the developing nervous system can exceed those of the adult nervous system.

Oxygen deprivation can occur during development in a variety of ways. Before birth, a child may experience reduced oxygen because the placenta (which allows blood to pass from the mother to the child) may be underdeveloped or damaged, or because the mother doesn't have adequate oxygen herself (e.g., as a result of anemia). During birth, damage to the placenta or entanglement of the umbilical cord may reduce the oxygen supply to the infant. After birth, some populations of infants, such as those born very prematurely, are at risk for anoxia because their lungs are not developed enough for breathing (Spreen et al., 1984; for a review of the implications of oxygen deprivation at birth, see Blackman, 1989).

Children who have an anoxic episode early in life are at increased risk for later mental retardation (Lipper et al., 1986) and **cerebral palsy,** which is an umbrella term for many motor disorders resulting from nonprogressive damage to neural structures important for motor control (e.g., K. B. Nelson & Ellenberg, 1986). Yet, mental retardation is not an inevitable consequence of anoxia early in life, and some children, such as those with congenital heart problems, may exhibit substantial improvement if interventions are enacted to increase the oxygen supply to the brain (e.g., O'Dougherty, Wright, Loewenson, & Torres, 1985). The outcome appears to depend on the degree of perinatal lack of oxygen. Whereas those with moderate anoxia show deficits on tests of memory, perceptual-motor skills, and frontal lobe function, those with only mild hypoxia do not (Maneru et al., 2001).

• *MALNUTRITION* •

Malnutrition either prenatally or postnatally can have serious consequences for later development because without enough nutrition, the child's organ systems, including the brain, will be underdeveloped (for a discussion of how undernutrition affects brain development and its effects on cognitive development, see Georgieff & Rao, 2001). In some situations, children receive adequate nutrition as long as they are breast-fed, but thereafter they may be in an environment in which their diet is deficient. Starvation due to a lack of protein in the diet, known as **kwashiorkor,** and starvation due to a deficiency in caloric intake, known as **marasmus,** are problems seen especially in developing countries (Spreen et al.,

1984). Children with these disorders often have much edema, which accounts for the rounded faces and greatly bloated stomachs that we commonly see in journalists' pictures of children who live in famine-stricken regions of the world. Compounding the problem is that such nutritional deficiency often coexists with other conditions, such as inadequate medical care and impoverished social and physical environments that also have negative consequences for intellectual development (e.g., Ricciuti, 1993). In the more developed world, preterm infants who are in a neonatal intensive care unit often exhibit signs of malnutrition, due to their undeveloped systems, and these effects can last more than a year. Although inadequate nutrition often leads to mental retardation (e.g., Hoorweg & Stanfield, 1976), proper nutrition after early starvation (e.g., Bartel et al., 1977), combined with a stimulating environment, may diminish or even overcome such effects. Although the earlier the intervention the better, it appears that recovery of function can occur even well beyond the period of rapid brain growth by increasing the supply of protein and energy sources for the brain (e.g., Pollitt, 1996). Unfortunately, the effects of a lack of certain substances, such as iodine, selenium, folate, and vitamin A, which are critical for brain development during the first 12 weeks post-conception, cannot be remedied.

Adult Outcomes of Developmental Disorders

So far we have discussed the effects of developmental disorders on children but not the level of functioning that these children show as adults. For some of the disorders we discussed, the outcome is relatively straightforward. For instance, individuals who exhibit mental retardation or pervasive developmental disorders as children also exhibit intellectual impairment as adults. But what about some of the more specific learning disabilities such as dyslexia and ADHD? Do children outgrow these disorders, or are they impaired for life?

One theory put forth to explain specific learning disabilities was the **maturational lag hypothesis,** which postulated that individuals with learning disabilities were slower to mature than their peers and that with time they would outgrow the problem much the way that children shed baby fat. This idea was fueled in part by observations that learning disabilities appear to become less severe with age in certain subpopulations of children. For example, some children with ADHD appear to become less impulsive around age 12 years, which is when children typically show an increase in attentional abilities. However, a change in the manifestation of the disorder with age does not imply that the problem has disappeared. Although at age 12 a child with ADHD may be able to sit in his chair in a classroom, something he could not do at age 7, the disorder may simply be manifesting itself differently—for example, as an inability to "sit with" a homework problem, rather than physically sitting in a chair.

Given our increasing knowledge regarding the neural bases for these disorders, the idea that these learning disabilities miraculously disappear at adulthood seems improbable. For the most part, learning disabilities in childhood also manifest in adulthood but in a different form and manner. Since the diagnostic criteria for these disorders usually refer to behaviors manifested in childhood, it may be challenging to diagnose disorders in an adult whose problems have previously gone unaddressed. One of the current challenges for researchers and clinicians alike is to determine how the diagnostic criteria for some of these disorders change over the life span and whether there is a core deficit that manifests itself regardless of developmental stage (see, for example, Faraone, 2000).

The fact that learning disabilities can endure across the life span is supported by both anatomical and behavioral evidence. Let's consider dyslexia as an example. As mentioned previously, atypical cell migration or atypical myelination occurs prenatally. These anatomical anomalies remain for the individual's entire life. The question then arises as to whether the brain can reorganize itself, despite this atypical substrate, to allow normal behavioral development. Such reorganization apparently isn't possible. Adults with dyslexia are still impaired on tests that emphasize phonologic processing as compared with neurologically intact adults. A difference is observed even if the individuals with dyslexia and the control individuals are matched for socioeconomic status (which is important, because a poor reading ability may limit job opportunities for persons with dyslexia, leading to a lower than average socioeconomic status). Furthermore, neuropsychological test results for adults with dyslexia exhibit a profile that is suggestive of dysfunction of left hemisphere language areas, similar to that of individuals who acquire alexia as a result of brain injury (see Chapter 9, page 303, for a discussion of alexia). Moreover, adults who had poor reading scores as children exhibit little focal activation (as measured by regional cerebral blood flow) of these left parietal regions during reading (Bigler, 1992). All these findings suggest that the brain of a person with dyslexia is unable to compensate for certain aspects of the neural disorganization that occurred early in development.

In addition, developmental syndromes may have consequences for functioning in realms different than those affected in childhood. For instance, because of their social inadequacy, children with nonverbal learning disabilities may exhibit mental health difficulties as adults. In one study, seven of eight adults who had been diagnosed with a nonverbal learning disability were prone to depression, four of them so severely as to require hospitalization. In addition, all were working at lower-status jobs than would have been anticipated on the basis of their schooling (Rourke, Young, Strang, & Russell, 1985). Likewise, as mentioned previously, children with ADHD may have problems that evolve into antisocial behavior, especially in the later teen and adult years.

As we learn in the next section, the brain has a large potential for reorganizing itself in response to trauma and deprivation. This plasticity may account for some of the diminution in learning disabilities that can occur as a child ages. Yet it does not occur either in the manner or to the degree necessary to prevent learning disorders from manifesting themselves. We now turn our attention to an examination of the reorganization and plasticity of the brain.

Recovery of Function

Our discussion so far has centered on the development of the brain and the anomalies that may occur in the course of that development. We now need to examine how the brain reacts when it sustains a specific insult (e.g., a gunshot wound). First, we describe, in a general manner, the brain's responses to injury on a neurophysiological level. Then we discuss the possible mechanisms for recovery. Finally, we compare the differences in recovery of function between adults and children.

Neurophysiological Responses to Insult

Damage to the brain sets a number of physiological processes in motion, some of which occur directly at the site of the lesion and others of which occur at more distant points. At the site of the lesion, cells begin to die, a process called **necrosis.** This process not only affects neurons, but also the glia that form the myelin sheath around a neuron. In some cases, cell loss may extend past the actual site of damage to more distal neurons, a process called **transneuronal degeneration.** Such degeneration occurs because neurons require an optimal level of stimulation and/or certain chemical (probably nutritional) factors from other nerve cells. Thus, if a substantial proportion of a neuron's inputs are damaged, that cell may die. Transneuronal degeneration can occur across more than one synapse, having a domino-like effect. For example, if the optic nerve is cut, cells of the lateral geniculate body degenerate completely. Then, as the lateral geniculate begins to degenerate, cells in the visual cortex may degenerate as well. Often transneuronal degeneration is accompanied by accumulations of calcium, a process known as **calcification,** which can easily be detected by brain imaging techniques such as computerized axial tomography (CAT) scanning.

Dead cells are engulfed and broken down (a process known as *phagocytosis*) by astrocytes and microglia. Because neurons have a far more limited capacity to regenerate than other cells in the body, fluid now fills the spaces where cells once resided. New capillaries may form in the region as well. The process of phagocytosis and capillary formation may continue for several months until only glial cells remain, a process known as **gliosis.** Astrocytes mark off the region, forming a scar.

In addition to changes in the neurons themselves, other processes occur with damage. One of these, **edema,** is the swelling of tissue after trauma, which occurs in the brain just as it does in any other part of the body. Swelling of the brain involves dangers not associated with swelling of tissue in other body parts. When other body parts swell, they just take up more space under your clothing. But the brain shares a confined space with cerebrospinal fluid within the skull, and when it is bruised, the situation is similar to that of having a badly bruised toe that must be shoved into your shoe. The edema associated with brain trauma leads to an increase in intracranial pressure, because more fluid now occupies the same amount of space. This increased pressure can interfere with neuronal function not only at the site of damage, but elsewhere as well. When the edema exerts pressure on brainstem regions controlling vital functions, it can cause a person to become comatose, or, in more severe cases, die. Hence, cortisone, a steroid, is often given after cerebral trauma to help reduce edema. Because edema may last for some time (e.g., weeks), the behavioral consequences of a lesion may not be apparent shortly after damage because such consequences are difficult to disentangle from the effects of generalized edema.

In addition to the changes just discussed, some of the basic aspects of a brain's functioning, such as its metabolic rate, neurotransmitter release, and oxygen consumption, may also be disrupted by a lesion (for a recent review and a discussion of how these problems might be clinically managed, see Verma, 2000). Generally, after brain damage, there is an early period of about five days post-injury in which some individuals actually exhibit increased metabolism. Between 5 to 28 days post-injury there is a decrease in overall metabolism, which generally normalizes by one month post-injury (Bergsneider et al., 2001).

Brain trauma may also cause changes in neurotransmitter levels and in oxygen supply to the brain. The lack of oxygen means that the brain has a reduced energy supply. One of the main goals of pharmacological interventions after brain trauma is to spare the use of energy. For example, immediately after damage, there may be the release of too much glutamate, an excitatory neurotransmitter. This over-release can lead to cell death by overexcitation (Kolb & Whishaw, 1990). As an acute intervention immediately after brain trauma, drugs are given to inhibit glutamate release (Verma, 2001).

At present, we still do not know the best intervention to ameliorate the effects of brain damage. Take, for example, the decrease in brain metabolism that typically occurs 5 to 30 days post-injury. There is some evidence from animal studies that in the first few days after brain injury to sensorimotor areas, use of the affected limb can *increase* neuronal damage (Humm et al., 1998). It is possible, then, that the period of decreased metabolism is one in which the brain is particularly vulnerable, even to early rehabilitative efforts. Yet, animal studies also suggest that the time period of decreased metabolism may provide a window of opportunity for pharmacological intervention, such as the administration of amphetamine, that will reduce neurological impairment. Obviously, it is difficult to know which time periods are critical in humans by extrapolating from data obtained on other species. Also, ethical considerations prohibit a researcher from engaging in a study of the effects of rehabilitation if there is any possibility of negative consequences. Thus, at present, we do not have know enough about the time-dependent aspects of changes following brain insult to allow for the design of more effective treatments.

Given these multiple changes in brain function in response to injury and the long time span during which they manifest themselves, you can begin to appreciate why the clinician often cannot immediately assess the degree of damage sustained from an injury. If swelling is extensive, the person may show severe impairments at first but significant improvement as the edema decreases. On the other hand, responses immediately after oxygen deprivation may lead one to overestimate later levels of functioning because the detrimental effects of the oxygen deprivation continue to accrue. Thus, measures based on the person's behavior immediately after injury can only crudely predict the prognosis for functioning a month or even a year into the future (we discuss one of these measures, the Glasgow Coma Scale, in Chapter 14).

Mechanisms for Recovery of Function

Once the brain sustains an insult, the central nervous system uses various processes to attempt to compensate for the loss. Some of these mechanisms occur at the cellular level, whereas others involve larger regions of brain tissue. These changes, in which the brain tries to override and adapt its typical organization in the face of damage, trauma, or unusual circumstances (e.g., sensory deprivation), are known as **reorganization.** This process is observed both in developing organisms (i.e., children) and in adults. Reorganization can occur at a very gross level, such as the pattern of gyri and sulci of the brain (if the damage is inflicted in utero) (Goldman-Rakic & Rakic, 1984), or on a neuronal level. As we learn in the following sections, reorganization of the brain that occurs after damage early in life is usually more profound than that which can occur later in life. Although scientists originally believed that little if any reorganization was possible in the adult brain, that notion is fading. With these general concepts in mind, we now examine in more detail the changes that occur in the nervous system in response to injury.

• *CELLULAR PROCESSES* •

At the cellular level, a number of changes occur that may aid in recovery of function. Although **regeneration,** the reestablishment of a prior connection by a damaged nerve fiber, can occur in the peripheral nervous system, once a connection in the central nervous system is lost, it cannot be regenerated (in part because glial cells appear to inhibit neural growth (see Bahr & Bonhoeffer, 1994). Other processes that occur in response to damage in both the central and peripheral nervous systems involve neurochemical adaptations. One of these is **denervation supersensitivity,** in which intact cells become hypersensitive to stimulation. This process is thought to occur when there are reductions in the level of neurotransmitters, such as dopamine. The number of receptors on the remaining cells increases so that the same amount of neurotransmitter can produce a much larger result. Such a mechanism may help to explain why deficits are not observed in people with Parkinson's disease until the vast majority of the dopamine-producing neurons have been destroyed (see Chapter 5, in which we discussed this disease). Responses to brain damage may also involve changes in the rate of synthesis or release of neurotransmitters or decreases in the rate at which transmitters are inactivated.

Two other cellular mechanisms for recovery are rerouting and sprouting. In **rerouting,** a neuron that has lost its target seeks a new target and connects with it instead. This process is distinct from **sprouting,** in which the nerve fiber grows, becomes bushier, and makes new connections. Thus, sprouting involves not only rerouting, but a proliferation of nerve growth as well. Sprouting may occur not only near an injury, but also at other sites far away (see Feinberg, Mazlin, & Waldman, 1989, for a discussion of the relevance of these mechanisms in humans).

One possible means by which regeneration, sprouting, and rerouting may occur is through a substance known as nerve growth factor (NGF), which is transported to nerve cells from glia. NGF was discovered in the 1940s by Rita Levi-Montalcini and colleagues, a discovery for which she received the Nobel Prize (for an interesting account of how doing experiments in a closet while hiding from the Nazis during World War II led her to this discovery, read her autobiography, entitled *In Praise of Imperfection*). NGF has a large effect on three classes of neurons, only one of which is located within the central nervous system: cholinergic neurons of the basal forebrain and septum. Injecting NGF into the ventricle immediately after cutting the septal cholinergic neurons leading into the hippocampus decreases neuronal death, suggesting that NGF may be an important substance in sustaining neurons, especially after injury (Jessell, 1991). An interesting point to note is that neurons in the basal forebrain are markedly degenerated in cases of Alzheimer's disease (see Chapter 14 for more on Alzheimer's disease). Hence, a reduction in NGF may be one of the mechanisms whereby cell death occurs in individuals with this syndrome (e.g., Hefti & Weiner, 1986).

The efficacy of these various cellular mechanisms in promoting neuronal responses after injury is important, because neuronal elaboration after injury appears to be linked to the degree to which behavior is restored. In a series of studies, Kolb and colleagues examined the consequences of unilateral damage to various areas of a rat's cortex. Afterward, the rats were given the equivalent of a rodent neuropsychological test battery to determine their degree of impairment on species-specific behavioral tasks (such as grooming and exploring) and more cognitive and novel tasks, such as maze learning. These investigators found that the recovery of skill was always accompanied by extensive dendritic arborization in the remaining intact cortex (Kolb, 1989).

• *REGIONAL PROCESSES* •

Not only can damage to the nervous system cause changes at the cellular level, but it can also cause regional changes in brain organization. Probably the best evidence that brain reorganization can occur in adult mammals comes from studies in which the brain loses specific types of sensory input or in which sensory regions are destroyed. Accordingly, we discuss these animal studies first and then examine whether similar effects can occur in humans after brain trauma.

Some of the most compelling research for reorganization in the adult mammalian brain comes from a series of studies done by Merzenich and colleagues, who demonstrated changes in the organization of somatosensory cortex in the adult monkey as a result of drastic changes in environmental input. In each animal, they first determined the map of the somatosensory cortex isolating the regions of brain that receive sensory input from each of the digits on the hand (Figure 13.13A). Such a map indicates clear borders between the regions responsible for sensory input from each finger. Then these researchers drastically changed the input into the brain's somatosensory region in a number of ways. In one study, they amputated the middle digit (such a manipulation is clearly not done lightly; it provides information on brain reorganization that is difficult to obtain otherwise, and helps in the treatment of humans who have lost a limb). Two months later, the brain region that had previously received information from the middle digit now responded to sensory input from the two adjacent digits (Figure 13.13B). In another study, these researchers "fused" two digits by sewing them together. This made the somatosensory input they received very similar. As a result there was a blurring of the border between the regions in somatosensory areas that were sensitive to each digit. Finally, the researchers trained monkeys for a long period (i.e., months) on a task that caused only particular parts of the hand to receive tactile input, and found that the representation of the often-used digits was greatly increased. Moreover, after the monkey ceased performing the behavior frequently, the map reverted to its original state. In sum, these studies demonstrate that the organization of the brain in adulthood can flexibly adapt to environmental input (Jenkins, Merzenich, & Recanzone, 1990).

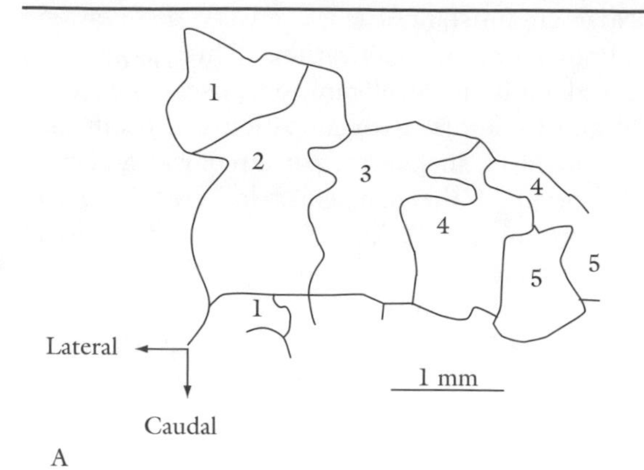

B

FIGURE 13.13 Changes in maps of somatosensory cortex in the monkey in response to changes in sensory information received. These maps indicate the areas of the brain that are sensitive to touch for the first (1) through fifth (5) digits (A) prior to amputation and (B) 62 days after amputation of the third digit. The region of brain tissue that previously was sensitive to touch from the third digit is now sensitive to tactile information from the second and fourth digits. The change between the map depicted in A and that depicted in B indicates the ability of the brain to reorganize even during adulthood.

These researchers also demonstrated that such reorganization can occur after brain damage. Unilateral lesions to somatosensory cortex caused the use of the contralateral hand to be limited to gross grasping behaviors such as climbing bars, with a loss of fine motor manipulation for tasks such as grasping food, which relies on somatosensory feedback. As the animal's abilities improved, there were concomitant changes in the somatosensory map.

When the brain tissue was first destroyed, portions of the contralateral hand were not represented anywhere in somatosensory cortex. With time, however, these same regions of skin surface became represented in the cortex surrounding the area that been lesioned (Jenkins, Merzenich, & Recanzone, 1990). This study provides strong proof of reorganization of function after brain lesions, which appears to be linked to recovery of function.

Evidence from humans who have a limb amputated, either accidentally or for medical reasons (e.g., gangrene), suggests a similar capacity for the reorganization of brain maps. Some individuals who undergo amputation of either the upper limb or a digit of the hand report feelings of the amputated limb when the face is stimulated (Ramachandran, Rogers-Ramachandran, & Steward, 1992). The regions of somatosensory cortex receiving information from the face and the hand are located next to each other and typically have a discrete boundary. After amputation, however, these regions reorganize so that the brain region previously sensitive solely to the hand has connections with neurons receiving information from the face. The result is that a touch to the face can cause a sensation of touch from the amputated (phantom) limb. An unfortunate consequence of such reorganization may be phantom-limb pain. The greater the reorganization that occurs between the face and hand areas, the greater the phantom-limb pain (Flor et al., 1995).

Such reorganization can also occur in response to less severe environmental input, that which is either long-lasting or more short-lived. For example, the region of the somatosensory cortex that responds to tactile information from the second through fifth digits of the left hand was found to be shifted in musicians of string orchestra instruments as compared with nonmusicians. However, no such difference was observed for the right hand, and that for the thumb of the left hand was much smaller. Thus, it appears that one to two hours a day of practice over 10 years of moving the second through fifth fingers of the left hand, as required by the musical performance of these individuals, influenced the cortical organization in primary somatosensory cortex of their brains. No such shifts were observed regarding the thumb of the left hand, because it was merely grasping the neck of the instrument, nor for the right hand, which grasps the bow (Elbert et al., 1995). Even practicing a simple motor sequence for 10–20 minutes a day over a period of four weeks can cause a change in the brain region supporting performance of a task. Compared to a novel, non-practiced sequence, the practiced sequence leads to greater activation of primary motor cortex, suggesting recruitment of additional cortex to support the skill (Karni et al., 1995).

It should also be noted that the *lack* of environment input can lead to changes in brain organization. This effect has been vividly demonstrated in a study involving blind and sighted individuals. When TMS is applied over the occipital lobe of sighted individuals, it does not disrupt their ability to identify Roman or Braille letters by touch. Such a result is not surprising since application of TMS to this region of the brain of sighted individuals interferes with visual processing. In contrast, TMS over the same location in blind individuals renders them unable to discriminate these forms! This finding indicates that their occipital cortex was recruited to process somatsensory information as a result of their blindness, which deprived them of visual input (Cohen et al., 1997).

Our discussion has focused on changes in brain organization that occur in sensorimotor regions. Clearly, a critical question for the rehabilitation of mental function after brain injury is the degree to which such mechanisms also work for cognitive functions, and the degree to which previously uninvolved brain regions can be recruited to aid in a task. Several examples of such reorganization exist, and we discuss them next.

A number of studies suggest that the undamaged hemisphere can aid in taking over the functions of the damaged one, both in childhood and adulthood. In one study, activation of the brain, as measured by fMRI, was examined in individuals who had suffered unilateral damage to the sensorimotor cortex either during or shortly after birth. Movement of the fingers of either the ipsilateral or contralateral hand produced an equivalent degree of brain activation over the intact hemisphere, suggesting that this region had taken over the functions of the damaged hemisphere (Cao et al., 1994).

Similar findings occurred in individuals who had sustained a stroke during adulthood. When tapping fingers on the hand contralateral to the lesion, they activated regions around the lesion in the affected hemisphere, and also activated a greater extent of cortex in the undamaged hemisphere than did neurologically intact individuals (Cramer et al., 1997). This study also suggests a reorganization of function in the intact tissue, both in the damaged hemisphere and the intact one.

Other examples of reorganization of function come from studies examining the reacquisition of language after brain damage. In one case, an individual sustained a left temporoparietal lesion that caused him to make semantic substitutions when using concrete words (e.g., saying "cherry" for "raspberry" and "ballet" instead of "theater") and left him unable to repeat pronounceable nonwords. When he performed semantic tasks, such as detecting a specific word from among several words (e.g. "bird"), there was a focal increase in activity in the right middle temporal region. In contrast, he could never make correct phonetic judgments, and no concomitant increase in activation in the right middle temporal region occurred during this task (Cardebat et al., 1994).

Other evidence for a right hemisphere role in recovery of function comes from the combined use of evoked potentials (EP) to a sensory probe, such as a flash of light or tone, and some additional task. Typically, when the additional task is verbal, the EP to the sensory probe is attenuated over the left hemisphere relative to a baseline condition in which the sensory probe is presented alone. This finding suggests that the left hemisphere is otherwise engaged in the verbal task and cannot respond to the sensory stimulus. Conversely, when the task is nonverbal, the EP is attenuated over the right hemisphere, which suggests that the right hemisphere is otherwise engaged in the nonverbal task. Whereas neurologically intact individuals and those with right hemisphere damage show a greater attenuation of the EP over the left hemisphere when engaged in a verbal task, individuals with left hemisphere brain damage did not. They showed greater attenuation over the right hemisphere, suggesting that it had taken over some aspects of processing language (Papanicolaou et al., 1988).

TABLE 13.4 Factors Likely to Influence Recovery

Severity of insult
Number of insults
Spacing of insults
Age at time of insult
Premorbid cognitive status
Extent to which one function can be taken over by another
Overall brain integrity
Individual differences in brain structure
Motivation
Emotional factors
Extent and quality of rehabilitation

Factors Influencing Recovery of Function in Adults

Although these studies provide evidence of possible brain reorganization after trauma, there are many unanswered questions regarding the degree to which recovery from nonprogressive brain damage is possible. At present, we do not know all of the parameters that limit the extent of reorganization and recovery, nor do we know exactly how to manipulate conditions to make such reorganization possible. What is clear, however, is that there are multiple factors that influence recovery, and that more recovery is possible in adults than has been traditionally thought. The multiple factors that influence recovery are listed in Table 13.4. One of the more interesting factors is the premorbid cognitive status of the individual. It is thought that individuals with higher intelligence and education may recover better. As said by a noted scientist over 60 years ago, "It is not only the kind of head injury that matters but the kind of head" (Symonds, 1937). However, the reason for this better recovery is unclear. On the one hand, more intelligent people may have a greater reserve of capacity so that suffering a brain insult does not diminish their overall capacity as much as it does in a less intelligent person. Another possibility is that more intelligent people are better at learning or devising strategies to overcome their disabilities.

Traditionally, when discussing recovery from brain damage, theorists differentiate between the restoration of a lost function and a substitution or compensation of function (e.g., Kolb, 1995). Some theorists have suggested that restitution of function occurs after relatively small lesions, whereas compensatory processes are more likely to occur after larger lesions. Furthermore, the time course of recovery may be more rapid for functions that can be subserved by multiple circuits, such as those that can cause unilateral neglect, as compared with those for which there are fewer alternative circuits, such as occurs in hemianopia (Robertson, cited in Wilson, 1998).

Not surprisingly, therapies aimed at individuals who have sustained brain trauma are similarly divided into two major camps: those aimed at restoration and those aimed at compensation. The goal of **restorative rehabilitation** is to gain increased function by repetitive exercise. This type of therapy can be considered the equivalent of "pumping iron" for the mind. The idea is that if you use it over and over again, you will redevelop a mental muscle. Such therapy has been found effective in reducing hemiparesis of the arm after stroke. It involves keeping the good limb constrained in a sling 90 percent of the time and providing six to seven hours of behaviorally relevant arm movements for two weeks (Taub & Uswatte, 2000). The result appears to be reorganization of motor cortex, as regions adjacent to the damaged areas are recruited to control the affected limb (Liepert et al., 1998) (for a good review of how animal experimentation led to the use of this application to humans, see Taub, Uswatte, & Pidikiti, 1999). Such an approach, however, does not tend to work as well with cognitive functions such as language and memory. There is no clear evidence that repetitive drills improve performance, nor that practice on specific drills generalizes to other tasks within the same cognitive domain (e.g., language). Nevertheless, such an approach may be useful if a patient suffers from a very specific, limited, and isolated deficit (Wilson, 1997).

The goal of **compensatory rehabilitation** is to provide a strategy that generally would not be used to perform a task but is invoked to minimize the loss of a specific skill. **Compensatory strategies** usually do not represent reorganization, because they rely on intact brain regions that are distinct from those used to perform the task prior to injury, or they rely on an external device, such as a computer or personal digital assistant. For example, a patient who becomes amnesic as a result of temporal lobe damage might carry a notebook with a picture of her car and a written note on where she parked it. Such a strategy is compensatory; it is not the approach people usually employ, and it is designed specifically to counteract her memory loss. Furthermore, this strategy does not rely on the brain region that typically is used to remember a car's identity and location, the hippocampus and entorhinal regions, but instead probably depends on the angular gyrus of the left hemisphere (for reading) and portions of the ventral visual-processing stream (for object recognition).

An **alternative strategy** is one that falls within the realm of everyday behavior but is distinct from the way in which the individual typically performed the task prior to injury. It may allow for good performance without the need for brain reorganization. As one example, a person may learn to navigate using a verbally mediated and landmark-based method (e.g., "I go four blocks to the gas station and turn right, continuing until I reach the bakery"), when prior to injury he or she would have just relied on the direction of travel (e.g., to the northeast).

Not surprisingly, because of the different ways that rehabilitation can be invoked and the heterogeneity of patients, there is some debate as to how useful cognitive rehabilitation really is. Although some studies indicate that individuals can improve on certain tests or narrowly defined tasks, one would also like to demonstrate that rehabilitation improves the ability of individuals to perform general activities of daily life, such as self-care (e.g., bathing and dressing) and self-sustenance (e.g., cooking, grocery shopping), as well as improving self-esteem and social interactions. Overwhelming evidence for improvement in these arenas is lacking (see Carney et al., 1999, for a review), yet there are some notable instances of success. A paging system has been found to improve the ability of brain-injured adults to remember to carry out important daily tasks, such as taking medication and going to work (e.g., Wilson et al., 1997), and strong verbal feedback to actions has been found to ameliorate executive deficits (e.g., Alderman, 1996). (For an excellent short review of issues regarding recovery of function, see Wilson, 1998).

Recovery of Function in Children

The recovery of function in children is distinct from that in adults because of the greater plasticity of the developing nervous system. We now turn to some specific issues regarding this topic.

Probably the most dramatic difference between adults and children after brain insult is the seemingly miraculous recovery that children appear to make. For example, lesions that would leave adults with little or no capacity for language do not have such dire consequences for children. For decades, scientists have thought that the earlier in life damage is sustained, the better the recovery. This maxim became known as the **Kennard principle,** named after the individual who first proposed such an effect (Kennard, 1936, 1942). As we learn in this section, it is now known that although the Kennard principle holds true in some cases, it does not in others.

When damage occurs early in life, the reorganizational capacity of the brain is large. One example of the huge potential for structural reorganization is provided by work with monkeys who received lesions in utero. In response to these lesions, drastic changes were noted in the gyral patterns of the brain, indicative of massive reorganization (Figure 13.14) (Goldman-Rakic & Rakic, 1984). Such drastic reorganization can have positive behavioral consequences. For example, damage early in life to the primary visual cortex in cats causes the enhancement of particular visual pathways and the retention of other pathways that usually disappear with age (Figure 13.15).

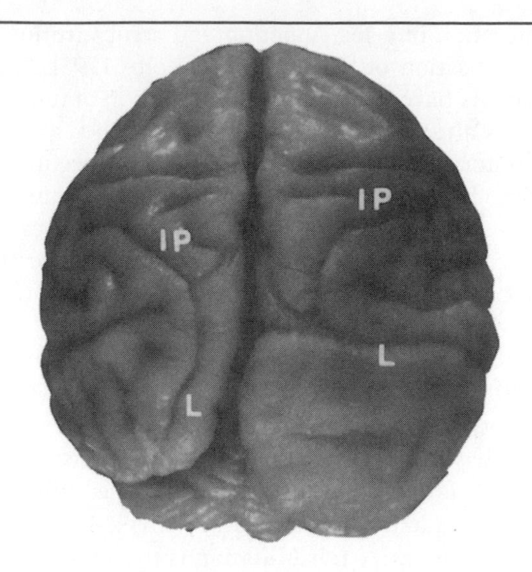

FIGURE 13.14 Massive reorganization in brain structure resulting from insult very early in life. Shown here is reorganization of the left hemisphere of a rhesus monkey whose left occipital lobe was removed at gestational day 83 (note the lack of cortical mass at the back of the brain on the left-hand side). Changes in brain organization can be seen by comparing the size of the inferior parietal lobule in each hemisphere. The right hemisphere's inferior parietal lobule is the normal size and extends from the intraparietal (IP) sulcus to the lunate (L) sulcus. In the left hemisphere, the inferior parietal lobule extends from the intraparietal sulcus all the way to the back of the brain and is almost twice as large as normal.

Moreover, these changes in neuronal wiring have important behavioral consequences. In adult cats, bilateral removal of visual cortex results in deficits in pattern discrimination, depth perception, and visual orienting, whereas removal of these same regions shortly after birth causes much less severe deficits. Similar trends are observed for visual function in both monkeys and humans, who have better abilities if a lesion to visual cortex occurs earlier rather than later in life (Payne & Cornwell, 1994). Thus, in these cases, the Kennard principle is correct: Early damage does lead to better reorganization and recovery.

Such is not the case for all functions. Recent studies attempting to replicate Kennard's findings that motor behaviors are less disrupted by early lesions have not been successful (e.g., Passingham, Perry, & Wilkinson, 1983). The Kennard principle also may not hold in humans with regard to cognitive skills, because damage at an early age does not always lead to better recovery (e.g., Woods, 1980). However, obtaining a clear picture of the effects of early damage in humans is complicated by a number of factors. First, findings from studies of monkeys and humans indicate that the consequences of early damage to the nervous system may not be revealed immediately but may become apparent only some time later (Goldman, 1974). Hence, researchers must consider not only the age at which a child sustains a lesion, but also the age at which the child is being assessed and the amount of time that has passed since the injury. Second, the type of task used to

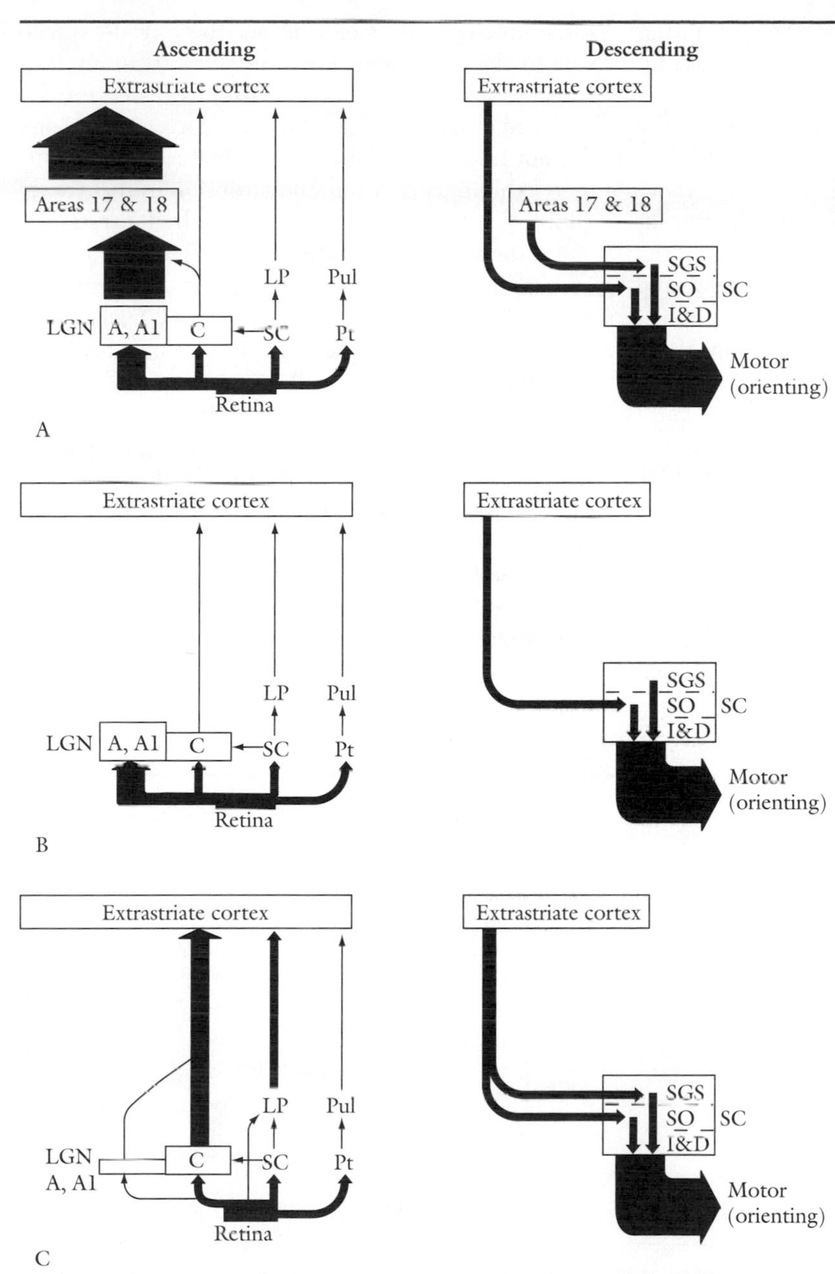

FIGURE 13.15 Comparison of the degree of brain reorganization after damage in adulthood and after damage in infancy. The ascending pathways from the retina to the extrastriate cortex and the descending pathways from extrastriate cortex to the superior colliculus (SC) in the cat are depicted for (A) intact adults, and those with ablation of the primary visual cortex during (B) adulthood and (C) infancy. In these diagrams, the width of the arrow indicates the size of the connection. After a lesion in infancy, the ascending pathway from the C layer of the lateral geniculate nucleus (LGN) to extrastriate cortex increases in size (large thick arrow), as does the pathway from the retina through the superior colliculus and the lateral posterior (LP) nucleus. Furthermore, two novel pathways not observed in intact animals are formed: an ascending pathway from the retina to the lateral posterior nucleus and a descending pathway from extrastriate cortex to the stratum griseum superficiale (SGS) of the superior colliculus. In contrast, none of these changes are seen after lesions in adult animals, a finding that demonstrates the greater plasticity of the immature nervous system. A and A1, layers A and A1; Pul, pulvinar nucleus; Pt, pretectum; SO, stratum opticum; I & D, intermediate and deep layers.

assess cognitive ability is important, whether it measures general intellectual ability, as in the case of IQ tests, or a specific skill, such as language. To illustrate some of the complicated ways in which these factors interact, let's discuss one study in which this author participated (Banich, Levine, Kim, & Huttenlocher, 1990; S. C. Levine, Huttenlocher, Banich, & Duda, 1987).

In this study, children who sustained unilateral brain damage were assessed, at some time after their brain injury, on a variety of neurological and intellectual tasks. The children were divided into two groups, those who had sustained damage either before or during birth, known as the *congenital group,* and those who had sustained damage later on (average age at insult was three years), known as the *acquired group.* To understand what factors contributed to subsequent intellectual ability, a number of variables were examined, including the age at which the lesion occurred, the size of the lesion, the location of the lesion, the child's age at testing, and how much time had elapsed since the child sustained the damage (for the congenital group, these last two factors were the same, whereas for the acquired group they were not). My colleagues and I also assessed a wide range of cognitive abilities, including reading, mathematical skills, vocabulary, and general intelligence.

In one respect, we found evidence for the Kennard principle: early damage led to maximal reorganization. Regardless of lesion location, all the children with congenital lesions acquired language and basic social skills. Thus, there seemed to be enough neural reorganization to support almost all cognitive functions, regardless of whether the initial damage was to the right hemisphere or the left. In another respect, however, we did not find evidence for the Kennard principle. Children with congenital lesions did not have maximal recovery. Instead, these children exhibited a substantial disruption in their overall intellectual abilities as measured by IQ tests.

Furthermore, the factor that influenced performance in each group differed. For the acquired group, the best predictor of subsequent IQ was lesion size (Figure 13.16A): The larger the lesion, the lower the child's IQ was, regardless of the time elapsed since the lesion had occurred and the age at which it occurred. In contrast, for the congenital group, there was no good predictor of IQ for children younger than age six years, but after that point, a strong negative relationship was seen between the time since the lesion had been sustained (also equivalent to the child's age) and IQ: The longer the time since lesion had been sustained (and hence the older the child), the lower the IQ (Figure 13.16B), regardless of lesion size.

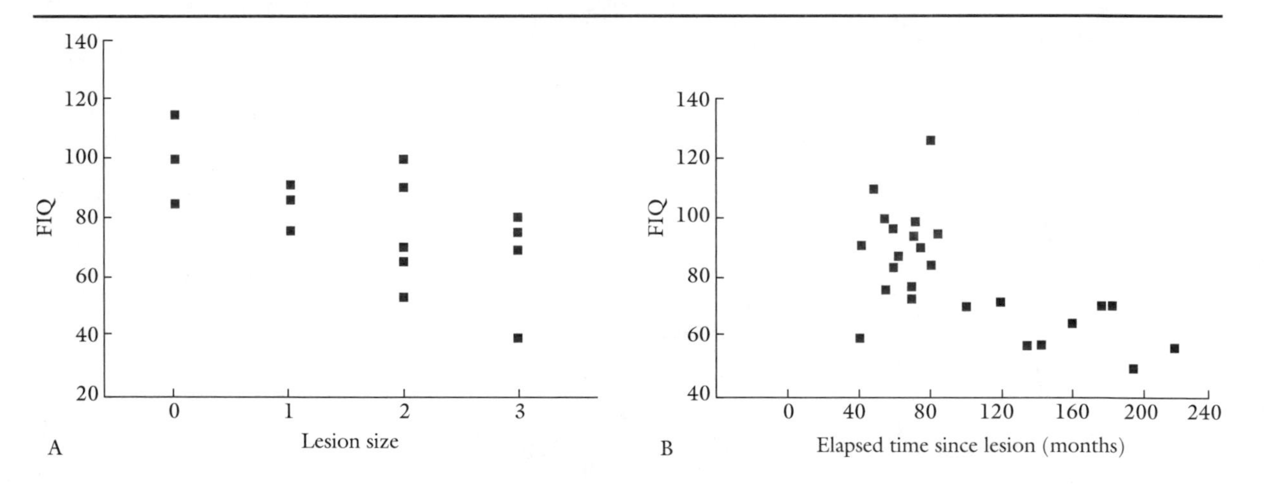

FIGURE 13.16 Relationship between neurological factors and intellectual status in children who sustain unilateral brain lesions. (A) For children who sustain a lesion after birth (acquired group), lesion size (0 = small, 3 = extensive) predicts subsequent intellectual status, indicated by full-scale IQ (FIQ): The larger the lesion, the lower the IQ ($r = -.669$). (B) For children who sustain a lesion prior to or at birth (congenital group) a significant relationship exists between FIQ and the elapsed time since the lesion (which is equivalent to the child's age when tested), such that older age is associated with poorer intellectual performance ($r = -.648$). Note, however, that this relationship holds only for children older than approximately age 70 months. The factors predicting the intellectual performance of children who sustain lesions after birth differ substantially from those for children who sustain damage before or during birth.

How are we to interpret these results with regard to reorganization of function? The pattern in the children who sustained damage at birth may be explained by the **crowding hypothesis** (e.g., Teuber & Rudel, 1962). According to this hypothesis, the young brain compensates for early damage by instituting a maximal rewiring of the available neural space and thus, no loss in cognitive ability is apparent at first. Although this reorganization works well initially, consequences develop later in life because the system cannot adapt to or does not have the capacity to acquire those later developing mental skills. In contrast, when lesions are acquired later in life, the brain has had time to organize normally prior to the lesion. Thus, what predicts subsequent IQ is the size of the lesion: larger cognitive deficits are associated with larger lesions because more regions of brain tissue are affected.

Because our study assessed performance only at one point in time, it provides just a "snapshot" of the effects of brain damage on cognitive function in children. Longitudinal studies that follow children who have sustained early brain damage over time suggest that the pattern of deficits can change quite drastically depending on the child's age and degree of development. These findings have formed the basis of the notion that the brain organization for a specific task, such as language, emerges over the lifetime. The suggestion here is that the brain is neither totally pre-wired at birth for specific cognitive function, nor is the cortex equipotent, with all areas able to assume all tasks. Rather, brain regions are pluripotent, meaning that they can take on a wide variety of functions, with varying degrees of success, which depend on the type, degree, and nature of information that is received (Bates, 1999). These studies and others we have discussed underscore the degree to which the human brain is designed to take in information from the environment to sculpt and resculpt its form over the lifetime.

Programs of Rehabilitation

Arguably, the single most important issue for anyone who has sustained brain damage is the degree to which rehabilitation and therapy can aid in recovery of function. Fortunately, a strong scientific basis supports the assumption that rehabilitation programs can have a positive effect. Research with animals provides evidence that the environment into which they are placed after sustaining damage can influence recovery. Moreover, research with humans suggests that a better quality of life and a higher level of cognitive performance can be attained when appropriate interventions are provided after brain damage (see Cope, 1995, for a recent review evaluating the effectiveness of rehabilitation after brain injury, and Rattok et al., 1992, for an example of how the efficacy of a treatment program is evaluated).

To examine the effect of an environment on recovery of function after brain damage, researchers typically compare the anatomical, physiological, and behavioral responses of two groups of animals: those placed in an isolated environment after damage and those placed in an enriched environment. The enriched environments are those with many interesting objects and the chance for social interaction, essentially similar to those conditions that can lead to more extensive dendritic elaboration in neurologically intact rats. Damage is generally induced either by surgery, by exposure to toxins (such as alcohol, lead, or radiation), by metabolic disruption, or by malnutrition. Although every study does not find this effect, enriched environments have been shown to attenuate the effects of brain damage. Unfortunately, the optimal conditions for such an attenuation are not completely known, although some principles are beginning to emerge (see Kolb & Gibb, 2001, for a recent review). Furthermore, other therapies after brain damage, such as brain-cell grafts, may be effective only when coupled with an enriched environment (e.g., Kelche et al., 1995).

It is difficult to extrapolate directly from these studies of animals to humans. For instance, what would constitute an "enriched" environment for a person? Clearly, we couldn't simply place people with lesions in an environment with complex objects and lots of people. In fact, too high a degree of complexity may be confusing to the patient with brain injury. Additionally, the patient, unlike the laboratory animal, must learn to negotiate not only a complex cognitive world, but a socially complex one. Let's now examine the factors involved in rehabilitating patients with brain injury.

CAN DEPRIVATION LEAD THE BRAIN TO REORGANIZE IN A WAY THAT PRODUCES EXTRAORDINARY ABILITIES?

In this chapter we have discussed how the brain's plasticity allows it to reorganize in response to insult or atypical environments (e.g., sensory deprivation), in some cases allowing it to attain or reacquire a normal complement of abilities. Now we discuss the intriguing possibility that reorganization might actually enhance the brain's processing capacity. In at least one study, congenitally deaf individuals showed a superior ability to direct attention to particular regions of space as compared with hearing counterparts.

It had been known for quite some time that deprivation from birth of a particular sensory input, such as auditory input, does not enhance basic perceptual processing in the remaining sensory modalities, such as the threshold at which light can be detected. These findings suggested that little, if any, reorganization occurs in primary sensory cortex. Yet the possibility remained that higher-level sensory processing areas or multimodal regions of the brain might reorganize in response to deprivation. To examine this issue, Helen Neville and colleagues examined individuals who were deaf from birth because they lacked the peripheral receptor, the cochlea, that is required to transduce sound waves into electrical signals. Nonetheless, their nervous systems, including the auditory portions, were perfectly intact,

In trying to address this issue, Neville and colleagues faced a difficult problem. Most, if not all, of these individuals learn American Sign Language (ASL). As discussed in Chapter 9 (see page 310), ASL is a visually based language that requires attention to a large expanse of visual space in front of an individual and sensitivity to movement within that space. Hence any extraordinary visual abilities relative to hearing individuals exhibited by these deaf speakers of ASL might occur either because their brains had reorganized to handle visual information more efficiently or because years of training and practice in ASL made them especially keen observers of the visual world. To solve the dilemma of distinguishing between those two causes, the researchers included a third group of individuals in their study: hearing individuals who, because their parents were deaf, learned ASL at a young age. If deaf signers performed better than not only the regular hearing individuals but also

Some experts have argued that an adequate rehabilitation program must have three components: one that addresses changes in cognitive capacity; one that addresses emotional changes, such as reactions to the trauma and any changes in personality resulting from brain damage; and one that addresses changes in behavior that will affect the person's lifestyle, such as pain and diminished energy (O'Hara, 1988). Not only must one consider what specific cognitive capacities have been lost (e.g., language output), but what other cognitive abilities tend to be diminished after brain damage. One of the most pervasive problems with these patients is their lack of self-awareness and lack of self-evaluatory capabilities (e.g., Prigatano, 1991). In addition, these individuals are likely to interpret information in the most concrete of manners and have difficult generalizing information learned in one setting to another. Consequently, if they are in a situation even slightly different than the one they previously experienced (e.g., at home rather than in the hospital), they are likely to miss similarities that exist (e.g., Thomas & Trexler, 1982).

Because their self-monitoring skills can be so poor and their thinking so concrete, individuals with brain damage must be given very specific feedback. Increased self-monitoring by these individuals can be accomplished by giving them formal checklists to use to evaluate their behavior; by making them view themselves on videotape; by having materials around the room, such as posters, that remind them of what they should be doing; and by having the staff be a "prosthetic conscience" telling the patient when he or she is behaving inappropriately.

Rehabilitation with regard to emotional functioning is especially important. Although you may be

than the hearing signers, then the researchers could deduce that the superior abilities of the congenitally deaf could be attributed to brain reorganization in response to deafness.

These three groups of individuals were tested with both behavioral and event-related potential (ERP) methods. Signers who were deaf were more than 100 ms faster to respond to peripheral stimuli than either hearing signers or hearing nonsigners. Moreover, individuals who were deaf exhibited an attention-related N_{150} over occipital regions that was much larger than that observed in either group of hearing individuals. These findings suggest an enhancement of visuospatial attention to peripheral regions in the deaf (See Neville, 1990, for a summary of this work, which was described in more detail in Neville & Lawson, 1987a–c).

More recently fMRI studies have helped to provide information on what parts of the brain seem to be related to these extraordinary abilities in the deaf. The superior performance of deaf individuals on directing attention to peripheral locations, as compared to hearing signers and nonsigners, is associated with increased activation in MT/MST (the motion area) and posterior parietal cortex (Bavelier et al., 2001). As we learned in Chapter 8, these regions are involved in the direction of spatial attention. Additionally, it appears that posterior parietal cortex becomes more functionally connected with sensory cortical areas, as if a more efficient highway emerged between these two regions to control attention (Bavelier et al., 2000). Also, deaf signers activated the posterior superior temporal sulcus to a greater degree than hearing individuals. As you may remember from Chapter 7, this region of the brain is sensitive to motion in biological systems (e.g., motion of the face). The picture to emerge from these studies is that brain regions involved in processing motion and in directing visual attention reorganize in response to deafness so as to provide extraordinary abilities.

Certainly more remains to be learned about such brain organization after early deprivation. Some studies suggest that the deaf may be better able to search for targets in a cluttered visual array even when they are within central vision (Stivalt et al., 1998). And other studies suggest that some of the enhanced ability to orient to peripheral targets may not emerge totally until adulthood (Rettenback, Diller, & Sireteanu, 1999). Regardless of future work, these studies confirm the capacity of the brain to reorganize, and in ways that can optimize performance. ■

tempted to think that cognitive and physical disabilities would be the most dire consequences of brain injury, a long-term study suggests that individuals who sustain head injury are most disabled by emotional and personality disturbances (Lezak, 1987). Regrettably, rehabilitation of emotional functioning is especially difficult. In typical psychotherapy, a person is encouraged to discuss the problems at hand. Such discussion requires a certain level of cognitive sophistication, good language and interpersonal conversational skills, and a capacity for self-evaluation. Clearly, these abilities are all taxed in individuals with brain injury.

A rehabilitation program also must address an individual's premorbid personality because this personality is likely to have a strong influence on emotional reactions after brain trauma. If someone was suspicious and withdrawn before brain trauma, that characteristic may be exaggerated and may cause the therapist to be viewed as an adversary rather than as an ally. In contrast, if the person was passive and dependent, after brain trauma he or she may be impulsive, inconsiderate, and egocentric. Generally, problem areas in personality (as well as family dynamics) are highlighted and enhanced by brain trauma (e.g., Lishman, 1973). Knowledge of a person's premorbid personality is also important because it can assist in designing more effective rehabilitation. For example, N. F. Cohen (1989) discussed a case in which rehabilitation of language difficulties, especially related to conversational skills, was helped along by having a young man who had been a "Trekkie" premorbidly watch and then verbally discuss *Star Trek* episodes.

The rehabilitation program must also address the patient's physical status. If a person is in severe pain or has reduced energy, her or his ability to concentrate for long periods may be diminished, and adjustments will need to be made. For example, even if the person has the cognitive capacity to return to work full-time, physical ailments may require an adjustment to part-time work, or a staggered schedule may be required so that the person does not become too exhausted. Clearly, sensory and motor deficits, such as loss of vision and paralysis, are also likely to influence the nature and type of rehabilitation employed.

These three components—the cognitive, emotional, and physical—must be considered simultaneously because they are interrelated. For example, the inability to cognitively evaluate a situation may interfere with emotional processing. We often use cognitive judgments about a situation to determine our emotional reaction, such as judging whether or not to feel hurt after hearing a comment that might be either sincere or sarcastic. Changes in emotional processing, especially personality, will in turn affect cognitive capacity. For example, damage to frontal areas can lead to impulsivity or depression. Likewise, an individual's physical condition will influence both cognition and emotion. For example, chronic pain is likely to affect a person's emotional state and to induce a negative bias pervading much of that person's thinking (L. Miller, 1992).

The final factor that must be considered in any rehabilitation plan is the nature of the support system available to the patient. If an individual has a caring family who is economically stable, a greater chance exists that a therapeutic intervention can continue at home and that additional problems imposed by the brain damage can be minimized. Nonetheless, the quality of life for family members is profoundly altered (e.g., Lezak, 1978) and by some estimates so negatively that 50 percent of all family members resort to taking prescription drugs to reduce anxiety (Panting & Merry, 1972).

Although various models of how to treat brain injury exist (see D. C. Burke, 1995, for a review), probably the most common one is an integrated multidisciplinary approach that is organized as a small "therapeutic community" in which the different domains affected by the injury (i.e., cognitive, emotional, family, social, behavioral, and vocational) are addressed simultaneously. For example, a treatment program might include training using hierarchically organized computer tasks to alleviate attentional disorders, individualized remediation of cognitive skills (including eye-hand coordination, constructional praxis, visual information processing, and logical reasoning), small-group interpersonal communication exercises, therapeutic-community activities, and personal counseling. If an individual makes sufficient progress, vocational counseling might be added (see, for example, Ben-Yishay & Diller, 1983; Ben-Yishay & Prigatano, 1990). As you can see, rehabilitation of brain-injured individuals is an involved and demanding process, involving resources at multiple levels. Thus, as we discuss in the next chapter, one of the most effective avenues that can be taken is to invoke preventative measures that will avoid or minimize brain injury, such as the use of seatbelts or helmets for certain activities.

Changes in the Brain with Aging

Changes in brain functioning occur not only during childhood and as a result of brain damage, but also as a result of the aging process. These changes become more noticeable as a person approaches the later adult years. In this last section of the chapter, we consider some of the cognitive changes that accompany old age and the degree to which they may be neurologically based. Before we turn to this discussion, however, we should note that one of the most prominent neuropsychological issues with regard to abnormal aging and cognition is that of dementia, such as accompanies Parkinson's and Alzheimer's disease. In the present chapter, we discuss changes associated with normal aging and leave issues of dementia for the final chapter of the book.

Theories of Cognitive Changes with Aging

At present there are two major theoretical camps with regard to how cognitive functions change with age. One camp argues that with age there is a general decline across all abilities. This decline is believed to represent a general reduction in the mental resources that can be brought to bear on a problem (e.g., Craik & Byrd, 1982) or a general slowing in the speed of processing (e.g., Salthouse, 1996). Evidence for this theory comes from comparing the performance of young adults and older adults (usually early retirement age or older) across a variety of tasks from different experiments. Generally, older individuals perform more poorly than younger persons, and this difference is accentuated for tasks that place more demands on central aspects of processing (e.g., memory search) than on peripheral aspects of processing in perceptual tasks (e.g., quickly identifying viewed items) (Cerella, 1985). The assumption derived from these types of data is that aging diminishes the ability to process tasks, especially those that are complex.

In contrast, the second camp argues that the deficits that emerge with age are not general, but rather more specific, such as a specific deficit in inhibitory processes (e.g., Hasher & Zacks, 1988). And still other researchers find a more variable picture of performance with age, in which some aspects of processing are compromised in older persons but other aspects are not (e.g., Kramer, Larish, & Strayer, 1995).

Given these conflicting viewpoints of cognitive changes with aging, is there any way that neuropsychological evidence can help disentangle them? As we review next, neuropsychological evidence is much more consistent with the hypothesis that aging is associated with specific cognitive deficits rather than general slowing. Tasks that show declines with age depend on particular brain regions, such as the frontal lobes and posterior association areas, whereas tasks relying on other areas tend not to be affected. Furthermore, the types of processes that are compromised, such as aspects of inhibitory control, tend to rely on the regions (e.g., frontal regions) that exhibit more severe changes during old age. We now turn our attention to the physiological and behavioral evidence that certain brain regions are more affected by aging than are others.

Brain Regions Most Susceptible to the Effects of Aging

The regions of the brain that appear to be most affected by aging are those that support higher-order associative functions, namely frontal and parietal cortices, and to a lesser degree, medial temporal regions.

• *FRONTAL REGIONS* •

Physiological evidence suggests that frontal regions are one of the brain regions most susceptible to change as a result of increasing age. With age, they show the greatest reduction in blood flow (R. C. Gur et al., 1987; Shaw et al., 1984; L. R. Warren, Butler, Katholi, & Halsey, 1985), and the greatest loss of neural tissue (along with regions to which they connect, such as the basal ganglia and the thalamus) (e.g., Haug et al., 1983; Raz et al., 1993).

These physiological changes in brain function appear to have behavioral consequences. Cognitive functions supported by frontal regions are particularly compromised with age. Older adults exhibit deficits on a battery of tests involving tasks described in prior chapters as dependent on frontal areas, such as the self-ordered pointing task, the Wisconsin Card Sorting Test, verbal and design fluency, and the Stroop task (Daigneault, Braun, & Whitaker, 1992). More importantly, these deficits are selective and are not observed to as great a degree for tasks dependent on other brain regions (e.g., Mittenberg, Seidenberg, O'Leary, & DiGiulio, 1989). Older individuals show clear declines in memory tasks that rely on frontal regions. These include working-memory tasks; "metamemory" tasks, such as knowing the temporal order in which information was received (Parkin, Walter, & Hunkin, 1995); prospective-memory tasks, in which you have to remember to carry out a function at a future time; and **source memory,** which is the ability to remember the specific circumstances or context in which particular information was learned (e.g., knowing that you learned that the earth orbits the sun in your third-grade class taught by Ms. Frost) (McIntyre & Craik, 1987). (See Grady and Craik, 2000, and West, 1996, for recent reviews on this subject.)

Neuroimaging studies reveal that the pattern of activation in frontal regions varies between younger and older adults. The changes in older adults can go in one of two directions: decreased activation or increased activation. In some cases, older adults perform more poorly than younger adults on a task, such as remembering temporal order, and concomitantly exhibit reduced activation in the specific brain region that supports that task (i.e., right prefrontal areas) relative to younger adults (e.g., Cabeza et al., 2000). These findings suggest that the necessary neural processors for the task have been compromised, leading to poor performance. For other tasks, such as remembering specific items, older adults show increased activation in prefrontal regions relative to their younger counterparts (e.g., Cabeza et al., 2000), suggesting that these areas must be engaged to a greater extent, or work doubly hard, to support a reasonable level of performance relative to younger adults.

• *PARIETAL REGIONS* •

Some evidence suggests that tasks dependent on the parietal regions are also susceptible to aging effects, although these findings are not as strong as those for frontal regions. With age, decrements are found on certain tasks whose performance is disrupted by parietal lesions, most notably constructional and visuomotor tasks (e.g., Ardila & Rosselli, 1989; Farver & Farver, 1982). There are some hints (e.g., Farver & Farver, 1982) that the right parietal lobe may be more vulnerable to aging effects than the left is, and in fact some researchers have suggested that overall the right hemisphere is more susceptible to aging effects (e.g., Klisz, 1978). However, an important caveat is in order. Many tests on which older persons show right hemisphere deficits are those on which speedy motor responses lead to high scores. To the degree that these more peripheral processes (e.g., motoric actions) are slowed with age, they will hinder the level of performance on such tasks. Other studies have yielded no evidence of selective deficits on right hemisphere tasks when the tasks do not emphasize motor skills but instead emphasize problem-solving skills (e.g., determining how to reassemble disassembled parts into a whole) (e.g., Libon et al., 1994).

• *TEMPORAL REGIONS* •

As we learned in Chapter 10, the temporal lobes, and particularly the hippocampus, are critically important for creating new long-term memories of the declarative sort, memories that allow information to be used flexibly and in a variety of contexts. By the sixth and seventh decades of life, healthy older adults begin to perform more poorly than younger individuals on direct tests of declarative memory. Older persons especially have problems with recall and on tasks that require an organized search through memory to retrieve information as compared with structured situations in which a person merely recognizes information (Craik, 1989).

The inability to remember information has been associated with loss of hippocampal tissue. This effect is found not only for individuals who suffer from Alzheimer's disease (de Leon et al., 1997) (which we discuss in more detail in the next chapter) but also in elderly individuals who exhibit mild cognitive impairments in daily tasks yet don't meet the clinical criteria for Alzheimer's or some other dementing disorder (Convit et al., 1995). (For a review of changes in these brain regions with age and concomitant declines in cognitive functions, see Greenwood, 2000.)

■ Global Changes in Patterns of Brain Activation with Aging

Aging affects not only the integrity of processing of specific brain regions, but can also affect the global pattern of activation across the brain. One prominent theory is that **dedifferentiation** causes the localization of function to become less defined with age (for a review, see Li & Lindenberger, 1999). Prominent evidence for such a viewpoint comes from studies showing that correlations between how well an individual performs on a task and activation of particular brain regions are much more diffuse for older than younger adults (e.g., Madden et al., 1999).

These findings, however, do not mean that the elderly brain becomes one large, undifferentiated mush. Rather, the elderly may need to recruit more or additional brain regions to attain the same level of performance as younger adults, or they may recruit the same set of brain regions but in different proportions. In a perceptual-memory task, older individuals showed significant increases in activation in medial temporal and dorsolateral prefrontal cortices that were not engaged by younger participants (McIntosh et al., 1999). In this case, the dorsolateral activation may have reflected that the elderly found the task more attentionally demanding than younger adults.

In fact, one elegant series of studies suggests that these additional activations may be due to increasing demand. Unlike younger adults, who activate left prefrontal regions during verbal working-memory tasks and right prefrontal regions during spatial working-memory tasks, elderly adults tend to exhibit bilateral activation for both verbal and spatial working memory (Reuter-Lorenz et al., 2001). This pattern of bilateral activation is seen across a variety of tasks (Cabeza, 2001) (see Color insert 13.1). To determine whether this pattern represents a breakdown, or dedifferentiation, of performance, or instead a compensatory mechanism, the researchers turned to behavioral techniques. They suggested that the bilateral pattern of performance might indicate that the elderly adults needed to engage both hemispheres because of reduced abilities in each hemisphere (as predicted by the theory of Banich, 1998). As we discussed in Chapter 4, it is advantageous to have the hemispheres couple their performance under demanding conditions. Indeed, the hemispheres of elderly adults coupled their performance at lower levels of task demands than did the younger adults, suggesting that this bilateral pattern of activation in the working-memory tasks reflects a compensatory strategy (Reuter-Lorenz, Stanczak, & Miller, 1999).

In other cases, the relative activation of brain regions within a network will change with age. For example, in the Stroop task, in which an individual must identify the ink color of a word, younger individuals show large activation of dorsolateral prefrontal regions, with lesser activation of inferior frontal regions, on incongruent (e.g., the word *blue* in red ink) versus neutral trials (e.g., the word *bond* in red ink). It is thought that the dorsolateral prefrontal regions are involved in attentional control; they enable one to pay attention to the ink color rather than the word. In contrast, inferior prefrontal regions help to hold online the task-relevant information (e.g., that the ink color was red).

The elderly tend to show increased interference on incongruent trials and less activation in dorsolateral prefrontal regions, indicating that these regions cannot exert as large a degree of attentional control as in younger individuals. However, they show increased activation in inferior prefrontal regions, as if they are unable to select the exact task-relevant information and are trying to hold online multiple pieces of information (i.e., the concept of blue from the word and the concept of red from the ink color) (Milham et al., 2002).

Another possible reason why the pattern of activation might change in the elderly is that there is a greater disconnection between brain regions as a result of a loss of myelin (Guttmann et al., 1998). This greater disconnection would explain in part why executive control by frontal regions is compromised by aging. Older people would be less able to exert their top-down attentional control over other parts of the brain, unable to rev up activation of brain regions involved in processing task-relevant information (e.g., in the Stroop task those involved in color identification), while dampening down activation of brain regions involved in processing task-irrelevant information (e.g., in the Stroop task those involved in word reading).

Slowing the Effects of Aging

Just as Ponce de Leon went searching for the fountain of youth, scientists have embarked on a voyage to determine what can help keep the elderly mentally "young." Two factors have emerged as helping to impede or slow the effects of aging: aerobic exercise and keeping mentally challenged. Our knowledge of the importance of these factors was initially gleaned from animal research and then shown to be equally important for people. Each factor helps to sustain the brain by a distinct mechanism. Aerobic exercise produces a greater proliferation of blood vessels to the brain, resulting in enhanced oxygen supply. And, as we discussed earlier, a mentally stimulating environment produces an elaboration of dendritic trees, allowing for more numerous and varied synaptic connections. We discuss each in turn.

Animal research has indicated that exercising leads to greater proliferation of the blood supply to the brain (e.g., Black et al., 1990). Oxygen insufficiency, whether caused by pulmonary disease, cigarette smoking, or being on a high mountaintop, can lead to deterioration in neuropsychological functioning (Hjalmarsen et al., 1999; Kramer, Coyne, & Strayer, 1993). It is not surprising, therefore, that individuals who engage in aerobic exercise have better neurocognitive functioning than their nonexercising peers (van Boxtel et al., 1997). Furthermore, those individuals who exercise into old age perform better on mental tasks than those who don't (Clarkson-Smith & Hartley, 1989). An issue with such findings, however, is that these individuals might be particularly blessed physical specimens, which is why they retain their mental faculties and can continue to exercise into old age.

To examine whether exercise can aid the average individual, my colleagues and I (Kramer et al., 1999) selected people aged 60–75 who did not exercise, being "couch potatoes" who preferred to watch TV or read. We enrolled them in a six-month program of either light aerobic exercise (e.g., 30 minutes of brisk walking three times a week) or a toning and stretching program that involved no aerobic exercise (e.g., 30 minutes of stretching exercises three times a week). At the end of the six-month period, the aerobic-exercise group showed fewer age-related deficits on attentional and some memory functions that rely on prefrontal regions of the brain than did the stretching and toning group. Although one might have guessed that exercise would be helpful, the study was notable because it demonstrated that the effect was specific to aerobic exercise in particular, and that even relatively low levels of such exercise can have significant effects.

There is also evidence that a stimulating environment may stave off some of the more negative effects of aging. For example, in a long-term study of more than 5,000 adults it was found that being involved in activities that are intellectually stimulating and challenging, both at work and at home, reduces the risk of cognitive decline in old age. These activities include having a job involving high complexity and low routine, participating in continuing education, having a habit of extensive reading, being active in social groups, and engaging in travel (Schaie, 1994). Such an effect is also found when biological factors are kept constant. A study of twins discordant for dementia (one has dementia, one doesn't) found that the twin with a low level of education (e.g., didn't graduate high school) and who tended not be mentally active was more likely to get Alzheimer's disease (Gatz et al., 2001).

Another recently discovered mechanism that may help to stave off the effects of cognitive decline typically observed in old age is neurogenesis, the formation of new neurons (for a discussion, see Gould, Tanapat, Hastings, & Shors, 1999). Until very recently, it was taken as gospel that at birth people had all the neurons they would ever have, and that it was all downhill from there. Scientists presumed that unlike skin, which replaces itself every three days or so, no additional neurons would be created after birth, and those that existed at birth would need to be retained over a lifetime. If neurons came and went, then so might memory and learning from earlier in your life! Instead recent research suggests that the adult brains of both animals (Kuhn, Dickinson-Anson, & Gage, 1996) and humans (Eriksson et al., 1998) have a limited ability to form new neurons. This effect has been demonstrated most clearly in the hippocampus. These new cells first appear as undifferentiated *stem cells* (which are primordial cells from which all of tissue derives) and then evolve into neurons. A certain proportion of these neurons never become functional, probably because they do not make adequate connections with other neurons (similar to the pruning process in development).

Aerobic exercise and an enriched environment have also each been implicated as affecting neurogenesis, albeit in different ways: aerobic exercise affects the production of stem cells whereas an enriched environment affects their survival. Rats given aerobic exercise produce more of these stem cells than rats that are not given exercise. Because the exercising rats have more stem cells to begin with, they end up with more new neurons (e.g., Van Praag, Kempermann, & Gage, 1999). In contrast, mice in an enriched environment don't produce any more new stem cells than mice in a less stimulating environment, but not as many of the stem cells die while transforming into functional neurons, presumably because they have made useful functional connections (e.g., Kempermann, Kuhn, & Gage, 1997). The issue of neurogenesis is one of the more controversial and exciting topics in cognitive neuroscience today, not only because it has turned decades-old thinking on its head, but because it points to greater possibilities for recovery or effective intervention than were previously presumed to exist.

SUMMARY

Developmental Cognitive Neuroscience & Neuropsychology

- Nerve cells proliferate during gestation, whereas glia proliferate after birth.
- Physiological changes during childhood include an increase in the brain's metabolic rate, a greater coherence in electrical activity, and an overproduction and then pruning of synaptic connections.
- Developmental changes in brain structure and function are accompanied by changes in the cognitive skills of the child that occur in an orderly fashion, such as crawling before walking.
- The environment can have profound effects on the developing brain, especially during sensitive periods, during which information from the environment has a lifelong effect on the brain's organization and capacity.

Developmental Disorders

- Developmental disorders are syndromes in which the developing nervous system never acquires specific skills or acquires them in a less than optimal manner.
- Dyslexia is an inability to read despite adequate intelligence in other domains and schooling in the reading process. It is associated with atypical anatomy and function of language regions of the left hemisphere, and possibly poor integration of information between brain regions.
- Nonverbal learning disabilities, which are associated with right-hemisphere dysfunction, involve difficulty with spatial relations, geographic orientation, and puzzle construction, as well as difficulty with social relations and peer interaction.
- Autism and pervasive developmental disorders are characterized by a profound lack of desire to interact emotionally or socially with other people, and profound delays and disturbances in cognitive functioning, especially those that relate to communication and language. These disorders are thought to involve a large number of brain regions that may include the temporal and frontal lobes, portions of the limbic system and the cerebellum.
- Children with attention-deficit hyperactivity disorder (ADHD) have difficulty concentrating, are physically restless, cannot focus their attention on a task, and tend to be impulsive. Dysregulation of the dopaminergic system is implicated in this disorder, as well as prefrontal regions of the brain, the basal ganglia, and possibly the anterior cingulate.
- Mental retardation is characterized by a lack of intellectual ability across a wide range of cognitive skills. It is caused by various factors including infections, genetic disorders, toxins, anoxia, and malnutrition.
- Children with learning disabilities rarely outgrow them as the disorder manifests itself differently in adulthood. For example, while a hyperactive child might have trouble sitting in a chair in class, a hyperactive adult might not be able to "sit with" a problem.

Recovery of Function

- A vast physiological response occurs to brain injury, including the degeneration and death of nerve cells, the cleaning up of debris by glia, swelling (known as edema), and eventually the formation of a scar.
- In addition, lesions may disrupt other aspects of brain functioning, such as metabolic rate, neurotransmitter release, and oxygen consumption.
- At the cellular level, compensatory mechanisms for neural injury include an increased sensitivity to neurotransmitters and the formation of new connections by rerouting and sprouting.
- At the regional level, the brain has the capacity to reorganize its functional maps in response to extreme changes in environmental input or injury.
- Factors influencing recovery of function in adults include the premorbid status of the individual,

SUMMARY

repetitive training, and the use of compensatory or alternative strategies.

- Although the Kennard principle posited that recovery of function in children was superior to that in adults, recent studies suggest that the deficits observed after brain damage in children may emerge or recede depending on the time since the lesion and the developmental stage at which a function is examined.
- Many rehabilitation programs take a multifaceted approach in which cognitive, emotional, social, and vocational issues are dealt with simultaneously.
- Making the patient aware of his or her deficits is often a critical component of a successful rehabilitation program.

Changes in the Brain with Aging

- Some theories posit a general slowing or overall reduction in capacity with age, but evidence from cognitive neuroscience suggests that the changes with age are more specific.
- Brain regions most susceptible to the effects of aging include the frontal, parietal, and temporal regions.
- With aging, the brain appears to exhibit less localization of function, which may occur because older individuals attempt to recruit more brain areas to compensate for lost function.
- Engaging in aerobic exercise and being in a stimulating environment appear to stave off the effects of aging, possibly because both processes aid in the formation of new neurons in the adult brain.

KEY TERMS

alternative strategy 463
attention-deficit hyperactivity disorder (ADHD) 449
autism 447
calcification 457
cerebral palsy 455
compensatory rehabilitation 463
compensatory strategy 463
crowding hypothesis 467
dedifferentiation 472
denervation supersensitivity 459
developmental dysphasia 446
developmental milestones 439
Down syndrome 452
dyslexia 447
edema 457
elimination of synapses 436
experience-dependent systems 438
experience-expectant systems 438
fetal alcohol effects 454
fetal alcohol syndrome (FAS) 454
fragile X syndrome 452
gliosis 457
Kennard principle 464
kwashiorkor 454
learning disabilities 443
marasmus 454
maturational lag hypothesis 456
mental retardation 450
necrosis 457
neurogenesis 434
nonverbal learning disabilities 446
pervasive developmental disorders 447
phenylketonuria (PKU) 452
phonological awareness 444
plasticity 432
regeneration 459
reorganization 459
rerouting 459
restorative rehabilitation 463
risk factors 450
sensitive period 442
source memory 471
sprouting 459
synaptogenesis 434
transneuronal degeneration 457
Turner's syndrome 453

CHAPTER 14

GENERALIZED COGNITIVE DISORDERS

A strong and determined woman, L.F. immigrated to the United States from Italy in the early 1900s when she was in her 20s. She came alone, without family or friends—a journey that few women dared to make at that time, especially under such circumstances. After arriving in the United States, she bucked tradition, setting out on her own and not marrying immediately, even though she was already considered an "old maid." Eventually she met a fellow Italian immigrant who suited her taste, and they married.

Their life together started out well. Her husband was a successful small businessman, and along came four children, the last two of whom were born when L.F. was in her 40s. However, when the financial markets collapsed at the beginning of the Depression, the debt her husband had incurred building multifamily dwellings caused him to lose everything. Determined that all her children would nonetheless get a college education (which they all eventually did), L.F. worked 10- to 14-hour days for years as a seamstress, doing intricate embroidery and beadwork for numerous garment makers in New York City. Despite the family's dire poverty, she instilled in her children a strong work ethic, a love of learning, and a sense of pride.

When she was in her early 80s, L.F. and her husband were forced to leave the apartment building and neighborhood in which they had lived for the past 40 years. The property had been sold to a new owner and was to be converted into a bank. So they went to live with their second eldest daughter's family. L.F.'s memory had been deteriorating for some time, and moving into a new home was exceedingly difficult for her. Beset by forgetfulness and disorientation, this once vibrant, resourceful, and proud woman, who had traveled the streets of New York City with ease, now had difficulty navigating from one room to the next. She was disoriented not only with regard to space, but also with regard to time, often confusing whether it was morning or night. L.F. would wander aimlessly around the house, especially at night, searching for an item whose location she couldn't remember. On rare occasions she would even have a brief bout of paranoia. Once, for example, while her daughter was adjusting her seat belt for a trip to the grocery store, L.F. muttered in Italian that her ungrateful daughter was taking her to be killed.

The strain on L.F.'s daughter's family was great. The house was small, and L.F.'s wanderings, especially at night, disrupted everyone in the house. During these jaunts, she would move various items all over the house, open and close cabinets, turn lights on and off, and sometimes leave her dentures in bizarre locations. Because she found the world so confusing, it was important to keep the house as orderly as possible. This degree of order was sometimes difficult for her grandchildren to maintain. They were still in grade school and junior high, so just keeping their own rooms clean was a challenge! And L.F.'s grandchildren found it difficult to have their friends come over to play because L.F.'s paranoia might cause her to follow their friends around the house to ensure that they weren't stealing anything.

About nine months later, L.F. and her husband moved to the other half of the duplex in which their eldest daughter and family lived. These new living arrangements were much more suitable for the couple. L.F. could wander without disturbing others and the house could be organized specifically to accommodate her mental deterioration. Because her daughter's family was next door, L.F.'s husband, who was also in his 80s, received generous help whenever he had difficulty handling her or the daily chores. However, even with these new arrangements, L.F.'s ability to care for herself continued to decline. Eventually she needed almost constant care, although she was never institutionalized because of the love and patience of her husband of more than 50 years. He outlived his wife, and, unlike her, remained intellectually sharp and physically active until a few weeks before his death at the age of 90 years. ■

THE CASE HISTORY described in the opening vignette is that of my maternal grandmother and describes, in part, the nine-month period when she lived with my family. Although the disease was never formally diagnosed, my grandmother surely had Alzheimer's, multi-infarct, or some similar dementia. In many ways, her case was typical, characterized by loss of memory, difficulties in spatial processing, disorientation, and changes in personality, especially paranoia. The course was unremittingly downward, although she died from heat stroke before becoming totally bedridden.

In this chapter, we discuss disorders such as Alzheimer's disease that are distinct from the neuropsychological syndromes that were the focus of most of this book. In our discussions so far, we have emphasized the breakdown of specific cognitive functions, such as item recognition, and precisely described the circumscribed nature of the deficits. For example, in the case of visual object agnosia, we noted the specificity of the disruption, an inability in visually identifying objects because of perceptual difficulties that prevent visual form from being linked to meaning. Yet in many syndromes that the neuropsychologist encounters, such as Alzheimer's disease, the breakdown of function is not restricted to one cognitive domain but rather affects multiple cognitive abilities simultaneously. We refer to these syndromes as **generalized (nonspecific) disorders.**

You should not be surprised to learn that the causes of generalized disorders vary significantly from those of the specific disorders we discussed in Chapters 5 through 12. Specific disorders usually result from focal damage to the brain, such as that caused by bullet wounds and strokes, which confine damage to the path of the projectile and the brain regions deprived of oxygen, respectively. In contrast, the causes of generalized disorders include closed head injury (which results from falls, vehicular accidents, assaults, and sports injuries), dementing disorders (which result from pathological changes in the brain), demyelinating diseases (which result from damage to the myelin sheath surrounding neurons), and exposure to toxins, all of which are likely to have more distributed, rather than focal, effects on brain tissue.

Even though all these causes of brain damage are likely to influence more than one cognitive system at the same time, their effects are not identical, so subtle but important differences in their neuropsychological manifestations can be observed. We now turn to a more detailed discussion of these various etiologies and the nature of the generalized cognitive disorders that they produce.

Closed Head Injury

Closed head injury occurs when the brain sustains damage because the head forcefully comes into contact with another object (e.g., a car windshield, the ground, or a blunt instrument such as a baseball bat), but no object penetrates the brain. This type of injury is a significant source of neuropsychological dysfunction with approximately 1 million new cases a year in the United States alone (Thurman & Guerrero, 1999). It may surprise you to learn that this rate is higher than the combined rate of three other well-known neuropsychological disorders: Alzheimer's disease, multiple sclerosis, and Parkinson's disease.

Closed head injury is most common in adolescents and young adults 15–24 years of age, caused mainly by motor vehicle, bicycle or vehicle-pedestrian accidents. In older individuals (65 years or older), closed head injury is predominantly attributed to falls. Other causes include assault, and sport-related injuries (which we discuss later). Alcohol tends to be involved in over half of the incidents of closed head injury, either with regard to the person causing the injury, the person injured, or both (NIH Consensus Panel, 1999). The brain injury is typically diffuse, as is seen most commonly after motor vehicle accidents, but it may also have focal elements, as is usually the case with falls (Alberico et al., 1987). We now briefly discuss the mechanisms by which both diffuse and focal damage can occur in closed head injury and then discuss the neuropsychological consequences of such damage.

Etiology and Neuropsychological Consequences

The main mechanism of damage in closed head injury is a rapid acceleration of the head followed by a deceleration; hence it is sometimes referred

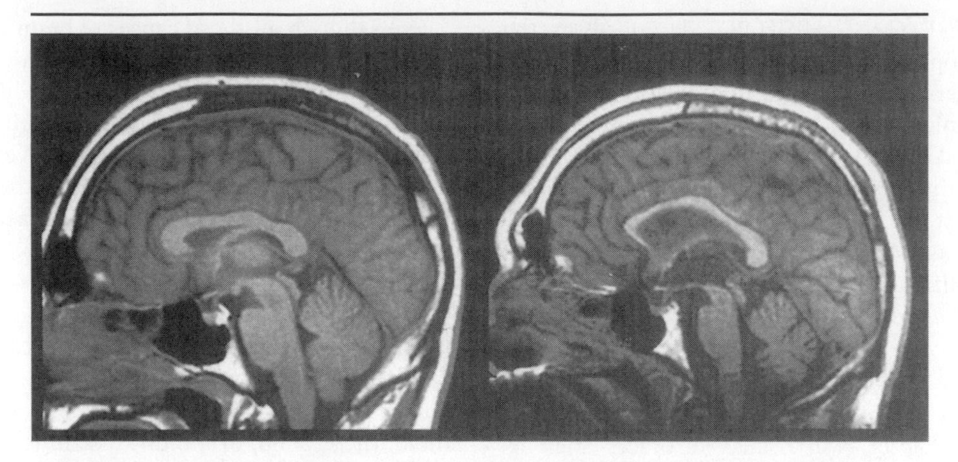

FIGURE 14.1 Effects of closed head injury on long myelinated nerve-fiber tracts in the brain. Compared with an age- and gender-matched neurologically intact individual (A), an individual who sustained a closed head injury (B) exhibits a neuronal loss in white matter that is especially prominent in the corpus callosum as shown in these midsagittal MRI images.

to as **acceleration-deceleration injury.** The energy imparted to the brain causes it to move within the skull. This movement can lead to diffuse damage as a result of the twisting and shearing of neurons, as well as focal damage due to the impact of the brain with the hard inner surface of the skull. The neurons most vulnerable to twisting are those that compose white-matter tracts, which have long axons and connect distant brain regions (e.g., Adams, Graham, Murray, & Scott, 1982). At the time of injury, such diffuse damage is not readily revealed by anatomical brain imaging studies because it does not result in a focal lesion. Instead, the major telltale sign of closed head injury that can be detected at the time of injury is edema (i.e., swelling). As time passes, a diffuse loss of neural tissue may be detected as an enlargement of the ventricles and a loss of volume in large myelinated tracts such as the corpus callosum. Some of these anatomical changes, such as ventricular enlargement (e.g., Levin, Meyers, Grossman, & Sarwar, 1981) and the degree of damage to specific white-matter tracts (e.g., Gale, Johnson, Bigler, & Blatter, 1995) have been found to correlate with the degree of intellectual impairment observed (Figure 14.1).

The brain regions most likely to sustain focal injury are the orbitofrontal and temporal regions, because the bones at these points in the skull are rough and protrude (e.g., Adams, Graham, Murray, & Scott, 1982). Focal damage at the site of impact is known as a **coup injury,** whereas focal damage opposite the site of impact is known as a **contrecoup injury.** For example, if the head strikes a windshield, a coup injury in the frontal areas might be sustained, as well as a contrecoup injury at occipital sites. In sum, closed head injury involves diffuse damage to neurons throughout the brain, especially those with long axons, as well as possible localized damage, either at or opposite the site of impact (Grafman & Salazar, 1987).

One of the most prominent clinical signs of closed head injury is a significant alteration in consciousness. As you may remember from Chapter 1 (see page 13), basic aspects of wakefulness and consciousness are controlled by the brainstem. Consequently, the degree to which the injury interferes with these aspects of brain-stem function can serve as a proxy for the overall impact on the brain. For this reason, scales such as the **Glasgow Coma Scale (GCS)** (Teasdale & Jennett, 1974), which assess the level of consciousness, are widely used in emergency rooms around the world to provide a gross method for classifying the severity of damage in someone who just sustained a head injury. This

TABLE 14.1 Glasgow Coma Scale Used to Predict Severity of Brain Trauma

RESPONSE	POINTS	INDEX OF WAKEFULNESS
Eye opening		
None	1	Not attributable to ocular swelling
To pain	2	Pain stimulus is applied to chest or limbs
To speech	3	Nonspecific response to speech or shout, but does not imply the patient obeys command to open eyes
Spontaneous	4	Eyes are open, but this does not imply intact awareness
Motor response		
No response	1	Flaccid
Extension	2	"Decerebrate." Adduction, internal rotation of shoulder, and pronation of the forearm
Abnormal flexion	3	"Decorticate." Abnormal flexion, adduction of the shoulder
Withdrawal	4	Normal flexor response; withdraws from pain stimulus with abduction of the shoulder
Localizes pain	5	Pain stimulus applied to supraocular region or fingertip causes limb to move so as to attempt to remove it
Obeys command	6	Follows simple commands
Verbal response		
No response	1	(Self-explanatory)
Incomprehensible	2	Moaning and groaning, but no recognizable words
Inappropriate	3	Intelligible speech (e.g., shouting or swearing), but no sustained or coherent conversation
Confused	4	Patient responds to questions in a conversational manner, but the responses indicate varying degrees of disorientation and confusion
Oriented	5	Normal orientation to time, place, and person

An individual's consciousness is assessed in three separate arenas: visual responsiveness, motor capabilities, and verbal responsiveness. The scores obtained in each of these three arenas are totaled to provide the overall score. Scores less than or equal to 8 indicate severe head injury, scores of 9 to 12 indicate moderate head injury, and scores of 13 or greater indicate mild head injury.

scale, which is shown in Table 14.1, evaluates three realms of functioning: visual responsiveness, motor capabilities, and verbal responsiveness.

Scores on the GCS are divided into three general categories: severe injury (a score of 8 or less), moderate injury (a score of 9–12), and mild injury (a score of 13–15). Medical personnel find the GCS score useful because it has prognostic value for survival rates and the future level of functioning. For example, six hours after injury, an individual whose GCS score is 8 or less (i.e., a severe head injury) has a 35–50 percent chance of dying within the next six months (although most of these individuals die within three days), a 1–5 percent chance of remaining in a persistent vegetative state, a 20–30 percent chance of being so disabled that he or she can manage only basic self-care or employment in a sheltered workshop, and only a 25 percent chance of independent functioning, although not at the same level as prior to the injury (e.g., the person would probably have to work at a less demanding job). Furthermore, gradations of scores even within the three basic categories of head injury are important for predicting outcome. For example, individuals with a GCS score of 3 have a fourfold greater chance of dying than those with a GCS score of 7 (Eisenberg & Weiner, 1987).

The profile of neuropsychological deficits observed in individuals who have closed head injury can vary widely due to dissimilarities in the nature of the damage (e.g., Thomas & Trexler, 1982). Nonetheless, certain difficulties are commonly observed, most notably in memory and attention. In the realm of memory, such individuals tend to have posttraumatic amnesia (which is the inability to acquire new information for events after the injury; see page 325, Chapter 10) (e.g., Levin & Grossman, 1978). The initial presentation of these memory problems tends to be predictive of the severity of injury and the subsequent level of functioning. For example, posttraumatic amnesia extending longer than three weeks is associated with a poor level of subsequent cognitive functioning. Some of the memory problems may arise from damage to the cholinergic system (see Chapter 2, page 49), which tends to be more compromised by closed head injury than other neurotransmitter systems (Schmidt & Grady, 1995). We will revisit the role of the cholinergic system in memory later in the chapter when we discuss Alzheimer's disease.

Another one of the commonly affected abilities is attentional functioning. Although individuals with closed head injury maintain vigilance and alertness, they have particular difficulty in selective attention and divided attention (Zoccolotti et al., 2000), especially with regard to inhibiting responses and being cognitively flexible. Their behavioral control is often poor, and they appear impulsive, impatient, and distractible. In addition, the ability to plan toward a goal, or the motivation to do so, is compromised. This latter difficulty can be related to emotional changes after injury such as depression or the person's lack of appreciation of his or her deficits, which are often prominent after closed head injury. Deficits in executive function and abstract thought or conceptualization are common (e.g., Levin, High, et al., 1987). In addition, deficits in cognitive functions performed by the brain region at the site of coup or contrecoup injuries are likely to be observed (Orsini, Van Gorp, & Boone, 1988).

Mild head injury, also known as concussion, occurs when individuals have a change in consciousness (but not necessarily unconsciousness) for 2 to 30 minutes and do not have other gross signs of neurological damage. Behaviors that are often associated with concussion are listed in Table 14.2.

Even such mild damage can have consequences for mental functioning. Complaints tend to fall into three major areas. First, difficulties in cognition are noted, especially with regard to concentration and memory. Second, the person experiences somatic symptoms, such as dizziness, blurred vision, sensitivity to noise and bright lights, sleep disturbances, fatigue, headaches, lightheadedness, alterations in taste and smell, and changes in appetite. Third, the individual undergoes emotional changes, including depression, anxiety, loss of patience, and increased temper (Levin, Gary, et al., 1987). Despite apparent recovery as evidenced on neuropsychological tests, some of these symptoms, such as irritability, anxiety, depression, insomnia, and fatigue, may remain (e.g., Binder, 1986).

Not only does closed head injury have consequences in and of itself, but it is a risk factor for various subsequent neuropsychological problems.

TABLE 14.2 Frequently Observed Behaviors Associated with Mild Head Injury

Vacant stare	Befuddled facial expression
Delayed responses	Slower to answer questions or follow instructions
Inability to focus	Easily distracted; unable to follow through with normal activities
Disorientation	Unaware of time, date, place; walking in wrong direction
Atypical speech	Slurred speech; incoherent, disjointed, or incomprehensible statements
Gross incoordination	Stumbling; inability to walk a straight line
Hyperemotionality	Acting distraught; crying for no reason
Memory deficits	Asking the same question; inability to remember what happened five minutes ago
Loss of consciousness	Nonresponsiveness to stimuli

First, having a closed head injury puts an individual at higher risk for sustaining another head injury (see Salcido & Costich, 1992), increasing the risk four to six times more than someone who has never had a head injury (e.g., Zemper, 1994). The subsequent head injury may occur, in part, because these individuals have certain personality and social characteristics (e.g., risk taking, alcohol abuse) that predispose them to accidents (e.g., Tsuang, Boor, & Fleming, 1985). However, decrements in attention and poor judgment associated with the initial head injury may also predispose these individuals to another head injury (e.g., not noticing a change in the color of a traffic light might lead to another motor vehicle accident). The risk of additional head injury is problematic, as the effects, both neuropsychological (Gronwall & Wrightson, 1975) and neurophysiological (Jordan & Zimmerman, 1990), are cumulative, even when the injuries are separated by months or years.

Closed head injury is also associated with posttraumatic epilepsy, which does not always manifest itself immediately but may begin more than a year after the head injury. (Later in the chapter, we discuss epilepsy in more detail.) If closed head injury occurs in early adulthood, it is associated with a significant increase in the risk of depression over an individual's lifetime (Holsinger et al., 2002). And even a mild closed head injury may put an individual at higher risk for dementing disorders such as Alzheimer's disease (e.g., Mortimer, French, Hutton, & Schuman, 1985; Nemetz et al., 1999).

Closed Head Injury and Sports

Closed head injury is a common occurrence in sports, as can be attested to by any fan of Canadian or U.S. football. Although a commentator may reassure the audience that a player who receives a hard hit was "just shook up on the play and will be back soon," as a student of neuropsychology you should know that if the hit caused any alteration in consciousness, the story is much more complicated. Even though the symptoms associated with mild head injury dissipate enough to let the player return to competition within a week or so, questions remain as to whether that individual will have longer-term effects (for a wealth of information on brain injury and sports, see the September 8, 1999, issue of the *Journal of the American Medical Association*).

Probably the clearest case of sports-related head trauma occurs in boxing in the syndrome known as *dementia pugilistica,* or *chronic posttraumatic encephalopathy.* This syndrome, which begins to exhibit itself at the end of a boxing career or soon thereafter, initially manifests as tremors, difficulties in speaking, and abnormal reflexes (due to damage to the cerebellum and other motor areas). Insidiously, these difficulties become worse, and disorders in thinking and emotion manifest, indicative of the extensive nature of damage to more wide-ranging regions of the brain. Regardless of whether a boxer is a professional or an amateur, heavyweight or lightweight, the probability of exhibiting such symptoms is related to the number of bouts in which the person fought (Mortimer & Pirozzolo, 1985). In fact, so clear is the association between head trauma sustained in the ring and subsequent neurological deficits that over 20 years ago, the American Academy of Neurology called for a ban on the sport (American Academy of Neurology, 1983).

A wide variety of sports are associated with head injury. Some of these are sports in which no protective headgear is worn, such as men's and women's soccer (called football outside the United States), field hockey, and wrestling. But others, such as football, hockey, lacrosse, and baseball/softball, are associated with head injury despite the use of helmets. (If you are interested in the rates of concussion for your particular college sport, see Dick, 1994, or for high school sports, see Powell & Barber-Foss, 1999). For the most part these injuries tend to be associated with collisions among players, explaining why U.S. football accounts for over half the reported injuries (Powell & Barber-Foss, 1999). To appreciate the frequency of such injury, consider the following: In one study of college football players, researchers found that 1 in 10 players received a head injury within any given season and that more than 40 percent of the athletes sustained at least one head injury during their high school and college careers (Barth et al., 1989).

Other sporting activities associated with significant rates of head trauma are those in which individuals collide with other objects, such as equestrian sports, in which riders hit objects after falling off or being thrown from horses, and skiing, in which individuals collide with trees, other skiers, boulders, ski-lift equipment, or ice. Here is the self-evaluation by a 42-year-old neurosurgeon of how his mental abilities were changed after a fall while skiing caused him to hit his head and lose consciousness for no more than a few seconds (for an interesting collection of self-reports of various types of brain trauma by medical personnel, see Kapur, 1997).

> Upon returning home, the neurosurgeon noted that he was a bit more distractible than was his norm and he had a great deal of difficulty remembering recent events, including particularly the location of objects necessary for work, such as a dictaphone, briefcase, and keys. List making in order to recall meetings scheduled and tasks to be performed becamc necessary, whereas they were not necessary before. Referencing articles from memory storage was difficult: authors were frequently transposed and dates incorrectly recalled. Information processing did not appear to be affected, but the ability to attend to a task required a higher level of energy expenditure than previously. These symptoms persisted, but improved gradually over a period of approximately 18 months. . . . Function as judged by others remains good, but is not optimal. (L. F. Marshall & Ruff, 1989.)

Even when individuals feel that most all of the symptoms have subsided, the effect of mild head injury can still be detected in the laboratory. One such example is a study of professional football players in Australia (Cremona-Meteyard & Geffen, 1994), who had suffered a mild head injury, defined as any 2- to 20-minute change in consciousness with no accompanying gross signs of neurological damage, and a posttraumatic amnesia that lasted less than 24 hours. The players were tested both two weeks after the injury and one year later. Two weeks post-injury they exhibited, not surprisingly, a slowing of overall reaction time (RT) and an inability to direct attention to a cued location. A year later, when the players claimed that all the behavioral signs of the concussion had disappeared, overall RT had returned to normal but the deficit in directing visual attention remained. These findings suggest that even mild head injuries may be associated with long-term consequences that may go unnoticed by the people who sustain these injuries.

The long-term effects of mild head injury are not limited to the orienting or directing of visual attention, but can affect more central aspects of processing as well. Individuals who have mild head injury as a result of contact sports, including rugby, soccer, and wrestling can exhibit a decrease in the amplitude of the P_{300} component, which is taken to index more central aspects of attentional control. The amount of the decrease was related to the degree of post-concussive symptoms (Dupuis et al., 2000). And the statistics on amateur soccer, which involves over 200 million individuals worldwide, are equally sobering. In a recent study, one out of every four serious amateur soccer players (playing on average four hours a week for over 15 years) were moderately impaired on tests of memory, and four out of ten were impaired on executive function as measured by the Wisconsin Card Sorting Test (WCST) (Matser, Kessels, Lezak, & Jordan, 1999).

Given the deleterious effects of even mild closed head injury, it is a worthwhile endeavor to determine what can be done to minimize its effect. In this case, an ounce of prevention is worth a ton of cure, because most closed head injuries are avoidable. One of the best preventive measures is to use seat belts and to have cars equipped with air bags. They do not allow the driver's or the passenger's head to come into contact with the windshield, and they help prevent individuals from being thrown from a car, events that greatly increase the chance of head injury. A second preventive measure is to emphasize the responsible consumption of alcoholic beverages, because a clear association exists between alcohol intoxication and accidents. A third measure is to train individuals to carefully evaluate the risks of the activities or behavior in which they engage; a predisposing factor for head injury is risk taking and reckless behavior. Another simple measure is to wear protective headgear whenever two-wheeled transportation is involved, regardless of whether it is a bicycle, a motor scooter, or a motorcycle. Although helmet use is compulsory in some countries, such as Australia and New Zealand, it is not as widely adopted elsewhere even though it has been proved to reduce brain injury (Attewell, Glase, & McFadden,

2001). It must be stressed, however, that wearing a helmet does not make one invulnerable and that risky riding behavior should still be avoided.

A similar approach can be taken to avoid closed head injury associated with sports. Protective gear is more or less the norm in some sports, such as lacrosse, hockey, and football, and its use is increasing in others. For example, headgear is worn by windsurfers sailing in stiff winds (because the mast or the wishbone holding the sail might hit a person's head forcefully enough to cause a loss of consciousness), by mountain-bike enthusiasts (in case they fly over the handlebars or otherwise awkwardly dismount from the bicycle), and by skiers, both children and adults (to minimize head injuries associated with collisions and falls). To provide perspective on how much these measures would help, consider the results of an epidemiological study which found that (1) three quarters of the individuals who sustained a brain injury in a motor vehicle accident were not wearing seat belts; (2) 84 percent of the persons who sustained a brain injury in a bicycle or motorcycle accident were not wearing a helmet; and (3) half of all individuals were intoxicated at the time of the accident (e.g., W. A. Gordon, Mann, & Willer, 1993).

Dementing Diseases

Dementia is a debilitating syndrome involving a loss of cognitive functions, sometimes accompanied by personality changes, that interferes significantly with work or social activities. Although a person can become demented after an acute neurological incident (i.e., very severe head injury), dementias typically progress in stages, generally termed *mild, moderate,* and *severe,* and eventually lead to death. In mild dementia, the person retains judgment, can live alone, and can maintain adequate personal hygiene, although work or social activities are significantly impaired. As the disease progresses to the moderate stage, independent living becomes hazardous (e.g., the individual forgets to turn off the stove) and some degree of supervision becomes necessary. In severe dementia, the person's abilities are so impaired that he or she requires constant supervision (e.g., the person is mute or cannot maintain minimal personal hygiene).

Dementia is a growing problem because the average life span of individuals continues to lengthen and the risk of dementia increases with age. Estimates from many countries, including France, Japan, Sweden, and the United States, are that 5 percent of individuals age 75 have dementia, 9 percent of those age 80, 16 percent of those age 85, and 30 percent of those age 90. As you can see, the rate almost doubles with every five years of increasing age (Brookmeyer, Gray, & Kawas, 1998).

Although all dementias lead to the same depressing end, there are different varieties that manifest in somewhat distinct ways, both with regard to the specific constellation of cognitive functions affected and with regard to the course of decline. Typically, dementias are divided into three major varieties loosely based on the region of the brain most affected: those that mainly affect cortical regions, those that mainly affect subcortical regions, and those that affect both, which are referred to as *mixed-variety dementias.* The cortical dementias—Alzheimer's disease, Pick's disease, and Creutzfeldt-Jakob disease—manifest as the co-occurrence of many deficits with which we are already familiar, such as aphasia, apraxia, agnosia, acalculia, spatial deficits, and memory problems. They generally have an insidious onset in which the first symptoms are difficulty remembering events, disorientation in familiar surroundings, problems finding the correct words to use or difficulty naming objects, and changes in personality and mood. The cognitive decline thereafter is steady, and except for Creutzfeldt-Jakob disease, is slow. In contrast, subcortical dementias, which occur in Huntington's disease and Parkinson's disease, do not result in specific and striking cognitive deficits, such as aphasia and apraxia. Instead, they are much more likely to manifest first as changes in personality, slowness in the speed of cognitive processing, lapses in attention, and difficulties in goal-directed tasks or tasks that require formation of a strategy (see Cummings & Benson, 1984, for a review). Moreover, people with subcortical dementias have relatively few difficulties on recognition tasks, showing impairment mainly on recall. Table 14.3 lists the major features that distinguish cortical and subcortical dementias.

Mixed-variety dementias are disorders in which both cortical and subcortical involvement seems to

TABLE 14.3 Major Characteristics That Distinguish Cortical and Subcortical Dementias

CHARACTERISTIC	TYPE OF DEMENTIA	
	SUBCORTICAL	CORTICAL
Mental status		
Language	No aphasia	Aphasia
Memory	Forgetful (difficulty retrieving learned material)	Amnesia (difficulty learning new material)
Cognition	Impaired (poor problem solving produced by slowness, forgetfulness, and impaired strategy and planning)	Severely disturbed (based on agnosia, aphasia, acalculia, and amnesia)
	Slow processing time	Response time relatively normal
Personality	Apathetic	Unconcerned or euphoric
Mood	Affective disorder common (depression or mania)	Normal
Motor system		
Speech	Dysarthric	Normal*
Posture	Abnormal	Normal, upright*
Gait	Abnormal	Normal*
Motor speed	Slow	Normal*
Movement disorder	Common (chorea, tremor, rigidity, ataxia)	Absent
Anatomy		
Cortex	Largely spared	Involved
Basal ganglia, thalamus, mesencephalon	Involved	Largely spared
Metabolism		
Fluorodeoxyglucose scan	Subcortical hypometabolism (cortex largely normal)	Cortical hypometabolism (subcortical metabolism less involved)
Neurotransmitters preferentially involved	Huntington's disease: γ-aminobutyric acid Parkinson's disease: dopamine	Alzheimer's disease: acetylcholine

*Motor system involvement occurs late in the course of Alzheimer's disease and Pick's disease.

occur, such as vascular dementia (previously referred to as *multi-infarct dementia*) and the dementia associated with AIDS. These dementias manifest as patterns of cognitive performance that are midway between those observed in cortical and subcortical dementias. We now turn our attention to a more detailed discussion of each syndrome.

Cortical Dementias

For each of the major cortical dementias—Alzheimer's, Pick's, and Creutzfeldt-Jakob—we first discuss its neuropsychological profile, then its neurophysiological bases and putative causes.

• *ALZHEIMER'S DISEASE* •

The average person associates Alzheimer's disease with memory loss, which is reasonable considering that the best measure for distinguishing between a mildly demented individual and a healthy older adult is the ability to remember a 10-item word list after a delay (e.g., Welsh et al., 1991). Yet the consequences of the disease reach far beyond memory. **Alzheimer's disease** (or, as it is often called, **dementia of the Alzheimer's type [DAT]**) is defined by a decline not only in memory but in many other aspects of cognitive function including at least one of the following: language, visuospatial skills, abstract thinking, motor performance, and judgment. In addition, emotional dysfunction and personality changes, which at first are subtle but later become profound, are typically observed as well. As we learn later, the damage sustained to the brain is diffuse, which accounts for the broad nature of the cognitive deficits observed.

Because Alzheimer's disease has been estimated to account for more than half of all cases of dementia observed in older persons, researchers are intensely examining it in an attempt to understand both its neuropsychological consequences and its causes (R. B. Knight, 1992). Generally, Alzheimer's disease is considered to comprise two subsyndromes. One, known as *early onset Alzheimer's,* is characterized by onset of the disease before age 65 years and progresses rapidly. The other, known as *late-onset Alzheimer's,* is characterized by an onset after age 65 years and is usually associated with a slower decline [American Psychiatric Association, *Diagnostic and Statistical Manual of Mental Disorders,* 4th ed. (*DSM-IV),* 1994]. As we discuss later on, different genetic factors are thought to be linked to each of these syndromes.

At present, no specific physiological test exists that can reveal the presence of Alzheimer's disease in living individuals. Although some fanfare was given to a test (Scinto et al., 1994) that purported to diagnose Alzheimer's disease by measuring the response of the pupil (as an index of cholinergic function, whose importance we will discuss later), subsequent studies have not found it to be a valid measure (e.g., Caputo et al., 1998). Because the defining characteristics of the disease, specific neuroanatomical changes to the brain (which we discuss later), can be determined only by postmortem examination of brain tissue, a probable diagnosis is made on the basis of behavior. When other causes of dementia have been ruled out (e.g., dementia due to substance abuse) and the person's behavioral pattern is consistent with the disease, a diagnosis of Alzheimer's disease is made. These behavioral criteria do quite well, in the best cases agreeing with the diagnosis at autopsy as much as 90 percent of the time (e.g., Blacker et al., 1994).

From its typically gradual onset, the course of the disease is progressively downward. Because of the variability of impairment seen at different stages of the disease, scales are widely used to quantify the degree to which the abilities of patients with Alzheimer's disease are compromised. One such scale, The Global Deterioration Scale (e.g., Reisberg, Ferris, deLeon, & Crook, 1988; Reisberg et al., 1989) uses an interview to examine memory, orientation to the world, and self-care skills to provide a seven-stage rating (from 1, no decline, to 7, very severe decline). An overview of the characteristics of each stage and its typical duration is provided in Table 14.4.

• ***Neuropsychological Profile*** • Now let us examine some of the more specific neuropsychological deficits associated with Alzheimer's disease, starting with memory impairment, which is one of the most prominent aspects of the disease. Individuals with Alzheimer's disease show a severe anterograde amnesia that is global. Thus, like patients with amnesia, they cannot acquire new information. Not surprisingly, they have significant discrepancies between their IQ score (which tends to rely more on previously acquired information) and their scores on tests such as the Wechsler Memory Scale (which measure the acquisition of new memories) (e.g., Weingartner et al., 1981). Often family members will not realize how debilitated a loved one is because the patient instinctively remains in familiar environments and engages in behaviors that are routine, so that new information need not be acquired. The severity of the deficit becomes unmasked only when the person is confronted with unfamiliar circumstances, such as those encountered on a vacation away from home or with the institution of new procedures at work.

Patients with Alzheimer's disease also exhibit a retrograde amnesia. Their ability to recall information from various periods in their lifetime prior to the onset of their disorder is worse than that of neurologically intact elderly individuals (e.g., Beatty et al., 1988). Furthermore, they show a temporal gradient in such effects (e.g., Kopelman, 1989). Finally, difficulties in short-term memory, such as those assessed by digit-span tasks, may sometimes be observed, especially in later stages of the disease (e.g., R. S. Wilson, Bacon, Fox, & Kaszniak, 1983).

Thus, individuals with Alzheimer's disease exhibit a pattern of memory impairment that differs in

TABLE 14.4 A Typical Rating Scale for Alzheimer's Dementia (AD)

STAGE	DIAGNOSIS	CHARACTERISTICS	ESTIMATED DURATION*
1	Normal adult	No decrement noted	
2	Normal older adult	Subjective deficit in word finding noted	
3	Compatible with incipient AD	Deficits noted on demanding job-related tasks	7 years
4	Mild AD	Assistance required for complex tasks (e.g., handling finances, planning a dinner party)	2 years
5	Moderate AD	Assistance required for choosing attire	18 months
6	Moderately severe AD	a. Assistance required for dressing	5 months
		b. Assistance required for bathing properly	5 months
		c. Assistance required with mechanics of toileting (e.g., flushing, wiping)	5 months
		d. Urinary continence lost	4 months
		e. Fecal continence lost	10 months
7	Severe AD	a. Speech ability limited to about one-half dozen intelligible words	12 months
		b. Intelligible vocabulary limited to a single word	18 months
		c. Ambulatory ability lost	12 months
		d. Ability to sit up lost	12 months
		e. Ability to smile lost	18 months
		f. Ability to hold up head lost	Unknown

*In subjects who survive and progress to the next stage.

important ways from patients with amnesia (see page 330, Chapter 10). First, patients with Alzheimer's disease do not have the spared procedural knowledge that is observed in individuals with amnesia. As we discussed in Chapter 10, procedural memory is independent of the hippocampal system and depends on activating the same cortical processors that were used in the acquisition of a skill. Procedural knowledge is affected in Alzheimer's disease to the degree that a particular cortical processor is affected by the disease. For example, Alzheimer's patients are not biased to complete a stem (e.g., *mot*) with a word that they recently read in a list of words (e.g., *motel*), (e.g., A. P. Shimamura, Salmon, Squire, & Butters, 1987). Such a task requires knowledge about language and word meaning, presumably relying on frontal and parietotemporal regions that are often compromised in Alzheimer's disease. In contrast, they exhibit intact perceptual priming for visual form, which presumably relies on occipital regions that are relatively spared in the disease process (Keane et al., 1991). Second, patients with Alzheimer's disease exhibit an extensive retrograde amnesia, whereas most patients with non-Korsakoff's amnesia exhibit only a limited retrograde amnesia. Third, patients in the later stages of Alzheimer's disease may have short-term memory problems, whereas patients with amnesia do not (for a short review of the characteristics of long-term memory in Alzheimer's disease, see Fleischman & Gabrieli, 1999; for a longer review, see Carlesimo & Oscar-Berman, 1992).

Toward the later stages of the disease, language problems, such as aphasia, usually become prominent, affecting semantic aspects of language more than syntax or phonology. At this time, the patient's speech becomes sparse and empty of meaning. For example, when asked to name an orange pictured in a photograph, a moderately demented patient replied, "Same thing, this is no, no, they may be this here and it didn't get here, but it got there, there, there" (Bayles, 1982, p. 276). Despite the lack of content, the syntactic structure of these individuals' language remains intact (e.g., Hier, Hagenlocker, & Shindler, 1985), and they show few phonemic disturbances or articulatory problems (e.g., Appell, Kertesz, & Fisman, 1982).

They also exhibit difficulty in other functions, such as visuospatial processing and the conceptual aspects of motor behavior one often observes in apraxic individuals. The exact functions compromised, especially in the early phases of the disorder, vary from individual to individual and tend to be predicted by regional decreases in brain metabolism (e.g., Haxby et al., 1990). For example, low metabolism in right parietal regions is associated with disturbances in spatial functions, whereas low metabolism in left parietal regions is associated with apraxia symptoms and language problems (S. Hart & Semple, 1990).

Alzheimer's disease also causes changes in emotional functioning and personality. Relative to their premorbid personality, caregivers rate the patients as more neurotic, vulnerable, and anxious; less extroverted; more passive; less agreeable; less open to new ideas; and more depressed although not profoundly so. Individuals with Alzheimer's disease tend not to exhibit odd or socially inappropriate behaviors, which are more common in people with subcortical dementias. For the most part, personality changes are not correlated with the duration of the illness and may begin to manifest relatively early in the disease. In some cases, the patients may exhibit psychiatric symptoms. For example, at later stages of the disease, delusions, especially of persecution, infidelity, and theft, may occur. However, these delusions tend not to be elaborate and pass quickly. The more atypical an individual's personality before she or he is diagnosed with the disease, the more likely the person is to exhibit psychiatric symptoms such as depression and paranoid delusions (Chatterjee, Strauss, Smyth, & Whitehouse, 1992).

• ***Neurophysiological Bases*** • Now that we discussed the neuropsychological profile of impairment in Alzheimer's disease, we turn our attention to its neurophysiological bases and some of its possible causes. The defining symptoms of the disease are a brain riddled with large numbers of neurofibrillary tangles and amyloid plaques. **Neurofibrillary tangles** are twisted pairs of helical filaments found within the neuron. They are similar to but distinct from microtubules, which are normal cell structures that allow neurotransmitters and other proteins made within the cell body to be transported to other regions of the cell. Because of their structure, neurofibrillary tangles are thought to disrupt a neuron's structural matrix. Although these tangles can be found in the brain of the average healthy older individual, they are greatly increased in the cortex of an individual with Alzheimer's disease (e.g., Tomlinson, 1980, 1982), and their number predicts the severity of the dementia (e.g., Bierer et al., 1995; Nagy et al., 1995) (see Figure 14.2). Large numbers of neurofibrillary tangles are not unique to Alzheimer's disease but are also observed in other neurological conditions such as Down syndrome, dementia from boxing, and Parkinson's disease resulting from encephalitis. These tangles are not equally distributed throughout the brain but have an affinity

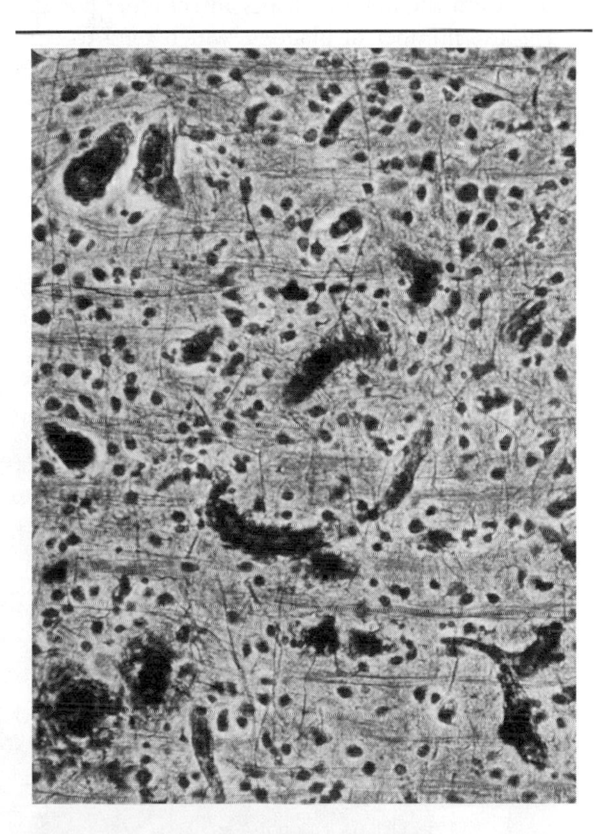

FIGURE 14.2 Neurofibrillary tangles that are typically observed in Alzheimer's disease. Shown here is a section of cortex from a patient with Alzheimer's disease. The neurofibrillary tangles are the dark crescent-shaped objects.

for medial temporal, inferior parietal, and frontal regions, while sparing primary motor and sensory areas (e.g., Kemper, 1984).

Amyloid plaques are deposits consisting of aluminum silicate and amyloid peptides, meaning that they are basically a buildup or a conglomeration of proteins (Figure 14.3). These plaques often include tau protein, and apolipoprotein E (ApoE), which, as we will soon learn, are implicated in the genetic aspects of Alzheimer's disease. The plaques, typically surrounded by neurons containing neurofibrillary tangles, are believed to cause vascular damage and neuronal cell loss. As with neurofibrillary tangles, amyloid plaques can be observed in the brain of the average older individual without dementia. What distinguishes individuals with Alzheimer's disease from the neurologically intact older population is the number of plaques, which tend to concentrate in the cortex and the hippocampus. Like neurofibrillary tangles, plaques are not unique to Alzheimer's disease. They are observed in other brain diseases, such as amyotrophic lateral sclerosis (ALS), a demyelinating disease. There is usually evidence of inflammation in the vicinity of the plaque (Aisen & Davis, 1994) and a deficiency of nerve growth factor (Tonnaer & Dekker, 1994). These findings will become important later on when we discuss potential therapeutic interventions to slow the course of the disease.

The net result of all these tangles and amyloid deposits is the loss of synapses and then the loss of cells. At later stages of the disease the cell loss is very visible on anatomical brain images, as the cortex is atrophied and the ventricles enlarged (Figure 14.4). As might be expected from the description of the location of tangles and plaques, cell loss in cortical regions is greatest in frontal, anterior temporal, and parietal regions. The subcortical and midbrain structures most affected include the hippocampus, amygdala, and olfactory system. Not surprisingly, the degree of tissue loss predicts behavior. For example, the degree of tissue loss in temporal regions predicts the degree to which new information cannot be remembered (Wilson et al., 1996).

With regard to neurotransmitter systems, the cholinergic system is most affected, and the disruption

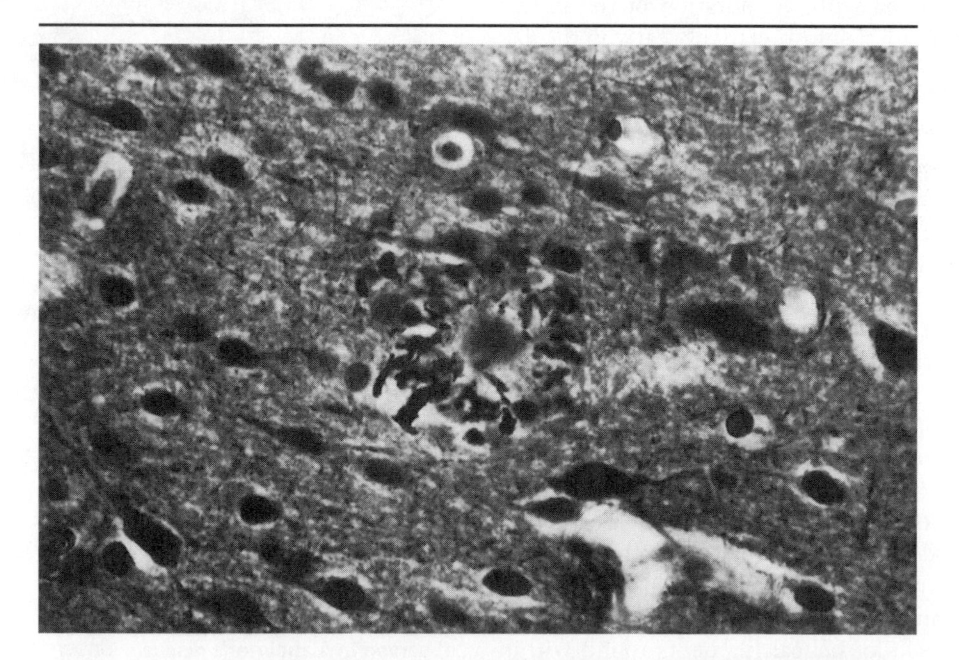

FIGURE 14.3 Amyloid plaques that are observed in Alzheimer's disease. Shown here is an amyloid plaque (large round sphere), which is composed of proteins, in the cortex of a patient with Alzheimer's disease.

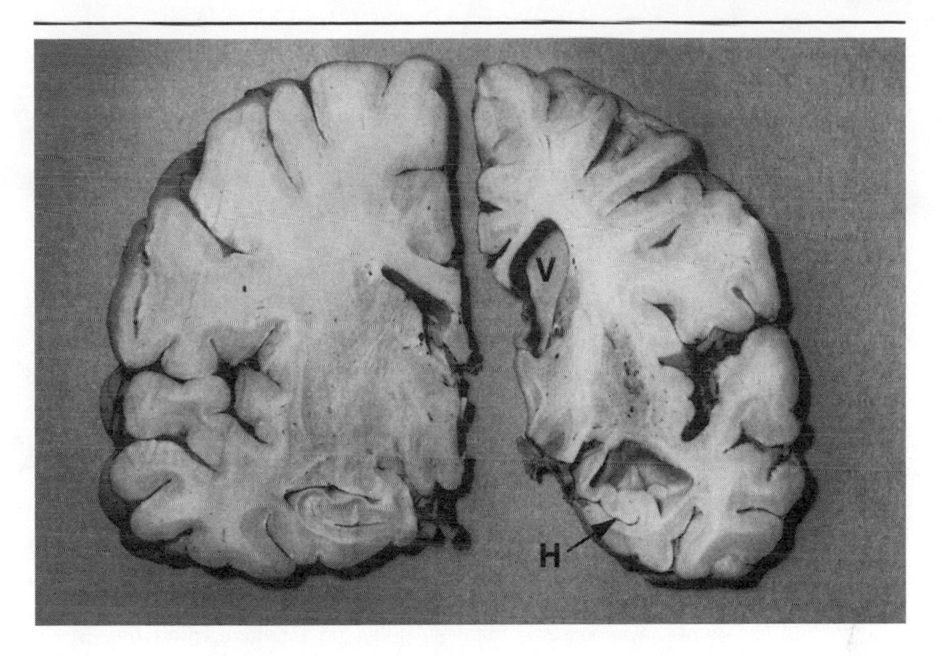

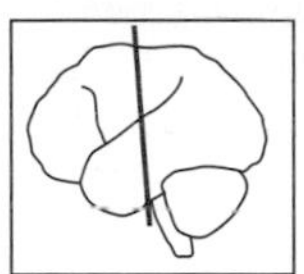

FIGURE 14.4 Cell loss due to Alzheimer's disease. (Left) Coronal postmortem hemisection taken from the brain of a neurologically intact older person. (Right) Coronal postmortem hemisection taken from the brain of a 75-year-old patient with Alzheimer's disease who died approximately 5 years after the onset of the disease. Note the extensive atrophy of this patient's brain, especially that of the hippocampus (H). Also note that the ventricles (V) are extremely enlarged because as cortical cells die, cerebrospinal fluid fills the remaining space.

to this system correlates with the severity of dementia (Wilcock, Esiri, Bowen, & Smith, 1982). The main route for cholinergic input to the cortex and hippocampus is lost as up to 90 percent of cells are destroyed in the *nucleus basalis of Meynert* (e.g., Whitehouse et al., 1981, 1982). Figure 14.5A shows the location of the nucleus basalis of Meynert in relation to midbrain structures, and Figure 14.5B depicts cholinergic projections from this region to cortical areas. Although cholinergic transmission is most affected, the noradrenergic and serotonergic systems are also compromised. To a lesser extent, reductions can also be observed in levels of glutamate and dopamine (Parnetti, Senin, & Mecocci, 1997).

• ***Genetic Bases and Risk Factors*** • Much research has examined the genetic factors that are related to Alzheimer's disease. One set of genetic factors are those that involve mutations that *lead* to Alzheimer's disease. They are associated with Alzheimer's dementia of early onset and all involve increased production of the amyloid beta protein. Another set of genes is associated with the *risk* of late-onset Alzheimer's disease, either increasing or decreasing the likelihood of disease. These genetic contributions to Alzheimer's disease are outlined in Table 14.5. We now discuss them in a bit more detail.

A number of genes have been found to cause the early-onset varieties of Alzheimer's disease. One is a mutation of the gene on chromosome 21 coding for amyloid precursor protein (Goate et al., 1991). Aberrant catabolism of amyloid precursor protein is linked to the formation of amyloid deposits. Interestingly, by the age of 30, individuals with Down syndrome, which involves an extra copy of chromosome 21, have pathology of the brain similar to that seen in people with Alzheimer's disease and

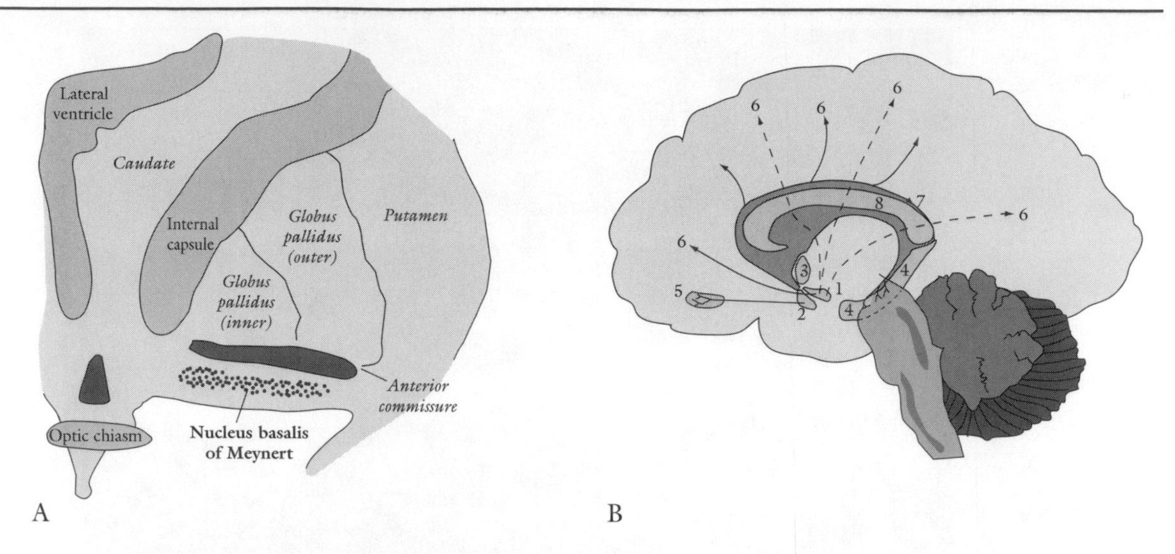

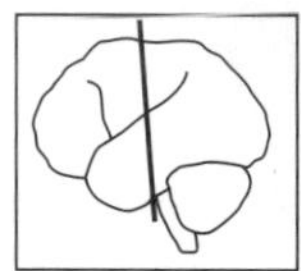

FIGURE 14.5 The nucleus basalis of Meynert and cholinergic projections, which are affected by Alzheimer's disease. (A) A coronal section at the level of the optic chiasm illustrating the position of the nucleus basalis of Meynert relative to the striatum, and anterior commissure. (B) A midsagittal view of the brain showing the major cholinergic projections to the cortex, including those from the nucleus basalis of Meynert. 1, Nucleus basalis of Meynert; 2, nucleus of the diagonal band of Broca; 3, medial septal nucleus; 4, hippocampus; 5, olfactory bulb; 6, neocortex; 7, cingulate cortex; 8, corpus callosum.

start to exhibit dementia with increasing age (Wisniewski, Wisniewski, & Wen, 1985). Two genes that code for presinilin are also linked to early-onset Alzheimer's. The gene on chromosome 1 that codes for presilin 2 has been found in a small group of German families that migrated to the Volga region of Russia (Levy-Lahad et al., 1995), and the gene on chromosome 14 that codes for presenilin 1 has been linked to the majority of cases of early-onset Alzheimer's disease (Sherrington et al., 1995). It should be noted that these early-onset varieties of Alzheimer's disease account for less than 5 percent of all patients with Alzheimer's dementia.

Another gene, the ApoE gene, is linked to the vulnerability of getting Alzheimer's disease. Commonly it has three alleles (i.e., possible forms), e-2,

TABLE 14.5 Genetic Associations for Alzheimer's Dementia (AD)

GENE	CHROMOSOME	EFFECT
Mutations causing AD		
Presenilin 2	1	Disease typically occurs between age 30 and 40 years, but can be wide-ranging
Presenilin 1	14	Disease occurs between age 50 and 65 years
Trisomy 21 (Down's syndrome)	21	Disease occurs between age 30 and 40 years
Amyloid precursor protein	21	Disease occurs between age 40 and 50 years
Factors modulating AD		
Apolipoprotein—ApoE-4 allele	19	Increased risk of late-onset AD
Apolipoprotein—ApoE-2 allele	19	Decreased risk of late-onset AD

e-3, and e-4. The ApoE-4 allele is associated with an increased risk of Alzheimer's (Corder et al., 1993). The brains of individuals with this allele exhibit increased plaques and a deficiency in the cholinergic system (Gomez-Isla et al., 1996). In contrast, individuals with the ApoE-2 allele have a decreased risk for Alzheimer's (Duara et al., 1996).

Factors other than genes have been linked to the risk of getting Alzheimer's. Nongenetic risk factors include smoking (Merchant et al., 1999), cardiovascular disease (Stewart, 1998), diabetes mellitus (Leibson et al., 1997), having a first-degree relative who had dementia (Van Diujn et al., 1991) and as we have mentioned earlier, head injury. Interestingly, boxers who have an ApoE-4 allele show greater neuropsychological deficits, indicating the interplay between genetic and environmental factors in producing dementia (Barry et al., 1997).

And on the other side of the coin, a number of factors are associated with decreased risk of Alzheimer's disease. These include the use of nonsteroidal anti-inflammatory drugs (McGeer, Schulzer, & McGeer, 1996), having higher education and being involved in mentally challenging work and activities (Stern et al., 1994), and receiving estrogen replacement therapy (Ohkura et al., 1994). Increased estrogen levels in older women can have a positive effect on mental performance. For example, even in women with Alzheimer's disease, those who weigh more are more cognitively intact than those who weigh less. Increased weight is associated with higher levels of estrogen because fat is estrogen-producing (Buckwalter et al., 1997) (for a good review of these studies and other aspects of Alzheimer's disease, see Cummings et al., 1998).

• *Therapeutic Interventions* • The vast majority of therapeutic interventions for Alzheimer's disease attempt to influence the cholinergic system because acetylcholine levels are linked to the severity of memory loss and dementia (for a nice review of cholinergic activity and cognitive decline, see Gallagher & Colombo, 1995). In fact, drugs that block acetylcholine, such as scopolamine, cause memory impairment in neurologically intact young adults (e.g., Caine et al., 1981). This effect of scopolamine has been known since ancient times when it was used in witchcraft rituals and in obstetrics to produce "twilight sleep" with amnesia for painful events (e.g., Drachmann, 1978; Warburton, 1979).

The main approaches to treating Alzheimer's disease have focused on boosting the amount of acetylcholine in the system. Initial drug trials attempted to increase acetylcholine levels by providing more precursors to acetylcholine, such as lecithin and choline. This approach did not meet with much success and has been abandoned because the level of the enzyme needed to create acetylcholine from these precursors, choline acetyltransferase, is also reduced in the disease. More successful are drugs that inhibit the action of acetylcholinesterase, the enzyme that breaks down acetylcholine in the synaptic cleft. The first widely used drug of this nature in the United States was tacrine, which was shown to result in better mental performance for those taking the drug than those who received a placebo (Knapp et al., 1993). However, this drug has adverse effects. Its effect on the cholinergic system also produces symptoms such as nausea, diarrhea, dizziness, and muscle weakness that make it hard to tolerate. Even more problematic, it can lead to liver damage, and its short half-life means that the medication must be taken often.

The second drug available for treatment in the United States was donepezil, which has a longer half-life and less toxicity. Next came rivastigmine, and then clinical trials with metrifonate, eptastigmine, extended-release physostigmine, and galanthamine. There is variability across patients in their response to such drugs. In some cases, less than half the patients show significant effects. The drugs tend to be most effective when they can be given in an adequate dosage without cholinergic side effects.

None of these drugs stops the progression of Alzheimer's disease; they just slow its course. In one study, long-term treatment with tacrine significantly extended the time needed before an individual was placed in a nursing home (Knopman et al., 1996). Although this benefit may seem at first glance to be rather trivial, a delay in nursing home placement can be of great importance. For the affected individual and his or her family, it provides the time needed to make necessary financial, living, social, and emotional adjustments for the affected person's decline. For society as a whole it can mean a savings of about $1 billion dollars a year, resulting both from direct costs, such as nursing home, acute, and in-home care, and indirect costs, which would include unpaid home care provided by family and friends (Brookmeyer, Gray, & Kawas, 1998).

In addition to the drugs just discussed, other substances are also being tried experimentally. Four promising candidates are estrogen, nonsteroidal anti-inflammatory drugs, and free radical inhibitors (also known as antioxidants), and neurotrophic factors. As we have already learned, estrogen and nonsteroidal anti-inflammatory drugs have been suggested to be protective factors against getting Alzheimer's disease. Estrogen is thought to be helpful because it has multiple effects: improving the transport of glucose to the hippocampus, enhancing choline uptake, increasing cerebral blood flow, promoting neuronal viability and synaptic integrity, and decreasing the amount of amyloid beta protein formed from the precursor protein (for a review of the effects of estrogen on the central nervous system, see Woolley, 1999).

Anti-inflammatory drugs such as indomethacin and prednisone are thought to be useful because plaque formation is associated with inflammatory processes. Antioxidants are drugs or compounds that prevent damage to cells produced by free radicals, which are by-products of a disruption in oxidative metabolism. Increased production of free radicals, which damage cell membrane and tissue, is thought to underlie many neurodegenerative disorders (see Beal, 1996). Recent evidence suggests that antioxidants, such as vitamin E & C, selegiline, and flavinoids (which are contained in many fruits and vegetables, including blueberries, strawberries, broccoli, spinach, and garlic) can slow or reduce aging effects in the central nervous system (see Cantuti-Castelvetri, Shukitt-Hale, & Joseph, 2000).

At present there exists a debate as to whether these two processes, free radical formation and inflammatory disease, are the by-product or the cause of amyloid overproduction (see, for example, Roses, 2000). According to the latter viewpoint, the amyloid buildup is a by-product of the "real" cause, much the way a fever doesn't cause the flu but always accompanies it. Thus, at least some researchers are skeptical that treatment with anti-inflammatory drugs or antioxidants will effectively treat the causative factor in Alzheimer's disease. They view such substances as just treating the symptoms. Neurotrophic compounds, such as nerve growth factor (NGF), are being used to prevent or retard the loss of cholinergic cells and thereby reduce the magnitude of acetylcholine depletion. Such an approach is being investigated because, as we learned in Chapter 13 (see page 459), the *basal forebrain system* (of which the nucleus basalis is a part) is the main site in the cortex that has receptors for NGF (see Farlow & Evans, 1998, and Cutler & Sramek, 2001, for very good reviews of the different current and potential pharmacological treatments of Alzheimer's disease).

Before we leave our discussion of possible treatments of Alzheimer's disease it is worth mentioning that some researchers have suggested that the "treatment" could start long before the symptoms are evident. These researchers posit that Alzheimer's disease results from the cumulative effect of a lifetime's worth of neurotoxic processes. For example, in one study of elderly nuns, the complexity of an individual's writing exhibited 50 years prior when she first entered the convent predicted her likelihood of getting Alzheimer's. The researchers suggested that the processes leading to Alzheimer's may have started at an early age and accumulated over a lifetime (Snowdon et al., 1996). On the other hand, such patterns might also provide evidence for *cognitive reserve*, which is the idea that individuals with greater mental reserves can sustain more insult before exhibiting symptoms. Some individuals may just be genetically endowed with a greater than average elaboration of dendritic branching and synaptic density. Their brains can sustain more degradation before the matrix of their synaptic connections makes them incapable of handling complex cognitive thought.

It is also interesting to consider whether increased cognitive reserve might be something that an individual could create over a lifetime by continually engaging in complex mental activities. It may be that you can start making choices now in your 20s that will reduce your chances of getting Alzheimer's in your 80s!

Because Alzheimer's disease is so debilitating and so prevalent (the fourth leading cause of death among older individuals), scientists are working diligently to try to understand it. The segment of the world's population older than age 65 years is increasing drastically. With advances in health care extending the average life span, the care and management of individuals with Alzheimer's disease will be a significant problem in the years to come. In addition to its devastating effects on the individual, Alzheimer's disease, like other dementias, places a severe strain on those persons who must care for the afflicted individuals (for a review of the effects on caregivers, see Dunkin & Anderson-Hanley, 1998).

• *FRONTOTEMPORAL DEMENTIA* •

Another type of cortical dementia is **frontotemporal dementia,** of which Pick's disease is one. This disorder accounts for about 15–20 percent of all dementias (Jackson & Lowe, 1996) and rarely has an onset after the age of 75. Unlike the initial symptom in Alzheimer's disease, which tends to be memory impairment, the first symptoms of frontotemporal dementia usually occur in the realm of social-emotional functioning. Generally such persons have difficulty modulating their behavior, especially in a socially appropriate manner. These individuals will lack inhibition and be impulsive, doing things such as swearing at inappropriate times, having outbursts of frustration, and impulsively grabbing what they want, such as snatching food off someone's plate or shoplifting. Their lack of concern for social norms will extend to a lack of concern for their personal appearance, so they often are unkempt. In some cases, they may also exhibit inappropriate sexual behaviors. Furthermore, they have no insight into the inappropriateness of their behavior. Another characteristic that is sometimes observed is a preoccupation with repetitive or routinized behavior. They may read the same book over and over again or always take a walk to the same place. In addition, they tend to be hyperoral, overeating and obsessively focusing on food. Mood changes can occur as well, tending toward depression and anxiety. In addition to these behavioral changes there are cognitive changes that mainly manifest in the domain of language. People with frontotemporal dementia tend to have difficulty in verbal expression and in naming of persons and things. With time their speech has less and less content, and eventually they can become practically mute. Difficulties in reading and writing also develop. Later in the disease they can have Parkinson-like motor difficulties with tremor and rigidity.

Other aspects of mental functioning, however, remain surprising intact. For example, their ability to do spatial processing and higher-order motor programming is fine. In one case report, a former computer engineer took to wandering miles from his home to collect cans, never having any trouble returning home. However, his wife had to start managing such behavior when he started peering into people's windows in search of his prized cans. Memory problems are less prominent at first, as these individuals, at least in the initial stages of the disease, tend to be oriented to time and place and are able to keep track of recent events (Kaye, 1998; McKhann et al., 2001).

The physiological characteristics of frontotemporal dementia also differ from those of Alzheimer's disease. Imaging studies suggest atrophy and lack of activation of frontal and anterior temporal regions, but intact parietal lobes, whereas the parietal lobes tend to be affected in Alzheimer's disease. An example of the severe atrophy of the frontal regions in frontotemporal dementia is shown in Figure 14.6. Cellular characteristics also distinguish frontotemporal dementias from Alzheimer's disease. For example, Pick's disease is characterized by two main features: pale neurons swollen as if they had "ballooned," and clumps of fibers in the cytoplasm that are stained by silver and are known as *Pick's bodies.* These fibers are distinguishable from the neurofibrillary tangles seen in Alzheimer's disease because they are straight rather than paired and helical (see Scully, 1986, for a particularly vivid case report of Pick's disease). Finally, when genes are linked to frontotemporal dementia, they involve a different chromosome, 17, (Spillantini, Bird, and Ghetti, 1998) than the ones implicated in Alzheimer's disease.

• *CREUTZFELDT-JAKOB DISEASE* •

Creutzfeldt-Jakob disease, which is quite rare (1 in every 1 million persons), is unlike the two cortical dementias discussed so far in that it has a known

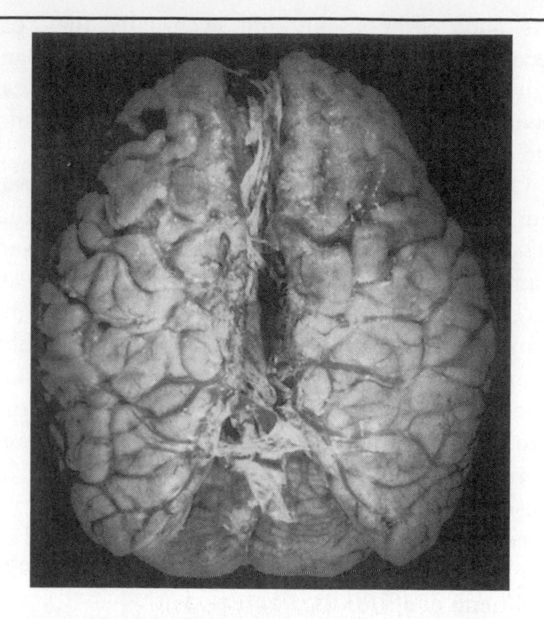

FIGURE 14.6 Brain atrophy in Pick's disease. Shown here is the brain, as viewed from above, of an individual with Pick's disease. Note the amount of degeneration in the frontal regions relative to that in other areas of the cortex.

cause: a group of transmissible protein agents known as *prions* (*pro*teinaceous *in*fectious particles) (e.g., Gibbs et al., 1968). They cause disease when a prion protein, which is a normal brain protein, undergoes a change of shape that makes it insoluble. Once insoluble it can no longer be broken down, so it accumulates, leading to cell death. The incubation period for Creutzfeldt-Jakob disease can be quite long; it is not uncommon for symptoms to manifest years to decades after the individual is infected (for a good brief review of prion diseases, see Fleminger & Curtis, 1997). The prion responsible for this disorder is highly transmissible. It can be transmitted from one person to the next during medical procedures, such as corneal implants, injections of human growth factor, and the implantation of intracranial electroencephalography (EEG) electrodes. It can even be contracted from contact with brain tissue during dissection if gloves are not worn. Although the actual prion causing the disease has not been isolated, it is known to be hardy (unlike the HIV virus) because it is resistant to boiling, formalin, alcohol, and ultraviolet radiation. Fortunately, the prion can be inactivated by autoclaving or by bleach.

Creutzfeldt-Jakob disease has characteristics that easily distinguish it from Alzheimer's and frontotemporal dementia. This dementia is accompanied by involuntary movements and a characteristic EEG pattern consisting of periodic sharp, synchronous spikes at a rate of 0.5 to 2 Hz. In addition, it typically involves a course of decline that is much quicker than that of frontotemporal or Alzheimer's dementia. Although Creutzfeldt-Jakob disease may occur at any age, it manifests most frequently in the 50s or 60s. The initial complaints tend to be fatigue, anxiety, problems in concentration, difficulties with appetite or sleep, and occasionally an elated mood. Because of these symptoms, individuals are sometimes given a psychiatric diagnosis. Several weeks later, these symptoms are typically followed by motor symptoms, such as contractions of muscle groups, which then may be followed by a lack of coordination, involuntary movements, difficulty in gait, and altered vision. A swift and progressive neurological collapse, of which dementia is invariably a component, follows (e.g., P. Brown, Cathala, Sadowski, & Gajdusek, 1979; *DSM-IV*, 1994; Will & Matthews, 1984). The overall course of the disease, once manifest, is usually not longer than one year; the median duration is four months from the onset of the dementia. The decline is so rapid that it can be seen week by week, or in some cases even day by day (e.g., R. Knight, 1989). Neuropathologically, the changes seen in the cortex are widespread neuronal loss and a proliferation of glial cells. In addition, the brain appears "spongy," which is why this disease is sometimes referred as to as *spongiform encephalopathy.*

Recently a new variant of this disorder has been identified in the United Kingdom and France. This variant has afflicted individuals younger than the age of 40, including some adolescents. In these cases, the initial presentation tends to be behavioral changes, and the decline is more protracted (up to 22 months), with dementia occurring only later on. The characteristic EEG abnormalities are not observed, and although there are sparse spongy cells, with damage mainly in the basal ganglia and thalamus, plaques, typically absent in standard Creutzfeldt-

Jakob disease, are observed in the cortex and cerebellum (for a good review, see Weissman & Aguzzi, 1997).

It is thought that people obtained this disorder by eating cattle infected with a variant form of it, bovine spongiform encephalopathy, also known as *mad cow disease.* Observed first in British cattle starting in 1986, the disorder appears to have been transmitted across species from cattle to humans through butchering practices that allowed brain and spinal tissue to taint the meat prepared for consumption. Because of such concerns, other European countries banned the importing of British meat during the spring of 1996 (Epstein & Brown, 1997). This bovine disorder has now been found in countries outside Europe, including Japan. Scientists are currently trying to determine how its transmission can be stopped.

Subcortical Dementias

Patients with subcortical dementias display a pattern of cognitive disabilities that are distinct from those observed in patients with cortical dementias. Thought tends to be slowed, and symptoms related to frontal lobe dysfunction are prominent. These latter difficulties probably result because the main subcortical regions affected in these dementias have intimate connections with frontal regions. We will now discuss two subcortical diseases: Huntington's and Parkinson's.

• *HUNTINGTON'S DISEASE* •

As we discussed in Chapter 5, Huntington's disease is an inherited, progressive neurological disease that generally first manifests around age 35–42 and inevitably leads to death about 14–17 years later. The incidence of this disease is about 5 cases per 100,000 people. As we discussed in some detail in Chapter 5, the disease destroys GABAergic (and cholinergic) neurons in the striatum (caudate nucleus and putamen) and to some degree the globus pallidus (see Figure 14.7), leading to a movement

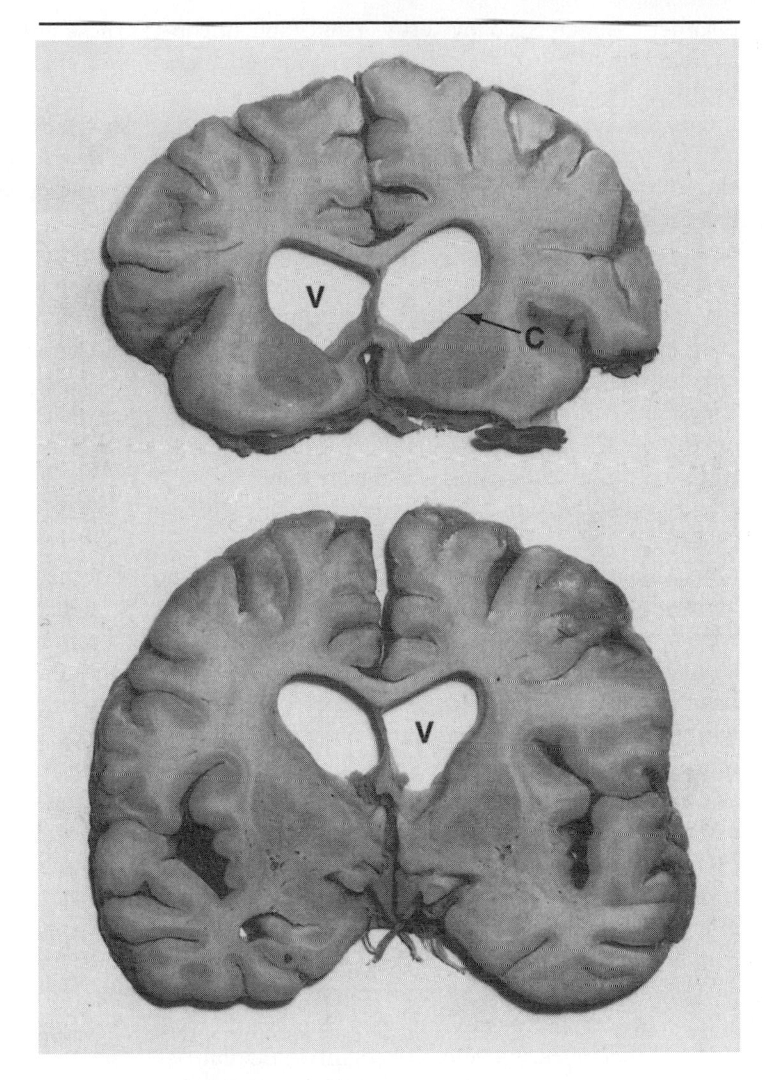

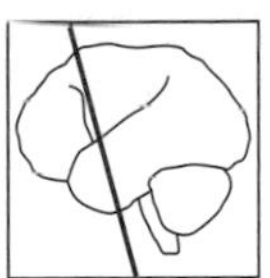

FIGURE 14.7 Neurological degeneration in Huntington's disease. Coronal postmortem slices from a 65-year-old individual who had Huntington's dementia. The caudate (C) nucleus has shrunk to only a small thin strip below the ventricle (top slice), and the ventricles (V) have become greatly enlarged (both slices). To compare how these structures look in a neurologically intact older person, refer to the left-hand portion of Figure 14.4. Also note that the main area of neural degeneration in Huntington's disease is distinct from that in Alzheimer's disease (see the right-hand portion of Figure 14.4).

disorder characterized by jerky, rapid, and uncontrollable movements (i.e., choreiform movements). In this section, we examine the intellectual impairments that accompany the disease.

The decline in cognitive functioning in individuals with Huntington's disease approximately parallels their decline in motor functioning, with practically all patients eventually becoming demented (Lieberman et al., 1979). These people have difficulty with executive aspects of attention (e.g., Josiassen, Curry, & Mancall, 1982), with processing spatial information (e.g., Brouwers et al., 1984), and with retrieving information from memory (e.g., Butters et al., 1985). The foregoing symptoms are often accompanied by disorganized speech and changes in personality and emotional functioning. As with other subcortical dementias, profound aphasia and apraxia are rare, a factor that allows clinicians to easily differentiate between Alzheimer's disease (or other cortical dementias) and Huntington's disease (or other subcortical dementias). We now examine the constellation of cognitive and emotional deficits in Huntington's disease in more detail (for a good review, see Brandt, 1991).

One broad domain of cognitive dysfunction observed in Huntington's disease is in the realm of executive control and other abilities mediated by the frontal lobe. Patients with this disease have specific difficulties in initiating behavior, selecting a response, selecting a stimulus on the basis of particular attributes, and switching mental sets. In addition, they have reduced verbal fluency, perseverative tendencies, and a loss of cognitive flexibility. Such deficits are manifest on tasks such as the Wisconsin Card Sorting Test (WCST) and the Stroop test. The existence of such deficits is not surprising if you consider that the head of the caudate nucleus, which is damaged by Huntington's disease, receives much input from the dorsolateral and orbital frontal cortex. The disintegration of the connections between the frontal lobe and the basal ganglia manifests early in the course of the disease. One of the most common early complaints of individuals with Huntington's disease is that they have difficulty planning their activities and scheduling their lives.

A second broad domain affected in this disorder is spatial processing. One might speculate that because spatial tests often emphasize motor speed, these difficulties are a consequence of the motor difficulties associated with Huntington's disease rather than a specific deficit in spatial processing. Arguing against such a conclusion, however, is the fact that deficits are even observed on tasks in which motor demands are not prominent, especially on tasks of spatial learning. Such findings are consistent with research performed on monkeys in which damage to the caudate nucleus has been found to cause difficulty on spatial learning tasks, such as spatial alternation (e.g., respond to the left stimulus on Trial 1, to the right stimulus on Trial 2, to the left stimulus on Trial 3, etc.).

A third domain in which patients with Huntington's disease often exhibit problems is in certain aspects of memory. In fact, these are often one of the earliest signs of cognitive impairment. The memory disorder is characterized by two main features, each of which distinguishes it from the memory problems observed in patients with Alzheimer's disease. The first main feature of memory dysfunction in patients with Huntington's disease is that they are much better at recognition than at recall. In contrast, patients with Alzheimer's disease are equally impaired at both. These findings suggest that although patients with Huntington's disease can store new information, they have difficulty making the kind of self-guided search through memory that is required to recall (rather than recognize) information. Indicating that the information has been indeed successfully stored in memory, though, they are able to retrieve it when given cues, such as those provided in multiple-choice recognition memory tasks.

The second main feature of memory dysfunction in patients with Huntington's disease is the lack of a temporal gradient to the memory impairment. Unlike patients in the early stages of Alzheimer's disease, who have better memory for historical events that occurred earlier in life (e.g., when they were 20 or 30 years old) than for events that occurred more recently (e.g., when they were 40, 50, or 60 years old), patients with Huntington's disease show closer to equal memory impairment across all time periods (e.g., Beatty et al., 1988) (Figure 14.8).

Besides being affected cognitively, over 80 percent of all individuals with Huntington's disease manifest changes in their emotional functioning (Lieberman et al., 1979). About half of all individuals

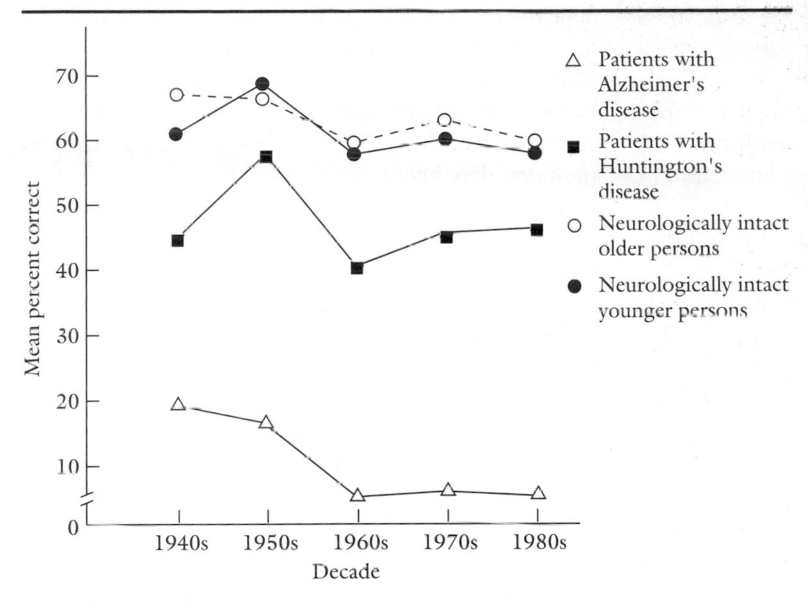

FIGURE 14.8 Memory across life span of patients with Huntington's disease. This graph depicts the performance of individuals with Huntington's disease (blue squares), Alzheimer's disease (triangles), young neurologically intact individuals (black circles), and older neurologically intact individuals (white circles) on tasks requiring the free recall of famous faces and public events pertaining to different decades of the 20th century. Two trends are noticeable. First, the memory deficit of patients with Huntington's disease is not as severe as that of patients with Alzheimer's disease. Second, the pattern of remembering in patients with Huntington's disease is similar to that of neurologically intact individuals and is distinct from that shown by patients with Alzheimer's disease, who have better memory for more remote events than for more recent events.

with this disease have major depressive episodes or exhibit a depressed mood. You might think that such a reaction is a normal response to dealing with a fatal illness. However, the depression can often precede motor symptoms and is similar to that observed in individuals with Parkinson's disease, whose prognosis for subsequent functioning is not as bleak. Hence, the depression in both Huntington's and Parkinson's is probably caused by dysfunction in striatal-frontal regions.

Patients with Huntington's disease can also be irritable, apathetic, impulsive, aggressive, and emotionally labile. At times they even exhibit psychotic symptoms such as delusions (e.g., thinking you are being persecuted by the FBI or that you are Napoleon reincarnated). Hallucinations (e.g., hearing voices) are rarer. These patients often act in socially inappropriate ways that are reminiscent of the behavior of individuals with frontal lobe damage (Cummings & Benson, 1988).

Because it is known that Huntington's disease is caused by changes to the striatum, researchers have examined the relationship between behavioral deficits and anatomical and functional changes in the basal ganglia. Atrophy or metabolically decreased function of the caudate nucleus is a good predictor of performance, especially with regard to psychomotor and executive attentional tasks (e.g., Bamford et al., 1995). It has also been shown that individuals who carry the Huntington's gene but are asymptomatic with regard to motor signs exhibit poorer cognitive performance than noncarriers on tests such as set-switching (Lawrence et al., 1998a). Furthermore, these cognitive deficits are associated with reduced dopamine binding in the striatum (Lawrence et al., 1998b). Thus, it appears that Huntington's disease has a progressive degenerative effect even before the onset of motor symptoms (for a recent review of deficits in Huntington's patients, see Brandt & Butters, 1996).

Because there is no cure for Huntington's disease, the aim of treatment is generally to treat the motor and psychiatric symptoms. An attempt has been made to implant human fetal tissue from an individual without Huntington's disease into the striatum of a patient with the disease in the hope that it may graft on to the patient's brain to counteract the loss of tissue (Hauser, 2002). The degree to which such transplantation will work as an effective cure remains an open question.

• *PARKINSON'S DISEASE* •

As we learned in Chapter 5, patients with Parkinson's disease have a specific cell loss in the substantia nigra, the major source of dopaminergic neurons in the brain, and to a lesser degree in the locus ceruleus. Along with the motor symptoms that accompany the disease, dementia manifests in approximately 30 percent of these individuals (Tison et al., 1995). The cardinal neuropsychological symptoms of Parkinson's disease are a dysfunction of executive processes, slowing in motor and thought processes, and impairment in memory retrieval (but not retention) (see McPherson & Cummings, 1996, for a good review).

Like individuals with Huntington's disease, patients with Parkinson's disease exhibit cognitive dysfunction in the realm of executive function (e.g., Dalrymple, Kalders, Jones, & Watson, 1994). For example, these patients have difficulty with the WCST, not so much because they act in a perseverative manner but because they are not able to think abstractly, being deficient at identifying the categories into which the cards should be sorted. They exhibit deficits in switching between categories, in overriding stereotypic responses, in responding in novel situations, and in developing plans of action (e.g., Henik, Singh, Beckley, & Rafal, 1993) (See Color insert 14.1).

The second area of cognitive compromise exhibited by individuals with Parkinson's disease is the slowing of motor and thought processes known as **bradyphrenia.** Although patients with Parkinson's disease can arrive at a correct answer, they do so slowly, seeming to need to overcome some sort of mental inertia. Such slowing is more likely to occur on tasks requiring planning (e.g., Tower of London) than on simpler tasks. This slowness may influence a variety of mental functions, contributing to poor performance in other domains, such as language and visuospatial functioning. For example, this slowing can reduce the ability to name items and can disrupt articulatory capacities. Some of the slowing of mental and motoric functions may also be exacerbated by the depression that often accompanies the disease.

A third area in which these patients manifest difficulty is in certain aspects of memory, specifically in retrieving information in nonstructured situations and in spatial working memory (Postle et al., 1997). As with Huntington's disease, the ability to plan a strategic search through memory, which is required by recall, is impaired. However, long-term memory for both verbal and visuospatial material appears to be intact when recognition procedures are used (e.g., "Have you seen this item before?"). The pattern of memory functions observed in Parkinson's disease suggests that memory functions dependent on the temporal lobes are spared, whereas memory dependent on the integrity of the frontal lobes is more severely compromised (e.g., memory for recency). Finally, working memory is generally spared in Parkinson's disease, although performance deteriorates if a distracting stimulus intervenes, probably because of difficulties in attentional processes rather than difficulties in working memory (e.g., Pillon, Deweer, Agid, & Dubois, 1993).

In sum, the cognitive deficits exhibited by these individuals involve executive functions, speed of processing (which affects tasks such as word naming, word fluency, and certain visuospatial tasks), and memory tasks that require frontal regions (e.g., estimates of recency and temporal order). Although this profile is consistent with that of a selective impairment in frontal functioning, the pattern observed in patients with Parkinson's disease differs in subtle ways from that of patients with frontal lobe damage. For example, individuals with Parkinson's disease are less likely to perseverate (Owen et al., 1993), to lack insight into their behavior, or to be disinhibited than are patients with frontal lobe damage (Dubois, Boller, Pillon, & Agid, 1991).

Patients with Parkinson's disease also show changes in emotional functioning. Estimates of depression in these patients range from 12 percent to 90 percent with an average of 46 percent. This depression appears to be more linked to the neurobiological substrate of the disease than the disabilities imposed by the illness. Levels of depression in patients with Parkinson's disease are higher than those observed in patients with other debilitating motor impairments, such as paraplegia and hemiplegia. Also, the depression may precede motor symptoms and be uncorrelated with their severity.

Compromise of the dopaminergic system, which is associated with reward, may explain some of the apathy and lack of pleasure associated with depression in these patients. Furthermore, compromise of the serotonergic system may lead to depression. Low concentrations of serotonin have been found in the striatal-pallidal complex, hippocampus, frontal cortex, cingulate cortex, and entorhinal cortex of patients with Parkinson's disease who are depressed. Moreover, the main metabolite of serotonin is found in lower concentrations in the cerebrospinal fluid of depressed than non-depressed Parkinson's patients.

In addition to mood changes, other aspects of emotional function are compromised. One prominent symptom of the disease is the **Parkinsonian mask,** which is an expressionless face. This masklike facial appearance may, in part, reflect a dampening of motor movements because the patients can identify which facial expression should go with an emotional situation and can produce a particular facial expression when asked (although they rarely do so spontaneously). In part, though, it seems to reflect a dampening of emotional responsiveness. The facial expressions and tone of voice of people with Parkinson's disease lack emotional intensity, even in response to pictures with strong affective value.

Parkinson's appears to be caused by a combination of genetic and environmental factors. First-degree relatives of individuals with Parkinson's are between 2 and 10 times more likely to get the disease than individuals with no affected relatives; and siblings are likely to get the disorder at a similar age. From the environmental side, increased risk has been associated with a rural or farming environment, drinking well water, exposure to pesticides or herbicides, head trauma, and exposure to industrial pollutants (Maher et al., 2002). For example, long-term exposure to metals such as manganese, copper, iron, and lead, which are occupational hazards for pipe fitters, electrical workers, engineers, chemists, machinists, firefighters, steam-fitters, and toolmakers, has been linked to neuropsychological disorders such as Parkinson's disease. It is thought that these metals can lead to the generation of free radicals, which, as we discussed earlier, are neurotoxic (Gorell et al., 1997).

The standard treatment for Parkinson's has been to try to offset the dopamine deficiency by giving patients L-dopa, a precursor to dopamine that can cross the blood-brain barrier. This drug can improve at least some of the cognitive deficits associated with Parkinson's by influencing dopamine levels in the prefrontal cortex (e.g., Cools et al., 2002). Unfortunately, it is associated with dyskinesias in about 35 percent of patients, hallucinations in some patients, and there is a loss of drug efficacy over time. Consequently, dopamine agonists are now preferred for early stages of the disorder when they are effective, with L-dopa reserved for later stages when the dopamine agonists are ineffective (Jenner, 2002).

In cases in which the patient becomes resistant to L-dopa and the symptoms are extremely problematic, ablation of the thalamus or the internal portion of the globus pallidus is used, as is deep brain stimulation of these structures via an implanted electrode. Although these procedures are thought to improve motor functioning, controversy exists at present as to whether they have any positive cognitive consequences (Fields & Troster, 2000; Hugdahl & Wester, 2000). Moreover, in some cases, specific negative effects on mental processes have been documented (e.g., Scott et al., 2002). A final therapeutic and very infrequently used approach is fetal transplants into the substantia nigra (see Olanow, Kordower, & Freeman, 1996, for a review). Because the number of individuals who undergo this treatment is so small, it is not yet possible to determine whether it has any positive effects on cognition (Diederich & Goetz, 2000).

■ Mixed-Variety Dementias

Mixed-variety dementias are characterized by a substantial degree of both cortical and subcortical damage, which makes the clinical profile of these disorders an amalgam of the cortical and subcortical dementias. At present, our ability to characterize the constellation of the two main types of mixed-variety dementias, vascular dementia and AIDS dementia, is not as clear-cut as for the other types of dementia we discussed. One reason for this murkiness is that the mixed-variety dementias affect the nervous system in a heterogeneous manner. In vascular dementia, the regions of the circulatory system that fail may vary from person to person. In the case of AIDS dementia, the profile of some aspects of neuropsychological functioning may vary between different groups of individuals (e.g., gay or bisexual men vs. intravenous drug users; e.g., E. M. Martin et al., 1995).

• *VASCULAR (MULTI-INFARCT) DEMENTIA* •

Vascular dementia, which formerly was known as *multi-infarct dementia,* is the second most common form of dementia. It results not from a single stroke, which tends to compromise a specific mental capacity (e.g., speech output), but from the cumulative effects of many small strokes that tend to create both cortical and subcortical lesions. In some cases, the vascular damage is mainly cortical, and in such cases there is a higher frequency of lesions in the frontal lobes than in other lobes of the cortex (e.g., Erkinjuntti, Haltia, Palo, & Paetau, 1988). In other cases, especially with hypertension, lesions occur in the small blood vessels supplying subcortical areas, primarily those that supply the basal ganglia, internal capsule, thalamus, and pons. When the damage is restricted to the subcortical white matter, the dementia is sometimes referred to as *Binswanger's disease* (e.g., Libon, Scanlon, Swenson, & Coslet, 1990).

The presentation of patients with vascular dementia is often similar to that of patients with Alzheimer's disease. Ways to distinguish between the two include the patient's medical history, brain imaging, and neuropsychological testing. Regarding medical history, evidence for a vascular contribution to dementia comes from a long-standing history of arterial hypertension, focal neurological signs (such as weakness of an extremity) that are suggestive of a stroke, and MRI scans revealing specific and multiple infarcts of the cortex in either the white or gray matter. Typically, vascular dementia occurs with a relatively abrupt onset (due to a stroke), is accompanied by a stepwise rather than gradual course (because the effects are compounded by each additional stroke), and is not restricted to an onset in the later years. This pattern contrasts with that observed in Alzheimer's disease, which has an insidious onset, slow progression, an unremittingly downward course, and tends to occur later in life. Finally, because vascular dementia is associated with stroke, the pattern of impairment can fluctuate, being worse initially and then improving. Moreover, treating hypertension may help prevent further progression of the disease, factors that do not characterize or influence Alzheimer's disease (*DSM-IV,* 1994).

In terms of their neuropsychological profile, individuals with vascular dementia usually demonstrate the same type of pattern observed in patients with Alzheimer's disease, except they are more likely to exhibit deficits on tasks relying on frontal lobe function and to display a pattern suggestive of subcortical involvement (e.g., Kertesz & Clydesdale, 1994). For example, patients with vascular dementia and Alzheimer's disease usually perform similarly on tests assessing visuospatial ability, language, and memory, but patients with vascular dementia usually perform more poorly on tests measuring executive function, verbal fluency, and attention, all of which are believed to rely on the frontal lobes (see Almkvist, 1994, for a review). Consistent with the idea of greater subcortical involvement in vascular dementia than in Alzheimer's disease, patients with vascular dementia tend to exhibit slowing of performance on motor tasks and, to a lesser degree, on cognitive tasks in general (Almkvist, Backman, Basun, & Wahlund, 1993).

• *AIDS DEMENTIA* •

AIDS is a viral disease that is passed through the exchange of blood or bodily fluids (mainly contracted during sexual relations between male-female, male-male, and possibly female-female partners) and that acts to devastate the immune system, eventually leading to death. Because no cure exists for the disease, prevention is paramount, requiring the one-time use or bleaching of hypodermic needles, the wearing of latex gloves to protect against contamination by infected blood, the practice of "safe sex," in which a barrier is used to prevent the exchange of bodily fluids, adherence to monogamy with a noninfected partner, or abstinence from any sexual activity that involves the exchange of bodily fluids.

As AIDS ravages the systems of the body, it does so evenhandedly, not sparing the brain. Studies suggest that brain pathology exists in 75–90 percent of all individuals who have died of AIDS. Some of the effects are direct. As soon as a few weeks after infection, HIV can be found in cerebrospinal fluid; therefore, we know that it crosses the blood-brain barrier, although the exact mechanism whereby it does so is not yet clear. Once in the brain, it appears to cause neuronal death, as evidenced by a reduction in the density of neurons, and to destroy oligodendrocytes, leading to a loss of the brain's white matter. Brain imaging studies suggest that AIDS is associated with both cortical atrophy and subcortical damage, especially the white matter and subcortical structures, and in particular the striatum and the thalamus (Navia, Cho, Petito, & Price, 1986). This pattern of regional brain atrophy significantly influences the nature of the neuropsychological disorders that accompany AIDS.

AIDS dementia, which affects 6–30 percent of all adult AIDS patients, almost always occurs in the late stages of the disease when immunosuppression exists and other AIDS-defining illnesses manifest (e.g., Kaposi's sarcoma) (e.g., J. J. Day et al., 1992). As with any dementia, it causes serious declines in cognitive functioning. The most notable consequences are slowing of mental and motor functions, disruptions in concentration and attention, and memory disturbances. In contrast, naming and vocabulary are more likely to be spared. Often, AIDS dementia is also accompanied by changes in affect. Emotionally, individuals tend toward a flattened affect manifesting as apathy, reduced spontaneity, social withdrawal, increased irritability, and emotional lability. Depression is often noted as well. As in patients with Parkinson's and Huntington's disease, the changes in mood for people with AIDS dementia, especially apathy and irritability, appear to be linked to frontal-subcortical dysfunction rather than just being a response to having a terminal illness. These mood changes tend to be associated with deficits in dual-task performance and attentional control in the face of salient distracting information (Castellon, Hinkin, & Myers, 2000). Hence, the profile of neuropsychological dysfunction has components that are observed both in cortical and subcortical dementias. The progression of the dementia is variable, and at present no good predictors of its course are known (e.g., Maj, 1990; Navia, Jordan, & Price, 1986).

The effects of AIDS on neuropsychological function may not be limited to cases in which it causes dementia. Because the HIV virus affects the brain so early in the course of the disease, much research has focused on trying to determine whether asymptomatic individuals who are infected with HIV exhibit any neuropsychological impairment. These studies have revealed that the greater the degree of immunological compromise, the greater the neuropsychological impairment.

The rates of impairment for asymptomatic individuals who are seropositive but asymptomatic are about three times higher than those for individuals who were seronegative (i.e., 35 percent vs. 12 percent) (White, Heaton, Monsch, & the HNRC Group, 1995). Tests on which asymptomatic individuals who are seropositive are likely to perform poorly include those requiring speeded psychomotor or mental functioning and those that require new learning (e.g., R. A. Bornstein et al., 1993; Heaton et al., 1995). At the symptomatic stage, a 44 percent rate of impairment in mildly symptomatic individuals (Class B) and a 56 percent rate in the AIDS group (Class C) have been reported (Heaton et al., 1995). These data have implications for everyday functioning, as those individuals who have some neuropsychological impairment are more likely to have difficulty in performing their job (Heaton et al., 1996) and to be involved in motor vehicle accidents, as indicated by results of driving-simulation tasks (Marcotte et al., 1997). The rates of neuropsychological compromise are even higher in children, with 75–90 percent exhibiting neuropsychological deficits (Levenson & Mellins, 1992).

As the disease progresses, measures of frontal lobe function (e.g., perseverative errors on the WCST, verbal fluency) are more likely to be impaired (e.g., R. A. Bornstein et al., 1993; Heaton et al., 1995). These frontal impairments are accompanied by a lack of insight into the degree of cognitive compromise (Rourke, Halman, & Bassel, 1999). The findings among asymptomatic and symptomatic individuals suggest that the early neuropsychological manifestations of HIV infection reflect compromise of subcortical structures and that the later stages of the disease affect frontal and frontal-striatal regions.

Although at one point there was little or nothing that could be done for individuals with AIDS, a variety of drug therapies have emerged. One of the first was zidovudine (AZT). This drug seems to have little long-term effect in ameliorating the cognitive decline associated with the disorder (Llorente et al., 2001). Recently, highly active antiretroviral therapy (HAART) has been used to restore immune function. These drugs seem to substantially elongate the time from diagnosis to that at which neuropsychological impairment is observed. For example, before the introduction of highly active antiretroviral therapy, half of all individuals exhibited neuropsychological impairment within a year and a half from diagnosis. In contrast, three years from diagnosis, only 20 percent of individuals on retroviral drugs are exhibiting neuropsychological impairment (Deutsch et al., 2001). In some cases these antiviral drugs actually can improve performance. In one study, neuronal damage (measured by *N*-acetyl-aspartate) was found to decrease, especially in frontal regions and the subcortical areas to which they connect, along with a concomitant increase in cognitive performance of individuals who had previously been assessed as being cognitively impaired (Stankoff et al., 2001) (for a good short review of the neurological and neuropsychological effects of HIV, see Grant et al., 1999).

Demyelinating Diseases

One of the most common neurological diseases of nontraumatic origin that compromises the neuropsychological functioning of young and middle-age adults is **multiple sclerosis (MS),** so named because it is characterized by multiple discrete areas, ranging in size from 1 mm to several centimeters, in which neurons have a complete absence of myelin. In addition to the lack of myelin, there is inflammation of neurons as well as neuronal degeneration. It has been speculated that this axonal injury helps to contribute to irreversible neurological damage, as neurons seem to be able to adapt somewhat to the lack of myelin to keep neuronal transmission intact. The destruction of myelin in MS is thought to result from an immunological disruption in which the body incorrectly identifies part of its own system as a foreign agent or invader and attacks it (i.e., an autoimmune disorder). Such demyelinated areas interfere or block neural transmission and cause symptoms specific to the location of these areas. Although the sites affected tend to be diffuse and multifocal, certain sites, such as those in the periventricular (*peri,* "near"; *ventricular,* "having to do with the ventricles") regions tend to be more affected.

MS occurs in approximately 85 of every 100,000 individuals, affecting women about twice as often as men (Noonan, Kathman, & White, 2002). Its etiology is unknown, although evidence suggests both an environmental and a genetic contribution. In general, MS is linked to geographical locale; it is much less prevalent near the equator and more prevalent as you move geographically toward the poles. Individuals who change their geographical location after the age of 15 years retain the risk rate associated with their birthplace, which has led some researchers to suggest that the causative agent may be a slow virus that is more common in temperate and colder locales (Kurtzke, 1980). A genetic risk for the disease is suggested by findings that one in five patients with MS have a family member with the disease and that a higher concordance rate (20–30 percent) occurs in monozygotic twins (who share identical genetic material) than in dizygotic twins (2–5 percent) (who have only half their genetic endowment in common). Furthermore, researchers have found similarities among individuals with MS with regard to genes that influence the immunologic response of the body, most notably the human lymphocyte antigen (HLA) gene on the short arm of chromosome 6. The genetic risk factor appears to be independent of the environmental factor because, for example, the incidence rate among the Japanese is low regardless of whether they live in Japan, Hawaii, or the Pacific Coast of the United States (R. Martin & McFarland, 1993).

Because of the diffuse nature of the lesions in MS and the variability of their location, MS has multiple manifestations. Initially, it tends to manifest as weakness in the extremities or as difficulty in some aspect of sensory processing. These sensory and motor tracts are often myelinated because information must travel long distances from the peripheral receptor to the brain or from the brain to the muscle. Thus, it is not surprising that they are affected considering that MS selectively disrupts white-matter tracts. For the individual, the first manifestations of the disease can be petrifying. Common initial symptoms include a blurring or loss of vision, persistent tingling or numbness of a body part, weakness of a body part, or difficulty in coordination. Unlike many of the other syndromes we have discussed in this chapter, the course of MS is highly variable. A person can have an acute flare-up that results in a hemianopsia, only to have the hemianopsia dissipate and remit. But then a subsequent attack could leave the person with a permanent visual loss. Because MS usually affects individuals in the prime of their lives and its progression is highly unpredictable, the disease is extremely stressful for those who have it, as well as for their families. An individual never knows whether he or she will have the next attack 20 years later or if a series of exacerbations will lead to permanent blindness or paralysis in the near future.

Some individuals with MS exhibit little if any cognitive disability, whereas others show clear cognitive compromise. Researchers have estimated that cognitive deficits occur in 40–60 percent of all MS patients (e.g., S. M. Rao, Leo, Bernardin, & Unverzagt, 1991). When cognitive difficulties do occur, they tend to be variable and not affect as large a range of function as observed in patients with dementia. If a typical pattern of cognitive disability exists in MS, it involves difficulty in memory and conceptual reasoning along with a general sparing of knowledge systems. On memory tasks, individuals with MS have difficulty recalling information but display good recognition memory, which suggests an impairment of memory search patterns. Consistent with such an interpretation, they also tend to have difficulty in verbal fluency, which also requires an atypical search through memory. In terms of conceptual skills, patients with MS have difficulty on the types of tasks that require abstraction. They may also exhibit deficits on visuospatial tasks. However, many of these tasks rely on either speeded performance or manual dexterity. Hence, the clinician may have difficulty disentangling the degree to which such deficits result from peripheral sensory and motoric consequences of MS and the degree to which they arise from more cognitively based difficulties. The pattern of neuropsychological difficulties and the affinity of the disease for periventricular white matter suggest a disruption of processing involving both subcortical structures (such as the thalamus and the basal ganglia) and the cortex, mainly the frontal lobes (S. Rao, 1986), as well as the connections between these regions.

The cognitive changes in MS are usually accompanied by changes in mood and personality. The most common disorder in MS is depression, occurring in 30 to 60 percent of all affected individuals (Aikens, Fischer, Namey, & Rudick, 1997). These mood changes are difficult to interpret because they could be normal reactions to having a lifelong debilitating disease, as patients with MS have a normal life expectancy, or they could reflect the fatigue that is often associated with the disorder. They also may, in part, reflect some of the organic changes that accompany the disease, although no clear connection has yet been found (see S. M. Rao, Huber, & Bornstein, 1992, for a review).

With the advent of magnetic resonance imaging (MRI), which allows fine resolution between white and gray matter, research has been directed at attempting to determine whether the pattern and degree of white-matter destruction in MS can be linked to specific patterns of cognitive disabilities. If such correlations exist, they could be of great prognostic value. Unfortunately, at present no clear-cut relationships have emerged (Rovaris & Filippi, 2000). Not surprisingly, however, a relationship has been found between the total amount of brain tissue affected and the degree of cognitive decline, especially on memory tests and tasks of abstract or conceptual reasoning. Another notable finding is that the size of the corpus callosum predicts declines on tasks that involve quick processing speed and attention (e.g., mental arithmetic). This finding may result either because rapid problem solving requires quick integration among brain regions, which is compromised by demyelination (S. M. Rao et al., 1989), or because the corpus callosum plays an important role in attentional functioning (e.g., Banich, 1998).

No cure exists yet for MS. Traditionally, drugs were given to reduce the severity of the disease or the associated symptoms. For example, drugs were given to suppress the immune system and reduce tissue inflammation. Drugs of this nature are ACTH (adrenocorticotropic hormone), which both modulates immunological function and has anti-inflammatory properties, and methylprednisolone administered intravenously. Neither drug, however, changes the long-term course of the disease. Both can be used in conjunction with other drugs such as antidepressants, to treat specific symptoms.

A recent and very promising therapy that has just undergone large-scale clinical trials is interferon beta-1b. Interferons are proteins produced by the body that have antiviral characteristics and modulate the immune response (you may have heard of them in regard to treating patients with cancer). Unlike other therapies, which just stay the course of the disease, interferon appears to actually reduce exacerbations of the disease (Jacobs, Munschauer, & Pullicino, 1993). Over a period of a year or more, interferon beta-1b was found to have a beneficial effect on cognitive performance for individuals with a relapsing-remitting, rather than continually progressive, form of MS. In particular, it was found to aid visual memory, learning, memory, problem solving, and complex attentional control, skills that tend to decline over a similar time period in individuals that do not receive such medication (Barak & Achiron, 2000; Fischer et al., 2000).

Brain Syndromes Resulting from Substance Abuse and Exposure to Toxins

In the preceding sections we have discussed generalized neuropsychological disorders that occur as a result of a specific disease. Yet there are many substances to which we are exposed, either where we work or where we live, or that we ingest voluntarily that can have harmful effects on mental functions. We now discuss some of these agents and outline their neuropsychological effects.

Substance Abuse

A variety of substances that individuals abuse can have neuropsychological consequences. Getting a clear picture of the deficits associated with a particular substance can be difficult for various reasons. First, these substances have both acute effects, which occur during or soon after exposure, and cumulative effects, which accrue with prolonged abuse. The contribution of each is difficult to tease apart. Typically, researchers try to determine a substance's long-term effects by testing abusers only after they go through a detoxification program for two to three weeks, which is a time period considered adequate to preclude the possibility of acute effects. Second, individuals often abuse more than one substance, so obtaining a clear picture of the effect of a particular drug is difficult. Third, substance abuse may be associated with other variables that can adversely affect neuropsychological function and may either precede or exist concomitantly with the substance abuse, such as a history of childhood learning disabilities (e.g., Tarter & Alterman, 1984). Fourth, although researchers try to control for such variables, obtaining a sample of substance abusers and control individuals who are matched with regard to all the relevant factors is often impossible. All these difficulties are worth mentioning because, as we learn in a moment, discrepancies in results can sometimes be found across studies. Nonetheless, clear evidence indicates that the abuse of certain substances can have deleterious effects on neuropsychological functioning.

One of the most widely abused substances in the world is alcohol. The number of cases of alcoholism in the United States alone is estimated at 9 million. The approximate cost of this alcohol abuse, including costs from hospitalization, institutionalization, motor vehicle crashes, and crime, is $85.8 billion (Rice, Kelman, & Miller, 1991). Generally, patients with chronic alcoholism exhibit a profile of cognitive deficits that includes difficulties in learning, memory, and executive functioning along with deficits in visuospatial functioning. Overall functioning tends to be not much compromised, with, for example, little decrease in overall IQ.

Patients with chronic alcoholism exhibit deficits on tests of executive functioning that are compromised by frontal lobe damage and concomitantly exhibit decreased cerebral metabolism in these regions. For example, they do poorly on the WCST, and have difficulty switching between categories, such as on Part B of the Trail Making Test (responding by connecting A to 1 to B to 2, etc.). Their memory problems manifest as subtle deficits on tasks such as the serial list-learning tasks, paired-associate learning tasks, and immediate and delayed recall tests (e.g., Errico, Parsons, & King, 1991; Parsons, Butters, & Nathan, 1987). Difficulties in spatial processing tend to be exhibited on tasks such as the Block Design subtest of the WAIS-III and tests in which spatial information must be disembedded from the context in which it appears, as shown in

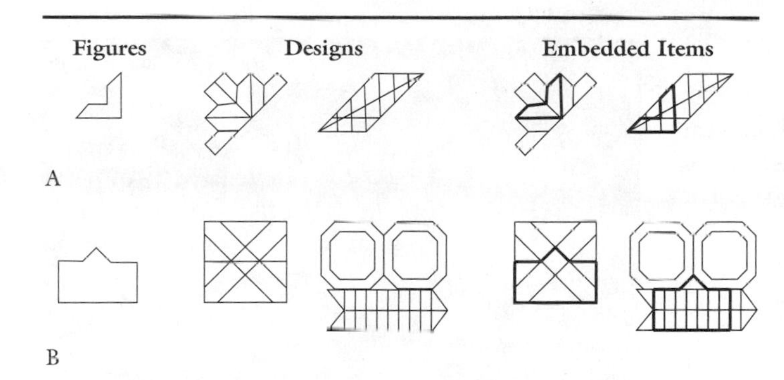

FIGURE 14.9 Example of a visuospatial task that can be compromised by long-term alcohol abuse. Shown here are two sample items from the Embedded Figures Test. The object of the test is to find the small figure that is embedded within the larger one.

Figure 14.9 (for a review of neuropsychological deficits associated with alcoholism, see Rourke & Lørberg, 1996).

Although less research has been directed toward the neuropsychological deficits associated with the use of other drugs, other agents also have been found to have negative neuropsychological consequences. For instance, marijuana has acute effects 12 to 24 hours after use, including decrements in attention, short-term memory, and psychomotor skills. Although some research suggests attentional problems in long-term users of marijuana (e.g., Page, Fletcher, & True, 1988), debate continues as to whether long-term use is associated with significant neuropsychological deficits (for a review, see Pope, Gruber, & Yurgelun-Todd, 1995).

Other drugs are associated with more clear-cut long-term deficits. For example, difficulties in temporal aspects of visual processing and increased visual sensitivity have been found to remain two to three years after the use of LSD (Abraham & Wolf, 1988), and individuals followed up four to six years after being treated for abuse of sedative or hypnotic agents, although improved, still exhibit neuropsychological deficits (Bergman, Borg, Engelbrekston, & Viker, 1989). Like chronic alcoholic abuse, chronic cocaine abuse has been associated with difficulties in attention and memory (e.g., O'Malley, Adamse, Heaton, & Gawin, 1992). Conceptual flexibility, abstracting abilities, visuospatial skills, and psychomotor performance may also be affected.

Another drug that is beginning to be abused in large amounts is (±) 3,4-methylenedioxymethamphetamine (MDMA), more commonly known as *"ecstasy."* In animals, this substance has been shown to be toxic to serotonergic neurons; therefore, research has examined whether similar effects are associated with its use in humans. As we have learned previously, the serotonergic system is associated with mood, memory, and attentional control. Evidence suggests that ecstasy depletes serotonin, leading to alterations in affect, depressed mood, elevated anxiety, increased impulsivity and hostility. Cognitive declines are observed in the areas of memory, working memory, and attention. For example, heavy users of ecstasy (those who have used it an average of 200 times during their life) show significant declines on a variety of memory tasks, including those that measure verbal and spatial memory as well as working and long-term memory. Even moderate users (those who have used it an average of 70 times during their life) show evidence of memory impairment, most specifically with nonverbal material. In addition, these individuals show evidence of compromise of the serotonergic system (Verkes et al., 2001). Although still tentative, after six months of abstinence these cognitive effects may dissipate, whereas the mood changes may take a year to diminish (for a good review, see Morgan, 2000).

Not surprisingly, individuals who abuse multiple substances show more impairments than individuals who abuse just one, especially in the areas of short-term memory, long-term memory, and visuospatial abilities (e.g., Selby & Azrin, 1998). It should be noted that, however paradoxical it may seem, there have been some reports that certain substances abused in tandem result in *fewer* neuropsychological deficits than when a substance is abused alone. Two such examples are the combination of alcohol and marijuana as compared to alcohol alone (Nixon, 1999), and cocaine and alcohol as compared to cocaine alone (Robinson, Heaton, & O'Malley, 1999). The reasons for these findings are not clear but may depend on the way the substances interact.

For example, cocaine and alcohol may have opposite effects on the vascular system.

Currently, much effort has been directed at trying to determine whether the neuropsychological impairments associated with substance abuse can be reversed by abstinence. The findings are mixed. For example, neuropsychological performance can be within normal limits for alcoholics who refrain from drinking if they are relatively young (ages 18–35 years) and had a drinking problem of relatively short duration (e.g., 6 years as opposed to 30) (Eckardt et al., 1995). Such findings offer hope that early intervention and treatment that enable the individual to cease drinking can stave off long-lasting deleterious effects. Yet other studies do not provide evidence of such recovery (e.g., Beatty, Katzung, Moreland, & Nixon, 1995).

Similarly, rcsearchers debate whether abstinence reduces deficits in memory and concentration in persons who abuse cocaine. Some findings indicate that deficits remain (e.g., Berry et al., 1993), whereas other findings provide some evidence of recovery of function (e.g., Azrin, Millsaps, Burton, & Mittenberg, 1992). The discrepancies among studies may arise because of differences in the premorbid status of particular samples (e.g., IQ and educational background, history of depression or attention-deficit hyperactivity disorder, family history of substance abuse) as well as their current status (e.g., age and amount of time abstinent).

Although many substances of abuse, such as cocaine and alcohol, are thought to induce generalized brain dysfunction, there is some evidence that their effects may differentially influence frontal-limbic areas. For example, alcoholics exhibit reductions in cerebral blood flow to these areas for as long as four months after abstinence (e.g., Volkow et al., 1992) (for an overview of the neuropsychological effects of substance abuse, see Carlin & O'Malley, 1996). Correlations of behavior, morphology, and brain activation reveal that dysfunction in chronic alcoholics is most related to dorsolateral and medial regions of the frontal lobe (see Figure 14.10). For example, poor performance on attentional tasks, such as the Stroop task, and the inability to guide behavior in novel ways, as assessed by verbal fluency, is associated with a lack of activation of these frontal areas (Dao-Castellana et al., 1998).

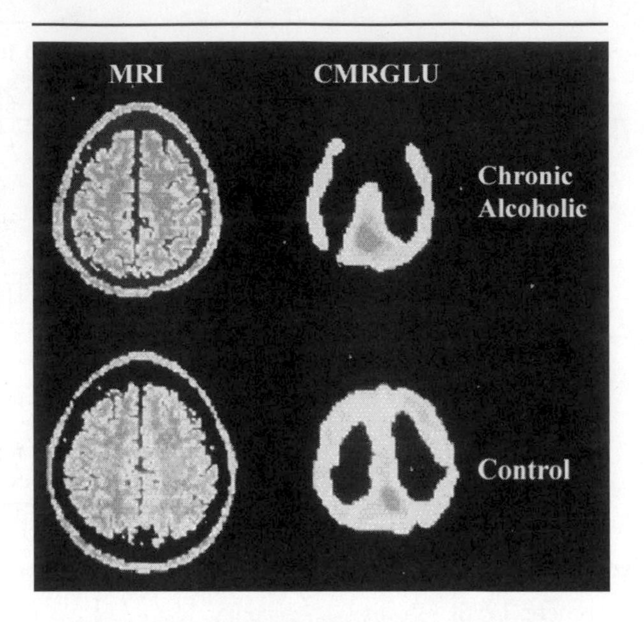

FIGURE 14.10 Changes in brain metabolism in alcoholics. Notice that although the alcoholic individual shows relatively little brain atrophy on the MRI scan relative to the control individual (left), there is a clear reduction in brain activation in frontal areas as measured by PET (right). CMRGLU = Cerebral metabolic rate of glucose.

One reason that frontal regions may be differentially affected in substance abuse is that these regions have receptors for dopamine, which as we learned earlier, is important for reward. Certain models of addiction assume that this reward system can be "hijacked," either by a substance of abuse or by some other stimulus, such as would occur in compulsive gambling. Certain individuals may be genetically predisposed to such hijacking, as certain alleles of genes that code for the expression of dopaminergic receptors have been found to be linked to substance abuse (for a short review, see Duaux, Krebs, Loo, & Poirier, 2000).

Given the prominent role that frontal regions play in substance abuse, it follows that executive functions are often compromised. This connection may explain in part the cycle of addiction. For example, individuals who abuse substances will have impaired ability to realize the consequences of their actions, such as understanding that having another drink will lead them to act aggressively or will impair their ability to drive. These actions may lead to fights or vehicular accidents that will cause head injury, further compromising executive abilities (e.g., Solomon & Malloy, 1992).

In addition, some researchers have suggested that the effects can go in the opposite direction—that is, individuals with poor executive skills are at risk for substance abuse (e.g., Giancola & Tarter, 1999). Thus, the effects can be mutually reinforcing: poor executive skills can lead to substance abuse, which in turn can further compromise the executive control that would be needed to break out of the cycle of addiction.

Toxins

Toxins are substances that have the ability to destroy neural tissue; hence they are another means by which the brain can incur nonspecific damage. Toxins take various forms, but in this section we focus our discussion on the neurotoxic effects and neuropsychological consequences of metals, organic solvents, and pesticides. Exposure to these materials can take place in a variety of settings but usually occurs in the workplace. Consequently, exposure to toxins is an occupational hazard for 20 million workers in the United States alone and a substantial number of individuals in other countries.

• *METALS* •

Many heavy metals (known as such because of their atomic weight) have been found to be toxic. Probably the best known of these is lead, because its effect on mental function has historical significance. Drinking from lead vessels may have led to the deranged behavior of certain Roman emperors. Our exposure to lead continues today with smelting and steel plants, battery-reprocessing plants, and the continued use of leaded gasoline in some countries.

Lead has damaging effects on both cognitive and emotional functioning that vary with the degree of exposure. These effects may be observed after only a few weeks or a few months of exposure. At low levels of exposure, emotional or nonspecific complaints are most common. These include fatigue, depression, and apathy. At higher levels of exposure, more specific neuropsychological complaints are manifest. These tend to center around difficulties in memory, visuospatial abilities, and visuomotor functions. In addition, reductions in psychomotor speed and manual dexterity are noted. Severe exposure is associated with increased memory deficits as well as deficits in attention, concentration, and abstract thought, along with complaints of depression, anger, and tension. Also, with extreme exposure, dementia can result (Hartman, 1987). Although removing an individual from an environment in which he or she is exposed to lead (such as a foundry) can reduce the emotional symptoms for about one-fifth to one-third of the individuals, performance on memory and psychomotor tasks does not improve (E. L. Baker, White, & Murawski, 1985).

Lead poisoning in children has received much attention because it leads to mental retardation and can easily occur when children eat paint chips in older buildings, which contain as much as 50 percent lead. Even when the level of lead in a child's blood is below that considered toxic, she or he will show significant slowing in reaction time, and the higher the lead level, the more severe the dysfunction. Children with high levels of lead have been found to exhibit difficulties in a wide variety of domains, including problem solving, perceptual-motor tasks, visuomotor tasks, and visuospatial tasks. These children also exhibit depressed performance on subtests of the Wechsler Intelligence Scale for Children (WISC) that are highly correlated with overall IQ, such as the Information, Comprehension, and Vocabulary subtests, and may exhibit hyperactivity.

Clearly, not every child will show all these symptoms, but the evidence suggests that lead toxicity can compromise intellectual functioning in many ways. Because lead exposure in children is associated with certain living conditions (e.g., living in an older building), which in turn may be associated with other factors that have injurious effects on neuropsychological function (e.g., poor socioeconomic status, an impoverished environment), researchers have been careful to evaluate the effects of lead independent of these other factors. Even when such factors are considered, exposure to lead appears to cause cognitive decline (Hartman, 1987).

HOW TO DETECT MALINGERING

As we learned in this chapter, a number of nonspecific cognitive disorders, including mild head injury, exposure to organic solvents, and sports-related injury, can present signs that are vague and diffuse (e.g., amorphous difficulties in memory and concentration). Such symptoms can sometimes impede the clinical neuropsychologist's ability to determine the consequences of these injuries, especially when she or he must do so for legal purposes. For example, closed head injury may be a consequence of an automobile accident in which a driver is being sued for negligence, or exposure to toxic substances at work may lead a person to sue for disability insurance. How is a neuropsychologist to distinguish between the individual who has a legitimate disability and one who is faking it?

The exaggeration or creation of symptoms for personal gain, either for money or to avoid responsibility for personal actions, is referred to as **malingering.** An important point about malingering is that the perpetrator's symptoms disappear when having them is no longer advantageous. You may have been a malingerer on occasion yourself. For example, to avoid going to elementary school one day you may have presented with all the symptoms of a severe stomachache only to have them miraculously disappear when the other children came home from school and it was time to go out and play.

Neuropsychologists generally have a number of ways to detect the presence of malingering, the most prominent of which is based on the analysis of the response pattern that an individual exhibits on standard tests of mental function. Malingerers act the way that they *think* they should act given their complaints. However, because they generally do not know much about neuropsychology, their common wisdom generates a profile of impairment that is at odds with that which is typically observed.

Some general telltale signs can alert the clinical neuropsychologist to the fact that he or she is dealing with a malingerer (for an example case study, see Orsini, Van Gorp, & Boone, 1988). One of the most obvious signs is a pattern of performance that is grossly inconsistent across situations. One suspicious pattern would be an inability to remember one's age, location of birth, or degree of schooling, but a good memory for the accident for which compensation is desired. Another example would be a sharp mismatch between the person's test performance and performance in everyday life. For example, a red flag should be raised by the case of a person who does extremely poorly on tests of executive function and spatial abilities but manages to take the bus to the hospital for neuropsychological testing without any problems. Another tip-off that an individual is malingering is a systematic pattern of incorrect responses—for example, answers to mental arithmetic problems that are always off by a certain number (e.g., the answer is always one number greater than the true answer), or puzzles that are always solved correctly except for one item.

Yet another clue to malingering is a pattern that is highly atypical from a neuropsychological perspective. One example would be poorer performance on tests of recognition memory than on tests of recall.

• *ORGANIC SOLVENTS* •

Organic solvents are toxic materials derived from naturally occurring substances. Individuals are exposed to them in the workplace (as in the case of carbon disulfide or carbon monoxide) or voluntarily abuse them, as in the case of toluene, which is the solvent found in glue and in cans of spray paint. Exposure to organic solvents tends to have large effects on the motor system, affecting the cerebellum, cranial nerves, and pyramidal motor system. Signs indicative of cerebellar compromise include disturbances in gait, poor control over the vocal apparatus, eye flutter, hearing loss, and poor arm coordination.

As with other toxic substances, deficits in processing appear to be related to the level of exposure. At low levels, individuals complain of fatigue, irritability, depression, and anxiety, as in the case of heavy metals. Few if any deficits are observed on standard neuropsychological tests. With higher levels of exposure, changes in mood, personality, and impulse control are found, along with intellectual deficits in memory, learning, concentration, and psychomotor functions. The most severe exposure, more commonly reported with substance abuse rather than exposure in the workplace, leads to pervasive neuropsychological dysfunction and dementia (Hartman, 1987).

As we know from our discussion of memory disorders and generalized cognitive disorders, recall is usually worse than recognition, or in the case of cortical dementia, they are equally affected. Another example would be an inability to count to 10 or to recite the days of the week, which can be preserved even in patients with severe dementia. Still another atypical pattern is one of relatively mild injury (e.g., mild head injury) with complaints of symptoms whose onset is some time after the injury and whose duration is longer than would be expected. In fact, it has been found that late-onset symptoms are disproportionately found among individuals seeking some sort of compensation (Binder & Rohling, 1996).

Unless someone is showing an obvious sign of malingering it may be hard to detect his or her duplicity just by examining the pattern of performance across neuropsychological tests (e.g., McKinzey & Russell, 1997; vanGorp et al., 1999). Thus, when faced with a potential malingerer, neuropsychologists adopt particular indices or administer tests specifically designed to detect malingering. One approach is to examine performance on a series of items that even the most compromised individuals answer correctly, such as is used by the rarely missed index for the Wecshler Memory Scale-III (e.g., Killgore & DellaPietra, 2000). A variation on this theme is to examine whether the individual is performing below chance on a forced-choice memory task. Let's say that a person is given a test with three possible answers for each question. If the person has serious memory impairment, she or he should perform at chance (which would be 33 percent). However, if performance is significantly below chance (only 5-10 percent of the questions answered correctly), it indicates a deliberate selection of the incorrect answer.

Another way to detect malingering is to make the task seem difficult when in actuality it is very easy. For example, in one such test, a person is given a series of 15 items and told to memorize them. The examiner emphasizes that 15 items far exceed the normal memory span. However, the items can be easily categorized into five conceptual groups of three (e.g., 1 2 3; a b c), which should make the list relatively easy to learn. Thus, if the individual being tested has an inability to recall at least three groups of items, she or he is likely to be malingering. Another test involves presenting individuals with five-digit numbers, and after a 5, 10 or 15-second delay, asking the individual which one of two five-digit numbers was the one previously viewed. As the incorrect answer always begins and ends with a different number than the correct answer, the test is relatively simple (Hiscock & Hiscock, 1989). If the person performs below chance, he or she is likely to be malingering.

Because malingering represents a particular level of cognitive sophistication, including strategy formation and goal-directed behavior, the individual's neuropsychological functioning cannot be very compromised. Nonetheless, the ability to malinger does not preclude the possibility that the individual does indeed have some disability. It is useful for the clinical neuropsychologist to emphasize to the individual being tested that honest cooperation is likely to prove a better approach than deception because neuropsychological testing can provide exactly the type of information that would bolster a legitimate claim. ■

When exposure to an organic solvent in the workplace ceases, about half of the exposed individuals show improvements in neuropsychological performance. However, half remain at the same level of functioning or show deterioration. The distinguishing factor between these two groups is not their level of neuropsychological functioning prior to removal from the hazardous environment, but rather whether they had a brief but intense peak exposure to the solvent that required treatment or hospitalization. Such exposure is associated with poorer performance (L. A. Morrow, Ryan, Hodgson, & Robin, 1991).

• *PESTICIDES* •

The use of pesticides is commonplace in farming and agriculture, and 2 to 5 million workers in the United States are exposed to pesticides each year. Of these individuals, about 1,200 experience acute pesticide poisoning annually. Yet the effects of pesticides are not limited to farmers or even home gardeners. Many people are unknowingly being exposed to high levels of pesticides because these substances are seeping into the groundwater supply that provides drinking water for agricultural communities. Exposure to these agents is also a concern in many developing countries where pesticides outlawed in the West are routinely sold.

Because pesticides are clearly designed to be deadly to certain life forms, such as insects, the fact that they can have negative effects on humans is not surprising. One particularly large class of pesticides, organophosphates, is derived from the highly toxic nerve gases developed during World War II. Pesticides differ from these nerve gases mainly in potency and function. Many of the organophosphate pesticides are lipid soluble, meaning that, like alcohol, they can dissolve fats. This characteristic allows them to be easily absorbed through the skin, eyes, and respiratory tract. Generally, they have toxic effects by inhibiting acetylcholinesterase, which results in a buildup of acetylcholine in the synapse. With exposure to large amounts of these pesticides, a person can die. Other pesticides, such as fungicides, contain manganese, which is toxic because it interferes with catecholamine metabolism in the central nervous system.

Various cognitive dysfunctions are associated with an acute episode of overexposure to pesticides, including reduced concentration, slowing of psychomotor function, memory problems, and language disturbances. Emotional changes, such as depression, anxiety, irritability, and personality changes have also been reported. Bodily symptoms include headaches, dizziness, stomach problems, cardiorespiratory problems, weakness, and weight loss. These symptoms may continue for as long as 11 years following pesticide exposure. Furthermore, they can be observed even when levels of acetylcholinesterase in the blood are within normal limits (Reidy, Bowler, Rauch, & Pedroza, 1992). Pesticides other than organophosphates, such as dichlorodiphenyltrichloroethane (DDT), have also been associated with neuropsychological decline, especially on tasks that measure attentional control and sequencing abilities (de Joode et al., 2001).

There currently is some debate as to whether long-term chronic exposure to organophosphates without an acute episode of poisoning leads to much neuropsychological dysfunction beyond a general slowing in reaction time (Fiedler, Kipen, Kelly-McNeil, and Fenske, 1997). Some researchers have argued that their effects may be manifest in more subtle ways such as premature aging or a compromised ability of the nervous system to handle additional toxic challenges that occur with aging (Weiss, 2000). Furthermore, individuals who do not experience the negative neuropsychological consequences of an acute attack of poisoning may not realize that long-term exposure to these substances can adversely affect them, as there is little relationship between the neuropsychological effects of acute and long-term exposure to organophosphates (Stephens, Spurgeon, & Berry, 1996).

• *OTHER SUBSTANCES* •

So far we have discussed metals, organic solvents, and pesticides, which are toxins that individuals either abuse or are exposed to during employment. However, sometimes people voluntarily take toxins for legitimate (rather than abusive) reasons. For example, lithium carbonate, a metal, is considered the drug of choice in treating manic-depression. Nonetheless, at high levels lithium is toxic and can lead to disintegration of neuropsychological function. Likewise, popular minor tranquilizers such as Valium, which comes from a family of medications known as benzodiazepines (named after their chemical structure), steroids, and drugs used to fight cancer, have all been shown to have neuropsychological sequelae. For example, tranquilizers affect short-term memory and learning, and steroid use (popularized by athletes) leads to declines in cognitive performance. Thus, the neuropsychologist must know not only an individual's occupational history, but also his or her current medical status to determine whether declines in cognitive functioning might be caused by either toxins or drugs.

Epilepsy

Throughout much of history, epilepsy has had a negative connotation; epileptic seizures have been referred to as "fits," and individuals with epilepsy have been stigmatized. We now know that such characterizations are unfair and that the disease is indicative of a neurological problem that does not reflect on the person's character. Epilepsy is a disease in which seizure activity is recurrent but intermittent. **Epileptic seizures** are episodes in which synchronous activity of nerve cells increases so that a gigantic hyperpolarization of neurons spreads over a large area in an atypical and abnormal manner. On

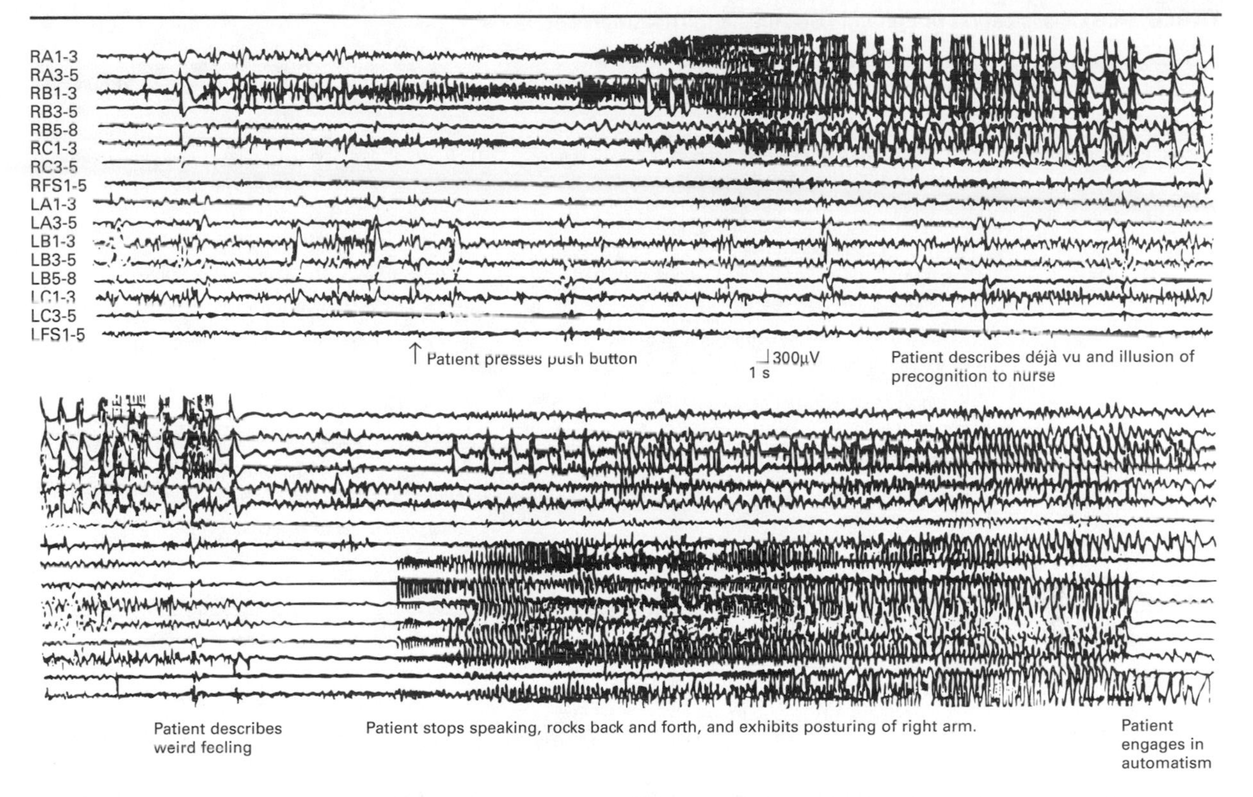

FIGURE 14.11 Spiking of electrical brain activity that typically accompanies epileptic seizure. Reproduced here are recordings from eight electrodes over each hemisphere (R, right hemisphere; L, left hemisphere). The behavioral manifestations of the seizure are listed below the recordings. The spiking activity can be seen most prominently over the right hemisphere soon after the beginning of the seizure, but it manifests over the left hemisphere only when the patient stops speaking and begins to rock back and forth.

the EEG record these gigantic hyperpolarizations are seen as "spikes," as shown in Figure 14.11. Seizures for which a cause is known are termed *symptomatic.* Typical causes include head trauma, metabolic disorders, infection, toxins, and tumors. For example, approximately 20 percent of all individuals who sustain a penetrating brain injury develop epilepsy. This "silent interval" between a central nervous system insult, such as infection or trauma, and the first appearance of seizures, which can be years, suggests that the imbalance leading to seizure activity builds over time. (See Dalmady-Israel & Zasler, 1993, for a review of issues related to posttraumatic seizures.) Seizures that occur for no apparent reason are known as *idiopathic.*

Seizures come in many varieties, but are divided into two major classes. One major class is *generalized seizures,* so called because they involve the entire body. The second class is *focal seizures,* in which the activity starts in a particular region of the brain and then spreads. During seizure activity, consciousness is disturbed. The major types of seizures, along with their motoric effects and usual changes in consciousness, are outlined in Table 14.6.

Epileptic seizures can be triggered by a variety of stimuli, with the agent most likely to evoke a seizure varying from individual to individual. It often takes an affected individual some time to determine exactly what the exacerbating stimulus is. Once identified, the individual will try to avoid the situation or stimulus that leads to a seizure. Stressful situations, especially those induced by sleep deprivation, can lead to seizure activity. In fact, so potent is sleep deprivation in bringing on seizure

TABLE 14.6 Classification of Epileptic Seizures and Their Manifestations

TYPE OF SEIZURE	MOTOR MANIFESTATIONS	CHANGES IN CONSCIOUSNESS
Generalized seizures		
Grand mal (tonic-clonic)	1. *Tonic phase:* The person shouts or makes a loud noise and falls. Then the person exhibits upward or sideways turning of the eyes and tonic tension of the muscles in which the whole body stiffens and breathing stops.	1. *Tonic phase:* The person loses conscious control of movement and loses consciousness.
	2. *Clonic phase:* Rhythmic jerking of body parts begins and continues for minutes.	2. *Clonic phase:* Disorientation or comatose behavior is exhibited following clonic motor activity.
Clonic	Same as clonic phase of grand mal seizures described above.	Same as clonic phase of grand mal seizures described above.
Tonic	Same as tonic phase of grand mal seizures described above.	Same as tonic phase of grand mal seizures described above.
Petit mal	A slight movement of the eyes or turning of the head can be observed.	A brief change in consciousness occurs, which is often overlooked by untrained individuals. The person seems to "space out" briefly (i.e., is unresponsive for about 10 seconds).
Focal seizures		
Jacksonian (originate in a specific region of the motor strip but sometimes in other regions such as the somatosensory strip)	The seizure starts as a clonic movement of one specific body part. The seizure spreads in an orderly progression down the motor strip to neighboring regions, involving more and more body parts; this progression is known as a Jacksonian march.	Little impairment of consciousness occurs.
Complex partial seizures (originate in the temporal or frontal lobe)	*During seizures:* The person engages in automatisms—repetitive motions including buttoning and unbuttoning the same button, lip smacking, swallowing, and chewing. This phase may then be followed by one in which the person seems catatonic, or frozen.	*Preceding seizures:* The person experiences an aura, which is a feeling, sensation, smell, or taste that signals the onset of the seizure. In some cases, these auras can be elaborate and may involve mood changes, feelings of déjà vu, hallucinations, repetitive thoughts, or a warping of the sense of time and place. *During seizures:* A limited clouding of consciousness occurs.

activity that neurologists will evaluate the likelihood of a diagnosis of epilepsy by recording an individual's EEG after he or she has gone without a night's sleep. Seizures may also be triggered by certain sensory stimuli, such as flashing lights; particular sounds; reading or laughing; certain classes of drugs, including alcohol; specific foods; and hormonal changes. For example, hormonal changes at puberty often cause a seizure (Kolb & Whishaw, 1990; Spreen et al., 1984).

Epilepsy impairs cognitive and psychosocial functioning in about half of all cases (Binnie, 1994). Clearly, consciousness is disrupted during the seizure and this disruption impairs cognition, but there are *interictal* (i.e., between-seizure) consequences that occur as well. Some neuropsychological deficits reflect dysfunction of the area from where the seizure originates, such as the memory problems and word-finding difficulties associated with temporal lobe seizures. Other difficulties are more generalized. These include poor sustained attention, compromised executive function, and lengthening of reaction time.

Epilepsy is sometimes associated with psychiatric disorders that occur postictally or chronically. Individuals may show psychotic features similar to those observed in schizophrenics except that they retain interpersonal skills and appropriate emotional affect. Other commonly observed psychiatric symptoms are anxiety and depression. It has also been suggested that individuals with temporal lobe epilepsy are likely to exhibit an odd constellation of personality traits interictally. The characteristics of this syndrome are an interpersonal "stickiness," in which the person doesn't know when to disengage from interaction with someone else; empty, verbose, and pedantic speech; a preoccupation with religious concepts, though not usually of an organized nature; and excessive writing, such as excessive note-taking or writing in diaries. The existence of such a syndrome, however, is controversial (see Blumer, 1999, and Devinsky & Najjar, 1999 for differing viewpoints). (For a review of the neuropsychological consequences of epilepsy, see Dodrill, 1992 and Thompson & Trimble, 1996; for a discussion of some of the psychiatric sequalae, see Perrine & Kiobasa, 1999).

The two main forms of therapy for epilepsy are drug therapy and surgery. The first step in any treatment involves the administration of anticonvulsant medication, which reduces the likelihood of epileptic discharges. Three major classes of drugs are used. One class, which includes barbiturates, mimics the neurotransmitter, GABA, or potentiates its transmission. GABA, as we learned in Chapter 2, is the main inhibitory neurotransmitter in the brain. Such drugs include phenobarbitol, a barbiturate, which was the first anti-epileptic drug. Another class of anticonvulsants, known as hydantoins, including phenytoin (Dilanin) and carbamazepine (Tegretol), acts to block the influx of sodium into the neuron, which reduces the ability of neurons to fire at high rates.

More recent anti-epileptic drugs work by attenuating glutamate release, which, as you may remember from Chapter 2, is the main excitatory neurotransmitter in the brain. Such drugs include lamotrigine (Ketter, Post, & Theodore, 1999; Julien, 2000). As with all other drugs, they can have side effects, such as excessive sedation, and when given in too large a dose can impair cognition (for a review of the side effects of anticonvulsant medication, see Nichols, Meador, & Loring, 1993). Therefore, drug administration must be *titrated*, that is, adjusted bit by bit, so that the physician can find the dosage that has the greatest efficacy against seizures with the fewest side effects on cognition (Bannister, 1992).

If the focal origin for the seizure is clear, the physician and the patient may opt for surgery to remove the source of the seizure activity, especially if it seems to be recruiting previously healthy areas. As we discussed in the preceding section, focal seizures are most often localized to temporal and frontal areas. Especially when the focus is in the temporal areas, resection of epileptiform tissue may be associated with memory loss.

SUMMARY

Closed Head Injury

- Closed head injury, which occurs when the head hits or is hit by a blunt object as happens in vehicular accidents, falls, and sport-related injuries, is generally associated with loss of consciousness.
- Acute consequences of head injury include difficulties in concentration, attentional problems, and posttraumatic amnesia, whereas more long-term effects include difficulties in abstract thought, anxiety, depression, and anger.

SUMMARY

- Ways to avoid head injury include wearing protective headgear, using seat belts, equipping cars with air bags, responsibly consuming alcohol, and not engaging in risky or reckless behavior.

Dementing Diseases

- Cortical dementias compromise a wide range of mental functions including memory, language, spatial abilities, and object recognition.
- The main feature of Alzheimer's disease is prominent memory impairment, with compromise of other cognitive functions as well.
- Alzheimer's disease is associated with specific neuroanatomical changes: the presence of neurofibrillary tangles and amyloid plaques in brain tissue.
- There is evidence of both a genetic and environmental contribution to Alzheimer's disease.
- Drug therapies designed to delay the effects of Alzheimer's disease concentrate on boosting the amount of acetylcholine in the nervous system.
- Fronto-temporal dementia is characterized by difficulty with language and changes in personality.
- Creutzfeldt-Jakob disease, which leads to a fast decline in cognitive function, is caused by a prion that is easily transmissible, although symptoms typically do not appear until decades after exposure.
- Subcortical dementias are characterized by difficulty with tasks related to motor functioning, attention, and executive control, along with poor memory recall but intact recognition, and symptoms of depression.
- Huntington's disease is characterized by a constellation of cognitive disturbances in executive functioning, spatial processing, and retrieving information from memory, along with emotional symptoms including depression, irritability, impulsivity and aggression.
- In Parkinson's disease, there is a general slowing of both motor functioning and thinking, dysfunction of executive processes, difficulty in memory retrieval, apathy and depression.
- Therapies for Parkinson's disease are aimed at ameliorating the loss of dopamine.
- Mixed-variety dementias have symptoms that are a blend of those seen in cortical and subcortical dementias.
- Vascular dementia, which results from the cumulative effect of many small strokes, has a variable profile of neuropsychological dysfunction depending on the brain regions affected.
- Individuals with AIDS dementia have difficulties in attention, problem solving, and memory, and may exhibit psychiatric symptoms. Mild neuropsychological dysfunction may occur in individuals who are infected with HIV but asymptomatic.

Demyelinating Diseases

- The most common demyelinating disease is multiple sclerosis (MS), which seems to be caused by a genetic vulnerability combined with exposure to an environmental pathogen, which, as yet, is undefined.
- Because the regions of brain tissue affected differ among individuals, some variability in the cognitive dysfunction is observed, although sensory and motor deficits, along with difficulties in memory, conceptual reasoning, and attention, are common.

Brain Syndromes Resulting from Substance Abuse and Exposure to Toxins

- Patients who abuse alcohol and other substances, even those who have abstained for some time, typically exhibit deficits on visuospatial functioning, learning, memory, and executive functioning.
- Toxins, such as metals, organic solvents, and pesticides, lead to diffuse complaints, including problems in attention and memory, slow psychomotor speed, as well as increased depression and irritability.

Epilepsy

- Epilepsy, which is caused by synchronous and atypical firing of nerve cells, usually results from exposure to toxins, head injury, or metabolic disturbances.

- Cognitive deficits are usually seen on tasks dependent on the region from which the seizures originate. Sometimes changes in personality occur as well.
- Typically, epilepsy is treated by drugs that dampen down the activity of the nervous system, while in more severe cases, surgery is employed when the focus of the seizure can be clearly defined.

KEY TERMS

acceleration-deceleration injury 480
Alzheimer's disease 486
amyloid plaques 490
bradyphrenia 500
closed head injury 479
contrecoup injury 480
coup injury 480
Creutzfeldt-Jakob disease 495
dementia 485
dementia of the Alzheimer's type (DAT) 486
epileptic seizures 512
frontotemporal dementia 495
generalized (nonspecific) disorders 479
Glasgow Coma Scale (GCS) 480
malingering 510
mild head injury 482
multiple sclerosis (MS) 504
neurofibrillary tangles 489
Parkinsonian mask 501
vascular dementia 501

SUMMARY

GLOSSARY

2½-D representation—A more elaborate representation of the visual world than the primal sketch. It contains information about the relative depth of surfaces.

3-D representation—A volumetric representation of an object that truly describes its 3-D characteristics so that the object can be identified regardless of the orientation from which it is viewed.

Acceleration-deceleration injury—See *Closed head injury.*

Acetylcholine—The neurotransmitter of the cholinergic system, which is composed of acetate and choline bound together.

Acetylcholinesterase—Enzyme in the synaptic cleft that divides acetylcholine into its two constituent parts, choline and acetate.

Action potential—The firing of a neuron in which the charge of the cell increases from the resting potential to +40 mV, then becomes more negative than the resting potential, and finally rebounds to the resting potential.

Action tremor (intention tremor)—A tremor causing movement to occur in a staggered manner during a motor act. It is typically associated with cerebellar damage and is distinct from the tremors usually observed in Parkinson's disease, which occur at rest.

Activating-orienting model—The idea that perceptual asymmetries arise from hemispheric differences in activation. The underlying assumption is that depending on the task demands (e.g., verbal vs. spatial), one hemisphere will become more activated than the other. This activation will cause an attentional bias to the side of space contralateral to the more activated hemisphere, which will lead to better processing of information on that side of space.

Affective prosody—The aspect of an utterance that communicates the emotional context or tone. For example, "My mother is coming to dinner" could be stated in a way that expresses elation or in a way that expresses dismay.

Agnosia—A modality-specific deficit occurring after brain damage that results in an inability to recognize objects even though basic sensory processing in that modality and memory are intact.

Agonist—A chemical that facilitates the effect of a neurotransmitter on a target neuron.

Agrammatic aphasia—An aphasia characterized by an inability to produce and comprehend the correct grammatical markers. The lesion causing it is generally located in left frontal regions.

Agraphia—The inability to write as a result of brain damage, usually to the left parietal region.

Akathisia—Compulsive, hyperactive, fidgety movements of the legs.

Akinesia—The lack of spontaneous movement. One of the main symptoms of Parkinson's disease.

Alertness and arousal—The basic aspects of attention that enable a person to extract information from the environment or to select a particular response.

Alexia—The inability to read as a result of brain damage, usually to the left parietal region.

Alien limb syndrome—A disorder in which a person feels unable to control the movements of a body part, believes the limb is alien, or believes that the body part has its own personality. It is typically associated with lesions in the supplementary motor area or those affecting blood flow to the anterior regions of the corpus callosum and the anterior cingulate cortex.

Alpha suppression—A decrease in the electroencephalographic (EEG) activity in the 9- to 12-Hz range (alpha activity) that generally accompanies mental activity.

Alternative strategy—An approach to a task that falls within the realm of everyday behavior but is distinct from the way in which the individual typically performs the task.

Altitudinal neglect—Disregard for one-half of vertical space (e.g., the upper half).

Alzheimer's disease—A cortical dementia that results in a decline in many aspects of cognitive functioning. It is characterized by a prominent impairment in memory along with at least one of the following: aphasia, apraxia, agnosia, and disturbance in executive functioning. It is sometimes called *dementia of the Alzheimer's type (DAT).*

Amino acids—Smallest and most basic building block of proteins, some of which (GABA, glycine, glutamate, and aspartate) act as neurotransmitters.

Amnesia—A memory deficit, including both anterograde and retrograde components, for facts and data (i.e., for declarative memory). It is caused by damage to the medial temporal lobes, midline diencephalic brain regions, or both.

Amyloid plaques—Deposits of aluminum silicate and amyloid peptides, which are basically a buildup or a conglomeration of proteins, that are not in the neurons themselves. They are believed to cause vascular damage and neuronal cell loss. Like neurofibrillary tangles, they are much more numerous in patients with Alzheimer's disease than in neurologically intact older individuals.

Anosognosia—A condition observed after hemiplegia in which a person denies, with both verbal and nonverbal behaviors, that his or her limb is paralyzed.

Antagonist—A chemical that opposes or diminishes the effect of a neurotransmitter on a target neuron.

Anterior—Located toward the front of the brain (by the face).

Anterior cingulate cortex—A region of the brain located below the cingulate sulcus but above the corpus callosum that is important for motor control, especially when it involves novel responses to a stimulus (e.g., pressing the gas pedal when a red light appears).

Anterograde amnesia—The impairment of memory for information acquired after the onset of amnesia.

Anxious apprehension—An uncontrollable tendency to worry and ruminate about self-relevant issues that is concerned primarily with future events.

Anxious arousal—An acute state of anxiety associated with many physiological symptoms such as increased heart rate, temperature, and feelings of panic.

Aphasia—A class of syndromes, resulting from brain damage, that are characterized by a deficit in language processing.

Apperceptive agnosia—A type of visual agnosia in which a fundamental difficulty in forming a percept exists. Although basic visual information is processed (e.g., areas of light and dark), it cannot be bound together so that a meaningful whole is perceived.

Apraxia—An inability to perform skilled, purposeful movement even though the affected individual has intact motor innervation of the muscles, can spontaneously coordinate sensorimotor actions, and can comprehend what is being asked. It is generally observed bilaterally and is typically associated with lesions to the parietal region of the left hemisphere.

Aprosodia—Difficulty with prosody, usually as a result of brain damage.

Aprosodic—Lacking prosody.

Association Area—An area of the brain where information from multiple sensory modalities is processed.

Associative agnosia—A type of visual agnosia in which basic visual information can be integrated to form a meaningful perceptual whole but that particular perceptual whole cannot be linked to knowledge stored in memory.

Athetosis—Involuntary writhing contractions and twisting of the body into abnormal postures. It is a symptom of Huntington's disease.

Attention—A psychological process that allows us, because of the limited capacity of the human brain, to select only certain types of information and not others.

Attentional dyslexia—A syndrome in which an individual can recognize a single letter or a single word in isolation but cannot recognize the same letter or word if it is presented along with items of the same kind (i.e., other letters or other words).

Attentional set—Mental set that designates which information is relevant for the task at hand.

Attention-deficit hyperactivity disorder (ADHD)—A developmental disorder in which a child is more distractible and inattentive, sometimes with a tendency to be hyperactive and impulsive, compared to a child of the same age.

Auditory agnosia—A condition in which basic aspects of auditory stimuli can be processed but the person is unable to link that sensory information to meaning, despite the fact that memory, as assessed through other modalities, appears to be normal.

Auditory nerve—The conduit whereby information is carried from the ear to the brain.

Auditory-verbal working memory—Memory that allows us to hold and repeat verbatim the contents of the immediately preceding verbal utterance. It is sometimes called the *phonological store.*

Autism—A type of pervasive development disorder that is characterized by particularly profound social deficits as well as difficulties in learning.

Autoreceptors—Receptors located on the presynaptic neuron that bind to the same transmitter released by that neuron. They work as a part of a feedback mechanism to control the amount of neurotransmitter released by the presynaptic cell.

Axon—The appendage of the cell along which a large electrical signal, the action potential, is propagated.

Axon hillock—The region of the cell near the cell body at which excitatory and inhibitory postsynaptic potentials summate to cause an action potential.

Balint's syndrome—A disorder in which individuals have difficulty localizing items in space, groping for objects as if blind. These individuals have optic ataxia, ocular apraxia, and simultanagnosia. The syndrome is sometimes referred to as *dorsal simultanagnosia* because it is generally seen after bilateral lesions to the dorsal occipitoparietal region and because the individual is unable to pay attention to two points in space simultaneously.

Ballistic movement—A movement that occurs so quickly that little or no time is available for it to be modified by feedback while it is being performed. The cerebellum controls this type of movement.

Barbiturates—Class of central nervous system depressants derived from barbituric acid. These bind to GABA receptors and can induce sedation and sleep as well as reduce seizure activity.

Basal ganglia—A group of subcortical structures, including the putamen and the caudate nucleus (known collectively as the *striatum*) and the globus pallidus (or *pallidum*), located near the thalamus, that are responsible for motor control. The substantia nigra and the subthalamic nucleus are two other nuclei associated with the basal ganglia.

Benzodiazepines—Class of central nervous system depressants that bind to GABA receptors. They are used to treat anxiety, promote sleep and muscle relaxation, and reduce seizure activity.

Bilateral—Pertaining to both sides of the brain (or space).

Bilateral presentation—A method in divided visual field studies in which two items are presented, one in each visual field.

Binocular disparity—The difference in the retinal images received by each eye that aids in determining the relative depth of items.

Blood-brain barrier—An impediment that prevents nutrients and other elements (including harmful substances such as toxins) that are in the bloodstream from entering neurons directly. It is created by a tight packing of glia between blood vessels and neurons.

Body schema—A conceptual spatial framework of the body that allows for an understanding of the spatial relationships among different body parts.

Bradykinesia—Slowness of movement. One of the main symptoms of Parkinson's disease.

Bradyphrenia—The slowing of motor and thought processes that typically accompanies Parkinson's disease.

Broca's Aphasia—A syndrome in which fluent speech is lost even though the person's speech comprehension is relatively spared. It is caused by a lesion to posterior regions of the left frontal lobe located directly in front of the face area of the motor strip.

Brodmann map—A neuroanatomical map of the cortex. It differentiates brain regions based on the nature of cells within a region and their laminar organization.

Calcification—Accumulations of calcium that are associated with transneuronal degeneration.

Callosal apraxia—An apraxia resulting from damage to the corpus callosum that prevents motor plans devised in the left hemisphere from reaching the right hemisphere. Skilled motor movements cannot be executed with the left hand because the right hemisphere cannot receive information about the motor program.

Callosal relay model—The idea that perceptual asymmetries arise because of degradation of information as it is transferred across the corpus callosum. The underlying assumption is that information received by a hemisphere less suited for a task is transferred to the opposite hemisphere through the corpus callosum and that the fidelity of the information is reduced during that transfer.

Caloric stimulation—The introduction of 20 ml of water that is at least 7 °C warmer or colder than body temperature into the ear canal during the course of 15 s. It has been found to reduce neglect but cannot be used as a therapy because its effects dissipate with time and because of its side effects (e.g., nausea).

Cannon-Bard theory—The idea that an emotion is produced when an event or an object is perceived by the thalamus, which conveys this information simultaneously to the cerebral cortex and to the skeletal muscles and autonomic nervous system.

Catastrophic interference—Interference during the acquisition of new memories, occurring between those new memories and already existing items, and destroying representations for the preexisting items.

Catastrophic reaction—A condition in which patients are described to be emotionally volatile and especially prone to depression and crying. It occurs most frequently after left-hemisphere damage.

Catecholamines—Group of monoamines synthesized in a common pathway from the same amino acid precursor, tyrosine. Dopamine and norepinephrine are catecholamines.

Categorical spatial relations—One position in relation to another (e.g., above vs. below, top vs. bottom, front vs. back, left vs. right). This type of spatial relation is believed to rely on left-hemisphere mechanisms and to be independent of a system in the right hemisphere that is believed to compute metric spatial relations.

Category-specific deficit—An inability to recognize a particular subclass of items, such as fruits and vegetables, while the ability to recognize other classes of items, such as human-made objects, remains relatively intact. This difficulty seems to reflect a disruption in the organization of semantic memory rather than a problem in linking specific perceptual forms to meaning.

Caudal—Located toward an animal's tail.

Caudate nucleus—A portion of the basal ganglia that, along with the putamen, receives all the input into the basal ganglia. It degenerates in Huntington's disease.

Cell body—The part of the neuron containing the nucleus and other cellular apparatus responsible not only for manufacturing proteins and enzymes that sustain cell functioning, but also for producing neurotransmitters.

Central executive—The portion of working memory that performs the mental work of controlling subsystems that store or maintain information on-line.

Central fissure—The main fissure that divides anterior and posterior sections of the brain. It is sometimes called the *Rolandic fissure.*

Central nervous system—The portion of the nervous system that consists of the brain and the spinal cord.

Cerebellum—The brain region posterior to the medulla that is important for regulating muscle tone, guiding motor activity, and allowing motor skills to be learned.

Cerebral dominance—The idea that one hemisphere dominates or leads mental thought. In the late 19th and early 20th centuries, the left hemisphere was considered the dominant hemisphere because it is involved with language processing (and language was equated with thought).

Cerebral hemisphere—One half of the cortex. It is the region of the brain that plays a primary role in most of our mental skills, such as language, attention, and artistry.

Cerebral palsy—A disorder of motor functioning that occurs as a result of motor system damage during or preceding birth rather than from a progressive disease.

Cerebrospinal fluid (CSF)—The substance, similar in composition to blood plasma, in which the spinal cord and brain float. It cushions these structures from their bony encasements and transports nutrients to neurons.

Chorea—A variety of jerky movements that appear to be well-coordinated but are performed involuntarily, ceaselessly, and in an irregular manner. It is one of the main symptoms of Huntington's disease.

Chronic vegetative state—A state of consciousness that occurs after coma, in which the person regains a normal sleep-wake cycle, may follow people with his or her eyes, and responds with primitive reflexes but has no additional awareness of the external world or internal needs.

Cingulate cortex—The interface between subcortical and cortical brain regions that imparts emotional significance to information that has captured attention. It is involved when attention must be used to override automatic motor responses.

Closed head injury—Brain damage sustained when the head forcefully comes into contact with another object (e.g., a car windshield, the ground, a blunt instrument such as a baseball bat), but no object penetrates the brain. It is also called *acceleration-deceleration injury* because the damage usually occurs when a rapid acceleration of the head is followed by a rapid deceleration.

Coarticulation—Variations in the production of sounds by the vocal muscles depending on the preceding sounds.

Cognitive estimation—Using known information to make reasonable judgments or deductions about the world.

Cognitive neuroscience—The branch of science that investigates how mental functions are linked to neural processes.

Cogwheel rigidity—The stiffness observed in Parkinson's disease due to increased muscle tone in extensor and flexor muscles. The increased tone causes the limbs to move in specific rigid steps, much as a cogwheel does.

Coma—An impaired state of consciousness in which individuals are seemingly unresponsive to most external stimuli, lying with their eyes closed. In severe cases, they may not even exhibit defensive movements to noxious or painful stimuli, although in less severe cases they will do so.

Compensatory rehabilitation—Rehabilitation that is designed to gain increased function by providing a strategy that generally would not be used to perform a task but is invoked to minimize the loss of a specific skill.

Compensatory strategy—An approach to a task that generally would not be used to perform the task but is invoked to minimize the loss of a specific skill.

Components—Characteristics portions of the event-related potential (ERP) waveform that have been linked to certain psychological processes, such as attention and memory.

Computational model—A computer model, which has neuron-like properties, that is used to simulate how the brain processes information.

Computerized axial tomography—A technique for imaging the brain with x-rays that provides information on the density of brain structures. It is also known as *CAT* or *CT.*

Conduction aphasia—A syndrome in which a person can comprehend and produce speech but cannot repeat what was just said. It is associated with damage to the region between Wernicke's and Broca's areas, damage that has been conceptualized as preventing information from Wernicke's area from being conducted forward to Broca's area for speech output.

Connectionist networks—Neural networks that are composed of interconnected layers of units that exhibit neuronlike behavior.

Consolidation—The process by which a memory is strengthened over time.

Constructional apraxia—Difficulty with spatial aspects of motor functioning. It may not be considered a true apraxia because the difficulty seems to arise not so much from motor problems as from spatial problems.

Constructional praxis—The ability to motorically produce or manipulate items so that they have a certain spatial relationship.

Contention scheduling—The cognitive system that allows for automatic processing. This automaticity is engendered over time, because stimuli or situations become linked to actions, routines, or schemata, and then groups of these become linked to one another.

Contextual fear conditioning—Conditioning in which the fear response is selective to the context, or environment, in which conditioning occurs.

Contingent negative variation (CNV)—An electroencephalographic (EEG) signal often recorded after the brain receives a warning signal that puts the brain in an alert state to receive information. This potential is thought to involve the reticular activating system, which then activates the rest of the cortex: first prefrontal areas, then more posterior regions.

Contralateral—On the opposite side from.

Contrecoup injury—Focal damage that occurs opposite the site of impact in closed head injury.

Coronal view—A plane that divides the front of the brain from the back.

Corpus callosum—The massive neural tract of more than 250 million nerve fibers that connects the cerebral hemispheres.

Corticobulbar pathway—The motor pathway that connects motor cortex to the face region and is important for motor control of the face.

Corticospinal pathway—The motor pathway that connects motor cortex to the spinal cord. Two major tracts within it are the lateral corticospinal tract and the ventral corticospinal tract.

Coup injury—Focal damage that occurs at the site of impact in closed head injury.

Cranial nerves—The nerves responsible for receipt of sensory information and motor control of the head as well as for neural control of internal organs.

Creutzfeldt-Jakob disease—A rare cortical dementia caused by an infectious agent, a prion. The initial symptoms, which are psychiatric, are followed by motor symptoms, then a swift mental decline and death.

Crossed aphasia—Aphasia in a right-handed individual that results from a right-hemisphere lesion. It occurs very rarely.

Crowding hypothesis—The theory that the young brain compensates for early damage by instituting a maximal rewiring of the available neural space. Although this reorganization works well initially, deleterious consequences are seen later in life because the system cannot adapt to or acquire later developing mental skills.

Cued recall—A direct (explicit) test of memory that samples the ability to recover items from memory in response to direct cues, such as the name of the actor who starred in the first Batman movie or the word from the study list that was an example of a vehicle.

Customized neuropsychological assessment—An approach in which a small set of standard tests is used to assess general intelligence, after which the administrator generates hypotheses about the nature of an individual's deficits and tests the hypotheses by using specialized tests to assess specific abilities.

Declarative memory—A memory system, which is dependent on the hippocampus and related structures, that supports a fundamentally relational form of memory that allows it to be retrieved and used flexibly in a number of contexts.

Decomposition of movement—The breakdown of complex, multijoint movement into single, serial movements. This phenomenon is often observed after cerebellar damage.

Dedifferentation—Process in which localization of function in the brain becomes less defined.

Deep alexia—A syndrome similar to phonologic alexia in that the phonologic route from print to meaning is disrupted. However, additional symptoms include misreading words as those with similar meaning (e.g., reading *ship* as "boat"), difficulty in reading words that serve as grammatical markers, and difficulty in reading abstract words (e.g., *faith*) although reading concrete words (e.g., *chair*) is preserved.

Deep cerebellar nuclei—Three nuclei (fastigial, interpositus, and dentate) embedded within the cerebellum, each of which connects to a different region of the cerebellum.

Delayed nonmatch-to-sample task—A task in which an animal must remember the identity of recently presented objects. Each trial of the task consists of a sample phase and a match phase.

Dementia—A debilitating syndrome involving a loss of cognitive funtions, sometimes accompanied by personality changes, that interferes significantly with work or social activities.

Dementia of the Alzheimer's type (DAT)—See *Alzheimer's disease.*

Dendritic tree—The part of the neuron that receives input from other cells.

Denervation supersensitivity—A process occurring after damage or cell loss by which the remaining intact cells become hypersensitive to stimulation.

Dentate nucleus—One of the deep cerebellar nuclei. It receives input from the lateral zone of the cerebellum.

Developmental dysphasia—A disorder of expressive language in which children have difficulty understanding and producing speech.

Developmental milestones—Specific changes in behavior and skills that manifest at certain ages during development.

Diathesis-stress model—A model of psychopathology in which environmental factors (the stressors) interact with or exacerbate a biological predisposition (the diathesis).

Dichaptic presentation—A method for testing lateralization of function in the tactile modality, in which an individual feels two items simultaneously, one in each hand, and then must identify these items in some manner. A superiority in processing by one hand is believed to indicate a superiority of the contralateral hemisphere.

Dichotic presentation—A method for examining hemispheric differences in the auditory modality in which *different* information is presented simultaneously to each ear. An advantage for information presented to one ear is believed to indicate a superiority of the contralateral hemisphere.

Diencephalon—The hypothalamus and the thalamus.

Digit span task—A task in which an individual has to report back in order digits read one at a time. The person's digit span is the number of items they can recall, usually in the range of 7 ± 2 items.

Dipole—A small region of electrical current with a relatively positive end and a relatively negative end produced by the common alignment and firing of dendritic fields in the brain.

Direct access theory—The idea that perceptual asymmetries arise because the hemispheres have differing competencies and any information received by a hemisphere is processed by that hemisphere. From this perspective, perceptual asymmetries arise because the hemisphere more suited for a task will exhibit superior processing of the information received than the hemisphere that is less suited for the task will.

Direct route to reading—The method of linking print to meaning without a phonologic intermediary.

Direct (explicit) tests of memory—Tests of memory that depend upon conscious recollection of the learning event and refer the subject to a particular study episode or learning event.

Disconnection syndrome—A disruption in cognitive function that occurs when a brain region is damaged, not because that region controls the function but because fibers connecting two brain regions critical to the function are destroyed.

Distal—Located toward the periphery or toward the end of a limb.

Divided visual field technique—A method whereby information is presented separately in each visual field. By comparing performance for information presented in the right visual field (received by the left hemisphere) and performance for that presented in the left visual field (received by the right hemisphere), researchers can determine hemispheric differences in processing.

Dopamine—Monoamine (and catecholamine) that is the neurotransmitter of the dopaminergic system. Linked to working memory, schizophrenic and psychotic symptoms, motor control, emotion, and impulsiveness.

Dorsal—Located toward an animal's back (in people sometimes toward the top as in the case of the brain).

Dorsal simultanagnosia—See *Balint's syndrome.*

Double dissociation—A method for determining that two cognitive functions are independent of each other. It occurs when lesions have converse effects on two distinct cognitive functions: One brain lesion causes a disruption in Cognitive Function A but not Cognitive Function B, whereas a different lesion causes a disruption in Cognitive Function B but not Cognitive Function A.

Double simultaneous stimulation technique—A method in which the patient is confronted with two similar items on each side of space simultaneously and is asked how many items have been presented. Under these conditions, a patient with neglect typically says that she or he sees, hears, or feels only a single item. However, if the same item is presented in isolation on the neglected side of space, it will be noticed.

Down syndrome—One of the leading genetic causes of mental retardation. It occurs because of a defective egg, a defective sperm, or defects in cell division; gene translocation; or trisomy 21, in which the 21st pair of chromosomes contains an extra (third) chromosome. This disorder is associated with maternal age older than 35 years.

Dressing apraxia—Difficulty performing the correct spatial manipulations and motor actions required to dress yourself. Like constructional apraxia, it may not be considered a true apraxia because the difficulty seems to arise not so much from difficulties in motor processing as from difficulties in spatial processing.

Dyslexia—The inability to learn to read at an age-appropriate level, despite adequate opportunity, training, and intelligence. It is sometimes called *a specific reading disability.*

Dysprosodic—Having disordered intonation.

Dystonia—Painful, continual muscle spasms.

Early-selection viewpoint—The idea that selection occurs early in the stream of processing, soon after the receipt of sensory information and before an item is identified.

Echolalia—The compulsion to repeat what was just said. It is common in individuals with transcortical motor and transcortical sensory aphasia.

Edema—Tissue swelling after trauma.

Electrical potential—The summed or superimposed signal of the electrical activity of fields of neuronal dendrites that are all similarly aligned. It is typically recorded at the scalp.

Electroconvulsive therapy (ECT)—A series of treatments for the relief of severe depressive illness. When it is performed bilaterally, in which electrical current is applied across two electrodes placed on the surface of the head, it produces an amnesia that dissipates with time.

Electroencephalography (EEG)—A method of recording the electrical signals produced by the synchronous firing of neurons that provides information on the frequency at which neurons are firing.

Elimination of synapses—The process whereby numerous synaptic connections are lost during development. It allows pruning of neural connections after their proliferation early in life.

Emotional semantics—The ability to label emotions and to understand the link between certain situations and specific emotions. It is thought to depend partly on the left hemisphere.

Endogenous components—Event-related potential (ERP) components that are independent of stimulus characteristics, driven by internal cognitive states, and typically occur later in the waveform.

Environmental dependency syndrome—A disorder in which objects in the environment trigger individuals with executive dysfunction to act, even though the actions are inappropriate.

Enzymatic deactivation—Process in which an enzyme cleaves a neurotransmitter so that it becomes incapable of binding to the receptor.

Enzyme—Any molecule that controls a chemical reaction, either by binding together two substances or cleaving a substance into parts.

Epileptic seizure—A pathological neural phenomenon in which a vast number of neurons misfire in great bursts, or volleys, called *spikes.*

Episodic memory—Memory containing autobiographic records of personally experienced events occurring in specifiable temporal and spatial contexts.

Error-related negativity (ERN)—An event-related potential, negative in polarity, that occurs approximately 100 ms after an error has been made.

Estimate of premorbid functioning—An approximation of the level at which a person was functioning before a brain injury.

Euphoric-indifference reaction—A condition in which patients are inappropriately cheerful, prone to laughter, and display a lack of awareness with regard to their disabilities and other consequences of changes wrought by brain damage. It occurs most frequently after right-hemisphere damage.

Event-related potentials (ERPs)—Recordings of the brain's electrical activity that are linked to the occurrence of an event.

Excitatory postsynaptic potentials (EPSPs)—Small graded electrical potentials induced in a postsynaptic neuron after the binding of neurotransmitters to its membrane that serve to make the electrical charge of the postsynaptic cell more positive than the resting potential.

Excitotoxicity—Excessive activity of neurons that leads to their death from too much stimulation. Linked to excessive release of glutamate.

Executive functions—A family of functions that include the ability to plan actions toward a goal, to use information flexibly, to realize the ramifications of behavior, and to make reasonable inferences based on limited information. They can be compromised by damage to a variety of brain regions but most commonly occur after frontal lobe damage.

Exogenous components—Event-related potential (ERP) components linked to the physical characteristics of a stimulus. They usually occur early in the waveform.

Experience-dependent systems—Those brain systems that are vary in plasticity throughout the lifetime and depend on the specific experience of an organism, such as the acquisition of musical skill.

Experience-expectant systems—Those brain systems designed to be plastic across all individuals so that appropriate information can be gleaned from the environment, such as occurs with language.

Extended digit span—The number of digits that can be repeated verbatim if a person is given multiple repetitions of the same digit string with an additional digit added to extend the span. It provides an index of long-term memory.

Eye-movement monitoring techniques—Methods in which the eye movements of individuals are recorded.

Fastigial nucleus—One of the deep cerebellar nuclei. It receives input from the vermis.

Fear conditioning—Conditioning in which a stimulus comes to invoke fear because it is paired with an aversive event.

Fetal alcohol effects—Negative consequences of alcohol intake by the mother during pregnancy that are not severe enough to be characterized as fetal alcohol syndrome.

Fetal alcohol syndrome (FAS)—A disorder characterized by mental retardation as well as stunted growth and congenital defects of the face and cranium. It is caused by excessive alcohol intake by the mother during pregnancy.

Fiber tract—A group of cells whose axons all project to the same region of the brain.

Figure-ground separation—The process of distinguishing a visual object from the background against which it is embedded. Color is an attribute that aids in such separation.

Finger agnosia—The bilateral inability of a person to recognize or localize his or her own fingers that is often associated with left-right confusion and is typically caused by a lesion to the left parietal cortex.

Fissure—A particularly deep sulcus.

Forward model—Model of what will happen forward in time as a consequence of motor movements.

Fragile X syndrome—A common form of mental retardation that is inherited. It is caused by a fragile section of the X chromosome; therefore, it has a much higher incidence rate in males than in females. It is sometimes called *Martin-Bell syndrome.*

Free recall—A direct (explicit) test of memory that samples the ability to recover items from memory in response to only a general cue about an event or a circumstance, such as the names of all the students in a particular class or the words on a given study list.

Frontal eye field—A region of the brain located anterior to the supplementary motor area and dorsal to Broca's area. It is important for the control of voluntary eye movements.

Frontal lobe—The region of cortex in front of the central fissue.

Frontotemporal dementia—A cortical dementia characterized by poor social-emotional functioning, poor language skills, and motor difficulties.

Functional magnetic resonance imaging (fMRI)—A method, using magnetic resonance imaging (MRI) techniques, for assessing brain metabolism either through use of a magnetic contrast agent that enables blood flow to be determined or through measures of relative blood oxygenation.

G protein (guanylyl nucleotide-binding protein)—Proteins linked to metabotropic receptors. When a receptor binds to a metabotropic receptor, it causes the alpha subunit of the G protein to break away. That subunit then causes an additional reaction in the cell, either affecting an ion channel or activating an enzyme.

GABA (gamma-aminobutyric acid)—One of the primary inhibitory amino acid neurotransmitters in the central nervous system.

Generalized (nonspecific) disorders—Syndromes in which the loss of function is not restricted to one cognitive domain but affects multiple cognitive abilities simultaneously.

Gerstmann syndrome—A disorder that was proposed to be caused by damage to the left parietal cortex and behaviorally characterized by four major attributes: right-left disturbances, finger agnosia, dysgraphia (an inability to write), and dyscalculia (the inability to perform arithmetic). Although these four symptoms can co-occur, they do not do so with such frequency that they represent a unique syndrome.

Glasgow Coma Scale (GCS)—A metric for assessing a person's level of consciousness that is widely used to provide a gross method for classifying the severity of damage in someone who just sustained a head injury.

Glia—The basic support cells of the central nervous system.

Gliosis—The filling in of a site of damage by glial cells.

Global aphasia—The inability to produce and comprehend language. It is usually associated with extensive left-hemisphere damage.

Global precedence—An idea advanced by the gestalt psychologists in the early 20th century, which says that the overall shape or relation among parts may be analyzed before the parts themselves.

Global processing—Analysis of the overall form, or gestalt, of objects. It is thought to rely on right-hemisphere mechanisms, most likely those in temporal regions.

Globus pallidus—The region of the basal ganglia from which almost all outputs emanate. It connects with the thalamus. It is sometimes called the *pallidum.*

Glutamate—One of the primary amino acid neurotransmitters in the central nervous system; it has an excitatory effect.

Gradient field—A magnetic field that varies in intensity over the area being imaged and provides the ability to localize the points in space from which different portions of the signal are emanating.

Grandmother cell theory—The idea that a small set of particular cells would fire only in response to a highly specific object, such as your grandmother's face, and no other objects. These cells alone would be responsible for recognizing your grandmother. They would fire in response to her face because they received information from other cells that analyzed the parts of her face (e.g., cells that recognized her nose, her hair, her eyes, her chin line) and then conjoined the information.

Grapheme-to-phoneme correspondence rules—The guidelines that let us know how each grapheme should sound and how graphemes should be combined. Graphemes are the smallest units of written language that are combined to form words (e.g., "c").

Group studies—Neuropsychological investigations in which individuals with brain damage who have similar characteristics (e.g., lesions in similar areas) are studied as a group.

Gyrus—A ridge or mound of cortical tissue.

Habit learning—Type of skill learning that while gradual and incremental, may not necessarily generalize to new exemplars.

Hemi-inattention—See *Hemineglect.*

Hemineglect—The lack of attention to one side of space, usually the left, as a result of parietal lobe damage. It occurs despite intact sensory and motor functioning and is sometimes called *hemi-inattention.*

Hemiplegia—Paralysis on one entire side of the body. It typically results from damage to primary motor cortex and the basal ganglia.

Hemispherectomy—The surgical removal of an entire cerebral hemisphere.

Hemispheric specialization—The specialization of each cerebral hemisphere for different aspects of cognitive and emotional functioning. It is also referred to as *lateralization of function.*

Heschl's gyrus—The superior portion of the posterior temporal lobe in which primary auditory cortex is located.

Hippocampal system—The hippocampus, amygdala, and adjoining regions of cortex (parahippocampal and entorhinal gyri), whose damage results in amnesia.

Homonymous hemianopsia—The loss of vision in one entire visual field.

Homovanillic acid (HVA)—A by-product of dopamine synthesis.

Horizontal view—A plane in which the top of the brain is separated from the bottom.

Human neuropsychology—An area of study that is devoted to understanding how the neurological organization of the brain influences the way that people think, feel, and act.

Huntington's disease—A rare inherited neurologic disease caused by degeneration of the striatum that produces abnormal movements, cognitive deficits (eventually dementia), and psychiatric symptoms. It eventually leads to death.

Hyperkinesias—Involuntary undesired movements. They are observed in Huntington's disease.

Hypothalamus—The brain region that is responsible for regulatory behaviors, such as eating and drinking, that maintain the integrity of bodily systems.

Ideational apraxia—Difficulty performing a movement when the "idea" of the movement is lost. According to Liepmann, who proposed this concept, it occurs when individuals can perform simple one-step movements but not multistep movements.

Ideomotor apraxia—Difficulty performing a movement when a disconnection occurs between the idea of a movement and its execution. According to Liepmann, who proposed this concept, simple movements of an abstract nature are most affected.

Indirect (implicit) tests of memory—Tests of memory in which participants are referred to a previously experienced task but aren't required to consciously recall a specific learning experience. Changes in performance on the task as a consequence of prior experience are considered indices of memory.

Inference—The ability to "fill in the blanks" and make assumptions about material that is implied.

Inferior—Located toward the bottom of the brain.

Inferior colliculus—A structure in the midbrain that is important for integrating head and eye movements in response to sounds and for localizing sounds.

Inhibitory postsynaptic potentials (IPSPs)—Small graded electrical potentials induced in a postsynaptic neuron after the binding of neurotransmitters to its membrane that serve to make the electrical charge of the postsynaptic cell more negative than the resting potential.

Input phonologic buffer—Working-memory store that holds auditory-verbal information received by the listener online while an utterance is being parsed.

Intermediate zone of the cerebellum—The region of the cerebellum that is located between the vermis and the lateral zone. It is important for smooth, nonrigid limb movements.

Interpositus nucleus—One of the deep cerebellar nuclei. It receives input from the intermediate zone of the cerebellum.

Intralaminar nucleus of the thalamus—A nucleus of the thalamus that affects attention by modulating the level of arousal of the cortex.

Inverse model—Model of the desired states at each point along a trajectory, which is then translated into specific motor commands.

Inversion effect—Greater difficulty remembering inverted stimuli than upright stimuli. It is thought to assess the degree to which configural properties of an item are important for recognition and is greater for faces than for other mono-oriented stimuli.

Ionotropic receptors—Receptor sites connected to an ion channel; ionotropic receptors work directly to either open or close an ion channel.

Ipsilateral—On the same side as.

Irregular words—Words that do not follow the standard English grapheme-to-phoneme correspondence rules and thus require the direct route to reading.

Ischemia—Specific form of brain damage in which neurons die due to lack of oxygen, most typically after the blockage of a blood vessel in the brain.

James-Lange theory—The idea that each emotion is caused by a specific physical response to a stimulus (e.g., we feel afraid because we see a snake and tremble).

Kennard principle—The maxim suggesting that the earlier in life damage is sustained, the better the recovery. This generalization is now known not to be entirely true.

Korsakoff's amnesia—Amnesia related to chronic alcoholism. A gradual worsening of cognitive abilities is followed by acute hemorrhaging of midline diencephalic structures of the brain, which results in amnesia.

Kwashiorkor—Starvation due to a protein-deficient diet.

Lateral—Located toward the outside of the brain (away from the brain's midline).

Lateral corticospinal tract—The tract within the corticospinal pathway that is important for the control of distal muscles. When it is damaged, the ability to grasp and manipulate items with the far extremities is disrupted.

Lateral geniculate nucleus—The area of the thalamus onto which visual information from the optic tract synapses.

Lateralization of function—See *Hemispheric specialization.*

Lateral zone of the cerebellum—The most lateral region of the cerebellum. It is important for ballistic movements, multijoint movements, motor learning, and the timing of actions. It has been implicated in both motor and cognitive behaviors.

Late-selection viewpoint—The idea that selection occurs later in processing, only after information is identified and categorized.

L-Dopa—A precursor to dopamine that can cross the blood-brain barrier when given orally. It is used to treat Parkinson's disease.

Learning disabilities—Syndromes in which a child has difficulty acquiring cognitive skills in only one particular domain or area.

Left visual field—The portion of space that falls to the left of the fixation point of gaze and projects to primary visual cortex of the right hemisphere.

Lesion method—The method of inferring that a mental function is supported by a particular region of brain tissue if that function is lost after damage to that region.

Letter-by-letter reading—A syndrome caused by damage to the left ventral occipital area, in which individual letters can be identified but they cannot be integrated to form a word. It is sometimes referred to as *spelling dyslexia* or *pure alexia.*

Lexical agraphia—A writing disorder in which the ability to use the direct route from meaning to writing is lost but the ability to use the phonologic route remains intact.

Limb apraxia—Difficulty performing voluntary movements with a limb, such as manipulating scissors, using a key to open a door, or waving good-bye.

Limbic system—A series of subcortical structures, including the amygdala, hypothalamus, cingulate cortex, anterior thalamus, mammillary bodies, hippocampus, and parahippocampal gyrus, that are thought to play a prominent role in emotional functions. However, they are also involved in many other diverse functions, including motor control, attention, and memory.

Localization of function—The idea that particular mental functions are carried out by particular brain regions.

Local processing—Analysis of the features or details of objects. It is thought to rely on left-hemisphere mechanisms, most likely those in temporal regions.

Longitudinal fissure—The fissure that separates the right cerebral hemisphere from the left.

Long-term potentiation (LTP)—Phenomenon in which brief, patterned activation of particular pathways produces a stable increase in synaptic efficacy lasting for hours to weeks.

Macrosomatagnosia—A disturbance of body schema in which a person perceives a portion of his or her body as being too big. It is usually associated with the auras that precede epileptic seizures.

Magnetic resonance imaging (MRI)—A brain imaging technique that relies on electromagnetic radiation to provide highly precise anatomical images of the brain. The images can be tuned to different substances, such as water or fat, to emphasize different regions of brain tissue.

Magnetoencephalography (MEG)—Method of indexing the time course of brain activity by recording magnetic potentials at the scalp, which are a result of electrical activity within the brain.

Malingering—The exaggeration or creation of symptoms for personal gain, either for money or to avoid responsibility for personal actions.

Mammillary bodies—The hypothalamic nuclei typically damaged in diencephalic amnesia.

Marasmus—Starvation due to a lack of adequate caloric intake.

Mass action—The idea that all regions of the brain contribute to almost all functions.

Material-specific memory disorders—Selective impairment of memory for a particular type of material. Impairment in remembering verbal material is observed after left-hemisphere damage, whereas impairments in remembering nonverbal material is observed after right-hemisphere damage.

Maturational lag hypothesis—The theory that individuals with learning disabilities are slower to mature than their peers and that with time they will outgrow the problem.

Medial—Located toward the middle of the brain.

Medial dorsal nucleus of the thalamus—A nucleus of the thalamus that affects attention by modulating the level of arousal of the cortex.

Medial geniculate of the thalamus—The thalamic relay station for auditory information.

Medulla—The section of the brain directly superior to the spinal cord that contains many of the cell bodies of the cranial nerves. It is also the region of the brain where motor information crosses from one side of the body to the other. It is important not only for the control of many essential functions, such as respiration and heart rate, but also for overall arousal and attention.

Memory consolidation—Processes that occur during the time after learning to increase resistance to disruption of surviving memories.

Mental retardation—An inability to acquire intellectual abilities across practically all cognitive domains in the rate and manner expected during normal development. It is also characterized by difficulties in adaptive functioning, such as self-care.

Mesocortical system—Subsystem of the dopaminergic system that begins in the ventral tegmental area and projects to the prefrontal cortex. Influences a variety of mental functions, including working memory, planning, strategy preparation, and problem solving.

Mesolimbic system—Subsystem of the dopaminergic system that begins in the ventral tegmental area and projects to several areas of the limbic system. Important for processing reward and punishment.

Metabotropic receptors—Receptors that indirectly control an ion channel; linked to a G protein.

Metamemory—The abilities that allow for the strategic use, deployment, and retrieval of memories.

Method of converging operations—Examination of the same research question by using various methods and different subject populations to determine whether the results all converge on the same conclusion regarding a particular brain-behavior relationship.

Metric (coordinate) spatial relations—The distance between two locations. This type of spatial relation is thought to rely on right-hemisphere mechanisms and to be independent of a system in the left hemisphere that is thought to compute categorical spatial relations.

Microsomatagnosia—A disturbance of body schema in which a person perceives a portion of his or her body as being too small. It is usually associated with the auras that precede epileptic seizures.

Midbrain—A major section of the nervous system containing nuclei of the cells for some of the cranial nerves. It is the location of the inferior and superior colliculi, which are important for allowing a person to orient eye and head movements in response to auditory and visual stimuli, respectively.

Midline diencephalic region—Structures along the medial aspect of the thalamus and the hypothalamus. Damage to this region (particularly the dorsomedial nucleus of the thalamus and the mammillary bodies of the hypothalamus) results in amnesia.

Midsagittal—A medial, or middle, slice down the center of the brain, separating the left side from the right side.

Mild head injury—A head injury that results in a change in consciousness for 2 to 30 minutes but is unaccompanied by other gross signs of neurologic damage.

Mirror-reading task—A task in which mirror-image text must be read aloud as quickly and accurately as possible. It is an example of a perceptual skill that can be learned normally despite amnesia.

Mirror tracing task—A task that requires the outline of a figure to be traced when visual information is conveyed only by means of a mirror. It is an example of a perceptual-motor skill that patients with amnesia can learn normally.

Mixed auditory agnosia—An auditory agnosia in which the ability to attach meaning to both verbal and nonverbal sounds is affected.

Modality specific—Manifesting in one sensory modality (e.g., vision) but not in others (e.g., hearing, touch).

Monoamines—Subset of the biogenic amines. Includes dopamine, norepinephrine, and serotonin.

Morris water maze—A test in which rats must learn and remember the spatial location of an escape platform submerged just below the surface of milky water in a circular tank or pool. Profound impairment on this task is seen following hippocampal system damage.

Motor program—An abstract representation of an intended movement that contains a plan for both general and specific aspects of an action. It is created before a complex motor act begins.

Motor unit—Motor neuron and the muscle fibers it innervates.

Multiple-case study approach—A neuropsychological investigation technique in which findings are obtained for a series or a group of patients, each of whom is also treated as a single-case study.

Multiple-resource theory—The viewpoint that attention consists of a limited set of attentional pools of resources. The capacity of the system to process information is greater when tasks draw from distinct resource pools rather than from the same one.

Multiple sclerosis (MS)—An autoimmune disorder that is characterized by multiple discrete areas, ranging in size from 1 mm to several centimeters, in which neurons have a complete absence of myelin. The cognitive concommitants include difficulty in memory and conceptual reasoning along with a general sparing of verbal and language skills.

Myelin—The fatty sheath around neurons formed by specific glial cells that causes increased conduction velocity of an action potential.

Narrative—The construction or understanding of a story line.

Necrosis—A process in which cells die at a site of damage.

Neglect dyslexia—A syndrome associated with parietal lobe damage, in which an individual consistently misreads a specific portion of words (e.g., just the beginning).

Neologisms—Sounds produced by persons with aphasia that follow the rules by which sounds are produced in a language but do not comprise a real word (e.g., "galump," "trebbin").

Neural networks—Computer modeling techniques designed to simulate the action of the brain and its processes.

Neurofibrillary tangles—Twisted pairs of helical filaments found within neurons in neurologically intact older individuals and patients with Alzheimer's disease. These tangles tend to displace the cell body and are much more numerous in the cortex of a person with Alzheimer's disease than in a neurologically intact individual.

Neurogenesis—Formation of new neurons.

Neuromuscular junction—The place at which a neuron synapses on a muscle. When the neuron fires, the muscle contracts.

Neurons—The cells in the nervous system that are responsible for transmitting information by means of a combination of electrical and chemical signals.

Neuropsychological assessment—An evaluation of a person's cognitive, behavioral, and emotional functioning, which a neuropsychologist performs to determine the degree to which central nervous system damage may have compromised the person's abilities.

Neuropsychological test battery—A large number of neuropsychological tests that are designed to assess a range of sensory and cognitive abilities.

Neurotransmitters—The chemical substances that neurons use to communicate with one another.

Nigrostriatal bundle—The nerve-fiber tract that runs from the substantia nigra to the basal ganglia.

Nigrostriatal system—Subsystem of the dopaminergic system that begins in the substantia nigra and projects to the neostriatum. Important in motor control, especially the initiation and cessation of motor behaviors; this system is affected in Parkinson's disease.

Nodes of Ranvier—Gaps between myelinated sections of an axon.

Nonverbal affect lexicon—A knowledge base that stores nonverbal information about the meaning of emotion. It is thought to reside in the right hemisphere.

Nonverbal auditory agnosia—An auditory agnosia in which the ability to attach meaning to words is intact, but the ability to do so for nonverbal sounds is disrupted.

Nonverbal learning disabilities—Specific learning disabilities in which a child has difficulty with nonverbal and spatial skills but not verbal skills. They have been linked to right-hemisphere dysfunction.

Norepinephrine (noradrenaline)—Monoamine (and catecholamine) that is the neurotransmitter of the noradrenergic system. Linked to attention, working memory, and sexual and feeding behaviors.

Nuclei—Distinct groups of neurons whose cell bodies are all situated in the same region of the nervous system.

Nucleus accumbens—Portion of the basal ganglia.

Object-based viewpoint of attention—The idea that attention is directed toward particular objects.

Object-centered representation—A representation of an object that is based on a coordinate system with regard to the object's main attributes (center of mass, overall size, principle axis of elongation or principle axis of symmetry). This representation is invariant regardless of the direction from which the person views the object and hence allows the object to be recognized as equivalent across many orientations.

Occipital lobe—The region of cortex behind the endpoint of the Sylvian fissure and below the parietal lobe.

Ocular apraxia—The inability to voluntarily shift your gaze toward a new visual stimulus. It is one of the three main symptoms of Balint's syndrome.

Olfactory bulb—The region of the brain that is responsible for processing information about odors.

Oligodendrocytes—Glia in the central nervous system responsible for creating a myelin sheath around neurons.

Optic ataxia—The inability to point to a target under visual guidance. It is one of the three main symptoms of Balint's syndrome.

Optic chiasm—The point at which information from the nasal hemiretinae crosses the midline to the opposite side of the brain.

Optic nerve—The axons of retinal ganglion cells that serve as the conduit whereby information is carried from the eye to the brain.

Optic tract—The portion of axons of the ganglion cells of the retina past the optic chiasm that synapse in the lateral geniculate nucleus of the thalamus. The portion of the axons situated before the optic chiasm is referred to as the optic nerve.

Optical imaging—Method of determining both the source and the time course of neural activity by positioning a laser source of near infrared light on the scalp and detecting how the light is altered as it passes through the brain.

Oral (buccofacial) apraxia—Difficulty performing voluntary movements with the tongue, lip, cheek, and muscles of the larynx, such as blowing a kiss or sucking on a straw.

Orientation invariant—The situation in which the relationships among an object's parts can be specified regardless of the angle from which the object is viewed.

Output phonological buffer—Working memory store that holds the phonological code online as a speaker is preparing his or her own utterance.

Paired-associate learning—The ability to learn word pairs or pairs of other objects that have no preexisting association. This type of learning is profoundly impaired in amnesia.

Paraphasias—Speech errors made by an individual with aphasia.

Parietal lobe—The region of cortex directly behind the central fissure but above the Sylvian fissure.

Parkinsonian mask—The expressionless face that typically accompanies Parkinson's disease.

Parkinson's disease—A syndrome associated with degeneration of the substantia nigra that leads to a slowness in movements, muscle rigidity, tremors, and cognitive dysfunction.

Pattern completion—Process whereby one piece of an event is used to reconstitute all the other aspects of information that were bound to that event. It is thought that this is how the hippocampus aids in memory retrieval.

Perceptual asymmetries—Differences in the perception of sensory information that are interpreted as reflecting differences in hemispheric processing.

Perceptual categorization—The ability to classify an object as the same item despite variations in the information received by the sensory system, such as variations in size, color, and position.

Peripheral nervous system—All neural processes beyond the central nervous system, such as neurons that receive sensory information or synapse on muscle, and those that relay information to or from the spinal cord or the brain.

Perseverate—To engage in the same behavior or thought pattern repeatedly.

Perseveration—The tendency to engage in repetitive behavior.

Pervasive developmental disorders—Developmental disorders that have four basic characteristics: qualitative impairment in social interaction; delays and abnormalities in language as well as other aspects of communication; restricted, repetitive, and stereotyped patterns of behaviors, interests, or activities; and an onset of the problems in at least one of these three areas before the age of 3 years.

Phenylketonuria (PKU)—A genetic disorder that leads to mental retardation. It is caused by the lack of phenylalanine hydroxylase, an enzyme that breaks down the amino acid, phenylalanine. Its effects can be minimized by an appropriate diet beginning at birth.

Phonemic paraphasia—A paraphasia in which a similar-sounding word is substituted for another (e.g., "table" becomes "trable" or "fable").

Phonological agraphia—A writing disorder in which the ability to use the phonological route from meaning to writing is lost but the ability to use the direct route remains intact.

Phonological alexia—A reading disorder in which the ability to use the phonological route from print to meaning is lost but the ability to use the direct route remains intact.

Phonological awareness—Ability to identify, think about, and manipulate the individual sounds in words.

Phonological loop—A portion of working memory that maintains auditory verbal information in support of speech perception and production.

Phonological route to reading—The method of linking the written word to meaning by using sound as the intermediary.

Phonology—The set of rules governing the sounds of lan guage. It is one of the three fundamental components of language.

Place of articulation—The location in the vocal tract where airflow is obstructed during the production of consonants.

Place fields—The regions of space that cause hippocampal cells to fire preferentially when they are traversed by an animal.

Planum temporale—The temporal plane; the region of the brain at the end of the Sylvian fissure that has been implicated in language processing. It is often larger in the left hemisphere than in the right.

Plasticity—The ability of the brain to change, especially in response to environmental input.

Pons—A major section of the nervous system located directly superior to the medulla and anterior to the cerebellum. It is involved in vestibular functions, auditory functions and in relaying information to the cerebellum.

Positron emission tomography (PET)—A method of investigating the metabolic activity of the brain by introducing a radioactive substance, which emits a positron that causes the substance to go from a radioactive state to a nonradioactive one. After being emitted, the positron is annihilated by an electron, and two photons of light, which travel in 180-degree opposite directions, are produced. Regions of high metabolic activity are determined by a series of light detectors placed around the head that detect the coincident arrival of photons.

Posterior—Located toward the back of the brain.

Post-traumatic amnesia—Amnesia for events following a brain injury.

Praxis—A system that is proposed to control all aspects of motor planning, including speech production, nonspeech oral movements, and limb movements. It is thought to be specialized to the left hemisphere.

Premotor area—Area of the brain located just in front of the motor area that is responsible for selecting the types of movements (e.g., a grasp).

Primal sketch—A "rough draft" of information in the visual world that is easily derived from the basic information that reaches the retina. This sketch contains information about things such as light-dark contrast, edges, and lines.

Primary motor cortex—A region of the cortex that is the final exit point for neurons controlling the fine motor control of the body's muscles.

Primary sensory cortex—The first region of cortex to receive information about a particular sensory modality (e.g., visual information).

Procedural learning—The memory system that supports the acquisition and expression of skill.

Procedural memory—A memory system, operating independently of the hippocampal system, in which information is stored in an inflexible manner related to the context in which it was first acquired.

Propositional prosody—The aspect of an utterance that communicates lexical or semantic information—for example, "What's that in the road ahead?" versus "What's that in the road, a head?"

Proprioception—The perception of the position of body parts and their movements.

Prosody—The intonation pattern, or sound envelope, of an utterance.

Prosopagnosia—A selective inability to recognize or differentiate among faces, although other objects in the visual modality can be correctly identified.

Proximal—Located near the trunk or center.

Psychological inertia—The tendency if at rest, to stay at rest, or if in motion, to stay in motion, unless acted on by an outside force. It is the resistance or disinclination to motion, action, or change. Such inertia must be overcome to initiate action or to cease an ongoing course of action.

Pulse sequence—A magnetic field that is quickly applied and then stopped in a pulsing manner. These pulses perturb the static field, and are tuned to the energy of the atom under investigation. They cause these specific atoms, but not others, to flip 180 degrees.

Pulvinar—A nucleus of the thalamus that aids in attentional processing by filtering out specific information from the barrage of information that constantly impinges upon our sensory systems.

Pure-tone audiometry—A method in which an individual is tested for the ability to perceive a tone that consists of only one frequency (e.g., 1000 Hz). In the test, numerous trials are given so that the ability to process pure tones is assessed over the range of frequencies that humans can detect (e.g., ~125–8000 Hz).

Pure-word deafness—see *Verbal auditory agnosia.*

Putamen—A portion of the basal ganglia that, along with the caudate nucleus, receives all the input into the basal ganglia. It degenerates in Huntington's disease.

Pyramidal cell—Specific type of neuron in the brain involved in controlling muscle movement.

Quadranopsia—The loss of vision in one half of a visual field (a quadrant of visual space).

Receiver coil—The coil that picks up the signal from the atoms as they return to their static state after the pulse sequence.

Receptive field—The region of the sensory world to which a cell will respond if an appropriate stimulus appears within that region.

Receptor sites—Specific places on the postsynaptic dendritic tree that have a particular configuration allowing neurotransmitters to bind there, much as a key fits into a lock.

Recognition—A direct (explicit) test of memory that samples the ability to make judgments about a previous occurrence or to distinguish between items that were and items that were not previously encountered.

Regeneration—The reestablishment of a prior connection by a damaged nerve fiber. This mechanism of recovery of function is limited to the peripheral nervous system.

Relational learning—Learning that occurs in tasks or situations where performance depends on memory for the relations among items, especially items associated only arbitrarily or accidentally.

Relay center—A brain region in which the neurons from one area of the brain synapse onto other neurons that then go on to synapse somewhere else in the brain.

Reorganization—Changes in which the brain tries to override and adapt its typical organization in the face of damage, trauma, or unusual circumstances.

Repetition priming—An item-specific facilitation of performance based on previous experience. It is preserved in amnesia and is an indirect (implicit) test of memory.

Rerouting—A process by which a given neuron seeks and connects with a new target after losing an old one.

Resources—The components of attention, or the effort, that must be devoted to processing certain information.

Resting potential—The resting state of the cell in which the electrical charge inside the cell is −70 mV relative to the charge outside the cell.

Restorative rehabilitation—Rehabilitation that is designed to gain increased function through repetitive exercise.

Reticular activating system (RAS)—A brain system whose cell bodies are located in the medulla and other brain regions. It is responsible for alerting and arousal aspects of attention and for regulation of sleep-wake cycles. Damage to this system causes coma.

Reticular nuclei—Nuclei in the thalamus that affects attention by modulating the level of arousal of the cortex.

Retrograde amnesia—The impairment of memory for information that was acquired normally prior to the onset of amnesia.

Reuptake—The rapid removal of neurotransmitter from the synaptic cleft back into the terminal bouton by special transporter molecules embedded in the presynaptic membrane.

Reversal learning—A situation in which a previously learned set of responses must be reversed (e.g., learning to press the right-hand key when a yellow light appears and the left-hand key when a blue light appears after previously having learned to press the right-hand key when a blue light appeared and the left-hand key when a yellow light appeared).

Ribot's Law—The law, posited by Theodule Ribot in the late 19th century, which states that the most recently acquired memories are most susceptible to disruption by brain damage.

Right visual field—The portion of space that falls to the right of the fixation point of gaze and projects to primary visual cortex of the left hemisphere.

Risk factors—Factors that, although they increase the likelihood that a syndrome will be observed, do not ensure that it will occur.

Rostral—Located toward an animal's head.

Rotary pursuit—A task requiring manual tracking of a circularly moving target. It is an example of a perceptual-motor skill that patients with amnesia can learn normally.

Rubrospinal pathway—The motor pathway that is important for control of forearm and hand movement independent from trunk movement. This pathway is less important in humans than in other species.

Saccade—An eye movement in which the eyes jump from one position to the next (rather than moving smoothly) with seemingly no processing of the intervening visual information.

Sagittal view—A plane that divides the brain along a left-right dimension.

Scotomas—Particular regions in the visual field in which light-dark contrast cannot be detected.

Selective attention—The aspect of attention that is used to select either specific incoming information or specific responses for priority in processing.

Self-ordered pointing task—A test requiring the ability to keep track of which items in an array were already selected because the subject must point to a new item each time the array is viewed. It depends on the integrity of frontal lobe systems.

Semantic memory—Memory of world knowledge that is stored in a context-free fashion.

Semantic paralexias—Reading errors in which a word is misread as a word with a related meaning.

Semantic paraphasia—A paraphasia in which a semantically related word is substituted for the desired word (e.g., "barn" for "house").

Semantics—The meaning of language. It is one of the three fundamental components of language.

Sensitive period—A developmental time period, which has a specific onset and offset, when the organism is especially sensitive to specific external stimuli. After this period ends, any organization that has occurred is generally irreversible.

Serotonin—Monoamine group (and indolamine) that is the neurotransmitter of the serotonergic system. Linked to a wide range of behaviors, including arousal, mood, anxiety and aggression, the control of eating, sleeping and dreaming, pain, sexual behavior, and memory.

Simultanagnosia—An inability to perceive different pieces of information in the visual field simultaneously because the person cannot direct attention to more than one small location in the visual world at a time. The person can recognize individual elements of a scene but not the scene as a whole. It is one of the three main symptoms of Balint's syndrome.

Single-case studies—Neuropsychological investigations in which researchers intensively study the performance of a single person with brain damage on a variety of neuropsychological tests.

Skill learning—The gradual acquisition of new skills such as motor, perceptual, and cognitive skills. These skills are generally preserved in amnesia.

Somatoparaphrenia—A relatively rare condition occurring in hemineglect in which the individual claims that a limb on the neglected side belongs to someone else.

Somatosensory agnosia—A condition in which a person is unable to recognize an item by touch but can recognize it in other modalities. As with other agnosias, memory is intact. It is also called *tactile agnosia* or *astereognosia.*

Source memory—Ability to remember the specific circumstances or context in which particular information was learned.

Space-based viewpoint of attention—The idea that attention is directed toward a particular point in space and that the information at this location is processed more fully.

Spatial frequency hypothesis—The idea that hemispheres differ in their ability to process visual information, depending on spatial frequency. The left hemisphere is posited to excel at processing information of high spatial frequency and the right at processing information of low spatial frequency.

Spinal cord—The portion of the central nervous system where most (but not all) sensory neurons synapse on their way to the brain and whereby motor commands output from the brain are sent to the muscles.

Split-brain procedure—An operation in which the corpus callosum and other cortical commissures are severed precluding any communication between the cerebral hemispheres at the cortical level. Individuals who underwent this procedure are known as *patients with the split-brain syndrome.* It is sometimes referred to as *commissurotomy.*

Sprouting—A process in which a nerve fiber grows, becomes bushier, and makes new connections. It involves not only rerouting, but also a proliferation of nerve growth.

Static field—A magnetic field of high field strength that causes all the atoms to spin and orient in the same direction. Magnets are classified according to the strength of this field, such as 1.5 tesla.

Stereopsis—Depth perception.

Stupor—A state of consciousness in which the individual can be aroused when shaken vigorously or called by name but cannot speak rationally and falls back into unconsciousness quickly.

Subsequent memory effect—The phenomenon that subsequently remembered items are associated with greater brain activation at encoding than items that are not subsequently remembered.

Substantia nigra—A midbrain nucleus that is associated with the basal ganglia. The cell bodies of dopaminergic neurons are located there. This structure degenerates in Parkinson's disease.

Subthalamic nucleus—Portion of the basal ganglia.

Sulcus—A valley between gyri.

Superior—Located toward the top of the brain.

Superior colliculus—A structure in the midbrain that is important for allowing a person to orient her or his eyes to large moving objects in the periphery of the visual field. It allows a person to move his or her focus of attention.

Supervisory attentional system—The cognitive system required to effortfully direct attention.

Supplementary motor area (SMA)—A region of the frontal lobe located on the medial surface of each hemisphere (in the longitudinal fissure) anterior to the region of primary motor cortex and dorsal to the cingulate sulcus. It is important for planning, preparing, and initiating movements.

Surface alexia—A reading disorder in which the ability to use the direct route from print to meaning is lost but the ability to use the phonologic route remains intact.

Sylvian (lateral) fissure—The fissure that divides the temporal lobe from the rest of the brain.

Synapses—The points at which neurons connect with one another.

Synaptic vesicles—Little packages filled with neurotransmitters and located at the terminal, or buton, of the axon.

Synaptogenesis—The process whereby a neuron makes new connections (synapses) with other neurons.

Syntax—The grammar of language. It is one of the three fundamental components of language.

Tactile agnosia—See *Somatosensory agnosia.*

Tactile asymbolia—A form of tactile agnosia in which an individual can form a percept in the tactile modality but cannot link it to meaning (e.g., the 1.5-in.-long metal object that is big at the top and thin at the bottom with a jagged edge on one side cannot be linked to the concept of a key).

Tardive dyskinesia—A movement disorder that occurs in 20 to 40% of all individuals who are long-term users of antipsychotic drugs that block dopamine. It is characterized by increased motor movements, especially of the face and lips.

Telegraphic speech—Speech that contains content words, such as nouns and verbs, but is devoid of function words and word endings. It is characteristic of the speech output of patients with anterior lesions of the left hemisphere.

Temporal gradient—A gradient in memory loss in which recent memories are affected to a greater degree than more remote memories.

Temporal lobe—The region of cortex below the Sylvian fissure.

Temporally limited retrograde amnesia—An amnesia that extends backward in time from the onset of injury for a period of only several months or years.

Thalamus—A brain region that helps to regulate and organize information from the outer reaches of the nervous system as it ascends to the cortex. It also modifies information descending from the cortex.

Theory of mind—The ability to represent mental states of others, such as their beliefs and intentions.

Tics—Repetitive involuntary movements such as compulsive twitching of facial or limb muscles.

Tonotopic—A spatial organization of structures with regard to a tone's frequency.

Topographical disorientation—Difficulty remembering the way around the world after brain trauma. It may affect either the ability to learn routes in a new environment, such as a hospital, or the ability to remember routes through familiar places.

Topographical memory—Thc spatial memory that enables an individual to store information about his or her way around a new environment and to remember routes through familiar places.

Tourette's syndrome—A relatively rare disorder that manifests as a variety of motor and vocal tics. It has its onset in childhood, usually before the age of 11 years.

Transcortical motor aphasia—A syndrome in which an individual loses the ability to produce spontaneous speech but retains the ability to repeat. It is associated with damage that is either anterior or superior to Broca's area.

Transcortical sensory aphasia—A syndrome in which an individual loses the ability to comprehend language but retains the ability to repeat. It is associated with damage to regions posterior to Wernicke's area.

Transcranial magnetic stimulation (TMS)—Method of modulating brain activity by using pulsating magnetic fields on the scalp to interfere with the normal electrical activity of neurons in the brain.

Transneuronal degeneration—A process in which neuronal loss extends past the site of damage to more distal cells.

Tremors—Rhythmic, oscillating movements, usually of a limb or the head. One of the main symptoms of Parkinson's disease.

Turner's syndrome—A genetic disorder in which a female inherits just one X chromosome (XO) rather than two (XX). It is associated with especially poor spatial and perceptual skills.

Two-factor theory—The idea that emotional experience is the outcome of physiological arousal and the attribution of a cause for that arousal.

Unilateral—Pertaining to only one side of the brain (or space).

Unilateral presentation—A method in divided visual field studies in which a single item is presented in only one visual field.

Valence theory—The idea that the emotional state of one hemisphere has a particular valence (e.g., positive), whereas the emotional state of the other hemisphere has the opposite valence (e.g., negative).

Vascular dementia—A mixed-variety dementia that results from the cumulative effects of many individual strokes that tend to involve both cortical and subcortical lesions, with a higher frequency of lesions in the frontal lobes than in other cortical lobes. It was previously called *multi-infarct dementia.*

Ventral—Located toward an animal's stomach (in people sometimes toward the bottom as in the case of the brain).

Ventral corticospinal tract—The tract within the corticospinal pathway that is important for control of the trunk and upper legs. When it is damaged, locomotion and posture are disrupted.

Ventral visual system—Regions of the occipital and temporal lobes that respond only to visual stimuli and are important for object recognition. This system is often referred to as the *"what" visual system.*

Ventromedial pathway—The motor pathway that controls the trunk and proximal limb muscles. It is important for various functions including posture, coordination of eye movements with movements of the trunk and head, autonomic functions, and walking.

Verbal auditory agnosia—An auditory agnosia in which words cannot be understood but the ability to attach meaning to nonverbal sounds is intact. It is sometimes called *pure word deafness.*

Vermis—The medial region of the cerebellum that is important for postural adjustments and walking.

Viewer-centered representation—A representation of an object that is based on the coordinate system of information falling on the retina. As the viewer's position changes relative to an object, so does the representation of the object.

Vigilance—The ability to maintain alertness continuously without "tuning in" and "tuning out." It is also called *sustained attention.*

Visual agnosia—An inability to recognize an object from information provided in the visual modality. It cannot be attributed either to a basic deficit in processing visual information or to a pervasive memory disorder. Furthermore, the deficit is modality specific because the item can be recognized through other sensory channels.

Visual-verbal working memory—Memory that allows us to hold visual-verbal information "on-line" during reading while language processing occurs.

Visuospatial scratch pad—Memory that allows us to hold nonverbal visual information while we perceptually analyze the stimulus array.

Voicing—The timing between the release of air for a stop consonant and the vibration of the vocal cords. When a sound is voiced, the release of air and vocal cord vibration coincide, whereas when a sound is unvoiced, the vocal cords don't begin to vibrate until after the release.

Volumetric representation—A true 3-D representation of an object that describes its volumetric properties, including its center of mass, its overall size (mean diameter or volume), and the principle axis of elongation or principle axis of symmetry.

Wada technique—A method used with patients about to undergo surgery for the removal of epileptic tissue to determine the hemisphere responsible for speech output. It involves injecting a barbiturate into the carotid artery to anesthetize one hemisphere.

Watershed lesion—A lesion caused by lack of oxygen to brain regions that are more susceptible to oxygen deprivation because they fall between the main "watershed" areas for the arterial blood supply. The cause of Balint's syndrome.

Wernicke's aphasia—A syndrome in which speech comprehension is disrupted but speech output is fluent although nonsensical. It is associated with a lesion to the temporal lobe typically near the junction with parietal and occipital regions.

Wisconsin Card Sorting Test (WCST)—A test often used to assess executive dysfunction. It requires individuals to discover which of three attributes (color, number, or shape) should be used to sort cards and to flexibly change the attribute used for sorting.

Word-stem completion task—An indirect (implicit) test of memory in which the completion of three-letter word stems into whole words is influenced by recent study of words composed of the same stems.

Working memory—Short-term memory. The memory that we use to hold information for a brief amount of time or to hold information "on-line" as we perform a task.

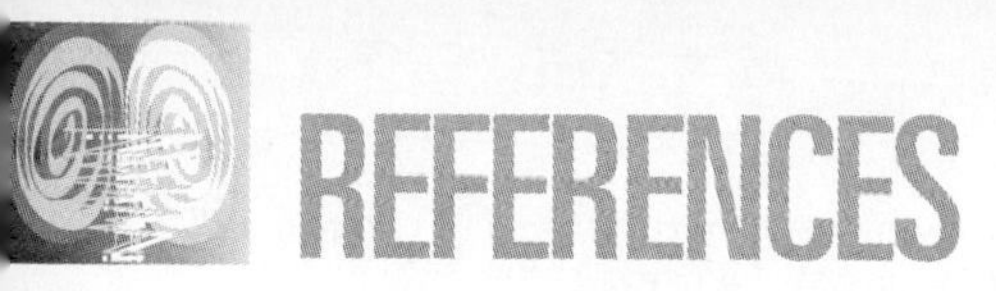

REFERENCES

Abraham, H. D., & Wolf, E. (1988). Visual function in past users of LSD: Psychophysical findings. *Journal of Abnormal Psychology, 97,* 443–447.

Adams, J. H., Graham, D. I., Murray, L. S., & Scott, G. (1982). Diffuse axonal injury due to nonmissile head injury in humans: An analysis of 45 cases. *Annals of Neurology, 12,* 557–563.

Adams, K. M. (1980). In search of Luria's battery. A false start. *Journal of Consulting and Clinical Psychology, 48,* 511–516.

Adolphs, R., Cahill, L., Schul, R., & Babinsky, R. (1997). Impaired declarative memory for emotional material following bilateral amygdala damage in humans. *Learning & Memory, 4,* 291–300.

Adolphs, R., Tranel, D., & Damasio, A. R. (1998). The human amygdala in social judgment. *Nature, 393,* 470–474.

Adolphs, R., Tranel, D., & Damasio, H. (2001). Emotion recognition from faces and prosody following temporal lobectomy. *Neuropsychology, 15,* 396–404.

Adolphs, R., Tranel, D., Damasio, H., & Damasio, A. R. (1995). Fear and the human amygdala. *Journal of Neuroscience, 15*(9), 5879–5891.

Adolphs, R., Tranel, D., Damasio, H., & Damasio, A. (1994). Impaired recognition of emotion in facial expressions following bilateral damage to the human amygdala. *Nature, 372*(6507), 669–672.

Aggelton, J. P., Bland, J. M., Kentridge, R. W., & Neave, N. J. (1994). Handedness and longevity: Archival study of cricketers. *British Medical Journal, 309,* 1681–1684.

Aggleton, J. P., & Young, A. W. (2000). The enigma of the amygdala: On its contribution to human emotion. In R. D. Lane, & L. Nadel (Eds.), *Cognitive neuroscience of emotion* (pp. 106–128). New York: Oxford University Press.

Aglioti, S., Smania, N., Manfredi, M., & Berlucchi, G. (1996). Disownership of left hand and objects related to it in a patient with right brain damage. *Neuroreport, 8*(1), 293–296.

Aguirre, G. K., Zarahn, E., & D'Esposito, M. (1998). An area within human ventral cortex sensitive to 'building' stimuli: Evidence and implications. *Neuron, 21,* 373–383.

Ahern, G. L., & Schwartz, G. E. (1979). Differential lateralization for positive versus negative emotion. *Neuropsychologia, 17,* 693–698.

Ahlfors, S. P., Simpson, G. V., Dale, A. M., Belliveau, J. W., Liu, A. K., Korvenoja, A., Virtanen, J., Huotilainen, M., Tootell, R. B. H., Aronen, H. J., & Ilmoniemi, R. J. (1999). Spatiotemporal activity of a cortical network for processing visual motion revealed by MEG and fMRI. *Journal of Neurophysiology, 82,* 2545–2555.

Aikens, J. E., Fischer, J. S., Namey, M., & Rudick, R. A. (1997). A replicated prospective investigation of life stress, coping, and depressive symptoms in multiple sclerosis. *Journal of Behavioral Medicine, 20,* 433–445.

Aisen, P. S., & Davis, K. L. (1994). Inflammatory mechanisms in Alzheimer's disease: Implications for therapy. *American Journal of Psychiatry, 151,* 1105–1113.

Akshoomoff, N. A., & Courchesne, E. (1992). A new role for the cerebellum in cognitive operations. *Behavioral Neuroscience, 106*(5), 731–738.

Alberico, A. M., Ward, J. M., Choi, S. C., Marmarou, A., & Young, H. F. (1987). Outcome after severe head injury: Relationship to mass lesions, diffuse injury, and ICP course in pediatric and adult patients. *Journal of Neurosurgery, 67,* 648–656.

Albert, M. L. (1973). A simple test of visual neglect. *Neurology, 23,* 658–664.

Albert, M. L., & Bear, D. (1974). Time to understand: A case study of word deafness with reference to the role of time in auditory comprehension. *Brain, 97,* 373–384.

Albert, M. S., Butters, N., & Levin, J. (1979). Temporal gradients in the retrograde amnesia of patients with Korsakoff's disease. *Archives of Neurology, 36,* 211.

Albin, R. L., Young, A. B., & Penney, J. B. (1989). The functional anatomy of basal ganglia disorders. *Trends in Neurosciences, 12,* 366–375.

Alderman, N. (1996). Central executive deficit and response to operant conditioning methods. *Neuropsychological Rehabilitation, 6,* 161–186.

Alexander, G. E., & Crutcher, M. D. (1990). Functional architecture of basal ganglia circuits: Neural substrates of parallel processing. *Trends in Neurosciences, 13,* 266–271.

Alexander, G. E., DeLong, M. R., & Strick, P. L. (1986). Parallel organization of functionally segregated circuits linking basal ganglia and cortex. *Annual Review of Neuroscience, 9,* 357–381.

Alivisatos, B. (1992). The role of the frontal cortex in the use of advance information in a mental rotation paradigm. *Neuropsychologia, 30,* 145–159.

Alivisatos, B., & Milner, B. (1989). Effects of frontal or temporal lobectomy on the use of advance information in a choice reaction time task. *Neuropsychologia, 27,* 495–503.

Alivisatos, B., & Petrides, M. (1997). Functional activation of the human brain during mental rotation. *Neuropsychologia, 35,* 111–118.

Allen, L. F., Palomares, R. S., DeForest, P., Sprinkle, B., & Reynolds, C. R. (1991). The effects of intrauterine cocaine exposure: Transient or teratogenic? *Archives of Clinical Neuropsychology, 6*(3), 133–146.

Allen, L. S., Richey, M. F., Chai, Y. M., & Gorski, R. A. (1991). Sex differences in the corpus callosum of the living human being. *Journal of Neuroscience, 11,* 933–942.

Allison, T., McCarthy, G., Nobre, A., Puce, A., & Belger, A. (1994). Human extrastriate visual cortex and the perception of faces, words, numbers, and colors. *Cerebral Cortex, 5,* 544–554.

Allison, T., Puce, A., & McCarthy, G. (2000). Social perception from visual cues: Role of the STS region. *Trends in Cognitive Sciences, 4*(7), 267–278.

Allmann, J. M., Hakeen, A., Erwin, J. M., Nimchinsky, E., & Hof, P. (2001). The anterior cingulate cortex: The evolution of an interface between emotion and cognition. In A. R. Damasio, A. Harrington, J. Kagan, B. S. McEwen, H. Moss, & R. Shaikh (Eds.), *Unity of knowledge: The convergence of natural and human science. Annals of the New York Academy of Sciences, Vol. 935* (pp. 107–117). New York: The New York Academy of Sciences.

Allport, A., Styles, E., & Hsieh, S. (1994). Non-spatial orienting of attention: Exploring the dynamic control of tasks. In *Attention and performance XV.* Umilta, C. A., & Moscovitch, M. (Eds.). *Conscious and nonconscious information processing.* Cambridge, MA: The MIT Press.

Almkvist, O. (1994). Neuropsychological deficits in vascular dementia in relation to Alzheimer's disease: Reviewing evidence for functional similarity or divergence. *Dementia, 5,* 203–209.

Almkvist, O., Backman, L., Basun, H., & Wahlund, L. O. (1993). Patterns of neuropsychological performance in Alzheimer's disease and vascular dementia. *Cortex, 29,* 661–673.

Althoff, R. R., & Cohen, N. J. (2000). Eye-movement-based memory effect: A reprocessing effect in face perception. *Journal of Experimental Psychology: Learning, Memory, & Cognition, 25,* 997–1010.

Althoff, R. R., Maciukenas, M., & Cohen, N. J. (1993). Indirect assessment of memory using eye movement monitoring. *Society for Neuroscience Abstracts, 19,* 439.

Alvarez, P., & Squire, L. R. (1994). Memory consolidation and the medial temporal lobe: A simple network model. *Proceedings of the National Academy of Science, USA, 91*(15), 7041–7045.

Alyward, E. H., Henderer, J. D., McArthur, J. C., Brettschneider, P. D., Barta, P. E., & Pearlson, G. D. (1993). Reduced basal ganglia volume in HIV-1 associated dementia: Results from quantitative neuroimaging. *Neurology, 43,* 1099–2104.

American Academy of Neurology (1983). The American Academy of Neurology opposes the practice of boxing (policy statement). Executive Board Meeting, May 1983.

American Psychiatric Association. (1994). *Diagnostic and statistical manual of mental disorders* (4th ed.). Washington, DC: Author.

Andersen, R. A. (1988). The neurobiological basis of spatial cognition: Role of the parietal lobe. In J. Stiles-Davis, M. Kritchevsky, & U. Bellugi (Eds.), *Spatial cognition: Brain bases and development* (pp. 57–80). Hillsdale, NJ: Erlbaum.

Andersen, R. A., & Mountcastle, V. B. (1983). The influence of the angle of gaze upon the excitability of the light-sensitive neurons of the posterior parietal cortex. *Journal of Neuroscience, 3,* 532–548.

Andersen, R. A., Snyder, L. H., Bradley, D. C., & Xing, J. (1997). Multimodal representation of space in the posterior parietal cortex and its use in planning movements. *Annual Review of Neuroscience, 20,* 303–330.

Anderson, S. W., Bechara, A., Damasio, H., Tranel, D., & and Damasio, A. R. (1999). Impairment of social and moral behavior related to early damage in human prefrontal cortex. *Nature Neuroscience, 2,* 1032–1037.

Anderson, S. W., Damasio, H., Jones, R. D., & Tranel, D. (1991). Wisconsin Card Sorting Test performance as a measure of frontal lobe damage. *Journal of Clinical and Experimental Neuropsychology, 13,* 909–922.

Andreasen, N. (1989). Nuclear magnetic resonance imaging. In N. Andreasen (Ed.), *Brain imaging: Applications in psychiatry* (pp. 67–121). Washington, DC: American Psychiatric Press.

Andreassi, J. L. (1989). *Psychophysiology: Human behavior and physiological response* (2nd ed.). Hillsdale, NJ: Erlbaum.

Andrew, R. D., & MacVicar, B. A. (1994). Imaging cell volume changes and neuronal excitation in the hippocampal slice. *Neuroscience, 62,* 371–383.

Angrilli, A., Mauri, A., Palomba, D., Flor, H., Birbaumer, N., Sartori, G., & di Paola, F. (1996). Startle reflex and emotion modulation impairment after a right amygdala lesion. *Brain, 119,* 1991–2000.

Anilo-Vento, L., Luck, S. J., & Hillyard, S. A. (1998). Spatio-temporal dynamics of attention to color: Evidence from human electrophysiology. *Human Brain Mapping, 6,* 216–238.

Annett, M. (1985). *Left, right, hand and brain: The right shift theory.* London: Lawrence Erlbaum Associates.

Annett, M. (1995). The right shift theory of a genetic balanced polymorphism for cerebral dominance and cognitive processing. *Current Psychology of Cognition, 14,* 427–480.

Anton, P. S., Granger, R., & Lynch, G. (1993). Simulated dendritic spines influence reciprocal synaptic strengths and lateral inhibition in the olfactory bulb. *Brain Research, 628*(1–2), 157–165.

Appell, J., Kertesz, A., & Fisman, M. (1982). A study of language functioning in Alzheimer patients. *Brain and Language, 17,* 73–91.

Aquirre, G. K., Detre, J. A., Alsop, D. C., & D'Esposito, M. (1996). The parahippocampus subserves topographical learning in man. *Cerebral Cortex, 6,* 823–829.

Aram, D. M., & Eisele, J. A. (1994). Intellectual stability in children with unilateral brain lesions. *Neuropsychologia, 32,* 85–95.

Ardila, A., & Rosselli, M. (1989). Neuropsychological characteristics of normal aging. *Developmental Neuropsychology, 5,* 307–320.

Aretz, A. J. (1991). The design of electronic map displays. *Human Factors, 33,* 85–101.

Aretz, A. J., & Wickens, C. D. (1992). The mental rotation of map displays. *Human Performance, 5,* 303–328.

Arnsten, A. F. T. (1998). Catecholamine modulation of prefrontal cortical cognitive function. *Trends in Cognitive Sciences, 2,* 436–447.

Ashbridge, E., Walsh, V., & Cowey, A. (1997). Temporal aspects of visual search studies by transcranial magnetic stimulation. *Neuropsychologia, 35,* 1121–1131.

Askil, J. (1979). *Physics of musical sounds.* New York: Van Nostrand.

Atkinson, J., & Egeth, J. (1973). Right hemisphere superiority in visual orientation matching. *Canadian Journal of Psychology, 27,* 152–158.

Attewell, R. G., Glase, K., & McFadden, M. (2001). Bicycle helmet efficacy: A meta-analysis. *Accident Analysis and Prevention, 33,* 345–352.

Auerbach, S. H., Allard, T., Naeser, M., Alexander, M. P., & Albert, M. L. (1982). Pure word deafness: Analysis of a case with bilateral lesions and a defect at the prephonemic level. *Brain, 105,* 271–300.

Austin, M. P., Mitchell, P., & Goodwin, G. M. (2001). Cognitive deficits in depression: Possible implications for functional neuropathology. *British Journal of Psychiatry, 178,* 200–206.

Azrin, R. L., Millsaps, C. L., Burton, D. B., & Mittenberg, W. (1992). Recovery of memory and intelligence following chronic cocaine abuse. *Clinical Neuropsychologist, 6,* 344–345.

Bachevalier, J. (1994). Medial temporal lobe structures and autism: A review of clinical and experimental findings. *Neuropsychologia, 32,* 627–648.

Baddeley, A. (1992). Working memory. *Science, 255*(5044), 556–559.

Baddeley, A. (1996). The fractionation of working memory. *Proceedings of the National Academy of Science, USA, 93*(24), 13468–13472.

Baddeley, A. D. (1986). *Working memory.* Oxford, England: Oxford University Press.

Baddeley, A. D., & Hitch, G. (1974). Working memory. In G. A. Bower (Ed.), *The psychology of learning and motivation (Vol. 8)* (pp. 47–90). New York: Academic Press.

Bahr, M., & Bonhoeffer, F. (1994). Perspectives on axonal regeneration in the mammalian CNS. *Trends in Neurosciences, 17,* 473–478.

Baillargeon, R. (1994). How do infants learn about the physical world? *Current Directions in Psychological Science, 3,* 133–139.

Baker, D. P., Chabris, C. F., & Kosslyn, S. M. (1999). Encoding categorical and coordinate spatial relations without input-output correlations: New simulation models. *Cognitive Science, 23,* 33–51.

Baker, E., Blumstein, S. E., & Goodglass, H. (1981). Interaction between phonological and semantic factors in auditory comprehension. *Neuropsychologia, 19,* 1–16.

Baker, E. L., White, R. F., & Murawski, B. J. (1985). Clinical evaluation of neurobehavioral effects of occupational exposure to organic solvents and lead. *British Journal of Mental Health, 14,* 135–158.

Bakker, D. J. (1973). Hemispheric specialization and stages in the learning-to-read process. *Bulleting of the Orton Society, 23,* 15–27.

Ball, M., Braak, H., Coleman, P., Dickson, D., Duyckaerts, C., Gambetti, P., Hansen, L., Hyman, B., Jellinger, K., Markesbery, W., Perl, D., Powers, J., Price, J., Trojanowski, J. Q., Wisniewski, H., Phelps, C., Khachaturian, Z. (1997). Consensus recommendations for the postmortem diagnosis of Alzheimer's disease. *Neurobiology of Aging, 18*(4), S1–S2.

Bamford, K. A., Caine, E. D., Kido, D. K., Cox, C., & Shoulson, I. (1995). A prospective evaluation of cognitive decline in early Huntington's disease: Functional and radiographic correlates. *Neurology, 45*(10), 1867–1873.

Banich, M. T. (1995a). Interhemispheric interaction: Mechanisms of unified processing. In F. L. Kitterle (Ed.), *Hemispheric communication: Mechanisms and models* (pp. 271–300). Hilldale, NJ: Erlbaum.

Banich, M. T. (1998). The missing link: The role of interhemispheric interaction in attentional processing. *Brain & Cognition, 36*(2), 128–157.

Banich, M. T. (2003). Interaction between the hemispheres and its implications for the processing capacity of the brain. In R. Davidson, & K. Hugdahl (Eds.), *Brain asymmetry* (2nd ed.) (pp. 261–302). Cambridge, MA: MIT Press.

Banich, M. T., & Belger, A. (1990). Interhemispheric interaction: How do the hemispheres divide and conquer a task? *Cortex, 26,* 77–94.

Banich, M. T., & Brown, W. S. (2000). A life-span perspective on interaction between the cerebral hemispheres. *Developmental Neuropsychology, 18*(1), 1–10.

Banich, M. T., & Federmeier, K. D. (1999). Categorical and metric spatial processes distinguished by task demands and practice. *Journal of Cognitive Neuroscience, 11,* 153–166.

Banich, M. T., Heller, W., & Levy, J. (1989). Aesthetic preference and picture asymmetries. *Cortex, 25,* 187–196.

Banich, M. T., & Karol, D. L. (1992). The sum of the parts does not equal the whole: Evidence from bihemispheric processing. *Journal of Experimental Psychology: Human Perception and Performance, 18,* 763–784.

Banich, M. T., Levine, S. C., Kim, H., & Huttenlocher, P. (1990). The effects of developmental factors on IQ in hemiplegic children. *Neuropsychologia, 28,* 35–47.

Banich, M. T., Milham, M. P., Atchley, R. A., Cohen, N. J., Webb, A., Wszalek, T., Kramer, A. F., Liang, Z.-P., Barad, V., Gullett, D., Shah, C., & Brown, C. (2000) Prefrontal regions play a predominant role in imposing an attentional "set": Evidence from fMRI. *Cognitive Brain Research, 10,* 1–9.

Banich, M. T., Milham, M. P., Atchley, R. A., Cohen, N. J., Webb, A., Wszalek, T., Kramer, A. F., Liang, Z.-P., Wright, A., Shenker, J., Magin, R., Barad, V., Gullett, D., Shah, C., & Brown, C. (2000). fMRI studies of Stroop tasks reveal unique roles of anterior and posterior brain systems in attentional selection. *Journal of Cognitive Neuroscience, 12,* 988–1000.

Banich, M. T., Passarotti, A. M., & Janes, D. (2000). Interhemispheric interaction during childhood: I. Neurologically intact children. *Developmental Neuropsychology, 18*(1), 33–51.

Banich, M. T., Passarotti, A. M., White, D. A., Nortz, M. J., & Steiner, R. D. (2000). Interhemsipheric interaction during childhood: II. Children with early-treated phenylketonuria. *Developmental Neuropsychology, 18,* 53–71.

Banich, M. T., & Scalf, P. E. (2003). The neurocognitive bases of developmental reading disorders. In Banich, M. T., & Mack, M. (Eds.), *Mind, brain, and language: Multidisciplinary perspectives* (pp. 283–306). Mahwah, NJ: Lawrence Erlbaum Associates.

Banich, M. T., & Shenker, J. I. (1994a). Dissociations in memory for item identity and item frequency: Evidence from hemispheric interactions. *Neuropsychologia, 32,* 1179–1194.

Banich, M. T., & Shenker, J. I. (1994b). Investigations of interhemispheric processing: Methodological considerations. *Neuropsychology, 8*(2), 263–277.

Banich, M. T., Stokes, A., & Elledge, V. C. (1989). Neuropsychological evaluation of aviators: A review.

Aviation Space and Environmental Medicine, 60, 361–366.

Banich, M. T., Stolar, N., Heller, W., & Goldman, R. (1992). A deficit in right-hemisphere performance after induction of a depressed mood. *Neuropsychiatry, Neuropsychology and Behavioral Neurology, 5,* 20–27.

Banks, G., Short, P., Martinez, A. J., Latchaw, R., Ratcliff, G., & Boller, F. (1989). The alien hand syndrome: Clinical and postmortem findings. *Archives of Neurology, 46,* 456–459.

Bannister, R. (1992). *Brain and Bannister's clinical neurology* (7th ed.). Oxford, England: Oxford University Press.

Barak, Y., & Achiron, A. (2000). Effect of interferon-beta-1b on cognitive functions in multiple sclerosis. *Annals of Neurology, 48*(6), 885–892.

Barbizet, J. (1970). *Human memory and its pathology.* San Francisco: Freeman.

Barkley, R. A. (1977). The effects of methylphenidate on various measures of activity level and attention in hyperkinetic children. *Journal of Abnormal Child Psychology, 5,* 351–369.

Barkley, R. A. (1998). Attention-deficit hyperactivity disorder. *Scientific American, 279,* 66–71.

Barkley, R. A., Grodzinsky, G., & DuPaul, G. J. (1992). Frontal lobe functions in attention deficit disorder with and without hyperactivity: A review and research report. *Journal of Abnormal Child Psychology, 20,* 163–188.

Barkley, R. A., Karlsson, J., Pollard, S., & Murphy, J. V. (1985). Developmental changes in the mother–child interactions of hyperactive boys: Effects of two dose levels of Ritalin. *Journal of Child Psychology and Psychiatry and Allied Disciplines, 24,* 705–715.

Barlow, D. H. (1991). Disorders of emotion. *Psychological Inquiry, 2,* 58–71.

Barlow, H. B. (1985). The twelfth Bartlett Memorial Lecture: The role of single neurons in the psychology of perception. *Quarterly Journal of Experimental Psychology, 37A,* 121–145.

Baron-Cohen, S. (1995). *Mindblindness: An essay on autism and theory of mind.* Cambridge, MA: The MIT Press.

Barry, J., Relkin, N., Ravdin, L., Jacobs, A. R., Bennett, A., & Gandy, S. (1997). Apolipoprotein E epsilon 4 associated with chronic traumatic brain injury in boxing. *JAMA, 278,* 136–140.

Bartel, P. R., Burnett, L. S., Griesel, R. D., Freiman, I., Rosen, E. G., & Grefhuysen, G. (1977). The effects of kwashiorkor on performance on tests of neuropsychological function. *Psychologia Africana, 17,* 153–160.

Bartels, A., & Zeki, S. (2000). The neural basis of romantic love. *Neuroreport, 11,* 3829–3834.

Barth, J. T., Alves, W. M., Ryan, T. V., Macchiocchi, S. N., Rimel, R. W., Jane, J. A., & Nelson, W. E. (1989). Mild head injury in sports: Neuropsychological sequelae and recovery of function. In H. S. Levin, H. M. Eisenberg, & A. L. Benton (Eds.), *Mild head injury.* New York: Oxford University Press.

Bartus, R. T. (2000). On neurodegenerative diseases, models, and treatment strategies: Lessons learned and lessons forgotten a generation following the cholinergic hypothesis. *Experimental Neurology, 163,* 495–529.

Bates, E. (1999). Plasticity, localization, and language development. In S. H. Broman, & J. M. Fletcher (Eds.). *The changing nervous system* (pp. 214–253). New York: Oxford University Press.

Bates, E., Wulfeck, B., & MacWhinney, B. (1991). Cross-linguistic research in aphasia: An overview. *Brain and Language, 41,* 123–148.

Baum, S. R., & Pell, M. D. (1999). The neural bases of prosody: Insights from lesion studies and neuroimaging. *Aphasiology, 13,* 581–608.

Bavelier, D., Brozinsky, C., Tomann, A., Mitchell, T., Neville, H., & Liu, G. (2001). Impact of early deafness and early exposure to sign language on the cerebral organization for motion processing. *Journal of Neuroscience, 21,* 8931–8942.

Bavelier, D., Tomann, A., Hutton, C., Mitchell, T., Corina, D., Liu, G., & Neville, H. (2000). Visual attention to the periphery is enhanced in congenitally deaf individuals. *Journal of Neuroscience, 20,* RC93, 1–6

Baxter, L. R., Schwartz, J. M., Phelps, M. E., Mazziotta, J. C., Guze, B. H., Selin, C. E., Gerner, R. H., & Sumida, R. M. (1989). Reduction of prefrontal cortex glucose metabolism common to three types of depression. *Archives of General Psychiatry, 46,* 243–250.

Bayles, K. A. (1982). Language function in senile dementia. *Brain and Language, 16,* 265–280.

Beal, M. F. (1996). Mitochondria, free radicals, and neurodegeneration. *Current Opinion in Neurobiology, 6,* 661–666.

Bear, D. M. (1986). Hemispheric asymmetries in emotional function: A reflection of lateral specialization in cortical-limbic connections. In B. K. Doane, & K. E. Livingston (Eds.), *The limbic system: Functional organization and clinical disorders* (pp. 29–42). New York: Raven Press.

Bearden, C. E., Woodin, M. F., Wang, P. P., Moss, E., McDonald-McGinn, D., Zackai, E., Emmanuel, B., & Cannon, T. D. (2001). The neurocognitive phenotype of the 22q11.2 deletion syndrome: selective deficit in visual-spatial memory. *Journal of Clinical and Experimental Neuropsychology, 23,* 447–464.

Beats, B. C., Sahakian, B. J., & Levy, R. (1996). Cognitive performance in tests sensitive to frontal lobe dysfunction in the elderly depressed. *Psychological Medicine, 26,* 591–603.

Beatty, J. (1995). *Principles of behavior neuroscience.* Madison, WI: Brown & Benchmark.

Beatty, W. W., Katzung, V. M., Moreland, V. J., & Nixon, S. J. (1995). Neuropsychological performance of recently abstinent alcoholics and cocaine abusers. *Drug and Alcohol Dependence, 37,* 247–253.

Beatty, W. W., Salmon, D. P., Butters, N., Heindel, W. C., & Granholm, E. L. (1988). Retrograde amnesia in patients with Alzheimer's disease or Huntington's disease. *Neurobiology of Aging, 9,* 181–186.

Beaubrun, G., & Gray, G. E. (2000). A review of herbal medicines for psychiatric disorders. *Psychiatric Services, 51,* 1130–1134.

Beaumont, J. G. (1985). Lateral organization and aesthetic preference: The importance of peripheral visual asymmetrics. *Neuropsychologia, 23,* 103–113.

Beauregard, M., Chertkow, H., Bub, D., Murtha, S., Dixon, R., & Evans, A. (1997). The neural substrate for concrete, abstract, and emotional word lexica: A positron emission tomography study. *Journal of Cognitive Neuroscience, 9,* 441–461.

Beauvois, M.-F., & Derouesne, J. (1981). Lexical or ortho graphic dysgraphia. *Brain, 104,* 21–50.

Bechara, A., Damasio, A. R., Damasio, H., & Anderson, S. W. (1994). Insensitivity to future consequences following damage to human prefrontal cortex. *Cognition, 50,* 7–15.

Bechara, A., Damasio, H., & Damasio, A. R. (2000). Emotion, decision making and the orbitofrontal cortex. *Cerebral Cortex, 10,* 295–307.

Bechara, A., Tranel, D., Damasio, H., Adolphs, R., Rockland, C., & Damasio, R. A. R. (1995). Double dissociation of conditioning and declarative knowledge relative to the amygdala and hippocampus in humans. *Science, 269*(5227), 1115–1118.

Beck, D. M., Rees, G., Frith, C. D., & Lavie, N. (2001). Neural correlates of change detection and change blindness. *Nature Neuroscience, 4,* 645–650.

Beckwith, L., Rodning, C., Norris, D., Phillipsen, L., Khandabi, P., & Howard, J. (1994). Spontaneous play in two-year-olds born to substance-abusing mothers. *Infant Mental Health Journal, 15*(2), 189–201.

Beeman, M. (1993). Semantic processing in the right hemisphere may contribute to drawing inferences during comprehension. *Brain and Language, 44,* 80–120.

Beeman, M. (1997). Discourse comprehension and coarse semantic coding. In M. Beeman & C. Chiarello (Eds.), *Right hemisphere language comprehension: Perspectives from cognitive neuroscience.* Hillsdale, NJ: Erlbaum.

Beeman, M. (1998). Coarse semantic coding and discourse comprehension. In M. Beeman & C. Chiarello (Eds.), *Right hemisphere language comprehension: Perspectives from cognitive neuroscience* (pp. 255–285). Mahwah, NJ: Lawrence Erlbaum.

Beeman, M. J., & Chiarello, C. (1998a). Complementary right- and left-hemisphere language comprehension. *Current Directions in Psychological Science, 7*(1), 2–8.

Beeman, M. J., & Chiarello, C. (Eds.) (1998b). *Right hemisphere language comprehension: Perspectives from cognitive neuroscience.* Mahwah, NJ: Lawrence Erlbaum & Associates., Inc.

Beeman, M., Friedman, R. B., Grafman, J., Perez, E., Diamond, S., & Lindsay, M. B. (1994). Summation priming and coarse semantic coding in the right hemisphere. *Journal of Cognitive Neuroscience, 6,* 26–45.

Behrens, S. (1988). The role of the right hemisphere in the production of linguistic stress. *Brain and Language, 33,* 104–127.

Behrmann, M. (2000). The mind's eye mapped onto the brain's matter. *Current Directions in Psychological Science, 9,* 50–54.

Behrmann, M., & Moscovitch, M. (1994). Object-centered neglect in patients with unilateral neglect. *Journal of Cognitive Neuroscience, 6,* 1–16.

Behrmann, M., Moscovitch, M., & Winocur, G. (1994). Intact visual imagery and impaired visual perception in a patient with visual agnosia. *Journal of Experimental Psychology: Human Perception and Performance, 20,* 1068–1087.

Beiderman, I. (1987). Matching image edges to object memory. From *Proceedings of the IEEE First International Conference on Computer Vision,* 364–392.

Belger, A., & Banich, M. T. (1992). Interhemispheric interaction affected by computational complexity. *Neuropsychologia, 30,* 923–931.

Belger, A., & Banich, M. T. (1998). Costs and benefits of integrating information between the cerebral hemispheres: A computational perspective. *Neuropsychology, 12*(3), 380–988.

Belleza, T., Rappaport, M., Hopkins, H. K., & Hall, K. (1979). Visual scanning and matching dysfunction in brain-damaged patients with drawing impairment. *Cortex, 15,* 19–36.

Belliveau, J. W., Kennedy, D. N., McKinstry, R. C., Buchbinder, B. R., Weisskoff, R. M., Cohen, M. S., Vevea, J. M., Brady, T. J., & Rosen, B. R. (1991). Functional mapping of the human visual cortex by magnetic resonance imaging. *Science, 254,* 716–718.

Belmont, L., & Birch, H. G. (1963). Lateral dominance and right-left awareness in normal children. *Child Development, 34,* 257–270.

Bench, C. J., Friston, K. J., Brown, R. G., Scott, L. C., Frackowiak, R. S., & Dolan, R. J. (1992). The anatomy of melancholia: Focal abnormalities of cerebral blood flow in major depression. *Psychological Medicine, 22,* 607–615.

Bench, C. J., Frith, C. D., Grasby, P. M., Friston, K. J., Paulesu, P., Frackowiak, R. S. J., & Dolan, R. J. (1993). Investigations of the functional anatomy of attention using the Stroop test. *Neuropsychologia, 31,* 907–922.

Bender, B. G., Linden, M. G., & Robinson, A. (1994). Neurocognitive and psychosocial phenotypes associated with Turner syndrome. In S. H. Broman & J. Grafman (Eds.), *Atypical cognitive deficits in developmental disorders* (pp. 197–216). Hillsdale, NJ: Erlbaum.

Benishin, C. G., Lee, R., Wang, L. C. H., & Liu, H. J. (1991). Effects of ginsenoside Rb_1 on central cholinergic metabolism. *Pharmacology, 42,* 223–229.

Benjamin, J., Li, L., Patterson, C., Greenberg, B. D., Murphy, D. L., & Hamer, D. H. (1996). Population and familial association between the D4 dopamine receptor gene and measures of Novelty Seeking. *Nature Genetics, 12,* 81–84.

Benowitz, L. I., Bear, D. M., Rosenthal, R., Mesulam, M.-M., Zaidel, E., & Sperry, R. W. (1983). Hemispheric specialization in nonverbal communication. *Cortex, 19,* 5–12.

Benson, D. F. (1985). Aphasia. In K. M. Heilman & E. Valenstein (Eds.), *Clinical neuropsychology* (2nd ed.). New York: Oxford University Press.

Benson, D. F., & Geschwind, N. (1967). Shrinking retrograde amnesia. *Journal of Neurology, Neurosurgery and Psychiatry, 30*(6), 539–544.

Benson, D. F., & Geschwind, N. (1972). Aphasia and related disturbances. In A. B. Baker (Ed.), *Clinical neurology.* New York: Harper and Row.

Benson, D. F., & Greenberg, J. P. (1969). Visual form agnosia. *Archives of Neurology, 20,* 82–89.

Benton, A. (1986). Reaction time in brain disease: Some reflections. *Cortex, 22,* 129–140.

Benton, A. L. (1961). The fiction of the Gerstmann syndrome. *Journal of Neurology, Neurosurgery and Psychiatry, 24,* 176–181.

Benton, A. L. (1967). Constructional apraxia and the minor hemisphere. *Confinia Neurologica, 29,* 1–16.

Benton, A. L. (1969). Disorders of spatial orientation. In P. J. Vinken & G. W. Bruyn (Eds.), *Handbook of clinical neurology.* Amsterdam: North Holland.

Benton, A. L. (1985). Body schema disturbances: Finger agnosia and right-left disorientation. In K. M. Heilman & E. Valenstein (Eds.), *Clinical neuropsychology* (2nd ed.). New York: Oxford University Press.

Benton, A. L., Hannay, H. J., & Varney, N. R. (1975). Visual perception of line direction in patients with unilateral brain disease. *Neurology, 25,* 907–910.

Benton, A. L., & Hécaen, H. (1970). Stereoscopic vision in patients with unilateral cerebral disease. *Neurology, 20,* 1084–1088.

Benton, A. L., Levin, H. S., & Van Allen, M. W. (1974). Geographic orientation in patients with unilateral cerebral disease. *Neuropsychologia, 12,* 183–191.

Benton, S., Allison, T., Puce, A., Perez, E., & McCarthy, G. (1996). Electrophysiological studies of face perception in humans. *Journal of Cognitive Neuroscience, 8,* 551–565.

Ben-Yishay, Y., & Diller, L. (1983). Cognitive remediation. In E. A. Griffith, M. Bond, & J. Miller (Eds.), *Rehabilitation of the head injured adult* (pp. 367–380). Philadelphia: F A Davis.

Ben-Yishay, Y., & Prigatano, G. (1990). Cognitive remediation. In M. Rosenthal, E. R. Griffith, M. R. Bond, & J. D. Miller (Eds.), *Rehabilitation of the adult and child with traumatic brain injury* (pp. 393–409). Philadelphia: F A Davis.

Berg, L. (1988). Clinical Dementia Rating (CDR). *Psychopharmacology Bulletin, 24,* 637–639.

Bergman, J., Borg, S., Engelbrekston, K., & Viker, B. (1989). Dependence on sedative-hypnotics: Neuropsychological impairment, field dependence and clinical course in a 5-year follow-up study. *British Journal of Addiction, 84,* 547–553.

Bergsneider, M., Hovda, D. A., McArthur, D. L., Etchepare, M., Huang, S.-C., Sehati, N., Satz, P., Phelps, M. E. & Becker, D. (2001). Metabolic recovery following human traumatic brain injury based on FDG-PET: Time course and relationship to neurological disability. *Journal of Head Trauma Rehabilitation, 16,* 135–148.

Berlucchi, G. & Aglioti, S. (1997). The body in the brain: Neural bases of corporeal awareness. *Trends in Neuroscience, 20,* 560–564.

Bernheimer, H., Birkmayer, W., Hornykiewicz, O., Jellinger, K., & Seitelberg, F. (1973). Brain dopamine and the syndromes of Parkinson and Huntington: Clinical, morphological and neurochemical correlations. *Journal of Neuroscience, 20,* 415–455.

Bernstein, A. S., Riedel, J. A., & Graae, F. (1988). Schizophrenia is associated with altered orienting activity. *Journal of Abnormal Psychology, 97,* 3–12.

Berquier, A., & Ashton, R. (1992). Language lateralization in bilinguals: More not less is needed. A reply to Paradis (1990). *Brain and Language, 43,* 528–533.

Berquin, P. C., Giedd, J. N., Jacobsen, L. K., Hamburger, S. D., Krain, A. L., Rapoport, J. L., & Castellanos, F. X. (1998). Cerebellum in attention-deficit hyperactivity disorder. *Neurology, 50,* 1087–1093.

Berry, J., Van Gorp, W. G., Herzberg, D. S., Hinkin, C., Boone, K., Steinman, L., & Wilkins, J. N. (1993). Neuropsychological deficits in abstinent cocaine abusers: Preliminary findings after two weeks of abstinence. *Drug and Alcohol Dependence, 32,* 231–237.

Berti, A., & Rizzolatti, G. (1992). Visual processing without awareness: Evidence from unilateral neglect. *Journal of Cognitive Neuroscience, 4,* 345–351.

Bertolino, A., Esposito, G., Callicott, J. H., Mattay, V. S., Van Horn, J. D., Frank, J. A., Berman, K. F., & Weinberger, D. R. (2000). Specific relationship between prefrontal neuronal *N*-Acetylaspartate and activation of the working memory cortical network in schizophrenia. *American Journal of Psychiatry, 157,* 26–33.

Bertoncini, J., Morais, J., Bijeljac-Babic, R., McAdams, S., Peretz, I., & Mehler, J. (1989). Dichotic perception and laterality in neonates. *Brain and Language, 37,* 591–605.

Best, C. T. (1988). The emergence of cerebral asymmetries in early human development: A literature review and a neuroembryological model. In D. L. Molfese & S. J. Segalowitz (Eds.), *Brain lateralization in children: Developmental implications* (pp. 5–34). New York: Guilford Press.

Best, C. T., Hoffman, H., & Glanville, B. B. (1982). Development of infant ear asymmetries for speech and music. *Perception and Psychophysics, 31*(1), 75–85.

Bettleheim, B. (1967). *The empty fortress.* New York: Free Press.

Bever, T., & Chiarcllo, R. (1974). Cerebral dominance in musicians and nonmusicians. *Science, 185,* 137–139.

Bickford, R. G., Mulder, D. W., Dodge, H. W., Svien, H. J., & Rome, H. P. (1958). Changes in memory function produced by electrical stimulation of the temporal lobe in man. *Research Publications—Association for Research in Nervous and Mental Disease, 36,* 227–243.

Biederman, I. (1987). Recognition by components: A theory of human image understanding. *Psychological Review, 94,* 115–147.

Biederman, J., & Spencer, T. (1999). Attention-deficit/hyperactivity disorder (ADHD) as a noradrenegic disorder. *Biological Psychiatry, 46,* 1234–1242.

Bierer, L. M., Aisen, P. S., Davidson, M., Ryan, T. M., Schmeidler, J., & Davis, K. L. (1994). A pilot study of clonidine plus physostigmine in Alzheimer's disease. *Dementia, 5,* 243–246.

Bierer, L. M., Hof, P. R., Purohit, D. P., Carlin, L., Schmeidler, J., Davis, K. L., & Perl, D. P. (1995). Neocortical neurofibrillary tangles correlate with dementia severity in Alzheimer's disease. *Archives of Neurology. 52,* 81–88.

Bigler, E. D. (1992). The neurobiology and neuropsychology of adult learning disorders. *Journal of Learning Disabilities, 25,* 488–506.

Binder, J. R., Frost, J. A., Hammeke, T. A., Cox, R. W., Rao, S. M., & Pricto, T. (1997). Human brain language areas identified by functional magnetic resonance imaging. *The Journal of Neuroscience, 17,* 353–362.

Binder, J. R., Frost, J. A., Hammeke, T. A., Rao, S. M., & Cox, R. W. (1996). Function of the left planum temporale in auditory and linguistic processing. *Brain, 119,* 1239–1247.

Binder, L. M. (1986). Persisting symptoms after mild head injury: A review of the post-concussive syndrome. *Journal of Clinical and Experimental Neuropsychology, 8,* 323–346.

Binder, L. M. & Rohling, M. L. (1996). Money matters: A meta-analytic review of the effects of financial incentives on recovery after closed-head injury. *American Journal of Psychiatry, 153,* 7–10.

Binnie, C. D. (1994). Cognitive impairment: Is it inevitable? *Seizure, 3*(Suppl. A), 17–22.

Birchall, J. D., & Chappel, J. S. (1988). Aluminum, chemical physiology, and Alzheimer's disease. *Lancet, 2,* 1008–1010.

Birnbaum, S. G., Gobeske, K. T., Auerbach, J., Taylor, J. R., & Arnsten, A. F. T. (1999). A role for norepinephrine in stress-induced cognitive deficits: Alpha-1-adrenoceptor mediation in prefrontal cortex. *Biological Psychiatry, 46,* 1266–1274.

Bishop, D., Carlyon, R., Deeks, J., & Bishop, S. (1999). Auditory temporal processing impairment: Neither necessary nor sufficient for causing language impairment in children. *Journal of Speech, Language, and Hearing Research, 42,* 1295–1310.

Bisiach, E., Capitani, E., & Porta, E. (1985). Two basic properties of space representation in the brain. *Journal of Neurology, Neurosurgery and Psychiatry, 48,* 141–144.

Bisiach, E., Geminiani, G., Berti, A., & Rusconi, M. L. (1990). Perceptual and premotor factors of unilateral neglect. *Neurology, 40,* 1278–1281.

Bisiach, E., & Luzzatti, C. (1978). Unilateral neglect of representational space. *Cortex, 14,* 129–133.

Bisiach, E., & Rusconi, M. L. (1990). Break-down of perceptual awareness in unilateral neglect. *Cortex, 24,* 643–649.

Bisiach, E., Rusconi, M. L., & Vallar, G. (1991). Remission of somatoparaphrenic delusion through vestibular stimulation. *Neuropsychologia, 29,* 1029–1031.

Black, F. W., & Strub, R. L. (1976). Constructional apraxia in patients with discrete missile wounds of the brain. *Cortex, 12,* 212–220.

Black, J. E., Isaacs, K. R., Anderson, B. J., Alcantara, A. A., & Greenough, W. T. (1990). Learning causes synaptogenesis, whereas motor activity causes angiogenesis, in cerebellar cortex of adult rats. *Proceedings of the National Academy of Science, USA, 87*(14), 5568–5572.

Blacker, D., Albert, M. S., Bassett, S. S., Go, R. C. P., Harrell, L. E. & Folstein, M. F. (1994). Reliability and validity of NINCDS-ADRDA criteria for Alzheimer's disease: The National Institute of Mental Health Genetics Initiative. *Archives of Neurology, 51,* 1198–1024.

Blackman, J. A. (1989). The relationship between inadequate oxygenation of the brain at birth and developmental outcome. *Topics in Early Childhood Special Education, 9,* 1–13.

Blair, R. J. R., Morris, J. S., Frith, C. D., Perrett, D. I., & Dolan, R. J. (1999). Dissociable neural responses to facial expressions of sadness and anger. *Brain, 122,* 883–893.

Blakemore, S. J., Wolpert, D. M., & Frith, C. D. (1998). Central cancellation of self-produced tickle sensation. *Nature Neuroscience, 1,* 635–640.

Bleier, R. (1984). *Science and gender.* New York: Pergamon Press.

Blumer, D. (1999). Evidence supporting the temporal lobe epilepsy personality syndrome. *Neurology, 53 (Suppl. 2),* S9–S12.

Blumstein, S. (1991). Phonological aspects of aphasia. In M. Sarno (Ed.), *Acquired aphasia* (pp. 129–155). New York: Academic Press.

Blumstein, S. E., Baker, E., & Goodglass, H. (1977). Phonological factors in auditory comprehension in aphasia. *Neuropsychologia, 15,* 19–30.

Blumstein, S. E., Cooper, W. E., Zurif, E., & Caramazza, A. (1977). The perception and production of voice-onset time in aphasia. *Neuropsychologia, 15,* 371–383.

Blumstein, S. E., Tartar, V. C., Nigro, G., & Statlender, S. (1984). Acoustic cues for perception of place of articulation in aphasia. *Brain and Language, 22,* 128–149.

Boder, E. (1973). Developmental dyslexia: A diagnostic approach based on three reading-spelling patterns. *Developmental Medicine and Child Neurology, 15,* 663.

Bogen, J. (1979). The callosal syndrome. In K. E. Heilman & E. Valenstein (Eds.), *Clinical neuropsychology.* New York: Oxford University Press.

Boll, T. J. (1981). The Halstead-Reitan Neuropsychological Battery. In S. B. Filskov & T. J. Boll (Eds.), *Handbook of clinical neuropsychology.* New York: Wiley Interscience.

Bookheimer, S. Y., Zeffiro, T. A., Blaxton, T., Gaillard, W., & Theodore, W. (1995). Regional cerebral blood flow during object naming and word reading. *Human Brain Mapping, 3,* 93–106.

Borchgrevink, H. M. (1980). Cerebral lateralization of speech and singing after intracarotid amytal injection. In M. T. Samo & O. Hook (Eds.), *Aphasia: Assessment and treatment.* Stockholm: Almqvist and Wiksell.

Bornstein, B. (1963). Prosopagnosia. In L. Hapern (Ed.), *Problems of dynamic neurology* (pp. 283–318). Jerusalem: Hadassah Medical School.

Bornstein, B., Sroka, M., & Munitz, H. (1969). Propsoagnosia with animal face agnosia. *Cortex, 5,* 164–169.

Bornstein, R. A., Nasrallah, H. A., Para, M. F., Whitacre, C. C., Rosenberger, P., & Fass, R. J. (1993). Neuropsychological performance in symptomatic and asymptomatic HIV infection. *AIDS, 7,* 519–524.

Borod, J., Goodglass, H., & Kaplan, E. (1980). Normative data on the Boston Diagnostic Aphasia Examination Parietal Lobe Battery, and the Boston Naming Test. *Journal of Clinical Neuropsychology, 2,* 209–216.

Borod, J. C. (1993). Cerebral mechanisms underlying facial, prosodic, and lexical emotional expression: A review of neuropsychological studies and methodological issues. *Neuropsychology, 7,* 445–463.

Borod, J. C., Carper, M., Naeser, M., & Goodglass, H. (1985). Left-handed and right-handed aphasics with left hemisphere lesions compared on nonverbal performance measures. *Cortex, 21,* 81–90.

Borod, J. C., Cicero, B. A., Obler, L. K., Welkowitz, J., Erhan, H. M., Santschi, C., Grunwald, I. S., Agosti, R. M., &

Whalen, J. R. (1998). Right hemisphere emotional perception: Evidence across multiple channels. *Neuropsychology, 12,* 446–458.

Bottini, G., Corcoran, R., Sterzi, R., Paulesu, E., Schenone, P., Scarpa, P., Frackowiak, R. S., & Frith, C. D. (1994). The role of the right hemisphere in the interpretation of figurative aspects of language. A positron emission tomography activation study. *Brain, 117,* 1241–1253.

Botvinick, M., Nystrom, L. E., Fissell, K., Carter, C. S., & Cohen, J. D. (1999) Conflict monitoring versus selection-for-action in anterior cingulate cortex. *Nature, 402*(6758), 179–181.

Boutros, N., Belger, A, Campbell, D., D'Souza, C., & Krystal, J. (1999). Comparison of four components of sensory gating in schizophrenia and normal subjects: A preliminary report. *Psychiatry Research, 88*(2), 119–130.

Bowers, D., Bauer, R. M., Coslett, H. B., & Heilman, K. M. (1985). Processing of faces by patients with unilateral hemispheric lesions. I. Dissociations between judgements of facial affect and facial identity. *Brain and Cognition, 4,* 258–272.

Bowers, D., Bauer, R. M., & Heilman, K. M. (1993). The nonverbal affect lexicon: Theoretical perspectives from neuropsychological studies of affect perception. *Neuropsychology, 7,* 433–444.

Bradley, M. M., & Lang, P. J. (2000). Measuring emotion: Behavior, feeling, and physiology. In R. D. Lane, & L. Nadel (Eds.), *Cognitive neuroscience of emotion* (pp. 242–276). New York: Oxford University Press.

Bradshaw, J. L., Phillips, J. G., Dennis, C., Mattingley, J. B., Andrewes, D., Chiu, E., Pierson, J. M., & Bradshaw, J. A. (1992). Initiation and execution of movement sequences in those suffering from and at-risk of developing Huntington's disease. *Journal of Clinical and Experimental Neuropsychology, 14,* 179–192.

Brandt, J. (1991). Cognitive impairments in Huntington's disease: Insights into the neuropsychology of the striatum. In F. Boller & J. Grafman (Eds.), *Handbook of neuropsychology* (Vol. 5, pp. 241–264). New York: Elsevier.

Brandt, J., & Butters, N. (1986). The neuropsychology of Huntington's disease. *Trends in Neurosciences, 9,* 118–120.

Brandt, J., & Butters, N. (1996). Neuropsychological characteristics of Huntington's disease. In I. Grant, & K. M. Adams (Eds.), *Neuropsychological assessment of neuropsychiatric disorders* (2nd ed.) (pp. 312–341). New York: Oxford University Press.

Braver, T. S., Barch, D. M., Gray, J. R., Molfese, D. L., & Snyder, A. (2001). Anterior cingulate cortex and response conflict: Effects of frequency, inhibition and errors. *Cerebral Cortex, 11,* 825–836.

Breedlove, S. M. (1992). Sexual differentiation of the brain and behavior. In J. B. Becker, S. M. Breedlove, & D. Crews (Eds.), *Behavioral endocrinology* (pp. 39–68). Cambridge, MA: MIT Press.

Breggin, P. R. (1993). Parallels between neuroleptic effects and lethargic encephalitis: The production of dyskinesias and cognitive disorders. *Brain and Cognition, 23,* 8–27.

Breiter, H. C., Etcoff, N. L., Whalen, P. J., Kennedy, W. A., Rauch, S. L., Buckner, R. L., Strauss, M. M., Hyman, S. E., & Rosen, B. R. (1996). Response and habituation of the human amygdala during visual processing of facial expression. *Neuron, 17*(5), 875–887.

Brewer, J. B., Zhao, Z., Desmond, J. E., Glover, G. H., & Gabrieli, J. D. (1998). Making memories: brain activity that predicts how well visual experience will be remembered. *Science, 281*(5380), 1151–1152.

Brinkman, C. (1984). Supplementary motor area of the monkey's cerebral cortex: Short- and long-term deficits after unilateral ablation and the effects of subsequent callosal section. *Journal of Neuroscience, 4,* 918–929.

Broadbent, D. E. (1958). *Perception and communication.* London: Pergamon Press.

Brodal, A. (1981). *Neurological anatomy in relation to clinical medicine* (3rd ed.). New York: Oxford University Press.

Brodal, P. (1998). *The central nervous system: Structure and function* (2nd ed). Oxford University Press: New York.

Brontë, C. (1962). *Jane Eyre.* New York: Macmillan.

Brookmeyer, R., Gary, S., & Kawas, C. (1998). Projections of Alzheimer's disease in the United States and the public health impact of delaying disease onset. *American Journal of Public Health, 88,* 1337–1342.

Brooks, D. N., & Baddeley, A. (1976). What can amnesic patients learn? *Neuropsychologia, 14,* 111–122.

Brouwers, P., Cox, C., Martin, A., Chase, T. N., & Fedio, P. (1984). Differential perceptual-spatial impairment in Huntington's and Alzheimer's dementias. *Archives of Neurology, 41,* 1073–1076.

Brown, J. (1977). *Mind, brain and consciousness.* New York: Academic Press.

Brown, P., Cathala, F., Sadowski, D., & Gajdusek, D. (1979). Creutzfeldt-Jakob disease in France: II. Clinical characteristics of 124 consecutively verified cases during the decade 1968–1977. *Annals of Neurology, 6,* 430–437.

Brown, W. T., Jenkins, E., Cohen, I. L., Fisch, G. S., Wolf-Schein, E. G., Gross, A., Waterhouse, L., Fein, D., Mason-Brothers, A., Ritvo, E., Ruttenberg, B., Bentley, W., & Castells, S. (1986). Fragile X and autism: A multi-center survey. *American Journal of Medical Genetics, 23,* 341–352.

Brownell, H. (1988). Appreciation of metaphoric and connotative word meaning by brain-damaged patients. In C. Chiarello (Ed.), *Right hemisphere contributions to lexical semantics* (pp. 19–31). New York: Springer-Verlag.

Brownell, H. H., Michel, D., Powelson, J. A., & Gardner, H. (1983). Surprise but not coherence: Sensitivity to verbal humor in right hemisphere patients. *Brain and Language, 18,* 20–27.

Brownell, H. H., Simpson, T. L., Bihrle, A. M., Potter, H. H., & Gardner, H. (1990). Appreciation of metaphorical alternative word meanings by left and right brain-damaged patients. *Neuropsychologia, 28,* 375–383.

Brozoski, T. J., Brown, R. M., Rosvold, H. E., & Goldman, P. S. (1979). Cognitive deficit caused by regional depletion of dopamine in prefrontal cortex of rhesus monkey. *Science, 205,* 929–932.

Bruder, G. E., Fong, R., Tenke, C. E., Leite, P., Towey, J. P., Stewart, J. E., McGrath, P. J., & Quitkin, F. M. (1997). Regional brain asymmetries in major depression with or without an anxiety disorder: A quantitative EEG study. *Biological Psychiatry, 41,* 939–948.

Bruder, G. E., Quitkin, F. M., Stewart, J. W., Martin, C., Voglmaier, M. M., & Harrison, W. M. (1989). Cerebral laterality and depression: Differences in perceptual asymmetry among diagnostic subtypes. *Journal of Abnormal Psychology, 98,* 177–186.

Bruder, G. E., Stewart, J. W., McGrath, P. J., Ma, G. G. J., Wexler, B. E., & Quitkin, F. M. (2002). Atypical depression: Enhanced right hemispheric dominance for perceiving emotional chimeric faces. *Journal of Abnormal Psychology, 111,* 446–451.

Bruder, G. E., Tenke, C. E., Stewart, J. W., McGrath, P. J., & Quitkin, F. M. (1999). Predictors of therapeutic response to treatments for depression: A review of electrophysiologic and dichotic listening studies. *CNS Spectrums, 4,* 30–36.

Bruyer, R., Laterre, C., Seron, X., Feyereisen, P., Strypstein, E., Pierrard, E., & Rectem, D. (1983). A case of prosopagnosia with some preserved covert remembrance of familiar faces. *Brain and Cognition, 2,* 257–284.

Bryden, M. P. (1965). Tachistoscopic recognition, handedness, and cerebral dominance. *Neuropsychologia, 3,* 1–8.

Bryden, M. P. (1976). Response bias and hemispheric differences in dot localization. *Perception and Psychophysics, 19,* 23–28.

Bryden, M. P., & Allard, F. (1976). Visual hemifield differences depend on typeface. *Brain and Language, 3,* 191–200.

Bryden, M. P., McManus, I. C., & Bulman-Fleming, M. B. (1995). GBG, hormones, genes, and anomalous dominance: A reply to commentaries. *Brain and Cognition, 27,* 94–97.

Buchanan, L., Pavlovic, J., Rovet, J. (1998). A reexamination of the visuospatial deficit in Turner syndrome: Contributions of working memory. *Developmental Neuropsychology, 14*(2–3), 341–367.

Buchanan, T. W., Lutz, K., Mirzazade, S., Specht, K., Shah, N. J., Zilles, K., & Jancke, L. (2000). Recognition of emotional prosody and verbal components of spoken language: An fRMI study. *Cognitive Brain Research, 9,* 227–238.

Buchsbaum, M. S. (1990). Frontal lobes, basal ganglia, temporal lobes—Three sites for schizophrenia? *Schizophrenia Bulletin, 16,* 379–390.

Buchsbaum, M. S., Wu, J., Haier, R., Hazlett, E., Ball, R., Katz, M., Sokolski, K., Lagunas-Solar, M., & Langer, D. (1987). Positron emission tomography assessment of effects of benzodiazepines on regional glucose metabolic rate in patients with anxiety disorder. *Life Sciences, 40,* 2393–2400.

Buchtel, H., Campari, F., De Risio, C., & Rota, R. (1978). Hemispheric differences in discriminative reaction time to facial expressions. *Italian Journal of Psychology, 5,* 159–169.

Buchtel, H. A., & Stewart, J. D. (1989). Auditory agnosia: Apperceptive or associative disorder? *Brain and Language, 37,* 12–25.

Buckner, R., Petersen, S. E., Ojemann, J. G., Miezin, F. M., Squire, L. R., & Raichle, M. E. (1995). Functional anatomical studies of explicit and implicit memory retrieval tasks. *Journal of Neuroscience,* 15, 19–29.

Buckner, R. L. (1996). Beyond HERA: Contributions of specific prefrontal brain areas to long-term memory retrieval. *Psychonomic Bulletin & Review, 3*(2), 149–158.

Buckner, R. L., & Koutstaal, W. (1998). Functional neuroimaging studies of encoding, priming, and explicit memory retrieval. *Proceedings of the National Academy of Science, USA, 95*(3), 891–898.

Buckner, R. L., & Wheeler, M. E. (2001). The cognitive neuroscience of remembering. *Nature Reviews Neuroscience, 2*(9), 624–634.

Buckner, R. L., Koutstaal, W., Schacter, D. L., Wagner, A. D., & Rosen, B. R. (1998). Functional-anatomic study of episodic retrieval using fMRI. I. Retrieval effort versus retrieval success. *Neuroimage, 7*(3), 151–162.

Buckner, R. L., Wheeler, M. E., & Sheridan, M. A. (2001). Encoding processes during retrieval tasks. *Journal of Cognitive Neuroscience, 13*(3), 406–415.

Buckwalter, J. G., Schneider, L. S., Wilshire, T. W., Dunn, M. E., & Henderson, V. W. (1997). Body weight, estrogen and cognitive functioning in Alzheimer's disease: An analysis of the Tacrine Study Group data. *Archives of Gerontology and Geriatrics, 24,* 261–267.

Buhot, M.-C. (1997) Serotonin receptors in cognitive behaviors. *Current Opinion in Neurobiology, 7,* 243–254.

Buhot, M.-C., Martin, S., & Segu, L. (2000). Role of serotonin in memory impairment. *Annals of Medicine, 32,* 210–221.

Burgess, C., & Simpson, G. B. (1988). Cerebral hemispheric mechanisms in the retrieval of ambiguous word meanings. *Brain and Language, 33,* 86–103.

Burke, D. C. (1995). Models of brain injury rehabilitation. *Brain Injury, 9,* 735–743.

Burke, K. A., Letsos, A., & Butler, R. A. (1994). Asymmetric performances in biaural localization of sound in space. *Neuropsychologia, 32,* 1409–1417.

Burton, L. A., Wagner, N., Lim, C., & Levy, J. (1992). Visual field differences for clockwise and counterclockwise mental rotation. *Brain and Cognition, 18,* 192–207.

Bush, G., Frazier, J. A., Rauch, S. L., Seidman, L. J., Whalen, P. J., Jenike, M. A., Rosen, B. R., & Biederman, J. (1999). Anterior cingulate cortex dysfunction in attention-deficit/hyperactivity disorder revealed by fMRI and the counting Stroop, *Biological Psychiatry, 45,* 1542–1552.

Bush, G., Luu, P., & Posner, M. I. (2000). Cognitive and emotional influences in anterior cingulate cortex. *Trends in Cognitive Sciences, 4,* 215–222.

Butler, R. A. (1994). Asymmetric performances in monaural localization of sound in space. *Neuropsychologia, 32,* 221–229.

Butler, R. W., Rorsman, I., Hill, J. M., & Tuma, R. (1993). The effects of frontal brain impairment on fluency: Simple and complex paradigms. *Neuropsychology, 7,* 519–529.

Butters, N., & Cermak, L. S. (1986). A case study of the forgetting of autobiographical knowledge: Implications for the study of retrograde amnesia. In D. C. Rubin (Ed.), *Autobiographical memory* (pp. 253–272). Cambridge, England: Cambridge University Press.

Butters, N., Soeldner, C., & Fedio, P. (1972). Comparison of parietal and frontal lobe spatial deficits in man: Extrapersonal vs. personal (egocentric) space. *Perceptual and Motor Skills, 34,* 27–34.

Butters, N., Wolfe, J., Martone, M., Granholm, E., & Cermak, L. S. (1985). Memory disorders associated with Huntington's disease: Verbal recall, verbal recognition, and procedural memory. *Neuropsychologia, 23,* 729–743.

Byne, W., Bleier, R., & Houston, L. (1988). Variations in human corpus callosum do not predict gender: A study using magnetic resonance imaging. *Behavioral Neuroscience, 102,* 222–227.

Cabeza, R. (2002). Hemispheric asymmetry reduction in older adults: The HAROLD model. *Psychology & Aging, 17,* 85–100.

Cabeza, R., Anderson, N. D., Mangels, J. A., Nyberg, L., & Houle, S. (2000). Age-related differences in neural activity during item and temporal order memory retrieval: A positron emission tomography study. *Journal of Cognitive Neuroscience, 12*(1), 197–206.

Cahill, L., Babinsky, R., Markowitsch, H. J., & McGaugh, J. L. (1995). The amygdala and emotional memory. *Nature, 377*(6547), 295–296.

Cahill, L., Haier, R. J., Fallon, J., Alkire, M. T., Tang, C., Keator, D., Wu, J., & McGaugh, J. L. (1996). Amygdala activity at encoding correlated with long-term, free recall of emotional information. *Proceedings of the National Academy of Science, USA, 93*(15), 8016–8021.

Cahill, L., Pham, C. A., & Setlow, B. (2000). Impaired memory consolidation in rats produced with beta-adrenergic blockade. *Neurobiology of Learning & Memory, 74,* 259–266.

Cahill, L., Weinberger, N. M., Roozendaal, B., & McGaugh, J. L. (1999). Is the amygdala a locus of "conditioned fear"? Some questions and caveats. *Neuron, 23*(2), 227–228.

Caine, E. D., Weingartner, H., Ludlow, C. L., Cudahy, E. A., & Wehry, S. (1981). Qualitative analysis of scopolamine-induced amnesia. *Psychopharmacology, 74,* 74–80.

Calvanio, R., Petrone, P. N., & Levine, D. M. (1987). Left visual spatial neglect is both environment-centered and body-centered. *Neurology, 37,* 1179–1183.

Campbell, R. (1978). Asymmetries in interpreting and expressing a posed facial expression. *Cortex, 19,* 327–342.

Canadian Study of Health and Aging. (1994). The Canadian Study of Health and Aging: Risk factors for Alzheimer's disease in Canada. *Neurology, 44,* 2073–2080.

Cancelliere, A., & Kertesz, A. (1990). Lesion localization in acquired deficits of emotional expression and comprehension. *Brain and Cognition, 13,* 133–147.

Cannon, W. B. (1927). The James-Lange theory of emotions: A critical examination and an alternative theory. *American Journal of Psychology, 39,* 106–124.

Cannon, W. B. (1931). Again the James-Lange and the thalamic theories of emotion. *Psychological Review, 38,* 281–295.

Cantuti-Castelvetri, I., Shukitt-Hale, B., & Joseph, J. A. (2000). Neurobehavioral aspects of antioxidants in aging. *International Journal of Developmental Neuroscience, 18,* 367–381.

Cao, Y., Vikingstad, E. M., Huttenlocher, P. R., Towle, V. L., & Levin, D. N. (1994). Functional magnetic resonance imaging studies of the reorganization of the human hand sensorimotor area after unilateral brain injury in the perinatal period. *Proceedings of the National Academy of Sciences, USA, 91,* 9612–9616.

Caplan, D. (1987). *Neurolinguistics and linguistic aphasiology.* Cambridge, England: Cambridge University Press.

Cappa, S., Sterzi, R., Vallar, G., & Bisiach, E. (1987). Remission of hemineglect and anosognosia during vestibular stimulation. *Neuropsychologia, 25,* 775–782.

Caputo, L., Casartelli, M., Perrone, C., Santori, M., Annoni, G., & Vergani, C. (1998). The 'eye test' in recognition of late-onset Alzheimer's disease. *Archives of Gerontology and Geriatrics, 27,* 171–177.

Caramazza, A., & Badecker, W. (1989). Patient classification in neuropsychological research. *Brain and Cognition, 10,* 256–295.

Caramazza, A., & Hillis, A. (1990). Spatial representation of words in the brain implied by studies of a unilateral neglect patient. *Nature, 346,* 267–269.

Caramazza, A., Hillis, A. E., Rapp, B. C., & Romani, C. (1990). The multiple semantics hypothesis: Multiple confusions? *Cognitive Neuropsychology, 7,* 161–189.

Caramazza, A., Miceli, G., Silveri, M. C., & Laudanna, A. (1985). Reading mechanisms and the organization of the lexicon: Evidence from acquired dyslexia. *Cognitive Neuropsychology, 2,* 81–114.

Caramazza, A., & Shelton, J. R. (1998). Domain-specific knowledge systems in the brain: The animate-inanimate distinction. *Journal of Cognitive Neuroscience, 10,* 1–34.

Cardebat, D., Demonet, J.-F., Celsis, P., Puel, M., Viallard, G., & Marc-Vergnes, J.-P. (1994). Right temporal compensatory mechanisms in a deep dysphasic patient: A case report with activation study by SPECT. *Neuropsychologia, 32,* 97–103.

Cardoso, F., & Jankovic, J. (1997). Dystonia and dyskinesia. *The Psychiatric Clinics of North America, 20,* 821–838.

Carey, S., & Diamond, R. (1977). From piecemeal to configurational representation of faces. *Science, 195,* 312–314.

Carlesimo, G. A., & Oscar-Berman, M. (1992). Memory deficits in Alzheimer's patients: A comprehensive review. *Neuropsychologia, 3,* 119–169.

Carlin, A. S., & O'Malley, S. (1996). Neuropsychological consequences of drug abuse. In I. Grant, & K. M. Adams (Eds.), *Neuropsychological assessment of neuropsychiatric disorders* (pp. 486–503). New York: Oxford University Press.

Carlson, N. (1986). *Physiology of behavior* (3rd ed.). Boston: Allyn & Bacon.

Carlson, N. (1994). *Physiology of behavior.* (5th ed.). Boston: Allyn & Bacon.

Carmon, A., & Bechtoldt, H. P. (1969). Dominance of the right cerebral hemisphere for stereopsis. *Neuropsychologia, 7,* 29–39.

Carney, N., Chesnut, R., Hugo, M., Mann, N. C., Patterson, P., & Helfand, M. (1999). Effect of cognitive rehabilitation on outcomes for persons with traumatic brain injury: A systematic review. *Journal of Head Trauma Rehabilitation, 14,* 277–307.

Carpenter, M. B. (1976). *Human neuroanatomy* (7th ed.). Baltimore: Williams & Wilkins.

Carpenter, P., Just, M., Keller, T., Eddy, W., & Thulborn, K. (1999). Graded functional activation in the visuospatial system in the amount of task demand. *Journal of Cognitive Neuroscience, 11,* 9–24.

Carpenter, P. A., Just, M. A., & Reichle, E. D. (2000). Working memory and executive function: Evidence from neuroimaging. *Current Opinion in Neurobiology, 10,* 195–199.

Carter, C. S., Botvinick, M. M., & Cohen, J. D. (1999). The contribution of the anterior cingulate cortex to executive processes in cognition. *Reviews in the Neurosciences, 10,* 49–57.

Carter, C. S., Braver, T. S., Barch, D. M., Botvinick, M. M., Noll, D., & Cohen, J. D. (1998). Anterior cingulate cortex, error detection, and the online monitoring of performance. *Science, 280,* 747–749.

Carter, C. S., Macdonald, A. M., Botvinick, M., Ross, L. L., Stenger, V. A., Noll, D., & Cohen, J. D. (2000). Parsing executive processes: Strategic vs. evaluative functions of the anterior cingulate cortex. *Proceedings of the National Academy of Sciences, 97,* 1994–1998.

Carter, C. S., Mintun, M., & Cohen, J. D. (1995). Interference and facilitation effects during selective attention—an $H_2{}^{15}O$ PET study of Stroop task performance. *Neuroimage,* 2(4), 264–272.

Carter, W. R., Johnson, M. C., & Borkovec, T. D. (1986). Worry: An electrocortical analysis. *Advances in Behavioral Research and Therapy, 8,* 193–204.

Caselli, R. J. (1993). Ventrolateral and dorsomedial somatosensory association cortex damage produces distinct somesthetic syndromes in humans. *Neurology, 43,* 762–771.

Casey, D. E. (2000). Tardive dyskinesia: Pathophysiology and animal models. *Journal of Clinical Psychiatry, 61*(Suppl. 4), 5–9.

Castellon, S. A., Hinkin, C. H., & Myers, H. F. (2000). Neuropsychiatric disturbance is associated with executive dysfunction in HIV-1 infection. *Journal of the International Neuropsychological Society, 6,* 336–347.

Cavalli, M., DeRenzi, E., Faglloni, P., & Vitale, A. (1981). Impairment of right brain-damaged patients on a linguistic cognitive task. *Cortex, 17,* 545–556.

Cerhan, J. R., Folsom, A. R., Potter, J. D., & Prineas, R. J. (1994). Handedness and mortality risk in older women. *American Journal of Epidemiology, 140,* 368–374.

Cerella, J. (1985). Information processing rates in the elderly. *Psychological Bulletin, 98,* 67–83.

Cerella, J. (1990). Aging and information processing rate. In J. Birren & K. Schaic (Eds.), *Handbook of psychology and aging* (pp. 201–221). New York: Academic Press.

Cermak, L. S., Lewis, R., Butters, N., & Goodglass, H. (1973). Role of verbal mediation in performance of motor tasks by Korsakoff patients. *Perceptual and Motor Skills, 37,* 259–262.

Cermak, L. S., & O'Connor, M. (1983). The anterograde and retrograde retrieval ability of a patient with amnesia due to encephalitis. *Neuropsychologia, 21,* 213–234.

Chabris, C. F., & Kosslyn, S. M. (1998). How do the cerebral hemispheres contribute to encoding spatial relations? *Current Directions in Psychological Science, 7*(1), 8–14.

Chastain, G. (1987). Visually presented letter strings are encoded phonologically: Some converging evidence. *Journal of Experimental Psychology: General, 114,* 147–156.

Chatterjee, A., Strauss, M. E., Smyth, K. A., & Whitehouse, P. J. (1992). Personality changes in Alzheimer's disease. *Archives of Neurology, 49,* 486–491.

Chee, M. W. L., Tan, E. W. L., & Thiel, T. (1999). Mandarin and English single-word processing studied with functional magnetic resonance imaging. *The Journal of Neuroscience, 19,* 3050–3056.

Chess, S., Fernandez, P., & Korn, S. (1979). Behavioral consequences of congenital rubella. *Annual Progress in Child Psychiatry and Child Development,* 467–475.

Chiarello, C. (1991). Interpretation of word meanings by the cerebral hemispheres: One is not enough. In P. J. Schwanenflugel (Ed.), *The psychology of word meanings* (pp. 251–278). Hillsdale, NJ: Earlbaum.

Chiarello, C., & Beeman, M. (1997). Toward a veridical interpretation of right-hemisphere processing and storage. *Psychological Science, 8*(4), 343–344.

Christman, S. (1989). Perceptual characteristics in visual field research. *Brain and Language, 11,* 238–257.

Christman, S., Kitterle, F. L., & Hellige, J. B. (1991). Hemispheric asymmetry in the processing of absolute versus relative spatial frequency. *Brain and Cognition, 16,* 62–73.

Christoff, K., & Gabrieli, J. D. E. (2000). The frontopolar cortex and human cognition: Evidence for a rostrocaudal hierarchical organization within the human prefrontal cortex. *Psychobiology, 28*(2), 168–186.

Chugani, H. T., Phelps, M. E., & Mazziotta, J. C. (1987). Positron emission tomography study of human brain functional development. *Annals of Neurology, 22*(4), 487–497.

Cianchetti, C., Sannio-Fancello, G., Fratta, A. L., Manconi, F., Orano, A., Pischedda, M. P., Pruna, D., Spinicci, G., Archidiacono, N., & Filippi, G. (1991). Neuropsychological, psychiatric, and physical manifestations in 140 members from 18 fragile X families. *American Journal of Medical Genetics, 40,* 234–243.

Cicerone, K., Lazar, R., & Shapiro, W. (1983). Effects of frontal lobe lesions on hypothesis sampling during concept formation. *Neuropsychologia, 21,* 513–524.

Cicone, M., Wapner, W., & Gardner, H. (1980). Sensitivity to emotional expressions and situations in organic patients. *Cortex, 16,* 145–158.

Clark, V. P., & Hillyard, S. A. (1996). Spatial selective attention affects early extrastriate but not striate components of the visual evoked potential. *Journal of Cognitive Neuroscience, 8,* 387–402.

Clarke, S., Assal, G., & de Tribolet, N. (1993). Left hemisphere strategies in visual recognition, topographical orientation and time planning. *Neuropsychologia, 31,* 99–113.

Clarkson-Smith, L., & Hartley, A. A. (1989). Relationships between physical exercise and cognitive abilities in older adults. *Psychology and Aging, 4,* 183–189.

Cohen, J. C., Braver, T. S., & O'Reilly, R. C. (1996). A computational approach to prefrontal cortex, cognitive control, and schizophrenia: Recent developments and current challenges. *Philosophical Transactions of the Royal Society of London, B, 351,* 1515–1527.

Cohen, J. D., & Tong, F. (2001). The face of controversy. *Science, 293,* 2405–2407.

Cohen, L. G., Celnik, P., Pscual-Leonie, A., Corwell, B., Falz, L., Damrosia, J., Honda, M., Sadato, N., Gerloff, C., Catalan, M. D., & Halett, M. (1997). Functional relevance of cross-modal plasticity in blind humans. *Nature, 389,* 180–183.

Cohen, L., Dehaene, S., Naccache, L., Lehéricy, S., Dehacne-Lambertz, G., Hénaff, M.-A., & Michel, F. (2000). The visual word form area: Spatial and temporal characterization of an initial stage of reading in normal subjects and posterior split-brain patients. *Brain, 123,* 291–307.

Cohen, N. F. (1989). Staying in the community after a head injury. In E. Perecman (Ed.), *Integrating theory and practice in clinical neuropsychology.* Hillsdale, NJ: Erlbaum.

Cohen, N. J. (1981). *Neuropsychological evidence for a distinction between procedural and declarative knowledge in human memory and amnesia.* Unpublished doctoral dissertation, University of California, San Diego.

Cohen, N. J. (1984). Preserved learning capacity in amnesia: Evidence for multiple memory systems. In L. R. Squire & N. Butters (Eds.), *Neuropsychology of memory* (pp. 83–103). New York: Guilford Press.

Cohen, N. J., Althoff, R. R., Webb, J. M., McConkie, G. W., Holden, J. A., & Noll, E. L. (1995). *Eye movement monitoring as an indirect measure of memory.* Manuscript submitted for publication.

Cohen, N. J., Banich, M. T., Kramer, A. F., Morris, H. D., Lauterbur, P. C., Potter, C. S., Cao, Y., & Levin, D. N. (1993). Assessing test-retest reliability of functional MRI data. *Society for Neuroscience Abstracts, 23,* 1494.

Cohen, N. J., & Eichenbaum, H. E. (1993). *Memory, amnesia, and the hippocampal system.* Cambridge, MA: MIT Press.

Cohen, N. J., Eichenbaum, H. E., Deacedo, B. S., & Corkin, S. (1985). Different memory systems underlying acquisition of procedural and declarative knowledge. *Annals of the New York Academy of Sciences, 444,* 54–71.

Cohen, N. J., Ramzy, C., Hu, Z., Tomaso, H., Strupp, J., Erhard, P., Anderson, P., & Ugurbil, K. (1994). Hippocampal activation in fMRI evoked by demand for declarative memory-based binding of multiple streams of information. *Society for Neuroscience Abstracts, 20,* 1290.

Cohen, N. J., Ryan, J., Hunt, C., Romine, L., Wszalek, T., & Nash, C. (1999). Hippocampal system and declarative (relational) memory: Summarizing the data from functional neuroimaging studies. *Hippocampus, 9*(1), 83–98.

Cohen, N. J., & Squire, L. R. (1980). Preserved learning and retention of pattern-analyzing skill in amnesia: Dissociation of knowing how and knowing that. *Science, 210,* 207–210.

Cohen, N. J., & Squire, L. R. (1981). Retrograde amnesia and remote memory impairment. *Neuropsychologia, 19*(3), 337–356.

Cohen, R. A., Kaplan, R. F., Zuffante, P., Moser, D. J., Jenkins, M. A., Salloway, S., & Wilkinson, H. (1999). Alteration of intention and self-initiated action associated with bilateral anterior cingulotomy. *Journal of Neuropsychiatry & Clinical Neurosciences, 11,* 444–453.

Cohen, R. M., Semple, W. E., Gross, M., Holcomb, H. J., Dowling, S. M., & Nordahl, T. E. (1988). Functional localization of sustained attention. *Neuropsychiatry, Neuropsychology and Behavioral Neurology, 1,* 3–20.

Colby, C. L., Duhamel, J.-R., & Goldberg, M. E. (1996). Visual, presaccadic and cognitive activation of single neurons in monkey lateral intraparietal area. *Journal of Neurophysiology, 76,* 2841–2852.

Colby, C. L., & Zeffiro, T. (1990). Cortical activation in humans during visual and oculomotor processing measured by positron emission tomography (PET). *Society for Neuroscience Abstracts, 16,* 621.

Cole, M., Schutta, H. S., & Warrington, E. K. (1962). Visual disorientation in homonymous half fields. *Neurology, 12,* 257–263.

Coleman, M. (1987). The search for neurological subgroups in autism. In E. Schopler & G. Mesibov (Eds.), *Neurobiological issues in autism* (pp. 163–178). New York: Plenum Press.

Coltheart, M. (1980). Reading, phonological recoding and deep dyslexia. In M. Coltheart, K. E. Patterson, & J. C. Marshall (Eds.), *Deep dyslexia* (pp. 197–226). London: Routledge.

Coltheart, M. (1982). The psycholinguistic analysis of acquired dyslexias: Some illustrations. *Philosophical Transactions of the Royal Society of London, B298,* 151–164.

Compton, R. J., Heller, W., Banich, M. T., Palmieri, P. A., & Miller, G. A. (2000). Responding to threat: Effects of hemispheric asymmetry and interhemispheric division of input. *Neuropsychology, 14,* 254–264.

Compton, R. J., Williamson, S., Murphy, S. G., & Heller, W. (2002). Hemispheric differences in affective response: Effects of mere exposure. *Social Cognition, 20*(1), 1–17.

Conturo, T. E., Lori, N. F., Cull, T. S., Akbudak, E., Synder, A. Z., Shimony, J. S., McKinstry, R. C., Burton, H., & Raichle, M. E. (1999). Tracking neuronal fiber pathways in the living human brain. *Proceedings of the National Academy of Sciences, 96,* 10422–10427.

Convit, A., de Leon, M. J., Tarshish, C., De Santi, S., Kluger, A., Rusinek, H., & George, A. E. (1995). Hippocampal volume losses in minimally impaired elderly. *Lancet, 345,* 266.

Cook, E. H., Stein, M. A., Krasowski, M. D., Cox, N. J., Olkon, D. M., Kieffer, J. E., & Leventhal, B. L. (1995). Association of attention-deficit disorder and the dopamine transporter gene. *American Journal of Human Genetics, 56,* 993–998.

Cools, R., Stefanova, E., Barker, R. A., Robbins, T. W., & Owen, A. M. (2002). Dopaminergic modulation of high-level cognition in Parkinson's disease: The role of the prefrontal cortex revealed by PET. *Brain, 125,* 584–594.

Cope, D. N. (1995). The effectiveness of traumatic brain injury rehabilitation: A review. *Brain Injury, 9,* 649–670.

Corballis, M., & McLaren, R. (1984). Winding one's *p*'s and *q*'s: Mental rotation and mirror image discrimination. *Journal of Experimental Psychology: Human Perception and Performance, 10,* 318–327.

Corballis, M., & Sergent, J. (1989). Hemispheric specialization for mental rotation. *Cortex, 25,* 15–25.

Corballis, M. C. (1991). Memory, growth, evolution, and laterality. In W. E. Hockley, & S. Lewandowsky (Eds.), *Relating theory and data: Essays on human memory in* honor of Bennet B. Murdock (pp. 23–38). Hillsdale, NJ: Lawrence Erlbaum & Associates, Inc.

Corballis, M. C. (1997). The genetics and evolution of handedness. *Psychological Review, 104,* 714–727.

Corbetta, M., Miezin, F. M., Dobmeyer, S., Shulman, G. L., & Petersen, S. E. (1991). Selective and divided attention during visual discriminations of shape, color, and speed: Functional anatomy by positron emission tomography. *Journal of Neuroscience, 11,* 2383–2402.

Corbetta, M., Miezin, F. M., Shulman, G. L., & Petersen, S. E. (1993). A PET study of visuospatial attention. *Journal of Neuroscience, 13,* 1202–1226.

Corder, E. H., Saunders, A. M., Strittmatter, W. J., Schmechel, D. E., Gaskell, P. C., Small, G. W., Roses, A. D., Haines, J. L., Pericak-Vance, M. A. (1993). Gene dose of apolipoprotein E Type 4 allele and the risk of Alzheimer's disease in late onset families. *Science, 261,* 921–923.

Coren, S., & Halpern, D. F. (1991). Left-handedness: A marker for decreased survival fitness. *Psychological Bulletin, 109,* 90–106.

Coren, S., & Halpern, D. F. (1993). A replay of the baseball data. *Perceptual and Motor Skills, 76,* 403–406.

Corina, D. P., Poizner, H., Bellugi, U., Feinberg, T., Dowd, D., & O'Grady-Batch, L. (1992). Dissociations between linguistic and nonlinguistic gestural systems: A case for compositionality. *Brain and Language, 43,* 414–447.

Corina, D. P., Vaid, J., & Bellugi, U. (1992). The linguistic basis of left hemisphere specialization. *Science, 255,* 1258–1260.

Corkin, S. (1968). Acquisition of motor skill after bilateral medial temporal-lobe excision. *Neuropsychologia, 6,* 255–265.

Corkin, S. (1982). Some relationships between global amnesias and the memory impairments in Alzheimer's disease. In S. Corkin, K. L. Davis, J. H. Growdon, & E. Usdin (Eds.), *Alzheimer's disease: A report of progress in research* (pp. 149–164). New York: Raven Press.

Corkin, S. (1984). Lasting consequences of bilateral medial temporal lobectomy: Clinical course and experimental findings in H. M. *Seminars in Neurology, 4,* 249–259.

Corkin, S. (2002). What's new with the amnesic patient H. M.? *Nature Reviews Neuroscience, 3*(2), 153–160.

Corkin, S., Milner, B., & Rasmussen, T. (1970). Somatosensory thresholds: Contrasting effects of postcentral gyrus and posterior parietal-lobe excisions. *Archives of Neurology, 23,* 41–58.

Corkin, S., Rosen, T. J., Sullivan, E. V., & Clegg, R. A. (1989). Penetrating head injury in young adulthood exacerbates cognitive decline in later years. *Journal of Neuroscience, 9,* 3876–3883.

Coslett, H. B., Bowers, D., & Heilman, K. M. (1987). Reduction in cerebral activation after right hemisphere stroke. *Neurology, 37,* 957–962.

Coull, J. T., & Nobre, A. C. (1998). Where and when to pay attention: The neural systems for directing attention to spatial locations and to time intervals as revealed by both PET and fMRI. *Journal of Neuroscience, 18,* 7426–7435.

Coull, J. T., Middleton, H. C., Robbins, T. W., & Sahakian, B. J. (1995) Clonidine and diazepam have differential effects on tests of attention and learning. *Psychopharmacology, 120,* 322–332.

Coull, J. T., Nobre, A. C., & Frith, C. D. (2001). The noradrenergic α_2 agonist clonidine modulates behavioural and neuroanatomical correlates of human attentional orienting and alerting. *Cerebral Cortex, 11,* 73–84.

Coull, J. T., Sahakian, B. J., Middleton, H. C., Young, A. H., Park, S. B., McShane, R. H., Cowen, P. J., & Robbins, T. W. (1995). Differential effects of clonidine, haloperidol, diazepam, and tryptophan depletion on focused attention and attentional search. *Psychopharmacology, 121,* 222–230.

Courchesne, E. (1997). Brainstem, cerebellar and limbic neuroanatomical abnormalities in autism. *Current Opinion in Neurobiology, 7,* 269–278.

Courchesne, E., Yeung-Courchesne, R., Press, G. A., Hesselink, J. R., & Jernigan, T. L. (1988). Hypoplasia of cerebellar vermis lobules VI and VII in autism. *New England Journal of Medicine, 138,* 1349–1354.

Court, J., Perry, E., Johnson, M., Piggott, M., Kerwin, J., Perry, R., & Ince, P. (1993). Regional patterns of cholinergic and glutamate activity in the developing and aging human brain. *Developmental Brain Research, 74,* 73–82.

Courchesne, E., Yeung-Courchesne, R., Press, G. A., Hesselink, J. R., & Jernigan, T. L. (1988). Hypoplasia of cerebellar vermal lobules VI and VII in autism. *New England Journal of Medicine, 318,* 1349–1354.

Craft, S., Gourovitch, M. L., Dowton, S. B., Swanson, J., & Bonforte, S. (1992). Lateralized deficits in visual attention in early treated PKU. *Neuropsychologia, 30,* 341–351.

Craik, F. I. M. (1989). In R. Wurtman (Ed.), *Alzheimer's disease: Advances in basic research and therapy.* Cambridge, MA: Center for Brain Sciences.

Craik, F. I. M., & Byrd, M. (1982). Aging and cognitive deficits: the role of attentional resources. In F. I. M. Craik, & S. Trehub (Eds.), *Aging and cognitive processes* (pp. 191–211). New York: Plenum Press.

Craik, F. I. M. & McDowd, J. M. (1987). Age differences in recall and recognition. *Journal of Experimental Psychology: Learning, Memory, and Cognition, 13,* 474–479.

Craik, F. I. M., Morris, L. W., Morris, R. G., & Loewen, E. R. (1990). Relations between source amnesia and frontal lobe functioning in older adults. *Psychology and Aging, 5,* 148–151.

Cramer, S. C., Nelles, G., Benson, R. R., Kaplan, J. D., Parker, R. A., Kwong, K. K., Kennedy, D. N., Finklestein, S. P., & Rosen, B. R. (1997). A functional MRI study of subjects recovered from hemiparetic stroke. *Stroke, 28,* 2518–2527.

Crawford, J. R. (1992). Current and premorbid intelligence measures in neuropsychological assessment. In J. R. Crawford, D. M. Parker, & W. W. McKinlay (Eds.), *A handbook of neuropsychological assessment.* Hillsdale, NJ: Erlbaum.

Creem, S. H., & Proffitt, D. R. (2001). Defining the cortical visual systems: "What," "where," and "how." *Acta Psychologica, 107*(1–3), 43–68.

Cremona-Meteyard, S. L., & Geffen, G. M. (1994). Persistent visuospatial attention deficits following mild head injury in Australian Rules football players. *Neuropsychologia, 32,* 649–662.

Critchley, H., Daly, E., Phillips, M., Brammer, M., Bullmore, E., Williams, S., Van Amelsvoort, T., Robertson, D., David, A., & Murphy, D. (2000). Explicit and implicit neural mechanisms for processing of social information from facial expressions: A functional magnetic resonance imaging study. *Human Brain Mapping, 9,* 93–105.

Critchley, M. (1970). *Developmental dyslexia.* Springfield, IL: Charles C Thomas.

Crowder, R. G., Serafine, M. L., & Repp, B. (1990). Physical interaction and association by contiguity in memory for the words and melodies of songs. *Memory and Cognition, 18,* 469–476.

Crowne, D. P., Novotny, M. F., Maier, S. E., & Vitols, R. (1992). Effects of unilateral parietal lesions on spatial localization in the rat. *Behavioral Neuroscience, 106*(5), 808–819.

Cumming, W. J. K. (1988). The neurobiology of body schema. *British Journal of Psychiatry, 153*(Suppl. 2), 7–11.

Cummings, J. (1998). Current perspectives in Alzheimer's disease. *Neurology, 51*(Suppl. 1), S2–S17.

Cummings, J. L. (1991). Behavioral complications of drug treatment in Parkinson's disease. *Journal of the American Geriatrics Society, 39,* 708–716.

Cummings, J. L., & Benson, D. F. (1983). *Dementia: A clinical approach.* Boston: Butterworth.

Cummings, J. L., & Benson, D. F. (1984). Subcortical dementia: Review of an emerging concept. *Archives of Neurology, 41,* 874–879.

Cummings, J. L., & Benson, D. F. (1988). Psychological dysfunction accompanying subcortical dementias. *Annual Review of Medicine, 39,* 53–61.

Cummings, J. L., Benson, D. F., Hill, M. A., & Read, S. (1985). Aphasia in dementia of the Alzheimer type. *Neurology, 35,* 394–397.

Cummings, J. L., & Duchen, L. W. (1981). Kluver-Bucy syndrome in Pick's disease: Clinical and pathologic correlations. *Neurology, 31,* 1415–1422.

Curran, T. (2000). Brain potentials of recollection and familiarity. *Memory and Cognition 28,* 923–938.

Cutler, N. R., & Sramek, J. J. (2001). Review of the next generation of Alzheimer's diseasetherapeutics: Challenges for drug development. *Progression in Neuro-psychopharmacology and Biological Psychiatry, 25,* 27–57.

Daigncault, S., Braun, C. M. J., & Whitaker, H. A. (1992). Early effects of normal aging on perseverative and non-perseverative prefrontal measures. *Developmental Neuropsychology, 8,* 99–114.

Dalmady-Israel, C., & Zasler, N. D. (1993). Post-traumatic seizures: A critical review. *Brain Injury, 7,* 263–273.

Dalrymple, A. J. C., Kalders, A. S., Jones, R. D., & Watson, R. W. (1994). A central executive deficit in patients with Parkinson's disease. *Journal of Neurology, Neurosurgery and Psychiatry, 57,* 360–367.

Damasio, A. R. (1985). Disorders of complex visual processing: Agnosia, achromatopsia, Balint's syndrome, and related difficulties of orientation and construction. In M.-M. Mesulam (Ed.), *Principles of behavioral neurology* (pp. 259–288). Philadelphia: F A Davis.

Damasio, A. R. (1989). The brain binds entities and events by multiregional activation from convergence zones. *Neural Computation, 1,* 123–132.

Damasio, A. R., Damasio, H., & Chui, H. C. (1980). Neglect following damage to frontal lobe or basal ganglia. *Neuropsychologia, 18,* 123–132.

Damasio, A. R., Damasio, H., & Van Hoesen, G. W. (1982). Prosopagnosia: Anatomical basis and behavioral mechanisms. *Neurology, 32,* 331–341.

Damasio, A. R., & Maurer, R. G. (1978). A neurological model for childhood autism. *Archives of Neurology, 35,* 777–786.

Damasio, H., & Damasio, A. R. (1989). *Lesion analysis in neuropsychology.* New York: Oxford University Press.

Damasio, H. C. (1991a). Neuroanatomical correlates of the aphasias. In M. T. Sarno (Ed.), *Acquired aphasia* (2nd ed., pp. 45–70). New York: Academic Press.

Damasio, H. C. (1991b). Neuroanatomy of frontal lobe in vivo: A comment on methodology. In J. S. Levin, H. M. Eisenberg, & A. L. Benton (Eds.), *Frontal lobe function and dysfunction.* New York: Oxford University Press.

Daniel, W. F., & Yeo, R. A. (1994). Accident proneness and handedness. *Biological Psychiatry, 35,* 499.

Danly, M., & Shapiro, B. (1982). Speech prosody in Broca's aphasia. *Brain and Language, 16,* 171–190.

Danta, G., Hilton, R. C., & O'Boyle, D. J. (1978). Hemisphere function and binocular depth perception. *Brain, 101,* 569–590.

Dao-Castellana, M. H., Samson, Y., Legault, F., Martinot, J. L., Aubin, H. J., Crouzel, C., Feldman, L., Barrucand, D., Rancurel, G., Feline, A., & Syrota, A. (1998). Frontal dysfunction in neurologically normal chronic alcoholic subjects: Metabolic and neuropsychological Findings. *Psychological Medicine, 28,* 1039–1048.

Davidson, R. J. (1984). Affect, cognition, and hemispheric specialization. In C. E. Izard, J. Kagan, & R. Zajonc (Eds.), *Emotion, cognition, and behavior* (pp. 320–365). New York: Cambridge University Press.

Davidson, R. J. (1992). Emotion and affective style: Hemispheric substrates. *Psychological Science, 3,* 39–43.

Davidson, R. J. (1993). Parsing affective space: Perspectives from neuropsychology and psychophysiology. *Neuropsychology, 7,* 464–475.

Davidson, R. J. (1998). Affective style and affective disorders: Perspectives from affective neuroscience. *Cognition and Emotion, 12,* 307–330.

Davidson, R. J. (2000). Affective style, psychopathology, and resilience: Brain mechanisms and plasticity. *American Psychologist, 55,* 1196–1214.

Davidson, R. J. (2001). Toward a biology of personality and emotion. In A. R. Damasio, A. Harrington, J. Kagan, B. S. McEwen, H. Moss, & R. Shaikh (Eds.) *Unity of knowledge: The convergence of natural and human science: Annals of the New York Academy of Sciences, Vol. 935* (pp. 191–207). New York: The New York Academy of Sciences.

Davidson, R. J., Chapman, J. P., & Chapman, L. J. (1987). Task-dependent EEG asymmetry discriminates between depressed and non-depressed subjects. *Psychophysiology, 24,* 585.

Davidson, R. J., & Hugdahl, K. (1995). *Brain asymmetry.* Cambridge, MA: MIT Press.

Davidson, R. J., Pizzagalli, D., Nitschke, J. B., & Putnam, K. M. (2002). Depression: Perspectives from affective neuroscience. *Annual Review of Psychology. 53,* 545–574.

Davidson, R. J., & Tomarken, A. J. (1989). Laterality and emotion: An electrophysiological approach. In F. Boller & J. Grafman (Eds.), *Handbook of neuropsychology* (pp. 419–441). Amsterdam: Elsevier.

Davies, P., Anderton, B., Kirsch, J., Konnerth, A., Nitsch, R., & Sheetz, M. (1998). First one in, last one out: The role of gabinergic transmission in generation and degeneration. *Progress in Neurobiology, 55,* 651–658.

Davies, P., & Maloney, A. J. F. (1976). Selective loss of central cholinergic neurons in Alzheimer's disease. *Lancet, 2,* 1403.

Davis, H., Cohen, A., Gandy, M., Colombo, P., Van Dusseldorp, G., Simolke, N., & Romano, J. (1990). Lexical priming deficits as a function of age. *Behavioral Neuroscience, 104,* 288–297.

Davis, K. D., Hutchinson, W. D., Lozano, A. M., Tasker, R. R., & Dostrovsky, J. O. (2000). Human anterior cingulated cortex neurons modulated by attention-demanding tasks. *Journal of Neurophysiology, 83,* 3575–3577.

Davis, K. D., Taylor, S. J., Crawley, A. P., Wood, M. L., & Mikulis, D. J. (1997). Functional MRI of pain- and attention-related activations in human cingulated cortex. *Journal of Neurophysiology, 77,* 3370–3380.

Davis, M. (1992). The role of the amygdala in fear and anxiety. *Annual Review of Neuroscience, 15,* 353–375.

Davis, M. (1994). The role of the amygdala in emotional learning. *International Review of Neurobiology, 36,* 225–266.

Davis, M., & Whalen, P. J. (2001). The amygdala: Vigilance and emotion. *Molecular Psychiatry, 6,* 13–34.

Day, J. J., Grant, I., Atkinson, J. H., Brysk, L. T., McCutchan, J. A., Hesselink, J. R., Heaton, R. K., Weinrich, J. D., Spector, S. A., & Richman, D. D. (1992). Incidence of dementia in a two year follow-up of AIDS and ARC patients on an initial Phase II AZT placebo-controlled study: San Diego Cohort. *Journal of Neuropsychiatry, 4,* 15–20.

Day, N. L. (1992). Effects of prenatal alcohol exposure. In I. S. Zagon & T. A. Slotkin (Eds.), *Maternal substance abuse and the developing nervous system* (pp. 27–44). New York: Academic Press.

Day, N. L., & Richardson, G. A. (1993). Cocaine use and crack babies: Science, the media, and miscommunication. *Neurotoxicology and Teratology, 15*(5), 293–294.

Dee, H. L., Benton, A. L., & Van Allen, M. W. (1970). Apraxia in relation to hemisphere locus of lesion and aphasia. *Transactions of the American Neurological Association, 95,* 147–148.

Decety, J., Perani, D., Jeannerod, M., Bettindardi, V., Tadary, B., Wood, R., Mazziotla, J. C., & Fazio, F. (1994). Mapping motor representations with positron emission tomography. *Nature, 371,* 600–602.

deFockert, J. W., Rees, G., Frith, C. D., & Lavie, N. (2001). The role of working memory in visual selective attention. *Science, 291,* 1803–1806.

DeFries, J. C. (1985). Colorado reading project. In D. B. Gray & J. F. Kavanaugh (Eds.), *Biobehavioral measures of dyslexia,* Parkton, MD: York Press.

Degl'Innocenti, A., Agren, H. & Backman, L. (1998). Executive deficits in major depression. *Acta Psychiatrica Scandinavica, 97,* 182–188.

De Haan, E. H., Young, A., & Newcombe, F. (1987). Faces interfere with name classification in a prosopagnosic patient. *Cortex, 23,* 309–316.

Dehaene, S., & Naccache, L. (2001). Towards a cognitive neuroscience of consciousness: basic evidence and a workspace framework. *Cognition, 79,* 1–37.

Dehaene, S., Dupoux, E., Mehler, J., Cohen, L., Perani, D., van de Moortele, P. F., Lehérici, S., & LeBihan, D. (1997). Anatomical variability in the cortical representation of first and second languages. *Neuroreport, 17,* 3809–3815.

Dehaene, S., Naccache, L., Le Clec'H, G., Koechlin, E., Mueller, M., Dehaene-Lambertz, van de Moortele, P. F., & Le Bihan, D. (1998). Imaging unconscious semantic priming. *Nature, 395,* 597–600.

Dehaene, S., Posner, M. I. & Tucker, D. M. (1994). Localization of a neural system for error detection and compensation. *Psychological Science, 5,* 303–305.

de Joode, B. V., Wesseling, C., Kromhout, H., Monge, P., Garcia, M., & Mergler, D. (2001). Chronic nervous-system effects of long-term occupational exposure to DDT. *Lancet, 357*(9261), 1014–1016.

DeKosky, S. T., Heilman, G. E., Bowers, D., & Valenstein, I. (1980). Recognition and discrimination of emotional faces and pictures. *Brain and Language, 9,* 206–214.

deLacoste, C., Kirkpatrick, J. B., & Ross, E. D. (1985). Topography of the human-corpus callosum. *Journal of Neuropathology and Experimental Neurology, 44,* 578–591.

deLacoste-Utamsing, C., & Holloway, R. L. (1982). Sexual dimorphism in the human corpus callosum. *Science, 216,* 1431–1432.

Deldin, P. J., Keller, J., Gergen, J. A., & Miller, G. A. (2000). Right-posterior face processing anomaly in depression. *Journal of Abnormal Psychology, 109,* 116–121.

de Leon, M. J., George, A. E., Golomb, J., Tarshish, C., Convit, A., Kluger, A., De Santi, S., McRae, T., Ferris, S. H., Reisberg, B., Ince, C., Rusinek, H., Bobinski, M., Quinn, B., Miller, D. C., & Wisniewski, H. M. (1997). Frequency of hippocampal formation atrophy in normal aging and Alzheimer's disease. *Neurobiology of Aging, 18,* 1–11.

Delis, D. C., Robertson, L. C., & Efron, R. (1986). Hemispheric specialization of memory for visual hierarchical stimuli. *Neuropsychologia, 24,* 205–214.

Delis, D. C., Squire, L. R., Bihrle, A., & Massman, P. (1992). Componential analysis of problem-solving ability: Performance of patients with frontal lobe damage and amnesic patients on a new sorting test. *Neuropsychologia, 30,* 683–697.

Delis, D. C., Wapner, W., Gardner, H., & Moses, J. A. (1983). The contribution of the right hemisphere to the organization of paragraphs. *Cortex, 19,* 43–50.

Della Malva, C. L., Stuss, D. T., D'Alton, J., & Willmer, J. (1993). Capture errors and sequencing after frontal brain lesions. *Neuropsychologia, 31,* 363–372.

Demb, J. B., Desmond, J. E., Wagner, A. D., Stone, M., Lee, A. T., Glover, G. H., & Gabrieli, J. D. E. (1994). A functional MRI (fMRI) student of semantic encoding and memory in the left inferior frontal gyrus. *Society for Neuroscience Abstracts, 20,* 1290.

Denckla, M. B. (1979). Childhood learning disabilities. In K. M. Heilman & E. Valenstein (Eds.), *Clinical neuropsychology.* New York: Oxford University Press.

Dennett, D. C., & Kinsbourne, M. (1992). Time and the observer: The where and when of consciousness in the brain. *Behavioral and Brain Sciences, 17,* 175–180.

Dennis, M., & Kohn, B. (1975). Comprehension of syntax in infantile hemiplegics after cerebral hemidecortication: Left-hemisphere superiority. *Brain and Language, 2,* 472–482.

Dennis, M., & Whitaker, W. (1976). Language acquisition following hemidecortication: Linguistic superiority of left over right hemisphere. *Brain and Language, 3,* 404–433.

DeRenzi, E. (1980). The Token Test and the Reporter's Test: A measure of verbal input and a measure of verbal output. In M. T. Sarno & O. Hook (Eds.), *Aphasia: Assessment and treatment.* New York: Masson.

DeRenzi, E. (1986). Current issues in prosopagnosia. In H. D. Ellis, M. A. Jeeves, F. Newcombe, & Y. A. (Eds.), *Aspects of face processing.* Dordrecht, The Netherlands: Martinus Nijhoff.

DeRenzi, E. (2000). Prosopagnosia. In M. J. Farah, & T. E. Feinberg (Eds.), *Patient-based approaches to cognitive neuroscience* (pp. 85–95). Cambridge, MA: MIT Press.

DeRenzi, E., Faglioni, P., & Previdi, P. (1977). Spatial memory and hemispheric locus of lesion. *Cortex, 13,* 424–433.

DeRenzi, E., & Lucchelli, F. (1988). Ideational apraxia. *Brain, 111,* 1173–1188.

DeRenzi, E., Motti, F., & Nichelli, P. (1980). Imitating gestures: A quantitative approach. *Archives of Neurology, 37,* 6–10.

DeRenzi, E., & Nichelli, P. (1975). Verbal and non-verbal short-term memory impairment following hemispheric damage. *Cortex, 11,* 341–354.

DeRenzi, E., Perani, D., Carlesimo, G. A., Silveri, M. C., & Fazio, F. (1994). Prosopagnosia can be associated with damage confined to the right hemisphere—An MRI and PET study and review of the literature. *Neuropsychologia, 32,* 893–902.

DeRenzi, E., Pieczuro, A., & Vignolo, L. A. (1968). Ideational apraxia: A quantitative study. *Neuropsychologia, 6,* 41–52.

DeRenzi, E., & Spinnler, H. (1966). Visual recognition in patients with unilateral cerebral disease. *Journal of Nervous and Mental Disease, 142,* 513–525.

Desimone, R., Albright, T. D., Gross, C. G., & Bruce, C. (1984). Stimulus selective properties of inferior temporal neurons in the macaque. *Journal of Neuroscience, 4,* 2051–2062.

Desimone, R., & Duncan, J. (1995). Neural mechanisms of selective visual attention. *Annual Review of Neuroscience, 18,* 193–222.

Desimone, R., & Gross, C. G. (1979). Visual areas in the temporal cortex of the macaque. *Brain Research, 178,* 363–380.

Desmedt, J. E., & Robertson, D. (1977). Differential enhancement of early and late components of the cerebral somatosensory evoked potentials during forced-paced cognitive tasks in man. *Journal of Physiology (London), 271,* 761–782.

Desmond, J. E., & Fiez, J. A. (1998). Neuroimaging studies of the cerebellum: Language, learning and memory. *Trends in Cognitive Science, 2,* 355–362.

Desmurget, M., Epstein, C. M., Turner, R. S., Prablanc, C., Alexander, G. E., & Grafton, S. T. (1999). Role of the posterior parietal cortex in updating reaching movements to a visual target. *Nature Neuroscience, 2,* 563–567.

Deutsch, D., Ellis, R., McCutchan, J. A., Marcotte, T. D., Letendre, S., & Grant, I. (2001). AIDS-associated mild neurocognitive impairment is delayed in the era of highly active antiretroviral therapy. *AIDS, 15,* 1898–1899.

Deutsch, G., Bourbon, W., Papanicolaou, A., & Eisenberg, H. (1988). Visuospatial tasks compared during activation of regional cerebral blood flow. *Neuropsychologia, 26,* 445–452.

Deutsch, J. A., & Deutsch, D. (1963). Attention: Some theoretical considerations. *Psychological Review, 70,* 80–90.

Devinsky, O., & Najjar, S. (1999). Evidence against the existence of temporal lobe epilepsy personality syndrome. *Neurology, 53*(Suppl. 2), S13–S25.

Diamond, A. (1990). Developmental time course in human infants and infant monkeys, and the neural bases of inhibitory control in reading. *Annals of the New York Academy of Sciences, 608,* 637–676.

Diamond, A., Prevor, M. B., Callender, G., & Druin, D. P. (1997). Prefrontal cortex cognitive deficits in children treated early and continuously for PKU. *Monographs of the Society for Research in Child Development, 62,* 1–205.

Diamond, D. M., & Weinberger, N. M. (1986). Classical conditioning rapidly induces specific changes in frequency receptive fields of single neurons in secondary and ventral ectosylvian cortical fields. *Brain Research, 372,* 357–360.

Diamond, R., & Carey, S. (1986). Why faces are and are not special: An effect of expertise. *Journal of Experimental Psychology: General, 115,* 107–117.

Dick, R. W. (1994). A summary of head and neck injuries in collegiate athletics using the NCAA Injury Surveillance System. In Horner, E. F. (Ed.), *Head and neck injuries in sports.* Philadelphia, PA: American Society for Testing and Materials.

Diederich, N. J., & Goetz, C. G. (2000). Neuropsychological and behavioral aspects of transplants in Parkinson's Disease and Huntington's Disease. *Brain and Cognition 42,* 294–306.

Dimond, S. J., & Beaumont, J. G. (1973). Difference in the vigilance performance of the right and left hemisphere. *Cortex, 9,* 259–265.

Ditunno, P., & Mann, V. (1990). Right hemisphere specialization for mental rotation in normals and brain damaged subjects. *Cortex, 26,* 177–188.

Dodrill, C. B. (1992). Neuropsychological aspects of epilepsy. *Psychiatric Clinics of North America, 15,* 383–394.

Dolan, R. J., & Morris, J. S. (2000). The functional anatomy of innate and acquired fear: Perspectives from neuroscience. In R. D. Lane, and L. Nadel (Eds.) *Cognitive neuroscience of emotion* (pp. 156–191). New York: Oxford University Press.

Dolan, R. J., Fletcher, P., Morris, J., Kapur, N., Deakin, J. F. W., & Frith, C. D. (1996). Neural activation during covert processing of positive emotional facial expressions. *Neuroimage, 4,* 194–200.

Donaldson, D. I., Petersen, S. E., & Buckner, R. L. (2001). Dissociating memory retrieval processes using fMRI: Evidence that priming does not support recognition memory. *Neuron, 31*(6), 1047–1059.

Donchin, E. (1981) Surprise! … Surprise? *Psychophysiology, 18,* 493–513.

Donchin, E. (1984). Report of Panel III: Preparatory processes. In E. Donchin (Ed.), *Cognitive psychophysiology* (pp. 179–219). Hillsdale, NJ: Erlbaum.

Donchin, E., & Coles, M. (1988). Is the P_{300} component a manifestation of context updating? *Behavioral and Brain Sciences, 11,* 406–417.

Doody, R. S., & Jankovic, J. (1992). The alien hand and related signs. *Journal of Neurology, Neurosurgery and Psychiatry, 55,* 806–810.

Dove, A., Pollmann, S., Schubert, T., Wiggins, C. J., & von Cramon, D. Y. (2000). Prefrontal cortex activation in task switching: An event-related fMRI study. *Cognitive Brain Research, 9,* 103–109.

Downing, P., Liu, J., Kanwisher, N. (2001). Testing cognitive models of visual attention with fMRI and MEG. *Neuropsychologia, 39*(12 Special Issue SI), 1329–1342.

Downing, P. E., Jiang, Y., Shuman, M., & Kanwisher, N. (2001). A cortical area selective for visual processing of the human body. *Science, 293,* 2470–2473.

Doyon, J., & Milner, B. (1991). Right temporal-lobe contribution to global visual processing. *Neuropsychologia, 29,* 343–360.

Drachman, D. A. (1978). Memory, dementia, and the cholinergic system. In R. Katzman, R. D. Terry, & K. L. Bick (Eds.), *Alzheimer's disease: Senile dementia and related disorders* (pp. 141–148). New York: Raven Press.

Drachman, D. A., & Arbit, J. (1966). Memory and hippocampal complex. II. Is memory a multiple process? *Archives of Neurology, 15,* 52–61.

Drachman, D. A., & Leavitt J. (1974). Human memory and the cholinergic system. *Archives of Neurology, 30,* 113–121.

Driver, J., Baylis, G., Goodrich, S. J., & Rafal, R. D. (1994). Axis-based neglect of visual shapes. *Neuropsychologia, 32,* 1353–1365.

Dror, I. E., Kosslyn, S. M., & Waag, W. L. (1993). Visual-spatial abilities of pilots. *Journal of Applied Psychology, 78,* 763–773.

Duara, R., Barker, W. W., Lopez-Alberola, R. Loewenstein, D. A., Grau, L. B., Gilchrist, D., Sevush, S., St George-Hyslop, S. (1996). Alzheimer's disease: Interaction of apolipoprotein E genotype, family history of dementia, gender, education, ethnicity, and age of onset. *Neurology, 46,* 1575–1579.

Duaux, E., Krebs, M. O., Loo, H., & Poirier, M. F. (2000). Genetic vulnerability to drug abuse. *European Psychiatry, 15,* 109–114.

Dubner, R., & Zeki, S. M. (1971). Response properties and receptive fields of cells in an anatomically defined region of the superior temporal sulcus in the monkey. *Brain Research, 35,* 528–532.

Dubois, B., Boller, F., Pillon, B., & Agid, Y. (1991). Cognitive deficits in Parkinson's disease. In F. Boller & J. Grafman (Eds.), *Handbook of neuropsychology* (Vol. 5, pp. 195–240). New York: Elsevier.

Dubovsky, S. L., & Thomas, M. (1995). Serotonergic mechanisms and current and future psychiatric practice. *Journal of Clinical Psychiatry, 56,* 38–48.

Duncan, J. (1986). Disorganisation of behavior after frontal lobe damage. *Cognitive Neuropsychology, 3,* 271–290.

Duncan, J. & Owen, A. M. (2000). Cognitive regions of the human frontal lobe recruited by diverse cognitive demands. *Trends in Neurosciences, 23,* 475–483.

Duncan, J. J., & Anderson-Hanley, C. (1998). Dementia caregiver burden: A review of the literature and guidelines for assessment and intervention. *Neurology, 51*(Suppl 1), S53–S60.

Dupuis, F., Johnston, K. M., Lavoie, M., Lepore, F., & Lassonde, M. (2000). Concussions in athletes produce brain dysfunction as revealed by event-related potentials. *Neuroreport. An International Journal for the Rapid Communication of Research in Neuroscience, 11*(18), *4087–4092.*

Dusek, J. A., & Eichenbaum, H. (1997). The hippocampus and memory for orderly stimulus relations. *Proceedings of the National Academy of Science, USA, 94*(13), 7109–7114.

Eckardt, M. J., Stapleton, J. M., Rawlings, R. R., Davis, E. Z., & Grodin, D. M. (1995). Neuropsychological functioning in detoxified alcoholics between 18 and 35 years of age. *American Journal of Psychiatry, 152*(1), 45–52.

Edwards, B. (1989). *Drawing on the right side of the brain: A course in creativity and artistic confidence.* Los Angeles: Jeremy P Tarcher.

Ehrlichman, H., & Weinberger, A. (1978). Lateral eye movements and hemispheric asymmetry: A critical review. *Psychological Bulletin, 85,* 1080–1101.

Eichenbaum, H. (1994). The hippocampal system and declarative memory in humans and animals: Experimental analysis and historical origins. In D. L. Schacter & E. Tulving (Eds.), *Memory systems 1994.* Cambridge, MA: MIT Press.

Eichenbaum, H. (1997). How does the brain organize memories? *Science, 277*(5324), 330–332.

Eichenbaum, H. (1999). Neurobiology. The topography of memory. *Nature, 402*(6762), 597–599.

Eichenbaum, H. (2000). A cortical-hippocampal system for declarative memory. *Nature Reviews Neuroscience, 1*(1), 41–50.

Eichenbaum, H., & Cohen, N. J. (2001). *From conditioning to conscious recollection: Memory systems of the brain.* New York: Oxford University Press.

Eichenbaum, H., Dudehenko, P., Wood, E., Shapiro, M., & Tanila, H. (1999). The hippocampus, memory, and place cells: Is it spatial memory or a memory space? *Neuron, 23*(2), 209–226.

Eichenbaum, H., Otto, T., & Cohen, N. J. (1994). Two component functions of the hippocampal memory system. *Behavioral and Brain Sciences, 17,* 449–517.

Eichenbaum, H., Stewart, C., & Morris, R. G. M. (1990). Hippocampal representation in spatial learning. *Journal of Neuroscience, 10,* 331–339.

Eichhorn, S. K. (1982). Congenital cytomegalovirus infection: A significant cause of deafness and mental deficiency. *American Annals of the Deaf, 127*(7), 838–843.

Eidelberg, D., & Galaburda, A. M. (1984). Inferior parietal lobule: Divergent architectonic asymmetries in the human brain. *Archives of Neurology, 41*, 843–852.

Eisenberg, H. M., & Weiner, R. L. (1987). Input variables: How information from the acute injury can be used to characterize groups of patients for studies of outcome. In H. S. Levin, J. Grafman, & H. M. Eisenberg (Eds.), *Neurobehavioral recovery from head injury.* New York: Oxford University Press.

Ekman, P., Hager, J. C., & Friesen, W. V. (1981). The symmetry of emotional and deliberate facial actions. *Psychophysiology, 18*, 101–106.

Elbert, T., Pantev, C., Wienbruch, C., Rockstroh, B., & Taub, E. (1995). Increased cortical representation of the fingers of the left hand in string players. *Science, 270*(5234), 305–307.

Eldridge, L. L., Knowlton, B. J., Furmanski, C. S., Bookheimer, S. Y., & Engel, S. A. (2000). Remembering episodes: A selective role for the hippocampus during retrieval. *Nature Reviews Neuroscience, 3*(11), 1149–1152.

Elliott, R., Baker, S. C., Rogers, R. D., O'Leary, D. A., Paykel, E. S., Frith, C. D., Dolan, R. J., & Sahakian, B. J. (1997). Prefrontal dysfunction in depressed patients performing a complex planning task: A study using positron emission tomography. *Psychological Medicine, 27*, 931–942.

Elliott, R., Frith, C. D., & Dolan, R. J. (1997). Differential neural response to positive and negative feedback in planning and guessing tasks. *Neuropsychologia, 35*, 1395–1404.

Elliott, R., Sahakian, B. J., McKay, A. P., Herrod, J. J., Robbins, T. W., & Paykel, E. S. (1996). Neuropsychological impairments in unipolar depression: The influence of perceived failure on subsequent performance. *Psychological Medicine, 26*, 975–990.

Ellis, A. W., Flude, B. M., & Young, A. W. (1987). "Neglect dyslexia" and the early visual processing of letters in words. *Cognitive Neuropsychology, 4*, 439–464.

Ellis, H. D., & Gunter, H. L. (1999). Asperger syndrome: A simple matter of white matter? *Trends in Cognitive Sciences, 3*, 192–200.

Entus, A. K. (1977). Hemispheric asymmetry in processing of dichotically presented speech and nonspeech stimuli by infants. In S. J. Segalowitz & F. A. Gruber (Eds.), *Language development and neurological theory* (pp. 64–73). New York: Academic Press.

Epstein, L., & Brown, P. (1997). Bovine spongiform encephalopathy and a new variant of Cretuzfeldt-Jakob disease. *Neurology, 48*, 569–571.

Epstein, R., Harris, A., Stanley, D., & Kanwisher, N. (1999). The parahippocampal place area: Recognition, navigation or encoding? *Neuron, 23*, 115–125.

Eriksson, P. S., Perfilieva, E., Björk-Eriksson, T., Alborn, A. M., Nordborg, C., Peterson, D. A., & Gage, F. H. (1998). Neurogenesis in adult human hippocampus. *Nature Medicine, 4*, 1313–1317.

Erkinjuntti, T., Haltia, M., Palo, J., & Paetau, A. (1988). Accuracy of the clinical diagnosis of vascular dementia: A prospective clinical and post-mortem neuropathological study. *Journal of Neurology, Neurosurgery and Psychiatry, 51*, 1037–1044.

Errico, A. L., Parsons, O. A., & King, A. C. (1991). Assessment of verbosequential and visuospatial cognitive abilities in chronic alcoholics. *Psychological Assessment, 3*, 693–696.

Eschweiler, G. W., Wegerer, C., Scholotter, W., Spandl, C., Stevens, A., Bartels, M., & Buchkremer, G. (2000). Left prefrontal activation predicts therapeutic effects of repetitive transcranial magnetic stimulation (rTMS) in major depression. *Psychiatry Research: Neuroimaging, 9*, 161–172.

Eslinger, P. J., & Grattan, L. M. (1993). Frontal lobe and frontal-striatal substrates for different forms of human cognitive flexibility. *Neuropsychologia, 31*, 17–28.

Etcoff, N. (1989). Asymmetries in recognition of emotion. In F. Boller & J. Grafman (Eds.), *Handbook of neuropsychology: Vol. 3. Emotional behavior and its disorders* (pp. 363–382). New York: Elsevier.

Etcoff, N. L. (1984). Selective attention to facial identity and facial emotion. *Neuropsychologia, 22*, 281–295.

Everall, I. P., & Lantos, P. L. (1991). The neuropathology of HIV: A review of the first 10 years. *International Review of Psychiatry, 3*, 307–320.

Fabiani, M., & Donchin, E. (1995). Encoding processes and memory organization: A model of the von Restorff effect. *Journal of Experimental Psychology: Learning, Memory, & Cognition, 21*(1), 224–240.

Falzi, G., Perrone, P., & Vignolo, L. (1982). Right-left asymmetry in anterior speech region. *Archives of Neurology, 39*, 239–240.

Farah, M. J. (1984). The neurological basis of mental imagery: A componential analysis. *Cognition, 18*, 245–272.

Farah, M. J. (1988). Is visual imagery really visual? Overlooked evidence from neuropsychology. *Psychological Review, 95*, 307–317.

Farah, M. J. (1990). *Visual agnosia: Disorders of object recognition and what they tell us about normal vision.* Cambridge, MA: MIT Press.

Farah, M. J. (2000). *The cognitive neuroscience of vision.* Malden, MA: Blackwell Publishers.

Farah, M. J., & Feinberg, T. E. (2000). Visual object agnosia. In M. J. Farah, & T. E. Feinberg (Eds.), *Patient-based approaches to cognitive neuroscience* (pp. 79–84). Cambridge, MA: MIT Press.

Farah, M. J., Gazzaniga, M. S., Holtzman, J. D., & Kosslyn, S. M. (1985). A left hemisphere basis for visual imagery? *Neuropsychologia, 23*, 115–118.

Farah, M. J., Hammond, K. M., Mehta, Z., & Ratcliff, G. (1989). Category-specificity and modality-specificity in semantic memory. *Neuropsychologia, 27*, 193–200.

Farah, M. J., Levine, D. N., & Calvanio, R. (1988). A case study of a mental imagery deficit. *Brain and Cognition, 8*, 147–164.

Farah, M. J., & McClelland, J. L. (1991). A computational model of semantic memory impairment: Modality-specificity and emergent category-specificity. *Journal of Experimental Psychology: General, 120*, 339–357.

Farah, M. J., O'Reilly, R. C., & Vecera, S. P. (1993). Dissociated overt and covert recognition as an emergent property of a lesioned neural network. *Psychological Review, 100*, 571–588.

Farah, M. J., Rabinowitz, C., Quinn, G. E., & Liu, G. T. (2000). Early commitment of neural substrates for face recognition. *Cognitive Neuropsychology, 17,* 117–123.

Farah, M. J., Soso, M. J., & Dasheiff, R. M. (1992). Visual angle of the mind's eye before and after unilateral occipital lobectomy. *Journal of Experimental Psychology: Human Perception and Performance, 18,* 241–246.

Faraone, S. V. (2000). Attention deficit hyperactivity disorder in adults: Implications for theories of diagnosis. *Current Directions in Psychological Science, 9,* 33–36.

Farlow, M., & Evans, R. (1998). Pharmacologic treatment of cognition in Alzheimer's disease. *Neurology,* 51 (Suppl. 1), S36–S44.

Farver, P. F., & Farver, T. B. (1982). Performance of normal older adults on tests designed to measure parietal lobe functioning. *American Journal of Occupational Therapy, 36,* 444–449.

Fauth, C., Meyer, B. U., Prosiegel, M., Zihl, J., & Conrad, B. E. (1992). Seizure induction and magnetic stimulation after stroke. *Lancet, 339,* 362.

Fein, D., Pennington, B., Markowitz, P., Braverman, M., & Waterhouse, L. (1986). Towards a neuropsychological model of infantile autism: Are the social deficits primary? *Journal of the American Academy of Child Psychiatry, 25*(2), 198–212.

Feinberg, T. E., Mazlin, S. E., & Waldman, G. E. (1989). Recovery from brain damage: Neurologic considerations. In E. Perecman (Ed.), *Integrating theory and practice in clinical neuropsychology* (pp. 49–73). Hillsdale, NJ: Erlbaum.

Feinberg, T. E., Schindler, R. J., Ochoa, E., Kwan, P. C., & Farah, M. J. (1994). Associative visual agnosia and alexia without prosopagnosia. *Cortex, 30,* 395–411.

Feldman Barrett, L., & Russell, J. A. (1999). The structure of current affect: Controversies and emerging consensus. *Current Directions in Psychological Science, 8,* 10–14.

Fernandez, G., Effern, A., Grunwald, T., Pezer, N., Lehnertz, K., Dumpelmann, M., Van Roost, D., & Elger, C. E. (1999). Real-time tracking of memory formation in the human rhinal cortex and hippocampus. *Science, 285*(5433), 1582–1585.

Ferraro, F. R., Balota, D. A., & Connor, L. T. (1993). Implicit memory and the formation of new associations in nondemented Parkinson's disease individuals and individuals with senile dementia of the Alzheimer type: A serial reaction time (SRT) investigation. *Brain and Cognition, 21*(2), 163–180.

Fiedler, N., Kipen, H., Kelly-McNeil, K., & Fenske, R. (1997). Long-term use of organophosphates and neuropsychological performance. *American Journal of Industrial Medicine, 32,* 487–496.

Fields, J. A., & Troster, A. I. (2000). Cognitive outcomes after deep brain stimulation for Parkinson's Disease: A review of initial studies and recommendations for future research. *Brain and Cognition, 42,* 268–293.

Fiez, J., Petersen, S. E., Cheney, M. K., & Raichle, M. E. (1992). Impaired non-motor learning and error detection associated with cerebellar damage: A single case study. *Brain, 115,* 155–178.

Fiez, J. A., (1997). Phonology, semantics, and the role of the left inferior prefrontal cortex. *Human Brain Mapping, 5,* 79–83.

Fiez, J. A., & Petersen, S. E. (1993). PET as part of an interdisciplinary approach to understanding processes involved in reading. *Psychological Science, 4,* 287–293.

Fiez, J. A., & Petersen, S. E. (1998). Neuroimaging studies of word reading. *Proceedings of the National Academy of Sciences, USA, 95,* 914–921.

Fiez, J. A., Tallal, P., Raichle, M. E., Miezin, F. M., Katz, W. F., & Petersen, S. E. (1995). PET studies of auditory and phonological processing: Effects of stimulus characteristics and task demands. *Journal of Cognitive Neuroscience, 7,* 357–375.

Fink, G. R., Dolan, R. J., Halligan, P. W., Marshall, J. C., & Frith, C. D. (1997). Space-based and object-based visual attention: shared and specific neural domains. *Brain, 120,* 2013–2028.

Fisch, G. S. (1992). Is autism associated with the fragile X syndrome? *American Journal of Medical Genetics, 43,* 47–55.

Fischer, J. S., Priore, R. L., Jacobs, L. D., Cookfair, D. L., Rudick, R. A., Herndon, R. M., Richert, J. R., Salazar, A. M., Goodkin, D. E., Granger, C. V., Simon, J. H., Grafman, J. H., Lezak, M. D., O'Reilly Hovey, K. M., Perkins, K. K., Barilla-Clark, D., Schacter, M., Shucard, D. W., Davidson, A. L., Wende, K. E., Bourdette, D. N., & Kooijmans-Coutinho, M. F. (2000). Neuropsychological effects of interferon beta-1a in relapsing multiple sclerosis. Multiple Sclerosis Collaborative Research Group. *Annals of Neurology, 48*(6), 885–892.

Fitzpatrick, S. M., & Rothman, D. L. (2000). Meeting report: Transcranial magnetic stimulation and studies of human cognition. *Journal of Cognitive Neuroscience, 12,* 704–709.

Flament, D., Ellermann, J. M., Kim, S.-G., Ugurbil, K., & Ebner, T. J. (1996). Functional magnetic resonance imaging of cerebellar activation during the learning of a visuomotor dissociation task. *Human Brain Mapping, 4*(3), 210–226.

Fleischman, D. A., & Gabrieli, J. (1999). Long-term memory in Alzheimer's disease. *Current Opinion in Neurobiology, 9,* 240–244.

Fleminger, S., & Curtis, D. (1997). Prion diseases. *British Journal of Psychiatry, 170,* 103–105.

Fletcher, P. (1998). The missing link: A failure of fronto-hippocampal integration in schizophrenia. *Nature Neuroscience, 1,* 266–267.

Fletcher, P. C., & Henson, R. N. A. (2001). Frontal lobes and human memory: Insights from functional neuroimaging. *Brain, 124,* 849–881.

Flicker, C., Ferris, S. H., Crook, T., & Bartus, R. T. (1987). Implications of memory and language dysfunction in the naming deficit of senile dementia. *Brain and Language, 31,* 187–200.

Flicker, C., Ferris, S. H., Crook, T., Bartus, R. T., & Reisberg, B. (1986). Cognitive decline in advanced age: The psychometric differentiation of normal and pathological age changes in cognitive function. *Developmental Neuropsychology, 2,* 309–322.

Flor, H., Elbert, T., Knecht, S., Wienbruch, C., Pantev, C., Birbaumer, N., Larbig, W., & Taub, E. (1995). Phantom-limb pain as a perceptual correlate of cortical reorganization following arm amputation. *Nature, 375,* 482–484.

Fodor, J. (1985). The modularity of mind. *Behavioral and Brain Sciences, 8,* 1–42.

Foldi, N. S. (1987). Appreciation of pragmatic interpretation of indirect commands: Comparison of right and left brain-damaged patients. *Brain and Language, 31,* 88–108.

Fontenot, D. J. (1973). Visual field differences in the recognition of verbal and nonverbal stimuli in man. *Journal of Comparative and Physiological Psychology, 85,* 564–569.

Ford, J. M., Sullivan, E. V., Marsh, L., White, P. M., et al. (1994). The relationship between P_{300} amplitude and regional gray matter volumes depends upon the attentional system engaged. *Electroencephalography and Clinical Neurophysiology, 90,* 214–228.

Forss, N., Makela, J. P., Keranen, T., & Hari R. (1995). Trigeminally triggered epileptichemifacial convulsions. *Neuroreport, 6*(6), 918–920.

Foundas, A. L., Leonard, D. M., Gilmore, R., Fennell, E., & Heilman, K. M. (1994). Planum temporale asymmetry and language dominance. *Neuropsychologia, 10,* 1225–1231.

Fowler, J. S., Wang, G. J., Volkow, N. D., Logan, J., Franceschi, D., Franceschi, M., MacGregor, R., Shea, C., Garza, V., Liu, N., & Ding, Y. S. (2000). Evidence that gingko biloba extract does not inhibit MAO A and B in living human brain. *Life Science, 66,* 141–146.

Fox, P. T., Raichle, M. E., Mintun, M. A., & Dence, C. (1988). Nonoxidative glucose consumption during focal physiologic neural activity. *Science, 241,* 462–464.

Franco, L., & Sperry, R. W. (1977). Hemisphere lateralization for cognitive processing of geometry. *Neuropsychologia, 15,* 107–114.

Frassinetti, F., Rossi, M., & Ladavas, E. (2001). Passive limb movements improve visual neglect *Neuropsychologia, 39,* 725–733.

Fredrikson, M., Gustav, W., Greitz, T., Erikson, L., Stone-Elander, S., Ericson, K., & Sedvall, G. (1993). Regional cerebral blood flow during experimental phobic fear. *Psychophysiology, 30,* 126–130.

Freedman, R., Waldo, M. C., Bickford-Wimer, P., & Nagamoto, H. (1991). Elementary neuronal dysfunctions in schizophrenia. *Schizophrenia Research, 4*(2), 233–243.

Freeman, E. A. (1991). Coma arousal therapy. *Clinical Rehabilitation, 5,* 241–249.

Freiberg, L., Olsen, T. S., Roland, P. E., Paulson, O. B., & Lassen, N. A. (1985). Focal increase of blood flow in the cerebral cortex of man during vestibular stimulation. *Brain, 108,* 609–623.

Freimuth, M., & Wapner, S. (1979). The influence of lateral organization on the evaluation of paintings. *British Journal of Psychology, 70,* 211–218.

Fried, I., Mateer, C., Ojemann, G., Wohns, R., & Fedio, P. (1982). Organization of visuospatial functions in human cortex. *Brain, 105,* 349–371.

Friederici, A. D., Hahne, A., & Mecklinger, A. (1996). Temporal structure of syntactic parsing: Early and late event-related brain potential effects. *Journal of Experimental Psychology: Learning, Memory, and Cognition, 22,* 1219–1248.

Friederici, A. D., Optiz, B., & von Cramon, D. Y., (2000). Segregating semantic and syntactic aspects of processing in the human brain: An fMRI investigation of different word types. *Cerebral Cortex, 10,* 698–705.

Friedman, A., & Polson, M. C. (1981). The hemispheres as independent resource systems: Limited capacity processing and cerebral specialization. *Journal of Experimental Psychology: Human Perception and Performance, 7,* 1031–1058.

Friedman, A., Polson, M. C., Dafoe, C. G., & Gaskill, S. J. (1982). Dividing attention within and between hemispheres: Testing a multiple resources approach to limited-capacity information processing. *Journal of Experimental Psychology: Human Perception and Performance, 8,* 625–650.

Friedman-Hill, S. R., Robertson, L. C., & Treisman, A. M. (1995). Parietal contributions to visual feature binding: Evidence from a patient with bilateral lesions. *Science, 269,* 853–855.

Frisk, V., & Milner, B. (1990). The role of the left hippocampal region in the acquisition and retention of story content. *Neuropsychologia, 28*(4), 349–359.

Friston, K. J., Frith, C. D., Fletcher, P., Liddle, P. F., & Frackowiak, R. S. J. (1996). Functional topography: Multidimensional scaling and functional connectivity in the brain. *Cerebral Cortex, 6,* 156–164.

Friston, K. J., Frith, C. D., Passingham, R. E., Liddle, P. F., & Frackowiak, R. S. (1992). Motor practice and neurophysiological adaptation in the cerebellum: A positron tomography study. *Proceedings of the Royal Society of London, Series B, Biological Sciences, 248*(1323), 223–228.

Frith, C. D., Friston, K. J., Liddle, P. F., & Frackowiak, R. S. J. (1991). A PET study of word finding. *Neuropsychologia, 29,* 1137–1148.

Frost, J. A., Binder, J. R., Springer, J. A., Hammeke, T. A., Bellgowan, P. S. F., Rao, S. M., & Cox, R. W. (1999). Language processing is strongly lateralized in both sexes: Evidence from functional MRI. *Brain, 122,* 199–208.

Fudin, R., Renninger, L., Lembessis, E., & Hirshon, J. (1993). Sinistrality and reduced longevity: Reichler's 1979 data on baseball players do not indicate a relationship. *Perceptual and Motor Skills, 76,* 171–182.

Fulton, J. F. (1935). A note on the definition of the "motor" and "premotor" areas. *Brain, 58,* 311–316.

Funahashi, S., Bruce, C. J., & Goldman-Rakic, P. S. (1989). Mnemonic coding of visual space in the monkey's dorsolateral prefrontal cortex. *Journal of Neurophysiology, 61*(2), 331–349.

Funahashi, S., Bruce, C. J., & Goldman-Rakic, P. S. (1991). Neuronal activity related to saccadic eye movements in the monkey's dorsolateral prefrontal cortex. *Journal of Neurophysiology, 65*(6), 1464–1483.

Funahashi, S., Bruce, C. J., & Goldman-Rakic, P. S. (1993). Dorsolateral prefrontal lesions and oculomotor delayed-response performance: Evidence for mnemonic "scotomas." *Journal of Neuroscience, 13*(4), 1479–1497.

Furey, M. L., Pietrini, P., & Haxby, J. V. (2000). Cholinergic enhancement and increased selectivity of perceptual processing during working memory. *Science, 290,* 2315–2319.

Fuster, J. M. (1985). The prefrontal cortex, mediator of cross-temporal contingencies. *Human Neurobiology, 4,* 169–179.

Fuster, J. M. (1989). *The prefrontal cortex* (2nd ed.). New York: Raven Press.

Fuster, J. M., & Alexander, G. E. (1971). Neuron activity related to short-term memory. *Science, 173*(997), 652–654.

Gabrieli, J. D. (1995). A systematic view of human memory processes. *Journal of the International Neuropsychological Society, 1*(1), 115–118.

Gabrieli, J. D. (1998). Cognitive science of human memory. *Annual Review of Psychology, 49*, 87–115.

Gabrieli, J. D., Cohen, N. J., & Corkin, S. (1988). The impaired learning of semantic knowledge following bilateral medial temporal-lobe resection. *Brain and Cognition, 7*(2), 157–177.

Gabrieli, J. D., E., Fleischman, D. A., Keane, M. M., Reminger, S. L., & Morrell, F. (1995). Double dissociation between memory systems underlying explicit and implicit memory in the human brain. *Psychological Science, 6*(2), 76–82.

Gadow, K. D. (1981). Drug therapy for hyperactivity: Treatment procedures in natural settings. In K. D. Gadow & J. Loney (Eds.), *Psychosocial aspects of drug treatment for hyperactivity* (pp. 325–378). Boulder, CO: Westview Press.

Gaffan, D. (1974). Recognition impaired and association intact in the memory of monkeys after transection of the fornix. *Journal of Comparative and Physiological Psychology, 86*, 1100–1109.

Gaffan, D. (1977). Monkey's recognition memory for complex pictures and the effects of fornix transection. *Quarterly Journal of Experimental Psychology, 29*, 505–514.

Gainotti, G. (1972). Emotional behavior and hemisphere side of lesion. *Cortex, 8*, 41–55.

Gainotti, G. (1989). Disorders of emotions and affect in patients with unilateral brain damage. In F. Boller & J. Grafman (Eds.), *Handbook of neuropsychology* (pp. 345–361). Amsterdam: Elsevier.

Gainotti, G., Cianchetti, C., & Tiacci, C. (1972). The influence of hemispheric side of lesions on non-verbal tasks of finger localization. *Cortex, 8*, 364–381.

Galaburda, A. M., LeMay, M., Kemper, T. L., & Geschwind, N. (1978). Right-left asymmetries in the brain. *Science, 199*, 852–856.

Galaburda, A. M., Sherman, G. F., Rosen, G. D., Aboitiz, F., & Geschwind, N. (1985). Developmental dyslexia: Four consecutive patients with cortical anomalies. *Annuals of Neurology, 18*, 222–233.

Gale, S. D., Johnson, S. C., Bigler, E. D., & Blatter, D. D. (1995). Nonspecific white matter degeneration following traumatic brain injury. *Journal of the International Neuropsychological Society, 1*, 17–28.

Gallagher, M., & Colombo, P. J. (1995). Aging: The cholinergic hypothesis of cognitive decline. *Current Opinion in Neurobiology, 5*, 161–168.

Gannon, P. J., Holloway, R. L., Broadfield, D. C., & Braun, A. R. (1998). Asymmetry of chimpanzee planum temporale: Human-like brain pattern of Wernicke's area homolog. *Science, 279*, 220–221.

Garavan, H., Ross, T. J., & Stein, E. A. (1999). Right hemispheric dominance of inhibitory control: An event-related functional MRI study. *Proceedings of the National Academy of Sciences, USA, 96*, 8301–8306.

Gardner, H. (1974). *The shattered mind.* New York: Vintage Books.

Gardner, H. (1983). *Frames of mind.* New York: Basic Books.

Gardner, H., Brownell, H. H., Wapner, W., & Michelow, D. (1983). Missing the point: The role of the right hemisphere in the processing of complex linguistic materials. In E. Perecman (Ed.), *Cognitive processing in the right hemisphere* (pp. 169–191). New York: Academic Press.

Gardner, H., King, P. K., Flamm, L., & Silverman, J. (1975). Comprehension and appreciation of humorous material following brain damage. *Brain, 98*, 399–412.

Gardner, H., Silverman, J., Denes, G., Semenza, C., & Rosenstiel, A. K. (1977). Sensitivity to musical denotation and connotation in organic patients. *Cortex, 13*, 242–256.

Garrett, M. F. (1975). The analysis of sentence production. In G. H. Bower (Ed.), *The psychology of learning and motivation* (pp. 133–177). New York: Academic Press.

Gasne, M., Millot, J-L., Brand, G., & Math, F. (2001). Intercorrelations among tests of lateralisation in the BALB/c mouse. *Laterality, 6*(1), 89–96.

Gasquoine, P. G. (1993). Alien hand sign. *Journal of Clinical and Experimental Neuropsychology, 15*, 653–667.

Gatz, M., Svedberg, P., Pedersen, N. L., Mortimer, J. A., Berg, S., & Johansson, B. (2001). Education and the risk of Alzheimer's disease: Findings from the study of dementia in Swedish twins. *Journal of Gerontology Series B—Psychological Sciences & Social Sciences, 56B*, 292–300.

Gauggel, S. (1996). *Control of action after frontal lobe damage.* Manuscript submitted for publication.

Gauthier, I., Skudlarski, P., Gore, J. C., & Anderson, A. W. (2000). Expertise for cars and birds recruits brain areas involved in face recognition. *Nature Neuroscience, 3*, 191–197.

Gauthier, I., Tarr, M. J., Anderson, A. W., Skudlarski, P., & Gore, J. C. (1999). Activation of the middle fusiform 'face area' increases with expertise in recognizing novel objects. *Nature Neuroscience, 2*, 568–573.

Gaze, R. M. (1982). R. W. Sperry and the neuronal specificity hypothesis. *Trends in Neurosciences, 5*(10), 330–332.

Gazzaniga, M. S. (1970). *The bisected brain.* New York: Appleton-Century-Crofts.

Gazzaniga, M. S. (1983a). Reply to Levy and Zaidel. *American Psychologist, 38*, 547–549.

Gazzaniga, M. S. (1983b). Right hemisphere language following brain bisection: A 20-year perspective. *American Psychologist, 38*, 525–537.

Gazzaniga, M. S. (2000). Cerebral specialization and interhemispheric communication: Does the corpus callosum enable the human condition. *Brain, 123*, 1293–1326.

Gazzaniga, M. S., Bogen, J. E., & Sperry, R. W. (1962). Some functional effects of sectioning the cerebral commissures in man. *Proceedings of the National Academy of Science, USA, 48*, 1765–1769.

Gazzaniga, M. S., Ivry, R., & Mangun, G. (1998). *Cognitive Neuroscience—Biology of the Mind.* New York: Norten.

Gazzaniga, M. S., & LeDoux, J. E. (1978). *The integrated mind.* New York: Plenum Press.

Geffen, G., Bradshaw, J. L., & Wallace, G. (1971). Interhemispheric effects on reaction time to verbal and nonverbal visual stimuli. *Journal of Experimental Psychology, 87*, 415–422.

Gehring, W. J. & Knight, R. T. (2000). Prefrontal-cingulate interactions in action monitoring. *Nature Neuroscience, 3,* 516–520.

Gehring, W. P., Goss, B., Coles, M. G. H., Meyer, D. E., and Donehin, E. (1993). A neural system for error detection and compensation. *Psychological Science, 4*(6), 385–390.

George, M. S., Ketter, T. A., Gill, D. S., Haxby, J. V., Ungerleider, L., Herscovitch, P., & Post, R. M. (1993). Brain regions involved in recognizing facial emotion or identity: An O_{15} PET study. *Journal of Neuropsychiatry and Clinical Neuroscience, 5,* 384–394.

George, M. S., Ketter, T. A., Parekh, P. I., Rosinsky, N., Ring, H. A., Pazzaglia, P. J., Marangell, L. B., Callahan, A. M., & Post, R. M. (1997). Blunted left cingulate activation in mood disorder subjects during a response interference task (the Stroop). *Journal of Neuropsychiatry, 9,* 55–63.

George, M. S., Ketter, T. A., Parekh, P., Gill, D. S., Huggins, T., Marangell, L., Pazzaglia, P. J., & Post, R. M. (1994). Spatial ability in affective illness: Differences in regional brain activation during a spatial matching task. *Neuropsychiatry, Neuropsychology and Behavioral Neurology, 7,* 143–153.

George, M. S., Parekh, P. I., Rosinsky, N., Ketter, T. A., Kimbrell, T. A., Heilman, K. M., Herscovitch, P., & Post, R. M. (1996). Understanding emotional prosody activates right hemisphere regions. *Archives of Neurology, 53,* 665–670.

George, M. S., Wasserman, E. M., Kimbrell, T. A., Little, J. T., Williams, W. E., Danielson, A. L., Greenberg, B. D., Hallett, M., & Post, R. M. (1997). Mood improvement following daily left prefrontal repetitive transcranial magnetic stimulation in patients with depression: A placebo-controlled crossover trial. *American Journal of Psychiatry, 154,* 1752–1756.

Georgieff, M. K., & Rao, R. (2001). The role of nutrition in cognitive development. In C. Nelson, & M. Luciana (Eds.), *Handbook of developmental cognitive neuroscience* (pp. 491–504). Cambridge, MA: The MIT Press.

Georgopoulos, A. P. (2000). Neural aspects of cognitive motor control. *Current Opinion in Neurobiology, 10,* 238–241.

Georgopolous, A. P., Lurito, J. T., Petrides, M., Schwartz, A. B., & Massey, J. T. (1989). Mental rotation of the neuronal population vector. *Science, 243,* 234–236.

Georgopoulos, A. P., Schwartz, A. B., & Kettner, R. E. (1986). Neuronal population coding of movement direction. *Science, 233,* 1416–1419.

Gerardin, E., Sirigu, A., Lehéricy, S., Poline, J.-B., Gaymard, B., Marsault, C., Agid, Y., & Le Bihan, D. (2000). Partially overlapping neural networks for real and imagined hand movements. *Cerebral Cortex, 10,* 1093–1104.

Gershberg, F. B., & Shimamura, A. P. (1995). Impaired use of organizational strategies in free recall following frontal lobe damage. *Neuropsychologia, 33*(10), 1305–1333.

Gerstmann, J. (1957). Some notes on the Gerstmann syndrome. *Neurology, 7,* 866–869.

Gerstner, W., Kempter, R., van Hemmen, J. L., & Wagner, H. (1996). A neuronal learning rule for submillisecond temporal coding. *Nature, 383*(6595), 76–78.

Geschwind, N., & Galaburda, A. M. (1985a). Cerebral lateralization: Biological mechanisms, associations, and pathology: I, A hypothesis and a program for research. *Archives of Neurology, 42,* 428–459.

Geschwind, N., & Galaburda, A. M. (1985b). Cerebral lateralization: Biological mechanisms, associations, and pathology: II. A hypothesis and a program for research. *Archives of Neurology, 42,* 521–552.

Geschwind, N., & Galaburda, A. M. (1985c). Cerebral lateralization: Biological mechanisms, associations, and pathology: III. A hypothesis and a program for research. *Archives of Neurology, 42,* 634–654.

Geschwind, N., & Levitsky, W. (1968). Human brain: Left-right asymmetrics in temporal speech region. *Science, 161,* 186–187.

Giancola, P. R., & Tarter, R. E. (1999). Executive functioning and risk for substance abuse. *Psychological Science, 10,* 203–205.

Gibbs, C. J., Gajdusek, D. C., Asher, D. M., Alpers, M. P., Beck, E., Daniel, P. M., & Matthews, W. B. (1968). Creutzfeldt-Jakob disease (spongiform encephalopathy): Transmission to the chimpanzee. *Science, 161,* 388–389.

Gibson, C., & Bryden, M. P. (1983). Dichaptic recognition of shapes and letters in children. *Canadian Journal of Psychology, 37,* 132–143.

Giedd, J. N., Blumenthal, J., Jeffries, N. O., Castellanos, F. X., Lui, H., Zijdenbos, A., Paus, T., Evans, A. C., & Rapoport, J. L. (1999). Brain development during childhood and adolescence: A longitudinal MRI study. *Nature Neuroscience, 2*(10), 861–863.

Giedd, J. N., Rumsey, J. M., Castellanos, F. X., Rajapakse, J. C., Kaysen, D., Vaituzis, A. C., Vauss, Y. C., Hamburger, S. D., & Rapoport, J. L. (1996). A quantitative MRI study of the corpus callosum in children and adolescents. *Development Brain Research, 91,* 274–280.

Gilger, J. W., Pennington, B. F., Green, P., Smith, S. M., & Smith, S. D. (1992). Reading disability, immune disorders and non-right-handedness: Twin and family studies of their relations. *Neuropsychologia, 30,* 209–227.

Gillberg, C. (1999). Neurodevelopmental processes and psychological functioning in autism. *Development and Psychopathology, 11,* 567–587.

Gladstone, M., Best, C. T., & Davidson, R. J. (1989). Anomalous bimanual coordination among dyslexic boys. *Developmental Psychology, 25,* 236–246.

Glick, S. D., Ross, A. D., & Hough, L. B. (1982). Lateral asymmetry of neurotransmitters in human brain. *Brain Research, 234,* 53–63.

Glisky, E. L., & Schacter, D. L. (1987). Acquisition of domain-specific knowledge in organic amnesia: Training for computer-related work. *Neuropsychologia, 25*(6), 893–906.

Glisky, E. L., Schacter, D. L., & Tulving, E. (1986). Computer learning by memory-impaired patients: Acquisition and retention of complex knowledge. *Neuropsychologia, 24*(3), 313–328.

Glosser, G., & Friedman, R. B. (1990). The continuum of deep/phonological alexia. *Cortex, 26,* 343–359.

Gluck, M. A. (1996). Computational models of hippocampal function in memory. *Hippocampus, 6*(6), 643–653.

Glucksberg, S., & Keysar, B. (1990). Understanding metaphorical comparisons: Beyond similarity. *Psychological Review, 97,* 3–18.

Goate, A., Chartierharlin, M. C., Mullan, M., Brown, J., Crawford, F., Fidani, L., Giuffra, L., Haynes, A., Irving, N., James, L., Mant, R., Newton, P., Rooke, K., Roques, P., Talbot, C., Pericakvance, M., Roses, A., Williamson, R., Rossor, M., Owen, M., & Hardy, J. (1991). Segregation of a missense mutation in the amyloid precursor protein gene with familial Alzheimer's disease. *Nature, 349,* 704–706.

Godwin-Austen, R. B. (1965). A case of visual disorientation. *Journal of Neurology, Neurosurgery and Psychiatry, 28,* 453–458.

Goetz, C. G., Tanner, C. M., Stebbins, G. T., Leipzig, G., & Carr, W. C. (1992). Adult tics in Gilles de la Tourette's syndrome: Description and risk factors. *Neurology, 42,* 784–788.

Golby, A. J., Gabrieli, J. D. E., Chiao, J. Y., & Eberhardt, J. L. (2001). Differential responses in the fusiform region to same-race and other-race faces. *Nature Neuroscience, 4,* 845–850.

Goldberg, G. (1985). Supplementary motor area structure and function: Review and hypotheses. *Behavioral and Brain Sciences, 8,* 567–616.

Golden, C. J. (1981). A standardized version of Luria's neuropsychological tests. In S. Filskov & T. J. Boll (Eds.), *Handbook of clinical neuropsychology.* New York: Wiley Interscience.

Golden, C. J., Hammeke, T. A., & Purisch, A. D. (1978). Diagnostic validity of a standardized neuropsychological test battery derived from Luria's neuropsychological tests. *Journal of Consulting and Clinical Psychology, 46,* 1258–1265.

Golden, G. S. (1990). Tourette syndrome: Recent advances. *Pediatric Neurology, 8,* 705–714.

Goldman, P. (1974). An alternative to developmental plasticity: Heterology of CNS structures in infants and adults. In D. G. Stein, J. J. Rosen, & N. Butters (Eds.), *Plasticity and recovery from brain damage* (pp. 149–174). New York: Academic Press.

Goldman-Rakic, P. S. (1987). Circuitry of the prefrontal cortex and the regulation of behavior by representational knowledge. In F. Plum & V. Mountcastle (Eds.), *Handbook of physiology, Vol. 5.* Bethesda, MD: American Physiological Society.

Goldman-Rakic, P. S. (1988). Topography of cognition: Parallel distributed networks in primate association cortex. *Annual Review of Neuroscience, 11,* 137–156.

Goldman-Rakic, P. S. (1990). Cellular and circuit basis of working memory in prefrontal cortex of nonhuman primates. *Progress in Brain Research, 85,* 325–336.

Goldman-Rakic, P. S. (1995). Anatomical and functional circuits in prefrontal cortex of nonhuman primates. Relevance to epilepsy. *Advances in Neurology, 66,* 51–63.

Goldman-Rakic, P. S. (1996). The prefrontal landscape: Implications of functional architecture for understanding human mentation and the central executive. *Philosophical Transactions of the Royal Society of London, B Biological Sciences, 351*(1346), 1445–1453.

Goldman-Rakic, P. S. (1998). The prefrontal landscape: Implications of functional architecture for understanding human mentation and the central executive. In A. C. Roberts, & T. W. Robbins (Eds.), *The prefrontal cortex: Executive and cognitive functions* (pp. 87–102). New York: Oxford University Press.

Goldman-Rakic, P. S., & Rakic, P. (1984). Experimental modification of gyral patterns. In N. S. Geschwind & A. M. Galaburda (Eds.), *Cerebral dominance: The biological foundations.* Cambridge, MA: Harvard University Press.

Gomez-Isla, T., West, H. L., Rebeck, G. W., Harr, S. D., Growdon, J. H., Locascio, J. J., Perls, T. T., Lipsitz, L. A., Hyman, B. T. (1996). Clinical and pathological correlates of apolipoprotein E e-4 in Alzheimer's disease. *Annals of Neurology, 39,* 62–70.

Goodale, M. A., & Humphrey, G. K. (1998). The objects of action and perception. *Cognition, 67,* 181–207.

Goodale, M. A., & Milner, A. D. (1992). Separate visual pathways for perception and action. *Trends in Neurosciences, 15,* 20–25.

Goodglass, H. (1976). Agrammatism. In H. Whitaker & H. A. Whitaker (Eds.), *Studies in neurolinguistics* (pp. 237–260). New York: Academic Press.

Gooding, D. C., Luh, K. E., & Tallent, K. A. (2001). Evidence of schizophrenia patients' reduced perceptual biases in response to emotion chimera. *Schizophrenia Bulletin, 27,* 709–716.

Goodlett, C. R., & West, J. R. (1992). Fetal alcohol effects: Rat model of alcohol exposure during the brain growth spurt. In I. S. Zagon & T. A. Slotkin (Eds.), *Maternal substance abuse and the developing nervous system* (pp. 45–76). New York: Academic Press.

Gordon, H. W. (1980). Degree of ear asymmetries for perception of dichotic chords and for illusory chord localization in musicians of different levels of competence. *Journal of Experimental Psychology: Human Perception and Performance, 6,* 516–527.

Gordon, J. W., & Bogen, J. E. (1974). Hemispheric lateralization of singing after intracarotid sodium amylobarbitone. *Journal of Neurology, Neurosurgery and Psychiatry, 37,* 727–738.

Gordon, W. A., Mann, N., & Willer, B. (1993). Demographic and social characteristics of the traumatic brain injury model system database. *Journal of Head Trauma Rehabilitation, 8,* 26–33.

Gorell, J. M., Johnson, C. C., Rybicki, B. A., Peterson, E. L., Kortsha, G. X., Brown, G. G., & Richardson, R. J. (1997). Occupational exposure to metals as risk factors for Parkinson's disease. *Neurology, 48,* 650–658.

Gould, E., Tanapat, P., Hastings, N. B., & Shors, T. J. (1999). Neurogenesis in adulthood: A possible role in learning. *Trends in Cognitive Sciences, 3,* 186–192.

Grady, C. L., & Craik, F. I. M. (2000). Changes in memory processing with age. *Current Opinion in Neurobiology, 10,* 224–231.

Grady, C. L., Haxby, J. V., Horwitz, B., Schapiro, M. B., Rapoport, S. I., Ungerleider, L. G., Mishkin, M., Carson, R. E., & Herscovitch, P. (1992). Dissociation of object and spatial vision in human extrastriate cortex: Age-related changes in activation of regional cerebral blood flow measured with (-sup-I-sup-5O)water and positron emission tomography. *Journal of Cognitive Neuroscience, 4*(1), 23–34.

Graf, P., & Schacter, D. L. (1985). Implicit and explicit memory for new associations in normal and amnesic subjects.

Journal of Experimental Psychology: Learning, Memory, and Cognition, 11(3), 501–518.

Graf, P., Squire, L. R., & Mandler, G. (1984). The information that amnesic patients do not forget. *Journal of Experimental Psychology: Learning, Memory, and Cognition, 10*(1), 164–178.

Grafman, J. (1989). Plans, actions, and mental sets: managerial knowledge units in the frontal lobes. In E. Perecman (Ed.), *Integrating theory and practice in clinical neuropsychology* (pp. 93–138). Hillsdale, NJ: Erlbaum.

Grafman, J., Jones, B., & Salazar, A. (1990). Wisconsin Card Sorting Test performance based on location and size of neuroanatomical lesion in Vietnam veterans with penetrating head injury. *Perceptual and Motor Skills, 71*, 1120–1122.

Grafman, J., & Salazar, A. (1987). Methodological considerations relevant to the comparison of recovery from penetrating and closed head injury. In H. S. Levin, J. Grafman, & H. M. Eisenberg (Eds.), *Neurobehavioral recovery from head injury* (pp. 43–54). New York: Oxford University Press.

Grafman, J., Sirigu, A., Spector, L., & Hendler, J. (1993). Damage to the prefrontal cortex leads to decomposition of structured event complexes. *Journal of Head Rehabilitation, 8*, 73–87.

Grafton, S. T., Hazeltine, E., & Ivry, R. (1995). Functional mapping of sequence learning in normal humans. *Journal of Cognitive Neuroscience, 7*(4), 497–510.

Grafton, S. T., Mazziotta, J. C., Presty, S., Friston, K. J., Frackowiak, R. S., & Phelps, M. E. (1992). Functional anatomy of human procedural learning determined with regional cerebral blood flow and PET. *Journal of Neuroscience, 12*(7), 2542–2548.

Grafton, S. T., Woods, R. P., & Mazziotta, J. C. (1993). Within-arm somatotopy in human motor areas determined by positron emission tomography imaging of cerebral blood flow. *Experimental Brain Research, 95*(1), 172–176.

Grafton, S. T., Woods, R. P., & Tyszka, M. (1994). Functional imaging of procedural motor learning: Relating cerebral blood flow with individual subject performance. *Human Brain Mapping, 1*(3), 221–234.

Graham, C. J., & Cleveland, E. (1995). Left-handedness as an injury risk factor in adolescents. *Journal of Adolescent Health, 16*(1), 50–52.

Grant, I., Marcotte, T. D., Heaton, R. K., & HNRC Group (1999). Neurocognitive complications of HIV disease. *Psychological Science, 10*, 191–195.

Grant, I., Olshen, R. A., Atkinson, J. H., Heaton, R. K., Nelson, J., McCutchan, J. A., & Weinrich, J. D. (1993). Depressed mood does not explain neuropsychological deficits in HIV-infected persons. *Neuropsychology, 7*, 53–61.

Grasby, P. M., Fletcher, P., Frith, C. D., Liddle, P. F., Frackowiak, R. S., & Dolan, R. J. (1994). Anterior cingulate rCBF responses in volunteers and schizophrenic patients. *Schizophrenia Research, 11*, 170–179.

Gratton, G., & Fabiani, M. (1998). Dynamic brain imaging: Event-related optical signal (EROS) measures of the time course and localization of cognitive-related activity. *Psychonomic Bulletin & Review, 5*, 535–563.

Gray, D. P. (1998). Forty-seven minutes a year for the patient. *British Journal of General Practice, 48*(437), 1816–1817.

Gray, J. A. (in press). The contents of consciousness: A neuropsychological conjecture. *Behavioral and Brain Sciences.*

Gray, J. R., & Braver, T. S. (2002). Personality predicts working-memory-related activation in caudal anterior cingulate cortex. *Cognitive, Affective & Behavioral Neuroscience, 2*, 64–75.

Gray, J. R., Braver, T. S., & Raichle, M. E. (2002). Integration of emotion and cognition in the lateral prefrontal cortex. *Proceedings of the National Academy of Sciences of the United States of America, 99*, 4115–4120.

Graybiel, A. M. (1990). Neurotransmitters and neuromodulators in the basal ganglia. *Trends in Neurosciences, 13*, 246.

Graybiel, A. M., Aosaki, T., Flaherty, A. W., & Kimura, M. (1994). The basal ganglia and adaptive motor control. *Science, 265*, 1826–1831.

Greenblatt, S. H. (1973). Alexia without agraphia or hemianopia. Anatomical analysis of an autopsied case. *Brain, 96*, 307–316.

Greenough, W., Black, J., & Wallace, C. (1987). Experience and brain development. *Child Development, 58*, 539–559.

Greenough, W. T. (1975). Experiential modification of the developing brain. *American Scientist, 63*, 37–46.

Greenough, W. T. (1987). Experience effects on the developing and the mature brain: Dendritic branching and synaptogenesis. In N. A. Krasnegor, E. Blass, M. Hofer, & W. P. Smotherman (Eds.), *Perinatal development: A psychobiological perspective* (pp. 195–221). New York: Academic Press.

Greenough, W. T., & Chang, F.-L. F. (1988). Plasticity of synaptic structure in the cerebral cortex. In A. Peters & E. G. Jones (Eds.), *Cerebral cortex* (pp. 391–439). New York: Plenum Publishing.

Greenwald, A. G., McGhee, J. L., & Schwartz, J. L. (1998). Measuring individual differences in social cognition: The Implicit Association Test. *Journal of Personality and Social Psychology, 74*, 1464–1480.

Greenwood, P. M. (2000). The frontal aging hypothesis evaluated. *Journal of International Neuropsychological Society, 6*, 705–726.

Grigorenko, E. L. (2001). Developmental dyslexia: An update on genes, brains, and environments. *Journal of Child Psychology and Psychiatry, 42*, 91–125.

Grill-Spector, K., Kushnir, T., Edelman, S., Itzchak, Y., & Malach, R. (1998). Cue-invariant activation in object-related areas of the human occipital lobe. *Neuron, 21*, 191–202.

Gronwall, D., & Wrightson, P. (1975). Cumulative effect of concussion. *Lancet, 2*(7943), 995–997.

Gross, C. G. (1992). Visual stimuli and the inferior temporal cortex. *Philosophical Transactions of the Royal Society of London, B335*, 3–10.

Gross, C. G., Bender, D. B., & Rocha-Miranda, C. E. (1969). Visual receptive fields of neurons in inferotemporal cortex of the monkey. *Science, 166*, 1303–1306.

Gross, C. G., & Mishkin, M. (1977). The neural basis of stimulus equivalence across retinal translation. In S. Harnad, R. Doty, J. Jaynes, L. Goldstein, & G. Krauthamer (Eds.), *Lateralization in the nervous system* (pp. 109–122). New York: Academic Press.

Gross, C. G., Rocha-Miranda, C. E., & Bender, D. B. (1972). Visual properties of neurons in inferotemporal cortex of the macaque. *Journal of Neurophysiology, 35*, 96–111.

Grossman, M. (1988). Drawing deficits in brain-damaged patients' freehand pictures. *Brain and Cognition, 8*, 192–213.

Grote, C. L., Wierenga, C., & Smith M. C. (1999). Wada difference a day makes: Interpretive cautions regarding same-day injections. *Neurology, 52*, 1577–1582.

Grote, C. L., Wierenga, C., Smith, M. C., Kanner, A. M., Bergen, D. C., Geremia, G., Greenlee, W. (1999). Wada difference a day makes: Interpretive cautions regarding same-day injections. *Neurology, 52*(8), 1577–1582.

Groves, P. M., & Rebec, G. V. (1988). *Introduction to biological psychology* (3rd ed.). Dubuque, IA: William C. Brown.

Guariglia, C., & Antonucci, G. (1992). Personal and extrapersonal space: A case of neglect dissociation. *Neuropsychologia, 30*(11), 1001–1009.

Guitton, D., Buchtel, H. A., & Douglas, R. M. (1985). Frontal lobe lesions in man cause difficulties in suppressing reflexive glances and in generating goal-directed saccades. *Experimental Brain Research, 58*, 455–472.

Gunderson, C. H. (1990). *Essentials of clinical neurology.* New York: Raven Press.

Gur, R. C., Gur, R. E., Obrist, W. D., Skolnick, B. E., & Reivitch, M. (1987). Age and regional cerebral blood flow at rest and during cognitive activity. *Archives of General Psychiatry, 44*, 617–621.

Gur, R. C., Mozley, L. H., Mozley, P. D., Resnick, S. M., Karp, J. S., Alvai, B., Arnold, S. E., & Gur, R. E. (1995). Sex differences in regional cerebral glucose metabolism during a resting state. *Science, 267*, 528–531.

Gur, R. E. (1978). Left hemisphere dysfunction and left hemisphere overactivation in schizophrenia. *Journal of Abnormal Psychology, 87*, 226–238.

Gusella, J. G., Wexler, N. S., Conneally, P. A., Naylor, S. L., Anderson, M. A., Tanzi, R. E., Watkins, P. C., Ottina, K., Wallace, M. R., Sakaguchi, A. Y., Young, A. B., Shoulson, I., Bonillo, E., & Martin, J. B. (1983). A polymorphic DNA marker genetically linked to Huntington's disease. *Nature, 306*, 234–238.

Guttmann, C., Jolesz, F., Kikinis, R., Killiany, R., Moss, M., Sandor, T., & Albert, M. (1998). White matter changes with normal aging. *Neurology, 50*, 972–978.

Habib, M., Gayraud, D., Oliva, A., Regis, J., Salamon, G., & Khalil, R. (1991). Effects of handedness and sex on the morphology of the corpus callosum: A study with brain magnetic resonance imaging. *Brain and Cognition, 16*, 41–61.

Habib, M., & Sirigu, A. (1987). Pure topographical disorientation: A definition and anatomical basis. *Cortex, 23*, 73–85.

Habib, R., & Lepage, M. (2000). Novelty assessment in the brain. In E. Tulving (Ed.), *Memory, consciousness, and the brain: The Tallinn Conference* (pp. 265–277). Philadelphia, PA: Psychology Press/Taylor & Francis.

Hagoort, P. & Brown, C. (2000a). ERP effects of listening to speech: Semantic ERP effects. *Neuropsychologia, 38*(11), 1518–1530.

Hagoort, P. & Brown, C. (2000b). ERP effects of listening to speech compared to reading: The P600/SPS to syntactic violations in spoken sentences and rapid serial visual presentation. *Neuropsychologia, 38*(11), 1531–1549.

Hagoort, P., & Brown, C. (1994). Brain responses to lexical ambiguity resolution and parsing. In Clifton, Jr., C., Frazier, L., & Rayner, K. (Eds.), *Perspectives on sentence processing* (pp. 45–80). Hillsdale NJ: Lawrence Erlbaum.

Hagoort, P., Indefrey, P., Brown, C., Herzog, H., Steinmetz, H., & Seitz, R. J. (1999). The neural circuitry involved in the reading of German words and pseudowords: A PET study. *Journal of Cognitive Neuroscience, 11*(4), 383–398.

Haist, F., Shimamura, A. P., & Squire, L. R. (1992). On the relationship between recall and recognition memory. *Journal of Experimental Psychology: Learning, Memory, and Cognition, 18*(4), 691–702.

Halgren, E. (1984). Human hippocampal and amygdal recording and stimulation: Evidence for a neural model of recent memory. In L. R. Squire, & N. Butters (Eds.), *The neuropsychology of memory* (pp. 165–182). New York: Guilford Press.

Halgren, E., Raij, T., Marinkovic, K., Jousmaki, V., & Hari, R. (2000). Cognitive response profile of the human fusiform face area as determined by MEG. *Cerebral Cortex, 10*, 69–81.

Halligan, P. W., Marshall, J. C., & Wade, D. T. (1993). Three arms: A case study of supernumerary phantom limb after right hemisphere stroke. *Journal of Neurology, Neurosurgery, and Psychiatry, 56*, 159–166.

Halpern, D. F., & Coren, S. (1993). Left-handedness and life span: A reply to Harris. *Psychological Bulletin, 114*, 235–241.

Hamann, S. B., Stefanacci, L., Squire, L. R., Adolphs, R., Tranel, D., Damasio, H., & Damasio, A. (1996). Recognizing facial emotion. *Nature, 379*(6565), 497.

Hamilton, C. R., & Vermeire, B. A. (1988). Complementary hemispheric specialization in monkeys. *Science, 242*(4886), 1691–1694.

Hannay, H. J., Rogers, J. P., & Durant, R. F. (1976). Complexity as a determinant of visual field effects for random forms. *Acta Psychologica (Amsterdam), 40*, 29–34.

Hannay, H. J., Varney, N., & Benton, A. L. (1976). Visual localization in patients with unilateral cerebral brain disease. *Journal of Neurology, Neurosurgery and Psychiatry, 39*, 307–313.

Hansch, E. C., & Pirozzolo, F. J. (1980). Task relevant effects on the assessment of cerebral specialization for facial emotion. *Brain and Language, 10*, 51–59.

Hardy, J. A., & Higgins, G. A. (1992). Alzheimer's disease: The amyloid cascade hypothesis. *Science, 25*, 184–185.

Harmony, T. (1989). Psychophysiological evaluation of children's neuropsychological disorders. In C. R. Reynolds & E. Fletcher-Janzen (Eds.), *Handbook of clinical child neuropsychology* (pp. 265–270). New York: Plenum Press.

Harnadek, M. C. S., & Rourke, B. P. (1994). Principal identifying features of the syndrome of nonverbal learning disabilities in children. *Journal of Learning Disabilities, 27*, 144–154.

Harris, L. J. (1993a). Do left-handers die sooner than right-handers? Commentary on Coren and Halpern's (1991) "Left-handedness: A marker for decreased survival fitness." *Psychological Bulletin, 114*, 203–234.

Harris, L. J. (1993b). "Left-handedness and life span": Reply to Halpern and Coren. *Psychological Bulletin, 114,* 242–247.

Harrison, P. J. (1999). The neuropathology of schizophrenia: A critical review of the data and their interpretation. *Brain, 122,* 593–624.

Harrison, P. J., & Roberts, G. W. (1991). "Life, Jim, but not as we know it?" Transmissible dementias and the prion protein. *British Journal of Psychiatry, 158,* 457–470.

Hart, J., Berndt, R. S., & Caramazza, A. (1985). Category-specific naming deficit following cerebral infarction. *Nature, 316,* 439–440.

Hart, S., & Semple, J. M. (1990). *Neuropsychology and the dementias.* London: Ehrlbaum.

Hartman, D. E. (1987). Neuropsychological toxicology: Identification and assessment of neurotoxic syndromes. *Archives of Clinical Neuropsychology, 2,* 45–65.

Harwood, K., & Wickens, C. D. (1991). Frames of reference for helicopter electronic maps: The relevance of spatial cognition and componential analysis. *International Journal of Aviation Psychology, 1,* 5–23.

Hasher, L., & Zacks, R. (1988). Working memory, comprehension, and aging: A review and a new view. In G. Bower (Ed.), *The psychology of learning and motivation* (pp. 193–225). New York: Academic Press.

Hatta, T. (1977). Functional hemisphere asymmetries in an inferential thought task. *Psychologia, 20,* 145–150.

Haug, H., Barmwater, U., Eggers, R., Fischer, D., Kuhl, S., & Sass, N. L. (1983). Anatomical changes in aging brain: Morphometric analysis of the human prosencephalon. In J. Cerbos-Navarro & H. I. Sarkander (Eds.), *Neuropharmacology: Vol. 21. Aging* (pp. 1–12). New York: Raven Press.

Hauser, R. A., Freeman, T. B., Snow, J. B., Nauert, M., Gauger, L., Kordower, J. H., & Olanow, W. (1999). Long-term evaluation of bilateral fetal nigral transplantation in Parkinson disease. *Archives of Neurology, 56,* 179–187.

Hauser, R. A., Furtado, S., Cimino, C. R., Delgado, H., Eichler, S., Schwartz, S., Scott, D., Nauert, G. M., Soety, E., Sossi, V., Holt, D. A., Sanberg, P. R., Stoessl, A. J., & Freeman, T. B. (2002). Bilateral human fetal striatal transplantation in Huntington's disease. *Neurology, 58,* 687–695.

Hauser, T. (1991). *Muhammad Ali: His life and times.* New York: Simon & Schuster.

Hawrylak, N., & Greenough, W. T. (1995). Plasticity of astrocytes: A review and hypothesis.

Haxby, J. V., Gobbini, M. I., Furey, M. L., Ishai, A., Shouten, J. L., & Pietrini, P. (2001). Distributed and overlapping representations of faces and objects in ventral temporal cortex. *Science, 293,* 2425–2430.

Haxby, J. V., Grady, C. L., Koss, E., Horwitz, B., Heston, L., Scapiro, M., Friedland, R. P., & Rapoport, S. I. (1990). Longitudinal study of cerebral metabolic asymmetries and associated neuropsychological patterns in early dementia of the Alzheimer type. *Archives of Neurology, 47,* 753–760.

Haxby, J. V., Hoffman, E. A., & Gobbini, M. I. (2000). The distributed human neural system for face perception. *Trends in Cognitive Sciences, 4,* 223–232.

Haxby, J. V., Horwitz, B., Ungerleider, L. G., Maisog, J. M., Pietrini, P., & Grady, C. L. (1994). The functional organization of human extrastriate cortex: A PET-rCBF study of selective attention to faces and locations. *Journal of Neuroscience, 14*(11), 6336–6353.

Hazeltine, E., Grafton, S. T., & Ivry, R. (1997). Attention and stimulus characteristics determine the locus of motor-sequence encoding. A PET study. *Brain, 120*(Pt. 1), 123–140.

Heath, M., Roy, E. A., Westwood., D, Black, S. E. (2001). Patterns of apraxia associated with the production of intransitive limb gestures following left and right hemisphere stroke. *Brain & Cognition, 46,* 165–169.

Heaton, R. K., Grant, I., Butters, N., White, D. A., Kirson, D., Atkinson, J. H., McCutchan, J. A., Taylor, M. J., Kelly, M. D., Ellis, R. J., Wolfson, T., Velin, R., Marcotte, T. D., Hesselink, J. R., Jernigan, T. L., Chandler, J., Wallace, M., Abramson, I., & Group, T. H. (1995). The HNRC 500—Neuropsychology of HIV infection at different disease stages. *Journal of the International Neuropsychological Society, 1,* 231–251.

Heaton, R. K., Marcotte, T. D., White, D. A., Ross, D., Meredith, K., Taylor, M. J., Kaplan, R., & Grant, I. (1996). Nature and vocational significance of neuropsychological impairment associated with HIV infection. *The Clinical Neuropsychologist, 10,* 1–14.

Hebben, N., Corkin, S., Eichenbaum, H., & Shedlack, K. (1985). Diminished ability to interpret and report internal states after bilateral medial temporal resection: Case H. M. *Behavioral Neuroscience, 99*(6), 1031–1039.

Hécaen, H. (1962). Clinical symptomology in right and left hemisphere lesions. In V. B. Mountcastle (Ed.), *Interhemispheric relations and cerebral dominance* (pp. 215–243). Baltimore: Johns Hopkins University Press.

Hécaen, H., & Kremin, H. (1976). Neurolinguistic research on reading disorder from left hemisphere lesions: Aphasic and "pure" alexias. In H. A. Whitaker & H. Whitaker (Eds.), *Studies in neurolinguistics II* (pp. 269–329). New York: Academic Press.

Hécaen, H., & Rondot, P. (1985). Apraxia as a disorder of signs. In E. Roy (Ed.), *Neuropsychological studies of apraxia and related disorders.* Amsterdam: Elsevier-North Holland.

Heekers, S., Rauch, S. L., Goff, D., Savage, C. R., Schacter, D. L., Fischman, A. J., & Alpert, N. M. (1998). Impaired recruitment of the hippocampus during conscious recollection in schizophrenia. *Nature Neuroscience, 1,* 318–323.

Hefti, E., & Weiner, W. J. (1986). Nerve growth factor and Alzheimer's disease. *Annals of Neurology, 20,* 275–281.

Heilman, K., Bowers, D., Speedie, L., & Coslett, H. B. (1984). Comprehension of affective and nonaffective prosody. *Neurology, 34,* 917–921.

Heilman, K. M., Bowers, D., Coslett, H. B., Whelan, H., & Watson, R. T. (1985). Directional hypokinesia: Prolonged reaction times for leftward movements in patients with right hemisphere lesions and neglect. *Neurology, 35,* 855–859.

Heilman, K. M., Rothi, L. J., & Valenstein, E. (1982). Two forms of ideomotor apraxia. *Neurology, 32,* 342–346.

Heilman, K. M., & Rothi, L. J. G. (1985). Apraxia. In K. M. Heilman & E. Valenstein (Eds.), *Clinical neuropsychology* (2nd ed., pp. 131–150). New York: Oxford University Press.

Heilman, K. M., Scholes, R., & Watson, R. T. (1975). Auditory affective agnosia: Disturbed comprehension of affective speech. *Journal of Neurology, Neurosurgery and Psychiatry, 38,* 69–72.

Heilman, K. M., & Valenstein, E. (1972). Frontal lobe neglect in man. *Neurology, 22,* 660–664.

Heilman, K. M., Watson, R. T., & Valenstein, E. (1985). Neglect and related disorders. In K. M. Heilman & E. Valenstein (Eds.), *Clinical neuropsychology* (2nd ed.). New York: Oxford University Press.

Heinze, H. J., Luck, S. J., Mangun, G. R., & Hillyard, S. A. (1990). Visual event-related potentials index focused attention within bilateral stimulus arrays: 1. Evidence for early selection. *Electroencephalography & Clinical Neurophysiology, 75*(6), 511–527.

Heinze, H. J., Mangun, G. R., Burchert, W., Hinrichs, H., Scholz, M., Munte, T. F., Cos, A., Scherg, M., Johannes, S., Hudeshagen, J., Gazzaniga, M., & Hillyard, S. A. (1994). Combined spatial and temporal imaging of brain activity during visual selective attention in humans. *Nature, 372,* 543–546.

Heit, G., Smith, M. E., & Halgren, E. (1988). Neural encoding of individual words and faces by the human hippocampus and amygdala. *Nature, 333*(6175), 773–775.

Heller, W. (1986). *Cerebral organization of emotional function in children.* Unpublished doctoral dissertation, University of Chicago.

Heller, W. (1987). Lateralization of emotional content in children's drawings. *Scientific proceedings of the annual meeting of the American Academy of Child and Adolescent Psychiatry, 3,* 63.

Heller, W. (1988). Asymmetry of emotional judgements in children. *Journal of Clinical and Experimental Neuropsychology, 10,* 36.

Heller, W. (1990). The neuropsychology of emotion: Developmental patterns and implications for psychopathology. In N. Stein, B. L. Leventhal, & T. Trabasso (Eds.), *Psychological and biological approaches to emotion* (pp. 167–211). Hillsdale, NJ: Erlbaum.

Heller, W. (1991). New territory: Creativity and brain injury. *Creative Woman, 11,* 16–18.

Heller, W. (1993a). Gender differences in depression: Perspectives from neuropsychology. *Journal of Affective Disorders, 29,* 129–143.

Heller, W. (1993b). Neuropsychological mechanisms of individual differences in emotion, personality, and arousal. *Neuropsychology, 7,* 476–489.

Heller, W. (1994). Cognitive and emotional organization of the brain: Influences on the creation and perception of art. In D. Zaidel (Ed.), *Neuropsychology* (pp. 271–292). San Diego: Academic Press.

Heller, W., Etienne, M., & Miller, G. A. (1995). Patterns of perceptual asymmetry in depression and anxiety: Implications for neuropsychological models of emotion and psychopathology. *Journal of Abnormal Psychology, 104,* 327–333.

Heller, W., Hopkins, J., & Cox, S. (1991). Effects of lateralized brain damage on infant socioemotional development. *Journal of Clinical and Experimental Neuropsychology, 13,* 64.

Heller, W., & Levy, J. (1981). Perception and expression of emotion in right-handers and left-handers. *Neuropsychologia, 19,* 263–272.

Heller, W., & Nitschke, J. B. (1997). Regional brain activity in emotion: A framework for understanding cognition in depression. *Cognition and Emotion, 11,* 637–661.

Heller, W., & Nitschke, J. B. (1998). The puzzle of regional brain activity in depression and anxiety: The importance of subtypes and comorbidity. *Cognition and Emotion, 12,* 421–447.

Heller, W., Nitschke, J. B., & Lindsay, D. L. (1997). Neuropsychological correlates of arousal in self-reported emotion. *Cognition and Emotion, 11,* 383–402.

Heller, W., Schmidtke, J. I., Nitschke, J. B., Koven, N. S., & Miller, G. A. (2002). States, traits, and symptoms: Investigating the neural correlates of emotion, personality, and psychopathology. In D. Cervone, & W. Mischel (Eds.), *Advances in personality science* (pp. 106–126). New York: The Guilford Press.

Hellige, J. B. (1993a). *Hemispheric asymmetry: What's right and what's left.* Cambridge, MA: Harvard University Press.

Hellige, J. B. (1993b). Unity of thought and action: Varieties of interaction between the left and right cerebral hemispheres. *Current Directions in Psychological Science, 2,* 21–25.

Hellige, J. B., & Cox, P. J. (1976). Effects of concurrent verbal memory on recognition of stimuli from the left and right visual fields. *Journal of Experimental Psychology: Human Perception and Performance, 2,* 210–221.

Hellige, J. B., & Michimata, C. (1989). Categorization versus distance: Hemispheric differences for processing spatial information. *Memory and Cognition, 17,* 770–776.

Hellige, J. B., Taylor, A. K., & Eng, T. L. (1989). Interhemispheric interaction when both hemispheres have access to the same stimulus information. *Journal of Experimental Psychology: Human Perception and Performance, 15,* 711–722.

Hellige, J. B., & Webster, R. (1979). Right hemisphere superiority for initial stages of letter processing. *Neuropsychologia, 17,* 653–660.

Helm-Estabrooks, N. (1983). Exploiting the right hemisphere for language rehabilitation: Melodic intonation therapy. In E. Perecman (Ed.), *Cognitive processing in the right hemisphere.* New York: Academic Press.

Henderson, A. S. (1988). The risk factors for Alzheimer's disease: A review and hypothesis. *Acta Psychiatrica Scandinavica, 78,* 257–275.

Henik, A., Singh, J., Beckley, R. J., & Rafal, R. D. (1993). Disinhibition of automatic word reading in Parkinson's disease. *Cortex, 29,* 589–599.

Henke, K., Buck, A., Weber, B., & Weiser, H. G. (1997). Human hippocampus establishes associations in memory. *Hippocampus, 7*(3), 249–256.

Henke, P. G. (1982). Telencephalic limbic system and experimental gastric pathology: A review. *Neuroscience and Biobehavioral Reviews, 6,* 381–390.

Henriques, J. B., & Davidson, R. J. (1991). Left frontal hypoactivation in depression. *Journal of Abnormal Psychology, 100,* 535–545.

Henson, R. N., Rugg, M. D., Shallice, T., Josephs, O., & Dolan, R. J. (1999). Recollection and familiarity in recognition memory: An event-related functional magnetic resonance imaging. *Journal of Neuroscience, 19*(10), 3962–3972.

Herbster, A. N., Mintun, M. A., Nebes, R. D., Becker, J. T. (1997). Regional cerebral blood flow during word and nonword reading. *Human Brain Mapping, 5,* 84–92.

Hess, R. F., Baker, C. L., & Zihl, J. (1989). The motion-blind patient: Low-level spatial and temporal filters. *Journal of Neuroscience, 9,* 1628–1640.

Heumann, D., & Leuba, G. (1983). Neuronal death in the development and aging of the cerebral cortex of the mouse. *Neuropathology and Applied Neurobiology, 9,* 297–311.

Hicks, R. A., Johnson, C., Cuevas, T., Deharo, D., & Bautista, J. (1994). Do right-handers live longer? An updated assessment of baseball player data. *Perceptual and Motor Skills, 78*(3, Pt. 2), 1243–1247.

Hicks, R. A., Pass, K, Freeman, H., Bautista, J., et al. (1993). Handedness and accidents with injury. *Perceptual and Motor Skills, 77*(3, Pt. 2), 1119–1122.

Hier, D. B., Hagenlocker, K., & Shindler, A. G. (1985). Language disintegration in dementia: Effects of etiology and severity. *Brain and Language, 25,* 117–133.

Hiller, W., Zaudig, M., & Rose, M. (1989). The overlap between depression and anxiety on different levels of psychopathology. *Journal of Affective Disorders, 16,* 223–231.

Hilliger, L. A., & Koenig, O. (1991). Separable mechanisms in face processing: Evidence from hemispheric specialization. *Journal of Cognitive Neuroscience, 3,* 42–58.

Hillis, A. E., & Caramazza, A. (1991). Deficit to stimulus-centered, letter shape representations in a case of "unilateral neglect." *Neuropsychologia, 29*(12), 1223–1240.

Hillyard, S. A., Hink, R. F., Schwent, V. L., & Picton, T. W. (1973). Electrical signs of selective attention in the human brain. *Science, 182,* 177–180.

Hillyard, S. A., & Kutas, M. (1983). *Annual Review of Psychology, 34,* 33–61.

Hinton, G. E. (1992). How neural networks learn from experience. *Scientific American, 267*(3), 145–151.

Hirshkowitz, M., Earle, J., & Paley, B. (1978). EEG alpha asymmetry in musicians and non-musicians: A study of hemispheric specialization. *Neuropsychologia, 16,* 125–128.

Hirst, W., Johnson, M. K., Kim, J. K., Phelps, E. A., Risse, G., & Volpe, B. T. (1986). Recognition and recall in amnesics. *Journal of Experimental Psychology: Learning, Memory, and Cognition, 12,* 445–451.

Hirst, W., & Volpe, B. T. (1984). Automatic and effortful encoding in amnesia. In M. S. Gazzaniga (Ed.), *Handbook of cognitive neuroscience.* New York: Plenum Press.

Hiscock, M., & Hiscock, C. K. (1989). Refining the forced-choice method for the dedection of malingering. *Journal of Clinical and Experimental Neuropsychology, 11,* 967–974.

Hiscock, M., Inch, R., Jacek, C., Hiscock-Kalil, C., & Kalil, K. M. (1994). Is there a sex difference in human laterality? I. An exhaustive survey of auditory laterality studies from six neuropsychology journals. *Journal of Clinical and Experimental Neuropsychology, 16,* 423–435.

Hiscock, M., Israelian, M., Inch, R., Jacek, C., Hiscock-Kalil, C. (1995). Is there a sex difference in human laterality? II. An exhaustive survey of visual laterality studies from six neuropsychology journals. *Journal of Clinical and Experimental Neuropsychology, 17,* 590–610.

Hjalmarsen, A., Waterloo, K., Dahl, A., Rolf, J., & Viitanen, M. (1999). Effect of long-term oxygen therapy on cognitive and neurological dysfunction in chronic obstructive pulmonary disease. *European Neurology, 42,* 27–35.

Hochberg, F., & LeMay, M. (1975). Arteriographic correlates of handedness. *Neurology, 25*(3), 218–222.

Hodges, J. R., Salmon, D. P., & Butters, N. (1992). Semantic memory impairment in Alzheimer's disease: Failure of access or degraded knowledge? *Neuropsychologia, 30,* 301–314.

Hoffman, E., & Haxby, J. (2000). Distinct representations of eye gaze and identity in the distributed human neural system for face perception. *Nature Neuroscience, 3,* 80–84.

Hoffman, J. E. (1990). Event-related potentials and automatic and controlled processes. In J. W. Rohrbaugh, R. Parasuraman, & R. Johnson (Eds.), *Event-related brain potentials: Basic issues and applications* (pp. 145–157). New York: Oxford University Press.

Holland, A. L., McBurney, D. H., Mossy, J., & Reinmuth, O. M. (1985). The dissolution of language in Pick's disease with neurofibrillary tangles: A case study. *Brain and Language, 24,* 36–58.

Hollerman, J. R., & Schultz, W. (1998). Dopamine neurons report an error in the temporal prediction of reward during learning. *Nature Neuroscience, 1,* 304–309.

Holloway, R. L. (1980). Indonesian "solo" (Ngandong) endocranial reconstructions: Some preliminary observations and comparisons with Neanderthal and Homo erectus groups. *American Journal of Physical Anthropology, 53,* 285–295.

Holmes, G. (1919). Disturbances of visual orientation. *British Journal of Ophthalmology, 2,* 449–468, 506–518.

Holsinger, T., Steffens, D. C., Phillips, C., Helms, M., Havlik, R. J., Brietner, J. C. S., Guralnik, J. M., & Plassman, B. L. (2002). Head injury in early adulthood and the lifetime risk of depression. *Archives of General Psychiatry, 59,* 17–22.

Holtzman, J. D., & Gazzaniga, M. S. (1982). Dual task interactions due exclusively to limits in processing resources. *Science, 218,* 1325–1327.

Hoorweg, J., & Stanfield, J. P. (1976). The effects of protein energy malnutrition in early childhood on intellectual and motor abilities in later childhood and adolescence. *Developmental Medicine and Child Neurology, 18,* 330–350.

Hopkins, W. D. (1997). Hemispheric specialization for local and global processing of hierarchical visual stimuli in chimpanzees (Pan troglodytes). *Neuropsychologia, 35*(3), 343–348.

Hopkins, W. D., Marino, L., Rilling, J. K., & MacGregor, L. A. (1998). Planum temporale asymmetries in great apes as revealed by magnetic resonance imaging (MRI). Neuroreport: An International Journal for the Rapid

Communication of Research in *Neuroscience, 9*(12), 2913–2918.

Hornak, J. (1992). Ocular exploration in the dark by patients with visual neglect. *Neuropsychologia, 30,* 547–552.

Hosford, D. A., Clark, S., Cao, Z., Wilson, W. A. Jr., Lin, F. H., Morriset, R. A., & Huin, A. (1992). The role of $GABA_B$ receptor activation in absence seizures of lethargic (lh/lh) mice. *Science, 257,* 398–401.

Hough, M. S. (1990). Narrative comprehension in adults with right and left hemisphere brain-damage: Theme organization. *Brain and Language, 38,* 253–277.

Howard, D., Patterson, K., Wise, R., Brown, W. D., Friston, K., Weiller, C., & Frackowiak, R. (1992). The cortical localization of the lexicons. *Brain, 115,* 1769–1782.

Hubel, D. H., & Wiesel, T. N. (1970). The period of susceptibility to the physiological effects of unilateral eye closure in kittens. *Journal of Physiology, 206,* 419–436.

Huber, S. J., Christy, J. A., & Paulson, G. W. (1991). Cognitive heterogeneity associated with clinical subtypes of Parkinson's disease. *Neuropsychiatry, Neuropsychology and Behavioral Neurology, 4,* 147–157.

Hugdahl, K., & Wester, K. (2000). Neurocognitive correlates of stereotactic thalamotomy and thalamic stimulation in Parkinsonian patients. *Brain and Cognition, 42,* 231–252.

Hughes, H. C., Fendrich, R., & Reuter-Lorenz, P. A. (1990). Global versus local processing in the absence of low spatial frequencies. *Journal of Cognitive Neuroscience, 2,* 272–282.

Huijbregts, S. C. J., de Sonneville, L. M. J., Licht, R., van Spronsen, F. J., Verkerk, P. H., & Sergeant, J. A. (2002). Sustained attention and inhibition of cognitive interference in treated phenylketonuria: Associations with concurrent and lifetime phenylalanine concentrations. *Neuropsychologia, 40,* 7–15.

Humm, J. L., Kozlowski, D. A., James, D. C., Gotts, J. E., & Schallert, T. (1998). Use-dependent exacerbation of brain damage occurs during an early post-lesion vulnerable period. *Brain Research, 783*(2), 286–292.

Hummel, J. E., & Stankiewicz, B. J. (1996). An architecture for rapid, hierarchical structural description. In T. Inui, & J. McClelland (Eds.), *Attention and performance XVI* (pp. 93–121). Cambridge, MA: MIT Press.

Humphreys, G. W. (1996). Object recognition: The man who mistook his dog for a cat. *Current Biology, 6,* 821–824.

Humphreys, G. W., & Riddoch, M. J. (1984). Routes to object constancy: Implications from neurological impairments of object constancy. *Quarterly Journal of Experimental Psychology: Human Experimental Psychology, 36A*(3), 36A, 385–415.

Humphreys, P., Kaufmann, W. E., & Galaburda, A. M. (1990). Developmental dyslexia in women: Neuropathological findings in three patients. *Annuals of Neurology, 28,* 727–738.

Hunter, K. E., Blaxton, T. A., Bookheimer, S. Y., Figlozzi, C., Gaillard, W. D., Grandin, C., Anyanwu, A., & Theodore, W. H. (1999). (15)O water position emission tomography in language localization: A study comparing positron emission tomography visual and computerized region of interest analysis with the Wada test. *Annals of Neurology, 45*(5), 662–665.

Huttenlocher, P., & Dabholkar, A. (1997). Regional differences in synaptogenesis in human cerebral cortex. *Journal of Comparative Neurology, 387,* 167–178.

Huttenlocher, P., & de Courten, C. (1987). The development of synapses in striate cortex of man. *Human Neurobiology, 6,* 1–9.

Huttenlocher, P. R. (1979). Synaptic density in human frontal cortex: Developmental changes and effects of aging. *Brain Research, 163,* 195–205.

Huttenlocher, P. R. (1990). Morphometric study of human cerebral cortex development. *Neuropsychologia, 28,* 517–527.

Huttenlocher, P. R. (1994). Synaptogenesis in human cerebral cortex. In G. Dawson & K. W. Fischer (Eds.), *Human behavior and the developing brain* (pp. 137–152). New York: Guilford Press.

Hynd, G. W., & Cohen, M. (1983). *Dyslexia: Neuropsychological theory, research, and clinical differentiation.* New York: Grune & Stratton.

Hynd, G. W., Hall, J., Novey, E. S., Eliopulos, D., Black, K., Gonzalez, J. J., Edmonds, J. E., Riccio, C., & Cohen, M. (1995). Dyslexia and corpus callosum morphology. *Archives of Neurology, 52,* 32–38.

Hynd, G. W., & Semrud-Clikeman, M. (1989). Dyslexia and brain morphology. *Psychological Bulletin, 106,* 447–482.

Iacoboni, M., Woods, R. P., & Mazziota, J. C. (1996). Brain-behavior relationships: Evidence from practice effects in spatial stimulus-response compatibility. *Journal of Neurophysiology, 76,* 321–331.

Iacoboni, M., Woods, R. P., Brass, M., Bekkering, H., Mazziotta, J. C., & Rizzolatti, G. (1999). Cortical mechanisms of human imitation. *Science, 286,* 2526–2528.

Iidaka, T., Omori, M., Murata, T., Kosaka, H., Yonekura, Y., Okada, T., & Sadato, N. (2001). Neural interaction of the amygdala with the prefrontal and temporal cortices in the processing of facial expressions as revealed by fMRI. *Journal of Cognitive Neuroscience, 13,* 1035–1047.

Illes, J., Francis, W. S., Desmond, J. E., Gabrieli, J. D. E., Glover, G. H., Poldrack, R., Lee, C. J., & Wagner, A. D. (1999). Convergent cortical representation of semantic processing in bilinguals. *Brain and Language, 70,* 347–363.

Ilmoniemi, R. J., Ruohonen, J., & Karhu, J. (1999). Transcranial magnetic stimulation—A new tool for functional imaging of the brain. *Critical Reviews in Biomedical Engineering, 27,* 241–284.

Imaizumi, S., Mori, K., Kiritani, S., Kawashima, R., Sugiura, M., Fukuda, H., Itoh, K., Kato, T., Nakamura, A., Hatano, K., Kojima, S., & Nakamura, K. (1997). Vocal identification of speaker and emotion activates different brain regions. *NeuroReport, 8,* 2809–2812.

Imamizu, H., Miyauchi, S., Tamada, T., Sasaki, Y., Takino, R., Pütz, B., Yoshioka, T. & Kawato, M. (2000). Human cerebellar activity reflecting an acquired internal model of a new tool. *Nature, 403,* 192–195.

Incisa della Rocchetta, A., Cipolotti, L., & Warrington, E. K. (1996). Topographical disorientation: Selection impairment of locomotor space. *Cortex, 32,* 727–735.

Indefrey, P. I., Kleinschmidt, A., Merboldt, K D., Krüger, G., Brown, C., Hagoort, P., & Frahm, J. (1997). Equivalent responses to lexical and nonlexical visual stimuli in occipital cortex: A functional magnetic resonance imaging study. *Neuroimage, 5,* 78–81.

Irwin, S. A., Galvez, R., & Greenough, W. T. (2000). Dendritic spine structural anomalies in Fragile-X mental retardation syndrome. *Cerebral Cortex, 10,* 1038–1044.

Irwin, W., Davidson, R. J., Lowe, M. J., Mock, B. J., Sorenson, J. A., & Turski, P. A. (1996). Human amygdala activation detected with echo-planar functional magnetic resonance imaging. *NeuroReport, 7,* 1765–1769.

Ishai, A., Ungerleider, L. G., & Haxby, J. V. (2000). Distributed neural systems for the generation of visual images. *Neuron, 28*(3), 979–990.

Ivry, R. (1997). Cerebellar timing systems. *International Review of Neurobiology, 41,* 555–573.

Ivry, R. (1997). The many manifestations of a cerebellar timing system. *International Review of Neurobiology, 41,* 555–573.

Ivry, R. B. (1996). The representation of temporal information in perception and motor control. *Current Opinion in Neurobiology, 6,* 851–857.

Ivry, R., & Keele, S. (1989). Timing functions of the cerebellum. *Journal of Cognitive Neuroscience, 1,* 136–152.

Ivry, R. B., & Lebby, P. C. (1993). Hemispheric differences in auditory perception are similar to those found in visual perception. *Psychological Science, 4*(1), 41–45.

Ivry, R. B., & Robertson, L. C. (1998). *The Two Sides of Perception.* Cambridge, MA: MIT Press.

Jackson, M., & Lowe, J. (1996). The new neuropathology of degenerative frontotemporal dementias. *Acta Neuropathologica, 91,* 127–134.

Jacobs, L., Munschauer, F. E., & Pullicino, P. (1993). Current treatment strategies and perspectives of multiple sclerosis. In U. Halbreich (Ed.), *Multiple sclerosis: A neuropsychiatric disorder.* Washington, DC: American Psychiatric Press.

Jacoby, L. L. (1984). Incidental versus intentional retrieval: Remembering and awareness as separate issues. In L. R. Squire & N. Butters (Eds.), *Neuropsychology of memory* (pp. 145–156). New York: Guilford Press.

Jakobson, L. S., Archibald, Y. M., Carey, D. P., & Goodale, M. A. (1991). A kinematic analysis of reaching and grasping movements in a patient recovering from optic ataxia. *Neuropsychologia, 29,* 803–809.

James, W. (1890). *The principles of psychology.* New York: Holt.

Janowsky, J. S., Shimamura, A. P., & Squire, L. R. (1989). Source memory impairment in patients with frontal lobe lesions. *Neuropsychologia, 27*(8), 1043–1056.

Jenkins, I. H., Brooks, D. J., Nixon, P. D., Frackowiak, R. S., & Passingham, R. E. (1994). Motor sequence learning: A study with positron emission tomography. *Journal of Neuroscience, 14*(6), 3775–3790.

Jenkins, W. M., Merzenich, M. M., & Recanzone, G. (1990). Neocortical representational dynamics in adult primates: Implications for neuropsychology. *Neuropsychologia, 28,* 573–584.

Jenner, P. (2002). Pharmacology of dopamine agonists in the treatment of Parkinson's disease. *Neurology, 58,* S1–S8.

Jernigan, T. L., & Ostergaard, A. L. (1993). Word priming and recognition memory are both affected by mesial temporal lobe damage. *Neuropsychology, 7,* 14–26.

Jessell, T. M. (1991). Reactions of neurons to injury. In E. R. Kandel, J. H. Schwartz, & T. M. Jessell (Eds.), *Principles of neural science* (3rd ed., pp. 258–282). New York: Elsevier.

Jetter, W., Poser, U., Freeman, R. B. J., & Markowitsch, H. J. (1986). A verbal long term memory deficit in frontal lobe damaged patients. *Cortex, 22,* 229–242.

Johnson, J. S., & Newport, E. L. (1989). Critical period effects in second language learning: The influence of maturational state on the acquisition of English as a second language. *Cognitive Psychology, 21*(1), 60–99.

Jones-Gotman, M. (1986a). Memory for designs: The hippocampal contribution. *Neuropsychologia, 24,* 193–203.

Jones-Gotman, M. (1986b). Right hippocampal excision impairs learning and recall of a list of abstract designs. *Neuropsychologia, 24,* 659–670.

Jones-Gotman, M., & Milner, B. (1977). Design fluency: The invention of nonsense drawings after focal cortical lesions. *Neuropsychologia, 15,* 653–674.

Jonides, J., Smith, E. E., Koeppe, R. A., Awh, E., Minoshima, S., & Mintun, M. A. (1993). Spatial working memory in humans as revealed by PET. *Nature, 363,* 623–625.

Jordan, B. D., & Zimmerman, R. D. (1990). Computed tomography and magnetic resonance imaging comparisons in boxers. *Journal of the American Medical Association, 263,* 1670–1674.

Josiassen, R. C., Curry, L. M., & Mancall, E. L. (1982). Patterns of intellectual deficit in Huntington's disease. *Journal of Clinical Neuropsychology, 4,* 173–183.

Julesz, B. (1964). Binocular depth perception without familiarity cues. *Science, 145,* 356.

Julien, R. M. (2001). *A primer of drug action* (9th ed.). New York: Worth Publishers.

Jung, R. E., Yeo, R. A., Chiulli, S. J., Sibitt, W. L. Jr., Weers, D. C., Hart, B. L., & Brooks, W. M. (1999). Biochemical markers of cognition: a proton MR spectroscopy study of normal human brain. *Neuroreport, 10,* 3327–3331.

Juraska, J. (1991). Sex difference in "cognitive" regions of the rat brain. *Psychoneuroendocrinology, 16,* 105–119.

Juraska, J. M., Henderson, C., & Muller, J. (1984). Differential rearing experience, gender, and radial maze performance. *Developmental Psychobiology, 17,* 209–215.

Kahle, Leonhardt, & Platzer. *Color atlas and textbook of human anatomy: Vol. 3. Nervous system and sensory organs.* Chicago: Year Book Medical.

Kahneman, D. (1973). *Attention and effort.* Englewood Cliffs, NJ: Prentice Hall.

Kalat, J. W. (1992). *Biological psychology* (4th ed.). Belmont, CA: Wadsworth.

Kalivas, P. W., & Nakamura, M. (1999). Neural systems for behavioral activation and reward. *Current Opinion in Neurobiology, 9,* 223–227.

Kandel, E. R., Schwartz, J. H., & Jessell, T. M. (Eds.). (1991). *Principles of neural science* (3rd ed.). New York: Elsevier.

Kandel, E. R., Schwartz, J. H., & Jessell, T. M. (1995). *Essentials of neural science and behavior.* Norwalk, CT: Appleton & Lange.

Kanwisher, N. (2000). Domain specificity in face perception. *Nature Neuroscience, 3,* 759–763.

Kanwisher, N., McDermott, J., & Chun, M. M. (1997). The fusiform face area: A module in human extrastriate cortex specialized for face perception. *Journal of Neuroscience, 17,* 4302–4311.

Kaplan, E., Fein, D., Morris, R., & Delis, D. C. (1991). *Manual for the WAIS-R as a neuropsychological instrument.* San Antonio, TX: Psychological Corporation.

Kaplan, J. A., Brownell, H. H., Jacobs, J. R., & Gardner, H. (1990). The effects of right hemisphere damage on the pragmatic interpretation of conversational remarks. *Brain and Language, 38,* 315–333.

Kapur, N. (1993). Focal retrograde amnesia in neurological disease: A critical review. *Cortex, 29*(2), 217–234.

Kapur, N. (Ed.) (1997). Injured brains of medical minds. New York: Oxford University Press.

Kapur, N., & Brooks, D. J. (1999). Temporally-specific retrograde amnesia in two cases of discrete bilateral hippocampal pathology. *Hippocampus, 9*(3), 247–254.

Kapur, S., & Seeman, P. (2001). Does fast dissociation from the dopamine D(2) receptor explain the action of atypical antipsychotics? A new hypothesis. *The American Journal of Psychiatry, 158*(3), 360–369.

Karlinsky, H. (1986). Alzheimer's disease and Down's syndrome: A review. *Journal of the American Geriatrics Society, 34,* 728–734.

Karnath, H.-O., Christ, K., & Hartje, W. (1993). Decrease of contralateral neglect by neck muscle vibration and spatial orientation of trunk midline. *Brain, 116,* 383–396.

Karnath, H.-O., Sievering, D., & Fetter, M. (1994). The interactive contribution of neck muscle proprioception and vestibular stimulation to subjective 'straight ahead' orientation in man. *Experimental Brain Research, 101,* 140–146.

Karni, A., Meyer, G., Jezzard, P., Adams, M. M., Turner, R., & Ungerleider, L. G. (1995). Functional MRI evidence for adult motor cortex plasticity during motor skill learning. *Nature, 377,* 155–158.

Karni, A., Meyer, G., Jezzard, P., Adams, M. M., Turner, R., & Ungerleider, L. G. (1998). The acquisition of skilled motor performance: Fast and slow experience-driven changes in primary motor cortex. *Proceedings of the National Academy of Sciences, USA, 95,* 861–868.

Kassel, J. (1997). Smoking and attention: A review and reformulation of the stimulus-filter hypothesis. *Clinical Psychology Review, 17,* 451–478.

Kastner, S., DeWeerd, P., Desimone, R., & Ungerleider, L. G. (1998). Mechanisms of directed attention in the human extrastriate cortex as revealed by functional MRI. *Science, 282,* 108–111.

Kastner, S., Pinsk, M. A., De Weerd, P., Desimone, R., & Ungerleider, L. G. (1999). Increased activity in human visual cortex during directed attention in the absence of visual stimulation. *Neuron, 22,* 751–761.

Katon, W., & Roy-Byrne, P. P. (1991). Mixed anxiety and depression. *Journal of Abnormal Psychology, 100,* 337–345.

Katzman, R. (1993). Education and the prevalence of Alzheimer's disease. *Neurology, 43,* 13–20.

Kaufmann, W. E., & Moser, H. W (2000). Dendritic anomalies in disorders associated with mental retardation. *Cerebral Cortex, 10,* 981–991.

Kawahata, N., Nagata, K., & Shishido, F. (1988). Alexia with agraphia due to the left posterior inferior temporal lobe lesion—Neuropsychological analysis and its pathogenetic mechanisms. *Brain and Language, 33,* 296–310.

Kawamura, M., Hirayama, K., Hasegawa, K., Takahashi, N., & Yamaura, A. (1987). Alexia with agraphia of kanji (Japanese morphograms). *Journal of Neurology, Neurosurgery and Psychiatry, 50,* 1125–1129.

Kawasaki, H., Adolphs, R., Kaufman, O., Damasio, H., Damasio, A. R., Granner, M., Bakken, H., Hori, T., & Howard, M., III. (2001). Single-neuron responses to emotional visual stimuli recorded in human ventral prefrontal cortex. *Nature Neuroscience, 4,* 15–16.

Kawashima, R., Naitoh, E., Matsumura, M., Itoh, H., Ono, S., Satoh, K., Gotoh, R., Koyama, M., Inoue, K., Yoshioka, S., & Fukuda, H. (1996). Topographic representation in human intraparietal sulcus of reaching and saccade. *NeuroReport, 7,* 1253–1256.

Kay, D. W. K., Henderson, A. S., Scott, R., Wilson, J., Rickwood, D., & Grayson, D. A. (1985). Dementia and depression among the elderly living in the Hobart community: The effect of the diagnostic criteria on the prevalence rates. *Psychological Medicine, 15,* 771–788.

Kaye, J. (1998). Diagnostic challenges in dementia. *Neurology, 51*(Suppl. 1), S45–S52.

Kayser, J., Bruder, G. E., Tenke, C. E., Stuart, B. K., Amador, X. F., & Gorman, J. M. (2001). Event-related brain potentials (ERPs) in schizophrenia for tonal and phonetic oddball tasks. *Biological Psychiatry, 49,* 832–847.

Keane, M. M., Clarke, H., & Corkin, S. (1992). Impaired perceptual priming and intact conceptual priming in a patient with bilateral posterior cerebral lesions. *Society for Neuroscience Abstracts, 18,* 386.

Keane, M. M., Gabrieli, J. D., Fennema, A. C., Growdon, J. H., & Corkin, S. (1991). Evidence for a dissociation between perceptual and conceptual priming in Alzheimer's disease. *Behavioral Neuroscience, 105*(2), 326–342.

Keele, S. (1968). Movement control in skilled motor performance. *Psychological Bulletin, 70,* 387–403.

Kelche, C., Roeser, C., Jeltsch, H., Cassel, J. C., & Will, B. (1995). The effects of intrahippocampal grafts, training, and postoperative housing on behavioral recovery after septohippocampal damage in the rat. *Neurobiology of Learning and Memory, 63,* 155–166.

Kelley, W. M., Miezin, F. M., McDermott, K. B., Buckner, R. L., Raichle, M. E., Cohen, N. J., Ollinger, J. M., Akbudak, E., Conturo, T. E., Snyder, A. Z., & Petersen, S. E. (1998). Hemispheric specialization in human dorsal frontal cortex and medial temporal lobe for verbal and nonverbal memory encoding. *Neuron, 20*(5), 927–936.

Kelly, J. P. & Rosenberg, J. H. (1997). Diagnosis and management of concussion in sport. *Neurology, 48,* 575–580.

Kelly, J. P. (1991). The neural basis of perception and movement. In E. R. Kandel, J. H. Schwartz, & T. M. Jessell (Eds.), *Principles of neural science.* (pp. 283–295). New York: Elsevier.

Kemper, T. (1984). Neuroanatomical and neuropathological changes in normal aging and dementia. In M. A. Albert (Ed.), *Clinical neurology of aging.* New York: Oxford University Press.

Kempermann, G., Kuhn, H. G., and Gage, F. H. (1997). More hippocampal neurons in adult mice living in an enriched environment. *Nature, 386,* 493–495.

Kendrick, K. M., & Baldwin, B. A. (1987). Cells in temporal cortex of conscious sheep can respond preferentially to the sight of faces. *Science, 236,* 448–450.

Kennard, M. A. (1936). Age and other factors in motor recovery from precentral lesions in monkeys. *Journal of Neurophysiology, 1,* 477–496.

Kennard, M. A. (1942). Cortical reorganization of motor function. *Archives of Neurological Psychiatry, 48,* 227–240.

Kent, R. D., & Rosenbek, J. (1982). Prosodic disturbance and neurologic lesion. *Brain and Language, 15,* 259–291.

Kertesz, A., & Clydesdale, S. (1994). Neuropsychological deficits in vascular dementia vs. Alzheimer's disease: Frontal lobe deficits prominent in vascular dementia. *Archives of Neurology, 51,* 1226–1231.

Kertesz, A., Ferro, J. U., & Shewan, C. M. (1984). Apraxia and aphasia: The functional anatomical basis for their dissociation. *Neurology, 34,* 40–47.

Kesler-West, M. L., Andersen, A. H., Smith, C. D., Avison, M. J., Davis, C. E., Kryscio, R. J. & Blonder, L. X. (2001). Neural substrates of facial emotion processing using fMRI. *Cognitive Brain Research, 11,* 213–226.

Kessels, R. P. C., de Hann, E. H. F., Kappelle, L. J., & Postma, A. (2001). Varieties of human spatial memory: A meta-analysis on the effects of hippocampal lesions. *Brain Research Reviews, 35,* 295–303.

Kessels, R. P. C., Postma, A., Kappelle, L. J., & de Haan, E. H. F. (2000). Spatial memory impairment in patients after tumour resection: Evidence for a double dissociation. *Journal of Neurology, Neurosurgery, and Psychiatry, 69,* 389–391.

Ketter, T. A., Post, R. M., & Theodore, W. H. (1999). Positive and negative psychiatric effects of antiepileptic drugs in patients with seizure disorders. *Neurology, 53*(Suppl. 2), S53–S67.

Kiehl, K. A., Laurens, K. R., Duty, T. L., Forster, B. B., & Liddle, P. F. (2001). Neural sources involved in auditory target detection and novelty processing: An event-related fMRI study. *Psychophysiology, 38,* 133–142.

Kiehl, K. A., Liddle, P. F., & Hopfinger, J. B. (2000). Error processing and the rostral anterior cingulate: An event-related fMRI study. *Psychophysiology, 37,* 216–223.

Kihlstrom, J. F., & Schacter, D. L. (1995). Functional disorders of autobiographical memory. In A. D. Baddeley, & B. A. Wilson (Eds.), *Handbook of memory disorders* (pp. 337–364). New York: John Wiley & Sons.

Killgore, W. D. S., & DellaPietra, L. (2000). Using the WMS-III to detect malinger: Empirical validation of the Rarely Missed Index (RMI). *Journal of Clinical and Experimental Neuropsychology, 22,* 761–771.

Kim, K. H. S., Relkin, N. R., Lee, K.-M., & Hirsch, J. (1997). Distinct cortical areas associated with native and second languages. *Nature, 388,* 171–174.

Kim, S. G., Ugurbil, K., & Strick, P. L. (1994). Activation of a cerebellar output nucleus during cognitive processing. *Science, 265,* 949–951.

Kimberg, D. Y., Aguirre, G. K., & D'Esposito, M. (2000). Modulation of task-related neural activity in task-switching: An fMRI study. *Cognitive Brain Research, 10,* 189–196.

Kimberg, D. Y., & Farah, M. J. (1993) A unified account of cognitive impairments following frontal lobe damage: The role of working memory in complex, organized behavior. *Journal of Experimental Psychology: General, 122,* 411–428.

Kimble, D. P. (1990). Functional effects of neural grafting in the mammalian central nervous system. *Psychological Bulletin, 108,* 462–479.

Kimura, D. (1967). Functional asymmetry of the brain in dichotic listening. *Cortex, 3,* 164–178.

Kimura, D. (1969). Spatial localization in left and right visual fields. *Canadian Journal of Psychology, 23,* 445–458.

Kimura, D. (1977). Acquisition of a motor skill after left hemisphere damage. *Brain, 100,* 337–350.

Kimura, D. (1980). Neuromotor mechanisms in the evolution of human communication. In H. D. Steklis & M. J. Raleigh (Eds.), *Neurobiology of social communication in primates: An evolutionary perspective.* New York: Academic Press.

Kimura, D. (1982). Left-hemisphere control of oral and brachial movements and their relation to communication. *Philosophical Transactions of the Royal Society of London, B298,* 135–149.

Kimura, D. (1993). *Neuromotor Mechanisms in Human Communication.* New York: Clarendon Press/Oxford University Press.

Kimura, D., & Faust, R. (1987). Spontaneous drawing in an unselected sample of patients with unilateral brain damage. In D. Ottoson (Ed.), *Duality and unity of the brain: Unified functioning and specialisation of the hemispheres* (pp. 114–146). New York: Plenum Press.

Kimura, D., & Hampson, E. (1994). Cognitive pattern in men and women is influenced by fluctuations in sex hormones. *Current Directions in Psychological Science, 3,* 57–61.

Kimura, D., & Watson, N. (1989). The relation between oral movement control and speech. *Brain and Language, 37,* 565–590.

King, F. L., & Kimura, D. (1972). Left-ear superiority in dichotic perception of vocal nonverbal sounds. *Canadian Journal of Psychology, 26,* 111–116.

Kinomura, S., Larsson, J., Gulyas, B., & Roland, P. E. (1996). Activation by attention of the human reticular formation and thalamic intralaminar nuclei. *Science, 271,* 512–515

Kinsbourne, M. (1974). Lateral interaction in the brain. In M. Kinsbourne & W. L. Smith (Eds.), *Hemispheric disconnections and cerebral function* (pp. 239–259). Springfield, IL: Charles C Thomas.

Kinsbourne, M. (1975). The mechanisms of hemispheric control of the lateral gradient of attention. In P. M. A. Rabbitt & S. Dornic (Eds.), *Attention and performance.* New York: Academic Press.

Kinsbourne, M. (1993). Orientational bias model of unilateral neglect: evidence from attentional gradients within hemispace. In I. H. Robertson, & J. C. Marshall (Eds), *Unilateral neglect: Clinical and experimental studies* (63–86). Hillsdale, NJ: Lawrence Erlbaum.

Kinsbourne, M., & Warrington, E. K. (1962). A study of finger agnosia. *Brain, 85,* 47–66.

Kircher, T. T. J., Brammer, M., Andreu, N. T., Steven C. R. Williams, S. C. R., & McGuire, P. K. (2001). Engagement of right temporal cortex during processing of linguistic context. *Neuropsychologia, 39*(8), 798–809.

Kirchhoff, B. A., Wagner, A. D., Maril, A., & Stern, C. E. (2000). Prefrontal-temporal circuitry for episodic encoding and subsequent memory. *Journal of Neuroscience, 20(16)*, 6173–6180.

Kirk, A., & Kertesz, A. (1989). Hemispheric contributions to drawing. *Neuropsychologia, 27*, 881–886.

Kirk, A., & Kertesz, A. (1993). Subcortical contributions to drawing. *Brain and Cognition, 21*, 57–70.

Kitterle, F. L., Hellige, J. B., & Christman, S. (1992). Visual hemispheric asymmetries depend on which spatial frequencies are task relevant. *Brain and Cognition, 20*, 308–314.

Kleim, J. A., Lussnig, E., Schwarz, E. R., Comery, T. A., & Greenough, W. T. (1996). Synaptogenesis and Fos expression in the motor cortex of the adult rat after motor skill learning. *Journal of Neuroscience, 16*(14), 4529–4535.

Klein, D., Moscovitch, M., & Vigna, C. (1976). Attentional mechanisms and perceptual asymmetrics in tachistoscopic recognition of words and faces. *Neuropsychologia, 14*, 335–338.

Kling, A. S., & Brothers, L. A. (1992). The amygdala and social behavior. In J. P. Aggleton (Ed.), *The amygdala: Neurobiological aspects of emotion, memory, and mental dysfunction* (pp. 353–377). New York: Wiley-Liss.

Klingberg, T., Hedehus, M., Emple, E., Satz, T., Gabrieli, J. D. E., Moseley, M. E., & Poldrack, R. A. (2000). Microstructure of temporo-parietal white matter as a basis for reading ability: Evidence from diffusion tensor magnetic resonance imaging. *Neuron, 25*, 493–500.

Klisz, D. (1978). Neuropsychological evaluation of older persons. In M. Storandt (Ed.), *The clinical psychology of aging* (pp. 71–95). New York: Plenum Press.

Klüver, H., & Bucy, P. C. (1937). "Psychic blindness" and other symptoms following bilateral temporal lobectomy in rhesus monkeys. *American Journal of Physiology, 119*, 352–353.

Klüver, H., & Bucy, P. C. (1939). Preliminary analysis of the functions of the temporal lobes in monkeys. *Archives of Neurology and Psychiatry, 42*, 979–1000.

Knapp, M. J., Knopman, D. S., Solomon, P. R., Pendelbury, W. W., Davis, C. S., & Gracon, S. I. (1993). A 30-week randomized controlled trial of high-dose tacrine in patient with Alzheimer's disease. *Journal of the American Medical Association, 271*, 985–991.

Knight, R. (1989). Creutzfeldt-Jakob disease. *British Journal of Hospital Medicine, 41*, 165–171.

Knight, R. B. (1992). *The neuropsychology of degenerative brain diseases.* Hillsdale, NJ: Erlbaum.

Knight, R. T. (1991). Evoked potential studies of attention capacity in human frontal lobe lesions. In H. S. Levin, H. M. Eisenberg, & A. L. Benton (Eds.), *Frontal lobe function and dysfunction* (pp. 139–153). New York: Oxford University Press.

Knight, R. T., Scabini, D., Woods, D. L., & Clayworth, C. C. (1989). Contribution of temporal-parietal junction to the human auditory P_3. *Brain Research, 502*, 109–116.

Knopman, D., Schneider, L., Davis, K., Talwalker, S., Smith, F., Hoover, T., et al., (1996). Long-term tacrine (Cognex) treatment: Effects on nursing home placement and mortality. *Neurology, 47*, 166–177.

Knott, V. J., & Lapierre, Y. D. (1987). Electrophysiological and behavioral correlates of psychomotor responsivity in depression. *Biological Psychiatry, 22*, 313–324.

Knowlton, B. J., Mangels, J. A., & Squire, L. R. (1996). A neostriatal habit learning system in humans. *Science, 273*(5280), 1399–1402.

Knowlton, B. J., Ramus, S. J., & Squire, L. R. (1992). Intact artificial grammar learning in amnesia: Dissociation of classification learning and explicit memory for specific instances. *Psychological Science, 3*, 172–179.

Knowlton, B. J., & Squire, L. R. (1993). The learning of categories: Parallel brain systems for item memory and category knowledge. *Science 262*(5140), 1747–1749.

Knowlton, B. J., & Squire, L. R. (1994). The information acquired during artificial grammar learning: Item similarity vs. grammaticality. *Journal of Experimental Psychology: Learning, Memory, and Cognition, 20*, 79–91.

Koechlin, E., Basso, G., Pietrini, P., Panzer, S., & Grafman, J. (1999). The role of the anterior prefrontal cortex in human cognition. *Nature, 399*, 148–151.

Koepp, M. J., Gunn, R. N., Lawrence, A. D., Cunningham, V. J., Dagher, A., Jones, T., Brooks, D. J., Bench, C. J., & Grasby, P. M. (1998). Evidence for striatal dopamine release during a video game. *Nature, 393*, 266–268.

Kohn, B., & Dennis, M. (1974). Selective impairments of visuospatial abilities in infantile hemiplegics after right cerebral hemidecortication. *Neuropsychologia, 12*, 505–512.

Kolb, B. (1989). Brain development, plasticity, and behavior. *American Psychologist, 44*, 1203–1212.

Kolb, B. (1995). *Brain plasticity and behavior.* Hillsdale, NJ: Lawrence Erlbaum.

Kolb, B., & Fantie, B. (1989). Development of the child's brain and behavior. In C. R. Reynolds & E. Fletcher-Janzen (Eds.), *Handbook of clinical child neuropsychology* (pp. 17–39). New York: Plenum Press.

Kolb, B., & Gibb, R. (2001). Early brain injury, plasticity, and behavior. In C. A. Nelson, & M. Luciana (Eds.), *Handbook of developmental cognitive neuroscience* (pp. 75–190). Cambridge, MA: MIT Press.

Kolb, B., & Milner, B. (1981). Performance of complex arm and facial movements after focal brain lesions. *Neuropsychologia, 19*, 291–308.

Kolb, B., & Taylor, L. (1981). Affective behavior in patients with localized cortical excisions: Role of lesion site and side. *Science, 214*, 89–91.

Kolb, B., & Whishaw, I. Q. (1985). *Fundamentals of human neuropsychology* (2nd ed.). New York: Freeman.

Kolb, B., & Whishaw, I. Q. (1990). *Fundamentals of human neuropsychology* (3rd ed.). New York: Freeman.

Kolb, B., & Whishaw, I. Q. (2001). *An introduction to brain and behavior.* New York: Worth Publishing.

Komatsu, H., & Wurtz, R. H. (1988). Relation of cortical areas MT and MST to pursuit eye movements. I. Localization and visual properties of neurons. *Journal of Neurophysiology, 60*, 580–603.

Kondo, K., Niino, M., & Shido, K. (1994). A case-control study of Alzheimer's disease in Japan: Significance of lifestyles. *Dementia, 5*, 314–326.

Konishi, S., Nakajima, K., Uchida, I., Kikyo, H., Kameyama, M., & Miyashita, Y. (1999). Common inhibitory mechanism in human inferior prefrontal cortex revealed by event-related functional MRI. *Brain, 122,* 981–991.

Konishi, S., Wheeler, M. E., Donaldson, D. I., & Buckner, R. L. (2000). Neural correlates of episodic retrieval success. *NeuroImage, 12*(3), 276–286.

Koopmans, R. A., Li, D. K., Grochowski, E., Cutler, P. J., & Paty, D. W. (1989). Benign versus chronic progressive multiple sclerosis: Magnetic resonance imaging features. *Annals of Neurology, 25,* 74–81.

Kopelman, M. D. (1989). Remote and autobiographical memory, temporal context memory and frontal atrophy in Korsakoff and Alzheimer patients. *Neuropsychologia, 27,* 437–460.

Kopelman, M. D. (2000). Focal retrograde amnesia and the attribution of causality: An exceptionally critical review. *Cognitive Neuropsychology, 17*(7), 585–621.

Kopelman, M. D., Stanhope, N., & Kingsley, D. (1999). Retrograde amnesia in patients with diencephalic, temporal lobe or frontal lesions. *Neuropsychologia, 37*(8), 939–958.

Koranyi, E. K. (1988). The cortical dementias. *Canadian Journal of Psychiatry, 33,* 838–845.

Kosslyn, S. M. (1973). Scanning visual images. Some structural implications. *Perception and Psychophysics, 14,* 90–94.

Kosslyn, S. M. (1987). Seeing and imagining in the cerebral hemispheres: A computational approach. *Psychological Review, 94,* 148–175.

Kosslyn, S. M. (1990). Mental imagery. In D. N. Osherson, S. M. Kosslyn, & J. M. Hollerbach (Eds.), *Visual cognition and action* (pp. 73–97). Cambridge, MA: MIT Press.

Kosslyn, S. M., Alpert, N. M., Thompson, W. L., Maljkovic, V., Weise, S. B., Chabris, C. F., Hamilton, S. E., Rauch, S. L., & Buonanno, F. S. (1993). Visual mental imagery activates topographically organized visual cortex: PET investigations. *Journal of Cognitive Neuroscience, 5,* 263–287.

Kosslyn, S. M., Chabris, C. F., Marsolek, C. J., & Koenig, O. (1992). Categorical versus coordinate spatial relations: Computational analyses and computer simulations. *Journal of Experimental Psychology: Human Perception and Performance, 18,* 562–577.

Kosslyn, S. M., Holtzman, J. D., Farah, M. J., & Gazzaniga, M. S. (1985). A computational analysis of mental image generation: Evidence from functional dissociations in split-brain patients. *Journal of Experimental Psychology: General, 114,* 311–341.

Kosslyn, S. M., Koenig, O., Barrett, A., Cave, C., Tang, J., & Gabrieli, J. D. E. (1989). Evidence for two types of spatial representations: Hemispheric specialization for categorical and coordinate relations. *Journal of Experimental Psychology: Human Perception and Performance, 15,* 723–735.

Kosslyn, S. M., & Ochsner, K. N. (1994). In search of occipital activation during visual mental imagery. *Trends in Neurosciences, 17,* 290–292.

Kosslyn, S. M., Pascual-Leone, A., Felician, O., Camposano, S., Keenan, J. P., Thompson, W. L., Ganis, G., Sukel, K. E., & Alpert, N. M. (1999). The role of Area 17 in visual imagery: Convergent evidence from PET and rTMS. *Science, 284*(5411), 167–170.

Kosslyn, S. M., Thompson, W. L., & Alpert, N. M. (1997) Neural systems shared by visual imagery and visual perception: A positron emission tomography study, *NeuroImage, 6*(4), 320–334.

Kosslyn, S. M., Thompson, W. L., Gitelman, D. R., & Alpert, N. M. (1998). Neural systems that encode categorical versus coordinate spatial relations: PET investigations. *Psychobiology, 26,* 333–347.

Kosslyn, S. M., Thompson, W. L., Kim, I. J., & Alpert, N. M. (1995). Topographical representations of mental images in primary visual cortex. *Nature, 378*(6556), 496–498.

Kourtzi, Z., & Kanwisher, N. (2000). Cortical regions involved in perceiving object shape. *Journal of Neuroscience, 20,* 3310–3318.

Koyama, S., Kakigi, R., Hoshiyama, M., & Kitamura, Y. (1998). Reading of Japanese Kanji (morphograms) and Kana (syllabograms): A magnetoencephalographic study. *Neuropsychologia, 36*(1), 83–98.

Kramer, A., Larish, J., & Strayer, D. (1995). Training strategies for attentional control in dual-task settings: A comparison of young and old adults. *Journal of Experimental Psychology: Applied, 1,* 50–76.

Kramer, A. F., Coyne, J. T., & Strayer, D. L. (1993). Cognitive function at high altitude. *Human Factors, 35,* 329–344.

Kramer, A. F., Hahn, S., Cohen, N. J., Banich, M. T., McAuley, E., Harrison, C. R., Chason, J., Vakil, E., Bardell, L., Boileau, R. A., & Colcombe, A. (1999). Aging, fitness and neurocognitive function. *Nature, 400*(6743), 418–419.

Kramer, A. F., Wickens, C. D., & Donchin, E. (1985). Processing of stimulus properties: Evidence for dual-task integrality. *Journal of Experimental Psychology: Human Perception & Performance, 11*(4), 393–408.

Kramer, A. F., Wickens, C. D., & Donchin, E. (1985). Processing of stimulus properties: Evidence for dual-task integrity. *Journal of Experimental Psychology: Human Perception and Performance, 11,* 393–408.

Kraus, J. (1987). Epidemiology of head injury. In P. R. Cooper (Ed.), *Head injury.* Baltimore: Williams & Wilkins.

Kreiman, G., Koch, C., & Fried, I. (2000). Category-specific visual responses of single neurons in the human medial temporal lobe. *Nature Neuroscience, 3,* 946–953.

Kretschmann, H. J., Kammradt, G., Krauthausen, I., Sauer, B., & Wingert, F. (1986). Brain growth in man. *Bibliotheca Anatomica, 28,* 1–26.

Kroll, N. E. A., Knight, R. T., Metcalfe, J., Wolf, E. S., & Tulving, E. (1995). *Cohesion failure as a source of memory illusions.* Manuscript submitted for publication.

Kubie, J. L., & Ranck, J. B., Jr. (1984). Hippocampal neuronal firing, context, and learning. In L. R. Squire & N. Butters (Eds.), *Neuropsychology of memory* (pp. 417–423). New York: Guilford Press.

Kubota, K., & Niki, H. (1971). Prefrontal cortical unit activity and delayed alternation performance in monkeys. *Journal of Neurophysiology, 34*(3), 337–347.

Kuhn, H. G., Dickinson-Anson, H., & Gage, F. H. (1996). Neurogenesis in the dentate gyrus of the adult rat: Age-related decrease of neuronal progenitor proliferation. *Journal of Neuroscience, 16,* 2027–2033.

Kuhl, P. K., Williams, K. A., Lacerda, F., Stevens, K. N., & Lindblom, B. (1992). Linguistic experience alters phonetic perception in infants by 6 months of age. *Science, 255,* 606–608.

Kumar, A., Ghosal, S., & Bigl, V. (1997). Systematic administration of defined extracts from *Withania somnifera* (Indian Ginseng) and Shilajit differentially affects cholinergic but not glutamatergic and GABAergic markers in rat brain. *Neurochemistry International, 30,* 181–190.

Kurlan, R., Behr, J., Medved, L., Shoulson, I. Pauls, D. L., Kidd, J. R., & Kidd, K. K. (1986). Familial Tourette's syndrome: Report of a large pedigree and potential for linkage analysis. *Neurology, 36,* 772–776.

Kurtzke, J. F. (1980). Epidemiologic contributions to multiple sclerosis: An overview. *Neurology, 30,* 61–79.

Kutas, M., & Hillyard, S. A. (1980). Reading senseless sentences: Brain potentials reflect semantic incongruity. *Science, 207,* 203–205.

Kwong, K. K., Belliveau, J. W., Chesler, D. A., Goldberg, I. E., Weisskoff, R. M., Poncelet, B. P., Kennedy, P. N., Hoppel, B. E., Cohen, M. S., Turner, R., Cheng, H.-M., Brady, T. J., & Rosen, B. R. (1992). Dynamic magnetic resonance imaging of human brain activity during primary sensory stimulation. *Proceedings of the National Academy of Sciences, USA, 89,* 5675–5679.

LaBerge, D., & Buchsbaum, M. S. (1990). Positron emission tomographic measurements of pulvinar activity during an attention task. *Journal of Neuroscience, 10,* 613–619.

LaBerge, D. L. (1990). Attention. *Psychological Science, 1,* 156–162.

Ladavas, E. (1987). Is the hemispatial deficit produced by right parietal lobe damage associated with retinal or gravitational coordinates? *Brain, 110,* 167–180.

Ladavas, E., Nicoletti, R., Umilta, C., & Rizzolatti, G. (1984). Right hemisphere interference during negative affect: A reaction time study. *Neuropsychologia, 22,* 479–485.

Ladavas, E., Petronio, A., & Umilta, C. (1990). The deployment of visual attention in the intact field of hemineglect patients. *Cortex, 26,* 307–317.

Ladavas, E., Umilta, C., & Ricci-Bitti, P. E. (1980). Evidence for sex differences in right hemisphere dominance for emotions. *Neuropsychologia, 18,* 361–367.

Laeng, B. (1994). Lateralization of categorical and coordinate spatial functions: A study of unilateral stroke patients. *Journal of Cognitive Neuroscience, 6,* 189–203.

LaHoste, G. J., Swanson, J. M., Wigal, S. B., Glabe, C., Wigal, T., King, N., & Kennedy, J. L. (1996). Dopamine D4 receptor gene polymorphism is associated with attention deficit hyperactivity disorder. *Molecular Psychiatry, 1,* 21–124.

Lakoff, G. (1987). *Women, fire, and dangerous things: What categories reveal about the mind.* Chicago: University of Chicago Press.

LaMantia, A. S., & Rakic, P. (1990). Axon overproduction and elimination in the corpus callosum of the developing rhesus monkey. *Journal of Neuroscience, 10,* 2156–2175.

Laming, P. R., Kimelberg, H., Robinson, S., Salm, A., Hawrylak, N., Mueller, C., Roots, B., & Ng, K. (2000). Neuronal-glial interactions and behavior. *Neuroscience & Biobehavioral Reviews, 24,* 295–340.

Landis, T., Assal, G., & Perret, E. (1979). Opposite cerebral hemispheric superiorities for visual associative processing of emotional facial expressions and objects. *Nature, 278,* 739–740.

Landis, T., Cummings, J. L., Benson, D. F., & Palmer, E. P. (1986). Loss of topographic familiarity: An environmental agnosia. *Archives of Neurology, 43,* 132–136.

Lane, R. D. (2000). Neural correlates of conscious emotional experience. In R. D. Lane, & L. Nadel (Eds.), *Cognitive neuroscience of emotion* (pp. 345–370). New York: Oxford University Press.

Lane, R. D., Chua, P. M.-L., & Dolan, R. J. (1999). Common effects of emotional valence, arousal and attention on neural activation during visual processing of pictures. *Neuropsychologia, 37,* 989–997.

Lane, R. D., Reiman, E. M., Ahem, G. L., Schwartz, G. E., & Davidson, R. J. (1997). Neuroanatomical correlates of happiness, sadness, and disgust. *American Journal of Psychiatry, 154,* 926–933.

Lange, C. C., & James, W. (1967). *The emotions.* New York: Hafner.

Lange, C. S. (1887). The emotions. W. James & C. G. Lange (Trans.). Baltimore: Williams & Wilkins. (Original work published 1887)

Larrabee, G. J., Kane, R. L., Morrow, L., & Goldstein, G. (1982). Differential drawing size associated with unilateral brain damage. In *Paper presented at the tenth annual meeting of the International Neuropsychological Society,* Pittsburgh, PA.

Lashley, K. (1950). In search of the engram. *Symposia of the Society of Experimental Biology, 4,* 454–482.

Lashley, K. S. (1929). *Brain mechanisms and intelligence.* Chicago: University of Chicago Press.

Lavergne, J., & Kimura, D. (1987). Hand movement asymmetry during speech: No effect of speaking topic. *Neuropsychologia, 25,* 689–693.

Lawrence, A., & Sahakian, B. (1995). Alzheimer's disease, attention, and the cholingergic system. *Alzheimer's Disease Association Disorder, 9*(Suppl. 2), 43–49.

Lawrence, A. D., Hodges, J. R., Rosser, A. E., Kershaw, A., French-Constant, C., Rubinstein, D. C., Robbins, T. W., Sahakian, B. J. (1998a). Evidence for specific cognitive deficits in preclinical Huntington's disease. *Brain, 121*(7), 1329–1341.

Lawrence, A. D., Weeks, R. A., Brooks, D. J., Andrews, T. C., Watkins, L. H., Harding, A. E., Robbins, T. W., & Sahakian, B. J. (1998b). The relationship between striatal dopamine receptor binding and cognitive performance in Huntington's disease. *Brain, 121*(7), 1343–1355.

Lawrence, D. G., & Kuypers, G. J. M. (1968). The functional organization of the motor system in the monkey. II. The effects of lesions of the descending brain-stem pathways. *Brain, 91,* 15–36.

Lawrie, S. M., & Abukmeil, S. S. (1998). Brain abnormality in schizophrenia: A systematic and quantitative review of volumetric magnetic resonance imaging studies. *British Journal of Psychiatry, 172,* 110–120.

LeBars, P. L., Katz, M. M., Berman, N., Itil, T. M., Freedman, A. M., & Schatzberg, A. F. (1997). A placebo-controlled, double blind, randomized trial of an extract of Ginkgo biloba for dementia. North American EGb study group. *Journal of the American Medical Association, 278,* 1327–1332.

Lechevalier, B., Petit, M. C., Eustache, F., Lambert, J., Chapon, F., & Vaider, F. (1989). Regional cerebral blood flow during comprehension and speech (in cerebrally healthy subjects). *Brain and Language, 37,* 1–11.

Leckman, J. F., & Riddle, M. A. (2000). Tourette's syndrome: When habit-forming systems form habits of their own? *Neuron, 28,* 349–354.

LeDoux, J. (1996). *The emotional brain: The mysterious underpinnings of emotional life.* New York: Touchstone.

LeDoux, J. (2000). Cognitive-emotional interactions: Listen to the brain. In R. D. Lane, & L. Nadel (Eds.), *Cognitive neuroscience of emotion* (pp. 129–155). New York: Oxford University Press.

LeDoux, J. E. (1989). Cognitive-emotional interactions in the brain. *Cognition and Emotion, 3,* 267–289.

LeDoux, J. E. (1992). Brain mechanisms of emotion and emotional learning. *Current Opinion in Neurobiology, 2*(2), 191–197.

LeDoux, J. E. (1993). Emotional networks in the brain. In M. Lewis & J. M. Haviland (Eds.), *Handbook of emotions* (pp. 109–118). New York: Guilford Press.

LeDoux, J. E. (1994). Emotion, memory and the brain. *Scientific American, 270*(6), 50–57.

Lee, G. P., Loring, D. W., Meador, K. J., & Brooks, B. B. (1990). Hemispheric specialization for emotional expression: A reexamination of results from intracarotid administration of sodium amobarbital. *Brain and Cognition, 12,* 267–280.

Lee, G. P., Loring, D. W., Meador, K. J., Flanigin, H. F., & Brooks, B. S. (1988). Severe behavioral complications following intracarotid sodium amobarbital injection: Implications for hemispheric asymmetry of emotion. *Neurology, 38,* 1233–1236.

Leehey, S. C., Carey, S., Diamond, R., & Cahn, A. (1978). Upright and inverted faces: The right hemisphere knows the difference. *Cortex, 14,* 411–419.

Lees, A. (1990). Tics. *Behavioural Neurology, 3,* 99–108.

Lehmkuhl, G., & Poeck, K. (1981). A disturbance in the conceptual organization of actions in patients with ideational apraxia. *Cortex, 17,* 153–158.

Leibson, C. L., Rocca, W. A., Hanson, V. A., Cha, R., Kokmen, E., O'Brien, P. C., Palumbo, P. J. (1997). Risk of dementia among persons with diabetes mellitus: A population based cohort study. *American Journal of Epidemiology, 145,* 301–308.

Leiguarda, R. C., & Marsden, C. D. (2000). Limb apraxias: Higher-order disorders of sensorimotor integration. *Brain, 123,* 860–879.

LeMay, M. (1976). Morphological cerebral asymmetries of modern man, fossil man, and nonhuman primate. *Annals of the New York Academy of Sciences, 280,* 349–366.

Lembessis, E., & Rudin, R. (1994). Sinistrality and reduced longevity: Reply to Coren and Halpern's replay. *Perceptual and Motor Skills, 78,* 579–582.

Lenneberg, E. H. (1967). *Biological foundations of language.* New York: Wiley.

Lepage, M., Habib, R., & Tulving, E. (1998). Hippocampal PET activations of memory encoding and retrieval: The HIPER model. *Hippocampus, 8*(4), 313–322.

Leung, C. M., Chan, Y. W., Chang, C. M., Yu, Y. L., & Chen, C. N. (1992). Huntington's disease in Chinese: A hypothesis of its origin. *Journal of Neurology, Neurosurgery and Psychiatry, 55,* 681–684.

LeVay, S., Wiesel, T. N., & Hubel, D. H. (1980). The development of ocular dominance columns in normal and visually deprived monkeys. *Journal of Comparative Neurology, 191,* 1–51.

Levenson, R. L., & Mellins, C. A. (1992). Pediatric HIV and disease: What psychologists need to know. *Professional Psychology: Research and Practice, 23,* 410–415.

Levenson, R. W., Eckman, P., & Friesen, W. V. (1990). Voluntary facial action generates emotion-specific autonomic nervous system activity. *Psychophysiology, 27,* 363–383.

Leveroni, C. Seidenberg, M., Mayer, A. R., Mead, L. A., Binder, J. R., & Rao, S. M. (2000). Neural systems underlying the recognition of familiar and newly learned faces. *Journal of Neuroscience, 20,* 876–886.

Levin, H. S., Gary, H. E., High, W. M., Mattis, S., Ruff, R. M., Eisenberg, H. M., Marshall, L. F., & Tabaddor, K. (1987). Minor head injury and the postconcussional syndrome: Methodological issues in outcomes studies. In H. S. Levin, J. Grafman, & H. M. Eisenberg (Eds.), *Neurobehavioral recovery from head injury* (pp. 262–275). New York: Oxford University Press.

Levin, H. S., Goldstein, F. C., Williams, D. H., & Eisenberg, H. M. (1991). The contribution of frontal lobe lesions to the neurobehavioral outcome of closed head injury. In H. S. Levin, H. M. Eisenberg, & A. L. Benton (Eds.), *Frontal lobe function and dysfunction* (pp. 318–338). New York: Oxford University Press.

Levin, H. S., & Grossman, R. G. (1978). Behavioral sequelae of closed head injury. *Archives of Neurology, 35,* 720–727.

Levin, H. S., High, W. M., Goethe, K. E., Sisson, R. A., Overall, J. E., Rhoades, H. M., Eisenberg, H. M., Kalisky, Z., & Gary, J. (1987). The Neurobehavioural Rating Scale: Assessment of the behavioural sequelae of head injury by the clinician. *Journal of Neurology, Neurosurgery and Psychiatry, 50,* 183–193.

Levin, H. S., Meyers, C. A., Grossman, R. G., & Sarwar, M. (1981). Ventricular enlargement after closed head injury. *Archives of Neurology, 38,* 623–629.

Levine, D. N., Kaufman, K. J., & Mohr, J. P. (1978). Inaccurate reaching associated with a superior parietal lobe tumor. *Neurology, 28,* 556–561.

Levine, S. C. (1984). Developmental changes in right-hemisphere involvement in face recognition. In C. Best (Ed.), *Hemispheric function and collaboration in the child* (pp. 157–191). New York: Academic Press.

Levine, S. C., & Banich, M. T. (1982). Lateral asymmetries in the naming of words and corresponding line drawings. *Brain and Language, 17,* 34–45.

Levine, S. C., Banich, M. T., & Koch-Weser, M. (1988). Face recognition: A general or specific right hemisphere capacity? *Brain and Cognition, 8,* 303–325.

Levine, S. C., Huttenlocher, P., Banich, M. T., & Duda, E. (1987). Factors affecting cognitive functioning of hemiplegic children. *Developmental Medicine and Child Neurology, 29,* 27–35.

Levy, J. (1976). Lateral dominance and aesthetic preference. *Neuropsychologia, 14,* 431–445.

Levy, J. (1983). Language, cognition, and the right hemisphere: A response to Gazzaniga. *American Psychologist, 38,* 538–541.

Levy, J. (1988). Cerebral asymmetry and aesthetic experience. In I. Rentschler, B. Herzberger, & D. Epstein (Eds.), *Beauty and the brain* (pp. 219–242). Basel, Switzerland: Birkhäuser Verlag.

Levy, J., Heller, W., Banich, M. T., & Burton, L. A. (1983a). Are variations among right-handed individuals in perceptual asymmetries caused by characteristic arousal differences between hemispheres? *Journal of Experimental Psychology: Human Perception and Performance, 9,* 329–359.

Levy, J., Heller, W., Banich, M. T., & Burton, L. A. (1983b). Asymmetry of perception in free viewing of chimeric faces. *Brain and Cognition, 2,* 404–419.

Levy, J., & Kueck, L. (1986). A right hemispatial field advantage on a verbal free-vision task. *Brain and Language, 27,* 24–37.

Levy, J., & Trevarthen, C. W. (1976). Metacontrol of hemispheric function in human split-brain patients. *Journal of Experimental Psychology: Human Perception and Performance, 2,* 299–312.

Levy, J., & Trevarthen, C. W. (1977). Perceptual, semantic and phonetic aspects of elementary language processes in split-brain patients. *Brain, 100,* 105–118.

Levy, J., Trevarthen, C. W., & Sperry, R. W. (1972). Perception of bilateral chimeric figures following "hemispheric deconnexion." *Brain, 95,* 61–78.

Levy-Lahad, E., Wasco, W., Poorkaj, P., Romano, D. M., Oshima, J., Pettingell, W. H., Yu, C. E., Jondro, P. D., Schmidt, S. D., Wang, K., Crowley, A. C., Fu, Y. H., Guenette, S. Y., Galas, D., Nemens, E., Wijsman, E. M., Bird, T. D., Schellenberg, G. D., & Tanzi, R. E. (1995). Candidate gene for the chromosome 1 familial Alzheimer's disease locus. *Science, 269,* 973–977.

Ley, R. G., & Bryden, M. P. (1979). Hemispheric differences in processing emotions and faces. *Brain and Language, 7,* 127–138.

Ley, R. G., & Bryden, M. P. (1982). A dissociation of right and left hemispheric effects for recognizing emotional tone and verbal content. *Brain and Cognition, 1,* 3–9.

Lezak, M. D. (1978). Living with the characterologically altered brain injured patient. *Journal of Clinical Psychiatry, 39,* 63–72.

Lezak, M. D. (1983). *Neuropsychological assessment* (2nd ed.). New York: Oxford University Press.

Lezak, M. D. (1987). Relationships between personality disorders, social disturbances, and physical disability following traumatic brain injury. *Journal of Head Trauma Rehabilitation, 2,* 57–69.

Lezak, M. D. (1995). *Neuropsychological assessment* (3rd ed.). New York: Oxford University Press.

Lhermitte, F. (1983). "Utilization behavior" and its relation to lesions of the frontal lobes. *Brain, 106,* 237–255.

Lhermitte, F. (1986). Human autonomy and the frontal lobes: Part II. Patient behavior in complex and social situations: The "Environmental Dependency Syndrome." *Annals of Neurology, 19*(4), 335–343.

Lhermitte, F., Pillon, B., & Serdaru, M. (1986). Human autonomy and the frontal lobes: Part I. Imitation and utilization behavior: A neuropsychological study of 75 patients. *Annals of Neurology, 19,* 326–334.

Lhermitte, F., & Signoret, J.-L. (1976). The amnesic syndromes and the hippocampal-mammillary system. In M. Rosenzweig & E. L. Bennett (Eds.), *Neural mechanisms of learning and memory* (pp. 49–56). Cambridge, MA: MIT Press.

Li, S.-C., & Lindenberger, U. (1999). Cross level unification: A computational exploration of the link between deterioration of neurotransmitter systems and dedifferentiation of cognitive abilities in old age. In L.-G. Nilsson, & H. J. Markowitsch (Eds.), *Cognitive neuroscience of memory* (pp. 103–146). Seattle, WA: Hogrefe & Huber Publishers.

Libon, D. J., Glosser, G., Malamut, B. L., Kaplan, E., Goldberg, E., Swenson, R., & Sand, L. P. (1994). Age, executive functions, and visuospatial functioning in healthy older adults. *Neuropsychology, 8,* 38–43.

Libon, D. J., Scanlon, M., Swenson, R., & Coslet, H. B. (1990). Binswanger's disease: Some neuropsychological considerations. *Journal of Geriatric Psychiatry and Neurology, 3,* 31–40.

Liddle, P. F., Kiehl, K. A., & Smith, A. M. (2001). Event-related fMRI study of response inhibition. *Human Brain Mapping, 12,* 100–109.

Lidow, M. S., Williams, G. V., & Goldman-Rakic, P. S. (1998). The cerebral cortex: A case for a common site of action of antipsychotics. *Trends in Pharmacological Science, 19,* 136–140.

Lieberman, A., Dziatolowski, M., Neophytides, A., Kupersmith, M., Aleksic, S., Serby, M., Koerin, J., & Goldstein, H. (1979). Dementias of Huntington's and Parkinson's disease. In T. N. Chase, N. Wexler, & A. Barbeau (Eds.), *Advances in neurology* (pp. 273–289). New York: Raven Press.

Liepert, J., Miltner, W. H. R., Bauder, H., Sommer, M., Dettmers, C., Taub, E., & Weiler, C. (1998). Motor cortex plasticity during constraint-induced movement therapy in stroke patients. *Neuroscience Letters, 250,* 5–8.

Lilienfeld, A. M. (1969). *Epidemiology of mongolism.* Baltimore: Johns Hopkins University Press.

Lipper, E. G., Voorhies, T. M., Ross, G., Vannucci, R. C., & Auld, P. A. M. (1986). Early predictors of one-year outcome for infants asphyxiated at birth. *Developmental Medicine and Child Neurology, 28,* 303–309.

Lipsey, J. R., Robinson, R. G., Pearlson, G. D., Rao, K., & Price, T. R. (1983). Mood change following bilateral hemisphere brain injury. *British Journal of Psychiatry, 143,* 266–273.

Lishman, W. A. (1973). The psychiatric sequelae of head injury: A review. *Psychological Medicine, 3,* 304–318.

Llorente, A. M., Van Gorp, W. G., Stern, M. J., George, L., Satz, P., Marcotte, T. D., Calvillo, G. M., & Hinkin, C. H. (2001). Long-term effects of high-dose zidovudine treatment on neuropsychological performance in mildly symptomatic HIV-positive patients: Results of a randomized, double-blind, placebo-controlled investigation. *Journal of the International Neuropsychological Society, 7,* 27–32.

Logsdon, R. G., Teri, L., Williams, D. E., Vitiello, M. V., & Prinz, P. N. (1989). The WAIS-R profile: A diagnostic tool for Alzheimer's disease? *Journal of Clinical and Experimental Neuropsychology, 11,* 892–898.

Longden, K., Ellis, C., & Iversen, S. D. (1976). Hemispheric differences in the discrimination of curvature. *Neuropsychologia, 14,* 195–202.

Lou, H. D., Henriksen, L., Bruhn, P., Borner, H., & Nielsen, J. G. (1989). Striatal dysfunction in attention deficit and hyperkinetic disorder. *Archives of Neurology, 46,* 48–52.

Lounasmaa, O. V., Hämäläinen, M., Hari, R., & Salmelin, R. (1996). Information processing in the human brain: Magnetoencephalographic approach. *Proceedings of the National Academy of Sciences, USA, 93,* 8809–8815.

Lu, Z.-L., Williamson, S. J., & Kaufmann, L. (1992). Behavioral lifetime of human auditory sensory memory predicted by physiological measures. *Science, 258,* 1668–1670.

Luck, S. J., & Hillyard, S. A. (1994). Spatial filtering during visual search: Evidence from human electrophysiology. *Journal of Experimental Psychology: Human Perception and Performance, 20,* 1000–1014.

Luh, K., & Levy, J. (1995). Interhemispheric cooperation. Left is left and right is right, but sometimes the twain shall meet. *Journal of Experimental Psychology: Human Perception and Performance, 21,* 1243–1258.

Lundberg, G. D. (1994). Let's stop boxing in the Olympics and the United States Military. *Journal of the American Medical Association, 271,* 1790.

Luria, A. R. (1966). *Higher cortical functions in man.* New York: Basic Books.

Luu, P., Collins, P., & Tucker, D. M. (2000). Mood, personality, and self-monitoring: Negative affect and emotionality in relation to frontal lobe mechanisms of error monitoring. *Journal of Experimental Psychology General, 129,* 43–60.

Luu, P., Flaisch, T., & Tucker, D. M. (2000). Medial frontal cortex in action monitoring. *Journal of Neuroscience, 20,* 464–469.

Lynch, J. C. (1980). The functional organization of posterior parietal association cortex. *Behavioral and Brain Sciences, 3,* 485–534.

Lynch, J. C., Mountcastle, V. B., Talbot, W. H., & Yin, T. C. (1977). Parietal lobe mechanisms for directed visual attention. *Journal of Neurophysiology, 40,* 362–389.

MacDonald, A. W., Cohen, J. D., Stenger, V. W., & Carter, C. S. (2000). Dissociating the role of the dorsolateral prefrontal and anterior cingulated cortex in cognitive control. *Science, 288,* 1835–1838.

Mack, M. (in press). The phonetic systems of bilinguals. In M. T. Banich, & M. Mack (Eds.), *Mind, brain, and language: Multidisciplinary perspectives.* Mahwah, NJ: Lawrence Erlbaum Associates.

MacLean, P. D. (1949). Psychosomatic disease and the "visceral brain": Recent developments' bearing on the Papez theory of emotion. *Psychosomatic Medicine, 11,* 338–353.

MacLean, P. D. (1952). Some psychiatric implications of physiological studies on frontotemporal portion of limbic system (visceral brain). *Electroencephalography and Clinical Neurophysiology, 4,* 407–418.

MacLean, P. D. (1967). The brain in relation to empathy and medical education. *Journal of Nervous and Mental Disease, 144,* 374–382.

MacNiven, E. (1994). Increased prevalence of left-handedness in victims of head trauma. *Brain Injury, 8*(5), 457–462.

Madden, D. J., Gottlob, L. R., Denny, L. L., Turkington, T. G., Provenzale, J. M., Hawk, T. C., & Coleman, R. E. (1999). Aging and recognition memory: Changes in regional cerebral blood flow associated with components of reaction time distributions. *Journal of Cognitive Neuroscience, 11,* 511–520.

Maddock, R. J. (1999). The retrosplenial cortex and emotion: New insights from functional neuroimaging of the human brain. *Trends in Neuroscience, 22,* 310–316.

Maess, B., Koelsch, S., Gunter, T. C., & Friederici, A. D. (2001). Musical syntax is processed in Broca's area: An MEG study. *Nature Neuroscience, 4,* 540–545.

Maguire, E. A. (1997) Hippocampal involvement in human topographical memory: Evidence from functional imaging. *Philosophical Transaction of the Royal Society of London, B, 352,* 1475–1480.

Maguire, E. A., Frackowiak, R. S. J., & Frith, C. D. (1996). Learning to find your way—A role for the human hippocampal region. *Proceedings of the Royal Society of London, B, 263,* 1745–1750.

Maguire, E. A., Frackowiak, R. S., & Frith, C. D. (1997). Recalling routes around London: Activation of the right hippocampus in taxi drivers. *Journal of Neuroscience, 17*(18), 7103–7110.

Maher, N. E., Golbe, L. I., Lazzarini, M. A. M., Mark, M. H., Currie, J. L. J., Wooten, G. F., Saint-Hilaire, M., Wilk, J. B., Volejak, J., Maher, J. E., Feldman, J. R. J., Guttman, M., Lew, M., Schuman, S., Suchowersky, O., Lafontaine, A. L., Labelle, N., Vieregge, P., Pramstaller, P. P., Klein, C., Hubble, J., Reider, C., Growdon, J., Watts, R., Montgomery, E., Baker, K., Singer, C., Stacy, M., & Myers, R. H. (2002). Epidemiologic study of 203 sibling pairs with Parkinson's disease. The *Gene*PD study. *Neurology, 58,* 79–84.

Maier, S. E., & West, J. R. (2001). Drinking patterns and alcohol-related birth defects. *Alcohol Research & Health, 25,* 168–174.

Maj, M. (1990). Psychiatric aspects of HIV-1 infection and AIDS. *Psychological Medicine, 20,* 547–563.

Majovski, L. V. (1989). Higher cortical functions in children: A developmental perspective. In C. R. Reynolds & E. Fletcher-Janzen (Eds.), *Handbook of clinical child neuropsychology* (pp. 41–67). New York: Plenum Press.

Malloy, P. (1987). Frontal lobe dysfunction in obsessive-compulsive disorder. In E. Perecman (Ed.), *The frontal lobes revisited* (pp. 207–224). New York: IRBN Press.

Mancuso, G., Andres, P., Ansseau, M., & Tirelli, E. (1999). Effects of nicotine administered via a transdermal delivery system on vigilance: A repeated measure study. *Psychopharmacology, 142,* 18–23.

Maneru, C., Junque, C., Botet, F., Tallada, M., & Guardia, J. (2001). Neuropsychological long-term sequelae of perinatal asphyxia. *Brain Injury, 15,* 1029–1039.

Mangun, G. R., Buonocore, M. H., Girelli, M., & Jha, A. P. (1998). ERP and fMRI measures of visual spatial selection attention. *Human Brain Mapping, 6,* 383–389.

Mangun, G. R., & Hillyard, S. A. (1988). Spatial gradients of visual attention: Behavioral and electrophysiological evidence. *Electroencephalography and Clinical Neurophysiology, 70,* 417–428.

Mangun, G. R., & Hillyard, S. A. (1990). Electrophysiological studies of visual selective attention in humans. In A. R. Scheibel & A. F. Wechsler (Eds.), *Neurobiology of higher cognitive function* (pp. 271–295). New York: Guilford Press.

Mangun, G. R., Hopfinger, J. B., & Heinze, H.-J. (1998). Integrating electrophysiology and neuroimaging in the study of human cognition. *Behavior Research Methods, Instruments and Computers, 30,* 118–130.

Marcotte, T. D., Heaton, K. R. K., Alhassoon, O., Taylor, J. M. J., Arffa, K., Grant, I., & HNRC Group (1997). Mild HIV-related cognitive impairment is associated with reduced performance on a driving simulator. *Journal of the International Neuropsychological Society, 3,* 14.

Marin-Padilla, M. (1970). Prenatal and early postnatal ontogenesis of the motor cortex: A Golgi study. 1. The sequential development of cortical layers. *Brain Research, 23,* 167–183.

Mark, V. W., Kooistra, C. A., & Heilman, K. M. (1988). Hemispatial neglect affected by non-neglected stimuli. *Neurology, 38,* 1207–1211.

Markee, T., Brown, W. S., Moore, L. H., & Theberge, D. C. (1996). Callosal function in dyslexia: Evoked potential interhemispheric transfer time and bilateral field advantage. *Developmental Neuropsychology, 12,* 409–428.

Marr, D. (1971). Simple memory: A theory for archicortex. *Philosophical Transactions of the Royal Society of London, B, Biological Sciences, 262*(841), 23–81.

Marr, D. (1982). *Vision.* San Francisco: Freeman.

Marr, D., & Nishihara, H. K. (1978). Visual information processing: Artificial intelligence and the sensorium of sight. *Technology Review, 81,* 2–23.

Marsden, C., Merton, P., Morton, H., Hallett, M., Adam, J., & Rushton, D. (1977). Disorders of movement in cerebellar disease in man. In F. Rose (Ed.), *Physiological aspects of clinical neurology* (pp. 179–199). Oxford, England: Blackwell.

Marsden, C. D. (1986). Movement disorders and the basal ganglia. *Trends in Neurosciences, 9,* 512–515.

Marshall, J. C., & Halligan, P. W. (1988). Blindsight and insight in visuospatial neglect. *Nature, 336,* 766–767.

Marshall, L. F., & Ruff, R. M. (1989). Neurosurgeon as victim. In H. S. Levin, H. M. Eisenberg, & A. L. Benton (Eds.), *Mild head injury.* New York: Oxford University Press.

Marsolek, C. J., Kosslyn, S. M., & Squire, L. R. (1992). Form-specific visual priming in the right cerebral hemisphere. *Journal of Experimental Psychology: Learning, Memory and Cognition, 18*(3), 492–508.

Martin, A., Wiggs, C. L., Ungerleider, L. G., & Haxby, J. V. (1996). Neural correlates of category-specific knowledge. *Nature, 379,* 649–652.

Martin, E. M., Pitrak, D. L., Pursell, K. J., Mullane, K. M., & Novak, R. M. (1995). Delayed recognition memory span in HIV-1 infection. *Journal of the International Neuropsychological Society, 1,* 575–580.

Martin, G. M., Harley, C. W., Smith, R. A. R., Hoyles, E. S., & Hynes, C. A. (1997). Spatial disorientation blocks reliable goal location on a plus maze but does not prevent goal location in the Morris maze. *Journal of Experimental Psychology: Animal Behavior Processes, 23*(2), 183–193.

Martin, M. (1979). Hemispheric specialization for local and global processing. *Neuropsychologia, 17,* 33–40.

Martin, R., & McFarland, H. F. (1993). Role of genetic factors for the autoimmune pathogenesis of multiple sclerosis. In U. Halbreich (Ed.), *Multiple sclerosis: A neuropsychiatric disorder* (pp. 73–96). Washington, DC: American Psychiatric Press.

Martinez, A., Anllo-Vento, L., Sereno, M. I., Frank, L. R., Buxton, R. B., Dubowitz, D. J., Wong, E. C., Hinrichs, H., Heinze, H. J., & Hillyard, S. A. (1999) Involvement of striate and extrastriate visual cortical areas in spatial attention. *Nature Neuroscience, 2,* 364–369.

Martinot, J. L., Hardy, P., Feline, A., Huret, J. D., Mazoyer, B., Attar-Levy, D., Pappata, S., & Syrota, A. (1990). Left prefrontal glucose hypometabolism in the depressed state: A confirmation. *American Journal of Psychiatry, 147,* 1313–1317.

Martone, M., Butters, N., Payne, M., Becker, J. T., & Sax, D. (1984). Dissociations between skill learning and verbal recognition in amnesia and dementia. *Archives of Neurology, 41*(9), 965–970.

Masterton, R. B. (1992). Role of the central auditory system in hearing: The new direction. *Trends in Neurosciences, 15*(8), 280–285.

Matser, E. J. T., Kessels, A. G., Lezak, M. D., & Jordan, B. D. (1999). Neuropsychological impairment in amateur soccer players. *Journal of the American Medical Association, 282,* 971–973.

Matsumura, M., Kawashima, R., Naito, E., Satoh, K., Takahashi, T., Yanagisawa, T., & Fukuda, H. (1996). Changes in rCBF during grasping in humans examined by PET. *NeuroReport, 7,* 749–452.

Matthews, W. S. (1988). Attention deficit and learning disabilities in children with Tourette's syndrome. *Psychiatric Annals, 18,* 414–416.

Mattis, S., French, J. H., & Rapin, I. (1975). Dyslexia in children and young adults: Three independent neuropsychological syndromes. *Developmental Medicine and Child Neurology, 17,* 150.

Mattson, S. N., Schoenfeld, A. M., & Riley, E. P. (2001). Teratogenic effects of alcohol on brain and behavior. *Alcohol Research & Health, 25,* 185–191.

Mauk, M. D., Medina, J. F., Nores, W. L., & Ohyama, T. (2000). Cerebellar function: Coordination, learning or timing? *Current Biology, 10,* R522–R525.

Maunsell, J. H. R., & Newsome, W. T. (1987). Visual processing in monkey extrastriate cortex. *Annual Review of Neuroscience, 10,* 365, 367.

Mayes, A. R., Meudell, P. R., & Pickering, A. (1985). Is organic amnesia caused by a selective deficit in remembering contextual information? *Cortex, 21,* 167–202.

Mayes, L. C., Grillon, C., Granger, R., & Schottenfeld, R. (1998). Regulation of arousal and attention in preschool children exposed to cocaine prenatally. *Annals of the New York Academy of Science, 846,* 126–143.

Mayes, R. A. R., Downes, J. J., McDonald, C., Poole, V., Rooke, S., Sagar, H. J., & Meudell, P. R. (1994). Two tests for assessing remote public knowledge: A tool for assessing retrograde amnesia. *Memory, 2*(2), 183–210.

Mazer, J. A., & Gallant, J. L. (2000). Object recognition: Seeing us seeing shapes. *Current Biology, 10,* R668–R670.

Mazzoni, M., Pardossi, L., Cantini, R., Giorgetti, V., & Arena, R. (1990). Gerstmann syndrome: A case report. *Cortex, 26,* 459–467.

McArthur, D., & Adamson, L. B. (1996). Joint attention in preverbal children: Autism and developmental language disorder. *Journal of Autism and Developmental Disorders, 26,* 481–496.

McCarley, R. W., Shenton, M. E., O'Donnell, B. F., Faux, S. F., Kikinis, R., Nestor, P. G., & Jolesz, F. A. (1993). Auditory P_{300} abnormalities and left posterior superior temporal gyrus volume reduction in schizophrenia. *Archives of General Psychiatry, 50,* 190–197.

McCarthy, G., Puce, A., Gore, J. C., & Allison, T. (1997). Face-specific processing in the human fusiform gyrus. *Journal of Cognitive Neuroscience, 9,* 605–610.

McCarthy, R. A., & Warrington, E. K. (1990). *Cognitive neuropsychology: A clinical introduction.* New York: Academic Press.

McClelland, J. L., McNaughton, B. L., & O'Reilly, R. C. (1995). Why there are complementary learning systems in the hippocampus and neocortex: Insights from the successes and failures of connectionist models of learning and memory. *Psychological Review, 102*(3), 419–457.

McCloskey, M., & Cohen, N. J. (1989). Catastrophic interference in connectionist networks: The sequential learning problem. In G. H. Bower (Ed.), *The psychology of learning and motivation* (Vol 24) (pp. 109–174). San Diego: Academic Press.

McDermott, K. B., Buckner, R. L., Peterson, S. E., Kelley, W. M., & Sanders, A. L. (1999). Set- and code-specific activation in the frontal cortex: An fMRI study of encoding and retrieval of faces and words. *Journal of Cognitive Neuroscience, 11*(6), 631–640.

McFie, J., Piercy, M. F., & Zangwill, O. L. (1950). Visual spatial agnosia associated with lesions of the right cerebral hemisphere. *Brain, 73,* 167–190.

McFie, J., & Zangwill, O. L. (1960). Visual-constructive disabilities associated with lesions of the left cerebral hemisphere. *Brain, 83,* 242–260.

McGaugh, J. L., & Herz, M. J. (1972). *Memory consolidation.* San Francisco: Albion.

McGeer, P. L., Schulzer, M., & McGeer, E. G. (1996). Arthritis and anti-inflammatory agents as possible protective factors for Alzheimer's disease: A review of 17 epidemiological studies. *Neurology, 47,* 425–432.

McGlinchey-Berroth, R., Milberg, W. P., Verfaellie, M., Alexander, M., & Kilduff, P. T. (1993). Semantic processing in the neglected visual field: Evidence from a lexical decision task. *Cognitive Neuropsychology, 10,* 79–108.

McGlone, J. (1980). Sex differences in human brain asymmetry: A critical survey. *Behavioral and Brain Sciences, 3*(2), 215–263.

McGrew, W. C., & Marchant, L. F. (1999). Laterality of hand use pays off in foraging success for wild chimpanzees. *Primates, 40*(3), 509–513.

McIntosh, A. R., Sekular, A. B., Penpeci, C., Rajah, M. N., Grady, C. L., Sekular, R., & Bennett, P. J. (1999). Recruitment of unique neural systems to support visual memory in normal aging. *Current Biology, 9,* 1275–1278.

McIntyre, J. S., & Craik, F. I. M. (1987). Age differences in memory for item and source information. *Canadian Journal of Psychology, 41,* 175–192.

McKeever, W. F., & Dixon, M. S. (1981). Right-hemisphere superiority for discriminating memorized from nonmemorized faces: Affective imagery, sex, and perceived emotionally effects. *Brain and Language, 12,* 246–260.

McKhann, M. G. M., Albert, M., Grossman, M., Miller, B., Dickson, D., & Trojanowski, J. Q. (2001). Clinical and pathological diagnosis of frontotemporal dementia: Report of the work group on frontotemporal dementia and Pick's disease. *Archives of Neurology, 58,* 1803–1809.

McKinzey, K. R. K. & Russell, E. W. (1997). A partial cross-validation of a Halstead-Reitan battery malingering formula. *Journal of Clinical and Experimental Neuropsychology, 19,* 484–488.

McLaughlin, J. P., Dean, P., & Stanley, P. (1983). Aesthetic preference in dextrals and sinistrals. *Neuropsychologia, 21,* 147–153.

McLeod, P., Shallice, T., & Plaut, D. C. (2000) Attractor dynamics in word recognition: Converging evidence from errors by normal subjects, dyslexic patients and a connectionist model. *Cognition, 74*(1), 91–113.

McManus, I. C. (1985). Handedness, language dominance and aphasia: A genetic model. *Psychological Medicine, 8*(Suppl.), 1–40.

McManus, I. C., & Bryden, M. P. (1991). Geschwind's theory of cerebral lateralization: Developing a formal, causal model. *Psychological Bulletin, 110,* 237–253.

McNally, R. J. (1998). Information-processing abnormalities in anxiety disorders: Implications for cognitive neuroscience. *Cognition and Emotion, 12,* 479–495.

McNaughton, B. L., & Morris, R. G. (1987). Hippocampal synaptic enhancement and information storage within a distributed memory system. *Trends in Neurosciences, 10(10),* 408–415.

McNeil, J. E., & Warrington, E. K. (1993). Prosopagnosia: A face-specific disorder. *Quarterly Journal of Experimental Psychology, 46A,* 1–10.

McPherson, S., & Cummings, J. L. (1996). Neuropsychological aspects of Parkinson's disease and Parkinsonism. In G. Igor, & K. M. Adams (1996), *Neuropsychological assessment of neuropsychiatric disorders* (2nd ed.) (pp. 288–311). New York: Oxford University Press.

Mead, A. M., & McLaughlin, J. P. (1992). The roles of handedness and stimulus asymmetry in aesthetic preference. *Brain and Cognition, 20,* 300–307.

Meerwaldt, J. D., & Van Harskamp, F. (1982). Spatial disorientation in right-hemisphere infarction. *Journal of Neurology, Neurosurgery and Psychiatry, 45,* 586–590.

Mehta, Z., & Newcombe, F. (1991). A role for the left hemisphere in spatial processing. *Cortex, 27,* 153–167.

Melzack, R. (1990). Phantom limbs and the concept of a neuromatrix. *Trends in Neuroscience, 13*(3), 88–92.

Menard, M. T., Kosslyn, S. M., Thompson, W. L., Alpert, N. M., & Rauch, S. L. (1996). Encoding words and pictures: A positron emission tomography study. *Neuropsychologia, 34,* 185–194.

Mendez, M. F., & Geehan, G. R. (1988). Cortical auditory disorders: Clinical and acoustic features. *Journal of Neurology, Neurosurgery and Psychiatry, 51,* 1–9.

Mendez, M. F., Underwood, K. L., Zander, B. A., Mastri, A. R., et al. (1992). Risk factors in Alzheimer's disease: A clinicopathologic study. *Neurology, 42,* 770–775.

Mennemeier, M., Wertman, E., & Heilman, K. M. (1992). Neglect of near peripersonal space. *Brain, 115,* 37–50.

Menon, D. K., Owen, A. M., Williams, E. J., Minhas, P. S., Allen, C. M. C., Boniface, S. J., Pickard, J. D. & the Wolfson Brain Imaging Centre Team. (1998). Cortical processing in the vegetative state. *Lancet, 352,* 200.

Merchant, C., Tang, M. X., Albert, S., Manly, J., Stern, Y., & Mayeux, R. (1999). The influence of smoking on the risk of Alzheimer's disease. *Neurology, 52,* 1408–1412.

Merckelbach, H., Muris, P., & Kop, W. J. (1994). Handedness, symptom reporting, and accident susceptibility. *Journal of Clinical Psychology, 50,* 389–392.

Mertens, I., Siegmund, H., & Gruesser, O. J. (1993). Gaze motor asymmetries in the perception of faces during a memory task. *Neuropsychologia, 31*(9), 989–998.

Merzenich, M. M., Recanzone, G. H., Jenkins, W. M., & Grajski, K. A. (1990). Adaptive mechanisms in cortical networks underlying cortical contributions to learning and nondeclarative memory. In *Cold Spring Harbor Symposia on Quantitative Biology: Vol. 55: The brain.* New York: Cold Spring Harbor Laboratory.

Messerli, P., Pegna, A., & Sordet, N. (1995). Hemispheric dominance for melody recognition in musicians and non-musicians. *Neuropsychologia, 33,* 395–405.

Mesulam, M.-M. (1981). A cortical network for directed attention and unilateral neglect. *Annals of Neurology, 10,* 309–325.

Mesulam, M.-M. (Ed.). (1985). *Principles of behavioral neurology.* Philadelphia: F A Davis.

Meyer, D., Schvaneveldt, R., & Ruddy, M. G. (1974). Functions of graphemic and phonemic codes in visual word recognition. *Memory and Cognition, 2,* 309–321.

Miall, R. C., Reckess G. Z., & Imamizu, H. (2001). The cerebellum coordinates eye and hand tracking movements. *Nature Neuroscience, 4,* 638–644.

Miceli, G. (1982). The processing of speech sounds in a patient with cortical auditory disorder. *Neuropsychologia, 20,* 5–20.

Miceli, G., Gainotti, G., Caltagirone, C., & Masullo, C. (1980). Some aspects of phonological impairment in aphasia. *Brain and Language, 11,* 159–169.

Middleton, F. A., & Strick, P. L. (2000). Basal ganglia and cerebellar loops: Motor and cognitive circuits. *Brain Research Reviews, 31,* 236–250.

Milham, M. P., Banich, M. T., Webb, A., Barad, V., Cohen, N. J., Wszalek, T., & Kramer, A. F. (2001). The relative involvement of anterior cingulate and prefrontal cortex in attentional control dependson nature of conflict. *Cognitive Brain Research, 12,* 467–473.

Milham, M. P., Erickson, K. I., Banich, M. T., Kramer, A. F., Webb, A., Wszalek, T., & Cohen, N. J. (2002). Attentional control in the aging brain: Insights from an fMRI study of the Stroop task. *Brain and Cognition, 49,* 277–296.

Miller, E. K., & Cohen, J. D. (2001). An integrative theory of prefrontal cortex function. *Annual Review of Neuroscience, 24,* 167–202.

Miller, L. (1992). Cognitive rehabilitation, cognitive therapy, and cognitive style: Toward an integrative model of personality and psychotherapy. *Journal of Cognitive Rehabilitation, 10,* 18–29.

Miller, L. A. (1992). Impulsivity, risk-taking, and the ability to synthesize fragmented information after frontal lobectomy. *Neuropsychologia, 31,* 69–79.

Mills, D. L., Coffey-Corina, S. A. & Neville, H. J. (1997). Language comprehension and cerebral specialization from 13 to 20 months. *Developmental Neuropsychology, 13,* 397–445.

Milner, A. D., Perrett, D. I., Jonston, R. S., Benson, P. J., Jordan, T. R., Heeley, D. W., Bettucci, D., Mortara, F., Mutani, R., & Terazzi, E. (1991). Perception and action in "visual form agnosia." *Brain, 114,* 405–428.

Milner, B. (1962a). Laterality effects in audition. In V. B. Mountcastle (Ed.), *Interhemispheric relations and cerebral dominance* (pp. 177–195). Baltimore: Johns Hopkins Press.

Milner, B. (1962b). Les Troubles de la mémoire accompagnat des lésions hippocampiques bilatérales. In P. Passouant (Ed.), *Physiologic de l'hippocampe* (pp. 257–272). Paris: Centre National de la Recherche Scientifique.

Milner, B. (1964). Some effects of frontal lobectomy in man. In J. M. Warren & K. Akert (Eds.), *Frontal granular cortex and behavior* (pp. 313–331). New York: McGraw-Hill.

Milner, B. (1965). Visually-guided maze learning in man: effects of bilateral hippocampal, bilateral frontal and unilateral cerebral lesions. *Neuropsychologia, 3,* 317–338.

Milner, B. (1966). Amnesia following operation on the temporal lobes. In C. W. M. Whitty & O. L. Zangwill (Eds.), *Amnesia* (pp. 109–133). London: Butterworth.

Milner, B. (1968). Visual recognition and recall after temporal lobe excisions in man. *Neuropsychologia, 6,* 191–209.

Milner, B. (1971). Interhemispheric differences in the localization of psychological processes in man. *British Medical Bulletin, 27,* 272–277.

Milner, B. (1978). Clues to the cerebral organization of memory. In P. Buser & A. Rougeul-Buser (Eds.), *Cerebral correlates of conscious experience.* Amsterdam: Elsevier.

Milner, B. (1982). Some cognitive effects of frontal-lobe lesions in man. *Philosophical Transactions of the Royal Society of London, B298,* 211–226.

Milner, B., Corkin, S., & Teuber, H. L. (1968). Further analysis of the hippocampal amnesia syndrome. *Neuropsychologia, 6,* 215–234.

Milner, B., Corsi, P., & Leonard, G. (1991). Frontal-lobe contribution to recency judgements. *Neuropsychologia, 29,* 601–618.

Milner, B., & Petrides, M. (1984). Behavioural effects of frontal-lobe lesions in man. *Trends in Neurosciences, 7,* 403–407.

Milner, B., Taylor, L., & Sperry, R. W. (1968). Lateralized suppression of dichotically presented digits after commissural section in man. *Science, 161,* 184–185.

Mink, J. W., & Thach, W. T. (1993). Basal ganglia intrinsic circuits and their role in behavior. *Current Opinion in Neurobiology, 3,* 952.

Mishkin, M. (1978). Memory in monkeys severely impaired by combined but not separate removal of the amygdala and hippocampus. *Nature, 273,* 297–298.

Mishkin, M. (1982). A memory system in the monkey. *Philosophical Transactions of the Royal Society of London, B298,* 85–95.

Mishkin, M., & Delacour, J. (1975). An analysis of short-term visual memory in the monkey. *Journal of Experimental Psychology: Animal Behavior Processes, 104,* 326–334.

Mishkin, M., Ungerleider, G., & Macko, K. A. (1983). Object vision and spatial vision: Two cortical pathways. *Trends in Neurosciences, 6,* 414–417.

Mittenberg, W., Seidenberg, M., O'Leary, D. S., & DiGiulio, D. V. (1989). Changes in cerebral functioning associated with normal aging. *Journal of Clinical and Experimental Neuropsychology, 11,* 918–932.

Miwa, H., Iijima, M., Tanaka, S., & Mizuno, Y. (2001). Generalized convulsions after consuming a large amount of gingko nuts. *Epilepsia, 42,* 280–281.

Mize, K. (1980). Visual hallucinations following viral encephalitis: A self report. *Neuropsychologia, 18,* 193–202.

Moffat, S. D., & Hampson, E. (1996). A curvilinear relationship between testosterone and spatial cognition in humans: Possible influence of hand preference. *Psychoneuroendocrinology, 21,* 323–337.

Mohanty, A., & Heller, W. (2002). The neuropsychology of mood disorders: Affect, cognition, and neural circuitry. In H. D'haenen, J. A. den Boer, H. Westenberg, & P. Willner (Eds.), *Textbook of biological psychiatry, Vol. 2* (pp. 791–802). Hoboken, NJ: John Wiley & Sons.

Molfese, D., & Molfese, V. J. (1994). Short-term and long-term developmental outcomes: The use of behavioral and electrophysiological measures in early infancy as predictors. In G. Dawson & K. W. Fischer (Eds.), *Human behavior and the developing brain* (pp. 493–517). New York: Guilford Press.

Molfese, D. L., Freeman, R. B., & Palermo, D. S. (1975). The ontogeny of brain lateralization for speech and nonspeech stimuli. *Brain and Language, 2,* 356–368.

Molfese, D. L., & Molfese, V. J. (1997). Discrimination of language skills at five years of age using event-related potentials recorded at birth. *Developmental Neuropsychology, 13,* 135–156.

Molfese, D. L., Molfese, V. J., & Espy, K. A. (1999). The predictive use of event-related potentials in language development and the treatment of language disorders. *Developmental Neuropsychology, 13,* 373–377.

Money, J. A. (1976). *A standardized road map test of directional sense. Manual.* San Rafael, CA: Academic Therapy Publications.

Monrad-Krohn, G. H. (1947). Dysprosady of altered "melody of language." *Brain, 70,* 405–415.

Monsch, A. U., Bondi, M. W., Butters, N., Paulsen, J. S., Salmon, D. P., Brugger, P., & Swenson, M. R. (1994). A comparison of category and letter fluency in Alzheimer's disease and Huntington's disease. *Neuropsychology, 8,* 25–30.

Moonen, C. T. W., & Bandettini, P. A. (2001). *Functional MRI. Medical radiology diagnostic imaging and radiation oncology.* New York: Springer.

Moran, J., & Desimone, R. (1985). Selective attention gates visual processing in the extrastriate cortex. *Science, 229,* 782–784.

Moray, N. (1959). Attention in dichotic listening: Affective cues and the influence of instruction. *Quarterly Journal of Experimental Psychology, 11,* 56–60.

Morgan, M. J. (2000). Ecstasy (MDMA): A review of its possible persistent psychological effect. *Psychopharmacology, 152*(3), 230–248.

Morgenstern, H., Glazer, W. M., Niedzwiecki, D., & Nourjah, P. (1987). The impact of neuroleptic medication on tardive dyskinesia: A meta-analysis of published studies. *American Journal of Public Health, 77,* 717–724.

Morris, J. S., Ohman, A., & Dolan, R. J. (1998). Conscious and unconscious emotional learning in the human amygdala. *Nature, 393,* 467–470.

Morris, P. L., Robinson, R. G., de Carvalho, M. L., Albert, P., Wells, J. C., Samuels, J. F., Eden-Fetzer, D., & Price, T. R. (1996). Lesion characteristics and depressed mood in the Stroke Data Bank study. *Journal of Neuropsychiatry and Clinical Neurosciences, 8,* 153–159.

Morris, P. L., Robinson, R. G., Raphael, B., & Hopwood, M. J. (1996). Lesion location and poststroke depression. *Journal of Neuropsychiatry and Clinical Neurosciences, 8,* 399–403.

Morris, R. G., Ahmed, S., Syed, G. M., & Toone, B. K. (1993). Neural correlates of planning ability: Frontal lobe activation during the Tower of London test. *Neuropsychologia, 31,* 1367–1378.

Morris, R. G. M. (1981). Spatial localization does not require the presence of local cues. *Learning and Motivation, 12,* 239–260.

Morrow, L., Ratcliff, G., & Johnston, C. S. (1985). Externalising spatial knowledge in patients with right hemisphere lesions. *Cognitive Neuropsychology, 2,* 265–273.

Morrow, L., Vrtunski, P. B., Kim, Y., & Boller, F. (1981). Arousal responses to emotional stimuli and laterality of lesions. *Neuropsychologia, 19,* 65–71.

Morrow, L. A., Ryan, C. M., Hodgson, M. J., & Robin, N. (1991). Risk factors associated with persistence of neuropsychological deficits in persons with organic solvent exposure. *Journal of Nervous and Mental Disease, 9,* 540–545.

Morselli, P. L., & Lloyd, K. G. (1985). Mechanisms of action of antiepileptic drugs. In R. J. Porter & P. L. Morselli (Eds.), *The epilepsies* (pp. 40–81). Boston: Butterworth.

Mortimer, J. A., French, L. M., Hutton, D. J., & Schuman, L. M. (1985). Head trauma as a risk factor for Alzheimer's disease. *Neurology, 35,* 264–267.

Mortimer, J. A., & Pirozzolo, F. J. (1985). Remote effects of head trauma. *Developmental Neuropsychology, 1,* 215–229.

Mortimer, J. A., van Duijn, C. M., Chandra, V., Fratiglioni, L., Graves, A. B., Heyman, A., Jorm, A. F., Kokmen, E., Konda, K., Rocca, W. A., Shalat, S. L., Soininen, H., & Hofman, A. (1991). Head trauma as a risk factor for Alzheimer's disease: A collaborative re-analysis of case-control studies. *International Journal of Epidemiology, 20*(Suppl. 2), S28–S35.

Moscovitch, M. (1979). Information processing and the cerebral hemispheres. In M. S. Gazzaniga (Ed.), *Handbook of behavioral neurobiology: Neuropsychology.* New York: Plenum Press.

Moscovitch, M. (1994). Memory and working-with-memory: A component process model based on modules and central systems. In D. L. Schacter & E. Tulving (Eds.), *Memory systems 1994.* Cambridge, MA: MIT Press.

Moscovitch, M. (1995). Confabulation. In D. Schacter (Ed.), *Memory distortions: How minds, brains, and societies reconstruct the past* (pp. 226–251). Cambridge, MA: Harvard University Press.

Moscovitch, M., Behrmann, M., & Winocur, G. (1994). Do PETS have long or short ears? Mental imagery and neuroimaging. *Trends in Neurosciences, 17,* 292–294.

Moscovitch, M., & Radzins, M. (1987). Backward masking of lateralized faces by noise, pattern, and spatial frequency. *Brain and Cognition, 6,* 72–90.

Moscovitch, M., Winocur, G., & Behrmann, M. (1997). What is special about face recognition? Nineteen experiments on a person with visual object agnosia and dyslexia but normal face recognition. *Journal of Cognitive Neuroscience, 9,* 555–604.

Moscovitch, M., Winocur, G., & McLachlan, D. (1986). Memory as assessed by recognition and reading time in normal and memory-impaired people with Alzheimer's disease and other neurological disorders. *Journal of Experimental Psychology: General, 115*(4), 331–347.

Mosimann, U. P., Rihs, T. A., Engeler, J., Fisch, H.-U., & Schlaepfer, T. E. (2000). Mood effects of repetitive transcranial magnetic stimulation of left prefrontal cortex in healthy volunteers. *Psychiatry Research, 94,* 251–256.

Moss, A. D., & Turnbull, O. H. (1996). Hatred of the hemiparetic limbs (misoplegia) in a 10-year-old child. *Journal of Neurology, Neurosurgery and Psychiatry, 61,* 210–211.

Mostofsky, S. H., Mazzocco, M. M. M., Aakalu, G., Warsofsky, I. S., Denckla, M. B., & Reiss, A. L. (1998). Decreased cerebellar posterior vermis size in fragile-X syndrome: Correlation with neurocognitive performance. *Neurology, 50,* 121–130.

Motter, B. C., & Mountcastle, V. B. (1981). The functional properties of light-sensitive neurons of the posterior parietal cortex studies in waking monkeys: Foveal sparing and opponent vector organization. *Journal of Neuroscience, 1,* 3–26.

Mountcastle, V. B., Lynch, J. C., Georgopoulos, A., Sakata, H., & Acuna, C. (1975). Posterior parietal association cortex of the monkey: Command functions for operations within extrapersonal space. *Journal of Neurophysiology, 38,* 871–908.

Moya, K. L., Benowitz, L. I., Levine, D. N., & Finklestein, S. (1986). Covariant defects in visuospatial abilities and recall of verbal narrative after right hemisphere stroke. *Cortex, 22,* 381–397.

Mozaz, M. J. (1992). Ideational and ideomotor apraxia: A qualitative analysis. *Behavioral Neurology, 5,* 11–17.

Mozer, M. C. & Sitton, M. (1998). Computational modeling of spatial attention. In H. Pashler (Ed.) *Attention.* (pp. 341–395). Hove: Psychology Press.

Mozer, M. C., Halligan, P. W., & Marshall, J. C. (1997). The end of the line for a brain-damaged model of unilateral neglect. *Journal of Cognitive Neuroscience, 9*(2), 171–190.

Muir J. L., Everitt B. J., Robbins, T. W. (1994). AMPA-induced excito toxic lesions of the basal forebrain—A significant role for the cortical cholinergic system in attentional function. *Journal of Neuroscience, 14,* 2313–2326.

Muller, R. U., Kubic, J. L., & Ranck, J. B., Jr. (1987). Spatial firing patterns of hippocampal complex spike cells in a fixed environment. *Journal of Neuroscience, 7.*

Mumenthaler, M. S., Taylor, J. L., O'Hara, R., & Yesavage, J. A. (1998). Influence of nicotine on simulator flight performance in non-smokers. *Psychopharmacology, 140,* 38–41.

Murray, M. (1994, February 13). Nancy Wexler's test. *The New York Times Magazine,* p. 28.

Musen, G., & Squire, L. R. (1993). Implicit learning of color-word associations using a Stroop paradigm. *Journal of Experimental Psychology. Learning, Memory, and Cognition, 19*(4), 789–98.

Myklebust, H. R. (1975). Nonverbal learning disabilities: Assessment and intervention. In H. R. Myklebust (Ed.), *Progress in learning disabilities: Vol. 3* (pp. 85–121). New York: Grune & Stratton.

Myles-Worsley, M., Johnston, W. A., & Simons, M. A. (1988). The influence of expertise on x-ray image processing. *Journal of Experimental Psychology: Learning, Memory, and Cognition, 14,* 553–557.

Myslobodsky, M. S. (1983). Epileptic laughter. In M. S. Myslobodsky (Ed.), *Hemisyndromes: Psychobiology, neurology, psychiatry.* New York: Academic Press.

Myslobodsky, M. S., & Horesh, N. (1978). Bilateral electrodermal activity in depressive patients. *Biological Psychiatry, 6,* 111–120.

Naatanen, R., Gaillard, A. W. K., & Mantysalo, S. (1978). The N_1 effect of selective attention reinterpreted. *Acta Psychologica (Amsterdam), 42,* 313–329.

Nader, K., & LeDoux, J. (1999). Inhibition of the mesoamygdala dopaminergic pathway impairs the retrieval of conditioned fear associations. *Behavioral Neuroscience, 113,* 891–901.

Naeser, M. A., & Borod, J. C. (1986). Aphasia in left-handers: Lesion site, lesion side and hemispheric asymmetries on CT. *Neurology, 36,* 471–488.

Nagahama, Y., Okada, T., Katsumi, Y., Hayashi, T., Yamauchi, H., Oyangi, C., Konishi, J., Fukuyama, H., & Shibasaki, H. (2001). Dissociable mechanisms of attentional control within the human prefrontal cortex. *Cerebral Cortex, 11,* 85–92.

Nagy, Z., Esiri, M. M., Jobst, K. A., Morris, J. H., King, E. M. F., McDonald, B., Litchfield, S., Smith, A., Barnetson, L., & Smith, A. D. (1995). Relative roles of plaques and tangles in the dementia of Alzheimer's disease: Correlations using three sets of neuropathological criteria. *Dementia, 6,* 21–31.

Nakamura, K., Kawashima, R., Sato, N., Nakamura, A., Sugiura, M., Kato, T., Hatano, K., Ito, K., Fukuda, H., Schormann, T., & Zilles, K. (2000). Functional delineation of the human occipito-temporal areas related to face and scene processing: A PET study. *Brain, 123,* 1903–1912.

Nakanishi, A. (1980). *Writing systems of the world.* Tokyo: Charles E. Tuttle.

Nass, R. (1997). Language development in children with congenital strokes. *Seminars in Pediatric Neurology, 4,* 109–116.

Nass, R., Peterson, H., & Koch, D. (1989). Differential effects of congenital left and right brain injury on intelligence. *Brain and Cognition, 9,* 258–266.

National Institute of Health Consensus Development Panel on Rehabilitation of Persons With Traumatic Brain Injury (1999). Rehabilitation of persons with traumatic brain injury. *Journal of the American Medical Association, 282, 974–983.*

Nauta, W. (1971). The problem of the frontal lobe: A reinterpretation. *Journal of Psychiatric Research, 8,* 167–187.

Naveh-Benjamin, M. (1990). Coding of temporal order information: An automatic process? *Journal of Experimental Psychology: Learning, Memory, and Cognition, 16,* 117–126.

Navia, B. A., Cho, E., Petito, C. K., & Price, R. W. (1986). The AIDS dementia complex: II. Neuropathology. *Annals of Neurology, 19,* 525–535.

Navia, B. A., Jordan, B. D., & Price, R. W. (1986). The AIDS dementia complex: I. Clinical features. *Annals of Neurology, 19,* 517–524.

Navon, D. (1977). Forest before trees: The precedence of global features in visual perception. *Cognitive Psychology, 9,* 353–383.

Naya, Y., Yoshida, M., & Miyashita, Y. (2001). Backward spreading of memory-retrieval signal in the primate temporal cortex. *Science, 291*(5504), 661–664.

Neary, J. T. & Bu, Y. (1999). Hypericum LI 160 inhibits uptake of serotonin and norepinephrine in astrocytes. *Brain Research, 816,* 358–363.

Nebes, R. D. (1978). Direct examination of cognitive function in the right and left hemispheres. In M. Kinsbourne (Ed.), *Asymmetrical function of the brain* (pp. 99–137). Cambridge, England: Cambridge University Press.

Neill, W. T. (1977). Inhibition and facilitation processes in selective attention. *Journal of Experimental Psychology: Human Perception and Performance, 3,* 444–450.

Nelson, H. E. (1982). *National Adult Reading Test: Test manual.* Windsor, England: NFER-Nelson.

Nelson, K. B., & Ellenberg, J. H. (1986). Antecedents of cerebral palsy: Multivariate analysis of risk. *New England Journal of Medicine, 315,* 81–86.

Nemetz, P. N., Leibson, C., Naessens, J. M., Beard, M., Kokmen, E., Annegers, J. F., & Kurland, L. T. (1999). Traumatic brain injury and the time to onset of Alzheimer's disease: A population-based study. *American Journal of Epidemiology, 149,* 32–40.

Nespoulous, J. L., Joanette, Y., Béland, R., Caplan, D., & Lecours, A. R. (1984). Phonological disturbances in aphasia: Is there a "markedness" effect in aphasic phonemic errors? In F. C. Rose (Ed.), *Progress in aphasiology: Advances in neurology, Vol. 42.* New York: Raven Press.

Netley, C., & Rovet, J. (1982). Verbal deficits in children with 47,XXY and 47,XXX karyotypes: A descriptive and experimental study. *Brain and Language, 17,* 58–72.

Neville, H. J. (1990). Intermodal competition and compensation in development: Evidence from studies of the visual system in congenitally deaf adults. *Annals of the New York Academy of Sciences, 608,* 71–91.

Neville, H. J., Bavelier, D., Corina, D., Rauschecker, J., Karni, A., Lalwani, A., Braun, A., Clark, V., Jezzard, P., & Turner, R. (1998). Cerebral organization for language in deaf and hearing subjects: Biological constraints and effects of experience. *Proceedings of the National Academy of Sciences, USA, 95,* 922–929.

Neville, H. J., & Lawson, D. (1987a). Attention to central and peripheral visual space in movement detection task: An event-related potential and behavioral study. I. Normal hearing adults. *Brain Research, 405,* 253–267.

Neville, H. J., & Lawson, D. (1987b). Attention to central and peripheral visual space in movement detection task: An event-related potential and behavioral study. II. Congenitally deaf adults. *Brain Research, 405,* 268–283.

Neville, H. J., & Lawson, D. (1987c). Attention to central and peripheral visual space in movement detection task: An event-related potential and behavioral study. III. Separate effects of auditory deprivation and acquisition of a visual language. *Brain Research, 405,* 284–294.

Newcombe, F. (1969). *Missile wounds of the brain: A study of psychological deficits.* Oxford, England: Oxford University Press.

Newcombe, F. (1985). Neuropsychology of consciousness: A review of human clinical evidence. In D. A. Oakley (Ed.), *Brain and mind* (pp. 152–196). New York: Methuen.

Newcombe, F., & Russell, W. R. (1969). Dissociated visual perceptual and spatial deficits in focal lesions of the right hemisphere. *Journal of Neurology, Neurosurgery and Psychiatry, 32,* 73–81.

Newman, A. J., Bavelier, D., Corina, D., Jezzard, P., & Neville, H. J. (2002). A critical period for right hemisphere recruitment in American Sign Language processing. *Nature Neuroscience, 5*(1), 76–80.

Ng, V. W. K., Bullmore, E. T., de Zubicaray, G. I., Cooper, A., Suckling, J., & Williams, S. C. R. (2001). Identifying rate-limiting nodes in large-scale cortical networks for visuospatial processing: An illustration using fMRI. *Journal of Cognitive Neuroscience, 13,* 537–545.

Nichelli, P., Grafman, J., Pietrini, P., Clark, K. Lee, K. Y., & Miletich, R. (1995). Where the brain appreciates the moral of a story. *NeuroReport, 6,* 2309–2313.

Nichols, M. E., Meador, K. J., & Loring, D. W. (1993). Neuropsychological effects of antiepileptic drugs: A current perspective. *Clinical Neuropharmacology, 16,* 471–484.

Nigg, J. T. (2001). Is ADHD a disinhibitory disorder? *Psychological Bulletin, 127,* 571–598.

Niki, H., & Watanabe, M. (1976). Prefrontal unit activity and delayed response: Relation to cue location versus direction of response. *Brain Research, 105,* 79–88.

Nishimura, T., Sugita, Y., & Takeda, M. (1999). Different neural substrates for Kanji and Kana writing: A PET study. *Neuroreport, 10*(16), 3315–3319.

Nissen, M. J., & Bullemer, P. (1987). Attentional requirements of learning: Evidence from performance measures. *Cognitive Psychology, 19*(1), 1–32.

Nitschke, J. B., Heller, W., & Miller, G. A. (2000). Anxiety, stress, and cortical brain function. In J. C. Borod (Ed.), *The neuropsychology of emotion* (pp. 298–319). New York: Oxford University Press.

Nitschke, J. B., & Heller, W. (2002). The neuropsychology of anxiety disorders: Affect, cognition, and neural circuitry. In H. D'haenen, J. A. den Boer, H. Westenberg, & P. Willner (Eds.), *Textbook of biological psychiatry, Vol. 2* (pp. 975–988). Hoboken, NJ: John Wiley & Sons.

Nixon, S. J. (1999). Neurocognitive performance in alcoholics: Is polysubstance abuse important? *Psychological Science, 10,* 181–185.

Nobre, A. C., Allison, T., McCarthy, G. (1994). Word recognition in the human inferior temporal lobe. *Nature, 372,* 260–263.

Nobre, A. C., Gitelman, D. R., Sebestyen, G. N., Meyer, J., Frackowiak, R. S. J., Frith, C. D., & Mesulam, M. M. (1997). Functional localization of the system for visuospatial attention using positron emission tomography. *Brain, 120,* 515–553.

Nolen-Hocksema, S. (1987). Sex differences in unipolar depression: Evidence and theory. *Psychological Bulletin, 101,* 259–282.

Nolte, J. (1999), *The Human Brain: An Introduction to its Functional Anatomy.* (4 ed.). St. Louis: Mosby.

Noonan, W. C. W., Kathman, S. J., & White, C. M. C. (2002). Prevalence estimates for MS in the United States and evidence of an increasing trend for women. *Neurology, 58,* 136–138.

Northoff, G., Richter, A., Gessner, M., Schlagenhauf, F., Fell, J., Baumgart, F., Kaulisch, T., Kotter, R., Stephan, K. E., Leschinger, A., Hagner, T., Bargel, B., Witzel, T., Hinrichs, H., Bogerts, B., Scheich, H., & Heinze, H.-J. (2000). Functional dissociation between medial and lateral prefrontal cortical spatiotemporal activation in negative and positive emotions: A combined fMRI/MEG study. *Cerebral Cortex, 10,* 93–107.

Novelly, R. A. (1992). The debt of neuropsychology to the epilepsies. *American Psychologist, 47,* 1126–1129.

Nudo, R. J., Milliken, G. W., Jenkins, W. M., & Merzenich, M. M. (1996). Use-dependent alterations of movement representations in primary motor cortex of adult squirrel monkeys. *Journal of Neuroscience, 16*(2), 785–807.

Nyberg, L., Cabeza, R., & Tulving, E. (1996). PET studies of encoding and retrieval: The HERA model. *Psychonomic Bulletin & Review, 3*(2), 135–148.

Nyberg, L., McIntosh, R. A. R., Cabeza, R., Nilsson, L. G., Houle, S., Habib, R., & Tulving, E. (1996). Network analysis of positron emission tomography regional cerebral blood flow data: Ensemble inhibition during episodic memory retrieval. *Journal of Neuroscience, 16*(11), 3753–3759.

Obler, L. K., & Albert, M. (1981). Language and aging: A neurobiological analysis. In D. S. Beasley & G. A. Davis (Eds.), *Aging: Communication processes and disorders* (pp. 107–121). New York: Grune & Stratton.

O'Boyle, M. W., Van Wyhe-Lawler, F., & Miller, D. A. (1987). Recognition of letters traced in the right and left palms: Evidence for a process-oriented tactile asymmetry. *Brain and Cognition, 6,* 474–494.

O'Craven, K. M., & Kanwisher, N. (2000). Mental imagery of faces and places activates corresponding stimulus-specific brain regions. *Journal of Cognitive Neuroscience, 12*(6), 1013–1023.

O'Craven, K., Downing, P., & Kanwisher, N. (1999). fMRI evidence for objects as the units of attentional selection. *Nature, 401,* 584–587.

O'Doherty, J., Kringelbach, M. L., Rolls, E. T., Hornak, J., & Andrews, C. (2001). Abstract reward and punishment representations in the human orbitofrontal cortex. *Nature Neuroscience, 4,* 95–102.

O'Dougherty, M., Wright, F. S., Loewenson, R. B., & Torres, F. (1985). Cerebral dysfunction after chronic hypoxia in children. *Neurology, 35,* 42–46.

Ogden, J. A. (1985). Antero-posterior interhemispheric differences in the loci of lesions producing visual hemineglect. *Brain and Cognition, 4,* 59–75.

O'Hara, C. (1988). Emotional adjustment following minor head injury. *Cognitive Rehabilitation, 6,* 26–33.

Ohkura, T., Isse, K., Akazawa, K., Hamamoto, M., Yaoi, Y., & Hagino, N. (1994). Evaluation of estrogen treatment in female patients with dementia of the Alzheimer type. *Endocrine Journal, 41,* 361–371.

Ohta, H., Ni, J.-W., Matsumoto, K., Watanabe, H., & Shimizu, M. (1993). Peony and its major constituent, paeoniflorin, improve radial maze performance impaired by scopolamine in rats. *Pharmacology, Biochemistry, and Behavior, 45,* 719–723.

Ojemann, G. A. (1983). Brain organization for language from the perspective of electrical stimulation mapping. *Behavioral and Brain Sciences, 6,* 189–230.

Ojemann, G. A. (1991). Cortical organization for language. *Journal of Neuroscience, 11,* 2281–2287.

Ojemann, G. A., Ojemann, J., Lettich, E., & Berger, M. (1989). Cortical language localization in left, dominant hemisphere. *Journal of Neurosurgery, 71,* 316–326.

Oke, A., Keller, R., Mefford, I., & Adams, R. (1978). Lateralization of norepinephrine in human thalamus. *Science, 200,* 1411–1413.

O'Keefe, J., & Burgess, N. (1996). Geometric determinants of the place fields of hippocampal neurons. *Nature, 381*(6581), 425–428.

O'Keefe, J., & Conway, D. H. (1978). Hippocampal place units in the freely moving rat: Why they fire where they fire. *Experimental Brain Research, 31*(4), 573–590.

O'Keefe, J., & Dostrovsky, J. (1971). The hippocampus as a spatial map. Preliminary evidence from unit activity in the freely-moving rat. *Brain Research, 34*(1), 171–175.

O'Keefe, J. A. (1976). Spatial memory within and without the hippocampal system. In W. Seifert (Ed.), *Neurobiology of the hippocampus.* New York: Academic Press.

O'Keefe, J. A., & Nadel, L. (1978). *The hippocampus as a cognitive map.* London: Oxford University Press.

O'Keefe, J. A., & Speakman, A. (1987). Single unit activity in the rat hippocampus during a spatial memory task. *Experimental Brain Research, 68,* 1–27.

Okubo, Y., Suhara, T., Suzuki, K., Kobayashi, K., Inoue, O., Terasaki, O., Someya, Y., Sassa, T., Sudo, Y., Matsushima, E., Iyo, M., Tateno, Y., & Toru, M. (1997). Decreased prefrontal dopamine D1 receptors in schizophrenia revealed by PET. *Nature, 385,* 634–636.

O'Kusky, J., & Colonnier, M. (1982). Postnatal changes in the number of neurons and synapses in the visual cortex

(A17) of the macaque monkey. *Journal of Comparative Neurology, 210,* 291–296.

Olanow, C. W., Kordower, J. H., & Freeman, T. B. (1996). Fetal nigral transplantation as a therapy for Parkinson's disease. *Trends in Neurosciences, 19,* 102–109.

Oliver, C., & Holland, A. J. (1986). Down's syndrome and Alzheimer's disease: A review. *Psychological Medicine, 16,* 307–322.

Oliveri, M., Rossini, P. M., Traversa, R., Cicinelli, P., Filippi, M. M., Pasqualetti, P., Tomaiuolo, F., & Caltagirone, C. (1999). Left frontal transcranial magnetic stimulation reduces contralesional extinction in patients with unilateral right brain damage. *Brain, 122,* 1731–1739.

Olson, I. R., Chun, M. M., & Allison, T. (2001). Contextual guidance of attention: Human intracranial event-related potential evidence for feedback modulation in anatomically early, temporally late stages of visual processing. *Brain, 124,* 1417–1425.

Olson, R. K. (1999). Genes, environment, and reading disabilities. In R. J. Stemberg & L. Spear-Swerling (Eds.), *Perspective on learning disabilities* (pp. 3–21). Boulder, CO: Westview Press.

O'Malley, S., Adamse, M., Heaton, R. K., & Gawin, F. H. (1992). Neuropsychological impairment in chronic cocaine abusers. *American Journal of Drug and Alcohol Abuse, 18,* 131–144.

O'Reilly, R. C., & Munakata, Y. (2000). *Computational explorations in cognitive neuroscience: Understanding the mind by stimulating the brain.* Cambridge, MA: The MIT Press.

O'Reilly, R. C., & Rudy, J. W. (2000) Computational principles of learning in the neocortex and hippocampus. *Hippocampus, 10*(4), 389–397.

Orsini, D. L., Van Gorp, W. G., & Boone, K. B. (1988). *The neuropsychology casebook.* New York: Springer-Verlag.

Orton, S. T. (1937). *Reading, writing and speech problems in children.* New York: Norton.

Ostergaard, A. L. (1987). Episodic, semantic, and procedural memory in a case of amnesia at an early age. *Neuropsychologia, 25*(2), 341–357.

Osterhout, L., & Holcomb, P. J. (1992). Event-related potentials elicited by syntactic anomaly. *Journal of Memory and Language, 31,* 785–806.

Osterhout, L., McLaughlin, J., & Bersick, M. (1997). Event-related brain potentials and human language. *Trends in Cognitive Sciences, 1,* 203–209.

Owen, A. M. (1997). The functional organization of working memory processes within human lateral frontal cortex: The contribution of functional neuroimaging. *European Journal of Neuroscience, 9*(7), 1329–1339.

Owen, A. M., Doyon, J., Dagher, A., Sadikot, A., & Evans, A. C. (1998). Abnormal basal ganglia outflow in Parkinson's disease identified with PET: Implications for higher cortical functions. *Brain, 121,* 949–965.

Owen, A. M., Roberts, A. C., Hodges, J. R., Summers, A. B. A., Polkey, C. E., & Robbins, T. W. (1993). Contrasting mechanisms of impaired attentional set-shifting in patients with frontal lobe damage or Parkinson's disease. *Brain, 116*(5), 1159–1175.

Owen, A. M., Roberts, A. C., Polkey, C. E., Sahakian, B. J., & Robbins, T. W. (1991). Extra-dimensional versus intra-dimensional set shifting performance following frontal lobe excisions, temporal lobe excisions or amygdalo-hippocampectomy in man. *Neuropsychologia, 29,* 993–1006.

Packard, M. G., & McGaugh, J. L. (1996). Inactivation of hippocampus or caudate nucleus with lidocaine differentially affects expression of place and response learning. *Neurobiology of Learning and Memory, 65*(1), 65–72.

Page, J. B., Fletcher, J., & True, W. R. (1988). Psychosocial perspectives on chronic cannabis use: The Costa Rican follow-up. *Journal of Psychoactive Drugs, 20,* 57–65.

Pall, E. (1995, September 24). Starting from scratch. *The New York Times Magazine,* pp. 39–43.

Paller, K. A., Kutas, M., & Mayes, R. A. R. (1987). Neural correlates of encoding in an incidental learning paradigm. *Electroencephalography and Clinical Neurophysiology, 67*(4), 360–371.

Panting, A., & Merry, P. (1972). The long term rehabilitation of severe head injuries with particular reference to the need for social and medical support for the patient's family. *Rehabilitation, 38,* 33–37.

Papagno, C., della Sala, S. D., & Basso, A. (1993). Ideomotor apraxia without aphasia and aphasia without apraxia: The anatomical support for a double dissociation. *Journal of Neurology, Neurosurgery and Psychiatry, 56,* 286–289.

Papanicolaou, A. C., Moore, B. D., Deutsch, G., Levin, H. S., & Eisenberg, H. M. (1988). Evidence for right-hemisphere involvement in recovery from aphasia. *Archives of Neurology, 45,* 1025–1029.

Papez, J. W. (1937). A proposed mechanism of emotion. *Archives of Neurological Psychiatry, 38,* 725–743.

Paradis, A. L., Cornilleau-Peres, V., Droulez, J., Van de Moortele, P. F., Lobel, E., Berthoz, A., Le Bihan, D., & Poline, J. B. (2000). Visual perception of motion and 3-D structure from motion: An fMRI study. *Cerebral Cortex, 10*(3), 772–783.

Paradis, M. (1977). Bilingualism and aphasia. In H. Whitaker & H. A. Whitaker (Eds.), *Studies in neurolinguistics* (pp. 65–122). New York: Academic Press.

Paradis, M. (1990). Language lateralization in bilinguals: Enough already! *Brain and Language, 39,* 576–586.

Paradis, M. (1992). The Loch Ness Monster approach to bilingual language lateralization: A response to Berquier and Ashton. *Brain and Language, 43,* 534–537.

Paradis, M., Goldblum, M. C., & Abidi, R. (1982). Alternate antagonism with paradoxical translation behavior in two bilingual aphasic patients. *Brain and Language, 15,* 55–69.

Paradis, M., Hagiwara, H., & Hildebrandt, N. (1985). *Neurolinguistic aspects of the Japanese writing system.* New York: Academic Press.

Paradiso, S., Lamberty, G. J., Garvey, M. J., & Robinson, R. G. (1997). Cognitive impairment in the euthymic phase of chronic unipolar depression. *Journal of Nervous and Mental Disease, 185,* 748–754.

Pardo, J. V., Fox, P. T., & Raichle, M. E. (1991). Localization of a human system for sustained attention by positron emission tomography. *Nature, 349,* 61–64.

Pardo, J. V., Pardo, P. J., Janer, K. W., & Raichle, M. E. (1990). The anterior cingulate cortex mediates processing selection in the Stroop attentional conflict paradigm.

Proceedings of the National Academy of Science, USA, 87, 256–259.

Parkin, A. J. (1987). *Memory and amnesia.* Oxford, England: Basil Blackwell.

Parkin, A. J. (1996). Focal retrograde amnesia: A multi-faceted disorder? *Acta Neurological Belgica, 96*(1), 43–50.

Parkin, A. J., Walter, B. M., & Hunkin, N. M. (1995). Relationships between normal aging, frontal lobe function, and memory for temporal and spatial information. *Neuropsychology, 9*, 304–312.

Parnetti, L., Senin, U., & Mecocci, P. (1997). Cognitive enhancement therapy for Alzheimer's disease. *Drugs, 53*, 752–768.

Parsons, O. A., Butters, N., & Nathan, P. (Eds.). (1987). *Neuropsychology of alcoholism: Implications for diagnosis and treatment.* New York: Guilford Press.

Parsons, O. A., & Farr, S. P. (1981). The neuropsychology of alcohol and drug use. In S. B. Filskov & T. J. Boll (Eds.), *Handbook of clinical neuropsychology* (pp. 320–365). New York: Wiley.

Pascual-Leone, A., Gates, J. R., & Dhuna, A. (1991). Induction of speech arrest and counting errors with rapid rate transcranial magnetic stimulation. *Neurology, 41*, 697–702.

Pascual-Leone, A., Grafman, J., Clark, K., Stewart, M., Massaquoi, S., Lou, J. S., & Hallett, M. (1993). Procedural learning in Parkinson's disease and cerebellar degeneration. *Annals of Neurology, 34(4)*, 594–602.

Passingham, R. E., Perry, V. H., & Wilkinson, F. (1983). The long-term effects of removal of sensorimotor cortex in infant and adult rhesus monkeys. *Brain, 106*, 675–705.

Patel, A. J. (1983). Undernutrition and brain development. *Trends in Neurosciences, 6*(4), 151–154.

Patterson, K. (1982). Reading and phonological coding. In A. W. Ellis (Ed.), *Normality and pathology in cognitive functions* (pp. 77–112). New York: Academic Press.

Patterson, K. E., & Kay, J. (1982). Letter-by-letter reading: Psychological descriptions of a neurological syndrome. *Quarterly Journal of Experimental Psychology, 34A*, 411–441.

Patterson, K. E., Seidenberg, M. S., & McClelland, J. L. (1989). Connections and disconnections: Acquired dyslexia in a computational model of reading processes. In R. G. M. Morris (Ed.), *Parallel distributed processing: Implications for psychology and neurobiology* (pp. 131–181). Oxford, England: Oxford University Press.

Paulesu, E., Frith, C. D., & Frackowiak, R. S. J. (1993). The neural correlates of the verbal component of working memory [see comments]. *Nature, 362*, 342–345. Comment in *Nature, 363*, 583–584.

Paulesu, E., Frith, U., Snowling, M., Gallagher, A., Morton, J., Frackowiak, R. S. J., & Frith, C. D. (1996). Is developmental dyslexia a disconnection syndrome? Evidence from PET scanning. *Brain, 119*, 143–157.

Paus, T. (1996). Location and function of the human frontal eye-field: A selective review. *Neuropsychologia, 34*, 475–483.

Paus, T., Collins, D. L., Evans, A. C., Pike, L. B., & Zijdenbos, A. (2001). Maturation of white matter in the human brain: A review of magnetic resonance studies. *Brain Research Bulletin, 54*, 255–266.

Paus, T., Jech, R., Thompson, C. J., Comeau, R., Peters, T., & Evans, A. (1997). Transcranial magnetic stimulation during positron emission tomography: A new method for studying connectivity of the human cerebral cortex. *Journal of Neuroscience, 17*, 3178–3184.

Paus, T., Kalina, M., Patockova, L., Angerova, Y., Cerny, R., Mecir, P., Bauer, J., & Krabec, P. (1991). Medial versus lateral frontal lobe lesions and differential impairment of central-gaze fixation maintenance in man. *Brain, 114*, 2051–2067.

Paus, T., Koski, L., Caramanos, Z., & Westbury, C. (1998). Regional differences in the effects of task difficulty and motor output on blood flow response in the human anterior cingulate cortex: A review of 107 PET activation studies. *NeuroReport, 9*, R37–R47.

Paus, T., Petrides, M., Evans, A. C., & Meyer, E. (1993). Role of the human anterior cingulate cortex in the control of oculomotor, manual, and speech responses: A positron emission tomography study. *Journal of Neurophysiology, 70*, 1–18.

Paus, T., Zatorre, R. J., Hofle, N., Caramanos, Z., Gotman, J., Petrides, M., & Evans, A. C. (1997). Time-related changes in neural systems underlying attention and arousal during the performance of an auditory vigilance task. *Journal of Cognitive Neuroscience, 9*, 392–408.

Pavlides, C., & Winson, J. (1989). Influences of hippocampal place cell firing in the awake state on the activity of these cells during subsequent sleep episodes. *Journal of Neuroscience, 9*(8), 2907–2918.

Payne, B. R., & Cornwell, P. (1994). System-wide repercussions of damage to the immature visual cortex. *Trends in Neurosciences, 17*(3), 126–130.

Pedersen, J. R., Johannsen, P., Bak, C. K., Kofoed, B., Saermark, K., & Gjedde, A. (1998). Origin of human motor readiness field linked to left middle frontal gyrus by MEG and PET. *NeuroImage, 8*, 214–220.

Pell, M. D. (1999). Fundamental frequency encoding of linguistic and emotional prosody by right hemisphere-damaged speakers. *Brain and Language, 69*, 161–192.

Pell, M. D., & Baum, S. R. (1997). The ability to perceive and comprehend intonation in linguistic and affective contexts by brain-damaged adults. *Brain and Language, 57*, 80–99.

Pelosi, L., Slade, T., Blumhardt, L. D., & Sharma, V. K. (2000). Working memory dysfunction in major depression: An event-related potential study. *Clinical Neurophysiology, 111*, 1531–1543.

Penfield, W., & Perot, P. (1963). The brain's record of auditory and visual experience. *Brain, 86*, 595–696.

Penfield, W., & Rasmussen, T. (1950). *The cerebral cortex of man: A clinical study of localization of function.* New York: Macmillan.

Pennington, B., Puck, M., & Robinson, A. (1980). Language and cognitive development in 47, XXX females followed since birth. *Behavior Genetics, 10*, 31–41.

Pennington, B. F., Lefly, D. L., Van Orden, G. C., Bookman, M. O., & Smith, S. D. (1987). Is phonology bypassed in normal or dyslexic development? *Annals of Dyslexia, 37*, 62–89.

Perani, D., Cappa, S. F., Bettinardi, V., Bressi, S., Gorno-Tempini, M., Matarrese, M., & Fazio, F. (1995). Different neural systems for the recognition of animals and man-made tools. *NeuroReport, 6,* 1637–1641.

Perani, D., Dehaene, S., Grassi, F., Cohen, L., Cappa, S. F., Dupoux, E., Fazio, F., & Mehler, J. (1996). Brain processing of native and foreign languages. *NeuroReport, 7,* 2439–2444.

Perani, D., Paulesu, E., Galles, N. S., Dupoux, E., Dehaene, S., Bettinardi, V., Cappa, S. F., Fazio, F., & Mehler, J. (1998). The bilingual brain: Proficiency and age of acquisition of the second language. *Brain, 121,* 1841–1852.

Perrett, D. I., & Mistlin, A. J. (1990). Perception of facial attributes. In W. C. Stebbins, & M. A. Berkley (Eds.), *Comparative perception, complex signals, Vol. 2* (pp. 187–215). New York: Wiley.

Perrett, D. I., Mistlin, A. J., & Chitty, A. J. (1987). Visual neurones responsive to faces. *Trends in Neurosciences, 10,* 358–364.

Perrett, D. I., Smith, P. A. J., Potter, D. D., Mistlin, A. J., Head, A. S., Milner, A. D., & Jeeves, M. A. (1985). Visual cells in the temporal cortex sensitive to face view and gaze direction. *Proceedings of the Royal Society of London, B, 223,* 293–317.

Perrine, K., & Kiolbasa, T. (1999). Cognitive deficits in epilepsy and contribution to psychopathology. *Neurology, 53*(Suppl. 2), S39–S48.

Perry, E. K., Tomlinson, B. E., & Blessed, G. (1978). Correlation of cholinergic abnormalities with senile plaques and mental test scores in senile dementia. *British Medical Journal, 2,* 1457–1459.

Perry, N., Court, G., Bidet, N., & Court, J. (1996). European herbs with cholinergic activities: Potential in dementia therapy. *International Journal of Geriatric Psychiatry, 11,* 1063–1069.

Persson, P. G., & Allebeck, P. (1994). Do left-handers have increased mortality? *Epidemiology, 5,* 337–340.

Peterson, B. S., Leckman, J. F., Scahill, L., Naftolin, F., Keege, D., Charest, N. J., & Cohen, D. J. (1992). Hypothesis: Steroid hormones and sexual dimorphisms modulate symptom expression in TS. *Psychoneuroendocrinology, 17,* 553–563.

Petersen, M. R., Zoloth, S. R., Beecher, M. D., Green, S., Marler, P. R., Moody, D. B., & Provins, K. A. (1997). Handedness and speech: A critical reappraisal of the role of genetic and environmental factors in the cerebral lateralization of function. *Psychological Review, 104,* 554–571.

Petersen, S. E., Fox, P. T., Posner, M. I., Mintun, M., & Raichle, M. E. (1988). Positron emission tomographic studies of the cortical anatomy of single-word processing. *Nature, 331,* 585–589.

Petersen, S. E., Fox, P. T., Posner, M. I., Mintun, M., & Raichel, M. E. (1989). Positron emission tomography studies of the processing of single words. *Journal of Cognitive Neuroscience, 1,* 153–170.

Petersen, S. E., Fox, P. T., Snyder, A. Z., & Raichle, M. E. (1990). Activation of extrastriate and frontal cortical areas by visual words and word-like stimuli. *Science, 249,* 1041–1044.

Petito, L. A., Zatorre, R. J., Gauna, K., Nikelski, E. J., Dostie, D., & Evans, A. C. (2000). Speech-like cerebral activity in profoundly deaf people processing signed languages: Implications for the neural basis of human language. *Proceedings of the National Academy of Sciences, USA, 97,* 13961–13966.

Petrides, M. (1995). Functional organization of the human frontal cortex for mnemonic processing. In J. Grafman, & K. J. Holyoak (Eds.), *Structure and functions of the human prefrontal cortex* (pp. 85–96). New York: New York Academy of Sciences.

Petrides, M. (2000). The role of the mid-dorsolateral prefrontal cortex in working memory. *Experimental Brain Research, 133,* 44–54.

Petrides, M., & Milner, B. (1982). Deficits on subject-ordered tasks after frontal- and temporal-lobe lesions in man. *Neuropsychologia, 20,* 249–262.

Petruzzello, S. J., & Landers, D. M. (1994). State anxiety reduction and exercise: Does hemispheric activation reflect such changes? *Medicine and Science in Sports and Exercise, 26,* 1028–1035.

Pettinati, H. M. (1988). *Hypnosis and memory.* New York: Guilford Press.

Peyser, J. M., & Poser, C. M. (1986). Neuropsychological correlates of multiple sclerosis. In S. B. Filskov & T. J. Boll (Eds.), *Handbook of clinical neuropsychology* (pp. 364–398). New York: Wiley.

Phelps, E. A., O'Connor, K. J., Cunningham, W. A., Funayama, E. S., Gatenby, J. C., Gore, J. C., & Banaji, M. R. (2000). Performance on indirect measures of race evaluation predicts amygdala activation. *Journal of Cognitive Neuroscience, 12,* 729–738.

Phelps, E. A., O'Connor, K. J., Gatenby, J. C., Gore, J. C., Grillon, C., & Davis, M. (2001). Activation of the left amygdala to a cognitive representation of fear. *Nature Neuroscience, 4,* 437–441.

Phillips, J. G., Bradshaw, J. L., Iansek, R., & Chiu, E. (1993). Motor functions of the basal ganglia. *Psychological Research, 55,* 175–181.

Pigott, S., & Milner, B. (1993). Memory for different aspects of complex visual scenes after unilateral temporal- or frontal-lobe resection. *Neuropsychologia, 31,* 1–15.

Pigott, S., & Milner, B. (1994). Capacity of visual short-term memory after unilateral frontal or anterior temporal-lobe resection. *Neuropsychologia, 32, 969–981.*

Pillon, B., Deweer, B., Agid, Y., & Dubois, B. (1993). Explicit memory in Alzheimer's, Huntington's, and Parkinson's diseases. *Archives of Neurology, 50,* 374–379.

Pinek, B., Duhamel, J.-R., Cave, C., & Brouchon, M. (1989). Audio-spatial deficits in humans: Differential effects associated with left versus right hemisphere parietal damage. *Cortex, 25,* 175–186.

Pizzamiglio, L., Zoccolotti, P., Mammucari, A., & Cesaroni, R. (1983). The independence of face identity and facial expression recognition mechanisms: Relation to sex and cognitive style. *Brain and Cognition, 2,* 176–188.

Plaut, D. C. (in press). Connectionist modeling of language: Examples and implications. In M. T. Banich, & M. Mack (Eds.), *Mind, brain, & language: Multidisciplinary perspectives.* Mahwah, NJ: Lawrence Erlbaum Associates.

Plaut, D. C., & Farah, M. J. (1990). Visual object representation: Interpreting neurophysiological data within a computational framework. *Journal of Cognitive Neuroscience, 2,* 320–343.

Plum, F., & Posner, J. B. (1980). *The diagnosis of stupor and coma* (3rd ed.). Philadelphia: F A Davis.

Poeck, K. (1986). The clinical examination for motor apraxia. *Neuropsychologia, 24,* 129–134.

Poeck, K., & Lehmkuhl, G. (1980). Das Syndrom der ideatorischen Apraxie und seine Localisation. *Nervenarzt, 51,* 217–225.

Pohl, W. (1973). Dissociation of spatial discrimination deficits following frontal and parietal lesions in monkeys. *Journal of Comparative and Physiological Psychology, 82,* 227–239.

Poirier, P., Lassonde, M., Villemure, J.-G., Geoffroy, G., & Lepore, F. (1994). Sound localization in hemispherectomized patients. *Neuropsychologia, 32,* 541–553.

Poizner, H., Klima, E. S., & Bellugi, U. (1987). *What the hands reveal about the brain.* Cambridge, MA: MIT Press.

Poldrack, R. A., Clark, J., Pare-Blagoev, E. J., Shohamy, D., Moyano, J. C., Myers, C., & Gluck, M. A. (2001). Interactive memory systems in the human brain. *Nature, 414*(6863), 546–550.

Poldrack, R. A., Desmond, J. E., Glover, G. H., & Gabrieli, J. D. (1998). The neural basis of visual skill learning: An fMRI study of mirror reading. *Cerebral Cortex 8*(1), 1–10.

Poldrack, R. A., & Gabrieli, J. D. (1998). Memory and the brain: What's right and what's left? *Cell, 93*(7), 1091–1093.

Poldrack, R. A., & Gabrieli, J. D. (2001). Characterizing the neural mechanisms of skill learning and repetition priming: Evidence from mirror reading. *Brain, 124*(Pt 1), 67–82.

Poldrack R. A., Prabhakaran V., Seger, C. A., & Gabrieli, J. D. E. (1999). Striatal activation during acquisition of a cognitive skill. *Neuropsychology, 13,* 564–574.

Pollitt, E. (1996). Timing and vulnerability in research on malnutrition and cognition. *Nutrition Research, 54,* S49–S55.

Polson, M. C., & Friedman, A. (1988). Task-sharing within and between hemispheres: A multiple-resources approach. *Human Factors, 30,* 633–643.

Pope, H. G., Gruber, A. J., & Yurgelun-Todd, T. D. (1995). The residual neuropsychological effects of cannabis: The current status of research. *Drug and Alcohol Dependence, 38,* 25–34.

Posner, M. I. (1973). *Cognition: An introduction.* Glenview, IL: Scott, Foresman.

Posner, M. I. (1980). Orienting of attention. *Quarterly Journal of Experimental Psychology, 32,* 3–25.

Posner, M. I. (1992). Attention as a cognitive and neural system. *Current Directions in Psychological Science, 1,* 11–14.

Posner, M. I., & DiGirolamo, G. J. (1998). Executive attention: Conflict, target detection, and cognitive control. In R. Parasuraman (Ed), *The attentive brain* (pp. 401–423). Cambridge, MA: The MIT Press.

Posner, M. I., Inhoff, A. W., Friedrich, F. J., & Cohen, A. (1987). Isolating attentional systems: A cognitive-anatomical analysis. *Psychobiology, 15,* 107–121.

Posner, M. I., & McCandliss, B. D. (1993). Converging methods for investigating lexical access. *Psychological Science, 4,* 305–309.

Posner, M. I., & Petersen, S. E. (1990). The attention system of the human brain. *Annual Review of Neuroscience, 13,* 25–42.

Posner, M. I., Petersen, S. E., Fox, P. T., & Raichle, M. E. (1988). Localization of cognitive operations in the human brain. *Science, 240,* 1627–1631.

Posner, M. I., & Raichle, M. E. (1994). *Images of mind.* New York: Freeman.

Posner, M. I., Sandson, J., Dhawan, M., & Shulman, G. L. (1989). Is word recognition automatic? *Journal of Cognitive Neuroscience, 1,* 50–60.

Posner, M. I., Walker, J. A., Friedrich, F. J., & Rafal, R. D. (1984). Effects of parietal injury on covert orienting of attention. *The Journal of Neuroscience, 4,* 1863–1874.

Postle, R. B. R., Jonides, J., Smith, E. E., Corkin, S., Growdon, J. H. (1997). Spatial, but not object, delayed response is impaired in early Parkinson's disease. *Neuropsychology, 11,* 171–179.

Potts, G. F., Liotti, M., Tucker, D. M., & Posner, M. I. (1996) Frontal and inferior temporal cortical activity in visual target detection: Evidence from high spatially sampled event-related potentials. *Brain Topography, 9*(1), 3–14.

Powell, J. W. & Barber-Foss, K. D. (1999). Traumatic brain injury in high school athletes. *Journal of the American Medical Association, 282,* 958–963.

Price, C. J. (1998). The functional anatomy of word comprehension and production. *Trends in Cognitive Sciences, 2,* 281–288.

Price, C. J., Moore, C. J., Humphreys, G. W., Wise, R. J. S. (1997). Segregating semantic from phonological processes during reading. *Journal of Cognitive Neuroscience, 9,* 727–733.

Price, C. J., Wise, R. J. S., & Frackowiak, R. S. J. (1996). Demonstrating the implicit processing of visually presented words and pseudowords. *Cerebral Cortex, 6,* 62–70.

Price, C. J., Wise, R. J. S., Watson, J. D. G., Patterson, K., Howard, D., & Frackowiak, R. S. J. (1994). Brain activity during reading: The effects of exposure duration and task. *Brain, 117,* 1255–1269.

Prigatano, G. P. (1991). Disturbances of self-awareness of deficit after traumatic brain injury. In G. P. Prigatano & D. L. Schacter (Eds.), *Awareness of deficit after brain injury* (pp. 111–126). Oxford, England: Oxford University Press.

Prigatano, G. P., Altman, I. M., & O'Brien, K. P. (1990). Behavioral limitations that traumatic-brain-injured patients tend to underestimate. *Clinical Neuropsychologist, 4,* 163–176.

Prigatano, G. P., & Schacter, D. L. (1991) *Awareness of deficit after brain injury.* Oxford, England: Oxford University Press.

Provins, K. A. (1997). Handedness and speech: A critical reappraisal of the role of genetic and environmental factors in the cerebral lateralization of function. *Psychological Review, 104,* 554–571.

Ptito, A., & Zatorre, R. J. (1988). Impaired stereoscopic detection thresholds after left or right temporal lobectomy. *Neuropsychologia, 26,* 547–554.

Ptito, A., Zatorre, R. J., Petrides, M., Frey, S., Alivisatos, B. & Evans, A. C. (1993). Localization and lateralization of stereoscopic processing in the human brain. *Neuroreport, 4,* 1155–1158.

Puce, A., & Allison, T. (1999). Differential processing of mobile and static faces by temporal cortex. *NeuroImage, 9,* S801.

Pugh, K. R., Shaywitz, B. A., Shaywitz, S. E., Constable, R. T., Skudlarksi, P., Fulbright, R. K., Bronen, R. A., Shankweiler, D. P., Katz, L., Fletcher, J. M., & Gore, J. C. (1996). Cerebral organization for component processes in reading. *Brain, 119,* 1221–1238.

Purves, D., Augustine, G. J., Fitzpatrick, D., Katz, L. C., La Mantia, A. S., McNamara, J. O., & Williams, S. M. (2001). *Neuroscience* (2nd ed.). Sunderland MA: Sinauer Associates Inc.

Pylyshyn, Z. W. (1973). What the mind's eye tells the mind's brain: A critique of mental imagery. *Psychological Bulletin, 80,* 1–24.

Pylyshyn, Z. W. (1981). The imagery debate: Analogue media versus tacit knowledge. *Psychological Review, 87,* 16–45.

Qian, N. (1995). Generalization and analysis of the Lisberger-Sejnowski VOR model. *Neural Computation, 7*(4), 735–752.

Rabinowicz, T., Courten-Myers, G., Petetot, J., Xi, G., & Los Reyes, E. (1996). Human cortex development: Estimates of neuronal numbers indicate major loss during gestation. *Journal of Neuropathology and Experimental Neurology, 55,* 320–328.

Rafal, R., & Posner, M. I. (1987). Deficits in human visual spatial attention following thalamic lesions. *Proceedings of the National Academy of Sciences, USA, 84,* 7349–7353.

Rafal, R. D., Posner, M. I., Friedman, J. H., Inhoff, A. W., & Bernstein, E. (1988). Orienting of visual attention in progressive supranuclear palsy. *Brain, 111,* 267–280.

Raichle, M., Fiez, J., Videen, T. O., MacLeod, A. M. K., Pardo, J. V., Fox, P. T., & Petersen, S. E. (1994). Practice-related changes in human brain functional anatomy during nonmotor learning. *Cerebral Cortex, 4,* 8–26.

Raichle, M. E. (1994). Images of the mind: Studies with modern imaging techniques. *Annual Review of Psychology, 45,* 333–356.

Raichle, M. E., Fiez, J. A., Videen, T. O., MacLeod, A.-M. K., Pardo, J. V., Fox, P. T., & Petersen, S. E. (1994). Practice-related changes in human brain functional anatomy during nonmotor learning. *Cerebral Cortex, 4*(1), 8–26.

Rakie, P. (1981). Developmental events leading to laminar and areal organization of the neocortex. In F. O. Schmitt, F. G. Worden, G. Adelman, & S. G. Dennis (Eds.), *The organization of the cerebral cortex* (pp. 7–28). Cambridge, MA: MIT Press.

Rakic, P. (1991). Plasticity of cortical development. In S. E. Brauth, W. S. Hall, & R. J. Dooling (Eds.), *Plasticity of development* (pp. 127–161). Cambridge, MA: MIT Press.

Ramachandran, V. S., Rogers-Ramachandran, D., & Steward, M. (1992). Perceptual correlates of massive cortical reorganization. *Science, 258,* 1159–1160.

Randolph, C., Braun, A. R., Goldberg, T. E., & Chase, T. N. (1993). Semantic fluency in Alzheimer's, Parkinson's and Huntington's disease: Dissocation of storage and retrieval failures. *Neuropsychology, 7,* 82–88.

Ranganath, C., & D'Esposito, M. (2001). Medial temporal lobe activity associated with active maintenance of novel information. *Neuron, 31*(5), 865–873.

Rao, S. (1986). Neuropsychology of multiple sclerosis: A critical review. *Journal of Clinical and Experimental Neuropsychology, 8,* 503–542.

Rao, S. C., Rainer, G., & Miller, E. K. (1997). Integration of what and where in the primate prefrontal cortex. *Science, 276*(5313), 821–824.

Rao, S. M., Huber, S. J., & Bornstein, R. A. (1992). Emotional changes with multiple sclerosis and Parkinson's disease. *Journal of Consulting and Clinical Psychology, 60,* 369–378.

Rao, S. M., Leo, G. J., Bernardin, L., & Unverzagt, F. (1991). Cognitive dysfunction in multiple sclerosis: 1. Frequency, patterns, and prediction. *Neurology, 41,* 685–691.

Rao, S. M., Leo, G. J., Haughton, V. M., St. Aubin-Faubert, P., & Bernardin, L. (1989). Correlation of magnetic resonance imaging with neuropsychological testing in multiple sclerosis. *Neurology, 39,* 161–166.

Rapesak, S. Z., Cimino, C. R., & Heilman, K. M. (1988). Altitudinal neglect. *Neurology, 38,* 277–281.

Rapin, I., Allen, D. A., & Dunn, M. A. (1992). Developmental language disorders. In S. J. Segalowitz & I. Rapin (Eds.), *Handbook of neuropsychology: Vol. 7. Child Neuropsychology* (pp. 111–137). New York: Elsevier.

Rapoport, J. L. (1990). Obsessive compulsive disorder and basal ganglia dysfunction. *Psychological Medicine, 20,* 465–469.

Raskin, S. A., Borod, J. C., & Tweedy, J. (1990). Neuropsychological aspects of Parkinson's disease. *Neuropsychology Review, 1,* 185–221.

Rasmussen, T., & Milner, B. (1977a). The role of early left-brain injury in determining lateralization of cerebral speech function. *Annals of the New York Academy of Sciences, 299,* 355–369.

Rasmussen, T., & Milner, B. (1977b). The role of early left-brain injury in determining lateralization of cerebral speech functions. In S. Dimond & D. Blizzard (Eds.), *Evolution and lateralization of function in the brain.* New York: New York Academy of Sciences.

Ratcliff, G. (1979). Spatial thought, mental rotation and the right cerebral hemisphere. *Neuropsychologia, 17,* 49–54.

Ratcliff, G., & Davies-Jones, G. A. B. (1972). Defective visual localization in focal brain wounds. *Brain, 95,* 49–60.

Ratcliff, G., Dila, C., Taylor, L., & Milner, B. (1980). The morphological asymmetry of the hemispheres and cerebral dominance for speech: A possible relationship. *Brain and Language, 11,* 87–98.

Ratcliff, G., & Newcombe, F. (1973). Spatial orientation in man: Effects of left, right, and bilateral cerebral lesions. *Journal of Neurology, Neurosurgery and Psychiatry, 36,* 448–454.

Ratcliff, G., & Newcombe, F. (1982). Object recognition: Some deductions from the clinical evidence. In A. W. Ellis (Ed.), *Normality and pathology in cognitive functions* (pp. 147–171). London: Academic Press.

Rattok, J., Ben-Yishay, Y., Ezrachi, O., Lakin, P., Piasetsky, E., Ross, B., Silver, S., Vakil, E., Zide, E., & Diller, L. (1992). Outcome of different treatment mixes in a multidimensional neuropsychological rehabilitation program. *Neuropsychology, 6,* 395–415.

Rayman, J., & Zaidel, E. (1991). Rhyming and the right hemisphere. *Brain and Language, 40,* 89–105.

Raz, S. (1993). Structural cerebral pathology in schizophrenia: Regional or diffuse? *Journal of Abnormal Psychology, 102,* 445–452.

Raz, N., Torres, I. J., Spencer, W. D., Baertschie, J. C., Millman, D., & Sarpel, G. (1993). Neuroanatomical correlates of age-sensitive and age-invariant cognitive abilities: An in vivo MRI investigation. *Intelligence, 17,* 407–422.

Recanzone, G. H., Merzenich, M. M., & Jenkins, W. M. (1992). Frequency discrimination training engaging a restricted skin surface results in an emergence of a cutaneous response zone in cortical area 3a. *Journal of Neurophysiology, 67*(5), 1071–1091.

Recanzone, G. H., Schreiner, C. E., & Merzenich, M. M. (1993). Plasticity in the frequency representation of primary auditory cortex following discrimination training in adult owl monkeys. *Journal of Neuroscience, 13*(1), 87–103.

Reed, C. L., & Caselli, R. J. (1994). The nature of tactile agnosia: A case study. *Neuropsychologia, 32,* 527–539.

Reed, C. L., Caselli, R. J., & Farah, M. J. (1996). Tactile agnosia: Underlying impairment and implications for normal tactile recognition. *Brain, 199,* 875–888.

Rees, G., Frith, C. D., & Lavie, N. (1997). Modulating irrelevant motion perception by varying attentional load in an unrelated task. *Science, 278,* 1616–1619.

Rees, G., Wojciulik, E., Clarke, K., Husain, M., Frith, C., & Driver, J. (2000). Unconscious activation of visual cortex in the damaged right hemisphere of a parietal patient with extinction. *Brain, 123,* 1624–1633.

Reed, J. M., & Squire, L. R. (1998). Retrograde amnesia for facts and events: Findings from four new cases. *Journal of Neuroscience, 18*(10), 3943–3954.

Rehak, A., Kaplan, J. A., & Gardner, H. (1992). Sensitivity to conversational deviance in right-hemisphere-damaged patients. *Brain and Language, 42,* 203–217.

Reidy, T. J., Bowler, R. M., Rauch, S. S., & Pedroza, G. I. (1992). Pesticide exposure and neuropsychological impairment in migrant farm workers. *Archives of Clinical Neuropsychology, 7,* 85–95.

Reiman, E. M., Fusselman, M. J., Fox, P. T., & Raichle, M. E. (1989). Neuroanatomical correlates of anticipatory anxiety. *Science, 243,* 1071–1074.

Reiman, E. M., Raichle, M. E., Butler, F. K., Herscovitch, P., & Robins, E. (1984). A focal brain abnormality in panic disorder, a severe form of anxiety. *Nature, 310,* 683–685.

Reisberg, B. (1986). Dementia: A systematic approach to identifying reversible causes. *Geriatrics, 41,* 30–46.

Reisberg, B., Ferris, S. H., deLeon, M. J., & Crook, T. (1988). Global Deterioration Scale (GDS). *Psychopharmacology Bulletin, 24,* 661–663.

Reisberg, B., Ferris, S. H., deLeon, M. J., Kluger, A., Franssen, E., Borenstein, J., & Alba, R. C. (1989). The stage-specific temporal course of Alzheimer's disease: Functional and behavioral concomitants based upon cross-sectional and longitudinal observation. *Progress in Clinical and Biological Research, 317,* 23–41.

Reisenhuber, M., & Poggio, T. (2000). Models of object recognition. *Nature Neuroscience, 3,* 1199–1204.

Reiss, A. L., Abrams, M. T., Singer, H. S., Ross, J. L., & Denckla, M. B. (1996). Brain development, gender and IQ in children. A volumetric imaging study. *Brain, 119,* 1763–1774.

Reist, C., Duffy, J. G., Fujimoto, K., & Cahill, L. (2001). Beta-Adrenergic blockade and emotional memory in PTSD. *International Journal Neuropsychopharmacology, 4,* 377–383.

Reite, M., Adams, M., Simon, J., Teale, P., Sheeder, J., Richardson, D., & Grabbe, R. (1994). Auditory M100 component 1: Relationship to Heschl's gyri. *Cognitive Brain Research, 2,* 13–20.

Reite, M., Sheeder, J., Teale, P., Adams, M., Richardson, D., Simon, J., Jones, R., & Rojas, D. (1997). Magnetic source imaging evidence of sex differences in cerebral lateralization in schizophrenia. *Archives of General Psychiatry, 54,* 433–440.

Rettenback, R., Diller, G., & Siretcanu, R. (1999). Do deaf people see better? Texture segmentation and visual search compensate in adult but not in juvenile subjects. *Journal of Cognitive Neuroscience, 11,* 560–583.

Reuter-Lorenz, P. A., & Brunn, J. L. (1990). A pre-lexical basis for letter-by-letter reading: A case study. *Journal of Cognitive Neuropsychology, 7,* 1–20.

Reuter-Lorenz, P. A., Kinsbourne, M., & Moscovitch, M. (1990). Hemispheric control of spatial attention. *Brain and Cognition, 12,* 240–266.

Reuter-Lorenz, P. A., & Miller, A. C. (1998). The cognitive neuroscience of human laterality: Lessons from the bisected brain. *Current Directions in Psychological Science, 7,* 15–20.

Reuter-Lorenz, P. A., Marshuetz, C., Jones, J., Smith, E. E., Hartley, A., & Koeppe, R. (2001). Neurocognitive ageing of storage and executive processes. *European Journal of Cognitive Psychology, 13,* 257–278.

Reuter-Lorenz, P. A., & Posner, M. I. (1990). Components of neglect from right-hemisphere damage: An analysis of line bisection. *Neuropsychologia, 28,* 327–333.

Reuter-Lorenz, P. A., Stanczak, L. M., & Miller, A. C. (1999). Neural recruitment and cognitive aging: Two hemispheres are better than one, especially as you age. *Psychological Science, 10*(6), 494–500.

Reynolds, C. R., & Fletcher-Jansen, E. (1989). *Handbook of clinical child neuropsychology.* New York: Plenum Press.

Reynolds, J. H., Chelazzi, L., & Desimone, R. (1999). Competitive mechanisms subserve attention in macaque areas V2 and V4. *Journal of Neuroscience, 19,* 1736–1753.

Rhodes, G., Tan, S., Brake, S., & Taylor, K. (1989). Expertise and configural coding in face recognition. *British Journal of Psychology, 80,* 313–331.

Ribot, T. (1881/1882). *Diseases of memory.* New York: Appleton.

Ricciuti, H. N. (1993). Nutrition and mental development. *Current Directions in Psychological Science, 2,* 43–46.

Rice, D. P., Kelman, S., & Miller, L. S. (1991). The economic cost of alcohol abuse. *Alcohol Health and Research World, 15*(4), 307–316.

Richardson, G. A., Conroy, M. L., & Day, N. L. (1996). Prenatal cocaine exposure: Effects on the development of school-age children. *Neurotoxicology and Teratology, 18,* 627–634.

Richardson-Klaven, A., & Bjork, R. A. (1988). Measures of memory. *Annual Review of Psychology, 39,* 475–543.

Richter, W., Somorjai, R., Summers, R., Jarmasz, M., Menon, R. S., Gati, J. S., Georgopoulos, A. P., Tegeler, C., Ugurbil, K., & Kim, S. G. (2000). Motor area activity during mental rotation studied by time-resolved single-trial fMRI. *Journal of Cognitive Neuroscience, 12*(2), 310–20.

Riddoch, M. J., & Humphreys, G. W. (1983). The effect of cueing on unilateral neglect. *Neuropsychologia, 21,* 589–599.

Riedel, W. M., Klaassen, T., Deutz, N. E. P., van Someren, A., & van Praag, H. M. (1999) Tryptophan depletion in normal volunteers produces selective impairment in memory consolidation. *Psychopharmacology, 141,* 362–369.

Riesenhuber, M., & Poggio, T. (2000). Models of object recognition. *Nature Neuroscience, 3*(Suppl), 1199–1204.

Ringo, J. L., Doty, R. W., Demeter, S., & Simard, P. Y. (1994). Time is of the essence: A conjecture that hemispheric specialization arises from interhemispheric conduction delay. *Cerebral Cortex, 4,* 331–343.

Riva, D., & Cazzaniga, L. (1986). Late effect of unilateral brain lesions sustained before and after age one. *Neuropsychologia, 24,* 423–428.

Rizzolatti, G., & Arbib, M. A. (1998). Language within our grasp. *Trends in Neurosciences, 21,* 188–194.

Roberts, G. W., Gentleman, S. M., Lynch, A., Murray, L., et al. (1994). β Amyloid protein deposition in the brain after severe head injury: Implications for the pathogenesis of Alzheimer's disease. *Journal of Neurology, Neurosurgery and Psychiatry, 57,* 419–425.

Robertson, L. C., & Ivry, R. (2000). Hemispheric asymmetries: Attention to visual and auditory primitives. *Current Directions in Psychological Science, 9,* 59–63.

Robertson, L. C., & Lamb, M. R. (1991). Neuropsychological contributions to part-whole organization. *Cognitive Psychology, 23,* 299–332.

Robertson, L. C., Lamb, M. R., & Knight, R. T. (1988). Effects of lesions of temporal-parietal junction on perceptual and attentional processing in humans. *Journal of Neuroscience, 8,* 3757–3769.

Robertson, S. D., Zelanznik, H. M., Lantero, D. A., Bojczyk, K. D., Spencer, R. M., Doffin, J. G., & Schneidt, T. (1999). Correlations for timing consistency among tapping and drawing tasks: Evidence against a single timing process for motor control. *Journal of Experimental Psychology: Human Perception and Performance, 25,* 1316–1330.

Robichon, F., & Habib, M. (1998). Abnormal callosal morphology in male adult dyslexics: Relationships to handedness and phonological ability. *Brain & Language, 62,* 127–146.

Robin, D. A., Klouda, G., & Hug, L. N. (1991). Neurogenic disorder of prosody. In M. Cannito & D. Vogel (Eds.), *Treating disordered speech motor control: For clinicians by clinicians* (pp. 241–271). Austin, TX: PRO-ED.

Robin, D. A., Tranel, D., & Damasio, H. (1990). Auditory perception of temporal and spectral events in patients with focal left and right cerebral lesions. *Brain and Language, 39,* 539–555.

Robinson, J. E., Heaton, K. R. K., & O'Malley, S. S. (1999). Neuropsychological functioning in cocaine abusers with and without alcohol dependence. *Journal of the International Neuropsychological Society, 5,* 10–19.

Robinson, R. G., Kubos, K. L., Starr, L. B., Rao, K., & Price, T. R. (1984). Mood disorders in stroke patients. Importance of location of lesion. *Brain, 107,* 81–93.

Robinson, R. G., & Szetela, B. (1981). Mood change following left hemisphere brain injury. *Annals of Neurology, 9,* 447–453.

Rode, G., Charles, N., Perenin, M. T., Vighetoo, A., Trillet, M., & Aimard, G. (1992). Partial remission of hemiplegia and somatoparaphrenia through vestibular stimulation in a case of unilateral neglect. *Cortex, 28*(2), 203–208.

Rodel, M., Cook, N. D., Regard, M., & Landis, T. (1992). Hemispheric dissociation in judging semantic relations: Complementarity for close and distant associates. *Brain and Language, 43,* 448–459.

Roediger, H. L., III. (1990). Implicit memory. Retention without remembering. *American Psychologist, 45*(9), 1043–1056.

Roeltgen, D. P., & Heilman, K. M. (1984). Lexical agraphia: Further support for the two strategy hypothesis of linguistic agraphia. *Brain, 107,* 811–827.

Rogers, R. D., Andrews, T. C., Grasby, P. M., Brooks, D. J., & Robbins, T. W. (2000). Contrasting cortical and subcortical activations produced by attentional-set shifting and reversal learning in humans. *Journal of Cognitive Neuroscience, 12,* 142–162.

Rogers, R. D., & Monsell, S. (1995). Costs of a predictable switch between simple cognitive tasks. *Journal of Experimental Psychology: General, 124,* 207–231.

Rogers, R. D., Sahakian, B. J., Hodges, J. R., Polkey, C. E., Kennard, C., & Robbins, T. W. (1998). Dissociating executive mechanisms of task control following frontal lobe damage and Parkinson's disease. *Brain, 121(5),* 815–842.

Roland, P. E., Larsen, B., Lassen, N. A., & Skinhøj, E. (1980). Supplementary motor area and other cortical areas in organization of voluntary movements in man. *Journal of Neurophysiology, 43,* 118–136.

Rolls, E. T. (1999). *The brain and emotion.* Oxford: Oxford University Press.

Rolls, E. T., Hornak, J., Wade, D., & McGrath, J. (1994). Emotion-related learning in patients with social and emotional changes associated with frontal lobe damage. *Journal of Neurology, Neurosurgery, & Psychiatry, 57,* 1518–1524.

Romani, G. L., Williamson, S. J., & Kaufman, L. (1982). Tonotopic organization of the human auditory cortex. *Science, 216,* 1339–1340.

Roper, S. N., Levesque, M. F., Sutherling, W. W., & Engel, J., Jr. (1993). Surgical treatment of partial epilepsy arising from the insular cortex. Report of two cases. *Journal of Neurosurgery, 79*(2), 266–269.

Rose, F. D. (1988). Environmental enrichment and recovery of function following brain damage in the rat. *Medical Science Research, 16,* 257–263.

Rosenzweig, M. R., Bennett, E. L., & Diamond, M. C. (1972). Brain changes in response to experience. *Scientific American, 226,* 22–29.

Rosenzweig, M. R., & Leiman, A. L. (1989). *Physiological psychology* (2nd ed.). New York: Random House.

Roses, A. D. (2000). Causes or consequences of inflammation and pathological signs of Alzheimer disease. *Neurobiology of Aging, 21,* 423–425.

Ross, C. A., McInnis, M. G., Margolis, R. L., & Li, S. (1993). Genes with triplet repeats: Candidate mediators of neuropsychiatric disorders. *Trends in Neurosciences, 16*(7), 254–260.

Ross, E. D. (1981). The aprosodias: Functional-anatomic organization of the affective components of language in the right hemisphere. *Archives of Neurology, 38,* 561–569.

Ross, E. D., & Mesulam, M.-M. (1979). Dominant language functions of the right hemisphere? Prosody and emotional gesturing. *Archives of Neurology, 36,* 144–148.

Ross, E. D., Orbelo, D. M., Cartwright, J., Hansel, S., Burgard, M., Testa, J. A., & Buck, R. (2001). Affective-prosodic deficits in schizophrenia: Profiles of patients with brain damage and comparison with relation to schizophrenic symptoms. *Journal of Neurology, Neurosurgery, and Psychiatry, 70,* 597–604.

Rourke, B. P., Bakker, D. J., Fisk, J. L., & Strang, J. D. (1983). *Child neuropsychology: An introduction to theory, research, and clinical practice.* New York: Guilford Press.

Rourke, B. P., & Finlayson, M. A. J. (1978). Neuropsychological significance of variations in patterns of academic performance: Verbal and visual-spatial abilities. *Journal of Clinical Neuropsychology, 6,* 121–133.

Rourke, B. P., Young, G. C., Strang, J. D., & Russell, D. L. (1985). Adult outcomes of central processing deficiencies in childhood. In I. Grant & K. M. Adams (Eds.), *Neuropsychological assessment in neuropsychiatric disorder: Clinical methods and empirical findings* (pp. 244–257). New York: Oxford University Press.

Rourke, S. B., Halman, M. H., & Bassel, C. (1999). Neuropsychiatric correlates of memory-metamemory dissociations in HIV infection. *Journal of Clinical and Experimental Neuropsychology, 21,* 757–768.

Rourke, S. B., & Lørberg, T. (1996). The neurobehavioral correlates of alcoholism. In I. Grant, & K. M. Adams (Eds.), *Neuropsychological assessment of neuropsychiatric disorders* (2nd ed.) (pp. 423–485). New York: Oxford University Press.

Rousselle, C., & Wolff, P. H. (1991). The dynamics of bimanual coordination in developmental dyslexia. *Neuropsychologia, 29,* 907–924.

Rovaris, M., & Filippi, M. (2000). MRI correlates of cognitive dysfunction in multiple sclerosis patients. *Journal of Neurovirology, 6*(Suppl. 2). S172–S175.

Rowe, A. D., Bullock, P. R., Polkey, C. E., & Morris, R. G. (2001). 'Theory of mind' impairments and their relationship to executive functioning following frontal lobe excisions. *Brain, 124,* 600–616.

Royet, J.-P., Zald, D., Versace, R., Costes, N., Lavenne, F., Koenig, O., & Gervais, R. (2000). Emotional responses to pleasant and unpleasant olfactory, visual, and auditory stimuli: A positron emission tomography study. *Journal of Neuroscience, 20,* 7752–7759.

Rubens, A. B. (1985). Caloric stimulation and unilateral visual neglect. *Neurology, 35,* 1019–1024.

Rubens, A. B., Geschwind, N., Mahowald, M. W., & Mastri, A. (1977). Posttraumatic cerebral hemispheric disconnection syndrome. *Archives of Neurology, 34,* 750–755.

Rubens, A. B., Mahowald, M. W., & Hutton, J. T. (1976). Asymmetry of lateral (Sylvian) fissure in man. *Neurology, 26,* 620–624.

Rubenstein, J. S. (1993). *Executive control of cognitive processes in task switching.* Unpublished manuscript.

Rubia, K., Overmeyer, S., Taylor, E., Brammer, M., Williams, S. C. R., Simmons, A., & Bullmore, E. T. (1999). Hypofrontality in attention deficit hyperactivity disorder during higher-order motor control: A study with functional MRI. *American Journal of Psychiatry, 156*(6), 891–896.

Rubia, K., Russell, T., Overmeyer, S., Brammer, M. J., Bullmore, E. T., Sharma, T., Simmons, A., Williams, S. C. R., Giampietro, V., Andrew, C. M., & Taylor, E. (2001). Mapping motor inhibition: Conjunctive brain activations across different versions of go/no-go and stop tasks. *NeuroImage, 13,* 250–261.

Rubin, P., Holm, S., Friberg, L., Videbech, P., Andersen, H. S., Bendsen, B. B., Stromso, N., Larsen, J. K., Lassen, N. A., & Hemmingsen, R. (1991). Altered modulation of prefrontal and subcortical brain activity in newly diagnosed schizophrenia and schizophreniform disorder. *Archives of General Psychiatry, 48,* 987–995.

Ruff, R. M., Hersh, N. A., & Pribram, K. H. (1981). Auditory spatial deficits in the personal and extrapersonal frames of reference due to cortical lesions. *Neuropsychologia, 19,* 435–443.

Rugg, M. D., & Coles, M. G. H. (Eds.). (1995). *Electrophysiology of mind: Event-related brain potential and cognition.* New York: Oxford University Press.

Rumsey, J. M., Andreason, P., Zametkin, A. J., Aquino, T., King, A. C., Hamburger, S. D., Pikus, A., Rapoport, J. L., & Cohen, R. M. (1992). Failure to activate the left temporoparietal cortex in dyslexia: An oxygen 15 positron emission tomographic study. *Archives of Neurology, 54,* 1481–1489.

Rumsey, J. M., Horwitz, B., Donohue, B. C., Nace, K. L., Maisog, J. M., & Andreason, P. (1999). A functional lesion in developmental dyslexia: Left angular gyral blood flow predicts severity. *Brain and Language, 70,* 187–204.

Rumsey, J. M., Horwitz, B., Donohue, B. C., Nace, K., Maisog, J. M., & Andreason, P. (1997). Phonological and orthographic components of word recognition: A PET-rCBF study. *Brain, 120,* 739–759.

Rushworth, M. F. S., & Walsh, V. (Eds.) (1999). *Neuropsychologia* (special issue: *TMS in Neuropsychology*), *37*(2), 125–251.

Russell, J. A. (1979). Affective space is bipolar. *Journal of Personality and Social Psychology, 37,* 345–356.

Russell, W. R., & Nathan, P. W. (1946). Traumatic amnesia. *Brain, 68,* 280–300.

Rutten, G. J. M., Ramsey, N. F., van Rijen, P. C., Noordmans, H. J., & van Veelen, C. W. M. (2002). Development of a functional magnetic resonance imaging protocol for intraoperative localization of critical temporoparietal language areas. *Annals of Neurology, 51,* 350–360.

Rutter, M. (1983). Cognitive deficits in the pathogenesis of autism. *Journal of Child Psychology and Psychiatry, 24,* 513–531.

Ryan, J. D., Althoff, R. R., Whitlow, S., & Cohen, N. J. (2000). Amnesia is a deficit in relational memory. *Psychological Science, 11*(6), 454–461.

Rybash, J. M., & Hoyer, W. J. (1992). Hemispheric specialization for categorical and coordinate spatial representation: A reappraisal. *Memory and Cognition, 20,* 271–276.

Sackeim, H. A., Greenberg, M. S., Weiman, A. L., Gur, R. C., Hungerbuhler, J. P., & Geschwind, N. (1982). Hemispheric asymmetry in the expression of positive and negative emotions: Neurological evidence. *Archives of Neurology, 39,* 210–218.

Sackheim, H. A., Gur, R. C., & Saucy, M. C. (1978). Emotions are expressed more intensely on the left side of the face. *Science, 202,* 434.

Sacks, O. (1985). *The man who mistook his wife for a hat.* New York: Summit Books.

Safer, M. A., & Leventhal, H. (1977). Ear differences in evaluating emotional tones of voice and verbal content. *Journal of Experimental Psychology: Human Perception and Performance, 3,* 75–82.

Sagar, H. J., Cohen, N. J., Corkin, S., & Growdon, J. H. (1985). Dissociations among processes in remote memory. *Annals of the New York Academy of Sciences, 444,* 533–535.

Sagar, H. J., Cohen, N. J., Sullivan, E. V., Corkin, S., & Growdon, J. H. (1988). Remote memory function in Alzheimer's disease and Parkinson's disease. *Brain, 111,* 185–206.

Sahakian, B. J., & Coull, J. T. (1994). Nicotine and tetrahroaminoarcridine: Evidence for improved attention in patients with dementia of the Alzheimer's type. *Drug Development Research, 31,* 80–88.

Saito, H. A., Yukic, M., Tanaka, K., Hikosaka, K., Fukada, Y., & Iwai, E. (1986). Integration of direction signals of image motion in the superior temporal sulcus of the macaque monkey macaca-fuscafa. *Journal of Neuroscience, 6,* 147–157.

Sakai, K., & Miyashita, Y. (1991). Neural organization for the long-term memory of paired associates. *Nature, 354,* 152–155.

Sakata, H., Shibutani, H., & Kawano, K. (1983). Functional properties of visual tracking neurons in posterior parietal association cortex of the monkey. *Journal of Neurophysiology, 49,* 1364–1380.

Sakata, H., Shibutani, H., Kawano, K., & Harrington, T. L. (1985). Neural mechanism of space vision in the parietal association cortex of the monkey. *Vision Research, 25,* 453–463.

Sakurai, Y., Momose, T., Iwata, M., Sudo, Y., Ohtomo, K., & Kanazawa, I. (2000). Different cortical activity in reading Kanji words, Kana words and Kana nonwords. *Cognitive Brain Research, 9*(1), 111–115.

Salamy, A. (1978). Commissural transmission: Maturational changes in humans. *Science, 200,* 1409–1411.

Salcido, R., & Costich, J. F. (1992). Recurrent traumatic brain injury. *Brain Injury, 6,* 293–298.

Salive, M. E., Guralnik, J. M., & Glynn, R. J. (1993). Left-handedness and mortality. *American Journal of Public Health, 83,* 265–267.

Salmon, D. P., & Butters, N. (1995). Neurobiology of skill and habit learning. *Current Opinion in Neurobiology, 5*(2), 184–190.

Salthouse, T. (1985). Speed of behavior and its implications for cognition. In J. Birren & K. Schaie (Eds.), *Handbook of the psychology of aging* (pp. 400–426). New York: Van Nostrand Reinhold.

Salthouse, T. A. (1996). The processing-speed theory of adult age differences in cognition. *Psychological Review, 103,* 403–428.

Sampson, G. W. (1985). *Writing systems.* Stanford, CA: Stanford University Press.

Samson, S., & Zatorre, R. J. (1988). Melodic and harmonic discrimination following unilateral cerebral excision. *Brain and Cognition, 7,* 348–360.

Samson, S., & Zatorre, R. J. (1991). Recognition memory for text and melody of songs after unilateral temporal lobe lesion: Evidence for dual encoding. *Journal of Experimental Psychology: Learning, Memory, and Cognition, 17,* 793–804.

Samuelsson, S. (2000). Converging evidence for the role of occipital regions in orthographic processing: A case of developmental surface dyslexia. *Neuropsychologia, 38*(4), 351–362.

Sanders, A. L., Wheeler, M. E., & Buckner, R. L. (2000). Episodic recognition modulates frontal and parietal cortex activity. *Journal of Cognitive Neuroscience, (Suppl).* 50A.

Sanders, H. I., & Warrington, E. K. (1971). Memory for remote events in amnesic patients. *Brain, 94*(4), 661–668.

Sandman, C. A., O'Halloran, J. P., & Isenhart, R. (1984). Is there an evoked vascular response? *Science, 224,* 1355–1367.

Saron, C. D., & Davidson, R. J. (1989). Visual evoked potential measures of interhemispheric transfer time in humans. *Behavioral Neuroscience, 103,* 1115–1138.

Sarter, M., & Bruno, J. P. (1997). Cognitive functions of cortical acetylcholine: Toward a unifying hypothesis. *Brain Research Reviews, 23,* 28–46.

Sasanuma, S. (1980). Acquired dyslexia in Japanese: Clinical features and underlying mechanisms. In M. Coltheart, K. E. Patterson, & J. C. Marshall (Eds.), *Deep dyslexia* (pp. 91–118). London: Routledge & Kegan Paul.

Sawaguchi, T., & Goldman-Rakic, P. S. (1991). D1 dopamine receptors in prefrontal cortex: Involvement in working memory. *Science, 251,* 947–950.

Schacter, D. L. (1987a). Implicit memory: History and current status. *Journal of Experimental Psychology: Learning, Memory, and Cognition, 13,* 501–518.

Schacter, D. L. (1987b). Memory, amnesia, and frontal lobe dysfunction. *Psychobiology, 15,* 21–36.

Schacter, D. L., Curran, T., Galluccio, L., Milberg, W. P., & Bates, J. F. (1996). False recognition and the right frontal lobe: A case study. *Neuropsychologia, 34*(8), 793–808.

Schacter, D. L., & Tulving, E. (1994). Memory, amnesia, and the episodic/semantic distinction. In R. L. Isaacson & N. E. Spear (Eds.), *Expressions of knowledge.* New York: Plenum Press.

Schacter, D. L., & Wagner, A. D. (1999). Medial temporal lobe activations in fMRI and PET studies of episodic encoding and retrieval. *Hippocampus, 9*(1), 7–24.

Schacter, S., & Singer, J. E. (1962). Cognitive, social, and physiological determinants of emotional state. *Psychological Review, 69,* 379–399.

Schaffer, C. E., Davidson, R. J., & Saron, C. (1983). Frontal and parietal electroencephalogram asymmetry in depressed and nondepressed subjects. *Biological Psychiatry, 18,* 753–762.

Schaie, K. W. (1994). The course of adult intellectual development. *American Psychologist, 49,* 304–313.

Schank, R. (1982). *Dynamic memory: A theory of reminding and learning in computers and people.* Cambridge, England: Cambridge University Press.

Scheffers, M. K., Coles, M. G. H., Bernstein, P., Gehring, W. J., & Donchin, E. (1996). Event-related brain potentials and error-related processing: An analysis of incorrect responses to go and no-go stimuli. *Psychophysiology, 33,* 42–53.

Scheibel, A. B. (1984). A dendritic correlate of human speech. In N. Geschwind & A. M. Galaburda (Eds.), *Cerebral dominance: The biological foundations* (pp. 43–52). Cambridge, MA: Harvard University Press.

Schenck, F., & Morris, R. G. M. (1985). Dissociation between components of spatial memory in rats after recovery from the effects of retrohippocampal lesions. *Experimental Brain Research, 58,* 11–28.

Scherg, M. (1992). Functional imaging and localization of electromagnetic brain activity. *Brain Topography, 5,* 103–111.

Schiller, P. H., Sandell, J. H., & Maunsell, J. H. R. (1987). The effect of frontal eye field and superior colliculus lesions on saccadic latencies in the rhesus monkey. *Journal of Neurophysiology, 57,* 1033–1049.

Schiller, P. H., True, S. D., & Conway, J. L. (1980). Deficits in eye movements following frontal eye field and superior colliculus ablations. *Journal of Neurophysiology, 44,* 1175–1189.

Schlag-Rey, M., Schlag, J., & Dassonville, P. (1992). How the frontal eye field can impose a saccade goal on superior colliculus neurons. *Journal of Neurophysiology, 67,* 1003–1005.

Schlaug, G., Jancke, L., Huang, Y., Staiger, J. F., & Steinmetz, J. (1995). Increased corpus callosum size in musicians. *Neuropsychologia, 33,* 1047–1055.

Schlaug, G., Jancke, L., Huang, Y., & Steinmetz, H. (1995). In vivo evidence of structural brain asymmetry in musicians. *Science, 267,* 699–701.

Schmahmann, J. D. (1998). Dysmetria of thought: Clinical consequences of cerebellar dysfunction on cognition and affect. *Trends in Cognitive Science, 2,* 362–371.

Schmidt, R. H., & Grady, M. S. (1995). Loss of forebrain cholinergic neurons following fluid percussion injury. *Journal of Neurosurgery, 83,* 496–502.

Schneiderman, E. I., Murasugi, K. G., & Saddy, J. D. (1992). Story arrangement ability in right-brain damaged patients. *Brain and Language, 43,* 107–120.

Schoenberg, B. S., Kokmen, E., & Okazaki, H. (1987). Alzheimer's disease and other dementing illnesses in a defined United States population: Incidence rates and clinical features. *Annals of Neurology, 22,* 724–729.

Schroder, J., Buchsbaum, M. S., Siegel, B. V., Geider, F. J., & Niethammer, R. (1995). Structural and functional correlates of subsyndromes in chronic schizophrenia. *Psychopathology, 28,* 38–45.

Schulder, M., Maldjian, J. A., Liu, W. C., Holodny, A. I., Kalnin, A. T., Mun, I. K., & Carmel, P. W. (1998). Functional image-guided surgery of intracranial tumors located in or near the sensorimotor cortex. *Journal of Neurosurgery, 89*(3), 412–418.

Schwartz, M. F., Mayer, N. H., FitzpatrickDeSalme, E. J., & Montgomery, M. W. (1993). Cognitive theory and the study of everyday action disorders after brain damage. *Journal of Head Trauma and Rehabilitation, 8,* 59–72.

Scinto, L. F. M., Daffner, K. R., Dressler, D., Ransil, B. I., Rentz, D., Weintraub, S., Mesulam, M., & Potter, H. (1994). A potential noninvasive neurobiological test for Alzheimer's disease. *Science, 266,* 1051–1054.

Scott, R. B., Harrison, J., Boulton, C., Wilson, J., Gregory, R., Parkin, S., Bain, P. G., Joint, C., Stein, J., & Aziz, T. Z. (2002). Global attentional-executive sequelae following surgical lesions to globus pallidus interna. *Brain, 125,* 562–574.

Scott, S. H. (2000). Population vectors and motor cortex: Neural coding or epiphenomenona? *Nature Neuroscience, 3,* 307–308.

Scoville, W. B., & Milner, B. (1957). Loss of recent memory after bilateral hippocampal lesions. *Journal of Neurology, Neurosurgery and Psychiatry, 20,* 11–12.

Scully, R. E. (1986). Case records of the Massachusetts General Hospital. Case 16–1986. *New England Journal of Medicine, 314,* 1101–1111.

Segalowitz, S., & Gruber, F. (Eds.). (1977). *Language development and neurological theory.* New York: Academic Press.

Seidenberg, M. S., & McClelland, J. L. (1989). A distributed, developmental model of word recognition and naming. *Psychological Review, 96*(4), 523–568.

Seitz, R. J., & Roland, E. (1992). Learning of sequential finger movements in man: A combined kinematic and positron emission tomography (PET) study. *European Journal of Neuroscience, 4,* 154–165.

Seitz, R. J., Canavan, A. G., Yaguez, L., Herzog, H., Tellmann, L., Knorr, U., Huang, Y., & Homberg, V. (1994). Successive roles of the cerebellum and premotor cortices in trajectorial learning. *NeuroReport, 5*(18), 2541–2544.

Seitz, R. J., Roland, E., Bohm, C., Greitz, T., & Stone-Elander, S. (1990). Motor learning in man: A positron emission tomographic study. *NeuroReport, 1*(1), 57–60.

Selby, J. M. J., & Azrin, R. L. (1998). Neuropsychological functioning in drug abusers. *Drug and Alcohol Dependence, 50,* 39–45.

Semmes, J. (1965). A non-tactual factor in astereognosis. *Neuropsychologia, 3,* 295–315.

Semmes, J. (1968). Hemispheric specialization: A possible clue to mechanism. *Neuropsychologia, 6,* 11–26.

Semmes, J., Weinstein, S., Ghent, L., & Teuber, H.-L. (1955). Spatial orientation: 1. Analysis of locus of lesion. *Journal of Psychology, 39,* 227–244.

Semmes, J., Weinstein, S., Ghent, L., & Teuber, H.-L. (1963). Impaired orientation in personal and extrapersonal space. *Brain, 86,* 747–772.

Semrud-Clikeman, M., & Hynd, G. W. (1990). Right hemisphere dysfunction in nonverbal learning disabilities: Social, academic and adaptive functioning in adults and children. *Psychological Bulletin, 107*(2), 196–209.

Sereno, M. I., Dale, A. M., Reppas, J. B., Kwong, K. K., Belliveau, J. W., Brady, T. J., Rosen, B. R., & Tootell, R. B. H. (1995). Borders of multiple visual areas in humans revealed by functional magnetic resonance imaging. *Science, 268,* 889–893.

Sergent, J. (1982a). About face: Left-hemisphere involvement in processing physiognomies. *Journal of Experimental Psychology: Human Perception and Performance, 8,* 1–14.

Sergent, J. (1982b). The cerebral balance of power: Confrontation or cooperation. *Journal of Experimental Psychology: Human Perception and Performance, 8,* 253–272.

Sergent, J. (1983). The role of the input in visual hemispheric asymmetries. *Psychological Bulletin, 93,* 481–514.

Sergent, J. (1985). Influence of task and input factors on hemispheric involvement in face processing. *Journal of Experimental Psychology: Human Perception and Performance, 11,* 846–861.

Sergent, J. (1990). Furtive incursions into bicameral minds. *Brain, 113,* 537–568.

Sergent, J. (1991). Judgments of relative position and distance on representations of spatial relations. *Journal of Experimental Psychology: Human Perception and Performance, 91,* 762–780.

Sergent, J. (1993). Music, the brain and Ravel. *Trends in Neurosciences, 16,* 168–172.

Sergent, J. (1994). Brain-imaging studies of cognitive functions. *Trends in Neurosciences, 17*(6), 221–227.

Sergent, J., Ohta, S., & MacDonald, B. (1992). Functional neuroanatomy of face and object processing. *Brain, 115,* 15–36.

Sergent, J., & Signoret, J.-L. (1992a). Functional and anatomical decomposition of face processing: Evidence from prosopagnosia and PET study of normal subjects. *Philosophical Transactions of the Royal Society of London, B335,* 55–62.

Sergent, J., & Signoret, J.-L. (1992b). Varieties of functional deficits in prosopagnosia. *Cerebral Cortex, 2,* 375–388.

Sergent, J., Zuck, E., Terriah, S., & MacDonald, B. (1992). Distributed neural network underlying musical sight-reading and keyboard performance. *Science, 257,* 106–109.

Shallice, T. (1981). Phonological agraphia and the lexical route in writing. *Brain, 104,* 413–429.

Shallice, T. (1982). Specific impairments of planning. *Philosophical Transactions of the Royal Society of London, B298,* 199–209.

Shallice, T. (1988). *From neuropsychology to mental structure.* Cambridge, England: Cambridge University Press.

Shallice, T., & Evans, M. E. (1978). The involvement of frontal lobes in cognitive estimation. *Cortex, 13,* 294–303.

Shallice, T., & Warrington, E. K. (1977). The possible role of selective attention in acquired dyslexia. *Neuropsychologia, 15,* 31–41.

Shallice, T., & Warrington, E. K. (1979). Auditory-verbal short-term memory impairment and conduction aphasia. *Brain and Language, 4,* 479–491.

Shallice, T., Warrington, E. K., & McCarthy, R. (1983). Reading without semantics. *Quarterly Journal of Experimental Psychology, 35,* 111–138.

Shapiro, B. E., Grossman, M., & Gardner, H. (1981). Selective processing deficits in brain damaged populations. *Neuropsychologia, 19,* 161–169.

Shapiro, M. L., Heikki, T., & Eichenbaum, H. (1997). Cues that hippocampal place cells encode: Dynamic and hierarchical representation of local and distal stimuli. *Hippocampus, 7*(6), 624–642.

Shaw, T. G., Mortel, K. F., Meyer, J. S., Rogers, R. L., Hardenberg, J., & Cutaia, M. M. (1984). Cerebral blood flow changes in benign and cerebrovascular disease. *Neurology, 34,* 855–862.

Shaywitz, B. A., Shaywitz, S. E., Pugh, K. R., Constable, R. T., Skudlarski, P., Fulbright, R. K., Bronen, R. A., Fletcher, J. M., Shankweiler, D. P., Katz, L., & Gore, J. C. (1995). Sex differences in the functional organization of the brain for language. *Nature, 373,* 607–609.

Shaywitz, S. E., Shaywitz, B. A., Pugh, K. R., Fulbright, R. K., Constable, R. T., Mencl, W. E., Shankweiler, D. P., Liberman, A. M., Skudlarsi, P., Fletcher, J. M., Katz, L., Marchione, K. E., Lacadie, C., Gatenby, C., & Gore, J. C. (1998). Functional disruption in the organization of the brain for reading in dyslexia. *Proceedings of the National Academy of Sciences of the United States of America, 95,* 2636–2641.

Shelton, P. A., Bowers, D., & Heilman, K. M. (1990). Peripersonal and vertical neglect. *Brain, 113,* 191–205.

Shelton, R. C., Keller, M. B., Gelenberg, A., Dunner, D. L., Hirschfeld, R., Thase, M. E., Russeel, J., Lydiard, R. B., Crits-Cristoph, P., Gallop, R., Todd, L., Hellerstein, D., Goodnick, P., Keitner, G., Stahl, S. M., & Halbreich, U. (2001). Effectiveness of St. John's wort in major depression. *Journal of the American Medical Association, 285,* 1978–1986.

Shen, L., & Alexander, G. E. (1997). Neural correlates of a spatial sensory-to-motor transformation in the primary motor cortex. *Journal of Neurophysiology, 77,* 1171–1194.

Shenker, J. I., Banich, M. T., & Klipstein, S. (1993). Unpublished observations.

Shepard, R. (1988). The role of transformations in spatial cognition. In J. Stiles-Davis, M. Kritchevsky, & U. Bellugi (Eds.), *Spatial cognition: Brain bases and development* (pp. 81–110). Hillsdale, NJ: Erlbaum.

Shepard, R. N., & Cooper, L. A. (1982). *Mental images and their transformations.* Cambridge, MA: MIT Press.

Sherrington, R., Rogaev, E. I., Liang, Y., Rogacva, E. A., Levesque, G., Ikeda, M., Chi, H., Lin, C., Li, G., Holman, K., Tsuda, T., Mar, L., Foncin, J. F., Bruni, A. C., Montesi, M. P., Sorbi, S., Rainero, I., Pinessi, L., Nee, L., Chumakov, I., Pollen, D., Brookes, A., Sanseau, P., Polinsky, J. R. J., Wasco, W., Dasilva, H. A. R., Haines, J. L., Pericakvance, M. A., Tanzi, R. E., Roses, A. D., Fraser, P. E., Rommens, J. M., & Stgeorgehyslop, P. H. (1995). Cloning of a gene bearing missense mutations in early-onset familial Alzheimers-disease. *Nature, 375,* 754–760.

Shimamura, A. (1990). Aging and memory disorders: A neuropsychological analysis. In M. L. Howe, M. J. Stones, & C. J. Brainerd (Eds.), *Cognitive and behavioral performance factors in atypical aging.* New York: Springer-Verlag.

Shimamura, A., & Jurica, P. J. (1994). Memory interference effects and aging: Findings from a test of frontal lobe function. *Neuropsychology, 8,* 408–412.

Shimamura, A. P., Janowsky, J. S., & Squire, L. R. (1990). Memory for the temporal order of events in patients with frontal lobe lesions and amnesic patients. *Neuropsychologia, 28*(8), 803–813.

Shimamura, A. P., Jernigan, T. L., & Squire, L. R. (1988). Korsakoff's syndrome: Radiological (CT) findings and neuropsychological correlates. *Journal of Neuroscience, 8,* 4400–4410.

Shimamura, A. P., Salmon, D. P., Squire, L. R., & Butters, N. (1987). Memory dysfunction and word priming in dementia and amnesia. *Behavioral Neuroscience, 101,* 347–351.

Shin, L. M., Dougherty, D. D., Orr, S. P., Pitman, R. K., Lasko, M., Macklin, M. L., Alpert, N. M., Fischman, A. J., & Rauch, S. L. (2000). Activation of anterior paralimbic structures during guilt-related script-driven imagery. *Biological Psychiatry, 48,* 43–50.

Sidtis, J. J., & Volpe, B. T. (1988). Selective loss of complex-pitch or speech discrimination after unilateral lesion. *Brain and Language, 34,* 235–245.

Sidtis, J. J., Volpe, B. T., Watson, D. H., Rayport, M., & Gazzaniga, M. S. (1981). Variability in right hemisphere language after callosal section: Evidence for a continuum of generative capacity. *Journal of Neuroscience, 1,* 323–331.

Sieg, K. G., Gaffney, G. R., Preston, D. F., & Hellings, J. A. (1995). SPECT brain imaging abnormalities in attention deficit hyperactivity disorder. *Clinical Nuclear Medicine, 20,* 55–60.

Sigman, M. (1994). What are the core deficits in autism? In S. H. Broman & J. Grafman (Eds.), *Atypical cognitive deficits in developmental disorders* (pp. 139–157). Hillsdale, NJ: Erlbaum.

Silberman, E. K., & Weingarner, H. (1986). Hemispheric lateralization of functions related to emotion. *Brain and Cognition, 5,* 322–353.

Silverberg, R., Bentin, S., Gaziel, T. Obler, L. K., & Albert, M. L. (1979). Shift of visual field preference for English words in native Hebrew speakers. *Brain and Language, 8,* 184–190.

Simion, F., Bagnaro, S., Bisiachi, P., Roncata, S., & Umilta, C. (1980). Laterality effect, levels of processing and stimulus properties. *Journal of Experimental Psychology: Human Perception and Performance, 6,* 184–195.

Sirigu, A., Duhamel, J.-R., Cohen, L., Pillon, B., Dubois, B., & Agid, Y. (1996). The mental representation of hand movements after parietal cortex damage. *Science, 273,* 1564–1568.

Sirviö, J. (1999). Strategies that support declining cholinergic neurotransmission in Alzheimer's disease patients. *Gerontology, 45,(Suppl. 1),* 3–14.

Sitaram, N., Weingartner, H., & Gillin, J. C. (1978). Human serial learning: Enhancement with arechline and choline and impairment with scopolamine. *Science, 201,* 274–276.

Skaggs, W. E., & McNaughton, B. L. (1996). Replay of neuronal firing sequences in rat hippocampus during sleep following spatial experience. *Science, 271*(5257), 1870–1873.

Skottun, B. C. (2000). The magnocellular deficit theory of dyslexia: The evidence from contrast sensitivity. *Vision Research, 40,* 111–127.

Skuse, D. H., James, R. S., Bishop, D. V. M., Coppin, B., Dalton, P., Aarnodt-Leeper, G., Bacarese-Hamilton, M., Creswell, C., McGurk, R., & Jacobs, P. A. (1997). Evidence from Turner's syndrome of an imprinted X-linked locus affecting cognitive function. *Nature, 387,* 705–708.

Slaghuis, W., & Ryan, J. (1999). Spatio-temporal contrast sensitivity, coherent motion, and visible persistence in developmental dyslexia. *Vision Research, 39,* 651–668.

Slotnick, S. D., Moo, L. R., Tesoro, M. A., & Hart, J. (2001). Hemispheric asymmetry in categorical versus coordinate visuospatial processing revealed by temporary cortical deactivation. *Journal of Cognitive Neuroscience, 13*(8), 1088–1096.

Small, G. W., Mazziotta, J. C., Collins, M. T., Baxter, L. R., Phelps, M. E., Mandelkern, M. A., Kaplan, A., La Rue, A., Adamson, C. F., Chang, L., Guze, B. H., Corder, E. H., Saunders, A. M., Haines, J. L., Pericak-V., M. A., & R., Allen D. (1995). Apolipoprotein E type 4 allele and cerebral metabolism in relatives at risk for familial Alzheimer's disease. *Journal of the American Medical Association, 273,* 942–947.

Small, D. M., Zatorre, R. J., Dagher, A., Evans, A. C., & Jones-Gotman, M. (2001). Changes in brain activity related to eating chocolate: From pleasure to aversion. *Brain, 124,* 1720–1733.

Smith, A., & Nutt, D. (1996). Noradrenaline and attention lapses. *Nature, 380,* 291.

Smith, A. S., Boutrous, N. N., & Schwarzkopf, S. B. (1994). Reliability of P50 auditory event-related poential indices of sensory gating. *Psychophysiology, 31,* 495–502.

Smith, E. E., & Jonides, J. (1999). Storage and executive processes in the frontal lobes. *Science, 283*(5408), 1657–1661.

Smith, E. E., Jonides, J., & Koeppe, R. A. Dissociating verbal and spatial working memory using PET. *Cerebral Cortex, 6,* 11–20.

Smith, E. E., Jonides, J., Koeppe, R. A., Awh, E., Schumacher, E. H., & Minoshima, S. (1995). Spatial versus object working memory: PET investigations. *Journal of Cognitive Neuroscience, 7,* 337–356.

Smith, M. A., Brandt, J., & Shadmehr, R. (2000). Motor disorder in Huntington's disease begin as a dysfunction in error feedback control. *Nature, 403,* 544–549.

Smith, M. L., & Milner, B. (1981). The role of the right hippocampus in the recall of spatial location. *Neuropsychologia, 19*(6), 781–793.

Smith, M. L., & Milner, B. (1984). Differential effects of frontal-lobe lesions on cognitive estimation and spatial memory. *Neuropsychologia, 22,* 697–705.

Smith, M. L., & Milner, B. (1988). Estimation of frequency of occurrence of abstract designs after frontal or temporal lobectomy. *Neuropsychologia, 26*(2), 297–306.

Snowdon, D. A., Kemper, S. J., Mortimer, J. A., Greiner, L. H., Wekstein, D. R., & Markesbery, W. R. (1996). Linguistic ability in early life and cognitive function and Alzheimer's Disease in late life. Findings from the Nun Study. *Journal of the American Medical Association, 275,* 528–532.

Snyder, L. H., Grieve, K. L., Brotchie, P., & Andersen, R. A. (1998). Separate body- and world-referenced representations of visual space in parietal cortex. *Nature, 394,* 887–891.

Snyder, P. J., & Harris, L. J. (1998). Lexicon size and foot preference in the African grey parrot (Psittacus erithacus). *Brain & Cognition, 37,* 160–163.

Solomon, D., & Malloy, P. F. (1992). Alcohol, head injury, and neuropsychological function. *Neuropsychology Review, 3,* 249–280.

Spanagel, R., & Weiss, F. (1999). The dopamine hypothesis of reward: Past and current status. *Trends in Neurosciences, 22,* 521–527.

Speer, A. M., Kimbrell, T. A., Wassermann, E. M., Repella, J., Willis, M. W., Herscovitch, P., & Post, R. M. (2000). Opposite effects of high and low frequency rTMS on regional brain activity in depressed patients. *Biological Psychiatry, 48*(12), 1133–1141.

Spencer, K. M., Dien, J., & Donchin, E. (1999). A componential analysis of the ERP elicited by novel events using a dense electrode array. *Psychophysiology, 36*(3), 409–414.

Spencer, W. D., & Raz, N. (1994). Memory for facts, source, and context: Can frontal lobe dysfunction explain age-related differences? *Psychology and Aging, 9,* 149–159.

Sperry, R. W. (1964). The great cerebral commissure. *Scientific American.*

Sperry, R. W. (1974). Lateral specialization in the surgically separated hemispheres. In F. Schmitt & F. Worden (Eds.), *The neurosciences: Third study program.* Cambridge, MA: MIT Press.

Sperry, R. W., Zaidel, E., & Zaidel, D. (1979). Self recognition and social awareness in the deconnected minor hemisphere. *Neuropsychologia, 17,* 153–166.

Spillane, J. A., White, Goodhart, Flack, Borden, & Davison. (1977). Selective vulnerability of neurones in organic dementia. *Nature, 266,* 558–559.

Spillantini, M. G., Bird, T. D., & Ghetti, B. (1998). Frontotemporal dementia and parkinsonism linked to choromosome 17: A new group of tauopathies. *Brain Pathology, 8,* 387–402.

Sponheim, S. R., Clementz, B. A., Iacono, W. G., & Beiser, M. (2000). Clinical and biological concomitants of resting-state EEG power abnormalities in schizophrenia. *Biological Psychiatry, 48,* 1088–1097.

Spreen, O., Tupper, D., Risser, A., Tuokko, H., & Edgell, D. (1984). *Human developmental neuropsychology.* New York: Oxford University Press.

Springer, J. A., Binder, J. R., Hammeke, T. A., Swanson, S. J., Frost, J. A., Bellgowan, P. S. F., Brewer, C. C., Perry, H. M., Morris, G. L., & Mueller, W. M. (1999). Language dominance in neurologically normal and epilepsy subjects: A functional MRI study. *Brain, 122,* 2033–2045.

Springer, S. P., & Deutsch, G. (1993). *Left brain, right brain.* New York: Freeman.

Squire, L. R. (1982). Comparisons between forms of amnesia: Some deficits are unique to Korsakoff's syndrome. *Journal of Experimental Psychology: Learning, Memory, and Cognition, 8*(6), 560–571.

Squire, L. R. (1984). The neuropsychology of memory. In P. Marler & H. Terrace (Eds.), *The biology of learning (Dablem-Konferenzen).* Berlin: Springer-Verlag.

Squire, L. R. (1987). *Memory and brain.* New York: Oxford University Press.

Squire, L. R. (1992). Memory and the hippocampus: A synthesis from findings with rats, monkeys, and humans. *Psychological Review, 99*(2), 195–231.

Squire, L. R., & Cohen, N. J. (1979). Memory and amnesia: Resistance to disruption develops for years after learning. *Behavioral and Neural Biology, 25,* 115–125.

Squire, L. R., & Cohen, N. J. (1982). Remote memory, retrograde amnesia, and the neuropsychology of memory. In L. S. Cermak (Ed.), *Human memory and amnesia.* Hillsdale, NJ: Erlbaum.

Squire, L. R., & Cohen, N. J. (1984). Human memory and amnesia. In G. Lynch, J. L. McGaugh, & N. M. Weinberger (Eds.), *Neurobiology of learning and memory* (pp. 3–64). New York: Guilford Press.

Squire, L. R., Cohen, N. J., & Nadel, L. (1984). The medial temporal region and memory consolidation: A new hypothesis. In H. Weingartner & E. Parker (Eds.), *Memory consolidation* (pp. 185–210). Hillsdale, NJ: Erlbaum.

Squire, L. R., Cohen, N. J., & Zouzounis, J. A. (1984). Preserved memory in retrograde amnesia: Sparing of a recently acquired skill. *Neuropsychologia, 22*(2), 145–152.

Squire, L. R., Ojemann, J. G., Miezin, F. M., Petersen, S. E., Videen, T. O., & Raichle, M. E. (1992). Activation of the hippocampus in normal humans: A functional anatomical study of memory. *Proceedings of the National Academy of Sciences, USA, 89,* 1837–1841.

Stankoff, B., Tourbah, A., Suarez, S., Turell, E., Stievenart, J. L., Payan, C., Coutellier, A., Herson, S., Baril, L., Bricaire, F., Calvez, V., Cabanis, E. A., Lacomblez, L., & Lubetzki, C. (2001). Clinical and spectroscopic improvement in HIV associated cognitive impairment. *Neurology, 56,* 112–115.

Starkstein, S. E., Brandt, J., Folstein, S., Strauss, M., Berthier, M. L., Pearlson, G. D., Wong, D., McDonnell, A., & Folstein, M. (1988). Neuropsychological and neuroradiological correlates in Huntington's disease. *Journal of Neurology, Neurosurgery and Psychiatry, 51,* 1259–1263.

Starkstein, S. E., & Robinson, R. G. (1988). Lateralized emotional response following stroke. In M. Kinsbourne (Ed.), *Cerebral hemisphere function in depression* (pp. 23–48). Washington, DC: American Psychiatric Press.

Stebbins, W. C. (1984). Neural lateralization of vocalizations by Japanese macaques: Communicative significance is more important than acoustic structure. *Behavioral Neuroscience, 98(5),* 779–790.

Steckler, T., & Sahgal, A. (1995). The role of serotonergic-cholinergic interactions in the mediation of cognitive behavior. *Behavioral Brain Research, 67,* 165–199.

Steenhuis, R. E., Østbye, T., & Walton, R. (2001). An examination of the hypothesis that left-handers die earlier: The Canadian Study of Health and Aging. *Laterality, 6,* 69–75.

Stein, J. F. (1991). Space and the parietal association areas. In J. Paillard (Ed.), *Brain and space* (pp. 185–222). New York: Oxford University Press.

Stein, J. F. (1994). A visual deficit in dyslexics? In A. Fawcett, & R. Nicolson, (Eds.), *Dyslexia in children: Multidisciplinary perspectives.* Hemel Hampstead: Harvester Wheatsheaf.

Stein, J., & Walsh, V. (1997). To see but not to read: The magnocellular theory of dyslexia. *Trends in Neuroscience, 20,* 147–152.

Stein, J., Talcott, J., & Walsh, V. (2000). Controversy about the visual magnocellular deficit in developmental dyslexics. *Trends in Cognitive Sciences, 4,* 209–211.

Steinmetz, H., Volkmann, J., Jancke, L., & Freund, H. J. (1991). Anatomical left right asymmetry of language-related temporal cortex is different in left- and right-handers. *Annals of Neurology, 29,* 315–319.

Stephens, R., Spurgeon, A., and Berry, H. (1996). Organophosphates: The relationship between chronic and acute exposure effects. *Neurotoxicology and Teratology, 18,* 449–453.

Stern, C. E., Sherman, S. J., Kirchhoff, B. A., & Hasselmo, M. E. (2001). Medial temporal and prefrontal contributions to working memory tasks with novel and familiar stimuli. *Hippocampus, 11*(4), 337–346.

Stern, L. D. (1981). A review of theories of amnesia. *Memory and Cognition, 9,* 247–262.

Stern, Y., Gurland, B., Tatemichi, K., Tang, M. X., Wilder, D., & Mayeux, R. (1994). Influence of education and occupation on the incidence of Alzheimer's disease. *Journal of the American Medical Association, 271,* 1004–1010.

Sternberg, S. S., Monsell, S., Knoll, R. L., & Wright, C. E. (1978). The latency and duration of rapid movement sequences: Comparisons of speech and type-writing. In G. E. Stelmach (Ed.), *Information processing in motor control and learning* (pp. 118–152). New York: Academic Press.

Stewart, R. (1998). Cardiovascular factors in Alzheimer's disease. *Journal of Neurology, Neurosurgery and Psychiatry, 65,* 143–147.

St. George, M., Kutas, M., Martinez, A., & Sereno, M. I. (1999). Semantic integration in reading: Engagement on the right hemisphere during discourse processing. *Brain, 122,* 1317–1325.

Stivalet, P., Moreno, V., Richard, J., Barraud, P.-A., & Raphel, C. (1998). Differences in visual search tasks between congenitally deaf and normally hearing adults. *Cognitive Brain Research, 6,* 227–232.

Stokes, A., Banich, M. T., & Elledge, V. C. (1991). Testing the tests—An empirical evaluation of screening tests for the detection of cognitive impairment in aviators. *Aviation Space and Environmental Medicine, 62,* 783–788.

Stolar, N., Berenbaum, H., Banich, M. T., and Barch, D. (1994). Neuropsychological correlates of alogia and affective flattening in schizophrenia. *Biological Psychiatry, 35,* 164–172.

Strang, J. D., & Rourke, B. P. (1985). Arithmetic disability subtypes: The neuropsychological significance of specific arithmetic impairment in childhood. In B. P. Rourke (Ed.), *Neuropsychology of learning disabilities* (pp. 302–330). New York: Guilford Press.

Strauss, E., Hunter, M., & Wada, J. (1995). Risk factors for cognitive impairment in epilepsy. *Neuropsychology, 9,* 457–463.

Strauss, E., LaPointe, J. S., Wada, J. A., Gaddes, W., & Kosaka, B. (1985). Language dominance: Correlation of radiological and functional data. *Neuropsychologia, 23,* 415–420.

Strauss, E., & Moscovitch, M. (1981). Perception of facial expressions. *Brain and Language, 13,* 308–332.

Streissguth, A. P. (1992). Fetal alcohol syndrome and fetal alcohol effects: A clinical perspective of later developmental consequences. In I. S. Zagon & T. A. Slotkin (Eds.), *Maternal substance abuse and the developing nervous system* (pp. 5–26). New York: Academic Press.

Stromswold, K., Caplan, D., Alpert, N., & Rauch, S. (1996). Localization of syntactic comprehension by positron emission tomography. *Brain and Language, 52,* 452–473.

Studdert-Kennedy, M., & Shankweiler, D. (1970). Hemispheric specialization for speech perception. *Journal of the Acoustical Society of America, 48,* 579–594.

Stuss, D. T. (1987). Contribution of frontal lobe injury to cognitive impairment after closed head injury: Methods of assessment and recent findings. In H. S. Levin, J. Grafman, & H. M. Eisenberg (Eds.), *Neurobehavioral recovery from head injury* (pp. 166–177). New York: Oxford University Press.

Stuss, D. T., & Benson, D. F. (1986). *The frontal lobes.* New York: Raven Press.

Suberi, M., & McKeever, W. F. (1977). Differential right hemispheric memory storage of emotional and non-emotional faces. *Neuropsychologia, 15,* 757–768.

Stuss, D. T., Shallice, T., Alexander, M. P., & Pieton, T. W. (1995). A multidisciplinary approach to anterior attentional functions. In J. Grafman, K. J. Holyoak, & F. Boller, (Eds.), *Structure and functions of the human prefrontal cortex. Annals of the New York Academy of Sciences, Vol. 769* (pp. 191–211). New York, NY: New York Academy of Sciences.

Sutherland, R. J., Whishaw, I. Q., & Kolb, B. (1983). A behavioral analysis of spatial localization following electrolytic, kainate- or colchicine-induced damage to the hippocampal formation in the rat. *Behavioral Brain Research, 7,* 133–153.

Sutton, S. K. (2002). Incentive and threat reactivity: Relations with anterior cortical activity. In D. Cervone, & W. Mischel, (Eds.), *Advances in personality science* (pp. 127–150). New York: The Guilford Press.

Sutton, S. K., Ward, R. T., Larson, C. L., Holden, J. E., Perlman, S. B., & Davidson, R. J. (1997). Asymmetry in prefrontal glucose metabolism during appetitive and aversive emotional states: An FGD-PET study. *Psychophysiology, 34,* S89.

Swanson, J., Posner, M. I., Cantwell, D., Wigal, S., Crinella, F., Filipek, P. A., Emerson, J., Tucker, D., & Nalcioglu, O. (1998). Attention-deficit hyperactivity disorder: symptom domain, cognitive processes and neural networks. In R. Parasuraman, (Ed.), *The attentive brain* (pp. 445–460). Cambridge, MA: The MIT Press.

Swanson, J. M., Flodman, P., Kennedy, J. M., Spence, M. A., Moyzis, R., Schuck, S., Murias, M., Moriarity, J., Barr, C., Smith, M., & Posner, M. (2000). Dopamine genes and ADHD. *Neuroscience and Biobehavioral Reviews, 24,* 21–25.

Swillen, A., Vandeputte, L., Cracco, J., Maes, B., Ghesquiere, P., Devridendt, K., & Fryns, J. P. (1999). Neuropsychological, learning and psychosocial profile of primary school aged children with the velocardio-facial syndrome (22q11 deletion): Evidence for a nonverbal learning disability? *Neuropsychology, Development, and Cognition, Section C: Child Neuropsychology, 5*(4), 230–241.

Swirsky-Sacchetti, T., Mitchell, D. R., Seward, J., Gonzales, C., Lublin, F., Knobler, R., & Field, H. L. (1992). Neuropsychological and structural brain lesions in multiple sclerosis: A regional analysis. *Neurology, 42,* 1291–1295.

Symonds, G. P. (1937). Mental disorder following head injury. *Proceedings of the Royal Society of Medicine, 30,* 1081–1094.

Taft, M. (1982). An alternative to grapheme-phoneme conversion rules? *Memory and Cognition, 10,* 465–474.

Tagamets, M. A., Novick, J. M., Chalmers, M. L., & Friedman, R. B. (2000). A parametric approach to orthographic processing in the brain: An fMRI study. *Journal of Cognitive Neuroscience, 12,* 281–297.

Taira, M., Mine, S., Georgopoulos, A. P., Murata, A., & Sakata, H. (1990). Parietal cortex neurons of the monkey related to the visual guidance of hand movement. *Experimental Brain Research, 83,* 29–36.

Tallal, P., Miller, S. L., Bedi, G., Byma, G., Wang, X., Nagarajan, S. S., Schreiner, C., Jenkins, W. M., & Merzenich, M. M. (1996). Language comprehension in language-learning impaired children improved with acoustically modified speech. *Science, 271,* 81–84.

Tallal, P., Sainburg, R. L., & Jernigan, T. (1991). The neuropathology of developmental dysphasia: Behavioral, morphological, and physiological evidence for a pervasive temporal processing disorder. *Reading and Writing, 3,* 363–377.

Talland, G. A. (1965). *Deranged memory.* New York: Academic Press.

Tanguay, P. E. (2000). Pervasive developmental disorders: A 10-year review. *Journal of the American Academy of Child and Adolescent Psychiatry, 39,* 1079–1095.

Tanji, J., Taniguchi, K., & Saga, T. (1980). Supplementary motor area: neuronal response to motor instructions. *Journal of Neurophysiology, 43,* 60–68.

Tarr, M. J. & Bülthoff, H. H. (1998). Image-based object recognition in man, monkey, and machine. *Cognition, 67,* 1–20.

Tarr, M. J., & Gauthier, I. (2000). FFA: A Flexible Fusiform Area for subordinate-level visual processing automatized by expertise. *Nature Neuroscience, 3*(8), 764–769.

Tarter, R. E., & Alterman, A. I. (1984). Neuropsychological deficits in alcoholics: Etiological considerations. *Journal of Studies on Alcohol, 45,* 1–9.

Tatemichi, T. K. (1990). How acute brain failure becomes chronic: A view of the mechanisms of dementia related to stroke. *Neurology, 40,* 1652–1659.

Taub, E. (2000). Constraint-induced movement therapy and massed practice. *Stroke, 31(4),* 986–988.

Taub, E., & Uswatte, G. (2000). Constraint-induced movement therapy based on behavioral neuroscience. In R. G. Frank, & T. R. Elliott, (Eds.), *Handbook of rehabilitation psychology* (pp. 475–496). Washington, DC: American Psychological Association.

Taub, E., Uswatte, G., & Pidikiti, R. (1999). Constraint-induced movement therapy: A new family of techniques with broad application to physical rehabilitation—A clinical review. *Journal of Rehabilitation Research and Development, 36,* 237–251.

Teasdale, G., & Jennett, B. (1974). Assessment of coma and impaired consciousness: A practical scale. *Lancet, 2,* 81–84.

Tecce, J. J., & Cole, J. O. (1974). Amphetamine effects in man: Paradoxical drowsiness and lowered electrical brain activity (CNV). *Science, 185,* 451–453.

Tecce, J. J., Cole, J. O., Mayer, J., & Lewis, D. C. (1977). Barbiturate effects on brain functioning (CNV) and attention performance in normal men. *Psychopharmacology Bulletin, 13,* 64–66.

Teuber, H. L. (1955). Physiological psychology. *Annual Review of Psychology, 6,* 267–296.

Teuber, H. L., & Rudel, R. G. (1962). Behavior after cerebral lesions in children and adults. *Developmental Medicine and Child Neurology, 3,* 3–20.

Teyler, T. J., & DiScenna, P. (1986). The hippocampal memory indexing theory. *Behavioral Neuroscience, 100*(2), 147–154.

Thach, W. T. (1998). What is the role of the cerebellum in motor learning and cognition? *Trends in Cognitive Science, 2,* 331–337.

Thach, W. T., Goodkin, H. G., & Keating, J. G. (1992). Cerebellum and the adaptive coordination of movement. *Annual Review of Neuroscience, 15,* 403–442.

Thach, W. T., Jr. (1992). The cerebellum: Coordination and adaptation of movement. In K. W. Brocklehurst (Ed.), *Neuropsychology: The neuronal basis of cognitive function* (pp. 113–130). New York: Thieme.

Thomas, D. L., Lythgoe, M. F., Calamante, F., Gadian, D. G., & Ordidge, R. J. (2001). Simultaneous noninvasive measurement of CBF and CBV using double-echo FAIR (DEFAIR). *Magnetic Resonance in Medicine, 45*(5), 853–863.

Thomas, J. D., & Trexler, L. E. (1982). Behavioral and cognitive deficits in cerebrovascular accident and closed head injury: Implications for cognitive rehabilitation. In L. E. Trexler (Ed.), *Cognitive rehabilitation: Conceptualization and intervention* (pp. 27–62). New York: Plenum Press.

Thompson, P. (1980). Margaret Thatcher: A new illusion. *Perception, 9,* 483–484.

Thompson, P. J., & Trimble, M. R. (1996). Neuropsychological aspects of epilepsy. In G. Igor, & K. M. Adams, (1996). *Neuropsychological assessment of neuropsychiatric disorders,* 2nd ed, (pp. 263–287). New York: Oxford University Press.

Thurman, D, & Guerrero, J. (1999). Trends in hospitalization associated with traumatic brain injury. *Journal of the American Medical Association, 282,* 954–957.

Thurstone, L., & Thurstone, T. (1943). *The Chicago Tests of Primary Mental Abilities.* Chicago: Science Research Associates.

Thut, G., Schultz, W., Roelcke, U., Nienhusmeier, M., Missiner, J., Maguire, R. P., & Leenders, K. L. (1997). Activation of the human brain by monetary reward. *NeuroReport, 8,* 1225–1228.

Tian, J. R., Zee, D. S., Lasker, A. G., & Folstein, S. E. (1991). Saccades in Huntington's disease: Predictive tracking and interaction between release of fixation and initiation of saccades. *Neurology, 41,* 875–881.

Tipper, S. P. (1985). The negative priming effect: Inhibitory effects of ignored primes. *Quarterly Journal of Experimental Psychology, 37A,* 571–590.

Tison, F., Dartigues, J. F., Auriacombe, S., Letenneur, L., Boller, F., & Alperovitch, A. (1995). Dementia in Parkinson's disease: A population-based study in ambulatory and institutionalized individuals. *Neurology, 45,* 705–708.

Todorov, E. (2000). Direct cortical control of muscle activation in voluntary arm movements: A model. *Nature Neuroscience, 3,* 391–398.

Tognola, G., & Vignolo, L. A. (1980). Brain lesions associated with oral apraxia in stroke patients: A clinicoeuroradiological investigation with CT scan. *Neuropsychologia, 18,* 257–272.

Tokunaga, H., Nishikawa, T., Ikejiri, Y., Nakagawa, Y., Yasuno, F., Hashikawa, K., Nishimura, T., Sugita, Y., & Takeda, M. (1999). Different neural substrates for Kanji and Kana writing: A PET study. *NeuroReport, 10*(16), 3315–3319.

Tomlinson, B. E. (1980). The structural and quantitative aspects of the dementias. In P. Roberts (Ed.), *Biochemistry of dementia* (pp. 15–52). London: Wiley.

Tomlinson, B. E. (1982). Plaques, tangles and Alzheimer's disease. *Psychological Medicine, 12,* 449–459.

Tompkins, C., & Flowers, C. R. (1985). Perception of emotional intonation by brain-damaged adults: The influence of task processing levels. *Journal of Speech and Hearing Research, 28,* 527–538.

Tompkins, S. S. (1984). Affect theory. In K. R. Scherer & P. Ekman (Eds.), *Approaches to emotion* (pp. 163–195). Hillsdale, NJ: Erlbaum.

Tonnaer, J. A., & Dekker, W. C. (1994). Nerve growth factor, neurotrophic agents and dementia. In D. G. Nicholson (Ed.), *Anti-dementia agents: Research and prospects for therapy* (pp. 139–165). London: Academic Press.

Tootell, R. B. H., Reppas, J. B., Kwong, K. K., Malach, R., Born, R. T., Brady, T. J., Rosen, B. R., & Belliveau, J. W. (1995b). Functional analysis of human MT and related visual cortical areas using magnetic resonance imaging. *Journal of Neuroscience, 15,* 3215–3230.

Tranel, D., Damasio, A., & Damasio, H. (1988). Intact recognition of facial expression, gender, and age in patients with impaired recognition of face identity. *Neurology, 38,* 690–696.

Tranel, D., & Damasio, A. R. (1988). Non-conscious face recognition in patients with face agnosia. *Behavioral Brain Research, 30,* 235–249.

Tranel, D., Damasio, H., & Damasio, A. R. (1997). A neural basis for the retrieval of conceptual knowledge. *Neuropsychologia, 35,* 1319–1327.

Treadway, M., McCloskey, M., Gordon, B., & Cohen, N. J. (1992). Landmark life events and the organization of memory: Evidence from functional retrograde amnesia. In S.-A. Christianson (Ed.), *The handbook of emotion and memory: Research and theory* (pp. 389–410). Hillsdale, NJ: Lawrence Erlbaum Associates, Inc.

Treisman, A., & Gelade, G. (1980). A feature integration theory of attention. *Cognitive Psychology, 12,* 97–136.

Treisman, A. M., & Kanwisher, N. G. (1998). Perceiving visually presented objects: Recognition, awareness and modularity. *Current Opinion in Neurobiology, 8,* 218–226.

Treisman, A. M., & Schmidt, H. (1982). Illusory conjunctions in the perception of objects. *Cognitive Psychology, 14,* 107–141.

Treves, A., & Rolls, E. T. (1994). Computational analysis of the role of the hippocampus in memory. *Hippocampus, 4*(3), 374–391.

Trichard, C., Martinot, J. L., Alagille, M., Masure, M. C., Hardy, P., Ginestet, D., & Feline, A. (1995). Time course of prefrontal lobe dysfunction in severly depressed inpatients: A longitudinal neuropsychological study. *Psychological Medicine, 25,* 79–85.

Trimble, M. R. (1988). Body image and the temporal lobes. *British Journal of Psychiatry, 153*(Suppl. 2), 12–14.

Trimble, M. R., & Rogers, D. (1987). The neurobiology of schizophrenia. In L. DeLisi & F. Henn (Eds.), *Handbook of schizophrenia* (pp. 439–466). Amsterdam: Elsevier.

Tsuang, M. T., Boor, M., & Fleming, J. A. (1985). Psychiatric aspects of traffic accidents. *American Journal of Psychiatry, 142,* 538–546.

Tucker, D., & Williamson, P. (1984). Asymmetric neural control systems in human self-regulation. *Psychological Review, 91*(2), 185–215.

Tucker, D. M. (1981). Lateral brain function, emotion, and conceptualization. *Psychological Bulletin, 89,* 19–46.

Tucker, D. M., Antes, J. R., Stenslie, C. E., & Barnhardt, T. M. (1978). Anxiety and lateral cerebral function. *Journal of Abnormal Psychology, 87,* 380–383.

Tucker, D. M., Roth, R. S., Arneson, B. A., & Buckingham, V. (1977). Right hemisphere activation during stress. *Neuropsychologia, 15,* 697–700.

Tucker, D. M., Watson, R. T., & Heilman, K. M. (1977). Discrimination and evocation of affectively intoned speech in patients with right parietal disease. *Neurology, 27,* 947–958.

Tulving, E. (1972). Episodic and semantic memory. In E. Tulving & W. Donaldson (Eds.), *Organization of memory* (pp. 382–403). New York: Academic Press.

Tulving, E. (1994). Organization of memory: *Quo vadis?* In M. S. Gazzaniga (Ed.), *The cognitive neurosciences* (pp. 839–853). Cambridge, MA: MIT Press.

Turner, A. M., & Greenough, W. T. (1985). Differential rearing effects on rat visual cortex synapses: I. Synaptic and neuronal density and synapses per neuron. *Brain Research, 329,* 195–203.

Tyler, A., Morris, M., Lazarou, L., Meredith, L., Myring, J., & Harper, P. (1992). Presymptomatic testing for Huntington's disease in Wales: 1987–90. *British Journal of Psychiatry, 161,* 481–488.

Tyler, S. K., & Tucker, D. M. (1982). Anxiety and perceptual structure: Individual differences in neuropsychological function. *Journal of Abnormal Psychology, 91,* 210–220.

Umbricht, D., Degreef, G., Barr, W. B., Lieberman, J. A., Pollack, S., & Schaul, N. (1995). Postictal and chronic psychoses in patients with temporal lobe epilepsy. *American Journal of Psychiatry, 152,* 224–231.

Umilta, C., Bagnara, S., & Simion, F. (1978). Laterality effects for simple and complex geometrical figures and nonsense patterns. *Neuropsychologia, 16,* 43–49.

Umilta, C., Rizzolatti, G., Marzi, C. A., Zamboni, G., Franzini, C., Camarda, R., & Berlucchi, G. (1974). Hemispheric differences in the discrimination of line orientation. *Neuropsychologia, 12,* 165–174.

Ungerleider, L. G. (1994). Transient and enduring effects of experience: Functional studies of visual and motor cortex. *Society for Neuroscience Abstracts, 20,* 124.

Ungerleider, L. G. (1995). Functional brain imaging studies of cortical mechanisms for memory. *Science, 270*(5237), 769–775.

Ungerleider, L. G., & Mishkin, M. (1982). Two cortical visual systems. In D. J. Ingle, M. A. Goodale, & R. J. W. Mansfield (Eds.), *Analysis of visual behavior* (pp. 549–586). Cambridge, MA: MIT Press.

Vaidya, C. J., Austin, G., Kirkorian, G., Ridlehuber, H. W., Desmond, J. E., Glover, G. H., & Gabrieli, J. D. E. (1998). Selective effects of methylphenidate in attention deficit hyperactivity disorder: A functional magnetic resonance study. *Proceedings of the National Academy of Science, USA, 95,* 14494–14499.

Vaina, L. M., LeMay, M., Bienfang, D. C., Choi, A. Y., & Nakayama, K. (1990). Intact "biological motion" and "structure from motion" perception in a patient with impaired motion mechanisms: A case study. *Visual Neuroscience, 5,* 353–369.

Valenstein, E. S. (1986). *Great and desperate cures: The rise and decline of psychosurgery and other radical treatments for mental illness.* New York: Basic Books.

Vallar, G. (1998). Spatial neglect in humans. *Trends in Cognitive Sciences, 2,* 87–97.

Vallar, G., & Baddeley, A. (1984a). Fractionation of working memory: Neuropsychological evidence for a phonological short-term store. *Journal of Verbal Learning and Verbal Behavior, 23,* 151–162.

Vallar, G., & Baddeley, A. (1984b). Phonological short-term store, phonological processing, and sentence comprehension: A neuropsychological case study. *Cognitive Neuropsychology, 1,* 121–141.

Vallar, G., Guariglia, C., & Rusconi, M. L. (1997). Modulation of neglect syndrome by sensory stimulation. In P. Their, & H. O. Karnath, (Eds.) *Parietal lobe contributions to orientation* in *3D-space (pp. 401–429).* Heidelberg: Springer-Verlag.

Vallar, G., & Perani, D. (1986). The anatomy of unilateral neglect after right-hemisphere stroke lesions. A clinical CT/scan study in man. *Neuropsychologia, 24,* 609–622.

Vallar, G., Sterai, R., Bottini, G., Cappa, S., & Rusconi, M. L. (1990). Temporary remission of left hemi-anesthesia after vestibular stimulation. A sensory neglect phenomenon. *Cortex, 26,* 121–131.

van Boxtel, M. P., Paas, F. G., Houx, P. J., Adam, J. J., Teeken, J. C., & Jolles, J. (1997). Aerobic capacity and cognitive performance in a cross-sectional aging study. *Medicine and Science in Sports and Exercise, 29,* 1357–1365.

van der Knaap, M. S. & Valk, J. (1990). MR imaging of the various staes of normal myelination during the first year of life. *Neuroradiology, 31,* 459–470.

Van Duijn, C. M., Clayton, D., Chandra, V., Fratiglioni, L., Graves, A. B., Heyman, A., Jorm, A. F., Kokmen, E., Kondo, K., & Mortimer, J. A. (1991). Familial aggregation of Alzheimer's disease and related disorders: A collaborative re-analysis of case-control studies: Eurodem risk factors research group. *International Journal of Epidemiology, 20*(Suppl. 2), S13–S20.

Van Gorp, W. G., Humphrey, L. A., Kalechstein, A., Brumm, V. L., McMullen, W. J., Stoddard, M., & Pachana, N. A. (1999). How well do standard clinical neuropsychological tests identify malingering? A preliminary analysis. *Journal of Clinical and Experimental Neuropsychology, 21,* 245–250.

van Haaren, F., van Hest, A., & Heinsbroek, R. P. (1990). Behavioral differences between male and female rats: Effects of gonadal hormones on learning and memory. *Neuroscience and Biobehavioral Reviews, 14,* 23–33.

Vanier, M., & Caplan, D. (1985). CT scan correlates of surface dyslexia. In K. E. Patterson, J. C. Marshall, & M. Coltheart (Eds.), *Surface dyslexia: Neuropsychological and cognitive studies of phonological reading* (pp. 511–525). Hove, London: Erlbaum.

Van Kleeck, M. H. (1989). Hemispheric differences in global versus local processing of hierarchical visual stimuli by normal subjects: New data and a meta-analysis of previous studies. *Neuropsychologia, 27,* 1165–1178.

Van Lancker, D., & Sidtis, J. J. (1992). The identification of affective-prosodic stimuli by left and right brain damaged subjects: All errors are not created equal. *Journal of Speech and Hearing Research, 35,* 963–970.

Van Lancker, D. R., Kreiman, J., & Cummings, J. (1989). Voice perception deficits: Neuroanatomical correlates of phonagnosia. *Journal of Clinical and Experimental Neuropsychology, 11,* 665–674.

van Leeuwen, F. W. & Hol, E. M. (1999). Molecular misreading of genes in Down syndrome as a model for the Alzheimer type of neurodegneration. *Journal of Neural Transmission, 57,* 137–159.

van Praag, H., Kempermann, G., & Gage, F. H. (1999). Running increases cell proliferation and neurogenesis in the adult mouse dentate gyrus. *Nature Neuroscience, 2,* 266–270.

Van Strien, J. W., Heijt, R. (1995). Altered visual field asymmetries for letter naming and letter matching as a result of concurrent presentation of threatening and nonthreatening words. *Brain and Cognition, 29,* 187–203.

Van Voorhis, S., & Hillyard, S. A. (1977). Visual evoked potentials and selective attention to points in space. *Perception and Psychophysics, 22,* 54–62.

van Wendel de Joode, B., Wesseling, C., Kromhout, H., Monge, P., García, M., & Mergler, D. (2001). Chronic nervous-system effects of long-term occupational exposure to DDT. *Lancet, 357,* 1014–1016.

Vargha-Khadem, F., Isaacs, E., & Muter, V. (1994). A review of cognitive outcome after unilateral lesions sustained during childhood. *Journal of Child Neurology, 9,* 2S67–2S73.

Vega, A., Jr., & Parsons, O. A. (1967). Cross-validation of the Halstead-Reitan tests for brain damage. *Journal of Consulting Psychology, 31,* 619–623.

Vellurino, F. R. (1987). Dyslexia. *Scientific American, 256,* 34–41.

Verkes, J. R. J., Gijsman, H. J., Pieters, M. S. M., Schoemaker, R. C., de Visser, S., Kuijpers, M., Pennings, E. J. M., de Bruin, D., Van de Wijngaart, G., Van Gerven, J. M. A., & Cohen, A. F. (2001). Cognitive performance and serotonergic function in users of ecstasy. *Psychopharmacology, 153,* 196–202.

Verma, A. (2000). Opportunities for neuroprotection in traumatic brain injury. *Journal of Head Trauma Rehabilitation, 15,* 1149–1161.

Verma, A. (2001). "Low-tech" neuroprotection for brain injury. *Journal of Head Trauma Rehabilitation, 16,* 206–209.

Vidal, F., Hasbroucq, T., Grapperon, J., & Bonnet, M. (2000). Is the 'error negativity' specific to errors? *Biological Psychology, 51,* 109–128.

Videbech, P. (2000). PET measurements of brain glucose metabolism and blood flow in major depressive disorder: A critical review. *Acta Psychiatrica Scandinavica, 101,* 11–20.

Villardita, C., Cultrera, S., Cupone, V., & Mejia, R. (1985). Neuropsychological test performances and normal aging. *Archives of Gerontology and Geriatrics, 4,* 311–319.

Vogt, B. A., Absher, J. R., & Bush, G. (2000). Human retrosplenial cortex: Where is it and is it involved in emotion? *Trends in Neurosciences, 23,* 195–196.

Vogt, B. A., Finch, D. M., & Olson, C. R. (1992). Functional heterogeneity in cingulated cortex: The anterior executive and posterior evaluative regions. *Cerebral Cortex, 2,* 435–443.

Volkow, N. D., Chang, L., Wang, G. J., Fowler, J. S., Leonido-Yee, M., Franceschi, D., Sedler, M. J., Gatley, S. J., Hitzemann, R., Ding, Y. S., Logan, J., Wong, C., & Miller, E. N. (2001). Association of dopamine transporter reduction with psychomotor impoairment in methamphetamine abusers. *American Journal of Psychiatry, 158*(3), 377–382.

Volkow, N. D., Hitzemann, R., Wang, G. J., Fowler, J. S., Wolf, A. P., Dewey, S. L., & Handlesman, L. (1992). Long-term frontal brain metabolic changes in cocaine abusers. *Synapse, 11,* 183–190.

von Stockert, T. R., & Bader, A. L. (1976). Some relations of grammar and lexicon in aphasia. *Cortex, 12,* 49–60.

Voytko, M., Olton, D., Richardson, R., Gorman, L., Tobin, J., & Price, D. (1994). Basal forebrain lesions in monkeys disrupt attention but not learning and memory. *Journal of Neuroscience, 14,* 167–186.

Vuilleumier, P., Sagiv, N., Hazeltine, E., Poldrack, R. A., Swick, D., Rafal, R. D., & Gabrieli, J. D. E. (2001). Neural fate of seen and unseen faces in visuospatial neglect: A combined event-related functional MRI and event-related potential study. *Proceedings of the National Academy of Sciences, USA, 98, 3495–3500.*

Wachsmuth, E., Oram, M. W., & Perrett, D. I. (1994). Recognition of objects and their component parts: Responses of single units in the temporal cortex of the macaque. *Cerebral Cortex, 5,* 509–522.

Wada, J. A., Clarke, R., & Hamm, A. (1975). Cerebral hemispheric asymmetry in humans. *Archives of Neurology, 32,* 239–246.

Wagner, A. D. (1999). Working-memory contributions to human learning and remembering. *Neuron, 22*(1), 19–22.

Wagner, A. D., Desmond, J. E., Glover, G. H., & Gabrieli, J. D. (1998). Prefrontal cortex and recognition memory. Functional-MRI evidence for context-dependent retrieval processes. *Brain, 121*(10), 1985–2002.

Wagner, A. D., Maril, A., Bjork, R. A., & Schacter, D. L. (2001). Prefrontal contributions to executive control: fMRI evidence for functional distinctions within lateral prefrontal cortex. *NeuroImage, 14,* 1337–1347.

Wagner, H. N., Burns, D. H., Dannais, R. F., Wong, D. F., Langstrom, B., Duefler, T., Frost, J. J., Ravert, H. T., Links, J. M., Rosenbloom, S. B., Lucas, S. E., Kramer, A. V., & Kuhlar, M. J. (1983). Imaging dopamine receptors in the human brain by positron tomography. *Science, 221,* 1264–1266.

Wake, G., Court, J., Pickering, A., Lewis, R., Wilkins, R., & Perry, E. (2000). CNS acetylcholine receptor activity in European medicinal plants traditionally used to improve failing memory. *Journal of Ethnopharmacology, 69,* 105–114.

Waldie, K. E., & Mosley, J. L. (2000). Developmental trends in right hemispheric participation in reading. *Neuropsychologia, 38*(4), 462–474.

Walker, B. B., & Sandman, C. A. (1979). Human visual evoked responses are related to heart rate. *Journal of Comparative and Physiological Psychology, 93,* 717–729.

Wallesch, C. W., Henriksen, L., Kornhuber, H. H., & Paulson, O. B. (1985). Observations on regional cerebral blood flow in cortical and subcortical structures during language production in normal man. *Brain and Language, 25,* 224–233.

Walsh, V., Ellison, A., Battelli, L., & Cowey, A. (1998). Task-specific impairments and enhancements induced by magnetic stimulation of human visual area V5. *Proceedings of the Royal Society of London, B, 265,* 537–543.

Wapner, W., Hamby, S., & Gardner, H. (1981). The role of the right hemisphere in the apprehension of complex linguistic materials. *Brain and Language, 14,* 15–33.

Warburton, D. M. (1979). Neurochemical basis of consciousness. In K. Brown & S. J. Cooper (Eds.), *Chemical influences on behavior* (pp. 421–462). New York: Academic Press.

Warburton, D. M., & Rusted, J. M. (1993). Cholinergic control of cognitive resources. *Neuropsychobiology, 28,* 43–46.

Warren, K. R. & Foudin, L. L. (2001). Alcohol-related birth defects—The past, present, and future. *Alcohol Research and Health, 25,* 153–158.

Warren, L. R., Butler, R. W., Katholi, C. R., & Halsey, J. H. (1985). Age differences in cerebral blood flow during rest and during mental activation measurements with and without monetary incentive. *Journal of Gerontology, 40,* 53–59.

Warren, S. T., & Nelson, D. L. (1994). Advances in molecular analysis of fragile X syndrome. *Journal of the American Medical Association, 271*(7), 536–542.

Warrington, E. K. (1975). The selective impairment of semantic memory. *Quarterly Journal of Experimental Psychology, 27,* 187–199.

Warrington, E. K. (1982). Neuropsychological studies of object recognition. *Philosophical Transactions of the Royal Society of London, B298,* 15–33.

Warrington, E. K. (1985). A disconnection analysis of amnesia. *Annals of the New York Academy of Sciences, 444,* 72–77.

Warrington, E. K., & James, M. (1986). Visual object recognition in patients with right-hemisphere lesions: Axes or features? *Perception, 15,* 355–366.

Warrington, E. K., & James, M. (1988). Visual apperceptive agnosia: A clinico-anatomical study of three cases. *Cortex, 24,* 13–32.

Warrington, E. K., James, M., & Kinsbourne, M. (1966). Drawing disability in relation to laterality of cerebral lesion. *Brain, 89,* 53–82.

Warrington, E. K., & McCarthy, R. A. (1987). Categories of knowledge: Further fractionations and an attempted integration. *Brain, 110,* 1273–1296.

Warrington, E. K., & McCarthy, R. A. (1994). Multiple meaning systems in the brain: A case for visual semantics. *Neuropsychologia, 32,* 1465–1473.

Warrington, E. K., & Rabin, P. (1970). Perceptual matching in patients with cerebral lesions. *Neuropsychologia, 8,* 475–487.

Warrington, E. K., & Shallice, T. (1980). Word-form dyslexia. *Brain, 103,* 99–112.

Warrington, E. K., & Shallice, T. (1984). Category specific semantic impairments. *Brain, 107,* 829–854.

Warrington, E. K., & Taylor, A. M. (1973). The contribution of the right parietal lobe to object recognition. *Cortex, 9,* 152–164.

Warrington, E. K., & Taylor, A. M. (1978). Two categorical stages of object recognition. *Perception, 7,* 695–705.

Warrington, E. K., & Weiskrantz, L. (1968). A new method of testing long-term retention with special reference to amnestic patients. *Nature, 217,* 972–974.

Warrington, E. K., & Weiskrantz, L. (1970). The amnesic syndrome: Consolidation or retrieval? *Nature, 228,* 628–630.

Wasserman, E. M. (1998). Risk and safety of repetitive transcranial magnetic stimulation: Report and suggested guidelines from the international workshop on the safety of repetitive transcranial magnetic stimulation, June 5–7, 1996. *Electroencephalography and Clinical Neurophysiology, 198,* 1–16.

Wasserman, E. M., Cohen, L. G., Flitman, S. S., Chen, R., & Hallett, M. (1996). Seizure in healthy people with repeated 'safe' trains of transcranial magnetic stimulation. *Lancet, 347,* 825–826.

Watson, R. T., Heilman, K. M., Cauthen, J. C., & King, F. A. (1973). Neglect after cingulectomy. *Neurology, 23,* 1003–1007.

Watson, R. T., Miller, B. D., & Heilman, K. M. (1978). Nonsensory neglect. *Annals of Neurology, 3,* 505–508.

Watson, R. T., Valenstein, E., & Heilman, K. M. (1981). Thalamic neglect. *Archives of Neurology, 38,* 501–506.

Webb, S. J., Monk, C. S., & Nelson, C. A. (2001). Mechanisms of postnatal neurobiological development: Implications for human development. *Developmental Neuropsychology, 19,* 147–171.

Webb, T. P., Bundey, S. E., Thake, A. I., & Todd, J. (1986). Population incidence and segregation ratios in the Martin-Bell syndrome. *American Journal of Medical Genetics, 23,* 573–580.

Weber-Fox, C., & Neville, H. J. (1996). Maturational constraints on functional specializations for language processing: ERP and behavioral evidence in bilingual speakers. *Journal of Cognitive Neuroscience, 8,* 231–256.

Wechsler adult intelligence scale, third edition: Technical manual (1997). New York: The Psychological Corporation.

Wechsler, D. (1981). *Manual for the Wechsler Adult Intelligence Scale—Revised.* San Antonio, TX: Psychological Corporation.

Wechsler, D. (1989). *Manual for the Wechsler Preschool and Primary Scale of Intelligence—Revised.* San Antonio, TX: Psychological Corporation.

Wechsler, D. (1991). *Manual for the Wechsler Intelligence Scale for Children—Third Edition.* San Antonio, TX: Psychological Corporation.

Weinberger, D. R., Berman, K. F., & Illowsky, B. P. (1988). Physiological dysfunction of dorsolateral prefrontal cortex in schizophrenia: III. A new cohort and evidence for a monoaminergic mechanism. *Archives of General Psychiatry, 45,* 609–615.

Weinberger, N. M., Javid, R., & Lepan, B. (1995). Heterosynaptic long-term facilitation of sensory-evoked responses in the auditory cortex by stimulation of the magnocellular medial geniculate body in guinea pigs. *Behavioral Neuroscience, 109*(1), 10–17.

Weiner, W. J., & Goetz, C. G. (Eds.), (1989). *Neurology for the non-neurologist* (2nd ed.). Philadelphia: Lippincott.

Weingartner, H., Kaye, W., Smallberg, S. A., Ebert, M. H., Gillin, J. C., & Sitaram, N. (1981). Memory failures in progressive idiopathic dementia. *Journal of Abnormal Psychology, 90,* 187–196.

Weingartner, H., Grafman, J., Boutelle, W., & Martin, P. (1983). Forms of cognitive failures. *Science, 221,* 380–382.

Weintraub, S., & Mesulam, M. (1987). Right cerebral dominance in spatial attention. *Archives of Neurology, 44,* 621–625.

Weintraub, S., Mesulam, M.-M., & Kramer, L. (1981). Disturbances in prosody: A right hemisphere contribution to language. *Archives of Neurology, 38,* 742–744.

Weiskrantz, L. (1985). On issues and theories of the human amnesic syndrome. In N. Weinberger, J. L. McGaugh, & G. Lynch (Eds.), *Memory systems of the brain* (pp. 380–418). New York: Guilford Press.

Weiss, B. (2000). Vulnerability to pesticide neurotoxicity is a lifetime issue. *Neurotoxicology, 21*(1–2), 67–73.

Weissman, C., & Aguzzi, A. (1997). Bovine spongiform encephalopathy and early onset variant Creutzfeldt-Jakob disease. *Current Opinion in Neurobiology, 7,* 695–700.

Weissman, D. H. & Banich, M. T. (2000). The cerebral hemispheres cooperate to perform complex but not simple tasks. *Neuropsychology, 14*(1), 41–59.

Weissman; M. M., Leaf, P. J., Holzer, C. E. I., Myers, J. K., & Tischler, G. L. (1984). The epidemiology of depression: An update on sex differences in rates. *Journal of Affective Disorders, 7,* 179–188.

Welsh, K. A., Butters, N., Hughes, J., Mohs, R., & Heyman, A. (1991). Detection of abnormal memory decline in mild cases of Alzheimer's disease using CERAD neuropsychological measures. *Archives of Neurology, 48,* 278–281.

Wesnes, K. A., Ward, T., McGinty, A., & Petrini, O. (2000). The memory-enhancing effects of a *Ginkgo biloba/Panax ginseng* combination in healthy middle-aged volunteers. *Psychopharmacology, 152,* 353–361.

Wesnes, K., & Warburton, D. M. (1984). Effects of scopolamine and nicotine on human rapid information-processing performance. *Psychopharmacology, 82*(3), 147–150.

West, R. L., (1996). An application of prefrontal cortex function theory to cognitive aging. *Psychological Bulletin, 120,* 272–292.

Westwood, D. A., Schweizer, T. A., Heath, M. D., Roy, E. A., Dixon, M. J., & Black, S. (2001). Transitive gesture production in apraxia: Visual and nonvisual sensory contributions. *Brain & Cognition, 46,* 300–304.

Wettstein, A. (2000). Cholinesterase inhibitors and Gingko extracts—Are they comparable in the treatment of dementia? Comparison of published placebo-controlled efficacy studies of at least six months' duration. *Phytomedicine, 6,* 393–401.

Whalen, C. K., Henker, B., & Dotemoto, S. (1981). Teacher response to methylphenidate (Ritalin) versus placebo status of hyperactive boys in the classroom. *Child Development, 52,* 1005–1014.

Whalen, P. J. (1998). Fear, vigilance, and ambiguity: Initial neuroimaging studies of the human amygdala. *Current Directions in Psychological Science, 7,* 177–188.

Whalley, L. J. (1989). Drug treatment of dementia. *British Journal of Psychiatry, 155,* 595–611.

Wheeler, M. A., Stuss, D. T., & Tulving, E. (1995). Frontal lobe damage produces episodic memory impairment. *Journal of the International Neuropsychological Society, 1*(6), 525–536.

Wheeler, M. E., Petersen, S. E., & Buckner, R. L. (2000). Memory's echo: Vivid remembering reactivates sensory-specific cortex. *Proceedings of the National Academy of Science, USA, 97*(20), 11125–11129.

Whelihan, W. M., & Lesher, E. (1985). Neuropsychological changes in frontal functions with aging. *Developmental Neuropsychology, 1,* 371–380.

Whishaw, I. Q., Cassel, J. C., & Jarrad, L. E. (1995). Rats with fimbria-fornix lesions display a place response in a swimming pool: A dissociation between getting there and knowing where. *Journal of Neuroscience, 15*(8), 5779–5788.

White, D., Heaton, R. K., Monsch, A. U., & the HNRC Group (1995). Neuropsychological studies of asymptomatic human immunodeficiency virus-type-1 infected individuals. *Journal of the International Neuropsychological Society, 1,* 304–315.

White, N. M., & McDonald, R. J. (1993). Acquisition of a spatial conditioned place preference is impaired by amygdala lesions and improved by fornix lesions. *Behavioral Brain Research, 55*(2), 269–281.

Whitehouse, P. J., Price, D. L., Clark, A. W., Coyle, J. T., & DeLong, M. R. (1981). Alzheimer disease: Evidence for selective loss of cholinergic neurons in the nucleus basalis. *Annals of Neurology, 10,* 122–126.

Whitehouse, P. J., Price, D. L., Stubble, R. G., Clark, A. W., Coyle, J. T., & DeLong, M. R. (1982). Alzheimer's disease and senile dementia: Loss of neurons in the basal forebrain. *Science, 215,* 1237–1239.

Whitlow, S. D., Althoff, R. R., & Cohen, N. J. (1995). Deficit in relational (declarative) memory in amnesia. *Society for Neuroscience Abstracts, 21,* 754.

Wickens, C., Kramer, A., Vanasse, L., & Donchin, E. (1983). Performance of concurrent tasks: A psychophysiological analysis of the reciprocity of information-processing resources. *Science, 221,* 1080–1082.

Wickens, C. D. (1980). The structure of attentional resources. In R. Nickerson & R. Pew (Eds.), *Attention and performance VIII.* Hillsdale, NJ: Erlbaum.

Wiggins, S., Whyte, P., Higgins, M., Adam, S., Theilmann, J., Bloch, M., Sheps, S. B., Schechter, M. T., & Hayden, M. R. (1992). The psychological consequences of predictive testing for Huntington's disease. *New England Journal of Medicine, 327,* 1401–1405.

Wigstrom, H., & Gustafsson, B. (1985). On long-lasting potentiation in the hippocampus: A proposed mechanism for its dependence on pre- and postsynaptic activity. *Acta Psychologia Scandinavica, 123,* 519–522.

Wilcock, G. K. (1994). The role of growth factors and neuropeptides in Alzheimer's disease. *Human Psychopharmacology Clinical and Experimental, 9,* 353–356.

Wilcock, G. K., Esiri, M. M., Bowen, D. M., & Smith, C. C. T. (1982). Alzheimer's disease: Correlation of cortical choline acetyltransferase activity with the severity of dementia and histological abnormalities. *Journal of Neurological Sciences, 57,* 407–417.

Wilkins, W. K., & Wakefield, J. (1995). Brain evolution and neurolinguistic preconditions. *Behavioral & Brain Sciences Special Issue: Second Annual "Controversies in Neuroscience" Conference, 18*(1), 161–226

Will, R. G., & Matthews, W. B. (1984). A retrospective study of Creutzfeld-Jakob disease in England and Wales, 1970–1979. I. Clinical features. *Journal of Neurology, Neurosurgery and Psychiatry, 47,* 134–140.

Williams, G. V., & Goldman-Rakie, P. S., (1995) Modulation of memory fields by dopamine D1 receptors in prefrontal cortex. *Nature, 376,* 572–575.

Williamson, P. D., French, J. A., Thadani, V. M., Kim, J. H., Novelly, R. A., Spencer, S. S., & Mattson, R. H. (1993). Characteristics of medial temporal lobe epilepsy: II. Interictal and ictal scalp electroencephalography, neuropsychological testing, neuroimaging, surgical results, and pathology. *Annals of Neurology, 34,* 781–787.

Willingham, D. B., & Koroshetz, W. J. (1993). Evidence for dissociable motor skills in Huntington's disease patients. *Psychobiology, 21*(3), 173–182.

Wilson, B., Kaszniak, A. W., & Fox, J. H. (1981). Remote memory in senile dementia. *Cortex, 17,* 41–48.

Wilson, B. A. (1997). Cognitive rehabilitation: How it is and how it might be. *Journal of the International Neuropsychological Society, 3,* 487–496.

Wilson, B. A. (1998). Recovery of cognitive functions following nonprogressive brain injury. *Current Opinion in Neurobiology, 8,* 281–287.

Wilson, B. A., Evans, J. J., Emslie, H., & Malinke, V. (1997). Evaluation of NeuroPage: A new memory aid. *Journal of Neurology, Neurosurgery, and Psychiatry, 63,* 113–115.

Wilson, F. A., O Scalaidhe, S. P., & Goldman-Rakie, P. S. (1993). Dissociation of object and spatial processing domains in primate prefrontal cortex. *Science, 260,* 1955–1958.

Wilson, M. A., & McNaughton, B. L. (1994). Reactivation of hippocampal ensemble memories during sleep. *Science, 265*(5172), 676–679.

Wilson, R. S., Bacon, L. D., Fox, J. H., & Kaszniak, A. W. (1983). Primary memory and secondary memory in dementia of the Alzheimer type. *Journal of Clinical Neuropsychology, 5,* 337–344.

Wilson, R. S., Sullivan, M., de Toledo-Morrell, L., Stebbin, G. T., Bennett, D. A., & Morrell, P. (1996). Association of memory and cognition in Alzheimer's disease with volumetric estimate of temporal lobe structures. *Neuropsychology, 10,* 459–463.

Winner, E. (1982). *Invented worlds: The psychology of the arts.* Cambridge, MA: Harvard University Press.

Winner, E., & Gardner, H. (1977). The comprehension of metaphor in brain-damaged patients. *Brain, 100,* 719–727.

Winocur, G. (1980). The hippocampus and cue utilization. *Physiological Psychology, 8*(2), 280–288.

Wirshing, W. C., & Cummings, J. (1990). Tardive movement disorders. *Neuropsychiatry, Neuropsychology and Behavioral Neurology, 3,* 23–35.

Wisniewski, K. E., Wisniewski, H. M., & Wen, G. Y. (1985). Occurrence of neuropathological changes and dementia of Alzheimer's disease in Down's syndrome. *Annals of Neurology, 17,* 278–282.

Witelson, S. F. (1974). Hemisphere specialization for linguistic and nonlinguistic tactual perception using a dichotomous stimulation technique. *Cortex, 10,* 3–17.

Witelson, S. F. (1977). Early hemisphere specialization and inter-hemispheric plasticity: An empirical and theoretical review. In S. J. Segalowitz & F. A. Gruber (Eds.), *Language development and neurological theory* (pp. 213–289). New York: Academic Press.

Witelson, S. F., & Goldsmith, C. H. (1991). The relationship of hand preference to anatomy of the corpus callosum in men. *Brain Research, 545,* 175–182.

Witelson, S. F., & Nowakowski, R. S. (1991). Left out axons make men right: A hypothesis for the origin of handedness and functional asymmetry. *Neuropsychologia, 29,* 327–333.

Witelson, S. F., & Pallie, W. (1973). Left hemisphere specialization in the newborn: Anatomical evidence of asymmetry. *Brain, 96,* 641–646.

Witte, E. A., Davidson, M. C., & Marrocco, R. T. (1997). Effects of altering brain cholinergic activity on covert orienting of attention: Comparison of monkey and human performance. *Psychopharmacology, 132,* 324–334.

Wittling, W. (1990). Psychophysiological correlates of human brain asymmetry: Blood pressure changes during lateralized presentation of an emotionally laden film. *Neuropsychologia, 28,* 457–470.

Wittling, W., & Pflüger, M. (1990). Neuroendocrine hemisphere asymmetries: Salivary cortisol secretion during lateralized viewing of emotion-related and neutral films. *Brain and Cognition, 14,* 243–265.

Woelk, H. (2000). Comparison of St John's wort and imipramine for treating depression: Randomised controlled trial. *British Medical Journal, 321,* 536–539.

Wojeiulik, E., & Kanwisher, N. (1999). The generality of parietal involvement in visual attention. *Neuron, 23,* 747–764.

Wojeiulik, E., Kanwisher, N., & Driver, J. (1998). Covert visual attention modulates face-specific activity in the human fusiform gyrus: fMRI study. *Journal of Neurophysiology, 79,* 1574–1578.

Wolf, S. S., Jones, D. W., Knable, M. B., Gorey, J. G., Less, K. S., Hyde, T. M., Coppola, R., & Weinberger, D. R. (1996). Tourette syndrome: Prediction of phenotypic variation in monozygotic twins by caudate nucleus D_2 receptor binding. *Science, 273,* 1225–1227.

Wolff, P. H., Cohen, C., & Drake, C. (1984). Impaired motor timing control in specific reading retardation. *Neuropsychologia, 22,* 587–600.

Wolpert, D. M., & Ghahramani, Z. (2000). Computational principles of movement neuroscience. *Nature Neuroscience, 3*(Suppl), 1212–1217.

Wong, D. F., Wagner, H. N., Tune, L. E., Dannals, R. F., et al. (1986). Positron emission tomography revealed elevated D2 receptors in drug-naive schizophrenics. *Science, 234,* 1558–1563.

Wong, E. H. F., Reynolds, G. P., Bonhaus, D. W., Hsu, S., & Eglen, R. M. (1996). Characterization of [3H]GR 113808 binding to 5-HT_4 receptors in brain tissues from patients with neurodegenerative disorders. *Behavioral Brain Research, 73,* 249–252.

Wood, E. R., Dudchenko, P. A., & Eichenbaum, H. (1999). The global record of memory in hippocampal neuronal activity. *Nature, 397*(6720), 613–616.

Woods, B. T. (1980). The restricted effects of right-hemisphere lesions after age one: Wechsler test data. *Neuropsychologia, 18,* 65–70.

Woolley, C. (1999). Effects of estrogen in the CNS. *Current Opinion in Neurobiology, 9,* 349–354.

Wright, B. A., Bowen, R. W., & Zecker, S. G. (2000). Nonlinguistic perceptual deficits associated with reading and language disorders. *Current Opinion in Neurobiology, 10,* 482–486.

Wright, C. E. (1990). Controlling sequential motor activity. In D. N. Osherson, S. M. Kosslyn, & J. M. Hollerbach (Eds.), *Visual cognition and action* (pp. 285–316). Cambridge, MA: MIT Press.

Wright, P., Williams, J., Currie, C., & Beattie, T. (1996). Left-handedness increases injury risk in adolescent girls. *Perceptual & Motor Skills, 82*(3, Pt 1), 855–858.

Wurtz, R. H., & Goldberg, M. E. (1972). Activity of superior colliculus in behaving monkey: III. Cells discharging before eye movements. *Journal of Neurophysiology, 35,* 575–586.

Wurtz, R. H., & Goldberg, M. E. (Eds.). (1988). *The neurobiology of saccadic eye movements.* Amsterdam: Elsevier.

Yakovlev, P. I., & Lecours, A. R. (1967). The myelogenetic cycles of regional maturation of the brain. In A. Minkowski (Ed.), *Regional development of the brain in early life* (pp. 3–65). Oxford, England: Blackwell.

Yamaguchi, S., & Knight, R. T. (1991). Anterior and posterior association cortex contributions to the somatosensory P_{300}. *Journal of Neuroscience, 11,* 2039–2054.

Yin, R. K. (1970). Face recognition by brain-injured patients: A dissociable ability? *Neuropsychologia, 8,* 395–402.

Yokoyama, K., Jennings, R., Ackles, P., Hood, P., & Boller, F. (1987). Lack of heart rate changes during an attention-demanding task after right hemisphere lesions. *Neurology, 37,* 624–630.

Young, A. W., Aggleton, J. P., Hellawell, D. J., Johnson, M., Broks, P., & Hanley, J. R. (1995). Face processing impairments after amygdalotomy. *Brain, 118*(1), 15–24.

Young, A. W., DeHaan, E. H. F., Newcombe, F., & Hay, D. C. (1990). Facial neglect. *Neuropsychologia, 28,* 391–415.

Young, A. W., Hellawell, D. J., & Welch, J. (1992). Neglect and visual recognition. *Brain, 115,* 51–71.

Yurgelun-Todd, D. A., Renshaw, P. F., & Cohen, B. M. (1995). Functional MRI of schizophrenics and normal controls during word production. *Schizophrenia Research, 15,* 104–111.

Zahrt, J., Taylor, J. R., Mathew, R. G., & Arnsten, A. F. T. (1997). Supranormal stimulation of dopamine D1 receptors in the rodent prefrontal cortex impairs spatial working memory performance. *Journal of Neuroscience, 17,* 8525–8535.

Zaidel, D. W., & Kasher, A. (1989). Hemispheric memory for surrealistic versus realistic paintings. *Cortex, 25,* 617–641.

Zaidel, E. (1978). Auditory language comprehension in the right hemisphere following cerebral commissurotomy and hemispherectomy: A comparison with child language and aphasia. In A. Caramazza & E. B. Zurif (Eds.), *Language acquisition and language breakdown: Parallels and divergencies* (pp. 229–275). Baltimore: Johns Hopkins University Press.

Zaidel, E. (1983a). Disconnection syndrome as a model for laterality effects in the normal brain. In J. B. Hellige (Ed.), *Cerebral hemisphere asymmetry: Method, theory and application* (pp. 95–151). New York: Praeger.

Zaidel, E. (1983b). A response to Gazzaniga: Language in the right hemisphere, convergent perspectives. *American Psychologist, 38,* 542–546.

Zaidel, E. (1990). The saga of right-hemisphere reading. In C. Trevarthen (Ed.), *Brain circuits and functions of the mind: Essays in honor of Roger W. Sperry* (pp. 304–319). Cambridge, England: Cambridge University Press.

Zajonc, R. B. (1980). Feeling and thinking: Preferences need no inferences. *American Psychologist, 35,* 151–175.

Zajonc, R. B. (1984). On the primacy of affect. *American Psychologist, 39,* 117–123.

Zametkin, A. J., Liebenauer, L. L., Fitzgerald, G. A., King, A. C., Minkunas, D. V., Herscovitch, P., Yamada, E. M., & Cohen, R. M. (1993). Brain metabolism in teenagers with attention deficit hyperactivity disorder. *Archives of General Psychiatry, 50,* 333–340.

Zangwill, O. L. (1960). La problème de l'apraxie idéatoire. *Revue Neurologique (Paris), 102,* 595–603.

Zatorre, R. J. (1984). Musical perception and cerebral function: A critical review. *Music Perception, 2,* 196–221.

Zatorre, R. J. (1985). Discrimination and recognition of tonal melodies after unilateral cerebral excisions. *Neuropsychologia, 23,* 31–41.

Zatorre, R. J. (1988). Pitch perception of complex tones and human temporal-lobe function. *Journal of the Acoustical Society of America, 84,* 566–572.

Zatorre, R. J., Evans, A. C., Meyer, E., & Gjedde, A. (1992). Lateralization of phonetic and pitch discrimination in speech processing. *Science, 256,* 846–849.

Zatorre, R. J., Meyer, E., Gjedde, A., & Evans, A. C. (1996). PET studies of phonetic processing of speech: Review, replication, and reanalysis. *Cerebral Cortex, 6,* 21–30.

Zatorre, R. J., & Samson, S. (1991). Role of the right temporal neocortex in retention of pitch in auditory short-term memory. *Brain, 114,* 2403–2417.

Zeki, S. (1980). The representation of colours in the cerebral cortex. *Nature, 284,* 412–418.

Zeki, S., & Shipp, S. (1988). The functional logic of cortical connections. *Nature, 335,* 311–317.

Zeki, S., Watson, J. D. G., Lueck, C. J., Friston, K. J., Kennard, C., & Frackowiak, R. S. J. (1991). A direct demonstration of functional specialization in human visual cortex. *Journal of Neuroscience, 11,* 641–649.

Zemper, E. (1994). Analysis of cerebral concussion frequency with the most commonly used models of football helmets. *Journal of Athletic Training, 29,* 33–50.

Zigmond, M. J., Abercrombie, E. D., Berger, T. W., Grace, A. A., et al. (1990). Compensations after lesions of central dopaminergic neurons: Some clinical and basic implications. *Trends in Neurosciences, 13,* 290–296.

Zihl, J., Von Cramon, D., & Mai, N. (1983). Selective disturbance of movement vision after bilateral brain damage. *Brain, 106,* 313–340.

Zipser, D., & Andersen, R. A. (1988). A backpropagation programmed network that simulates response properties of a subset of posterior parietal neurons. *Nature, 331,* 679–684.

Zoccolotti, P., Matan, A., Deloche, G., Cantagallo, A., Passadori, A., Leclercq, M., Braga, L., Cremel, N., Pittau, P., Renom, M., Rousseaux, M., Truche, A., Fimm, B., & Zimmermann, P. (2000). Patterns of attentional impairment following closed head injury: A collaborative European study. *Cortex, 36,* 93–107.

Zola-Morgan, S., Cohen, N. J., & Squire, L. R. (1983). Recall of remote episodic memory in amnesia. *Neuropsychologia, 21*(5), 487–500.

Zola-Morgan, S., & Squire, L. R. (1985). Medial temporal lesions in monkeys impair memory on a variety of tasks sensitive to human amnesia. *Behavioral Neuroscience, 99,* 22–34.

Zurif, E. B., Gardner, J., & Brownell, H. H. (1989). The case against the case against group studies. *Brain and Cognition, 10,* 237–255.

CREDITS

Chapter 1

6 Adapted from Kolb & Whishaw, 2001, p. 83. Worth Publishers © 2001. **7** Adapted from Rosenzweig & Leiman, 1989, p. 29. **8** Adapted from Rosenzweig & Leiman, 1989, p. 30; Purves, 2001, p. 32. **9** Adapted from Kolb & Whishaw, 1990, p. 26. **11** Adapted from Kandel et al., 1991, p. 8; Kolb & Whishaw, 1990, p. 13. **12** Adapted from Kandel et al., 1991, p. 7. **13** Adapted from Groves & Rebec, 1988, p. 103; Kalat, 1992, p. 110. **15** Adapted from Kalat, 1992, p. 109. **17** A, Adapted from Carlson, 1994, p. 93; B, Adapted from Kandel et al., 1991, p. 648. **18** Adapted from Kalat, 1992, p. 112; Kandel et al., 1991, p. 736; Gazzaniga et al., 1998, p. 56. **20** Adapted from Carlson, 1994, p. 89. **21** Adapted from Kandel et al., 1991, p. 372; Posner & Raichle, 1994, p. 14. **22** Adapted from Kandel et al., 1991, p. 372; Posner & Raichle, 1994, p. 14. **26** Adapted from Kalat, 1992, p. 235; Kandel et al., 1991, p. 432. **29** Adapted from Kalat, 1992, p. 201. **30** A, Adapted from Romani et al., 1982; B, Adapted from Purves et al., 2001. **31** Adapted from Groves & Rebec, 1988, p. 103; Kandel et al., 1991, p. 517. **33** A, Adapted from Damasio, 1991b, p. 103; B, Adapted from McCarthy & Warrington, 1990, p. 357.

Chapter 2

42 Adapted from Carlson, 2001, p. 45. **43** Adapted from Kandel et al., 1991, p. 19. **45** From Purves et al., 2001. **46** Adapted from Kolb & Whishaw, 2001, p. 197. **49** Adapted from Purves et al., 2001, p. 121. **50** Adapted from Kolb, 1992, p. 72. **59** Adapted from Carlson, 1994, p. 27; Kahle et al., p. 31.

Chapter 3

70 Adapted from Jernigan & Ostergaard, 1993, p. 19. **73** From *Lesion Analysis in Neuropsychology* by Hana Damasio and Antonio R. Damasio. Copyright © 1989 by Oxford University press, Inc. Used by permission of Oxford University Press Inc.. **74–75** A, From *Lesion Analysis in Neuropsychology* by Hana Damasio and Antonio R. Damasio. Copyright © 1989 by Oxford University Press, Inc. Used by permission of Oxford University Press Inc.; B, Adapted from Damasio & Damasio, 1989, pp. 56, 57. **76–77** Adapted from Damasio & Damasio 1989, pp. 190, 191. **78** Reprinted with permission from "Introduction and Overview," by E. D. Bigler, R. A. Yeo, and F. Turkheimer, in *Neuropsychological Function and Brain Imaging* (p. 10), edited by E. D. Bigler, R. A. Yeo, and F. Turkheimer, 1989, New York, Plenum Press. **80** Adapted from Posner & Raichle, 1994, pp. 19, 63. **83** Adapted from Moonen et al, 2000, p. 158. **85** Sandro Miller/Getty Images. **86** From Allison, T., Puce, A., & McGarthy, G. (2000). Social perception from visual cues: role of the STS region. *Trends in Cognitive Sciences, 4*(7), p. 272. **87** Adapted from Kandel et al., 1991, p. 779. **88–89** A, From *Epilepsy and the Functional Anatomy of the Human Brain,* by W. Penfield and H. H. Jasper, 1954, Boston, Little Brown. Reprinted by permission of Lippincott, Williams, & Wilkins; B, From *A Primer of Electroencephalography*, by G. D. Vander Ark and L. G. Kemp, 1970. Copyright © 1970 by Hoffmann-Laroche. **90** Adapted from Hillyard & Kurtas, 1983, p. 35. **93 (left)** From Clark & Hillyard, 1996, p. 392; **(right)** B, Modified from Hämäläinen et al., 1993, p. 417, figs. 4 & 5. **94** From Proc. Natl. Acad. Sci. USA, Vol. 93, p. 8810. **95** Adapted from Gratton & Fabiani, 1998, p. 544. **97** Adapted from Ilmoniemi et al., 1999, p. 247. **107** From Pashler, 1998, p. 325.

Chapter 4

113 From Carrie Newcomer, c/o Windchime Promotions, P.O. Box 3040, West Lafayette, IN 47906. Reprinted with permission. **114** A, Adapted from Hellige, 1993a, p. 116; B & C, Adapted from Kolb & Whishaw, 1990, p. 349. **117** B, Adapted from Sperry, 1964. **118** From Levy, Trevarthan, & Sperry, 1972. **122–123** Adapted from Kalat, 1992, p. 201. **125** Adapted from Ivry & Lebby, 1993, p. 42. **127** Adapted from Levy & Trevarthen, 1976. **128** Reprinted from *Neuropsychologia,*24. D. Delis, L. Robertson, & R. Efron, "Hemispheric Specialization of Memory for Visual Hierarchical Stimuli," pp. 205–214, Copyright © 1986, with permission from Elsevier Science Ltd., The Boulevard, Langford Lane, Kidlington OX5 1GB, UK. **129** Adapted from deLacoste et al., 1985. **130** Adapted from Sperry, 1964. **131** Adapted from Saron & Davidson, 1989, p. 1120.

Chapter 5

148 Adapted from Beatty, 1995, p. 253. **149** Adapted from *Physiology of Behavior* (3rd ed., p. 308), by N. Carlson, 1986, Boston: Allyn & Bacon. **150–151** Adapted from Carlson, 1986, pp. 304, 306. **153** A, Adapted from Kandel et al., 1995, p. 538; B, Adapted from Kandel et al., 1991, p. 629. **154** Reprinted from *International Review of Neurobiology, 41.* Richard Ivey,. "Cerebellar Timing Systems," 558. Copyright © 1997 with permission from Elsevier Science. **155** Adapted from Thach et al., 1992, pp. 429, 431. **156** Adapted from Ivry, 1996, p. 853. **158** A & C, Adapted from Rosenzweig & Leiman, 1989, p. 64; B, Adapted from Kandel et al., 1991, p. 648. **159** Adapted from Graybiel, 1990, p. 246; Mink & Thach, 1993, p. 952. **160** From Phillips et al., 1993. p. 179. **161** Adapted from Kolb & Whishaw, 1990, p. 464. **168** Adapted from Kolb & Whishaw, 1990, p. 16. **182** Adapted from Kolb & Whishaw, 1990, p. 309.

Chapter 6

187 (top) Adapted from Maunsell & Newsome, 1987, pp. 365, 367; **(bottom)** "Visual Properties of Neurons in Inferotemporal Cortex of the Macaque," by C. G. Gross, C. E. Rocha-Miranda, and D. B. Bender, 1972, *Journal of Neurophysiology, 35,* p. 104. **190** From Haxby et al., 2001,

p. 2426, fig. 1. **193** From Beiderman, I., 1987. "Matching Image Edges to Object Memory. From *Proceedings of the IEEE First International Conference on Computer Vision,* pp. 364–392. **195 (top)** D. F. Benson and J. P. Greenberg, "Visual Form Agnosia," from *Archives of Neurology, 20,* pp. 82–89. Copyright © 1969 by the American Medical Association. Reprinted by permission; **(bottom)** From Landis et al., 1982, p. 59. **196** A, From "Visual Object Recognition in Patients with Right Hemisphere Lesions," by E. K. Warrington and M. James, 1986, first published in *Perception, 14,* pp. 355–366, fig. 2. Reprinted by permission of Pion Limited, London. **197 (left)** Adapted from Marr & Nishihara, 1978, p. 19; **(right)** "Object Recognition: Some Deductions from the Clinical Evidence," by Graham Ratcliff & Frida Newcombe, in *Normality and Pathology in Cognitive Functions* (p. 162), edited by A. W. Ellis, 1982, London, Academic Press. **204** After "Margaret Thatcher: A New Illusion," by P. Thompson, 1980, *Perception, 9,* pp. 483–484. **205** Adapted from Allison et al., 1994, p. 548. **207** Adapted from Kreiman et al., 2000, p. 947, fig. 2, and p. 949, fig. 4. **209** Adapted from Myles-Worsley et al., 1988, p. 556. **211** From Gauthier et al., 1999, p. 569, fig. 1. **213** top, Reuters/Corbis-Bettmann; middle, UPI/Corbis-Bettmann; bottom, Reuters/Bettmann. **218** Adapted from Reed & Caselli, 1994.

Chapter 7

224 Adapted from Maunsell & Newsome, 1987, pp. 365, 367. **225** Adapted from Mishkin et al., 1983, p. 415. **227** Adapted from Kimura, 1969, pp. 447, 452. **229** From *Contributions to Neurological Assessment: A Clinical Manual,* by A. L. Benton, K. D. Hamsher, N. R. Varney, and O. Spreen, 1983, New York: Oxford University Press. **232** From *Mental Images and Their Transformations* (p. 35), by R. N. Shepard and L. A. Cooper, 1986, Cambridge, MA: MIT Press. Copyright © 1986 by The MIT Press. Reprinted by permission.; B. Adapted from Corballis & Sergent, 1989, p. 20. **233** From Carpenter, P. A., et al. (1999). Graded functional activation in the visuospatial system and the amount of task demand. *Journal of Cognitive Neuroscience, 11*(1), p. 14. **234** From *Neuropsychological Assessment* (2nd ed., p. 396), by M. D. Lezak, 1983, Oxford, England: Oxford University Press; B. Adapted with permission from "The Role of the Right Cerebral Hemisphere in Evaluating Configurations," by L. I. Benowitz, S. Finkelstein, D. N. Levine, and K. Moya, as appeared in *Brain Circuits and Functions of the Mind* (p. 327), edited by C. Trevarthen, Copyright © 1990, Reprinted by permission of Cambridge University Press. **236** Adapted from Milner, B. 1962b, 257–272. **237** Adapted from Morrow et al., 1985, pp. 269, 270. **240 (left)** Adapted from DeRenzi et al., 1977, p. 426; **(right)** Reprinted from *Neuropsychologia,*. 32, S. Pigott and B. Milner, "Capacity of Visual Short-Term Memory After Unilateral Frontal or Anterior Temporal-Lobe Resection," p. 975, Copyright 1994, with permission from Elsevier Science Ltd., The Boulevard, Langford Lane, Kidlington OX5 1GB, UK. **241** From E. E. Smith et al., 1996. "Dissociating Verbal and Spatial Working Memory Using PET," *Cerebral Cortex,6,* p. 12. Reprinted by permission of Oxford University Press and the author. **244** Adapted from Farah, 1990, p. 18. **249** A, From "Seeing and Imagining in the Cerebral Hemispheres: A Computational Approach," by S. M. Kosslyn, 1987, *Psychological Review, 94,* p. 164. Copyright © 1987 by the American Psychological Association. Reprinted with permission; B, From *Memory and Cognition, 17,* 1989, p. 772, reprinted by permission of Psychonomic Society, Inc.

Chapter 8

258 Adapted from Kelly, 1991, pp. 283–295. **259** From Farah, 2000, p. 198, Blackwell. **263** Adapted from Andreassi, 1989, p. 124. **269** From Vallar, 1998, p. 93, fig 5. **271** Adapted from Heilman et al., 1985, p. 246. **273** Adapted from Bisiach & Luzzatti, 1978, p. 130. **280** Reprinted with permission from "Asymmetry of Perception in Free Viewing of Chimeric Faces," by J. Levy, W. Heller, M. T. Banich, and L. A. Burton, 1983, *Brain and Cognition, 2,* p. 406.

Chapter 9

288 Adapted from Damasio, 1991a, p. 56. **290** A, Adapted from Damasio & Damasio, 1989, p. 184; B, Adapted from Damasio, 1981, p. 33. **291** A, Adapted from Damasio & Damasio, 1989, p. 184; B, Adapted from Damasio, 1981, p. 31. **292 (left)** Adapted from Damasio, 1991a, p. 57; **(right)** A, Adapted from Damasio & Damasio, 1989, p. 184; B, Adapted from Damasio, 1981, p. 34. **293 (left)** Adapted from Damasio, 1991a, p. 59; **(right)** Adapted from Damasio, 1991a, p. 47. **294** Adapted from Benson, 1985, p. 32. **298** Data from Rasmussen & Milner, 1997a, p. 359. **299** Adapted from Ojemann et al., 1989, pp. 318, 320. **302** A, From Hagoort & Brown, 2000a, p. 1523, fig. 2; B, From Hagoort & Brown, 2000b, p. 1535, fig. 1. **310** A, Reprinted with permission from *Writing Systems of the World* (p. 94), by A. Nakanishi, 1980, Rutland, VT: Charles E. Tuttle; B, Adapted with permission from *Writing Systems* (p. 178), by G. Sampson, 1985, Stanford, CA: Stanford University Press. **311 (left)** Adapted from Poizner et al., 1987, p. 4; **(right)** Adapted from Poizner et al., 1987, p. 52. **312** Adapted from Poizner et al., 1987, p. 15.

Chapter 10

326 Adapted from Kolb & Whishaw, 2001, p. 499, fig. 13–8. **328** Adapted from Squire & Cohen, 1979, p. 118. **329** Adapted from Barbizet, 1970. **330** Left, Adapted from Squire & Cohen, 1982, p. 289; Right, Adapted from Albert et al., 1979, p. 211. **334** A, N. J. Cohen and H. E. Eichenbaum, *Memory, Amnesia, and the Hippocampal System* (pp. 38–39), Copyright © 1993 by the MIT Press. Reprinted with permission. **335** From "Priming Effects in Picture Fragment Completion: Support for the Perceptual Closure Hypothesis," by J. G. Snodgrass and K. Feenan, 1990, *Journal of Experimental Psychology: General, 119,* p. 280. Copyright © 1990 by the American Psychological Association. Reprinted with permission. **336** Adapted from Graf et al., 1984. **339** Courtesy of Neal J. Cohen; used by permission. **341** A, Adapted from Eichenbaum et al., 1990; B & C, Adapted from Eichenbaum, 1994,

p. 162. **343** A, Adapted from O'Keefe, 1976, p. 377; B, Adapted from O'Keefe & Speakman, 1987; C, Adapted from Muller et al., 1987. **345 (top)** From Paul H. Mussen, ed., *Handbook of Child Psychology* Fourth Edition. Copyright © 1983 This material is used by permission of John Wiley & Sons, Inc; **(bottom)** Adapted from Funahashi et al., 1989, p. 335. **350** Adapted from Cohen & Eichenbaum, 1993, p. 255. **352** "Neural Organization for the Long-Term Memory of Paired Associates," by K. Sakai and Y. Miashita. Reprinted with permission from *Nature* (354, pp. 152–155). Copyright © 1991 by Macmillan Magazines Limited. **361** Adapted from Nolte, 1999, p. 454; Gazzaniga et al., 2002, p. 85.

Chapter 11

366 Adapted from M. D. Lezak (1983). *Neuropsychological Assessment,* 2nd ed., pp. 39–40. New York: Oxford University Press. **370** From "Human Autonomy and the Frontal Lobes: Part II. Patient Behavior in Complex and Social Situations. The 'Environmental Dependency Syndrome'" by F. Lhermitte, 1986. *Annals of Neurology,* 19(4), pp. 339, 340. Copyright © 1986 by the American Neurological Association. Used with permission of Lippincott-Raven Publishers, Philadelphia, PA. **371** Adapted from Delis et al., 1992, p. 688. **374** From Spencer et al., 1999, p. 411, fig. 1. **380** From "Specific Impairments of Planning," by T. Shallice, 1982, *Philosophical Transactions of the Royal Society of London, B298,* p. 204. **381** Adapted from Owen et al., 1991. **382** Reprinted from *Neuropsychologia, 21,* L. Cicerone, R. Lazar, and W. Shapiro, "Effects of Frontal Lobe Lesions on Hypothesis Sampling During Concept Formation," p. 515, Copyright © 1983, with permission from Elsevier Science, Ltd., The Boulevard, Langford Lane, Kidlington OX5 1GB, UK. **383** Reprinted from *Neuropsychologia, 30,* B. Alivisatos, "The Role of Frontal Cortex in the Use of Advance Information in a Mental Rotation Paradigm," p. 151, Copyright © 1992, with permission from Elsevier Science Ltd., The Boulevard, Langford Lane, Kidlington OX5 1GB, UK. **385** From Gehring, W. J., Goss, B., Coles, M. G. H., Meyer, D. E., & Donchin, E., "A Neural System for Error Detection and Compensation" from *Psychological Science* 4(6) November 1993, p. 387. Reprinted by permission of Blackwell Publishers.

Chapter 12

397 Adapted with permission from "Autonomic Nervous System Activity Distinguishes Among Emotions," by P. Ekman, R. W. Levenson, and W. V. Friesen, 1983, *Science, 221* p. 1209. Copyright © 1983 American Association for the Advancement of Science. **398** Adapted from Purves et al., 2001, p. 633. **399** Adapted from MacLean, 1967, p. 377. **403** From Davis, K. D., Taylor, S. J., Crawley, A.P., Wood, M. L., & Mikulis, D. J., "Functional MRI of pain- and attention-related activations in human cingulated cortex," from *Journal of Neurophysiology, 77,* Copyright © 1997, p. 3374. Reprinted by permission. **407** A, Adapted from Lipsey et al., 1983, p. 266; B, Adapted from Robinson et al., 1984, p. 81. **410** Adapted from Strauss & Moscovitch, 1981, p. 314. **414** A & B, Corbis-Bettmann; C & D, UPI/Corbis-Bettmann. **415** Reprinted with permission from "Emotions Are Expressed More Intensely on the Left Side of the Face," by H. A. Sackeim, R. C. Gur, M. C. Saucy, 1978, *Science, 202,* p. 434. Copyright © 1978 American Association for the Advancement of Science. **417** From *Neuropsychology, 7,* pp. 477–489. Copyright © 1993 by the American Psychological Association. Reprinted with permission. **420** From Paradiso S., Lamberty, G. J., Garvey, M. J., & Roboinson, R. G., "Cognitive Impairment in the Euthymic Phase of Chronic Unipolar Depression," *Journal of Nervous and Mental Disease, 185,* pp. 748–754, fig. 1. Reprinted by permission. **426** From Heckers, S., Rauch, S. L., Goff, D., Savage, C. R., Schacter, D. L., Fischman, A. J., and Alpert, N. M. "Impaired recruitment of the hippocampus during conscious recollection in schizophrenia," *Nature Neuroscience, 1,* (1998), 318–323, fig. 2, p. 321. Reprinted with permission of the publisher and the author.

Chapter 13

432 Adapted from *Child Neuropsychology: An Introduction to Theory, Research, and Clinical Practice* (pp. 343–350), by B. P. Rourke, D. J. Bakker, J. L. Fisk, and J. D. Strang, 1983, New York: Guildford Press. **433** Adapted from Reynolds & Fletcher-Jansen, 1989, p. 19; Spreen et al., 1984, p. 25. **434** Modified from the work of Conel, A, 1947; B, 1955; and C, 1959. With the permission of Dr. Karl H. Pribram. **435** From Paus et al., 2001, p. 37; van der Knapp & Valk, 1990, pp. 459–470. **436** From "Positron Emission Tomography Study of Human Brain Functional Development," by H. T. Chugani, M. E. Phelps, and J. C. Mazziotta, 1987, *Annals of Neurology,* 22(4), p. 492. Copyright © 1987 by the American Neurological Association. Used with permission of Lippincott-Raven Publishers, Philadelphia, PA. **437** Reprinted from *Neuropsychologia, 28,* P. R. Huttenlocher, "Morphometric Study of Human Cerebral Cortex Development," p. 519, Copyright © 1990, with permission from Elsevier Science Ltd., The Boulevard, Langford Lane, Kidlington OX5 1GB, UK. **439** Adapted from Kalat, 1992, p. 317; Kandel, 1991. **440** Adapted from Spreen et al., 1984, pp. 32–33. **442** From *Biological Psychology,* by J. W. Kalat. Copyright © 1992, 1988, 1984, 1981 Wadsworth, Inc. By permission of Brooks/Cole Publishing Company, Pacific Grove, CA 93950, a division of International Thomson Publishing Inc. **443** Adapted from Johnson & Newport, 1989, pp. 79, 80. **444** Adapted from Bigler, 1992, p. 489. **451 (top)** Data from American Psychiatric Association, 1994; **(bottom)** Data from American Psychiatric Association, 1994. **453** A, Cindy Karp/Picture Quest, B, Reprinted with permission from "Advances in Molecular Analysis of Fragile X Syndrome," by S. T. Warren and D. L. Nelson, 1994, *Journal of the American Medical Association, 271*(7), p. 537. Copyright © 1994, American Medical Association. **454** Adapted from Warren & Foudin, 2001, p. 155. **460** Adapted from Jenkins et al., 1990, p. 577. **462** Adapted from Wilson, 1998, p. 281. **464** Reprinted with permission of the publisher from *Cerebral Dominance: The Biological Foundations,* edited by A. M. Galaburda and N. S. Geschwind, Cambridge, Mass.: Harvard University Press, Copyright © 1984 by the President and Fellows of

Harvard College. **465** "System-wide Repercussions of Damage to the Immature Visual Cortex," by B. R. Payne and P. Cornwell, *Trends in Neuroscience, 17*(3), p. 127, Copyright © 1994, with permission from Elsevier Science Ltd., The Boulevard, Langford Lane, Kidlington OX5 1GB, UK. **466** Reprinted from *Neuropsychologia 28,* M. T. Banich, S. C. Levine, H. Kim, and P. Huttenlocher, "The Effects of Developmental Factors on IQ in Hemiplegic Children," pp. 40, 42. Copyright © 1990, with permission from Elsevier Science Ltd., The Boulevard, Langford Lane, Kidlington OX5 1GB, UK.

Chapter 14

480 From Nonspecific White Matter Degeneration Following Traumatic Brain Injury," by S. D. Gale, S. C. Johnson, E. D. Bigler, and D. D. Blatter, 1995, *Journal of the International Neuropsychological Society, 1,* p. 26. Copyright © 1995 Cambridge University Press, Reprinted with the permission of Cambridge University Press. **481** Adapted from Kolb & Whishaw, 1990, p. 820. **482** Adapted from Kelly & Rosenberg, 1997, 575–580. **486** Adapted from Cummings & Benson, 1984, p. 875. **488** Adapted from Reisbert, 1986, pp. 30–46. **489** CNRI/SPL/Photo Researchers, Inc. **490** From *Neuropsychology and the Dementias* (p. 32), by S. Hart and J. M. Semple, 1990, London, Erlbaum. Copyright © 1990. Reprinted by permission of Erlbaum (UK) Taylor & Francis. **491** From *Neuropsychology and the Dementias* (p. 30), by S. Hart and J. M. Semple, 1990, London, Erlbaum. Copyright © 1990. Reprinted by permission of Erlbaum (UK) Taylor & Francis. **492** A, Adapted from Kandel et al., 1991, p. 980; B, Adapted from Hart & Semple, 1990, p. 48. **496** From "Case Records of the Massachusetts General Hospital: Case 16–1986," by R. E. Scally, 1986, *New England Journal of Medicine,* 314, p. 1108. Copyright © 1986, Massachusetts Medical Society. Reprinted by permission of *The New England Journal of Medicine.* **497** From *Neuropsychology and the Dementias* (p. 39), by S. Hart and J. M. Semple, 1990, London, Erlbaum. Copyright © 1990. Reprinted by permission of Erlbaum (UK) Taylor & Francis. **499** Adapted from Beatty et al., 1988, p. 182. **507** Adapted from Talland, 1965. **508** Adapted from Dao-Castellana et al., (1998). Frontal dysfunction in neurologically normal chronic alcoholic subjects: Metabolic and neuropsychological findings. *Psychological Medicine, 28,* p. 1045, © 1998 Cambridge University Press. **513** "Neurobiological Substrates of Ictal Behavioral Changes," by P. Gloor, in *Advances in Neurology: Vol. 55, Neurobehavioral Problems in Epilepsy,* edited by D. B. Smith, D. M. Treiman, and M. R. Trimble, 1991, New York: Raven Press. Reprinted by permission.

Color insert

1 (top) From Volkow et al., 2001. Association of dopamine transporter reduction with psychomotor impairment in methamphetamine abusers. *American Journal of Psychiatry, 158*(3) p. 378; **(bottom)** From Louanasmaa et al., 1996. Information processing in the human brain: Magnetoencephalographic approach. *Proceedings of the National Academy of Sciences, USA, 93,* p. 8814. **2 (top)** A, From Milham et al, 2001, The relative involvement of anterior cingulate and prefrontal cortex in attentional control depends on nature of conflict. *Cognitive Brain Research, 12,* p. 471, fig.1; B, Braver et al., 2001, Anterior cingulate cortex and response conflict: Effects of frequency, inhibition and errors. *Cerebral Cortex, 11*(9), p. 831, fig.3B; **(middle)** From Gauthier, et al, 2000, Expertise for cars and birds recruits brain areas involved in face recognition. *Nature Neuroscience, 3*(2), p. 195; **(bottom)** From Paradis et al., 2000, Visual perception of motion and 3-D structure from motion: An fMRI study. *Cerebral Cortex, 10*(3), p. 776, fig. 4. **3 (top)** From Maguire, E. A. 1997. Hippocampal involvement in human topographical memory: Evidence from functional imaging, *Philosophical Transactions of the Royal Society of London, B, 352*: p. 1476; **(middle)** From Mangun et al., 1998. ERP and fMRI measures of visual spatial selection attention. *Human Brain Mapping, 6,* p. 386, fig. 1; **(bottom)** From Rees et al., 2000. Unconscious activation of visual cortex in the damaged right hemisphere of a parietal patient with extinction, *Brain, 123,* p. 1629, fig. 2. **4 (top)** From Cohen et al., 2000. The visual word form area: Spatial and temporal characterization of an initial stage of reading in normal subjects and posterior split-brain patients. *Brain, 123,* p. 29, fig. 5; **(bottom)** From Petito et al., 2000. Speech-like cerebral activity in profoundly deaf people processing signed languages: Implications for the neural basis of human language. *Proceedings of the National Academy of Sciences, USA, 97,* p. 13964, fig. 1.1. **5 (top)** A, From Maess et al., 2001. Musical syntax is processed in Broca's area: An MEG study, *Nature Neuro science, 4*(5), p. 542, fig. 4; B, From Maess et al., 2001. p. 543, fig. 5; **(bottom)** From Kim et al., 1997, Distinct cortical areas associated with native and second languages, *Nature, 388*: p. 173, fig. 4. **6 (top)** From Smith & Jonides, 1999, Storage and executive processes in the frontal lobes, *Science,* 283, p. 1660, fig. 4; **(bottom)** A, From Liddle et al., 2001. Event-related fMRI study of response inhibition. *Human Brain Mapping, 12,* p. 106, fig. 1; B & C, From Konishi et al., 1999. Common inhibitory mechanism in human inferior prefrontal cortex revealed by event-related functional MRI. *Brain, 122,* p. 985, figs. 3b, 3c. **7 (top)** From Banich et al., 2000. fMRI studies of Stroop tasks reveal unique roles of anterior and posterior brain systems in attentional selection. *Journal of Cognitive Neuroscience, 12*(6), p. 990, fig. 1a; **(middle)** From Phelps et al., 2000. Performance on indirect measures of race evaluation predicts amygdala activation. *Journal of Cognitive Neuroscience, 12*(5), p. 732; **(bottom)** From Bush et al., 2000, Cognitive and emotional influences in anterior cingulate cortex. *Trends in Cognitive Sciences, 4,* p. 217. **8 (top)** From Kesler-West et al., 2001. Neural substrates of facial emotion processing using fMRI, *Cognitive Brain Research, 11,* p. 220; **(bottom left)** From Cabeza, R., 2002. Hemispheric asymmetry reduction in older adults: The HAROLD model. *Psychology and Aging, 17,* p. 87; **(bottom right)** Adapted from Owen et al., 1998. Abnormal basal ganglia outflow in Parkinson's disease identified with PET: Implications for higher cortical functions, *Brain, 121,* p. 955.

NAME INDEX

SUBJECT INDEX

Methods Used in Cognitive Neuroscience and Neuropsychology

METHODS OF ASSESSING BRAIN ANATOMY

	Information Provided	Spatial Resolution	Temporal Resolution
CAT (computerized axial tomography)	Anatomical image of brain density	0.5–1.0 cm	Not available
MRI (magnetic resonance imaging)	Anatomical image of the distribution of a certain substance, such as water or fat	1mm	Not available

METHODS OF ASSESSING BRAIN PHYSIOLOGY

Functional Brain Imaging

	Information Provided	Spatial Resolution	Temporal Resolution
PET (positron emission tomography)	Functional image of physiological activity for various substances, including glucose, oxygen, and neurotransmitters	5–10 mm	40 seconds–1 hour
fMRI (functional MRI)	Functional image of relative blood oxygenation or blood flow	3–7 mm	2 seconds

Methods of Assessing Electromagnetic Activity

	Information Provided	Spatial Resolution	Temporal Resolution
Single Cell	Electrical signal that provides information about the firing rate of a cell	1/100th mm	1–2 Milliseconds (1 thousandth of a second)
EEG (electroencephalography)	Electrical signal that provides information about the summed post-synaptic dendritic activity (typically provided in frequency, Hz)	Poor	1–2 Milliseconds
ERP (event-related potentials)	Electrical signal that provides a record of the averaged electrical activity that is time-locked to an event	Poor	1–2 Milliseconds
MEG (magnetoencephalography)	Magnetic potentials that provide information derived from the electrical activity of neurons	5 mm	1–2 Milliseconds

Optical Imaging

	Information Provided	Spatial Resolution	Temporal Resolution
Slow Signal (metabolic)	Laser light provides information on the concentration of oxygenated and deoxygenated blood	1–5 mm	1–2 seconds
Fast Signal–EROS (event-related optical signal)	Laser light provides information on the deformation of neurons that accompanies neuronal firing	1–5 mm	1–2 milliseconds

METHODS OF MODULATING BRAIN ACTIVITY

	Means of Modulating Activity	Spatial Resolution	Temporal Resolution
TMS (transcranial magnetic stimulation)	Pulsed magnetic field induces an electric field causing neurons to fire in a random pattern	Currently ambiguous, probably 10–15 mm	Currently ambiguous, probably 20–50 ms